STATUTORY HISTORY
OF THE
UNITED STATES

LABOR
ORGANIZATION

STATUTORY HISTORY
OF THE
UNITED STATES

LABOR
ORGANIZATION

Editor
Robert F. Koretz
Syracuse University College of Law

CHELSEA HOUSE PUBLISHERS
In Association with
McGRAW-HILL BOOK CO.
New York   Toronto   London   Sydney

PREFACE

Man-made legislation is far older than most people realize. As I write this, I have before me a commemorative cone in which Lipit-Ishtar, King of Isin in ancient Sumeria (twenty-third century B.C.), refers to his promulgation of a law code for Sumer and Akkad. And we know of codes issued even centuries earlier in the ancient world. For all we know, indeed, man the legislator may appear virtually as soon as he displays the characteristics that distinguish him from other species.

At the same time, it is fair to say that not until modern times did legislation begin to play the positive role in ordering the society to which we have become accustomed. The change in this respect is usually associated with the name of Jeremy Bentham. Prodded by his *Philippics* (which make our current diatribes seem bland and amiable), Parliament consciously used its legislative power to regulate the economic, social, and political systems. Statute-law was the main weapon in the Benthamite armory; for the first time, legislation became the great instrument of advance.

During the past century, Benthamism came to the United States—and with a vengeance. And in this country, as in Benthamite Britain, the essential governmental instrument has been statute-law enacted by the national legislature. More and more, acts of Congress have been asserting control over matters formerly deemed outside the range of governmental concern.

The primary place of legislation in the governmental system has made it appropriate to publish the *Statutory History of the United States*. The series will include the principal subjects dealt with by federal legislation. Each volume will contain in historical order the important statutes on the subject covered, as well as their legislative history, including detailed extracts from the congressional debates and other pertinent materials, such as committee reports and Presidential messages. In addition, major Supreme Court decisions which bear upon the history of the statutes will be given. All of these materials will be carefully compiled by the editors of the respective volumes, who will also explain the statutes and their legislative history in commentaries interspersed throughout the volumes.

The *Statutory History* will make available legislative materials that are missing in most libraries. This series will also enable the reader to trace, in workable compass, the legislative history of all important statutes in the fields covered. As such, it should serve as a useful tool which is at present wholly lacking to those interested in law and legislation in this country.

Bernard Schwartz
Edwin D. Webb Professor of Law
New York University
June 1969

CONTENTS

THE ORIGINS

THE DEBATE

THE DECISIONS

CONCLUSION   *793*

INDEX   *795*

INTRODUCTION:
COLLECTIVE BARGAINING AND FREE ENTERPRISE

COLLECTIVE BARGAINING AND FREE ENTERPRISE

Labor law in the broadest sense embraces the entire range of legal problems that may arise when one person engages to work for another. It covers such diverse matters as health and welfare benefits, sanitary and safety conditions, wages and hours of work, workmen's compensation, and many other aspects of employee-employer relations. At the heart of our national labor policy, however, is a commitment to free collective bargaining that would leave to the parties involved the resolution of most, if not all, of the problems growing out of the multi-faceted employment relationship. Paradoxically, as Benjamin Aaron has pointed out in his article "Labor Relations Law": "Although the national labor policy is the commitment to 'free' collective bargaining in the private sector, the United States has a more comprehensive and bewildering array of restrictive laws regulating the relations between employer and unions than does any other industrialized society." Moreover, even though United States labor law has its origins in the decisions of the English and American courts of common law, in nearly every significant respect our contemporary labor law is founded in statutory rather than judicial creativity.

This statutory foundation is of recent origin and is essentially a product of the agitation for social reform that culminated in the New Deal. By far the most important statutes are those of the Federal Government, for they have preempted to a large degree the regulation of collective bargaining by the states. This body of law involving trade unionism and collective bargaining is our primary concern in this statutory history.

Nineteenth-Century Courts

Until well into the twentieth century, the predominant effect of judge-made labor law was the repression of collective action by workers. Borrowing from the doctrines of English common law, early nineteenth-century American courts generally applied the theory that the organizing of employees to raise wages was a criminal conspiracy. In the famous *Philadelphia Cordwainers'* case decided in 1806, the judge, Recorder Levy, reflected the prevailing sentiment: "A combination of workmen to raise their wages may be considered in a two-fold point of view; one is to benefit themselves . . . the other is to injure those who do not join their society. The rule of law condemns both." The jury agreed and the tiny union of journeymen cordwainers who sought to raise the price of their labor through a "turnout," or strike, was effectively destroyed.

Frustrated by the courts in their efforts to organize, irate workingmen held mock trials of judges and hung them in effigy. The public outcry against prosecution of workers under the criminal conspiracy doctrine was enough in some instances to cause juries to find for the defendants. In

1

1842 Massachusetts Chief Justice Lemuel Shaw all but killed the doctrine in *Commonwealth* v. *Hunt,* 45 Mass. 111 (1842), when he dismissed a conspiracy indictment against The Boston Journeymen Bootmakers' Society for a strike to force the dismissal of a nonmember. Shaw held that the indictment did not set forth any agreement to engage in a criminal act. Combination, the judge declared, might be employed for honorable purposes as well as dangerous and pernicious ones. Since it is natural for workers to seek improvement of their conditions under our industrial system, the purpose of the combination was a lawful one, and a combination of workingmen for a lawful purpose was not prohibited by law. Following Shaw's opinion American courts rarely invoked the conspiracy doctrine to control labor unions.

Although workers needed no longer fear being jailed for merely joining a union, *Commonwealth* v. *Hunt* did leave it to the courts to declare the conduct of a union socially injurious or oppressive. As a result, the law dealing with civil wrongs—tort law—became the instrument through which union activity was controlled. Often developing new doctrines as they went, many courts of common law declared illegal various forms of union economic pressures that did not fall within recognized tort categories such as assault or trespass. As Justice Oliver Wendell Holmes put the matter in a famous dissent written as a judge of the Massachusetts Supreme Court: "The true grounds of decision are considerations of policy and social advantage." [*Vegelahn* v. *Guntner,* 167 Mass. 92 (1896)] Many judges, however, based their decisions on their personal views of desirable social policy, and under the guise of one or more legal theories condemned many forms of the strike or boycott. This process culminated toward the end of the nineteenth century in the "equitable" remedy, or the injunction, considered by Charles Gregory as "a device for the control of labor disputes that really worked."

As an anti-labor device the injunction came into prominence after a long period of industrial development and, consequently, one of vast social change. In 1860, at a time when there were only 1½ million industrial wage earners, slightly more than a billion dollars was being invested in manufacturing. By 1900, capital had increased to over 12 billion dollars, while the number of wage earners rose to 5½ million. The period was not, however, without its crippling panics and depressions. The entrepreneurs responded to the great economic fluctuations by seeking security in corporations, while the working people turned to unionization as an answer to their problems.

Worker efforts at organization met great resistance. The forty years from the Civil War to the turn of the century were marked by the wreckage of many great unions—the Knights of St. Crispin, a powerful union of shoemakers destroyed by the panic of 1873 and by the introduction of machinery that undercut their traditional skills; the Trainmen's Union, wrecked along with the Pennsylvania Railroad's roundhouse in Pittsburgh by fire, riot, and the state militia in the Great Upheavel of 1877; the Knights of Labor, destroyed in 1886 by Jay Gould and the aftermath of the Haymarket Riot in Chicago; the Amalgamated Association of Iron and Steel Workers, whose members fought and defeated the dreaded Pinkerton strikebreakers at Carnegie's Homestead works in 1892 only to lose their struggle in the courts, where, as labor historian Samuel Yellen has noted, "The leadership of the men was buried beneath bail bonds"; and the American Railway Union, led by Eugene Victor Debs, defeated by railroad management, federal troops, and the injunction.

The so-called Debs Rebellion began as a boycott of Pullman Cars by railroad workers in sympathy with fellow workers on strike at the Pullman works near Chicago. Despite having made promises of "no reprisal" when the workingmen had sought a meeting, paternalistic George M. Pullman had fired the members of an employee grievance committee. This precipitated a mass downing of tools by his employees on May 10, 1894. After the failure of repeated attempts at mediation, an American Railway Union convention in June voted to back the strike by not handling Pullman Cars. By June 28, 125,000 railroad workers had joined the boycott and were successfully disrupting service on every Middle Western railroad. Management countered by loading United States mail onto Pullman Cars and then charging illegal interference with the mail against the striking workers. When the railroad men and their sympathizers continued to block the trains, Governor Altgeld called in the state militia. Bayonet wielding soldiers led charges into the crowds, who were incited by *agents provocateurs* into throwing rocks and harassment. The violence reached its peak on July 7 when the soldiers opened fire on a crowd and killed some thirty persons.

What finally ended the strike, however, was an injunction issued by President Grover Cleveland under the Sherman Anti-Trust Act of 1890, ordering the union leaders and members to refrain from interference with the operation of the railroads. Debs and other strike leaders were arrested for violating the injunction and jailed for contempt. The strike was broken.

While judicial restraint in the form of an injunction undoubtedly may serve a useful purpose in protecting the individual or firm from actual or threatened invasion of property rights, the use of the injunction in labor disputes gave rise to many abuses. The Debs case [*In re Debs,* 158 U.S. 564 (1895)], of course, is the classic. It certainly encouraged the widespread use of the injunction to curb labor disputes following the Pullman Strike. Temporary restraining orders came to be issued without proper notice to the unions or their members; injunctions were granted upon stereotyped complaints and based upon unreliable affidavit proof; court decrees were frequently "dragnet" in nature, purporting to bind "others whose names are not known," and couched in such legal gobbledegook as to be unintelligible; and jail sentences for contempt of court were often not even related to any alleged "crime."

The courts, moreover, went far beyond simple condemnation of many forms of union behavior now regarded as commonplace. They attached legal privilege to a wide range of antiunion conduct by employers. Until quite recently, for example, employers were privileged to threaten discrimination against employees for union activity, to blacklist with impunity union activists, to sponsor company-dominated employee associations, to engage in surveillance and espionage, and to refuse to bargain with the freely chosen representatives of their employees.

Increased Labor Activity

The Sherman Anti-Trust Act contains the following provision: "Every contract, combination in the form of trust or otherwise, or conspiracy, in restraint of trade or commerce among the several States, or with foreign nations, is hereby declared to be illegal." Enacted primarily to limit the social and economic depredations of massed corporate capital, the act, following its use in the Debs case, became a prime weapon in the war of capital against labor. The manner of its application is succinctly described in a latter-day decision of the Supreme Court: "Federal court injunctions were freely issued against all manner of strikes and boycotts under rulings that condemned virtually every collective activity of labor as unlawful restraint of trade." [*National Woodwork Manufacturers Association* v. *N. L. R. B.* 356 U.S. 612 (1967)] Or, as Mr. Dooley once quoted Capital as having said to Labor in a card game: "I've got ye beat . . . I've got a Supreme Court full of injunctions."

But injunctions were not the sole form of legal weaponry under the Sherman Act. In March, 1902, the United Hatters of North America called a strike against Dietrich Loewe and Company and boycotted its products. Although the strike was not very successful, the boycott apparently hurt enough for the company to sue the 240 hatters of Danbury for treble damages of $240,000 under the Sherman Act. After many years of legal wrangling—and $98,756.02 in legal fees—the Court upheld the company's right to sue in *Loewe* v. *Lawloe,* 208 U.S. 224 (1908).

The judgment must have made many workers think twice before joining unions, for fear of being sued as individuals for their collective actions. The American Federation of Labor was thus forced to drop the boycott as a defense against antiunion employers. The apogee of the employers' legal freedom as regards unionism, however, is perhaps best exemplified in a 1917 United States Supreme Court decision upholding "yellow-dog" contracts. [*Hitchman Coal & Coke Co.* v. *Mitchell,* 245 U.S. 229] By 1906, the United Mine Workers had a relatively secure foothold in the bituminous coal fields of Ohio, Indiana, Illinois, and much of Pennsylvania. But armed mine guards, deputized as sheriffs, successfully kept UMW organizers out of the southern fields, especially those of West Virginia, an exception being the unionized Hitchman mine in the West Virginia panhandle. When the UMW called a bituminous strike in 1906, Hitchman asked its employees to continue working at the old rate with a promise of a retroactive adjustment if the other operators raised their rates. For tactical reasons the UMW refused to permit the local union to accept. Roughly six weeks later, impoverished by the strike, the Hitchman miners returned to work as individuals. The mine owner insisted that they sign a so-called "yellow-dog" contract, an agreement *not* to join the union while employed by Hitchman. When union organizers approached the Hitchman employees about rejoining the union, the company secured an injunction barring the union from inducing Hitchman miners into breaking their "contract" with the company. The injunction was upheld by the U.S. Supreme Court on May 28, 1914. The decision reads in part: "This court repeatedly has held that the employer is as free to make non-membership in a union a condition of employment, as the working man is free to join the union, and that this is a part of the constitutional rights of personal liberty and private property, not to be taken away even by legislation, unless through some proper exercise of the paramount police power."

The *Hitchman* case, along with the *Danbury Hatters'* case still in the courts at the time, evoked vehement protests from organized labor, prompted its growing involvement in politics, and heightened the call for federal legislation to alleviate labor's difficulties. The first such effort resulted in the enactment of the Clayton Anti-Trust Act in 1914. Section 6 of that act provides: "That the labor of a human being is not a commodity or article of commerce. Nothing contained in the antitrust laws shall be construed to forbid the existence and operation of labor . . . organizations, instituted for the purposes of mutual help . . . or to forbid or restrain individual members of such organizations from lawfully carrying out the legitimate objects thereof. . . ." Section 20 bars federal court injunctions "in any case between an employer and employees, or between employers and employees," involving a dispute concerning terms and conditions of employment. It specifically prohibits injunctions against activities such as quitting work and persuading others to do so. It concludes, "nor shall any of the acts specified . . . be considered or held to be violations of any law of the United States."

The Clayton Act was hailed by organized labor as an "industrial Magna Carta." American Federation of Labor President Samuel Gompers jubilantly proclaimed that "those words [labor . . . is not a commodity] are sledge hammer blows to the wrongs and injustices so long inflicted upon the workers" by the courts. But labor's hopes and expectations were frustrated by the subsequent course of judicial decisions. The first blow fell upon the International Association of Machinists, which had organized three of the four major manufacturers of printing press machinery in the United States. The union shops enjoyed high wages and an eight-hour day; the nonunion Duplex Printing Press Company of Battle Creek, Michigan, paid lower wages and maintained a ten-hour day. The three unionized firms gave notice that they would not deal any further with the union unless it either lowered the scale or organized Duplex. A strike at the Duplex plant was unsuccessful, but the union then instituted a series of actions putting pressure on the company. Customers, trucking companies, and repair shops were all warned to curtail business with Duplex. A union business agent, Emil J. Deering, even attempted to block the showing of Duplex presses at a New York City trade show.

The company went to court and secured an *ex parte* injunction without a hearing. A lower court voided the injunction, but *Duplex* v. *Deering,* 254 U.S. 443 (1921), was carried to the Supreme Court by the company. A majority of the court held that Section 20 of the Clayton Act immunized only union activities directed against an employer by his own employees, and that a "secondary boycott" which interfered with Duplex's interstate trade was a violation of the Sherman Act. Again in *Bedford Cut Stone Co.* v. *Journeymen Stone Cutters' Association of North America,* 274 U.S. 37 (1927), the Court condemned a similar interstate boycott, even though the refusal of union members to handle Bedford stone was purely defensive, following a long course of company misdealings with the union, including a lockout of union members, and the establishment of what plainly appears to have been a company-dominated union. Both the *Duplex* and *Bedford* decisions evoked powerful dissent from Justices Brandeis and Holmes, who would have given Section 20 a broader reading of statutory intent, thus justifying the unions' conduct on the basis of economic self-interest.

The Court also denied immunity under Section 20 to certain types of "primary" union activity. In the two *Coronado Coal* cases, the Court handed down two seemingly contradictory opinions. The events leading up to them began in 1914 when Franklin Bache, an engineer and mine operator, decided to run his then unionized Arkansas mines as an open shop. To this end he shut down his mines, erected "no trespassing" signs, and hired nonunion workers from Tennessee. When Bache attempted to reopen his mines, the local mine workers and their neighbors marched to the pit head, shouting and hurling fists at Bache's hired armed guards. Bache secured an injunction and had U.S. marshals brought in. The conflict continued, and after two strikebreakers were shot and a powerhouse burned down, federal troops were summoned to restore peace. Bache subsequently sued the United Mine Workers, claiming $427,820.77 in damages.

The first time the case reached the Supreme Court, it was decided that in the absence of a showing that the union intended to restrain commerce the Sherman Act had not been violated. When, upon retrial, it was argued that the union intended to close interstate markets to nonunion coal and thereby eliminate competition with union-dug coal, the Court reversed itself and found that what had been an "indirect" effect was now "direct" and indeed a violation of the Sherman Act. In subsequent decisions in similar cases, the Court held that it did not matter that the alleged restraint was accomplished by peaceful economic pressures.

Felix Frankfurter and Nathan Green, in their perceptive work *The Labor Injunction,* commented on the foregoing development: "The Clayton Act was the product of twenty years of voluminous agitation. It came as clay into the hands of the federal courts, and we have attempted a portrayal of what they made of it. The result justifies an application of a familiar bit of French cynicism: the more things are legislatively changed, the more they remain the same judicially."

Executive and Legislative Action

Hostile courts forced the unions to turn to the legislative branch for relief. There the unions were encouraged by the changes taking place through their efforts in related fields. Worker agitation had won the support of the middle-class reformers, who secured legislation limiting the length of the workday and regulating the use of child labor. As early as the 1830's, workingmen's parties won the enactment of legislation to establish the ten-hour day as well as mechanic-lien laws in most of the industrial states of the time. President Martin Van Buren, in 1840, responded to labor pressures by establishing a ten-hour day for Naval Yard workers. In 1868, Congress enacted the first federal eight-hour law, which was limited, however, to laborers, workmen, and mechanics employed by or on behalf of the United States Government. Federal and state legislative efforts to limit the hours of work and to fix minimum wages in private industry were less successful, often being opposed as unconstitutional. Although the Supreme Court did, in 1915, sustain in *Bunting* v. *Oregon,* 273 U.S. 246, a state statute limiting the hours of work for adult males, and in 1917, in *New York Capital Railroad* v. *White,* 243 U.S. 188, ruled that workmen's compensation laws were a proper exercise of the police power of the state, it nevertheless ruled, as late as 1923, in *Adkins* v. *Children's Hospital,* 261 U.S. 525, that a District of Columbia minimum wage law for women violated the due process clause of the Fifth Amendment. The law, the Court maintained, took away the liberty of employers and workers to include any terms they wished in their employment contract. It wasn't until 1937 that the Court finally upheld the constitutionality of minimum wage legislation. [*West Coast Hotel Company* v. *Parrish,* 300 U.S. 39]

The establishment of the Department of Labor in the Executive Branch reflected the growing political and economic strength of trade unionism. It also underscored the reliance of organized labor on federal action to protect its interests. William H. Sylvis, the first outstanding figure of the American labor movement and a founder of the National Moulders' Union, suggested in the late 1860's that a department of labor be added to the federal government. The Knights of Labor took up the idea as did other trade unionists, and in 1884 a Bureau of Labor was established in the Department of the Interior. In 1889 it was merged into the newly created Department of Labor and headed by a commissioner without cabinet rank. In 1903, Congress created the Department of Commerce and Labor, the secretary of which was made a member of the Cabinet. Finally, in 1913, (a year, incidentally, of great labor ferment), the present United States Department of Labor was established by Act of Congress. The enabling statute provides:

There shall be an executive department in the Government called the Department of Labor, with a Secretary of Labor who shall be head thereof, to be appointed by the President, by and with the advice and consent of the Senate, and whose tenure of office shall be like that of the heads of the other executive departments. . . . The purpose of the Department of Labor shall be to foster, promote, and develop the welfare of the wage earners of the United States, to improve their working conditions, and to advance their opportunities for profitable employment. . . .

To carry out this mandate, the Department over the years has developed a wide range of services, bureaus, and divisions embracing nearly all aspects of labor from apprenticeships to workmen's compensation. The growth of these services, however, was often hampered by adverse court decisions until the coming of the New Deal.

The New Deal and Federal Legislation

There were numerous attempts in both state and federal legislatures around the turn of the century to ameliorate the legal plight of organized labor. In addition to the effort to limit the application of the antitrust laws and the injunction, there were statutes striking at the "yellow-dog" contract, the blacklisting of unionists, and other antiunion devices and strategems. Positive measures were also introduced, such as the protection of the union label and statutes providing for the mediation and arbitration of labor disputes. As Thomas R. Brooks points out in his history of American labor, *Toil and Trouble,* "Populist agitation combined with labor strife and Protestant conscience to prod the middle class into action. A wave of political reform washed over the entrenched political machines of the day. The 'Wisconsin idea' of reform through legislation and administrative advances, as in the income tax and railroad legislation, spread. . . ." This development was bolstered by the growing recognition of the political power of organized labor, as well as the gradual acceptance of unionism as an institution in American society. The American Federation of Labor, founded in 1886, barely numbered 550,000 members at the turn of the century; by 1914 it had reached the 2 million mark, and by 1920 had peaked at 5 million.

Nonetheless, the early gains of labor were not only sporadic, but, as we have seen, often nullified by judicial interpretation. With the increasing acceptance of unionism, however, it was inevitable that there should be changes in the legal rules surrounding union activity. Although union membership dropped during the 1920's to a low in 1933 of 2.9 million, it shot up rapidly within a decade to over 10 million, and to 15 million by the end of World War II. Over the last decade union membership has fluctuated around 18 million.

Since the beginning of the New Deal era in 1933 we have witnessed profound changes in the legislative treatment of trade union activity. Casual and scattered legislative efforts were superseded by a comprehensive legislative approach, reflecting the fact that contemporary policy making is centered in the legislatures rather than in the courts. And it is plain that the courts, particularly those in the federal system, have come to exhibit far greater sympathy and understanding for the workingman in their interpretations of legislative intent than their nineteenth-century predecessors.

THE RAILWAY LABOR ACT

Modern federal labor legislation is rooted in the experience of the railroads, our first national industry. Here the major nineteenth-century labor struggles took place. Clashes of near revolutionary fervor, they pitted the workers, farmers, and even the urban merchants against the railroads' monopolistic power. During the great upheaval of 1877, for instance, the townspeople of Pittsburgh set fire to the roundhouse, destroyed 104 locomotives, 2,152 cars, 79 buildings, and drove out the state militia. A strike by the Trainmen's Union protesting a 10 per cent pay cut grew into a seven-state uprising that had to be quelled by federal troops. The union was temporarily crushed, but despite such failures, railroad workers continued their efforts at unionization. In 1884, railroad shopmen in Denver, under the aegis of the Knights of Labor, precipitated a system-wide strike that eventually forced the powerful Union Pacific to terms. A year later, the Knights won an even greater victory by compelling Jay Gould to accede to favorable wage settlements on his railroads. Such successes account for the Knights' unprecedented growth from fifty thousand to over seven hundred thousand members in less than three years (1883–1886). However, the railroads that had set the stage for the dramatic rise of the union were also responsible for its destruction.

On March 1, 1886, the Knights called a strike against Jay Gould's Southwestern Railroad System. The strike, covering five thousand miles of track, stretched into Missouri, Kansas, Arkansas, Nebraska, and the Indian Territory. Involving some nine thousand shopmen, yardmen, and section hands, it ended abruptly when unsympathetic engineers, firemen, and brakemen refused to join the walkout. Gould quickly turned the tables on the Knights, blacklisted their leaders, and all but broke the union. Unfortunately, this failure came at nearly the same time that a general strike in Chicago for an eight-hour day was turning into the disastrous Haymarket Riot incident. The Knights could not survive the concurrent calamities.

As a result of over a decade of such railroad labor conflict, Congress enacted the Arbitration Act of 1888. Generally considered the first federal labor relations law, the act provided for the voluntary arbitration of railway labor disputes and for Presidential boards to investigate the causes of such disputes. The arbitration provisions of this statute were never used and the investigation provision was tried only once when President Grover Cleveland set up a temporary commission in 1894 to examine the causes of the famous Pullman Strike. The ensuing report is significant in American labor history. In it, the commission castigated Pullman, pointing out that: "The policy of both the Pullman Company and the Railway Managers' Association in reference to application to arbitrate, closed the door to all attempts at conciliation and settlement of differences. . . . A different policy would have prevented the loss of life and great loss of property and wages occasioned by the strike."

The commission recommended that the states consider adopting a conciliation and arbitration system and outlawing "yellow-dog" contracts. It urged employers to recognize labor organizations and deal with them through their representatives. President Cleveland submitted the report to Congress in 1895 and Representative Jacob Erdman [Dem., Pa.] introduced a bill based on its recommendations. With the support of the railroad brotherhoods, the operating craft unions, and the newly created Interstate Commerce Commission, the bill finally passed in 1898. The Erdman Act initiated a policy of governmental mediation in the railroad industry by providing that upon application of "either party to the controversy," the chairman of the Interstate Commerce Commission and the Commissioner of Labor were required to "put themselves in communication with the parties to such controversy, and shall use their best efforts, by mediation and conciliation, to amicably settle the same." If such efforts proved unsuccessful, the officials were to endeavor to induce the parties voluntarily to submit their dispute to arbitration in accordance with detailed procedures specified by the statute.

Under the act labor organizations were lawfully recognized as representatives of rail employees and brought into the mediation and conciliation process. Section 10 outlawed the "yellow-dog" contract on the railroads and prohibited discrimination against employees because of union membership. With a few exceptions, however, the statute fell into disuse, largely because the railroads refused to mediate whenever disputes arose. The Supreme Court struck down Section 10 in *Adair* v. *United States,* 208 U.S. 161 (1908), on two grounds: (1) Congress had stretched its power over interstate commerce too far in regulating railway labor relations; and (2) the prohibition of employer discrimination violated the Fifth Amendment due process clause, thus constituting "an arbitrary interference with the liberty of contract." In a similar case, *Coppage* v. *Kansas,* 236 U.S. 1 (1915), the Court, relying on the due process clause of the Fourteenth Amendment, held unconstitutional a Kansas statute outlawing "yellow-dog" contracts.

The Erdman Act was succeeded by the 1913 Newlands Act, which created a four-member permanent board of mediation and conciliation appointed by the President. The Newlands Act provided for mediation upon the initiative of the board, which could also recommend arbitration if mediation failed. The statutory arbitration provisions remained similar to those contained in the Erdman Act. Again, a number of cases were settled by mediation and arbitration under the act's provisions. Between 1913 and 1918 the Board settled 58 out of the 71 controversies which came before it. But the statute's provisions were not strong enough to settle a 1916 dispute over hours. A rail stoppage threat by the four operating brotherhoods, followed by President Woodrow Wilson's intervention, resulted in the passage of the Adamson Act, which established an eight-hour day and time-and-a-half for overtime for all interstate railroad employees. The Supreme Court upheld its constitutionality in *Wilson* v. *New,* 243 U.S. 332 (1917).

World War I brought about labor shortages, labor crises, and the seizure of the railroads by the government. From December, 1917 to April, 1920, the federal government operated the railroads and fostered collective bargaining. The President created the Board of Railroad Wages and Working Conditions, composed of equal representation from labor and management, for advisory purposes. In addition, three national adjustment boards were established to deal with secondary disputes arising from interpretations of existing agreements. Perhaps of greater significance was a general order of the Railroad Administration which prohibited discrimination in hiring, tenure, and other conditions of employment because of union membership or nonmembership. As a result of these measures wages improved as did hours, work rules, and other employment conditions. The railroad unions flourished.

On April 8, 1918, President Woodrow Wilson established the most important of war agencies, the National War Labor Board. The board acted as a court of last resort in settling controversies by mediation and voluntary arbitration in areas directly or indirectly related to the effective conduct of the war. Frank P. Walsh and ex-President Taft were named co-chairmen. Among the principles adopted was: "The right of workers to organize in trade unions and to bargain collectively, through chosen representatives, is recognized and affirmed. This right shall not be denied, abridged, or interfered with by the employers in any manner whatever. . . . Employers shall not discharge workers for membership in trade unions, nor for legitimate trade union activities."

However, the National War Labor Board's policies were not carried over to the postwar period, nor were they applied effectively to the largely non-union, mass-production industries. Freed from wartime restraints, employers returned to their union-busting activities. The steel industry, for example, successfully smashed a major organization drive in 1919 and set a repression pattern that lasted until 1937. Labor membership fell from 5 million in 1919 to 2.9 million in 1933. Only the rail unions continued to enjoy federal protection of their bargaining rights. When Congress transferred the railroads back into private hands on March 1, 1920, it made specific provision for continuing the wartime system of union recognition and bargaining. Title III of the Transportation Act of 1920 (Esch-Cummins

Act) directed representatives of the carriers and their employees to exert every reasonable effort to avoid interruption of service and to settle all disputes by direct conference if possible. The establishment of a bipartisan adjustment board by agreement of the parties was authorized for the settlement of disputes concerning grievances, rules, and working conditions, but not wages. If settlement could not be had in conference, the dispute could be referred to such an adjustment board at the request of either party, upon its own initiative, or at the request of the Railway Labor Board, a tripartite agency created by the act. Failing adjustment, the dispute was to be taken to the new Railway Labor Board for a hearing and decision. Empowered to decide wage disputes pursuant to criteria provided in the 1920 statute, the board could suspend wage agreements if, in its opinion, an increase would necessitate a substantial readjustment of a carrier's rates. The Supreme Court, in *Pennsylvania Railroad Company* v. *United States,* 261 U.S. 72 (1923), held that the board's orders were not legally enforceable, the only sanction being public opinion. Although the 1920 act made no reference to employees' rights to organize without company interference, the board foreshadowed the future of our national labor relations policy by articulating this principle in an early decision.

The absence of statutory enforcement sanctions, and the fact that the Railway Labor Board made wage decisions in a period of industrial depression, contributed to the board's ultimate ineffectiveness, and both management and labor often settled disputes by a show of force rather than submitting to the board's machinery. The inadequacies of the Transportation Act were recognized during a 1922 shopmen's strike. Four years later, Congress passed a new law intended to remedy these shortcomings.

A series of conferences held between railway executives and union officials early in 1926 hammered out a basis for new railway labor legislation. A bill was drafted and submitted to Congress under the sponsorship of Senator James Watson [R., Ind.] and Congressman James Parker [R., N. Y.], chairmen of the respective Commerce committees, and it passed the House by a vote of 321 to 13, and the Senate by a vote of 69 to 13. President Calvin Coolidge signed it into law on May 20, 1926. Having the support of both labor and management, the 1926 Railway Labor Act represented an effort to incorporate the best features of earlier legislation. It emphasized collective bargaining and mediation over settlement of wage disputes by a federal board, and provided for all disputes to be considered and decided in conference between the parties' representatives. Declaring the right of employers and employees to designate representatives without interference, influence, or coercion, the new statute replaced the former Labor Board with the Board of Mediation, an independent agency consisting of five members appointed by the President.

The 1926 act distinguished between what has come to be known as "minor" disputes, those arising out of "grievances or out of the interpretation or application of agreements concerning rates of pay, rules, or working conditions," and "major" disputes, those "concerning changes in rates of pay, rules, or working conditions." For such minor disputes, the act provided for the creation of adjustment boards by agreement. As to major disputes, the act required first a thirty-day notice of intended change. The parties then were required to agree within ten days upon the time and place for a conference. Failing settlement by negotiation, the statute provided for mediation by the new board, which, if its efforts failed, was to urge arbitration, acceptance of which was voluntary. If the parties rejected arbitration and an emergency then arose, the mediation board could bring this to the President's attention. He could then name an emergency board to investigate and report within thirty days. The statute provided that for thirty days after the report no change, except by agreement, could be made by either party in the conditions from which the dispute arose.

Questions as to the construction and constitutionality of certain provisions of the 1926 Act came before the Supreme Court in *Texas & New Orleans Railroad Company* v. *Brotherhood of Railway Clerks,* 281 U.S. 548 (1930). The majority opinion written by Chief Justice Charles Evans Hughes presaged a new era in judicial construction of federal labor legislation. [*supra,* p. 140.] Briefly stated, the Court, after thoroughly reviewing the background and legislative history of the 1926 act, held that the statutory declaration of the right to designate representatives freely imposed a definite obligation enforceable by legal proceedings, and that the statutory prohibition of interference with that right remained within the constitutional authority of Congress.

A number of weaknesses in the 1926 act, including the necessity for agreement in the creation of adjustment boards for minor disputes, and the ineffectualness of the protection of the right to self-organization, led to the enactment of the 1934 amendments to the Railway Labor Act. To decide minor disputes, this legislation created the four-divisioned National Railroad Adjustment Board. Next, the amendments substituted the National Mediation Board for the Board of Mediation. The new board mediated disputes other than the "minor" disputes arising out of existing contracts. It also had the important function of deciding representation disputes. The protection of the rights of self-organization and collective bargaining were clarified and strengthened. For the first time there was explicit statutory recognition of the principle of majority rule: "The majority of any craft or class of employees shall have the right to determine who shall be the representative of the craft or class for the purposes of this Act." The law now prohibited carriers from interfering in any way with self-organization, including maintaining or assisting labor organizations, or influencing or coercing employees regarding union membership. And carriers were directed to "treat with" the certified representative of the craft or class.

In a second landmark decision under the act, *Virginia Railway Company v. System Federation No. 40,* 300 U.S. 515 (1937), the Supreme Court held that: "the statute does not undertake to compel agreement between the employer and employees, but it does command those preliminary steps without which no agreement can be reached. It at least requires the employer to meet and confer with the authorized representative of its employees, to listen to their complaints, to make reasonable effort to compose differences . . . It imposes the affirmative duty to treat only with the true representative, and hence the negative duty to treat with no other." The Court sustained the constitutionality of the statute in the face of claims to the contrary under the commerce clause and the due process clause of the Fifth Amendment.

Since 1934 there have been several amendments to the Railway Labor Act, two of which require mention. In 1936 most of the provisions were made applicable to interstate air carriers. In 1951 the act was amended to authorize union security agreements as well as the check-off, subject to conditions quite similar to those which had been made applicable to other interstate industries by the Taft-Hartley Act of 1947.

THE RAILWAY LABOR ACT (As Amended)
April 10, 1936

Being An Act To provide for the prompt disposition of disputes between carriers and their employees and for other purposes

(U.S. Code, Title 45, Chapter 8)[1]

Be it enacted by the Senate and House of Representatives of the United States of America in Congress assembled,

TITLE I[2]

DEFINITIONS

SEC. 1. When used in this Act and for the purposes of this Act—

First. The term "carrier" includes any express company, sleeping-car company, carrier by railroad, subject to the Interstate Commerce Act, and any company which is directly or indirectly owned or controlled or under common control with any carrier by railroad and which operates any equipment or facilities or performs any service (other than trucking service) in connection with the transportation, receipt, delivery, elevation, transfer in transit, refrigeration or icing, storage, and handling of property transported by railroad, and any receiver, trustee, or other individual or body, judicial or otherwise, when in the possession of the business of any such "carrier": *Provided, however,* That the term "carrier" shall not include any street, interurban, or suburban electric railway, unless such railway is operating as a part of a general steam-railroad system of transportation but shall not exclude any part of the general steam-railroad system of transportation now or hereafter operated by any other motive power. The Interstate Commerce Commission is hereby authorized and directed upon request of the Mediation Board or upon complaint of any party interested to determine after hearing whether any line operated by electric power falls within the terms of this

---

[1](Public Law 257, 69th Cong.) (H.R. 9463); (Approved May 20, 1926), The Railway Labor Act (44 Stat. L. 577.)

(Public Law 442, 73rd Cong.) (H.R. 9861), An Act to amend the Railway Labor Act approved May 20, 1926. (Approved June 21, 1934.)

That Section 1 of the Railway Labor Act is amended to read as follows: (Followed by text governing carriers by railroad and related transportation agencies.) (48 Stat. L. 926.)

[2]Title II, (Public Law 487, 74th Cong.) (S. 2496), An Act to amend the Railway Labor Act. (Approved Apr. 10, 1936.)

That the Railway Labor Act, approved May 20, 1926, as amended, herein referred to as "Title I" is hereby further amended by inserting after the enacting clause the caption "Title I" and by adding the following Title II. (Followed by Title II governing air carriers.) (48 Stat. L. 1185.)

proviso. *The term "carrier" shall not include any company by reason of its being engaged in the mining of coal, the supplying of coal to carrier where delivery is not beyond the tipple, and the operation of equipment or facilities therefor, or any of such activities.

Second. The term "Adjustment Board" means the National Railroad Adjustment Board created by this Act.

Third. The term "Mediation Board" means the National Mediation Board created by this Act.

Fourth. The term "commerce" means commerce among the several States or between any State, Territory, or the District of Columbia and any foreign nation, or between any Territory or the District of Columbia and any State, or between any Territory, and any other Territory, or between any Territory and the District of Columbia, or within any Territory or the District of Columbia, or between points in the same State but through any other State or any Territory or the District of Columbia or any foreign nation.

Fifth. The term "employee" as used herein includes every person in the service of a carrier (subject to its continuing authority to supervise and direct the manner of rendition of his service) who performs any work defined as that of an employee or subordinate official in the orders of the Interstate Commerce Commission now in effect, and as the same may be amended or interpreted by orders hereafter entered by the Commission pursuant to the authority which is hereby conferred upon it to enter orders amending or interpreting such existing orders: *Provided, however,* That no occupational classification made by order of the Interstate Commerce Commission shall be construed to define the crafts according to which railway employees may be organized by their voluntary action, nor shall the jurisdiction or powers of such employee organizations be regarded as in any way limited or defined by the provisions of this Act or by the orders of the Commission.** The term "employee" shall not include any individual while such individual is engaged in the physical operations consisting of the mining of coal, the preparation of coal, the handling (other than movement by rail with standard locomotives) of coal not beyond the mine tipple, or the loading of coal at the tipple.

Sixth. The term "representative" means any person or persons, labor union, organization, or corporation designated either by a carrier or group of carriers or by its or their employees, to act for it or them.

Seventh. The term "district court" includes the Supreme Court of the District of Columbia; and the term "circuit court of appeals" includes the

---

*Final paragraphs to Section 1 First and 1 Fifth marked by asterisks are amendments by the Act of Aug. 13, 1940 (Public Law 764).

(Public Law 914, 81st Cong.) (S. 3295); (Approved Jan. 10, 1951) providing for union membership. (See Sec. 2, Eleventh.)

**Added by amendment by the Act of Aug. 13, 1940 (Public Law 764).

Court of Appeals of the District of Columbia.

This Act may be cited as the "Railway Labor Act."

GENERAL PURPOSES

SEC. 2. The purposes of the Act are: (1) To avoid any interruption to commerce or to the operation of any carrier engaged therein; (2) to forbid any limitation upon freedom of association among employees or any denial, as a condition of employment or otherwise, of the right of employees to join a labor organization; (3) to provide for the complete independence of carriers and of employees in the matter of self-organization; (4) to provide for the prompt and orderly settlement of all disputes concerning rates of pay, rules, or working conditions; (5) to provide for the prompt and orderly settlement of all disputes growing out of grievances or out of the interpretation or application of agreements covering rates of pay, rules, or working conditions.

GENERAL DUTIES

First. It shall be the duty of all carriers, their officers, agents, and employees to exert every reasonable effort to make and maintain agreements concerning rates of pay, rules, and working conditions, and to settle all disputes, whether arising out of the application of such agreements or otherwise, in order to avoid any interruption to commerce or to the operation of any carrier growing out of any dispute between the carrier and the employees thereof.

Second. All disputes between a carrier or carriers and its or their employees shall be considered, and, if possible, decided, with all expedition, in conference between representatives designated and authorized so to confer, respectively, by the carrier or carriers and by the employees thereof interested in the dispute.

Third. Representatives, for the purposes of this Act, shall be designated by the respective parties without interference, influence, or coercion by either party over the designation of representatives by the other; and neither party shall in any way interfere with, influence, or coerce the other in its choice of representatives. Representatives of employees for the purposes of this Act need not be persons in the employ of the carrier, and no carrier shall, by interference, influence, or coercion seek in any manner to prevent the designation by its employees as their representatives of those who or which are not employees of the carrier.

Fourth.[3] Employees shall have the right to organize and bargain collectively through representatives of their own choosing. The majority of any craft or class of employees shall have the right to determine who shall be the representative of the craft or class for the purposes of this Act. No

---

[3] Amended by Public Law 914, 81st Cong. (See Sec. 2, Eleventh.)

carrier, its officers or agents, shall deny or in any way question the right of its employees to join, organize, or assist in organizing the labor organization of their choice, and it shall be unlawful for any carrier to interfere in any way with the organization of its employees, or to use the funds of the carrier in maintaining or assisting or contributing to any labor organization, labor representative, or other agency of collective bargaining, or in performing any work therefor, or to influence or coerce employees in an effort to induce them to join or remain or not to join or remain members of any labor organization or to deduct from the wages of employees any dues, fees, assessments, or other contributions payable to labor organizations, or to collect or to assist in the collection of any such dues, fees, assessments, of other contributions: *Provided,* That nothing in this Act shall be construed to prohibit a carrier from permitting an employee, individually, or local representatives of employees from conferring with management during working hours without loss of time, or to prohibit a carrier from furnishing free transportation to its employees while engaged in the business of a labor organization.

Fifth.[4]   No carrier, its officers, or agents shall require any person seeking employment to sign any contract or agreement promising to join or not to join a labor organization; and if any such contract has been enforced prior to the effective date of this Act, then such carrier shall notify the employees by an appropriate order that such contract has been discarded and is no longer binding on them in any way.

Sixth.   In case of a dispute between a carrier or carriers and its or their employees, arising out of grievances or out of the interpretation or application of agreements concerning rates of pay, rules, or working conditions, it shall be the duty of the designated representative or representatives of such carrier or carriers and of such employees, within ten days after the receipt of notice of a desire on the part of either party to confer in respect to such dispute, to specify a time and place at which such conference shall be held: *Provided,* (1) That the place so specified shall be situated upon the line of the carrier involved or as otherwise mutually agreed upon; and (2) that the time so specified shall allow the designated conferees reasonable opportunity to reach such place of conference, but shall not exceed twenty days from the receipt of such notice: *And provided further,* That nothing in this Act shall be construed to supersede the provisions of any agreement (as to conferences) then in effect between the parties.

Seventh.   No carrier, its officers, or agents shall change the rates of pay, rules, or working conditions of its employees, as a class as embodied in agreements except in the manner prescribed in such agreements or in Section 6 of the Act.

Eighth.   Every carrier shall notify its employees by printed notices in such

---

[4]Amended by Public Law 914, 81st Cong. (See Sec. 2, Eleventh.)

form and posted at such times and places as shall be specified by the Mediation Board that all disputes between the carrier and its employees will be handled in accordance with the requirements of this Act, and in such notices there shall be printed verbatim, in large type, the third, fourth, and fifth paragraphs of this section. The provisions of said paragraphs are hereby made a part of the contract of employment between the carrier and each employee, and shall be held binding upon the parties, regardless of any other express or implied agreements between them.

Ninth.   If any dispute shall arise among a carrier's employees as to who are the representatives of such employees designated and authorized in accordance with the requirements of this Act, it shall be the duty of the Mediation Board, upon request of either party to the dispute, to investigate such dispute and to certify to both parties, in writing, within thirty days after the receipt of the invocation of its services, the name or names of the individuals or organizations that have been designated and authorized to represent the employees involved in the dispute, and certify the same to the carrier. Upon receipt of such certification the carrier shall treat with the representative so certified as the representative of the craft or class for the purposes of this Act. In such an investigation, the Mediation Board shall be authorized to take a secret ballot of the employees involved, or to utilize any other appropriate method of ascertaining the names of their duly designated and authorized representatives in such manner as shall insure the choice of representatives by the employees without interference, influence, or coercion exercised by the carrier. In the conduct of any election for the purposes herein indicated the Board shall designate who may participate in the election and establish the rules to govern the election, or may appoint a committee of three neutral persons who after hearing shall within ten days designate the employees who may participate in the election. The Board shall have access to and have power to make copies of the books and records of the carriers to obtain and utilize such information as may be deemed necessary by it to carry out the purposes and provisions of this paragraph.

Tenth.   The willful failure or refusal of any carrier, its officers, or agents to comply with the terms of the third, fourth, fifth, seventh, or eighth paragraph of this section shall be a misdemeanor, and upon conviction thereof the carrier, officer, or agent offending shall be subject to a fine of not less than $1,000 nor more than $20,000 or imprisonment for not more than six months, or both fine and imprisonment, for each offense, and each day during which such carrier, officer, or agent shall willfully fail or refuse to comply with the terms of the said paragraphs of this section shall constitute a separate offense. It shall be the duty of any district attorney of the United States to whom any duly designated representative of a carrier's employees may apply to institute in the proper court and to prosecute under the direction of the Attorney General of the United States, all necessary proceedings for the enforcement of the provisions of this section, and for the punishment of all violations thereof and the costs and expenses of such prosecution shall be paid out of the appropriation for the expenses of the courts of the United States: *Provided,* That nothing in this Act shall be construed to require an individual employee to render labor or service without his consent, nor shall anything in this Act be construed to make the quitting of his labor by an individual employee an illegal act; nor shall any court issue any process to compel the performance by an individual employee of such labor or service, without his consent.

Eleventh.[5]   Notwithstanding any other provisions of this Act, or of any other statute or law of the United States, or Territory thereof, or of any State, any carrier or carriers as defined in this Act and a labor organization or labor organizations duly designated and authorized to represent employees in accordance with the requirements of this Act shall be permitted—

(a) To make agreements, requiring, as a condition of continued employment, that within sixty days following the beginning of such employment, or the effective date of such agreements, whichever is the later, all employees shall become members of the labor organization representing their craft or class: *Provided,* That no such agreement shall require such condition of employment with respect to employees to whom membership is not available upon the same terms and conditions as are generally applicable to any other member or with respect to employees to whom membership was denied or terminated for any reason other than the failure of the employee to tender the periodic dues, initiation fees, and assessments (not including fines and penalties) uniformly required as a condition of acquiring or retaining membership.

(b) To make agreements providing for the deduction by such carrier or carriers from the wages of its or their employees in a craft or class and payment to the labor organization representing the craft or class of such employees, of any periodic dues, initiation fees, and assessments (not including fines and penalties) uniformly required as a condition of acquiring or retaining membership: *Provided,* That no such agreement shall be effective with respect to any individual employee until he shall have furnished the employer with a written assignment to the labor organization of such membership dues, initiation fees, and assessments, which shall be revocable in writing after the expiration of one year or upon the termination date of the applicable collective agreement, whichever occurs sooner.

(c) The requirement of membership in a labor organization in an agreement made pursuant to subparagraph (a) shall be satisfied, as to both a present or future employee in engine, train, yard, or hostling service, that is, an employee engaged in any of the services or capacities covered in Section

---

[5]Added by amendment (Public Law 914, 81st Cong.)   (S. 3295); (Approved Jan. 10, 1951).

3, First (h) of this Act defining the jurisdictional scope of the First Division of the National Railroad Adjustment Board, if said employee shall hold or acquire membership in any one of the labor organizations, national in scope, organized in accordance with this Act and admitting to membership employees of a craft or class in any of said services; and no agreement made pursuant to subparagraph (b) shall provide for deductions from his wages for periodic dues, initiation fees, or assessments payable to any labor organization other than that in which he holds membership: *Provided, however,* That as to an employee in any of said services on a particular carrier at the effective date of any such agreement on a carrier, who is not a member of any one of the labor organizations, national in scope, organized in accordance with this Act and admitting to membership employees of a craft or class in any of said services such employee, as a condition of continuing his employment, may be required to become a member of the organization representing the craft in which he is employed on the effective date of the first agreement applicable to him: *Provided, further,* That nothing herein or in any such agreement or agreements shall prevent an employee from changing membership from one organization to another organization admitting to membership employees of a craft or class in any of said services.

(d) Any provisions in paragraphs Fourth and Fifth of Section 2 of this Act in conflict herewith are to the extent of such conflict amended.

NATIONAL BOARD OF ADJUSTMENT; GRIEVANCES; INTERPRETATION AGREEMENTS

SEC. 3. First. There is hereby established a Board to be known as the "National Railroad Adjustment Board", the members of which shall be selected within thirty days after approval of this Act, and it is hereby provided—

(a) That the said Adjustment Board shall consist of thirty-six members, eighteen of whom shall be selected by the carrier and eighteen by such labor organizations of the employees, national in scope, as have been or may be organized in accordance with the provisions of Section 2 of this Act.

(b) The carriers, acting each through its board of directors or its receiver or receivers, trustee or trustees, or through an officer or officers designated for that purpose by such board, trustee or trustees, or receiver or receivers, shall prescribe the rules under which its representatives shall be selected and shall select the representatives of the carriers on the Adjustment Board and designate the division on which each such representative shall serve, but no carrier or system of carriers shall have more than one representative on any division of the Board.

(c) The national labor organizations, as defined in paragraph (a) of this section, acting each through the chief executive or other medium designated by the organization or association thereof, shall prescribe the rules under which the labor members of the Adjustment Board shall be selected and shall select such members and designate the division on which each member shall serve; but no labor organization shall have more than one representative on any division of the Board.

(d) In case of a permanent or temporary vacancy on the Adjustment Board, the vacancy shall be filled by selection in the same manner as in the original selection.

(e) If either the carriers or the labor organizations of the employees fail to select and designate representatives to the Adjustment Board, as provided in paragraphs (b) and (c) of this section, respectively, within sixty days after the passage of this Act, in case of any original appointment to office of a member of the Adjustment Board, or in a case of vacancy in any such office within thirty days after such vacancy occurs, the Mediation Board shall thereupon directly make the appointment and shall select an individual associated in interest with the carriers or the group of labor organizations of employees, whichever he is to represent.

(f) In the event a dispute arises as to the right of any national labor organization to participate as per paragraph (c) of this section in the selection and designation of the labor members of the Adjustment Board, the Secretary of Labor shall investigate the claim of such labor organization to participate, and if such claim in the judgment of the Secretary of Labor has merit, the Secretary shall notify the Mediation Board accordingly, and within ten days after receipt of such advice the Mediation Board shall request those national labor organizations duly qualified as per paragraph (c) of this section to participate in the selection and designation of the labor members of the Adjustment Board to select a representative. Such representative, together with a representative likewise designated by the claimant, and a third or neutral party designated by the Mediation Board, constituting a board of three, shall within thirty days after the appointment of the neutral member investigate the claims of the labor organization desiring participation and decide whether or not it was organized in accordance with Section 2 hereof and is otherwise properly qualified to participate in the selection of the labor members of the Adjustment Board, and the findings of such boards of three shall be final and binding.

(g) Each member of the Adjustment Board shall be compensated by the party or parties he is to represent. Each third or neutral party selected under the provisions of (f) of this section shall receive from the Mediation Board such compensation as the Mediation Board may fix, together with his necessary traveling expenses and expenses actually incurred for subsistence, or per diem allowance in lieu thereof, subject to the provisions of law applicable thereto, while serving as such third or neutral party.

(h) The said Adjustment Board shall be composed of four divisions, whose proceedings shall be independent of one another, and the said divisions as well as the number of their members shall be as follows:

First division: To have jurisdiction over disputes involving train-and-yard service employees of carriers; that is, engineers, firemen, hostlers, and outside hostler helpers, conductors, trainmen, and yard-service employees. This division shall consist of ten members, five of whom shall be selected and designated by the carriers and five of whom shall be selected and designated by the national labor organizations of the employees.

Second division: To have jurisdiction over disputes involving machinists, boilermakers, blacksmiths, sheetmetal workers, electrical workers, carmen, the helpers and apprentices of all the foregoing, coach cleaners, power-house employees, and railroad-shop laborers. This division shall consist of ten members, five of whom shall be selected by the carriers and five by the national labor organizations of the employees.

Third division: To have jurisdiction over disputes involving station, tower, and telegraph employees, train dispatchers, maintenance-of-way men, clerical employees, freight handlers, express, station, and store employees, signalmen, sleeping-car conductors, sleeping-car porters, and maids and dining-car employees. This division shall consist of ten members, five of whom shall be selected by the carriers and five by the national labor organizations of employees.

Fourth division. To have jurisdiction over disputes involving employees of carriers directly or indirectly engaged in transportation of passengers or property by water, and all other employees of carriers over which jurisdiction is not given to the first, second, and third divisions. This division shall consist of six members, three of whom shall be selected by the carriers and three by the national labor organizations of the employees.

(i) The disputes between an employee or group of employees and a carrier or carriers growing out of grievance or out of the interpretation or application or agreements concerning rates of pay, rules, or working conditions, including cases pending and unadjusted on the date of approval of this Act, shall be handled in the usual manner up to and including the chief operating officer of the carrier designated to handle such disputes; but, failing to reach an adjustment in this manner, the disputes may be referred by petition of the parties or by either party to the appropriate division of the Adjustment Board with a full statement of the facts and all supporting data bearing upon the disputes.

(j) Parties may be heard either in person, by counsel, or by other representatives, as they may respectively elect, and the several divisions of the Adjustment Board shall give due notice of all hearings to the employee or employees and the carrier or carriers involved in any disputes submitted to them.

(k) Any division of the Adjustment Board shall have authority to empower two or more of its members to conduct hearings and make findings upon disputes, when properly submitted, at any place designated by the division: *Provided, however,* That final awards as to any such disputes must be made by the entire division as hereinafter provided.

(1) Upon failure of any division to agree upon an award because of a deadlock or inability to secure a majority vote of the division members, as provided in paragraph (n) of this section, then such division shall forthwith agree upon and select a neutral person, to be known as "referee", to sit with the division as a member thereof and make an award. Should the division fail to agree upon and select a referee within ten days of the date of the deadlock or inability to secure a majority vote, then the division, or any member thereof, or the parties or either party to the dispute may certify that fact to the Mediation Board, which Board shall, within ten days from the date of receiving such certificate, select and name the referee to sit with the division as a member thereof and make an award. The Mediation Board shall be bound by the same provisions in the appointment of these neutral referees as are provided elsewhere in this Act for the appointment of arbitrators and shall fix and pay the compensation of such referees.

(m) The awards of the several divisions of the Adjustment Board shall be stated in writing. A copy of the awards shall be furnished to the respective parties to the controversy, and the awards shall be final and binding upon both parties to the dispute. In case a dispute arises involving an interpretation of the award the division of the Board upon request of either party shall interpret the award in the light of the dispute.

(n) A majority vote of all members of the division of the Adjustment Board shall be competent to make an award with respect to any dispute submitted to it.

(o) In case of an award by any division of the Adjustment Board in favor of petitioner, the division of the Board shall make an order, directed to the carrier, to make the award effective and, if the award includes a requirement for the payment of money, to pay to the employee the sum to which he is entitled under the award on or before a day named.

In the event any division determines that an award favorable to the petitioner should not be made in any dispute referred to it, the division shall make an order to the petitioner stating such determination.[6]

(p) If a carrier does not comply with an order of a division of the Adjustment Board within the time limit in such order, the petitioner, or any person for whose benefit such order was made, may file in the District Court of the United States for the district in which he resides or in which is located the principal operating office of the carrier, or through which the carrier operates, a petition setting forth briefly the causes for which he claims relief, and the order of the division of the Adjustment Board in the premises. Such

---

[6](Public Law 456, 89th Cong.) (H.R. 706); (Approved June 20, 1966).

suit in the District Court of the United States shall proceed in all respects as other civil suits, except that on the trial of such suit the findings and order of the division of the Adjustment Board shall be conclusive on the parties[7] and except that the petitioner shall not be liable for costs in the district court nor for costs at any subsequent stage of the proceedings, unless they accrue upon his appeal, and such costs shall be paid out of the appropriation for the expenses of the courts of the United States. If the petitioner shall finally prevail he shall be allowed a reasonable attorney's fee, to be taxed and collected as a part of the costs of the suit. The district courts are empowered, under the rules of the court governing actions at law, to make such order and enter such judgment, by writ of mandamus or otherwise, as may be appropriate to enforce or set aside the order of the division of the Adjustment Board: *Provided, however,* That such order may not be set aside except for failure of the division to comply with the requirements of this Act, for failure of the order to conform, or confine itself, to matters within the scope of the division's jurisdiction, or for fraud or corruption by a member of the division making the order[7]

(q) If any employee or group of employees, or any carrier, is aggrieved by the failure of any division of the Adjustment Board to make an award in a dispute refered to it, or is aggrieved by any of the terms of an award or by the failure of the division to include certain terms in such award, then such employee or group of employees or carrier may file in any United States district court in which a petition under paragraph (p) could be filed, a petition for review of the division's order. A copy of the petition shall be forthwith transmitted by the clerk of the court to the Adjustment Board. The Adjustment Board shall file in the court the record of the proceedings on which it based its action. The court shall have jurisdiction to affirm the order of the division or to set it aside, in whole or in part, or it may remand the proceeding to the division for such further action as it may direct. On such review, the findings and order of the division shall be conclusive on the parties, except that the order of the division may be set aside, in whole or in part, or remanded to the division, for failure of the division to comply with the requirements of this Act, for failure of the order to conform, or confine itself, to matters within the scope of the division's jurisdiction, or for fraud or corruption by a member of the division making the order. The judgment of the court shall be subject to review as provided in Sections 1291 and 1254 of title 28, United States Code.[7]

(r) All actions at law based upon the provisions of this section shall be begun within two years from the time the cause of action accrues under the award of the division of the Adjustment Board, and not after.

(s) The several divisions of the Adjustment Board shall maintain head-

---

[7](Public Law 456, 89th Cong.) (H.R. 706); (Approved June 20, 1966).

quarters in Chicago, Illinois, meet regularly, and continue in session so long as there is pending before the division any matter within its jurisdiction which has been submitted for its consideration and which has not been disposed of.

(t) Whenever practicable, the several divisions or subdivisions of the Adjustment Board shall be supplied with suitable quarters in any Federal building located at its place of meeting.

(u) The Adjustment Board may, subject to the approval of the Mediation Board, employ and fix the compensations of such assistants as it deems necessary in carrying on its proceedings. The compensation of such employees shall be paid by the Mediation Board.

(v) The Adjustment Board shall meet within forty days after the approval of this Act and adopt such rules as it deems necessary to control proceedings before the respective divisions and not in conflict with the provisions of this section. Immediately following the meeting of the entire Board and the adoption of such rules, the respective divisions shall meet and organize by the selection of a chairman, a vice chairman, and a secretary. Thereafter each division shall annually designate one of its members to act as chairman and one of its members to act as vice chairman: *Provided, however,* That the chairmanship and vice chairmanship of any division shall alternate as between the groups, so that both the chairmanship and vice chairmanship shall be held alternately by a representative of the carriers and a representative of the employees. In case of a vacancy, such vacancy shall be filled for the unexpired term by the selection of a successor from the same group.

(w) Each division of the Adjustment Board shall annually prepare and submit a report of its activities to the Mediation Board, and the substance of such report shall be included in the annual report of the Mediation Board to the Congress of the United States. The reports of each division of the Adjustment Board and the annual report of the Mediation Board shall state in detail all cases heard, all actions taken, the names, salaries, and duties of all agencies, employees, and officers receiving compensation from the United States under the authority of this Act, and an account of all moneys appropriated by Congress pursuant to the authority conferred by this Act and disbursed by such agencies, employees, and officers.

(x) Any division of the Adjustment Board shall have authority, in its discretion, to establish regional adjustment boards to act in its place and stead for such limited period as such division may determine to be necessary. Carrier members of such regional boards shall be designated in keeping with rules devised for this propose by the carrier members of the Adjustment Board and the labor members shall be designated in keeping with rules devised for this purpose by the labor members of the Adjustment Board. Any such regional board shall, during the time for which it is appointed, have the same authority to conduct hearings, make findings upon disputes, and adopt the same procedure as the division of the Adjustment Board appointing it, and its decisions shall be enforceable to the same extent and under the same processes. A neutral person, as referee, shall be appointed for service in connection with any such regional adjustment board in the same circumstances and manner as provided in paragraph (1) hereof, with respect to a division of the Adjustment Board.

Second. Nothing in this section shall be construed to prevent any individual carrier, system, or group of carriers and any class or classes of its or their employees, all acting through their representatives, selected in accordance with the provisions of this Act, from mutually agreeing to the establishment of system, group, or regional boards of adjustment for the purpose of adjusting and deciding disputes of the character specified in this section. In the event that either party to such a system, group, or regional board of adjustment is dissatisfied with such arrangement, it may upon ninety days' notice to the other party elect to come under the jurisdiction of the Adjustment Board.

If written request is made upon any individual carrier by the representative of any craft or class of employees of such carrier for the establishment of a special board of adjustment to resolve disputes otherwise referable to the Adjustment Board, or any dispute which has been pending before the Adjustment Board for twelve months from the date the dispute (claim) is received by the Board, or if any carrier makes such a request upon any such representative, the carrier or the representative upon whom such request is made shall join in an agreement establishing such a board within thirty days from the date such request is made. The cases which may be considered by such board shall be defined in the agreement establishing it. Such board shall consist of one person designated by the carrier and one person designated by the representative of the employees. If such carrier or such representative fails to agree upon the establishment of such a board as provided herein, or to exercise its rights to designate a member of the board, the carrier or representative making the request for the establishment of the special board may request the Mediation Board to designate a member of the special board on behalf of the carrier or representative upon whom such request was made. Upon receipt of a request for such designation the Mediation Board shall promptly make such designation and shall select an individual associated in interest with the carrier or representative he is to represent, who, with the member appointed by the carrier or representative requesting the establishment of the special board, shall constitute the board. Each member of the board shall be compensated by the party he is to represent. The members of the board so designated shall determine all matters not previously agreed uopn by the carrier and the representative of the employees with respect to the establishment and jurisdiction of the board. If they are unable to agree such matters shall be determined by a neutral member of the board selected or appointed and compensated in the same manner as is hereinafter provided with respect to situations where the members of the board are unable to agree upon an award. Such neutral member shall cease to be a member of the board when he has determined such matters. If with respect to any dispute or group of disputes the members of the board designated by the carrier and the representative are unable to agree upon an award disposing of the dispute or group of disputes they shall by mutual agreement select a neutral person to be a member of the board for the consideration and disposition of such dispute or group of disputes. In the event the members of the board designated by the parties are unable, within ten days after their failure to agree upon the award, to agree upon the selection of such neutral person, either member of the board may request the Mediation Board to appoint such neutral person and upon receipt of such request the Mediation Board shall promptly make such appointment. The neutral person so selected or appointed shall be compensated and reimbursed for expenses by the Mediation Board. Any two members of the board shall be competent to render an award. Such awards shall be final and binding upon both parties to the dispute and if in favor of the petitioner, shall direct the other party to comply therewith on or before the day named. Compliance with such awards shall be enforceable by proceedings in the United States district courts in the same manner and subject to the same provisions that apply to proceedings for enforcement of compliance with awards of the Adjustment Board.[8]

NATIONAL MEDIATION BOARD

SEC. 4. First. The Board of Mediation is hereby abolished, effective thirty days from the approval of this Act and the members, secretary, officers, assistants, employees, and agents thereof, in office upon the date of the approval of this Act, shall continue to function and receive their salaries for a period of thirty days from such date in the same manner as though this Act had not been passed. There is hereby established, as an independent agency in the executive branch of the Government, a board to be known as the "National Mediation Board," to be composed of three members appointed by the President, by and with the advice and consent of the Senate, not more than two of whom shall be of the same political party. Each member of the Mediation Board in office on January 1, 1965, shall be deemed to have been appointed for a term of office which shall expire on July 1 of the year his term would have otherwise expired. The terms of office of all successors shall expire three years after the expiration of the terms for which their predecessors were appointed; but any member appointed to fill a vacancy occurring prior to the expiration of the term for which his predecessor was appointed shall be appointed only for the unexpired term of his predecessor. Vacancies in the Board shall not impair the powers nor affect the duties of

---

[8](Public Law 456, 89th Cong.) (H.R. 706); (Approved June 20, 1966).

the Board nor of the remaining members of the Board. Two of the members in office shall constitute a quorum for the transaction of the business of the Board. Each member of the Board shall receive a salary at the rate of $10,000[9] per annum, together with necessary traveling and subsistence expenses, or per diem allowance in lieu thereof, subject to the provisions of law applicable thereto, while away from the principal office of the Board on business by this Act. No person in the employment of or who is pecuniarily or otherwise interested in any organization of employees or any carrier shall enter upon the duties of or continue to be a member of the Board. Upon the expiration of his term of office a member shall continue to serve until his successor is appointed and shall have qualified.[10]

All cases referred to the Board of Mediation and unsettled on the date of the approval of this Act shall be handled to conclusion by the Mediation Board.

A member of the Board may be removed by the President for inefficiency, neglect of duty, malfeasance in office or ineligibility, but for no other cause.

Second.   The Mediation Board shall annually designate a member to act as chairman. The Board shall maintain its principal office in the District of Columbia, but it may meet at any other place whenever it deems it necessary so to do. The Board may designate one or more of its members to exercise the functions of the Board in mediation proceedings. Each member of the Board shall have power to administer oaths and affirmations. The Board shall have a seal which shall be judically noticed. The Board shall make an annual report to Congress.

Third.   The Mediation Board may (1) appoint such experts and assistants to act in a confidential capacity and, subject to the provisions of the civil service laws, such other officers and employees as are essential to the effective transaction of the work of the Board; (2) in accordance with the Classification Act of 1923,[11] fix the salaries of such experts, assistants, officers, and employees; and (3) make such expenditures (including expenditures for rent and personal services at the seat of government and elsewhere, for law books, periodicals, and books of reference, and for printing and binding, and including expenditures for salaries and compensation, necessary traveling expenses and expenses actually incurred for subsistence, and other necessary expenses of the Mediation Board, Adjustment Board, Regional Adjustment Boards established under paragraph (x) of Section 3, and boards of arbitration, in accordance with the provisions of this section and Sections 3 and 7, respectively) as may be necessary for the execution of the functions vested

---

[9](Public Law 88—542, 88th Cong.)   (H.R. 8344); (Approved Aug. 31, 1964).
[10]The salary of the Chairman changed to $28,500 and of the members to $27,000 per annum by Public Law 426, 88th Cong. (H.R. 11049); (Approved Aug. 14, 1964).
[11]Superseded by "Classification Act of 1949" (Public Law 829, 81st Cong.)   (H.R. 5931); (Approved Oct. 28, 1949).

in the Board, in the Adjustment Board and in the boards of arbitration, and as may be provided for by the Congress from time to time. All expenditures of the Board shall be allowed and paid on the presentation of itemized vouchers therefor approved by the chairman.

Fourth. The Mediation Board is hereby authorized by its order to assign, or refer, any portion of its work, business, or functions arising under this or any other Act of Congress, or referred to it by Congress or either branch thereof, to an individual member of the Board or an employee or employees of the Board to be designated by such order for action thereon, and by its order at any time to amend, modify, supplement, or rescind any such assignment or reference. All such orders shall take effect forthwith and remain in effect until otherwise ordered by the Board. In conformity with and subject to the order or orders of the Mediation Board in the premises, any such individual member of the Board or employee designated shall have power and authority to act as to any of said work, business, or functions so assigned or referred to him for action by the Board.

Fifth. All officers and employees of the Board of Mediation (except the members thereof whose offices are hereby abolished) whose services in the judgment of the Mediation Board are necessary to the efficient operation of the Board are hereby transferred to the Board, without change in classification or compensation; except that the Board may provide for the adjustment of such classification or compensation to conform to the duties to which such officers and employees may be assigned.

All unexpended appropriations for the operation of the Board of Mediation that are available at the time of the abolition of the Board of Mediation shall be transferred to the Mediation Board and shall be available for its use for salaries and other authorized expenditures.

FUNCTIONS OF MEDIATION BOARD

SEC. 5. First. The parties, or either party, to a dispute between an employee or group of employees and a carrier may invoke the services of the Mediation Board in any of the following cases:

(a) A dispute concerning changes in rates of pay, rules, or working conditions not adjusted by the parties in conference.

(b) Any other dispute not referable to the National Railroad Adjustment Board and not adjusted in conference between the parties or where conferences are refused.

The Mediation Board may proffer its services in case any labor emergency is found by it to exist at any time.

In either event the said Board shall promptly put itself in communication with the parties to such controversy, and shall use its best efforts, by mediation, to bring them to agreement. If such efforts to bring about an amicable settlement through mediation shall be unsuccessful, the said Board shall at once endeavor as its final required action (except as provided in paragraph third of this section and in Section 10 of this Act) to induce the parties to submit their controversy to arbitration, in accordance with the provisions of this Act.

If arbitration at the request of the Board shall be refused by one or both parties, the Board shall at once notify both parties in writing that its mediatory efforts have failed and for thirty days thereafter, unless in the intervening period the parties agree to arbitration, or an emergency board shall be created under Section 10 of this Act, no change shall be made in the rates of pay, rules, or working conditions or established practices in effect prior to the time the dispute arose.

Second. In any case in which a controversy arises over the meaning or the application of any agreement reached through mediation under the provisions of this Act, either party to the said agreement, or both, may apply to the Mediation Board for an interpretation of the meaning or application of such agreement. The said Board shall upon receipt of such request notify the parties to the controversy, and after a hearing of both sides give its interpretation within thirty days.

Third. The Mediation Board shall have the following duties with respect to the arbitration of disputes under Section 7 of this Act:

(a) On failure of the arbitrators named by the parties to agree on the remaining arbitrator or arbitrators within the time set by Section 7 of this Act, it shall be the duty of the Mediation Board to name such remaining arbitrator or arbitrators. It shall be the duty of the Board in naming such arbitrator or arbitrators to appoint only those whom the Board shall deem wholly disinterested in the controversy to be arbitrated and impartial and without bias as between the parties to such arbitration. Should, however, the Board name an arbitrator or arbitrators not so disinterested and impartial, then, upon proper investigation and presentation of the facts, the Board shall promptly remove such arbitrator.

If an arbitrator named by the Mediation Board, in accordance with the provisions of this Act, shall be removed by such Board as provided by this Act, or if such an arbitrator refuses or is unable to serve, it shall be the duty of the Mediation Board promptly to select another arbitrator in the same manner as provided in this Act for an original appointment by the Mediation Board.

(b) Any member of the Mediation Board is authorized to take the acknowledgment of an agreement to arbitrate under this Act. When so acknowledged, or when acknowledged by the parties before a notary public or the clerk of a district court or a circuit court of appeals of the United States, such agreement to arbitrate shall be delivered to a member of said Board or transmitted to said Board to be filed in its office.

(c) When an agreement to arbitrate has been filed with the Mediation

Board, or with one of its members as provided by this section, and when the said Board has been furnished the names of the arbitrators chosen by the parties to the controversy, it shall be the duty of the Board to cause a notice in writing to be served upon said arbitrators, notifying them of their appointment, requesting them to meet promptly to name the remaining arbitrator or arbitrators necessary to complete the board of arbitration, and advising them of the period within which, as provided by the agreement to arbitrate, they are empowered to name such arbitrator or arbitrators.

(d) Either party to an arbitration desiring the reconvening of a board of arbitration to pass upon any controversy arising over the meaning or application of an award may so notify the Mediation Board in writing, stating in such notice the question or questions to be submitted to such reconvened board. The Mediation Board shall thereupon promptly communicate with the members of the board of arbitration, or a subcommittee of such board appointed for such purpose pursuant to a provision in the agreement to arbitrate, and arrange for the reconvening of said board of arbitration or subcommittee, and shall notify the respective parties to the controversy of the time and place at which the board, or the subcommittee, will meet for hearings upon the matters in controversy to be submitted to it. No evidence other than that contained in the record filed with the original award shall be received or considered by such reconvened board or subcommittee, except such evidence as may be necessary to illustrate the interpretations suggested by the parties. If any member of the original board is unable or unwilling to serve on such reconvened board or subcommittee thereof, another arbitrator shall be named in the same manner and with the same powers and duties as such original arbitrator.

(e) Within sixty days after the approval of this Act every carrier shall file with the Mediation Board a copy of each contract with its employees in effect on the 1st day of April 1934, covering rates of pay, rules, and working conditions. If no contract with any craft or class of its employees has been entered into, the carrier shall file with the Mediation Board a statement of that fact including also a statement of the rates of pay, rules, and working conditions applicable in dealing with such craft or class. When any new contract is executed or change is made in an existing contract with any class or craft of its employees covering rates of pay, rules, or working conditions, or in those rates of pay, rules, and working conditions of employees not covered by contract, the carrier shall file the same with the Mediation Board within thirty days after such new contract or change in existing contract has been executed or rates of pay, rules, and working conditions have been made effective.

(f) The Mediation Board shall be the custodian of all papers and documents heretofore filed with or transferred to the Board of Mediation bearing upon the settlement, adjustment, or determination of disputes between carriers and their employees or upon mediation or arbitration proceedings held under or pursuant to the provisions of any Act of Congress in respect thereto; and the President is authorized to designate a custodian of the records and property of the Board of Mediation until the transfer and delivery of such records to the Mediation Board and to require the transfer and delivery to the Mediation Board of any and all such papers and documents filed with it or in its possession.

SEC. 6. Carriers and representatives of the employees shall give at least thirty days' written notice of an intended change in agreements affecting rates of pay, rules, or working conditions, and the time and place for the beginning of conference between the representatives of the parties interested in such intended changes shall be agreed upon within ten days after the receipt of said notice, and said time shall be within the thirty days provided in the notice. In every case where such notice of intended change has been given, or conferences are being held with reference thereto, or the services of the Mediation Board has been requested by either party, or said Board has proffered its services, rates of pay, rules, or working conditions shall not be altered by the carrier until the controversy has been finally acted upon as required by Section 5 of this Act, by the Mediation Board, unless a period of ten days has elapsed after termination of conferences without request for or proffer of the services of the Mediation Board.

ARBITRATION

SEC. 7. First. Whenever a controversy shall arise between a carrier or carriers and its or their employees which is not settled either in conference between representatives of the parties or by the appropriate adjustment board or through mediation, in the manner provided in the preceding sections, such controversy may, by agreement of the parties to such controversy, be submitted to the arbitration of a board of three (or, if the parties to the controversy so stipulate, of six) persons: *Provided, however,* That the failure or refusal of either party to submit a controversy to arbitration shall not be construed as a violation of any legal obligation imposed upon such party by the terms of this Act or otherwise.

Second. Such board of arbitration shall be chosen in the following manner:

(a) In the case of a board of three, the carrier or carriers and the representatives of the employees, parties respectively to the agreement to arbitrate, shall each name one arbitrator; the two arbitrators thus chosen shall select a third arbitrator. If the arbitrators chosen by the parties shall fail to name the third arbitrator within five days after their first meeting, such third arbitrator shall be named by the Mediation Board.

(b) In the case of a board of six, the carrier or carriers and the representatives of the employees, parties respectively to the agreement to arbitrate, shall each name two arbitrators; the four arbitrators thus chosen shall, by a majority vote, select the remaining two arbitrators. If the arbitrators chosen by the parties shall fail to name the two arbitrators within fifteen days after their first meeting, the said two arbitrators, or as many of them as have been named, shall be named by the Mediation Board.

Third. (a) When the arbitrators selected by the respective parties have agreed upon the remaining arbitrator or arbitrators, they shall notify the Mediation Board, and, in the event of their failure to agree upon any or upon all of the necessary arbitrators within the period fixed by this Act, they shall, at the expiration of such period, notify the Mediation Board of the arbitrators selected, if any, or of their failure to make or to complete such selection.

(b) The board of arbitration shall organize and select its own chairman and make all necessary rules for conducting its hearings: *Provided, however,* That the board of arbitration shall be bound to give the parties to the controversy a full and fair hearing, which shall include an opportunity to present evidence in support of their claims, and an opportunity to present their case in person, by counsel, or by other representatives as they may respectively elect.

(c) Upon notice from the Mediation Board that the parties, or either party, to an arbitration desire the reconvening of the board of arbitration (or a subcommittee of such board of arbitration appointed for such purpose pursuant to the agreement to arbitrate) to pass upon any controversy over the meaning or application of their award, the board, or its subcommittee, shall at once reconvene. No question other than, or in addition to, the questions relating to the meaning or application of the award, submitted by the party or parties in writing, shall be considered by the reconvened board of arbitration or its subcommittee.

Such rulings shall be acknowledged by such board or subcommittee thereof in the same manner, and filed in the same district court clerk's office, as the original award and become a part thereof.

(d) No arbitrator, except those chosen by the Mediation Board, shall be incompetent to act as an arbitrator because of his interest in the controversy to be arbitrated, or because of his connection with or partiality to either of the parties to the arbitration.

(e) Each member of any board of arbitration created under the provisions of this Act named by either party to the arbitration shall be compensated by the party naming him. Each arbitrator selected by the arbitrators or named by the Mediation Board shall receive from the Mediation Board such compensation as the Mediation Board may fix, together with his necessary traveling expenses and expenses actually incurred for subsistence, while serving as an arbitrator.

(f) The board of arbitration shall furnish a certified copy of its award to the respective parties to the controversy, and shall transmit the original, together with the papers and proceedings and a transcript of the evidence taken at the hearings, certified under the hands of at least a majority of the arbitrators, to the clerk of the district court of tthe United States for the district wherein the controversy arose or the arbitration is entered into, to be filed in said clerk's office as hereinafter provided. The said board shall also furnish a certified copy of its award, and the papers and proceedings, including testimony relating thereto, to the Mediation Board, to be filed in its office; and, in addition a certified copy of its award shall be filed in the office of the Interstate Commerce Commission: *Provided, however,* That such award shall not be construed to diminish or extinguish any of the powers or duties of the Interstate Commerce Commission, under the Interstate Commerce Act, as amended.

(g) A board of arbitration may, subject to the approval of the Mediation Board, employ and fix the compensation of such assistants as it deems necessary on the arbitration proceedings. The compensation of such employees, together with their necessary traveling expenses and expenses actually incurred for subsistence, while so employed, and the necessary expenses of boards of arbitration, shall be paid by the Mediation Board.

Whenever practicable, the board shall be supplied with suitable quarters in any Federal building located at its place of meeting or at any place where the board may conduct its proceedings or deliberations.

(h) All testimony before said board shall be given under oath or affirmation, and any member of the board shall have the power to administer oaths or affirmations. The board of arbitration, or any member thereof, shall have the power to require the attendance of witnesses and the production of such books, papers, contracts, agreements, and documents as may be deemed by the board of arbitration material to a just determination of the matters submitted to its arbitration, and may for that purpose request the clerk of the district court of the United States for the district wherein said arbitration is being conducted to issue the necessary subpoenas, and upon such request the said clerk or his duly authorized deputy shall be, and he hereby is, authorized, and it shall be his duty, to issue such subpoenas. In the event of the failure of any person to comply with such subpoena, or in the event of the contumacy of any witness appearing before the board of arbitration, the board may invoke the aid of the United States courts to compel witnesses to attend and testify and to produce such books, papers, contracts, agreements, and documents to the same extent and under the same conditions and penalties as provided for in the Act to regulate commerce approved February 4, 1887, and the amendments thereto.

Any witness appearing before a board of arbitration shall receive the same fees and mileage as witnesses in courts of the United States, and be paid by the party securing the subpoena.

SEC. 8.[12] The agreement to arbitrate—

(a) Shall be in writing;

(b) Shall stipulate that the arbitration is had under the provisions of this Act;

(c) Shall state whether the board of arbitration is to consist of three or of six members;

(d) Shall be signed by the duly accredited representatives of the carrier or carriers and the employees, parties respectively to the agreement to arbitrate, and shall be acknowledged by said parties before a notary public, the clerk of a district court or circuit court of appeals of the United States, or before a member of the Mediation Board, and, when so acknowledged, shall be filed in the office of the Mediation Board;

(e) Shall state specifically the questions to be submitted to the said board for decision; and that, in its award or awards, the said board shall confine itself strictly to decisions as to the questions so specifically submitted to it;

(f) Shall provide that the questions, or any one or more of them, submitted by the parties to the board of arbitration may be withdrawn from arbitration on notice to that effect signed by the duly accredited representatives of all the parties and served on the board of arbitration;

(g) Shall stipulate that the signatures of a majority of said board of arbitration affixed to their award shall be competent to constitute a valid and binding award;

(h) Shall fix a period from the date of the appointment of the arbitrator or arbitrators necessary to complete the board (as provided for in the agreement) within which the said board shall commence its hearings;

(i) Shall fix a period from the beginning of the hearings within which the said board shall make and file its award: *Provided,* That the parties may agree at any time upon an extension of this period;

(j) Shall provide for the date from which the award shall become effective and shall fix the period during which the award shall continue in force;

(k) Shall provide that the award of the board of arbitration and the evidence of the proceedings before the board relating thereto, when certified under the hands of at least a majority of the arbitrators, shall be filed in the clerk's office of the district court of the United States for the district wherein the controversy arose or the arbitration was entered into, which district shall be designated in the agreement; and, when so filed, such award and proceedings shall constitute the full and complete record of the arbitration;

(l) Shall provide that the award, when so filed, shall be final and conclusive upon the parties as to the facts determined by said award and as to the merits of the controversy decided;

(m) Shall provide that any differences arising as to the meaning, or the

---

[12]Section 8 as contained in Railway Labor Act; (Approved May 20, 1926).

application of the provisions, of an award made by a board of arbitration shall be referred back for a ruling to the same board, or, by agreement, to a subcommittee of such board; and that such ruling when acknowledged in the same manner, and filed in the same district court clerk's office, as the original award, shall be a part of and shall have the same force and effect as such original award; and

(n) Shall provide that the respective parties to the award will each faithfully execute the same.

The said agreement to arbitrate, when properly signed and acknowledged as herein provided, shall not be revoked by a party to such agreement: *Provided, however,* That such agreement to arbitrate may at any time be revoked and canceled by the written agreement of both parties, signed by their duly accredited representatives, and (if no board of arbitration has yet been constituted under the agreement) delivered to the Mediation Board or any member thereof; or, if the board of arbitration has been constituted as provided by this Act, delivered to such board of arbitration.

SEC. 8.[13] If any section, subsection, sentence, clause, or phrase of this Act is for any reason held to be unconstitutional, such decision shall not affect the validity of the remaining portions of this Act. All Acts or parts of Acts inconsistent with the provisions of this Act are hereby repealed.

SEC. 9. First.   The award of a board of arbitration, having been acknowledged as herein provided, shall be filed in the clerk's office of the district court designated in the agreement to arbitrate.

Second. An award acknowledged and filed as herein provided shall be conclusive on the parties as to the merits and facts of the controversy submitted to arbitration, and unless, within ten days after the filing of the award, a petition to impeach the award, on the grounds hereinafter set forth, shall be filed in the clerk's office of the court in which the award has been filed, the court shall enter judgment on the award, which judgment shall be final and conclusive on the parties.

Third. Such petition for the impeachment or contesting of any award so filed shall be entertained by the court only on one or more of the following grounds:

(a) That the award plainly does not conform to the substantive requirements laid down by this Act for such awards, or that the proceedings were not substantially in conformity with this Act;

(b) That the award does not conform, nor confine itself, to the stipulations of the agreement to arbitrate; or

(c) That a member of the board of arbitration rendering the award was guilty of fraud or corruption; or that a party to the arbitration practiced

---

[13]Section 8 as contained in Public Law 442, 73rd Cong. (H.R. 9861, amendment to Railway Labor Act (Approved June 21, 1934).)

fraud or corruption which fraud or corruption affected the result of the arbitration: *Provided, however,* That no court shall entertain any such petition on the ground that an award is invalid for uncertainty; in such case the proper remedy shall be a submission of such award to a reconvened board, or subcommittee thereof, for interpretation, as provided by this Act: *Provided, further,* That an award contested as herein provided shall be construed liberally by the court, with a view to favoring its validity, and that no award shall be set aside for trivial irregularity or clerical error, going only to form and not to substance.

Fourth. If the court shall determine that a part of the award is invalid on some ground or grounds designated in this section as a ground of invalidity, but shall determine that a part of the award is valid, the court shall set aside the entire award: *Provided, however,* That, if the parties shall agree thereto, and if such valid and invalid parts are separable, the court shall set aside the invalid part, and order judgment to stand as to the valid part.

Fifth. At the expiration of ten days from the decision of the district court upon the petition filed as aforesaid, final judgment shall be entered in accordance with said decision, unless during said ten days either party shall appeal therefrom to the circuit court of appeals. In such case only such portion of the record shall be transmitted to the appellate court as is necessary to the proper understanding and consideration of the questions of law presented by said petition and to be decided.

Sixth. The determination of said circuit court of appeals upon said questions shall be final, and, being certified by the clerk thereof to said district court, judgment pursuant thereto shall thereupon be entered by said district court.

Seventh. If the petitioner's contentions are finally sustained, judgment shall be entered setting aside the award in whole or, if the parties so agree, in part; but in such case the parties may agree upon a judgment to be entered disposing of the subject matter of the controversy, which judgment when entered shall have the same force and effect as judgment entered upon an award.

Eighth. Nothing in this Act shall be construed to require an individual employee to render labor or service without his consent, nor shall anything in this Act be construed to make the quitting of his labor or service by an individual employee an illegal act; nor shall any court issue any process to compel the performance by an individual employee of such labor or service, without his consent.

EMERGENCY BOARD

SEC. 10. If a dispute between a carrier and its employees be not adjusted under the foregoing provisions of this Act and should, in the judgment of the Mediation Board, threaten substantially to interrupt interstate commerce to a degree such as to deprive any section of the country of essential transportation service, the Mediation Board shall notify the President, who may thereupon, in his discretion, create a board to investigate and report respecting such dispute. Such board shall be composed of such number of persons as to the President may seem desirable: *Provided, however,* That no member appointed shall be pecuniarily or otherwise interested in any organization of employees or any carrier. The compensation of the members of any such board shall be fixed by the President. Such board shall be created separately in each instance and it shall investigate promptly the facts as to the dispute and make a report thereon to the President within thirty days from the date of its creation.

There is hereby authorized to be appropriated such sums as may be necessary for the expenses of such board, including the compensation and the necessary traveling expenses and expenses actually incurred for subsistence, of the members of the board. All expenditures of the board shall be allowed and paid on the presentation of itemized vouchers therefor approved by the chairman.

After the creation of such board and for thirty days after such board has made its report to the President, no change, except by agreement, shall be made by the parties to the controversy in the conditions out of which the dispute arose.

GENERAL PROVISIONS

SEC. 11. If any provision of this Act, or the application thereof to any person or circumstances, is held invalid, the remainder of the Act, and the application of such provision to other persons or circumstances, shall not be affected thereby.

SEC. 12. There is hereby authorized to be appropriated such sums as may be necessary for expenditure by the Mediation Board in carrying out the provisions of this Act.

SEC. 13. (a) Paragraph "Second" of subdivision (b) of Section 128 of the Judicial Code, as amended, is amended to read as follows: "Second. To review decisions of the district courts, under Section 9 of the Railway Labor Act."

(b) Section 2 of the Act entitled "An Act to amend the Judicial Code, and to further define the jurisdiction of the circuit court of appeals and of the Supreme Court, and for other purposes," approved February 13, 1925, is amended to read as follows:

SEC. 2. "That cases in a circuit court of appeals under Section 9 of the Railway Labor Act; under Section 5 of 'An Act to create a Federal Trade Commission; to define its powers and duties, and for other purposes,' approved September 26, 1914; and under Section 11 of 'An Act to supplement existing laws against unlawful restraints and monopolies, and for other purposes,' approved October 15, 1914, are included among the cases to which Sections 239 and 240 of the Judicial Code shall apply."

SEC. 14. Title III of the Transportation Act, 1920, and the Act approved July 15, 1913, providing for mediation, conciliation, and arbitration, and all Acts and parts of Acts in conflict with the provisions of this Act are hereby repealed, except that the members, secretary, officers, employees, and agents of the Railroad Labor Board, in office upon the date of the passage of this Act, shall receive their salaries for a period of 30 days from such date, in the same manner as though this Act had not been passed.

TITLE II[14]

SEC. 201. All of the provisions of Title I of this Act, except the provisions of Section 3 thereof, are extended to and shall cover every common carrier by air engaged in interstate or foreign commerce, and every carrier by air transporting mail for or under contract with the United States Government, and every air pilot or other person who performs any work as an employee or subordinate official of such carrier or carriers, subject to its or their continuing authority to supervise and direct the manner of rendition of his service.

SEC. 202. The duties, requirements, penalties, benefits, and privileges prescribed and established by the provisions of Title I of this Act, except Section 3 thereof, shall apply to said carriers by air and their employees in the same manner and to the same extent as though such carriers and their employees were specifically included within the definition of "carrier" and "employee," respectively, in Section 1 thereof.

SEC. 203. The parties or either party to a dispute between an employee or a group of employees and a carrier or carriers by air may invoke the services of the National Mediation Board and the jurisdiction of said Mediation Board is extended to any of the following cases:

(a) A dispute concerning changes in rates of pay, rules, or working conditions not adjusted by the parties in conference.

(b) Any other dispute not referable to an adjustment board, as hereinafter provided, and not adjusted in conference between the parties, or where conferences are refused.

The National Mediation Board may proffer its services in case any labor emergency is found by it to exist at any time.

The services of the Mediation Board may be invoked in a case under this title in the same manner and to the same extent as are the disputes covered by Section 5 of Title I of this Act.

SEC. 204. The disputes between an employee or group of employees and

---

[14](Public Law 487, 74th Cong.) (S. 2496); An Act to amend the Railway Labor Act (Approved Apr. 10, 1936).

a carrier or carriers by air growing out of grievances, or out of the interpretation or application of agreements concerning rates of pay, rules, or working conditions, including cases pending and unadjusted on the date of approval of this Act before the National Labor Relations Board, shall be handled in the usual manner up to and including the chief operating officer of the carrier designated to handle such disputes; but, failing to reach an adjustment in this manner, the disputes may be referred by petition of the parties or by either party to an appropriate adjustment board, as hereinafter provided, with a full statement of the facts and supporting data bearing upon the disputes.

It shall be the duty of every carrier and of its employees, acting through their representatives, selected in accordance with the provisions of this title, to establish a board of adjustment of jurisdiction not exceeding the jurisdiction which may be lawfully exercised by system, group, or regional boards of adjustment, under the authority of Section 3, Title I, of this Act.

Such boards of adjustment may be established by agreement between employees and carriers either on any individual carrier, or system, or group of carriers by air and any class or classes of its or their employees; or pending the establishment of a permanent National Board of Adjustment as hereinafter provided. Nothing in this Act shall prevent said carriers by air, or any class or classes of their employees, both acting through their representatives selected in accordance with provisions of this title, from mutually agreeing to the establishment of a National Board of Adjustment of temporary duration and of similarly limited jurisdiction.

SEC. 205. When, in the judgment of the National Mediation Board, it shall be necessary to have a permanent national board of adjustment in order to provide for the prompt and orderly settlement of disputes between said carriers by air, or any of them, and its or their employees, growing out of grievances or out of the interpretation or application of agreements between said carriers by air or any of them, and any class or classes of its or their employees, covering rates of pay, rules, or working conditions, the National Mediation Board is hereby empowered and directed, by its order duly made, published, and served, to direct the said carriers by air and such labor organizations of their employees, national in scope, as have been or may be recognized in accordance with the provisions of this Act, to select and designate four representatives who shall constitute a board which shall be known as the National Air Transport Adjustment Board. Two members of said National Air Transport Adjustment Board shall be selected by said carriers by air and two members by the said labor organizations of the employees, within thirty days after the date of the order of the National Mediation Board, in the manner and by the procedure prescribed by Title I of this Act for the selection and designation of members of the National Railroad Adjustment Board. The National Air Transport Adjustment Board shall meet within forty days after the date of the order of the National Mediation Board directing the selection and designation of its members and shall organize and adopt rules for conducting its proceedings, in the manner prescribed in Section 3 of Title I of this Act. Vacancies in membership or office shall be filled, members shall be appointed in case of failure of the carriers or of labor organizations of the employees to select and designate representatives, members of the National Air Transport Adjustment Board shall be compensated, hearings shall be held, findings and awards made, stated, served, and enforced, and the number and compensation of any necessary assistants shall be determined and the compensation of such employees shall be paid, all in the same manner and to the same extent as provided with reference to the National Railroad Adjustment Board by Section 3 of Title 1 of this Act. The powers and duties prescribed and established by the provisions of Section 3 of Title I of this Act with reference to the National Railroad Adjustment Board and the several divisions thereof are hereby conferred upon and shall be exercised and performed in like manner and to the same extent by the said National Air Transport Adjustment Board, not exceeding, however, the jurisdiction conferred upon said National Air Transport Adjustment Board by the provisions of this title. From and after the organization of the National Air Transport Adjustment Board, if any system, group, or regional board of adjustment established by any carrier or carriers by air and any class or classes of its or their employees is not satisfactory to either party thereto, the said party, under ninety days' notice to the other party, may elect to come under the jurisdiction of the National Air Transport Adjustment Board.

SEC. 206. All cases referred to the National Labor Relations Board, or over which the National Labor Relations Board shall have taken jurisdiction, involving any dispute arising from any cause between any common carrier by air engaged in interstate or foreign commerce or any carrier by air transporting mail for or under contract with the United States Government, and employees of such carrier or carriers, and unsettled on the date of approval of this Act, shall be handled to conclusion by the Mediation Board. The books, records, and papers of the National Labor Relations Board and of the National Labor Board pertinent to such case or cases, whether settled or unsettled, shall be transferred to the custody of the National Mediation Board.

SEC. 207. If any provision of this title or application thereof to any person or circumstances is held invalid, the remainder of the Act and the application of such provision to other persons or circumstances shall not be affected thereby.

SEC. 208. There is hereby authorized to be appropriated such sums as may be necessary for expenditure by the Mediation Board in carrying out the provisions of this Act.

Approved, April 10, 1936.

THE ORIGINS

Report of the House Committee on Interstate
and Foreign Commerce, February 19, 1926

JOHN COOPER [R., OHIO] submitted the Report.

The Committee on Interstate and Foreign Commerce, to whom was referred the bill (H. R. 9463) to provide for the prompt disposition of disputes between carriers and their employees, and for other purposes, having considered the same, report thereon with a recommendation that it pass.

The bill was introduced as the product of negotiations and conferences between a representative committee of railroad presidents and a representative committee of railroad labor organization executives, extending over several months, which were concluded with the approval of the bill, respectively, by the Association of Railway Executives and by the executives of 20 railroad labor organizations. As introduced, it represented the agreement of railway managements operating over 80 per cent of the railroad mileage and labor organizations representing an overwhelmingly majority of the railroad employees.

During the hearings conducted by the committee it was conceded by all concerned that the enactment of this agreement into law would impose upon the parties to the agreement the moral obligation to settle their differences in the manner provided by law, so as to insure to the public continuity and efficiency of interstate transportation service, and to protect the public from the injuries and losses consequent upon any impairment or interruption of interstate commerce through failures of managers and employees to settle peaceably their controversies. There are also legal obligations which would be accepted by and imposed upon the parties by the proposed law that afford further guaranties of improved and continuous transportation service and protection of the public interest therein.

The principal point impressed upon the committee during the hearings was the desirability of giving the managers and employees of this most important national industry the aid and cooperation of the legislative, executive, and judicial power of the Government in the settlement of industrial controversies by the means which practical men, who have devoted their lives to this industry, believe are best adapted to maintain satisfactory relations between employers and employees.

The need for an impetus given to the proposed legislation are clearly indicated in the following extracts from the Republican and Democratic platforms in the national election of 1924 and from the three messages of the President to Congress in December of 1923, 1924, and 1925.

The Republican platform of 1924:

The labor board provision of the present law should be amended whenever it appears necessary to meet changed conditions. Collective bargaining, mediation, and voluntary arbitration are the most important steps in the maintaining peaceful labor relations and should be encouraged. We do not believe in compulsory action at any time in the settlement of disputes. Public opinion must be the final arbiter in any crisis which so vitally affects public welfare as the suspension of transportation. Therefore the interests of the public require the maintenance of an impartial tribunal which can in an emergency make an investigation of the facts and publish its conclusion. This is essential as the basis for popular judgment.

The Democratic platform of 1924:

The labor provisions of the act (transportation act, 1920) have proven unsatisfactory in settling differences between employer and employee. . . . It must therefore be so rewritten so that the high purposes which the public welfare demands may be accomplished.

The President's message, December 6, 1923:

The settlement of railroad labor disputes is a matter of grave public concern. The labor board is not altogether satisfactory to the public, the employees, or the companies. If a substantial agreement can be reached among the groups interested there should be no hesitation in enacting such an agreement into law.

The President's message, December 3, 1924:

Another matter before the Congress is legislation affecting the labor sections of the transportation act. Much criticism has been directed at the workings of this section and experience has shown that some useful amendment could be made to these provisions.

It would be helpful if a plan could be adopted which, while retaining the practice of systematic collective bargaining with conciliation and voluntary arbitration of labor differences, could also provide simplicity in relations and more direct local responsibility of employees and managers. But such legislation will not meet the requirements of the situation unless it recognizes the principle that the public has a right to the uninterrupted service of transportation, and therefore a right to be heard when there is danger that the nation may suffer a great injury through the interruption of operations because of labor disputes. If these elements are not comprehended in proposed legislation, it would be better to gain further experience with the present organization dealing with these questions before undertaking a change.

The President's message, December 5, 1925:

I am informed that the railroad managers and their employees have reached a substantial agreement as to what legislation is necessary to regulate and improve their relationship. Whenever they bring forward such proposals, which seem sufficient also to protect the interests of the public, they should be enacted into law.

It is gratifying to report that both the railroad managers and railroad employees are providing boards for the mutual adjustment of differences in harmony with the principles of conferences, conciliation, and arbitration. The solution of these problems ought to be an example to all other industries. Those who ask the protection of civilization should be ready to use the methods of civilization. . . .

The manifest inclination of the managers and employees of the railroads to adopt a policy of action in harmony with these principles mark a new epoch in our industrial life.

On January 7, 1926, representatives of the carriers and the employees informally reported to the President that they had agreed upon the draft of legislation embodying a substitute for Title III of the transportation act, 1920. And on January 8, identical bills expressing this agreement of the parties were introduced in the House and Senate, respectively, by the chairman of the Committee on Interstate and Foreign Commerce of the House and the chairman of the Committee on Interstate Commerce of the Senate.

The committee has held extended hearings giving ample opportunity to the proponents and opponents of the bill to present their views. In addition to the representatives of the carriers and their employees, the chairman of the executive council of the National Civic Federation presented testimony in support of the bill. The American Short Line Railroad Association offered a statement to the effect that the short-line railroads did not oppose the enactment of the proposed law.

Representatives of various associations of manufacturers presented suggestions for a few amendments which were given careful consideration. The bill provides in brief as follows:

1. It is made the duty of all railroad managers and employees to exert every reasonable effort to make and maintain agreements.

2. All disputes shall be considered first in conference between representatives designated and authorized so to confer respectively by the carriers and by the employees thereof interested in the dispute.

3. Representatives shall be designated in such manner as the parties themselves shall determine "without interference, influence, or coercion exercised by either party over the self-organization or designation of representatives by the other."

4. Disputes between employers and employees are divided into three classes:

   a. Disputes over grievances or the interpretation or application of agreements.

   b. Disputes over proposed changes in agreements concerning rates of pay, rules of working conditions.

   c. All other disputes.

5. All disputes must be considered first in conference, but if not settled in conference disputes in class *b* and *c* are considered directly by the Government board of mediation. Disputes in class *a* if not settled in conference must be referred to an adjustment board and are only considered by the

board of mediation if not decided by the adjustment board.

6. Boards of adjustment must be created by agreement, which may be between an individual carrier and its employees or between a group of carriers and employees or between all the carriers and their employees.

7. The bill provides for a machinery of contract and adjustment between the parties, but also leaves them free to set up "such machinery of contract and adjustment as they may mutually establish." If, however, they are unable to settle their differences either under the machinery provided in the bill or an alternative machinery agreed upon, the bill provides that either party may invoke the aid of the board of mediation—a public body—or the board of mediation may intervene of its own motion, in order to promote the public interest in the settlement of disputes.

8. A board of mediation is created, composed of five members appointed by the President by and with the advice and consent of the Senate, with the duty to intervene at the request of either party or on its own motion in any unsettled dispute, whether it be a (class *a*) dispute not decided in conference or by the appropriate adjustment board, or a dispute over changes in rates of pay, rules or working conditions (class *b*) or any other dispute (class *c*) not settled in conference.

9. If the board of mediation is unable to bring about a settlement, it is required to seek to induce the parties to submit the controversy to arbitration.

10. Boards of arbitration are provided for when the parties consent to arbitrate. The provisions of an arbitration agreement, the methods of selecting arbitrators, and the arbitration procedure are written in detail in the text of the bill. The bill provides that an arbitration award shall be made the judgment of the court, which judgment shall be final and conclusive on the parties.

11. In the event that a dispute is not settled under the foregoing provisions of the bill, it is provided that the board of mediation, if in its judgment the dispute threatens substantially to interrupt interstate commerce, shall notify the President, who is thereupon authorized, in his discretion, to create a board to investigate and report to the President within 30 days from the date of its creation. It is also provided that after the creation of such a board and for 30 days after it has made its report to the President, no change except by agreement shall be made by the parties to the controversy in the conditions out of which the dispute arose.

The proponents of this bill have assured the committee of their conviction that the methods for voluntary settlement of disputes with the aid of Government mediators are so well adapted to insure the adjustment of differences, either through conference, mediation, or arbitration, that it should be seldom, if ever necessary for the President to exercise the power conferred upon him to appoint an emergency board. The records of the success of mediation and arbitration under the Erdman and Newlands Acts considerably justify this conviction, which is also supported by the obvious good faith, the spirit of fair play, and of genuine regard for the public interest which characterized the negotiations of the parties and their presentations before the committee.

If, however, the full expectations of the proponents of the bill are not realized, and controversy threatens the interruption of interstate commerce, there is assurance of the protection of the public interest in this bill greater than has ever been offered in previous legislation. The President is empowered to create a board of outstanding representatives of the public who can investigate, with the aid of the permanent board of mediation, the Interstate Commerce Commission, the Department of Labor, and all other agencies of government, and bring to bear upon the parties the pressure of the highest governmental authority either to adjust their differences by voluntary agreement or to consent to submit them to arbitration. If this pressure shall fail to in itself bring about a setlement, this Emergency Board will then be able in its report to give to the public adequate and intelligible information regarding the merits of the contentions of the parties, and to crystallize public opinion in support of that party or that program which should be supported in the public interest.

The temporary emergency board will be able to express and to mobilize public opinion to an extent impossible to any permanent board or any agency of Government which has been heretofore created for that purpose. It is also highly important to point out that during the period of investigation and for 30 days thereafter the parties to the controversy are bound under the proposed law to maintain unchanged the conditions out of which the dispute arose, thereby assuring the parties and the public that the emergency board will have the full and unembarrassed opportunity to exert its authority and fulfill its important function.

This bill is recommended for passage as both the most practical and advanced legislation for the settlement of industrial controversies that has been presented for the consideration of Congress.

Report of the Senate Committee on Interstate Commerce, April 16, 1926

JAMES WATSON [R., IND.] submitted the Report.

The Committee on Interstate Commerce, to whom was referred the bill (H. R. 9463) to provide for the prompt disposition of disputes between carriers and their employees, and for other purposes, after holding hearings and giving consideration to the bill, recommends that it do pass without amendment.

The bill is almost identical with Senate bill 2306, heretofore favorably reported to the Senate from this committee on February 26, 1926.

Briefly stated, the bill provides—

1. That it shall be the duty of the parties to exert every reasonable effort to make and maintain agreements.

2. That any and all disputes shall first be considered in conference between the parties directly interested.

3. That adjustment boards shall be established by agreement, which shall be either between an individual carrier and its employees, or regional or national, such adjustment boards to have jurisdiction over disputes relating to grievances or to the interpretation or application of existing agreements but having no jurisdiction over changes in rates of pay, rules, or working conditions. It is, however, provided that nothing in the act shall be construed to prohibit an individual carrier and its employees from agreeing upon a settlement of disputes through such machinery of contract and adjustment as they may mutually establish.

4. A board of mediation is created, to consist of five members appointed by the President, by and with the advice and consent of the Senate, none of whom shall be in the employment of or pecuniarily or otherwise interested in any organization of employees or any carrier. The duty is imposed upon this board of mediation to intervene, at the request of either party or on its own motion, in any unsettled labor dispute, whether it be a grievance, or a difference as to the interpretation or application of agreements not decided in conference, or by the appropriate adjustment board, or a dispute over changes in rates of pay, rules, or working conditions not adjusted in conference between the parties. If it is unable to bring about an amicable adjustment between the parties, it is required to make an effort to induce them to consent to arbitration.

5. Boards of arbitration are provided for, when both parties consent to arbitration. The method of selecting members of the boards and the arbitration procedure are also set out. It is provided that the award of the arbitrators shall be binding upon the parties and shall be filed in the appropriate district court of the United States and become a judgment of the court, which judgment shall be binding upon the parties.

6. In the possible event that a dispute between a carrier and its employees is not settled under any of the foregoing methods, provision is made that the board of mediation, if in its judgment the dispute threatens to substantially interrupt interstate commerce, shall notify the President, who is thereupon authorized, in his discretion, to create a board, known as an emergency board, to investigate and report to him within 30 days from the date of the creation of the board. It is also provided that after the creation of such a board and for 30 days after it has made its report to the President,

no change, except by agreement, shall be made by the parties to the controversy in the conditions out of which the dispute arose.

The bill abolishes the Railroad Labor Board and repeals Title III of the transportation act, 1920, and the act of July 15, 1913, known as the Newlands Act, which latter provides for mediation, conciliation, and arbitration.

This bill had its origin in conferences and a resulting agreement between a large majority of Class I railroads and their employees.

It was submitted to a meeting of the Association of Railway Executives, at which 52 roads with 199 votes, representing 167,915.69 miles, favored it; and 20 roads with 48 votes, representing 36,564.67 miles, opposed it. This was out of a total membership of 107 roads with 288 votes, representing 222,842.84 miles. Of these, 32 roads with 38 votes, representing 18,134.45 miles, were absent; and 3 roads with 3 votes, representing 228.03 miles, did not vote.

The railroads favoring the bill appeared before the committee through their representatives and advocated it. None of the railroads opposing the bill appeared either in person or by any representative.

The bill was agreed to also by all the organizations known as "standard recognized railway labor organizations," 20 in number, and these appeared by their representatives before the committee in advocacy of the bill.

The conferences referred to were invited by the President in more than one message to Congress, the first of these being his message of December 6, 1923, in which he said:

The settlement of railroad labor disputes is a matter of grave public concern. The labor board was established to protect the public in the enjoyment of continuous service by attempting to insure justice between the companies and their employees. It has been a great help, but is not altogether satisfactory to the public, the employees, or the companies. If a substantial agreement can be reached among the groups interested, there should be no hesitation in enacting such agreement into law. If it is not reached, the labor board may very well be left for the present to protect the public welfare.

Again, in his message to Congress of December 3, 1924, a similar suggestion of change in existing law was made.

It should also be noted that dissatisfaction with the method of adjusting disputes between carriers and their employees now provided by the provisions of the transportation act relating to labor was expressed in the platforms adopted in 1924 by both the Republican and Democratic Parties.

The Republican platform contained the following provision:

The labor-board provision of the present law should be amended whenever it appears necessary to meet changed conditions. Collective bargaining, mediation, and voluntary arbitration are the most important steps in the maintaining peaceful labor relations and should be encouraged. We do not believe in compulsory action at any time in the settlement of disputes. Public opinion must be the final arbiter in any crisis which so vitally affects public welfare as the suspension of transportation. Therefore the interests of the public require the maintenance of an impartial tribunal which can in an emergency make an investigation of the facts and publish its conclusion. This is essential as the basis for popular judgment.

The Democratic platform contained the following:

The labor provisions of the act (transportation act, 1920) have proven unsatisfactory in settling differences between employer and employee. . . . It must therefore be so rewritten so that the high purposes which the public welfare demands may be accomplished.

Pursuant to the suggestions of the President, representatives of the railroads and representatives of their employees, after the adjournment of the last session of Congress, began conferences to ascertain whether or not there was a basis on which they could agree and present a plan for the adjustment of disputes. These conferences were long continued and resulted in the agreement set out in the form of the bill now under consideration.

As stated, both parties to this agreement have appeared before the committee in advocacy of the bill and have represented to the committee that in their belief the bill, if enacted into law, will promote peaceful relationships between the carriers and their employees, will prevent interruptions of transportation, and will amply protect the paramount interests of the public in every way.

The committee has been impressed by the evident earnestness and sincerity of both parties directly interested, as both have represented to the committee that if the plan on which they have agreed is enacted into law they will each feel under moral obligations to see that the law works, that it will avoid interruptions of commerce, and will protect the paramount public interest.

The first fundamental question with which the committee was confronted was whether or not the provisions of the present labor law, as contained in the transportation act, 1920, should be repealed and the Railroad Labor Board abolished.

In view of the fact that the employees absolutely refuse to appear before the labor board and that many of the important railroads are themselves opposed to it, that it has been held by the Supreme Court to have no power to enforce its judgments, that its authority is not recognized or respected by the employees and by a number of important railroads, that the President has suggested that it would be wise to seek a substitute for it, and that the party platforms of both the Republican and Democratic Parties in 1924 clearly indicated dissatisfaction with the provisions of the transportation act relating to labor, the committee concluded that the time had arrived when the labor board should be abolished and the provisions relating to labor in the transportation act, should be replaced.

The question was consequently presented whether the substitute should consist of a compulsory system with adequate means provided for its enforcement, or whether it was in the public interest to create the machinery for amicable adjustment of labor disputes agreed upon by the parties and to the success of which both parties were committed.

Manifestly, it is unwise to commingle the two. One plan or the other should be adopted.

The committee is of opinion that it is in the public interest to permit a fair trial of the method of amicable adjustment agreed upon by the parties, rather than to attempt under existing conditions to use the entire power of the Government to deal with these labor disputes. If the plan proposed by the parties does not work, it will then be proper to consider what other methods are essential to protect the public interest in adequate and uninterrupted transportation.

The only interest which, through its representatives, appeared in opposition to the bill was certain associations of industrial and manufacturing concerns. It is to be noted that these opponents of the bill did not advocate the retention of the labor board or oppose the repeal of the labor provisions of the transportation act of 1920.

They proposed certain amendments to the pending bill, which they urged would be in the public interest.

These amendments related, except in one particular hereinafter to be mentioned, to paragraph (8) of Section 9, which deals with prohibitions against the use of legal process to make an individual employee work against his will, and to section 10 of the bill, which relates to the emergency board.

As to paragraph (8) of Section 9, it was urged that it should be clarified so as certainly to apply only to the use of legal process against an individual employee and so as not to apply to combinations or conspiracies between several employees, or groups of employees, to interrupt interstate commerce.

It was frankly stated by the advocates of the bill, both those representing the carriers and those representing the employees, that the purpose of the paragraph was to deal merely with individual employees, to express only the constitutional right of individuals against involuntary servitude, and was not intended to deal with combinations, conspiracies, or group action. This construction has been made abundantly clear by an amendment to the bill by which the word "individual" has been inserted before the word "employee" wherever the latter word appears in the paragraph.

It was further objected that Section 10 of the bill should not make the action of the President dependent upon a report from the board of mediation, that it should authorize the emergency board to issue compulsory process to obtain evidence, and that it should provide in express terms that no strike should occur until 30 days after the report of the emergency board to the President.

The committee is of opinion that there is no danger to the public interest in requiring a report from the board of mediation to the President prior to the exercise by him of his discretion as to the appointment of an emergency board. The board of mediation is a body composed entirely of representatives of the public with no connection with either party, and it is inconceivable that this board would fail to notify the President in case of a threatened interruption of commerce. Its members are subject to removal by him for malfeasance in office, and it would undoubtedly be malfeasance in office for the board to neglect to notify the President in case of public emergency. Moreover, the provision referred to is a means of protecting the President from unnecessary urgency on the part of the parties in cases not requiring the exercise of Executive action.

It is not deemed by the committee necessary to invest the emergency board with the compulsory power to secure testimony. The period of 30 days at the end of which the board is to make its report to the President, the practical fact that the merits of the case will turn upon large and easily ascertained considerations, and that neither party could decline to give all the information desired by the board without the certainty of the concentration of public opinion against that party, convince the committee that it is not essential to bestow the power to issue subpoenas upon the emergency board. It is not expected that the board will go into a long drawn out inquiry into details, for that, besides being unnecessary to intelligently inform public opinion on the larger and controlling features of the controversy, would preclude a very desirable class of men from accepting appointment to such an exacting and prolonged duty.

The objection that the bill should in express terms forbid strikes during the period of the inquiry by the emergency board and for 30 days thereafter is successfully met, in the opinion of the committee, by the contention that in forbidding a change in the conditions out of which a dispute arose, one of which and a very fundamental one is the relationship of the parties, it already forbids any interruption of commerce during the period referred to; and if strikes were in express terms forbidden for a given period there might be an implication that after that period strikes to interfere with the passage of the United States mails and with continuous transportation service might be made legal. In the opinion of the committee, this possible implication should be avoided.

The remaining objection above referred to was that the power of the Labor Board, under Section 307 of the existing labor act, to suspend agreements between the parties as to wages the result of which would have an effect upon rates should be in substance preserved by creating that power in the Interstate Commerce Commission or in some other public body.

This was objected to on the part of the representatives of the employees for a number of reasons, among which was that the power to control agreements as to wages between the employer and the employee is, as they contend, unconstitutional in the case of *Wilson* v. *New,* 243 U. S. 332 (1917).

However this may be, there is an objection, which the committee deems conclusive, to giving the Interstate Commerce Commission jurisdiction over agreements as to wages. That, in the committee's opinion, would involve the commission in a field of fierce controversy, which might, and probably would, impair its usefulness.

Undoubtedly, under Section 15a of the interstate commerce act, the Interstate Commerce Commission has jurisdiction, in fixing rates, to examine into the carriers' expenditures of all sorts, and not to increase rates to provide for extravagant expenditures, whether for labor or for any other purpose.

In addition to the reasons above given, there was a fundamental objection to making changes of a substantive character in the agreement which the parties had reached. The proposals above mentioned for amendments suggested that in the arrangement there should be included provisions looking to force or compulsion. Viewed from that standpoint, they are clearly inadequate for the purposes of compulsion, and, if compulsion is to be resorted to, it clearly should be of an adequate character. If agreement is to be resorted to, the committee is of opinion that the agreement should not be destroyed by placing in the act provisions which would have that effect.

The committee was informed that in agreeing to the emergency board the representatives of the employees had gone further than they had ever gone before in the history of their organizations, that they could go no further as a matter of agreement, and that, if what they had agreed to was changed, the proposal would be deprived of the attributes of agreement and the success of it would have to rest on the legislation and not upon the agreement of the parties.

In the course of the hearings it was urged in opposition to the bill that the argument in favor of the method proposed in it for adjustment of disputes based on the fact of agreement between the carriers and their employees lost its force when it is remembered that both the Erdman Act and the Newlands Act were based on agreements, and it was argued that neither of these worked satisfactorily. While neither of these acts may have worked perfectly, it must be admitted that each of them served a very important public service when the results of the two acts are reviewed. A review of the results under the Erdman Act will be found on page 37 and of the Newlands Act on pages 50 and 51 of the Bulletin of the United States Bureau of Labor Statistics, No. 303, published in 1922.

Under all the circumstances, the committee is of opinion that the public interest will best be promoted by the enactment of the bill in its present form, and it attaches value to the fact that it establishes good will and amicable relations between the parties and places upon them the responsibility of seeing that it works so as to avoid any impairment of the public interest. If it does not so work, Congress will be unembarrassed in adopting any means it sees fit to protect the public interest.

It will be noted that the President, in his message to Congress delivered at the opening of the present session, having been informed that the railroad managers and their employees had reached a substantial agreement as to what legislation is necessary to regulate and improve their relationship, said:

It is gratifying to report that both the railroad managers and railroad employees are providing boards for the mutual adjustment of differences in harmony with the principles of conference, conciliation, and arbitration. The solution of their problems ought to be an example to all other industries. Those who ask the protection of civilization should be ready to use the methods of civilization.

A strike in modern industry has many of the aspects of war in the modern world. It injures labor and it injures capital. If the industry involved is a basic one it reduces the necessary economic surplus and, increasing the cost of living, it injures the economic welfare and general comfort of the whole people. It also involves a deeper cost. It tends to embitter and divide the community into warring classes and thus weakens the unity and power of our national life.

Labor can make no permanent gains at the cost of the general welfare. All the victories won by organized labor in the past generation have been won through the support of public opinion. The manifest inclination of the managers and employees of the railroads to adopt a policy of action in harmony with these principles marks a new epoch in our industrial life.

THE DEBATE

House of Representatives—69th Congress, 1st Session
February 24–25, 1926

JOHN COOPER [R., OHIO]. Mr. Chairman and Members of the House, we are beginning the consideration today of H. R. 9463, a bill for the prevention and settlement of disputes between the railroad carriers and their employees.

There is no subject which in my humble opinion is more worthy of the earnest and careful attention of Congress. I believe that it was the late President Wilson who once said that "the railroads are the arteries through which flow the lifeblood of our Nation." It is vital to the country that the operation of its railroads be uninterrupted, that the owners of the same receive a fair return on capital invested and that the pay and working conditions of the employees be adequate and just in order that the operation of our transportation systems shall be efficient and that the people and their goods may be carried safely and promptly from place to place.

To my mind this bill is one of the most favorable signs that has appeared in the troubled field of industrial relations for many years. I believe it marks the end of some very distressing and troublesome differences between the railroad managers and their employees as to the best method of facing and solving the problems of employment, conditions of service, and wage adjustments.

More than that, I believe that this measure establishes a model for the solution of these great questions which if followed in other lines of industry will open the way for lasting industrial peace and prosperity and the settlement of differences between employers and employees through the exercise of reason, mutual consideration, and cooperation rather than by the methods of strife and force. Congress by making this bill law, will have placed its stamp of approval on the great principle that the interests of employers and employees are mutual and not conflicting and that the only sensible and effective way for them to settle their differences is to meet together at the conference table in a spirit of fellowship and forbearance rather than for either side to attempt to compel the other by resorting to methods of industrial warfare. [Applause.]

Congress and the country have spent several years arguing over world courts and leagues of nations and the best method of advancing the cause of world peace, but here today we have the opportunity of furthering the equally great cause of industrial peace. We must not let this wonderful opportunity pass by. If we can help capital and labor to settle their age-old differences and misunderstandings, then we will have promoted such an era

58

of good feeling among men that international peace and cooperation will follow naturally and of its own accord.

Mr. Chairman, it is with a feeling of peculiar personal pleasure that I urge the enactment of this bill into law. For many years my lot was cast among the railroad workers who with their quick intelligence and cool judgment safely guide the train loads of precious human and commercial freight through rain and shine, over the mountains, and across the rivers of this broad land of ours, or who feed with the brawn of their muscle and the sweat of their brow the boilers which furnish the power by which the railroads operate. I know their trials and their troubles, and I understand, to some extent at least, their point of view. This bill means much to those men. It means assurance that they can receive fair pay and fair treatment without being compelled to live under the constant shadow that some day they may be called upon to enforce their rights by quitting their jobs, losing their means of livelihood, and their rights of service and chance of advancement. If I can be of material service in securing the enactment of this bill into law I shall feel that my service in Congress has been justified better, perhaps, than by any other single accomplishment since I first came to Washington, because I know that I will have helped to do something which will be of the greatest benefit to my old fellow workers, as well as the railroad management and the public. [Applause.]

Mr. Chairman, the bill which is now before us like most good things, is simple and easy to understand. It is a return to fundamental principles and does not offer any quick remedy for curing all conceivable labor troubles. But an analysis of it will show that it is a decided forward step toward peaceful settlement of labor disputes. Representatives of both the railroad managers and employees have assured the Committee on Interstate and Foreign Commerce that it establishes machinery which will remove practically all danger of strikes and tie-ups of transportation, and I may say in this connection that it is the spirit of cooperation which evidently inspired the representatives of the railroad companies and their employees in getting together behind this bill, which, to my mind, is the best possible assurance that the measure will be effective as law.

The railroad labor bill proposes to prevent and settle serious railroad labor disputes by a method of conference, mediation, and arbitration. I have myself introduced several bills similar in principle to this bill, and therefore I am especially glad that the railroads and their employees have united in advocating the plan outlined in this measure.

Before we commence to discuss in detail the provisions of the bill it is necessary, in order to understand it and the railroad labor situation better, to refer briefly to the history of railroad labor legislation and the movement resulting in this bill.

Before the Government took over the operation of the railroads during the World War, provision was made under the Newlands law so that the Board of Mediation and Conciliation established by this act could intervene when a stoppage of traffic was threatened on any railroad operating in interstate commerce by labor difficulties. During the war railroad labor questions were handled by a series of national adjustment boards located in Washington.

When the time came for the return of the railroads by the Government to their owners there was a wide range of opinion in and out of Congress as to what labor provisions should be inserted in the transportation act of 1920. Finally, Title III of the transportation act creating the present Railroad Labor Board was adopted as a compromise by the conferees. Congress had to take the Railroad Labor Board or nothing.

I had serious doubts from the beginning about the practicability of the board, and so did most others who had studied the question. These doubts were soon confirmed, and on several occasions since 1920 I introduced bills to abolish the board, proposing to re-establish the machinery of mediation, conciliation, and arbitration provided in the Newlands law.

The Railroad Labor Board has not been satisfactory to either the railroad managers, the employees, or the public, but has only been a source of trouble since it was established. Some railway managers and employees have refused to recognize the board and then again at times both railway managers and employees would refuse to assume the responsibility of making labor settlements, but would "pass the buck" to the board, which has become simply an agency for airing petty grievances of all kinds.

It has become generally recognized that Title III of the transportation act, which created the Railroad Labor Board, should be changed.

The national Republican Party platform of 1924 contained the following provision:

> The labor provisions of the present law should be amended whenever it appears necessary to meet changed conditions. Collective bargaining, mediation, and voluntary arbitration are the most important steps in maintaining peaceful labor relations and should be encouraged. We do not believe in compulsory action at any time in the settlement of disputes. Public opinion must be the final arbiter in any crisis which so vitally affects public welfare as the suspension of transportation. Therefore the interests of the public require the maintenance of an impartial tribunal which can in an emergency make an investigation of the facts and publish its conclusions. This is essential as the basis for popular judgment.

This plank in the Republican Party platform of 1924 is identical in principle with the provisions of the bill which we are now considering.

The Democratic platform of 1924 contains the following:

> The labor provisions of the transportation act of 1920 have proven unsatisfactory in settling differences between employer and employees. . . .

. . . It must therefore be rewritten that the high purposes which the public welfare demands may be accomplished.

President Coolidge, in his message to Congress, December 6, 1920 said:

The settlement of railroad-labor disputes is a matter of grave public concern. The Labor Board . . . is not altogether satisfactory to the public, the employees, or the companies. If a substantial agreement can be reached among the groups interested there should be no hesitation in enacting such agreement into law.

The President in his message to Congress, December 3, 1924, again touched on this question as follows:

Another matter before the Congress is legislation affecting the labor sections of the transportation act. Much criticism has been directed at the workings of this section. . . . It would be helpful if a plan could be adopted, which, while retaining the practice of systematic collective bargaining with conciliation and voluntary arbitration of labor differences, could also provide simplicity in relations and more direct local responsibility of employees and managers. But such legislation will not meet the requirements of the situation unless it recognizes the principle that the public has a right to the uninterrupted services of transportation, and therefore the right to be heard when there is danger that the Nation may suffer a great injury through the interruption of operations because of labor disputes.

I believe at this point I can say without any feeling of partisanship that the position of President Coolidge had a great influence in bringing the railroad managers and the representatives of the employees together on the subject of railroad labor legislation. [Applause.] He urged that they come to an understanding and that they should cooperate, and it is his excellent advice that has been followed and has borne fruit in the provision of the bill now before us.

It was not the easiest task in the world to bring the railroad executives and the labor officials together and agree upon the draft of a bill. But they did get together, however, and it took months of hard work by the biggest, broadest, and wisest leaders on both sides to accomplish the result.

During the year 1925 the railroad executives and the officials of the railroad labor organizations held conferences to consider plans for changing the present labor section of the transportation act. A subcommittee was created which was instructed to draft a bill and report back to the full committees as soon as possible. Too much credit can not be given to the subcommittee for the important work it accomplished in the drafting of the bill.

In due time the subcommittee reported to the full committees of railroad executives and labor officials, and the draft of the bill was approved and indorsed by the executives representing 80 per cent of the railroad mileage of the country and the officials of 20 railroad labor organizations.

I desire to say a word about the four men who, I understand, constituted the subcommittee. I believe they should be congratulated and that they deserve recognition for the splendid service they have performed.

It has been my good fortune to have been personally acquainted with three of them for years. The subcommittee consisted of Mr. David Robertson, president of the Brotherhood of Locomotive Firemen and Enginemen, and Mr. William N. Doak, vice president of the Brotherhood of Railroad Trainmen, representing the employees; Mr. Elisha Lee, vice president of the Pennsylvania Railroad system, and Mr. J. G. Walber, vice president of the New York Central Railroad system, representing the railway executives. I have known Mr. Robertson for many years. We were boys together out in Youngstown, Ohio, and worked together on the railroad. We have not always agreed on economic questions, but I have always held him in high regard and recognized his ability, sterling honesty, and deep convictions, knowing he was working for what he believed to be for the best interests of the members of the great labor organizations of which he is the president.

When I first came to Congress 11 years ago I met William N. Doak, who was the other labor representative on the subcommittee, and I want to say I have never met a fairer, wiser, or broader representative of labor in my legislative or other experience. [Applause.] The representatives of the executives on the subcommittee, Mr. Lee and Mr. Walber, are well known by the American people for their honesty, integrity, and ability in all questions relating to our great transportation systems.

The report of the subcommittee and the draft of the bill was approved by the full committee of railroad executives and the railroad labor organizations. Whereupon representatives of the carriers and their employees reported to the President that they had agreed upon the draft of legislation embodying a substitute for Title III of the transportation act of 1920. At this point I want to call your attention to the message of the President to Congress on December 8, 1925, in which he said:

I am informed that the railroad managers and their employees have reached a substantial agreement as to what legislation is necessary to regulate and improve their relationship. Whenever they bring forward such proposals, which seem sufficient also to protect the interests of the public, they should be enacted into law.

It is gratifying to report that both the railroad managers and railroad employees are providing boards for the mutual adjustment of differences in harmony with the principles of conference, conciliation, and arbitration. The solution of these problems ought to be an example to all other industries. Those who ask the protections of civilization should be ready to use the methods of civilization. . . .

The manifest inclination of the managers and employees of the railroads to adopt a policy of action in harmony with these principles marks a new epoch in our industrial life.

On January 8, 1926, identical bills expressing this agreement of the parties were introduced in the House and Senate, respectively, by the chairman of the Committee on Interstate and Foreign Commerce of the House and the chairman of the Committee on Interstate Commerce of the Senate.

The House committee has held extended hearings giving ample opportunity to the proponents and opponents of the bill to present their views. In addition to the representatives of the carriers and their employees the chairman of the executive council of the National Civic Federation presented testimony in support of the bill. The American Short Line Railroad Association offered a statement to the effect that the short-line railroads did not oppose the enactment of the proposed law. Representatives of various associations of manufacturers presented suggestions for a few amendments, which were given careful consideration.

The principal point impressed upon the committee during the hearings was the desirability of giving the managers and employees of this most important national industry the aid and cooperation of the legislative, executive, and judicial power of the Government in the settlement of industrial controversies by the means which practical men, who have devoted their lives to this industry, believe are best adapted to maintain satisfactory relations between employers and employees.

Both Senate and House committees have been holding hearings on the bill for several weeks. The House committee has reported the bill out substantially as introduced with the recommendation that it be passed. That brings us to a consideration of the provisions of the bill. The bill provides it shall be the duty of all carriers, their officers, agents, and employees to exert every reasonable effort to make and maintain agreements concerning rates of pay, rules, and working conditions, and to settle all disputes, whether arising out of applications of such agreements or otherwise, in order to avoid any interruption to commerce.

The provisions of the bill require, in the first place, that all disputes between carriers and their employees shall be adjusted by agreement if possible; that the relations of the parties shall be controlled by agreements; that there shall be created boards of adjustment, composed of equal representatives of managers and employees.

This is not a new procedure. For years it has been the custom of many railroads and of their employees to adjust disputes that might arise from time to time by boards of adjustment, members of which understand the problems by reason of their technical knowledge of the industry. These boards may be established by an individual carrier and its employees of any class, or they can be regional or national in scope, as may be agreed upon. These adjustment boards are established not for the purpose of having jurisdiction over the question of changes in wages and working conditions, but of grievances or disputes growing out of a misunderstanding of the interpretation or application of agreements concerning rates of pay, rules, or working conditions.

The adjustment boards must be chosen by each party in such a way as they may determine. They are not Government boards, but boards chosen by the parties and paid by them.

The bill also provides that all questions relating to change in wages and working conditions shall be first considered by the parties in conference. If no agreement is reached in conference, the matter shall then be taken up by the Board of Mediation, which is created by the bill and is composed of five members appointed by the President, by and with the advice and consent of the Senate. This is a Government board and paid by the Government, and no person in the employment of or who is pecuniarily or otherwise interested in any organization of employees or any carrier is eligible to be a member of the board, or in other words the membership of the board is composed entirely of representatives of the public.

The parties, or either party, to a dispute between employees and a carrier, if unable to agree or settle the dispute in conference, may invoke the services of the board of mediation, or the board of mediation may proffer its services in any dispute arising out of grievances or out of the interpretation or application of agreements concerning rates of pay, rules, or working conditions not adjusted by the parties in conference; or a dispute which is not settled in conference between the parties in respect to changes in the rates of pay, rules, or working conditions. If a dispute should arise between a carrier and its employees of a serious character, it is the duty of the mediation board to promptly put itself in touch with the parties to the controversy, and to use its best efforts by mediation to bring them to agreement. If such efforts to bring about an amicable adjustment of the dispute or controversy through mediation are unsuccessful, it is the duty of the board of mediation to try and induce the parties to submit to arbitration. I have great faith in mediation for the settlement of labor disputes. The Newlands Act of 1913 provided for mediation, which plan was in effect until Title III of the transportation act became law in 1920.

More than 90 per cent of the cases that came before the board of mediation under the Newlands Act were adjusted and approved by both sides to the dispute.

In the four-year period ending June 30, 1917, the board of mediation created under the Newlands Act had before it 71 controversies. Fifty of these were settled wholly by mediation, 6 by mediation and arbitration, 3 by contestants without the aid of mediation, and 1 by an act of Congress.

If the parties to dispute fail to agree and if the board of mediation is unable to bring them together and arbitration is agreed upon, then the board of arbitration is created by each party selecting one or two representatives, as they may prefer, as the board may consist of three or six. The parties themselves select the one or two neutral arbitrators, if they can do so. If the parties can not agree, then the board of mediation must select the neutral arbiter. If the parties agree to arbitrate, then the award of the board of arbitration shall be conclusive on the parties as to the merits and facts of the controversy submitted to arbitration, and unless within 10 days after the filing of the award a petition is filed to impeach the award on the grounds set forth in the bill, the court shall enter judgment on the award, which judgment shall be final and conclusive on the parties.

If a dispute between a carrier and its employees be not adjusted through the process of conference, adjustment, mediation, or arbitration, the President is empowered to create a board of outstanding representatives of the public who can investigate, with the aid of the permanent Board of Mediation, the Interstate Commerce Commission, the Department of Labor, and all other agencies of Government, and bring to bear upon the parties the pressure of the highest governmental authority either to adjust their differences by voluntary agreement or to consider to submit them to arbitration. If this pressure shall fail in itself to bring about a settlement, this emergency board will then be able in its report to give to the public adequate and intelligible information regarding the merits of the contentions of the parties, and to crystallize public opinion in support of that party or that program which should be supported in the public interest. This temporary emergency board will be able to express and to mobilize public opinion to an extent impossible to any permanent board or any agency of Government which has been heretofore created for that purpose. It is also highly important to point out that during the period of investigation and for 30 days thereafter the parties to the controversy are bound under the proposed law to maintain unchanged the conditions out of which the dispute arose, thereby assuring the parties and the public that the emergency board will have the full and unembarrassed opportunity to exert its authority and fulfill its important function.

Mr. Chairman, in conclusion I desire to say that the one thing that impressed me more than anything else during the hearings held by the committee on this bill was the spirit of the railway managers and employees, and their earnest desire to cooperate, in promoting industrial peace and harmony, by securing the enactment into law of provisions which will enable them to settle their differences in conference. I am confident that nearly every industrial dispute can be settled if both sides will sit down in a spirit of fairness and justice to discuss matters at issue around the council table.

The Committee on Interstate and Foreign Commerce presents this bill to the House for your consideration, recommends its passage as both the most practical and advanced legislation for the settlement of labor controversies that has ever been presented to Congress. [Applause.] . . .

THOMAS BLANTON [DEM., TEX.]. May I say that if all of the 600,000 railroad employees most vitally affected by this bill were as fair and reasonable and honest and capable and efficient and as splendid gentlemen as are the gentleman from Ohio [Mr. Cooper] and our colleague from Minnesota [Mr. Carrs], we would not need any law and would not have any strikes. But I want to say this to the gentleman. The Erdman Act in 1898 provided the machinery which required the status quo to be maintained during arbitration and required the parties in arbitration to agree to faithfully accept the award and abide by it. It provided a court of equity to enforce it, as far as equity provisions would allow, and it gave to the public other rights, for it prevented the men from changing the status quo for at least three months without giving 30 days' notice, and also provided that the award should last for one year, and all the men and all the railroads agreed to that legislation, and yet it did not bring about the desired results, did it?

MR. COOPER. Can the gentleman name me any one serious strike except one, since the Erdman Act was passed?

MR. BLANTON. I will name the gentleman one. President Cleveland stopped the Debs strike in 1894 with troops. But peaceful conditions lasted until 1913, and then there was a condition similar to the one that exists today, only it was more intense. The employees said to Congress that if you do not pass the Newlands Act just like we have agreed to it with the railroads there will be a strike. . . . I want to ask if in 1913 they did not come in with the Newlands Act and say that if Congress did not pass the law as it was written —if they changed the dotting of an "i" or the crossing of a "t" there is going to be a strike—and was not the Newlands Act pushed thus through?

MR. COOPER. No; I did not know that.

MR. BLANTON. The Record shows that.

ALBEN BARKLEY [DEM., KY.]. I will answer it; they did not.

MR. BLANTON. The Record shows that, and if the gentleman will look at the excerpts of the debate which I have copied from the statements of Members in the Senate and House, and published in Monday's Record, they will show that condition prevailed. . . .

CHARLES KEARNS [R., OHIO]. There have been a great many protests, the gentleman knows, that have come from various parts of the country, claiming that this bill does not properly take care of the public interest. Will the gentleman for a moment direct his attention to that proposition and tell the House whether this bill does protect the public interest, and wherein?

MR. COOPER. The bill creates a board of mediators composed entirely of public members appointed by the President, by and with the advice and consent of the Senate, and, in addition, it creates an emergency board appointed by the President.

MR. KEARNS. The board is composed of five members.

MR. COOPER. The Board of Mediation; yes.

Furthermore, let me say that the bill surely is as good as what we have at the present time. There is no change I can see when it comes to protecting the public.

MR. KEARNS. Let me ask the gentleman this question: Under this bill the employer and employee can get together and rearrange their wage schedule in any way that would be agreeable to both parties?

MR. COOPER. Certainly.

MR. KEARNS. That would necessitate, or it might necessitate, a raise in the freight rates?

MR. COOPER. Possibly it might.

MR. KEARNS. Under this bill would the railroads have the right in that event to raise the freight rates and passenger rates to meet that increase?

MR. COOPER. That would be a question that would have to be passed upon by the Interstate Commerce Commission.

MR. KEARNS. That is what I wanted to know.

MR. COOPER. It is their duty to protect the public. The question of fixing an agreement on wages is primarily private, and the Interstate Commerce Commission and no other public body can interfere with that private contract.

The Supreme Court of the United States has already ruled on that; but when it comes to the question of rates, that is a public question, and the Interstate Commerce Commission will fix that.

EUGENE BLACK [DEM., TEX.]. If the gentleman holds that position, why does he object to the Hoch amendment, which makes the situation perfectly clear?

MR. COOPER. Did you hear me say I was opposed to the Hoch amendment?

MR. BLACK. No.

MR. COOPER. I am not for it. Now let me read to the gentleman from Texas what the Supreme Court has said on the question of wage agreements. There was placed on all of our desks this morning a paper sent out by one of the farm organizations, and I want to read to you what it says. I read:

Under the present law the Railroad Labor Board can not make a wage award without the approval of one of the representatives of the public on the board. If the railroad managers and their employees make an agreement about wages, the board can suspend the agreement until it finds out what effect it will have upon railroad rates. That is a clear-cut, definite protection which Congress gave six years ago to prevent new and excessive burdens being put upon railroad service. Now, in the bill you are about to consider it is proposed to abolish the Railroad Labor Board and permit the parties signatory thereto to make wage agreements, without any public body having control over such agreements.

There is not a man in this House but knows that the Railroad Board can not suspend any wage agreement made between the railroad managers and the employees.

MR. BLACK. This would leave us without such protection.

MR. COOPER. I say they have no power to suspend an agreement.

MR. BLACK. They have the power under the present law.

MR. COOPER. Where do they have the power under the present law to suspend agreements?

MR. BLACK. Section 307 so states. That is the section, as I now remember it.

MR. COOPER. The Supreme Court says in its ruling that they have not that power.

MR. BLACK. It would be within the province of Congress to amend the railway labor act.

MR. COOPER. The Supreme Court of the United States said this in its ruling:

> It is also equally true that, as the right to fix by agreement between the carrier and its employees a standard of wages to control their relations is primarily private, the establishment and giving effect of an agreed-on standard is not subject to be controlled or to be prevented by public authority. . . .

HOMER HOCH [R., KAN.]. Of course, the gentleman realizes that the Supreme Court was passing upon the question of the right to set aside a private contract. The amendment which I propose does not in any way infringe upon that proposition.

MR. COOPER. I did not say it did.

MR. HOCH. I do not propose to lodge any power in the Interstate Commerce Commission to set aside a contract, but I propose to retain now in the Interstate Commerce Commission the power they now have to say if you make a contract, the contract with the railroad shall control. . . .

WALTER NEWTON [R., MINN.]. There is nothing in the bill as it is drawn that in any way impairs or modifies the present powers of the Interstate Commerce Commission to do that very thing.

MR. COOPER. I think that is right.

MR. HOCH. If that be true, what objection can there be to making it clear that we reserve the right to the Interstate Commerce Commission to say that it comes within reasonable expenditures in passing that burden on to the public? . . .

JOHN NELSON [R., ME.]. Mr. Chairman and gentlemen of the committee, I find myself in the unpleasant situation of differing very materially in thought from my esteemed associates on the Interstate Commerce Committee. I realize that this reflects on my good judgment, and that it must be I, rather than the rest of the regiment, that is out of step. However, I have attended the hearings on this bill, listened to the witnesses, studied the testimony, given the matter my careful and prayerful attention: and there are considerations here that appeal to me so strongly, the interests of my State are so involved, that I desire briefly to express my views on this legislation, relying somewhat on that spirit of charity and forbearance that characterizes and enriches our associations in this body.

I come from a State situated in the extreme northeastern section of this great country, where the transportation problem is today a very vital issue. It is a long haul from the source of raw materials to our mills; it is a long haul back to market. Transportation charges today are such that the growth of my State is retarded, its industries threatened with extinction, and the welfare of our great agricultural and industrial classes imperiled. At the present time there is pending before the Interstate Commerce Commission a request for increased freight charges in eastern Maine, the result of which if granted, I can only contemplate with dismay.

The railroads of my State, at peace with their employees, have just begun to turn the corner, just begun to recover from the effects of war-time operation, and we in Maine had begun to believe that, in a time not too far removed for joyful hope, the increased prosperity of those roads might be reflected in a much-needed and beneficial reduction of freight charges.

Now, I am in sympathy with organized labor, its needs, and aspirations. I believe that we should safeguard their every essential right. I would go with them as far as any legislator can honestly go, and that is to a point where I believe that the interests of the minority conflicts with the interests of the whole. To go further than that would be to justify the suspicion, somewhat prevalent, that organized minorities and selfish interests play a disproportionate part in the shaping of legislation here, and that the great mass of our people are not truly represented.

The situation that challenges our attention to-day is this: A railway labor bill is presented here for enactment that, in my opinion, wipes out every existing public safeguard [applause], and coincident with its presentation comes a demand from railroad labor for wage increases variously estimated at from $250,000,000 to $500,000,000. My friends, I do not know what sort of farm relief legislation we are going to pass at this Congress; but, in my opinion, if this bill is enacted agriculture is going to need relief more than ever before.

I believe a study of the situation will convince the investigator that the carriers in favor of this measure, with possibly a few exceptions, represent principally the larger and the more prosperous eastern roads, roads subject to the recapture clause, roads that are able and willing to purchase industrial peace by distributing to their employees the money that would otherwise be returned to the Government.

With the roads of my State, with most of the roads in the West and South, the situation is far different. The proposed wage demands, if granted, would indefinitely postpone freight reductions, if they did not necessitate freight increases.

As has been stated, there are three parties interested in these railroad labor disputes—the carriers, their employees, and the public. Some months ago representatives of the first two parties held a disarmament conference and unanimously voted to disarm the third party [laughter], retaining at the same time all their own weapons of offense and defense. You may study the provisions of the bill as you will and you will find that statement to be true.

MR. BLANTON. Will the gentleman permit an interruption right there?

MR. NELSON. I will, but I hope to be able to finish in the time allotted to me.

MR. BLANTON. This will be the only interruption I will make. They not only retained all their own arms but they took over all the arms of the public.

MR. NELSON. I so understand it.

The carriers and their employees entered upon a composition of their difficulties and upon the drafting of this bill under the mistaken assumption that the matter was one of personal contract between themselves. The public was not represented in that conference and had no voice. It is said that each group made substantial concessions to the other, all predicated, however, on the proposition that Congress in return should wipe from the statute books all the public safeguards now existing for the benefit of that great unorganized majority which, in the final analysis, must pay all the bills.

In the course of the discussion of this measure such a variety of opinion was manifest as to what were the rights of the public in interstate commerce, what was the authority of Congress, and what was the efficacy of existing laws, that I want to say just a word on that subject, although I do not claim to speak with authority.

The founders of this Republic, those worthy men who formulated and penned the Constitution of the United States, recognized the rights of the public in interstate commerce and gave expression to that right in the clause which confers upon Congress the power to regulate and control interstate commerce. The courts have sustained that constitutional authority even to the point of holding that we may, by appropriate legislation, provide for compulsory arbitration of these labor difficulties. Subsequent acts of Congress have recognized and given expression to that right. By a process of evolution the accepted conception of the public interest has broadened with the years.

The first national act passed for the settlement of railroad labor disputes constituted a recognition of the right of the public to continuous and uninterrupted service, and the right, in case of critical labor disputes, to know the true facts of the controversy. The Erdman Act, passed in 1898, marked a distinct step in advance in the recognition and protection of the public interest; in that, beside providing for conciliation, mediation, and voluntary arbitration, it contained the drastic antistrike and antilockout clause that has already been referred to.

You are told by the proponents of this measure that never before has labor made such concessions as in the present bill. The Erdman Act was indorsed by the railroad labor organizations and contained this antistrike clause, compared to which the ambiguous status quo clause of the present bill is but a pale preliminary. [Applause.]

Some of you who have had no opportunity of reading the hearings on this measure may be laboring under the impression that here, in the case of this bill, for the first time have the carriers and their employees met, compromised, agreed, and asked Congress to enact that agreement into law, promising to abide by it if enacted without change. As has already been suggested, such is not the fact, nor is this law dignified by any such distinction. The Newlands Act was presented to Congress in 1913 exactly as this bill is now presented by the same parties, with the same representations, the same demands, the same rosy promises. On page 237 of the committee hearings appears a part of the then discussion in the Senate, in the course of which Senator Pomerene, of Ohio, made these statements:

> Mr. President, I am in favor of this bill as it is written, and though in some respects I would prefer to see a change, I will not vote to change a single word in it, and for the reasons I shall state: It appears that before the committee the railway companies, through their presidents and representatives, and the railway men's organizations, through their chiefs, said that this bill represented months of work; that while there were slight differences of opinion, they all agreed to accept it as a solution of the problem. A number of the witnesses, when interrogated before the committee, said, in substance, that if the bill was passed as it was written they did not believe there would be a single railroad or a single organization that would refuse to accept the plan of settlement here adopted.
>
> It stands to reason that when they come before the Congress asking that this plan be incorporated into a statute no one of these parties would be in a position where he could honorably say, "I will not accept the plan of mediation or of arbitration which is therein contained."

Here is an absolute echo of the words spoken in the committee room during the consideration of this bill. The Newlands Act was not a solution of the problem. No problem is solved until it is rightly solved, and you can not solve a problem involving three equations by absolutely ignoring one of them.

Reverting for a moment to the three laws passed between 1888 and 1913, it will be noted that public thought had not during that time progressed beyond the conception that the only interest the public had in interstate commerce was the right of continuous and uninterrupted service. With the passage of the transportation act of 1920 we find for the first time statutory expression of the concept that the public has an interest, not only in uninterrupted service, but in the amount of wages paid as reflected in freight rates. [Applause.]

Section 307, Title III, of the transportation act authorizes the Railroad

Labor Board to suspend an agreement between parties with respect to wages until it can determine whether or not the proposed increase would require a readjustment of transportation rates. . . .

JAMES PARKER [R., N.Y.]. Has any such suspension ever been asked or granted?

MR. NELSON. The very fact that such a law exsists, whether legal or illegal, is a deterrent upon the attempted making of uncontrolled wage agreements. I believe the law is constitutional and effective. The bill was reported out of two great committees of the House and Senate containing excellent constitutional lawyers, with able chairmen. It is the law and has been the law for six years. It has never been successfully questioned, and I believe it is the law of the land to-day, and a very excellent law.

Title III provides something more than that—it provides that one member of the public group must join in any wage award made by the board. If you pass this bill without amendment, you repeal Title III of the transportation act; you destroy the only existing preventive remedy against uncontrolled wage agreements; you remove the representative of the public from wage negotiations; and at a time like the present, when there is a universal demand and need for reduced freight rates, and a pending demand for increased wages, you deprive the public of any voice or control in matters that are to them of supreme importance. [Applause.]

If you pass this bill, as I assume you will, and repeal Title III, the only surviving hope the public has is in the power of the Interstate Commerce Commission to refuse to recognize an unreasonable wage agreement as a proper element of cost of service in fixing freight and passenger rates. As suggested by the Hoch amendment, even this provision is endangered by the pending bill. Section 9 of this act, paragraph 2, provides that in the case of an arbitration the award shall be filed in the office of the appropriate district court and judgment entered thereon. Thus the decision becomes a decree of a Federal court. It was suggested during the hearings that under the full faith and credit provision of the Constitution a quasi Federal court like the Interstate Commerce Commission could not refuse to give full faith and credit to a decree of a Federal district court; that such refusal to consider in rate making a wage charge thus fixed on the carrier by law would constitute confiscatory legislation and be null and void. The proponents of this measure stated that they had no desire to curtail this power of the Interstate Commerce Commission. Their attention was called to this danger by the gentleman from Kansas [Mr. Hoch]. They refused to allow an amendment to the effect that nothing in the act should preclude the Interstate Commerce Commission from considering the merits of any such arbitration award when determining freight or passenger rates, and they refused a clause allowing the commission to intervene in the public interest before the award became a court judgment.

In my opinion, if you pass this bill without amendment, you destroy every existing public safeguard that time and experience have given us. . . .

MR. BLANTON. Is it not a fact that this board of mediation has nothing in the world to do with fixing wage schedules, and is it not a further fact that it has no power of compulsory investigation?

MR. NELSON. I am coming to that. I think all that is true, and even more than that. . . .

I say if you pass this act in its present form, without amendment, you destroy at one blow all those public safeguards that time and experience have given us. You deny public rights never before questioned. You declare public interest a myth, and public control a failure. You reverse the enlightened thought and policy of preceding Congresses, and turn back the hands on the clock of recorded progress in public interest 40 years. . . .

BENJAMIN MURPHY [R., OHIO]. I am not going to ask a frivolous question. I am very serious about this. The gentleman has made the statement several times in the course of his remarks that the public is losing what it now has. Will the gentleman please be specific and tell us one thing that the public loses by the adoption of this bill?

MR. NELSON. I thought that I had already done that.

MR. MURPHY. I wish the gentleman would pin his remarks to one thing that the public will lose.

MR. NELSON. I believe that Title III of the transportation act is sound law and of great public benefit and protection. That law as drafted has existed for six years and has never been upset by any court. It provides that the Railroad Labor Board may suspend an unreasonable agreement as to wages. It also provides that one member of the public group must join in any wage award made by the board. As the law stands to-day the Interstate Commerce Commission can refuse to consider in the making of rates an unreasonable wage agreement, and I maintain that even this last provision is endangered by the present bill.

I believe in self-government in industry. I would encourage these parties to set up their own machinery of adjustment and to use it. I would assist them in any legitimate agreement, subject only to the paramount rights of the public. In any dispute I would allow them to exhaust their every last remedy before governmental interference. But when those remedies are exhausted, when their machinery has broken down, when disaster threatens the whole social structure, then I believe this Government should exercise the power inherent in it and take every proper and reasonable step to avert a great national catastrophe. . . .

SCHUYLER MERRITT [R., CONN.]. By averting a national catastrophe, does the gentleman mean that he thinks that by law 100,000 men can be compelled to work if they do not want to?

MR. NELSON. I never have believed in such procedure. I never have suggested it, and I do not believe that any true American would countenance the attempt. I believe that compulsory arbitration even is repugnant to our concepts of government; but I believe that compulsory investigation is in entire harmony with the genius of American institutions, and that on an occasion of that sort, in the case of a great national emergency, it should be resorted to for these purposes: To focus public attention, to create an intelligent and informed public opinion, to bring to bear upon the offending party the compelling influence of public disapprobation. . . .

MR. PARKER. What does Section 10 of this bill do?

MR. NELSON. Nothing. I shall come to that in a moment.

This idea of compulsory investigation is no new one. President Roosevelt in 1905, and again in 1906, urged upon Congress the necessity of creating machinery for compulsory investigation of critical labor controversies. President Wilson, in 1916, facing a threatened paralysis of transportation, made practically the same request to Congress. The Howell-Barkley bill of last year, as amended in the Senate, provided for compulsory investigation. The Railroad Labor Board, which it is proposed to abolish, to-day possesses this power. President Coolidge, in his December message, in dealing with the coal situation, emphasized the need of machinery for compulsory investigation in labor difficulties.

In these messages of three great Presidents of the United States we see expressed the universally admitted thought, that when industrial disputes threaten the national welfare, then the people are entitled to know the full facts of the controversy, and it is the duty of Congress to provide the machinery for obtaining those facts.

Section 10 of this act provides for the appointment by the President of an emergency board. Its sole purpose is to discover and report the facts, a purpose of extreme importance, as upon those facts the President may act, or Congress legislate. This bill gives the emergency board no power whatever to compel the attendance of witnesses or the production of evidence. Its proponents refuse to allow such an amendment. In time of national emergency, tremendous responsibility is placed upon the President. He may appoint this board for the purpose of investigation, but they go forth not clothed in any sovereign power of the United States, but go forth as suppliants taking what they can get. . . .

MR. BLANTON. It would not be authorized to force the production of a document or the presence of a witness.

MR. NELSON. Not one. I say that this board is appointed simply for the purpose of discovering and reporting evidence, and then its hands are tied.

I believe we could have a pretty fair bill here if we would simply add to it the provisions of existing statutes for the protection of the public rights. Transfer to the Interstate Commerce Commission the power of review and suspension of wage agreements now possessed by the Railroad Labor Board;

amend Section 9 so that it shall not preclude the Interstate Commerce Commission from considering the merits of any award in making rates; give to the emergency board the power of compulsory investigation; and we would have a bill here that I believe any man could vote for without misgivings or misapprehension. . . .

MR. BLANTON. Why should we not give the President's emergency board the same power that the Board of Arbitration has?

MR. NELSON. I have not been able to ascertain.

MR. BLANTON. Has the committee ever been able to explain why it is not able to do that?

CARROLL BEEDY [R., ME.]. If the gentleman will permit, the answer is that the two parties in this three-sided matter have gotten together and said that they do not want it.

MR. BLANTON. They do not want the public to have any rights in it?

MR. BEEDY. Yes; that is their agreement. This is not the legislation of this Congress or of any member of this committee. This is an agreement that they allow us to make a gesture of in the way of having it printed and having us go through the form of voting for it. . . .

MR. BARKLEY. Mr. Chairman [applause] and gentlemen of the committee, I shall not limit myself as to time because I want to be free to discuss this bill in as much detail as possible; but I hope not to consume more time than the House is willing patiently to listen. We have before us today a measure which involves probably as vitally and as intimately the welfare of the people of the United States as any measure which Congress can possibly consider. This bill affects not only the fundamental rights of the American people; it affects the fundamental rights of the transportation systems of the United States as well as the men who operate those transportation systems.

I desire to make some comparisons between the bill now before us and the measures which have heretofore been enacted, and especially some comparisons between it and the present law. I wish also to discuss the question which has been injected here, and which seems to be in the minds of many of the Members, the rights of the public, not only from a legalistic standpoint, not only from the standpoint of the power that may be conferred upon the Congress by the commerce clause of the Constitution, but I desire to discuss that right from its fundamental standpoint independent of any power to deal with it that may be conferred upon Congress by the Constitution.

Before I undertake to discuss the details of this bill I desire briefly to outline the history of labor legislation which led up to the passage of the present transportation act and its labor provisions, beginning in 1888. For many years prior to the enactment of the first law which undertook, in a feeble and timid way, to provide for the adjustment of railroad labor disputes, there had been much agitation throughout the country upon this subject and many bills had been introduced in the House and in the Senate. I think, probably, beginning back in 1873 Congress began to give its attention to the problem of providing some way by which labor disputes arising upon our railroads might be amicably adjusted so as to prevent interference with interstate commerce and at the same time provide a just method of setting disputes so as to grant to the carriers and their employees the rights to which they were entitled.

The first bill, however, which ever became a law was enacted by Congress in 1888. That law provided that both sides to any controversy, if they agreed to arbitrate the question, were to appoint one representative, and that these two representing each side should appoint a third, all of whom were to be impartial and disinterested.

The third appointee was to be the president of the board of arbitration, and any two members of that board might render a decision. They were supposed to meet and organize as soon as possible after their appointment, to hear and determine the controversy, sign their decision, and file it in the office of the Commissioner of Labor, who at that time occupied the position which was subsequently enlarged into the present Department of Labor. Each member of this board was to receive $10 a day for his services during the time actually consumed in the settlement of any dispute. The President was authorized in the same law of 1888 to appoint two commissioners, one of whom was to be a resident of the State where the dispute existed, and who, with the Commissioner of Labor, were to investigate the causes of any dispute and suggest a settlement or remedy, the result to be reported to the President and Congress, whereupon the commission ceased to exist. The President was authorized to tender the services of this commission to settle any dispute either on his own motion or on the application of either side or upon the application of the executive of the State in which the dispute existed. The President could direct the commission to visit the scene of the controversy, and it had all the powers given to a board of arbitration. It was to hear and consider the disputes, make its report, and file that with the Commissioner of Labor, as the board of arbitration, which I have already mentioned, was to do.

That law was in existence from 1888 to 1898, but during its entire 10 years on the statutes not one controversy was ever settled by the arbitration provisions of that early law, and only one dispute was ever considered by the investigating commission referred to in the latter provisions of the law, and that was the famous Pullman strike which occurred in Chicago in 1894 while Grover Cleveland was President, in which Eugene V. Debs and others were enjoined from interfering with interstate commerce or with the transportation of the mails. President Cleveland sent troops out to Chicago to preserve order and to prevent interference with the transportation of the mails.

It was recognized during the existence of this law that it was inadequate, and there began a movement for its amendment; various bills were introduced in the House and in the Senate.

In 1898 the sentiment which had crystallized for some amendments to this law took form in the House and in the Senate by the enactment of the law now known as the Erdman Act. The Erdman Act was limited in its application to employees who were engaged in actual train service and had no application to the settlement of disputes arising among any other class of railroad employees. It did not provide for any investigation, as authorized in the act of 1888, but provided for mediation and conciliation, for which the former law did not provide in terms, although the committee of investigation authorized to be appointed by the President might be said to correspond in some degree to the Board of Mediation and Conciliation provided in the Erdman Act.

Under the Erdman Act in case of any controversy over wages, hours of labor, or conditions of employment the chairman of the Interstate Commerce Commission and the Commissioner of Labor were to communicate with both sides and try to settle it by mediation and conciliation. In the event they failed to bring about a settlement by mediation and conciliation they were to endeavor to bring about arbitration through a board of three, one of whom was to be named by the road or roads involved in the controversy, another by the employees involved in the dispute, and these two were to name a third, and a majority of this commission of three or board of arbitration might render a decision.

Under the terms of the Erdman Act any agreement to arbitrate was to be submitted in writing, under certain stipulations which the law provided, which I need not detail. After the award was made it was to be filed in the office of the clerk of the United States circuit court in the district where the dispute arose or where the arbitration was entered into, and was to go into effect within 10 days from its filing. Exceptions might be filed by either side within 10 days to the award, and it was to be tried out in the circuit court of the United States.

If the report of the award was sustained by the court it was to become binding and, under the terms of the Erdman Act, no employer could discharge an employee pending the settlement or for three months after the settlement without 30 days' notice, and the employees could not terminate their employment by any concerted action upon their part except under the same conditions. There was no penalty attached in this statute which would punish either side for a violation of that provision.

The law also provided that all members of any corporation should cease to be members in case they used force to bring about the settlement of any railroad dispute, but a corporation was not liable for the acts of its members, nor the members for the acts of the corporation. The corporations referred to evidently were not only the railroads but the labor organizations, which were incorporated in certain cases.

Contracts prohibiting any employee from joining an organization were declared to be void. This provision was afterwards declared unconstitutional by the Supreme Court.

Under the terms of the Erdman Act all the provisions of the act of 1888 were repealed.

For eight years and a half after the passage of the Erdman Act only one attempt was made to use it, and this attempt failed; but during the remainder of its existence, which was until the Newlands Act was enacted in 1913, 61 disputes arising upon the railroads of this country between the carriers and their employees were settled and adjusted under its provisions. No award ever made under this act was ever repudiated by either side, and only one appeal was ever taken to the courts of the United States as a result of awards made under the operation of the Erdman law.

One of the greatest improvements of this act over that of 1888 was a provision for a permanent Board of Mediation and Conciliation instead of a temporary board appointed for each particular emergency, but during all the existence of this law agitation became widespread throughout the country and in both Houses of Congress for its further amendment, and many bills were introduced by Members of the Senate and by Members of the House.

The result of this, in 1913, was the law which has since been known as the Newlands Act, which was in fact a mere amendment and extension of the Erdman Act, but which was afterwards known as the Newlands law and which repealed the provisions of the Erdman Act.

This law, like the Erdman law, applied only to employees engaged in actual train service. In the event there was a dispute between the roads and their employees over wages, hours of labor, or conditions of employment, either side might request, as in the Erdman Act, this permanent Board of Mediation, which was provided for in the law, to make an effort to bring about a settlement. If the Board of Mediation was unable to bring about a settlement, the law provided for an arbitration by another board of three, one to be appointed by each side and one by the two, or if they failed to make the appointment, the third member was to be appointed by the Board of Mediation and Conciliation; or they might have, if they desired and preferred, a board of six, in which event two were to be appointed by each side and the other two by the four, or if they failed to appoint within 15 days, then the other two might be appointed by the Board of Mediation and Conciliation.

There was also provided in the law that there should be, in case of failure to settle the dispute by the Board of Mediation, an agreement to arbitrate, and this agreement had to be signed by both sides and had to contain certain stipulations as to what the award was to provide for. I believe there were 12 different things that the agreement had to stipulate. The award was likewise to be filed in the United States circuit court, and exception might be filed within 10 days to its provisions, to be tried out by the circuit court, and after they were tried out by the circuit court, if the award was sustained, it likewise became binding upon both parties. If there were no exceptions filed, the award became binding after 10 days.

In the agreement to arbitrate both sides had to agree that they would abide by the results of the arbitration, which, of course, was subject to be nullified on grounds of fraud or that it did not comply with the law or the terms of arbitration.

In addition to this, the President was to appoint a commissioner of mediation and conciliation, who was made a permanent officer of the United States, and in addition to this commissioner he was to designate two other officers already in the Government service, who were to compose the board of three to be known as the Board of Mediation and Concilliation, with the commissioner of mediation as the chairman, who was to receive, I believe, a salary of $7,500 per annum. It provided also for an assistant commissioner of mediation and conciliation, and the old law of 1898 was likewise repealed.

That was in 1913, and the Newlands Act was in force from that time until the Government took over the railroads in the latter part of 1917. During that four and a half years up to June 30, 1917, many controversies were adjusted and settled. In all I believe 71 separate and distinct controversies between the railroads and the employees arising out of dispute over wages, hours of service, and conditions of labor were settled and adjusted under the Newlands Act, and in all a total of 148 cases were brought to consideration, some of which were withdrawn or otherwise disposed of.

Then, in 1916 the Adamson law was enacted, which provided for an eight-hour day, which I need not take the time to discuss and which many Members will remember, and which did not apply to any settlement of dispute by mediation and conciliation because the dispute was settled by act of Congress.

During the operation of the railroads by the Government a different method was set up for adjusting railroad disputes. In fact, when the Government took over the roads there was a dispute pending between the railroad employees and the carriers which had been pending for several weeks or months, but was settled some time after they were taken over, and the director general gave out a statement in which he said this dispute which existed at the time the Government took the roads over and inherited it would be settled, and that the men should go on with the work and depend on the Government to bring about a method of settlement which would be just and fair to both sides.

Acting under that statement, the director general appointed a commission composed of four members; that commission held hearings for many months and considered the disputes and finally brought in a report which recommended a certain increase in wages. That report, with very slight changes, was put into effect by the director general, and on account of the delay in bringing about that adjustment it was made retroactive, to take effect January 1, 1918.

After that dispute was settled, recognizing the fact that, as history had already demonstrated, other disputes were likely to arise in the operation of the roads between the carriers and the men, a board of railroad wages and working conditions was created, whose report had to be submitted to the director general before going into effect.

There are two sorts of disputes that arise on railroads. One kind is a dispute growing out of the interpretation of agreement as to wage scales or working conditions that already exist. These disputes might be termed grievances; they might affect a large number of men in some way and they might affect only a small number of men, or they might affect a single individual. Recognizing the difference between the character of these disputes, the director general instituted boards of adjustment which were not to deal with the questions involved in changes of wages, their increase or decrease or change in the working conditions or hours of service, but these boards were to deal with adjustments and were to be composed of the representatives of the men themselves and of the carriers, to be selected by the respective sides of the dispute, or if there was no dispute the boards were created and made permanent during the Government operation and they were to settle all grievances of every kind and character growing out of disputes that arose over the interpretation of existing agreements as to scales of wages and conditions of service.

The board on wages and working conditions was a board which after the first settlement was to settle all disputes arising with reference to increase or decrease in wages or changes in working conditions. The boards of adjustment were numbered adjustment board No. 1, dealing with one class of employees, and board No. 2, dealing with a different class of employees, and board No. 3, dealing with still other classes.

Not only the first director general but Walker D. Hines, who was subsequently appointed, the railroads themselves, the Department of Labor, and every organization and every agency that had any opportunity to observe the operation of this system of settlement have testified to its efficiency, to its fairness, and the wise methods which were adopted in the settlement of disputes.

When the railroads were turned back to the owners under the Esch-Cummins Act, which passed in February, 1920, a new method was set up for settling disputes arising between the railroads and employees. It seemed to be recognized by Congress, and by a large number of people, that the

railroads ought not to be turned back to the private owners without providing some method of adjusting disputes that might arise. During the latter
days of the operation of the Newlands Act there had grown up a wide-
spead belief among many people, and particularly among the employees of
the railroads, that the Newlands Act itself in many respects ought to be
amended and changed. In November, 1919, Mr. Esch, of Wisconsin, chairman of the Committee on Interstate and Foreign Commerce, introduced the
original Esch bill restoring the railroads to private operation, and in that
bill he provided a method by which disputes might be settled between the
roads and their employees, and that method was that conferences were enjoined by the act itself upon the employees and the carriers in an effort
to bring about an adjustment of their difficulties without interference from
the outside.

That bill passed in November, 1919. During its consideration the Anderson amendment introduced by the gentleman from Minnesota, Mr. Anderson, was substituted for the Esch provisions as introduced by the committee in the House in November. Even that amendment provided for conferences and the appointment of adjustment boards and for provision for
mediation and conciliation somewhat similar to the provisions of the Erdman
and Newlands Acts.

That bill went to the Senate with the Anderson amendment included
within it, as passed by the House. In the meantime, Senator Cummins, of
Iowa, had introduced a bill which was radically different from either the
Anderson amendment or the original text provision, and which provided
for compulsory arbitration, providing a drastic and stringent law that made
it unlawful for any two or more men to agree to quit their work prior to
the submission of a dispute to arbitration, pending the arbitration and after
it had been arbitrated. So that under the terms of that bill any two men,
father and son, brother and brother, at the breakfast table in the morning,
who were participants in a dispute with the railroad company, if they agreed,
talking things over at their breakfast, that they would quit, would violate
the law, and they might be punished by heavy fine and imprisonment.
When the House bill went to the Senate, after its consideration here, the
Cummins amendment was inserted and was passed by the Senate practically as introduced by Senator Cummins. When that bill came back here
from the Senate it provided for compulsory arbitration and for drastic antistrike provisions which punished by fines and imprisonment any two or
more railroad employees on any road engaged in interstate commerce and
subject to the act to regulate commerce, who got together and agreed to
quit. The bill was sent to conference. The conferees were engaged every
day for six weeks in undertaking to adjust the differences between the
House and the Senate, and after many laborious days of consultation and
conference, debate and dispute, the conferees brought back into the House

and into the Senate the Esch-Cummins law as it now exists. Two of the members of the conference, of whom I was one, refused to sign that report, and refused to vote for it upon its passage. Title III of the Esch-Cummins law provides that there shall be a conference between the railroads and their employees in an effort to bring about an adjustment of all disputes, not only involving grievances or the interpretation of existing contracts, but in order that all disputes arising out of controversies over increases or decreases of wages, or any change in the working conditions might be settled by a conference among these railroads and their employees.

The history of railroading in this country has demonstrated that the most satisfactory method of adjustment of all railroad disputes involving labor and working conditions has been when the men on both sides were permitted to sit down at a table and settle their own disputes without interference from the outside. [Applause.] But in the event that they could not settle their disputes by a conference, the present Esch-Cummins law provides that there shall be set up voluntary adjustment boards, to be composed of men on both sides. There is no compulsion, however, in the law relative to the setting up of these adjustment boards. They were supposed to take the place of the adjustment boards provided in the operation of the roads by the Federal Government, so that where conferences had not been able on the ground to settle these disputes they might be referred to these various boards of adjustment set up either in regions or in any locality by common consent of the roads and their employees. After the adoption of this law the railroad employees, from one end of this Nation to the other, offered to enter into agreements setting up these adjustment boards. They made these propositions not only nation-wide, but they made them to their individual employers upon the individual roads of the United States. Some of the railroads agreed to these adjustment boards, but many of them did not agree, and until this time many of the railroads have refused to enter into agreements with their employees establishing these adjustment boards either in the regions or upon individual roads, so that this particular part of the present law has been ineffective, for the sole reason that many railroad companies have refused to carry out the spirit even of the Esch-Cummins law in the formation of these adjustment boards.

The present law provides for the present Railroad Labor Board, composed of nine members, three of whom are to be appointed by the President from a list submitted by the railroad employees, three of whom are to be appointed by the President from lists submitted by railroads, and the other three to be appointed by the President from the public.

These nine men now form the Railroad Labor Board. So far as the labor provision in the Esch-Cummins law is concerned, I do not know yet where that particular title came from. It was brought into the conference committee somewhere from the outside. No employee was ever consulted with reference to its provisions. They were not permitted to come before the conference committee to express their desire with reference to labor legislation, but they have entered into the operation of the objectionable provision in a spirit of patriotism. They submitted their names to the President. It was contemplated that no dispute arising from disagreement as to the interpretation of existing wage scales and agreements should have to go to this Railroad Labor Board, except in cases where these adjustment boards referred to have been unable to reach an agreement. The Railroad Labor Board as now formed was intended to deal with larger questions—questions of wage increases or decreases, or the questions of changes in the fundamental conditions of labor that might apply upon the transportation systems of the country; but because many of the railroads and the employees have been unable to agree on the formation of these adjustment boards, the Labor Board, composed of nine men, sitting in Chicago, have been compelled not only to adjust differences involving the larger questions of railroad employment, but they have been compelled to consume their time in petty disputes arising on individual roads from the interpretation of a grievance, and even to take up their time adjusting individual disputes between individual men and the employers. As a result the Railroad Labor Board has been unable in many cases and unwilling in others so to function as to give satisfaction to either side in disputes arising.

The first three laws passed by Congress—that of 1888, the Erdman Act of 1898, and the Newlands Act of 1913—applied only to men actually engaged in the operation of trains. Recognizing that the people's primary interest in the problem concerned the service of continuous and uninterrupted transportation, Congress made no effort to include any except men in actual train service until the transportation act of 1920, and, although the latter applies to all employees of railroads, it made no effort to restrict or interfere with the fundamental right of private agreement as to wages or working conditions. And for that reason the laws which Congress enacted were limited to disputes and disagreements which might arise between the railroad companies and those who were engaged in the actual transportation of commodities in interstate commerce. During the life of the Newlands Act 148 disagreements between railroads and their employees were settled, and there was not a serious interruption of traffic nor a serious threat of interruption of traffic except in 1916, which resulted in the passage of the Adamson law.

I wish to call attention to the reason which made it impossible for that dispute to be adjusted under the terms of the Newlands Act. The heart of that contest, the thing around which the men and the roads disagreed, was the question of the 8-hour day. On about 15 per cent of the railroads of the United States the 8-hour day was in force, but upon about 85 per cent of the roads the 10-hour day as a standard of labor for the men engaged in the transportation of commerce was in effect. A dispute arose about the 8-hour day and about the allowance of overtime for work that was protracted beyond the 8-hour period, which was regarded as a fundamental right, as the 8-hour day had been established by the United States in the laws that applied to the public service and as the 8-hour day had been established in practically every other industry in the United States in response to the enlightened and progressive opinion of the people of our country.

It was generally agreed that in a hard and hazardous industry eight hours was as long as any man ought to be required to work as the standard of a day's labor. So the question arose over the arbitration of the 8-hour day. The employees contended that the 8-hour day ought not to be a subject of arbitration; that the 8-hour day had been accepted by civilized society as the standard of a man's work, and that they ought not to be required to go into arbitration over the question whether they should extend the hours of service beyond the period of time which society and our Government had recognized as wise and proper in the conservation of human energy. And so an impasse was reached between the railroads and their employees, and a serious strike which, if it had occurred, would not only have meant serious damage to labor and industry itself, but which might have resulted in the breaking down of our transportation system and might have resulted in hunger and want and starvation to the people of the United States, hung like a great cloud over the entire Nation. It was at that juncture that President Wilson called the two sides to Washington and asked them to confer with him over an amicable adjustment of this dispute. They came here, not of their own volition, but in response to his invitation. They conferred with him. Propositions were made back and forth, using him as an intermediary between the employees and the roads, and finally the employees said once and for all that they could not agree to arbitrate the 8-hour day, and President Wilson issued a public statement agreeing that they were right about that, and taking the position himself that the 8-hour day was a fundamental human right, and it was not subject to arbitration. [Applause.]

As a result of that situation he asked Congress to pass a law which recognized the 8-hour day as a standard for man's work in the United States on the transportation systems, and hence the Adamson law was enacted by Congress, and the strike, called by reason of the disagreement, was called off, and the Adamson law went into effect and has been in force from that time until now, and has been interpreted by the Supreme Court of the United States and held constitutional.

I shall not undertake to call attention in detail to the decision holding the Adamson law constitutional, but in view of the contention made by the opposition, which seems to have focused around one certain idea in connection with this legislation, I do desire to call attention to the question which was at the bar in that decision, and, if I have time, to read the language of the court in passing upon the thing which certain Members seem to hold as important in regard to this bill. You will recall that there was a disagreement on the part of the men and the roads; there was a failure of their minds to meet, and what is known as the Adamson law was intended to fill the gap between the two sides and make an agreement which they themselves were unable to arrive at; and in passing on the question of the constitutionality of the Adamson law the Supreme Court held that where there was a failure to agree, admitting that the parties had a primary and fundamental right to contract privately for fixed wages upon the railroads of the United States, where there was no agreement, where there was a gap between the minds on the two sides, Congress had the right to deal with the condition by passing a law that would bridge this gap and create an agreement by operation of the law in order that the people may have uninterrupted transportation.

But in that decision Chief Justice White over and over again reiterated and emphasized the principle that the rights of private agreement was one over which Congress had no power of control or restriction. In that decision, which is cited as *Wilson* v. *New* (243 U. S. 333), the court said:

It is also equally true that as the right to fix by agreement between the carrier and its employees a standard of wages to control their relations is primarily private, the establishment and giving effect to such an agreed-on standard is not subject to be controlled or to be prevented by public authority.

Then the court continues:

Conceding . . . the power between the parties employers and employees to agree as to a standard of wages free from legislative interference, that right in no way affects the lawmaking power to protect the public right and create a standard of wages resulting from a dispute as to wages and a failure thereby to establish by consent a standard.

This principle is reiterated time and again all through the decision.

I need not take the time of this committee to read that decision. It is a very lengthy decision, but if you have the time, especially those who are now contending for an amendment to this bill that shall give the public a right not only to representation when there is a dispute but which goes even further and says that the public has the right to sit in on any private agreement between the railroads and their men, because the public in the long run pays the bill, especially the Members who have that slant on this situation, it might be illuminative and instructive and valuable if you would study the lengthy decision of Chief Justice White in interpreting the Adamson Act in 1916.

So, my friends, every law that has been enacted in the United States, as well as the decisions which have been rendered in their interpretation, has started out upon the fundamental theory that a man who goes out in the night or in the day working upon the railroad or a man who works in a railroad shop or in any other capacity in interstate commerce has a fundamental, elemental, American right to have a voice in the price of his wage, and that he has the right to reach an agreement with his employer in respect of the amount of that wage and the working conditions under which it may be earned, and the law that is in existence now does not seek to take away that right.

In the very midst of the operation of the Newlands Act the war came on, and as a war measure the Government took over the railroads of the United States; but, of course, the taking over of the railroads did not operate to repeal the Newlands Act; and as a matter of fact, the passage of the transportation act itself did not in terms repeal the Newlands Act. So that some features of that law which have not been specifically repealed by the Constitution of the United States may even yet be in existence.

During the war, of course, the Government had the railroads, and we need not enter into any discussion about the merits of Government operation of railroads, but the experience of the Government during the operation of the railroads has been very valuable not only to the railroads but to the men themselves and to the Congress and all public authorities in undertaking to arrive at the psychology of labor situations and the psychology of labor rights and the rights of the public.

When the railroads were taken over by the Government in 1918—I believe, on January 1, 1918—there was a dispute then pending between the roads and their employees with reference to wages, and the United States Government inherited that dispute. The director general and the commissions which were operating with him—and, of course, he was advised not only by public authorities but by executives of railroads and by executives of railway labor organizations—created certain boards, some of them local, some of them regional, some of them national, for the purpose of adjusting these disputes that then existed between the railroads and their employees. For instance, a wage commission was appointed, which was nonpartisan, to settle the controversy then pending. I think Secretary Lane was on it; William Willcox, chairman of the Republican National Committee, was a member of it. I do not recall any of the other members. They heard the dispute, they heard all the testimony, and finally made a recommendation to the director general recommending certain increases in wages, and that recommendation was put into effect.

I want to say here, because I think probably it ought to be said, the man who was then director general of the railroads has received in one place and another very severe criticism for having increased the wages of the railroad employees after the railroads were taken over by the Government, but those increases were not made by him on his own initiative but were made in pursuance of a recommendation of a nonpartisan commission made up of Democrats and Republicans, who recommended these increases to the director general and they were put into effect as a result of that recommendation.

The war ended and we, of course, were confronted with a situation where we had to determine what was to be done with the railroads; whether there should be a continuation of Government operation for a year or two years or five years or whether there should be an immediate return of the roads to their owners. Congress decided the roads ought to be returned immediately. So they passed in 1920 what is now known as the transportation act, Title III of which deals with labor disputes.

I wish to give a little of the history of that legislation so that we may get a sufficient background and perspective and have an understanding about why its has been so ineffective in its settlement of disputes and in its enjoyment of confidence or lack of confidence among both sides to railroad disputes in the United States.

I must correct my good friend, the gentleman from Maine [Mr. Nelson], who suggested that Mr. Winslow, a great constitutional lawyer, was chairman of the Committee on Interstate and Foreign Commerce when the transportation act was passed. Mr. Winslow, of Massachusetts, as we all know, was a very delightful companion and very earnest in the advocacy of all his views, but I doubt if his warmest friend would contend he is a great constitutional lawyer. He is a business man and not a lawyer. But whether he is or not, he was not at that time chairman of the Committee on Interstate and Foreign Commerce. Mr. Esch, of Wisconsin, now a member of the Interstate Commerce Commission, was chairman of the Committee at that time, and I think our old friend from Tennessee, Judge Sims, was the ranking Democratic member on the committee.

As the bill passed the House it did little more than return the roads to the owners with certain technical amendments to the act to regulate commerce, except that it did try to set up some kind of machinery by which labor disputes might be adjusted. On the floor of the House, this provision which had been worked out laboriously and carefully in the committee, as the committee thought, was kicked out overwhelmingly and unceremoniously, and what was known as the Anderson amendment was substituted on the floor of the House and went to the Senate as a part of the Esch bill. This was in the fall of 1919.

In the Senate, the bill was considered by the Committee on Interstate Commerce, and all the language of the House bill was stricken out and the Senate rewrote the measure. Among other things it sought to deal with labor disputes. It set up a national board or transportation board. It undertook to set up adjustment boards; and in addition to the machinery by which they expected to settle disputes, they put in a rigid, automatic, and autocratic antistrike provision which provided if there was a dispute on the railroads, the men could not quit their employment before the dispute was submitted to arbitration, they could not quit while it was under submission, and they could not quit after it was decided. So an effective administration of it would have meant compulsory, lifetime employment on the part of the employees of the railroads, because they could not quit before, they could not quit during, and they could not quit after a dispute had arisen and had been settled. . . .

CLEVELAND NEWTON [R., MO.]. There was, of course, a provision permitting individual employees to quit at any time.

MR. BARKLEY. Yes; but it provided that no two men could agree to quit, and this meant that a father and son could not sit down at the breakfast table in the morning and agree they would not go back to work without subjecting themselves to a fine or imprisonment.

MR. NEWTON. Did the Senate amendment pass the Senate in that form?

MR. BARKLEY. Practically in that form. So when the bill went to conference the conferees had to adjust the differences between the House and the Senate. The Senate bill had a compulsory antistrike provision which made it a crime for two or more men to agree not to work, and that was the bone of contention so far as the labor provision was concerned. I think I am the only Member of the House who was then on the conference committee. The House conferees were Mr. Esch, Mr. Winslow, Mr. Hamilton of Michigan, Republicans, and Judge Sims and I were the Democratic conferees. We were in session in that conference for more than six weeks. On the Senate side, Senator Cummins, the author of the Cummins amendment, was chairman of the conferees, and the other conferees were the present minister to Peru, Senator Poindexter, the present Secretary of State, Mr. Kellogg, Senator Pomerene, of Ohio, and, I think, Senator Robinson, now the Democratic leader of the Senate.

In the labor title of that bill the present law was set up, and one of the first provisions of the title was that both sides should undertake to arrive at an agreement over wages. That law as it exists to-day does not take away from the parties the right to contract. That right was recognized; the only thing in that law that even squinted at the contrary is the provision to which I desire to refer a little later, but even that does not interfere with the right of the employees and the employers to make an agreement; even that does not give the Railroad Labor Board the power to suspend an agreement that has been reached by the men and the roads. All that does is to give the Labor Board the power to suspend its own decision if they believe that its own decision would result in a substantial increase of railroad rates in the United States. Of course, if they have the constitutional power to render a decision, they have the same power to suspend a decision, and perhaps set it aside. We are not dealing with that question now. . . .

FINIS GARRETT [DEM., TENN.]. I did not understand the gentleman's last statement—do I understand the gentleman to say that the only power given to the Labor Board is to suspend one of its own decisions?

MR. BARKLEY. The only power of suspension.

MR. GARRETT. The gentleman does not think the language of the act empowers the Labor Board to suspend an agreement reached voluntarily between the parties?

MR. BARKLEY. I do not think it does, and if it did, I do not think any such power would be constitutional. The language of the statute, giving the Labor Board the power of suspension, is as follows:

The Labor Board, (1) upon the application of the chief executive of any carrier or organization of employees or subordinate officials whose members are directly interested in the dispute; (2) upon a written petition signed by not less than 100 unorganized employees or subordinate officials directly interested in the dispute; or (3) upon the Labor Board's own motion if it is of the opinion that the dispute is likely substantially to interrupt commerce, shall receive for hearing, and as soon as practicable and with due diligence decide, all disputes with respect to the wages or salaries or employees or subordinate officials of carriers, not decided as provided in section 301. The Labor Board may upon its own motion within 10 days after the decision, in accordance with the provisions of section 301, of any dispute with respect to wages or salaries of employees or subordinate officials of carriers, suspend the operation of such decision if the Labor Board is of the opinion that the decision involves such an increase in wages or salaries as will be likely to necessitate a substantial readjustment of the rates of any carrier. The Labor Board shall hear any decision so suspended and as soon as practicable and with due diligence decide to affirm or modify such suspended decision.

Title III of the present transportation act was not, as my friend from Maine [Mr. Nelson] says, deliberated on here in the House of Representatives. It never came from any committee of this House. It was not put in the bill by any action of this House. All those who are now on the floor, who were Members then, will remember that the conference report came in here on the 21st of February—I believe that was the date—a little more than a week before the automatic adjournment of Congress on the 4th of March, and that there were many Members of this House who were fearful that if they voted against the conference report it would result in no legislation whatever, and that the Government would still maintain the operation of the roads for an indefinite period; and there were many who did not approve of it, who were afraid that if they voted against it that the vote might be interpreted as being in favor of Government ownership of railroads in the United States. So by reason of lack of time the conference report was rushed through the House, without any deliberation worthy of the importance of that great question, which had not been passed upon by the House or any committee that had jurisdiction of the legislation. . . .

MR. BEEDY. Mr. Chairman, referring to the question recently put by the minority leader, the gentleman from Tennessee [Mr. Garrett], and the reply of the gentleman from Kentucky that he does not think the present law gives the Labor Board any power to suspend decisions voluntarily arrived at by the employees and the railroad executives, if the gentleman from Kentucky has a copy of the transportation act of 1920 before him, may I ask him to turn to that section and tell me what this provision in that law means, which immediately follows the statement of the power of the board to suspend decisions:

The Labor Board shall hear any decision so suspended, and as soon as practicable and with due diligence decide to affirm or modify such suspended decision.

MR. BARKLEY. Of course, if after it has rendered a decision, facts are brought to it that would bring the matter within this provision, or if they think a wage increase, if there has been a wage increase, would materially increase rates upon railroads, and are convinced of that, then, of course, they would have the power to suspend their own decision.

That would not mean that the suspension should operate indefinitely. Both sides would have the right to be heard; first on the question of whether the increased wages materially increased rates, and second, whether it would be a justifiable increase and whether the wage itself is justified. Let me read again the whole section. Subsection (b) of Section 307 of the transportation act reads as follows:

(b) The Labor Board, (1) upon the application of the chief executive of any carrier or organization of employees or subordinate officials whose members are directly interested in the dispute, (2) upon a written petition signed by not less than 100 unorganized employees or subordinate officials directly interested in the dispute, or (3) upon the Labor Board's own motion if it is of the opinion that the dispute is likely substantially to interrupt commerce, shall receive for hearing, and as soon as practicable and with due diligence decide, all disputes with respect to the wages or salaries of employees or subordinate officials of carriers not decided as provided in section 301. The Labor Board may upon its own motion with 10 days after the decision, in accordance with the provisions of section 301, of any dispute with respect to wages or salaries of employees or subordinate officials of carriers, suspend the operation of such decision if the Labor Board is of the opinion that the decision involves such an increase in wages or salaries as will be likely to necessitate a substantial readjustment of the rates of any carrier.

It will be seen that the emphasis there is laid upon the fact that the dispute is liable to interrupt interstate commerce. That gives them the jurisdiction to take charge even on their own motion, without application from either side.

What decision is it they may suspend? Its own decision arrival at in one of the manners provided for in the previous language.

The Labor Board shall hear any decision so suspended and as soon as practicable and with due diligence decide to affirm or modify such suspended decision.

After it has made a decision upon a dispute between the carrier and its employees as to wages, and that decision is presumed to be upon the merits of the controversy, if they believe it involves such an increase in wages as would require a substantial increase in rates, they have the power to suspend their own decision; and after they have suspended it, of course, the provision is made that they hear both sides again as to whether the suspension shall be limited for a period of time or shall be made permanent, or allowed to stand indefinitely. Certainly it would have been an unfair thing to give them the right to suspend their own decision but to give them no right to reconsider their own decision of suspension.

MR. BEEDY. Before we leave this question, might it not be helpful to the House, inasmuch as specific reference is made to Section 301, to say that that section refers to such decisions as may be rendered through failure of a conference between the representatives of the parties in dispute.

MR. BARKLEY. That Section 301 is a general provision under the title which gives authority for adjustment.

MR. BEEDY. It refers to these decisions, does it not?

MR. BARKLEY. If the gentleman is prepared to contend—

MR. BEEDY. Oh, I am trying to bring out the facts for general information.

MR. BARKLEY. Let us admit for the sake of argument that this section could be read back into the whole of Section 301, and undertook to give the Railroad Labor Board power to suspend a private agreement between the railroads and their men. That attempt to confer that authority upon the Labor Board would be an interference with the right of private contract which the Supreme Court of the United States, in the case of Wilson *v.* New, which was a decision growing out of the Adamson law, said could not be done. Because in that decision they held, not only that Congress could not control the matter of a private agreement as to wages, but could not even restrict the right of the employer and the employee to enter into an agreement over wages and conditions of employment. But the transportation act confers no power on the Labor Board to suspend private agreements as to wages. . . .

RALPH LOZIER [DEM. MO.]. In the last analysis, does not this section refer to cases where there is an existing acute dispute, and not the cases where there has been an adjustment between the employees and the railroads?

MR. BARKLEY. Yes. Of course, the whole machinery set up not only by the present law, but all the machinery set up by every law that has been passed heretofore has been predicated upon the fact that they could not agree upon wages, and that in the absence of an agreement there ought to be some public functionary which could step into the gap and make an agreement or adjustment that would not interrupt interstate commerce. . . .

OTIS WINGO [DEM., ARK.]. I think possibly the gentleman may have overlooked one point in Section 301. Section 301 is so short, that, if the gentleman will permit, I shall read it before I ask the question I have in mind. Section 301 reads as follows:

SEC. 301. It shall be the duty of all carriers and their officers, employees, and agents to exert every reasonable effort and adopt every available means to avoid any interruption to the operation of any carrier growing out of any dispute between the carrier and the employees or subordinate officials thereof. All such disputes shall be considered and, if possible, decided in conference between representatives designated and authorized so to confer by the carriers, or the employees or subordinate officials thereof, directly interested in the dispute. If any dispute is not decided in such conference, it shall be referred by the parties thereto to the board which under the provisions of this title is authorized to hear and decide such dispute.

The question is this: In the section which the gentleman read, which is subsection (b), paragraph (3) of Section 307, is this language:

Upon the Labor Board's own motion if it is of the opinion that the dispute is likely substantially to interrupt commerce shall receive for hearing, and as soon as practical and with due diligence decide, all disputes with respect to the wages and salaries of employees or subordinate officials or of carriers, not decided as provided in section 301.

In other words, if there may not be any agreement as to wages between employees and the railroads that the Labor Board would be then authorized to suspend because they only come in with power when called into operation where the parties have failed to agree and where the board has made a decision and in itself wanted to suspend its own decision.

MR. BARKLEY. The gentleman is correct, but in emphasis of that I will say that reference in subsection (b) of Section 307 to the previous Section 301 is only made necessary because Section 301 in its last sentence uses this language. It provides for the settlement of disputes by this Labor Board where there is a disagreement which has not been settled by conference. If it were not for that last sentence, there would be no necessity for subsection (b) of Section 307 even to refer to Section 301 in providing for suspensions of the decisions of the Railway Labor Board. . . .

WILLIAM STEVENSON [DEM., S.C.]. If the gentleman will permit, that is the principle that has been established by this decision of the Supreme Court and various others that the Congress and its instrumentalities can prescribe the hours of labor, what constitutes a day's labor, the limitations of employment of laborers so as to conserve the safety of the public, but it can not undertake to say through any of its instrumentalities as to how much a laborer shall have for eight hours' labor. That is left entirely as a matter of contract, and neither can we do it here under the decision of the Supreme Court.

MR. BARKLEY. The gentleman is correct. But Congress has power under the commerce clause of the Constitution to make such regulations as necessary to conserve the health, safety, and welfare of the employees, and the manner in which interstate commerce may proceed, and under the commerce clause of the Constitution if there had never been a decision of the Supreme Court controlling the subject, we would know intuitively that we can not interfere with the private right of a man who labors in private industry to control the price of his own labor, and the fact that he works on a railroad, which is a public utility, does not deprive him of that right, and I dare say those who are contending here that this right ought to be abridged by Congress would not be willing to have such a restriction applied to their own private affairs. . . .

MR. BLANTON. Before the gentleman leaves the subject of the right of the board to suspend—

MR. BARKLEY. Just for a moment.

MR. BLANTON. Is it not also the fact that in making a private agreement in respect to wage schedules both the railroads and employees always recognize the fact that if they should make an unreasonable agreement the public still is safeguarded because it knows that the Interstate Commerce Commission would then refuse to pass that on to any increased freight rates, and is not that a deterrent upon the railroads to enter into anything that would be unreasonable and unfair?

MR. BARKLEY. I think the gentleman is correct. Now, in reference to all laws upon the subject of the regulation of the relationship of employer and employees, after they have exercised what is their fundamental and constitutional right the people have the Interstate Commerce Commission which is entitled, and it is made its duty even in the present law, to make inquiry into the economical management of every railroad to determine whether an increase of rates should be allowed, and of course that would be an element to be taken into consideration. . . .

MR. NEWTON. And under the proposed law it applies not only to an agreement between the parties but as to awards made by way of arbitration or in any other way?

MR. BARKLEY. Oh, yes. The Interstate Commerce Commission has absolutely free power to determine the elements which go into the economical management of railroads with the view of determining whether it shall have any weight in the application for increased rates. . . .

OLGER BURTNESS [R., N.D.]. Before leaving the question of power of the present Labor Board to suspend wage agreements, I want to get that clear. Do I understand the gentleman to claim that the present Labor Board has no power to suspend an agreement; that that would be lodged not in the Labor Board itself but in the labor adjustment board, provided for under the present transportation act?

MR. BARKLEY. The present transportation act does not provide for adjustment boards in settling wages, and the adjustment boards provided for in this bill are not to deal with the wage question, but technical disputes that only a technician could understand and which would require somebody to examine and know in reference to it, so the Labor Board would have no power to suspend agreements originating under any adjustment board, because such agreements do not deal with wages but with grievances.

MR. BURTNESS. The language that the gentleman from Arkansas [Mr. Wingo] did not read out of subdivision (b) of Section 306—just one sentence—is as follows:

The Labor Board may on its own motion, within 10 days after a decision, examine into the provisions of Section 301 in relation to any dispute, suspend the operation of such decision if the Labor Board is of the opinion that the decision involves such an increase of wages or salaries as will likely necessitate a substantial readjustment of the rates of a common carrier.

And, then, the last sentence in Section 301 reads as follows, after stating that it is the duty of the carrier and employees, and so on, to come together—

If any dispute is not decided in such conference it shall be referred by the parties thereto to the board which under the provisions of this title is authorized to hear and decide such dispute.

Now, is it the contention of the gentleman that the only decisions with reference to wages that can be suspended by the Railroad Labor Board are the decisions which the Labor Board itself makes?

MR. BARKLEY. That is my contention, because in this language here it refers to decisions all the way through, and to its own decision; and an agreement where there was no dispute would not be a decision. It would be a contract. . . .

MR. NEWTON. The gentleman referred to the jurisdiction of the adjustment board under Title III of the transportation act, and I think unduly restricted their jurisdiction in his remarks. My recollection is that the Railroad Labor Board is given appellate jurisdiction under Title III over the decisions of the adjustment board regarding grievances?

MR. BARKLEY. Yes. Either side has the right, even where adjustment boards are created, to appeal from the decisions of that board; but that appeal would not involve the question of wages, and therefore suspension of it would not be applicable.

MR. WINGO. In the same Section 307, subdivision (d), it says:

All the decisions of the Labor Board in respect to wages or salaries and of the Labor Board or an adjustment board in respect to working conditions of employees or subordinate officials of carriers shall establish rates of wages and salaries and standards of working conditions which in the opinion of the board are just and reasonable.

And so forth. Am I correct in my interpretation of that, that the decisions of the Labor Board are the only ones that cover wages that might be adjudicated and considered, and that the adjustment boards are restricted to working conditions of employees?

MR. BARKLEY. The adjustment boards were not even given the power to consider changes in working conditions. You see there are two kinds of disputes recognized on railroads. One is the interpretation of agreements already in existence, applying to discipline and small grievances that may not only come up with reference to groups of men but may arise with reference to a single man. These are all technical. They have nothing to do with the wages received, but they have to do with the technical interpretation of agreements that exist and the exercise of discipline between the management and employees.

MR. WINGO. I am not clear on this. We will cut out what it says about the Labor Board with respect to wages and salaries. "All the decisions of the Labor Board and adjustment board are with respect to working conditions of employees." What does that mean? I understood the gentleman from Kentucky to say that could not cover the question of working conditions.

MR. BARKLEY. You can imagine that any dispute over the interpretation of an agreement would involve some working condition. It might involve how long a man would work in a certain place or what work he should do. But a change in general working conditions and wages is a matter over which the adjustment board has no jurisdiction. The same idea is carried in this bill also. . . .

MR. GARRETT. The gentleman stated a moment ago that it is the duty of the Interstate Commerce Commission, in considering the question of rates, to take various matters into consideration, among other things economical administration and operation. Arguing from that, it could take wages into consideration, could it not? Am I correct in that?

MR. BARKLEY. They have the power to do that, and it is their duty, and they do it all the time.

MR. GARRETT. Well, if they take that into consideration, what can they do about it so far as rates are concerned?

MR. BARKLEY. For instance, if they should conclude that there had been an unreasonable increase of railroad wages by the railroads to their employees and the roads should ask that their rates be increased by reason of the increase of wages, the Interstate Commerce Commission would have the power to say, "You have increased the wages unreasonably, and therefore you must bear the burden yourself, and not pass it on to the public." They could do that; that is, in determining upon the question of economical management, and they have in the past done that very thing.

MR. GARRETT. Does not the gentleman think that might bring us into conflict with the confiscation provision of the Constitution? It is admitted by all of us that the right exists to enter into a private agreement.

MR. BARKLEY. I do not think the question of confiscation needs deter us. Of course, the railroads have the right to reasonable rates, and the Interstate Commerce Commission the power to go into that and determine what a reasonable rate should be.

Now, Mr. Chairman, I shall have to take more time than I intended if I yield further at this point.

MR. HOCH. Just one word on the question of confiscation. In the case mentioned by the gentleman from Tennessee [Mr. Garrett], if it were an unreasonable wage adjustment, it would not be a question of Government confiscation, but a question of the carrier itself confiscating, and therefore I think they would have the power to refuse. . . .

MR. BLANTON. The gentleman spoke of the efficacy of the Erdman Act and mentioned that for 15 years, or during its life, there were 61 adjustments.

MR. BARKLEY. I do not want to go back to that again. I have passed by that long ago.

MR. BLANTON. What I want to ask the gentleman is this: Could we write a better bill on behalf of the public than the Erdman Act?

MR. BARKLEY. Yes; and I think we have done it in this bill.

MR. BLANTON. I think the Erdman Act is the best act the public has ever had in respect to railroad legislation, and if we could get back to it, I think the country would be better off.

MR. BARKLEY. I think the gentleman from Texas is gradually yielding and will come over entirely to our side before we get through with the consideration of this bill.

We were talking when I was diverted about the Railroad Labor Board as set up by the present law. This board has been in existence now for the last six years, and this brings me to a discussion of the necessity and advisability of some legislation to take its place.

I have been asked by a number of the Members of the House, as well as by others, what is the ground for the dissatisfaction with the Railroad Labor Board which now exists. I do not think any man can truthfully deny that not only among the railway employees, but among the railway managers and the public generally, to say the least of it, the Railroad Labor Board has been a distinct disappointment. In the first place, an effort was made here to set up a piece of machinery that partook of two different principles.

Congress tried to convince a certain element of our people that they were putting compulsion in the law, and it tried to convince another element of our people that they were not putting in compulsion but were just putting in persuasion.

We passed this law in a hurry, and nobody who represented or understood the problem of railway labor had anything to do with the writing of Title III of the transportation act. I have already shown it was not considered by a committee of this House. It was not considered by the House itself. It was not recommended by anybody from any source who could remotely claim that he spoke for the employees or the employers on the transportation systems of our country. I am frank to say I do not know where Title III came from. It was injected into the conference between the House and the Senate during the six weeks in which they sat, but I have never yet learned what fertile mind produced the thought which resulted in the enactment of Title III.

Therefore it can not be said to represent what the railroad laborers wanted, and so far as we know it does not represent what the managers wanted. It was an effort on the part of inexperienced men in Congress, who did not understand the psychology of labor, to superimpose their will upon a great body of men who were loyally and faithfully, as they have always done, ministering to the wants of the American people in the transportation of commerce and passenger traffic.

This is one of the reasons it has been a failure. It assumed to have compulsion without any power of compulsion. It made of men who set themselves up as judges to decide a given difficulty also mediators, and whenever a judge settles a controversy between two disputants, he no longer can be a mediator between them, because his decision is bound to give dissatisfaction to one side or the other. After that he can not operate as a mediator between the same parties in disputes that may arise in the future. This is a matter, of course, of human nature, and I think it was Artemus Ward who said: "One man has about as much human nature in him as another, if not more." [Laughter.]

So we have had this Railroad Labor Board for the last six years, and in the exercise of their jurisdiction I need not undertake to impugn their motives, I need not undertake to criticize them severely, though I might be justified in doing that with respect to some members of it if I desired to inject their personality into this debate. But by the very nature of their creation, by the very nature of their functions and their duties, it was bound to fail because it was a hybrid organization, one part going that way and another part this way, and it was never able to enjoy the confidence of either side.

I said that this Labor Board had lost the confidence of both sides to railroad disputes. In the hearings before our committee—and I want to say on the floor of this House what I said in the committee—in my 14 years of membership on the Committee on Interstate and Foreign Commerce, I have never witnessed a more able or more courteous or more profound discussion of the great problems that confronted us than was engaged in by the men who participated in that discussion before our committee. If you examine the hearings, you will find those who spoke for the railroad labor employees announced that their confidence in this Labor Board, if it ever existed, had been completely destroyed. You will find that the representatives of the railroad managers and the presidents themselves said it would not be resorted to again by either side in controversies that may arise in the years to come. Why? Well, on the part of the employees because, if the Labor Board rendered a decision that was unfavorable to the railroads, the board had no power to compel their obedience, and in many cases railroads that did not like the decisions of the Labor Board ignored them, refused to abide by them, and the employees and the courts and the Government itself had no power to compel the railroads to obey the decisions of the Labor Board, and as a result nobody could do anything.

On the other hand, if the employees did not like the decision of the Labor Board, they had no recourse except voluntarily relinquish their employment, either as individuals or as groups, which would bring about a strike, or accept the will of their employer because the board had no power to compel the employee or employer to obey its decisions. Therefore it is not strange that the employees soon lost confidence in it, and they expressed in one way or another their dissent from its decisions, and then to make matters worse, unfortunately, the chairman of the board, who has flooded us in the last few days with a long letter protesting against this bill, went over the country making speeches in which he denounced members of the employee group because they were unwilling to abide by his decisions, whereas at the same time men on the other side were equally violating them, and the board had no power to compel obedience in either case. So that Mr. Alfred P. Thom—for whom I have a very high regard as a lawyer and as a man, representing the carriers—in the hearings said that in the future neither side will resort to the Railroad Labor Board in the settlement of railroad disputes and we know the same attitude is taken by the men who work upon these great transportation systems. If both sides state that they will not resort to the present machinery for settling their disputes, what are we to do? Shall we face this situation like men and try to solve it, or shall we refuse to act for the public interest or attempt to set up machinery that all parties believe will be successful?

We are confronted as Members of Congress with the situation where the present machinery has broken down, where it has been unsatisfactory to all who have dealt with it, and we must ask ourselves seriously whether, with the situation confronting us, we are willing to do something that will insure peace and harmony and insure uninterrupted transportation and bring a new era in the relations of railroad capital and railroad labor by the enactment of the law before us.

Now I want to outline the details of the law, without undertaking to read it. In the first place, hearings showed that not only did this condition of unsatisfactory adjudication exist in the Railroad Labor Board, but evidence of that dissatisfaction was manifest in every part of the country and in Congress during the last three or four years. When asked by members of the committee why the road executives had gone into conference and reached an agreement with the employees on the principles of this bill, the representative of the railroads stated that in the last Congress a bill had been introduced in the Senate and the House which became known as the Howell-Barkley bill. I do not propose to discuss that measure except in its bearing on the present situation.

This Howell-Barkley bill, among other things, proposed to abolish the Railroad Labor Board. It was reported out in the Senate by the Committee on Interstate Commerce and showed at least, without regard to the merits of other provision of the bill, that the Senate committee had agreed that the Railroad Labor Board as it now exists had outlived its usefulness, if it had ever had any. In the House the bill was taken from the Committee on Interstate and Foreign Commerce by a vote of the majority, indicating, without regard to any difference of opinion on other principles of the bill, that everybody was practically agreed that the Railroad Labor Board as it now exists ought to be abolished. Therefore, if the Senate committee took such action and believed that the Railroad Labor Board ought to be abolished, and if the House, in taking such action as it took, endeavored to express the view that the Railroad Labor Board ought to be abolished, we are bound to confront the situation wherein this Congress was likely to pass a bill that would abolish the Railroad Labor Board and adopt something which will take its place.

The bill we have before us does what the Howell-Barkley bill did and what the present law requires; it makes it the duty of both sides to make every effort to agree upon the wages and working conditions. It puts upon the railroads and the employees the legal obligation to exert themselves in every reasonable way to arrive at an agreement over wages and working conditions. So the bill does what the present law does, what the Erdman Act, what the Newlands Act, and what the first law ever passed by Congress did—recognized the right of private agreement between the railroads of this country and their employees with respect to wages and conditions of labor. It provides that it shall be the duty of the railroads and their employees to settle their own disputes. Who does not want them to do that? Who desires to superimpose the right of the Government to interfere with the right of both sides to consult themselves in composing their differences? Who is there who would advocate seriously that it is a wise public policy for Congress to undertake to interject itself into the situation where it may make it more difficult for men to agree, rather than to make it more easy for men to agree? So we provide that it shall be their first duty to get together and settle their own disputes. We provide that it shall be their duty to set up adjustment boards, not to consider questions of wages but disagreements over grievances, interpretations, discipline, and other technicalities that arise from time to time in the workshop and out on the tracks in the operation of the roads. One of the difficulties of the present law has been that while it provided that the men and the roads should form these adjustment boards, for one reason and another they were never able to get together. One said it was the fault of the other and the other said it was the fault of the one. They could not reach an understanding about the creation of these adjustment boards, and therefore they were not created.

The two sides now come forward in an agreement and say that they are ready to acknowledge the mistakes of the past, are ready to wipe the slate clean, are ready to agree that upon the passage of this bill all the railroads in the United States, practically speaking, and all the men who work on the railroads will be able to get together and create these adjustment boards which are provided for as the second step in the adjustment of the relationship of employer and employee.

We set up in addition to that the first public board for which the bill provides, and that is the board of mediation, which is composed entirely of men drawn from the public. Interest on the part of men on either side of a controversy disqualifies them from membership on the Board of Mediation, which is taken wholly from the public. Now, let us say that a dispute has arisen between the railroads and their employees over the question of wages. They have tried their conferences, which they have the right to engage in; they have tried to get together by such representation as they chose themselves by agreement, and have been unable to arrive at an agreement. There is danger of a dispute resulting in a nationwide tie-up of traffic in this country; then this Board of Mediation may be applied to by either side or may offer its services to bring the two sides together. Complaint is made here that the Board of Mediation is a board of persuaders, with no power of compulsion. My friends, you might as well make up your minds now that you have to take one side of two propositions. You have either got to go along on the theory of freedom of contract, of voluntary arbitration, of mediation and persuasion, or you must go to the other extreme of compulsory arbitration, compulsory decision, and antistrike legislation, which has never succeeded in any country in the world where it has ever been tried. If I had the time, I could show you that in France they tried antistrike legislation, and the only way they could ever enforce it was to draw all of the railroad employees into the army of France and then make them operate the trains as soldiers and not as workers.

I could show you that they tried the same thing in Canada, and that to-day the law is a dead letter, and they have publicly acknowledged their inability to enforce it, because you can not put 2,000,000 men in jail in the United States or elsewhere for violating a law that compels them to work against their will, and you need not think that that method will ever bring about satisfactory results in the adjustment of labor controversies. So that we have either to take the voluntary or the compulsory side of this proposition, and the only practical side, as demonstrated by all of the laws heretofore passed and by every nation which has ever dealt with it, is the voluntary side, where the agencies of government are at the disposal of the disputants in an effort to bring them together, in an effort to arrive at an agreement which both sides will respect, because both sides have had a hand in its creation; and that is the fundamental proposition with which we are confronted to-day and with which this bill undertakes to deal.

MR. BLANTON. Mr. Chairman, will the gentleman yield?

MR. BARKLEY. The gentleman must excuse me. If I yield to one, I have to keep it up, and I do not want to take up too much time. Let us suppose that these voluntary conferences and these adjustment boards with respect to grievances and the Board of Mediation have all been unable to bring the two sides together. Then the law provides for arbitration, and bear in mind that is also voluntary. There is no power of compulsion upon either side to make them arbitrate, but, my friends, there is a higher power than the strong arm of government, and that is the power of compulsion of public opinion and public duty, and at the same time the private interests of both sides. I venture to say that neither a railroad company nor a railroad employee ever brings about a strike unless it is the last resort, the last step in an effort to secure what they may think are their rights. Those who think that men go out of work and make their women and children suffer for the necessities of life because of any vicious desire to interrupt traffic do not understand the principles of human nature.

A strike is always the last resort to which men go in an effort to secure their rights. We will suppose that they have been unable to agree, that the Board of Mediation can not get them together. Then this Board of Arbitration is set up, each side naming one man, or, if they want six arbitrators, each side naming two, and then these two or four, as the case may be, agree on the others. If they can not agree on the neutral arbitrator or arbitrators, then the Board of Mediation, which is a board appointed not from the two sides but from the public, select the third arbitrator, and before they go into the arbitration both sides agree what is the cause of the dispute, both sides agree what is to be decided, and both sides agree in advance that they will abide by the result. When that result is arrived at the award is filed in the United States court and becomes binding upon both sides, with the same force and effect as if it were a judgment of a court of the United States.

I have been asked whether that binding judgment can be enforced. Of course, it can not be enforced to prevent an individual employee from stopping work if he desires to, but no law can ever be passed that will prevent a man from doing that; but where the controversy is between groups, as it will be, the binding effect of this judgment in the United States courts, which both sides have in advance agreed to abide by, becomes as enforcible against each group as if it were a judgment of a court without regard to arbitration. And so, gentlemen, there is the third step toward the settlement of these disputes. Let us suppose that all these methods have been adhered to and that even yet they can not get together. Of course, gentlemen will understand that if they ever arbitrate, that settles it, because one side is represented by one man and the other side by another, and the third man is taken from the public, and in all arbitrations the neutral arbitrator becomes the judge, because he settles it as an umpire, and even in a board of arbitration the public has the power to bring about a decision as between the parties on either side. If there is arbitration, that settles the dispute, but if they do not begin to arbitrate, and there is danger of a nation-wide strike or any serious interruption of public commerce, the Board of Mediation, appointed by the President, confirmed by the Senate, representing neither side, but representing the public interests, reports to the President the fact that they have been unable to bring about a settlement, and that there is serious danger of an interruption of traffic, and then the law provides that the President shall have the power to appoint an emergency board for the purpose of investigating the merits of the controversy and reporting to him upon it.

Complaint has been made here and will be made, perhaps, that this emergency board is not given any power to enforce its decisions. You will bear in mind that the duty of the emergency board is to get the parties together and to report to the President. That board is a presidential board which is to be selected not from either interest but by the President from the body of our public citizens. They will exercise whatever mediatory or persuasive powers they might possess. If they can not bring the parties together, then it is made their duty to make a report upon the merits of the controversy, and by means of that report the power of public opinion is brought to bear and focused upon the side which is recreant or blamable for what might be a public calamity. The public are to be given the facts, upon which they will form their own judgment. Complaint is made that this board has not even the power to serve a subpœna, to go out and drag witnesses before it, and bring documents for the purpose of investigation. My friends, let us imagine this situation: Whenever a dispute has become so acute as to require the services of this superboard, as it has been called, this emergency board, which is the last resort, we may well imagine that both sides to the controversy, having in view their desire to impress upon the public their sides of the dispute, the merits of their controversy, and the justice of their demands, will be anxious and impatient to lay before this board and the public every pertinent fact or circumstance without the intervention of a United States marshal. Either side that refused to do so would be pilloried before the bar of public opinion. We know that here in our committees in Congress we never have to send a sheriff to bring in witnesses whenever there is a controversy over the passage of a bill. Both sides are always glad to come and give Congress the facts. But if Congress should see fit to give this board power to summon witnesses and drag men in by the scruff of the neck and make them testify or produce some petty document, the result is that not only would there be no disposition to compose their respective differences and try to get together but it would drive them further apart, and the value of their report might be prejudiced in advance because of some petty exercise of authority.

You need not have any fear. Both sides will not only be glad but an-anxious to give to the public their side of the controversy in order that the public may judge of its merits. Now, that is the machinery which this bill sets up. Can you improve upon it?

I want to talk for just a moment about the right of the public. I have already said that in all the laws which have been passed heretofore Congress has never undertaken to exercise any right or restraint over a private contract. There is some opposition to this bill which is engendered from a so-called belief or fear—and I take it that it is sincere—that the railroads and the employees may get together and make some sort of collusive agreement so as to boost wages with the expectation that the Interstate Commerce Commission would be required to pass that increase on to the shoulders of the public. Well, while the railroads and employees have a common interest, there is nothing more competitive than their interest. Every railroad that agrees to an increase in wages knows first that they must either pay that increase out of their own treasury or they have to persuade the Interstate Commerce Commission, which represents the public, that that charge ought to be passed on to the public, and in either case there is no inducement for the railroad company entering into a collusive agreement with its employees in order to boost wages upon its system. Then they say that the Interstate Commerce Commission ought to be given the power to supervise or suspend any decision or agreement fixing wages, and I understand that an amendment is going to be offered here providing that the Interstate Commerce Commission shall have the power to suspend or regulate or nullify agreements that may be entered into between the railroads and the employees with respect to wages.

Now, my friends, in addition to the fact that we have no constitutional power to do that, no power to interfere with private agreements, there would be nothing more disastrous that could happen to the Interstate Commerce Commission, which enjoys public confidence, then to drag it into these labor disputes which may arise in the United States from time to time.

In 1919, when the House Committee on Interstate and Foreign Commerce was considering the question of the return of the railroads to their owners and the passage of some law to bring that about, Commissioner Clark, who was then, I believe, chairman of the Interstate Commerce Commission, who spoke before our committee on behalf of the entire commission when this matter was discussed, in referring to such a suggestion made at that time, used the following language:

> We think it would be an unsound public policy to place in one body the duty of regulating the activities of the carriers and their rates and charges from which their revenues are derived, and also the fixing of the largest item in the operating expenses of the railroads, to wit, the wages of the employees. Personally, I believe it would develop in a few years that it would be destructive of the influence and standing and opportunity for good of the entire plan, and of the body that administers it.

That was the chairman of the Interstate Commerce Commission, and in that document he recommended to Congress that we place no such burden upon that great commission which stands between the railroads and the public, and which is supposed to be impartial, and which is charged with the duty of investigating the matter of economical management and operation of the railroads in passing on questions of rates and charges; but we have placed upon it no power to supervise or interfere with or in any way to control or be involved in the settlement of railroad disputes between railroads and their employees. . . .

DAVID KINCHELOE [DEM., KY.]. The gentleman has stated what would happen when an award is made. Does the gentleman think under this bill, if it is not amended, if these operators of railroads would come before the Interstate Commerce Commission and ask for an increase of rates, would the commission be legally bound to take into consideration this award?

MR. BARKLEY. Of course they would not be justified in ignoring it as an element of operating cost. But they are not only not legally bound to raise the rates on account of it, but they are under no moral obligation to increase rates unless they are convinced that the award or agreement fixing wages enters into the economical management of the roads. In other words, if they find that an increase of wages should justly be taken out of the profits of the railroads they would not be expected nor justified in raising freight rates by reason of such increase in wages. The commission has the power and duty of giving this element of cost such weight as it may merit in determining rates.

MR. KINCHELOE. Then the gentleman thinks the amendment would not be necessary in the administration of this law?

MR. BARKLEY. No. If it were adopted, I will say to you frankly that it would be simply an invitation to everybody who desired to attack it to come before the Interstate Commerce Commission and undertake to convince them that even an award of the board of arbitrators was an unmeritorious increase. . . .

ROBERT MOORE [DEM., VA.]. I believe the gentleman stated to his colleague that the Interstate Commerce Commission was not only not bound to increase rates because of an increase of wages, but is restrained from allowing or maintaining any unreasonable and discriminatory rates?

MR. BARKLEY. Yes.

MR. MOORE. Does not the gentleman think this is a dangerous amendment from this point of view?—assuming that the Interstate Commerce Commission would not be compelled to raise rates because of an increase of wages, would not this amendment, if adopted, by implication say that the Interstate Commerce Commission, if it looked into the matter of an increase of wages and found that it was meritorious, then as a matter of course it would increase rates? Is not that the implication of this amendment? And does it not seem to the gentleman that that would operate injuriously?

MR. BARKLEY. I think it would. . . .

MR. NEWTON. I agree with the gentleman that the Hoch amendment would be injurious. I think it ought to be brought out that there is a clear distinction between the Hoch amendment and the proposed amendment that has been circulated around here, which goes very much further than the Hoch amendment.

MR. BARKLEY. That is true. That is the amendment that substitutes the Interstate Commerce Commission for the Railroad Labor Board, to suspend decisions, and proposes to give the Interstate Commerce Commission the power to suspend all arrangements and agreements and arbitrations between the railroads and their employees. And not only would that be an invitation to the commission to inject itself into every question of wages, but it would bring about such a degree of uncertainty between the railroads and their employees that they would never know when they had entered into an agreement or adjusted their difficulties by an award; they would never know whether it was settled or unsettled until the Interstate Commerce Commission had passed judgment upon it and declared it either unreasonable or reasonable, and hence they would never agree to settle a dispute by arbitration. . . .

CHARLES CRISP [DEM., GA.]. Would any rights now enjoyed by the public under the present laws be impaired by the enactment of this bill?

MR. BARKLEY. No. No rights that the public now enjoys would be infringed upon or lessened or interfered with by the enactment of this bill.

Now, that brings me to the discussion of what are the public rights. Fear has been expressed here about passing wage increases on to the public. We might as well admit and start out by assuming that the public has to pay the operating expenses of the railroads. There is no way to avoid that. And in addition to that we must also bear such expense as will result in a reasonable profit to the people who have invested their money in railroads.

We are bound to assume that the railroad man has just as much right to a just wage as any other man engaged in industry. The public has the right to uninterrupted commerce; it also has the right to bring about the powers of government to prevent strikes and interruption of traffic. The public in itself and per se, however, has no more right to say what a railroad man shall receive as his wage than to say what the shoemaker or the blacksmith or any other worker anywhere in the United States shall receive. [Applause.]

The right of the public enters when the public is about to be denied something that is necessary for its existence. The right of the public is to have an interest in the continuous and uninterrupted transportation of the necessaries of life and of industry, and therefore the public has a right to an interest in the prompt settlement of any dispute on the railroads of the country which threatens this continuous and uninterrupted transportation. And this is the extent to which either Congress or the courts have gone thus far in undertaking to interpret or safeguard the rights of the public in railroad wage disputes.

For example, if the freight from Boston to Washington on a pair of shoes that cost $10 is 5 cents, and two-thirds of that 5 cents is represented by labor, has the public any more right to say what the man shall receive who brings those shoes from Boston to Washington than it has to say what the man shall receive who made the shoes in Boston in the beginning? As an economic proposition and as a matter of moral justice, I assert that as such the public has no more right to a voice in the agreements between railroad men and their employers than it has in the agreements between shoe-makers or steel workers and their employers, or between the employers and employees of any other great industry in the fixing of the compensation paid in the employment of labor. [Applause.] . . .

BURTON FRENCH [R., IDA.]. I take issue for the reason the railroads are public-service institutions. Competition in rates on the one hand and in the matter of wages paid on the other is largely removed because of the public interest. Because of this wiping out of competition in a way that does not exist in such institutions as the manufacturing concerns to which the gentleman refers, the welfare of both the employers and the employers must be protected.

MR. BARKLEY. I am speaking now, of course, from an economic and moral standpoint. I realize that the commerce clause of the Constitution gives the Congress the power to regulate commerce and to regulate the instrumentalities of commerce; but I say the mere fact that the public pays the bill for hauling freight does not give it any more right to fix the wages of the laborers who carry the freight than to fix the wages of the men who create the freight in the beginning. . . .

Let me be a little more specific. In 1922 a report was made by the

Joint Congressional Commission of Agricultural Inquiry, which had been appointed to inquire into the conditions surrounding agriculture. Hon. Sidney Anderson, of Minnesota, until lately a Member of this House, was the chairman of that commission. The report consists of four volumes and goes into great detail with reference to all phases of agricultural conditions. Among other things, it reported on the proportion of the ultimate cost charged the consumer on a number of commodities that is represented by transportation charges. In illustration of the thought I have endeavored to express, I call attention to some of them set forth in the report.

Taking eight groups of trade-marked food products, it is shown that out of each $1 paid therefor by the public the transportation charges amount to 8.76 cents—less than 9 cents. In the sale of canned milk, 6 cents out of each dollar represented transportation charges. Of the 10 cents paid for a loaf of bread, one-third of a cent represents the cost of transporting the wheat to the mills and one-sixth of a cent the cost of bringing the flour to the baker. About 11 or 12 cents represents the transportation charge out of each dollar paid for rolled oats and corn flakes. On salt, transportation gets 18 cents out of each dollar paid by the consumer. For wheat cereals, 8 cents out of each dollar paid represents transportation. For soap it is seven and a half cents; for manufactured package food, 12 cents; for dressed beef it is less than 6 cents. For men's suits and shoes it is even less, the freight on an ordinary suit of clothes being about 6 cents for 300 miles and about 5 cents for a pair of shoes for the same distance, provided they are carried in bulk. The freight charge on 100 pounds of ham from Iowa to New York is about 75 cents. If dealers' purchases are made from supplies that are reasonably convenient, the freight charges do not exceed 1 cent per pound on sugar, coffee, oatmeal, potatoes, eggs, fresh meat, butter, or more than 25 other important articles of food. Of course, there are many heavier commodities, such as hardware, coal, iron, and steel, on which the freight charge is higher.

I am not seeking to create the impression that even the transportation charges to which I have referred are as low as they ought to be. I am convinced that on many articles of necessity in this country, and especially on some varieties of farm products, the rates are too high. But what I am seeking to emphasize is the fact that if the public has a right to fix the compensation of men who labor on railroads merely because the public ultimately pays the bill in freight rates, which are only a small portion of ultimate prices, then, if we follow that logic to its conclusion, the public would have the same right to fix the compensation of men who labor in the industries which produce the freight to be carried in commerce; and this, in turn, would put the public, through the agencies of government, into the fixing of all costs and of all prices, because in the end the public must pay all this in the price of what it buys. This would ultimately mean

Government operation of everything, which is unthinkable. [Applause.]

Therefore, as an economic proposition I maintain that the interest of the public is not in the fixing of wages but in continuous transportation, in bringing about agreements and settlements of disputes so that their rights will not be invaded by long-drawn-out controversies over wages and disputes.

MR. BLACK. If the gentleman will yield, will not the gentleman add to that the public have the right also to have this transportation at reasonable rates?

MR. BARKLEY. Yes; and it has the Interstate Commerce Commission to see that this right is exercised. [Applause.]

My friends, I do not know that I can add much more to what I have already said with reference to the merits of this measure. After the fight which engaged our attention in the last Congress, and in response to Executive suggestions in three separate messages, the railroad executives and their employees have come to an agreement under legislation involving their rights and interests. They come here and appeal to us to enact it into law. They say it will work. Their moral obligation is to see that it will work. If we accept the results of their deliberation and their sacrifices—and both sides have yielded on important questions—and then it fails to work successfully, the Congress will be here to make another effort to find a remedy for this great problem. I trust that if it ever seeks out of its own counsel to find a remedy of its own it may find one that will be more successful and beneficial than that which has been in effect for the last six years as a result of the enactment of Title III of the transportation act. [Applause.]

Complaint has been made that in this bill the public is deprived of something which it now enjoys under the present law. Those who make this contention misunderstand either the bill itself or the present law, and possibly both. Under the present law all that the public has in the way of representation is one-third of the membership of the present Railroad Labor Board. The public is given in the present law no representation on any adjustment boards that might be set up by agreement, and under the present law the public is not given any supervision over private agreements as to wages, and Congress is powerless to bring about supervision or control over private agreements.

Under the present bill, which we are about to pass, there are three separate boards set up in the various stages for the settlement of railroad disputes. First, the Board of Mediation, composed of five men appointed by the President and confirmed by the Senate; all of them are taken from the public. Not one of them can be interested on either side of any dispute.

After this, arbitration boards are provided for, if the Board of Mediation is unable to settle the dispute. The public has one-third of the membership of these boards of arbitration, and experience has shown that the neutral representatives on boards of arbitration usually decide the terms of any award of settlement, so that on these boards the public has the same representation it now has on the Railroad Labor Board.

In addition to these, the bill provides for an emergency board to be appointed by the President. This board is also taken entirely from the public, so that under this bill, of the three different kinds of boards set up, the public has the entire membership on two of them, and one-third of the membership on the other. I challenge, therefore, any man to point to any law that now exists, or that has heretofore existed, where the interests of the public are more completely safeguarded than in the provisions of this bill.

It gives me pleasure to support this measure. If my efforts in the past have contributed anything toward this happy consummation, I am grateful for the opportunity which was mine. I hope this measure will be enacted without serious amendments. Therefore, I hope that the amendments which have been suggested, which may interfere with the harmonious operation of this law, will all be defeated, and I trust that after the enactment of this legislation we shall have a new era of peace, harmony, and sincere cooperation between the railroads and their employees throughout the Nation, and that the interests of all the people, will be protected in the enjoyment of the right to the best as well as the cheapest transportation that it is possible to afford them. [Applause.] . . . .

MR. BARKLEY. The employees agreed to arbitrate all the matters of dispute except the eight-hour day.

MR. BLACK. I am simply rehearsing these facts which we are all agreed upon to emphasize the point that we might as well understand that this bill sets up no new plan on settlement. I hope it will be successful, but gentlemen who are predicting that the millenium has come in industrial relations will probably have cause to revise their remarks. These same optimistic predictions were made when the Newlands Act was passed in 1913. . . .

MR. BARKLEY. I want to call the gentleman's attention to the fact that except for the difficulty that resulted from the Adamson law, all the predictions were fulfilled.

MR. BLACK. Yes. But that was the "big heap" trouble of them all; that threatened a nation-wide paralysis of transportation.

MR. BARKLEY. Would the gentleman from Texas, if he was a laborer and believed in the principle of the eight-hour day, agree to submit it to arbitration?

MR. BLACK. Yes. If I believed my rights were so clearly understood by the country as the railroad brotherhood leaders asserted, I would be willing to risk my chances under the law that I had advocated when Congress passed it and promised by my leadership that we would obey and abide by it.

Senate—69th Congress, 1st Session
May 6, 1926

The Senate, as in Committee of the Whole, proceeded to consider the bill (H. R. 9463) to provide for the prompt disposition of disputes between carriers and their employees, and for other purposes. . . .

JAMES WATSON [R., IND.]. Mr. President, I claim for the measure that is now brought before the Senate for consideration that it is the best that can be passed at the present time and under existing conditions to preserve peace between the carriers and their employees in the United States.

The measure is the result of conferences held during the summer and fall of 1925 between representatives of employers and employees on the transportation system of the United States. Informal conversations between them began before the adjournment of the last Congress, but it was not until after that time that representatives were formally selected for the purpose of conferring upon some measure or some principle or some policy that might prevent strikes in the future and preserve peace as between the parties. In December last the bill was finally formulated. During these conferences the parties gradually grew closer together. There had been more or less of antagonism, more or less of suspicion, more or less of fear, but gradually it dawned upon each party that the other was impelled by the most sincere motives and that each side was determined, if possible, to make concessions so that some measure might finally be agreed upon that would preserve peace in this portion of the industrial world and in the future prevent strikes and lockouts on the railroads. . . .

Suffice it to say in general terms that 58 railroads were concerned in these negotiations and 20 railroad labor organizations. Fifty-eight railroads were favorable. When the final vote was taken 20 were against the proposition, but the railroads do not vote as units. They vote in their meetings by each thousand miles of railroad, 1 vote for each 1,000 miles. One hundred and ninety-nine votes were cast for the bill measured in that way and 48 against it. Twenty railroad labor organizations participated through their representatives in these conferences. No labor organization was hostile to the proposition at that time and indeed at the present time none is hostile, though one or two have been here asking to have some amendments adopted, in order that they may certainly be included in the provisions of the bill.

The measure passed the House, after full consideration by the Committee on Interstate and Foreign Commerce and by the House of Representatives itself, by a vote of 381 to 13. We had ample hearings before the Interstate Commerce Committee of the Senate. Practically everybody was heard who demanded to be heard, and it was quite significant at the time that no railroad company appeared in opposition to it, that no labor organization appeared in opposition to it, and that the sole opposition was voiced by Mr. James A. Emery, a very able and brilliant lawyer representing the National Association of Manufacturers, who appeared in the interest of certain amendments, which had full consideration by the committee. So that this is a good-faith effort on the part of the managers and on the part of labor to set up some machinery by which their differences may be adjusted and by which peace between them may be preserved.

This is no experiment in the way of legislation in the United States. The truth about it is that as far back as 1875 discussions in both Houses of Congress began as to whether or not railroad strikes might not be prevented by conciliation, by arbitration, and by those peaceful methods that we all so much favor when they can possibly achieve the desired result. Public sentiment, however, did not sweep up to a sufficient height and develop sufficient volume to bring about the passage of an act until 1888; but in that year Congress did pass an act providing only for arbitration.

Let me say, Senators—and this is essential in the consideration of this question—that there are two classes of disputes that arise in connection with the operation of railroads. One class is what are ordinarily called grievances. They may be of a personal nature; they may involve a great many employees; they may involve a few employees; they may involve but one employee. Of this class, also, are disputes rising out of the interpretation and application of existing agreements as to wages, hours of labor, or working conditions.

The second class are those which have reference directly to changes in the rates of pay, salaries, hours of service, or working conditions, and they are the ones that in the last analysis occasion the greatest difficulties and give rise to the most serious disagreements.

I wish to give Senators a brief history of this attempt to set up machinery to preserve peace in the transportation system of the United States. The first act, that of 1888, provided for arbitration only. It had no reference to either mediation or conciliation and had to do only with wages and rules and conditions of service. There was no attempt to settle what are ordinarily called grievances by the boards of arbitration thus set up. The President was authorized by the act to appoint two commissioners, one from the State in which the dispute arose and the other from any place the President might choose to find him. Those two commissioners were authorized to cooperate with the Commissioner of Labor for the purpose of constituting a board that might arbitrate the dispute or disagreement in which the railroad was involved. They could voluntarily offer to arbitrate, and the President had the right to offer their services in case of a dispute, because, Senators, all of this legislation is based upon the theory of the existence of a dispute. If there be no dispute, there is no occasion for arbitration; there is no occasion for any attempt at either conciliation or mediation. It is only in the case of disputes where difficulties that are irreconcilable arise that this machinery is set up for the purpose of establishing some method that will bring the disputants together and prevent strikes or lockouts. The act of 1888 also provided for arbitration. In case of a dispute each side could name one individual and those two could name a third. They were clothed with powers of arbitration—that is, the powers usually given to boards of arbitration.

The law was on the statute books for 10 years, but in that whole time not one single case was submitted to it for consideration. This is most significant to a proper understanding of the mechanism of this machinery. In the 10 years that that law remained on the statute books not one case was referred to it, for the reason that it had in it provisions for compulsory investigation; that is to say, the board appointed by the President, if cases were referred to it—and it all had to be voluntary—could take charge and force the attendance of witnesses, the production of papers, and so on. That was so distasteful to both sides at that time that nobody appealed to the board.

There was one tremendous strike that occurred while the board was in existence, and that was the celebrated Debs strike of 1894, during the course of which President Cleveland sent troops to Chicago to see that the transportation of the mails was not interfered with by those who were seeking to destroy railroad property. Yet no case was submitted for the consideration of the board of arbitration.

By 1898 Congress and the public believed that some law should be enacted, that some machinery should be set up, that some method should be adopted by which arbitration, mediation, and conciliation, without the use of force, might be employed in the settlement of all such disputes. So what is called the Erdman Act was passed in 1898. Some of us were Members of the House of Representatives at that time. My friend the Senator from Kansas [Mr. Curtis], the present majority leader, and one or two other Senators were then Members of the House of Representatives and voted for the Erdman Act.

The act of 1888 and the Erdman Act of 1898 applied only to wages, rules, and working conditions, and not to grievances. Those acts applied only to those employees who were engaged in the actual operation of the trains, those engaged in train service only. They did not cover any other branch or organization of railroad employees.

The Erdman Act provided for mediation and conciliation; that is to say, when a dispute arose it was the business of the disputants to get together and undertake by mediation and conciliation to settle their own differences and arrange their own difficulties. Then it provided for arbitration in the usual way in which arbitration comes about, each side appointing a man, and those two a third, the three to arbitrate the difficulty. After the question was submitted to arbitration the board so created then had the right to send for persons and for papers; in other words, there was provision for compulsory investigation; and the award was filed with the circuit court of the United States and judgment was rendered thereon.

For eight and a half years after that act was passed no dispute was submitted under it for mediation or arbitration or conciliation or to be dealt with in any other manner. But by that time public sentiment had become so aroused to the danger of strikes and the interruption of the transportation service of the country that cases began to be referred to these boards for settlement, and between 1906 and 1913, when the Erdman Act was repealed, there were submitted to it 61 cases involving wages, salaries, and conditions of service, which are the questions out of which grow the great strikes on the railroads of the country. Every case was adjusted peacefully without any resort to force—a most happy consummation of the desires of those who were responsible for that legislation.

Of the 61 cases thus settled 16 were disposed of by arbitration and the remainder by mediation. Not one single strike of any great consequence came upon the country during that time, and every case that was referred to these boards was adjusted. . . .

DUNCAN FLETCHER [DEM., FLA.]. Under what act was that?

MR. WATSON. The Erdman Act. But the public and Congress became somewhat dissatisfied, and as a result, in 1913, the Newlands Act was passed. Senators will remember Senator Newlands, of Nevada. He introduced a bill which took his name and became a law in 1913. The difference between the Newlands Act and Erdman Act was that the Newlands Act provided a permanent Board of Mediation and Conciliation. It provided that the President could appoint a board consisting of a special commissioner of mediation and two others who were in the Government service, holding office at that time. That board could offer its services in case of a dispute between the management and employees of the railroads. It would only consider, as in the case of the other two acts, questions involving wages, hours of labor, and conditions of service. It could not in any wise deal with grievances or those minor disputes which are characterized as grievances. During the life of the Newlands Act 148 disputes were submitted to these boards, and all but one were settled peacefully. That was the one out of which grew the Adamson law. That dispute was settled not by mediation or conciliation or by arbitration, but by direct act of Congress.

I may have occasion later on to refer to the Adamson Act. Seventy-one of the cases submitted under the Newlands Act had reference to wages and hours and conditions of labor, the most aggravating class of cases that arise, and yet all were adjusted harmoniously; all were settled by mediation, conciliation, or arbitration. At all events no force was employed; at all events no compulsion was used, but all of the difficulties which arose during that time were settled in accordance with the methods of peace, which we trust may be those that shall be adopted in the future.

So, Senators, we come now to 1918, when the railroads were taken over by the Government on the 1st day of January of that year. With the advent of Government operation a new system was set up. We may all remember that at the time the railroads were taken over by the Government there was a tremendous demand for increased wages, and at that very time Mr. McAdoo appointed a commission of four. Mr. Wilcox, who had been chairman of the Republican National Committee, was one of those commissioners.

The commission sat for many months in the effort to adjust that question, and after, I think, four months, they decided unanimously in favor of the railroad employees; their decision was concurred in by Mr. McAdoo, and the award was made retroactive to January 1, 1918. Knowing that other disputes and difficulties would arise, at the suggestion of Mr. McAdoo, provision was made for boards of adjustment, which was the first time they appeared in connection with legislation of this kind. Such boards of adjustment could be formed by the parties to a controversy, or they could be permanent.

I refer to them as provided in the law at that time because in character and in formation they were identical with those in the Esch-Cummins Act. That is to say, they might be established by a single railroad line, a number of carriers, or any number of organizations. They might be established by a group of railroads. They might be established by the railroads nationally. I will say that under Government operation these boards of adjustment were almost universally acquiesced in and established by the labor organizations, or offers were made to do so, although at that time they were not looked upon so kindly by railroad managements.

During that period many cases were referred to these boards of adjustment; but the boards of adjustment in that case, as in this bill provided, had to do only with grievances—that is to say, with the interpretation and the application of existing agreements as to wages, hours of labor, and conditions of service not as to wages, conditions of service, and hours of labor themselves, but as to the application and interpretation of existing contracts as to them. These boards of arbitration always are made up of those intimately acquainted with the conditions. Outsiders are not put on the boards. The problems are all of a technical nature, and therefore railroad men are required to decide them. So that in the measures providing for Government operation, as well as in the Esch-Cummins Act and in the measure before us, we provide for boards of adjustment to settle those technical questions that arise growing out of the interpretation and the application of existing agreements as to wages, hours of labor, and conditions of service, though they do not deal with the larger and the more drastic and the more dangerous problems of changes in the rates of pay or in the conditions of service or in the hours of work.

These boards of adjustment, as I say, were almost universally accepted; and in order that everybody might have an opportunity to have his case adjusted, however small his grievance, Adjustment Board No. 1, Adjustment Board No. 2, and Adjustment Board No. 3 were established, and dozens upon dozens of cases were submitted to them during the time of their existence. All of these cases were settled in a spirit of conciliation and of harmony, and no difficulty grew out of the service during the time of Government operation so far as mediation or conciliation could maintain the harmonious relations that existed.

When the roads were to be turned back to their owners, Mr. Esch, then chairman of the Interstate and Foreign Commerce Committee of the House and now an honored member of the Interstate Commerce Commission, introduced a bill providing for the method of their return. This bill provided for conciliation and arbitration and for mediation. Mr. Anderson of Minnesota, submitted an amendment to it, which was adopted, which went even further along the line of conciliation and mediation than the proposition of Mr. Esch. When the bill came over to the Senate, however, there was a new situation. The Senator from Iowa [Mr. Cummins], then the honored chairman of the Interstate Commerce Committee, a man of wide knowledge and great experience in dealing with these problems, brought in an entirely new proposition. I call the particular attention of those who believe that at this time we should have force and compulsion instead of mediation and conciliation in the settlement of these disputes to the act that was passed by the Senate of the United States upon the recommendation of the Interstate Commerce Committee at that time.

We provided for a Railroad Labor Board. As recommended by the Interstate Commerce Committee and passed by the Senate, it consisted of five persons, all to be appointed by the President, all representing the general public. None of them was to have anything to do with railroad operation or with railroad ownership or with membership in any railroad organization; but when the bill got over to the House, the House would have none of it. It completely changed the complexion of the Railroad Labor Board, and it sent back to us a proposition providing for a Railroad Labor Board consisting of nine members—three representing management, three representing labor, and three representing the general public. In other words, it sent back to us a proposition by the terms of which we have six lawyers and three jurors on the jury, in which we have six advocates and three judges on the bench; and that is one of the causes of the failure of the Railroad Labor Board at the present time. It has been brought to a condition, as I shall show you presently, where it is absolutely useless so far as the settlement or adjustment of any controversies submitted to it is concerned.

That is just a brief history of the results of the efforts of Congress in time gone by, aided partially only by management on one side and labor on the other, to set up machinery for the adjustment of the differences between management and laborers on the railroads of the country.

That brings us up to the present time. "Well," you say, "what is the occasion for the passage of this bill at this time"? The necessity for the passage of this measure at this time is the collapse of the Railroad Labor Board, not because of the personnel of the board—because there are on it men of high character, wide experience, and high motives—but because of the very complexion of the board, its constituent elements. As I have said before, it has on it three members representing management, three representing labor, and three representing the general public; and when any case comes before that board, immediately those who are in sympathy with the respective sides become advocates on the court. . . .

THE ORIGINS

Report of the Senate Committee on Interstate Commerce, May 10, 1934
(With a Minority Report)

CLARENCE DILL [DEM., WASH.] submitted the following Report.

Your committee, to whom was referred Senate bill 3266, has held hearings on the same, made certain amendments thereto and hereby report the bill favorably to the Senate with the recommendation that the bill as amended do pass.

This bill proposes to amend the Railway Labor Act by rewriting it and making several far-reaching and important changes in the operation of the adjustment boards to settle grievances and the work of the mediation board.

Congress passed the Railway Labor Act with the joint approval of both the representatives of the railroads and the railway labor organization. They believed it would enable them to settle their differences without the element of compulsion.

They have tried this act for nearly 8 years. It has served a most useful purpose and brought about many good results, but both the representatives of the railroads and of the employees agree that it needs improvement.

This bill is intended to provide the needed amendments.

The most important change in the bill is the creation of what is termed the "National Adjustment Board." This Board will have four divisions. Each division will have a neutral member, so that these divisions will be able to make decisions. The present regional boards have no neutral members and for that reason are often unable to arrive at decisions.

One of the principal weaknesses of the present law in practice has been that regional boards have not been set up in some sections of the country for settlement of the disputes in some of the crafts. Both representatives of the carriers and of the employees agree that the setting up of boards for the settlement of disputes should be made compulsory, when necessary. Representatives of the carriers proposed that the setting up of regional boards be made compulsory; representatives of most of the employees insisted that the setting up of the National Board of Adjustment with four divisions be made compulsory.

As introduced in the Senate, Senate bill 3266 provided only for the creation of a National Board. Your committee has amended the bill authorizing the divisions of the National Board of Adjustment to provide for regional boards whenever, in the discretion of any division, it is desirable to create a regional board. The regional boards will be created for temporary periods, but their members are to be chosen in the same manner as the members of

117

the National Board of Adjustment and their decisions are to be binding and enforceable in the courts in the same manner.

Your committee believes that this amendment is highly desirable for the satisfactory operation of the law.

The four divisions of the National Adjustment Board are to be independent of one another. Each division is to adjust the disputes and grievances of a certain group of crafts, as specified in the bill. It may be subdivided to take testimony, but the entire division makes the decision. Thus, there will in effect be 18 boards for the taking of testimony and 4 to make decisions.

Each division will be composed of an equal number of representatives of the railroads and employees respectively, and each will compensate its representatives. In case of a deadlock, the members of the division may select a neutral member. If they cannot agree, then the National Mediation Board will select the neutral member, and he will be paid by the Government.

The bill also provides for the establishment of regional or system boards of adjustment, if the railroads and the employees desire to set up such boards voluntarily. The ideal situation would be to have disputes and grievances settled by the men and management on the several properties without any recourse to adjudication by an outside tribunal. Some of those advocating this legislation believe the fact that there is a compulsory board to which grievances may be taken will greatly increase the settlement of disputes by voluntary adjustment boards between the employees and the railroads.

Another extremely important change from the present law which this bill provides is that it prohibits any carrier from providing financial assistance to any union of employees from funds of the carrier. It also prohibits the railroads from interfering in any manner whatsoever with employees joining or refusing to join any organization or union. The bill specifically provides that the choice of representatives of any craft shall be determined by a majority of the employees voting on the question.

This prohibition is not new. Congress has declared it three times; in the present Railway Labor Act, the Bankruptcy Act and the Emergency Transportation Act. But there are no penalties against its violation. This bill provides severe penalties for violation of the law.

Section 4 of this bill abolishes the present Board of Mediation, consisting of 5 members, and establishes a new board called the "National Mediation Board," consisting of 3 members.

The present board has many important accomplishments to its credit. It has had many difficult tasks to perform. Its powers are wholly persuasive. The fact that under this bill the National Adjustment Board will deal with many grievances now brought before the Board of Mediation, makes it unnecessary that the new Board shall have such a large membership.

This new and smaller Board will have power to select and appoint employees to act as mediators under the instruction of the Board with the same freedom to delegate its work as the Interstate Commerce Commission now possesses. This board will appoint the netural members when necessary to obtain decisions of the National Board of Adjustment and is also authorized to set up a neutral committee to determine what employees shall vote in the elections to determine the representative in any grievance.

This determination of what employees shall be allowed to vote is one of the most controversial subjects in the settlement of disputes. Your committee amended the bill so that if the Mediation Board found it might arouse antipathy on the part of the carriers or the employees in deciding questions of this kind, it could create a neutral committee to do that work, so its own usefulness of settling disputes that might arise thereafter might not be impaired.

Minority Report

Mr. McNary for Mr. Hastings, from the Committee on Interstate Commerce, submitted the following Minority Report.

A minority of the Committee on Interstate Commerce, to whom was referred the bill (S. 3266) to amend the Railway Labor Act, approved May 20, 1926, and to provide for the prompt disposition of disputes between carriers and their employees, having had the same under consideration, beg leave to report thereon as follows:

We report unfavorably thereon and recommend that the bill be not passed.

Briefly stated, there are the following objections to the bill:

1. It is not desired by a very large group of railroad employees.

2. Railroad management is unanimous in its opinion that it will not work.

3. Even its sponsor, the Federal Coordinator of Transportation, admits it is only an experiment.

4. If railroad employees desire a voice in the selection of the members of the tribunal set up by this bill to adjust their controversies, they will be compelled to join organizations not of their choosing, against their religious or other convictions, and, in this sense, would be deprived of their civil liberty.

5. It will abrogate contractual relations between employees and carriers which have satisfactorily existed for many years.

6. It will foment strife in the railroad world where peace has reigned for 8 years.

7. Its effect on railroad service will be adverse to the users thereof.

8. It is not in the public interest.

Its sponsor, the Federal Coordinator of Transportation, admits that it is an experiment, and it is obvious from its entire text that it will encourage and foment disputes and controversies and rivalries in the labor field, and tend to interruption of commerce and railroad operation. No other result can follow a bill which specifically prefers one class of employees and one class of organization over any other class or classes of employees and organizations.

As examples of the discriminatory provisions of this bill, see Section 3, first (a) and (c).

In order to compel adjustment boards, it is proposed by this bill to create a national board of 36 members, 18 to be selected by carriers and 18 to be selected by employees. Unfortunately at the very beginning of Section 3, a discriminatory and unfair provision and restriction is made. If, as a matter of fact, a national board is necessary for the purpose of securing conclusive, enforcible decisions, it is doubtless proper that half the board should be constituted of railroad employees. But it is highly improper and unfair to declare by law that no railroad employees are eligible for membership upon this board unless and except there are members of certain organizations.

A close review of S. 3266, as favored by the majority of this committee, inevitably leads to the conclusion that it will defeat the underlying principles of the Railway Labor Act of 1926.

Evidence of this is contained in the following attached copy of a communication:

Grand Lodge Brotherhood of Railroad Trainmen,
Cleveland, Ohio, May 21, 1934.

Secretaries, all lodges: chairmen and secretaries, general grievance committees, and legislative boards in the United States.

Dear Sirs and Brothers: We are informed that in the consideration of proposed amendments to the Railway Labor Act, the Senate Committee on Interstate Commerce has recommended certain changes proposed by the Federal Coordinator of Transportation which, if adopted, will seriously interfere with, if not destroy, fundamental rights labor has heretofore enjoyed.

In Section 2, under the caption "General Purposes," the Federal Coordinator has recommended an amendment which, if enacted, will probably prohibit strikes and deprive railway workers of what little democracy and freedom of action they now enjoy, and in lieu of suggestions made by the standard railway labor organizations the Senate committee has recommended amendments proposed by the Coordinator, known as paragraphs "fourth" and "fifth" of Section 2 which would destroy existing percentage or closed-shop agreements and prohibit such agreements in future, and in paragraph "ninth" of the same Section 2 the Coordinator has proposed an amendment which would have the effect of placing jurisdictional questions in the hands of the Federal Government for determination which the organizations heretofore have been free to adjust among themselves without interference by the Government.

There can be no question but that the Railway Labor Act is in need of amendment to correct its admitted weaknesses, but the railway employees of the United States would be far better off to have the law continue as it is than to be shackled by amendments such as above mentioned.

It is important that we make every possible effort to protect against reactionary changes in the law such as above referred to, and all concerned are urgently requested to write or wire their Senators and Congressmen vigorously protesting against the adoption of amendments to the Railway Labor Act recommended by "fourth," "fifth," and "ninth" of Section 2, and paragraph captioned "General purposes" in Section 2, of Senate bill S. 3266.

United States Senators and Congressmen, respectively, should be addressed in care of the Senate Office Building and the House Office Building, Washington, D.C.

Fraternally yours,

A. F. Whitney
President

Report of the House Committee on Interstate
and Foreign Commerce, June 11, 1934
(With a Minority Report)

ROBERT CROSSER [DEM., OHIO] submitted the following Report.

The Committee on Interstate and Foreign Commerce, to whom was referred the bill (H. R. 9861) to amend the Railway Labor Act approved May 20, 1926, and to provide for the prompt disposition of disputes between carriers and their employees, having considered the same, report thereon with a recommendation that it pass with the following amendments:

Page 8, line 6, after the word "reach" strike out the word "of."

Page 22, line 15, after the word "section" insert a period.

After the word "section" change the small "i" to capital "I" in the word "in."

The Committee on Interstate and Foreign Commerce, to whom was referred bill (H. R. 9861) to amend the Railway labor Act, approved May 20, 1926, and to provide for the prompt disposition of disputes between carriers and their employees, and for other purposes, having considered the same, report favorably thereon to the House and recommend that the bill do pass.

Extensive hearings were held on this bill and the views of railway managements, employees, Federal Coordinator, chairman of the United States Board of Mediation, and other interested parties were presented. All agreed that the present Railway Labor Act is in need of amendment. The 21 Standard Railroad Labor Organizations unanimously urge the enactment of this legislation.

The purposes of this bill are:

1. To prohibit any interference with freedom of association among employees and to prevent the denial of the right of employees to join a labor organization as a condition precedent to their employment.

2. To provide for the complete independence of carriers and of employees in regard to self-organization in order to carry out the purposes of this act.

3. To provide for the prompt and orderly settlement of all disputes growing out of grievances and out of the interpretation or application of agreements concerning rates of pay, rules, or working conditions, so as to avoid any interruption of commerce or of the proper operation of any carrier engaged therein.

ANALYSIS OF THE BILL

Section 2

1. The bill does not introduce any new principles into the existing Railway Labor Act, but it is designed to amend that act in order to correct the defects which have become evident as a result of 8 years of experience. It does not change the methods of conference, mediation, and voluntary arbitration to settle major disputes over wages and working conditions, which are provided in the Railway Labor Act of 1926, now in effect.

2. It provides that the employees shall be free to join any labor union of their choice and likewise be free to refrain from joining any union if that be their desire and forbids interference by the carriers' officers with the exercise of said rights.

3. While providing that labor unions shall be free from employer influence and control, it does not give preference to any particular union or class of unions.

4. Machinery is provided for the taking of a secret ballot to enable the Board of Mediation to determine what representatives the employees desire to have negotiate for them with the managements of the carriers in matters affecting their wages and working conditions.

5. It forbids the use of the carriers' funds to maintain, aid, or control the labor organizations of the employees and specifically prohibits carrier managements from requiring employees to sign "yellow-dog" contracts requiring them to join company unions.

6. The Railway Labor Act of 1926, now in effect, provides that representatives of the employees, for the purpose of collective bargaining, shall be selected without interference, influence, or coercion by railway management, but it does not provide the machinery necessary to determine who are to be such representatives. These rights of the employees under the present act are denied by railway managements by their disputing the authority of the freely chosen representatives of the employees to represent them. A considerable number of railway managements maintain company unions, under the control of the officers of the carriers, and pay the salary of the employees' representatives, a practice that is clearly contrary to the purpose of the present Railway Labor Act, but it is difficult to prevent it because the act does not carry specific language in respect to that matter. This bill is designed to correct that defect.

Section 3

7. The second major purpose of the bill is to provide sufficient and effective means for the settlement of minor disputes known as "grievances," which develop from the interpretation and/or application of the contracts between the labor unions and the carriers, fixing wages and working conditions. The present Railway Labor Act provides for the establishment of boards of adjustment by agreement. In many instances, however, the carriers and the employees have been unable to reach agreements to establish such boards. Further, the present act provides that when and if such boards are established by agreement, the employees and the carriers shall be equally represented on the board.

Many thousands of these disputes have been considered by boards established under the Railway Labor Act; but the boards have been unable to reach a majority decision, and so the proceedings have been deadlocked. These unadjusted disputes have become so numerous that on several occasions the employees have resorted to the issuance of strike ballots and threatened to interrupt interstate commerce in order to secure an adjustment. This had made it necessary for the President of the United States to intervene and establish an emergency board to investigate the controversies. This condition should be corrected in the interest of industrial peace and of uninterrupted transportation service. This bill, therefore, provides for the establishment of a national board of adjustment to which these disputes may be submitted if they shall not have been adjusted in conference between the parties. The provisions as to the national board of adjustment are as follows:

(a) The board is to consist of equal number of representatives of the employees and the carriers. The members of the board are to be paid by the parties they represent.

(b) The board is to be divided into four divisions, each functioning independently of one another.

(c) Division 1 is given the authority to hear and decide disputes involving train, engine, and yard service employees, such as engineers, firemen, conductors, trainmen, and switchmen.

(d) Division 2 is to hear and decide the disputes of the mechanical forces, such as machinists, boiler makers, blacksmiths, electrical workers, sheet-metal workers, carmen, stationary firemen, and oilers, and their apprentices and helpers, respectively.

(e) Division 3 is to hear and decide disputes of dispatchers, telegraphers, clerks, freight handlers, express, station, and storehouse employees, maintenance-of-way and section forces, Pullman conductors, maids, and porters, dining-car employees, and other miscellaneous groups.

(f) Division 4 is to hear and decide disputes of the employees engaged on the marine equipment, such as masters, mates, pilots, marine engineers, longshoremen, etc.

(g) If any division of the Board should deadlock on a dispute, then the representatives on the Board will endeavor to select a neutral or impartial person; and if they are unable to agree upon the selection of such neutral person, then the United States Board of Mediation will appoint a neutral person. The dispute will then be again considered and a majority decision reached.

(h) It is further provided that should the National Board in its discretion, find it advisable to establish subordinate boards in any particular section of the country in order to take care of its work, that may be done.

(i) Finally, the bill gives absolute freedom to the carriers and the employees to establish any other machinery upon which they may voluntarily agree. If such voluntary machinery should be established, then the parties are exempt from the jurisdiction of this National Board.

(j) There is no increase in expense to the Government provided for in this bill. At the present time the United States Board of Mediation maintains a staff of field men to aid the parties in adjusting these disputes when they are not decided by the adjustment boards. That method will no longer be necessary because these boards will now have a neutral person, which will make it possible to break deadlocks and reach decisions.

The committee is confident that this bill strengthens the Railway Labor Act, where it is necessary to do so, and feels sure that if the act is amended as proposed in this bill, it will provide effective and adequate machinery to adjust controversies between the carrier managements and employees. It will assure employees the right to bargain collectively and will contribute immeasurably to the establishment and maintenance of industrial peace.

As heretofore stated in this report, all of the standard railroad labor organizations, numbering 21, are supporting the bill and unanimously urge its passage. . . .

Minority Report

For reasons outlined below the minority is of opinion that the committee should have reported unfavorably on the bill and that the bill should not be passed.

The present Railway Labor Act was the result of an agreement reached between the companies and their employees. It had the support of all interests affected, and since its passage, in 1926, there has been peace between the employers and employees in the railroad world. There is at this time no prospect of strife unless it should be fomented by unwise legislation. H. R. 9861 is not a bill as to which the parties at interest reached a common ground—far from it. The railroad companies are unanimous in the view that it is not practicable or workable; large and important groups of railway employees are opposed to it, and the Federal Coordinator of Transportation takes the most emphatic exception to many important features.

The bill is obviously and frankly discriminatory in favor of so-called "national labor organizations" and against other labor organizations. It provides for no representation for employees on the national adjustment board except those employees belonging to the so-called "national organizations," although a very substantial part of all employees are not members of such organizations. In other ways there is an unfair and indefensible distinction drawn between so-called "standard organizations" and other legitimate labor organizations. In this connection we quote a letter from the Federal Coordinator to the chairman of the committee:

Federal Coordinator of Transportation,
Washington, June 7, 1934.

Hon. Sam Rayburn,
Chairman Committee on Interstate and Foreign Commerce.

My Dear Congressman: Mr. J. A. Farquharson, vice president and legislative representative of the Brotherhood of Railroad Trainmen, has left with me a copy of his brief filed with your committee in support of amendments of bill H. R. 9689 proposed by the Association of Railway Labor Executives in lieu of paragraphs 4 and 5 of Section 2 of the bill. There has also been presented to your committee an argument by Mr. R. K. Corkhill in support of certain other amendments proposed by so-called "independent" organizations. It may clarify the situation if I reply to these communications.

Paragraphs 4 and 5 of Section 2 of H. R. 9689 merely write into the permanent law and clarify provisions of the Bankruptcy Act and Emergency Railroad Transportation Act, 1933. The proposed amendments which Mr. Farquharson undertakes to defend are designed to protect certain so-called "percentage contracts" which his brotherhood has with some of the railroads. These contracts are so out of harmony with the whole spirit of railroad labor relations as contemplated by the Railway Labor Act, the Bankruptcy Act, and the Emergency Railroad Transportation Act, that I am frankly astonished by the persistency with which these amendments are urged. In my testimony before your committee, I pointed out that they are designed to permit the so-called "standard organizations" to enter into contracts or agreements with the carriers which are prohibited in the case of company unions, such contracts or agreements being of the closed shop or "yellow-dog" variety. No such distinction is made in the present labor provisions of the Emergency Act, which the standard organizations themselves wrote, and I am at a loss to know how it can be defended. It is not necessary to repeat here all that I said in my statement to the committee. However, the trainmen have cleared up with my organization a few points as to which I was not fully informed at the time of my statement.

1. None of the percentage contracts applies to the road-train service. Conductors demoted to trainmen's work on account of decrease in business displace trainmen, and trainmen are promoted to conductors' jobs without any friction between the organizations and without any percentage contracts. Under these circumstances a percentage contract for the trainmen in road service would be impossible.

2. The percentage contracts apply only to yard service; i.e., yard conductors, yard brakemen, and switchmen. The contracts provide that at least 75, 85, or 100 percent, as the case may be, of these classes of employees working in a yard must belong to the Brotherhood of Railroad Trainmen and that, in one instance at least, the carrier must, in the contract of employment, provide that the new employee shall join the trainmen's organization within a limited number of days from his employment. Thus the contract provides for a closed shop, in whole or in part, and has also all the essential features of the "yellow-dog" contract, denying freedom of choice to the employees.

3. The Brotherhood of Railroad Trainmen have the contract for the yard-service employees on between 140 and 150 class I railroads, but on only 23 roads of this total has the brotherhood been able to negotiate a percentage contract. On the remaining one hundred and twenty-odd roads where the trainmen have the yard contract, they are in position to make the yard-service jobs interchangeable with the road train service, protect their contracts, prevent illegal strikes, insure division seniority for yard-service employees, and generally make the organization much more flexible in the protection of their members and the railroad than under a percentage contract. This is so because the percentage is figured for each yard separately, and hence the men have no seniority rights elsewhere in case the operation of a yard is abandoned through consolidation, lengthening of divisions, or other operating change.

4. The Brotherhood of Railroad Trainmen could, without difficulty, re-

write the percentage contracts to conform with the yard contracts that they hold on the great majority of the roads.

5. The percentage contracts of the Brotherhood of Railroad Trainmen cover not more than 10,000 employees. This is approximately 1 percent of the total of railroad employees. The provisions of paragraphs 4 and 5 of Section 2 of the bill will affect the opportunity of freedom of choice in the selection of representatives by perhaps 400,000 employees heretofore included in "company union" groups. Is it any wonder that the railroads foster the contentions made by the trainmen in the hope of preventing the passage of the bill or imperiling its constitutionality? The committee members will appreciate the legal arguments that will be raised in behalf of the "company unions" if Congress should prohibit certain practices with respect to them, but permit the same practices with respect to other labor organizations.

6. In Mr. Farquharson's brief, attention is called to certain contracts of the Brotherhood of Locomotive Firemen and Enginemen in the South, whereby a certain percentage of men employed as firemen are promotable men. Apparently Mr. Farquharson would have it appear that these contracts of the firemen are similar to the percentage contracts of the trainmen. This, however, is not the case. All that the firemen's contracts provide is that a certain ratio between white and colored firemen shall be maintained for reasons having absolutely no relation to membership or nonmembership in labor organizations. The percentage contracts of the trainmen for yard service are the only "closed-shop" contracts known to the railroad industry.

7. Long experience has shown that whenever management is put into position to assist in the control of membership in a labor organization, it will find ways to control the policy and practices of that organization.

8. The importation of labor practices in other industry as a guide to Congress in framing railroad labor legislation presents an anomaly. Heretofore, the railroad labor leadership has set the model to which labor interests in other industries have sought to attain. Senator Wagner has joined with the Committee on Interstate Commerce in the Senate in recommending this legislation as it appears in H. R. 9689. Mr. Farquharson's brief is in error in asserting that the United Mine Workers write only closed-shop contracts. The fact is that while the check-off may be written into the miners' contracts, it applies only to the members of the union.

I am confident that the only real support for the proposed amendments is from a single organization. None of the other standard organizations has anything to gain from such changes in the bill. I sincerely hope that your committee will not imperil the legislation by adopting these amendments. They can cause only trouble and are incapable of any sound defense.

With respect to the statement filed with your committee by Mr. R. K.

Corkhill, I have not been favored with a draft of the amendments proposed by Mr. Todd which Mr. Corkhill supports. The bill as proposed gives every latitude to independent unions, organized in accordance with the bill, to ally themselves in national organizations and participate in the selection of the labor representatives on the National Adjustment Board. They are also given every opportunity to agree with management upon any other system of adjustment. To open up additional avenues for the further review of minor grievances than those provided in the bill as now drawn, would be defeating the very purposes for which it is proposed to amend the Railway Labor Act.

Respectfully yours,

Joseph B. Eastman

Legislation of this importance, dealing with such a delicate and intricate problem as the relationship between railroad companies and their employees, deserves the most careful and thorough-going consideration. We cannot escape the conclusion that this bill was rushed through the committee without a proper understanding of its implications. The spirit of the bill is not in accord with that of the original Railway Labor Act. In many respects, the bill is vague and uncertain and carries possibilities for misunderstanding and controversy. Mr. John G. Walber, vice president of the New York Central Railroad, speaking for all class I railroads, stated:

It is clearly obvious, from the presentations and changes that have been made, that the proponents of this bill are not satisfied with it.

It is certainly obvious from the testimony of the organizations that they are not in agreement among themselves and are not satisfied with the bill.

The managements of none of the railroads approve of the bill, and no railroad officer with whom I have discussed this bill knows just where it will lead.

I agree with a thought expressed by Colonel Winslow before the Senate as to method of revision and I likewise recommend to you that the same forces that united in the preparation and approval of the Railway Labor Act of 1926—that is, Labor and Management—again get together and definitely come to joint recommendations as to revisions of this act; and ask the Coordinator to present them to Congress.

Clearly this bill should not be passed unless Congress desires to make a complete departure from the course which was followed so successfully in the original Railway Labor Act. That act, as has been stated, was the result of conferences between the interested parties and final agreement by them. If it has become or should become desirable to amend the original Railway Labor Act in certain particulars, it is our view that the amendments should, so far as possible, be brought about as a result of agreement. The hearings afford every indication that such a course would afford a practicable and wise solution.

Schuyler Merritt

THE ENSUING DEBATE

House of Representatives—73rd Congress, 2nd Session
June 15—18, 1934

ROBERT CROSSER [DEM., OHIO]. Mr. Speaker, I move to suspend the rules and pass the bill (H. R. 9861) to amend the Railway Labor Act approved May 20, 1926, and to provide for the prompt disposition of disputes between carriers and their employees, as amended. . . .

. . . Mr. Speaker, the purpose of this bill is to amend the original Railway Labor Act, passed in 1926. Certain defects in that bill have become evident as a result of the operation of the measure during the last 8 years.

The original Railway Labor Act provided for establishment of adjustment boards consisting of members nominated by the railroads and by the employees in equal numbers to consider grievances. The fact is that in a great many instances they have been unable to reach any decision and have become deadlocked because there was no provision for a neutral member to break such a deadlock.

We provide in this bill a new plan for adjusting grievances. There is to be an adjustment board consisting of 36 men, 18 men to be nominated by the railroads and 18 by the employees. This board of 36 men is to be divided into 4 divisions, 3 of 10 members each and the fourth of 6 members. Each of these divisions is required to take up the particular grievances which may come within its jurisdiction in accordance with the terms of the bill. If the board is unable to reach an agreement in regard to the grievance in question, then the members are required to endeavor to agree upon a neutral person to be called a referee to break the deadlock. If, however, the members of the adjustment board division are unable to reach an agreement as to the appointment of a neutral person, then the United States Board of Mediation is required by the bill to nominate a referee. There will be, therefore, absolute certainty of decision in all cases whereas heretofore such has not been the case.

We believe that this is a great step in the right direction. We feel that it will do much toward the establishment of industrial peace on the railroads of the United States.

It is significant, it seems to me, that we have a greater degree of industrial peace and harmony in the railroad industry than in any of the other industries of the country. This is due in large measure to the fact that we have had in operation for the last 8 years the Railway Labor Act of 1926, defective as it is. . . .

ADOLPH SABATH [DEM., ILL.]. This bill attempts to make the act of 1926 workable and effective; is not that about all?

MR. CROSSER. That is it. All this bill does is to make the act of 1926 more workable. . . .

WILLIAM BANKHEAD [DEM., ALA.]. I received some little protest from some short-line railroads in Alabama. I do not know whether the other Members have received this complaint or not. They are fearful of the operation of this bill upon their employees, because of their limited finances, and so forth, but Mr. Eastman, the Coordinator of Railroads, when he was before the Rules Committee, explained that in the set-up and operation of the present bill there had been no difficulty whatever in adjusting these matters upon the short-line railroads, because the regular standard unions recognized, in a large measure, the necessity of the employees of these short-line railroads making their individual agreements with these lines. Is this the gentleman's understanding?

MR. CROSSER. The gentleman is correct; and I am sure that the Coordinator is right in what he says.

In addition to the features I have discussed the bill clarifies the provisions in the existing Railway Labor Act by making it perfectly clear what kind of unions are not permitted under the law. Men may organize as they see fit, but the bill prohibits the railroads from paying the expenses of any union from company funds, to maintain, aid, or control labor organizations. The bill does not permit railroads to pay the salaries of the employees as officers of company- or corporation-controlled unions. It gives employees the absolute freedom to establish unions of employees of a company if they so desire, provided that such union is not supported or controlled by the company.

JOHN MARTIN [DEM., COLO.]. They are prohibited from maintaining company unions.

MR. CROSSER. The bill prohibits railroad companies from deducting dues from men's wages to support so-called "unions" which the railways themselves have organized and fostered. It stops that, and it should stop it.

The bill when enacted into law will do much to establish industrial peace in this country. It provides for an appeal to reason rather than to force. It gives every man employed by railroads an opportunity to be heard by an impartial tribunal. It will set a precedent for labor of every kind in the United States for the establishment of the correct method to be pursued for the establishment of peace in industry. [Applause.]

SCHUYLER MERRITT [R., CONN.]. Mr. Speaker, it is rather a difficult position for a man to stand up here alone and express opposition to bills which so many able men favor, but I have to this bill primarily the same objection I have to the bill just passed, namely, that it seems to reach the point of absurdity for the House to pass a bill of such importance on so little debate and with so little information.

The bill, as has been explained, amends the Railroad Labor Act of 1926.

The labor act was enacted with the consent and cooperation of all the railroads and the railroad organizations and has worked extremely well. I think it safe to say that there has never been a time when there has been so much peace and cooperation between the railroads and their employees as during the last 8 years, since this railway act has been in operation. The reason is because there has been cooperation in the administration of the act. All sides have been consulted, and all sides agreed to the principles in the bill. This bill violates to a very considerable extent the underlying principles of that bill, because it involves a certain amount of force and coercion which does not tend to peace.

Another thing that the bill does which I think is extremely important is that it interferes with the liberty of a very large percentage of the employees, because it militates against what are called "company unions." Some of the great railroads are now operating peacefully and successfully under company unions, but this bill is so drawn that that liberty is taken away, because it forces, either directly or indirectly, all the employees into the national unions, and the national unions are apart from and often opposed to the railroads. They have operated very successfully under the existing Labor Act of 1926; but I think anyone who takes the time to study the matter carefully will see that this bill that we are proposing to pass will foment objections and litigation instead of quieting them.

I ask gentlemen to read carefully, if they will, the extracts in the minority report which I have made from a letter from Mr. Eastman, who is the Railroad Coordinator and who knows more about the operation of the Railway Act than any other man. He says, among other things:

The proposed amendments which Mr. Farquharson undertakes to defend are designed to protect certain so-called "percentage contracts," which his brotherhood has with some of the railroads. These contracts are so out of harmony with the whole spirit of railroad labor relations, as contemplated by the Railway Labor Act, the Bankruptcy Act, and the Emergency Railroad Transportation Act, that I am frankly astonished by the persistency with which these amendments are urged. In my testimony before your committee I pointed out that they are designed to permit the so-called "standard organizations" to enter into contracts or agreements with the carriers which are prohibited in the case of company unions.

That, you will see, is covered by the fifth paragraph, page 7 of the bill, which provides:

No carrier, its officers, or agents shall require any person seeking employment to sign any contract or agreement promising to join or not to join a company union; and if any such contract has been enforced prior to the effective date of this act, then such carrier shall notify the employees by an appropriate order that such contract has been discarded and is no longer binding on them in any way.

But they are not prohibited from requiring them to join a national union.

Then as to the formation of the adjustment boards, the bill provides in paragraph (c), page 12, Section 3:

The national labor organizations, as defined in paragraph (a) of this section, acting each through the chief executive or other medium designated by the organization or association thereof, shall prescribe the rules under which the labor members of the adjustment board shall be selected.

That is, you give the national unions full power to select the labor members of the organization board which rules the whole industry, and thus deprive a large percentage of employees of representation.

ROBERT RICH [R., PA.]. If the National Labor Board is given power to make selection, is it not going to control the situation so that you will have national labor unions, and there will be no permission of any kind granted for the employees, if they desire, to have company unions?

MR. MERRITT. Absolutely.

BERTRAND SNELL [R., N.Y.]. Is there any additional expense placed on the railroads in connection with this piece of legislation?

MR. MERRITT. I think not—nothing material, so far as expense goes. But I want you to listen to what the vice president of the New York Central Railroad, who spoke for all the class I railroads, said:

It is clearly obvious, from the presentations and charges that have been made that the proponents of this bill are not satisfied with it.

It is certainly obvious from the testimony of the organizations that they are not in agreement with the bill.

The managements of none of the railroads approve of the bill, and no railroad officer with whom I have discussed this bill knows just where it will lead.

It is another case of legislation of which no one, I think, on the committee would say that he knows where it will lead. It is kowtowing to national labor organizations and giving them power to control the situation.

MR. RICH. If the railroads are not permitted to collect anything from their employees for their own unions, are they supposed to collect funds for the organization of national unions?

MR. MERRITT. No; I believe the bill prohibits the railroad companies from contributing to any union. . . .

HARRY GRISWOLD [R., WIS.]. If under this bill they are prohibited from joining company unions, the railroads actually save the expense they are now put to in maintaining the company union.

MR. MERRITT. That is a very small amount.

MR. GRISWOLD. It amounts to considerable on some systems. Has the gentleman any record of it?

MR. MERRITT. No.

MR. GRISWOLD. It shows that it goes into the hundreds of thousands of dollars.

MR. MERRITT. That is small, compared with the millions involved. I do not think the matter of expense enters into it. The question is as to the operation of the railroads and whether they will be operated in a more friendly spirit as between the railroads and their employees. My view is that this bill is not in the interest of labor or in the interest of the railroads, and, therefore, I think it should not be passed without much more consideration than we are giving it.

MR. GRISWOLD. In relation to these percentage contracts of which the gentleman spoke, was there any objection from the railroad management or the employees before the gentleman's committee?

MR. MERRITT. Yes; these percentage contracts apply only to yardmen now.

MR. GRISWOLD. I understand that, but the management of the roads that now hold these contracts do not object?

MR. MERRITT. They do not object to existing contracts, no. . . .

CARL MAPES [R., MICH.]. Mr. Speaker, we are passing in a few minutes, within less than 2 hours, two bills of great interest, importance, and benefit to railroad employees. They come up in the closing hours of the session when there seems to be no other way to pass them except to do it promptly and without very much debate. Under the circumstances, some of us have to forego the privilege of entering into any very extensive discussion of the legislation.

Personally, I wish to express myself in favor of both pieces of legislation, the retirement legislation and this bill to amend the Labor Act, and in some respects the emergency railroad law which created the Coordinator of Railroads. I think that society and industry must provide, in their old age, for those who have spent their time and energies in industry during their active lives. I feel that this retirement legislation is equitable and that the bill reported by the House committee is very conservative. As the gentleman from California [Mr. Lea] stated, it is concededly somewhat experimental, but it is a step in the right direction. I want to go on record as favoring it.

The purpose of the pending bill is simply to amend and make more workable the act creating the Board of Mediation and the labor provisions in the emergency railroad law. It seems to me some people are overestimating some features of this bill. The bill does prohibit so-called "company unions" as defined in the bill, but the definition of a company union in the bill is one that is organized at the suggestion or with the aid of the company. I do not think any disinterested person favors such a company union or thinks that it serves any good purpose; but this bill does not, in terms, prevent the employees from forming a company union if they do it of their own volition and independent of help from the company.

One other provision of this bill is to provide by law for the appointment of a neutral referee on adjustment boards. Under existing law the representatives of the carriers and representatives of the employees act as adjustment boards; but for the most part they come to a head-on whenever there is a real dispute between them in those cases where the interested parties have named representatives, and they are more and more ceasing to appoint even their own representatives. There is no provision for the selection of a neutral referee under existing law. This bill provides for the appointment of such neutral referee so that there can be an actual decision when disputes arise between carriers and employees.

Those two provisions, as I understand the bill, are the main and fundamental provisions in the bill now before us. As I said in the beginning, it is largely for the purpose of making existing law workable that this bill is now before the House. [Applause.] . . . .

Senate—73rd Congress, 2nd Session
June 18, 1934

CLARENCE DILL [DEM., WASH.]. Mr. President, I move that the Senate proceed to the consideration of the bill (S. 3266) to amend the Railway Labor Act, approved May 20, 1926, and to provide for the prompt disposition of disputes between carriers and their employees. . . .

DANIEL HASTINGS [R., DEL.]. Mr. President, I desire to say to the Senator from Wisconsin that for the moment I propose only to show to the Senate the difficulties which are involved in the passage of this bill at this session of Congress. I shall not take a long time in doing it. But I do want the Senate to get a true picture of this situation. For that purpose I desire to call attention to the fact that there is no emergency involved at all in this legislation.

I desire to quote from Mr. Eastman's testimony, to be found on page 13 of the hearing, as follows:

The fact is that I have spent considerable time with the railroad executives on this matter, and their attitude has, on the whole, been very commendable. . . .

The Coordinator states:

The conditions have been improved very materially. The improvement has not been complete, but excellent progress has been and is being made. I do not now suggest legislation because of immediate need, but in order that the legislative situation may be clarified and stabilized, and proper provision made for the future.

Again I desire to call attention to this language on page 17:

The National Adjustment Board is to handle only the minor cases growing out of grievances, or out of the interpretation or application of agreements. Provision is also made so that deadlocks will be impossible.

Again on page 13 Mr. Eastman states:

I know that the railroads will present, before these hearings are through, very emphatic objections to the creation of this National Adjustment Board.

I may say that I conferred with the representatives of the railroads before making the report on this bill.

They will probably tell you that it is something like shooting sparrows with a 16-inch gun; that those minor disputes ought to be considered locally and not by a national board far removed from the seat of conflict; that this is especially true of discipline cases; that the very existence of a national board will prevent the local settlement of these cases as they ought to be settled; that the tendency for the parties will be to disagree and to "pass the buck" to the national board; and that the national board will bog down with a multitude of docketed but undecided cases, to the dissatisfaction and great expense of all concerned.

Now I do not wish to dismiss these objections as of no moment. On the contrary I think they have substance and that you ought to give them very careful consideration. Nevertheless, I believe that this experiment of a national adjustment board should be tried. In the first place, as I have already indicated, I regard the appointment of a neutral member to prevent deadlocks as a provision having the very greatest of importance.

I desire to call attention to these three points. In the first place the Coordinator, who knows about these matters, says: "I do not now suggest legislation because of immediate need" . . . I have before me the hearings, and I was depending upon the hearings in order to ascertain the coordinator's views.

May I call attention that, in the first place, he says there is no immediate need; in the second place, he says that the national adjustment board proposed to be created by this bill "is to handle only minor cases growing out of grievances or out of the interpretation or application of agreements"; and, in the third place, he calls attention to the fact that this is merely an experiment.

So we have from the Coordinator three statements which, to my mind, are very important. First, he says there is no immediate necessity for such legislation; secondly, that it is intended to apply only in minor cases; and third, after all, it is wholly an experiment. And the points to which I have called attention are important only for the purpose of determining whether this kind of legislation ought to be taken up this late in the session. I mean by "this late in the session," assuming that the Congress itself believes and the country as a whole believes that the Congress has been in session as long as it reasonably ought to be and it is desirable for the country that it shortly adjourn.

I agree that there are provisions in the pending railroad bill that are worthy of discussion. The railroad managements are not objecting to the whole of this bill; they would be delighted, as I understand, to have some provision whereby when they reach an agreement with their men its execution could be made compulsory; but, Mr. President, I desire to call especially the attention of the distinguished chairman of the committee to one other very great difficulty that is involved in the passage of this proposed legislation at this time. I call his attention to the fact that as the House passed this bill it has in it under paragraphs 4 and 5 of Section 2 provisions which the Coordinator bitterly opposes, and, if I understand his letter, he believes that it would be better to pass no bill than it would be to pass the kind of bill which the House of Representatives has passed. If the Senator from Washington has not examined the House provisions, I call his attention to the very great difference between the provisions of the bill as passed by the House and the bill which has been recommended by the Interstate Commerce Committee of the Senate; and I suggest that in connection with those differences it might take literally days, with everyone working as hard as he could, to reach an agreement, before an agreement could be reached.

In that connection I desire to read a letter in order that the Senate may know the differences. I desire to read a letter of date June to the Chairman of the Committee on Interstate and Foreign Commerce of the House of Representatives by Mr. Eastman, in which he points out the danger of so amending the bill which he had prepared. I want to call the Senate's attention to the fact that the House ignored his recommendation, and in the bill are the very provisions to which the Coordinator objects.

This letter, which is directed to Representative Rayburn calls attention to the fact that—

Mr. J. A. Farquharson, vice president and legislative representative of the Brotherhood of Railroad Trainmen, has left with me a copy of his brief filed with your committee in support of amendments of bill H.R. 9689 proposed by the Association of Railway Labor Executives in lieu of paragraphs 4 and 5 of Section 2 of the bill. There has also been presented to your committee an argument by Mr. R. K. Corkhill in support of certain other amendments proposed by so-called "independent" organizations. It may clarify the situation if I reply to these communications.

Paragraphs 4 and 5 of Section 2 of H.R. 9689 merely write into the permanent law and clarify provisions of the Bankruptcy Act and Emergency Railroad Transportation Act, 1933.

Mr. President, may I call attention to the fact with respect to the bill which was presented to the Senate by the Coordinator and which is now

before the Senate, that he bases his recommendations largely upon the fact
that this provision was in the Emergency Railroad Transportation Act, but,
in reply to that, it ought to be remembered that that act was to run for only
a short time and was not intended to be permanent, while this proposed
legislation is intended to be permanent.

But the Coordinator points out—

> The proposed amendments which Mr. Farquharson undertakes to defend are de-
> signed to protect certain so-called "percentage contracts" which his brotherhood has
> with some of the railroads. These contracts are so out of harmony with the spirit of
> railroad labor relations as contemplated by the Railroad Labor Act, the Bankruptcy
> Act, and the Emergency Railroad Transportation Act, that I am frankly astonished by
> the persistency with which these amendments are urged. In my testimony before your
> committee I pointed out that they are designed to permit the so-called "standard organi-
> zations" to enter into contracts or agreements with the carriers which are prohibited in
> the case of company unions, such contracts or agreements being of the closed-shop or
> "yellow dog" variety.

In other words, Mr. Eastman takes the position that there should be no
"yellow-dog" contracts of any kind, either on behalf of the railroads or on
behalf of the unions. As I understand, 21 unions operating in connection
with 21 class I railroads of this country have contracts with the corporations
whereby no person shall be employed unless he agrees beforehand to become a part of that union and to be bound by the rules and regulations of
that union. In other words, that is the "yellow-dog" contract which has
been condemned by every Senator on the floor of the Senate, so far as I
know, who has had anything to say about it. That statement refers to contracts by which industries employ a person and make him agree before his
employment that he will not join certain unions. That, as I recollect, is
called the "yellow-dog" contract. . . .

Mr. President, I have pointed out what the "yellow-dog" contract means
to most of us, and as I have said, Senators on this floor have condemned it
and have been willing to do anything they could to outlaw the "yellow-dog"
contract.

But the 21 railroad organizations have made a contract already with the
railroads which prohibits the railroads from employing persons, any kind
of persons, until those persons agree to abide by the rules and regulations
of the railroad organizations. It was that kind of a contract which Mr.
Eastman condemned, but it is that kind of contract which the House has
written into paragraphs 4 and 5 of Section 2.

If there be a difference of opinion between the House and Mr. Eastman
and if the Senate agrees with the recommendations of Mr. Eastman as the
committee did, then we have a serious conflict between the Senate and the
House which may not be ended, as I pointed out a moment ago, without
debate involving a very great length of time.

Mr. Eastman continued:

No such distinction is made in the present labor provisions of the Emergency Act, which the standard organizations themselves wrote, and I am at a loss to know how it can be defended. It is not necessary to repeat here all that I said in my statement to the committee. However, the trainmen have cleared up with my organization a few points as to which I was not fully informed at the time of my statement.

(1) None of the percentage contracts applies to the road-train service. Conductors demoted to trainmen's work on account of decrease in business displace trainmen, and trainmen are promoted to conductors' jobs without any friction between the organizations and without any percentage contracts. Under these circumstances a percentage contract for the trainmen in road service would be impossible.

(2) The percentage contracts apply only to yard service: i.e., yard conductors, yard brakemen, and switchmen. The contracts provide that at least 75, 85, or 100 percent, as the case may be, of these classes of employees working in a yard must belong to the Brotherhood of Railroad Trainmen and that, in one instance at least, the carrier must, in the contract of employment, provide that the new employee shall join the trainmen's organization within a limited number of days from his employment. Thus the contract provides for a closed shop, in whole or in part, and has also all the essential features of the "yellow-dog" contract, denying freedom of choice to the employees.

(3) The Brotherhood of Railroad Trainmen have the contract for the yard-service employees on between 140 and 150 class I railroads, but on only 23 roads of this total has the brotherhood been able to negotiate a percentage contract. On the remaining one hundred and twenty-odd roads where the trainmen have the yard contract, they are in position to make the yard-service jobs interchangeable with the road-train service, protect their contracts, prevent illegal strikes, insure division seniority for yard-service employees, and generally make the organization much more flexible in the protection of their members and the railroad than under a percentage contract. This is so because the percentage is figured for each yard separately, and hence the men have no seniority rights elsewhere in case the operation of a yard is abandoned through consolidation, lengthening of divisions, or other operating change.

(4) The Brotherhood of Railroad Trainmen could, without difficulty, rewrite the percentage contracts to conform with the yard contracts that they hold on the great majority of the roads.

(5) The percentage contracts of the Brotherhood of Railroad Trainmen cover not more than 10,000 employees. This is approximately 1 percent of the total of railroad employees. The provisions of paragraphs 4 and 5 of Section 2 of the bill will affect the opportunity of freedom of choice in the selection of representatives by perhaps 400,000 employees heretofore included in company-union groups. Is it any wonder that the railroads foster the contentions made by the trainmen in the hope of preventing the passage of the bill or imperiling its constitutionality? The committee members will appreciate the legal arguments that will be raised in behalf of the company unions if Congress should prohibit certain practices with respect to them, but permit the same practices with respect to other labor organizations.

(6) In Mr. Farquharson's brief, attention is called to certain contracts of the Brotherhood of Locomotive Firemen and Enginemen in the South, whereby a certain percentage of men employed as firemen are promotable men. Apparently Mr. Farquharson would have it appear that these contracts of the firemen are similar to the percentage contracts of the trainmen. This, however, is not the case. All that the firemen's contracts provide is that a certain ratio between white and colored firemen shall be maintained for

reasons having absolutely no relation to membership or nonmembership in labor organizations. The percentage contracts of the trainmen for yard service are the only closed-shop contracts known to the railroad industry.

(7) Long experience has shown that whenever management is put into position to assist in the control of membership in a labor organization, it will find ways to control the policy and practices of that organization.

(8) The importation of labor practices in other industry as a guide to Congress in framing railroad labor legislation presents an anomaly. Heretofore, the railroad labor leadership has set the model to which labor interests in other industries have sought to attain. Senator Wagner has joined with the Committee on Interstate Commerce in the Senate in recommending this legislation as it appears in H.R. 9689. Mr. Farquharson's brief is in error in asserting that the United Mine Workers write only closed-shop contracts. The fact is that while the check-off may be written into the miners' contracts, it applies only to the members of the union.

I am confident that the only real support for the proposed amendments is from a single organization. None of the other standard organizations has anything to gain from such changes in the bill. I sincerely hope that your committee will not imperil the legislation by adopting these amendments. They can cause only trouble and are incapable of any sound defense.

With respect to the statement filed with your committee by Mr. R. K. Corkhill, I have not been favored with a draft of the amendments proposed by Mr. Todd which Mr. Corkhill supports. The bill as proposed gives every latitude to independent unions, organized in accordance with the bill, to ally themselves in national organizations and participate in the selection of the labor representatives on the National Adjustment Board. They are also given every opportunity to agree with managements upon any other system of adjustment. To open up additional avenues for the further review of minor grievances than those provided in the bill as now drawn, would be defeating the very purposes for which it is proposed to amend the Railway Labor Act. . . .

THE DECISIONS

Texas & New Orleans Railroad Company v. *Brotherhood of Railway Clerks*
281 U.S. 548 (1930)

MR. CHIEF JUSTICE HUGHES delivered the opinion of the Court.

This suit was brought in the District Court by the Brotherhood of Railway and Steamship Clerks, Freight Handlers, Express and Station Employees, Southern Pacific Lines in Texas and Louisiana, a voluntary association, and H. W. Harper, General Chairman of its System Board of Adjustment, against the Texas and New Orleans Railroad Company, and certain officers and agents of that Company, to obtain an injunction restraining the defendants from interfering with, influencing or coercing the clerical employees of the Railroad Company in the matter of their organization and designation of representatives for the purposes set forth in the Railway Labor Act of May 20, 1926, c. 347, 44 Stat. 577; U. S. C., Tit. 45, Secs. 151–163.

The substance of the allegations of the bill of complaint was that the Brotherhood, since its organization in September, 1918, had been authorized by a majority of the railway clerks in the employ of the Railroad Company (apart from general office employees) to represent them in all matters relating to their employment; that this representation was recognized by the Railroad Company before and after the application by the Brotherhood in November, 1925, for an increase of the wages of the railway clerks and after the denial of that application by the Railroad Company and the reference of the controversy by the Brotherhood to the United States Board of Mediation; that, while the controversy was pending before that Board, the Railroad Company instigated the formation of a union of its railway clerks (other than general office employees) known as the "Association of Clerical Employees—Southern Pacific Lines"; and that the Railroad Company had endeavored to intimidate members of the Brotherhood and to coerce them to withdraw from it and to make the Association their representative in dealings with the Railroad Company, and thus to prevent the railway clerks from freely designating their representatives by collective action.

The District Court granted a temporary injunction. Thereafter the Railroad Company recognized the Association of Clerical Employees—Southern Pacific Lines as the representative of the clerical employees of the Company. The Railroad Company stated that this course was taken after a committee of the Association had shown authorizations signed by those who were regarded as constituting a majority of the employees of the described class. The subsequent action of the Railroad Company and its officers and agents was in accord with this recognition of the Association and the consequent non-recognition of the Brotherhood. In proceedings to punish for contempt, the District Court decided that the Railroad Com-

140

pany and certain of its officers who were defendants had violated the order of injunction and completely nullified it. The Court directed that, in order to purge themselves of this contempt, the Railroad Company and these officers should completely "disestablish the Association of Clerical Employees," as it was then constituted as the recognized representative of the clerical employees of the Railroad Company, and should reinstate the Brotherhood as such representative, until such time as these employees by a secret ballot taken in accordance with the further direction of the Court, and without the dictation or interference of the Railroad Company and its officers, should choose other representatives. The order also required the restoration to service and to stated privileges of certain employees who had been discharged by the Railroad Company. 24 F. (2d) 426. Punishment was prescribed in case the defendants did not purge themselves of contempt as directed.

On final hearing, the temporary injunction was made permanent. 25 F. (2d) 873. At the same time, a motion to vacate the order in the contempt proceedings was denied. 25 F. (2d) 876. The Circuit Court of Appeals affirmed the decree, holding that the injunction was properly granted and that, in imposing conditions for the purging of the defendants of contempt, the District Court had not gone beyond the appropriate exercise of its authority in providing for the restoration of the *status quo*. 33 F. (2d) 13. This Court granted a writ of certiorari. 280 U. S. 550.

The bill of complaint invoked subdivision third of Section 2 of the Railway Labor Act of 1926, c. 347, 44 Stat. 577, which provides as follows:

"Third. Representatives, for the purposes of this Act, shall be designated by the respective parties in such manner as may be provided in their corporate organization or unincorporated association, or by other means of collective action, without interference, influence, or coercion exercised by either party over the self-organization or designation of representatives by the other."

The controversy is with respect to the construction, validity and application of this statutory provision. The petitioners, the Railroad Company and its officers, contend that the provision confers merely an abstract right which was not intended to be enforced by legal proceedings; that, in so far as the statute undertakes to prevent either party from influencing the other in the selection of representatives, it is unconstitutional because it seeks to take away an inherent and inalienable right in violation of the First and Fifth Amendments of the Federal Constitution; that the granting of the injunction was prohibited by Section 20 of the Clayton Act, U. S. C., Tit. 29, Sec. 52; that in any event the action taken by the Railroad Company and its officers in the recognition of the Association of Clerical Employees, and in other proceedings following upon that recognition, was not contrary to law and that there was no warrant for the interposition of the court either in granting the injunction order or in the proceedings for punishment for the alleged contempt. . . .

It is unnecessary to review the history of the legislation enacted by Congress in relation to the settlement of railway labor disputes, as earlier efforts culminated in Title III of the Transportation Act, 1920, c. 91, 41 Stat. 456, 469, the purpose and effect of which have been determined by this Court. In *Pennsylvania Railroad Company* v. *United States Railroad Labor Board,* 261 U. S. 72, the question was whether the members of the Railroad Labor Board as constituted under the provisions of the Transportation Act, 1920, had exceeded their powers. The Court held that the Board had jurisdiction to hear and decide a dispute over rules and working conditions upon the application of either side, when the parties had failed to agree and an adjustment board had not been organized. The Board also had jurisdiction to decide who might represent the employees in the conferences contemplated by the statute and to make reasonable rules for ascertaining the will of the employees in this respect. Interference by injunction with the exercise of the discretion of the Board in the matters committed to it, and with the publication of its opinions, was decided to be unwarranted. The Court thought it evident that Congress considered it to be "of the highest public interest to prevent the interruption of interstate commerce by labor disputes and strikes," and that its plan was "to encourage settlement without strikes, first by conference between the parties; failing that, by reference to adjustment boards of the parties' own choosing," and, if this proved to be ineffective, "by a full hearing before a National Board" organized as the statute provided. But the Court added: "The decisions of the Labor Board are not to be enforced by process. The only sanction of its decision is to be the force of public opinion invoked by the fairness of a full hearing, the intrinsic justice of the conclusion, strengthened by the official prestige of the Board, and the full publication of the violation of such decision by any party to the proceeding." It was said to be the evident thought of Congress "that the economic interest of every member of the Public in the undisturbed flow of interstate commerce and the acute inconvenience to which all must be subjected by an interruption caused by a serious and widespread labor dispute, fastens public attention closely on all the circumstances of the controversy and arouses public criticism of the side thought to be at fault." *Id.* pp. 79, 80. The Court concluded that the Labor Board was "to act as a Board of Arbitration," but that there was "no constraint" upon the parties "to do what the Board decided they should do except the moral constraint of publication of its decision." *Id.* p. 84.

The provisions of Title III of the Transportation Act, 1920, were again before the Court in *Pennsylvania Railroad System and Allied Lines Federation No. 90* v. *Pennsylvania Railroad Company,* 267 U. S. 203. This was a suit by a union to enjoin the Railroad Company from carrying out an alleged conspiracy to defeat the provisions of the legislation establishing the Railroad Labor Board. The complainants, the Court said, sought "to enforce by mandatory injunction a compliance with a decision of the Board"; and the Court held that "such a remedy by injunction in a court, it was not the intention of Congress to provide." *Id.* p. 216. The Court pointed out that "the ultimate decision of the Board, it is conceded, is not compulsory, and no process is furnished to enforce it." It was in the light of these conclusions as to the purport of the Statute that the Court considered the freedom of action of the Railroad Company. The Court said that the Company was using "every endeavor to avoid compliance with the judgment and principles of the Labor Board as to the proper method of securing representatives of the whole body of its employees," that it was "seeking to control its employees by agreements free from the influence of an independent trade union," and, so far as concerned its dealing with its employees, was "refusing to comply with the decisions of the Labor Board." But the Court held that this conduct was within the strict legal rights of the Railroad Company and that Congress had not intended to make such conduct legally actionable. *Id.* p. 217.

It was with clear appreciation of the infirmity of the existing legislation, and in the endeavor to establish a more practicable plan in order to accomplish the desired result, that Congress enacted the Railway Labor Act of 1926. It was decided to make a fresh start. The situation was thus described in the report of the bill to the Senate by the Committee on Interstate Commerce (69th Cong., 1st Sess., Sen. Rep. No. 22): "In view of the fact that the employees absolutely refuse to appear before the labor board and that many of the important railroads are themselves opposed to it, that it has been held by the Supreme Court to have no power to enforce its judgments, that its authority is not recognized or respected by the employees and by a number of important railroads, that the President has suggested that it would be wise to seek a substitute for it, and that the party platforms of both the Republican and Democratic Parties in 1924 clearly indicated dissatisfaction with the provisions of the transportation act relating to labor, the committee concluded that the time had arrived when the labor board should be abolished and the provisions relating to labor in the transportation act, 1920, should be repealed."

The bill was introduced as the result of prolonged conferences between representative committees of railroad presidents and of executives of railroad labor organizations, and embodied an agreement of a large majority of both. The provisions of Title III of the Transportation Act, 1920, and also the Act of July 15, 1913, c. 6, 38 Stat. 103, which provided for mediation, conciliation and arbitration in controversies with railway employees, were repealed.

While adhering in the new statute for the policy of providing for the amicable adjustment of labor disputes, and for voluntary submissions to arbitration as opposed to a system of compulsory arbitration, Congress buttressed this policy by creating certain definite legal obligations. The outstanding feature of the Act of 1926 is the provision for an enforceable award in arbitration proceedings. The arbitration is voluntary, but the award pursuant to the arbitration is conclusive upon the parties as to the merits and facts of the controversy submitted. (Section 9.) The award is to be filed in the clerk's office of the District Court of the United States designated in the agreement to arbitrate, and unless a petition to impeach the award is filed within ten days, the court is to enter judgment on the award, and this judgment is final and conclusive. Petition for the impeachment of the award may be made upon the grounds that the award does not conform to the substantive requirements of the Act or to the stipulation of the parties, or that the proceedings were not in accordance with the Act or were tainted with fraud or corruption. But the court is not to entertain such a petition on the ground that the award is invalid for uncertainty, and in such case the remedy is to be found in a submission of the award to a reconvened board or to a sub-committee thereof for interpretation, as provided in the Act. Thus it is contemplated that the proceedings for the amicable adjustment of disputes will have an appropriate termination in a binding adjudication, enforceable as such.

Another definite object of the Act of 1926 is to provide, in case of a dispute between a carrier and its employees which has not been adjusted under the provisions of the Act, for the more effectual protection of interstate commerce from interruption to such a degree as to deprive any section of the country of essential transportation service. (Section 10.) In case the Board of Mediation established by the Act, as an independent agency in the executive branch of the Government, finds that such an interruption of interstate commerce is threatened, that Board is to notify the President, who may thereupon in his discretion create an emergency board of investigation to report, within thirty days, with respect to the dispute. The Act then provides that "After the creation of such board and for thirty days after such board has made its report to the President, no change, except by agreement, shall be made by the parties to the controversy in the conditions out of which the dispute arose." *Id.* This prohibition, in order to safeguard the vital interests of the country while an investigation is in progress, manifestly imports a legal obligation. The Brotherhood insists, and we think rightly, that the major purpose of Congress in passing the Railway Labor Act was "to provide a machinery to prevent strikes." Section 10 is described by counsel for the Brotherhood as "a provision limiting the right to strike," and in this view it is insisted that there "is no possible question that Congress intended to make the provisions of

Section 10 enforceable to the extent of authorizing any court of competent jurisdiction to restrain either party to the controversy from changing the existing status during the sixty-day period provided for the emergency board."

The provision of Section 10 is to be read in connection with the qualification in subdivision eighth of Section 9 that nothing in the Act shall be construed to require an individual employee to render labor without his consent or as making the quitting of service by an individual employee an illegal act, and that no court shall issue any process to compel the performance by an individual employee of labor without his consent. The purpose of this limitation was manifestly to protect the individual liberty of employees and not to affect proceedings in case of combinations or group action. The denial of legal process in the one case is significant with respect to its expected, appropriate use in the other.

It is thus apparent that Congress, in the legislation of 1926, while elaborating a plan for amicable adjustments and voluntary arbitration of disputes between common carriers and their employees, thought it necessary to impose, and did impose, certain definite obligations enforceable by judicial proceedings. The question before us is whether a legal obligation of this sort is also to be found in the provisions of subdivision third of Section 2 of the Act providing that "Representatives for the purposes of this Act, shall be designated by the respective parties . . . without interference, influence, or coercion exercised by either party over the self-organization or designation of representatives by the other."

It is at once to be observed that Congress was not content with the general declaration of the duty of carriers and employees to make every reasonable effort to enter into and maintain agreements concerning rates of pay, rules and working conditions, and to settle disputes with all expedition in conference between authorized representatives, but added this distinct prohibition against coercive measures. This addition can not be treated as superfluous or insignificant, or as intended to be without effect. *Ex parte Public National Bank,* 278 U. S. 101, 104. While an affirmative declaration of duty contained in a legislative enactment may be of imperfect obligation because not enforceable in terms, a definite statutory prohibition of conduct which would thwart the declared purpose of the legislation cannot be disregarded. The intent of Congress is clear with respect to the sort of conduct that is prohibited. "Interference" with freedom of action and "coercion" refer to well understood concepts of the law. The meaning of the word "influence" in this clause may be gathered from the context. *Noscitur a sociis. Virginia* v. *Tennessee,* 148 U. S. 503, 519. The use of the word is not to be taken as interdicting the normal relations and innocent communications which are a part of all friendly intercourse, albeit between employer and employee. "Influence" in this context plainly means pressure, the use of the authority or power of either party to induce action by the other in derogation of what the statute calls "self-organization." The phrase covers the abuse of relation or opportunity so as to corrupt or override the will, and it is no more difficult to appraise conduct of this sort in connection with the selection of representatives for the purposes of this Act than in relation to well-known applications of the law with respect to fraud, duress and undue influence. If Congress intended that the prohibition, as thus construed, should be enforced, the courts would encounter no difficulty in fulfilling its purpose, as the present suit demonstrates.

In reaching a conclusion as to the intent of Congress, the importance of the prohibition in its relation to the plan devised by the Act must have appropriate consideration. Freedom of choice in the selection of representatives on each side of the dispute is the essential foundation of the statutory scheme. All the proceedings looking to amicable adjustments and to agreements for arbitration of disputes, the entire policy of the Act, must depend for success on the uncoerced action of each party through its own representatives to the end that agreements satisfactory to both may be reached and the peace essential to the uninterrupted service of the instrumentalities of interstate commerce may be maintained. There is no impairment of the voluntary character of arrangements for the adjustment of disputes in the imposition of a legal obligation not to interfere with the free choice of those who are to make such adjustments. On the contrary, it is of the essence of a voluntary scheme, if it is to accomplish its purpose, that this liberty should be safeguarded. The definite prohibition which Congress inserted in the Act can not therefore be overridden in the view that Congress intended it to be ignored. As the prohibition was appropriate to the aim of Congress, and is capable of enforcement, the conclusion must be that enforcement was contemplated.

The absence of penalty is not controlling. The creation of a legal right by language suitable to that end does not require for its effectiveness the imposition of statutory penalties. Many rights are enforced for which no statutory penalties are provided. In the case of the statute in question, there is an absence of penalty, in the sense of specially prescribed punishment, with respect to the arbitral awards and the prohibition of change in conditions pending the investigation and report of an emergency board, but in each instance a legal obligation is created and the statutory requirements are susceptible of enforcement by proceedings appropriate to each. The same is true of the prohibition of interference or coercion in connection with the choice of representatives. The right is created and the remedy exists. *Marbury* v. *Madison,* 1 Cranch 137, 162, 163.

We entertain no doubt of the constitutional authority of Congress to enact the prohibition. The power to regulate commerce is the power to enact "all appropriate legislation" for its "protection and advancement" (*The*

Daniel Ball, 10 Wall. 557, 564); to adopt measures "to promote its growth and insure its safety" (*County of Mobile* v. *Kimball,* 102 U. S. 691, 691, 696, 697); to "foster, protect, control and restrain" (*Second Employers' Liability Cases,* 223 U. S. 1, 47). Exercising this authority, Congress may facilitate the amicable settlement of disputes which threaten the service of the necessary agencies of interstate transportation. In shaping its legislation to this end, Congress was entitled to take cognizance of actual conditions and to address itself to practicable measures. The legality of collective action on the part of employees in order to safeguard their proper interests is not to be disputed. It has long been recognized that employees are entitled to organize for the purpose of securing the redress of grievances and to promote agreements with employers relating to rates of pay and conditions of work. *American Steel Foundries* v. *Tri-City Central Trades Council,* 257 U. S. 184, 209. Congress was not required to ignore this right of the employees but could safeguard it and seek to make their appropriate collective action an instrument of piece rather than of strife. Such collective action would be a mockery if representation were made futile by interferences with freedom of choice. Thus the prohibition by Congress of interference with the selection of representatives for the purpose of negotiation and conference between employers and employees, instead of being an invasion of the constitutional right of either, was based on the recognition of the rights of both. The petitioners invoke the principle declared in *Adair* v. *United States,* 208 U. S. 161, and *Coppage* v. *Kansas,* 236 U. S. 1, but these decisions are inapplicable. The Railway Labor Act of 1926 does not interfere with the normal exercise of the right of the carrier to select its employees or to discharge them. The statute is not aimed at this right of the employers but at the interference with the right of employees to have representatives of their own choosing. As the carriers· subject to the Act have no constitutional right to interfere with the freedom of the employees in making their selections, they cannot complain of the statute on constitutional grounds. . . .

We do not find that the decree below goes beyond the proper enforcement of the provision of the Railway Labor Act.

Decree affirmed.

Virginian Railway Company v. *System Federation No. 40*
300 U.S. 515 (1937)

MR. JUSTICE STONE delivered the opinion of the Court.

This case presents questions as to the constitutional validity of certain provisions of the Railway Labor Act of May 20, 1926, c. 347, 44 Stat. 577, as amended by the Act of June 21, 1934, c. 691, 48 Stat. 1185, 45

U. S. C. §§ 151–163, and as to the nature and extent of the relief which courts are authorized by the Act to give.

Respondents are System Federation No. 40, which will be referred to as the Federation, a labor organization affiliated with the American Federation, of Labor and representing shop craft employees of petitioner railway, and certain individuals who are officers and members of the System Federation. They brought the present suit in equity in the District Court for Eastern Virginia, to compel petitioner, an interstate rail carrier, to recognize and treat with respondent Federation, as the duly accredited representative of the mechanical department employees of petitioner, and to restrain petitioner from in any way interfering with, influencing or coercing its shop craft employees in their free choice of representatives, for the purpose of contracting with petitioner with respect to rules, rates of pay and working conditions, and for the purpose of considering and settling disputes between petitioner and such employees.

The history of this controversy goes back to 1922, when, following the failure of a strike by petitioner's shop employees affiliated with the American Federation of Labor, other employees organized a local union known as the "Mechanical Department Association of the Virginian Railway." The Association thereupon entered into an agreement with petitioner, providing for rates of pay and working conditions, and for the settlement of disputes with respect to them, but no substantial grievances were ever presented to petitioner by the Association. It maintained its organization and held biennial elections of officers, but the notices of election were sent out by petitioner and all Association expenses were paid by petitioner.

In 1927 the American Federation of Labor formed a local organization, which, in 1934, demanded recognition by petitioner of its authority to represent the shopcraft employees, and invoked the aid of the National Mediation Board, constituted under the Railway Labor Act as amended, to establish its authority. The Board, pursuant to agreement between the petitioner, the Federation, and the Association, and in conformity to the statute, held an election by petitioner's shop craft employees, to choose representatives for the purpose of collective bargaining with petitioner. As the result of the election, the Board certified that the Federation was the duly accredited representative of petitioner's employees in the six shop crafts.

Upon this and other evidence, not now necessary to be detailed, the trial court found that the Federation was the duly authorized representative of the mechanical department employees of petitioner, except the carmen and coach cleaners; that the petitioner, in violation of § 2 of the Railway Labor Act, had failed to treat with the Federation as the duly accredited representative of petitioner's employees; that petitioner had sought to influence its employees against any affiliation with labor organizations other than an association maintained by petitioner, and to prevent its employees from exercising their right to choose their own representative; that for that purpose, following the certification by the National Mediation Board, of the Federation, as the duly authorized representative of petitioner's mechanical department employees, petitioner had organized the Independent Shop Craft Association of its shop craft employees, and had sought to induce its employees to join the independent association, and to put it forward as the authorized representative of petitioner's employees.

Upon the basis of these findings the trial court gave its decree applicable to petitioner's mechanical department employees except the carmen and coach cleaners. It directed petitioner to "treat with" the Federation and to "exert every reasonable effort to make and maintain agreements concerning rates of pay, rules and working conditions, and to settle all disputes, whether arising out of the application of such agreements or otherwise, . . ." It restrained petitioner from "entering into any contract, undertaking or agreement of whatsoever kind concerning rules, rates of pay or working conditions affecting its Mechanical Department employees, . . . except . . . with the Federation," and from "interfering with, influencing or coercing" its employees with respect to their free choice of representatives "for the purpose of making and maintaining contracts" with petitioner "relating to rules, rates of pay, and working conditions or for the purpose of considering and deciding disputes between the Mechanical Department employees" and petitioner. The decree further restrained the petitioner from organizing or fostering any union of its mechanical department employees for the purpose of interfering with the Federation as the accredited representative of such employees. 11 F. Supp. 621.

On appeal the Court of Appeals for the Fourth Circuit approved and adopted the findings of the district court and affirmed its decree. 84 F. (2d) 641. This Court granted certiorari to review the cause as one of public importance.

Petitioner here, as below, makes two main contentions: First, with respect to the relief granted, it maintains that § 2, Ninth, of the Railway Labor Act, which provides that a carrier shall treat with those certified by the Mediation Board to be the representatives of a craft or class, imposes no legally enforcible obligation upon the carrier to negotiate with the representative so certified, and that in any case the statute imposes no obligation to treat or negotiate which can be appropriately enforced by a court of equity. Second, that § 2, Ninth, in so far as it attempts to regulate labor relations between petitioner and its "back shop" employees, is not a regulation of interstate commerce authorized by the commerce clause because, as it asserts, they are engaged solely in intrastate activities; and that so far as it imposes on the carrier any obligation to negotiate with a labor union authorized to represent its employees, and restrain it from making agreements with any other labor organization, it is a denial of due process guaranteed by the Fifth Amendment. Other minor objections to the decree, so far as relevant to our decision, will be referred to later in the course of this opinion.

The concurrent findings of fact of the two courts below are not shown to be plainly erroneous or unsupported by evidence. We accordingly accept them as the conclusive basis for decision, *Texas & N. O. R. Co.* v. *Brotherhood of Railway & S. S. Clerks,* 281 U. S. 548, 558; *Pick Mfg. Co.* v. *General Motors Corp.,* 299 U. S. 3, 4, and address ourselves to the questions of law raised on the record.

First. The Obligation Imposed by the Statute. By Title III of the Transportation Act of February 28, 1920, c. 91, 41 Stat. 456, 469, Congress set up the Railroad Labor Board as a means for the peaceful settlement, by agreement or by arbitration, of labor controversies between interstate carriers and their employees. It sought "to encourage settlement without strikes, first by conference between the parties; failing that, by reference to adjustment boards of the parties' own choosing, and if this is ineffective, by a full hearing before a National Board . . ." *Pennsylvania R. Co.* v. *Railroad Labor Board,* 261 U. S. 72, 79. The decisions of the Board were supported by no legal sanctions. The disputants were not; "in any way to be forced into compliance with the statute or with the judgments pronounced by the Labor Board, except through the effect of adverse public opinion." *Pennsylvania Federation* v. *Pennsylvania R. Co.,* 267 U. S. 203, 216.

In 1926 Congress, aware of the impotence of the Board, and of the fact that its authority was generally not recognized or respected by the railroads or their employees, made a fresh start toward the peaceful settlement of labor disputes affecting railroads, by the repeal of the 1920 Act and the adoption of the Railway Labor Act. Report, Senate Committee on Interstate Commerce, No. 222, 69th Cong., 1st Sess. *Texas & N. O. R. Co.* v. *Brotherhood of Railway & S. S. Clerks, supra,* 563. By the new measure Congress continued its policy of encouraging the amicable adjustment of labor disputes by their voluntary submission to arbitration before an impartial board, but it supported that policy by the imposition of legal obligations. It provides means for enforcing the award obtained by arbitration between the parties to labor disputes. § 9. In certain circumstances it prohibited any change in conditions, by the parties to an unadjusted labor dispute, for a period of thirty days, except by agreement. § 10. It recognized their right to designate representatives for the purposes of the Act "without interference, influence or coercion exercised by either party over the self-organization or designation of representatives by the other." § 2, Third. Under the last-mentioned provision this Court held, in the *Railway Clerks* case, *supra,* that employees were free to organize and to make choice of their representatives without the "coercive interference" and "pressure" of a company union organized and maintained by the employer; and that the statute protected the freedom of choice of representatives, which was an essential of the statutory scheme, with a legal sanction which it was the duty of courts to enforce by appropriate decree.

The prohibition against such interference was continued and made more explicit by the amendment of 1934. Petitioner does not challenge that part of the decree which enjoins any interference by it with the free choice of representatives by its employees, and the fostering, in the circumstances of this case, of the company union. That contention is not open to it in view of our decision in the *Railway Clerks* case, *supra,* and of the unambiguous language of § 2, Third, and Fourth, of the Act, as amended.

But petitioner insists that the statute affords no legal sanction for so much of the decree as directs petitioner to "treat with" respondent Federation "and exert every reasonable effort to make and maintain agreements concerning rates of pay, rules and working conditions, and to settle all disputes whether arising out of the application of such agreements or otherwise." It points out that the requirement for reasonable effort to reach an agreement is couched in the very words of § 2, First, which were taken from § 301 of the Transportation Act, and which were held to be without legal sanction in that Act. *Pennsylvania Federation* v. *Pennsylvania R. Co., supra,* 215. It is argued that they cannot now be given greater force as reënacted in the Railway Labor Act of 1926, and continued in the 1934 amendment. But these words no longer stand alone and unaided by mandatory provision of the statute as they did when first enacted. The amendment of the Railway Labor Act added new provisions in § 2, Ninth, which makes it the duty of the Mediation Board, when any dispute arises among the carrier's employees, "as to who are the representatives of such employees," to investigate the dispute and to certify, as was done in this case, the name of the organization authorized to represent the employees. It commands that "Upon receipt of such certification the carrier shall treat with the representative so certified as the representative of the craft or class for the purposes of this Act."

It is, we think, not open to doubt that Congress intended that this requirement be mandatory upon the railroad employer, and that its command, in a proper case, be enforced by the courts. The policy of the Transportation Act of encouraging voluntary adjustment of labor disputes, made manifest by those provisions of the Act which clearly contemplated the moral force of public opinion as affording its ultimate sanction, was, as we have seen, abandoned by the enactment of the Railway Labor Act. Neither the purposes of the later Act, as amended, nor its provisions when read, as they must be, in the light of our decision in the *Railway Clerks* case, *supra,* lend support to the contention that its enactments, which are mandatory in form and capable of enforcement by judicial process, were intended to be without legal sanction.

Experience had shown, before the amendment of 1934, that when there was no dispute as to the organizations authorized to represent the employees, and when there was willingness of the employer to meet such representative for a discussion of their grievances, amicable adjustment of differences had generally followed and strikes had been avoided. On the other hand, a prolific source of dispute had been the maintenance by the railroads of company unions and the denial by railway management of the authority of representatives chosen by their employees. Report of House Committee on Interstate and Foreign Commerce, No. 1944, 73rd Cong., 2d Sess., pp. 1–2. Section 2, Ninth, of the amended Act, was specifically aimed at this practice. It provided a means for ascertaining who are the authorized representatives of the employees through intervention and certification by the Mediation Board, and commanded the carrier to treat with the representative so certified. That the command was limited in its application to the case of intervention and certification by the Mediation Board indicates not that its words are precatory, but only that Congress hit at the evil "where experience shows it to be most felt." *Keokee Coke Co.* v. *Taylor,* 234 U. S. 224, 227.

Petitioner argues that the phrase "treat with" must be taken as meaning "regard" or "act towards," so that compliance with its mandate requires the employer to meet the authorized representative of the employees only if and when he shall elect to negotiate with them. This suggestion disregards the words of the section, and ignores the plain purpose made manifest throughout the numerous provisions of the Act. Its major objective is the avoidance of industrial strife, by conference between the authorized representatives of employer and employee. The command to the employer to "treat with" the authorized representatives of the employees adds nothing to the 1926 Act, unless it requires some affirmative act on the part of the employer. Compare the *Railway Clerks* case, *supra.* As we cannot assume that its addition to the statute was purposeless, we must take its meaning to be that which the words suggest, which alone would add something to the statute as it was before amendment, and which alone would tend to effect the purpose of the legislation. The statute does not undertake to compel agreement between the employer and employees, but it does command those preliminary steps without which no agreement can be reached. It at least requires the employer to meet and confer with the authorized representative of its employees, to listen to their complaints, to make reasonable effort to compose differences—in short, to enter into a negotiation for the settlement of labor disputes such as is contemplated by § 2, First.

Petitioner's insistence that the statute does not warrant so much of the decree as forbids it to enter into contracts of employment with its individual employees is based upon a misconstruction of the decree. Both the statute and the decree are aimed at securing settlement of labor disputes by inducing collective bargaining with the true representative of the employees and by preventing such bargaining with any who do not represent them. The obligation imposed on the employer by § 2, Ninth, to treat with the true representative of the employees as designated by the Mediation Board, when read in the light of the declared purposes of the Act, and of the provisions of § 2, Third and Fourth, giving to the employees the right to organize and bargain collectively through the representative of their own selection, is exclusive. It imposes the affirmative duty to treat only with the true representative, and hence the negative duty to treat with no other. We think, as the Government concedes in its brief, that the injunction against petitioner's entering into any contract concerning rules, rates of pay and working conditions, except with respondent, is designed only to prevent collective bargaining with anyone purporting to represent employees, other than respondent, who has been ascertained to be their true representative. When read in its context it must be taken to prohibit the negotiation of labor contracts, generally applicable to employees in the mechanical department, with any representative other than respondent, but not as precluding such individual contracts as petitioner may elect to make directly with individual employees. The decree, thus construed, conforms, in both its affirmative and negative aspects, to the requirements of § 2.

Propriety of Relief in Equity. Petitioner contends that if the statute is interpreted as requiring the employer to negotiate with the representative of his employees, its obligation is not the appropriate subject of a decree in equity; that negotiation depends on desires and mental attitudes which are beyond judicial control, and that since equity cannot compel the parties to agree, it will not compel them to take the preliminary steps which may result in agreement.

There is no want of capacity in the court to direct complete performance of the entire obligation: both the negative duties not to maintain a company union and not to negotiate with any representative of the employees other than respondent and the affirmative duty to treat with respondent. Full performance of both is commanded by the decree in terms which leave in no uncertainty the requisites of performance. In compelling compliance with either duty it does far less than has been done in compelling the discharge of a contractual or statutory obligation calling for a construction or engineering enterprise, *New Orleans, M. & T. Ry. Co.* v. *Mississippi,* 112 U.S. 12; *Wheeling Traction Co.* v. *Board of Commissioners,* 248 Fed. 205; see *Gas Securities Co.* v. *Antero & Lost Park Reservoir Co.,* 259 Fed. 423, 433; *Board of Commissioners* v. *A. V. Wills & Sons,* 236 Fed. 362, 380; *Jones* v. *Parker,* 163 Mass. 564; 40 N. E. 1044, or in granting specific performance of a contract for the joint use of a railroad bridge and terminals, *Joy* v. *St. Louis,* 138 U. S. 1; *Union Pacific Ry. Co.* v. *Chicago, R. I. & P. Ry. Co.,* 163 U. S. 564; cf. *Prospect Park & Coney Island R. Co.* v. *Coney Island & Brooklyn R Co.,* 144 N. Y. 152; 39 N. E. 17. Whether an obligation has been discharged, and whether action taken or omitted is in good faith or reasonable, are everyday subjects of inquiry by courts in framing and enforcing their decrees. . . .

In considering the propriety of the equitable relief granted here, we cannot ignore the judgment of Congress, deliberately expressed in legislation, that where the obstruction of the company union is removed, the meeting of employers and employees at the conference table is a powerful aid to industrial peace. Moreover, the resources of the Railway Labor Act are not exhausted if negotiation fails in the first instance to result in agreement. If disputes concerning changes in rates of pay, rules or working conditions, are "not adjusted by the parties in conference," either party may invoke the mediation services of the Mediation Board, § 5, First, or the parties may agree to seek the benefits of the arbitration provision of § 7. With the coercive influence of the company union ended, and in view of the interest of both parties in avoiding a strike, we cannot assume that negotiation, as required by the decree, will not result in agreement, or lead to successful mediation or arbitration, or that the attempt to secure one or another through the relief which the district court gave is not worth the effort.

More is involved than the settlement of a private controversy without appreciable consequences to the public. The peaceable settlement of labor controversies, especially where they may seriously impair the ability of an interstate rail carrier to perform its service to the public, is a matter of public concern. That is testified to by the history of the legislation now before us, the reports of committees of Congress having the proposed legislation in charge, and by our common knowledge. Courts of equity may, and frequently do, go much farther both to give and withold relief in furtherance of the public interest than they are accustomed to go when only private interests are involved. *Pennsylvania* v. *Williams,* 294 U. S. 176, 185; *Central Kentucky Gas Co.* v. *Railroad Commission,* 290 U. S. 264, 270–273; *Harrisonville* v. *W. S. Dickey Clay Co.,* 289 U. S. 334, 338; *Beasley* v. *Texas & Pacific Ry. Co.,* 191 U. S. 492, 497; *Joy* v. *St. Louis, supra,* 47; *Texas & Pacific Ry. Co.* v. *Marshall,* 136 U. S. 393, 405–406; *Conger* v. *New York, W. S. & B. R. Co.,* 120 N.Y. 29, 32, 33; 23 N. E. 983. The fact that Congress has indicated its purpose to make negotiation obligatory is in itself a declaration of public interest and policy which should be persuasive in inducing courts to give relief. It is for similar reasons that courts, which traditionally have refused to compel performance of a contract to submit to arbitration, *Tobey* v. *Bristol, supra,* enforce statutes commanding performance of arbitration agreements. *Red Cross Line* v. *Atlantic Fruit Co.,*

264 U. S. 109, 119, 121; *Marine Transit Corp.* v. *Dreyfus,* 284 U. S. 263, 278.

The decree is authorized by the statute and was granted in an appropriate exercise of the equity powers of the court.

Second. Constitutionality of § 2 of the Railway Labor Act. (A) Validity Under the Commerce Clause. The power of Congress over interstate commerce extends to such regulations of the relations of rail carriers to their employees as are reasonably calculated to prevent the interruption of interstate commerce by strikes and their attendant disorders. *Wilson* v. *New,* 243 U. S. 332, 347–348. The Railway Labor Act, § 2, declares that its purposes, among others, are "To avoid any interruption to commerce or to the operation of any carrier engaged therein," and "to provide for the prompt and orderly settlement of all disputes concerning rates of pay, rules or working conditions." The provisions of the Act and its history, to which reference has been made, establish that such are its purposes, and that the latter is in aid of the former. What has been said indicates clearly that its provisions are aimed at the settlement of industrial disputes by the promotion of collective bargaining between employers and the authorized representative of their employees, and by mediation and arbitration when such bargaining does not result in agreement. It was for Congress to make the choice of the means by which its objective of securing the uninterrupted service of interstate railroads was to be secured, and its judgment, supported as it is by our long experience with industrial disputes, and the history of railroad labor relations, to which we have referred, is not open to review here. The means chosen are appropriate to the end sought and hence are within the congressional power. See *Railway Clerks* case, *supra,* 570; *Railroad Retirement Board* v. *Alton R. Co.,* 295 U. S. 330, 369.

But petitioner insists that the Act as applied to its "back shop" employees is not within the commerce power since their duties have no direct relationship to interstate transportation. Of the 824 employees in the six shop crafts eligible to vote for a choice of representatives, 322 work in petitioner's "back shops" at Princeton, West Virginia. They are there engaged in making classified repairs, which consist of heavy repairs on locomotives and cars withdrawn from service for that purpose for long periods (an average of 105 days for locomotives and 109 days for cars). The repair work is upon the equipment used by petitioner in its transportation service, 97% of which is interstate. At times a continuous stream of engines and cars passes through the "back shops" for such repairs. When not engaged in repair work, the back shop employees perform "store order work," the manufacture of material such as rivets and repair parts, to be placed in railroad stores for use at the Princeton shop and other points on the line.

The activities in which these employees are engaged have such a relation to the other confessedly interstate activities of the petitioner that they are to be regarded as a part of them. All taken together fall within the power of Congress over interstate commerce. *Baltimore & Ohio R. Co.* v. *Interstate Commerce Comm'n,* 221 U. S. 612, 619; cf. *Pedersen* v. *Delaware, L. & W. R. Co.,* 229 U. S. 146, 151. Both courts below have found that interruption by strikes of the back shop employees, if more than temporary, would seriously cripple petitioner's interstate transportation. The relation of the back shop to transportation is such that a strike of petitioner's employees there, quite apart from the likelihood of its spreading to the operating department, would subject petitioner to the danger, substantial, though possibly indefinable in its extent, of interruption of the transportation service. The cause is not remote from the effect. The relation between them is not tenuous. The effect on commerce cannot be regarded as negligible. See *United States* v. *Railway Employees' Department of the American Federation of Labor,* 290 Fed. 978, 981, holding participation of back shop employees in the nation-wide railroad shopmen's strike of 1922 to constitute an interference with interstate commerce. As the regulation here in question is shown to be an appropriate means of avoiding that danger, it is within the power of Congress.

It is no answer, as petitioner suggests, that it could close its back shops and turn over the repair work to independent contractors. Whether the railroad should do its repair work in its own shops, or in those of another, is a question of railroad management. It is petitioner's determination to make its own repairs which has brought its relations with shop employees within the purview of the Railway Labor Act. It is the nature of the work done and its relation to interstate transportation which afford adequate basis for the exercise of the regulatory power of Congress.

The *Employers' Liability Cases,* 207 U. S. 463, 498, which mentioned railroad repair shops as a subject beyond the power to regulate commerce, are not controlling here. Whatever else may be said of that pronouncement, it is obvious that the commerce power is as much dependent upon the type of regulation as its subject matter. It is enough for present purposes that experience has shown that the failure to settle, by peaceful means, the grievances of railroad employees with respect to rates of pay, rules or working conditions, is far more likely to hinder interstate commerce than the failure to compensate workers who have suffered injury in the course of their employment.

(B) *Validity of § 2 of the Railway Labor Act Under the Fifth Amendment.* The provisions of the Railway Labor Act applied in this case, as construed by the court below, and as we construe them, do not require petitioner to enter into any agreement with its employees, and they do not prohibit its entering into such contract of employment as it chooses, with its individual employees. They prohibit only such use of the company union as, despite the objections repeated here, was enjoined in the *Railway Clerks* case, *supra,* and they impose on petitioner only the affirmative duty of "treating with" the authorized representatives of its employees for the purpose of negotiating a labor dispute.

Even though Congress, in the choice of means to effect a permissible regulation of commerce, must conform to due process, *Railroad Retirement Board* v. *Alton R. Co., supra,* 347; *Chicago, R. I. & P. Ry. Co.* v. *United States,* 284 U. S. 80, 97; see *Louisville Joint Stock Land Bank* v. *Radford,* 295 U. S. 555, 589, it is evident that where, as here, the means chosen are appropriate to the permissible end, there is little scope for the operation of the due process clause. The railroad can complain only of the infringement of its own constitutional immunity, not that of its employees. *Erie R. Co.* v. *Williams,* 233 U. S. 685, 697; *Jeffrey Mfg. Co.* v. *Blagg,* 235 U. S. 571, 576; *Rail & River Coal Co.* v. *Yaple,* 236 U. S. 338, 349; cf. *Hawkins* v. *Bleakly,* 243 U. S. 210, 214. And the Fifth Amendment, like the Fourteenth, see *West Coast Hotel Co.* v. *Parrish,* decided this day, *ante,* p. 379, is not a guarantee of untrammeled freedom of action and of contract. In the exercise of its power to regulate commerce, Congress can subject both to restraints not shown to be unreasonable. Such are the restraints of the safety appliance act, *Johnson* v. *Southern Pacific Co.,* 196 U. S. 1; of the act imposing a wage scale on rail carriers, *Wilson* v. *New, supra;* of the Railroad Employers' Liability Act, *Second Employers' Liability Cases,* 223 U. S. 1; of the act fixing maximum hours of service for railroad employees whose duties control or affect the movement of trains, *Baltimore & Ohio R. Co.* v. *Interstate Commerce Comm'n, supra;* of the act prohibiting the prepayment of seamen's wages, *Patterson* v. *Bark Eudora,* 190 U. S. 169.

Each of the limited duties imposed upon petitioner by the statute and the decree do not differ in their purpose and nature from those imposed under the earlier statute and enforced in the *Railway Clerks* case, *supra.* The quality of the action compelled, is reasonableness, and therefore the lawfulness of the compulsion, must be judged in the light of the conditions which have occasioned the exercise of governmental power. If the compulsory settlement of some differences, by arbitration, may be within the limits of due process, see *Hardware Dealers Mutual Fire Ins. Co.* v. *Glidden Co.,* 284 U. S. 151, it seems plain that the command of the statute to negotiate for the settlement of labor disputes, given in the appropriate exercise of the commerce power, cannot be said to be so arbitrary or unreasonable as to infringe due process.

Adair v. *United States,* 208 U. S. 161, and *Coppage* v. *Kansas,* 236 U. S. 1, have no present application. The provisions of the Railway Labor Act invoked here neither compel the employer to enter into any agreement, nor preclude it from entering into any contract with individual employees. They do not "interfere with the normal exercise of the right of the carrier to select its employees or to discharge them." See the *Railway Clerks* case, *supra,* 571.

There remains to be considered petitioner's contentions that the certificate of the National Mediation Board is invalid and that the injunction granted is prohibited by the provisions of the Norris-LaGuardia Act, of March 23, 1932, c. 90, 47 Stat. 70; 29 U. S. C. §§ 101–115.

Validity of the Certificate of the National Mediation Board. In each craft of petitioner's mechanical department a majority of those voting cast ballots for the Federation. In the case of the blacksmiths the Federation failed to receive a majority of the ballots of those eligible to vote, although a majority of the craft participated in the election. In the case of the carmen and coach cleaners, a majority of the employees eligible to vote did not participate in the election. There has been no appeal from the ruling of the district court that the designation of the Federation as the representative of the carmen and coach cleaners was invalid. Petitioner assails the certification of the Federation as the representative of the blacksmiths because less than a majority of that craft, although a majority of those voting, voted for the Federation.

Section 2, Fourth, of the Railway Labor Act provides: "The majority of any craft or class of employees shall have the right to determine who shall be the representative of the craft or class for the purposes of this Act." Petitioner construes this section as requiring that a representative be selected by the votes of a majority of eligible voters. It is to be noted that the words of the section confer the right of determination upon a majority of those eligible to vote, but is silent as to the manner in which that right shall be exercised. Election laws providing for approval of a proposal by a specified majority of an electorate have been generally construed as requiring only the consent of the specified majority of those participating in the election. *Carroll County* v. *Smith,* 111 U. S. 556; *Douglass* v. *Pike County,* 101 U. S. 677; *Louisville & Nashville R. Co.* v. *County Court of Davidson County,* 1 Sneed (Tenn.) 637; *Montgomery County Fiscal Court* v. *Trimble,* 104 Ky. 629; 47 S. W. 773. Those who do not participate "are presumed to assent to the expressed will of the majority of those voting." *Cass County* v. *Johnston,* 95 U. S. 360, 369, and see *Carroll County* v. *Smith, supra.*

We see no reason for supposing that § 2, Fourth, was intended to adopt a different rule. If, in addition to participation by a majority of a craft, a vote of the majority of those eligible is necessary for a choice, an indifferent minority could prevent the resolution of a contest, and thwart the purpose of the Act, which is dependent for its operation upon the selection of representatives. There is the added danger that the absence of eligible voters may be due less to their indifference than to coercion by the employer. The opinion of the trial court discloses that the Mediation Board scheduled an election to be determined by a majority of the eligible voters, but that the Federation's subsequent protest that the Railway was influencing the men not to vote caused the Board to hold a new election to be decided by the ballots of a majority of those voting.

It is significant of the congressional intent that the language of § 2, Fourth, was taken from a rule announced by the United States Railroad Labor Board, acting under the labor provisions of the Transportation Act of 1920, Decision No. 119, *International Association of Machinists* v. *Atchison, T. & S. F. Ry.*, 2 Dec. U. S. Railroad Labor Board, 87, 96, par. 15. Prior to the adoption of the Railway Labor Act, this rule was interpreted by the Board, in Decision No. 1971, *Brotherhood of Railway & S. S. Clerks* v. *Southern Pacific Lines*, 4 Dec. U. S. Railroad Labor Board 625, where it appeared that a majority of the craft participated in the election. The Board ruled, p. 639, that a majority of the votes cast was sufficient to designate a representative. A like interpretation of § 2, Fourth, was sustained in *Association of Clerical Employees* v. *Brotherhood of Railway & S. S. Clerks* 85 F. (2d) 152.

The petitioner also challenges the validity of the certificate of the National Mediation Board in this case because it fails to state the number of eligible voters in each craft or class. The certificate states that respondent "has been duly designated and authorized to represent the mechanical department employees" of petitioner. It also shows on its face the total number of votes cast in each craft in favor of each candidate, but omits to state the total number of eligible voters in each craft. Petitioner insists that this is a fatal defect in the certificate, upon the basis of those cases which hold that where a finding of fact of an administrative officer or tribunal is prerequisite to the making of a rule or order, the finding must be explicitly set out. See *Panama Refining Co.* v. *Ryan*, 293 U. S. 388; *United States* v. *Chicago, M., St. P. & P .R. Co.*, 294 U. S. 499; *Atchison, T. & S. F. Ry Co.* v. *United States*, 295 U. S. 193.

The practice contended for is undoubtedly desirable, but it is not required by the present statute or by the authorities upon which petitioner relies. The National Mediation Board makes no order. The command which the decree of the court enforces is that of the statute, not of the Board. Its certificate that the Federation is the authorized representative of the employees is the ultimate finding of fact prerequisite to enforcement by the courts of the command of the statute. There is no contention that this finding is conclusive in the absence of a finding of the basic facts on which it rests—that is to say, the number of eligible voters, the number participating in the election and the choice of the majority of those who participate. Whether the certification, if made as to those facts, is conclusive, it is unnecessary now to determine. But we think it plain that if the Board omits to certify any of them, the omitted fact is open to inquiry by the court asked to enforce the command of the statute. See *Dismuke* v. *United States,* 297 U. S. 167, 171–173. Such inquiry was made by the trial court, which found the number of eligible voters and thus established the correctness of the Board's ultimate conclusion. The certificate, which conformed to the statutory requirement, was *prima facie* sufficient, and was not shown to be invalid for want of the requisite supporting facts.

Validity of the Injunction Under the Norris-LaGuardia Act. Petitioner assails the decree for its failure to conform to the requirements of § 9 of the Norris-LaGuardia Act, which provides: "every restraining order or injunction granted in a case involving or growing out of a labor dispute shall include only a prohibition of such specific act or acts as may be expressly complained of in the bill of complaint or petition filed in such case and as shall be expressly included in . . . findings of fact made and filed by the court." The evident purpose of this section, as its history and context show, was not to preclude mandatory injunctions, but to forbid blanket injunctions against labor unions, which are usually prohibitory in form, and to confine the injunction to the particular acts complained of and found by the court. We deem it unnecessary to comment on other similar objections, except to say that they are based on strained and unnatural constructions of the words of the Norris-LaGuardia Act, and conflict with its declared purpose, § 2, that the employee "shall be free from the interference, restraint, or coercion of employers of labor, or their agents, in the designation of such representatives or in self-organization or in other concerted activities for the purpose of collective bargaining or other mutual aid or protection."

It suffices to say that the Norris-LaGuardia Act can affect the present decree only so far as its provisions are found not to conflict with those of §2, Ninth, of the Railway Labor Act, authorizing the relief which has been granted. Such provisions cannot be rendered nugatory by the earlier and more general provisions of the Norris-LaGuardia Act. See the *Railway Clerks* case, *supra,* 571; cf. *Callahan* v. *United States,* 285 U. S. 515, 518; *Walla Walla* v. *Walla Walla Water Co.,* 172 U. S. 1, 22; *International Alliance* v. *Rex Theatre Corp.,* 73 F. (2d) 92, 93.

Affirmed.

THE NORRIS-LA GUARDIA ANTI-INJUNCTION ACT

For nearly half a century organized labor battled against what it called "government by injunction." Section 20 of the Clayton Anti-Trust Act, the first federal anti-injunction statute, was largely nullified by judicial interpretation which limited its application to disputes between employers and employees. When labor's Magna Carta evaporated as a result of the Supreme Court's decisions in *Duplex Co.* v. *Deering,* 254 U.S. 443 (1921) and similar cases, the unions sought relief again and again in Congress. Labor's efforts were rewarded in the Norris-LaGuardia Act of 1932. The temper of the times may be gauged by the vote in Congress where the House bill passed 363 to 13, and the Senate bill, 75 to 5.

Railway labor legislation aside, the Norris-LaGuardia Act may appropriately be dubbed the first of the modern statutes constituting our present federal labor policy. But, in fact, the act, as Professor Archibald Cox rightly points out, "introduced the only period of unqualified *laissez-faire* in labor relations." Up until then, the courts usually sided with employers to deny the unions basic rights; after Norris-LaGuardia the unions enjoyed the same freedom from injunctive interference that business associations had always enjoyed under common law. Professor Cox continues:

> The most important of [the reasons behind the act] was the proposition that judges were ill equipped to pass judgment upon the social and economic issues involved in labor disputes—that indeed judicial intervention served no useful purpose in labor disputes, save possibly to protect tangible property and preserve public order. According to this view, union organization, strikes, boycotts, and picketing were considered part of the competitive struggle for life, which society tolerated because the freedom is worth more than it costs.

Philosophically, the Norris-LaGuardia Act belongs to an earlier period in labor history. It recalls the nineteenth-century social Darwinists and their "survival of the fittest" economic theories. If Congress had stopped enacting labor legislation with the passage of the Norris-LaGuardia Act we would, in effect, have no federal collective bargaining regulations. Actually, the no-holds-barred period lasted but a year, until the enactment of the National Recovery Act, which, among other things, regulated the conduct of labor relations within the context of government encouragement of industrial self-regulation.

Although the Norris-LaGuardia Act is set forth in full below, some of its central features bear mentioning here as they indicate the *laissez-faire,* self-help bias underlying the act. It rejected the "yellow-dog" contract as the basis for legal or equitable relief for the employer, in part because this unfairly weighted the contest in favor of one side against the other. The act also defined in extremely broad fashion the term "labor dispute," extending

162

this concept far beyond a dispute between an employer and his immediate employees. As Frankfurter and Greene argue, such a definition "registers the implications of interdependence within American industry. It permits the collaboration of efforts between unions whom substantial interests make mutual allies. It withholds immunity from the chancellor's decree at a point where combination aims to include unions that have no economic bond but only a sympathetic interest."

Section 4 of the act denies jurisdiction to a federal court to enjoin a wide range of typical union self-help activities, not involving fraud or violence. Even where fraud or violence is involved, Section 7 denies injunctive jurisdiction except after a hearing and specified findings of fact, and even then, under Section 8, until other methods of settlement have been exhausted. These are the basic statutory provisions, and they have gone far to take the federal courts out of the business of granting labor injunctions. A considerable number of states have also passed anti-injunction laws substantially similar to Norris-LaGuardia.

The act is set forth in full below and is followed by other important materials relating to its history.

THE NORRIS-LA GUARDIA ANTI-INJUNCTION ACT
March 23, 1932

Be it enacted by the Senate and House of Representatives of the United States of America in Congress assembled,

SEC. 1. That no court of the United States, as herein defined, shall have jurisdiction to issue any restraining order or temporary or permanent injunction in a case involving or growing out of a labor dispute, except in a strict conformity with the provisions of this Act; nor shall any such restraining order or temporary or permanent injunction be issued contrary to the public policy declared in this Act.

SEC. 2. In the interpretation of this Act and in determining the jurisdiction and authority of the courts of the United States, as such jurisdiction and authority are herein defined and limited, the public policy of the United States is hereby declared as follows:

Whereas under prevailing economic conditions, developed with the aid of governmental authority for owners of property to organize in the corporate and other forms of ownership association, the individual unorganized worker is commonly helpless to exercise actual liberty of contract and to protect his freedom of labor, and thereby to obtain acceptable terms and conditions of employment, wherefore, though he should be free to decline to associate with his fellows, it is necessary that he have full freedom of association, self-organization, and designation of representatives of his own choosing, to negotiate the terms and conditions of his employment, and that he shall be free from the interference, restraint, or coercion of employers of labor, or their agents, in the designation of such representatives or in self-organization or in other concerted activities for the purpose of collective bargaining or other mutual aid or protection; therefore, the following definitions of, and limitations upon, the jurisdiction and authority of the courts of the United States are hereby enacted.

SEC. 3. Any undertaking or promise, such as is described in this section, or any other undertaking or promise in conflict with the public policy declared in section 2 of this Act, is hereby declared to be contrary to the public policy of the United States, shall not be enforceable in any court of the United States and shall not afford any basis for the granting of legal or equitable relief by any such court, including specifically the following:

Every undertaking or promise hereafter made, whether written or oral, express or implied, constituting or contained in any contract or agreement of hiring or employment between any individual, firm, company, association, or corporation, and any employee or prospective employee of the same, whereby

(a) Either party to such contract or agreement undertakes or promises not to join, become, or remain a member of any labor organization or of any employer organization; or

(b) Either party to such contract or agreement undertakes or promises that he will withdraw from an employment relation in the event that he joins, becomes, or remains a member of any labor organization or of any employer organization.

SEC. 4. No court of the United States shall have jurisdiction to issue any restraining order or temporary or permanent injunction in any case involving or growing out of any labor dispute to prohibit any person or persons participating or interested in such dispute (as these terms are herein defined) from doing, whether singly or in concert, any of the following acts:

(a) Ceasing or refusing to perform any work or to remain in any relation of employment;

(b) Becoming or remaining a member of any labor organization or of any employer organization, regardless of any such undertaking or promise as is described in section 3 of this Act;

(c) Paying or giving to, or withholding from, any person participating or interested in such labor dispute, any strike or unemployment benefits or insurance, or other moneys or things of value;

(d) By all lawful means aiding any person participating or interested in any labor dispute who is being proceeded against in, or is prosecuting, any action or suit in any court of the United States or of any State;

(e) Giving publicity to the existence of, or the facts involved in, any labor dispute, whether by advertising, speaking, patrolling, or by any other method not involving fraud or violence;

(f) Assembling peaceably to act or to organize to act in promotion of their interests in a labor dispute;

(g) Advising or notifying any person of an intention to do any of the acts heretofore specified;

(h) Agreeing with other persons to do or not to do any of the acts heretofore specified; and

(i) Advising, urging, or otherwise causing or inducing without fraud or violence the acts heretofore specified, regardless of any such undertaking or promise as is described in section 3 of this Act.

SEC. 5.   No court of the United States shall have jurisdiction to issue a restraining order or temporary or permanent injunction upon the ground that any of the persons participating or interested in a labor dispute constitute or are engaged in an unlawful combination or conspiracy because of the doing in concert of the acts enumerated in section 4 of this Act.

SEC. 6.   No officer or member of any association or organization, and no association or organization participating or interested in a labor dispute, shall be held responsible or liable in any court of the United States for the unlawful acts of individual officers, members, or agents, except upon clear proof of actual participation in, or actual authorization of, such acts, or of ratification of such acts after actual knowledge thereof.

SEC. 7. No court of the United States shall have jurisdiction to issue a temporary or permanent injunction in any case involving or growing out of a labor dispute, as herein defined, except after hearing the testimony of witnesses in open court (with opportunity for cross-examination) in support of the allegations of a complaint made under oath, and testimony in opposition thereto, if offered, and except after findings of fact by the court, to the effect—

(a) That unlawful acts have been threatened and will be committed unless restrained or have been committed and will be continued unless restrained, but no injunction or temporary restraining order shall be issued on account of any threat or unlawful act excepting against the person or persons, association, or organization making the threat or committing the unlawful act or actually authorizing or ratifying the same after actual knowledge thereof;

(b) That substantial and irreparable injury to complainant's property will follow;

(c) That as to each item of relief granted greater injury will be inflicted upon complainant by the denial of relief than will be inflicted upon defendants by the granting of relief;

(d) That complainant has no adequate remedy at law; and

(e) That the public officers charged with the duty to protect complainant's property are unable or unwilling to furnish adequate protection.

Such hearing shall be held after due and personal notice thereof has been given, in such manner as the court shall direct, to all known persons against whom relief is sought, and also to the chief of those public officials of the county and city within which the unlawful acts have been threatened or committed charged with the duty to protect complainant's property: *Provided, however,* That if a complainant shall also allege that, unless a temporary restraining order shall be issued without notice, a substantial and irreparable injury to complainant's property will be unavoidable, such a temporary restraining order may be issued upon testimony under oath, sufficient, if sustained, to justify the court in issuing a temporary injunction upon a hearing after notice. Such a temporary restraining order shall be effective for no longer than five days and shall become void at the expiration of said five days. No temporary restraining order or temporary injunction shall be issued except on condition that complainant shall first file an undertaking with adequate security in an amount to be fixed by the court sufficient to recompense those enjoined for any loss, expense, or damage caused by the improvident or erroneous issuance of such order or injunction, including all reasonable costs (together with a reasonable attorney's fee) and expense of defense against the order or against the granting of any injunctive relief sought in the same proceeding and subsequently denied by the court.

The undertaking herein mentioned shall be understood to signify an agreement entered into by the complainant and the surety upon which a decree may be rendered in the same suit or proceeding against said complainant and surety, upon a hearing to assess damages of which hearing complainant and surety shall have reasonable notice, the said complainant and surety submitting themselves to the jurisdiction of the court for that purpose. But nothing herein contained shall deprive any party having a claim or cause of action under or upon such undertaking from electing to pursue his ordinary remedy by suit at law or in equity.

SEC. 8.   No restraining order or injunctive relief shall be granted to any complainant who has failed to comply with any obligation imposed by law which is involved in the labor dispute in question, or who has failed to make every reasonable effort to settle such dispute either by negotiation or with the aid of any available governmental machinery of mediation or voluntary arbitration.

SEC. 9.   No restraining order or temporary or permanent injunction shall be granted in a case involving or growing out of a labor dispute, except on the basis of findings of fact made and filed by the court in the record of the case prior to the issuance of such restraining order or injunction; and every restraining order or injunction granted in a case involving or growing out of a labor dispute shall include only a prohibition of such specific act or acts as may be expressly complained of in the bill of complaint or petition filed in such case and as shall be expressly included in said findings of fact made and filed by the court as provided herein.

SEC. 10.   Whenever any court of the United States shall issue or deny any temporary injunction in a case involving or growing out of a labor dispute, the court shall, upon the request of any party to the proceedings and on his filing the usual bond for costs, forthwith certify as in ordinary cases the record of the case to the circuit court of appeals for its review. Upon the filing of such record in the circuit court of appeals, the appeal shall be heard and the temporary injunctive order affirmed, modified, or set aside with the greatest possible expedition, giving the proceedings precedence over all other matters except older matters of the same character.

SEC. 11.   In all cases arising under this Act in which a person shall be charged with contempt in a court of the United States (as herein defined) the accused shall enjoy the right to a speedy and public trial by an impartial jury of the State and district wherein the contempt shall have been committed: *Provided,* That this right shall not apply to contempts committed in the presence of the court or so near thereto as to interfere directly with the administration of justice or to apply to the misbehavior, misconduct, or disobedience of any officer of the court in respect to the writs, orders, or process of the court.

SEC. 12.   The defendant in any proceeding for contempt of court may file with the court a demand for the retirement of the judge sitting in the proceeding, if the contempt arises from an attack upon the character or conduct of such judge and if the attack occurred elsewhere than in the presence of the court or so near thereto as to interfere directly with the administration of justice. Upon the filing of any such demand the judge shall thereupon proceed no further, but another judge shall be designated in the manner as is provided by law. The demand shall be filed prior to the hearing in the contempt proceeding.

SEC. 13.   When used in this Act, and for the purposes of this Act—

(a) A case shall be held to involve or to grow out of a labor dispute when the case involves persons who are engaged in the same industry, trade, craft, or occupation; or have direct or indirect interests therein; or who are employees of the same employer; or who are members of the same or an affiliated organization of employers or employees; whether such dispute is (1) between one or more employers or associations of employers and one or more employees or associations of employees; (2) between one or more employers or associations of employers and one or more employers or associations of employers; or (3) between one or more employees or associations of employees and one or more employees or associations of employees; or when the case involves any conflicting or competing interest in a "labor dispute" (as hereinafter defined) of "persons participating or interested" therein (as hereinafter defined).

(b) A person or association shall be held to be a person participating or interested in a labor dispute if relief is sought against him or it, and if he or it is engaged in the same industry, trade, craft, or occupation in which such dispute occurs, or has a direct or indirect interest therein, or is a member, officer, or agent of any association composed in whole or in part of employers or employees engaged in such industry, trade, craft, or occupation.

(c) The term "labor dispute" includes any controversy concerning terms or conditions of employment, or concerning the association or representation of persons in negotiating, fixing, maintaining, changing, or seeking to arrange terms or conditions of employment, regardless of whether or not the disputants stand in the proximate relation of employer and employee.

(d) The term "court of the United States" means any court of the United States whose jurisdiction has been or may be conferred or defined or limited by Act of Congress, including the courts of the District of Columbia.

SEC. 14.   If any provision of this Act or the application thereof to any person or circumstance is held unconstitutional or otherwise invalid, the remaining provisions of the Act and the application of such provisions to other persons or circumstances shall not be affected thereby.

SEC. 15.   All Acts and parts of Acts in conflict with the provisions of this Act are hereby repealed.

THE ORIGINS

Report of the Senate Committee on the Judiciary
February 4, 1932

GEORGE NORRIS [R., NEB.] submitted the Report.

The Committee on the Judiciary, to which was referred the bill (S. 935) to amend the Judicial Code and to define and limit the jurisdiction of courts sitting in equity, and for other purposes, having had the same under consideration, beg leave to report as follows:

We recommend that the bill be amended as hereinafter set forth, and, as so amended, that the bill be passed. . . .

The Committee on the Judiciary has been considering the subject of injunctions in labor disputes for several years, and this bill is a result of such study and consideration.

In the Seventieth Congress, on December 12, 1927, the Senator from Minnesota, Mr. Shipstead, introduced a bill on the subject (S. 1482). From that time to the present the Judiciary Committee, in one form or another, has had under consideration the question of limiting the jurisdiction of Federal courts in granting injunctions in labor disputes.

In the Seventieth Congress the bill referred to (S. 1482) was referred to a subcommittee consisting of the Senator from Wisconsin, Mr. Blaine; the Senator from Montana, Mr. Walsh; and the writer. This subcommittee held extensive and unlimited public hearings upon the bill. No limit was placed upon the hearings, and those who favored the legislation and those who were opposed to the legislation were heard without limitation.

At the close of the hearings this subcommittee, in executive session, went over the hearings and discussed all phases of the proposed legislation. The subcommittee was unanimous in reaching the conclusion that some legislation on this subject was absolutely necessary in the public interest; but it likewise reached the conclusion that the bill under consideration did not fully meet the requirements.

After further consideration this subcommittee called into consultation economists and attorneys who had made a special study of this particular subject. They invited Prof. Felix Frankfurter, of the law school of Harvard University, Cambridge, Mass.; Herman Oliphant, former professor of law at Columbia University, now a member of the faculty of the institute of law, the Johns Hopkins University, Baltimore, Md.; Prof. Francis B. Sayre, law school of Harvard University, Cambridge, Mass.; Mr. Edwin E. Witte, chief of the legislative reference library, Madison Wis.; and Hon. Donald R. Richberg, attorney, of Chicago, Ill., to meet with the subcommittee for the purpose of giving further consideration to the subject and drafting proper legislation. As a result of such consultation and deliberation, the subcommittee prepared a substitute bill which, in its essential and material particulars, is practically the same as the bill now reported to the Senate (S. 935).

The subcommittee reported this substitute to the full Committee on the Judiciary. After this report was made and after considerable consideration by the full Committee, various attorneys representing interests opposed to the enactment of the proposed bill requested further hearings upon the substitute bill recommended by the subcommittee.

The Committee on the Judiciary, after considerable discussion, thereupon referred the entire matter back to the subcommittee, with instructions to hold further hearings upon the proposed substitute. In accordance with these directions, the subcommittee again held public hearings and gave to all persons who so desired an opportunity to be heard. At the close of the hearings, the subcommittee again reported the bill to the full committee, with the recommendation that the substitute be agreed to and that the bill, as thus amended, be favorably reported to the Senate.

The proposed bill was the subject of consideration and discussion in the full committee for several weeks, but no final action was taken by the full committee during that session of the Seventieth Congress. At the second or short session of the Seventieth Congress, the bill was again taken up by the full committee, but no conclusion was reached and at the final adjournment of the Congress the bill died upon the calendar of the committee without any action thereon.

At the beginning of the regular session of the Seventy-first Congress, on the 9th day of December, 1929, the Senator from Minnesota, Mr. Shipstead, again introduced his bill, this time known as S. 2497, which bill was in practically the same form as the bill, S. 1482, of the Seventieth Congress.

The Judiciary Committee referred the bill to the same subcommittee which had handled the matter in the Seventieth Congress. This subcommittee, having given such extensive hearings and consideration to the bill in the Seventieth Congress, did not feel that additional hearings were necessary. Nevertheless, upon application of attorneys representing corporations and organizations opposed to the enactment of this kind of legislation, limited hearings were again held and all interested parties were permitted to file written briefs.

The subcommittee, after giving further consideration to the subject, and after making several amendments to the substitute bill previously prepared by the subcommittee, again reported the bill to the full committee with the recommendation that the amended substitute be agreed to and that the bill, as thus amended, be favorably reported to the Senate.

After further consideration by the full committee upon the report of the subcommittee, the substitute proposed by the subcommittee was amended by the full committee in several respects, but, upon motion to report the bill to the Senate as amended by the proposed subcommittee substitute, with a recommendation that as thus amended the bill be passed, 7 members of the committee voted in favor of such report and 7 members voted against making the report (3 members not voting). Thus the motion to make a favorable report was defeated.

The proposed substitute bill, however, was again further considered by the full committee and, as a result thereof, by a majority vote of the committee, the proposed bill was submitted to the Attorney General with the request that he indicate to the committee his views concerning the constitutionality of the proposed legislation and also as to the effect the enactment of such legislation would have upon the United States in cases in which the Government may desire to apply to Federal courts for equitable relief by injunction. After giving the matter consideration, the Attorney General declined to comply with the committee's request and in an official communication so informed the committee.

At the next meeting of the committee the substitute bill was again taken up and, after further discussion, the committee, by a majority vote, decided to make an adverse report upon the bill. The majority report was made by Senator Steiwer on June 18 (calendar day, June 20), 1930 (71st Cong., 2d sess., Report No. 1060). The minority report was filed on the same day and is known as Report No. 1060, part 2.

No action, however, was taken by the Senate upon the bill thus adversely reported and the same died upon the calendar of the Senate upon the adjournment of the Seventy-first Congress.

Soon after the convening of the Seventy-second Congress, on December 9, 1931, the present bill [S. 935] was introduced in the Senate. [This bill, for all practical purposes, is the same as the substitute bill reported by the subcommittee in both the Seventieth and the Seventy-first Congresses.]

Immediately upon the introduction of the bill various interests opposed to the bill again applied to the committee for further hearings. The committee, however, after considering such applications, reached the conclusion that sufficient hearings had been had, but they did allow all persons interested who desired to do so, to file written briefs upon the subject, limiting the time for the filing of such briefs to the 25th day of January, 1932.

Thereupon the full committee again took up the consideration of the bill and, after many days of consideration in executive session, the amendments heretofore suggested were agreed upon by the committee and, as thus amended, the committee, by a vote of 11 to 6, ordered a favorable report made to the Senate. . . .

The limitation of the jurisdiction of Federal courts to issue injunctions in labor disputes has been a subject of public discussion for many years. It is fair to say that public sentiment on the subject has reached the conclusion that some such limitation is absolutely necessary. Both of the great political parties in their last national platforms have promised remedial legislation upon the subject. The last Republican National Convention at Kansas City adopted a plank on the subject as follows:

> The party favors freedom in wage contracts, the right of collective bargaining by free and responsible agents of their own choosing, which develops and maintains that purposeful cooperation which gains its chief incentive through voluntary agreement.
> We believe that injunctions in labor disputes have in some instances been abused and have given rise to a serious question for legislation.

Following this, the last Democratic National Convention at Houston, Tex., in its platform, made the following promises:

> (a) We favor the principle of collective bargaining and the Democratic principle that organized labor should choose its own representatives without coercion or interference.
> (b) Labor is not a commodity. Human rights must be safeguarded. Labor should be exempt from the operation of antitrust laws.
> (c) We recognize that legislative and other investigations have shown the existence of grave abuse in the issuance of injunctions in labor disputes. No injunctions should be granted in labor disputes except upon proof of threatened irreparable injury and after notice and hearing, and the injunction should be confined to those acts which do directly threaten irreparable injury. The expressed purpose of representatives of capital, labor, and the bar to devise a plan for the elimination of the present evils with respect to injunctions must be supported and legislation designed to accomplish these ends formulated and passed.

It is, therefore, a nonpartisan question, and, assuming that both of these great political parties in their national conventions were acting in good faith, it follows that either this bill or some other legislation of similar import, carrying out the pledges made to the people of the United States, should be promptly enacted.

The injunction process is an extremely harsh remedy. Particularly is this true when a restraining order is issued without any notice to any of the defendants; and in nearly every case in a labor dispute where an injunction is issued, the restraining order is the first step. The first knowledge which the defendant has is service of notice upon him that the restraining order has already been issued. Before he is given an opportunity to be heard, he is enjoined, and in most cases he is restrained from doing acts and things which seriously interfere with, and sometimes completely deny, his fundamental right of liberty of action, which belongs to every free citizen.

That there have been abuses of judicial power in granting injunctions in labor disputes is hardly open to discussion. The use of the injunction in such disputes has been growing by leaps and bounds.

It is impossible to report with accuracy the number of injunctions issued in either the State or Federal courts in connection with labor disputes in recent years. Only a small percentage of these injunction cases are reported officially. For example, approximately 300 were issued in connection with the railway shopmen's strike of 1922, but only 12 were officially reported (See Frankfurter on *The Labor Injunction,* p. 52).

In testimony before the committee the president of the American Federation of Labor submitted a partial list of 389 labor injunctions in State and Federal courts during the last decade, most of which are unreported. (Hearings, February, 1928, pp. 77–86.) Out of over 260 cases listed by the Massachusetts Bureau of Statistics in the period of 1898–1916, only 18 were officially reported (p. 51). A large majority of injunction proceedings are never carried beyond a restraining order or temporary injunction and, therefore, are unlikely ever to reach the stage of official reporting, which is concerned largely with final decrees and with decisions of appellate courts. Therefore, exact statistics can not be presented, but the statement can be safely made that since 1890, when labor injunctions are practically unknown, their issuance has steadily increased until there are few controversies of substantial importance between employers and employees in which one or more injunctions will not be issued out of either a State or a Federal court.

The right of wage earners to organize and to act jointly in questions affecting wages, conditions of labor, and the welfare of labor generally is conceded and recognized by all students of the subject. An increasing necessity for the organization of labor has been brought about by modern economic conditions and methods of doing business, which have in the main been developed by the aid of governmental authority.

It is obvious that existing conditions under which large employers of labor possess unprecedented power to dictate contracts and conditions of employment have been developed through governmental grants of authority to form corporations and organizations of corporations, whereby thousands of owners of property are enabled to combine hundreds of millions of dollars of capital and, in this way, substantially to control and sometimes to monopolize opportunities for employment. Such a power, unrestrained by the organization of labor, would permit employers arbitrarily to fix the wages and conditions of labor under which millions of men and women would find their only opportunity to earn a living.

A single laborer, standing alone, confronted with such far-reaching, overwhelming concentration of employer power, and compelled to labor for the support of himself and family, is absolutely helpless to negotiate or to exert any influence over the fixing of his wages or the hours and conditions of his labor. A man must work in order to live. If he can exercise no control over his conditions of employment, he is subjected to involuntary servitude.

The efforts of the workers to preserve their freedom of association and their freedom in association to influence the fixing of wages and working conditions present questions which are unique and demand specific legislative action. The situation has been very well described by Chief Justice Taft in the opinion of the court delivered by him in *American Foundries* v. *Tri-City Council* (257 U. S. 184, 209), reading in part as follows:

> ... Labor unions are recognized by the Clayton Act as legal when instituted for mutual help and lawfully carrying out their legitimate objects. . . . They were organized out of the necessities of the situation. A single employee was helpless in dealing with an employer. He was dependent ordinarily on his daily wage for the maintenance of himself and family. If the employer refused to pay him the wages that he thought fair, he was nevertheless unable to leave the employ and to resist arbitrary and unfair treatment. Union was essential to give laborers opportunity to deal on equality with their employer. . . . The right to combine for such a lawful purpose has in many years not been denied by any court. The strike became a lawful instrument in a lawful economic struggle or competition between employer and employees as to the share or division between them of the joint product of labor and capital. To render this combination at all effective, employees must make their combination extend beyond one shop. It is helpful to have as many as may be in the same trade in the same community united, because in the competition between employers they are bound to be affected by the standard of wages of their trade in the neighborhood.

The foregoing opinion is cited with approval in the unanimous opinion of the Supreme Court handed down May 26, 1930, in *Texas & New Orleans Railroad Co.* v. *Brotherhood of Railway & Steamship Clerks,* in support of the following statement in the opinion by Mr. Chief Justice Hughes:

> The legality of collective action on the part of employees in order to safeguard their proper interests is not to be disputed. It has long been recognized that employees are entitled to organize for the purpose of securing the redress of grievances and to promote agreements with employers relating to rates of pay and conditions of work (citing the Tri-City case). Congress was not required to ignore this right of the employees, but could safeguard it and seek to make their appropriate collective action an instrument of peace rather than of strife.

If we concede, as we must, that labor has the right to combine for the lawful purpose of securing employment and has likewise the right to combine for the purpose of securing increased wages or bettering conditions of labor, then it follows, as the late Chief Justice Taft has so well stated, that the strike becomes a lawful instrument in the economic struggle between employer and employee. It would be hypocrisy, however, to concede these rights to labor and then to prohibit any effective exercise of these rights by labor. The primary object of the proposed legislation is to protect labor in the lawful and effective exercise of its conceded rights—to protect, first, the right of free association and, second, the right to advance the lawful object of association.

No one will seriously doubt the right of Congress, under the Constitution, to limit the jurisdiction of Federal courts. The jurisdiction, for instance, of the district courts of the United States is given by act of Congress. All the courts of the United States except the Supreme Court could be entirely abolished by act of Congress, and, while Congress could not give to these inferior courts jurisdiction greater than is provided by the Constitution, it could, on the other hand, within the limits of the Constitution, give to the inferior courts such jurisdiction as Congress in its wisdom deems just. It follows, also, that having given this jurisdiction, it can, by act of Congress, take away all or any part of it. This has been clearly held by the Supreme Court of the United States in *Myers* v. *United States* (272 U. S. 52). At page 130 the Supreme Court said:

... It is clear that the mere establishment of a Federal inferior court does not vest that court with all the judicial power of the United States as conferred in the second section of Article III but only that conferred by Congress specifically on the particular court. It must be limited territorially and in the classes of cases to be heard; and the mere creation of the court does not confer jurisdiction except as it is conferred in the law of its creation or its amendments.

In an earlier case the Supreme Court held:

The judicial power of the United States, although it has its origin in the Constitution, is (except in enumerated instances, applicable exclusively to this court) dependent for its distribution and organization, and for the modes of its exercise, entirely upon the action of Congress, who possess the sole power of creating the tribunals (inferior to the Supreme Court) for the exercise of the judicial power, and of investing them with jurisdiction either limited, concurrent, or exclusive, and of withholding jurisdiction from them in the exact degrees and character which to Congress may seem proper for the public good. (*Cary* v. *Curtis,* 3 How. 235 at 244.)

In a fairly recent case, the Supreme Court, construing the power of the inferior Federal courts to exercise jurisdiction over controversies between citizens of different States, pointed out that:

The right of a litigant to maintain an action in a Federal court (on this ground) is not one derived from the Constitution of the United States, unless in a very indirect sense.

And continued:

Certainly, it is not a right granted by the Constitution. . . . The Constitution simply gives to the inferior courts the capacity to take jurisdiction in the enumerated cases, but it requires an act of Congress to confer it. . . . A right which thus comes into existence only by virtue of an act of Congress, and which may be withdrawn by an act of Congress after its exercise has begun, can not well be described as a constitutional right. (*Kline* v. *Burke Construction Co.,* 260 U.S. 226, 233.)

PUBLIC POLICY

Relief by injunction is an extraordinary and harsh remedy. It should not be resorted to except in cases where such action is imperatively demanded; and yet injunctive relief is often the only adequate and effective relief against many wrongs and to prevent many irreparable injuries in controversies of infinite variety.

It is not sought by this bill to take away from the judicial power any jurisdiction to restrain by injunctive process, unlawful acts or acts of fraud or violence. In order to assist the courts in the proper interpretation of the proposed legislation, it has been attempted to declare, by act of Congress, the public policy of the United States in relation to labor disputes and the issuing of injunctions in connection therewith. This is done in section 2 of the proposed substitute bill, as follows:

> ... Whereas under prevailing economic conditions, developed with the aid of governmental authority for owners of property to organize in the corporate and other forms of ownership association, the individual unorganized worker is commonly helpless to exercise actual liberty of contract and to protect his freedom of labor, and thereby to obtain acceptable terms and conditions of employment, wherefore it is necessary that he have full freedom of association, self-organization, and designation of representatives of his own choosing, to negotiate the terms and conditions of his employment, and that he shall be free from the interference, restraint, or coercion of employers of labor, or their agents, in the designation of such representatives or in self-organization or in other concerted activities for the purpose of collective bargaining or other mutual aid or protection.

It is believed that the public policy of the United States thus declared is free from any possible objection and fundamentally beyond criticism if we desire to give those who labor equal opportunity in the economic world with the employers of labor.

In the case of *Texas & New Orleans Railroad Co.* v. *Brotherhood of Railway & Steamship Clerks,* decided May 26, 1930, previously quoted, the court had under consideration the provision of the railway labor act, confirming in railway employees the right of self-organization "free from the interference, influence or coercion" of employers. It will be noted that this right of employees, written into the railway labor act, is the same right which is affirmed in the declaration of public policy in the proposed bill, which affirms, in section 2, the employee's "full freedom of association, self-organization and designation of representatives of his own choosing," and provides that the employee "shall be free from the interference, restraint, or coercion of employers of labor." Therefore, the decision of the Supreme Court of May 26, 1930, sustaining the constitutionality and the enforceability of this right of employees under the railway labor act, directly and conclusively sustains the constitutionality of the declaration of policy in the proposed bill and the provision of the proposed bill making contracts contrary to such public policy nonenforceable in the Federal courts. In this most recent opinion, the Supreme Court held:

> Such collective action (of employees) would be a mockery if representation were made futile by interferences with freedom of choice. Thus the prohibition by Congress

of interference with the selection of representatives for the purpose of negotiation and conference between employers and employees, instead of being an invasion of the constitutional right of either, was based on the recognition of the rights of both.

It is also equally clear that the Congress has the right to declare the public policy of the United States so long as the policy thus declared does not conflict with the Constitution.

Where Congress has not declared the public policy it is within the province of the court to decide what the public policy is, but when such public policy has been declared by Congress it is the duty of the courts to follow such policy and to decide litigated questions related thereto in accordance with the public policy thus declared.

In the case of the *People* v. *City of Chicago* (321 Ill. 466–475) the Supreme Court of Illinois said:

The public policy of a State is to be found embodied in its constitution, its statutes, and, when these are silent on the subject, in the decisions of its courts. The public policy of the State, when not fixed by the Constitution, is not unalterable but varies upon any given question with changing legislation thereon, and any action which, in the absence of legislation thereon, by the decisions of the courts has been held contrary to the public policy of the State, is no longer contrary to such public policy when such action is expressly authorized by legislative enactment.

Another Illinois case on this subject is *Union Trust & Savings Bank* v. *Telephone Co.* (258 Ill. 202). The Supreme Court of Illinois said:

While no statute has been enacted declaring such exclusive contracts criminal or giving a right of action to persons prejudiced by them, the courts have declared the public policy of the State, in accordance with the common law, to be opposed to such contracts which tend to put the power to render public service in the hands of one corporation and to take it away from all others. The legislature has the power to change this policy. It is a legislative question whether the public interest will be promoted by monopolistic rather than competitive service.

Chief Justice Marshall, in the case of *McCulloch* v. *Maryland* (4 Wheat. 315, 423), used the following language:

Where the law is . . . calculated to affect any of the objects intrusted to the Government, to undertake here to inquire into the degree of its necessity, would be to pass the line which circumscribes the judicial department, and to tread on legislative ground.

The Supreme Court has expressly upheld the jurisdiction of Congress to declare the public policy of the United States in the case of *Michaelson* v. *United States* (266 U. S. 42, 68). In that case, the following language was used:

The words of the act are plain and in terms inclusive of all classes of employment; and we find nothing in them which requires a resort to judicial construction. The reasoning of the court below really does not present a question of statutory construction, but rather an argument justifying the supposititious exception on the ground of necessity or of policy—a matter addressed to the legislative and not the judicial authority.

The decisions and opinions of the Supreme Court of the United States in *Bailey* v. *Alabama* (219 U. S. 219) are significant in this connection. In that case the majority of the court held that a statute although in terms punishing a man for fraud in violating a contract to work, had the "inevitable effect" of convicting him of a crime in simply refusing to work and thus enforced peonage. This was held to be unconstitutional, in conflict with the thirteenth amendment, which was intended, as held in the majority opinion by Mr. Justice Hughes:

... to make labor free, by prohibiting that control by which the personal service of one man is disposed of or coerced for another's benefit, which is the essence of involuntary servitude.

The opinion further stated:

There is no more important concern than to safeguard the freedom of labor upon which alone can enduring prosperity be based.

It is noteworthy in this case that the dissenting opinion by Mr. Justice Holmes proceeded on the ground that the contract in question (to render services in consideration of an advance payment) was in itself a legal one, and that therefore a man could be legally punished for obtaining money by making such a contract with a fraudulent intention of breaking it. He met the argument that the enforcement of such contracts would result in peonage by the pertinent comment: "If the contract is one that ought not to be made, prohibit it." Thus both opinions already support the right of Congress to declare contracts resulting practically in involuntary servitude to be contrary to public policy and to deny their enforceability or validity in the Federal courts.

The declaration of a public policy is not new to the Congress of the United States. Such a policy is explicitly declared in the present railway labor act, as previously noted. In this connection, it is exceedingly interesting to trace the history of that act. Originally, in the transportation act, it was provided that disputes between employers and employees should, if possible, be "decided in conference between representatives designated and authorized so to confer." In administering this law the labor board found great difficulty on account of the interference by employers with the free designation of representatives by the employees. The chairman of the board appeared before the Interstate Commerce Committee of the Senate and explained the trouble. (See Hearings, Interstate Commerce Committee of the

Senate on S. 2646, 68th Cong. 1st Sess.) On account of this difficulty, the present railway labor act included this specific provision:

Representatives, for the purposes of this act, shall be designated by the respective parties in such manner as may be provided in their corporate organization or unincorporated association, or by other means of collective action, without interference, influence, or coercion exercised by either party over the self-organization or designation of representatives by the other. (Par. 3, sec. 152, title 45, U.S.C.A., 1929 sup.)

This act definitely declared the same public policy in regard to railway employees as is declared in the proposed bill in regard to all employees, and this provision of the railway labor act has been sustained by the United States Supreme Court in *Texas & New Orleans Railroad Co.* v. *Brotherhood of Railroad & Steamship Clerks,* decided May 26, 1930, as previously cited.

Another instance in which Congress declared the public policy of the United States is found in section 15a of the interstate commerce act, passed as a part of the transportation act of 1920. The language referred to in that act is as follows:

Inasmuch as it is impossible (without regulation and control in the interest of the commerce of the United States considered as a whole) to establish uniform rates upon competitive traffic which will adequately sustain all the carriers which are engaged in such traffic and which are indispensable to the communities to which they render the service of transportation, without enabling some of such carriers to receive a net railway operating income substantially and unreasonably in excess of a fair return upon the value of their railway property held for and used in the service of transportation, it is hereby declared that any carrier which receives such an income so in excess of a fair return, shall hold such part of the excess, as hereinafter prescribed, as trustee for, and shall pay it to, the United States. (41 Stat. 489.)

The declaration by Congress of the public policy thus declared was interpreted and sustained by the Supreme Court of the United States in the case of *Dayton-Goose Creek Railway* v. *United States* (263 U. S. 456). The opinion of the court in this case shows that the act was interpreted and sustained upon grounds of the public policy thus declared by Congress. The court in that case said:

The new act seeks affirmatively to build up a system of railways prepared to handle promptly all the interstate traffic of the country. . . . To achieve this great purpose, it puts the railroad systems of the country more completely than ever under the fostering guardianship and control of the commission.

Title IV of the transportation act, embracing paragraphs 418 and 422, is carefully framed to achieve its expressly declared objects.

The public policy of the United States in regard to disputes between labor and employers of labor, having been declared as provided in the proposed bill, it will become the duty of the courts to carry out this policy and to uphold it in passing upon any litigated questions which may arise under the act. Such a declaration of public policy should be of great assistance to the courts in the adjudication of any controversies which may arise.

THE "YELLOW-DOG" CONTRACT

One of the very serious difficulties which has arisen in many of the injunctions which have been issued in labor disputes has been the so-called "yellow-dog" contract. This contract is one which requires the employee, as a condition of obtaining employment, to agree that he will not join a union while he is in such employment, or, that if he is then a member of a union, he will disassociate himself from it; that he recognizes the right of the employer to discharge him without notice; that he will not quit without giving to his employer notice sufficient to enable the employer to hire some one to take his place. Such contracts frequently require the employee to agree in advance to accept such conditions of labor, hours of labor, etc., as may from time to time be decided upon by his employer. Not all of these contracts are the same, but, in general, the conditions are such as those which have been briefly outlined. In all of them the employee waives his right of free association and genuine representation in connection with his wages, the hours of labor, and other conditions of employment. In other words, he surrenders his actual liberty of contract and to a great extent he enters into involuntary servitude. Yet the Supreme Court has held very recently that "collective action would be mockery if representation were made futile by interference with freedom of choice." (*Texas & New Orleans* case previously cited.)

It is no defense to say that he is not compelled to sign a contract, as is so clearly pointed out in the citation from Chief Justice Taft heretofore quoted. He is helpless in dealing with his employer. This was not always true. It is only under modern conditions where, under the law, employers organize; where large corporations control labor in an entire line of industry. He is dependent upon his daily wage and so is his family. Therefore, he must accept whatever wages and whatever conditions are laid down by the employer. He has no other course to pursue. Union on his part with his fellow workers is absolutely necessary to protect his own liberty and, if he signs away this right, to a great extent he becomes the slave of his master.

In sustaining the right of railway employers to organize the Supreme Court held:

Congress was not required to ignore this right of the employees but could safeguard it and seek to make their appropriate collective action an instrument of peace rather than of strife. (*Texas & New Orleans* case previously cited.)

This doctrine upholds the purpose of the proposed bill.

One of the objects of this legislation is to outlaw this "yellow-dog" contract. It has become necessary for Congress to take some action in regard to these contracts, because many of the injunctions which have been issued by Federal courts have been based wholly or in part upon such contracts on the assumption that they are valid and not contrary to public policy.

At first blush it would seem unnecessary to pass any legislation upon the subject, because it is difficult to see how any court could sustain such a contract even though there were no statute condemning it. Many of the most eminent jurists have always believed that such contracts were void for several reasons.

1. They are contrary to public policy. If these contracts are held to be legal in one type of litigation, it would follow that they must be held legal in all other controversies, and thus in order to sustain life and support families, laboring men may be compelled to enter into practical peonage. If men must agree in advance to surrender any real liberty of contract in order to attain employment they are, under coercion of necessity, forced into working under conditions of involuntary servitude.

2. These contracts should be held void because they are entered into without consideration. The employer on the one hand has his work which he wants done. The laborer on the other hand, as a consideration for his part of the contract, undertakes to perform the labor. In practically every case there is no hiring for a definite period; no assurance of either work or fixed wages. The employer gives up none of his freedom of action and furnishes no consideration for the promise of the employee that he will surrender ordinary rights of "liberty of contract" which are inherent in every free citizen.

3. Such contracts should be held void because they are signed by the employee under coercion. The employee is forced to accept all of these burdensome conditions in order to support himself and family, because no man will voluntarily deprive himself of his power of self-protection.

Nevertheless, since such contracts have been held by the courts to furnish a legal basis for preventing employees from organizing for self-help, it seems to be necessary that some legislative action should be taken to liberate workers from a servitude thus imposed. The bill declares that such contracts are:

. . . contrary to the public policy of the United States, shall not be enforceable and shall not afford any basis for the granting of legal or equitable relief by any court of the United States.

ABUSES OF INJUNCTIVE POWER

One of the indefensible things contained in a great many of the injunctions issued by Federal judges is the enjoining of any person, organization, or corporation from paying benefits to laborers who are engaged in carrying on a strike. As a rule, labor unions provide for a fund out of which they pay benefits to their members who are out on a strike. These injunctions prohibit them from paying such benefits, although the accumulation of this fund has been in part contributed by the very men who are on a strike and under the rules of the union they are, as a matter of fact, entitled to these benefits.

Some of these injunctions go still further. They not only prohibit the unions from paying any strike benefits to men who are on a strike, but they prohibit any person, whether a member of the union or not, from in any way giving any assistance to the persons who are on the strike. It is a common thing, in the operation of coal mines, for the owners of the mine to own the houses in which the laborers live. They make a contract with the laborer for the rental which shall be paid, providing also for the surrender of the premises under conditions named in the contract of lease.

If a dispute arises between the employer and the employee as to whether the contract has been violated and as to whether the owner is entitled to dispossess the employee, the question becomes one of forcible entry and detainer under the laws of the State where the property is located. These laws usually, if not always, provide for the trial of forcible entry and detainer cases before an inferior court. Either side, being dissatisfied with the decision of the court, has the right to take an appeal. If the appeal is taken by the tenant he must put up a bond, not only to pay the costs, but to pay a reasonable rental for the property in case the decision in the higher court is against him. This is a right given him under the State law. The State law is general and applies to every one. It is the only means by which the question in dispute between landlord and tenant can be fully decided. If a tenant is wrongfully withholding the property the landlord is protected by the bond which the tenant must give providing for the payment of rental if the case shall ultimately be decided against him. Yet, strange as it may seem, Federal judges have been in the habit of issuing injunctions restraining outsiders—usually the term used is "any person whomsoever"—from doing anything to assist the laborer in a forcible entry and detainer case pending in the State court.

All persons are enjoined from furnishing bonds to take those cases up on appeal. All persons are enjoined from paying any money in the way of expenses in connection with such litigation in the State courts. The injunctions often go far enough to prevent an attorney from giving any advice to the employee who is trying to hold possession of a house belonging to the employer. All persons are restrained from giving them any assistance while they are living in these houses, including food and fuel. Why the judges of the United States, by extending the extraordinary remedy of the injunction, should prohibit laboring men from litigating in State courts, under the law of the State, to sustain what they claim to be their rights, is almost beyond human comprehension. In truth, such a summary method of depriving persons of their "day in court" has never been held to be "due process of law" in any other class of cases.

The bill, under section 4, takes away from all Federal courts the power to issue such injunctions. It also, in the same section, prohibits the issuing of injunctions which restrain employees from—

> ... assembling peaceably to act or to organize to act in promotion of their interests in a labor dispute.

It prohibits Federal courts from issuing injunctions restraining anyone from inducing or advising without threat, fraud, or violence, any of these things regardless of whether the employee may have signed the so-called "yellow-dog" contract.

Section 4 also prohibits the granting of injunctions which would restrain strikers from giving publicity to the existence of or the facts involved in a labor dispute. One of the most recent injunctions in a labor dispute was issued in the District Court of the United States for the Northern District of Iowa. This injunction was issued on the 29th day of March, 1930, enjoining the defendants, among other things, from—

> ... printing, publishing, issuing, circulating and distributing, or otherwise communicating, directly or indirectly, in writing or verbally to any person, association of persons, or corporation, any statement or notice of any kind or character whatsoever, stating or representing:
>
> (1) That there is a strike at the mill or plant of complainant at Fort Dodge, Iowa; or that the strike of 1921 is still in existence; or that there is a controversy over wages or conditions of employment between complainant and its employees; or any false statement with reference to conditions of employment at complainant's plant.
>
> (2) That complainant is unfair to organized union labor, or that its products are or were unfair to organized labor, or are on an unfair list.
>
> (3) That complainant forces or requires its employees to sign or subscribe to the so-called "yellow-dog" contract.

The defendants in this case, it will be observed, were not allowed to tell anyone that a strike was in progress. They were not allowed to give any publicity in any way to the fact that a strike existed. They were not allowed to tell anyone that the complainant required its employees to sign the "yellow-dog" contract. In other words, their mouths were absolutely closed and "free speech" was forbidden. They could not, without violating this injunction, have sought advice from an attorney. The son would not be allowed to seek advice from his own father. And if the defendants violated this severe decree they would be liable for contempt of court, which means that they would be tried for an offense made illegal by the judge— an offense consisting of an act which would be perfectly lawful under the laws of the State where the controversy existed. They were not only forbidden to violate this judge-made statute, but, in case they did violate it, they would be tried by the man who made the statute. They would not be allowed a trial before a jury of their peers—a privilege granted to the vilest of criminals.

It has long been recognized by students of law and government that the power to make law and the power to enforce law should be separated as a protection against tyranny. To prevent executive tyranny, the legislative power has been carefully separated from the executive power in our scheme of government and to prevent judicial tyranny it is equally necessary to preserve the separation of the legislative power from the judicial power.

A warning against the growing exercise of legislative power by the courts in injunction cases was uttered long ago by the great commentator, Blackstone, in the following language:

In all tyrannical government, the supreme magistracy or the right of making and enforcing laws is vested in one and the same man, or one and the same body of men; and wherever these two powers are united together there can be no public liberty. (1 Blackstone 142.)

It is amazing to realize that in the last 40 years there has developed in the American courts the practice of writing a special law to fit the individual case by judges in issuing labor injunctions; and that thereupon the judge, who himself wrote the law, has undertaken to prescribe the penalty for its violation and to punish the violator without permitting the accused to enjoy a trial by jury or even to insist upon a trial before another judge. It can not be successfully claimed that the courts have not written into these injunction cases a new law of labor disputes, fitting the law to each particular case, and then enforcing this new law made by the court.

Pomeroy, perhaps the leading authority, describes the development of the law compactly in his *Equity Jurisprudence* in the following language:

The courts have thus been required to face such questions as the nature and extent of the capitalist's rights in the management of his business and of the workingman's property in his labor; to decide how far the employer shall be protected in his right to have labor and custom flow to him free from the interference of third parties and how far the laborer shall be protected from similar interference in his contract of employment or his right to secure employment; to determine what limits shall be placed upon the individuals and combinations of individuals in seeking their economic advancement at the expense of their fellows. All these and other problems have come before the courts in rapid succession. (5 Pomeroy, *Equity Jurisprudence* (4th Ed.) 4566, sec. 2018.)

There can be no question, therefore, that there has been created, as a result of writing law into injunction orders and then enforcing those orders by the same judge who wrote them without a grant of trial by jury, that condition of uniting the two powers of making and enforcing laws in one person or one body of men wherein, using the language of Blackstone, "there can be no public liberty."

It is difficult to see how any civilized people could indefinitely submit to such tyrannical procedure. It is not difficult to understand how such cruel laws, made not by any legislature but by a judge upon the bench, should bring our Federal courts into disrepute. Neither is it difficult to see how such injunctions, violating the conscience of civilization, should frighten persons against whom such injunctions are issued into desperation. What free American citizen is willing to submit to the violation of his sacred rights of human liberty and freedom?

RESPONSIBILITY FOR UNLAWFUL ACTS

Section 6 of the bill relates to damages for unlawful acts arising out of labor disputes. It is provided that officers and members of any labor organization, and officers and members of any employers' organization, shall not be held liable for damages unless it is proven that the defendant either participated in or authorized such unlawful acts, or ratified such unlawful acts after actual knowledge thereof.

To hold that officers or members of a labor organization, or the organization itself, should be liable for damages for unlawful acts committed while a strike is on, without clear, actual proof of authorization, participation in, or ratification of such unlawful acts, would go far toward the destruction of organized labor.

Moreover, it will be observed that this section, as do most all of the other prohibitive sections of the bill, applies both to organizations of labor and organizations of capital. The same rule throughout the bill, wherever it is applicable, applies both to employers and employees, and also to organizations of employers and employees.

In most cases where strikes occur involving a great many employers and employees and covering a comparatively large territory, there are often unlawful acts committed in the way of injury to property or to persons. It is not the intention of the bill to protect anybody, whether he be employer or employee, from punishment for the commission of unlawful acts either as against property or persons. But no person or organization should be held thus liable unless he or it caused the unlawful act or participated in it or ratified it. It has often occurred that employers themselves have secured the services of detectives who, under the guise of labor men, have gained admission into labor unions. When this happens these detectives are usually doing everything within their power to incite employees who are on strike to commit acts of violence, and such detectives, contrary to the definite instructions of labor union leaders, sometimes commit unlawful acts for the express and only purpose of laying the foundation for injunctive process, of bringing discredit upon the union, and of making its officers and members liable for damages.

In case of a strike, where the officers of the labor union are doing everything within their power to prevent acts of violence from being committed by any person, the law should fully protect them and save them and the members of their organization who are following their advice from liability in damages because of unlawful acts of persons who are either directly or indirectly connected with those who are trying to defeat the purposes of the strike.

Opposition to this section has been voiced on the ground that it seeks to establish a "new law of agency." In the first place, this section is concerned especially with establishing a rule of evidence. There is no provision made relieving an individual from responsibility for his acts, but provision is made that a person shall not be held responsible for an "unlawful act" except upon "clear proof" of participation or authorization or ratification. Thus a rule of evidence, not a rule of substantive law, is established. "The general power of every legislature to prescribe the evidence which shall be received and the effect of that evidence in the courts of its own government," has been repeatedly upheld by the Supreme Court. (See *Fong Yue Ting* v. *U.S.,* 149 U. S. 698, 749; *Bailey* v. *Alabama,* 219 U. S. 219, 238.)

But the argument is made that a man is held legally responsible for the acts of his agents taken in due course of employment. This argument is evidently based upon a doctrine of the civil law of negligence. It has no application to the criminal law. If a man is held responsible for an unlawful act, his responsibility rests on the basis of actual or implied participation. He is responsible for conspiring to do an unlawful act or for setting in motion forces intended to result, or necessarily resulting, in an unlawful act.

Strictly speaking, the legal relation of principal and agent does not exist in regard to the commission of criminal offenses. All who participate in the commission of such offense are either principals or accessories. (*Anderson* v. *State,* 22 Ohio State 305.)

But where the agent's criminal act is unauthorized and is not sanctioned or acquiesced in by the principal, especially where it is contrary to the principal's direct instructions, the latter can not be held criminally responsible therefor. (1 Clark and Skyles, *Law of Agency,* 1140.)

The distinction should be clear. A man operating a dangerous machine negligently injures someone, and the negligence is imputed to the employer. But, there is a distinction between the torts of an employee and the crimes of an employee, and criminal responsibility is not to be imputed. If the president of a corporation sends a bill collector to persuade a debtor to pay a bill, instructing him to collect it in a peaceable manner, he does not become responsible for an assault by his employee upon the debtor.

According to the same reasoning, why should an officer of a labor union, who has specifically advised members that violence must be avoided, become responsible for the hot-headed action of some member in perhaps assaulting a strike breaker? Again, the relationship between officers and members of labor unions and other members is not that of employer and employee. The officers chosen by a union are not employers of the membership. They have no control over their associates based upon the power of determining whether or not they will employ them. It may be accepted that if a group associated in common activities becomes controlled by a lawless majority, it may be necessary for law-abiding men to dissolve their association with lawbreakers; but the doctrine that a few lawless men can change the character of an organization whose members and officers are very largely law-abiding is one which has been developed peculiarly as judge-made law in labor disputes, and it is high time that, by legislative action, the courts should be required to uphold the long established law that guilt is personal and that men can only be held responsible for the unlawful acts of associates because of participation in, authorization or ratification of such acts. As a rule of evidence, clear proof should be required, so that criminal guilt and criminal responsibility should not be imputed but proven beyond reasonable doubt in order to impose liability.

There has been a distinct conflict of opinion in the courts as to the degree of proof required. Mere ex parte affidavits establishing a certain amount of lawless conduct in the prosecution of a strike have been held in some instances to establish a "presumption" that the entire union and its officers were engaged in an unlawful conspiracy; and, on the other hand, other courts have declined thus to substitute inference for proof, rejecting such a doctrine in language such as the following used in a New York case: "Is it the law that a presumption of guilt attaches to a labor union association?" Various examples of these different rulings are quoted in *The Labor Injunction,* by Frankfurter and Greene, pp. 74–75.

It is appropriate and necessary to define by legislation the proper rule of evidence to be followed in this matter in Federal courts. That is the only object of section 6.

PROCEDURE

The bill, in section 7, provides for the procedure which shall be followed in case application is made for a temporary restraining order or for a temporary or permanent injunction. It provides that no temporary or permanent injunction shall be issued except after hearing the testimony of witnesses, under oath, in open court. The court is also required, before it issues a temporary or permanent injunction, to permit the defendants to offer testimony in opposition to such injunction; and, before the court is authorized to issue the temporary or permanent injunction, it must find that unlawful acts have been threatened or committed and will be executed or continued unless restrained; that substantial and irreparable injury to complainant's property will follow, and that as to each item of relief granted greater injury will be inflicted upon complainant by the denial of relief than will be inflicted upon defendants by the granting of relief.

This procedure balances the effect of an order upon both parties, and while an injunction might be granted against certain unlawful acts the injury to complainant from such acts can not be made the basis of enjoining other acts from which complainant will suffer but little, but the prohibition of which may cause greater injury to the defendants. This is only statutory sanction of the best and long established practice in equity. (See Pomeroy, *Equity Jurisprudence* (4th ed.), sec. 1685.)

It is likewise provided in section 7 that in addition to the ordinary requirements applying to all applications for injunction, the court must find—

That the public officers charged with the duty to protect complainant's property have failed or are unable to furnish adequate protection.

This is an entirely new provision, but it is believed to be a just one.

These injunctions are issued upon an allegation, among other things that unless the order is issued complainant's property will be injured or destroyed. If the public officers whose duty it is to protect complainant's property are able and willing to give the protection required by law, there is no reason why the courts of equity should take over the functions of the executive department and undertake to police their districts and no reason why the extraordinary and one–sided remedy of an injunction should be resorted to. It seems, therefore, but fair that before the injunction is issued, the court should find from the evidence that such officers have failed or are unable to furnish the protection required by law.

Injunctions are often applied for and issued for the moral effect that such injunctions will have in disheartening and discouraging employees engaged in a strike, rather than because of any real necessity to protect property.

Provision is also made in the bill for the issuance of a temporary restraining order without notice. This can be done only if the complainant shall allege that such temporary restraining order is necessary and that if time is taken to give notice a substantial and irreparable injury to complainant's property will be unavoidable.

Before issuing such temporary restraining order, however, the court must take testimony under oath, and such testimony must be sufficient, if sustained, to justify the court in issuing a temporary injunction upon a hearing after notice.

Injunctions issued without notice to the defendants against whom the injunctive order is sought are always ex parte. No good reason exists why this evidence thus taken, without the presence of the defendant, should not be required to be sufficient, if sustained to sustain an order issued after notice and hearing. If the complainant can not make a prima facie case without notice, he certainly never would be able to make such a case after notice when the defendant was in court contesting the issuing of the injunction.

The bill provides that such temporary restraining order so issued without notice shall not be effective for a longer time than five days. This, however, is a reasonable requirement. The only object in issuing a temporary restraining order without notice is because it is alleged by the complainant that notice of such application would bring about destruction of his property. Therefore, the time that such an extraordinary process should be effective without notice should not be prolonged beyond the time that it would take to give notice, and it is difficult for any mind to conceive of a condition where notice could not be given and a hearing held within the 5-day limit.

It is provided in section 8 that no restraining order or injunctive relief shall be granted to any complainant who has not complied with any obligation imposed by law in regard to the settlement of any labor dispute. Neither shall such order issue unless the complainant has made every reasonable effort to settle such dispute, either by the aid of negotiation or with the aid of any available governmental machinery of mediation or voluntary arbitration. But where such negotiations are in progress and have not been completed, the court is not required, before issuing the writ, to await the outcome of such action if the court is satisfied that irreparable injury is threatened.

This section simply requires that a complainant shall not be entitled to injunctive relief who has failed to comply with any legal obligations which may exist, to be performed on his part. In other words, he must go into court with clean hands. This doctrine here announced is that persons have no right to seek the aid of Federal courts and impose upon them additional burdens who have not sought to do all within their power to avoid the aid of the courts and who are not themselves aggravating or causing the dispute by violation of legal obligations.

It has often occurred, where employers have refused to confer with their employees, as required by law; or where they have refused to comply with the requirements of the law for the protection of employees, that they have nevertheless sought to have the court restrain the employees from promoting their interests properly in the resulting dispute. An employer who has himself brought on a controversy by wrongful conduct is not entitled to the aid of equity in advancing his interests in the resulting conflict.

A court of equity acts only when and as conscience commands; and if the conduct of the plaintiff be offensive to the dictates of natural justice, then, whatever may be the rights he possesses, and whatever use he may make of them in a court of law, he will be held remediless in a court of equity. (*Deweese* v. *Reinhard,* 165 U.S. 386, 390.)

Other cases and authorities upholding this principle written into the proposed bill are cited in the recent opinion of the Supreme Court of Wisconsin in *Adler & Sons* v. *Maglio* (228 N. W. 123), where the court denied injunctive relief and dismissed the complaint of an employer whose conduct was described by the court as follows:

> Plaintiff pursued a course of conduct that precipitated a labor war. When the tide of battle seemed to be setting against it, the plaintiff sought to withdraw from the field to which it had deliberately gone, and appealed to a court of equity for protection from the consequences that naturally flowed from the course of conduct which it had deliberately pursued.
>
> A court of conscience will not extend its strong arm to protect one who has pursued such a course of conduct. It will leave such applicant for relief where it had deliberately chosen to place itself. (P. 125.)

Later the court further upheld application of the equitable rule in the following language:

> Its strict application to all labor controversies ought to admonish both parties to these modern industrial struggles that, while they may conduct their own affairs in any way that does not violate the law, neither can be guilty of conduct that invades the rights of the others in regard to, or all events connected with, the matter of litigation, so as to in some measure affect the equitable relations subsisting between the two parties without forfeiting all right to resort to the extraordinary powers of equity. (P. 126.) (See also *Cornelleir* v. *Haverhill Shoe Manufacturers Association,* 212 Mass. 554; *Weegham* v. *Killefer,* 215 Fed. 168; Pomeroy, *Equity Jurisprudence* (4th ed.), sec. 398.)

The bill also provides for a speedy appeal by any party to the case who may be dissatisfied with the action of the court, either in allowing or denying the injunction; and when a case is appealed to the circuit court of appeals, it becomes the duty of that court to consider the case with the greatest possible expedition and to give such cases precedence over all other matters except older matters of the same character.

JURY TRIAL IN CONTEMPT CASES

Section 11 of the bill provides that where a person is charged with indirect criminal contempt for violation of a restraining order or injunction, the defendant shall have the right to demand a speedy and public trial by a jury. This requirement does not apply to contempts committed in the presence of the court or so near thereto as to interfere directly with the administration of justice. Neither does it apply to misbehavior, misconduct, or disobedience of any officer of the court in respect to the writs, orders, or process of the court.

Section 12 provides that the defendant in any proceeding for contempt of court is authorized to file with the court a demand for the retirement of the judge sitting in the proceeding if the alleged contempt arose from an attack upon the character or the conduct of the judge and if the attack occurred otherwise than in open court. Upon the finding of such a demand another judge shall be designated to hear the contempt proceeding, as provided in section 21 of the Judicial Code.

It will be observed that sections 11 and 12 have a general application and are not confined to labor disputes.

The ordinary criminal laws provide that any person charged with a crime shall have the right to a jury trial. The person tried for contempt of court is tried for a criminal act. It is true this act has not been made criminal by a statute, but by the order of a judge. The judgment, however, can deprive the defendant of his liberty, can confine him to jail, and the length of the term of confinement is within the discretion of the judge who made the order. The judge becomes the legislature and, as such legislature, he makes something a crime that is not a crime under the general law. He then sits in judgment and tries the person who is charged with violating the law which he has enacted. What difference is it to the defendant, so far as his punishment is concerned, whether the law has been made by the judge or by the legislature? His suffering is just as great in one case as in the other. Why should he be deprived of a jury trial when the law is made by one man instead of by the regular legislative authority? And in addition to all this, what defense can be made of the law which provides that the defendant shall have no opportunity, not only for an impartial jury, but for an impartial judge as well? And when the charge is made that the contempt arises from an attack upon the character or the conduct of the judge, what principle of justice would permit this same judge to sit in judgment upon the accused? All sense of justice and all fair judicial procedure revolt at such a condition.

If an attack is made upon the character or the conduct of the judge by a writer in a newspaper, for instance, is it fair, is it compatible with our idea of jurisprudence, that the judge against whom the attack is made should preside at the trial of the offender? Suppose a judge were assaulted on the street by a common thug. Our procedure would not permit this judge to sit at the trial of the person charged with the assault and battery. He would be tried under the laws provided by the legislature. In an injunction case, the general laws of the legislature would not apply. The person assaulted would not only preside at the trial but he would fix the punishment without regard to statute but in accordance with his own idea as to what the punishment should be.

It is interesting to note that, severe as was ancient law, it was the prevailing practice in the English courts for centuries that trials for criminal contempt were tried by a jury. It is only in the American courts in the last century that such trials by the judge alone developed. And yet we live under a Constitution which provides that—

In all criminal prosecutions the accused shall enjoy the right to a speedy and public trial by an impartial jury of the State and district wherein the crime shall have been committed. (Amendment 6.)

Also—

The trial of all crimes, except in cases of impeachment, shall be by jury. (Art. III.)

The power of the Congress to require trial by jury in cases of indirect criminal contempt should not be now subject to serious question. Criminal contempt consists of disobedience of the orders of the court, obstructions to the administration of justice, which are punished as an offense against the court and differ from civil contempt in that the purpose of punishment is not to grant relief to a litigant but to maintain the dignity of the court and uphold the power of Government. Direct criminal contempt consists of misbehavior in the presence of the court or so near thereto as to interfere directly with the administration of justice. Such contempts are expressly excepted from the provisions of trial by jury. Indirect criminal contempt consists of violation of the orders of the court, which is exactly the same as the violation of law, except that the law is written in the order of the court instead of in a statute.

The Supreme Court sustained the right of trial by jury required by congressional enactment in the Clayton Act in cases of indirect criminal contempt in the case of *Michaelson* v. *United States* (266 U. S. 42), where the unanimous opinion of the Supreme Court, written by Mr. Justice Sutherland, reads as follows:

Contempts of the kind within the terms of the statute (criminal contempts described in the Clayton Act) partake of the nature of crimes in all essential particulars. "So truly are they crimes that it seems to be proved that in the early law they were punished only by the usual criminal procedure, 3 Transactions of the Royal Historical Society, N. S., p. 147 (1885), and that at least in England it seems that they still may be and preferably are tried in that way." *Gompers* v. *U.S.* (233 U.S., 604, 610-611). . . . The statutory extension of this constitutional right (trial by jury) to a class of contempts which are properly described as "criminal offenses" does not, in our opinion, invade the powers of the courts as intended by the Constitution or violate that instrument in any other way (pp. 66-67).

Section 13 of the bill defines various terms used in the act, and it is not believed that any criticism has been or will be made to these definitions.

The main purpose of these definitions is to provide for limiting the injunctive powers of the Federal courts only in the special type of cases, commonly called labor disputes, in which these powers have been notoriously extended beyond the mere exercise of civil authority and wherein the courts have been converted into policing agencies devoted in the guise of preserving peace, to the purpose of aiding employers to coerce employees into accepting terms and conditions of employment desired by employers.

The proposed bill is designed primarily as a practical means of remedying existing evils, and limitations are imposed upon the courts in that class of cases wherein these evils have grown up and become intolerable. This is a reasonable exercise of legislative power, and in order that the limitation may not be whittled away by refined definitions of what persons are to be regarded as legitimately involved in labor disputes, the bill undertakes specifically to designate those persons who are entitled to invoke the protections of the procedure required.

The other sections of the bill contain the usual provisions in regard to the possibility of the court's holding portions of the act invalid and in relation to the repeal of acts in conflict with the provisions of the proposed legislation.

Report of the House Committee on the Judiciary
March 2, 1932

FIORELLO LA GUARDIA [R., N. Y.] submitted the following Report.

The Committee on the Judiciary, to whom was referred the bill (H. R. 5315) to amend the Judicial Code and to define and limit the jurisdiction of courts sitting in equity, and for other purposes, after hearing (serial 3) and consideration, reports the same favorably with amendments and recommends that the bill as amended do pass. . . .

This bill is the so-called anti-injunction bill. It is the outgrowth of years of agitation in the Congress for restriction upon the powers of Federal equity courts in the issuance of injunctions in labor disputes. Hearings have been held by congressional committees over a period of years and the facts adduced have brought about an almost unanimity of opinion that such powers of the Federal courts have been exercised to the detriment of the public welfare and should be curbed.

The questions are sociologic and economic as well as legal and jurisdictional. . . .

The purpose of the bill is to protect the rights of labor in the same manner the Congress intended when it enacted the Clayton Act, October 15, 1914 (38 Stat. L., 738), which act, by reason of its construction and application by the Federal courts, is ineffectual to accomplish the congressional intent.

Section 1: Section 1 provides that no United States court shall have jurisdiction to issue an injunction in a case growing out of a labor dispute except in strict conformity with the provisions of the act, and further that no such injunction shall be issued contrary to the public policy declared in the act.

The Constitution of the United States in Article III, section 1, provides:

The judicial power of the United States shall be vested in one Supreme Court and in such inferior courts as the Congress may from time to time ordain and establish.

The provisions of the bill are expressly limited (sec. 13 (d)) to courts whose jurisdiction has been or may be conferred by the Congress, under the foregoing provision of the Constitution. The Congress having the power to establish, and confer jurisdiction upon, the courts in question, it can not be questioned that it has the power to restrict or curtail the exercise of their powers, as proposed in this bill. The Supreme Court of the United States has clearly recognized that this is the law in *Kline* v. *Burke Construction Co.* (260 U. S. 226, 234), (1922), wherein the court says that—

Only the jurisdiction of the Supreme Court is derived directly from the Constitution. Every other court created by the General Government derives its jurisdiction wholly from the authority of Congress. *That body may give, withhold or restrict such jurisdiction at its discretion* provided it be not extended beyond the boundaries fixed by the Constitution. (Italics supplied.)

This case involved the jurisdiction of the United States District Court in cases depending upon diverse citizenship; and the Court continued (p. 234) as follows:

The Constitution simply gives to the inferior courts the capacity to take jurisdiction in the enumerated cases, but it requires an act of Congress to confer it. (*Nashville* v. *Cooper,* 6 Wall. 247, 252, 18 L. ed. 851, 852.) And the jurisdiction, having been conferred, may, at the will of Congress, be taken away in whole or in part; and, if withdrawn without a saving clause, all pending cases, though cognizable when commenced, must fall.

Concerning the so-called inherent power of the courts to punish for contempt, the following is the state of the law:

The judiciary act of September 24, 1789, creating United States district courts, conferred upon them the power to punish for contempt in the following language:

The said courts shall have power to impose and administer all necessary oaths, and to punish, by fine or imprisonment at the discretion of the court, contempts of their authority.

As early as 1831 the Congress limited this power by the act of March 2, 1831, as follows:

The power of the several courts of the United States to issue attachments and inflict summary punishments for contempts of court shall not be construed to extend to any case except the misbehavior of any person or persons in the presence of the said courts, or so near thereto as to obstruct the administration of justice, the misbehavior of any of the officers of the said courts in their official transactions, and the disobedience or resistance by any officer of the said courts, party, juror, witness or any other person or persons to any lawful writ, process, order, rule, decree, or command of the said courts (4 Stat. L. 487).

which is now section 385, title 28, chapter 10, United States Code:

The said courts shall have power to impose and administer all necessary oaths, and to punish, by fine or imprisonment, at the discretion of the court, contempts of their authority. Such power to punish contempts shall not be construed to extend to any cases except the misbehavior of any person in their presence, or so near thereto as to obstruct the administration of justice, the misbehavior of any of the officers of said courts in their official transactions, and the disobedience or resistance by any such officer, or by any party, juror, witness, or other person to any lawful writ, process, order, rule, decree, or command of the said courts.

Speaking of the act of March 2, 1831, the Supreme Court, in *Ex parte Robinson* (19 Wall. 505, 513), said:

But the power has been limited and defined by the act of Congress of March 2, 1831. . . . It limits the power of these courts in this respect to three classes of cases: 1, where there has been misbehavior of a person in the presence of the courts, or so near thereto as to obstruct the administration of justice; 2, where there has been misbehavior of any officer of the courts in his official transactions; and, 3, where there has been disobedience or resistance by any officer, party, juror, witness or other person, to any lawful writ, process, order, rule, decree, or command of the court. As thus seen, the power of these courts in the punishment of contempts can only be exercised to insure order and decorum in their presence, to secure faithfulness on the part of their officers in their official transactions, and to enforce obedience to their lawful orders, judgments, and processes.

Section 21 of the Clayton Act (*supra,* sec. 386, title 28, U. S. C.) is as follows:

That any person who shall willfully disobey any lawful writ, process, order, rule, decree, or command of any district court of the United States or any court of the District of Columbia by doing any act or thing therein, or thereby forbidden to be done by him, if the act or thing so done by him be of such character as to constitute also a criminal offense under any statute of the United States, or under the laws of any State in which the act was committed, shall be proceeded against for his said contempt as hereinafter provided.

Sections 22, 23, and 24 of the Clayton Act (now secs. 387, 388, and 389, title 28, U. S. C.) provide for procedure in cases of contempt and grant to the accused a trial by jury; with the exception of contempts committed in the presence of the court, etc., as stated in section 385, title 28, United States Code, *supra.*

The Supreme Court reversing the Circuit Court of Appeals for the Sixth Circuit sustained the constitutionality of the provisions of the Clayton Act, now embodied in the United States Code, *supra,* in the case of *Michaelson* v. *U. S.* ex rel. *C.,* St. P., M. & O. R. Co. (266 U.S. 42, 69 L. Ed. 162).

This case involved proceedings, under the Clayton Act of October 15, 1914, for contempt of certain striking railroad employees in violating an injunction against picketing, etc., entered in an equity proceeding. Upon answer and return, the defendants applied for a jury trial under section 22 of the Clayton Act; this request was refused and the court proceeded without a jury; defendants were adjudged guilty of contempt and sentenced. The Circuit Court of Appeals affirmed this judgment, and upon writ of certiorari the Supreme Court considered the constitutionality of sections 21 and 22 of the Clayton Act, and held they were constitutional and that the provision for a jury trial in certain specified kinds of contempt was mandatory and not permissive.

In discussing the statute, and the so-called inherent power of courts to punish for contempt, the court said:

It is contended that the statute materially interferes with the inherent power of the courts, and is therefore invalid. That the power to punish for contempts is inherent in all courts has been many times decided and may be regarded as settled law. It is essential to the administration of justice. The courts of the United States, when called into existence and vested with jurisdiction over any subject, at once become possessed of the power. So far as the inferior Federal courts are concerned however, it is not beyond the authority of Congress; but the attributes which inhere in that power and are inseparable from it can neither be abrogated nor rendered practically inoperative. That it may be regulated within limits not precisely defined may not be doubted. The statute now under review is of the latter character. It is of narrow scope, dealing with the single class where the act or thing constituting the contempt is also a crime in the ordinary sense. It does not interfere with the power to deal summarily with contempts committed in the presence of the court, or so near thereto as to obstruct the administration of justice, and is, in express terms, carefully limited to the cases of contempt specifically defined. But the simple question presented is whether Congress may require a trial by jury upon the demand of the accused in an independent proceeding at law for a criminal contempt which is also a crime. In criminal contempts, as in criminal cases, the presumption of innocence obtains. Proof of guilt must be beyond reasonable doubt, and defendant may not be compelled to be a witness against himself. (*Gompers* v. *Buck's Stove & Range Co., supra,* 221 U.S. 418, 55 L. Ed. 797, 444.) The fundamental characteristics of both are the same. Contempts of the kind within the terms of the Statute partake of the nature of crimes in all essential particulars. The only substantial difference between such a proceeding as we have here, and a criminal prosecution by indictment or information, is that in the latter the act complained of is the violation of a law, and, in the former, the violation of a decree. In the case of the latter, the accused has a constitutional right of trial by jury, while in the former he has not. The statutory extension of this constitutional right to a class of contempts which are properly described as "criminal offenses" does not, in our opinion, invade the powers of the courts as intended by the Constitution, or violate that instrument in any other way.

Section 2: Section 2 sets forth the public policy of the United States for the guidance of the courts in their interpretation of this proposed law.

Congress has heretofore declared the public policy of the United States for the guidance of the court. Previous acts of Congress containing wide declarations of policy may be found in the following statutes: Packers and stockyards act, 1921, *Staffold* v. *Wallace* (258 U. S. 495); transportation act of 1920, *Dayton-Goose Creek Ry. Co.* v. *United States* (263 U. S. 456); railway labor act of 1926, *T. & N. O. Ry.* v. *Brotherhood of Railway Clerks* (281 U. S. 548); grain futures act (title 7, U. S. C., sec. 5 et seq.).

In the Clayton Act (title 29, U. S. C., sec. 52), Congress read into the law the declaration of policy that "The labor of a human being is not a commodity or article of commerce."

This statement of public policy as contained in the bill is in accordance with the general trend of enlightened public opinion and finds adequate support in the opinions of the Supreme Court of the United States. For example, in the case of *American Steel Foundries* v. *Tri-City Central Trades Council* (257 U. S. 184), the Supreme Court, in an opinion by the late Mr. Chief Justice Taft, uses language of marked similarity with the foregoing statement of public policy, as follows:

Labor unions are recognized by the Clayton Act as legal when instituted for mutual help and lawfully carrying out their legitimate objects. They have long been thus recognized by the courts. They were organized out of the necessities of the situation. A single employee was helpless in dealing with an employer. He was dependent ordinarily on his daily wage for the maintenance of himself and family. If the employer refused to pay him the wages that he thought fair, he was nevertheless unable to leave the employ and to resist arbitrary and unfair treatment. Union was essential to give laborers an opportunity to deal on equality with their employer. They united to exert influence upon him and to leave him in a body, in order, by this inconvenience, to induce him to make better terms with him. They were withholding their labor of economic value to make him pay what they thought it was worth. The right to combine for such a lawful purpose has, in many years, not been denied by any court. The strike became a lawful instrument in a lawful economic struggle or competition between employer and employees as to the share or division between them of the joint product of labor and capital. To render this combination at all effective, employees must make their combination extend beyond one shop. It is helpful to have as many as may be in the same trade in the same community united, because, in the competition between employers, they are bound to be affected by the standard of wages of their trade in the neighborhood.

The inclusion of a statement of public policy in the act itself is unobjectionable. It tends to remove doubt as to the purpose and intention of the Congress and is thereby of assistance to the courts in determining questions of interpretation. Moreover, it is the place to look for a statement of the public policy involved, because, as said by the Supreme Court, the public policy of a State must be ascertained from its laws. (*Vidal* v. *Girard,* 2 How. 127; *License Tax Cases,* 5 Wall. 462; *St. Louis Mining & M. Co.* v. *Montana Mining Co.,* 171 U. S. 650.)

Furthermore, the Congress has heretofore stated in legislation the public policy in similar manner. For example, as late as 1925 the Congress declared by statute what should be the true policy in rate making to be pursued by the Interstate Commerce Commission, to the effect that conditions which at any given time prevail in our several industries should be considered in so far as it is legally possible so to do, to the end that commodities may freely move (43 Stat. L., 80).

Section 3: Section 3 is designed to outlaw the so-called "yellow-dog" contract. This section provides that any promise which is described therein or which conflicts with the public policy declared in section 2, is contrary to public policy and shall be unenforceable in any court of the United States. This section includes specifically a promise contained in any agreement of hiring whereby either party promises not to join a labor organization or employer organization, or promises to withdraw from an employment relation in the event he joins any such organization.

This section in no wise is concerned with interstate commerce or the application of the Sherman Act and its amendments, but the Federal courts obtain jurisdiction in cases involving such contracts by virtue of diversity of citizenship; and injunctions have been issued in the Federal courts on the basis of such contracts of employment.

It is easy to say that an employee is not compelled to accept employment and that an employer has the right to make such conditions as he may see fit surrounding the employment. But, aside from the necessity of providing support for himself and family always immediately confronting the workingman, and always materially diminishing his freedom of contract, the vice of such contracts, which are becoming alarmingly widespread, is that if they are carried to their ultimate conclusion, they would abolish trade-unionism. Indeed that is undoubtedly their purpose, and the purpose of the organizations of employers opposing this bill. With this prospect in immediate view, upon the general adoption of the "yellow-dog" contract, the employee, as stated by the late Mr. Chief Justice Taft in the *American Steel Foundries* v. *Tri-City C. C.* case, *supra,* becomes "helpless in dealing with an employer"; and the "union," stated by the same authority as "essential to give laborers an opportunity to deal on equality with their employer," becomes a thing of the past.

Also, as stated in a more recent decision of the Supreme Court of the United States in the case of *Texas & N. O. Railroad Co.* v. *Brotherhood of Railway and Steamship Clerks et al.* (281 U. S. 548), the opinion being written by Mr. Chief Justice Hughes, "collective action would be a mockery," because collective action would be impossible so far as the employee is concerned by virtue of the necessity of signing the character of contract condemned, which prevents a man from joining with his fellows for collective action; and the statement contained in the same decision that "it has long been recognized that employees are entitled to organize for the purpose of securing the redress of grievances and to promote agreements with employers relating to rates of pay and conditions of work" would become an empty statement of historical fact.

Section 4: Section 4 provides that no United States court shall have jurisdiction to issue any injunction in any case involving a labor dispute to prohibit any person participating in such dispute from doing, whether singly or in concert, certain acts. These acts, briefly stated, which can not be enjoined, are the acts of ceasing to work, of becoming a member of a labor or employer organization, of paying any strike benefit, of aiding by lawful means persons participating in a labor dispute who are being proceeded against in a suit, of giving publicity to the facts involved in a labor dispute, whether by advertising, speaking, patrolling, or by any other method not involving fraud or violence, of assembling peaceably to act in promotion of the interests involved in a labor dispute, of advising any person of any intention to do any of these acts, of agreeing with other persons to do or not to do any of these acts, and of advising or urging without fraud or violence any of these acts regardless of any promise described in section 3 as hereinabove discussed.

These are the same character of acts which Congress in section 20 of the Clayton Act of October 15, 1914, sought to restrict from the operation of injunctions, but because of the interpretations placed by the courts on this section of the Clayton Act, the restrictions as contained therein have become more or less valueless to labor, and this section is intended by more specific language to overcome the qualifying effects of the decisions of the courts in this respect.

As an example of the manner in which the courts have interpreted this section of the Clayton Act which is responsible in part for this agitation for further legislation, we beg leave to cite the following cases.

In the case of *Duplex Printing Press Co.* v. *Deering* (254 U. S. 443), decided January 3, 1921, and being a 6 to 3 decision, the court held so far as pertinent to this particular discussion that this section of the Clayton Act provided a restriction upon the use of the injunctions in favor only of the immediate disputants and that other members of the union not standing in the proximate relation of employer and employee could be enjoined. Of course, it is fundamental that a strike is generally an idle gesture if confined only to the immediate disputants. This is intended to be remedied by the later provision in this act defining the meaning of the term, "person participating in a labor dispute," as to whom, as in the bill defined, the courts are deprived of jurisdiction to issue injunctions in the specified instances set forth in this section.

In the case of the *American Steel Foundries Co.* v. *Tri-City Central Trades Council, supra,* there was a strike, and, of course, a picket line. There was practically no fraud or violence but the persistent giving of publicity to the facts involved in the dispute and the persistent advising of other persons without fraud or violence not to work for the employer. It was thought by the labor union that section 20 prohibited an injunction against such acts, but the Supreme Court held that such acts could be enjoined, and, therefore, the legislation proposed specifically restricts the courts in this respect unless the acts are accompanied by fraud or violence.

Section 5: This section provides that no United States court shall have jurisdiction to issue an injunction upon the ground that the persons participating in a labor dispute are engaging in an unlawful combination because of the doing in concert of the acts enumerated in section 4.

This section is included principally because many of the objectionable injunctions have been issued under the provisions of the anti-trust laws, a necessary prerequisite for invoking the jurisdiction of which is a finding of the existence of a conspiracy or combination and without which no injunction could have been issued. For example, in the case of *Bedford Cut Stone Co.* v. *Journeymen Stone Cutters' Association* (274 U. S. 37), a 7 to 2 decision, where there was simply a rule by the association forbidding the members from working on the "unfair" stone of the complainant, the Supreme Court held that while it was lawful for members independently to refuse to work, when they refused in concert, it became a combination, and when this unreasonably interfered with interstate commerce, it could be enjoined under the antitrust laws, resulting in the members being enjoined from refusing to work.

Section 6: Section 6 provides that no employee of any organization and no organization participating in a labor dispute shall be held liable for the unlawful acts of individual members, except upon clear proof of actual authorization of such acts. This section speaks for itself and is desirable because both individuals and associations have been held liable for unlawful acts of overzealous members which acts were neither authorized nor ratified by the officer or association and were entirely without the scope of any authority committed by the officer or association of the offending member.

This provision does not affect the general law of agency, and it is necessary, under the circumstances, that the courts should know that Congress expects them not to hold officers or associations liable for the unlawful acts of a member without clear proof of actual participation in, or authorization of, any unlawful acts by the officer or association.

Section 7. This section is largely procedural and restrictive in character. The fairness of this section can not reasonably be disputed. It simply provides that no court shall have jurisdiction to issue an injunction in cases growing out of a labor dispute except after hearing the testimony of witnesses in open court with an opportunity for cross-examination and except after findings of fact by the court that unlawful acts have been committed and will be continued unless restrained, that irreparable injury to the complainant's property will follow, that as to each item of relief granted greater injury will be inflicted upon complainant by the denial of relief than will be inflicted upon defendants by the granting of relief, that complainant has no adequate remedy at law, and that the public officers charged with the duty of protecting complainant's proprety are unable or unwilling to furnish adequate protection.

As will be noted, this is to prevent courts from issuing injunctions without making a finding of facts or where the unlawful acts are only threatened and where no substantial injury will follow, or where the injury always done by granting the relief is outweighed by the injury which would be inflicted by the denial of the relief, or where the public officers fail in their duty. The last provision is considered desirable, because it often happens that complainants rush into a Federal court and obtain an injunction the enforcement of which requires the court to consider and punish acts which are and ought to be, under our system of government, cognizable in the local tribunals. Our Federal courts already are congested with cases ordinarily cognizable in the local police courts, for example, the multitude of cases growing out of the prohibition act; and the granting of injunctions in many cases results in further congestion because the Federal courts are required to punish as contempts acts which are clearly local police-court matters.

The other provisions of this section hardly require any particular discussion, because they relate to the giving of notice, the length of time that a temporary restraining order shall be effective, the necessity for giving an undertaking with surety, the recompense for damages caused by the erroneous issuance of injunctions, and the like; all of which are generally considered necessary and reasonable when the extraordinary injunctive arm of the court is brought into play with the serious consequences of injury which the improvident issuance of an injunction frequently produces.

Section 8: This section prohibits any injunctive relief where the parties have failed to make every reasonable effort to settle, or have failed to comply with any obligation imposed by law, or have failed to invoke the aid of any available governmental machinery for mediation. There can be no reasonable objection to this section because it is universally believed that disputes should be settled without resort to courts wherever possible, and the settlement of disputes by conciliation and arbitration, instead of by strikes, has become the rule rather than the exception.

Section 9: This section provides for findings of fact by the court which must be filed in the record of the case prior to the issuance of any injunctive order, and also provides that every injunctive order growing out of a labor dispute shall include only a prohibition of such specific acts as are expressly complained of and expressly included in the findings of fact made and filed by the court. This section is designed to require the court to find as a fact the existence of the acts enjoined and to prevent the enjoining of acts which are not complained of—clearly a deterrent to prevent the very harsh inclusive injunctive orders which are sometimes encountered and which go, by the embracive character of the decree, beyond allegations of the complaint or the facts adduced. This is clearly a reasonable restriction and unobjectionable.

Section 10: Section 10 provides for a speedy appeal, which is highly desirable in view of the extremely important issues which disputes of this kind involve. This section also gives these cases precedence in the appellate courts, and contains a provision somewhat similar to the provision of the statute in relation to the orders of the Interstate Commerce Commission, wherein it is provided that such proceedings shall be given precedence over all cases pending therein and shall be in every way expedited. (Sec. 21; title 15, U. S. C.)

Section 11: Section 11 provides that in cases in which a person shall be charged with contempt for violating injunctive orders the accused shall enjoy the right to a speedy and public trial by a jury and also provides that this right shall not apply to contempts committed in the presence of the court or so near thereto as to interfere directly with the administration of justice, etc. That Congress has authority to provide for such a trial by jury has been upheld by the Supreme Court of the United States in the case of *Michaelson* v. *U. S. ex rel. Chicago, St. Paul, Milwaukee & Omaha Railway Co.* (266 U. S. 42), wherein the Supreme Court upheld a similar provision contained in section 21 of the Clayton Act.

Section 12: Section 12 provides that the defendant in any contempt proceeding may file with the court a demand for the retirement of the judge, if the contempt arises from an attack upon the conduct of said judge, and occurred other than in the presence of the court or so near thereto as to interfere directly with the administration of justice, and that upon filing of any such demand the judge is compelled to proceed no further. This is desirable because in some instances the presiding judges have had such pronounced views in labor disputes as to make impossible a fair and impartial hearing.

Section 13: Section 13 contains definitions which speak for themselves. It is hardly necessary to discuss them other than to say that these definitions include, as hereinabove stated, a definition of a person participating in a labor dispute which is broad enough to include others than the immediate disputants and thereby corrects the law as announced in the case of *Duplex Printing Press Co.* v. *Deering, supra,* wherein the Supreme Court reversed the circuit court of appeals and held that the inhibition of section 20 of the Clayton Act only related to those occupying the position of employer or employee and no others. The Supreme Court held to the same effect in the case of the *American Steel Foundries Co.* v. *Tri-City Central Trades Council, supra.*

The definitions also, as above stated, limit the act to courts of the United States whose jurisdiction has been conferred or limited by act of Congress; that is to say, the inferior Federal courts.

Section 14: Section 14 is the usual provision to the effect that if any provision is held to be unconstitutional the remaining provisions shall not be affected thereby.

Section 15: Section 15 is the usual provision repealing acts in conflict with the provisions of this act.

STATES HAVING ENACTED ANTI-INJUNCTION LEGISLATION

In the following States legislation has been enacted governing the so-called "anti-injunction laws": Illinois, Kansas, Minnesota, Montana, New Jersey, North Dakota, Oregon, Pennsylvania, Utah, Washington, and Wisconsin.

In four of the States (Kansas, Minnesota, Pennsylvania, and Wisconsin) the law specifically provides that no injunction shall be issued without previous notice and an opportunity to be heard in open court. The State of Wisconsin, by chapter 376 of the acts of 1931, enacted a law defining the public policy of the State relative to collective bargaining. This act creates a new section relating to litigation growing out of the labor disputes and limiting the jurisdiction of courts sitting in equity. Section 268.23 concerns the conditions of issuance of injunctions and restraining orders. This section provides that no court shall have jurisdiction to issue an injunction in any case involving a labor dispute except after the testimony of witnesses in open court and with an opportunity for cross-examination.

On October 15, 1914, the Congress of the United States enacted the Clayton Act. Prior to the enactment of this law, several States had already enacted provisions similar to those contained in section 20 of the Clayton Act. The following States have similar provisions: North Dakota, Oregon, Utah, Washington, and Wisconsin.

In addition to the above States which have enacted laws restricting the use of injunctions, three other States (Illinois, Montana, and New Jersey) have enacted laws, although similar in many respects to the Clayton Act, which differ in the exact wording of the law. (Credit for the research of State statutes on the subject is due the Bureau of Labor Statistics of the United States Department of Labor.)

In conclusion, it is repeated that the proposed bill is designed primarily as a practical means of remedying existing evils, and limitations are imposed upon the courts in that class of cases wherein these evils have grown up and become intolerable. This is a reasonable exercise of legislative power, and in order that the limitation may not be whittled away by refined definitions of what persons are to be regarded as legitimately involved in labor disputes, the bill undertakes specifically to designate those persons who are entitled to invoke the protections of the procedure required.

Report of the House Committee of Conference
March 16, 1932

HATTON SUMNERS [DEM., TEX.] submitted the Report.

The committee of conference on the disagreeing votes of the two Houses on the amendment of the Senate to the bill (H. R. 5315) to amend the Judicial Code and to define and limit the jurisdiction of courts sitting in equity, and for other purposes, having met, after full and free conference have agreed to recommend and do recommend to their respective Houses, as follows:

That the House recede from its disagreement to the amendment of the Senate and agree to the same with an amendment, as follows: . . .

The managers on the part of the House at the conference on the disagreeing votes of the two Houses on the bill (H. R. 5315) to amend the Judicial Code and to define and limit the jurisdiction of courts sitting in equity, and for other purposes, submit the following statement in explanation of the effect of the action agreed upon by the conferees and recommended in the accompanying conference report:

Section 2 of the Senate amendment contains, in the statement of the policy of the legislation, the phrase "though he (the individual unorganized worker) should be free to decline to associate with his fellows." The phase is not employed in the corresponding provision in the House bill. The conference agreement adopts the Senate provision.

Section 3 of the House bill and of the Senate amendment are identical except for minor differences in punctuation. The conference agreement adopts the Senate amendment with minor changes in punctuation.

There are minor differences in the punctuation of section 4 (c) of the House bill and the Senate amendment. The conference agreement adopts the Senate provision.

Section 6 of the Senate amendment provides that no court of the United States shall have jurisdiction upon the hearing of an application for temporary restraining order or an interlocutory injunction to grant a mandatory injunction compelling the performance of an act in any case involving or growing out of any labor dispute as defined in the act. There is no corresponding provision in the House bill. The conference agreement omits the Senate provision.

Section 6 of the House bill provides that no officer or member of any association or organization, participating or interested in a labor dispute, shall be held responsible or liable in any United States court for the unlawful acts of individual officers, members, or agents except upon clear proof of actual participation in or authorization of, such acts, or of ratification, with actual knowledge, of such acts. The section further provides that the liability of any such association or organization for unlawful acts of its members shall be similarly limited. Under the corresponding provision of the Senate amendment (section 7), no officer or member of any association or organization, participating or interested in a labor dispute, or interested in a labor dispute, is to be held responsible or liable in a United States court for the unlawful acts of individual officers, members, or agents, except upon clear proof of actual participation in or authorization of, such acts, or of ratification of such acts after actual knowledge. The conference agreement adopts the Senate provision.

Section 7 (a) of the House bill, which deals with findings of fact necessary to be made by the court before a temporary or permanent injunction may be issued, prescribes as one of the classes of findings that unlawful acts have been threatened or committed and will be continued. The paragraph further provides that no injunction or restraining order shall be issued except against the person or persons, association, or organization making the threat or committing the unlawful act or authorizing or ratifying it after actual knowledge thereof.

The corresponding provision of the Senate amendment (section 8 (a)) requires a finding that unlawful acts have been threatened or committed and will be committed or continued unless restrained, and omits the provision including associations and organizations within the exception.

The conference agreement requires a finding that unlawful acts have been threatened and will be committed unless restrained or have been committed and will be continued unless restrained, and includes associations and organizations as does the House bill.

Under the House bill (second subdivision of sec. 7) notice of hearing must be given to the chief of those public officials of the county and city within which the unlawful acts have been threatened or committed. Under the corresponding provision of the Senate amendment (second subdivision of sec. 8) notice of hearing must be given to the chief of those public officers of the county and city within which the unlawful acts have been threatened or committed charged with the duty to protect the complainant's property. The conference agreement adopts the Senate provision except that "officials" is substituted for "officers."

The second subdivision of section 7 of the House bill expressly gives the court the power to fix the amount of the security in the undertaking filed by the complainant. There is no corresponding provision in the Senate amendment. The conference agreement adopts the provision of the House bill.

The third subdivision of section 7 of the House bill provides that the undertaking given by the complainant shall signify an agreement upon which a decree may be rendered upon a hearing to assess damages of which hearing the complainant and surety shall have reasonable notice. The corresponding provision of the Senate amendment (third subdivision of sec. 8) contains no such provision with respect to hearing and notice. The conference agreement adopts the House provision.

The House bill (sec. 10) provides that upon the request of any party to the proceedings the court shall forthwith certify the entire record of the case, including a transcript of the evidence taken, to the circuit court of appeals for its review. The Senate amendment (sec. 11) provides that upon the request of any party to the proceedings and on his filing the usual bond for costs, the court shall forthwith certify as in ordinary cases the record of the case to the circuit court of appeals for its review. The conference agreement adopts the provisions of the Senate amendment.

The House bill (sec. 11) provides that in cases arising under sections 3, 4, 5, 6, and 7 of this amendatory act in which a person is charged with criminal contempt of a court of the United States, the accused should enjoy a speedy public trial by jury. The corresponding provision of the Senate amendment (sec. 12) is broader in that it relates to all cases in which a person is charged with contempt in a court of the United States. The conference agreement applies only to cases arising under the act under consideration in which a person is charged with contempt in a court of the United States.

Section 12 of the House bill provides that the defendant in any proceeding for contempt of court may file a demand for the retirement of the judge sitting in the proceeding if the contempt arises from an attack upon the character or conduct of such judge and if the attack occurred otherwise than in open court. The corresponding provision of the Senate amendment (sec. 13) permits such demand if the contempt occurred elsewhere than in the presence of the court or so near thereto as to interfere directly with the administration of justice. The conference agreement retains the Senate provision except that "attack" is substituted for "contempt."

The separability clause of the Senate amendment (sec. 15) is broader than the corresponding provision of the House bill (sec. 14) in that separability with regard to persons and circumstances is included. The conference agreement adopts the Senate provision.

Hatton W. Sumners,
A. J. Montague,
L. C. Dyer,
Managers on the part of the House.

THE DEBATE

Senate—72nd Congress, 1st Session
February 23, 1932

GEORGE NORRIS [R., NEB.]. Mr. President, it is not my intention to-day to go into an exhaustive consideration of the bill. At a later time, probably several times while the bill is before the Senate and under discussion, I shall go into more detail. At the present time I desire only to review as briefly as I can some of the leading questions that are involved in the proposed legislation. I therefore ask that I be allowed to proceed without interruption. At the conclusion of my analysis and likewise during the remainder of the debate on the measure, I shall be very glad indeed to yield at any time and to answer any questions that I am able to answer.

Mr. President, the writ of injunction is always a harsh remedy. It is one which should never be resorted to except in cases where irreparable injury will result unless a restraining hand is put forth to prevent it. It should never be issued except in cases where the law will afford no relief. It is a remedy having application only to property rights. Whenever it is used to deny the fundamental rights and privileges of free citizens, it becomes tyrannous and oppressive.

The cruelty of the injunction has been especially apparent in disputes between labor and capital, and it has often occurred in such cases that the real object of the injunction is not to protect property but to restrain the constitutional rights of individuals and thus to interfere with human liberty. Its use in labor disputes has been a gradual growth, coincident with the gradual growth of immense combinations of wealth. As monopoly has increased its hold upon great business undertakings and operations, and as combinations of great wealth have been formed for the financial enrichment of those engaged in the monopoly, the power thus attained for its own enrichment has often been used to take away the freedom of laboring men who are compelled to toil for the support of themselves and those dependent upon them.

The ordinary laboring man is powerless to cope with such combinations, and he must accept employment upon the terms which monopoly offers or become a subject of charity and see his family and those immediately dependent upon him deprived of the ordinary comforts of life.

To prevent this result laboring men have organized into associations and unions in order that they may present a united front to the demands of combined wealth and great aggregations of capital. His right to do this has become universally recognized, but, by means of harsh, cruel, and misused injunctive process, monopoly, through the assistance of our courts, has interfered by means of injunctions, which, in their effect, have often

207

taken away the real right of labor to have a voice in the wage it shall receive, and the effect has often been involuntary servitude on the part of those who must toil in order that they and their families may live. Such conditions bring about involuntary servitude—a species of economic slavery—which can not permanently exist in a free country; and such economic slavery is as cruel, as merciless, and as effective as slavery based upon the color of the human skin. The man who, by force of economic conditions is compelled to toil against his wish and under conditions depriving him of his freedom, is a slave even though his skin may be white.

The tyranny of some of these injunctions, as I shall hereafter point out, has taken away the freedom and the liberty of many of our citizens as completely and as tyrannically as ever occurred in days when slavery was recognized by the Constitution.

The hardship and the injustice brought about by the issuing of injunctions by Federal judges in labor disputes have been the subject of discussion for a number of years. The evils arising from such injunctions have been universally recognized. A public sentiment for relief through these years has gradually grown until the universal opinion of the patriotic people has crystallized into a demand for legislative relief.

Both of the great political parties in their last national conventions took a definite stand in favor of the passage of legislation by Congress which would give relief to the evils and the wrongs brought about by the issuing of injunctions in labor disputes. The Republican National Convention at Kansas City adopted a plank on the subject as follows:

The party favors freedom in wage contracts, the right of collective bargaining by free and responsible agents of their own choosing, which develops and maintains that purposeful cooperation which gains its chief incentive through voluntary agreement.

We believe that injunctions in labor disputes have in some instances been abused and have given rise to a serious question for legislation.

The Democratic National Convention, a short time thereafter, at Houston, Tex., spoke as follows:

(a) We favor the principle of collective bargaining and the democratic principle that organized labor should choose its own representatives without coercion or interference.

(b) Labor is not a commodity. Human rights must be safeguarded. Labor should be exempt from the operation of antitrust laws.

(c) We recognize that legislative and other investigations have shown the existence of grave abuse in the issuance of injunctions in labor disputes. No injunctions should be granted in labor disputes except upon proof of threatened irreparable injury and after notice and hearing, and the injunction should be confined to those acts which do directly threaten irreparable injury. The expressed purpose of representatives of capital, labor, and the bar to devise a plan for the elimination of the present evils with respect to injunctions must be supported and legislation designed to accomplish these ends formulated and passed.

It therefore becomes a nonpartisan question, or rather a party question agreed to by both of the dominant political parties.

Must we assume that these great political parties are not in earnest? Were they attempting to deceive the people of the United States when they proclaimed these two planks upon this important question? And are they now, on the eve of another great national campaign, admitting that they were not sincere and were only trying to get votes at the general election?

I do not want to indulge in any such assumptions. I would rather go on the theory that both of these great political parties were honestly laying down propositions in which they believed, and which, if granted the power by the people, they would enact into law.

We ought to remember, also, that this is the only anti-injunction bill which has been proposed. If it is claimed that this bill is not correct and that those in power want to redeem the promise thus publicly made, then why are we not presented with some substitute? Why have we not been presented long before this with legislation on the subject?

I can not close my eyes to the fact that the party which won that election and which, until just a few months ago, was in complete control of both branches of the National Legislature and the executive departments has made no effort so far as I know to redeem this platform pledge.

This proposed legislation has not had the assistance of the present administration; but, on the other hand, it is fair to say that in general the opposition to this legislation has come from those who are recognized as being closely allied with the present administration.

This bill starts out by declaring a public policy of the United States in relation to labor disputes. This is the first time in the history of the United States that any attempt has been made to declare, through an act of Congress, the public policy of the United States in relation to the issuing of injunctions in labor controversies. The object of setting up such a policy is to assist the courts in the proper interpretation of the proposed legislation. Such a legislative procedure, so far as labor disputes are concerned, will be of great assistance whenever the proposed law or any part of it comes up for review and consideration by a court and will relieve the question of many of the difficulties which have heretofore existed when a court has been called upon to interpret the law. It will, I am sure, go far toward brushing aside any question of the constitutionality of the act or any part of it.

Section 1 of the bill under consideration declares:

That no court of the United States, as herein defined, shall have jurisdiction to issue any restraining order or temporary or permanent injunction in a case involving or growing out of a labor dispute, except in strict conformity with the provisions of this act, nor shall any such restraining order or temporary or permanent injunction be issued contrary to the public policy declared in this act.

This section is really a preamble to the public policy declared in section 2, which reads as follows:

In the interpretation of this act and in determining the jurisdiction and authority of the courts of the United States, as such jurisdiction and authority are herein defined and limited, the public policy of the United States is hereby declared as follows:

"Whereas under prevailing economic conditions, developed with the aid of governmental authority for owners of property to organize in the corporate and other forms of ownership association, the individual unorganized worker is commonly helpless to exercise actual liberty of contract and to protect his freedom of labor, and thereby to obtain acceptable terms and conditions of employment, wherefore, though he should be free to decline to associate with his fellows, it is necessary that he have full freedom of association, self-organization, and designation of representatives of his own choosing, to negotiate the terms and conditions of his employment, and that he shall be free from the interference, restraint, or coercion of employers of labor, or their agents in the designation of such representatives or in self-organization or in other concerted activities for the purpose of collective bargaining or other mutual aid or protection; therefore the following definitions of, and limitations upon, the jurisdiction and authority of the courts of the United States are hereby enacted."

If the act or any part of it should be involved in any litigation where an injunction was issued or asked for, the judge before whom such action was pending would be required to give full force and effect to the public policy thus declared by the act; and, having in mind the public policy thus declared, he would be able to so construe the various provisions of the act as to give full effect and validity to the public policy thus declared.

There is no doubt whatever but that the Congress has the constitutional right to declare the public policy of the United States upon any question upon which the Congress has the right to legislate; and when such policy is declared, it becomes the duty of all the courts to give effect to such policy and to carry it out in the enforcement of any law where such public policy has application.

Where Congress has not declared a public policy, it is within the province of the court to decide what the public policy is; but when such public policy has been declared by Congress, it is the duty of the court to follow such policy and to decide litigated questions related thereto in accordance with the policy thus declared by Congress. This doctrine has been repeatedly upheld by both State and Federal courts. In the case of *People* v. *City of Chicago* (321 Ill. 466–475) the Supreme Court of Illinois said:

The public policy of a State is to be found embodied in its constitution, its statutes, and, when these are silent on the subject, in the decisions of its courts. The public policy of the State, when not fixed by the constitution, is not unalterable, but varies upon any given question with changing legislation thereon, and any action which, in the absence of legislation thereon, by the decisions of the courts has been held contrary to the public policy of the State, is no longer contrary to such public policy when such action is expressly authorized by legislative enactment.

Another case decided by the Supreme Court of the State of Illinois directly on the point was the case of *Union Trust & Savings Bank* v. *Telephone Co.* (253 Ill. 202). In that case the court said:

While no statute has been enacted declaring such exclusive contracts criminal or giving a right of action to persons prejudiced by them, the courts have declared the public policy of the State, in accordance with the common law, to be opposed to such contracts which tend to put the power to render public service in the hands of one corporation and to take it away from all others. The legislature has the power to change this policy. It is a legislative question whether the public interest will be promoted by monopolistic rather than competitive service.

The Supreme Court of the United States has several times upheld this doctrine. In the case of *McCulloch* v. *Maryland* (4 Wheat. 316, 423), the court, speaking through Chief Justice Marshall, said:

Where the law is . . . calculated to affect any of the objects intrusted to the Government, to undertake here to inquire into the degree of its necessity would be to pass the line which circumscribes the judicial department and to tread on legislative ground.

Again, in the case of *Michaelson* v. *United States* (266 U. S. 42, 68), the Supreme Court expressly upheld the right of Congress to declare the public policy of the United States, in the following declaration:

The words of the act are plain and in terms inclusive of all classes of employment, and we find nothing in them which requires a resort to judicial construction. The reasoning of the court below really does not present a question of statutory construction but rather an argument justifying the supposititious exemption on the ground of necessity or of policy—

Note the words, "or of policy"—

a matter addressed to the legislative and not the judicial authority.

In the passage of the existing railway labor act Congress has already established a precedent of proclaiming a public policy by legislative enactment. In the third paragraph of section 2 of that act it is provided:

Representatives, for the purposes of this act, shall be designated by the respective parties in such manner as may be provided in their corporate organization or unincorporated association, or by other means of collective action, without interference, influence, or coercion exercised by either party over the self-organization or designation of representatives by the other. (Par. 3, sec. 152, title 45, U.S.C.A., 1929 sup.)

In effect, this declaration of public policy in regard to railway employees is the same as the declaration of public policy in the present bill in regard to all employees. The constitutionality of the railway labor act has been sustained by the Supreme Court in *Texas & New Orleans Railroad Co.* v.

Brotherhood of Railroad and Steamship Clerks, decided May 26, 1930 (281 U. S. 548). In that case the Supreme Court, through Chief Justice Hughes, declared:

Evidence in this case supports the conclusion of the courts below that the defendant railroad company and its officers were actually engaged in promoting the organization of an association of its clerical employees in the interest of the company and in opposition to the plaintiff labor organization, and that these activities constituted an actual interference with the liberty of the clerical employees in the selection of representatives for the purposes set forth in the railway labor act of May 20, 1926.

Further on the Chief Justice said:

The railway labor act of 1926, while elaborating a plan for amicable adjustments and voluntary arbitration of disputes between common carriers and their employees, imposed certain definite obligations enforceable by judicial proceedings, one of which is found in the provision of subdivision 3 of section 2, that "representatives, for the purposes of this act, shall be designated by the respective parties . . . without interference, influence, or coercion exercised by either party over the self-organization or designation of representatives by the other."

Further on in that case, on page 570, the Supreme Court said:

Congress was not required to ignore this right of the employees but could safeguard it and seek to make their appropriate collective action an instrument of peace rather than of strife. Such collective action would be a mockery if representation were made futile by interferences with freedom of choice. Thus the prohibition by Congress of interference with the selection of representatives for the purpose of negotiation and conference between employers and employees, instead of being an invasion of the constitutional right of either, was based on the recognition of the rights of both.

In the case of *Dayton-Goose Creek Railway* v. *United States* (263 U. S. 456), the opinion of the court shows that the act was interpreted and was sustained upon the grounds of a public policy declared by Congress. The court in that case said:

The new act seeks affirmatively to build up a system of railways prepared to handle promptly all the interstate traffic of the country. . . . To achieve this great purpose it puts the railroad systems of the country more completely than ever under the fostering guardianship and control of the commission.

Title IV of the transportation act, embracing paragraphs 418 and 422, is carefully framed to achieve its expressly declared objects.

As I have before stated, the public policy of the United States in labor disputes, having been thus declared by the Congress, acting under its constitutional right to make such a declaration, it will become the duty of the courts to construe the act and to enforce it with a view of giving effect to the carrrying out of the public policy thus declared.

In a great many of the injunctions which the courts have issued in labor disputes the basis for the injunction was a written contract of employment, signed by the employee when he accepted employment. This contract has become almost universally known as the "yellow-dog" contract. It requires the employee, as a condition of obtaining employment, to agree that he will not join a union while he is in the employment, or, that if he is then a member of a union, he will disassociate himself from it; that he recognizes the right of the employer to discharge him without notice; that he will not quit his employment without giving sufficient notice to his employer to enable him to hire some one to take his place. The employee in most of these contracts agrees in advance to accept such conditions of labor, hours of labor, and so forth, as may from time to time be decided upon by the employer. Not all of these contracts are the same. Other and similar conditions from those noted are sometimes added, but, in a general way, they all have the same effect. They take away from the laboring man the right to have anything to say about any of the conditions connected with his employment. The hours of labor, conditions under which the labor is to be performed, the right of the laborer to quit employment whenever he becomes dissatisfied, the amount of pay which he shall receive, the right of the employer to reduce the pay at any time without notice, and so forth—all these things are turned over entirely and solely to the corporation or individual owning or operating the business. The employee waives his right absolutely to free association and fair representation in connection with his hours of labor, and any other conditions of employment. In other words, he surrenders his actual liberty of contract and to a great extent enters into voluntary servitude.

I know it can be said, and always is said, that the man seeking work does not have to sign this contract; that he does not have to work under the conditions named in the contract, because he has the right to refuse to enter into any employment contrary to what he believes to be right.

But all this, as a practical proposition, is no defense whatever. If the man applying for labor refuses to sign this contract, he can go on to some other corporation doing the same kind of business and apply for a job. But when he does, he will be confronted with the same "yellow-dog" contract. As he goes from place to place in his attempt to get work in his chosen field, he will always be presented with the same conditions. For instance, if the man hunting a job is a coal miner, he presents himself at the office of the corporation, asks for a job, and he is at once presented with the "yellow-dog" contract and told to sign on the dotted line. If he declines to sign and goes to the next coal mine, he is presented with the same contract, and so on throughout the entire coal field.

The result is that by the combination of large corporations in a particular line of business, the laboring man must accept unconditionally the terms laid down by the employer. He is absolutely helpless under such contracts. His family can not have food to eat or clothes to wear unless he gets a job. If he gets a job, he must surrender his liberty. He must, for the time being, become a slave. He can not associate with his fellows. In connection with his fellows, he can not present a grievance to the employer. He has agreed to make no such demand. If conditions become unbearable, his only remedy is to go alone and face the big combination of perhaps millions of wealth. He must singly present any grievance he has. He must abide by the decision which is thus given him. He has no appeal. He has no opportunity to join with his fellows and make his demands effective. In effect, if he must live and support his family and clothe his children, he must surrender his liberty.

These conditions have grown up because of the combinations of great aggregations of wealth. The poor man, standing alone, is absolutely helpless. This bill declares that such contracts are—

. . . contrary to the public policy of the United States, shall not be enforceable and shall not afford any basis for the granting of legal or equitable relief by any court of the United States.

Many of the injunctions which have been issued in the past in labor disputes have been based wholly, or in a large part, upon such contracts, and upon the assumption that they are valid.

As I have briefly outlined, this bill sets up a public policy. One of the objects of this proposed legislation is to outlaw this unconscionable and indefensible contract; and some action by Congress in this respect is absolutely necessary, because, as I have said, many labor injunctions have been sustained on the theory that such contracts are legal.

In my own humble judgment, it does not seem to me that any legislation ought to be necessary. It seems clear to me that as a matter of common law, without any statute being necessary, such contracts instead of being enforced ought to have been declared null and void by our courts. Such a contract, in my judgment, should be held void—

1. As being contrary to public policy under the common law. If these contracts are sustained, then no labor organization can exist, and laboring men will be compelled to submit unconditionally to any terms laid down by the employer. If men must agree in advance to surrender any liberty of contract in order to obtain employment, they are under coercion of necessity forced into working under conditions of involuntary servitude.

2. These contracts should have been held void because they are entered into without consideration. The employer, on the one hand, has his work which he wants done. The laborer, on the other hand, as a consideration for his part of the contract, undertakes to perform the work. The employer gives up none of his freedom and action, and furnishes no con-

sideration for the promise of the employee that he will surrender his ordinary rights of "liberty of contract," which are inherent in every free citizen.

3. Such contracts should have been held void because they are signed under duress and coercion. The employee, as I have said, is forced to accept all of the burdensome and unreasonable and sometimes inhuman conditions imposed upon him in order to support himself and family. Nevertheless, since the courts have sometimes enforced those contracts and issued unmerciful injunctions on the theory of the legality of such contracts, it is necessary that Congress take some action; and this bill has for one of its main objects the outlawing of and the doing away with such contracts.

It must be remembered that up to this time we have had no statute declaring any public policy on the subject, and have had no statute which attempts to outlaw such contracts as these. There is no doubt in my mind but that courts ought to and will follow the declaration of Congress and absolutely refuse to enforce any such contract if this bill becomes a law.

In the case of *Bailey* v. *Alabama* (219 U. S. 219) the Supreme Court said that one of the objects of the thirteenth amendment was—

. . . to make labor free by prohibiting that control by which the personal service of one man is disposed of or coerced for another's benefit, which is the essence of involuntary servitude.

In the same case the court said:

There is no more important concern than to safeguard the freedom of labor upon which alone can enduring prosperity be based.

This case was decided by a divided court, two Justices dissenting. Those opposing this legislation dwell with a great deal of assurance upon the dissenting opinion in that case, written by Justice Holmes. But a careful reading of Justice Holmes's dissenting opinion will convince any fairminded man that there will be no conflict between the dissenting opinion of Justice Holmes and this bill now before the Senate. The Bailey case was based upon an Alabama statute, and Justice Holmes in his dissenting opinion assumed that the contract under this statute was a legal one because it was made in accordance with the statute which he believed to be constitutional, and that, therefore, a man could be legally punished for obtaining money by making such a contract with the fraudulent intention of breaking it. He met the argument that the terms of such contract would result in peonage with the pertinent comment: "If the contract is one that ought not to be made, prohibit it." In other words, a fair conclusion from the dissenting opinion of Justice Holmes will convince anyone that the legislative power had the right to prohibit the very contract in dispute.

That is what we are trying to do in this bill—to declare by statute a public policy of the United States; that the "yellow-dog" contract is in conflict with such public policy and that, therefore, it shall not be enforced in any Federal court in the United States.

No attempt will be made to defend the "yellow-dog" contract. Its inhumanity will be admitted by those who oppose this bill. But, they will say, it is a wrong which can not be remedied under our Constitution, and therefore that such contracts must be upheld by the courts, with all their evil consequences.

The evils which this bill attempts to remedy, especially in respect to the "yellow-dog" contracts, are admitted. They will not be denied in the course of this debate and most of those who oppose the bill will frankly admit not only that the "yellow-dog" contracts which this bill outlaws are in existence but that some method of relief in behalf of suffering humanity ought to be devised. Yet it will be claimed that the bill under consideration is unconstitutional for the very reason that it does outlaw these inhuman and barbarous contracts.

It will be said, also, that during the last three or four years, in which the remedies proposed in this bill have been under consideration and discussion, those who have continually fought the legislation and are still opposing it have so far made no attempt themselves to report any bill or to suggest any remedy for the evil which they admit exists.

By the abolition of these unconscionable contracts this bill sets on the hilltop a beacon of human liberty. It gives to those who toil, to those who are poor, to those who by the sweat of their faces contribute to the happiness of humble homes the enjoyment of that freedom and that liberty which is necessary in every free country for all of its citizens and not by one class of its people. It gives liberty to the downtrodden and the poor, and in this respect puts them on an equality with those who live in luxury and plenty.

Human liberty after all is just as precious to the man who toils in the darkness of the bottomless mine as it is to the man who controls a nation or who owns unlimited wealth. It gives hope to the little children of those who have no hope if liberty is blotted out. It brings joy and peace to the humble fireside in the weather-beaten cottage. It fills the breast with pride and with love of country and of all mankind. Let me quote one of the most beautiful tributes which has ever been paid to human liberty by one of the world's great writers:

We speak of liberty as one thing and of virtue, wealth, knowledge, invention, national strength, and national independence as other things. But of all these liberty is the source, the mother, the necessary condition. She is to virtue what light is to color, to wealth what sunshine is to grain, to knowledge what eyes are to sight. She is a genius of invention, the brawn of national strength, the spirit of national independence. Where liberty rises there virtue grows, wealth increases, knowledge expands, invention multiplies human powers, and in strength and spirit the freer nation rises among her neighbors as Saul amid his brethren—taller and fairer. Where liberty sinks there virtue fades, wealth diminishes, knowledge is forgotten, invention ceases, and empires once mighty in arms and arts become a helpless prey to freer barbarians. . . .

Liberty came to a race of slaves crouching under Egyptian whips and led them forth from the house of bondage. She hardened them in the desert and made of them a race of conquerors. The free spirit of the Mosaic law took their thinkers up to heights where they beheld the unity of God and inspired their poets with strains that yet phrase the highest exaltations of thought. Liberty dawned on the Phœnician coast and ships passed the Pillars of Hercules to plow the unknown sea. She shed a partial light on Greece and marble grew to shapes of ideal beauty, words became the instruments of subtlest thought, and against the scanty militia of free cities the countless hosts of the great king broke like surges against a rock. She cast her beam on the 4-acre farms of Italian husbandmen, and born of her strength, a power come forth that conquered the world. . . . Out of the night that followed her eclipse her slanting rays fell again on free cities and a lost learning revived, modern civilization began, a new world was unveiled; and as liberty grew, so grew art, wealth, power, knowledge and refinement. In the history of every nation we may read the same truth. It was the strength born of Magna Carta that won Crecy and Agincourt. It was the revival of liberty from the despotism of the Tudors that glorified the Elizabethan age. It was the spirit that brought a crowned tyrant to the block that planted here the seed of a mighty tree. It was the energy of ancient freedom that the moment it had gained unity made Spain the mightiest power of the world, only to fall to the lowest depth of weakness when tyranny succeeded liberty. . . .

Shall we not trust her?

In our time, as in times before, creep on the insidious forces that producing inequality destroy liberty. On the horizon the clouds begin to lower. Liberty calls to us again. We must follow her further; we must trust her fully. Either we must wholly accept her or she will not stay. It is not enough that men should vote; it is not enough that they should be theoretically equal before the law. They must have liberty to avail themselves of the opportunities and means of life; they must stand on equal terms with reference to the bounty of nature. Either this or liberty withdraws her light; either this or darkness comes on and the very forces that progress has evolved turn to powers that work destruction. This is the universal law. This is the lesson of the centuries. Unless its foundations be laid in justice the social structure can not stand.

One of the indefensible things contained in a great many of the labor injunctions issued by Federal judges is the enjoining of the defendants from exercising their legal right under State law, given them by a State statute.

Labor unions usually provide for a fund out of which benefits are paid to their members when they are out of employment, including the time when they are out of employment on account of a strike. The members of the union who are out of employment are entitled, under the rules of their organization, to these benefits. They have themselves contributed to this fund. They have a direct interest in it. The fund is accumulated by dues paid by the members and the object of it is to assist the members when they are out of employment in the support of themselves and their families. Some of these injunctions issued by Federal judges enjoin the unions from paying their members who are on strike any of the benefits to which they are entitled from these funds accumulated by their own contributions. In such cases the money in this fund is in the possession of the proper officers. Under the rules and regulations of the organization it is the duty of these officers to pay these benefits to their fellows who are out of work. They are willing and anxious to perform their duty, but the strong arm of a Federal injunction prevents them from doing this act, from complying with their agreement, from performing their duties as officers of the union.

These injunctions often go still farther. Not only do they prohibit the workmen from thus contributing to their fellows but the injunction prohibits anyone, whether he is a member of the union or not, from giving any assistance or contributing any funds or other money to men who are on a strike.

But many of these injunctions go still farther. It is a common thing in the operation of coal mines for laborers to live in houses owned by the corporation owning or operating the mines. These houses—in many cases it would be more proper to term them shacks—are leased to the laboring man under contract by which the laborer agrees to pay a certain amount monthly or otherwise as a rental for the occupation, and providing also for the surrender of the premises under conditions named in the contract of lease. If a dispute arises between the employer and the employee as to whether or not the contract has been violated and as to whether the owner has a right to dispossess the employee, the question at once becomes one of forcible entry and detainer under the laws of the State where the property is located. These laws invariably provide for the trial of forcible entry and detainer cases before a justice of the peace. Upon the trial before the justice either side is given the right to appeal to a higher court. If the judgment of the justice of the peace is against the laboring man, the tenant, if he desires to appeal his case, has to give bond, not only for the costs in the case, as is usual in all cases, but also for the payment of a reasonable rental in case the decision of the higher court is against him. This is a right given him under the State law. It is a right that is general and applies to all cases between landlord and tenant. If the tenant is wrongfully holding possession of the premises, no loss can come to the landlord because, before he can appeal he must put up a bond to pay both costs and rental.

Many of these injunctions issued in Federal courts by Federal judges enjoin the tenant from taking the appeal given to him under a State law. Not only is the defendant enjoined but every and all persons are enjoined from going on the bond or from giving any advice or assistance of any kind to the laboring man who is a defendant in such forcible entry and detainer cases. All persons, whether they belong to the union or not, or whether they are defendants in the case or not, are enjoined from paying any money in the way of expenses in behalf of the defendant in such a case. The injunction sometimes goes far enough to prevent anyone from acting as attorney or from giving any legal advice to an employee whom the company is trying to eject from one of these houses. And very often all persons are enjoined from furnishing any food or fuel or any other necessity of life to any one of these defendants who happens to be living in one of these houses and who is out on a strike. Such injunctions have often resulted in the greatest kind of hardship and misery suffered by these coal miners. Under these unconscionable orders relief of any kind can not be given. Sickness, hunger, and cold can not be relieved. I know of no other instances in jurisprudence where such hardships have been upheld and where such summary methods of depriving persons of their "day in court" have been held to be "due process of law." By no conceivable stretch of the imagination can such instances of judicial cruelty be condoned or defended.

The bill under consideration takes away from the Federal courts the power to issue such injunctions and in the same section (sec. 4) the bill prohibits the issuing of injunctions which restrain employees from—

(f) Assembling peaceably to act or to organize to act in promotion of their interests in a labor dispute.

It prohibits the issuing of injunctions restraining anyone from inducing, assisting, counseling, or advising, without fraud or violence, any of these things, regardless of whether or not the employee may have signed a "yellow-dog" contract.

Injunctions have been issued which restrain employees engaged in a strike from giving publicity to the existence of or the facts involved in any labor dispute. In these cases the strikers are prohibited from telling anyone that a strike is in existence or from telling anyone that the company requires its men to sign a "yellow-dog" contract.

One of the most recent injunctions in a labor dispute was issued in the District Court of the United States for the Northern District of Iowa. This injunction was issued on the 29th day of March, 1930. When I was furnished a copy of this injunction I did not believe that it was true. I could not believe that any judge would issue such a cruel document. I thought I was being imposed upon and I wrote a letter to the clerk of the court and asked him to certify to me a correct copy of the injunction which had been issued. I found that I had been correctly informed and that the first copy which had been furnished me was a true copy of the official document. This injunction enjoined the defendants from doing many things. Among others, it enjoined them from—

. . . printing, publishing, issuing, circulating, and distributing, or otherwise communicating, directly or indirectly, in writing or verbally, to any person, association of persons, or corporation, any statement or notice of any kind or character whatsoever, stating or representing:

(1) That there is a strike at the mill or plant of complainant at Fort Dodge, Iowa; or that the strike of 1921 is still in existence; or that there is a controversy over wages or conditions of employment between complainant and its employees; or any false statement with reference to conditions of employment at complainant's plant.

Let me invite your attention to that word "false," because some one will say the injunction is against false statements of this kind. Not at all. The statement may be absolutely true. The only case where the word "false" applies is "any false statement with reference to conditions of employment at complainant's plant."

I continue reading from the injunction:

(2) That complainant is unfair to organized union labor, or that its products are or were unfair to organized labor, or are on an unfair list.
(3) That complainant forces or requires its employees to sign or subscribe to the so-called "yellow-dog" contract.

It will be observed that in this case the defendants were not allowed to tell anyone a strike was in progress. When the laboring man went home at night to his family, if he told his wife that a strike was on, he would be liable for arrest for contempt of court and to be sent to jail as a punishment. These men were not allowed to give any publicity in any way to the fact that a strike existed; and, although they might know of their own personal knowledge that employees were required to sign the "yellow-dog" contract, yet they would not dare tell even members of their own families of this fact. Their mouths were absolutely closed, and free speech was absolutely forbidden. They could not be allowed in such a case to seek advice from an attorney. The son would not be allowed to consult with his father on the subject. When the laboring man did not go to his work in the morning he would not even be allowed to tell his own wife why.

Under the laws of the State it would be perfectly proper and a defendant would have a perfect right to go out on the street and tell everyone he met that a strike was in progress; or that he, before he could get a job, was compelled to sign the "yellow-dog" contract. He would have a perfect right, under the State law, to consult an attorney and to lay all the facts before him, and to ascertain from a legal standpoint what his rights were, but, under this cruel injunction order, all those rights were swept away. State laws were all nullified and the fundamental right of human liberty and freedom was absolutely and completely denied.

And suppose one of these defendants disobeyed this injunction? He would not be violating any State law! He would be doing only what every human being has a right to do! No statute of any State or the Federal Government would preclude him from giving full publicity to all of the facts. But, under this judge-made law, a new statute was put in force—not by the legislature of the State, not by anyone having authority to enact a statute, but by the judge sitting on the Federal bench.

And let us suppose, too, that for a violation of this order, one of the defendants was arrested. Where would he be tried? Would it be in the courts of the State where the offense is alleged to have been committed? No. It would be before the same judge who made the law. The judge who, acting as a legislator, made the law. He would sit as a judge to try an offense for violation of the judge-made law. In such a case the defendant would have committed a crime as defined by this arbitrary law in the shape of an injunction—not a crime under the State law, not a crime under any Federal law, but a crime made so by an arbitrary order of a judge, who is not supposed, under our Constitution and laws, to have any legislative authority. And if, when he was arrested, there was a dispute as to whether he had violated the order of the judge and thus committed a crime, would he have the right to lay his case before a jury of his peers? Would the constitution and the laws of the State where the alleged offense was committed control in such trial? No. No jury could sit in that case. Who would be the jury? The answer is, the judge—the same person who made the law, the same person who fixes the penalty. He would fix the punishment and he would render the judgment, and at his will the defendant would go to jail for a time limited only by the discretion of the same judge.

The vilest criminal, under our legal system, would not be deprived of these fundamental rights and privileges. The common hobo, the escaped convict—all are protected when they are charged with a crime by the right to have the matter settled by a jury, and they can not, under the law, be found guilty unless the evidence shows they are guilty beyond a reasonable doubt. But this judge, who made the law, who issued the order, who fixed the penalty, and who tries the case, would be guided by no rule of evidence known to our system of jurisprudence. There would be no one to tell the defendant that he was entitled to every reasonable doubt and that he must be acquitted unless proven guilty beyond a reasonable doubt.

The result is that the rights of defendants, under our system, are completely taken away. Something is made a crime which is not a crime under the law. The penalty is fixed, not by a legislature but by one man sitting on the bench. So far as I know, such arbitrary action very seldom occurs except in labor disputes. The defendants in such cases are poor. Sometimes many of them are uneducated. They have no money of their own to defend themselves, and these injunctions make it impossible for any of their friends or any sympathizing citizens to come to their assistance, financially or otherwise, or to even give them advice. They are thus singled out. They stand alone, faced on the one side by great combinations of wealth, unable to defend themselves and prevented from being defended by any other persons who might become interested in their welfare. They must take the punishment administered by the man who made the law and who has fixed the penalty.

It has long been recognized by students of the law and acknowledged by experts in government that the power to make a law and the power to enforce the law should be completely separate, and that such separation is absolutely necessary as a protection against tyranny. Those who wrote our Constitution were careful to keep the judicial power separate from the legislative power and the administrative power. But these injunctions do away with all those fundamental principles of government and put in the hands of one man the rights to make the law, the right to enforce the law, the right to fix a penalty, the right to try those who it is alleged have offended the law thus made, and the right to inflict at their own sweet will whatever punishment they believe should be administered. It was many years ago that the great legal writer Blackstone used the following language:

In all tyrannical government the supreme magistracy or the right of making and enforcing laws is vested in one and the same man or one and the same body of men, and wherever these two powers are united together there can be no public liberty. (1 Blackstone 142.)

Pomeroy, an acknowledged authority, in his *Equity Jurisprudence,* has this to say on the subject:

The courts have thus been required to face such questions as the nature and extent of the capitalist's rights in the management of his business and of the workingman's property in his labor; to decide how far the employer shall be protected in his right to have labor and custom flow to him free from the interference of third parties, and how far the laborer shall be protected from similar interference in his contract of employment or his right to secure employment; to determine what limits shall be placed upon individuals and combinations of individuals in seeking their economic advancement at the expense of their fellows. All these and other problems have come before the courts in rapid succession. (5 Pomeroy, *Equity Jurisprudence* (4th ed.) 4566, sec. 2018.)

Is it any wonder that there has grown up a feeling of resentment against some of the actions of some Federal judges? Is it any wonder that there has gradually grown up in the minds of ordinary people a feeling of prejudice against Federal courts? Is it surprising that there should develop a sentiment against life tenure for Federal trial judges? Can anyone doubt that such action on the part of the Federal judiciary has gradually developed in the minds of ordinary people a fear that where a system of jurisprudence prevails which enables one man, endowed with a life tenure of office, to write a law and then order its enforcement, and then, refusing a jury, to try alleged offenders and punish them at his own sweet will, it will eventually lead us to the common knowledge and belief that where such things exist, as Blackstone says, "There can be no public liberty."

It is difficult to see how any civilized people would indefinitely submit to such tyrannical treatment, and, indeed, it would undoubtedly be true that there would not have been submission if this procedure were general and applied to all classes of people. It is because it applies only to the poor, to laboring men in labor disputes, that the great bulk of our people have not yet realized the great evil to human liberty and to popular government which such procedure brings about.

It is not difficult to see how such injunctions, violating the spirit of a free government, should frighten persons against whom such injunctions are issued and drive them to desperation. What free American citizen, let me ask, is willing to submit to such a violation of his sacred rights, which most of us had supposed were fully protected by our Constitution and our laws?

The bill under discussion makes all such injunctions impossible, and, if enacted into law, this shameful picture of human suffering and human misery brought about by judge-made law will be an impossibility.

Wherever it can be done this bill applies equally to organizations of labor and to organizations of capital. Organizations of employees and organizations of capital are treated exactly the same. The bill does not protect anyone, whether he be an employer or an employee, from punishment for the commission of any unlawful act, either as against property or as against persons.

It sometimes happens that detectives representing large corporations have been employed for the purpose of conveying information concerning the activities of laboring men to the corporation employing them. A notable instance of this kind was in the case of the street-railway strike in Indianapolis, Ind. There, two men were employed by the company as such detectives. They applied for admission to the union and were admitted. Subsequent evidence disclosed that those men were the most active of any of the men of the union in favor of drastic action on the part of the laboring men. They did all they could to incite the men to the commission of all kinds of illegal and unreasonable acts, and then the strong hand of the injunction was brought forth with its usual effect of frightening and disheartening members of the union. And in that particular case, I think it is fair to say that the members of the subcommittee who held the hearings were dumbfounded at the way in which members of the union were tried and convicted for contempt of court, where it seemed on the face of the evidence that the men convicted were not only innocent of a violation of the order of the court, illegal though it probably was, but that they had done their best to prevent the men from taking any action which would in any way violate the injunctive order.

In that case the workers before they were organized asked that some one be sent from an organized union to come to Indianapolis for the purpose of organizing the street-car employees into a union. At their request two organizers were sent to the city. These men, when they reached the city, were arrested on various kinds of charges not in any way connected with the object of their visit. Charges were made against them, and they were arrested. They had to arrange for bail to keep themselves out of jail while waiting for their various trials. Being strangers in the city and most of the other laboring men being financially unable to go on their bonds, arrangements were made through some bonding company to furnish bail. It was necessary, of course, in the cases, for them to pay the bonding companies. Their cases were continued and were never, in fact, brought to trial. When one of the cases reached a stage where it could no longer be continued the case was dismissed and the men were rearrested on some other charge of a similar nature. In this way their finances were used up, and they were worn out.

I may add, speaking from memory of the hearings, though I think I remember them accurately, that these men were arrested fifty-one times in something like 60 days and were never once tried. When the case finally came to trial—perhaps there was a charge in a police court of vagrancy or some other charge for which there was no foundation—it was dismissed, but before the men got out of the courthouse they were arrested again on a similar charge.

Laboring men are not financially able to pay the expenses which are necessary to make proper defenses. They are confronted with corporations having unlimited means, with attorneys of the greatest ability, and in such cases, if they have to try their case before a judge who is unsympathetic, it is necessary for their cases to be appealed. The harsh way in which the men are treated and the severity of these terrible injunctions break them down, even before trial, and the greatest damages are often done in cases which never reach the higher courts. A man who is confronted with an order which deprives him of all legal assistance, from seeking sympathetic advice, especially if he is an uneducated and ignorant person, is broken down before the case reaches the stage of a trial. He realizes that the judge-made law is made for him alone. He realizes that the man who made the law will be the man who tries him for contempt, and he realizes that the same man will administer punishment—a punishment not in accordance with law but in accordance with his individual opinion and judgment.

It is impossible to report with accuracy the number of injunctions issued either in State or Federal courts. As I have said, only a small percentage of them are reported officially. Approximately 300 injunctions were issued in the railway shopmen's strike of 1922, but only 12 were officially reported. Evidence taken by the subcommittee of the Committee on the Judiciary was to the effect that 389 labor injunctions in State and Federal courts were issued during the last decade, and that the most of these are unreported. Out of over 260 cases listed by the Massachusetts Bureau of Statistics in the period of 1898–1916, only 18 were officially reported. This is because, as I have said, defendants in these cases are financially unable to defend themselves in court. Most of the injunction proceedings never go beyond a restraining order or at best beyond a temporary injunction.

Prior to 1890, injunctions in labor disputes were practically unknown, but the issuing of restraining orders and injunctions has rapidly increased since that time, until now it is seldom that any controversy of importance between capital and labor takes place without the issuing of one or more injunctions.

Mr. President, this bill, in section 7, provides for the procedure which shall be followed in case application is made for a restraining order or a temporary or permanent injunction. It provides that before a temporary or permanent injunction shall be issued there must be an opportunity for the defendants to be heard, and that at such hearing they shall have the right to cross-examine witnesses who testify in behalf of the issuing of such an order. The court must also permit the defendants to offer witnesses and to take their oral testimony in open court; and the court is not authorized to issue a temporary injunction after such hearing unless the court finds that unlawful acts have been committed and will be committed unless restrained; that as to each item of relief granted greater injury will be inflicted upon complainant by the denial of relief than will be inflicted upon defendants by the granting of relief; and that complainant has no adequate remedy at law. The bill also provides that no temporary or permanent injunction shall be issued unless the court finds that the public officers charged with the duty to protect complainant's property are unable or unwilling to furnish adequate protection.

The bill, however, permits a temporary restraining order but in order to secure this the judge issuing the order must take the testimony, under oath, of witnesses, and the evidence must be sufficient, if sustained, to justify the court in issuing an injunction upon hearing with notice. In other words, a restraining order without notice can not be issued except upon the sworn testimony of witnesses, and that testimony must be sufficient to sustain an injunction in case the same evidence were offered with notice.

This can be no hardship to the complainant in the case. If the plaintiff is not able to produce sufficient evidence without notice, certainly he would not be able to produce sufficient evidence with notice. The greatest danger of damage comes in cases where restraining orders or temporary injunctions are issued without any notice to the defendants. This, in effect, takes away the protection with which the law always tries to surround the defendant by requiring that a summons be served or a notice given before any judgment shall be rendered against him. It must also appear, before a temporary restraining order can be issued without notice, that the giving of the notice would of itself result in irreparable damage to the complainant's property.

A restraining order without notice, under the bill, shall not be in force longer than five days. The usual provision for the giving of bond before the issuing of such temporary order is also provided for.

It is also provided, in section 8, that no restraining order or injunction relief shall be granted to anyone who has failed to comply with any obligation imposed by law which is involved in the labor dispute in question or who has failed to make every reasonable effort to settle such dispute either by negotiation or with the aid of any governmental machinery provided for arbitration.

This bill provides that a person charged with contempt for the violation of a restraining order or injunction shall have the right to a trial by jury. There is one exception to this, however, and that is where alleged contempt is committed in the presence of the court or so near thereto as to directly interfere with the administration of justice. Then the defendant is not entitled to a jury trial.

As I have already stated, the effect of an injunction is to make something illegal which is not illegal under the law of the land. It makes something a crime which is not a crime under public law. The punishment for such a crime is just the same as the punishment for the violation of any criminal statute of any State or of the Federal Government. Why should a defendant be entitled to a jury trial in one case and not in the other? If a defendant is sent to jail for the violation of a statute made by the judge, his punishment is just as severe, his suffering is just as great as though he were sent to jail for the violation of a criminal statute. Why should the procedure be different in these two cases? If a laboring man meets his neighbor upon the street and strikes him down with his fist, he has committed a crime against the State law; but, when he is arrested, he has a right to a jury trial. If the same laboring man meets the same neighbor on the same street and tells him that a strike at a certain factory is in progress, or that laborers in a certain mill are required to sign a "yellow-dog" contract before they can get employment, or gives him any information of a like kind where a judge has issued an order making it a crime to give such information, then the defendant has no right to demand a jury trial. He is tried by the same judge who made the order. The author of the law sits in judgment in a case involving an alleged violation of a law which he himself has made. How can you distinguish between the two cases?

In each case the defendant is charged with a violation of law. One is a written law passed by the legislature of his State. The other is an order made by a Federal judge, making something a crime which was not a crime before. If there should be any difference, it ought to be just the reverse of what it is. If there is a reason for a man to have a jury trial when it is alleged he has violated some State statute, there is a double reason why he should have a jury trial when he has violated some judge-made law, especially where he is going to be tried before the same judge who made the law. If a defendant is charged with a crime which will take him to jail if he is found guilty, how can we say that under the law of the land he shall have a jury trial in one case and shall be denied a jury trial in the other?

A procedure which violates this fundamental right of a trial by jury in criminal cases, even though it be a case of contempt, violates every sense of common justice, of human freedom, and of personal liberty.

Section 12 of the bill under consideration gives to any defendant who is charged with contempt of court the right to file with the court a demand for the retirement of the judge sitting in the proceeding in all cases where the alleged contempt arose from an attack upon the character or conduct of the judge and where such attack occurred otherwise than in open court. When such a demand is filed under oath, the judge shall proceed no further, but another judge will be designated in the same manner as provided in other cases to hear and try the contempt charge.

It will be noted that this section is general. It has no specific relation to a labor dispute, but is intended more fully to reach the case where newspapers have been charged with contempt because it is alleged they have made improper remarks in their publications in regard to the conduct of a judge in any case pending before him. The conscience of the country was shocked a year or two ago when a newspaper publisher was haled into court by the judge for something he had said in his paper in the way of criticism. The same person against whom the criticism was made sat in judgment. He presided at the trial which took place without a jury, and the charge was improper conduct leveled against the man who was presiding in the case.

The bill does not attempt to relieve any newspaper publisher from anything which, under existing law, would make him liable. But we do believe that such publisher ought to have the right to a fair and impartial trial before a judge not having a direct, personal interest in the outcome of the case. There is no reason why, in such case, some unbiased judge should not sit upon the bench and preside in such a trial. There is every reason in the world why the judge who seemed to have been offended by what the newspaper stated should not sit in judgment upon his own case. This is nothing but common, ordinary justice. It is not any legal refinement. It is simply good, ordinary, common sense, and no legal ability is required to recognize its justice.

There are several other things in the bill; but, in my judgment, no serious conflict will arise with reference to them. I have discussed, I think, all of the provisions of the bill which are contested, or which, for any reason, are claimed to be unjust or constitutional.

What we ought to do is to have the same rule of law apply to the poor as to the rich; to the ignorant as well as to the wise; to the weak as well as to the strong. This bill does nothing more. It provides for no avenue of escape for anyone who is guilty of fraud or violence. It limits the injunction to such cases as common, ordinary justice demands it should be limited. It permits laboring men to organize for the purpose of improving their conditions. It recognizes their right to organize in defense of their rights and their labors. It prevents great aggregations of capital from combining against the weak and the poor in any way which would deprive them of the ordinary rights of free American citizens. It attempts to weigh in the scales of justice all the elements which ought to be considered in passing upon controversies between labor and capital. It asks for the laboring man nothing that it does not concede to the corporation. Its enactment into law will, I believe, do away with much of the criticism which is now made—justly, I think—against the Federal courts. After all, a court, to be effective, must be respected. It is the duty of all citizens to obey all of the orders and judgments of our courts, but the success of our courts and the perpetuity of our Government will be seriously affected and retarded if its orders are unjust and unfair.

I believe, therefore, that the enactment of this bill into law will not only prevent injustices in labor disputes but that its effect will be to place upon a higher plane all of our courts, and eventually bring faith in and respect for all our judiciary tribunals.

In conclusion, it seems to me it would be very appropriate to call to the attention of the Senate the record of Judge Wilkerson in the issuing of injunctions in labor disputes. This record is particularly applicable now, when the President of the United States has sent the name of this judge to the Senate in his effort to promote him to the circuit court of appeals. This nomination for such promotion is now pending before the Judiciary Committee of the Senate.

Judge Wilkerson was appointed as district judge by President Harding, under the advice and at the suggestion of Attorney General Harry M. Daugherty. Hardly was the ink on the commission dry before the same Attorney General applied to this judge and secured of him a sweeping injunction applying to many thousands of railroad employees. This injunction was issued at a time when the dispute between the railroads and their employees was in a fair way of settlement, and contained many of the obnoxious provisions which are almost invariably included in labor injunctions.

Incidentally, this case illustrates the close connection between the judge and the appointive power. After all, judges are human beings; and it is perhaps too much to expect that a judge just appointed to the bench, where he has a life tenure, should be able to resist the request of the Attorney

General whose recommendation probably brought him the appointment. Congress, therefore, should see to it that the law is so plain and so explicit that even the weaknesses of human nature would not be sufficient to lead the judge astray in such cases where the temptation is admittedly great.

Another illustration of a conscienceless injunction issued by Judge Wilkerson was the injunction issued in the case against the Chicago Federation of Musicians and others. This injunction was issued on the first day of September, 1928, at 10 o'clock in the forenoon. The then existing contracts of the musicians with motion-picture houses expired the very next day, September 3, which was Sunday, and new contracts had not been agreed upon. Negotiations had been pending for some time between these musicians and the theater houses, but no definite agreement had been made. The musicians were asking that certain conditions be included in the new contracts of employment, which the employers and receivers for some of these houses were resisting. At this time, while these negotiations were pending and the day before these contracts expired by their own terms, these theaters commenced this action against their employees, and without any notice to the defendants the judge issued another one of his famous restraining orders.

In this injunction, among other things, the defendants were restrained from enforcing certain provisions of their own by-laws. It seems that these musicians, in their own organizations, had various stipulations in their by-laws; and this judge, upon the filing of the complaint by the plaintiffs, and without any notice whatever that such an application was pending, issued an order restraining the defendants from in any way, directly or indirectly, enforcing the provisions of the by-laws. In other words, the injunction restrained the defendants from making the demands which they were making in their negotiations with their employees. In some instances, in effect, it required these musicians to amend their by-laws. It restrained them, also "from ordering, commanding, directing, or causing any strike . . ."

It likewise enjoined the defendants—

From leaving or threatening to leave the employment of said receivers, either by way of strike or otherwise, unless with the consent of said receivers . . .

The injunction also restrained the defendants—

From imposing upon or levying or ordering against any member of said union any fine, penalty, suspension, erasure, expulsion, or assessment of whatsoever character for failure to leave the employment of said receivers, for refusal to refrain from seeking or accepting employment of said receivers, for refusal to obey any command, order, rule, by-law, provision, direction, hint, suggestion, or request of whatsoever character of said union or any officer, committee, or member thereof that he leave or refrain from seeking or accepting such employment, or for refusal to do, perform, aid, assist, counsel, command, direct, or acquiesce in any act forbidden by this order.

In this wonderful injunction there is just one ray of hope. The injunction did contain a provision that the defendants should have a right to appear in court and petition the court for a modification of this drastic order. What a wonderful and merciful thing that was.

The injunction was issued at 10 o'clock on Saturday morning. I presume before it was served it was probably late in the afternoon of Saturday. The court was not in session, of course, on Sunday. The contracts expired on Sunday by their own terms and, by the terms of the decree, these defendants were restrained from quitting the employment of the plaintiffs unless the plaintiffs consented. If they continued to negotiate on new contracts, they were restrained in such negotiations from even asking their employers to put certain things in the contract for which the defendants had been contending. They were compelled to remain in the employment after the expiration of their written contracts and were not even allowed, in trying to get new contracts, to ask that anything should be put in those contracts which the employers did not want put in.

I wonder if anyone will contend that such an order issued by Judge Wilkerson is not, in effect, an order of involuntary servitude? Can anyone claim for a moment that it is not a decree of human slavery? This calls to our attention not only that we should likewise be careful in passing upon any nomination which the President may make in the appointment of a judge to sit in judgment upon the law we shall make. Not only is it necessary that the proper law be passed but it is equally important that no person should be selected to administer the law as judge whose bias and prejudice and whose inclination might lead him to find a loophole of some kind by which such unconscionable injunctions could be issued.

This case and the others which I have enumerated illustrate the necessity of passing a law which can not be nullified even by judges who have no sympathy with those who toil when their interests conflict with great aggregations of wealth. It brings to our minds the almost superhuman importance of an untarnished judiciary. A perfect law can be nullified by an unfair and biased judge. It is a source of great satisfaction to be able to say that the great majority of our judges are above reproach. But the method of their selection often makes it possible for political bosses, political machines, and wealthy corporations which have made political contributions to name Federal judges who shall sit during their lifetime as arbiters between those who toil and those who sit in high places and from their luxurious quarters of wealth sometimes name the President, who, in turn, will nominate the judges; and one of the ways in which their investment can be returned manyfold is the selection of judges who are either their abject tools or whose viewpoint is such that they honestly and conscientiously believe that monopoly is always right and that the toiling masses are always wrong.

This, very logically, leads us to the selection of a Chief Magistrate—a President of the United States. Under our antiquated Electoral College system, which has no more place in a free government than a fifth wheel on a wagon, a system has grown up by which the people have but little to say in the selection of a president. Under this illogical system, in order to be elected the President must first be nominated by one of the dominant political parties. We all know that, as a general rule, the people themselves have but little influence in a national party convention. Too often Presidents are nominated in the wee, small hours of the night, in a dingy, smoky atmosphere, where the musical tinkle of clinking glasses is heard amid the booming of flying corks. Too often the people at the general election have only a choice between two evils; but when the election is over and the preelection promises are redeemed, it sometimes occurs that the demands of those who have contributed the money to carry on the fake contest are sufficiently influential to place upon the Federal bench persons who, after all, are only the tools of the corporations which made them.

It is because we have now on the bench some judges—and undoubtedly we will have others—who lack that judicial poise necessary in passing upon the disputes between labor and capital that such a law as is proposed in this bill is necessary.

BRONSON CUTTING [R., N. MEX.]. Mr. President, I want to ask the Senator a question specifically concerning the provisions in regard to contempt of court, section 11 and section 12.

I understood from the Senator's remarks that section 11 was confined to cases of restraining orders or injunctions in labor disputes, and that section 12, on the other hand, included all cases of contempt of court. The Senator specifically mentioned cases of newspaper criticism of judges.

MR. NORRIS. Section 11 applies to labor disputes; section 12 is general and applies to any kind of a general proceeding.

MR. CUTTING. Section 12 merely allows a defendant to ask that another judge shall sit in the case, one other than the judge who has been criticized?

MR. NORRIS. Yes.

MR. CUTTING Whereas section 11 provides for a jury trial. I have been wondering whether a jury trial should not be granted to all defendants in contempt of court cases.

I personally have had exactly the experience which the Senator describes, of having been haled into court to justify criticism of a particular judge by the judge himself. My defense, of course, was the truth of the charges, which the judge rather naturally found were untrue.

I quite admit that it would have been a relief to some extent to have had some other judge sitting in the case; but I am sure the Senator will recognize that here is a certain feeling of solidarity between various judges which makes it rather difficult for any one of them to decide that his brother judge had been justly criticized.

To my mind, trial by jury is the only effective defense in these cases, and I should like at some time during the consideration of the bill to offer an amendment, which I hope the Senator will accept, to provide jury trial in all cases of indirect contempt; that is, of contempt not committed in the actual presence of the court.

MR. NORRIS. Does not the Senator think section 11 gives it?

MR. CUTTING. It provides:

In all cases in which a person shall be charged with contempt for violation of a restraining order or injunction issued by a court of the United States (as herein defined).

MR. NORRIS. I see the Senator's point. As far as I can see, I would not have any objection to amending section 11 so that it would apply to cases of indirect contempt.

MR. CUTTING. I shall draw an amendment and offer it at the proper time.

JOHN BLAINE [R., WIS.]. Mr. President, while this subject is before us, I would like to say that I see nothing in section 11 which does not make it applicable to all cases, whether labor cases or otherwise.

MR. NORRIS. It does apply to all cases, but the Senator from New Mexico calls our attention to the fact that it applies only in cases where the contempt is charged because of violation of an injunctive order. The contempt mentioned in section 12 is a different kind of contempt. It refers to cases where no order has issued to begin with. A newspaper, for instance, might make an attack on a judge, but would not be violating any order of injunction, and it would not come under section 11, because under that section one must violate an order a judge has made. The case for which the Senator from New Mexico wants to get a jury trial is one where there has been no order issued, but a court has cited some one for contempt without any order having been issued.

MR. BLAINE. I merely want to call the Senator's attention to the fact that the committee did consider that question in connection with a bill introduced by the junior Senator from Michigan [Mr. Vandenberg], but it was intended to cover all cases of indirect criminal contempt. I would assume that there would be no objection to making section 11 expressly applicable to all cases, whether there was a violation of a restraining order or injunction or not.

MR. CUTTING. That was my purpose.

WILLIAM BORAH [R., IDAHO]. But the Senator from New Mexico is interested in a proposition where no injunction order may have been issued at all. If a newspaper criticizes a court, whether the court has issued an injunction order or not, the court may cite the newspaper for contempt. The

Senator from New Mexico is interested in having such a case as that tried by jury.

MR. NORRIS. I am in entire sympathy with what the Senator wants to accomplish.

House of Representatives—72nd Congress, 1st Session
March 8, 1932

JOHN O'CONNOR [DEM., N.Y.]. Mr. Speaker, a few years ago one would never have seriously believed that a bill curtailing the powers of Federal courts in granting injunctions in labor disputes would come before the House of Representatives assured of passage after having been passed almost unanimously by the other body.

Such is progress in a democracy. Many proposals but a few years ago considered radical and paternalistic are accepted to-day by all political parties as worthy and beneficial to the progress of our Government.

I congratulate the distinguished gentleman from New York [Mr. LaGuardia] in his advocacy of H. R. 5315, and I congratulate the distinguished senior Senator from Minnesota for his earnest work for years in behalf of this measure. Yes; I said Minnesota, not Nebraska, because the anti-injunction bill was first introduced in the Senate and again year after year by Senator Shipstead, who deserves credit alongside the gentleman from New York. For five years the bill has been before the Senate and the House. Lengthy hearings have been held year after year.

I shall not occupy the few minutes I have yielded to myself in complete analysis of this important piece of legislation. The rule under consideration provides for four hours' general debate which, while it sounds like a long time, may not be ample to fully explain this somewhat intricate measure:

Briefly, the bill deals with two major subjects:

1. The granting by the Federal courts of injunctions in labor disputes. It of course has no application to or control over state courts. Eleven States have already adopted somewhat similar anti-injunction bills.

2. The bill also declares the "yellow-dog" contract void and against public policy.

It is generally admitted that the granting of injunctions by our Federal judges in labor disputes has developed into a scandalous abuse of judicial process.

The 1928 national conventions of both political parties denounced the abuse and promised remedial legislation.

The Democratic platform said:

We believe that injunctions in labor disputes have in some instances been abused and have given rise to a serious question for legislation.

The Republican platform said, in part:

We recognize that legislative and other investigations have shown the existence of grave abuse in the issuance of injunctions in labor disputes.

The untrammeled right of workers to organize and act jointly in matters affecting their wages and welfare has been recognized by all courts, including the Supreme Court of the United States, as necessary to meet the concentration of employing power.

If a worker is prohibited from exercising some control over the conditions of his employment, he is in a state of peonage.

Chief Justice Taft in the case of *American Foundries* v. *Tri-City Council* (257 U. S. 184, 209) said:

Labor unions . . . were organized out of the necessities of the situation. A single employee was helpless in dealing with an employer. . . . The right to combine for such a lawful purpose has in many years not been denied by any court.

Chief Justice Hughes said in the case of *Texas & New Orleans Railroad Co.* v. *Brotherhood of Railway and Steamship Clerks,* decided May 26, 1930:

The legality of collective action on the part of employees in order to safeguard their proper interests is not to be disputed.

The "strike" has been recognized by our highest court as a lawful agency in the economic disputes between employee and employer.

This bill proposes to limit the jurisdiction of the Federal courts in labor disputes. That Congress has such power over the Federal district courts and the Federal circuit courts of appeal follows from the power of Congress to create or abolish those courts.

This was held in the case of *Myers* v. *United States* (272 U. S. 52, 130) and other cases.

Contrary to the belief of some people, this bill does not attempt to take away from the Federal courts all power to restrain unlawful acts or acts of fraud or violence in labor disputes.

The bill, section 2, declares it to be the public policy of the United States that the employee shall have a free opportunity in lawfully dealing with his employer, that he shall have "full freedom of association, self-organization, and designation of representatives of his own choosing," and "shall be free from the interference, restraint, or coercion of employers." . . .

Among the many abuses of the issuance of injunctions in labor disputes has been forbidding the unions to pay any strike benefits to the strikers; forbidding any person, whether a member of the union or not, to give any aid or assistance to the strikers. Often the injunctions have gone so far as to forbid attorneys to advise the strikers as to their rights even in proceedings to dispossess the strikers from their homes. Again some injunctions have prohibited the strikers from giving any publicity to the existence of the strike or the reasosn for it or their justification of it. Such prohibitions are, of course, outrageous violations of the right of "free speech."

Yet there has been no legislative law for these extraordinary decrees of our courts. This judge-made law has developed in the past 40 years. The judges have themselves made the law and have themselves enforced the penalties for the violation of the laws made by them.

Such an uncivilized and tyrannical procedure can not possibly be longer endured. It is because of this development of law made on the bench that our Federal courts have lost a great deal of respect.

In fact, I hope this measure is but one step that Congress will take to regulate the jurisdiction of the Federal courts.

I never have been able to understand the real necessity for the inferior Federal courts. I have always been opposed to their existence as unnecessary. I believe they have no place in our democratic form of government, of course, except the Supreme Court of the United States. I believe that every issue that comes into the inferior Federal courts could be tried in the State courts.

I have often said that the Federal courts obtain jurisdiction by fraud, not fraud on the part of the court but on the part of the litigants. Take practically every matter that comes into the Federal courts, whether because of alleged diverse citizenship or on other grounds, every one could as well be tried in the State courts, and in most instances the acquisition of jurisdiction is ground in fraud, fabricated and manufactured to avoid the State courts and get into the Federal court for ulterior purposes. . . .

The bill also—section 6, which, like the other section of the bill, applies alike to organizations of employees as well as employers—remedies a grossly unfair practice that has grown up of holding officers and members of unions liable for damages for the acts of other members without proof of participation or direction or ratification of such acts. The bill merely requires actual proof of such participation, direction, or ratification before the officers or other members can be held liable. If this be a change in the "law of agency," as some claim, it is at most a change in the rule of evidence in civil cases only, a power well recognized as lodging in Congress. See *Bailey* v. *Alabama* (219 U. S. 219, 238).

One of the big features of the bill is that no restraining order can be granted, except in exceptional cases, without notice to the defendant and a hearing in open court of the testimony of sworn witnesses on both sides.

Section 7 also provides that before issuing an injunction against defendants' alleged unlawful acts the court must find—

That the public officers charged with the duty to protect claimant's property have failed or are unable to furnish adequate protection.

Surely the court should not exercise police power if the constituted authorities are willing and able to perform that function.

There are, however, exceptional cases in which the Federal courts may issue a temporary restraining order without notice, if necessary to prevent irreparable injury to property. The court must first, however, take testimony under oath rather than by affidavit, and such an order is effective for only five days.

Section 8 of the bill might be called the "clean-hands" provision of the measure. That section provides that a complainant shall not be entitled to an injunction if he has not complied with any contract or obligation on his part or has not made every reasonable effort to settle the dispute by the available methods of arbitration or mediation. Surely, this fundamental principle of equity that "he who seeks justice must do justice" should apply in labor disputes as well as in other judicial controversies.

The bill also provides for a speedy appeal to either party and a preference in the appellate courts.

Another outstanding and progressive feature of the bill is the granting of a speedy and public trial by jury to a person charged with contempt of court, not committed in the court's presence or proximity. For centuries the English courts have granted jury trials for criminal contempt, while in our courts the practice has grown up during the last century to have such important trials before a judge alone, when, in fact, they are criminal offenses carrying confinement in prison for a term within the discretion of the judge who was offended. In the Clayton Act Congress granted the right to trial by jury in contempt cases and the Supreme Court in *Michaelson* v. *United States* (266 U. S. 42) unanimously sustained the constitutionality of that provision.

There is also a provision in the bill that the person charged with contempt may demand his trial before a different judge from the one of whom he is charged to be in contempt. No one can reasonably complain that the complainant, the one offended, should not sit in judgment on the offender!

The necessity for this legislation, however, arises from the fact that the provisions of the Clayton Act have not been construed broadly enough by our courts to cover the general situation as to labor disputes as this bill does.

Now, Mr. Speaker, we come to what I believe to be one of the greatest and most far-reaching provisions of the bill—the death knell of the "yellow-dog" contract.

Many injunctions issued in labor disputes have been founded on an alleged violation by the employee of the provisions of such a "yellow-dog" contract.

The "yellow-dog" contract usually requires the worker to agree not to join a union, or if he is already a member, to leave the same; that his employer may fire him without notice, but that he can not leave without notice to the employer. Such contracts also usually provide that all conditions of labor, hours, and so forth, are entirely within the determination of the employer. Under such a contract the worker practically enters into "involuntary servitude."

It seems strange to many people that there should be any need of legislation to make such un-American contracts unenforceable, but many Federal courts have enforced them. On the other hand, one would think that any person, let alone a judge, would agree with the many eminent jurists who have maintained for years that such contracts were illegal and void, because—

1. They are obviously contrary to public policy, because under their terms the employee enters into practical peonage.

2. There is no consideration to the employee entering into the contract, and no mutuality of consideration between the employer and employee.

3. The employee practically signs the contract under coercion. To say he has a free choice overlooks the fact that he must work to live and support his family. By necessity, he is at the mercy of the work-offering agency in his community.

Mr. Speaker, this bill contains a new Declaration of Independence. It declares to the world that the "yellow-dog" contract is "contrary to the public policy of the United States, shall not be enforceable, and shall not afford any basis for granting of legal or equitable relief by any court of the United States."

It is a happy day, indeed, when with the passage of this far-reaching and progressive measure, that resounding declaration of liberty, can go out to our people. [Applause.]

EARL MICHENER [R., MICH.]. Mr. Speaker, I am going to support this bill as amended by the committee, with an amendment which I hope to offer, which has been submitted to the gentleman from New York [Mr. LaGuardia], the proponent of the bill, and which I believe will be accepted by those who are deeply concerned in the enactment of this legislation. But, understand me, I am not going to vote for this bill for the reasons given by my friend from New York [Mr. O'Connor]. He would abolish the Federal court. He hates the Federal courts. He has proclaimed his position on this floor time and time again. I believe in the Federal courts, I believe in the necessity for the Federal courts, and in voting for this legislation I believe I am voting to strengthen the Federal courts in the minds of the American people. The courts of the United States are our bulwark, and they are never going to be destroyed by the gentleman from New York. If the courts of the United States are ever destroyed, they are going to be destroyed because they destroy themselves.

Unfortunately we have had a few injunctions issued which should not have been issued, and in some of these instances the injunctions have been so ridiculous that there has been a feeling of repulsion against the Federal courts in general. These specific cases have been broadcast throughout the length and breadth of the land until in many sections there is a general feeling against all Federal courts. This legislation is not needed to protect against the many but to protect against the few.

This type of legislation has been before Congress for 14 years. To my personal knowledge this bill is the lineal descendant of the Shipstead bill, which was introduced in the Seventieth Congress. I could not agree with the terms of that bill. I opposed it in the committee as did a majority of the committee. However, the present bill is entirely different. It contains some provisions with which I am not in sympathy, yet it has seldom been my pleasure to vote for a piece of legislation which suited me in every particular. This legislation will give to organized labor the protection to which it feels it is entitled. In my judgment, it will do no injury to the employer. It deals entirely with disputes between employer and employee in labor matters only. Be it remembered that this bill does not attempt to legislate concerning Government employees. I do not believe that the enactment of this bill into law will take away from the Federal Government any rights which it has under existing law, to seek and obtain injunctive relief where the same is necessary for the functioning of the Government.

In the section of the country from which I come we have very little use for Federal injunctions in labor disputes. This bill in no way legislates in reference to State courts. The powers of these courts are left undisturbed, and so far as this legislation is concerned a State court is at liberty to issue any type of an injunction which is permitted in the State where the court has jurisdiction.

I dislike very much to find it necessary to curb the ancient and honorable power of our equity courts. Yet we must realize that it is sometimes essential to provide against the human frailties of possible well-meaning judges, and let us not forget that we are dealing entirely with the jurisdiction in equity, and are not imposing any limitation on the law side of the court.

I disapprove very much of placing a declaration of policy in our statute laws. Federal statutes should not be cluttered up with stump speeches or reasons why the law was enacted. These are matters for debate on the floor of the House, and for the report of the committees. However, we have already established the precedent and have made a declaration of policy in the Sherman Antitrust Act, in the Clayton Act, in the Farm Board act, and in some other acts. Therefore there is a precedent for this feature of the bill, and the proponents of the measure were very insistent upon the inclusion of this declaration of policy, and the majority of the Committee on the Judiciary yielded in this regard.

Often when legislation of this type is being considered, less attention is given to the legislation than to the prejudice for or against organized labor.

There are certain interests in the country whose representatives in Washington at least feel called upon to oppose any legislation sponsored by organized labor; and on the other hand, certain representatives of organized labor seem to find it necessary to oppose with all their might and main all legislation suggested by industry and the employer class. It seems too bad that this is the case, and it is wholesome to observe that the day is fast approaching when the rights of both capital and labor are being recognized, and that agreement instead of war is the order of the day. This legislation is not, in my judgment, inimical to the best interests of all our people or any group of our people, and on the other hand will guarantee to the employer and the employee the right to attain the legitimate purposes of their respective organizations without interfering with the rights of others. A careful reading of this bill is necessary to understand its full import.

I am sure that I have never been considered as radical and I surely believe in the perpetuity of our courts, and I do not believe that in suppporting this bill I am forsaking my previous position in regard to these matters.

Let me say to my very conservative friends that the mere fact that organized labor is supporting this measure is not sufficient cause for you to oppose it. It is not the radical labor leader not the radical hater of organized labor that is going to control on the floor of the House in the end. It is the broad-minded, thinking man, who recognizes the virtues and faults in either labor or capital. Personally, I believe in organized labor. Capital is organized, and labor should have the right to organize and should be protected in lawful organization. I am opposed to strikes and do not believe that this is a bill to authorize strikes. Using the word "strike" in its common acceptation, men should have the right to work or cease working, yet they should have no right to interfere with others. Whether or not organized labor is undesirable depends, of course, upon its leadership. I hold no brief for the American Federation of Labor, but I do hold a brief for them in one particular at least, and that is so far as their activities with reference to communists are concerned. The American Federation of Labor has done more than any other group or class of our people in maintaining peace and order during this depression. It has fought communism at every turn of the road, when, as a matter of fact, organized labor would have been the ideal vehicle to carry communism to our people, and without this restraining influence no one knows what our political and social situation might be to-day. I congratulate the American Federation of Labor. [Applause.]

I believe that there will be very little opposition to this bill, and with the amendment to which I have referred placed in the bill I am satisfied that the purposes of the authors of the bill will be realized and that the employer and the public will be protected. . . .

JAMES BECK [R., PA.]. Mr. Chairman and gentlemen of the committee, I never addressed myself to an argument with such a solemn sense of responsibility. In my judgment, this proposal is one of the gravest proposals that has ever been brought before Congress during the period that I have had the honor of serving as a Member of this House.

I doubt very much whether some of my colleagues fully appreciate all the possible implications of this bill and the contribution it will one day make, not only to great discontent between employer and employee, but to a situation of industrial anarchy.

If I consulted my personal interests, I would remain silent and simply content myself with voting no. But I am a member of the bar and have a peculiar relation to the administration of the law. Moreover, I am a citizen of the United States who, I trust, holds in equal regard the interest of both employer and employee. Whatever the consequences, I feel I should speak; for if I did not, for fear of political consequences, I would have in the remainder of my life an uneasy conscience.

I believe this bill, if it becomes a law, will do infinite harm to both classes, employer and employee, and even of more consequence, the innocent public.

It was said by the gentleman from New York in the argument on the rule that the prospective passage of this bill illustrated the beneficent education of democratic institutions, in that after many years of agitation, when Congress after Congress had rejected proposals of a more deserving character than those embodied in this bill, that now, as a result of this education, the House is prepared to strip the Federal courts of the most vital function of those courts in promoting justice in industrial disputes. I recognize the probable passage of this bill by the House, and let me say here that if I were the only man in the House to speak and vote against the bill, and if I knew it would cost me my political life, I would regard it the crowning service of my modest public service that I at least protested against a measure so unjust and impolitic, and in so doing voiced the sober conscience of millions of right-thinking men. [Applause.]

Referring again to what the gentleman from New York said, this probable enactment, far from illustrating the educational possibilities of democracy, illlustrates what I have often regarded as the fatalism of democracy, a fatalism that will surely—not in your lifetime or mine—spell the ultimate dissolution of democratic institutions. I can illustrate my meaning by the homely illustration of the young lady who, wearied of the importunate solicitations of a suitor, marries him to get rid of him; and this yielding to long-continued importunity has often been illustrated in the history of the American Congress. A militant and vociferous minority will press long enough for the enactment of legislation, and in disregard of the many times that the Congress of the United States may have rejected their proposition, they will ultimately secure their ends by the sheer importunity of their demands, not to speak of the concerted pressure upon weak and timid legislators.

This is illustrated in this case, because the Senate, that had repeatedly rejected more deserving proposals to regulate injunctions, have passed this bill by a very substantial majority, some Senators voting affirmatively with avowed shame; and I am told the House, with only four hours to discuss the fundamental liberties of American citizens, whether they are of the laboring class or the employer class, will probably pass this bill, and the only thing that will stand between this iniquitous stripping of the courts of equity of their ancient and most beneficent powers will be the possible veto of the President. . . .

I shall now briefly indicate seven specific objections of a very grave character to this bill.

First. Section 4: Injunctions are to be largely limited to "fraud or violence." Mass picketing, intimidations, trailing, besetting, importuning, libeling, and false statements are to be beyond the reach of injunctive relief.

Second. Section 4: No injunction shall be issued against the organization and maintenance of strikes even where said strikes are called in violation of contract, to extort graft, to compel the employer to commit a criminal act, to accomplish political purposes, to prevent freedom of press, to prevent the use of products which the public desire to use, to coerce Congress and the Executive.

Third. Section 7: Although injunctions are to be limited largely to acts of fraud and violence, no relief can be granted in such cases unless the complainant can show that he is being injured more by the fraud and violence than the defendant will be injured by stopping such fraud and violence. This is an unpracticable requirement.

Fourth. Section 8: Although the defendants may, without notice, organize industrial war through fraud, violence, and other unlawful acts, the plaintiff shall not receive injunctive relief unless he first endeavors "to settle such dispute either by negotiation or with the aid of any available governmental machinery of mediation or arbitration." The aggressor may act without notice, but the aggrieved may not defend himself by securing injunctive relief without tolerating the violence until he has gone through various steps of peaceful negotiation. While plaintiff is negotiating, the situation may become beyond any possibility of judicial relief.

Fifth. Section 7: No injunction shall issue without proof that public officials charged with the duty to protect property are unable or unwilling to furnish adequate protection. Such an inquiry would be an affront to the authorities of a State.

Sixth. Section 7: The court is deprived of all jurisdiction to issue a temporary restraining order to continue for more than five days in labor dispute cases. This, of course, conflicts with the earlier provision in the same section requiring the examination and cross-examination of witnesses to secure a preliminary injunction, as it is obvious that more than five days would be consumed in most cases of this character by the examination of witnesses. Moreover, it deprives the court of any discretion to extend the restraining order, even though the court were otherwise engaged or counsel were sick. The provisions in the Clayton Act, leaving such matters to the discretion of the court, are as they should be.

Seventh. Section 11: The bill provides for a jury trial of criminal contempts. This is quite distinct from the present provision of the law, sustained in the case of *Michaelson* v. *United States* (266 U. S. 42), wherein a jury trial for contempts was prescribed in cases where the acts of contempt were per se criminal. Under provisions of the pending bill, contempts for ignoring supœnas, jury summons, and so forth, would have to be tried by a jury as well as contempts for violation of the Volstead Act, as this section of the bill is not limited to labor cases.

If I try to discuss these in this oral argument my half hour would be very speedily consumed. I would rather address myself to the more fundamental objection that seems to me to underlie this bill, and as to which I may venture to offer an amendment, which will test the sincerity of some of the proponents of this legislation.

The difficulty with this bill, fundamentally, is that it takes no account whatever of the motives and purposes with which a nation-wide strike or boycott can be commenced and prosecuted.

Obviously, an industrial dispute can be made the means of compelling some action wholly disconnected with the causes or conditions of employment, and it can even be caused to bring about some political result and threaten the freedom of decision of the Congress itself. In other words, the industrial boycott or strike, when nation-wide in its extent, can become that which in England is called "direct action," and there is no provision in this bill that if there be an industrial dispute or a threat of an industrial dispute that may, for example, paralyze interstate transportation from the Atlantic to the Pacific, that a court of equity in such case would have the right or power to invoke the ancient and beneficent remedy of injunction.

The so-called educational process, that now seems to be in the process of culmination, began in 1894, 38 years ago, in a strike to which I wish to refer, as it will illustrate what may happen if the courts of the United States no longer have any power to issue injunctions except under conditions that are almost prohibitive.

You will remember in that case the Pullman Co. had a controversy with its immediate employees. With that the railroad brotherhoods or the American Railway Union, as it was then called, had no legitimate concern. Nevertheless, in order to compel the Pullman Co. to make terms—whether they were just or unjust I do not know—with the Pullman employees, the railroads entered upon a strike which was intended to paralyze all traffic into the city of Chicago, with the potential threat of denying even the children of that city the milk requisite for their life, and which was intended to obstruct and prevent and put an embargo upon all the foodstuffs that would leave Chicago in order to provide nourishment and maintenance to some 12,000,000 people outside of the city of Chicago.

Let me remind the gentlemen on the Democratic side of the aisle that one of the crowning achievements of that great and noble President, Grover Cleveland, was to instruct his Attorney General to go into the United States courts and there bring the parties that were trying to starve the people of the United States into compelling the Pullman Co. to accede to the demands of the Pullman workmen; and, as a result of that bill in equity, after a hearing in court a permanent injunction was entered, and for a time disobeyed, although that is another matter.

At all events, if there be one act of Cleveland's administration of which every Democrat who cherishes the maintenance of American freedom should be proud, it is his brave act in initiating this suit. Yet, if this bill had been the law then, while there is the exception that an injunction can issue in cases of fraud or violence, yet the fact is that a restraining order to permit irreparable harm could only be granted for five days, at the end of which a court of equity would have been impotent to preserve the status quo in order to determine the respective rights of the parties. Prior to that time there had never been a suggestion on the part of those who are the proponents of labor organizations for legislation of the kind before us. I belive quite as much as does the gentleman from Maine [Mr. Nelson] in the right of labor organizations; I share his splendid eulogy of the beneficent workings of those associations; I indorse his views that in this most acute crisis that our country possibly has ever known the conduct of the labor organizations has been beyond praise. I share all that he has said about their generosity and their public spirit in agreeing to a reduction of wages as their contribution to an alleviation of the terrible conditions of the hour. But, let it not be forgotten that a labor organization can be malevolent as well as beneficent. It can have proper purposes and it can have improper purposes, and the attempt in 1894 in a matter which did not concern them to starve the community and compel it to bring unreasonable pressure upon the freedom of the Pullman Co. and of such of its employees as were satisfied to work was a denial of freedom.

Let me give a second illustration before I go farther. I suppose some of us remember the year 1916, when the demands upon traffic were unprecedented, when it was vital to the industries of this country that interstate traffic should move, when it was not only vital to us but vital to those nations that subsequently became our allies that war supplies should be moved to the Atlantic seaboard. The four railroad brotherhoods took that time to enforce their demand, and did so on the eve of a presidential election, just as they are doing now; and for the same reason, viz, that there is less freedom of action on the part of Congress on the eve of a presidential election, they went to President Wilson and with watch in their hands demanded that unless within a specified time, which, as I recall, was only a few days, he insured the passage of a clearly unconstitutional law to give 12 hours' pay for an 8-hour day's work they would at once paralyze the interstate traffic of the United States from the Atlantic to the Pacific, to the ruin of millions and possibly to the starvation of millions, because there are many cities, like New York and Chicago, where, if you cut off their supplies for a week or 10 days, the people will be threatened with starvation. It is a humiliating fact to recall that President Wilson bowed to the insolent demand and thereupon appeared before the Congress and urged the passage of that unprecedented law, the Adamson law. Do not tell that because it was direct action for a political purpose, it was not an industrial dispute, because the method of compelling the Congress of the United States to abdicate its function under the Constitution was for every workingman to leave his locomotive and his train and stop the movement of interstate traffic.

The Congress yielded, I think, to its own disgrace, and the Supreme Court so far yielded, that while five of the judges did hold that the law could be sustained, one of the five held that it was only temporarily constitutional, upon the theory of an emergency, in order to enable the railroads and the brotherhoods to agree upon suitable wages. But five judges held that except as an emergency measure it was unconstitutional and void. Yet they validated the law for the time being and in the way that I have indicated. If this bill had been the law then, there would have been no power whatever, in that critical year of 1916, when we were preparing for a war into which we were about to be drawn, for President Wilson to have done as President Cleveland did—direct the Attorney General to enter a court of equity, get a restraining order for a limited and reasonable time until the parties could be brought before it, and then, after full hearing, grant an injunction against the destruction of interstate trade. A sovereign State can not place an embargo upon interstate trade; yet this organization of railroad employees, with their power to tie up traffic from the Atlantic to the Pacific and from the Lakes to the Gulf, can put on such an embargo. In the last analysis this bill is to shift the power of granting an injunction from the courts that may be trusted to hold the scales even between employer and employee, to those who are not judges but who are only the representatives of a class, and who can starve a community into submission of their demands unless there be power in a court of equity to draw about an innocent public that suffers most by such embargoes the solemn circle of the law and say, "Thus far and no farther."

I recall two illustrations that happened to me in 1920 and 1922 which I wish to call to the attention of the committee. In 1920 I was in London. The communists of London—and I am not classing American labor organizations with communists because I have already assented to the well-deserved eulogium of the gentleman from Maine—had hired Albert Hall, I think it was, for three meetings. They had held two meetings in which they had agitated for the destruction of all organized government. They had marched in with red flags, denouncing every existing institution which you and I hold dear—a government of laws and not of men, the church, the courts, and the legislature. Thereupon the owners of the hall, at the direction of Lloyd George, canceled the lease for the third meeting; and the labor organizations of London, that were not communistic at heart but who were engaged in supplying London with light, heat, and water, sent notice to Lloyd George that unless within 24 hours the hall was given over to the communists to hold their meeting there would be no light, no heat, no water in London.

Lloyd George promptly succumbed to prevent irreparable harm, rather than see London plunged into darkness and its people wanting in the necessity of water.

Two years later the Bolshevists were at the gates of Warsaw, and if they had captured Warsaw they would have entered Germany and a minority of the German people, in their despair, crushed as they are, would have probably joined a movement that absolutely threatened the existence of western civilization itself. What happened? Poland put its women and children in the trenches against that attack of the Russian Soviets and appealed to France and Belgium and England. France promptly sent its generals and supplies. In Belgium it was proposed to aid Poland by contributing artillery and other munitions of war, and then the labor organizations said to the Belgian Government, "Do this and there will be a general strike in Belgium." At once the cabinet succumbed and Hymans, Foreign Minister, with whom I had dined the night before, resigned in protest.

In England the same thing took place. England wanted to join France in defending Poland and western Europe against a greater peril than had existed in Europe since Attila stood at Chalons centuries ago. England wanted to help. At once the railroad brotherhoods and other transportation interests served notice on Lloyd George that the moment one rifle was given to the Poles there would be a general strike in England. Lloyd George yielded to the threat.

You will say those are illustrations in other nations. Let me give one in our country that is in my memory, although I had no special connection with it. I refer to the shopcraft strike of 1922, when I was Solicitor General. I can still remember the great map we had in the Department of Justice which 2,000 deputy marshals reported day by day and hour by hour some new and fresh outrage, which was marked on the map. If you doubt it, go to the Department of Justice and you will see the record there. There were 1,500 cases of violent assault with intent to kill; 65 accounts of kidnaping, accompanied by brutal assaults; 8 cases of tar and feathers; 51 cases of dynamiting and burning railroad bridges for the purpose of wrecking freight and passenger trains; 250 records of bombing of railroad property or homes of nonstriking employees; 50 cases of train wrecking or derailment; hundreds of flagrant practices of sabotage in the crippling of engines and cars. That is the story of what was happening when another President, this time a Republican President, instructed the Attorney General to enter the United States court at Chicago and stop these wholesale assaults and outrages—nay, it was war against the people of this country. An injunction was filed, and never did those responsible for that strike dare to come into court and say that one single allegation of the United States Government in that case was, as a matter of fact, untrue. That strike was dissolved by the beneficent power of the injunction.

I have told you all this because I wanted to call attention to what I regard as a fundamental defect of this law. There are many others, and by reference to one you must not understand that I am excluding those to which I shall refer under the privilege of revising and extending my remarks.

Section 5 reads:

No court of the United States shall have jurisdiction to issue a restraining order.

Mark you, a restraining order is only for a few days, to preserve the status quo. If you can not preserve the status quo of a litigation, the courts of equity in many cases are impotent, because the thing about which the controversy rages is irreparably destroyed, and without the power of a restraining order there would not, in many cases, be any equity done. I continue reading—

shall have jurisdiction to issue a restraining order or temporary or permanent injunction upon the ground that any of the persons participating or interested in the labor dispute constitute or are engaged in an unlawful combination or conspiracy because of the doing in concert of the acts enumerated in section 4 of this act.

The enumeration of those acts includes the ordinary methods outside of physical violence with which these nation-wide strikes are carried to successful result.

That strips the powers of a court of equity, even though the purpose of the industrial dispute is an ulterior one. It may be to do to another President what was done to President Wilson; to another Congress what was done to the Congress of 1916. It will be within the power of the great railroad brotherhoods of this country, although I am loath to think that they would use the power, but if there be anything in human liberty it is the fear of possible abuses of power—I say it would be within their power to do again in some industrial crisis what was done in 1916; that is, to say to the President and to the Congress, "You will do so and so, or there will be no interstate transportation in this country. We will see people starve unless we get our will." Now, in the last analysis that is what it means. No State court has sufficient sweep of jurisdiction to be helpful. A nation-wide strike on interstate traffic has the purpose of taking a community by the throat and saying to that community, "You must compel, through your legislative or executive representatives, the people with whom we have a dispute to do our bidding, and if you fail to do it, the consequence be on your head," even if it involve suffering, privation, and death to the public and the community who are innocent, who have no part in the contro-versy, who have not been in any way responsible either for high or low wages or conditions of employment, who have relied upon the solemn guaranty of the Constitution that interstate commerce shall be free.

I say under those circumstances, after having spiked the last cannon that can defend a community from intolerable suffering, you are simply trans-ferring the power of compelling action, not merely in an industrial dispute but of compelling action of any political nature.

When you have done that, what have you done? You have made a long march away from that Philadelphia where the Constitution of the United States was framed and in the direction of Moscow, and do not be oblivious of that fact. [Applause.] You will have enthroned the possible rule of the proletariat in free America.

THE DECISIONS

The New Negro Alliance v. *Sanitary Grocery Co., Inc.*
303 U.S. 552 (1938)

MR. JUSTICE ROBERTS delivered the opinion of the Court.

The matter in controversy is whether the case made by the pleadings involves or grows out of a labor dispute within the meaning of § 13 of the Norris-La Guardia Act.

The respondent, by bill filed in the District Court of the District of Columbia, sought an injunction restraining the petitioners and their agents from picketing its stores and engaging in other activities injurious to its business. The petitioners answered, the cause was heard upon bill and answer, and an injunction was awarded. The United States Court of Appeals for the District of Columbia affirmed the decree. The importance of the question presented and asserted conflict with the decisions of this and other federal courts moved us to grant certiorari.

As the case was heard upon the bill and a verified answer the facts upon which decision must rest are those set forth in the bill and admitted or not denied by the answer and those affirmatively set up in the answer.

The following facts alleged in the bill are admitted by the answer. Respondent, a Delaware corporation, operates 255 retail grocery, meat, and vegetable stores, a warehouse and a bakery in the District of Columbia and employs both white and colored persons. April 3, 1936, it opened a new store at 1936 Eleventh Street, N. W., installing personnel having an acquaintance with the trade in the vicinity. Petitioner, The New Negro Alliance, is a corporation composed of colored persons, organized for the mutual improvement of its members and the promotion of civic, educational, benevolent, and charitable enterprises. The individual petitioners are officers of the corporation. The relation of employer and employees does not exist between the respondent and the petitioners or any of them. The petitioners are not engaged in any business competitive with that of the respondent, and the officers, members, or representatives of the Alliance are not engaged in the same business or occupation as the respondent or its employees. . . .

The case, then, as it stood for judgment, was this: The petitioners requested the respondent to adopt a policy of employing Negro clerks in certain of its stores in the course of personnel changes; the respondent ignored the request and the petitioners caused one person to patrol in front of one of the respondent's stores on one day carrying a placard which said: "Do Your Part! Buy Where You Can Work! No Negroes Employed Here!"

248

and caused or threatened a similar patrol of two other stores of respondent. The information borne by the placard was true. The patrolling did not coerce or intimidate respondent's customers; did not physically obstruct, interfere with, or harass persons desiring to enter the store, the picket acted in an orderly manner, and his conduct did not cause crowds to gather in front of the store.

The trial judge was of the view that the laws relating to labor disputes had no application to the case. He entered a decree enjoining the petitioners and their agents and employees from picketing or patrolling any of the respondent's stores, boycotting or urging others to boycott respondent; restraining them, whether by inducements, threats, intimidation or actual or threatened physical force from hindering any person entering respondent's places of business, from destroying or damaging or threatening to destroy or damage respondent's property and from aiding or abetting others in doing any of the prohibited things. The Court of Appeals thought that the dispute was not a labor dispute within the Norris-LaGuardia Act because it did not involve terms and conditions of employment such as wages, hours, unionization or betterment of working conditions, and that the trial court, therefore, had jurisdiction to issue the injunction. We think the conclusion that the dispute was not a labor dispute within the meaning of the Act, because it did not involve terms and conditions of employment in the sense of wages, hours, unionization or betterment of working conditions is erroneous.

Subsection (a) of § 13 provides: "A case shall be held to involve or to grow out of a labor dispute when the case involves persons who are engaged in the same industry, trade, craft, or occupation; or have direct or indirect interests therein; . . . or when the case involves any conflicting or competing interests in a 'labor dispute' (as hereinafter defined) of 'persons participating or interested' therein (as hereinafter defined)." Subsection (b) characterizes a person or association as participating or interested in a labor dispute "if relief is sought against him or it and if he or it . . . has a direct or indirect interest therein, . . ." Subsection (c) defines the term "labor dispute" as including "any controversy concerning terms or conditions of employment, . . . regardless of whether or not the disputants stand in the proximate relation of employer and employee." These definitions plainly embrace the controversy which gave rise to the instant suit and classify it as one arising out of a dispute defined as a labor dispute. They leave no doubt that The New Negro Alliance and the individual petitioners are, in contemplation of the Act, persons interested in the dispute.

In quoting the clauses of § 13 we have omitted those that deal with disputes between employers and employees and disputes between associations of persons engaged in a particular trade or craft, and employers in the same industry. It is to be noted, however, that the inclusion in the definitions of such disputes, and the persons interested in them, serves to emphasize the fact that the quoted portions were intended to embrace controversies other than those between employers and employees; between labor unions seeking to represent employees and employers; and between persons seeking employment and employers.

The Act does not concern itself with the background or the motives of the dispute. The desire for fair and equitable conditions of employment on the part of persons of any race, color, or persuasion, and the removal of discriminations against them by reason of their race or religious beliefs is quite as important to those concerned as fairness and equity in terms and conditions of employment can be to trade or craft unions or any form of labor organization or association. Race discrimination by an employer may reasonably be deemed more unfair and less excusable than discrimination against workers on the ground of union affiliation. There is no justification in the apparent purposes or the express terms of the Act for limiting its definition of labor disputes and cases arising therefrom by excluding those which arise with respect to discrimination in terms and conditions of employment based upon differences of race or color. . . .

The legislative history of the Act demonstrates that it was the purpose of the Congress further to extend the prohibitions of the Clayton Act respecting the exercise of jurisdiction by federal courts and to obviate the results of the judicial construction of that Act. It was intended that peaceful and orderly dissemination of information by those defined as persons interested in a labor dispute concerning "terms and conditions of employment" in an industry or a plant or a place of business should be lawful; that, short of fraud, breach of the peace, violence, or conduct otherwise unlawful, those having a direct or indirect interest in such terms and conditions of employment should be at liberty to advertise and disseminate facts and information with respect to terms and conditions of employment, and peacefully to persuade others to concur in their views respecting an employer's practices. The District Court erred in not complying with the provisions of the Act.

The decree must be reversed and the cause remanded to the District Court for further proceedings in conformity with this opinion.

Reversed.

MR. JUSTICE CARDOZO took no part in the consideration or decision of this case.

MR. JUSTICE MC REYNOLDS, dissenting.

MR. JUSTICE BUTLER and I cannot accept the view that a "labor dispute" emerges whenever an employer fails to respond to a communication from A, B and C—irrespective of their race, character, reputation, fitness, previous or present employment—suggesting displeasure because of his choice of employees and their expectation that in the future he will not fail to select men of their complexion.

It seems unbelievable that, in all such circumstances, Congress intended to inhibit courts from extending protection long guaranteed by law and thus, in effect, encourage mobbish interference with the individual's liberty of action. Under the tortured meaning now attributed to the words "labor dispute," no employer—merchant, manufacturer, builder, cobbler, housekeeper or what not—who prefers helpers of one color or class can find adequate safeguard against intolerable violations of his freedom if members of some other class, religion, race or color demand that he give them precedence.

Design thus to promote strife, encourage trespass and stimulate intimidation, ought not to be admitted where, as here, not plainly avowed. The ultimate result of the view now approved to the very people whom present petitioners claim to represent, it may be, is prefigured by the grievous plight of minorities in lands where the law has become a mere political instrument.

Brotherhood of Railroad Trainmen v. *Chicago River & Indiana Railroad Co.*
353 U.S. 30 (1957)

MR. CHIEF JUSTICE WARREN delivered the opinion of the Court.

We are asked to interpret that provision of the Railway Labor Act which created the National Railroad Adjustment Board for the resolution of minor grievances in the event that the parties were unable to settle them by negotiation. The ultimate question is whether a railway labor organization can resort to a strike over matters pending before the Adjustment Board.

The Chicago River and Indiana Railroad Company operates the switching and yard facilities at the Chicago stockyards. A segment of the employees of the River Road were represented by the Brotherhood of Railroad Trainmen. A collective bargaining agreement between the Brotherhood and the River Road was in existence throughout the period covered by this case. The present disagreement arises from an accumulation of twenty-one grievances of members of the Brotherhood against the carrier. Nineteen of these were claims for additional compensation, one was a claim for reinstatement to a higher position, and one was for reinstatement in the employ of the carrier. When negotiations failed, the Brotherhood called a strike.

Because of the serious nature of the impending work stoppage, the National Mediation Board proffered its services. The mediator was unsuccessful, and upon his withdrawal, the River Road submitted the controversy to the Adjustment Board. The Brotherhood promptly issued a strike call for four days later.

The River Road then sought relief from a District Court. Because of the threatened irreparable injury to the carrier, its employees and the 600 industries and 27 railroads served by it, the complaint prayed for a preliminary injunction, and ultimately a permanent injunction, against a strike by the Brotherhood over the grievances pending before the Adjustment Board. A temporary restraining order was issued, but that order was vacated and the complaint dismissed upon the finding by the district judge that the Norris-LaGuardia Act was applicable and that the court lacked jurisdiction to grant the relief requested. The Court of Appeals for the Seventh Circuit reversed. 229 F. 2d 926. A permanent injunction was accordingly entered by the District Court and affirmed by the Seventh Circuit. We granted certiorari in order to resolve an important question concerning interpretation and application of the Railway Labor Act. 352 U. S. 865.

The grievances for which redress is sought by the Brotherhood are admittedly "minor disputes" as that phrase is known in the parlance of the Railway Labor Act. These are controversies over the meaning of an existing collective bargaining agreement in a particular fact situation, generally involving only one employee. § 2, Sixth. They may be contrasted with "major disputes" which result when there is disagreement in the bargaining process for a new contract. § 2, Seventh. See *Elgin, J. & E. R. Co.* v. *Burley,* 325 U. S. 711, 722–724.

The first step toward settlement of either kind of dispute is negotiation and conference between the parties. Section 3, First (i), provides that—

The disputes between an employee or group of employees and a carrier or carriers growing out of grievances or out of the interpretation or application of agreements concerning rates of pay, rules, or working conditions . . . shall be handled in the usual manner up to and including the chief operating officer of the carrier designated to handle such disputes. . . .

If the parties are unable to reach an agreement, the section continues—

. . . but, failing to reach an adjustment in this manner, the disputes may be referred by petition of the parties or by either party to the appropriate division of the National Railroad Adjustment Board with a full statement of the facts and all supporting data bearing upon the disputes.

Section 3, First (m), declares that—

The awards of the several divisions of the Adjustment Board . . . shall be final and binding upon both parties to the dispute . . . .

This language is unequivocal. Congress has set up a tribunal to handle minor disputes which have not been resolved by the parties themselves. Awards of this Board are "final and binding upon both parties." And either side may submit the dispute to the Board. The Brotherhood suggests that we read the Act to mean only that an Adjustment Board has been organized and that the parties are free to make use of its procedures if they wish to; but that there is no compulsion on either side to allow the Board to settle a dispute if an alternative remedy, such as resort to economic duress, seems more desirable. Such an interpretation would render meaningless those provisions in the Act which allow *one* side to submit a dispute to the Board, whose decision shall be final and binding on *both* sides. If the Brotherhood is correct, the Adjustment Board could act only if the union and the carrier were amenable to its doing so. The language of §3. First, reads otherwise and should be literally applied in the absence of a clear showing of a contrary or qualified intention of Congress.

Legislative history of the provisions creating the National Railroad Adjustment Board reinforces the literal interpretation of the Act. The present law is a composite of two major pieces of legislation. Most of the basic framework was adopted in 1926. In 1934, after eight years of experience, the statute was amended, and in that amendment the Adjustment Board was born.

The distinction between "major disputes" and "minor disputes" was found in the 1926 statute. Above the level of negotiation and conference, each was to follow a separate procedure. Section 3, First, of the Act called upon carriers or groups of carriers and their employees to agree to the formation of boards of adjustment, composed equally of representatives of labor and management, to resolve the "minor disputes." If this step were unsuccessful, these disputes along with the "major disputes" became a function of the Board of Mediation, predecessor of the National Mediation Board.

The obvious lack of any compulsion toward a settlement of disputes was a basic characteristic of the Act and proved to be a major weakness in the procedures for handling "minor disputes." As stated in the Report of the House of Representatives Committee on Interstate and Foreign Commerce, after hearings on the 1934 amendment: "In many instances . . . the carriers and the employees have been unable to reach agreements to establish such boards [of adjustment]." H. R. Rep. No. 1944, 73d Cong., 2d Sess. 3. This was not the only weakness, however. "Many thousands of these [minor] disputes have been considered by boards established under the Railway Labor Act; but the boards have been unable to reach a majority decision, and so the proceedings have been deadlocked." *Ibid.*

This condition was in marked contrast to the declared purpose of the 1926 Act ". . . . to settle all disputes, whether arising out of the application of . . . agreements or otherwise, in order to avoid any interruption to commerce or to the operation of any carrier growing out of any dispute between the carrier and the employees thereof." § 2, First. The Report continued:

These unadjusted disputes have become so numerous that on several occasions the employees have resorted to the issuance of strike ballots and threatened to interrupt interstate commerce in order to secure an adjustment. This has made it necessary for the President of the United States to intervene and establish an emergency board to investigate the controversies. This condition should be corrected in the interest of industrial peace and of uninterrupted transportation service. *Ibid.*

The means chosen to correct this situation are the present provisions of § 3, First, concerning the National Railroad Adjustment Board. The Board was set up by Congress, making it unnecessary for the parties to agree to establish their own boards. In case of a deadlock on the Adjustment Board, which continued the policy of equal representation of labor and management, the appropriate division is allowed to select a neutral referee to sit with them and break the tie. If the division cannot agree even on a referee, the Act provides that one shall be appointed by the National Mediation Board. Thus was the machinery built for the disposition of minor grievances.

The change was made with the full concurrence of the national railway labor organizations. Commissioner Joseph B. Eastman, Federal Coordinator of Transportation and principal draftsman of the 1934 bill, complimented the unions on conceding the right to strike over "minor disputes" in favor of the procedures of the Adjustment Board:

The willingness of the employees to agree to such a provision is, in my judgment, a very important concession and one of which full advantage should be taken in the public interest. I regard it as, perhaps, the most important part of the bill.

Asked if the Act made it a matter of discretion whether disputes would be submitted to the Adjustment Board, he replied in the negative. It was, he said, a matter of duty—

. . . and it is my understanding that the employees in the case of these minor grievances—and that is all that can be dealt with by the adjustment board—are entirely agreeable to those provisions of the law.

I think that it is a very important concession on their part. . . . [T]his law is in effect an agreement on the part of the parties to arbitrate all of these minor disputes.

The chief spokesman for the railway labor organizations was George M. Harrison. He appeared as chairman of the legislative committee of the Railway Labor Executives' Association before both the House of Representatives and the Senate Committees. This Association comprised the twenty-one standard railway labor groups, including the Brotherhood of Railroad Trainmen. He testified before the House Committee:

So, out of all of that experience and recognizing the character of the services given to the people of the country by our industry and how essential it is to the welfare of the country, these organizations have come to the conclusion that in respect to these minor-grievance cases that grow out of the interpretation and/or application of the contracts already made that they can very well permit those disputes to be decided, . . . by an adjustment board.

Later, before the Senate Committee, he declared:

Grievances are instituted against railroad officers' actions, and we are willing to take our chances with this national board because we believe, out of our experience, that the national board is the best and most efficient method of getting a determination of these many controversies that arise on these railroads between the officers and the employees.

These railway labor organizations have always opposed compulsory determination of their controversies. . . . [W]e are now ready to concede that we can risk having our grievances go to a board and get them determined, and that is a contribution that these organizations are willing to make.

The voice of labor was not unanimous in this concession. The representative of the International Brotherhood of Teamsters vehemently objected to the adoption of § 3, First.

We are unalterably opposed to paragraph M, . . . [which] brings about compulsory arbitration and prevents the use of the only weapon in the hands of organized labor. We believe that a very dangerous precedent would be established with the passage of this paragraph, and to the best of our knowledge it is the first time that any such measure has been enacted by the Congress of the United States.

This record is convincing that there was general understanding between both the supporters and the opponents of the 1934 amendment that the provisions dealing with the Adjustment Board were to be considered as compulsory arbitration in this limited field. Our reading of the Act is therefore confirmed, not rebutted, by the legislative history.

The only question which remains is whether the federal courts can compel compliance with the provisions of the Act to the extent of enjoining a union from striking to defeat the jurisdiction of the Adjustment Board. The Brotherhood contends that the Norris-LaGuardia Act has withdrawn the power of federal courts to issue injunctions in labor disputes. That limitation, it is urged, applies with full force to all railway labor disputes as well as labor controversies in other industries.

We hold that the Norris-LaGuardia Act cannot be read alone in matters dealing with railway labor disputes. There must be an accommodation of that statute and the Railway Labor Act so that the obvious purpose in the enactment of each is preserved. We think that the purposes of these Acts are reconcilable.

In adopting the Railway Labor Act, Congress endeavored to bring about stable relationship between labor and management in this most important national industry. It found from the experience between 1926 and 1934 that the failure of voluntary machinery to resolve a large number of minor disputes called for a strengthening of the Act to provide an effective agency, in which both sides participated, for the final adjustment of such controversies. Accumulation of these disputes had resulted in the aggregate being serious enough to threaten disruption of transportation. Hence, with the full consent of the brotherhoods, the 1934 amendment became law.

The Norris-LaGuardia Act, on the other hand, was designed primarily to protect working men in the exercise of organized, economic power, which is vital to collective bargaining. The Act aimed to correct existing abuses of the injunctive remedy in labor disputes. Federal courts had been drawn into the field under the guise either of enforcing federal statutes, principally the Sherman Act, or through diversity of citizenship jurisdiction. In the latter cases, the courts employed principles of federal law frequently at variance with the concepts of labor law in the States where they sat. Congress acted to prevent the injunctions of the federal courts from upsetting the natural interplay of the competing economic forces of labor and capital. Rep. LaGuardia, during the floor debates on the 1932 Act, recognized that the machinery of the Railway Labor Act channeled these economic forces, in matters dealing with railway labor, into special processes intended to comprise them. Such controversies, therefore, are not the same as those in which the injunction strips labor of its primary weapon without substituting any reasonable alternative.

In prior cases involving railway labor disputes, this Court has authorized the use of injunctive relief to vindicate the processes of the Railway Labor Act. *Virginian R. Co.* v. *System Federation No. 40,* 300 U. S. 515, was an action by the union to enjoin compliance with the Act's provisions for certification of a bargaining representative. The question raised was whether a federal court could issue an injunction in a labor dispute. The Court held:

> It suffices to say that the Norris-LaGuardia Act can affect the present decree only so far as its provisions are found not to conflict with those of § 2, Ninth, of the Railway Labor Act, authorizing the relief which has been granted. Such provisions cannot be rendered nugatory by the earlier and more general provisions of the Norris-Laguardia Act. *Id.,* at 563.

In *Brotherhood of Railroad Trainmen* v. *Howard,* 343 U. S. 768, and other similar cases, the Court held that the specific provisions of the Railway Labor Act take precedence over the more general provisions of the Norris-LaGuardia Act.

Our conclusion is that the District Court has jurisdiction and power to issue necessary injunctive orders to enforce compliance with the requirements of the Railway Labor Act notwithstanding the provisions of the Norris-LaGuardia Act. *Id.,* at 774.

This is a clear situation for the application of that principle.

The Brotherhood has cited several cases in which it has been held that the Norris-LaGuardia Act's ban on federal injunctions is not lifted because the conduct of the union is unlawful and under some other statute. We believe that these are inapposite to this case. None involved the need to accommodate two statutes, when both were adopted as a part of a pattern of labor legislation.

The judgment of the Court of Appeals must be affirmed.

It is so ordered.

THE WAGNER ACT

(National Labor Relations Act)

Commentary

World War I regulations and the railway labor legislation of the 1920's nurtured the rights to self-organization and collective bargaining. It is not surprising, then, that these concepts found their way into the New Deal economic measures. The idea of the government encouraging "mutual agreements" between employers and employees on hours, wages, and other conditions of employment fit the quasi-regulatory-cum-industrial, self-help philosophy underlying the National Industrial Recovery Act of 1933. Section 7 (a) of that statute neatly blends voluntary action and federal encouragement:

> Every code of fair competition, agreement, and license approved, prescribed, or issued under this title shall contain the following conditions: (1) That employees shall have the right to organize and bargain collectively through representatives of their own choosing, and shall be free from the interference, restraint, or coercion of employers of labor, or their agents, in the designation of such representatives or in self-organization or in other concerted activities for the purpose of collective bargaining or other mutual aid or protection; (2) That no employee and no one seeking employment shall be required as a condition of employment to join any company union or to refrain from joining, organizing, or assisting a labor organization of his own choosing; (3) That employers shall comply with the maximum hours of labor, minimum rates of pay, and other conditions of employment, approved or prescribed by the President.

This was the genesis of much of the New Deal's labor legislation. On August 5, 1933, President Franklin D. Roosevelt carried out the responsibility assigned to him by the N.I.R.A. and created by executive order a tripartite National Labor Board composed of three employer and three employee representatives and an impartial chairman, Senator Robert F. Wagner [Dem., N. Y.]. The board's work largely involved attempted settlements of strikes for wages above the code minimums and strikes caused by employers' refusal to recognize and deal with unions.

Meanwhile, sound trucks emblazoned "The President Wants You To Unionize" rolled through the coal towns of Kentucky, West Virginia, Pennsylvania, and Illinois, as well as in the garment centers of New York, Philadelphia, Cleveland, and Chicago. By November, 1933, the United Mine Workers' Union had added three hundred thousand members, the International Ladies' Garment Workers' Union one hundred thousand, and the Amalgamated Clothing Workers' Union fifty thousand. In Toledo, Ohio, National Guardsmen were summoned to protect strikebreakers at the Electric Autolite Company plant. When angry strikers began tossing bottles and bricks, the guardsmen retaliated with gunfire and tear gas. Two people were killed and many injured. A threat of a city-wide strike brought the company around, and federal mediation helped work out a settlement. On the West Coast federal intervention finally secured union recognition for striking longshoremen. Only after a bloody conflict in Minneapolis, involving several strikes and two deaths, were the Teamsters established in the Midwest. Federal mediation, along with effective pressure from the Governor, also helped resolve that crisis.

A major shortcoming of the new act was that its Section 7 (a) and (b) lacked bite. The National Labor Board could recommend collective bargaining but it could not enforce its policy in the courts. The law, in fact, favored the establishment of company unions, which flourished in the steel, rubber, petroleum, and chemical industries. Disillusioned workers began calling the NRA the "National Run Around."

Senator Wagner also came to the conclusion that something more was needed to secure labor peace. Early in 1934 he introduced a bill calling for a quasi-judicial tribunal modeled after the Federal Trade Commission. Initially, however, he received little support for his proposal. Instead, Congress, on June 19, 1934, reaffirmed the principle of Section 7 (a). Public Resolution No. 44 reads:

Resolved by the Senate and the House of Representatives of the United States of America in Congress assembled, that in order to further effectuate the policy of title I of the National Industrial Recovery Act, and in the exercise of the powers therein and herein conferred, the President is authorized to establish a board or boards authorized and directed to investigate issues, facts, practices, or activities of employers or employees in any controversies arising under section 7a of said Act or which are burdening or obstructing, or threatening to burden or obstruct, the free flow of interstate commerce, the salaries, compensation and expenses of the board or boards and necessary employees being paid as provided in section 2 of the National Industrial Recovery Act.

SEC. 2. Any board so established is hereby empowered, when it shall appear in the public interest, to order and conduct an election by a secret ballot of any of the employees of any employer, to determine by what person or persons or organization they desire to be represented in order to insure the right of employees to organize and to select their representatives for the purpose of collective bargaining as defined in Section 7a of said Act and now incorporated herein.

Pursuant to the resolution the President appointed a National Labor Relations Board of three members, superseding the earlier, ineffective National Labor Board. The new board possessed considerable organization with some twenty field offices. It adopted procedures similar to those later incorporated in the 1935 National Labor Relations Act, and issued over two hundred decisions involving interpretations of Section 7 (a) of the N.L.R.A. These later were to prove extremely useful in interpreting similar provisions of the act. Because of its meager powers, the Board had little success in enforcing its decisions in the brief period which preceded the Supreme Court's declaration of May 27, 1935, in *Schechter Poultry Corporation* v. *United States,* 295 U.S. 495, holding the N.L.R.A. unconstitutional. As a result, the Court left the Roosevelt Administration with little to campaign on in the year ahead. Both of its efforts to establish effective boards had failed.

Senator Wagner reintroduced his measure to strengthen a national collective bargaining policy and the so-called Wagner Act of 1935 became a part of a broad legislative package, which included higher income taxes, a new relief program under the Works Progress Administration, and the nation's first social security act. Together this legislation formed the foundation of what is commonly referred to as the Second New Deal.

J. Warren Madden, the first Chairman of the Wagner Act's National Labor Relations Board, relates his recollections of the Wagner Act as it passed through the legislative mill:

In the testimony, and later on the floor of both houses of Congress, there was much criticism of the bill because it did not forbid "coercion from any source," meaning, of course, coercion of workmen by fellow workers or union, to join unions. It was answered that the coercion of employees by employees, if it involved violence or threats of violence, was adequately covered by existing local law, and that to attempt to place these matters within the jurisdiction of a federal regulatory agency would convert the agency into a police court.

The opposition to the bill spoke fervently in favor of the "employee representation plans," and the deprivation of freedom of employees which would result if employing companies were not permitted to prepare such plans and encourage their employees to make use of them rather than join outside unions. The testimony of those who favored the bill, and the sense of reality of the Committee and of the members of Congress discounted the testimony as to the peaceful personnel relations in plants having company unions. If real two-sided negotiations as to wages and hours and working conditions are to take place, and if the employer, before the negotiations begin, suggests that the employees have no one at the bargaining table except their fellow employees, dependent upon the employers for their jobs, it would seem that that would be notice enough to the employees that they need some independent advice and leadership. It is very romantic to idealize the innate shrewdness of the everyday American workman, but how can he possibly know how much the employer can or will or ought to pay, when he knows little about the real state of the employer's finances, or of the labor market, and his conferences are with the highly skilled and experienced representatives chosen and trained for that purpose by the employer. He is flattered, of course, by having been chosen by his fellow-employees as the best man they have for the purpose.

As Lloyd Garrison put it to the Committee, employee representatives are subject to being fired at any moment, are looking for advancement and therefore subconsciously at least hoping to curry favor with their employers by being polite and courteous and not bringing up disagreeable matters. They like to sit around the table with the employer and smoke free cigars but when it comes to actually attempting to negotiate wages and hours for the plant they are absolutely helpless. When you have got a problem of fixing up the back stairs, or putting a new window in the top story, they do very well.

A section of the bill provided for elections to be held by the Board, and for the representatives selected by the majority to be the sole representatives of all the employees in the bargaining unit. The opponents to the bill strongly urged the rights of minorities. The issue was never a genuine one. Purporting to negotiate with several groups or their representatives at the same time about the same subject matter could produce nothing but confusion and impossibility of agreement.

The Senate Committee reported the Wagner bill with minor amendments on May 2, 1935. After a lengthy debate the Senate passed it two weeks later. That bill, with certain amendments, was reported by the House committee, recommitted, again reported on June 10, and after an extensive House debate, was passed on June 19. A conference committee considered and resolved the differences between the two bills and the reconciled version received approval by both houses on June 27.

As the following legislative materials—committee reports and selections from the congressional debates—indicate, the principal matters of congressional controversy involved questions concerning constitutionality, company unions, the closed shop, the source and content of prohibited coercion, the principle of majority rule, appropriate bargaining units, the duty to bargain collectively, and the relationship of the National Labor Relations Board to the Department of Labor.

President Roosevelt signed the bill on July 5, 1935, declaring:

This act defines, as a part of our substantive law, the right of self-organization of employees in industry for the purpose of collective bargaining, and provides methods by which the Government can safeguard that legal right. It establishes a National Labor Relations Board to hear and determine cases in which it is charged that this legal right is abridged or denied, and to hold fair elections to ascertain who are the chosen representatives of employees.

A better relationship between labor and management is the high purpose of this act. By assuring the employees the right of collective bargaining it fosters the development of the employment contract on a sound and equitable basis. By providing an orderly procedure for determining who is entitled to represent the employees, it aims to remove one of the chief causes of wasteful economic strife. By preventing practices which tend to destroy the independence of labor, it seeks, for every worker within its scope, that freedom of choice and action which is justly his.

The National Labor Relations Board will be an independent quasi-judicial body. It should be clearly understood that it will not act as mediator or conciliator in labor disputes. The function of mediation remains, under this act, the duty of the Secretary of Labor and of the Conciliation Service of the Department of Labor. It is important that the judicial function and the mediation function should not be confused. Compromise, the essence of mediation, has no place in the interpretation and enforcement of the law.

This act, defining rights, the enforcement of which is recognized by the Congress to be necessary as both an act of common justice and economic advance, must not be misinterpreted. It may eventually eliminate one major cause of labor disputes, but it will not stop all labor disputes. It does not cover all industry and labor, but is applicable only when violation of the legal right of independent self-organization would burden or obstruct interstate commerce. Accepted by management, labor, and the public with a sense of sober responsibility and of willing cooperation, however, it should serve as an important step toward the achievement of justice and peaceful labor relations in industry.

The 1935 National Labor Relations Act forms the foundation of our present national commitment to free collective bargaining as a matter of public policy. Although desperate, troubled times brought on its enactment, nonetheless, the shape, the very origins of our national labor policy owe much to Senator Wagner. Leon Keyserling, the economist who served as Senator Wagner's legislative assistant between 1933 and 1937, has said, "The Wagner Act in its final form was shaped by Senator Wagner and me to the extent that any two people can shape so important a piece of legislation." Mr. Keyserling then added:

> Based on my proximity to the history of the Wagner Act, one item of prime significance which sticks in my memory is the role played by Senator Wagner himself in connection with the statute which bears his name. While it is true that his proposal could not have become law in the political climate of 1928, nor perhaps in the climate of 1938, it is equally true that there would never have been a Wagner Act or anything like it if the Senator had not spent himself in this cause to a degree which almost defies description.

Whatever one may think of the Wagner Act provisions, this writer strongly believes that it was a superior piece of legislative draftsmanship. Remarkably clear and concise for a statute of its importance and impact, its heart rested in Sections 7, 8, and 9. Section 7 succinctly stated the fundamental right of employees "to self-organization, to form, join, or assist labor organizations, to bargain collectively through representatives of their own choosing, and to engage in concerted activities, for the purpose of collective bargaining or other mutual aid or protection." These rights were implemented in two principal ways. First, Section 8 listed five specific employer unfair labor practices: (1) the broad and residual prohibition against interference, restraint, and coercion; (2) a ban on domination, interference and support with respect to any labor organization; (3) a proscription of discrimination to encourage or discourage union membership; (4) a similar prohibition against discrimination for filing charges or giving testimony under the act; and (5) a prohibition against refusal to bargain with the employees' statutory representative. The second implementation of the employees' rights was through the provisions of Section 9, which established machinery for the selection of employee representatives. The central features of this mechanism were: (1) the establishment of the extremely important principle of majority rule, that is, that the representative designated by a majority of the employees in an appropriate bargaining unit is their exclusive representative; (2) the grant to the National Labor Relations Board of broad discretion to determine whether the unit appropriate "shall be the employer unit, craft unit, or subdivision thereof"; (3) the delegation to the N.L.R.B. of power to investigate questions of representation and to resolve them by election or other suitable method; and (4) a system of judicial review of N.L.R.B. representation determinations.

The remaining provisions largely supplemented the basic provisions. Thus, Section 1 consisted of findings and policy underlying the statute; Section 2 defined a number of important terms used throughout the statute; Sections 3, 4, 5, and 6 dealt with the creation of a National Labor Relations Board in which was vested the primary responsibility for administration of the statute; Section 10 prescribed procedures for the prevention of unfair labor practices, including a system of judicial review of board orders; Section 11 granted the board certain investigatory powers; and the remaining Sections, 13, 14, 15, and 16, contained miscellaneous limitations.

The prime and immediate legal question raised by the passage of the Wagner Act was constitutionality. Again quoting Chairman Madden, that story began as follows:

On September 5, 1935, just 9 days after the members of the Board were commissioned, the National Lawyers Committee of the American Liberty League issued its "Report on the Constitutionality of the National Labor Relations Act." The report was in the form of a legal brief, 132 pages long, but it did not of course speak for any litigant or client since there was no case pending either before the Board or the courts under the new law. The report was issued, then, *pro bono publico,* to advise the public of the constitutional status of the new statute. The summary at the beginning of the report concluded with this language:

"Considering the Act in the light of our history, the established form of government, and the decisions of our highest Court, we have no hesitancy in concluding that it is unconstitutional and that it constitutes a complete departure from our constitutional and traditional theories of government."

The National Lawyers Committee which sponsored the report consisted of 58 lawyers whose names and addresses were printed on the inside cover of the report. Lawyers from practically all of the principal cities of the country were in the list. And every one of those named was recognized in his area as a lawyer of distinction and success. There were in the list a former General and two former Solicitors General of the United States.

The issuance of the report, and its sponsorship, were unique. That so many successful and reputable lawyers, without the inducement of retainer by client, should be so deeply moved by respect for the Constitution and our form of government that they felt compelled to advise the country of the wrong that threatened it, was a remarkable example of the devotion of the bar to the service of the public, or was it? The effect of the advice upon the thousands of lesser lawyers who looked for leadership to the distinguished lawyers of the committee was what might be expected. Many of them regarded themselves as being in the fortunate position of engaging in a holy crusade, with pay, when they were employed to frustrate the efforts of the Board to administer the new law. And there was a place for judges in the ranks of the devout. If, as advised, the statute was unconstitutional, the county judge had sworn the same oath as the Justices of the Supreme Court, to protect and defend the Constitution. He therefore felt obliged, and privileged, to restrain by injunction the activities of these agents from Washington who came to his community to administer a law which was no law at all.

The members of the Lawyers Committee might well have concluded, after normal deliberation, that the statute would be held to be unconstitutional. But there were, in the precedents, enough conflicts and inconsistencies to give pause to the normally cautious lawyer. I think that not many of the members of the committee would have, in an advisory opinion to an important paying client, said, "I have no hesitancy in advising you that the Act is a nullity and that you may disregard it, in complete confidence that any ensuing litigation will terminate in your favor."

The expectations of the Liberty League lawyers were doomed to disappointment. As far back as 1897, the Jones & Laughlin Steel Corporation had driven the Amalgamated Iron, Steel and Tin Workers from its plants. In 1919, it had been one of the mills to escape the steel strike. Aliquippa, Pennsylvania, the site of Jones & Laughlin's largest plant, was a closed company town where strangers were not welcome. In October, 1934, Governor Gifford Pinchot sent state troopers to Aliquippa to maintain order so that trade unionists could hold a meeting. When the company discharged thirteen men for union activity, the steel union appealed to the N.L.R.B. After a preliminary investigation, a complaint was issued against the company. The steel firm challenged the proceedings on the grounds that the Wagner Act was unconstitutional. The Supreme Court heard arguments in February, 1937, and gave its five to four decision which upheld the constitutionality of the Wagner Act. A thirty-six-hour strike in mid-May established the Steel Workers Organizing Committee, Congress of Industrial Organization, as the union of Jones & Laughlin workers. Indeed, a turning point in the history of labor law and labor relations had been reached.

The significance of the Wagner Act cannot be overstated. Validation by the Supreme Court forced employers to accept collective bargaining, and great organizing drives in the mass production industries—auto, steel, rubber, and oil to name a few—mounted by the Congress of Industrial Organizations succeeded under the legal protection afforded by the act. Unions flourished and the violence that attended labor's early struggles receded and was largely replaced by peaceful picketing. This much we owe the Wagner Labor Act.

The original National Labor Relations Act (the Wagner Act) is reproduced in full below and is followed by other materials relevant to the legislative history of the statute.

THE WAGNER ACT
July 5, 1935

To diminish the cause of labor disputes burdening or obstructing interstate and foreign commerce, to create a National Labor Relations Board, and for other purposes.

Be it enacted by the Senate and House of Representatives of the United States of America in Congress assembled,

FINDINGS AND POLICY

SEC. 1. The denial by employers of the right of employees to organize and the refusal by employers to accept the procedure of collective bargaining lead to strikes and other forms of industrial strife or unrest, which have the intent or the necessary effect of burdening or obstructing commerce by (a) impairing the efficiency, safety, or operation of the instrumentalities of commerce; (b) occurring in the current of commerce; (c) materially affecting, restraining, or controlling the flow of raw materials or manufactured or processed goods from or into the channels of commerce, or the prices of such materials or goods in commerce; or (d) causing diminution of employment and wages in such volume as substantially to impair or disrupt the market for goods flowing from or into the channels of commerce.

The inequality of bargaining power between employees who do not possess full freedom of association or actual liberty of contract, and employers who are organized in the corporate or other forms of ownership association substantially burdens and affects the flow of commerce, and tends to aggravate recurrent business depressions, by depressing wage rates and the purchasing power of wage earners in industry and by preventing the stabilization of competitive wage rates and working conditions within and between industries.

Experience has proved that protection by law of the right of employees to organize and bargain collectively safeguards commerce from injury, impairment, or interruption, and promotes the flow of commerce by removing certain recognized sources of industrial strife and unrest, by encouraging practices fundamental to the friendly adjustment of industrial disputes arising out of differences as to wages, hours, or other working conditions, and by restoring equality of bargaining power between employers and employees.

It is hereby declared to be the policy of the United States to eliminate the causes of certain substantial obstructions to the free flow of commerce and to mitigate and eliminate these obstructions when they have occurred by encouraging the practice and procedure of collective bargaining and by protecting the exercise by workers of full freedom of association, self-organization, and designation of representatives of their own choosing, for the purpose of negotiating the terms and conditions of their employment or other mutual aid or protection.

DEFINITIONS

SEC. 2. When used in this Act—

(1) The term "person" includes one or more individuals, partnerships, associations, corporations, legal representatives, trustees, trustees in bankruptcy, or receivers.

(2) The term "employer" includes any person acting in the interest of an employer, directly or indirectly, but shall not include the United States, or any State or political subdivision thereof, or any person subject to the Railway Labor Act, as amended from time to time, or any labor organization (other than when acting as an employer), or anyone acting in the capacity of officer or agent of such labor organization.

(3) The term "employee" shall include any employee, and shall not be limited to the employees of a particular employer, unless the Act explicitly states otherwise, and shall include any individual whose work has ceased as a consequence of, or in connection with, any current labor dispute or because of any unfair labor practice, and who has not obtained any other regular and substantially equivalent employment, but shall not include any individual employed as an agricultural laborer, or in the domestic service of any family or person at his home, or any individual employed by his parent or spouse.

(4) The term "representatives" includes any individual or labor organization.

(5) The term "labor organization" means any organization of any kind, or any agency or employee representation committee or plan, in which employees participate and which exists for the purpose, in whole or in part, of dealing with employers concerning grievances, labor disputes, wages, rates of pay, hours of employment, or conditions of work.

(6) The term "commerce" means trade, traffic, commerce, transportation, or communication among the several States, or between the District of Columbia or any Territory of the United States and any State or other Territory, or between any foreign country and any State, Territory, or the District of Columbia, or within the District of Columbia or any Territory, or between points in the same State but through any other State or any Territory or the District of Columbia or any foreign country.

(7) The term "affecting commerce" means in commerce, or burdening or obstructing commerce or the free flow of commerce, or having led or tending to lead to a labor dispute burdening or obstructing commerce or the free flow of commerce.

(8) The term "unfair labor practice" means any unfair labor practice listed in section 8.

(9) The term "labor dispute" includes any controversy concerning terms, tenure or conditions of employment, or concerning the association or representation of persons in negotiating, fixing, maintaining, changing, or seeking to arrange terms or conditions of employment, regardless of whether the disputants stand in the proximate relation of employer and employee.

(10) The term "National Labor Relations Board" means the National Labor Relations Board created by section 3 of this Act.

(11) The term "old Board" means the National Labor Relations Board established by Executive Order Numbered 6763 of the President on June 29, 1934, pursuant to Public Resolution Numbered 44, approved June 19, 1934 (48 Stat. 1183), and reestablished and continued by Executive Order Numbered 7074 of the President of June 15, 1935, pursuant to Title I of the National Industrial Recovery Act (48 Stat. 195) as amended and continued by Senate Joint Resolution 133 approved June 14, 1935.

NATIONAL LABOR RELATIONS BOARD

SEC. 3. (a) There is hereby created a board, to be known as the "National Labor Relations Board" (hereinafter referred to as the "Board"), which shall be composed of three members, who shall be appointed by the President, by and with the advice and consent of the Senate. One of the original members shall be appointed for a term of one year, one for a term of three years, and one for a term of five years, but their successors shall be appointed for terms of five years each except that any individual chosen to fill a vacancy shall be appointed only for the unexpired term of the member whom he shall succeed. The President shall designate one member to serve as chairman of the Board. Any member of the Board may be removed by the President, upon notice and hearing, for neglect of duty or malfeasance in office, but for no other cause.

(b) A vacancy in the Board shall not impair the right of the remaining members to exercise all the powers of the Board, and two members of the Board shall, at all times, constitute a quorum. The Board shall have an official seal which shall be judicially noticed.

(c) The Board shall at the close of each fiscal year make a report in writing to Congress and to the President, stating in detail the cases it has heard, the decisions it has rendered, the names, salaries, and duties of all employees and officers in the employ or under the supervision of the Board, and an account of all moneys it has disbursed.

SEC. 4. (a) Each member of the Board shall receive a salary of $10,000 a year, shall be eligible for reappointment, and shall not engage in any other business, vocation, or employment. The Board shall appoint, without regard for the provisions of the civil service laws but subject to the

Classification Act of 1923, as amended, an executive secretary, and such attorneys, examiners, and regional directors, and shall appoint such other employees with regard to existing laws applicable to the employment and compensation of officers and employees of the United States, as it may from time to time find necessary for the proper performance of its duties and as may be from time to time appropriated for by Congress. The Board may establish or utilize such regional, local, or other agencies, and utilize such voluntary and uncompensated services, as may from time to time be needed. Attorneys appointed under this section may, at the direction of the Board, appear for and represent the Board in any case in court. Nothing in this Act shall be construed to authorize the Board to appoint individuals for the purpose of conciliation or mediation (or for statistical work), where such service may be obtained from the Department of Labor.

(b) Upon the appointment of the three original members of the Board and the designation of its chairman, the old Board shall cease to exist. All employees of the old Board shall be transferred to and become employees of the Board with salaries under the Classification Act of 1923, as amended, without acquiring by such transfer a permanent or civil service status. All records, papers, and property of the old Board shall become records, papers, and property of the Board, and all unexpended funds and appropriations for the use and maintenance of the old Board shall become funds and appropriations available to be expended by the Board in the exercise of the powers, authority, and duties conferred on it by this Act.

(c) All of the expenses of the Board, including all necessary traveling and subsistence expenses outside the District of Columbia incurred by the members or employees of the Board under its orders, shall be allowed and paid on the presentation of itemized vouchers therefor approved by the Board or by any individual it designates for that purpose.

SEC. 5. The principal office of the Board shall be in the District of Columbia, but it may meet and exercise any or all of its powers at any other place. The Board may, by one or more of its members or by such agents or agencies as it may designate, prosecute any inquiry necessary to its functions in any part of the United States. A member who participates in such an inquiry shall not be disqualified from subsequently participating in a decision of the Board in the same case.

SEC. 6. (a) The Board shall have authority from time to time to make, amend, and rescind such rules and regulations as may be necessary to carry out the provisions of this Act. Such rules and regulations shall be effective upon publication in the manner which the Board shall prescribe.

RIGHTS OF EMPLOYEES

SEC. 7. Employees shall have the right to self-organization, to form, join, or assist labor organizations, to bargain collectively through representatives of their own choosing, and to engage in concerted activities, for the purpose of collective bargaining or other mutual aid or protection.

SEC. 8. It shall be an unfair labor practice for an employer—

(1) To interfere with, restrain, or coerce employees in the exercise of the rights guaranteed in section 7.

(2) To dominate or interfere with the formation or administration of any labor organization or contribute financial or other support to it: *Provided,* That subject to rules and regulations made and published by the Board pursuant to section 6 (a), an employer shall not be prohibited from permitting employees to confer with him during working hours without loss of time or pay.

(3) By discrimination in regard to hire or tenure of employment or any term or condition of employment to encourage or discourage membership in any labor organization: *Provided,* That nothing in this Act, or in the National Industrial Recovery Act (U. S. C., Supp. VII, title 15, secs. 701–712), as amended from time to time, or in any code or agreement approved or prescribed thereunder, or in any other statute of the United States, shall preclude an employer from making an agreement with a labor organization (not established, maintained, or assisted by any action defined in this Act as an unfair labor practice) to require as a condition of employment membership therein, if such labor organization is the representative of the employees as provided in section 9 (a), in the appropriate collective bargaining unit covered by such agreement when made.

(4) To discharge or otherwise discriminate against an employee because he has filed charges or given testimony under this Act.

(5) To refuse to bargain collectively with the representatives of his employees, subject to the provisions of Section 9 (a).

REPRESENTATIVES AND ELECTIONS

SEC. 9. (a) Representatives designated or selected for the purposes of collective bargaining by the majority of the employees in a unit appropriate for such purposes, shall be the exclusive representatives of all the employees in such unit for the purposes of collective bargaining in respect to rates of pay, wages, hours of employment, or other conditions of employment: *Provided,* That any individual employee or a group of employees shall have the right at any time to present grievances to their employer.

(b) The Board shall decide in each case whether, in order to insure to employees the full benefit of their right to self-organization and to collective bargaining, and otherwise to effectuate the policies of this Act, the unit appropriate for the purposes of collective bargaining shall be the employer unit, craft unit, plant unit, or subdivision thereof.

(c) Whenever a question affecting commerce arises concerning the representation of employees, the Board may investigate such controversy and certify to the parties, in writing, the name or names of the representatives that have been designated or selected. In any such investigation, the Board shall provide for an appropriate hearing upon due notice, either in conjunction with a proceeding under section 10 or otherwise, and may take a secret ballot of employees, or utilize any other suitable method to ascertin[1] such representatives.

(d) Whenever an order of the Board made pursuant to section 10 (c) is based in whole or in part upon facts certified following an investigation pursuant to subsection (c) of this section, and there is a petition for the enforcement or review of such order, such certification and the record of such investigation shall be included in the transcript of the entire record required to be filed under subsections 10 (e) or 10 (f), and thereupon the decree of the court enforcing, modifying, or setting aside in whole or in part the order of the Board shall be made and entered upon the pleadings, testimony, and proceedings set forth in such transcript.

PREVENTION OF UNFAIR LABOR PRACTICES

SEC. 10. (a) The Board is empowered, as hereinafter provided, to prevent any person from engaging in any unfair labor practice (listed in section 8) affecting commerce. This power shall be exclusive, and shall not be affected by any other means of adjustment or prevention that has been or may be established by agreement, code, law, or otherwise.

(b) Whenever it is charged that any person has engaged in or is engaging in any such unfair labor practice, the Board, or any agent or agency designated by the Board for such purposes, shall have power to issue and cause to be served upon such person a complaint stating the charges in that respect, and containing a notice of hearing before the Board or a member thereof, or before a designated agent or agency, at a place therein fixed, not less than five days after the serving of said complaint. Any such complaint may be amended by the member, agent, or agency conducting the hearing or the Board in its discretion at any time prior to the issuance of an order based thereon. The person so complained of shall have the right to file an answer to the original or amended complaint and to appear in person or otherwise and give testimony at the place and time fixed in the complaint. In the discretion of the member, agent or agency conducting the hearing or the Board, any other person may be allowed to intervene in the said proceeding and to present testimony. In any such proceeding the rules of evidence prevailing in courts of law or equity shall not be controlling.

(c) The testimony taken by such member, agent or agency or the Board shall be reduced to writing and filed with the Board. Thereafter, in its discretion, the Board upon notice may take further testimony or hear argument. If upon all the testimony taken the Board shall be of the opinion that any person named in the complaint has engaged in or is engaging in any such unfair labor practice, then the Board shall state its findings of fact and shall issue and cause to be served on such person an order requiring such person to cease and desist from such unfair labor practice, and to take such affirmative action, including reinstatement of employees with or without back pay, as will effectuate the policies of this Act. Such order may further require such person to make reports from time to time showing the extent to which it has complied with the order. If upon all the testimony taken the Board shall be of the opinion that no person named in the complaint has engaged in or is engaging in any such unfair labor practice, then the Board shall state its findings of fact and shall issue an order dismissing the said complaint.

(d) Until a transcript of the record in a case shall have been filed in a court, as hereinafter provided, the Board may at any time, upon reasonable notice and in such manner as it shall deem proper, modify or set aside, in whole or in part, any finding or order made or issued by it.

(e) The Board shall have power to petition any circuit court of appeals of the United States (including the Court of Appeals of the District of Columbia), or if all the circuit courts of appeals to which application may be made are in vacation, any district court of the United States (including the Supreme Court of the District of Columbia), within any circuit or district, respectively, wherein the unfair labor practice in question occurred or wherein such person resides or transacts business, for the enforcement of such order and for appropriate temporary relief or restraining order, and shall certify and file in the court a transcript of the entire record in the proceeding, including the pleadings and testimony upon which such order was entered and the findings and order of the Board. Upon such filing, the court shall cause notice thereof to be served upon such person, and thereupon shall have jurisdiction of the proceeding and of the question determined therein, and shall have power to grant such temporary relief or restraining order as it deems just and proper, and to make and enter upon the pleadings, testimony, and proceedings set forth in such transcript a decree enforcing, modifying, and enforcing as so modified, or setting aside in whole or in part the order of the Board. No objection that has not been urged before the Board, its member, agent or agency, shall be considered by the court, unless the failure or neglect to urge such objection shall be excused because of extraordinary circumstances. The findings of the Board as to the facts, if supported by evidence, shall be conclusive. If either party shall apply to the court for leave to adduce additional evidence and shall show to the satisfaction of the court that such additional evidence is material and that there were reasonable grounds for the failure to adduce such evidence in the hearing before the Board, its member, agent, or agency, the court may order such additional evidence to be taken before the Board, its member, agent, or agency, and to be made a part of the transcript. The Board may modify its findings as to the facts, or make new findings, by reason of additional evidence so taken and filed, and it shall file such modified or new findings, which, if supported by evidence, shall be conclusive, and shall file its recommendations, if any, for the modification or setting aside of its original order. The jurisdiction of the court shall be exclusive and its judgment and decree shall be final, except that the same shall be subject to review by the appropriate circuit court of appeals if application was made to the district court as hereinabove provided, and by the Supreme Court of the United States upon writ of certiorari or certification as provided in sections 239 and 240 of the Judicial Code, as amended (U. S. C., title 28, secs. 346 and 347).

(f) Any person aggrieved by a final order of the Board granting or denying in whole or in part the relief sought may obtain a review of such order in any circuit court of appeals of the United States in the circuit wherein the unfair labor practice in question was alleged to have been engaged in or wherein such person resides or transacts business, or in the Court of Appeals of the District of Columbia, by filing in such court a written petition praying that the order of the Board be modified or set aside. A copy of such petition shall be forthwith served upon the Board, and thereupon the aggrieved party shall file in the court a transcript of the entire record in the proceeding, certified by the Board, including the pleading and testimony upon which the order complained of was entered and the findings and order of the Board. Upon such filing, the court shall proceed in the same manner as in the case of an application by the Board under subsection (e), and shall have the same exclusive jurisdiction to grant to the Board such temporary relief or restraining order as it deems just and proper, and in like manner to make and enter a decree enforcing, modifying, and enforcing as so modified, or setting aside in whole or in part the order of the Board; and the findings of the Board as to the facts, if supported by evidence, shall in like manner be conclusive.

(g) The commencement of proceedings under subsection (e) or (f) of this section shall not, unless specifically ordered by the court, operate as a stay of the Board's order.

(h) When granting appropriate temporary relief or a restraining order, or making and entering a decree enforcing, modifying, and enforcing as so modified or setting aside in whole or in part an order of the Board, as provided in this section, the jurisdiction of courts sitting in equity shall not be limited by the Act entitled "An Act to amend the Judicial Code and to define and limit the jurisdiction of courts sitting in equity, and for other purposes," approved March 23, 1932 (U. S. C., Supp. VII, title 29, secs. 101–115).

(i) Petitions filed under this Act shall be heard expeditiously, and if possible within ten days after they have been docketed.

INVESTIGATORY POWERS

SEC. 11. For the purpose of all hearings and investigations, which, in the opinion of the Board, are necessary and proper for the exercise of the powers vested in it by section 9 and section 10—

(1) The Board, or its duly authorized agents or agencies, shall at all reasonable times have access to, for the purpose of examination, and the right to copy any evidence of any person being investigated or proceeded against that relates to any matter under investigation or in question. Any member of the Board shall have power to issue subpoenas requiring the attendance and testimony of witnesses and the production of any evidence that relates to any matter under investigation or in question, before the Board, its member, agent, or agency conducting the hearing or investigation. Any member of the Board, or any agent or agency designated by the Board for such purposes, may administer oaths and affirmations, examine witnesses, and receive evidence. Such attendance of witnesses and the production of such evidence may be required from any place in the United States or any Territory or possession thereof, at any designated place of hearing.

(2) In case of contumacy or refusal to obey a subpoena issued to any person, any District Court of the United States or the United States courts of any Territory or possession, or the Supreme Court of the District of Columbia, within the jurisdiction of which the inquiry is carried on or within the jurisdiction of which said person guilty of contumacy or refusal to obey is found or resides or transacts business, upon application by the Board shall have jurisdiction to issue to such person an order requiring such person to appear before the Board, its member, agent, or agency, there to produce evidence if so ordered, or there to give testimony touching the matter under investigation or in question; and any failure to obey such order of the court may be punished by said court as a contempt thereof.

(3) No person shall be excused from attending and testifying or from producing books, records, correspondence, documents, or other evidence in obedience to the subpoena of the Board, on the ground that the testimony or evidence required of him may tend to incriminate him or subject him to a penalty or forfeiture; but no individual shall be prosecuted or subjected to any penalty or forfeiture for or on account of any transaction, matter, or thing concerning which he is compelled, after having claimed his privilege against self-incrimination, to testify or produce evidence, except that such individual so testifying shall not be exempt from prosecution and punishment for perjury committed in so testifying.

(4) Complaints, orders, and other process and papers of the Board, its member, agent, or agency, may be served either personally or by registered mail or by telegraph or by leaving a copy thereof at the principal

office or place of business of the person required to be served. The verified return by the individual so serving the same, setting forth the manner of such service shall be proof of the same, and the return post office receipt or telegraph receipt therefor when registered and mailed or telegraphed as aforesaid shall be proof of service of the same. Witnesses summoned before the Board, its member, agent, or agency, shall be paid the same fees and mileage that are paid witnesses in the courts of the United States, and witnesses whose depositions are taken and the persons taking the same shall severally be entitled to the same fees as are paid for like services in the courts of the United States.

(5) All process of any court to which application may be made under this Act may be served in the judicial district wherein the defendent or other person required to be served resides or may be found.

(6) The several departments and agencies of the Government, when directed by the President, shall furnish the Board, upon its request, all records, papers, and information in their possession relating to any matter before the Board.

SEC. 12. Any person who shall willfully resist, prevent, impede, or interfere with any member of the Board or any of its agents or agencies in the performance of duties pursuant to this Act shall be punished by a fine of not more than $5,000 or by imprisonment for not more than one year, or both.

LIMITATIONS

SEC. 13. Nothing in this Act shall be construed so as to interfere with or impede or diminish in any way the right to strike.

SEC. 14. Wherever the application of the provisions of section 7 (a) of the National Industrial Recovery Act (U. S. C., Supp. VII, title 15, sec. 707 (a)), as amended from time to time, or of section 77 B, paragraphs (1) and (m) of the Act approved June 7, 1934, entitled "An Act to amend an Act entitled 'An Act to establish a uniform system of bankruptcy throughout the United States' approved July 1, 1898, and Acts amendatory thereof and supplementary thereto" (48 Stat. 922, pars. (1) and (m)), as amended from time to time, or of Public Resolution Numbered 44, approved June 19, 1934 (48 Stat. 1183), conflicts with the application of the provisions of this Act, this Act shall prevail: *Provided,* That in any situation where the provisions of this Act cannot be validly enforced, the provisions of such other Acts shall remain in full force and effect.

SEC. 15. If any provision of this Act, or the application of such provision to any person or circumstance, shall be held invalid the remainder of this Act, or the application of such provision to persons or circumstances other than those as to which it is held invalid, shall not be affected thereby.

SEC. 16. This Act may be cited as the "National Labor Relations Act." Approved, July 5, 1935.

THE ORIGINS

Senator Wagner's Statement Regarding National Labor Relations Bill
February 21, 1935

The recovery program has sought to bestow upon the businessman and the worker a new freedom to grapple with the great economic challenges of our times. We have released the businessman from the undiscriminating enforcement of the antitrust laws, which had been subjecting him to the attacks of the price cutters and wage reducers—the pirates of industry. In order to deal out the equal treatment upon which a just democratic society must rest, we at the same time guaranteed the freedom of action of the worker. In fact, the now famous section 7 (a), by stating that employees should be allowed to cooperate among themselves if they desire to do so, merely restated principles that Congress has avowed for half a century.

Congress is familiar with the events of the past two years. While industry's freedom of action has been encouraged until the trade association movement has blanketed the entire country, employees attempting in good faith to exercise their liberties under section 7 (a) have met with repeated rebuffs. It was to check this evil that the President in his wisdom created the National Labor Board in August 1933, out of which has emerged the present National Labor Relations Board.

The Board has performed a marvelous service in composing disputes and sending millions of workers back to their jobs upon terms beneficial to every interest. But it was handicapped from the beginning, and it is gradually but surely losing its effectiveness, because of the practical inability to enforce its decisions. At present it may refer its findings to the National Recovery Administration and await some action by that agency, such as the removal of the Blue Eagle. We all know that the entire enforcement procedure of the NRA is closely interlinked with the voluntary spirit of the codes. Business in the large is allowed to police itself through the code authorities. This voluntarism is without question admirable in respect to provisions for fair competition that have been written by industry and with which business is in complete accord. But it is wholly unadapted to the enforcement of a specific law of Congress which becomes a crucial issue only in those very cases where it is opposed by the guiding spirits of the code authorities. Secondly, the Board may refer a case to the Department of Justice. But since the Board has no power to subpoena records or witnesses, its hearings are largely *ex parte* and its records so infirm that the Department of Justice is usually unable to act. Finally, the existence of numerous industrial boards whose interpretations of section 7 (a) are not subject to the co-ordinating influence of a supreme National Labor Relations Board, is creating a maze of confusion and contradictions. While there is a different code for each trade, there is only one section 7 (a), and no definite law written by Congress can mean something different in each industry. These difficulties are reducing section 7 (a) to a sham and a delusion.

The breakdown of section 7 (a) brings results equally disastrous to industry and to labor. Last summer it led to a procession of bloody and costly strikes, which in some cases swelled almost to the magnitude of national emergencies. It is not material at this time to inquire where the balance of right and wrong rested in respect to these various controversies. If it is true that employees find it difficult to remain acquiescent when they lose the main privilege promised them by the Recovery Act, it is equally true that employers are tremendously handicapped when it is impossible to determine exactly what their rights are. Everybody needs a law that is precise and certain.

There has been a second and even more serious consequence of the breakdown of section 7 (a). When employees are denied the freedom to act in concert even when they desire to do so, they cannot exercise a restraining influence upon the wayward members of their own groups, and they cannot participate in our national endeavor to coordinate production and purchasing power. The consequences are already visible in the widening gap between wages and profits. If these consequences are allowed to produce their full harvest, the whole country will suffer from a new economic decline.

The national labor relations bill which I now propose is novel neither in philosophy nor in content. It creates no new substantive rights. It merely provides that employees, if they desire to do so, shall be free to organize for their mutual protection or benefit. Quite aside from section 7 (a), this principle has been embodied in the Norris-LaGuardia Act, in amendments to the Railway Labor Act passed last year, and in a long train of other enactments of Congress.

There is not a scintilla of truth in the widespread propaganda to the effect that this bill would tend to create a so-called "labor dictatorship." It does not encourage national unionism. It does not favor any particular union. It does not display any preference toward craft or industrial organizations. Most important of all, it does not force or even counsel any employee to join any union if he prefers to deal directly or individually with his employers. It seeks merely to make the worker a free man in the economic as well as the political field. Certainly the preservation of long-recognized fundamental rights is the only basis for frank and friendly relations in industry.

The erroneous impression that the bill expresses a bias for some particular form of union organization probably arises because it outlaws the company-dominated union. Let me emphasize that nothing in the measure discourages employees from uniting on an independent- or company-union basis, if by these terms we mean simply an organization confined to the limits of one plant or one employer. Nothing in the bill prevents employers from maintaining free and direct relations with their workers or from participating in group insurance, mutual welfare, pension systems, and other such activities. The only prohibition is against the sham or dummy union which is dominated by the employer, which is supported by the employer, which cannot change its rules or regulations without his consent, and which cannot live except by the grace of the employer's whims. To say that that kind of a union must be preserved in order to give employees freedom of selection is a contradiction in terms. There can be no freedom in an atmosphere of bondage. No organization can be free to represent the workers when it is the mere creature of the employer.

Equally erroneous is the belief that the bill creates a closed shop for all industry. It does not force any employer to make a closed-shop agreement. It does not even state that Congress favors the policy of the closed shop. It merely provides that employers and employees may voluntarily make closed-shop agreements in any State where they are now legal. Far from suggesting a change, it merely preserves the status quo.

A great deal of interest centers around the question of majority rule. The national labor relations bill provides that representatives selected by the majority of employees in an appropriate unit shall represent all the employees within that unit for the purposes of collective bargaining. This does not imply that an employee who is not a member of the majority group can be forced to enter the union which the majority favors. It means simply that the majority may decide who are to be the spokesmen for all in making agreements concerning wages, hours, and other conditions of employment. Once such agreements are made the bill provides that their terms must be applied without favor or discrimination to all employees. These provisions conform to the democratic procedure that is followed in every business and in our governmental life, and that was embodied by Congress in the Railway Labor Act last year. Without them the phrase "collective bargaining" is devoid of meaning, and the very few unfair employers are encouraged to divide their workers against themselves.

Finally, the National Labor Relations Board is established permanently, with jurisdiction over other boards dealing with cases under section 7 (a) or under its equivalent as written into this bill. Nothing could be more unfounded than the charges that the Board would be invested with arbitrary or dictatorial or even unusual powers. Its powers are modeled upon those of the Federal Trade Commission and numerous other governmental agencies. Its orders would be enforceable not by the Board, but by recourse to the courts of the United States, with every affected party entitled to all safeguards of appeal.

The enactment of this measure will clarify the industrial atmosphere and reduce the likelihood of another conflagration of strife such as we witnessed last summer. It will stabilize and improve business by laying the foundations for the amity and fair dealing upon which permanent progress must rest. It will give notice to all that the solemn pledge made by Congress when it enacted section 7 (a) cannot be ignored with impunity, and that a cardinal principle of the new deal for all and not some of our people is going to be supported and preserved by the Government.

Report of the Senate Committee on Education and Labor
May 1, 1935

THOMAS WALSH [DEM., MONT.] submitted the following Report.

The Committee on Education and Labor, to whom was referred the bill (S. 1958) to promote equality of bargaining power between employers and employees, to diminish the causes of labor disputes, to create a National Labor Relations Board, and for other purposes, after holding hearings and giving consideration to the bill, report the same with amendments and recommend the passage of the bill as amended.

In view of the impending expiration on June 16, 1935, of the National Industrial Recovery Act, with its fair promise in section 7 (a) of promoting industrial peace by the recognition of the rights of employees to organize and bargain collectively, and of Public Resolution 44, Seventy-third Congress, under which the present National Labor Relations Board was created, the time has come for a clean decision either to withdraw that promise or to implement it by effective legislation. Under the conditions existing a year ago the Congress was perhaps justified in passing Public Resolution 44 in lieu of a comprehensive dealing with the problem. But the compelling force of another year's experience, demonstrating that the Government's promise in section 7 (a) stands largely unfulfilled, makes unacceptable any further temporizing measures. In the committee's judgment the present bill is a logical development of a philosophy and a consistent policy manifest in many acts of Congress dealing over a period of years with labor relations.

GENERAL OBJECTIVES OF THE BILL

(1) *Industrial peace.*—The first objective of the bill is to promote industrial peace. The challenge of economic unrest is not new. During the period from 1915 through 1921 there were on the average 3,043 strikes per year, involving the vacating of 1,745,000 jobs and the loss of 50,242,000 working days every 12 months. From 1922 through 1926 the annual average totaled 1,050 strikes, 775,000 strikers, and 17,050,000 working days

lost. From 1927 through 1931 the yearly average for disputes was 763, for employees leaving their work 275,000, and for days lost 5,665,000. In 1933 over 812,137 workers were drawn into strikes, and in 1934 the number rose to 1,277,344. In this 2-year period over 32,000,000 working days were lost because of labor controversies. While exactitude is impossible, reliable authority has it that over a long range of time the loss due to strikes in this country has amounted to at least $1,000,000,000 per year. And no one can count the cost in bitterness of feeling, in inefficiency, and in permanent industrial dislocation.

Prudence forbids any attempt by the Government to remove all the causes of labor disputes. Disputes about wages, hours of work, and other working conditions should continue to be resolved by the play of competitive forces, so far as the provisions of codes of fair competition are not controlling. This bill in no respect regulates or even provides for supervision of wages or hours, nor does it establish any form of compulsory arbitration.

But many of the most fertile sources of industrial discontent can be segregated into a single category susceptible to legislative treatment. Competent students of industrial relations have estimated that at least 25 percent of all strikes have sprung from failure to recognize and utilize the theory and practices of collective bargaining, under which are subsumed the rights of employees to organize freely and to deal with employers through representatives of their own choosing. Figures compiled by the Bureau of Labor Statistics of the United States Department of Labor confirm this estimate. And of the 6,355 new cases received by the regional agencies of the present National Labor Relations Board during the second half of 1934, the issue of collective bargaining was paramount in 2,330, or about 74 percent.

It is thus believed feasible to remove the provocation to a large proportion of the bitterest industrial outbreaks by giving definite legal status to the procedure of collective bargaining and by setting up machinery to facilitate it. Furthermore by establishing the only process through which friendly negotiations or conferences can operate in modern large-scale industry, there should be a tremendous lessening of the strife that has resulted from failure to adjust wage and hour disputes.

This opinion is substantiated by experience in the United States. For over half a century, beginning with the act of October 1, 1888 (25 Stat. 501), and culminating in the 1934 amendments to the Railway Labor Act (48 Stat. 1185), Congress has constantly elaborated and perfected its protection of collective bargaining in the railroad industry. Largely in consequence, our main arteries of commerce have been remarkably free from the paralyzing effect of industrial disputes since the great strike of 1894. During the World War, when it became imperative that production should be maintained without interruption, the Government set up the War Labor Board and without hesitation applied to industry generally the principles that had been tested upon the railroads. Not until after the armistice was a single award of the War Labor Board violated, and our country remained singularly free from the industrial strife that harassed the other belligerent nations. Only after the war, when the Government withdrew its support of the practice of collective bargaining, was the country faced with a rising tide of labor disputes. And in this connection it must not be overlooked that the present National Labor Relations Board and its predecessor, the National Labor Board, despite the handicaps under which they have operated, handicaps which the present bill is designed to remove, have succeeded in keeping over 1,000,000 men at work upon terms satisfactory to all.

For these reasons, the committee believes that the present bill, by promoting peace in industry, will confer mutual benefits upon employers, workers, and the general public.

(2) *Economic adjustment.*—The second major objective of the bill is to encourage, by developing the procedure of collective bargaining, that equality of bargaining power which is a prerequisite to equality and opportunity and freedom of contract. The relative weakness of the isolated wage earner caught in the complex of modern industrialism has become such a commonplace of our economic literature and political vocabulary that it needs no exposition. This relative weakness of position has been intensified by the technological forces driving us toward greater concentration of business, by the tendency of the courts to narrow the application of the antitrust laws, and more recently by the policy of the Government in encouraging cooperative activity among trade and industrial groups.

Congress long ago recognized that it must play some part in redressing this inequality of bargaining power. A ready example has been the extensive role played by the Federal Government in the railroad industry, to which this report has referred. Another instance is the Norris-La Guardia Act (U. S. C., title 29, secs. 101–115). And a marked enlargement of Federal activity in the field of labor relations was one of the consequences of the nationwide depression beginning in 1929.

Between 1929 and February 1933, the index of industrial production dropped from 119 to 63, while construction activities fell from 117 to 19, and commodity prices from 95.3 to 59.8. Pay rolls receded from 107 to 40. In the 3 years following 1929, the income received by individuals in the United States shrunk from 81 billion dollars to 49, a reduction of 40 percent. At the height of the crisis, from 12 to 16 million people were unemployed.

While neither economists nor statesmen agreed entirely as to the causes or remedies for the depression, the overwhelming preponderance acknowledged that the disregard of economic forces for State lines, the interpenetration of various industries throughout the country, and the nation-wide character of the prolonged calamity made national action essential. To speed business revival Congress therefore abetted Nation-wide cooperation among businessmen to outlaw unfair trade practices, to rationalize production, and to coordinate the distribution of goods. Supplementary to this, Congress accepted and acted upon the tested hypothesis that the depression had been provoked and accentuated by a long-continued and increasing disparity between production and consumption; that this disparity had resulted from a level of wages that did not permit the masses of consumers to relieve the market of an ever-increasing flow of goods; and that even businessmen who recognized these evils—and very many of them did—were powerless to act because of the uncontrolled competition in regard to wages and other working conditions. Having in mind both the temporary expediency of priming the pump of business and the permanent objective of crystallizing antidepressive forces for the future, Congress commenced the regulation of minimum wages and maximum hours to stabilize competitive conditions and to spread adequate consumer purchasing power throughout the nation at large.

Congress recognized at the outset, however, that governmental regulation of wages and working conditions was not a complete solution, and that far from being a substitute for self-help by industry and labor, it was merely a bedrock upon which both might build. In order that industry might help itself, there was some relaxation of the antitrust laws; in order that labor might help itself, the prospectus of collective bargaining was set forth in section 7 (a) of the National Industrial Recovery Act (48 Stat. 198), supplemented in June 1934 by Public Resolution 44 (48 Stat. 1183), providing for governmentally supervised elections of representatives of employees.

Whatever divergence of opinion there may be as to the validity of some of the steps in the program above discussed, the committee believes that the desirability of collective bargaining, as it bears upon industrial peace and equality of bargaining power, is sufficiently well established and sufficiently divorced from the temporary aspects of the present economic situation to justify its affirmance in adequate and permanent Federal law.

WEAKNESSES IN EXISTING LAW

It is not necessary to cite extensive evidence of the breakdown of section 7 (a) of the National Industrial Recovery Act and of Public Resolution 44. That fact is not only a matter of common knowledge, but has been admitted publicly by officials of the National Recovery Administration, by those connected with the National Labor Relations Board, and by many others whose experience merits attention.

A recital of the weaknesses in these laws, however, will indicate that the defects are neither intrinsic nor irremediable, but may be cured by the corrective steps taken in the present bill.

(1) *Ambiguity.*—The language of section 7 (a) has been subjected to a variety of interpretation by persons whose opinions weighed heavily with public opinion, either because they were specifically charged with the administration of that law or because they were intimately connected with some other phase of the Government's program. It is clear that both employers and employees are entitled to and will benefit by a greater precision and certainty in the law.

(2) *Excessive generality.*—While section 7 (a) states the principles of collective bargaining in general terms, it contains no particularities as to what practices are contrary to its purposes. This has greatly hampered not only administrative and enforcing agencies, but also all those subject to the law who wish to obey it.

(3) *Excessive diffusion of administrative responsibility.*—Today a wide variety of independent industrial boards, from 13 to 15 in number, are entrusted with the administration of section 7 (a). The present National Labor Relations Board has no appellate jurisdiction over any board established pursuant to an industrial code, either in respect to findings of fact or interpretations of law. And as there are now over a hundred codes which make some provisions for the creation of such boards, it could be only a matter of time until this diffusion of authority would reach extraordinary proportions.

None of these boards has any actual power within itself to enforce section 7 (a). And even if such power could be granted wisely to a multitude of agencies, these boards are unsuited to the purpose. Largely bipartisan in character, they live in an atmosphere of conciliation and compromise that may be admirably suited to the settlement of wage and hour disputes where shifting standards must be applied to variegated local needs. But section 7 (a) is a uniform national policy established by law of Congress. As such it must receive uniform interpretation everywhere; it must be enforced by a judicial process rather than broken by compromise; and its enforcement must reside with governmental rather than with quasi-private agencies.

(4) *Disadvantages of tie-up with codes of fair competition.*—The incorporation of section 7 (a) in codes of fair competition entrusts the enforcement of that section largely to the National Recovery Administration. For example, even after the National Labor Relations Board decides that 7 (a) has been violated, ultimate decision as to whether the Blue Eagle shall be removed and Government contracts canceled rests with the Recovery Administration.

This arrangement is undesirable because policies admirably suited to the administration of canons of fair competition that have been written largely with the advice and consent of industry are not suited at all to the enforcement of section 7 (a), which is a law of Congress that becomes of moment precisely when it is defied. The tendency is to force the Recovery Administration upon the horns of a dilemma where it must decide either to speak softly about 7 (a) or disturb the amicable atmosphere in which the cooperative formation and execution of codes of fair competition thrives.

This evil is accentuated because section 7 (a) is now applicable only to codified industries. Thus recalcitrants are in a strategic position to threaten constantly the abandonment of their code if 7 (a) is invoked against them.

(5) *No power vested in National Labor Relations Board.*—The present National Labor Relations Board, which is the primary agency entrusted with the safeguarding of section 7 (a), has no quasi-judicial power. It must seek enforcement through reference to the Department of Justice. Since the Board has no power of subpoena, except in connection with elections, the records which it builds up are based in many cases upon the testimony of complainants alone, supplemented at best by the testimony of such witnesses as the defendants voluntarily present. This makes it necessary for the Department of Justice, in any event, to make further investigations before bringing suit in court, and if suit is brought at all, it must commence entirely *de novo* in court, with the defendant having 30 days to answer, or moving to dismiss, or applying for a bill of particulars. Thus is defeated the very purpose of an administrative agency, which is to provide specialized treatment of the factual aspects of a specialized type of controversy.

(6) *Obstacles to elections.*—Under Public Resolution 44, any attempt by the Government to conduct an election of representatives may be contested *ab initio* in the courts, although such election is in reality merely a preliminary determination of fact. This means that the Government can be delayed indefinitely before it takes the first step toward industrial peace. After almost a year not a single case, in which a company has chosen to contest an election order of the Board, has reached decision in any circuit court of appeals.

This breakdown of the law is breeding the very evil which the law was designed to prevent. During the past year and a half the country has lived under the constant shadow of actual or impending warfare in factory and in mine. A large portion of this strife, which falls so heavily upon the general public, may be attributed to the evils enumerated above.

ANALYSIS OF THE BILL

SEC. 1. *Findings and declaration of policy.*—This section states the dual objective of Congress to promote industrial peace and equality of bargaining power by encouraging the practice of collective bargaining and protecting the rights upon which it is based.

SEC. 2. *Definitions.*—It will be sufficient to discuss the more important definitions.

The term "employer" excludes labor organizations, their officers, and agents (except in the extreme case when they are acting as employers in relation to their own employees). Otherwise the provisions of the bill which prevent employers from participating in the organizational activities of workers would extend to labor unions as well, and thus would deprive unions of one of their normal functions.

The term "employee" is not limited to the employees of a particular employer. The reasons for this are as follows: Under modern conditions employees, at times, organize along craft or industrial lines and form labor organizations that extend beyond the limits of a single-employer unit. These organizations at times make agreements or bargain collectively with employers, or with an association of employers. Through such business dealings, employees are at times brought into an economic relationship with employers who are not their employers. In the course of this relationship, controversies involving unfair labor practices may arise. If this bill did not permit the Government to exercise complete jurisdiction over such controversies (arising from unfair labor practices), the Government would be rendered partially powerless, and could not act to promote peace in those very widespread controversies where the establishment of peace is most essential to the public welfare.

The term "employee" also includes any individual whose work has ceased as a consequence of or in connection with any current labor dispute or because of any unfair labor practice, who has not attained any other regular or substantially equivalent employment. The bill thus observes the principle that men do not lose their right only to be considered as employees for the purposes of this bill merely by collectively refraining from work during the course of a labor controversy. Recognition that strikers may retain their status as employees has frequently occurred in judicial decisions. (See, for example, *Michaelson* v. *United States* (291 Fed. 940), reversed on other grounds in 266 U. S. 42.) To hold otherwise for the purposes of this bill would be to withdraw the Government from the field at the very point where the process of collective bargaining has reached a critical stage and where the general public interest has mounted to its highest point. And to hold that a worker who because of an unfair labor practice has been discharged or locked out or gone on strike is no longer an employee, would be to give legal sanction to an illegal act and to deny redress to the individual injured thereby.

For administrative reasons, the committee deemed it wise not to include under the bill agricultural laborers, persons in domestic service of any family or person in his home, or any individual employed by his parent or spouse. But after deliberation, the committee decided not to exclude employees working for very small employer units. The rights of employees should not be denied because of the size of the plant in which they work. Section 7 (a) imposes no such limitation. And in cases where the organization of workers is along craft or industrial lines, very large associations of workers fraught with great public significance may exist, although all the members therein work in very small establishments. Furthermore, it is clear that the limitation of this bill to events affecting interstate commerce is sufficient to prevent intervention by the Federal Government in controversies of purely local significance.

The term "labor organization" is phrased very broadly in order that the independence of action guaranteed by section 7 of the bill and protected by section 8 shall extend to all organizations of employees that deal with employers in regard to "grievances, labor disputes, wages, rates of pay, hours of employment, or conditions of work." This definition includes employee-representation committees and plans in order that the employers' activities in connection therewith shall be equally subject to the application of section 8.

The term "affecting commerce" is inserted as a short cut to prevent the repetition of lengthy jurisdictional phraseology throughout the bill. The bill limits Federal action to areas sanctioned by the commerce clause. The bill does not project the Federal Government into matters of purely intrastate concern. It applies only in matters which burden or affect or obstruct interstate commerce, or which have led or tend to lead to a labor dispute that might have such effect upon interstate commerce. (The more general discussion of constitutional questions is deferred until the last section of this report).

The term "labor dispute" includes cases where the disputants do not stand in the proximate relation of employer and employee. An identical provision is contained in section 13 (c) of the Norris-LaGuardia Act (U. S. C., title 29, secs. 101–115), and in most recent labor legislation dealing with disputes. This definition does not mean that the Government could intervene in a "dispute" between an employer and, let us say, a critical college professor; for jurisdiction under this bill depends upon the charge of an unfair labor practice affecting commerce, and there could be no such practice involving the employer and the college professor. But unfair labor practices may, by provoking a sympathetic strike for example, create a dispute affecting commerce between an employer and employees between whom there is no proximate relationship. Liberal courts and Congress have already recognized that employers and employees not in proximate relationship may be drawn into common controversies by economic forces.

There is no reason why this bill should adopt a narrower view, or prevent action by the Government when such a controversy occurs.

SEC. 3. *National Labor Relations Board.*—This section creates, as an independent agency in the executive branch of the Government, a board to be known as the National Labor Relations Board. The Board shall be composed of three members, appointed for 5-year terms by the President by and with the advice and consent of the Senate.

SEC. 4. *Organization of the Board.*—This section provides that members of the Board shall receive salaries of $10,000 a year each. It also provides for the appointment of employees, for the transfer to the Board of the cases, records, and employees of the present National Labor Relations Board, and for the method of paying the expenses of the Board. These provisions are all in accordance with commonly accepted practice in setting up administrative agencies.

It is of special import that the National Labor Relations Board is not empowered to engage in conciliation of wage and hour disputes insofar as that activity can be carried on by the Department of Labor. Duplication of services is thus avoided, and in addition the Board is left free to engage in quasi-judicial work that is essentially different from conciliation or mediation of wage and hour controversies. And of course the binding effect of the provisions of this bill forbidding unfair labor practices are not subjects for mediation or conciliation.

The committee does not believe that the Board should serve as an arbitration agency. Such work, like conciliation, might impair its standing as an interpreter of the law. In addition, there is at present no dearth of arbitration agencies in this country. If arbitration lags, it is only because parties are not ready to submit to it. And compulsory arbitration has not received the sanction of the American people.

SEC. 5. *Prosecution of inquiry.*—This section follows the customary policy of allowing the Board or its agencies to move to the scene of action, rather than compelling all parties at all times to come to Washington.

SEC. 6. *Rules and regulations.*—This section follows the customary policy of giving the Board the power to make and amend rules and regulations. Such rules and regulations become effective only upon publication and there are no criminal penalties attached to their breach.

RIGHTS OF EMPLOYEES—UNFAIR LABOR PRACTICES

SECS. 7 and 8. *Rights of employees—Unfair labor practices.*—These sections are designed to establish and protect the basic rights incidental to the practice of collective bargaining. At this juncture the committee wishes to emphasize two points. In the first place, the unfair labor practices under the purview of this bill are strictly limited to those enumerated in section 8. This is made clear by paragraph 8 of section 2, which provides that "The term 'unfair labor practice' means any unfair labor practice listed in section 8," and by section 10 (a) empowering the Board to prevent any unfair labor practice "listed in section 8." Unlike the Federal Trade Commission Act, which deals somewhat analogously with unfair trade practices, this bill is specific in its terms. Neither the National Labor Relations Board nor the courts are given any blanket authority to prohibit whatever labor practices in their judgment are deemed to be unfair. Secondly, as will be shown directly, the unfair labor practices listed in this bill are supported by a wealth of precedent in prior Federal law.

Employees shall have the right to self-organization, to form, join, or assist labor organizations, to bargain collectively through representatives of their own choosing, and to engage in concerted activities, for the purpose of collective bargaining or other mutual aid or protection.

In conjunction with section 7, the first unfair labor practice enumerated in section 8 makes it illegal for an employer—

To interfere with, restrain, or coerce employees in the exercise of the rights guaranteed in section 7.

This familiar statement calls to mind the language of section 7 (a) of the National Industrial Recovery Act (48 Stat. 198, U. S. C., title 15, sec. 707 (a)), which provides that—

Employees shall have the right to organize and bargain collectively through representatives of their own choosing, and shall be free from the interference, restraint, or coercion of employers of labor, or their agents, in the designation of such representatives or in self-organization or in other concerted activities for the purpose of collective bargaining or other mutual aid or protection.

Similarly section 2 of the Railway Labor Act of 1934 (48 Stat. 1185) provides:

The purposes of the Act are . . . (3) to provide for the complete independence of carriers and of employees in the matter of self-organization. . . . Employees shall have the right to organize and bargain collectively through representatives of their own choosing. . . . No carrier, its officers or agents, shall deny or in any way question the right of its employees to join, organize, or assist in organizing the labor organization of their choice. . . .

Similar statements will be found in section 2 of the Railway Labor Act of 1926 (44 Stat. 577, U. S. C., title 45, sec. 152); section 2 of the Norris-LaGuardia Act (47 Stat. 70, U. S. C., title 29, sec. 102); section 77 (p) and (q) of the 1933 amendments to the Bankruptcy Act (47 Stat. 1481, U. S. C., title 11, sec. 205 (p) and (q)); and section 7 (c) of the act creating the office of the Federal Coordinator of Transportation (48 Stat. 214, U. S. C., title 49, sec. 257 (e)).

The four succeeding unfair-labor practices are designed not to impose limitations or restrictions upon the general guaranties of the first, but rather to spell out with particularity some of the practices that have been most prevalent and most troublesome.

THE COMPANY-UNION PROBLEM

The second unfair labor practice deals with the so-called "company-union problem." It forbids an employer—

to dominate or interfere with the formation or administration of any labor organization or contribute financial or other support to it.

(The proviso will be discussed subsequently.)

With identical objectives in view, section 2 of the Railway Labor Act of 1934 provides:

The purposes of the Act are . . . (3) . . . it shall be unlawful for any carrier to interfere in any way with the organization of its employees. . . . (4) It shall be unlawful for any carrier . . . to use the funds of the carrier in maintaining or assisting or contributing to any labor organization, labor representative, or other agency of collective bargaining, or in performing any work therefor.

To the same effect are the provisions of the Bankruptcy Act as amended in 1933 and 1934, and section 7 (e) of the Emergency Railroad Transportation Act of 1933. Under these sections it is unlawful for a carrier (whether under control of a judge, trustee, receiver, or private management) or for a judge, trustee, or receiver in a corporate reorganization under the Bankruptcy Act—

. . . to interfere in any way with the organizations of employees or to use the funds of the (property) under his jurisdiction in maintaining so-called "company unions."

This bill does nothing to outlaw free and independent organizations of workers who by their own choice limit their cooperative activities to the limits of one company. Nor does anything in the bill interfere with the freedom of employers to establish pension benefits, outing clubs, recreational societies, and the like, so long as such organizations do not extend their functions to the field of collective bargaining, and so long as they are not used as a covert means of discriminating against or in favor of membership in any labor organization. Such agencies, confined to their proper sphere, have promoted amicable relationships between employers and employees and the committee earnestly hopes that they will continue to function.

The so-called "company-union" features of the bill are designed to prevent interference by employers with organizations of their workers that serve or might serve as collective bargaining agencies. Such interference exists when employers actively participate in framing the constitution or bylaws of labor organizations; or when, by provisions in the constitution or bylaws, changes in the structure of the organization cannot be made without the consent of the employer. It exists when they participate in the internal management or elections of a labor organization or when they supervise the agenda or procedure of meetings. It is impossible to catalog all the practices that might constitute interference, which may rest upon subtle but conscious economic pressure exerted by virtue of the employment relationship. The question is one of fact in each case. And where several of these interferences exist in combination, the employer may be said to dominate the labor organization by overriding the will of employees.

The committee feels justified, particularly in view of statutory precedents, in outlawing financial or other support as a form of unfair pressure. It seems clear that an organization or a representative or agent paid by the employer for representing employees cannot command, even if deserving it, the full confidence of such employees. And friendly labor relations depend upon absolute confidence on the part of each side in those who represent it.

But the committee has been extremely careful not to work injustice by carrying these strictures too far. To deny absolutely by law the right of employees to confer with management during working hours without loss of time or pay would interrupt the very negotiations which it is the object of this bill to promote. For these reasons, there is attached to the second unfair labor practice the following proviso:

That, subject to rules and regulations made and published by the Board pursuant to section 6 (a), an employer shall not be prohibited from permitting employees to confer with him during working hours without loss of time or pay.

This proviso is surrounded by adequate safeguards. Where the right to receive normal pay while conferring is bestowed upon favored employees or organizations rather than equally upon all, it will run up against many of the prohibitions of section 8. In addition, the proviso in entirety is made subject to the rules and regulations of the Board, thus enabling the Board to confine it to whatever extent may be necessary to effectuate the purpose of the bill.

The committee's decision to prevent company interference with employee organizations has been influenced by recent events.

Practically 70 percent of the employer-promoted unions have sprung up since the passage of section 7 (a) of the National Industrial Recovery Act. The testimony before the committee has indicated that the active entry of some employers into a vigorous competitive race for the organization of workers is not conducive to peace in industry. It is the wish of the committee to prevent insofar as possible the perpetuation of bitterness or strife.

The third unfair labor practice forbids an employer—

by discrimination in regard to hire or tenure of employment or any term or condition of employment to encourage or discourage membership in any labor organization.

(The proviso will be discussed subsequently.)

This provision rounds out the idea expressed in section 7 (a) of the National Industrial Recovery Act to the effect that—

No employee and no one seeking employment shall be required as a condition of employment to join any company union or to refrain from joining, organizing, or assisting a labor organization of his own choosing . . .

Of course nothing in the bill prevents an employer from discharging a man for incompetence; from advancing him for special aptitude; or from demoting him for failure to perform. But if the right to be free from employer interference in self organization or to join or refrain from joining a labor organization is to have any practical meaning, it must be accompanied by assurance that its exercise will not result in discriminatory treatment or loss of the opportunity for work.

PROBLEM OF THE CLOSED SHOP

The proviso attached to the third unfair labor practice deals with the question of the closed shop. Propaganda has been widespread that this proviso attaches special legal sanctions to the closed shop or seeks to impose it upon all industry. This propaganda is absolutely false. The reason for the insertion of the proviso is as follows: According to some interpretations; the provision of section 7 (a) of the National Industrial Recovery Act, assuring the freedom of employees "to organize and bargain collectively through representatives of their own choosing," was deemed to illegalize the closed shop. The committee feels that this was not the intent of Congress when it wrote section 7 (a); that it is not the intent of Congress today; and that it is not desirable to interfere in this drastic way with the laws of the several States on this subject.

But to prevent similar misconceptions of this bill, the proviso in question states that nothing in this bill, or in any other law of the United States, or in any code or agreement approved or prescribed thereunder, shall be held to prevent the making of closed-shop agreements between employers and employees. In other words, the bill does nothing to facilitate closed-shop agreements to or make them legal in any State where they may be illegal; it does not interfere with the *status quo* on this debatable subject but leaves the way open to such agreements as might now legally be consummated, with two exceptions about to be noted.

The assertion that the bill favors the closed shop is particularly misleading in view of the fact that the proviso in two respects actually narrows the now existent law regarding closed-shop agreements. While today an employer may negotiate such an agreement even with a minority union, the bill provides that an employer shall be allowed to make a closed-shop contract only with a labor organization that represents the majority of employees in the appropriate collective-bargaining unit covered by such agreement when made.

Secondly, the bill is extremely careful to forestall the making of closed-shop agreements with organizations that have been "established, maintained, or assisted" by any action defined in the bill as an unfair labor practice. And of course it is clear that no agreement heretofore made could give validity to the practices herein prohibited by section 8.

The fourth unfair labor practice, which prohibits the discharge of or discrimination against an employee for filing charges or giving testimony under the bill, is self-explanatory.

DUTY TO BARGAIN COLLECTIVELY

The fifth unfair labor practice makes it illegal for an employer—

to refuse to bargain collectively with the representatives of his employees, subject to the provisions of section 9 (a).

The committee wishes to dispel any possible false impression that this bill is designed to compel the making of agreements or to permit governmental supervision of their terms. It must be stressed that the duty to bargain collectively does not carry with it the duty to reach an agreement, because the essence of collective bargaining is that either party shall be free to decide whether proposals made to it are satisfactory.

But, after deliberation, the committee has concluded that this fifth unfair labor practice should be inserted in the bill. It seems clear that a guarantee of the right of employees to bargain collectively through representatives of their own choosing is a mere delusion if it is not accompanied by the correlative duty on the part of the other party to recognize such representatives as they have been designated (whether as individuals or labor organizations) and to negotiate with them in a bona fide effort to arrive at a collective bargaining agreement. Furthermore, the procedure of holding governmentally supervised elections to determine the choice of representatives of employees becomes of little worth if after the election its results are for all practical purposes ignored. Experience has proved that neither obedience to law nor respect for law is encouraged by holding forth a right unaccompanied by fulfillment. Such a course provokes constant strife, not peace.

Subsequently, in this report the committee adverts to proposals for including in the bill prohibitions against practices by employees.

THE MAJORITY RULE

SEC. 9. *Selection of representatives.*—Section 9 (a) sets forth the majority rule. It provides that—

Representatives designated or selected for the purpose of collective bargaining by the majority of the employees in a unit appropriate for such purposes, shall be the exclusive representatives of all the employees in such unit for the purpose of collective bargaining in respect to rates of pay, wages, hours of employment, or other conditions of employment.

(The proviso will be discussed later.)

The principle of majority rule has been applied successfully by governmental agencies and embodied in laws of Congress. It was promulgated by the National War Labor Board created by President Wilson in the spring of 1918. It has been followed without deviation by the Railway Labor Board, created by the Transportation Act of 1920. Public Resolution No. 44, approved June 1934, contemplated majority rule in that it provided for secret elections. The 1934 amendments to the Railway Labor Act provided:

The majority of any craft or class of employees shall have the right to determine who shall be the representative of the craft or class for the purposes of this act.

And the rule is sanctioned by our governmental practices, by business procedure, and by the whole philosophy of democratic institutions.

The object of collective bargaining is the making of agreements that will stabilize business conditions and fix fair standards of working conditions. Since it is well-nigh universally recognized that it is practically impossible to apply two or more sets of agreements to one unit of workers at the same time, or to apply the terms of one agreement to only a portion of the workers in a single unit, the making of agreements is impracticable in the absence of majority rule. And by long experience, majority rule has been discovered best for employers as well as employees. Workers have found it impossible to approach their employers in a friendly spirit if they remained divided among themselves. Employers likewise, where majority rule has been given a trial of reasonable duration, have found it more conducive to harmonious labor relations to negotiate with representatives chosen by the majority than with numerous warring factions.

Majority rule carries the clear implication that employers shall not interfere with the practical application of the right of employees to bargain collectively through chosen representatives by bargaining with individuals or minority groups in their own behalf, after representatives have been picked by the majority to represent all. But majority rule, it must be noted, does not imply that any employee can be required to join a union, except through the traditional method of a closed-shop agreement, made with the assent of the employer. And since in the absence of such an agreement the bill specifically prevents discrimination against anyone either for belonging or for not belonging to a union, the representatives selected by the majority will be quite powerless to make agreements more favorable to the majority than to the minority. In addition, the bill preserves at all times the right of any individual employee or group of employees to present grievances to their employer.

Another protection for minorities is that the right of a majority group through its representatives to bargain for all is confined by the bill to cases where the majority is actually organized "for the purposes of collective bargaining in respect to rates of pay, wages, hours of employment, or other conditions of employment." An organization which is not constructed to practice genuine collective bargaining cannot be the representative of all employees under this bill.

Section 9 (b) empowers the National Labor Relations Board to decide whether the unit appropriate for the purposes of collective bargaining shall be the employer unit, craft unit, plant unit, or other unit. Obviously, there can be no choice of representatives and no bargaining unless units for such purposes are first determined. And employees themselves cannot choose these units, because the units must be determined before it can be known what employees are eligible to participate in a choice of any kind.

This provision is similar to section 2 of 1934 amendments to the Railway Labor Act (48 Stat. 1185), which states that—

In the conduct of any election for the purpose herein indicated the Board shall designate who may participate in the election and establish the rules to govern the election.

ELECTIONS

Section 9 (c) empowers the National Labor Relations Board, whenever a question affecting commerce arises concerning the representation of employees, to conduct an investigation either by secret ballot or otherwise to determine such representatives. In any such investigation, an appropriate hearing must be held.

Section 9 (d) makes it absolutely clear that there shall be no right to court review anterior to the holding of an election. An election is the mere determination of a preliminary fact, and in itself has no substantial effect upon the rights of either employers or employees. There is no more reason for court review prior to an election than for court review prior to a hearing. But if subsequently the Board makes an order predicated upon the election, such as an order to bargain collectively with elected representatives, then the entire election procedure becomes part of the record upon which the order of the Board is based, and is fully reviewable by any aggrieved party in the Federal courts in the manner provided in section 10. And this review would include within its scope the action of the Board in determining the appropriate unit for purposes of the election. This provides a complete guarantee against arbitrary action by the Board.

PREVENTION OF UNFAIR LABOR PRACTICES

SEC. 10. *Procedure before the Board.*—This is the most important procedural section. Despite the widespread charges that the bill invokes novel procedure and vests unusual powers in an administrative agency, the bill is modeled closely upon numerous Federal Statutes setting up administrative regulatory bodies of a quasi-judicial character. The common procedure is so well known that the committee deems it unnecessary in substantiation of this statement to refer to any analogous statutes save the Federal Trade Commission Act, section 5.

The bill empowers the National Labor Relations Board to hold hearings, either itself or through its agents, upon charges of unfair labor practices. After such hearings the Board, and the Board alone, may issue orders requiring the person complained of to cease and desist from the unfair labor practice and to take such affirmative action, including reinstatement with or without back pay, as may be necessary to effectuate the policies of the bill. If no sufficient case is made out, the Board shall issue an order dismissing the complaint.

If an order of the Board is disobeyed, the Board may petition for enforcement in any circuit court of appeals of the United States in any circuit wherein the unfair labor practice in question occurred or wherein the disobedient person resides or transacts business or in the appropriate district court if all circuit courts are in vacation. In such instances, the court shall have power to grant temporary relief or a restraining order, and to make and file a decree enforcing, modifying, or setting aside in whole or in part the order of the Board. Any person aggrieved by a final order of the Board granting or denying in whole or in part the relief sought may likewise obtain review in the appropriate court.

Section 10 (a) gives the National Labor Relations Board exclusive jurisdiction to prevent and redress unfair labor practices, and, taken in conjunction with section 14, establishes clearly that this bill is paramount over other laws that might touch upon similar subject matters. Thus it is intended to dispel the confusion resulting from dispersion of authority and to establish a single paramount administrative or quasi-judicial authority in connection with the development of the Federal American law regarding collective bargaining.

INVESTIGATORY POWERS

SEC. 11. *Investigation.*—This section confers upon the Board the usual investigatory powers vested in administrative agencies, but these powers are limited to the functions imposed in sections 9 and 10.

SEC. 12. *Protection of Federal officials.*—This section imposes a criminal penalty, not exceeding imprisonment for more than 1 year, or a fine not exceeding $5,000, or both, upon any person who willfully interferes with any member or agent of the Board in the performance of duties pursuant to the bill. Neither this nor any other section of the bill provides any criminal penalty (other than the usual penalty for contempt) for engaging in an unfair labor practice, even after a court had ordered its cessation.

LIMITATIONS

SEC. 13. *The right to strike.*—This section provides that "nothing in this act shall be construed so as to interfere with or impede or diminish in any way the right to strike." It is taken in substance from section 6 of Public Resolution No. 44, Seventy-third Congress.

SEC. 14. *Relationship to other legislation.*—This section is designed to resolve conflicts between this bill and other laws.

SEC. 15. *Separability.*—This section contains the standard provision for separability in the event that the application of some part of the bill might be invalid.

SEC. 16. *Title.*—This section provides that the bill may be cited as the "National Labor Relations Act."

REASONS FOR CONFINING THE BILL TO UNFAIR LABOR PRACTICES BY EMPLOYERS

One suggestion in regard to this bill has been advanced so frequently that the committee deems it advisable to set forth its reason for rejecting it. This proposal is that employees and labor organizations, as well as employers, should be prohibited from interfering with, restraining, or coercing employees in their organization activities or their choice of representatives.

The argument most frequently made for this proposal is the abstract one that it is necessary in order to provide fair and equal treatment of employers and employees. The bill prohibits employers from interfering with the right of employees to organize. The corresponding right of employers is that they should be free to organize without interference on the part of employees; no showing has been made that this right of employers to organize needs Federal protection as against employees. Regulation of the activities of employees and labor organizations in regard to the organization of employees is no more germane to the purposes of this bill than would be regulation of activities of employers and employer associations in connection with the organization of employers in trade association.

This erroneously conceived mutuality argument is that since employers are to be prohibited from interfering with the organization of workers, employees and labor organizations should also be prohibited from engaging in such activities. To say that employees and labor organizations should be no more active than employers in the organization of employees is untenable; this would defeat the very objects of the bill.

There is an even more important reason why there should be no insertion in the bill of any provision against coercion of employees by employees or labor organizations. Courts have held a great variety of activities to constitute "coercion": A threat to strike, a refusal to work on material of nonunion manufacture, circularization of banners and publications, picketing, even peaceful persuasion. In some courts, closed-shop agreements or strikes for such agreements are condemned as "coercive." Thus to prohibit employees from "coercing" their own side would not merely outlaw the undesirable activities which the word connotes to the layman, but would raise in Federal law the ghosts of many much-criticized injunctions issued by courts of equity against activities of labor organizations, ghosts which it was supposed Congress had laid low in the Norris-LaGuardia Act.

Nor can the committee sanction the suggestion that the bill should prohibit fraud or violence by employees or labor unions. The bill is not a mere police court measure. The remedies against such acts in the State and Federal courts and by the invocation of local police authorities are now adequate, as arrests and labor injunctions in industrial disputes throughout the country will attest. The Norris-LaGuardia Act does not deny to employers relief in the Federal courts against fraud, violence or threats of violence. See 29 U. S. C. § 104 (e) and (i).

Racketeering under the guise of labor-union activity has been successfully enjoined under the antitrust laws when it affected interstate commerce. The latest case along these lines is *United States* v. *Local No. 167 et al.* (291 U. S. 293).

In addition, the procedure set up in this bill is not nearly so well suited as is existing law to the prevention of such fraud and violence. Deliberations and hearings by the Board, followed by orders that must be referred to the Federal courts for enforcement, are methods of procedure that could never be sufficiently expeditious to be effective in this connection.

The only results of introducing proposals of this sort into the bill, in the opinion of the committee, would be to overwhelm the Board in every case with countercharges and recriminations that would prevent it from doing the task that needs to be done. There is hardly a labor controversy in which during the heat of excitement statements are not made on both sides which, in the hands of hostile or unsympathetic courts, might be construed to come under the common-law definition of fraud, which in some States extends even to misstatements innocently made, but without reasonable investigation.

And if the Board should decide to dismiss such charges, its order of dismissal would be subject to review in the Federal courts.

Proposals such as these under discussion are not new. They were suggested when section 7 (a) of the National Industrial Recovery Act was up for discussion, and when the 1934 amendments to the Railway Labor Act were before Congress. In neither instance did they command the support of Congress.

CONSTITUTIONALITY

The committee is convinced that this proposal keeps within the confines of the constitutional power of Congress. The two main questions involved are: (1) Are the regulations of the employer-employee relationship herein contemplated within the boundaries of due process of law and (2) can Federal jurisdiction be sustained under the commerce clause.

On the due-process point, the case of *Texas & New Orleans Railroad* v. *Brotherhood* (281 U. S. 548) completely sustained the authority of Congress to protect full freedom of organization and to prevent employer domination of employee organizations. This was a suit by a railway brotherhood to restrain the railroad from interfering with the right of its employees to self-organization and the designation of representatives in violation of the Railway Labor Act of 1926. The decree of the lower court, which was sustained in full by the Supreme Court, compelled the company (1) to completely disestablish its company union as representative of its employees; (2) to reinstate the brotherhood (which was the recognized representative chosen by the majority before the company began its unlawful interference) as the representative of all employees until they should make another free choice; (3) to restore to service and to stated privileges certain employees who had been discharged for activities in behalf of the brotherhood. The opinion of a unanimous Court was written by the present Chief Justice.

Turning to the question of interstate commerce, the figures cited earlier in this report can leave no doubt that widespread industrial disturbances burden the flow of commerce. That fact has received recognition by our highest tribunal in such well-known cases as *In re Debs* (158 U. S. 564), *Duplex Printing Press Co.* v. *Deering* (254 U. S. 443), *American Steel Foundries* v. *Tri-City Central Trades Council* (257 U. S. 184), *Coronado Coal Co.* v. *United Mine Workers* (268 U. S. 295), and *Bedford Cut Stone Co.* v. *Stone Cutters Association* (274 U. S. 37). Equally true it is that failure to accept the procedure of collective bargaining has been the cause of some of the most violent of these industrial disputes. That issue was paramount in the *Debs* case, the *Coronado* case, and *International Organization* v. *Red Jacket C. C. & C. Co.* (18 Fed. 2d 839, cert. den. 275 U. S. 536). And the remedy has been as well recognized as the cause. Whenever given a fair trial, machinery for facilitating collective bargaining has promoted industrial peace.

It is clear, in addition, that unfair labor practices which tend to promote strife may be enjoined before the strife occurs. Civilized law is preventive as well as punitive. As Chief Justice Taft said in the first *Coronado* case (259 U. S. 344):

If Congress deems certain recurring practices, though not really part of interstate commerce, likely to obstruct, restrain, or burden it, it has the power to subject them to national supervision or restraint.

See also *Wilson* v. *New,* 243 U. S. 322; *United States* v. *Ferger* (250 U. S. 199); *Stafford* v. *Wallace* (258 U. S. 495); *Chicago Board of Trade* v. *Olson* (262 U. S. 1); *Texas & New Orleans Railroad* v. *Brotherhood, supra.*

Cases under the antitrust laws, cited for the proposition that the Federal Government cannot deal with the employer-employee relationship, are not in point. They turned not on any question of constitutional limitations, but upon statutory construction of the extent of equity jurisdiction over labor activities under the antitrust laws. But the Federal Government has power to prevent burdens upon interstate commerce that reaches beyond the intent of those laws in regard to labor disputes, and it is intended in this bill to exercise the full constitutional power of Congress to prevent the described unfair labor practices, which have no extenuating social values operating in their favor.

The committee is further of the opinion that congressional power to prevent these unfair labor practices exists and should be exercised even where the threat of strife is not imminent. In line with modern economic developments, the courts have recognized that unsound economic practices have a marked effect upon the volume and stability of commerce. This is illustrated in the cases prohibiting unfair methods of competition under the Federal Trade Commission Act. Again, the general proposition is aptly stated in *Chicago Board of Trade* v. *Olsen* (262 U. S. 1), upholding Federal regulation of future sales on grain exchanges, an activity in itself purely local. The court said:

The question of price dominates trade between the States. Sales of an article which affect the countrywide price of the article directly affect the countrywide commerce in it. For this reason, Congress has the power to provide the appropriate means adopted in this act by which this abuse may be restrained and avoided.

In effect upon commerce, wage levels are as significant as price levels, for the exchange of goods depends as much upon the consumer's income as upon the price which he must pay. Income and cost of living must be indexed in terms of each other. An analysis of the effect of a decline in mass purchasing power upon all commercial transactions forces the conclusion that the protection of Nation-wide commerce depends as much upon a floor for wages as upon a ceiling for prices. And in stabilizing wages, no factor plays a more important role than collective bargaining.

In the case of *Appalachian Coals, Inc.* v. *United States* (288 U. S. 344), Chief Justice Hughes wrote:

> The interests of producers and consumers are interlinked. When industry is grievously hurt, when producing concerns fail, when unemployment mounts, and communities dependent upon profitable production are prostrated, the wells of commerce go dry.

This statement is a landmark of contemporary realism in regard to the commerce power. While this bill, of course, does not intend to go beyond the constitutional power of Congress, as that power may be marked out by the courts, it seeks the full limit of that power in preventing these unfair labor practices. It seeks to prevent them, whether they burden interstate commerce by causing strikes, or by occurring in the stream of interstate commerce, or by overturning the balance of economic forces upon which the full flow of commerce depends.

Recommendation of the House Committee on Labor, June 10, 1935
(With a Minority View)

WILLIAM CONNERY [DEM., MASS.] submitted the Report.

The Committee on Labor, to whom was referred the bill (S. 1958) to promote equality of bargaining power between employers and employees, to diminish the causes of labor disputes, to create a National Labor Relations Board, and for other purposes, having had the same under consideration, report it back to the House with amendments and recommend that the bill, as amended, do pass. . . .

Minority View

At the very outset I want to make my position clear. I am wholeheartedly in favor of this bill. I believe it to be a great step for the protection of the rights of organized labor of the United States; and irrespective of whether or not the following suggestions are adopted I shall vote for the bill.

I find myself unable to agree with the decision of the committee to affiliate the National Labor Relations Board with the Department of Labor. It is clearly immaterial whether this affiliation is accomplished merely by providing generally that the Board shall be located in the Department of Labor, or by providing in detail that the Secretary of Labor shall control the personnel, the regional agencies, and the budget of the Board. Regardless of variations in language, if the Board is placed within the Department, the Secretary of Labor will control the purse strings, and that control will be the decisive factor in determining the extent and the character of the personnel, the nature of the work done, and the administrative setup of the Board, both in Washington and throughout the country. This in turn will be determinative of the major policies of the Board, as I shall presently discuss. On this issue there can be no compromise; either the Board must be completely independent or it must be reduced to the level of a departmental bureau.

I should have thought that even without regard for the past history of the National Labor Relations Board and the testimony before this committee, both of which seem to me compelling upon this point, precedent alone would have induced the establishment of the Board as an independent agency. The Board is to be solely a quasi-judicial body with clearly defined and limited powers. Its policies are marked out precisely by the law. That such an agency should be free from any other executive branch of the Government has been the recognized policy of Congress. Ready examples are the Interstate Commerce Commission, the Federal Trade Commission, the Communications Commission, the Securities and Exchange Commission, the National Mediation Board, and agencies that are even less judicial in character, such as the Federal Housing Administration and the Reconstruction Finance Corporation. It seems strange that this committee, which has built up so fine a record in the interests of labor, should be grudgingly unwilling to establish for the protection of labor's most basic rights an agency as dignified and independent, and as likely to attain the prestige that flows from such independence, as those which have been established to protect the interests of other groups.

The vital need for the complete independence of a quasi-judicial board that must enforce the law has been best illustrated by the collapse of section 7 (a) of the Recovery Act. That famous section broke down, not so much because the Recovery Act into which it was written did not contain adequate enforcement provisions, but because the actual enforcement of 7 (a) was tied up with the wrong agencies. The Labor Board, it is true, could make "decisions"; but actual enforcement rested with the National Recovery Administration and the Department of Justice. Since the NRA had other functions, such as code making, etc., which required constant cultivation of friendly and conciliatory feelings between the NRA and those with whom it had to deal, the NRA has been forced repeatedly to compromise and bargain away the specific rights guaranteed by section 7 (a), and the Department of Justice likewise has been reluctant to act upon this touchy subject, because of entirely extrinsic consideration of government policy that should have had nothing to do with section 7 (a). The complete frustration of the present National Labor Relations Board has resulted from this very simple failure to maintain the traditional and tested division between quasi-judicial bodies on the one hand and the general work of executive departments tied up with the governmental policy of a particular administration, on the other.

This anomalous situation would be perpetuated by placing the National Labor Relations Board in the Department of Labor. The Department is an executive arm of the Government. The Secretary of Labor is an officer of a particular administration, and I say this from the long-range point of view, and with due regard for the abilities of the present Secretary. The Department is thus quickly susceptible to political repercussions, and it is charged with many administrative duties involving constant compromise between industry and government. Thus the Board would quickly be swallowed up in the general policies of the Department of Labor.

These difficulties are not answered at all by insisting that the judicial decisions of the National Labor Relations Board would not be subject to review by the Secretary of Labor or by any officer in the executive branch of the Government. If, in fact, the Board were to be independent in its actions, there would be no reason for anyone wanting to set it up in the Department of Labor. But that is not the case; the final "judicial decisions" are only a small part of the work of such a Board, and by control over other stages in the enforcement process the Department of Labor would be the final arbiter of the policies of the Board.

For example, to be effective in enforcement, the Board must control complaints of unfair labor practices from their very inception. Yet this would not be the case were the Board in the Department. It is quite true that the proponents of placing the Board in the Department insist that there should be no mediation or conciliation done by the Board. But that does not preclude the possibility of mediation of an unfair labor practice by the Conciliation Service of the Department before the Board would act. And in the long run, that would inevitably result from locating the Board in the Department, while its advent would be hastened by an administration unsympathetic toward labor. This is the very worst kind of confusion of conciliation and quasi-judicial work, not in that the Board will do both but that both will be used at successive stages in attempting to enforce the law.

What will result from such a procedure? Conciliation at the source will not build up the kind of records that the Board might later refer to the courts for enforcement. Compromise of the law at the outset will constantly plague the Government when the time comes to vindicate the law. A wide variety of interpretations without any centralizing force will create uncertainty and distrust. The National Labor Relations Board will be called into operation only where there has been a record of failure rather than success; only when the prestige of the Government has already been impaired by the failure of its agencies. Moreover, the duplication of effort and the long delay before complaints of unfair practices finally reach the Board will wreak havoc upon workers' rights. The worker who is wronged must get help quickly if at all. The injury of the long delay can never be redressed. The occasion to protest by his own collective action, once let pass, can never be recalled. These are not fancied evils; they are present now because of the very policies which I do not wish to see continued.

To prevent unfair labor practices, the National Labor Relations Board must have control of enforcement not at the end of the trail but from the very beginning. It must follow the procedure that is followed by the Federal Trade Commission in preventing unfair trade practices. No one would suggest, when there is a claim of an unfair trade practice, that there should first be mediation by the Department of Commerce and then action by the Commission in the event of failure.

In addition, if the Department of Labor is to control the first steps in regard to the prevention of unfair practices, it will have the discretion to cut enforcement off its sources. "Judicial independence" will do the Board no good as to cases that never reach it.

Thus the issue raised is a very narrow one. If the purpose of placing the National Labor Relations Board in the Department of Labor is that the Department and the Board shall function jointly to protect the rights guaranteed by section 7 (a), then the whole enforcement mechanism will collapse because of dispersion of responsibility and because of an overlapping of conciliation and judicial work. And if the Board should operate independently of the Department, it is unfair to make it subject to departmental control over budget and personnel.

In view of these major considerations, which have proved controlling in every other case where the Government has set up a quasi-judicial body, the point that there might be some overlapping of statistical work by the Board and the Department of Labor is trivial and unrealistic. In fact, it is entirely appropriate to amend the bill, as has been done, to provide that the Board should not do any statistical work, mediation, or conciliation, when such services are available in the Department of Labor.

It should be repeated that the National Labor Relations Board is to be purely a quasi-judicial commission. Its prestige and efficacy must be grounded fundamentally in public approval and in equal confidence in its impartiality by Labor and Industry. If the Board is placed in the Department it will suffer ab initio from the suspicion that it is not a court, but an organ devoted solely to the interests of laboring groups. Far from helping labor, this will impair the work of the Board and render more difficult the sustaining of its supposedly impartial decisions by the Federal courts.

Finally, let me emphasize the paramount consideration that the inclusion of the Board in the Department of Labor will injure not only the Board, but the Department itself, and through it the interests of labor. The Department was not established to handle all the industrial relation problems of the Government. It was not established to covet impartial or quasi-judicial functions, or to interpret laws of Congress. It was founded, as is too often forgotten now, as a department for labor, and to "foster, promote, and develop the welfare of the wage earners of the United States, to improve their working conditions, and to advance their opportunities for profitable employment." There is more work of this type to be done than ever before and the Department is in no danger of lapsing into disuse if it is aware of its duties. I believe that labor would have fared better under the codes if the Department had remained true to its function as a militant organ for working people, rather than attempted to appear as a labor relations bureau of the Federal Government, representing all interests alike, and overzealous to guard itself against supposed encroachments. The effort to secure control over an impartial quasi-judicial board is a definite step by the Department away from those activities which can make it most useful to the working people of America.

The Senate bill very wisely has made the Board an independent agency. The House should follow the Senate on this very vital matter.

I also find myself unable to agree with the committee in its exclusion of agricultural workers. It is a matter of plain fact that the worst conditions in the United States are the conditions among the agricultural workers. They have been brought to the public attention many times; for example, by the investigations of the National Child Labor Committee into the horrible conditions, especially as affecting children, in the beet-sugar fields. The complete denial of civil liberty and the reign of terror in the Imperial Valley have been the subject of investigation by Government agents. Last summer saw a protracted and heroic strike by the terribly exploited union workers in the fertile fields of Hardin County, Ohio, against their employers. These workers were organized in a federal local of the A. F. of L. They were victims of the usual type of oppression which was called to public attention in the press.

However, the most conclusive proof that there must be Federal action to protect the right of agricultural workers to organize is to be found in the situation in Arkansas. In that State, within the last year, there has come into being an admirable union of agricultural workers, the Southern Tenant Farmers Union. It has been incorporated under the laws of the State. Its immediate demands are entirely reasonable and its methods have been extraordinarily peaceful. Yet that union is at present holding no meetings on advice of its counsel who says that it cannot be protected from terroristic attacks. Armed planters have patrolled the roads looking for the principal organizers of the union. The president of the union, a former rural school teacher, was driven out of the county by threats of lynching. Members of the union have been beaten up. Some of them have been cast in jail from which they were ultimately delivered but only in one or two cases after they had been confined on trumped charges for 45 days. Meetings have been forcibly broken up. The lawyer for the union is C. T. Carpenter, one of the outstanding lawyers of the State of Arkansas. He was waited on by an armed mob one night in his own home. He met them at the door with a pistol in his hand. The mob left but not without firing shots at the house.

What these people in Arkansas are organizing against is the most outrageous exploitation in America. The plantation system of itself is damnable. It combines the worst evils of feudalism and capitalism. The overseers on the plantations go armed.

A continuance of these conditions is preparing the way for a desperate revolt of virtual serfs. Unless the right to organize peacefully can be guaranteed we shall have a continuance of virtual slavery until the day of revolt. The union and the exploited victims of this system have shown an amazing willingness, or rather a deep-seated anxiety, to avoid bloodshed.

I, therefore, respectfully submit that there is not a single solitary reason why agricultural workers should not be included under the provisions of this bill. The same reasons urged for the adoption of this bill in behalf of the industrial workers are equally applicable in the case of the agricultural workers, in fact more so as their plight calls for immediate and prompt action.

Vito Marcantonio

Report of the House Committee of Conference
June 26, 1935

WILLIAM CONNERY [DEM., MASS.] submitted the following Conference Report.

The committee of conference on the disagreeing votes of the two Houses on the amendments of the House to the bill (S. 1958) to promote equality of bargaining power between employers and employees, to diminish the causes of labor disputes, to create a National Labor Relations Board, and for other purposes, having met, after full and free conference, have agreed to recommend and do recommend to their respective Houses as follows: . . .

STATEMENT OF THE MANAGERS ON THE PART OF THE HOUSE

The managers on the part of the House at the conference on the disagreeing votes of the two Houses on the bill (S. 1958) to create a National Labor Relations Board, and for other purposes, submit the following statement of the effect of the action agreed upon by the conferees and recommended in the accompanying conference report:

The conference agreement accepts the first House amendment, striking out from the caption to section 1 the words "declaration of," so that the caption now reads "findings and policy." The omitted words were superfluous.

The Senate receded from its disagreement to House amendment no. 2 and the conferees agreed upon the same with minor amendments. The House redrafting of section 1 was thought by the conferees to contain a better statement of the jurisdictional basis of the bill. The conference struck out the words "interstate and foreign" modifying the word "commerce" appearing at four places in the section. The word "commerce" is defined in subsection 6 of section 2 as meaning interstate and foreign commerce. It is therefore confusing to use the adjectives "interstate and foreign" in various places in section 1, especially when these adjectives are not consistently used each time the word "commerce" appears in the section. The slight verbal change at the end of section 1 simply uses the plural to conform to the use in the preceding paragraphs of the section and in conformity with the general statement of rights in section 7.

The conference agreement accepted House amendment no. 3 as constituting a more accurate definition of the term "commerce." As originally defined in subsection 6 of section 2 the term included "any transportation or communication relating thereto." This was thought to be too broad a statement.

House amendment no. 4 effects a minor change in subsection 7 of section 2 by removing a tautological phrase. The idea is preserved in the phrase "tending to lead to a labor dispute," etc. The conference agreement accepts this amendment.

When the Senate passed S. 1958 it was assumed that the bill would become a law before June 16, 1935, on which date the National Labor Relations Board, created pursuant to Public Resolution 44, Seventy-third Congress, expired. Meanwhile, the President by a new Executive order of June 15, 1935, reestablished and continued the Board in existence, pursuant to his authority under title I of the National Industrial Recovery Act, as amended. House amendment no. 5 makes it clear that the term "old Board" as defined in subsection 11 of section 2, describes the Board which is at present in existence. This amendment is important in view of the provision at the end of section 4 (b) transferring to the Board to be created by S. 1958 the unexpended funds and appropriations of the old Board. The conference agreement accepts this amendment.

Section 3 (a) of the Senate bill provided:

There is hereby created as an independent agency in the executive branch of the Government a board, to be known as the "National Labor Relations Board."

House amendment no. 6 strikes out the phrase "as an independent agency in the executive branch of the Government." The Board as contemplated in the bill is in no sense to be an agency of the executive branch of the Government. It is to have a status similar to that of the Federal Trade Commission, which, as the Supreme Court pointed out in the *Schechter* case, is a quasi-judicial and quasi-legislative body. The conference agreement accepts this amendment.

The conference agreement accepts House amendment no. 7, stating specifically the circumstances under which a member of the Board may be removed. This amendment is desirable in the light of the decision of the Supreme Court in *Rathbun* v. *U. S.,* decided May 27, 1935, involving the removal by the President of Commissioner Humphreys of the Federal Trade Commission. If Congress in creating the Board vests the appointing power in the President it might be implied that it is intended to vest also in the President a general power of removal as an incident to the power to appoint. This inference is negatived by an express provision stating the conditions under which a member of the Board may be removed. Similar provisions are found in the Railway Labor Act of 1934 and the Federal Trade Commission Act.

House amendment no. 8 strikes out from section 4 (b) the provision continuing the court proceedings and orders of the old Board. The conference agreement accepts this amendment. All cases of the old Board pending in the courts have already been dropped at the direction of the Attorney General, in view of the *Schechter* case which invalidated the codes of fair competition as having been founded upon an improper delegation of legislative power to the President. Section 7 (a) which was the basis of the old Board's activity became inoperative, because section 7 (a) was effective only insofar as its provisions were inserted in the codes.

Section 4 (b) of the Senate bill provided that all employees of the old Board should be transferred to and become employees of the Board "without acquiring by such transfer a permanent civil service status." House amendment no. 9 proposed to strike out this quoted phrase. The conference agreement rejects the House amendment and reinstates the language of the Senate bill. The result is that all employees of the old Board will be carried over as provided in the Senate bill but such transfer will not of itself confer a civil-service status upon such employees of the old Board as have not now such status. The conferees thought that employees of the old Board should not be blanketed into the civil service without the usual formalities provided by law.

The conference agreement accepted House amendment no. 10 as constituting a more accurate citation of the National Industrial Recovery Act.

House amendment no. 11, which redrafted section 9 (b), embodied two changes from the Senate bill. The first change undertook to express more explicitly the standards by which the Board is to be guided in deciding what is an appropriate bargaining unit. The conference agreement accepts this part of the amendment. The amendment also added a proviso designed to limit the otherwise broad connotation that might be put upon the phrase "or other unit." The proviso, however, was subject to some misconstructions, and the conferees have agreed that the simplest way to deal with the matter is to strike out the undefined phrase "other unit." It was also agreed to insert after "plant unit" the phrase "or subdivision thereof." This was done because the National Labor Relations Board has frequently had occasion to order an election in a unit not as broad as "employer unit," yet not necessarily coincident with the phrases "craft unit" or "plant unit"; for example, the "production and maintenance employees" of a given plant.

House amendment no. 12 inserts the phrase "upon due notice" in section 9 (c) providing for hearings by the Board on the issue of collective bargaining representation. The conference agreement accepted this amendment out of abundant caution; though it would perhaps be implied that a requirement of a hearing includes due notice to the parties.

House amendment no. 13 was accepted by the conference agreement. It is a purely formal matter. The appropriate term for the intervention of a person in a quasi-judicial person is "intervene" rather than "appear." House amendment no. 14 was accepted by the conference agreement as a verbal change to conform with the preceding amendment.

Section 10 (e) of the Senate bill provided that "if such person fails or neglects to obey such order of the Board while the same is in effect, the Board may" petition any circuit court of appeals, etc. House amendment no. 15 strikes out the quoted phrase and substitutes "The Board shall have power to" petition any circuit court of appeals, etc. The conference agreement accepts this amendment. The purpose is to provide for more expeditious procedure. Delay in enforcement procedure due to technicalities would be especially harmful under this act. It is the purpose of this amendment to authorize the Board to apply to the courts for an enforcement order, without encountering the delay resulting from certain court decisions (a small minority) under the Federal Trade Commission Act, requiring the Commission to show in every case that its order is being disobeyed before the court will even proceed to consider the matter on its merits, or render a decree enforcing the Board's order. As the majority of courts have declared under the Federal Trade Commission Act, neither the administrative body nor the courts are required to assume in the ordinary case that the unlawful practice in question, even though presently terminated will not be resumed in the future. If such practice is resumed there will be immediately available to the Board an existing court decree to serve as a basis for contempt proceedings.

House amendment no. 16 was accepted in the conference agreement as conforming to the language of the Federal Trade Commission Act, in using the language of authorization rather than mandatory language in empowering the court to enter the appropriate decree.

House amendment no. 17 is clarifying language to cover the contingency where the court has occasion to modify an order of the Board. In such case the court is given by the amendment the power to enforce the Board's order as modified, as fully as in the case where the court affirms the Board's order without modification.

The conference agreement accepts House amendment no. 18. This amendment to section 10 (f), applying to a case where a party petitions the Circuit Court of Appeals to review the order of the Board, brings that subsection in conformity with section 10 (e) as amended.

House amendment no. 19, adding the phrase "and enforcing as so modified" to section 10 (h) was accepted by the conference agreement as conforming to the changes in the previous amendments.

The conference agreement accepted House amendments nos. 20, 21, and 22, as constituting merely formal corrections in the citations of the various statutes.

House amendment no. 23 inserted a new section providing that—

Nothing in this act shall abridge the freedom of speech, or of the press, as guaranteed in the first amendment to the Constitution.

The conference agreement rejected this amendment as having no proper place in the bill. There is no reason why the Congress should single out this provision of the Constitution for special affirmation. The amendment could not possibly have had any legal effect, because it was merely a restatement of the first amendment to the Constitution, which remains the law of the land irrespective of congressional declaration.

House amendments nos. 24 and 25 merely renumbered the sections as made necessary by House amendment no. 23 inserting a new section. Since the conference agreement has stricken out House amendment no. 23, House amendments nos. 24 and 25 become unnecessary and are rejected by the conference agreement.

The conference agreement accepts the House amendment to the title of the bill, because it describes more accurately the jurisdictional basis for the bill.

THE DEBATE

Senate—73rd Congress, 2nd Session
May 15—16, 1935

The Senate resumed the consideration of the bill (S. 1958) to promote equality of bargaining power between employers and employees, to diminish the causes of labor disputes, to create a National Labor Relations Board, and for other purposes. . . .

ROBERT WAGNER [DEM., N. Y.]. Mr. President, the national labor relations bill does not break with our traditions. It is the next step in the logical unfolding of man's eternal quest for freedom. For 25 centuries of recorded time before the machine age we sought relief from nature's cruel and relentless tyranny. Only 150 years ago did this country cast off the shackles of political despotism. And today, with economic problems occupying the center of the stage, we strive to liberate the common man from destitution, from insecurity, and from human exploitation.

In this modern aspect of a time-worn problem the isolated worker is a plaything of fate. Caught in the labyrinth of modern industrialism and dwarfed by the size of corporate enterprise, he can attain freedom and dignity only by cooperation with others of his group. This truism has been paid at least the lip service of universal opinion. It is on the page of every treatise and in the platform of every political party.

In fact, this simple idea has become so embedded in our habits of thought that we find it difficult to realize that only a little over a century ago our law denied workers the right to combine for the purpose of raising wages. In the *Philadelphia Cordwainer's* case, decided in 1806 (Common and Gilmore, *Doc. Hist.,* vol. 3, pp. 59–249), it was said of such a combination:

> This measure is pregnant with public mischief and private injury . . . tends to demoralize the workmen . . . destroy the trade of the city, and leaves the pockets of the whole community to the discretion of the concerned. If these evils were unprovided for by the law now existing, it would be necessary that laws should be made to restrain them.

Fortunately, it was not long before the law became more sensitive to life. The cornerstone of industrial liberty was laid in Massachusetts in 1842 by the great Chief Justice Shaw. In *Commonwealth* v. *Hunt* (4 Metcalf 111) he said:

> We think, therefore, that associations may be entered into . . . and yet so far from being criminal or unlawful, the object may be highly meritorious and public spirited.

The classic modern statement was written by Chief Justice Taft in *American Steel Foundry* v. *The Tri-City Central Trades Council* (257 U. S. 184 (1921)). In that opinion trade unions received the following encomium:

> They were organized out of the necessities of the situation. A single employee was helpless in dealing with an employer. He was dependent ordinarily upon his daily wage for the maintenance of himself and family. If the employer refused to pay him the wages that he thought fair, he was, nevertheless, unable to leave the employ and to resist arbitrary and unfair treatment. Union was essential to give laborers opportunity to deal on equality with their employers.

As the increasing mechanization of industry and the flowering of the factory system built up larger and larger aggregates of capital, it became obvious that our cherished equality of opportunity could not be maintained merely by pious declarations or abstract guaranties of freedom. By the second half of the nineteenth century, the active intervention of the Government was necessary to prevent economic concentration from fostering economic despotism. In consequence, the year 1890 witnessed the enactment of the Sherman antitrust laws, designed to protect the laborer, the small businessman, and the consumer from the power of combination and the greed of monopoly.

It is not my intent to debate at this time why the antitrust laws withered under sustained assault in the courts. Whether it was due to the formidable battery of lawyers that the powerful could gather, or to the subconscious prejudices that judges carried over from their former associations, or to the fact that the laws themselves were not in harmony with the technique of modern industry are matters of relatively little moment today. The important fact is that the laws failed.

In the very first prosecution which came before the Supreme Court, *United States* v. *E. C. Knight & Co.* (156 U. S. 1 (1894)), it was held that a combination embracing 98 percent of the sugar-refinery capacity of the country was not in restraint of trade because manufacturing was not commerce. This decision, based upon Webster's dictionary rather than upon economic reality, practically inhibited further action by the Government for a decade and created the impression that combines of industrial concerns were virtually impregnable.

Hope for the vindication of the law rose in 1911, when the Court ordered the dissolution of the Standard Oil Co., *Standard Oil Co. of New Jersey* v. *United States* (221 U. S. 1). But the rule of reason enunciated in that famous case soon became a vehicle for substituting the economic opinions of the Court for the expressed policy of Congress. The copious expansiveness of the rule was portended in *United States* v. *United States*

Steel Corporation (251 U. S. 417 (1920)). In writing the opinion of the Court which sanctioned that combine, Mr. Justice McKenna said:

> The power attained was much greater than that possessed by any one competitor. It was not greater than that possessed by all of them.

Thus it was held in effect that a monster combination which controlled from 40 to 50 percent of the steel industry was not in violation of the public interest, since its holdings did not exceed those of all of its competitors. It was overlooked that a scattered field of small rivals might be completely overridden by a single adversary representing even 40 percent of the total national strength.

The Steel case was followed closely by *United Shoe Machinery Corporation* v. *United States* (258 U. S. 451 (1922)), which upheld restrictive tying clauses enabling one corporation to control more than 95 percent of the shoe-machinery business of the country. But the final quietus to the anti-trust laws was given in *United States* v. *International Harvester Co.* (74 U. S. 693 (1926)). Here the Court elaborated its fine distinction between good and bad trusts, and said:

> The law, however, does not make the mere size of a corporation, however impressive, or the existence of unexerted power on its part, an offense, when unaccompanied by unlawful conduct in the exercise of its power.

Thus the heavy hand of the courts paralyzed the enforcement of the antitrust laws. During the 40 years after their enactment an average of one person per year was imprisoned for violating their criminal sections, while only about $2,000,000 in fines were collected. Under the provisions for confiscation of goods shipped in interstate commerce by concerns violating the law, only 40 cartons of cigarettes were seized, and these were returned. Walton H. Hamilton, a distinguished economist and lawyer, who has made extensive studies on this subject, testified before the Senate Committee on Finance last month:

> In terms of its formal administration the number of cases is pitiful, the amount of fines assessed is pitiful, the number of people sent to jail for violation of this law is almost negligible as against the great course of the concentration of wealth which has occurred in this country in the last generation and a half.

When the final history of our times comes to be written, its most glaring paradox will be the manner in which the antitrust laws were swerved from the course marked out by Congress and were invoked to harass the activities of those very groups they had been designed to protect. It is interesting to note that another famous Federal statute, also enacted for the protection of the weak, was used even sooner in a manner foreshadowing future events. In the case of *Toledo A. A. & N. M. Railway Co.* v. *Penn-*

sylvania Co. (54 Fed. 730 (1893)), Judge Taft, later to become Chief Justice of the United States, held that under the Interstate Commerce Act of 1887 the Brotherhood of Locomotive Engineers could be enjoined from ordering employees to refuse to handle freight cars during the course of a strike. But the further extension of that act to the labor field was checked by the advent of the Sherman law.

Beginning in 1893, the lower Federal courts applied the antitrust laws regularly to the activities of labor organizations. This procedure was first sustained by the Supreme Court in the case of *Loewe v. Lawlor* (208 U. S. 274 (1908)), where it was said that Congress "made the interdictions include combinations of labor as well as of capital." This *Danbury Hatters* case, it is true, involved activities which were clearly interstate in their ramifications and powerful in their effects. But in short order notice was served of the meticulous exactitude with which the actions of employees were to be surveyed. Thus in *Gompers v. Buck Stove & Range* (221 U. S. 418 (1911)), the Supreme Court said that the antitrust laws prohibited restraints whether occasioned "by blacklist, boycott, coercion, threat, intimidation, and whether these be made effective, in whole or in part, by act, words, or printed matter." Meanwhile the lower courts maintained their vigilance. Although peaceful picketing had come to be recognized as a legitimate and necessary incident to collective bargaining, the case of *Atchison, Topeka & Santa Fe Railway Co. v. Gee* (139 Fed. 582 (1905)) held that "there is and can be no such thing as peaceful picketing, any more than there can be chaste vulgarity or peaceful mobbing or lawful lynching." Certainly the rule of reason did not smile upon the aspirations of working people.

Vexed by the double frustration of its intent, an awakened Congress in 1914 passed the Clayton Act, declaring that labor organizations should be allowed to pursue their lawful and legitimate objectives, and that no injunction should be issued in a dispute between an employer and employees except when necessary to prevent irreparable injury.

But captious verbalisms by the Court soon rendered the Clayton Act as ineffectual as its predecessors. In *Duplex Printing Press v. Deering* (254 U. S. 443 (1921)), upholding an injunction against a secondary boycott by employees, Mr. Justice Pitney argued that Congress, in excluding from the provisions of the antitrust laws all lawful activities of labor organizations, had intended to exclude only those acts which had theretofore been lawful under the antitrust laws. This highly elliptical reasoning was reiterated in *American Steel Foundry v. The Tri-City Central Trades Council,* supra, declaring that the Clayton Act "introduced no new principle into the equity jurisprudence of those courts. It is merely declaratory of what was the best practice always."

Ironically enough, it was cases after the passage of the Clayton Act that marked the high-water mark of judicial hostility to labor organizations. In the *Tri-City* case an employee organization was denied the right to place more than one peaceful picket near the entrance to a building, and the Court added that "the name picket indicated a militant purpose, inconsistent with peaceful persuasion." In *Bedford Cut Stone Co.* v. *Journeymen Stone Cutters Association* (275 U. S. 37 (1927)) the issue was whether a small group of craftsmen might refuse to work upon stone shipped into the State from quarries in another State where non-union labor was employed. A secondary boycott had already been declared legal by high courts in New York and California. *Bossert* v. *Dhuy* (221 N. Y. 342 (1917)) and *Pierce* v. *Stablemen's Union* (156 Calif. 70 (1909)). But the Supreme Court found a violation of the antitrust laws and sustained an injunction. The voice of Mr. Justice Brandeis was heard in protest:

The Sherman law was held, in *United States* v. *The United States Steel Corporation,* to permit capitalists to combine in a single corporation 50 percent of the steel industry of the United States, dominating the trade through its vast resources. The Sherman law was held in *United States* v. *The United Shoe Machinery Co.,* to permit competitors to combine in another corporation practically the whole shoe-machinery industry of the country, necessarily giving a position of dominance over shoe manufacturing in America. It would, indeed, be strange if Congress had by the same action willed to deny to members of a small class of workmen the right to cooperate in simply refraining from work, when that course was the only means of self-protection against a combination of militant and powerful employers.

While the courts were thus turning the heavy batteries of the antitrust laws against the activities of employees, they were spiking the statutes that Congress and the States framed expressly to protect these groups. In *Truax* v. *Corrigan* (257 U. S. 312 (1912)), an Arizona statute forbidding the issuance of a labor injunction except to prevent irreparable injury was declared unconstitutional by the Supreme Court. Mr. Justice Brandeis, accompanied by Justices Holmes and Pitney, dissented in the following language:

It is urged that the real motive in seeking the injunction was not ordinarily to prevent property from being injured nor to protect the owner in its use, but to endow property with active, militant power which would make it dominant over men. In other words, that under the guise of protecting property rights, the employer was seeking sovereign power.

In *Adair* v. *United States* (208 U. S. 161 (1907)), over the dissents of Mr. Justice Holmes and Mr. Justice McKenna, a statute seeking to outlaw the "yellow-dog" contract was declared unconstitutional. Seven years later, when the State of Kansas tried to achieve the same result, it was thwarted by

Cooperage v. *Kansas* (236) U. S. A. (1914). It was in the latter case that Mr. Justice Holmes supported Justice Day and the then Associate Justice Hughes in saying:

> In present conditions a workman not unnaturally may believe that only by belonging to a union can he secure a contract that shall be fair to him. . . . If that belief, whether right or wrong, may be held by a reasonable man, it seems to me that it may be enforced by law in order to establish the equality of position between the parties in which liberty of contract begins.

These cases which I have cited are not mere records of mock trials in moot courts. They are the external evidence of sweeping political and economic developments completely out of line with our professed desires to make opportunity equally available to all.

The fragile resistance of the antitrust laws did nothing to prevent the compounding of business into larger and larger units. In 1909 there was one small enterprise or manufacturing establishment for every 250 people in the Nation; by 1929 there was only one for every 900 people. In 1904, over 50 percent of the manufacturers in the United States were small enterprisers each producing less than $20,000 worth of goods per year. By 1929, these small enterprisers had shrunk in number to 32 percent of the total. During the same span of time, producers of goods valued at $100,000 or more per year rose from 16.9 percent of the total to 31.5 percent. And while only one-quarter of the workers in America were employed by million-dollar-a-year concerns in 1904, about three-fifths of the workers were employed by such concerns in 1929.

These technological changes doubled the productive capacity of the average worker between 1919 and 1933. In manufacturing alone, they increased his hourly product by 71 percent. They opened up new vistas of comfort and security to the average man. But despite reassuring discourse about profit sharing and employee participation in industry, the increasing size of business brought concentration of wealth in geometric ratio. By 1929, 200 huge corporations owned one-half of our total corporate wealth. Two years later, 100 general industrial corporations out of a total of 300,000 controlled one-third of the general industrial wealth of the Nation. As a natural corollary, the wage earners' share in the product created by manufacturing has declined steadily for nearly a century. Standing at 51 percent in 1849, it fell to 42 percent in 1919 and to 36 percent in 1933. The isolation of the individual worker has been reflected glaringly in the distribution of the Nation's goods.

The tremendous disparity between the few and the many became most pronounced in that glittering era which we regarded as the zenith of American prosperity. Between 1922 and 1929 the real wages of employees increased by slightly less than 10 percent. But during the same period industrial profits rose by 86 percent, while in the shorter span from 1926 to 1939 dividend payments mounted by 104 percent.

If we had succeeded in providing the minimum requirements of health and decency for every deserving person in the United States, we might have said that the maldistribution of income was a fair price to pay for our industrial efficiency. But we know that we suffered from the prevalence of poverty in a land of plenty. In 1929, 6,000,000 families, or more than 21 percent of our total population, had incomes of less than $1,000 per year. About 12,000,000 families, or more than 42 percent of the total, earned less than $1,500 yearly. Sixteen million families, or 60 percent of the people, had annual incomes below the $2,000 per year necessary for the basic requirements of health and decency. And nearly 20,000,000 families, constituting 71 percent of all America, received less than $2,500 a year. At the same time, in the highest income bracket, one-tenth of 1 percent of the families in the United States were earning as much as the 42 percent at the bottom. It is not surprising that in *America's Capacity to Consume,* the most complete study of family income ever presented to the general reader in this country, the statement is made without equivocation that during the past decade "inequality in the distribution of income has been accentuated."

Not only the preachments of moralists but also the teachings of economists have proved that this injustice wrought its hardships upon those who were temporarily favored as well as those who had been permanently neglected. The low level of income prevented the vast majority of consumers from draining the market of its flood of goods. This was particularly serious in an age of mass production, which had built 21,000,000 automobiles and over 20,000,000 radio sets. At the same time, the extraordinary concentration of income placed excessive savings in the hands of a few. While 60 percent of the families in America contributed only 1.6 percent to the total savings of the country, 2.3 percent of all families contributed 66⅔ percent to all savings, and 60,000 families at the top of the economic ladder saved almost as much as 25,000,000 families on the lower rungs. Corporate surpluses rose from $8,500,000,000 in 1923 to $16,000,000,000 in 1929. These accumulations of the few sought outlet through investments in plant facilities. Contrasted with the 10-percent rise in wages between 1922 and 1929, the production of machinery increased 91 percent and of capital equipment 70 percent. Production mounted beyond any possibilities of market absorption.

For a short while we staved off inevitable disaster by the pipe dream of installment selling and by lending Europe money with which to buy our own products. But when the domestic market finally closed to further investment, and foreign trade collapsed because our own people had no money with which to buy European goods, the crash came.

This thesis, which places the failure of purchasing power at the center of all explanations of depression, has long received recognition. It has been further substantiated this year in a stimulating book entitled *The Formation of Capital,* by Dr. H. G. Moulton. This volume states:

> The base of the economic pyramid is the production of consumption goods. The demand for plant and equipment is derived from the demand for consumption goods . . . A slight shrinkage at the base of the pyramid very nearly eliminates the top . . . The primary need is a larger flow of funds through consumptive channels.

During 4 long years after the depression came we clung to the same policies which had brought the calamity and which were prolonging its ravages. While the level of wages dropped 60 percent between 1929 and 1932, property income fell only 29 percent. The remarkable report of the Research and Planning Division of the National Recovery Administration shows that while wages stood at 44 percent of the 1926 level in 1932, and the national income at only 62 percent of that level, dividend payments remained as high as 142 percent of that level. And day by day the downward spiral gained in momentum.

It was only when over 15,000,000 people were unemployed, when banks were closed, when business was uprooted, and when our whole economic system hung perilously on the precipice, that we embarked upon a new program. This new program was projected in terms of recovery and reform. It was designated not merely to set the forces of revival in motion, but, above all, to eradicate permanently the evils that had done so much harm in the past.

The first hypothesis was that the interpenetration of all industries throughout the country, the nonconformity of economic organization to State lines, and the deep-seated and widespread character of the national calamity, made Nationwide action essential. For the purpose of rationalizing production, outlawing cutthroat competition, and bringing order into the distribution of goods, not only were the antitrust laws in part suspended but the Government itself embarked upon the diametrically opposed policy of stimulating coast-to-coast cooperation among business men. It was thought that in this manner a permanent equilibrium of the various factors in industry might be maintained.

In addition, there was a second phase of the program which struck at the very core of the depression. Congress determined to fix wages and hours at a level that might, by reemployment and higher pay, spread adequate purchasing power among the masses of consumers and thus prime the pump of business. Equally in the foreground was the intent to insure a decent measure of security and comfort to those who worked, while protecting the fair-minded employer from the cutthroat tactics of the exploiting few.

But the Government never for a moment proposed to set up a benevolent despotism, or to extend its arm into every nook and cranny of private business. It did not contemplate regulation of every scale of wages or supervision of every schedule of hours. Acting in an emergency, it desired only to create a solid foundation upon which might be built the mutual efforts of a revived industry and a rehabilitated labor. And if industry and labor were to act in unison, it was clear that they would need equal opportunities for intelligent and effective action. Just as industry was organized, so labor was to be allowed to organize. It was for this purpose that section 7 (a) was written into the National Industrial Recovery Act and reinforced last June by Public Resolution No. 44, providing for the election of representatives for the purpose of collective bargaining.

I think it may be safely said that whatever controversy now rages as to the wisdom of many phases of the recovery program, and of the National Industrial Recovery Act in particular, there is practically unanimous agreement in Congress that section 7 (a) was sound in inception, and that the right of employees to organize and bargain collectively through representatives of their own choosing should be safeguarded at all times. If Congress recognized that right for decades, Congress must shoulder the responsibility to protect it now that employers are more united than ever before in trade associations blanketing the entire country. The developments of the past two years have not given employees any guaranties to which they were not entitled. But the events of the past two years have intensified the social necessity of protecting these guaranties against repudiation.

Nor is there any disagreement about the fact that section 7 (a) has collapsed. General Johnson, the first Administrator of the National Industrial Recovery Act, in testifying last month before the Finance Committee of the Senate, said:

"I think section 7 (a) has substantially failed of its original purpose."

Mr. Francis Biddle, the brilliant Chairman of the National Labor Relations Board, on the same occasion referred to "the emptiness of a law which we know cannot be enforced." A very recent and exceedingly comprehensive study of the National Recovery Administration by the Brookings Institution says:

"Section 7 of the Recovery Act is uncertain in purpose, vague in contents, and ambiguous in language."

This breakdown of section 7 (a) has driven a dagger close to the heart of the recovery program. It was intended that the codes should be formulated with the "united action of labor and management." But with labor denied the opportunity to organize and bargain collectively, practically all of the codes have been conceived and drafted and presented for governmental approval by employers alone. This means that in the original formulation of the labor provisions no less than the trade practices, industry wrote the ticket. Labor came into the picture, not as the genuine party in interest that it should have been, but merely through the indirect representation of the Labor Advisory Board, an organ with no actual authority and with no bargaining power comparable to that of the trade associations.

The results of this defect are well illustrated by the difference between the normal run of codes and the few special codes formed by a process of collective bargaining. The normal codes usually provide a 40-hour week, while the special codes descend frequently to a 36- or 35-hour week. The special codes, such as in the coal, needle, and building trades, provide fairly scientific minimum-wage levels for the various skills, while the normal codes are generally filled with vague and uncertain exemptions and exceptions which make enforcement difficult and remove much of the legal force from the minimum-wage rates.

One specific example is particularly telling. The tobacco industry is one of the most profitable in the country; but since it has allowed collective bargaining no place, the increase in the average weekly wage between 1933 and 1934 was only 75 cents. But in the women's clothing industry, where section 7 (a) has been an actuality, the advance in pay was $3. The average weekly earnings during the last year in the cigarette trade were $11.84, in the women's clothing trade $18.82.

The cumulative effects of these shortcomings are reflected in economic tendencies at the present time. Unemployment is as great as it was a year ago. Average weekly hours of work, which stood at 37¼ when the codes were established in the fall of 1933, stand at 37½ today. The real income of the individual worker employed full time is less than in March 1933. The average worker's income in 1934 was $1,099, or $813 less than the amount required to maintain a family of five in health and decency. The realignment of profits and wages, which we contemplated so confidently in the spring of 1933, has not taken place.

In December 1934, pay rolls registered only 60 percent of the 1926 level, while dividend and interest payments were fixed at 150 percent of that level. Total wages have risen only 28 percent in the past two years, while 840 large companies have increased their profits from $471,000,000 in 1933 to $673,000,000 in 1934, a gain of 42 percent. Net profits of 1,435 manufacturing and trading companies increased from $640,000,000 in 1933 to $1,071,000,000 in 1934, or 64 percent, while their annual rate of return rose from 2.7 percent to 4.5 percent.

Furthermore, the history of the past two years makes it clear that failure to maintain a sane balance between wages and industrial returns will be attended by the same fatal consequences as in the past. The rise of business activity to 89 percent of normal in the precode booms of April and July 1933 collapsed after July because no adequate purchasing power had been built up to sustain it. The rise to 80 percent of normal in April and May

1934, rested on a surer foundation because of the increase in purchasing power provided through reemployment in the fall of 1933 and through public spending.

If the more recent quickening of business activity is not supported by rises in wages, either we shall have to sustain the market indefinitely by huge and continuous public spending or we shall meet the certainty of another collapse. With the evil and the remedy in such clear relief, Congress cannot hesitate to atone the error of allowing section 7 (a) to languish.

A study of the weaknesses in the existing law brings the conviction that the remedy is neither obscure nor unattainable. The patent ambiguity and excessive generality of section 7 (a) has led to a proliferation of interpretations and counterinterpretations. Consequently both employers and employees have been denied their basic right to a clear and certain law.

Turning at once from substance to procedure, the greatest difficulty with section 7 (a) has been that the present National Labor Relations Board, the cardinal agency for interpreting it, has not been vested with enforcement powers. The Board, after hearing cases, may refer them with recommendations to the National Recovery Administration. As was demonstrated in the recent *Colt* case, it is that administration rather than the Board which exercises final discretion in determining whether the Blue Eagle shall be removed or whether Government contracts shall be canceled.

Of course, the National Recovery Administration has adequate enforcement powers. But everyone knows that the whole tendency of that organization has been toward conciliation and compromise with industry in order that codes of fair competition may be administered smoothly and continuously. This approach may be laudable in dealing with standards of fair competition that have been written and proposed by industry itself. But it is totally unsuited to the enforcement of section 7 (a), which is a mandate of Congress, which becomes a crucial issue in those very cases where it is most flagrantly challenged, and which, like all analogous laws of Congress, must be vindicated by a judicial process. The confusion of the voluntarily submitted fair-practice provisions with section 7 (a) has put the Recovery Administration in the untenable position of conciliator and prosecutor at once. Not only has section 7 (a) been lost in the shuffle but the Recovery Administration itself has suffered from the misplaced burden. And this difficulty has been aggravated because, under present conditions, section 7 (a) is applicable only where there is a code of fair competition, which constantly puts recalcitrants in the position where they can threaten to surrender their codes in case section 7 (a) is enforced against them.

As an alternative, the present National Labor Relations Board may refer its recommendations to the Department of Justice for enforcement. But since the Board has no power of subpoena or investigation except in connection with elections, the records which it builds up are based in most cases upon the testimony of complainants alone, supplemented at best by the testimony of such witnesses as the defendant voluntarily presents. This makes it necessary for the Department of Justice in any event to make further investigations before bringing suit; and if the Department brings suit at all, it must commence entirely *de novo* in the courts, with the defendant having 30 days to answer, or moving to dismiss, or applying for a bill of particulars. Thus is defeated the very purpose of an administrative agency, which is to provide specialized treatment of the factual aspects of a specialized controversy.

Weak as it is, the present National Labor Relations Board has been subjected, in addition, to the corroding influence of various industrial boards, dealing according to their own lights with the same subject matter. At present from 13 to 15 boards have been established to handle 7 (a) cases, and over none of these has the national board jurisdiction, either as to fact or as to law. Since there are now over 100 codes which provide for the establishment of industrial boards, there exists the constant threat that dispersion of authority will transcend all reasonable bounds.

Quite aside from all question of scattered responsibility, these industrial boards are essentially unsuited to the handling of 7 (a) cases. Partisan in composition, living in an atmosphere of compromise and conciliation, they are well designed to adjust wage and hour controversies in accordance with the varying standards of different localities. The success of labor before an industrial board depends upon the strength of labor in that particular area. But section 7 (a) was written by Congress to protect the weak who could not protect themselves, and it was intended for universal application, not universal modification. The major effect of leaving its enforcement to a variety of industrial boards is to give the least protection to those who need it most.

Last June, in order to remedy the recognized weaknesses in section 7 (a), Congress passed Public Resolution No. 44. The main purpose of that resolution was to facilitate the holding of elections by the National Labor Relations Board; but a fatal loophole has rendered its effect nugatory. In providing that election orders of the Board might be reviewed in the courts prior to the holding of the election itself, the law afforded employers a shield to ward off action indefinitely. The most revealing commentary upon the joint resolution is contained in a letter disclosed by the Senate committee investigating munitions. Written last June by a vice president of one of America's largest corporations, it says:

My guess is that Congress will today pass the joint resolution proposed as an alternative to the Wagner bill, and that will end, for the time being, at least, many of our troubles in that respect. Personally, I view the passage of the joint resolution with equanimity. It means that temporary measures, which cannot last more than a year, will be substituted for the permanent legislation proposed in the original Wagner bill. I do not believe that there will again be as good a chance for the passage of the Wagner Act as exists now, and the trade is a mighty good compromise.

I have read carefully the joint resolution, and my personal opinion is that it is not going to bother us very much. For one thing, it would be necessary, if the newly created boards are to order and supervise elections in our plants, that they first set aside as invalid the elections just completed.

I do not think this can be done. If, in 1935, our elections should occur in the second half of June rather than in the first half, the board would automatically be legislated out of existence before that date.

If they try to horn in on us in any situation in the meantime, I think we have our fences pretty securely set up. Therefore, and for other reasons, I am in favor of compromising by not opposing passage of the joint resolution. This, of course, is my own personal opinion. I have not yet had a chance to clear it with our people here.

The present bill cures the defects in existing law. It clarifies and amplifies the provisions of section 7 (a), and it centralizes in a single permanent National Labor Relations Board the duty to protect the collective-bargaining rights of employees. The Board will, of course, have regional agencies throughout the country to handle violations initially at their source, and will be empowered to designate any existing industrial board for such purposes. In all cases, however, the findings and recommendations of these agencies will be transferred to the National Labor Relations Board for final action. After these appropriate hearings the Board will be empowered to issue orders forbidding violations of the law and making restitution to those who have been injured thereby. All such orders will be fully reviewable at the instance of any aggrieved party in the Federal courts.

The procedure set forth in this bill is so closely modeled upon other statutes, such as the Federal Trade Commission Act and the Interstate Commerce Act, that one is astounded to hear the charges circulated to the effect that this measure would sweep aside the courts and endow a new and queer kind of agency with dictatorial or arbitrary powers.

The power of the Board to hold elections is considerably clarified. An election is merely a preliminary determination of fact. There is no more reason why it should be subject to anterior court review than why a hearing should be deferred pending judicial action; but if any election is made the basis for an order of the Board related to an unfair labor practice, the whole procedure embracing the election will be fully reviewable in the appropriate Federal court.

Let us turn now to the substantive provisions of the bill dealing with unfair labor practices. I wish to emphasize at the outset how limited these provisions are in their scope, how simple they are in their language, and how thoroughly they are grounded in long-established congressional policy.

The first unfair-labor-practice provision, in substance, forbids an employer to interfere with, restrain, or coerce employees in the exercise of their right to self-organization, to form, join, or assist labor organizations, to bargain collectively through representatives of their own choosing, and to engage in concerted activities for the purpose of collective bargaining or other mutual aid or protection.

This language follows practically verbatim the familiar principles already embedded in our law by section 2 of the Railway Labor Act of 1926, section 2 of the Norris-LaGuardia Act, section 77 (p) and (p) of 1932 amendments to the Bankruptcy Act, section 7 (a) of the National Industrial Recovery Act, and section 7 (e) of the act creating the office of the Federal Coordinator of Transportation.

Experience over a considerable period of time, however, has made it clear that these general declarations of freedom have little effect unless they are accomplished by a specific catalog of forbidden practices. Therefore, the succeeding four unfair-labor-practice provisions, without narrowing in any way the widest possible application of the first, enunciate with particularity the concrete acts which have been the most fertile source of trouble in the past.

The second unfair-labor-practice provision deals with the so-called "company-union problem." It makes it unlawful for an employer to dominate or interfere with the formation or administration of any labor organization, or contribute financial or other support to it.

The intent here is to bring about in industry generally the same conditions which Congress decreed for the railways and businesses under trusteeship by the 1933 amendments to the Bankruptcy Act, the act creating the office of the Federal Coordinator of Transportation, and the 1934 amendments to the Railway Labor Act.

Anyone familiar with these laws will recognize at once that there is nothing in the pending bill which promotes a union monopoly, which places the stamp of governmental favor upon any particular type of union, or which outlaws the so-called "company union," if by that term is meant simply an entirely free and independent organization of workers who through their own volition confine their cooperative activities to the limits of one company. Nor is there anything in the bill which interferes with the benefits of pension or recreation plans when such benefits are extended equally to all employees, without discrimination tending to encourage or discourage union membership. The bill intends merely that those agencies designed to represent the workers for purposes of collective bargaining shall be free from the domination or even the interference of the other party.

The primary evil of the organization which is dominated or interfered with by the employer is that, sometimes because of express prohibition, more often because of its intrinsic composition, it is not well suited to extend its cooperative activities beyond the bounds of a single employer unit.

A thorough study of this subject has just been made by the Twentieth Century Fund, backed by an impressive array of scholars, employers, and professional men. It shows that even different company unions of the same employer rarely work in unity, and almost never is there even a loose and informal contact between company unions of different employers.

Limitations such as these run counter to the very core of the new-deal philosophy. Businessmen are being allowed to pool their information and experience in vast trade associations in order to make a concerted drive against the evil features of modern industrialism. If employees are denied similar privileges, they not only are unable to uphold their end of the labor bargain but, in addition, they cannot cope with any issues that transcend the boundaries of a single business. And under modern industrial conditions problems of wages and hours are regional or even national in scope. Order must exist everywhere if it is to exist at all.

In the second place, the employer who dominates or interferes with his workers sometimes, either by express provisions or more likely by subtle economic pressure, limits his employees' choice of representatives to those who work for him. A worker may be a complete master of his tools, but as a representative he is not an expert in industrial relations, and is likely to be entirely unable to take advantage of legitimate opportunities based upon knowledge of the labor market and general business conditions. More important, only representatives who are not subservient to the employer with whom they deal can act freely in the interest of the workers. Simple common sense tells us that a man does not possess this freedom when he bargains with those who control his source of livelihood.

The third defect of the company-dominated union is that it is supported, in whole or in part, by the employer. I cannot understand how those so well schooled in the doctrines of Americanism can sanction a practice whereby the person on one side of the bargaining table pays the attorney of those with whom he deals. Collective bargaining becomes a mockery when the spokesman of the employee is the marionette of the employer.

These few practices by no means cover the whole range of the abuses that constitute interference. The undue influence which the employer exerts over the supposedly free agent of his workers may take other forms. It may consist in employer interference with the formation of the constitution or bylaws of a labor organization. The essence of interference is that the workers' organization, instead of being absolutely free and independent as an organic entity, is subjected in some way to the employer's will.

The recent study to which I have referred affords ample evidence that the company union is the mere creature of the employer. Out of 125 company unions investigated, the plans for 53 of them were installed by executive order on the part of the employer. Only 22 of them were ratified by a representative vote of the employees. In only 10 cases out of 72 were the employees alone free to change their plan.

The severest indictment of these unions imposed from above is that they have blossomed forth since the passage of the very act which was designed to give workers full freedom of organization. According to the National Industrial Conference Board, the number of workers recruited into company unions rose from 432,000 in 1932 to 1,164,000 in 1933, representing a gain of 169 percent. More than 69 percent of the company unions now in existence have been inaugurated in the brief period since the passage of the Recovery Act.

Contrary to the argument that the company union has the virtue of insuring industrial peace, we know that this open entry of employers in the field of active organization of workers promotes strife and discord. Men versed in the tenets of freedom become restive when not allowed to be free. The sharp outbreaks of economic warfare in various parts of the country to a large extent attest the bitterness of feeling when company unionism raises its head. Most impartial students of industrial problems agree that the best records of mutual accomplishments have been made where the sham union has been driven from the scene, and where workers are free men in fact as well as in name.

While outlawing the organization that is interfered with by the employer, this bill does not establish the closed shop or even encourage it. The much-discussed closed-shop proviso merely states that nothing in any Federal law shall be held to illegalize the confirmation of voluntary closed-shop agreements between employers and workers. This insertion is necessary to prevent repetition of those mistaken interpretations which have held that Congress intended to outlaw the closed shop when it enacted section 7 (a) of the Recovery Act.

I hold no brief for or against the closed shop, but there are some who believe that it is a device which at times may be necessary to advance and preserve the living standards of employees. It is legal in many States, and there is no reason why Congress should make it illegal in those places where public policy now sustains it.

The virulent propaganda to the effect that this bill encourages the closed shop is outrageous in view of the fact that in two respects it actually narrows the now-existing law in regard to the closed-shop agreement. In the first place, while today an employer may sign a closed-shop contract even with a minority group, the bill provides that he shall be allowed to negotiate such an agreement only with an organization which represents the majority of employees in the appropriate collective bargaining unit covered by such agreement when made. Secondly, the bill is extremely careful to forestall the making of closed-shop agreements with unions that are interfered with or dominated by the company, or with any organization that has been tainted at any time in the past by practices which are now declared to be unfair. The closed-shop agreement is to be allowable only when an organization has been free from its inception.

The third unfair-labor-practice provision makes it illegal for an employer, by discrimination in regard to hire or tenure of employment or any term or condition of employment, to encourage or discourage membership in any labor organization.

This provision is merely a logical and imperative extension of that section of the Norris-LaGuardia Act which makes the "yellow-dog" contract unenforceable in the Federal courts. If freedom of organization is to be preserved the employees must have more than the knowledge that the courts will not be used to confirm injustice. They need protection most in those very cases where the employer is strong enough to impress his will without the aid of the law. And it is perfectly obvious that unfair pressure may be exercised by discrimination during employment as well as by actual discharge.

The fourth unfair-labor-practice provision, forbidding discharge or discrimination because an employee has filed charges or given testimony under this measure, is self-explanatory.

The final unfair-labor-practice provision makes it illegal for an employer to refuse to bargain collectively with the representatives of his employees.

Most emphatically this provision does not imply governmental supervision of wage or hour agreements. It does not compel anyone to make a compact of any kind if no terms are arrived at that are satisfactory to him. The very essence of collective bargaining is that either party shall be free to withdraw if its conditions are not met. But the right of workers to bargain collectively through representatives of their own choosing must be matched by the correlative duty of employers to recognize and deal in good faith with these representatives. The Government itself is held up to ridicule when the elections which it supervises are rendered illusory by failure to acknowledge their results. And, needless to say, such a contradictory course generates perpetual discontent and strife.

Just what the duty to bargain collectively implies was clearly set forth by the present National Labor Relations Board in the *Houde Engineering Corporation* case, decided on August 30, 1934. There the Board said:

Without this duty the right to bargain would be sterile. . . . The incontestably sound principle is that the employer is obligated by the statutes to negotiate in good faith with his employee's representatives; to match their proposals, if unacceptable, with counterproposals; and to make every reasonable effort to reach an agreement.

The sound result which the Labor Board reached by interpretation of a vague law should be confirmed and protected by a clear definition of congressional policy.

Further to facilitate the procedure of collective bargaining, the bill embraces the principle of majority rule. It states:

Representatives designated or selected for the purpose of collective bargaining by the majority of the employees in a unit appropriate for such purposes shall be the exclusive representatives of all employees in such unit for the purposes of collective bargaining in respect to rates of pay, wages, hours of employment, or other conditions of employment.

Collective bargaining is not an artificial procedure devoted to an unknown end. Its object is the making of agreements which will stabilize employment conditions and promote fair working standards. It is well nigh universally recognized that it is practically impossible to apply two or more sets of agreements to one unit of workers at the same time, or to apply the terms of one agreement to only a portion of the workers in a single unit. For this reason, collective bargaining means majority rule. This rule is conducive not only to agreements, but also to friendly relations. Workers find it easier to approach their employers in a spirit of good will if they are not torn by internal dissent. And employers, wherever majority rule has been given a fair chance, have discovered it more profitable to deal with a single group than to be harassed by a constant series of negotiations with rival factions.

Majority rule makes it clear that the guaranty of the right of employees to bargain collectively through representatives of their own choosing must not be misapplied so as to permit employers to interfere with the practical effectuation of that right by bargaining with individuals or minority groups in their own behalf after representatives have been picked by the majority to represent all.

At the same time, majority rule recognizes minority rights. It does not ever imply that any employee can be forced to join a union, except through the traditional method of a closed-shop agreement with the employer. And since, in the absence of such an agreement, the bill specifically prevents discrimination against anyone either for belonging or for not belonging to a union, the majority will be quite powerless to make an agreement more favorable to themselves than to the minority who remain without. In addition, the bill preserves the right of any individual or minority group to present grievances to its employer.

Anyone who analyzes the problems and who studies the history of industrial relations will be amazed at the current opposition to majority rule. Certainly it cannot be claimed that the rule is lacking solid precedent. It has been applied regularly by governmental agencies and recognized repeatedly by laws of Congress. It was followed by the National War Labor Board created by President Wilson in the spring of 1918. It has been applied consistently by the Railway Labor Board created by the Transportation Act of 1920. The 1934 amendments to the Railway Labor Act provided for it. Public Resolution No. 44, approved last June, in that it provided for elections, must have contemplated majority rule.

If we turn from governmental experience to private practice, what do we find? The platform adopted by the Congress of American Industry and the National Association of Manufacturers on December 5 and 6, 1934, and they are the ones who now oppose majority rule for workers, provides:

> Under appropriate safeguards, the approved competitive practices and prohibitions submitted by the properly defined majority of a group, trade, or industry shall be binding upon the minority.

The experience of the National Labor Relations Board has been that the very employers who decry majority rule today insisted upon majority rule alone when they were in control of the situation through their dominance over a company union. The animus behind the crocodile tears now being shed for the welfare of minorities was laid bare by the liberal dean of the Wisconsin Law School, Lloyd K. Garrison, a former Chairman of the National Labor Relations Board. Testifying before the Committee on Education and Labor upon this bill, he said:

> It seemed to me last summer, as I sat on the Board and listened to these cases, quite evident that the opposition to this rule came down simply to this, that the employer who opposed the rule merely wanted to avoid doing any collective bargaining at all so long as he could keep his responsibility diffused. So long as he could say, "I will bargain first with this group, then I will bargain with that group, and then I will run back to the first and see what they think about the proposals," and so on ad infinitum, he would end up by reaching no collective agreement at all. And that is why the majority rule is opposed.

Mr. Garrison has placed the matter in a nutshell. He has made it clear that democracy in industry must be based upon the same principles as democracy in government. Majority rule, with all its imperfections, is the best protection of workers' rights, just as it is the surest guaranty of political liberty that mankind has yet discovered.

It is appropriate that some reference should be made to the constitutional problems raised by this bill. There are two broad questions involved: First, does the regulation of the employer-employee relationship as herein provided violate due process of law; and, secondly, can Federal jurisdiction over this relationship be sustained under the commerce clause?

The authority of Congress to guarantee freedom of organization, to prohibit the company-dominated union, and to prevent employers from requiring membership or nonmembership in any union, has been completely upheld in *Texas & New Orleans Railroad Co.* v. *Brotherhood* (281 U. S. 548 (1930)). This was a suit by a labor union to restrain the railroad from interfering, in violation of the Railway Labor Act of 1926, with the right of its employees to self-organization and the designation of representatives. The decree of the lower court had provided that the railroad company should: first, completely disestablish its company union; second, reinstate the Brotherhood as representative until the employees by secret ballot should make a choice; third, restore to service and to stated privileges certain employees who had been discharged for activities in behalf of the Brotherhood. The Supreme Court, with Chief Justice Hughes writing for a unanimous Court sustaining the decree, said:

> The legality of collective action on the part of employees in order to safeguard their proper interests is not to be disputed. It has long been recognized that employees are entitled to organize for the purpose of securing the redress of grievances and to promote agreements with employers concerning rates of pay and conditions of work. . . . Congress was not required to ignore this right of the employees, but could safeguard it and seek to make their appropriate collective action an instrument of peace rather than of strife. Such collective action would be a mockery if representation were made futile by interference with freedom of choice.

Thus the Supreme Court sustained a decree prohibiting, in substance, all except the last of the unfair labor practices listed in this bill, and it is particularly significant that this decree was based upon a law containing only the first of these practices. Brushing aside the much-criticized earlier cases which had declared the prohibition of the "yellow-dog" contract unconstitutional, Chief Justice Hughes said:

> The petitioners invoke the principle declared in *Adair* v. *United States* (208 U.S. 1, 61) and *Coppage* v. *Kansas* (236 U.S. 1), but these decisions are inapplicable. The Railway Labor Act of 1926 does not interfere with the normal exercise of the right of the carrier to select its employees or to discharge them. The statute is not aimed at this right of the employers but at the interference with the right of employees to have representatives of their own choosing. As the carrier subject to the act has no constitutional right to interfere with the freedom of the employees in making their selections they cannot complain of the statute on constitutional grounds.

When we realize that this prevailing and unanimous opinion rendered by the Chief Justice followed precisely the line of reasoning that he had followed when dissenting in the Coppage case, and that the two are really identical in principle, we can have no doubt that Coppage against Kansas and Adair against United States have been overruled.

It is true that the Texas case involved the interests of railway workers. But its decision upon the question of due process is equally applicable wherever congressional jurisdiction over interstate commerce can be established. Let us now examine the grounds for Federal jurisdiction.

A vast number of strikes have arisen in protestation against the denial of the rights guaranteed by section 7 (a) of the Recovery Act and re-affirmed by the present bill. Certainly, many similar outbreaks will be prevented if these rights are secured, for whenever given a fair trial the protection of collective bargaining has promoted industrial peace. And that strikes burden commerce cannot be denied, in view of the recognition of this fact by such landmarks of our law as *In re Debs* (158 U. S. 564), *Duplex Printing Press Co.* v. *Deering* (254 U. S. 443), *American Steel Foundries* v. *Tri-City Central Trades Council* (257 U. S. 184), *Coronado Coal Co* v. *United Mine Workers* (268 U. S. 295), and *Bedford Cut Stone Co.* v. *Stone Cutters Association* (274 U. S. 37). Moreover, the courts which have enunciated so broad an interpretation of commerce when the result has been to frustrate the attempts of wage earners to better their economic conditions by collective action, will be constrained to take an equally broad view in order to diminish strikes by preventing the unfair labor practices which incite them.

Those cases under the antitrust laws which have been cited for the proposition that the Federal Government cannot deal with the employer-employee relationship are not applicable. For where the courts have refused to enjoin strikes under the antitrust laws, it has not been for lack of constitutional power but because the burden upon commerce was not deemed such as the antitrust laws intended to prohibit. Statutory construction of these laws fixed the boundaries of equity jurisdiction. But the Federal Government has the power under the Constitution to prevent any burden whatsoever upon interstate commerce. And there can be no doubt that Congress intends this power to be exercised in full to prevent unfair practices that cause or threaten to cause even the slightest burden.

It is clear that these practices may be enjoined even before the strike occurs. As Chief Justice Taft said in the first *Coronado* case (259 U. S. 344 (1922)):

> If Congress deems certain recurring practices, although not really part of interstate commerce, likely to obstruct, restrain, or burden it, it has the power to subject them to national supervision or restraint.

I want to emphasize ever more strongly the constitutional power and the intent of Congress to prevent these unfair labor practices even where they do not lead or threaten to lead to strikes. As economic conditions have changed, courts on the whole have shown an increasing willingness to recognize that unsound business practices are a direct burden upon the regularity and volume of commerce. One example is the line of cases dealing with unfair competition under the Federal Trade Commission Act. The principle is well stated in another connection in *Chicago Board of Trade* v. *Olsen* (262 U. S. 1 (1922)), upholding Federal regulation of future sales on grain exchanges, an activity in itself purely local. The Court said:

> The question of price dominates trade between the States. Sales of an article directly affect the country-wide commerce in it. For this reason Congress has the power to

provide the appropriate means adopted in this act by which this abuse may be restrained and avoided.

In effect upon commerce, wages are indistinguishable from prices. In fact, each is significant only in terms of the other. When wages sink to low levels, the decline in purchasing power is felt upon the marts of trade. And since collective bargaining is the most powerful single force in maintaining and advancing wage rates, its repudiation is likely to intensify the maldistribution of buying power, thus reducing standards of living, unbalancing the economic structure, and inducing depression with its devastating effect upon the flow of commerce.

In the more recent case of *Appalachian Coals, Inc.,* v. *United States* (288 U. S. 344 (1933)), Chief Justice Hughes said:

The interests of producers and consumers are interlinked. When industry is grievously hurt, when producing concerns fail, when unemployment mounts, and communities dependent upon profitable production are prostrated, the wells of commerce go dry.

This statement will long be a beacon light to guide those who are seeking to make our law consonant to the needs of our social and economic life. While the pending bill of course does not intend to go beyond the constitutional power of Congress, as that power may be marked out by the courts, it seeks the full limit of that power to prevent these unfair labor practices. It seeks to prevent them whether they affect interstate commerce by causing strikes, or by destroying the equality of bargaining power upon which the flow of commerce depends, or by occurring in interstate commerce.

The recent decision in the *Weirton* case is based upon Judge Nields' finding that the activities of the Weirton company did not interfere with the freedom of employees to organize, as guaranteed by section 7 (a) of the Recovery Act. It seems clear that this decision is far out of line with that of the United States Supreme Court in the *Texas* case (supra), which held that activities similar to those at Weirton were illegal under the Railway Labor Act of 1926, an act no more specific in its terms than section 7 (a). Not a single lawyer with whom I have talked has been able to explain Judge Nields' failure not only to distinguish, but even to refer to the Texas case. And even if it were to be conceded that Judge Nields correctly interpreted section 7 (a), his decision merely emphasized the need for strengthening that section and creating a permanent administrative tribunal, versed in the complexities of labor relations, to deal with such matters.

Since Judge Nields found that section 7 (a) did not outlaw the activities complained of at Weirton, his discussion of the constitutionality of that section was pure dictum. I cannot believe that this decision of a single district judge as to the extent of the power of Congress to regulate interstate commerce will weigh very heavily with this Senate, particularly since his limited conception of interstate commerce, while in line with many early decisions of the United States Supreme Court, is clearly at odds with later decisions which I have discussed and which are more responsive to the changing character of our national economic life.

It is even clearer that the recent decision of the Supreme Court in the Railway Pension case has absolutely no applicability to this bill. That case held, rightly or wrongly, that the retirement of superannuated workers had no recognizable relationship to the efficiency of interstate transportation. The opinion of Mr. Justice Roberts expressly distinguished the situation covered by the Texas case, supra, where a statute was designed to promote interstate commerce by preserving industrial peace.

This bill is designed to promote industrial peace. The bitterness and the heavy cost of economic conflicts between employers and workers in this country constitute a long and tragic story. Between 1915 and 1931 there were 4,856 strikes, involving the surrender of 2,795,000 jobs and the loss of 72,957,000 working days. At least $1,000,000,000 per year have been wasted because of these controversies.

This toll of private warfare cannot be measured by statistics alone, for it places the taint of hatred and the stain of bloodshed across the pathway to amicable and profitable business dealings. Nor can we be satisfied to allow these troubles to proceed unchecked to their bitter conclusion. A do-nothing procedure leaves the temporary victor as exhausted as the temporarily vanquished, and sows the seeds for recurrent strife when the competitors have rallied from their efforts.

One method of approach to the problem of industrial peace would be for the Government to invoke compulsory arbitration, or to dictate the terms of settlement whenever a controversy arises. Where this procedure has been tried in European nations it has met with only questionable success. In any event, it is so alien to our American traditions of individual enterprise that it would provoke extreme resentment and constant discord.

It is clear that in this country peace must be based upon reason rather than upon force. We have cherished always the ideal of employers and workers meeting together with friendly and open minds in order that they may exchange views and arrive at solutions based not upon compulsion but upon mutual concessions and mutual benefit. This may be termed the method of conference, of give and take, of free cooperation.

The best example of the conference or voluntary method of ironing out disagreements is the railway industry. Because of the vital connection between steady transportation and the very lives of our people, the Government early took steps to set up machinery for the peaceful adjustment of railway-labor disputes. The central idea of all these efforts has been to promote the making of collective agreements between employers and workers without exercising any compulsion upon either side.

In seeking these ends, however, the Government did not rely upon a policy of complete laissez faire. It soon saw the necessity of establishing by law the underlying conditions from which agreements might arise. It protected employees in their right to organize and bargain collectively. It applied to the railway industry the principle of majority rule and it abolished the union that was interfered with or financed by the company.

The application of these rules of fair play yielded the finest results. Not once since 1894 has serious strife upon the railroads hardened our arteries of trade. It was to be expected that such a record of success would be emulated elsewhere, and when our entry into the World War made it imperative to cement the bonds of cordiality between employers and workers the War Labor Board was established. This Board immediately applied the principles that governed the railway industry. It was remarkable that not a single strike or lock-out in defiance of an award of the War Labor Board occurred until after the armistice; and the United States was the only belligerent unvexed by major labor disturbances.

It is a matter of record that one of the most prolific causes of strikes has been the failure to apply to industry generally the rules of industrial democracy underlying the conference method. At least 25 percent of the labor disputes in recent years has resulted from denials of the procedure of collective bargaining. In regard to the steel strike of 1919, which was one of the severest and most disastrous affrays in recent history, the impartial commission of inquiry of the Interchurch World Movement said that both sides agreed that the occasion of the strike was the failure to recognize the friendly conference idea. Of the 3,655 new cases received by the regional agencies of the present National Labor Relations Board during the second half of 1934 and the first month of 1935, the issue of collective bargaining was paramount in 2,330 cases, or about 74 percent.

The pending bill is designed merely to apply to industry generally the benefits of our rich American experience. While it has been branded radical by some and ultraconservative by others, every one of its principles has been sanctioned by a long train of laws of Congress. While it has been called inopportune and hasty, it is responsive to the serious industrial disturbances of last summer, when blood ran freely in the streets and martial law was in the offing. While some think it one-sided and directed against industry, it is trained upon the solution of problems that have plagued industry as much as any other group. In its search for industrial peace combined with economic justice, it appeals to the conscience and intelligence of all those who know the history of our country and are imbued with its high ideals. In applying the healing balm of an upright, impartial, and peaceful forum to industry and labor it will benefit employers, workers, and the country at large.

During the delivery of Mr. Wagner's speech—

JOSEPH ROBINSON [DEM., ARK.]. Mr. President, I do not understand the statement of the Senator from New York that "all such orders will be fully reviewable by any aggrieved party in the Federal courts."

MR. WAGNER. Parties to the controversy, of course.

MR. ROBINSON. Yes; but what is meant by the term "by any aggrieved party"? I am asking for information.

MR. WAGNER. Suppose the Board orders an election, which is held. Then a controversy arises as to who was really elected by a majority of the workers, the company making one contention, and a representative of the workers making another contention. That controversy will be heard by the Board, evidence will be taken, and then, if either party is dissatisfied with the order of the Board, based upon the supposed violation of a legal right, such party may have a review in the courts.

MR. ROBINSON. The point I am asking about is, What is the meaning of the words "by any aggrieved party"? The language is not clear to me.

MR. WAGNER. The bill itself is clearer than my statement. I assume that the meaning is by parties to the controversy which is heard before the Board. . . .

EDWARD COSTIGAN [DEM., COLO.]. I did not hear all, but what I did hear of the able Senator's discussion of the proposed legislation deeply impressed me by its force, persuasiveness, and learning.

Is it fair to conclude that the proposed legislation will have important values for national and industrial development and peace, whether the National Industrial Recovery Act shall be continued or not?

MR. WAGNER. Of course, I answer in the affirmative, absolutely.

MR. COSTIGAN. Is it proper to say that the measure is designed to apply to all industries which affect commerce?

MR. WAGNER. That is the intent.

MR. COSTIGAN. Is it to be understood that the proposed legislation's admirable purposes are to be attained by authorized Federal investigations with a view to voluntary settlement of industrial disputes; by outlawing company unions; by the assurance of majority rule among workers organized to bargain collectively with employers; and by the maintenance of a permanent and impartial national relations board?

MR. WAGNER. Yes; and by the prohibition of certain unfair labor practices which are enumerated in the bill and which are intended to make the worker a free man, to decide for himself whether he wants an organization, and if he wants one, what the type of that organization shall be.

MR. COSTIGAN. With such features the proposed legislation evidently embodies some of the settled conclusions of our foremost industrial experts.

The measure is clearly intended to support recommendations both of acknowledged industrial leaders in America and of America's organized labor movement. Nor are such convictions new. Almost 20 years ago they were urged as the prevailing expert judgment of those best informed on industrial problems, appearing at that time before the United States Industrial Relations Commission, which surveyed the entire field of industrial relations for a couple of years by authority of Congress and with commissioners of ability appointed by President Woodrow Wilson. . . .

PATRICK MC CARRAN [DEM., NEV.]. I have admired the Senator's presentation. I am very favorable to his bill. What I desire to know, in keeping with the question propounded by the Senator from Colorado, is whether the continuation of the NRA is in anywise linked with the bill now before the Senate.

MR. WAGNER. It is not. Of course, the NIRA has section 7 (a) in it; but this bill proposes, in the first place, to define the rights of labor more clearly; and, secondly, to implement them by certain enforcement sanctions.

MR. MC CARRAN. Just one further inquiry. Am I correct in saying that even though the NRA should pass out of existence with section 7 (a) as it now stands in the NRA Act, we should have all the beneficial results that might flow from section 7 (a) if we should enact the pending bill?

MR. WAGNER. That is certainly a correct statement so far as section 7 (a) is concerned.

MR. MC CARRAN. I thank the Senator.

House of Representatives—74th Congress, 1st Session
June 3, 1935

WILLIAM CONNERY [DEM., MASS.]. Mr. Speaker, I have taken the floor at this time in order to get into the Record for the information of the Members of the House some questions in regard to the constitutionality of the Wagner-Connery bill, the labor relations bill. I know there will be a great deal of discussion about that, and I would like to have this in the Record before the bill comes up in the House, as we confidently hope it will within the near future.

The pending Wagner-Connery bill, creating a National Labor Relations Board, rests upon a constitutional basis which is not adversely affected by the recent decisions of the Supreme Court in the *Railway Retirement* and the *Schechter* cases. Upon the contrary, the implications of those decisions, and the specific holding of the Supreme Court in previous decisions now cited with approval, make it clear that what is sought to be done in the Wagner-Connery bill is within the constitutional power of Congress. In the present situation, the need for the Wagner-Connery bill, if anything, is enhanced rather than diminished.

Section 7 (a) of the National Industrial Recovery Act reads as follows:

> Every code of fair competition, agreement and license approved, prescribed, or issued under this title shall contain the following conditions: (1) That employees shall have the right to organize and bargain collectively through representatives of their own choosing, and shall be free from the interference, restraint, or coercion of employers of labor, or their agents, in the designation of such representatives or in self-organization or in other concerted activities for the purpose of collective bargaining or other mutual aid or protection; (2) that no employee and no one seeking employment shall be required as a condition of employment to join any company union or to refrain from joining, organizing, or assisting a labor organization of his own choosing; . . .

Section 7 (a) was not self-executing; it did not forthwith confer any new legal rights upon employees, nor impose any new legal duties upon employers. Until an employer became subject to a code of fair competition approved by the President, he could still, without violating any Federal law, discharge an employee for union activity or otherwise interfere with the self-organization of his employees for the purposes of collective bargaining. This was so, because section 7 (a) did not directly prohibit employers from interfering with the self-organization of employees, as Congress might well have done, but provided only that prohibitions of this type of conduct should be included in every code of fair competition.

The Supreme Court held that the code-making process under section 3 of the Recovery Act was invalid because it constituted an attempt by Congress to delegate legislative power to the President "to exercise an unfettered discretion to make whatever laws he thinks may be needed or advisable for the rehabilitation and expansion of trade or industry." The protection to employees which Congress sought to establish in section 7 (a) is nullified by the decision in the *Schechter* case, not because the subject matter of section 7 (a) is beyond the congressional power of regulation, but because the codes of fair competition, in each of which the provisions of section 7 (a) have been embodied, have been knocked out by that decision.

This difficulty on the score of improper delegation, which for the reasons stated indirectly resulted in the invalidation of section 7 (a), is entirely removed in the Wagner-Connery bill. In that bill Congress specifically prohibits certain unfair labor practices, which by fair interpretation would constitute infringements upon the substantive rights of employees declared in section 7 (a). These prohibitions, and the substantive rights are made applicable, to the extent of Congress' power under the commerce clause, to employers and employees irrespective of whether the industry in question is subject to a code of fair competition. The bill, therefore, is entirely independent of the code-making process, and stands on its own constitutional footing quite apart from the ultimate disposition of the pending legislation affecting the National Recovery Administration.

It is significant that throughout the decision in the *Schechter* case the Court drew a sharp distinction between the delegation of legislative power and the Executive procedure provided in the National Industrial Recovery Act, on the one hand, and the formulation, on the other hand, of a specific congressional policy to be administered by boards with procedure of a quasi-judicial nature, such as the Federal Trade Commission, the Interstate Commerce Commission, the Radio Commission, and the Federal Tariff Commission. Perhaps the most striking example given by the Court, and at the same time the closest analogy to the proposed National Labor Relations Board, is the Federal Trade Commission Act, which declared to be unlawful "unfair methods of competition," a phrase which, as the Court recognized, "does not admit of precise definition, its scope being left to judicial determination as controversies arise." The Court goes on to say:

> What are "unfair methods of competition" are thus to be determined in particular instances, upon evidence, in the light of particular competitive conditions and of what is found to be a specific and substantial public interest. . . .
> To make this possible, Congress set up a special procedure. A Commission, a quasi-judicial body, was created. Provision was made for formal complaint, for notice and hearing, for appropriate findings of fact supported by adequate evidence, and for judicial review to give assurance that the action of the Commission is taken within the statutory authority. . . .
> In providing for codes, the National Industrial Act dispenses with this administrative procedure and with any administrative procedure of an analogous character.

The Board set up under the Wagner-Connery bill is just such a tribunal as the court describes. It is a quasi-judicial body, which acts upon formal complaint, after due notice and hearing. Provision is made for appropriate findings of fact, supported by adequate evidence and for judicial review to give assurance that the action of the Board is taken within its statutory authority.

Furthermore, in view of the court's approval of the Federal Trade Commission Act, the constitutionality of the Wagner-Connery bill on the score of delegation is beyond question, because the unfair labor practices in section 8 of the bill are defined with precision, whereas the Federal Trade Commission Act broadly prohibits unfair methods of competition.

Turning now to the interstate commerce aspect, the Wagner-Connery bill is on firm ground as a permissible regulation within the commerce clause of the Constitution.

The decision in the railway retirement case did not turn on a distinction between intrastate and interstate commerce, as has been erroneously asserted, but proceeded on the ground, whether rightly or wrongly, that legislative provision for pensions to retired railway employees was so remotely related to the facilitation and promotion of interstate commerce as not to amount to a regulation thereof. The Court expressly affirmed its previous decision in *Texas & New Orleans R. R. Co.* v. *Railway Clerks,* 281 U. S. 548, coming up under the Railway Labor Act—

Upon the express ground that to facilitate the amicable settlement of disputes which threatened the service of the necessary agencies of interstate transportation tended to prevent interruption of service and was therefore within the delegated power of regulation.

In that case a railway brotherhood, composed of railway clerks who were not themselves physically engaged in interstate transportation, sued to restrain the railroad from interfering with the right of its employees to self-organization and to designate representatives for collective bargaining in violation of the Railway Labor Act of 1926. The lower court gave equitable relief of the sort contemplated in the Wagner-Connery bill by ordering the company (1) to disestablish its company union as representative of its employees; (2) to reinstate the brotherhood (which was the recognized representative chosen by the majority before the company began its unlawful interference) as the representative of all employees until they should make another free choice; and to restore to service and to stated privileges certain employees who had been discharged for activities in behalf of the Brotherhood. The Supreme Court in a unanimous opinion affirmed the decree of the lower court.

The decision in the *Schechter* case is limited, on the interstate commerce point, to the attempted regulation of wages, hours, and certain trade practices in the case of a New York company engaged in the business of slaughtering chickens, which were bought almost entirely in the State of New York and sold exclusively to buyers in the same State. The Supreme Court held that in such a business the attempted regulations had no direct relation to interstate commerce and were therefore invalid. The Wagner-Connery bill is not materially affected by this decision for two reasons: (1) The decision does not touch industries or businesses which are interstate in character; (2) the regulations in the bill are of an entirely different legal nature from those in the *Schechter* case and have many times been recognized by the Supreme Court itself as having a direct effect upon the free flow of interstate commerce.

1. The Schechter decision is confined, as stated above, to a business which was wholly intrastate in character. The Court, on the other hand, reaffirmed the undoubted power of Congress to regulate businesses and industries which are interstate in character. The Court expressly pointed out that not only were the instrumentalities of interstate commerce subject

to regulation but that those industries in which the products flowed in a continuous stream from State to State were likewise subject to regulation. It follows that any industry engaged in the transportation of goods between the States would be subject to the provisions of the bill. So also all the large manufacturing or processing industries, with widespread interstate ramifications, would be subject to the terms of the bill. In these industries raw materials are secured from all States of the Union or from foreign countries, and the products manufactured or processed are shipped out again to every State and to foreign countries. The whole process plainly constitutes a continuous movement of goods in interstate commerce within the meaning of the Court's decision.

2. Of perhaps greater significance is the second reason why the Wagner-Connery bill is not affected by the Schechter decision, namely, that the regulations provided in the bill are of a different legal character from those before the Court in the Schechter case. The bill thus rests upon a constitutional basis entirely different from that urged by the Government in the Schechter case and not considered by the Supreme Court in that case. The provisions of the bill are designed to remove burdens and obstructions to interstate commerce arising out of strikes and other forms of industrial unrest.

There can be no question but that industrial strife burdens the flow of commerce among the States. This fact has received express recognition by the Supreme Court itself in such well-known cases as *In re Debs* (158 U. S. 564); *Duplex Printing Press Co.* v. *Deering* (254 U. S. 443); *American Steel Foundries* v. *Tri-City Central Trades Council* (257 U. S. 184); *Coronado Coal Co.* v. *United Mine Workers* (268 U. S. 295); and *Bedford Cut Stone Co.* v. *Stone Cutters Association* (274 U. S. 37). Especially is the burden on interstate commerce of industrial strife significant in times of depression or periods of recovery. As recent experience has demonstrated, a single strike in a large industry at such a time raises grave dangers of throwing the whole economic system out of gear and retarding recovery by many months.

The provisions of the Wagner-Connery bill are aimed to remove these obstructions to interstate commerce. The bill accomplishes this result in two ways: First, it is a well-known fact that many of the most serious and violent industrial disturbances arise out of the resistance by employers to self-organization among their employees or out of the refusal by employers to accept the procedure of collective bargaining. These issues have been paramount in many cases which have come before the Supreme Court, including the *Debs* case, the *Coronado* case, and *International Organization* v. *Red Jacket C. C. & C. Co.* (18 Fed. 2d 839, cert. den. 275 U. S. 536). The bill by compelling employers to refrain from interference with self-organization of employees and to accept the procedure of collective bargaining thus directly eliminates the causes of much industrial strife. Second, other industrial disturbances arise out of the struggle between employers and employees over the terms of the wage bargain. The bill, by protecting employees in their designation of representatives and by compelling employers to sit down in conference with those representatives, establishes the machinery of a method of proved effectiveness for the amicable adjustments of disputes and grievances. So completely accepted has this conference procedure for avoiding industrial conflict become that it constitutes a vital part of virtually every effort in the States and foreign countries to set up machinery for the peaceful settlement of labor disputes.

The Supreme Court has recently expressly ruled that provisions similar to those embodied in the bill have, for the reasons stated, a direct relation to interstate commerce, and are therefore valid. In *Texas & New Orleans Railroad* v. *Brotherhood of Railway Clerks* (281 U. S. 548), which, as has already been noted, was cited with approval in the recent Railway Retirement case, the Court ruled that the provisions of the Railway Labor Act of 1926, applying to the railroad industry substantially the same regulations as provided in the Wagner-Connery bill, were valid regulations under the commerce power, not only as to employees actually engaged in interstate transportation but also to clerks, ticket sellers, and other employees not physically so engaged. The power of the Federal Government to regulate industrial relations as the means of avoiding obstructions to commerce has likewise been approved by the Supreme Court as to other industries in a number of decisions holding that a strike which threatens to burden interstate commerce is subject to regulation under the anti-trust laws. Two of these decisions—*Coronado Coal Co.* v. *United Mine Workers* (268 U. S. 295) and *Bedford Cut Stone Co.* v. *Stone Cutters Association* (274 U. S. 37)— were expressly reaffirmed by the Supreme Court in the Schechter decision. Thus, in the *Bedford* case, the stonecutters refused to work upon stone which had been shipped into the State from quarries in other States where nonunion labor was employed. The stone upon which the cutters refused to work was no longer in the stream of commerce or destined for use outside the State in which it rested. The Supreme Court held that the activities of the stonecutters constituted a combination prohibited by the Sherman Act. . . .

That the means adopted to bring about the contemplated restraint of commerce operated after physical transportation had ended is immaterial (citing cases). The product against which the strikes were directed, it is true had come to rest in the respective localities to which it had been shipped, so that it had ceased to be a subject of interstate commence . . . In other words, strikes against the local use of the product were simply the means adopted to effect the unlawful restraint.

In *Coronado Coal Co.* v. *United Mine Workers* (268 U. S. 295), another celebrated case under the antitrust law, there was a strike of union men in the Arkansas mines of the Coronado Coal Co. The company broke a union contract, declared an open shop (avowedly to reduce the cost of production), shut down the mine, ordered its union employees to vacate company houses, and reopened with nonunion men. Considerable violence followed. The Court found the strikers and the district officers of the union guilty of a conspiracy in restraint of interstate commerce, based upon evidence which the Court held sufficient to sustain a finding that the purpose of the defendants was to stop the production of nonunion coal and prevent its shipment to markets in other States, where it would by competition tend to reduce the price of the commodity and affect injuriously the maintenance of wages for union labor in competing mines. From the point of view of constitutional power, of course, if a strike has the intent or necessary effect indicated by the Court, it is immaterial whether the local means adopted were lawful or tortuous.

How is the Federal Government to deal with the vexing problems of industrial disturbance or strife which in fact burdens and obstructs commerce, whether so intended or not, and where, as is increasingly the case, such obstructions are traceable to the denial of the right of employees to organize, the refusal of employers to accept the procedure of collective bargaining, or the absence of machinery for the amicable adjustments of disputes over wages and working conditions? The solution lies neither in compulsory arbitration, which has never been acceptable to the American people, nor in government by labor injunction, now effectively restrained by the Norris-LaGuardia Act, nor in subjecting labor organizations to the shifting canons of the antitrust laws, which were never intended by Congress to be applied against them. The Wagner-Connery bill goes to the heart of the problem by eliminating specific well-recognized causes of industrial disturbances substantially burdening or obstructing commerce, and by mitigating or eliminating such obstructions where they have occurred.

It is clear that unfair labor practices which tend to provoke industrial strife substantially burdening interstate commerce may be enjoined before any actual obstruction to commerce arises. Civilized law is preventive as well as punitive. As Chief Justice Taft said in the first *Coronado* case (259 U. S. 344):

> If Congress deems certain recurring practices, though not really part of interstate commerce, likely to obstruct, restrain, or burden it, it has the power to subject them to national supervision or restraint.

For this reason the Wagner-Connery bill aims to eliminate practices on the part of employers that tend to provoke manifestations of industrial strife recognized in the *Bedford, Coronado,* and other cases as directly and substantially affecting interstate commerce, and to substitute the orderly processes of collective bargaining, thereby making the appropriate collective action of employees an instrument of peace rather than of strife, as the Supreme Court said in the *Texas* case. The appropriateness and success of such regulation as is here provided is amply demonstrated by the experience with the railroads of the country and the experience of the National War Labor Board during the World War.

To sum up the point on interstate commerce, the Schechter decision relates only to a business engaged solely in intrastate commerce and applies only to regulations of wages, hours, and certain trade practices in such intrastate business. It does not affect in any way the application of the Wagner-Connery bill to industries and businesses which are interstate in character and does not touch in any way the validity of regulations designed to remove obstructions to the free flow of commerce by eliminating and alleviating industrial strife and unrest.

I close with this observation: We are faced now with a barrage of propaganda from inspired sources to the effect that in view of the recent Court decisions the Congress has no alternative but to abandon its pending legislative program and go home. Implications are being read into those decisions in an endeavor to make them applicable to other situations and problems not before the Court. The President, in his press conference on Friday, painted a vivid picture of national impotence to cope with national problems which would be our plight, if the Supreme Court in future cases does not limit its decision in the Schechter case to the particular facts before the Court.

The Supreme Court, in Rathbun against United States, which case was decided on the same day that it handed down its opinion in the *Schechter* case, invoked the following language from the opinion of Chief Justice Marshall in *Cohens* v. *Virginia* (6 Wheat. 264, 399):

> It is a maxim, not to be disregarded, that general expressions, in every opinion, are to be taken in connection with the case in which those expressions are used. If they go beyond the case, they may be respected, but ought not to control the judgment in a subsequent suit when the very point is presented for decision. The reason of this maxim is obvious. The question actually before the Court is investigated with care and considered in its full extent. Other principles which may serve to illustrate it are considered in their relation to the case decided, but their possible bearing on all other cases is seldom completely investigated.

In view of this salutary reminder by the Supreme Court that its decisions are controlling only on the facts of the case before it, we are guilty of no disrespect for that tribunal in pressing for the passage of the Wagner-Connery Bill. I have no doubt that Congress believes in the principles and purposes of the bill, and this being so, the Congress would be shirking its plain duty if dubious, and I believe unwarranted implications from recent court decisions stampede it into an abandonment of its legislative functions. This is no time to yield to defeatist talk and haul down the flag.

EDWARD COX [DEM., GA.]. Mr. Speaker, I had not intended, until a few minutes ago, to have anything whatever to say about the Wagner-Connery bill consideration of which the pending rule is intended to make in order. I recognize, of course, that the bill raises an issue that must at some time be fought out, and I think it may as well be now as any other time. I have not, therefore, opposed the reporting of the rule by the Rules Committee, and do not and will not oppose the adoption of the rule in the House.

I have not had time to digest the bill as fully as I should like, but it must be apparent to everyone who has read it that it carries upon its face the most terrible threat—and I speak deliberately and advisedly—to our dual form of government that has thus far arisen. In this respect it is far more terrible than was the National Recovery Act. It is not what appears upon the face of the bill that disturbs me, it is the intent and purpose carried by the measure which the language used is intended to conceal.

The purpose of the measure, as all honest minds must confess, is to circumvent the effect of the recent ruling of the Supreme Court in the *Schechter* case. It is intended by this measure through the use of the commerce clause of the Constitution to sap and undermine that great document to the extent of ultimately striking down and destroying completely all State sovereignty. Here the attempt is made through the use of the commerce clause to extend Feceral control to the point of production and distribution, which the courts for more than a hundred years have uniformly held to be domestic questions.

If it be not the purpose of the bill to circumvent and to nullify the pronouncements of the Court in the case to which I have referred, then there should be no objection to amending the measure to make it clear that there is no purpose to push Federal control through legislative definitions or otherwise beyond the point fixed by the Court in the *Schechter* case which defines the limit of congressional power. There is the test of what is here sought to be done; for, of course, no one objects to collective bargaining. I am for insuring to and protecting labor in the free and unrestricted exercise of all their constitutional rights. [Applause.] . . .

CHARLES EATON [R., N. J.]. This resolution describes the legislation under consideration as—

A bill to promote equality of bargaining power between employers and employees, to diminish the causes of labor disputes, to create a National Labor Relations Board, and for other purposes.

As I read the bill, the exact opposite of this description would be more in accord with the truth. It destroys equality of bargaining power between

employer and employee. And it will increase enormously the causes of labor disputes. It will not cure the disease. It will aggravate and perpetuate
the disease.

This legislation strikes a fatal blow at organized labor as we have known
it in America. For it plucks the labor union out of the plane of free,
self-governing American institutions and places it under the supreme control and domination of a political bureaucracy in Washington.

Under this bill the labor union ceases to function as an economic instrumentality and becomes a mere cog in the vast political bureaucracy now
being built up in Washington for the purpose of bringing all American life
under Government control and management.

It takes from employers and employees alike their constitutional right to
develop their mutual relationships under local conditions and free from
bureaucratic political dictation. And it denies the great majority of American workers the right to work under conditions and leaderships of their
own choosing.

This and all similar legislation rests upon the absurd proposition that
all businessmen are dishonest and unfair and all employees are incapable
of self-determination or self-government. It places the relation of employer
and employee upon a permanent and unalterable war basis. It rests upon
the false assumption that the interests of employer and employee are by
their intrinsic nature absolutely irreconcilable. And it puts the employer in
the criminal class, subject to fine and imprisonment for a list of new
crimes fastened upon him under legal processes as unjust and unfair as they
will certainly turn out to be unconstitutional.

Believing as I do that organized industry is now the chief instrument of
civilization, I see small hope for our social future unless employer and employee quit fighting each other and join forces to meet the challenge that
confronts them. Under our American system there is only one way
to justly distribute wealth, and that is by high wages made possible by high
production at low unit cost. Wages and profits must be paid out of production. There is no other source from which they can be derived. And
high wages cannot come out of an industry conducted as an armed camp
with the vultures of bureaucracy darkening the sky.

The problem of human relationships in industry can never be solved
by law, and especially by class legislation which seeks to enthrone one class
while it enslaves another. The need of the hour is not more law and more
bureaucratic dictators. Our need is an awakened sense of moral obligation
among employers and employees and the people generally, which will make
fair industrial cooperation possible and leave us all free to act as self-
governing, self-respecting American citizens, with faith in ourselves and in
each other. . . .

ADOLPH SABATH [DEM., ILL.]. Mr. Speaker, if a majority of employers would be as fair to their employees as those who have been mentioned by the gentleman from New Jersey [Mr. Eaton], there would be no need for this pending legislation; but, unfortunately, such is not the case. In many instances many honest employers are being misled by propaganda on the part of industry.

I am satisfied that the employers described by the gentleman will not be found among those objecting to this legislation, but they will give it their wholehearted support and cooperation.

I have in my hand more than 400 letters and telegrams from men protesting against the passage of the bill, and a majority of these men, Mr. Speaker, draw from $50,000 to $100,000 a year in salary as president or as other officers of these corporations. Moreover, many of them draw from $50,000 to $250,000 a year in bonuses. These are the men who are fearful that something will be done that will be helpful and beneficial to the deserving workers of this country.

Mr. Speaker, I feel that if the men who have either wired or written to me had been well informed on this proposed legislation they would not have sent these telegrams and letters; but, unfortunately, the officers of these various manufactories and large corporations, with the organizations and lobbies which they employ, as the gentleman from New York [Mr. O'Connor] has stated, to keep their fat jobs, instigate this propaganda. This should be condemned and, for one, I shall continue to resent such activities of these men who are responsible for the thousands of telegrams and letters with which they are endeavoring to influence and browbeat us while we are in the performance of our duties.

As to the constitutionality of this measure, during the 29 years I have been here, every time we have had a bill in the interest of the deserving labor, I have heard the learned lawyers of the nation raise the question of constitutionality. When I introduced my first bill on workmen's compensation 29 years ago, what a hue and cry was raised against it. The question of its constitutionality was raised then, and, as I have stated, the same question has been raised in every instance with respect to legislation considered on the floor of this House in the interest of the masses and the laboring people of the country.

All this legislation contemplates is the setting up of a labor-relations board that would be helpful in effecting adjustments in disputes among employers and employees. It has been stated, and I know it will be used again on the floor, that the leaders of the American Federation of Labor are dictating this legislation. Some gentlemen resent and give as a reason for opposing this bill the statements of Mr. Green, the president of the American Federation of Labor. Anyway, if this legislation is enacted, it would benefit only about 3,000,000 of the 30,000,000 workers of our country.

Let me say very earnestly to the opponents who are using that as a pretext for opposing this legislation that were it not for the work of the American Federation of Labor, we would still have in this county our workers enslaved 10, 12, and even 14 hours a day at the starvation wage of a dollar a day. The present high status of the workers of America is due to the age-long struggle and accomplishments of, first, the Knights of Labor, and, later, the conservative American Federation of Labor.

The American Federation of Labor has for many years been a benefactor not only of the deserving workers of America but to America herself. That splendid organization, more than any other, has been instrumental in the improvement of living conditions and wages of the labor of this Nation.

If employers and industries have unrestrained right to organize, why should not the same privilege be accorded to the real producers of wealth? Attacks against that splendid organization, the American Federation of Labor, are unfair, unjust, and in many cases contemptible.

Anybody who is fair and familiar with the existing condition of labor these distressful times will, if he follows the dictates of his heart and conscience not vote against this generally helpful proposed legislation. . . .

THE DECISIONS
Commentary

As previously stated, the Wagner Act in 1935 created a list of specified unfair labor practices of employers. Since the landmark *Jones & Laughlin* decision which upheld the constitutionality of the act in 1937, a great volume of litigation has developed concerning the interpretation of the employer unfair-labor-practice provisions of the statute. Of the scores of such cases decided by the Supreme Court, a few have been selected to illustrate typical issues reaching the high Court. While some of these decisions are subsequent to the amendments to the National Labor Relations Act contained in the Taft-Hartley Act of 1947 and the Landrum-Griffin Act of 1959, they involve provisions which remain substantially unchanged since their original enactment in 1935.

N.L.R.B. v. *Jones & Laughlin Steel Corporation*
301 U.S. 1 (1937)

MR. CHIEF JUSTICE HUGHES delivered the opinion of the Court.

In a proceeding under the National Labor Relations Act of 1935 the National Labor Relations Board found that the respondent, Jones & Laughlin Steel Corporation, had violated the act by engaging in unfair labor practices affecting commerce. The proceeding was instituted by the Beaver Valley Lodge No. 200, affiliated with the Amalgamated Association of Iron, Steel and Tin Workers of America, a labor organization. The unfair labor practices charged were that the corporation was discriminating against members of the union with regard to hire and tenure of employment, and was coercing and intimidating its employees in order to interfere with their self-organization. The discriminatory and coercive action alleged was the discharge of certain employees.

The National Labor Relations Board, sustaining the charge, ordered the corporation to cease and desist from such discrimination and coercion, to offer reinstatement to ten of the employees named, to make good their losses in pay, and to post for thirty days notices that the corporation would not discharge or discriminate against members, or those desiring to become members, of the labor union. As the corporation failed to comply, the Board petitioned the Circuit Court of Appeals to enforce the order. The court denied the petition holding that the order lay beyond the range of federal power. 83 F. (2d) 998. We granted certiorari. . . .

The scheme of the National Labor Relations Act—which is too long to be quoted in full—may be briefly stated. The first section (29 U.S.C.A. § 151) sets forth findings with respect to the injury to commerce resulting from the denial by employers of the right of employees to organize and from the refusal of employers to accept the procedure of collective bargaining. There follows a declaration that it is the policy of the United States to eliminate these causes of obstruction to the free flow of commerce. The act then defines the terms it uses, including the terms "commerce" and "affecting commerce." Section 2 (29 U.S.C.A. § 152). It creates the National Labor Relations Board and prescribes its organization. Sections 3-6 (29 U.S.C.A. §§ 153–156). It sets forth the right of employees to self-organization and to bargain collectively through representatives of their own choosing. Section 7 (29 U.S.C.A. § 157). It defines "unfair labor practices." Section 8 (29 U.S.C.A. § 158). It lays down rules as to the representation of employees for the purpose of collective bargaining. Section 9 (29 U.S.C.A. § 159). The Board is empowered to prevent the described unfair labor practices affecting commerce and the act prescribes the procedure to that end. The Board is authorized to petition designated courts to secure the enforcement of its order. The findings of the Board as to the facts, if supported by evidence, are to be conclusive. If either party on application to the court shows that additional evidence is material and that there were reasonable grounds for the failure to adduce such evidence in the hearings before the Board, the court may order the additional evidence to be taken. Any person aggrieved by a final order of the Board may obtain a review in the designated courts with the same procedure as in the case of an application by the Board for the enforcement of its order. Section 10 (29 U.S.C.A. § 160). The Board has broad powers of investigation. Section 11 (29 U.S.C.A. § 161). Interference with members of the Board or its agents in the performance of their duties is punishable by fine and imprisonment. Section 12 (29 U.S.C.A. § 162). Nothing in the act is to be construed to interfere with the right to strike. Section 13 (29 U.S.C.A. § 163). There is a separability clause to the effect that, if any provision of the act or its application to any person or circumstances shall be held invalid, the remainder of the act or its application to other persons or circumstances shall not be affected. Section 15 (29 U.S.C.A. § 165). The particular provisions which are involved in the instant case will be considered more in detail in the course of the discussion.

The procedure in the instant case followed the statute. The labor union filed with the Board its verified charge.

The Board thereupon issued its complaint against the respondent, alleging that its action in discharging the employees in question constituted unfair labor practices affecting commerce within the meaning of section 8, subdivisions (1) and (3), and section 2, subdivisions (6) and (7), of the act. Respondent, appearing specially for the purpose of objecting to the jurisdiction of the Board, filed its answer. Respondent admitted the discharges, but alleged that they were made because of inefficiency or violation of rules or for other good reasons and were not ascribable to union membership or activities. As an affirmative defense respondent challenged the constitutional validity of the statute and its applicability in the instant case. Notice of hearing was given and respondent appeared by counsel. The Board first took up the issue of jurisdiction and evidence was presented by both the Board and the respondent. Respondent then moved to dismiss the complaint for lack of jurisdiction and, on denial of that motion, respondent in accordance with its special appearance withdrew from further participation in the hearing. The Board received evidence upon the merits and at its close made its findings and order.

Contesting the ruling of the Board, the respondent argues (1) that the act is in reality a regulation of labor relations and not of interstate commerce; (2) that the act can have no application to the respondent's relations with its production employees because they are not subject to regulation by the federal government; and (3) that the provisions of the act violate section 2 of article 3 and the Fifth and Seventh Amendments of the Constitution of the United States.

The facts as to the nature and scope of the business of the Jones & Laughlin Steel Corporation have been found by the Labor Board, and, so far as they are essential to the determination of this controversy, they are not in dispute. The Labor Board has found: The corporation is organized under the laws of Pennsylvania and has its principal office at Pittsburgh. It is engaged in the business of manufacturing iron and steel in plants situated in Pittsburgh and nearby Aliquippa, Pa. It manufactures and distributes a widely diversified line of steel and pig iron, being the fourth largest producer of steel in the United States. With its subsidiaries—nineteen in number—it is a completely integrated enterprise, owning and operating ore, coal and limestone properties, lake and river transportation facilities and terminal railroads located at its manufacturing plants. It owns or controls mines in Michigan and Minnesota. It operates four ore steamships on the Great Lakes, used in the transportation of ore to its factories. It owns coal mines in Pennsylvania. It operates towboats and steam barges used in carrying coal to its factories. It owns limestone properties in various places in Pennsylvania and West Virginia. It owns the Monongahela connecting railroad which connects the plants of the Pittsburgh works and forms an interconnection with the Pennsylvania, New York Central and Baltimore & Ohio Railroad systems. It owns the Aliquippa & Southern Railroad Company, which connects the Aliquippa works with the Pittsburgh & Lake Erie, part of the New York Central system. Much of its product is shipped to its warehouses in Chicago, Detroit, Cincinnati and Memphis,—to the last two places by means of its own barges and transportation equipment. In Long Island City, New York, and in New Orleans it operates structural steel fabricating shops in connection with the warehousing of semifinished materials sent from its works. Through one of its wholly-owned subsidaries it owns, leases, and operates stores, warehouses, and yards for the distribution of equipment and supplies for drilling and operating oil and gas mills and for pipe lines, refineries and pumping stations. It has sales offices in twenty cities in the United States and a wholly-owned subsidiary which is devoted exclusively to distributing its product in Canada. Approximately 75 per cent of its product is shipped out of Pennsylvania.

Summarizing these operations, the Labor Board concluded that the works in Pittsburgh and Aliquippa "might be likened to the heart of a self-contained highly integrated body. They draw in the raw materials from Michigan, Minnesota, West Virginia, Pennsylvania in part through arteries and by means controlled by the respondent; they transform the materials and then pump them out to all parts of the nation through the vast mechanism which the respondent has elaborated."

To carry on the activities of the entire steel industry, 33,000 men mine ore, 44,000 men mine coal, 4,000 men quarry limestone, 16,000 men manufacture coke, 343,000 men manufacture steel, and 83,000 men transport its product. Respondent has about 10,000 employees in its Aliquippa plant, which is located in a community of about 30,000 persons.

Respondent points to evidence that the Aliquippa plant, in which the discharged men were employed, contains complete facilities for the production of finished and semifinished iron and steel products from raw materials; that its works consist primarily of a by-product coke plant for the production of coke; blast furnaces for the production of pig iron; open hearth furnaces and Bessemer converters for the production of steel; blooming mills for the reduction of steel ingots into smaller shapes; and a number of finishing mills such as structural mills, rod mills, wire mills, and the like. In addition, there are other buildings, structures and equipment, storage yards, docks and an intraplant storage system. Respondent's operations at these works are carried on in two distinct stages, the first being the conversion of raw materials into pig iron and the second being the manufacture of semifinished and finished iron and steel products; and in both cases the operations result in substantially changing the character, utility and value of the materials wrought upon, which is apparent from the nature and extent of the processes to which they are subjected and which respondent fully describes. Respondent also directs attention to the fact that the iron ore which is procured from mines in Minnesota and Michigan and transported to respondent's plant is stored in stock piles for future use, the amount of ore in storage varying with the season but usually being enough to maintain operations from nine to ten months; that the coal which is procured from the mines of a subsidiary located in Pennsylvania and taken to the plant at Aliquippa is there, like ore, stored for future use, approximately two to three months' supply of coal being always on hand; and that the limestone which is obtained in Pennsylvania and West Virginia is also stored in amounts usually adequate to run the blast furnaces for a few weeks. Various details of operation, transportation, and distribution are also mentioned which for the present purpose it is not necessary to detail.

Practically all the factual evidence in the case, except that which dealt with the nature of respondent's business, concerned its relations with the employees in the Aliquippa plant whose discharge was the subject of the complaint. These employees were active leaders in the labor union. Several were officers and others were leaders of particular groups. Two of the employees were motor inspectors; one was a tractor driver; three were crane operators; one was a washer in the coke plant; and three were laborers. Three other employees were mentioned in the complaint but it was withdrawn as to one of them and no evidence was heard on the action taken with respect to the other two.

While respondent criticizes the evidence and the attitude of the Board, which is described as being hostile toward employers and particularly toward those who insisted upon their constitutional rights, respondent did not take advantage of its opportunity to present evidence to refute that which was offered to show discrimination and coercion. In this situation, the record presents no ground for setting aside the order of the Board so far as the facts pertaining to the circumstances and purpose of the discharge of the employees are concerned. Upon that point it is sufficient to say that the evidence supports the findings of the Board that respondent discharged these men "because of their union activity and for the purpose of discouraging membership in the union." We turn to the questions of law which respondent urges in contesting the validity and application of the act.

First. The Scope of the Act.—The act is challenged in its entirety as an attempt to regulate all industry, thus invading the reserved powers of the States over their local concerns. It is asserted that the references in the act to interstate and foreign commerce are colorable at best; that the act is not a true regulation of such commerce or of matters which directly affect it, but on the contrary has the fundamental object of placing under the compulsory supervision of the federal government all industrial labor relations within the nation. The argument seeks support in the broad words of the preamble (section 1) and in the sweep of the provisions of the act, and it is further insisted that its legislative history shows an essential universal purpose in the light of which its scope cannot be limited by either construction or by the application of the separability clause.

If this conception of terms, intent and consequent inseparability, were sound, the act would necessarily fall by reason of the limitation upon the federal power which inheres in the constitutional grant, as well as because of the explicit reservation of the Tenth Amendment. *Schechter Corporation* v. *United States,* 295 U. S. 495, 549, 550, 554, 55 S.Ct. 837, 851, 853, 79 L.Ed. 1570, 97 A.L.R. 947. The authority of the federal government may not be pushed to such an extreme as to destroy the distinction, which the commerce clause itself establishes, between commerce "among the several States" and the internal concerns of a state. That distinction between what is national and what is local in the activities of commerce is vital to the maintenance of our federal system. *Id.*

But we are not at liberty to deny effect to specific provisions, which Congress has constitutional power to enact, by superimposing upon them inferences from general legislative declarations of an ambiguous character, even if found in the same statute. The cardinal principle of statutory construction is to save and not to destroy. We have repeatedly held that as between two possible interpretations of a statute, by one of which it would be unconstitutional and by the other valid, our plain duty is to adopt that which will save the act. Even to avoid a serious doubt the rule is the same. *Federal Trade Commission* v. *American Tobacco Co.,* 264 U.S. 298, 307, 44 S.Ct. 336, 367, 68 L.Ed. 696, 32 A.L.R. 786; *Panama R. R. Co.* v. *Johnson,* 264 U.S. 375, 390, 44 S.Ct. 391, 395, 68 L.Ed. 748; *Missouri Pacific R. R. Co.* v. *Boone,* 270 U.S. 466, 472, 46 S.Ct. 341, 343, 70 L.Ed. 688; *Blodgett* v. *Holden,* 275 U.S. 142, 148, 276 U.S. 594, 48 S.Ct. 105, 107, 72 L.Ed. 206; *Richmond Screw Anchor Co.* v. *United States,* 275 U.S. 331, 346, 48 S.Ct. 194, 198, 72 L.Ed. 303.

We think it clear that the National Labor Relations Act may be construed so as to operate within the sphere of constitutional authority. The jurisdiction conferred upon the Board, and invoked in this instance, is found in section 10(a), 29 U.S.C.A. § 160(a), which provides:

"SEC. 10(a). The Board is empowered, as hereinafter provided, to prevent any person from engaging in any unfair labor practice (listed in section 8 [section 158]) affecting commerce."

The critical words of this provision, prescribing the limits of the Board's authority in dealing with the labor practices, are "affecting commerce." The act specifically defines the "commerce" to which it refers (section 2(6), 29 U.S.C.A. § 152 (6)):

"The term 'commerce' means trade, traffic, commerce, transportation, or communication among the several States, or between the District of Columbia or any Territory of the United States and any State or other Territory, or between any foreign country and any State, Territory, or the District of Columbia, or within the District of Columbia or any Territory, or between points in the same State but through any other State or any Territory or the District of Columbia or any foreign country."

There can be no question that the commerce thus contemplated by the act (aside from that within a Territory or the District of Columbia) is interstate and foreign commerce in the constitutional sense. The act also defines the term "affecting commerce" section 2(7), 29 U.S.C.A. § 152(7):

"The term 'affecting commerce' means in commerce, or burdening or obstructing commerce or the free flow of commerce; or having led or tending to lead to a labor dispute burdening or obstructing commerce or the free flow of commerce."

This definition is one of exclusion as well as inclusion. The grant of authority to the Board does not purport to extend to the relationship between all industrial employees and employers. Its terms do not impose collective bargaining upon all industry regardless of effects upon interstate or foreign commerce. It purports to reach only what may be deemed to burden or obstruct that commerce and, thus qualified, it must be construed as contemplating the exercise of control within constitutional bounds. It is a familiar principle that acts which directly burden or obstruct interstate or foreign commerce, or its free flow, are within the reach of the congressional power. Acts having that effect are not rendered immune because they grow out of labor disputes. See *Texas & N. O. R. Co.* v. *Railway & S. S. Clerks,* 281 U.S. 548, 570, 50 S.Ct. 427, 433, 434, 74 L.Ed. 1034; *Schechter Corporation* v. *United States, supra,* 295 U.S. 495, at pages 544, 545, 55 S.Ct. 837, 849, 79 L.Ed. 1570, 97 A.L.R. 947; *Virginian Railway Co.* v. *System Federation No. 40,* 300 U.S. 515, 57 S.Ct. 592, 81 L.Ed. 789, decided March 29, 1937. It is the effect upon commerce, not the source of the injury, which is the criterion. Second Employers' Liability Cases (*Mondou* v. *New York,* N. H. & H. R. Co.), 233 U.S. 1, 51, 32 S.Ct. 169, 56 L.Ed. 327, 38 L.R.A. (NS) 44. Whether or not particular action does affect commerce in such a close and intimate fashion as to be subject to federal control, and hence to lie within the authority conferred upon the Board, is left by the statute to be determined as individual cases arise. We are thus to inquire whether in the instant case the constitutional boundary has been passed.

Second. The Unfair Labor Practices in Question.—The unfair labor practices found by the Board are those defined in section 8, subdivisions (1) and (3). These provide:

"Sec. 8. It shall be an unfair labor practice for an employer—

"(1)' To interfere with, restrain, or coerce employees in the exercise of the rights guaranteed in section 7 [section 157 of this title]. . . .

"(3) By discrimination in regard to hire or tenure of employment or any term or condition of employment to encourage or discourage membership in any labor organization."

Section 8, subdivision (1), refers to section 7, which is as follows:

"Section 7. Employees shall have the right to self-organization, to form, join, or assist labor organizations, to bargain collectively through representatives of their own choosing, and to engage in concerted activities, for the purpose of collective bargaining or other mutual aid or protection."

Thus, in its present application, the statute goes no further than to safeguard the right of employees to self-organization and to select representatives of their own choosing for collective bargaining or other mutual protection without restraint or coercion by their employer.

That is a fundamental right. Employees have as clear a right to organize and select their representatives for lawful purposes as the respondent has to organize its business and select its own officers and agents. Discrimination and coercion to prevent the free exercise of the right of employees to self-organization and representation is a proper subject for condemnation by competent legislative authority. Long ago we stated the reason for labor organizations. We said that they were organized out of the necessities of the situation; that a single employee was helpless in dealing with an employer; that he was dependent ordinarily on his daily wage for the maintenance of himself and family; that, if the employer refused to pay him the wages that he thought fair, he was nevertheless unable to leave the employ and resist arbitrary and unfair treatment; that union was essential to give laborers opportunity to deal on an equality with their employer. *American Steel Foundries* v. *Tri-City Central Trades Council*, 257 U.S. 184, 209, 42 S.Ct. 72, 78, 66 L.Ed. 189, 27 A.L.R. 360. We reiterated these views when we had under consideration the Railway Labor Act of 1926, 44 Stat. 577. Fully recognizing the legality of collective action on the part of employees in order to safeguard their proper interests, we said that Congress was not required to ignore this right but could safeguard it. Congress could seek to make appropriate collective action of employees an instrument of peace rather than of strife. We said that such collective action would be a mockery if representation were made futile by interference with freedom of choice. Hence the prohibition by Congress of interference with the selection of representatives for the purpose of negotiation and conference between employers and employees, "instead of being an invasion of the constitutional right of either, was based on the recognition of the rights of both." *Texas & N. O. R. Co.* v. *Railway & S. S. Clerks, supra.* We have reasserted the same principle in sustaining the application of the Railway Labor Act as amended in 1934 (45 U.S.C.A. § 151 et seq.). *Virginian Railway Co.* v. *System Federation No. 40, supra.*

Third. The Application of the Act to Employees Engaged in Production. —The Principle Involved.—Respondent says that, whatever may be said of employees engaged in interstate commerce, the industrial relations and activities in the manufacturing department of respondent's enterprise are not subject to federal regulation. The argument rests upon the proposition that manufacturing in itself is not commerce. *Kidd* v. *Pearson*, 128 U.S. 1, 20, 21, 9 S.Ct. 6, 32 L.Ed. 346; *United Mine Workers* v. *Coronado Co.,*

259 U.S. 344, 407, 408, 42 S.Ct. 570, 581, 582, 66 L.Ed. 975, 27 A.L.R. 762; *Oliver Iron Co.* v. *Lord,* 262 U.S. 172, 178, 43 S.Ct. 526, 529, 67 L.Ed. 929; *United Leather Workers' International Union* v. *Herkert & Meisel Trunk Co.,* 265 U.S. 457, 465. 44 S.Ct. 623, 625, 68 L.Ed. 1104, 33 A.L.R. 566; *Industrial Association* v. *United States,* 268 U.S. 64, 82, 45 S.Ct. 403, 407, 69 L.Ed. 849; *Coronado Coal Co.* v. *United Mine Workers,* 268 U.S. 295, 310, 45 S.Ct. 551, 556, 69 L.Ed. 963; *Schechter Corporation* v. *United States, supra,* 295 U.S. 495, at page 547, 55 S.Ct. 837, 850, 79 L.Ed. 1570, 97 A.L.R. 947; *Carter* v. *Carter Coal Co.,* 298 U.S. 238, 304, 317, 327, 56 S.Ct. 855, 869, 875, 880, 80 L.Ed. 1160.

The government distinguishes these cases. The various parts of respondent's enterprise are described as interdependent and as thus involving "a great movement of iron ore, coal and limestone along well-defined paths to the steel mills, thence through them, and thence in the form of steel products into the consuming centers of the country—a definite and well-understood course of business." It is urged that these activities constitute a "stream" or "flow" of commerce, of which the Aliquippa manufacturing plant is the focal point, and that industrial strife at that point would cripple the entire movement. Reference is made to our decision sustaining the Packers and Stockyards Act. *Stafford* v. *Wallace,* 258 U.S. 495, 42 S.Ct. 397, 66 L.Ed. 735, 23 A.L.R. 229. The Court found that the stockyards were but a "throat" through which the current of commerce flowed and the transactions which there occurred could not be separated from that movement. Hence the sales at the stockyards were not regarded as merely local transactions, for, while they created "a local change of title," they did not "stop the flow," but merely changed the private interests in the subject of the current. Distinguishing the cases which upheld the power of the state to impose a nondiscriminatory tax upon property which the owner intended to transport to another state, but which was not in actual transit and was held within the state subject to the disposition of the owner, the Court remarked: "The question, it should be observed, is not with respect to the extent of the power of Congress to regulate interstate commerce, but whether a particular exercise of state power in view of its nature and operation must be deemed to be in conflict with this paramount authority." *Id.,* 258 U.S. 495, at page 526, 42 S.Ct. 397, 405, 66 L.Ed. 735, 23 A.L.R. 229. See *Minnesota* v. *Blasius,* 290 U.S. 1, 8, 54 S.Ct. 34, 36, 78 L.Ed. 131. Applying the doctrine of *Stafford* v. *Wallace, supra,* the Court sustained the Grain Futures Act of 1922 with respect to transactions on the Chicago Board of Trade, although these transactions were "not in and of themselves interstate commerce." Congress had found that they had become "a constantly recurring burden and obstruction to that commerce." *Board of Trade of City of Chicago* v. *Olsen,* 262 U.S. 1, 32, 43 S.Ct. 470, 476, 67 L.Ed. 839. Compare *Hill* v. *Wallace,*

259 U.S. 44, 69, 42 S.Ct. 453, 458, 66 L.Ed. 822. See, also, *Tagg Bros. & Moorhead* v. *United States,* 280 U.S. 420, 60 S.Ct. 220, 74 L.Ed. 524.

Respondent contends that the instant case presents material distinctions. Respondent says that the Aliquippa plant is extensive in size and represents a large investment in buildings, machinery and equipment. The raw materials which are brought to the plant are delayed for long periods and, after being subjected to manufacturing processes "are changed substantially as to character, utility and value." The finished products which emerge "are to a large extent manufactured without reference to pre-existing orders and contracts and are entirely different from the raw materials which enter at the other end." Hence respondent argues that, "If importation and exportation in interstate commerce do not singly transfer purely local activities into the field of congressional regulation, it should follow that their combination would not alter the local situation." *Arkadelphia Milling Co.* v. *St. Louis Southwestern R. Co.,* 249 U.S. 134, 151, 39 S.Ct. 237, 63 L.Ed. 517; *Oliver Iron Co.* v. *Lord, supra.*

We do not find it necessary to determine whether these features of defendant's business dispose of the asserted analogy to the "stream of commerce" cases. The instances in which that metaphor has been used are but particular, and not exclusive, illustrations of the protective power which the government invokes in support of the present act. The congressional authority to protect interstate commerce from burdens and obstructions is not limited to transactions which can be deemed to be an essential part of a "flow" of interstate or foreign commerce. Burdens and obstructions may be due to injurious action springing from other sources. The fundamental principle is that the power to regulate commerce is the power to enact "all appropriate legislation" for its "protection or advancement" (*The Daniel Ball,* 10 Wall. 557, 564, 19 L.Ed. 999); to adopt measures "to promote its growth and insure its safety" (*County of Mobile* v. *Kimball,* 102 U.S. 691, 696, 697, 26 L.Ed. 238); "to foster, protect, control, and restrain." (*Second Employers' Liability Cases, supra,* 223 U.S. 1, at page 47, 32 S.Ct. 169, 174, 56 L.Ed. 327, 38 L.R.A. (N.S.) 44). See *Texas & N. O. R. Co.* v. *Railway & S. S. Clerks, supra.* That power is plenary and may be exerted to protect interstate commerce "no matter what the source of the dangers which threaten it." Second Employers' Liability Cases, 223 U.S. 1, at page 51, 32 S.Ct. 169, 176, 56 L.Ed. 327, 38 L.R.A. (N.S.) 44; *Schechter Corporation* v. *United States, supra.* Although activities may be intrastate in character when separately considered, if they have such a close and substantial relation to interstate commerce that their control is essential or appropriate to protect that commerce from burdens and obstructions, Congress cannot be denied the power to exercise that control. *Schechter Corporation* v. *United States, supra.* Undoubtedly the scope of this power must be considered in the light of our dual system of government and may not be extended so as to embrace effects upon interstate commerce so indirect and remote that to embrace them, in view of our complex society, would effectually obliterate the distinction between what is national and what is local and create a completely centralized government. Id. The question is necessarily one of degree. As the Court said in *Board of Trade of City of Chicago* v. *Olsen, supra,* 262 U.S. 1, at page 37, 43 S.Ct. 470, 477, 67 L.Ed. 839, repeating what had been said in *Stafford* v. *Wallace, supra:* "Whatever amounts to more or less constant practice, and threatens to obstruct or unduly to burden the freedom of interstate commerce is within the regulatory power of Congress under the commerce clause, and it is primarily for Congress to consider and decide the fact of the danger and to meet it."

That intrastate activities, by reason of close and intimate relation to interstate commerce, may fall within federal control is demonstrated in the case of carriers who are engaged in both interstate and intrastate transportation. There federal control has been found essential to secure the freedom of interstate traffic from interference or unjust discrimination and to promote the efficiency of the interstate service. The *Shreveport Case (Houston, E. & W. T. R. Co.* v. *United States),* 234 U.S. 342, 351, 352, 34 S.Ct. 833, 58 L.Ed. 1341; *Railroad Commission of Wisconsin* v. *Chicago, B. & Q. R. Co.,* 257 U.S. 563, 588, 42 S.Ct. 232, 237, 66 L.Ed. 371, 33 A.L.R. 1086. It is manifest that intrastate rates deal *primarily* with a local activity. But in rate making they bear such a close relation to interstate rates that effective control of the one must embrace some control over the other. Id. Under the Transportation Act, 1920, Congress went so far as to authorize the Interstate Commerce Commission to establish a statewide level of intrastate rates in order to prevent an unjust discrimination against interstate commerce. *Railroad Commission of Wisconsin* v. *Chicago, B. & Q. R. R. Co., supra; Florida* v. *United States,* 282 U.S. 194, 210, 211, 51 S.Ct. 119, 123, 75 L.Ed. 291. Other illustrations are found in the broad requirements of the Safety Appliance Act (45 U.S.C.A. §§ 1–10) and the Hours of Service Act (45 U.S.C.A. §§ 61–64). *Southern Railway Co.* v. *United States,* 222 U.S. 20, 32 S.Ct. 2, 56 L.Ed. 72; *Baltimore & Ohio R. R. Co.* v. *Interstate Commerce Commission,* 221 U.S. 612, 31 S.Ct. 621, 55 L.Ed. 878. It is said that this exercise of federal power has relation to the maintenance of adequate instrumentalities of interstate commerce. But the agency is not superior to the commerce which uses it. The protective power extends to the former because it exists as to the latter.

The close and intimate effect which brings the subject within the reach of federal power may be due to activities in relation to productive industry although the industry when separately viewed is local. This has been abundantly illustrated in the application of the Federal Anti-Trust Act (15 U.S.C.A. § 1–7, 15 note). In the Standard Oil and American Tobacco Cases

(*Standard Oil Co.* v. *United States*), 221 U.S. 1, 31, S.Ct. 502, 55 L.Ed. 619, 34 L.R.A. (N.S.) 834, Ann. Cas. 1912D, 734; (*United States* v. *American Tobacco Co.*) 221 U.S. 106, 31 S.Ct. 632, 55 L.Ed. 663), that statute was applied to combinations of employers engaged in productive industry. Counsel for the offending corporations strongly urged that the Sherman Act had no application because the acts complained of were not acts of interstate or foreign commerce, nor direct and immediate in their effect on interstate or foreign commerce, but primarily affected manufacturing and not commerce. 221 U.S. 1, at page 5, 31 S.Ct. 502, 55 L.Ed. 619, 34 L.R.A. (N.S.) 834, Ann. Cas. 1912D, 734; 221 U.S. 106, at page 125, 31 S.Ct. 632, 55 L.Ed. 663. Counsel relied upon the decision in *United States* v. *E. C. Knight Co.,* 156 U.S. 1, 15 S.Ct. 249, 39 L.Ed. 325. The Court stated their contention as follows: "That the act, even if the averments of the bill be true, cannot be constitutionally applied, because to do so would extend the power of Congress to subject dehors the reach of its authority to regulate commerce, by enabling that body to deal with mere questions of production of commodities within the states." And the Court summarily dismissed the contention in these words. "But all the structure upon which this argument proceeds is based upon the decision in *United States* v. *E. C. Knight Co.,* 156 U.S. 1, 15 S.Ct. 249, 39 L.Ed. 425. The view, however, which the argument takes of that case, and the arguments based upon that view have been so repeatedly pressed upon this court in connection with the interpretation and enforcement of the Antitrust Act, and have been so necessarily and expressly decided to be unsound as to cause the contentions to be plainly foreclosed and to require no express notice" (citing cases). 221 U.S. 1, at pages 68, 69, 31 S.Ct. 502, 519, 55 L.Ed. 619, 34 L.R.A. (N.S.) 834, Ann.Cas. 1912D, 734.

Upon the same principle, the Anti-Trust Act has been applied to the conduct of employees engaged in production. *Loewe* v. *Lawlor,* 208 U.S. 274, 28 S.Ct. 301, 52 L.Ed. 488, 13 Ann. Cas. 815; *Coronado Coal Co.* v. *United Mine Workers, supra; Bedford Cut Stone Co.* v. *Stone Cutters Association,* 274 U.S. 37, 47, S.Ct. 522, 71 L.Ed. 916, 54 A.L.R. 791. See, also, Local 167, *International Brotherhood of Teamsters* v. *United States,* 291 U.S. 293, 297, 54 S.Ct. 396, 398, 78 L.Ed. 804; *Schechter Corporation* v. *United States, supra.* The decisions dealing with the question of that application illustrate both the principle and its limitation. Thus, in the first *Coronado* case, the Court held that mining was not interstate commerce, that the power of Congress did not extend to its regulation as such, and that it had not been shown that the activities there involved—a local strike—brought them within the provisions of the Anti-Trust Act, notwithstanding the broad terms of that Statute. A similar conclusion was reached in *United Leather Workers' International Union* v. *Herbert & Meisel Trunk Co., supra, Industrial Association* v. *United States, supra,* and *Lever-*

ing & Garrigues v. *Morrin,* 289 U.S. 103, 107, 53 S.Ct. 549, 550, 77 L.Ed. 1062. But in the first *Coronado* case the Court also said that "if Congress deems certain recurring practices though not really part of interstate commerce, likely to obstruct, restrain or burden it, it has the power to subject them to national supervision and restraint" 259 U.S. 344, at page 408, 42 S.Ct. 2, 66 L.Ed. 975, 27 A.L.R. 762. And in the second *Coronado* case the Court ruled that, while the mere reduction in the supply of an article to be shipped in interstate commerce by the illegal or tortious prevention of its manufacture or production is ordinarily an indirect and remote obstruction to that commerce, nevertheless when the "intent of those unlawfully preventing the manufacture or production is shown to be to restrain or control the supply entering and moving in interstate commerce, or the price of it in interstate markets, their action is a direct violation of the Anti-Trust Act." 268 U.S. 295, at page 310, 45 S.Ct. 551, 556, 69 L.Ed. 963. And the existence of that intent may be a necessary inference from proof of the direct and substantial effect produced by the employees' conduct. *Industrial Association* v. *United States,* 268 U.S. 64, at page 81, 45 S.Ct. 403, 407, 69 L.Ed. 849. What was absent from the evidence in the first *Coronado* case appeared in the second and the act was accordingly applied to the mining employees.

It is thus apparent that the fact that the employees here concerned were engaged in production is not determinative. The question remains as to the effect upon interstate commerce of the labor practice involved. In the *Schechter* case, *supra,* we found that the effect there was so remote as to be beyond the federal power. To find "immediacy or directness" there was to find it "almost everywhere," a result inconsistent with the maintenance of our federal system. In the *Carter* case, *supra,* the Court was of the opinion that the provisions of the statute relating to production were invalid upon several grounds,—that there was improper delegation of legislative power, and that the requirements not only went beyond any sustainable measure of protection of interstate commerce but were also inconsistent with due process. These cases are not controlling here.

Fourth. Effects of the Unfair Labor Practice in Respondent's Enterprise. —Giving full weight to respondent's contention with respect to a break in the complete continuity of the "stream of commerce" by reason of respondent's manufacturing operations, the fact remains that the stoppage of those operations by industrial strife would have a most serious effect upon interstate commerce. In view of respondent's far-flung activities, it is idle to say that the effect would be indirect or remote. It is obvious that it would be immediate and might be catastrophic. We are asked to shut our eyes to the plainest facts of our national life and to deal with the question of direct and indirect effects in an intellectual vacuum. Because there may be but indirect and remote effects upon interstate commerce in connection with a host of local enterprises throughout the country, it does not follow that other industrial activities do not have such a close and intimate relation to interstate commerce as to make the presence of industrial strife a matter of the most urgent national conern. When industries organize themselves on a national scale, making their relation to interstate commerce the dominant factor in their activities, how can it be maintained that their industrial labor relations constitute a forbidden field into which Congress may not enter when it is necessary to protect interstate commerce from the paralyzing consequences of industrial war? We have often said that interstate commerce itself is a practical conception. It is equally true that interferences with that commerce must be appraised by a judgment that does not ignore actual experience.

Experience has abundantly demonstrated that the recognition of the right of employees to self-organization and to have representatives of their own choosing for the purpose of collective bargaining is often an essential condition of industrial peace. Refusal to confer and negotiate has been one of the most prolific causes of strife. This is such an outstanding fact in the history of labor disturbances that it is a proper subject of judicial notice and requires no citation of instances. The opinion in the case of *Virginian Railway Co.* v. *System Federation No. 40, supra,* points out that, in the case of carriers, experience has shown that before the amendment, of 1934, of the Railway Labor Act, "when there was no dispute as to the organizations authorized to represent the employees, and when there was willingness of the employer to meet such representative for a discussion of their grievances, amicable adjustment of differences had generally followed and strikes had been avoided." That, on the other hand, "a prolific source of dispute had been the maintenance by the railroads of company unions and the denial by railway management of the authority of representatives chosen by their employees." The opinion in that case also points to the large measure of success of the labor policy embodied in the Railway Labor Act. But, with respect to the appropriateness of the recognition of self-organization and representation in the promotion of peace, the question is not essentially different in the case of employees in industries of such a character that interstate commerce is put in jeopardy from the case of employees of transportation companies. And of what avail is it to protect the facility of transportation, if interstate commerce is throttled with respect to the commodities to be transported!

These questions have frequently engaged the attention of Congress and have been the subject of many inquiries. The steel industry is one of the great basic industries of the United States, with ramifying activities affecting interstate commerce at every point. The Government aptly refers to the steel strike of 1919-1920 with its far-reaching consequences. The fact that there appears to have been no major disturbance in that industry in the more recent period did not dispose of the possibilities of future and like dangers to interstate commerce which Congress was entitled to foresee and to exercise its protective power to forestall. It is not necessary again to detail the facts as to respondent's enterprise. Instead of being beyond the pale, we think that it presents in a most striking way the close and intimate relation which a manufacturing industry may have to interstate commerce and we have no doubt that Congress had constitutional authority to safeguard the right of respondent's employees to self-organization and freedom in the choice of representatives for collective bargaining.

Fifth. The Means Which the Act Employs.—Questions under the Due Process Clause and Other Constitutional Restrictions.—Respondent asserts its right to conduct its business in an orderly manner without being subjected to arbitrary restraints. What we have said points to the fallacy in the argument. Employees have their correlative right to organize for the purpose of securing the redress of grievances and to promote agreements with employers relating to rates of pay and conditions of work. *Texas & N. O. R. Co.* v. *Railway S. S. Clerks, supra; Virginian Railway Co.* v. *System Federation No. 40.* Restraint for the purpose of preventing an unjust interference with that right cannot be considered arbitrary or capricious. The provision of section 9 (a) that representatives, for the purpose of collective bargaining, of the majority of the employees in an appropriate unit shall be the exclusive representatives of all the employees in that unit, imposes upon the respondent only the duty of conferring and negotiating with the authorized representatives of its employees for the purpose of settling a labor dispute. This provision has its analogue in section 2, Ninth, of the Railway Labor Act, as amended (45 U.S.C.A. § 152, subd. 9), which was under consideration in *Virginian Railway Co.* v. *System Federation No. 40, supra.* The decree which we affirmed in that case required the railway company to treat with the representative chosen by the employees and also to refrain from entering into collective labor agreements with any one other than their true representative as ascertained in accordance with the provisions of the act. We said that the obligation to treat with the true representative was exclusive and hence imposed the negative duty to treat with no other. We also pointed out that, as conceded by the government, the injunction against the company's entering into any contract concerning rules, rates of pay and working conditions except with a chosen representative was "designed only to prevent collective bargaining with any one purporting to represent employees" other than the representative they had selected. It was taken "to prohibit the negotiation of labor contracts, generally applicable to employees" in the described unit with any other representative than the one so chosen, "but not as precluding such individual contracts" as the company might "elect to make directly with individual employees." We think this construction also applies to section 9 (a) of the National Labor Relations Act (29 U.S.C.A. § 159 (a).

The act does not compel agreements between employers and employees. It does not compel any agreement whatever. It does not prevent the employer "from refusing to make a collective contract and hiring individuals on whatever terms" the employer "may by unilateral action determine." The act expressly provides in section 9 (a) that any individual employee or a group of employees shall have the right at any time to present grievances to their employer. The theory of the act is that free opportunity for negotiation with accredited representatives of employees is likely to promote industrial peace and may bring about the adjustments and agreements which the act in itself does not attempt to compel. As we said in *Texas & N. O. R. Co.* v. *Railway & S. S. Clerks, supra,* and repeated in *Virginian Railway Co.* v. *System Federation No. 40,* the cases of *Adair* v. *United States,* 208 U.S. 161, 28 S.Ct. 277, 52 L.Ed. 436, 13 Ann. Cas. 764, and *Coppage* v. *Kansas,* 236 U.S. 1, 35 S.Ct. 240, 59 L.Ed. 441, L.R.A. 1915C, 960, are inapplicable to legislation of this character. The act does not interfere with the normal exercise of the right of the employer to select its employees or to discharge them. The employer may not, under cover of that right, intimidate or coerce its employees with respect to their self-organization and representation, and, on the other hand, the Board is not entitled to make its authority a pretext for interference with the right of discharge when that right is exercised for other reasons than such intimidation and coercion. The true purpose is the subject of investigation with full opportunity to show the facts. It would seem that when employers freely recognize the right of their employees to their own organizations and their unrestricted right of representation there will be much less occasion for controversy in respect to the free and appropriate exercise of the right of selection and discharge.

The act has been criticized as one-sided in its application; that it subjects the employer to supervision and restraint and leaves untouched the abuses for which employees may be responsible; that it fails to provide a more comprehensive plan,—with better assurances of fairness to both sides and with increased chances of success in bringing about, if not compelling, equitable solutions of industrial disputes affecting interstate commerce. But we are dealing with the power of Congress, not with a particular policy or with the extent to which policy should go. We have frequently said that the legislative authority, exerted within its proper field, need not embrace all the evils within its reach. The Constitution does not forbid "cautious advance, step by step," in dealing with the evils which are exhibited in activities within the range of legislative power. *Carroll* v. *Greenwich Insurance Co.,* 199 U.S. 401, 411, 26 S.Ct. 66, 50 L.Ed. 246; *Koekee Coke Co.* v. *Taylor,* 234 U.S. 224, 227, 34 S.Ct. 856, 58 L.Ed. 1288; *Miller* v. *Wilson,* 236 U.S. 373, 384, 35 S.Ct. 342, 59 L.Ed. 628, L.R.A. 1915F, 829; *Sproles* v. *Binford,* 286 U.S. 374, 396, 52 S.Ct. 581, 588, 76 L.Ed. 1167. The question in such cases is whether the Legislature, in what it does prescribe, has gone beyond constitutional limits.

The procedural provisions of the act are assailed. But these provisions, as we construe them, do not offend against the constitutional requirements governing the creation and action of administrative bodies. See *Interstate Commerce Commission* v. *Louisville & Nashville R. Co.,* 227 U.S. 88, 91, 33 S.Ct. 185, 57 L.Ed. 431. The act establishes standards to which the Board must conform. There must be complaint, notice and hearing. The Board must receive evidence and make findings. The findings as to the facts are to be conclusive, but only if supported by evidence. The order of the Board is subject to review by the designated court, and only when sustained by the court may the order be enforced. Upon that review all questions of the jurisdiction of the Board and the regularity of its proceedings, all questions of constitutional right or statutory authority are open to examination by the court. We construe the procedural provisions as affording adequate opportunity to secure judicial protection against arbitrary action in accordance with the well-settled rules applicable to administrative agencies set up by Congress to aid in the enforcement of valid legislation. It is not necessary to repeat these rules which have frequently been declared. None of them appears to have been transgressed in the instant case. Respondent was notified and heard. It had opportunity to meet the charge of unfair labor practices upon the merits, and by withdrawing from the hearing it declined to avail itself of that opportunity. The facts found by the Board support its order and the evidence supports the findings. Respondent has no just ground for complaint on this score.

The order of the Board required the reinstatement of the employees who were found to have been discharged because of their "union activity" and for the purpose of "discouraging membership in the union." That requirement was authorized by the act. Section 10 (c), 29 U.S.C.A. § 160 (c). In *Texas & N. O. R. Co.* v. *Railway & S. S. Clerks, supra,* a similar order for restoration to service was made by the court in contempt proceedings for the violation of an injunction issued by the court to restrain an interference with the right of employees as guaranteed by the Railway Labor Act of 1926. The requirement of restoration to service of employees discharged in violation of the provisions of that act was thus a sanction imposed in the enforcement of a judicial decree. We do not doubt that Congress could impose a like sanction for the enforcement of its valid regulation. The fact that in the one case it was a judicial sanction, and in the other a legislative one, is not an essential difference in determining its propriety.

Respondent complains that the Board not only ordered reinstatement but directed the payment of wages for the time lost by the discharge, less amounts earned by the employee during that period. This part of the order was also authorized by the act. Section 10 (c). It is argued that the requirement is equivalent to a money judgment and hence contravenes the Seventh Amendment with respect to trial by jury. The Seventh Amendment provides that "In suits at common law, where the value in controversy shall exceed twenty dollars; the right of trial by jury shall be preserved." The amendment thus preserves the right which existed under the common law when the amendment was adopted. *Shields* v. *Thomas,* 18 How 253, 262, 15 L.Ed. 368; In re Wood, 210 U.S. 246, 258, 28 S.Ct. 621, 52 L.Ed. 1046; *Dimick* v. *Schiedt,* 293 U.S. 474, 476, 55 S.Ct. 296, 79 L.Ed. 603, 95 A.L.R. 1150; *Baltimore & Carolina Line* v. *Redman,* 295 U.S. 654, 657, 55 S.Ct. 890, 891, 79 L.Ed. 1636. Thus it has no application to cases where recovery of money damages is an incident to equitable relief even though damages might have been recovered in an action at law. *Clark* v. *Wooster,* 119 U.S. 322, 325, 7 S.Ct. 217, 30 L.Ed. 392; *Pease* v. *Rathbun-Jones Engineering Co.,* 243 U.S. 273, 279, 37 S.Ct. 283, 61 L.Ed. 715, Ann. Cas. 1918C, 1147. It does not apply where the proceeding is not in the nature of a suit at common law. *Guthrie National Bank* v. *Guthrie,* 173 U.S. 528, 537, 19 S.Ct. 513, 43 L.Ed. 796.

The instant case is not a suit at common law or in the nature of such a suit. The proceeding is one unknown to the common law. It is a statutory proceeding. Reinstatement of the employee and payment for time lost are requirements imposed for violation of the statute and are remedies appropriate to its enforcement. The contention under the Seventh Amendment is without merit.

Our conclusion is that the order of the Board was within its competence and that the act is valid as here applied. The judgment of the Circuit Court of Appeals is reversed and the cause is remanded for further proceedings in conformity with this opinion. It is so ordered.

Reversed and remanded.

Commentary

This was the first case to reach the Supreme Court under this section of the Act. It sealed the fate of the popular "employee representation plans," which had been created by employers in response to demands for collective representation of employees. The Court reviewed the evidence showing that the employer had sponsored the formation of the employees' association, had maintained control over the structure and functions of the association, and had assisted it financially and otherwise. In these circumstances the Board was justified in ordering the employer to withdraw recognition from the association as representative of the employees.

N.L.R.B. v. *Pennsylvania Greyhound Lines, Inc.*
303 U.S. 261 (1938)

MR. JUSTICE STONE delivered the opinion of the Court.

The main question for decision is whether, upon a finding that an employer has created and fostered a labor organization of employees and dominated its administration in violation of § 8 (1), (2) of the National Labor Relations Act of July 5, 1935 (c. 372, 49 Stat. 449, 29 U. S. C., § 151, *et seq.*), the National Labor Relations Board, in addition to ordering the employer to cease these practices, can require him to withdraw all recognition of the organization as the representative of his employees and to post notices informing them of such withdrawal.

Respondent Pennsylvania Greyhound Lines, Inc., is a corporation operating a passenger motor bus system between the Atlantic Coast and Chicago and St. Louis. Respondent Greyhound Management Company, an affiliate of the Pennsylvania Company, performs various services relating to employee personnel of the latter and its affiliated corporations. Together, respondents act as employers of those employees working at the Pittsburgh Garage of the Pennsylvania Company and together actively deal with labor relations of those employees.

Upon charges filed by Local Division No. 1063, Amalgamated Association of Street, Electric Railway and Motor Coach Employees of America, a labor organization, the Board issued its complaint, as permitted by § 10 (b) of the Act, charging that respondents had engaged in specified unfair labor practices affecting interstate commerce, in violation of §8. After notice to respondents, and hearing, the Board found that they had engaged in unfair labor practices by interfering with, restraining, and coercing employees in the exercise of their rights, guaranteed by § 7, in that they had dominated and interfered with the formation and administration of a labor organization of their employees, Employees Association of the Pennsylvania Greyhound Lines, Inc., and had contributed financial and other support to it in violation of § 8 (1), (2).

The Board ordered that respondents cease each of the specified unfair labor practices. It further ordered that they withdraw recognition from the Employees Association as employee representative authorized to deal with respondents concerning grievances, terms of employment, and labor disputes, and that they post conspicuous notices in all the places of business where such employees are engaged, stating that the "Association is so disestablished and that respondents will refrain from any such recognition thereof." 1 N. L. R. B. 1.

Upon the Board's petition under § 10 (e) to enforce the order, heard

April 1, 1936, the Court of Appeals for the Third Circuit gave judgment after a delay of one year and two months, during which there were three postponements and two rearguments. It struck from the order all provisions requiring the withdrawal by respondents of recognition of the Employees Association and publication of notice of withdrawal, and directed that in other respects the Board's order be enforced. 91 F. (2d) 178. The court thought that the Board was without authority to order the employers to withhold recognition from the Association, without notice to it and opportunity for a hearing, and without an election by the employees to choose a labor organization to represent them. We granted certiorari, 302 U. S. 676, the questions involved being of importance in the administration of the National Labor Relations Act.

Respondents do not assail the Board's findings of fact as without support in the evidence, and the principal questions for decision are of law, whether in the circumstances disclosed by the findings the Board acted within the authority conferred upon it by §§ 7, 8 and 10 of the Act. . . .

Notwithstanding the mandatory form of § 10 (c), its provisions in substance leave to the Board some scope for the exercise of judgment and discretion in determining, upon the basis of the findings, whether the case is one requiring an affirmative order, and in choosing the particular affirmative relief to be ordered. Hence, upon the challenge of the affirmative part of an order of the Board, we look to the Act itself, read in the light of its history, to ascertain its policy, and to the facts which the Board has found, to see whether they afford a basis for its judgment that the action ordered is an appropriate means of carrying out that policy.

The history of the Act and its language shows that its ruling purpose was to protect interstate commerce by securing to employees the rights established by § 7 to organize, to bargain collectively through representatives of their own choosing, and to engage in concerted activities for that and other purposes. *National Labor Relations Board* v. *Jones & Laughlin Steel Corp.,* 301 U. S. 1, 23, 33. This appears both from the formal declaration of policy in § 1 of the Act, *National Labor Relations Board* v. *Jones & Laughlin Steel Corp., supra,* 22–24, and from § 7, in itself a declaration of the policy which, in conjunction with § 10 (c), it adopts as the controlling guide to administrative action.

Before enactment of the National Labor Relations Act this Court had recognized that the maintenance of a "company union," dominated by the employer, may be a ready and effective means of obstructing self-organization of employees and their choice of their own representatives for the purpose of collective bargaining. Section 2 (3) of the Railway Labor Act of 1926, had provided that representatives, for the purposes of the Act, should be designated by employer and employees "without interference, influence, or coercion exercised by either party over the self-organization or designation of representatives by the other." We had held that in enforcing this provision, employer recognition of a company union might be enjoined and the union "disestablished," as an appropriate means of preventing interference with the rights secured to employees by the statute. *Texas & N. O. R. Co.* v. *Brotherhood of Railway & S. S. Clerks,* 281 U. S. 548, 560; see also *Virginian Ry. Co.* v. *System Federation No. 40,* 300 U. S. 515, 542 *et seq.*

Congress, in enacting the National Labor Relations Act, had in mind the experience in the administration of the Railway Labor Act, and declared that the former was "an amplification and further clarification of the principles" of the latter. Report of the House Committee on Labor, H. R. 1147, 74th Cong., 1st Sess., p. 3. It had before it the *Railway Clerks* case which had emphasized the importance of union recognition in securing collective bargaining, Report of the Senate Committee on Education and Labor, S. Rep. 573, 74th Cong., 1st Sess., p. 17, and there were then available data showing that once an employer has conferred recognition on a particular organization it has a marked advantage over any other in securing the adherence of employees, and hence in preventing the recognition of any other.[2] The National Labor Relations Act continued and amplified the policy of the Railway Labor Act by its declaration in § 7, and by providing generally in § 8 that any interferences in the exercise of the rights guaranteed by §7 and specifically the domination or interference with the formation or administration of any labor organization were unfair labor practices. To secure to employees the benefits of self-organization and collective bargaining through representatives of the employees' own choosing, the Board was authorized by § 10 (c) to order the abandonment of unfair labor practices and to take affirmative action which would carry out the policy of the Act.

In recommending the adoption of this latter provision the Senate Committee called attention to the decree which, in the *Railway Clerks* case, had compelled the employer to "disestablish its company union as representative of its employees." Report of the Senate Committee on Education and Labor, *supra.* The report of the House Committee on Labor on this feature of the Act, after pointing out that collective bargaining is "a sham when the employer sits on both sides of the table by supporting a particular organization with which he deals," declared: "The orders will of course be adapted to the need of the individual case; they may include such matters as refraining from collective bargaining with a minority group, recognition of the agency chosen by the majority for the purposes of collective bargaining, posting of appropriate bulletins, refraining from bargaining with an organization corrupted by unfair labor practices." Report of the House Committee on Labor, *supra,* pp. 18, 24.

It is plain that the challenged provisions of the present order are of a kind contemplated by Congress in the enactment of § 10 (c) and are within its terms. There remains the question whether the findings adequately support them.

The Board's subsidiary findings of fact fully sustain its conclusion that respondents had engaged in unfair labor practices, by active participation in the organization and administration of the Employees Association, which they dominated throughout its history, and to whose financial support they had contributed; and that they had interfered with, restrained and coerced their employees in the exercise of the rights confirmed by § 7 to form for themselves a labor organization and to bargain collectively through representatives of their own choosing.

It is unnecessary to repeat in full detail the facts disclosed by the findings. They show that before the enactment of the National Labor Relations Act, respondents, whose employees were unorganized, initiated a project for their organization under company domination. In the course of its execution officers or other representatives of respondent were active in promoting the plan, in urging employees to join, in the preparation of the details of organization, including the bylaws, in presiding over organization meetings, and in selecting employee representatives of the organization.

The bylaws and regulations provided that all motorbus operators, maintenance men and clerical employees, after three months service, automatically became members of the Association, and that only employees were eligible to act as employee representatives. No provisions were made for meetings of members, nor was a procedure established whereby employees might instruct their representatives, or whereby those representatives might disseminate information or reports. Grievances were to be taken up with regional committees with final review by a Joint Reviewing Committee made up of an equal number of regional chairmen and of management representatives, but review in those cases could not be secured unless there was a joint submission of the controversy by employee and management representatives.

Change of the bylaws without employer consent was precluded by a provision that amendment should be only on a two-thirds vote of the Joint Reviewing Committee, composed of equal numbers of employer and employee representatives. Employees paid no dues, all the Association expenses being borne by the management.

Although the Association was in terms created as a bargaining agency for the purpose of "providing adequate representation" for respondents' employees by "securing for them satisfactory adjustment of all controversial matters," it has functioned only to settle individual grievances. On the one recorded occasion when the employees sought a wage increase, the company representatives prevented its consideration by refusing to join in the submission to the Joint Reviewing Committee.

In May, 1935, shortly before the passage of the Act, certain of respondents' Pittsburgh employees organized a local union, Local Division No. 1063 of the Amalgamated Association of Street, Electric Railway and Motor Coach Employees of America, affiliated with the American Federation of Labor, and continued to hold meetings of the organization after the passage of the Act on July 5, 1935. Before and after that date, respondents' officers were active in warning employees against joining the union and in threatening them with discharge if they should join, and in keeping the union meetings under surveillance.

Section 10 (e) declares that the Board's findings of fact "if supported by evidence, shall be conclusive." Whether the continued recognition of the Employees Association by respondents would in itself be a continuing obstacle to the exercise of the employees' right of self-organization and to bargain collectively through representatives of their own choosing, is an inference of fact to be drawn by the Board from the evidence reviewed in its subsidiary findings. See *Swayne & Hoyt* v. *United States,* 300 U. S. 297.

We may assume that there are situations in which the Board would not be warranted in concluding that there was any occasion for withdrawal of employer recognition of an existing union before an election by employees under § 9 (c), even though it had ordered the employer to cease unfair labor practices. But here respondents, by unfair labor practices, have succeeded in establishing a company union so organized that it is incapable of functioning as a bargaining representative of employees. With no procedure for meetings of members or for instructing employee representatives, and with no power to bring grievances before the Joint Reviewing Committee without employer consent, the Association could not without amendment of its bylaws be used as a means of the collective bargaining contemplated by § 7; and amendment could not be had without the employer's approval.

In view of all the circumstances the Board could have thought that continued recognition of the Association would serve as a means of thwarting the policy of collective bargaining by enabling the employer to induce adherence of employees to the Association in the mistaken belief that it was truly representative and afforded an agency for collective bargaining, and thus to prevent self-organization. The inferences to be drawn were for the Board and not the courts. *Swayne & Hoyt* v. *United States, supra.* There was ample basis for its conclusion that withdrawal of recognition of the Association by respondents, accompanied by suitable publicity, was an appropriate way to give effect to the policy of the Act.

As the order did not run against the Association it is not entitled to notice and hearing. Its presence was not necessary in order to enable the Board to determine whether respondents had violated the statute or to make an appropriate order against them. See *General Investment Co.* v. *Lake Shore & M. S. Ry. Co.,* 260 U. S. 261, 285–286.

Respondents suggest that the case has become moot by reason of the fact that since the Board made its order it has certified the Brotherhood of Railroad Trainmen as representative of the motorbus drivers of the Pennsylvania company for purposes of collective bargaining and that in a pending proceeding under § 9 (c) for the certification of a representative of the other Pittsburgh employees, to which the Employees Association is not a party, the Pennsylvania company and Local Division No. 1063, who are parties, have made no objection to the proposed certification. But an order of the character made by the Board, lawful when made, does not become moot because it is obeyed or because changing circumstances indicate that the need for it may be less than when made.

We have considered but find it unnecessary to comment upon other objections to the order, of less moment.

Reversed.

Commentary

The balance of power between labor and management during a strike is of the utmost significance in our economy. In this early decision the Supreme Court was called upon to decide whether the Wagner Act prevented an employer from permanently replacing strikers whose strike action was not the result of any employer "act denounced by the statute." The employees had struck for better employment terms, and during the strike the employer had promised eleven of the replacements permanent employment. At the conclusion of the strike, however, only five of the replacements desired to continue. The employer allowed six of the strikers to return, but in making its selection denied reinstatement to the five strikers "most active in the union." The Court held that while the employer was privileged to replace the strikers, he committed an unfair labor practice when he discriminated on the basis of union activity in reinstating the strikers to existing vacancies.

N.L.R.B. v. Mackay Radio & Telegraph Co.
304 U.S. 333 (1938)

MR. JUSTICE ROBERTS delivered the opinion of the Court.

The Circuit Court of Appeals refused to decree enforcement of an order of the National Labor Relations Board. We granted certiorari because of an asserted conflict of decision.

The respondent, a California corporation, is engaged in the transmission and receipt of telegraph, radio, cable, and other messages between points in California and points in other States and foreign countries. It maintains an office in San Francisco for the transaction of its business wherein it employs upward of sixty supervisors, operators and clerks, many of whom are members of Local No. 3 of the American Radio Telegraphists Association, a national labor organization; the membership of the local comprising "point-to-point" or land operators employed by respondent at San Francisco. Affiliated with the national organization also were locals whose members are exclusively marine operators who work upon oceangoing vessels. The respondent, at its San Francisco office, dealt with committees of Local No. 3; and its parent company, whose headquarters were in New York, dealt with representatives of the national organization. Demand was made by the latter for the execution of agreements respecting terms and conditions of employment of marine and point-to-point operators. On several occasions when representatives of the union conferred with officers of the respondent and its parent company the latter requested postponement of discussion of the proposed agreements and the union acceded to the requests. In September 1935 the union pressed for immediate execution of agreements and took the position that no contract would be concluded by the one class of operators unless an agreement were simultaneously made with the others. Local No. 3 sent a representative to New York to be in touch with the negotiations and he kept its officers advised as to what there occurred. The local adopted a resolution to the effect that if satisfactory terms were not obtained by September 23 a strike of the San Francisco point-to-point operators should be called. The national officers determined on a general strike in view of the unsatisfactory state of the negotiations. This fact was communicated to Local No. 3 by its representative in New York and the local officers called out the employees of the San Francisco office. At midnight Friday, October 4, 1935, all the men there employed went on strike. The respondent, in order to maintain service, brought employees from its Los Angeles office and others from the New York and Chicago offices of the parent company to fill the strikers' places.

Although none of the San Francisco strikers returned to work Saturday, Sunday, or Monday, the strike proved unsuccessful in other parts of the country and, by Monday evening, October 7th, a number of the men became convinced that it would fail and that they had better return to work before their places were filled with new employees. One of them telephoned the respondent's traffic supervisor Monday evening to inquire whether the men might return. He was told that the respondent would take them back and it was arranged that the official should meet the employees at a downtown hotel and make a statement to them. Before leaving the company's office for this purpose, the supervisor consulted with his superior, who told him that the men might return to work in their former positions but that, as the company had promised eleven men brought to San Francisco they might remain if they so desired, the supervisor would have to handle the return of the striking employees in such fashion as not to displace any of the new men who desired to continue in San Francisco. A little later the supervisor met two of the striking employees and gave them a list of all the strikers, together with their addresses, and the telephone numbers of those who had telephones, and it was arranged that these two employees should telephone the strikers to come to a meeting at the Hotel Bellevue in the early hours of Tuesday, October 8th. In furnishing this list the supervisor stated that the men could return to work in a body but he checked off the names of eleven strikers who he said would have to file applications for reinstatement, which applications would be subject to the approval of an executive of the company in New York. Because of this statement the two employees, in notifying the strikers of the proposed meeting, with the knowledge of the supervisor, omitted to communicate with the eleven men whose names had been checked off. Thirty-six men attended the meeting. Some of the eleven in question heard of it and attended. The supervisor appeared at the meeting and reiterated his statement that the men could go back to work at once, but read from a list the names of the eleven who would be required to file applications for reinstatement to be passed upon in New York. Those present at the meeting voted on the question of immediately returning to work, and the proposition was carried. Most of the men left the meeting and went to the respondent's office Tuesday morning, October 8th, where on that day they resumed their usual duties. Then or shortly thereafter, six of the eleven in question took their places and resumed their work without challenge. It turned out that only five of the new men brought to San Francisco desired to stay.

Five strikers who were prominent in the activities of the union and in connection with the strike, whose names appeared upon the list of eleven, reported at the office at various times between Tuesday and Thursday. Each of them was told that he would have to fill out an application for employment; that the roll of employees was complete, and that his application would be considered in connection with any vacancy that might thereafter occur. These men not having been reinstated in the course of three weeks, the secretary of Local No. 3 presented a charge to the National Labor Relations Board that the respondent had violated § 8 (1) and (3) of the National Labor Relations Act. . . .

The subsidiary or evidentiary facts were found in great detail and, upon the footing of them, the Board reached conclusions of fact to the effect that Local No. 3 is a labor organization within the meaning of the Act; that "by refusing to reinstate to employment" the five men in question, "thereby discharging said employees," the respondent by "each of said discharges," discriminated in regard to tenure of employment and thereby discouraged membership in the labor organization known as Local No. 3, and, by the described acts "has interfered with, restrained, and coerced its employees in the exercise of the rights guaranteed by Section 7 of the National Labor Relations Act." As conclusions of law the Board found that the respondent had engaged in unfair labor practices affecting commerce within the meaning of § 8, subsections (1) and (3), and § 2, subsections (6) and (7) of the Act. It entered an order that respondent cease and desist from discharging, or threatening to discharge, any of its employees for the reason that they had joined or assisted Local No. 3 or otherwise engaged in union activities; from interfering with, restraining or coercing its employees in the exercise of the rights guaranteed by § 7 of the Act; offer the five men immediate and full reinstatement to their former positions, without prejudice to rights and privileges previously enjoyed, and make each of them whole for any loss of wages due to their discharge; post notices that the respondent would not discharge or discriminate against members of, or those desiring to become members of, the union, and keep the notices posted for thirty days. . . .

Upon the hearing before the Circuit Court of Appeals, one judge held that the action of the Board was within the power sought to be conferred upon it by the statute but that the grant of power violated the due process clause of the Fifth Amendment, and the award of back pay to the employees, without a jury trial, violated the Seventh Amendment. Another judge held that as the statute defined employees to include a person whose work had ceased "as a consequence of, or in connection with, any current labor dispute," and since there was no allegation, evidence, or finding as to such a dispute, the strikers had ceased to be employees within the meaning of the Act and the respondent's treatment of them could not violate the Act. One judge dissented, holding that the Board's order was within its statutory authority and did not violate the Constitution. A petition and supplemental petition for rehearing were granted and, after argument, the court reaffirmed its former decision. The judge who had previously declared the Board's action within the terms of the statute, but unconstitutional, construed the Act as not intended to work the unconstitutional result of compelling an employer to enter into a contract of employment against his will and, hence, as requiring only that the strikers be reinstated to the position of applicants for employment rather than employees. The other judges adhered to the views they had previously expressed. . . .

We hold that we have jurisdiction; that the Board's order is within its competence and does not contravene any provision of the Constitution. . . .

Under the findings the strike was a consequence of, or in connection with, a current labor dispute as defined in § 2 (9) of the Act. That there were pending negotiations for the execution of a contract touching wages and terms and conditions of employment of point-to-point operators cannot be denied. But it is said the record fails to disclose what caused these negotiations to fail or to show that the respondent was in any wise in fault in failing to comply with the union's demands; and, therefore, for all that appears, the strike was not called by reason of fault of the respondent. The argument confuses a current labor dispute with an unfair labor practice defined in § 8 of the Act. True there is no evidence that respondent had been guilty of any unfair labor practice prior to the strike, but within the intent of the Act there was an existing labor dispute in connection with which the strike was called. The finding is that the strike was deemed "advisable in view of the unsatisfactory state of the negotiations" in New York. It was unnecessary for the Board to find what was in fact the state of the negotiations in New York when the strike was called, or in so many words that a labor dispute as defined by the Act existed. The wisdom or unwisdom of the men, their justification or lack of it, in attributing to respondent an unreasonable or arbitrary attitude in connection with the negotiations, cannot determine whether, when they struck, they did so as a consequence of or in connection with a current labor dispute.

The strikers remained employees under § 2 (3) of the Act which provides: "The term 'employee' shall include . . . any individual whose work has ceased as a consequence of, or in connection with, any current labor dispute or because of any unfair labor practice, and who has not obtained any other regular and substantially equivalent employment, . . ." Within this definition the strikers remained employees for the purpose of the Act and were protected against the unfair labor practices denounced by it.

It is contended that the Board lacked jurisdiction because respondent was at no time guilty of any unfair labor practice. Section 8 of the Act denominates as such practice action by an employer to interfere with, restrain, or coerce employees in the exercise of their rights to organize, to form, join or assist labor organizations, and to engage in concerted activities for the purpose of collective bargaining or other mutual aid or protection, or "by discrimination in regard to . . . tenure of employment or any term or condition of employment to encourage or discourage membership in any labor organization: . . ." There is no evidence and no finding that the respondent was guilty of any unfair labor practice in connection with the negotiations in New York. On the contrary, it affirmatively appears that the respondent was negotiating with the authorized representatives of the union. Nor was it an unfair labor practice to replace the striking employees with others in an effort to carry on the business. Although § 13 provides, "Nothing in this Act shall be construed so as to interfere with or impede or diminish in any way the right to strike," it does not follow that an employer, guilty of no act denounced by the statute, has lost the right to protect and continue his business by supplying places left vacant by strikers. And he is not bound to discharge those hired to fill the places of strikers, upon the election of the latter to resume their employment, in order to create places for them. The assurance by respondent to those who accepted employment during the strike that if they so desired their places might be permanent was not an unfair labor practice nor was it such to reinstate only so many of the strikers as there were vacant places to be filled. But the claim put forward is that the unfair labor practice indulged by the respondent was discrimination in reinstating striking employees by keeping out certain of them for the sole reason that they had been active in the union. As we have said, the strikers retained, under the Act, the status of employees. Any such discrimination in putting them back to work is, therefore, prohibited by § 8.

The Board's findings as to discrimination are supported by evidence. We shall not attempt a discussion of the conflicting claims as to the proper conclusions to be drawn from the testimony. There was evidence, which the Board credited, that several of the five men in question were told that their union activities made them undesirable to their employer; and that some of them did not return to work with the great body of the men at 6 o'clock on Tuesday morning because they understood they would not be allowed to go to work until the superior officials had passed upon their applications. When they did apply at times between Tuesday morning and Thursday they were each told that the quota was full and that their applications could not be granted in any event until a vacancy occurred. This was on the ground that five of the eleven new men remained at work in San Francisco. On the other hand, six of the eleven strikers listed for separate treatment who reported for work early Tuesday morning, or within the next day or so, were permitted to go back to work and were not compelled to await the approval of their applications. It appears that all of the men who had been on strike signed applications for reemployment shortly after their resumption of work. The Board found, and we cannot say that its finding is unsupported, that, in taking back six of the eleven men and excluding five who were active union men, the respondent's officials discriminated against the latter on account of their union activities and that the excuse given that they did not apply until after the quota was full was an afterthought and not the true reason for the discrimination against them.

As we have said, the respondent was not bound to displace men hired to take the strikers' places in order to provide positions for them. It might have refused reinstatement on the ground of skill or ability, but the Board found that it did not do so. It might have resorted to any one of a number of methods of determining which of its striking employees would have to wait because five men had taken permanent positions during the strike, but it is found that the preparation and use of the list, and the action taken by respondent, were with the purpose to discriminate against those most active in the union. There is evidence to support these findings.

The Board's order does not violate the Fifth Amendment. The respondent insists that the relation of employer and employee ceased at the inception of the strike. The plain meaning of the Act is that if men strike in connection with a current labor dispute their action is not to be construed as a renunciation of the employment relation and they remain employees for the remedial purposes specified in the Act. We have held that, in the exercise of the commerce power, Congress may impose upon contractual relationships reasonable regulations calculated to protect commerce against threatened industrial strife. *National Labor Relations Board* v. *Jones & Laughlin Steel Corp., 301 U. S. 1, 48.* The Board's order there sustained required the reinstatement of discharged employees. The requirement interfered with freedom of contract which the employer would have enjoyed except for the mandate of the statute. The provision of the Act continuing the relationship of employer and employee in the case of a strike as a consequence of, or in connection with, a current labor dispute is a regulation of the same sort and within the principle of our decision.

The affirmative relief ordered by the Board was within its powers and its order was not arbitrary or capricious.

As we have held in *National Labor Relations Board* v. *Pennsylvania Greyhound Lines, 303 U. S. 261,* the relief which the statute empowers the Board to grant is to be adapted to the situation which calls for redress. On the basis of the findings, five men who took part in the strike were discriminated against in connection with a blanket offer to reinstate striking employees. The Board enjoined further discrimination against employees by reason of union affiliation, but it could not grant complete relief in respect of the five men short of ordering that the discrimination be neutralized by their being given their former positions and reimbursed for the loss due to their lack of employment consequent upon the respondent's discrimination. The order is criticized as arbitrary in that it is said to award back pay to date of reinstatement with deductions only for what was earned to the date of the order. We do not so read it, and the Board admits that credit must be given for all sums earned to date of reinstatement, and so construes the order. It is further said that the order arbitrarily and unreasonably requires the notices to be posted to state that respondent will not discharge its reinstated employees for any reason whatever. This clause of the order is inartificially drawn, and counsel for the Board admit that it should be read in connection with the remainder of the order forbidding discharge on the ground of union activity. . . .

The judgment of the Circuit Court of Appeals is reversed and the cause is remanded to that court for further proceedings in conformity with this opinion.

Reversed.

Commentary

A recurring and controversial problem is the question of the extent to which an employer may speak on unionism to his employees. In the following decision the Court deals with the delicate task of balancing employer interference and his right of free speech. The N. L. R. B. had found that the employer had violated the act by posting a bulletin appealing to the employees to bargain with it directly without the intervention of an "outside" union, and by delivering a speech urging the employees to organize independently of "outside" assistance. Reviewing the Board's order, the Court held that an employer is constitutionally protected in expressing his views on labor problems so long as the statements do not amount to "coercion." As to the employer's statements just mentioned, the Court found it "difficult to sustain a finding of coercion with respect to them alone," but indicated that they might support such a finding if considered as part of a coercive "course of conduct."

N.L.R.B. v. *Virginia Electric & Power Co.*
314 U.S. 469 (1941)

MR. JUSTICE MURPHY delivered the opinion of the Court.

Upon the usual proceedings had pursuant to § 10 of the National Labor Relations Act, the Board made substantially the following findings of fact:

For years prior to the events in the case the Virginia Electric and Power Company (hereinafter called the Company) was hostile to labor organizations. From 1922, when a strike was unsuccessfully called by a nationally affiliated union, until the formation of the Independent Organization of Employees (hereinafter called the Independent) in 1937, there was no labor organization among its employees. Shortly after the enactment of the National Industrial Recovery Act in 1933, Holtzclaw, the president of the Company, spoke to the employees and stated that any organization among them was "entirely unnecessary." Until his death, in May 1937, the Company utilized the services of one Walters, an employee of the Railway Audit and Inspection Company, who, prior to the effective date of the Act, admittedly furnished a report on the labor activity of the employees to the Company. In 1936, Bishop, Superintendent of Transportation in Norfolk, interrogated employees concerning union activities. On April 26, 1937, shortly after the Act was upheld, and an A. F. of L. organizer had appeared, the Company posted a bulletin throughout its operations, appealing to the employees to

---

The bulletin read as follows:

April 26, 1937.

To the Employees of the Company:

As a result of recent national labor organization activities and the interpretation of the Wagner Labor Act by the Supreme Court, employees of such companies such as

bargain with the Company directly, without the intervention of an "outside" union, and thereby coerced its employees. In response to this bulletin several requests for increased wages and better working conditions were received. The Company decided to withhold action on those requests, and directed its employees to select representatives to attend meetings at which Company officials would speak on the Wagner Act. These representatives met in Norfolk and Richmond on May 24, and were addressed by high Company officials, who read identical speeches stressing the desirability of forming a bargaining agency. At the Richmond meeting it was announced that any wage increase granted would be retroactive to June 1. By the substance of the speeches and the mechanics of the meetings, the Company gave impetus to, and assured the creation of, an "inside" organization, and coerced its employees in the exercise of their rights guaranteed by § 7 of the Act. Meetings, arranged with the cooperation of Company supervisors, on Company property, and, in some instances, on Company time, followed, at which the May 24 speeches were reported to the men who voted to form an "inside" organization and selected committees for that purpose. These committees met on Company property until June 15, when the constitution of the Independent was adopted.

While the Independent was in the process of organization, Edwards, a

---

ours may be approached in the near future by representatives of one or more such labor organizations to solicit their membership. Such campaigns are now being pressed in various industries and in different parts of the country and strikes and unrest have developed in many localities. For the last fifteen years this Company and its employees have enjoyed a happy relationship of mutual confidence and understanding with each other, and during this period there has not been any labor organization among our employees in any department, so far as the management is aware. Under these circumstances, we feel that our employees are entitled to know certain facts and have a statement as to the Company's attitude with reference to this matter.

The Company recognizes the right of every employee to join any union that he may wish to join, and such membership will not affect his position with the Company. On the other hand, we feel that it should be made equally clear to each employee that it is not at all necessary for him to join any labor organization, despite anything he may be told to the contrary. Certainly, there is no law which requires or is intended to compel you to pay dues to, or to join any organization.

This Company has always dealt with its employees in full recognition of the right of every individual employee, or group of employees, to deal directly with the Company with respect to matters affecting their interests. If any of you, individually or as a group, at any time, have any matter which you wish to discuss with us, any officer or department head will be glad, as they always have been, to meet with you and discuss them frankly and fully. It is our earnest desire to straighten out in a friendly manner, as we have done in the past, whatever questions you may have in mind. It is reasonable to believe that our interests are mutual and can best be promoted through confidence and cooperation.

J. G. Holtzclaw,
President.

supervisor, kept meetings of a rival C.I.O. union under surveillance and warned employees that they would be discharged for "messing with the C.I.O." On June 1, Mann, a member of the C.I.O. who had openly protested against an "inside" union at one of the May 11 meetings attended by Superintendent Bishop's son, Warren, was discharged for union activities.

On June 17, application cards for the Independent were distributed throughout the entire system of the Company, and many were signed on Company property and time. Within three weeks after the adoption of the constitution of the Independent, a majority of the employees filled out application cards. By July 13, the organization was complete, and permanent committeemen had been elected. A majority of those committeemen had been present at the May 24 meetings. On July 19, the Independent notified the Company that it represented a majority of the employees, and submitted a proposed contract. Negotiations were begun on July 30, and agreement was reached by midnight of the following day. The contract was formally executed on August 5, and provided, *inter alia,* for a closed shop, a check-off, and a wage increase. On August 20, the Company paid $3,784.50 to the Independent, although it had not yet deducted that entire amount from the employees' wages. On November 4, the date upon which the closed shop provision became effective, the Company discharged two employees, Staunton and Elliott, because they refused to join the Independent. In March, 1938, it discharged another employee, Harrell, for his membership and activity in an outside union.

Upon the basis of these findings and the entire record in the case, the Board concluded that the Company had committed unfair labor practices within the meaning of § 8 (1), (2) and (3) of the Act. Its order directed the Company to cease and desist from its unfair labor practices and from giving effect to its contract with the Independent, to withdraw recognition from and disestablish that organization, to reinstate with back pay the four wrongfully discharged employees, to reimburse each of its employees who was a member of the Independent in the amount of the dues and assessments checked off his wages by the Company on behalf of the Independent, and to post appropriate notices.

The Company and the Independent filed separate petitions in the court below to review and set aside the Board's order. The Board answered and requested enforcement of its order against the Company. The court below denied enforcement to any part of the Board's order, completely setting it aside. We granted the petition for writs of certiorari because the case was thought to present important questions in the administration of the Act. 312 U. S. 677. . . .

DOMINATION OF THE INDEPENDENT

The command of § 10 (e) of the Act that "the findings of the Board as to the facts, if supported by evidence, shall be conclusive," precludes an independent consideration of the facts. Bearing this in mind, we must ever guard against allowing our views to be substituted for those of the agency which Congress has created to administer the Act. But here the Board's conclusion that the Independent was a company-dominated union seems based heavily upon findings which are not free from ambiguity and doubt. We believe that the Board, and not this Court, should undertake the task of clarification.

The Board specifically found that the bulletin of April 26 and the speeches of May 24 "interfered with, restrained and coerced" the Company's employees in the exercise of their rights guaranteed by § 7 of the Act. The Company strongly urges that such a finding is repugnant to the First Amendment. Neither the Act nor the Board's order here enjoins the employer from expressing its view on labor policies or problems, nor is a penalty imposed upon it because of any utterances which it has made. The sanctions of the Act are imposed not in punishment of the employer but for the protection of the employees. The employer in this case is as free now as ever to take any side it may choose on this controversial issue. But, certainly, conduct, though evidenced in part by speech, may amount, in connection with other circumstances, to coercion within the meaning of the Act. If the total activities of an employer restrain or coerce his employees in their free choice, then those employees are entitled to the protection of the Act. And in determining whether a course of conduct amounts to restraint or coercion, pressure exerted vocally by the employer may no more be disregarded than pressure exerted in other ways. For "Slight suggestions as to the employer's choice between unions may have telling effect among men who know the consequences of incurring that employer's strong displeasure." *International Association of Machinists* v. *National Labor Relations Board,* 311 U. S. 72, 78.

If the Board's order here may fairly be said to be based on the totality of the Company's activities during the period in question, we may not consider the findings of the Board as to the coercive effect of the bulletin and the speeches in isolation from the findings as respects the other conduct of the Company. If the Board's ultimate conclusion is based upon a complex of activities, such as the anti-union background of the Company, the activities of Bishop, Edward's warning to the employees that they would be discharged for "messing with the C.I.O.," the discharge of Mann, the quick formation of the Independent, and the part which the management may have played in that formation, that conclusion would not be vitiated by the fact that the Board considered what the Company said in conjunction with what it did. The mere fact that language merges into a course of conduct does not put that whole course without the range of otherwise applicable administrative power. In determining whether the Company actually interfered with, restrained, and coerced its employees, the Board has a right to look at what the Company has said, as well as what it has done.

But, from the Board's decision, we are far from clear that the Board here considered the whole complex of activities, of which the bulletin and the speeches are but parts, in reaching its ultimate conclusion with regard to the Independent. The Board regarded the bulletin, on its face, as showing a marked bias against national unions by implying that strikes and unrest are caused by the organizational campaigns of such bodies, by stressing the "happy relationship of mutual confidence and understanding" prevailing in the absence of organization since the defeat of the Amalgamated in 1922, and by emphasizing the negative "right" of the employees to refrain from exercising their rights guaranteed under the Act, after paying "lip service" to those rights. Summing up its conclusions, the Board said: "We interpret the bulletin as an appeal to the employees to bargain with respondent directly, without the intervention of any "outside' union. We find that by posting the bulletin the respondent interfered with, restrained, and coerced its employees in the exercise of the rights guaranteed in Section 7 of the Act."

The Board was of the view that the speeches delivered in the meetings of May 24 provided the impetus for the formation of a system-wide organization, that they reemphasized the Company's distaste for "outside" organizations by referring to the bulletin, and that, after quoting the provision of the Act forbidding employer domination of labor organizations, they suggested that the employees select their "own" officers, and adopt their "own" bylaws and rules. The Board's finding was: "We find that at the May 24 meetings the respondent urged its employees to organize and to do so independently of 'outside' assistance, and that it thereby interfered with, restrained, and coerced its employees in the exercise of the rights guaranteed in Section 7 of the Act."

It is clear that the Board specifically found that those utterances were unfair labor practices, and it does not appear that the Board raised them to the stature of coercion by reliance on the surrounding circumstances. If the utterances are thus to be separated from their background, we find it difficult to sustain a finding of coercion with respect to them alone. The bulletin and the speeches set forth the right of the employees to do as they please without fear of retaliation by the Company. Perhaps the purport of these utterances may be altered by imponderable subtleties at work, which it is not our function to appraise. Whether there are sufficient findings and evidence of interference, restraint, coercion, and domination, without reference to the bulletin and the speeches, or whether the whole course of conduct, evidenced in part by the utterances, was aimed at achieving objectives forbidden by the Act, are questions for the Board to decide upon the evidence. Here, we are not sufficiently certain from the findings that the

Board based its conclusion with regard to the Independent upon the whole course of conduct revealed by this record. Rather, it appears that the Board rested heavily upon findings with regard to the bulletin and the speeches, the adequacy of which we regard as doubtful. We therefore remand the cause to the Circuit Court of Appeals with directions to remand it to the Board for a redetermination of the issues in the light of this opinion.

We do not mean to intimate any views of our own as to whether the Independent was dominated, or suggest to the Board what its conclusion should be when it reconsiders the case. Since the Board rested the remainder of its order in large part on its findings with respect to the domination of the Independent, we do not at this time reach the other parts of the Board's order. including the command that the checked-off dues and assessments should be refunded.

Reversed and remanded.

Commentary

The Wagner Act adopted the doctrine of majority rule, that is, that the representative designated by a majority of the employees in an appropriate bargaining unit is the exclusive representative of such employees. This doctrine has become a cardinal principle of labor relations in interstate industry. Its impact is reflected in the following case, in which the employer contended that individual employment contracts, not in themselves illegal, prevented him from dealing with a union in any manner affecting rights and obligations under the individual contracts while they remained in effect. The Court rejected this contention, holding that individual contracts could not defeat the procedures of the Act, nor could they forestall collective bargaining or limit the terms of the collective agreement.

N.L.R.B. v. J. I. Case Co.
321 U.S. 332 (1944)

MR. JUSTICE JACKSON delivered the opinion of the Court.

This cause was heard by the National Labor Relations Board on stipulated facts which so far as concern present issues are as follows:

The petitioner, J. I. Case Company, at its Rock Island, Illinois, plant, from 1937 offered each employee an individual contract of employment. The contracts were uniform and for a term of one year. The Company agreed to furnish employment as steadily as conditions permitted, to pay a specified rate, which the Company might redetermine if the job changed, and to maintain certain hospital facilities. The employee agreed to accept the provisions, to serve faithfully and honestly for the term, to comply with factory rules, and that defective work should not be paid for. About 75% of the employees accepted and worked under these agreements.

According to the Board's stipulation and finding, the execution of the contracts was not a condition of employment, nor was the status of individual employees affected by reason of signing or failing to sign the contracts. It is not found or contended that the agreements were coerced, obtained by any unfair labor practice, or that they were not valid under the circumstances in which they were made.

While the individual contracts executed August 1, 1941 were in effect, a C.I.O. union petitioned the Board for certification as the exclusive bargaining representative of the production and maintenance employees. On December 17, 1941 a hearing was held, at which the Company urged the individual contracts as a bar to representation proceedings. The Board, however, directed an election, which was won by the union. The union was thereupon certified as the exclusive bargaining representative of the employees in question in respect to wages, hours, and other conditions of employment.

The union then asked the Company to bargain. It refused, declaring that it could not deal with the union in any manner affecting rights and obligations under the individual contracts while they remained in effect. It offered to negotiate on matters which did not affect rights under the individual contracts, and said that upon the expiration of the contracts it would bargain as to all matters. Twice the Company sent circulars to its employees asserting the validity of the individual contracts and stating the position that it took before the Board in reference to them.

The Board held that the Company had refused to bargain collectively, in violation of § 8 (5) of the National Labor Relations Act; and that the contracts had been utilized, by means of the circulars, to impede employees in the exercise of rights guaranteed by § 7 of the Act, with the result that the Company had engaged in unfair labor practices within the meaning of § 8 (1) of the Act. It ordered the Company to cease and desist from giving effect to the contracts, from extending them or entering into new ones, from refusing to bargain and from interfering with the employees; and it required the Company to give notice accordingly and to bargain upon request.

The Circuit Court of Appeals, with modification not in issue here, granted an order of enforcement. The issues are unsettled ones important in the administration of the Act, and we granted certiorari. In doing so we asked counsel, in view of the expiration of the individual contracts and the negotiation of a collective contract, to discuss whether the case was moot. In view of the continuing character of the obligation imposed by the order we think it is not, and will examine the merits.

Contract in labor law is a term the implications of which must be determined from the connection in which it appears. Collective bargaining between employer and the representatives of a unit, usually a union, results in an accord as to terms which will govern hiring and work and pay in that unit. The result is not, however, a contract of employment except in rare cases; no one has a job by reason of it and no obligation to any individual ordinarily comes into existence from it alone. The negotiations between union and management result in what often has been called a trade agreement, rather than in a contract of employment. Without pushing the analogy too far, the agreement may be likened to the tariffs established by a carrier, to standard provisions prescribed by supervising authorities for insurance policies, or to utility schedules of rates and rules for service, which do not of themselves establish any relationships but which do govern the terms of the shipper or insurer or customer relationship whenever and with whomever it may be established. Indeed, in some European countries, contrary to American practice, the terms of a collectively negotiated trade agreement are submitted to a government department and if approved become a governmental regulation ruling employment in the unit.

After the collective trade agreement is made, the individuals who shall benefit by it are identified by individual hirings. The employer, except as restricted by the collective agreement itself and except that he must engage in no unfair labor practice or discrimination, is free to select those he will employ or discharge. But the terms of the employment already have been traded out. There is little left to individual agreement except the act of hiring. This hiring may be by writing or by word of mouth or may be implied from conduct. In the sense of contracts of hiring, individual contracts between the employer and employee are not forbidden, but indeed are necessitated by the collective bargaining procedure.

But, however engaged, an employee becomes entitled by virtue of the Labor Relations Act somewhat as a third party beneficiary to all benefits of the collective trade agreement, even if on his own he would yield to less favorable terms. The individual hiring contract is subsidiary to the terms of the trade agreement and may not waive any of its benefits, any more than a shipper can contract away the benefit of filed tariffs, the insurer the benefit of standard provisions, or the utility customer the benefit of legally established rates.

Concurrent existence of these two types of agreement raises problems as to which the National Labor Relations Act makes no express provision. We have, however, held that individual contracts obtained as the result of an unfair labor practice may not be the basis of advantage to the violator of the Act nor of disadvantage to employees. *National Licorice Co.* v. *Labor Board,* 309 U. S. 350. But it is urged that where, as here, the contracts were not unfairly or unlawfully obtained, the court indicated a contrary rule in *Labor Board* v. *Jones & Laughlin Steel Corp.,* 301 U. S. 1,

44–45, and *Virginian Ry. Co.* v. *System Federation,* 300 U.S. 515, without reviewing those cases in detail, it may be said that their decision called for nothing and their opinions contain nothing which may be properly read to rule the case before us. The court in those cases recognized the existence of some scope for individual contracts, but it did not undertake to define it or to consider the relations between lawful individual and collective agreements, which is the problem now before us.

Care has been taken in the opinions of the Court to reserve a field for the individual contract, even in industries covered by the National Labor Relations Act, not merely as an act or evidence of hiring, but also in the sense of a completely individually bargained contract setting out terms of employment, because there are circumstances in which it may legally be used, in fact, in which there is no alternative. Without limiting the possibilities, instances such as the following will occur: Men may continue work after a collective agreement expires and, despite negotiation in good faith, the negotiation may be deadlocked or delayed; in the interim express or implied individual agreements may be held to govern. The conditions for collective bargaining may not exist; thus a majority of the employees may refuse to join a union or to agree upon or designate bargaining representatives, or the majority may not be demonstrable by the means prescribed by the statute, or a previously existent majority may have been lost without unlawful interference by the employer and no new majority have been formed. As the employer in these circumstances may be under no legal obligation to bargain collectively, he may be free to enter into individual contracts.

Individual contracts, no matter what the circumstances that justify their execution or what their terms, may not be availed of to defeat or delay the procedures prescribed by the National Labor Relations Act looking to collective bargaining, nor to exclude the contracting employee from a duly ascertained bargaining unit; nor may they be used to forestall bargaining or to limit or condition the terms of the collective agreement. "The Board asserts a public right vested in it as a public body, charged in the public interest with the duty of preventing unfair labor practices." *National Licorice Co.* v. *Labor Board,* 309 U. S. 350, 364. Wherever private contracts conflict with its functions, they obviously must yield or the Act would be reduced to a futility.

It is equally clear since the collective trade agreement is to serve the purpose contemplated by the Act, the individual contract cannot be effective as a waiver of any benefit to which the employee otherwise would be entitled under the trade agreement. The very purpose of providing by statute for the collective agreement is to supersede the terms of separate agreements of employees with terms which reflect the strength and bargaining power and serve the welfare of the group. Its benefits and advantages are open to every employee of the represented unit, whatever the type or terms of his pre-existing contract of employment.

But it is urged that some employees may lose by the collective agreement, that an individual workman may sometimes have, or be capable of getting, better terms than those obtainable by the group and that his freedom of contract must be respected on that account. We are not called upon to say that under no circumstances can an individual enforce an agreement more advantageous than a collective agreement, but we find the mere possibility that such agreements might be made, no ground for holding generally that individual contracts may survive or surmount collective ones. The practice and philosophy of collective bargaining looks with suspicion on such individual advantages. Of course, where there is great variation in circumstances of employment or capacity of employees, it is possible for the collective bargain to prescribe only minimum rates or maximum hours or expressly to leave certain areas open to individual bargaining. But except as so provided, advantages to individuals may prove as disruptive of industrial peace as disadvantages. They are a fruitful way of interfering with organization and choice of representatives; increased compensation, if individually deserved, is often earned at the cost of breaking down some other standard thought to be for the welfare of the group, and always creates the suspicion of being paid at the long-range expense of the group as a whole. Such discriminations not infrequently amount to unfair labor practices. The workman is free, if he values his own bargaining position more than that of the group, to vote against representation; but the majority rules, and if it collectivizes the employment bargain, individual advantages or favors will generally in practice go in as a contribution to the collective result. We cannot except individual contracts generally from the operation of collective ones because some may be more individually advantageous. Individual contracts cannot subtract from collective ones, and whether under some circumstances they may add to them in matters covered by the collective bargain, we leave to be determined by appropriate forums under the laws of contracts applicable, and to the Labor Board if they constitute unfair labor practices.

It also is urged that such individual contracts may embody matters that are not necessarily included within the statutory scope of collective bargaining, such as stock purchase, group insurance, hospitalization, or medical attention. We know of nothing to prevent the employee's, because he is an employee, making any contract provided it is not inconsistent with a collective agreement or does not amount to or result from or is not part of an unfair labor practice. But in so doing the employer may not incidentally exact or obtain any diminution of his own obligation or any increase of those of employees in the matters covered by collective agreement.

Hence we find that the contentions of the Company that the individual contracts precluded a choice of representatives and warranted refusal to bargain during their duration were properly overruled. It follows that representation to the employees by circular letter that they had such legal effect was improper and could properly be prohibited by the Board. . . .

As so modified the decree is

Affirmed.

Commentary

Does an employer commit an unfair labor practice when he closes his entire business "because of distaste for unionism"? Is a partial closing so motivated governed by the same considerations? Not until 1965 did the Supreme Court answer these questions. As to the first question, the answer was an unqualified no. But, said the Court, a partial closing is an unfair labor practice "if motivated by a purpose to chill unionism in any of the remaining plants of the single employer and if the employer may reasonably have foreseen that such closing will likely have that effect."

Textile Workers of America v. *Darlington Manufacturing Co.*
N.L.R.B. v. *Darlington Mfg. Co.*
380 U.S. 263 (1965)

MR. JUSTICE HARLAN delivered the opinion of the Court.

We here review judgments of the Court of Appeals setting aside and refusing to enforce an order of the National Labor Relations Board which found respondent Darlington guilty of an unfair labor practice by reason of having permanently closed its plant following petitioner union's election as the bargaining representative of Darlington's employes.

Darlington Manufacturing Company was a South Carolina corporation operating one textile mill. A majority of Darlington's stock was held by Deering Milliken, a New York "selling house" marketing textiles produced by others. Deering Milliken in turn was controlled by Roger Milliken, president of Darlington, and by other members of the Milliken family. The National Labor Relations Board found that the Milliken family, through Deering Milliken, operated 17 textile manufacturers, including Darlington, whose products, manufactured in 27 different mills, were marketed through Deering Milliken.

In March 1956 petitioner Textile Workers Union initiated an organizational campaign at Darlington which the Company resisted vigorously in various ways, including threats to close the mill if the union won a representation election. On September 6, 1956, the union won an election by a narrow margin. When Roger Milliken was advised of the union victory, he decided to call a meeting of the Darlington board of directors to consider closing the mill. Mr. Milliken testified before the Labor Board:

> I felt as a result of the campaign that had been conducted and the promises and statements made in these letters that had been distributed [favoring unionization], that if before we had had some hope, possible hope of achieving competitive [costs] . . . by taking advantage of new machinery that was being put in, that this hope had diminished as a result of the election because a majority of the employees had voted in favor of the union. . . . (R. 457.)

The board of directors met on September 12 and voted to liquidate the corporation, action which was approved by the stockholders on October 17. The plant ceased operations entirely in November, and all plant machinery and equipment were sold piecemeal at auction in December.

The union filed charges with the Labor Board claiming that Darlington had violated §§ 8 (a) (1) and (3) of the National Labor Relations Act by closing its plant, and § 8 (a) (5) by refusing to bargain with the union after the election. The Board, by a divided vote, found that Darlington had been closed because of the anti-union animus of Roger Milliken, and held that to be a violation of § 8 (a) (3). The Board also found Darlington to be part of a single integrated employer group controlled by the Milliken family through Deering Milliken; therefore Deering Milliken could be held liable for the unfair labor practices of Darlington. Alternatively, since Darlington was a part of the Deering Milliken enterprise, Deering Milliken had violated the Act by closing part of its business for a discriminatory purpose. The Board ordered back pay for all Darlington employees until they obtained substantially equivalent work or were put on preferential hiring lists at the other Deering Milliken mills. Respondent Deering Milliken was ordered to bargain with the union in regard to details of compliance with the Board order. 139 N. L. R. B. 241.

On review, the Court of Appeals, sitting *en banc,* set aside the order and denied enforcement by a divided vote. 325 F. 2d 682. The Court of Appeals held that even accepting *arguendo* the Board's determination that Deering Milliken had the status of a single employer, a company has the absolute right to close out a part or all of its business regardless of anti-union motives. The court therefore did not review the Board's finding that Deering Milliken was a single integrated employer. We granted certiorari, 377 U. S. 903, to consider the important questions involved. We hold that so far as the Labor Relations Act is concerned, an employer has the absolute right to terminate his entire business for any reason he pleases, but disagree with the Court of Appeals that such right includes the ability to close part of a business no matter what the reason. We conclude that the cause must be remanded to the Board for further proceedings.

Preliminarily it should be observed that both petitioners argue that the

Darlington closing violated § 8 (a) (1) as well as § 8 (a) (3) of the Act. We think, however, that the Board was correct in treating the closing only under § 8 (a) (3). Section 8 (a) (1) provides that it is an unfair labor practice for an employer "to interfere with, restrain, or coerce employees in the exercise of" § 7 rights. Naturally, certain business decisions will, to some degree, interfere with concerted activities by employees. But it is only when the interference with § 7 rights outweighs the business justification for the employer's action that § 8 (a) (1) is violated. See, e. g., *Labor Board* v. *Steelworkers,* 357 U. S. 357; *Republic Aviation Corp.* v. *Labor Board,* 324 U. S. 793. A violation of § 8 (a) (1) alone therefore presupposes an act which is unlawful even absent a discriminatory motive. Whatever may be the limits of § 8 (a) (1), some employer decisions are so peculiarly matters of management prerogative that they would never constitute violations of § 8 (a) (1), whether or not they involved sound business judgment, unless they also violated § 8 (a) (3). Thus it is not questioned in this case that an employer has the right to terminate his business, whatever the impact of such action on concerted activities, if the decision to close is motivated by other than discriminatory reasons. But such action, if discriminatorily motivated, is encompassed within the literal language of § 8 (a) (3). We therefore deal with the Darlington closing under that section.

We consider first the argument, advanced by the petitioner union but not by the Board, and rejected by the Court of Appeals, that an employer may not go completely out of business without running afoul of the Labor Relations Act if such action is prompted by a desire to avoid unionization. Given the Board's findings on the issue of motive, acceptance of this contention would carry the day for the Board's conclusion that the closing of this plant was an unfair labor practice, even on the assumption that Darlington is to be regarded as an independent unrelated employer. A proposition that a single businessman cannot choose to go out of business if he wants to would represent such a startling innovation that it should not be entertained without the clearest manifestation of legislative intent or unequivocal judicial precedent so construing the Labor Relations Act. We find neither.

So far as legislative manifestation is concerned, it is sufficient to say that there is not the slightest indication in the history of the Wagner Act or of the Taft-Hartley Act that Congress envisaged any such result under either statute.

As for judicial precedent, the Board recognized that "[t]here is no decided case directly dispositive of Darlington's claim that it had an absolute right to close its mill, irrespective of motive." 139 N. L. R. B., at 250. The only language by this Court in any way adverting to this problem is found in *Southport Petroleum Co.* v. *Labor Board,* 315 U. S. 100, 106, where it was stated: "Whether there was a *bona fide* discontinuance and a true change of ownership—which would terminate the duty of reinstatement created by the Board's order—or merely a disguised continuance of the old employer, does not clearly appear . . . ."

The courts of appeals have generally assumed that a complete cessation of business will remove an employer from future coverage by the Act. Thus the Court of Appeals said in these cases: The Act "does not compel a person to become or remain an employee. It does not compel one to become or remain an employer. Either may withdraw from that status with immunity, so long as the obligations of any employment contract have been met." 325 F. 2d, at 685. The Eighth Circuit, in *Labor Board* v. *New Madrid Mfg. Co.,* 215 F. 2d 908, 914, was equally explicit:

But none of this can be taken to mean that an employer does not have the absolute right, at all times, to permanently close and go out of business . . . for whatever reason he may choose, whether union animosity or anything else, and without his being thereby left subject to a remedial liability under the Labor Management Relations Act for such unfair labor practices as he may have committed in the enterprise, except up to the time that such actual and permanent closing . . . has occurred.

The AFL–CIO suggests in its *amicus* brief that Darlington's action was similar to a discriminatory lockout, which is prohibited " 'because designed to frustrate organizational efforts, to destroy or undermine bargaining representation, or to evade the duty to bargain.' " One of the purposes of the Labor Relations Act is to prohibit the discriminatory use of economic weapons in an effort to obtain future benefits. The discriminatory lockout designed to destroy a union, like a "runaway shop," is a lever which has been used to discourage collective employee activities in the future. But a complete liquidation of a business yields no such future benefit for the employer, if the termination is bona fide. It may be motivated more by spite against the union than by business reasons, but it is not the type of discrimination which is prohibited by the Act. The personal satisfaction that such an employer may derive from standing on his beliefs and the mere possibility that other employers will follow his example are surely too remote to be considered dangers at which the labor statutes are aimed. Although employees may be prohibited from engaging in a strike under certain conditions, no one would consider it a violation of the Act for the same employees to quit their employment *en masse,* even if motivated by a desire to ruin the employer. The very permanence of such action would negate any future economic benefit to the employees. The employer's right to go out of business is no different.

We are not presented here with the case of a "runaway shop," whereby Darlington would transfer its work to another plant or open a new plant in another locality to replace its closed plant. Nor are we concerned with a shutdown where the employees, by renouncing the union, could cause the plant to reopen. Such cases would involve discriminatory employer action for the purpose of obtaining some benefit from the employees in the future. We hold here that only when an employer closes his business, even if the liquidation is motivated by vindictiveness toward the union, such action is not an unfair labor practice.

While we thus agree with the Court of Appeals that viewing Darlington as an independent employer the liquidation of its business was not an unfair labor practice, we cannot accept the lower court's view that the same conclusion necessarily follows if Darlington is regarded as an integral part of the Deering Milliken enterprise.

The closing of an entire business, even though discriminatory, ends the employer-employee relationship; the force of such a closing is entirely spent as to that business when termination of the enterprise takes place. On the other hand, a discriminatory partial closing may have repercussions on what remains of the business, affording employer leverage for discouraging the free exercise of § 7 rights among remaining employees of much the same kind as that found to exist in the "runaway shop" and "temporary closing" cases. See *supra*, pp. 272–273. Moreover, a possible remedy open to the Board in such a case, like the remedies available in the "runaway shop" and "temporary closing" cases, is to order reinstatement of the discharged employees in the other parts of the business. No such remedy is available when an entire business has been terminated. By analogy to those cases involving a continuing enterprise we are constrained to hold, in disagreement with the Court of Appeals, that a partial closing is an unfair labor practice under § 8 (a) (3) if motivated by a purpose to chill unionism in any of the remaining plants of the single employer and if the employer may reasonably have foreseen that such closing would likely have that effect.

While we have spoken in terms of a "partial closing" in the context of the Board's finding that Darlington was part of a larger single enterprise controlled by the Milliken family, we do not mean to suggest that an organizational integration of plants or corporations is a necessary prerequisite to the establishment of such a violation of § 8 (a) (3). If the persons exercising control over a plant that is being closed for antiunion reasons (1) have an interest in another business, whether or not affiliated with or engaged in the same line of commercial activity as the closed plant, of sufficient substantiality to give promise of their reaping a benefit from the discouragement of unionization in that business; (2) act to close their plant with the purpose of producing such a result; and (3) occupy a relationship to the other business which makes it realistically foreseeable that its employees will fear that such business will also be closed down if they persist in organizational activities, we think that an unfair labor practice has been made out.

Although the Board's single employer finding necessarily embraced findings as to Roger Milliken and the Milliken family which, if sustained by the Court of Appeals, would satisfy the elements of "interest" and "relationship" with respect to other parts of the Deering Milliken enterprise, that and the other Board findings fall short of establishing the factors of "purpose" and "effect" which are vital requisites of the general principles that govern a case of this kind.

Thus, the Board's findings as to the purpose and foreseeable effect of the Darlington closing pertained *only* to its impact on the Darlington employees. No findings were made as to the purpose and effect of the closing with respect to the employees in the other plants comprising the Deering Milliken group. It does not suffice to establish the unfair labor practice charged here to argue that the Darlington closing necessarily had an adverse impact upon unionization in such other plants. We have heretofore observed that employer action which has a foreseeable consequence of discouraging concerted activities generally does not amount to a violation of § 8 (a) (3) in the absence of a showing of motivation which is aimed at achieving the prohibited effect. See *Teamsters Local* v. *Labor Board,* 365 U. S. 667, and the concurring opinion therein, at 677. In an area which trenches so closely upon otherwise legitimate employer prerogatives, we consider the absence of Board findings on this score a fatal defect in its decision. The Court of Appeals for its part did not deal with the question of purpose and effect at all, since it concluded that an employer's right to close down his entire business because of distaste for unionism, also embraced a partial closing so motivated.

Apart from this, the Board's holding should not be accepted or rejected without court review of its single employer finding, judged, however, in accordance with the general principles set forth above. Review of that finding, which the lower court found unnecessary on its view of the cause, now becomes necessary in light of our holding in this part of our opinion, and is a task that devolves upon the Court of Appeals in the first instance. *Universal Camera Corp.* v. *Labor Board,* 340 U. S. 474.

In these circumstances, we think the proper disposition of this cause is to require that it be remanded to the Board so as to afford the Board the opportunity to make further findings on the issue of purpose and effect. See, *e. g., Labor Board* v. *Virginia Elec. & Power Co.,* 314 U. S. 469, 479–480. This is particularly appropriate here since the cases involve issues of first impression. If such findings are made, the cases will then be in a posture for further review by the Court of Appeals on all issues. Accordingly, without intimating any view as to how any of these matters should eventuate, we vacate the judgments of the Court of Appeals and remand the cases to that court with instructions to remand them to the Board for further proceedings consistent with this opinion.

It is so ordered.

THE FAIR LABOR STANDARDS ACT OF 1938
(As Amended)

Commentary

The Wagner Act, of course, was but one of a number of statutes passed during the New Deal focusing on labor conditions. But, in a sense, it was a culmination of years of employee attempts to establish minimum wages and maximum hours. As early as 1868, Congress had established a ten-hour day for employees on public works. Subsequently, the government's efforts to establish labor standards related largely to work conditions under public contract and to interstate mail transportation, although Congress did attempt to control child labor through its commerce and taxing powers. The idea was for the government to set an example for private employers to follow. But the inability to establish minimum working conditions through Congress also reflected labor's national political weakness. Workingmen's organizations were often much more successful at the state level. Child labor laws, for example, were enacted in the six New England states by the mid-nineteenth century, and by 1900 some twenty-eight states had at least minimal protection for child workers. Today, there exists in every state a considerable body of law covering the employment of women and children, sanitation, and safety. Much of this sort of legislation, both state and federal, was challenged in the courts by employers and often declared unconstitutional. Thus, the Supreme Court upheld in 1898 a state statute fixing maximum hours for male miners (*Holden* v. *Hardy,* 169 U.S. 366), but subsequently decided in 1905 that it was unconstitutional for a state to limit work hours in bakeries (*Lochner* v. *New York,* 198 U.S. 45). The Court similarly struck down in 1923 state legislation fixing minimum wages in *Adkins* v. *Children's Hospital,* 261 U.S. 525. Federal regulation fared no better. An effort to control child labor was nullified by the Court in 1922 (*Bailey* v. *Drexel Furniture Company,* 259 U.S. 20). Further, the early efforts of the New Deal to regulate labor standards through the National Industrial Recovery Act [*Schechter Poultry Corporation* v. *United States,* 295 U.S. 495 (1935)] and the Bituminous Coal Conservation Act [*Carter* v. *Carter Coal Company,* 298 U.S. 238 (1936)] suffered the same fate. But in 1937, the Court sustained the constitutionality of the Wagner Act and upheld a state minimum wage law, in *West Coast Hotel Company* v. *Parrish,* 300 U.S. 379. Decisions such as these quite plainly forecast Court approval of federal legislation in the area of wages and hours. The landslide reelection of President Roosevelt in 1936 did not go unobserved by the Court. As Mr. Dooley sagely observed, "No matter whether th' constitution follos th' flag or not, th' supreme coort follos th' iliction returns."

On May 24, 1937, President Roosevelt, whose Administration consistently urged wage and hour legislation as an anti-depression measure, sent Congress a special message: "To conserve our primary resources of manpower, Government must have some control over maximum hours, minimum wages, the evil of child labor, and the exploitation of unorganized labor." The President argued that Congress' power to act in these matters rested on the Constitution's commerce clause. On the same day, Senator Eugene Black (Dem., Tex.) and Representative Lawrence Connery (Dem., Mass.) introduced bills to implement the Presidential request. But more than a year of legislative activity passed before a law was enacted. Joint hearings were held before the House Committee on Labor and the Senate Committee on Education and Labor at which representatives of labor, industry, various trade associations, and other interested organizations gave their views. Business and labor groups raised considerable objections on opposite sides of the enforcement question. Although the bill, with amendment, was favorably reported by the Senate Committee and passed the Senate, consideration of the bill was blocked in the House by the Rules Committee for the First Session of the Seventy-fourth Congress. In November, 1937, President Roosevelt called a special session. This time the Rules Committee could not keep the bill from the House floor, and a bill passed the House on May 24, 1938. The original bill had provided for administration of the law by a Fair Labor Standards Board of five members. The bill as passed made no such provision, entrusting administration to the Secretary of Labor. The bill returned to the Senate, which disagreed with the House bill, and the matter went to a joint conference committee. The forthcoming compromise measure was approved by both houses and signed by the President on June 25, 1938, as Public Law No. 718, the Fair Labor Standards Act of 1938.

The new statute created a Wage and Hour Division in the Department of Labor under the supervision of an administrator. The statute regulated wages, hours, and child labor. More specifically, it provided for a minimum hourly wage of twenty-five cents for the first year, and thirty cents for the second year. A minimum of forty cents was to become effective after seven years, and a wage between thirty and forty cents could be ordered during the first seven years. As to hours, it sought to spread employment by overtime penalties: for the first year maximum straight-time hours were forty-four; for the second year, forty-two; and thereafter forty. The child labor provisions, similar to those previously declared unconstitutional by the Supreme Court, prohibited the interstate shipment of goods produced in an establishment employing child labor.

Consistent with the constitutional philosophy exhibited in the Supreme Court's decisions to uphold the Wagner and Railway Labor Acts, the Court, in *United States* v. *Darby,* 312 U.S. 100 (1941), sustained the constitutionality of the act against attacks based upon the commerce clause and due process clause of the Fifth Amendment.

The Fair Labor Standards Act has been amended on a number of occasions. The first major change in the law resulted from the Portal-to-Portal

Act of 1947, the enactment clause of which reads: "An Act to relieve employers from certain liabilities and punishments under the Fair Labor Standards Act of 1938, as amended, the Walsh-Healey Act, and the Bacon-Davis Act, and for other purposes."

John L. Lewis and his miners had shut down the coal mines in 1943, seeking pay adjustments in line with the accelerated cost-of-living during wartime. Faced with a wage freeze, the miners demanded portal-to-portal pay for the time spent traveling from the pithead to the coal face. A Presidential committee found that miners spent, on the average, an hour traveling—and in some cases as much as three hours. The wartime War Labor Board finally allowed the miners forty-five minutes extra pay each day. "You can't shovel coal with machine guns" Lewis had declared. The award was challenged in the courts, and the Supreme Court held that certain preliminary and postliminary activities, such as travel time between the place of entrance and the place of work in mines and manufacturing plants was compensable working time. [*Tennessee Coal, Iron & Railway Company* v. *Muscoda Local 123,* 321 U.S. 590 (1944); *Jewell Ridge Coal Corp.* v. *Local 6167,* 325 U.S. 161 (1945); *Anderson* v. *Mt. Clemens Pottery Company,* 328 U.S. 690 (1946)] As a consequence, other unions initiated employee suits totaling more than six billion dollars in claims under the Court's interpretation of the Fair Labor Standards Act. When employers screamed, Congress deemed legislation necessary for relief from most of these and future claims. (The miners were a special case, after all.)

Another famous Supreme Court decision, issued in 1948, spurred further amendment of the Fair Labor Standards Act. In *Bay Ridge Operating Company* v. *Aaron,* the Court considered a collective agreement providing for premium pay or "overtime" for work beyond the regular shifts. The Court rejected the employer's contention that these payments were a form of overtime and that to include them in the employees' "regular rate" would constitute "overtime on overtime." The Court held that these premiums were a part of the regular rate; it defined true overtime premium as "any additional sum received by an employee for work because of previous work for a specified number of hours in the workweek or workday." Congress reversed this interpretation in the Overtime on Overtime Pay Claims Act of 1949.

In the meantime, a number of proposals had been made for revision of the act. These culminated in what was called the "Fair Labor Standards Amendments of 1949" which, among other things, repealed the Overtime on Overtime Act and incorporated its provisions. It has been pointed out that "the Amendments of 1949 were a compromise between President Truman's desire for a broader law to cover all employees of employers engaged in covered business, raise standards, and restrict exemptions, and the aims of those who wished to narrow the coverage, broaden the exemptions, and tie the minimum wage to the cost-of-living index." In brief, the 1949 amendments narrowed the coverage of the statute, strengthened the child labor prohibitions, set forth in greater detail the overtime standards, revised certain exemptions, made certain administrative changes, and increased the minimum wage to seventy-five cents.

There have been a number of amendments since 1949, the most important of which have increased the minimum wage and broadened statutory coverage. By the most recent amendments, those of 1966, the minimum hourly rate of most covered employees will reach $1.60 on specified future dates. Coverage was extended by the 1961 amendments through a new concept, the covering of specified business enterprises as well as the activities of individual employees; in 1966 the enterprise concept was utilized to further broaden coverage. In 1963 equal pay provisions were added to the act for the purpose of eliminating wage differentials based upon sex.

While the Fair Labor Standards Act unquestionably is the most important American statute dealing with wages and hours, other federal legislation, dealing with standards for employees of government contractors or employees in specified industries and occupations, merit brief mention. First, there is the Walsh-Healey (Public Contracts) Act of 1936, which contains provisions for the establishment of minimum wage rates and for the payment of daily and weekly overtime, and prohibits the employment of child labor with respect to government contracts exceeding $10,000 for supplies and equipment. The Davis-Bacon Act of 1931 provides for fixing minimum standards on federal works projects. The Copeland (Anti-Kickback) Act of 1934 makes it illegal to require that employees on public works "kickback" any part of their wages. The Eight-Hour Law and Work Hours Act limit the work hours of laborers and mechanics employed by contractors on federal public works.

Finally, there are a number of special statutes fixing labor standards affecting specific industries and occupations. These include: the Motor Carrier Act, which delegates to the Interstate Commerce Commission the authority to establish qualifications and maximum hours for certain employees of motor carriers; Part I of the Interstate Commerce Act, which limits the hours of employees on interstate railroads; the Merchant Marine Eight-Hour Act, which relates to the hours of work of certain employees in the merchant marine; the Civil Aeronautics Act of 1938, which limits the hours of pilots and co-pilots engaged in interstate transportation; and the Sugar Act of 1948, which contains child labor and minimum wage standards.

The Fair Labor Standards Act, as amended, is set forth in full below, and is followed by the subsequent materials relevant to the legislative history of the statute.

THE FAIR LABOR STANDARDS ACT
As Amended June 25, 1938[1]

An Act to provide for the establishment of fair labor standards in employments in and affecting interstate commerce, and for other purposes.

Be it enacted by the Senate and House of Representatives of the United States of America in Congress assembled, That this Act may be cited as the "Fair Labor Standards Act of 1938."

FINDING AND DECLARATION OF POLICY

SEC. 2. (a) The Congress hereby finds that the existence, in industries engaged in commerce or in the production of goods for commerce, of labor conditions detrimental to the maintenance of the minimum standard of living necessary for health, efficiency, and general well-being of workers (1) causes commerce and the channels and instrumentalities of commerce to be used to spread and perpetuate such labor conditions among the workers of the several States; (2) burdens commerce and the free flow of goods in commerce; (3) constitutes an unfair method of competition in commerce; (4) leads to labor disputes burdening and obstructing commerce and the free flow of goods in commerce; and (5) interferes with the orderly and fair marketing of goods in commerce.

(b) It is hereby declared to be the policy of this Act, through the exercise by Congress of its power to regulate commerce among the several States and with foreign nations, to correct and as rapidly as practicable to eliminate the conditions above referred to in such industries without substantially curtailing employments or earning power.[2]

---

[1] 52 Stat. 1060, as amended by the Act of August 9, 1939 (53 Stat. 1266); by section 404 of Reorganization Plan No. II of 1939 (53 Stat. 1436); by sections 3(c)—3(f) of the Act of June 26, 1940 (54 Stat. 615); by the Act of October 29, 1941 (55 Stat. 756); by Reorganization Plan No. 2 of 1946 (60 Stat. 1095); by the Portal-to-Portal Act of 1947 (61 Stat. 84); by the Act of July 20, 1949 (63 Stat. 446); by the Fair Labor Standards Amendments of 1949 (63 Stat. 910); by Reorganization Plan No. 6 of 1950 (64 Stat. 1263); by the Fair Labor Standards Amendments of 1955 (69 Stat. 711); by the American Samoa Labor Standards Amendments of 1956 (70 Stat. 1118); by the Act of August 30, 1957 (71 Stat. 514); by the Act of August 25, 1958 (72 Stat. 844); by section 22 of the Act of August 28, 1958 (72 Stat. 948); by the Act of July 12, 1960 (74 Stat. 417); by the Fair Labor Standards Amendments of 1961 (75 Stat. 65); by the Equal Pay Act of 1963 (77 Stat. 56); and by the Fair Labor Standards Amendments of 1966 (80 Stat. 830). The original text of the Fair Labor Standards Act of 1938 as set forth in 52 Stat. 1060 has been revised in this publication to reflect the changes effected by the amendments listed in this footnote, which may be found in official text at the cited pages of the Statutes at Large. Added or amended language as enacted by the Fair Labor Standards Amendments of 1961 is shown in bold face type. Added or amended language as enacted by the Fair Labor Standards Amendments of 1966 is shown in italics. The footnotes in this revision show where prior changes have been made and refer to the specific amendments relied upon so that a comparison may be made with the official text.

This revised text has been prepared in the Office of the Solicitor, U.S. Department of Labor.

[2] As amended by section 2 of the Fair Labor Standards Amendments of 1949.

DEFINITIONS

SEC. 3. As used in this Act—

(a) "Person" means an individual, partnership, association, corporation, business trust, legal representative, or any organized group of persons.

(b) "Commerce" means trade, commerce, transportation, transmission, or communication among the several States or between any State and any place outside thereof.[3]

(c) "State" means any State of the United States or the District of Columbia or any Territory or possession of the United States.

(d) "Employer" includes any person acting directly or indirectly in the interest of an employer in relation to an employee but shall not include the United States or any State or political subdivision of a State *(except with respect to employees of a State or a political subdivision thereof, employed (1) in a hospital, institution, or school referred to in the last sentence of subsection (r) of this section, or (2) in the operation of a railway or carrier referred to in such sentence)*, or any labor organization (other than when acting as an employer), or anyone acting in the capacity of officer or agent of such labor organization.

(e) "Employee" includes any individual employed by an employer, *except that such term shall not, for the purposes of section 3(u) include—*

(1) any individual employed by an employer engaged in agriculture if such individual is the parent, spouse, child, or other member of the employer's immediate family, or

(2) any individual who is employed by an employer engaged in agriculture if such individual (A) is employed as a hand harvest laborer and is paid on a piece rate basis in an operation which has been, and is customarily and generally recognized as having been, paid on a piece rate basis in the region of employment, (B) commutes daily from his permanent residence to the farm on which he is so employed, and (C) has been employed in agriculture less than thirteen weeks during the preceding calendar year.

(f) "Agriculture" includes farming in all its branches and among other things includes the cultivation and tillage of the soil, dairying, the production, cultivation, growing, and harvesting of any agricultural or horticultural commodities (including commodities defined as agricultural commodities in section 15(g) of the Agricultural Marketing Act, as amended), the raising of livestock, bees, fur-bearing animals, or poultry, and any practices (including any forestry or lumbering operations) performed by a farmer or on a farm as an incident to or in conjunction with such farming operations, including preparation for market, delivery to storage or to market or to carriers for transportation to market.

---

[3]As amended by section 3(a) of the Fair Labor Standards Amendments of 1949.

(g) "Employ" includes to suffer or permit to work.

(h) "Industry" means a trade, business, industry, or branch thereof, or group of industries, in which individuals are gainfully employed.

(i) "Goods" means goods (including ships and marine equipment), wares, products, commodities, merchandise, or articles or subjects of commerce of any character, or any part or ingredient thereof, but does not include goods after their delivery into the actual physical possession of the ultimate consumer thereof other than a producer, manufacturer, or processor thereof.

(j) "Produced" means produced, manufactured, mined, handled, or in any other manner worked on in any State; and for the purposes of this Act an employee shall be deemed to have been engaged in the production of goods if such employee was employed in producing, manufacturing, mining, handling, transporting, or in any other manner working on such goods, or in any closely related process or occupation directly essential to the production thereof, in any State.[4]

(k) "Sale" or "sell" includes any sale, exchange, contract to sell, consignment for sale, shipment for sale, or other disposition.

(1) "Oppressive child labor" means a condition of employment under which (1) any employee under the age of sixteen years is employed by an employer (other than a parent or a person standing in place of a parent employing his own child or a child in his custody under the age of sixteen years in an occupation other than manufacturing or mining or an occupation found by the Secretary of Labor to be particularly hazardous for the employment of children between the ages of sixteen and eighteen years or detrimental to their health or well-being) in any occupation,[5] or (2) any employee between the ages of sixteen and eighteen years is employed by an employer in any occupation which the Secretary of Labor[6] shall find and by order declare to be particularly hazardous for the employment of children between such ages or detrimental to their health or well-being; but oppressive child labor shall not be deemed to exist by virtue of the employment in any occupation of any person with respect to whom the employer shall have on file an unexpired certificate issued and held pursuant to regulations of the Secretary of Labor[7] certifying that such person is above the oppressive child labor age. The Secretary of Labor[8] shall provide by regulation or by order that the employment of employees be-

---

[4]As amended by section 3(b) of the Fair Labor Standards Amendments of 1949.

[5]As amended by section 3(c) of the Fair Labor Standards Amendments of 1949.

[6]Reorganization Plan No. 2 of 1946 provided that the functions of the Children's Bureau and of the Chief of the Children's Bureau under the Act as originally enacted be transferred to the Secretary of Labor.

[7]Ibid.

[8]Ibid.

tween the ages of fourteen and sixteen years in occupations other than manufacturing and mining shall not be deemed to constitute oppressive child labor if and to the extent that the Secretary of Labor[9] determines that such employment is confined to periods which will not interfere with their schooling and to conditions which will not interfere with their health and well-being.

(m) "Wage" paid to any employee includes the reasonable cost, as determined by the Secretary of Labor,[10] to the employer of furnishing such employee with board, lodging, or other facilities, if such board, lodging, or other facilities are customarily furnished by such employer to his employees: *Provided,* **That the cost of board, lodging, or other facilities shall not be included as a part of the wage paid to any employee to the extent it is excluded therefrom under the terms of a bona fide collective-bargaining agreement applicable to the particular employee:** *Provided further,* **That the Secretary is authorized to determine the fair value of such board, lodging, or other facilities for defined classes of employees and in defined areas, based on average cost to the employer or to groups of employers similarly situated, or average value to groups of employees, or other appropriate measures of fair value. Such evaluations, where applicable and pertinent, shall be used in lieu of actual measure of cost in determining the wage paid to any employee.** *In determining the wage of a tipped employee, the amount paid such employee by his employer shall be deemed to be increased on account of tips by an amount determined by the employer, but not by an amount in excess of 50 per centum of the applicable minimum wage rate, except that in the case of an employee who (either himself or acting through his representative) shows to the satisfaction of the Secretary that the actual amount of tips received by him was less than the amount determined by the employer as the amount by which the wage paid him was deemed to be increased under this sentence, the amount paid such employee by his employer shall be deemed to have been increased by such lesser amount.*

(n) "Resale" shall not include the sale of goods to be used in residential or farm building construction, repair, or maintenance: *Provided,* That the sale is recognized as a bona fide retail sale in the industry.[11]

(o) Hours worked.—In determining for the purposes of sections 6 and 7 the hours for which an employee is employed, there shall be excluded any time spent in changing clothes or washing at the beginning or end of each workday which was excluded from measured working time during the week involved by the express terms of or by custom or practice under a bona fide collective-bargaining agreement applicable to the particular employee.[12]

---

[9]Ibid.

[10]As amended by Reorganization Plan No. 6 of 1950, set out under section 4(a).

[11][12]Section 3(d) of the Fair Labor Standards Amendments of 1949. (Original Language of section 3(n) restored by sec. 215, Fair Labor Standards Amendments of 1966.)

(p) "American vessel" includes any vessel which is documented or numbered under the laws of the United States.

(q) "Secretary" means the Secretary of Labor.

(r) "Enterprise" means the related activities performed (either through unified operation or common control) by any person or persons for a common business purpose, and includes all such activities whether performed in one or more establishments or by one or more corporate or other organizational units including departments of an establishment operated through leasing arrangements, but shall not include the related activities performed for such enterprise by an independent contractor: Provided, That, within the meaning of this subsection, a retail or service establishment which is under independent ownership shall not be deemed to be so operated or controlled as to be other than a separate and distinct enterprise by reason of any arrangement, which includes, but is not necessarily limited to, an agreement, (1) that it will sell, or sell only, certain goods specified by a particular manufacturer, distributor, or advertiser, or (2) that it will join with other such establishments in the same industry for the purpose of collective purchasing, or (3) that it will have the exclusive right to sell the goods or use the brand name of a manufacturer, distributor, or advertiser within a specified area, or by reason of the fact that it occupies premises leased to it by a person who also leases premises to other retail or service establishments.

For purposes of this subsection, the activities performed by any person or persons—

(1) in connection with the operation of a hospital, an institution primarily engaged in the care of the sick, the aged, the mentally ill or defective who reside on the premises of such institution, a school for mentally or physically handicapped or gifted children, an elementary or secondary school, or an institution of higher education (regardless of whether or not such hospital, institution, or school is public or private or operated for profit or not for profit), or

(2) in connection with the operation of a street, suburban or interurban electric railway, or local trolley or motorbus carrier, if the rates and services of such railway or carrier are subject to regulation by a State or local agency (regardless of whether or not such railway or carrier is public or private or operated for profit or not for profit),

shall be deemed to be activities performed for a business purpose.

(s) "Enterprise engaged in commerce or in the production of goods for commerce" means an enterprise which has employees engaged in commerce or in the production of goods for commerce, including employees handling, selling, or otherwise working on goods that have been moved in or produced for commerce by any person, and which—

(1) during the period February 1, 1967 through January 31, 1969, is

an enterprise whose annual gross volume of sales made or business done is not less than $500,000 (exclusive of excise taxes of the retail level which are separately stated) or is a gasoline service establishment whose annual gross volume of sales is not less than $250,000 (exclusive of excise taxes at the retail level which are separately stated), and beginning February 1, 1969, is an enterprise whose annual gross volume of sales made or business done is not less than $250,000 (exclusive of excise taxes at the retail level which are separately stated);

(2) is engaged in laundering, cleaning, or repairing clothing or fabrics;

(3) is engaged in the business of construction or reconstruction, or both; or

(4) is engaged in the operation of a hospital, an institution primarily engaged in the care of the sick, the aged, the mentally ill or defective who reside on the premises of such institution, a school for mentally or physically handicapped or gifted children, an elementary or secondary school, or an institution of higher education (regardless of whether or not such hospital, institution, or school is public or private or operated for profit or not for profit).

Any establishment which has as its only regular employees the owner thereof or the parent, spouse, child, or other member of the immediate family of such owner shall not be considered to be an enterprise engaged in commerce or in the production of goods for commerce or a part of such an enterprise, and the sales of such establishment shall not be included for the purpose of determining the annual gross volume of sales of any enterprise for the purpose of this subsection.

(t) "Tipped employee" means any employee engaged in an occupation in which he customarily and regularly receives more than $20 a month in tips.

(u) "Man-day" means any day during which an employee performs any agricultural labor for not less than one hour.

(v) "Elementary school" means a day or residential school which provides elementary education, as determined under State law.

(w) "Secondary school" means a day or residential school which provides secondary education, as determined under State law.

ADMINISTRATION[13]

SEC. 4. (a) There is hereby created in the Department of Labor a Wage and Hour Division which shall be under the direction of an Administrator, to be known as the Administrator of the Wage and Hour Division (in this Act referred to as the "Administrator"). The Administrator shall be ap-

---

[13]Heading revised to reflect changes made by Reorganization Plan No. 6 of 1950.

pointed by the President, by and with the advice and consent of the Senate, and shall receive compensation at the rate of $26,000[14] a year.

Excerpts From Reorganization Plan No. 6 of 1950, 64 Stat. 1263

"Except as otherwise provided [with respect to hearing examiners], there are hereby transferred to the Secretary of Labor all functions of all other officers of the Department of Labor and all functions of all agencies and employees of such Department . . . . The Secretary of Labor may from time to time make such provisions as he shall deem appropriate authorizing the performance by any other officer, or by any agency or employee, of the Department of Labor of any function of the Secretary, including any function transferred to the Secretary by the provisions of this reorganization plan."

(b) The Secretary of Labor[15] may, subject to the civil-service laws, appoint such employees as he deems necessary to carry out his functions and duties under this Act and shall fix their compensation in accordance with the Classification Act of 1949[16] as amended. The Secretary[17] may establish and utilize such regional, local, or other agencies, and utilize such voluntary and uncompensated services, as may from time to time be needed. Attorneys appointed under this section may appear for and represent the Secretary[18] in any litigation, but all such litigation shall be subject to the direction and control of the Attorney General. In the appointment, selection, classification, and promotion of officers and employees of the Secretary,[19] no political test or qualification shall be permitted or given consideration, but all such appointments and promotions shall be given and made on the basis of merit and efficiency.

(c) The principal office of the Secretary[20] shall be in the District of Columbia, but he or his duly authorized representative may exercise any or all of his power in any place.

(d) The Secretary[21] shall submit annually in January a report to the Congress covering his activities for the preceding year and including such information, data, and recommendations for further legislation in connection with the matters covered by this Act as he may find advisable. Such report shall contain an evaluation and appraisal by the Secretary of the minimum wages established by this Act, together with his recommendations to the Congress. In making such evaluation and appraisal, the Secretary shall

---

[14]Executive Order 11189 of Nov. 3, 1964, 3. F.R. (1964 Supp.) 215.

[15]As amended by section 404 of Reorganization Plan No. II of 1939 (53 Stat. 1436) and by Reorganization Plan No. 6 of 1950 (64 Stat. 1263).

[16]As amended by section 1106 of the Act of October 28, 1949 (63 Stat. 972).

[17]See footnote 15.

[18]Ibid.

[19]Ibid.

[20]As amended by Reorganization Plan No. 6 of 1950.

[21]Ibid.

take into consideration any changes which may have occurred in the cost of living and in productivity and the level of wages in manufacturing, the ability of employers to absorb wage increases, and such other factors as he may deem pertinent.[22]

(e) Whenever the Secretary has reason to believe that in any industry under this Act the competition of foreign producers in United States markets or in markets abroad, or both, has resulted, or is likely to result, in increased unemployment in the United States, he shall undertake an investigation to gain full information with respect to the matter. If he determines such increased unemployment has in fact resulted, or is in fact likely to result, from such competition, he shall make a full and complete report of his findings and determinations to the President and to the Congress: Provided, That he may also include in such report information on the increased employment resulting from additional exports in any industry under this Act as he may determine to be pertinent to such report.

SPECIAL INDUSTRY COMMITTEES FOR PUERTO RICO AND THE VIRGIN ISLANDS

SEC. 5.[23] (a) The Secretary of Labor[24] shall as soon as practicable appoint a special industry committee to recommend the minimum rate or rates of wages to be paid under section 6 to employees in Puerto Rico or the Virgin Islands, or in Puerto Rico and the Virgin Islands, engaged in commerce or in the production of goods for commerce **or employed in any enterprise engaged in commerce or in the production of goods for commerce,** or the Secretary[25] may appoint separate industry committees to recommend the minimum rate or rates of wages to be paid under section 6 to employees therein engaged in commerce or in the production of goods for commerce **or employed in any enterprise engaged in commerce or in the production of goods for commerce** in particular industries. An industry committee appointed under this subsection shall be composed of residents of such island or islands where the employees with respect to whom such committee was appointed are employed and residents of the United States outside of Puerto Rico and the Virgin Islands. In determining the minimum rate or rates of wages to be paid, and in determining classifications, such industry committees[26] shall be subject to the provisions of section 8.

---

[22]Section 2 of the Fair Labor Standards Amendments of 1955.

[23]Section 5 as amended by section 3(c) of the Act of June 26, 1940 (54 Stat. 615); by section 5 of the Fair Labor Standards Amendments of 1949; by section 4 of the Fair Labor Standards Amendments of 1961; and as further amended as noted. Paragraphs (b), (c), and (d) (except for the substitution of "Secretary" for "Administrator") read as in the original Act.

[24]See footnote 20.

[25]Ibid.

[26]As amended by section 5(a) of the Fair Labor Standards Amendments of 1955.

(b) An industry committee shall be appointed by the Secretary[27] without regard to any other provisions of law regarding the appointment and compensation of employees of the United States. It shall include a number of disinterested persons representing the public, one of whom the Secretary[28] shall designate as chairman, a like number of persons representing employees in the industry, and a like number representing employers in the industry. In the appointment of the persons representing each group, the Secretary[29] shall give due regard to the geographical regions in which the industry is carried on.

(c) Two-thirds of the members of an industry committee shall constitute a quorum, and the decision of the committee shall require a vote of not less than a majority of all its members. Members of an industry committee shall receive as compensation, for their services a reasonable per diem, which the Secretary[30] shall by rules and regulations prescribe, for each day actually spent in the work of the committee, and shall in addition be reimbursed for their necessary traveling and other expenses. The Secretary[31] shall furnish the committee with adequate legal, stenographic, clerical, and other assistance, and shall by rules and regulations prescribe the procedure to be followed by the committee.

(d) The Secretary[32] shall submit to an industry committee from time to time such data as he may have available on the matters referred to it, and shall cause to be brought before it in connection with such matters any witnesses whom he deems material. An industry committee may summon other witnesses or call upon the Secretary[33] to furnish additional information to aid it in its deliberations.

MINIMUM WAGES

SEC. 6. (a) Every employer shall pay to each of his employees who **in any workweek** is engaged in commerce or in the production of goods for commerce, *or is employed in an enterprise engaged in commerce or in the production of goods for commerce, wages at the following rates:*

(1) not less than $1.40 an hour during the first year from the effective date of the Fair Labor Standards Amendments of 1966 and not less than $1.60 an hour thereafter, except as otherwise provided in this section;[34]

---

[27]See footnote 20.
[28]Ibid.
[29]Ibid.
[30]Ibid.
[31]Ibid.
[32]Ibid.
[33]Ibid.
[34]$1.40 rate becomes effective February 1, 1967. Section 602 of the Fair Labor Standards Amendments of 1966.

(2) [35] if such employee is a home worker in Puerto Rico or the Virgin Islands, not less than the minimum piece rate prescribed by regulation or order; or, if no such minimum piece rate is in effect, any piece rate adopted by such employer which shall yield, to the proportion or class of employees prescribed by regulation or order, not less than the applicable minimum hourly wage rate. Such minimum piece rates or employer piece rates shall be commensurate with, and shall be paid in lieu of, the minimum hourly wage rate applicable under the provisions of this section. The Secretary of Labor,[36] or his authorized representative, shall have power to make such regulations or orders as are necessary or appropriate to carry out any of the provisions of this paragraph, including the power without limiting the generality of the foregoing, to define any operation or occupation which is performed by such home work employees in Puerto Rico or the Virgin Islands; to establish minimum piece rates for any operation or occupation so defined; to prescribe the method and procedure for ascertaining and promulgating minimum piece rates; to prescribe standards for employer piece rates, including the proportion or class of employees who shall receive not less than the minimum hourly wage rate; to define the term "home worker"; and to prescribe the conditions under which employers, agents, contractors, and subcontractors shall cause goods to be produced by home workers;[37]

(3) if such employee is employed in American Samoa, in lieu of the rate or rates provided by this subsection or subsection (b), not less than the applicable rate established by the Secretary of Labor in accordance with recommendations of a special industry committee or committees which he shall appoint in the same manner and pursuant to the same provisions as are applicable to the special industry committees provided for Puerto Rico and the Virgin Islands by this Act as amended from time to time. Each such committee shall have the same powers and duties and shall apply the same standards with respect to the application of the provisions of this Act to employees employed in American Samoa as pertain to special industry committees established under section 5 with respect to employees employed in Puerto Rico or the Virgin Islands. The minimum wage rate thus established shall not exceed the rate prescribed in paragraph (1) of this subsection:[38]

(4) if such employee is employed as a seaman on an American vessel, not less than the rate which will provide to the employee, for the

---

[35]Paragraph number changed from (5) to (2) by section 6(b) of the Fair Labor Standards Amendments of 1949.

[36]See footnote 20.

[37]Section 3(f) of the Act of June 26, 1940 (54 Stat. 616).

[38]Section 2 of the American Samoa Labor Standards Amendments of 1956, as amended by section 5 of the Fair Labor Standards Amendments of 1961.

period covered by the wage payment, wages equal to compensation at the hourly rate prescribed by paragraph (1) of this subsection for all hours during such period when he was actually on duty (including periods aboard ship when the employee was on watch or was, at the direction of a superior officer, performing work or standing by, but not including off-duty periods which are provided pursuant to the employment agreement); or

(5) if such employee is employed in agriculture, not less than $1 an hour during the first year from the effective date of the Fair Labor Standards Amendments of 1966, not less than $1.15 an hour during the second year from such date, and not less than $1.30 an hour thereafter.

(b)[39] Every employer shall pay to each of his employees (other than an employee to whom subsection (a) (5) applies) who in any workweek is engaged in commerce or in the production of goods for commerce, or is employed in an enterprise engaged in commerce or in the production of goods for commerce, and who in such workweek is brought within the purview of this section by the amendments made to this Act by the Fair Labor Standards Amendments of 1966, wages at the following rates:

(1) not less than $1 an hour during the first year from the effective date of such amendments,

(2) not less than $1.15 an hour during the second year from such date,

(3) not less than $1.30 an hour during the third year from such date,

(4) not less than $1.45 an hour during the fourth year from such date, and

(5) not less than $1.60 an hour thereafter.

(c) *(1)* The rate or rates provided by subsections (a) and (b) of this section shall be superseded in the case of any employee in Puerto Rico or the Virgin Islands only for so long as and insofar as such employee is covered by a wage order heretofore or hereafter issued by the Secretary pursuant to the recommendations of a special industry committee appointed pursuant to section 5.

(2) In the case of any such employee who is covered by such a wage order to whom the rate or rates prescribed by subsection (a) would otherwise apply, the following rates shall apply:

(A) The rate or rates applicable under the most recent wage order issued by the Secretary prior to the effective date of the Fair Labor Standards Amendment of 1966, increased by 12 per centum, unless such rate or rates are superseded by the rate or rates prescribed in a wage order issued by the Secretary pursuant to the recommendations of a review committee appointed under paragraph (C). Such rate or rates shall

---

[39]As amended by the Fair Labor Standards Amendments of 1961 and 1962. Previously this subsection related to the effective date of section 6 of the Fair Labor Standards Act of 1938 as originally enacted.

become effective sixty days after the effective date of the Fair Labor Standards Amendments of 1966 or one year from the effective date of the most recent wage order applicable to such employee theretofore issued by the Secretary pursuant to the recommendations of a special industry committee appointed under section 5, whichever is later.

(B) Beginning one year after the applicable effective date under paragraph (A), not less than the rate or rates prescribed by paragraph (A), increased by an amount equal to 16 per centum of the rate or rates applicable under the most recent wage order issued by the Secretary prior to the effective date of the Fair Labor Standards Amendments of 1966, unless such rate or rates are superseded by the rate or rates prescribed in a wage order issued by the Secretary pursuant to the recommendations of a review committee appointed under paragraph (C).

(C) Any employer, or group of employers, employing a majority of the employees in an industry in Puerto Rico or the Virgin Islands, may apply to the Secretary in writing for the appointment of a review committee to recommend the minimum rate or rates to be paid such employees in lieu of the rate or rates provided by paragraph (A) or (B). Any such application with respect to any rate or rates provided for under paragraph (A) shall be filed within sixty days following the enactment of the Fair Labor Standards Amendments of 1966 and any such application with respect to any rate or rates provided for under paragraph (B) shall be filed not more than one hundred and twenty days and not less than sixty days prior to the effective date of the applicable rate or rates under paragraph (B). The Secretary shall promptly consider such application and may appoint a review committee if he has reasonable cause to believe, on the basis of financial and other information contained in the application, that compliance with any applicable rate or rates prescribed by paragraph (A) or (B) will substantially curtail employment in such industry. The Secretary's decision upon any such application shall be final. Any wage order issued pursuant to the recommendations of a review committee appointed under this paragraph shall take effect on the applicable effective date provided in paragraph (A) or (B).

(D) In the event a wage order has not been issued pursuant to the recommendation of a review committee prior to the applicable effective date under paragraph (A) or (B), the applicable percentage increase provided by any such paragraph shall take effect on the effective date prescribed therein, except with respect to the employees of an employer who filed an application under paragraph (C) and who files with the Secretary an undertaking with a surety or sureties satisfactory to the Secretary for payment to his employees of an amount sufficient to compensate such employees for the difference between the wages they actually receive and the wages to which they are entitled under this subsection.

The Secretary shall be empowered to enforce such undertaking and any sums recovered by him shall be held in a special deposit account and shall be paid, on order of the Secretary, directly to the employee or employees affected. Any such sum not paid to an employee because of inability to do so within a period of three years shall be covered into the Treasury of the United States as miscellaneous receipts.

(3) In the case of any such employee to whom subsection (a) (5) or subsection (b) would otherwise apply, the Secretary shall within sixty days after the effective date of the Fair Labor Standards Amendments of 1966 appoint a special industry committee in accordance with section 5 to recommend the highest minimum wage rate or rates in accordance with the standards prescribed by section 8, but not in excess of the applicable rate provided by subsection (a) (5) or subsection (b), to be applicable to such employee in lieu of the rate or rates prescribed by subsection (a) (5) or subsection (b), as the case may be. The rate or rates recommended by the special industry committee shall be effective with respect to such employee upon the effective date of the wage order issued pursuant to such recommendation but not before sixty days after the effective date of the Fair Labor Standards Amendments of 1966.

(4) The provisions of section 5 and section 8, relating to special industry committees, shall be applicable to review committees appointed under this subsection. The appointment of a review committee shall be in addition to and not in lieu of any special industry committee required to be appointed pursuant to the provisions of subsection (a) of section 8, except that no special industry committee shall hold any hearing within one year after a minimum wage rate or rates for such industry shall have been recommended to the Secretary by a review committee to be paid in lieu of the rate or rates provided for under paragraph (A) or (B). The minimum wage rate or rates prescribed by this subsection shall be in effect only for so long as and insofar as such minimum wage rate or rates have not been superseded by a wage order fixing a higher minimum wage rate or rates (but not in excess of the applicable rate prescribed in subsection (a) or subsection (b)) hereafter issued by the Secretary pursuant to the recommendation of a special industry committee.[40]

(d)[41] (1) No employer having employees subject to any provisions of this section shall discriminate, within any establishment in which such employees are employed, between employees on the basis of sex by paying wages to employees in such establishment at a rate less than the rate at

---

[40]Subsection (c) was added by Act of June 26, 1940 (54 Stat. 616), and amended by the Fair Labor Standards Amendments of 1949, 1961, and 1966.

[41]Subsection (d) added by Equal Pay Act of 1963, 77 Stat. 56 (effective on and after June 11, 1964 except for employees covered by collective bargaining agreements in certain cases).

which he pays wages to employees of the opposite sex in such establishment for equal work on jobs the performance of which requires equal skill, effort, and responsibility, and which are performed under similar working conditions, except where such payment is made pursuant to (i) a seniority system; (ii) a merit system; (iii) a system which measures earnings by quantity or quality of production; or (iv) a differential based on any other factor other than sex: *Provided,* That an employer who is paying a wage rate differential in violation of this subsection shall not, in order to comply with the provisions of this subsection, reduce the wage rate of any employee.

(2) No labor organization, or its agents, representing employees of an employer having employees subject to any provisions of this section shall cause or attempt to cause such an employer to discriminate against an employee in violation of paragraph (1) of this subsection.

(3) For purposes of administration and enforcement, any amounts owing to any employee which have been withheld in violation of this subsection shall be deemed to be unpaid minimum wages or unpaid overtime compensation under this Act.

(4) As used in this subsection, the term "labor organization" means any organization of any kind, or any agency or employee representation committee or plan, in which employees participate and which exists for the purpose, in whole or in part, of dealing with employers concerning grievances, labor disputes, wages, rates of pay, hours of employment, or conditions of work.

(e) (1) Notwithstanding the provisions of section 13 of this Act (except subsections (a) (1) and (f) thereof), every employer providing any contract services (other than linen supply services) under a contract with the United States or any subcontract thereunder shall pay to each of his employees whose rate of pay is not governed by the Service Contract Act of 1965 (41 U.S.C. 351–357) or to whom subsection (a) (1) of this section is not applicable, wages at rates not less than the rates provided for in subsection (b) of this section.

(2) Notwithstanding the provisions of section 13 of this Act (except subsections (a) (1) and (f) thereof) and the provisions of the Service Contract Act of 1965, every employer in an establishment providing linen supply services to the United States under a contract with the United States or any subcontract thereunder shall pay to each of his employees in such establishment wages at rates not less than those prescribed in subsection (b), except that if more than 50 per centum of the gross annual dollar volume of sales made or business done by such establishment is derived from providing such linen supply services under any such contracts or subcontracts, such employer shall pay to each of his employees in such establishment wages at rates not less than those prescribed in subsection (a) (1) of this section.

MAXIMUM HOURS

SEC. 7[42]* (a) **(1)** Except as otherwise provided in this section, no employer shall employ any of his employees who **in any workweek** is engaged in commerce or in the production of goods for commerce, *or is employed in an enterprise engaged in commerce or in the production of goods for commerce,* for a workweek longer than forty hours, unless such employee receives compensation for his employment in excess of the hours above specified at a rate not less than one and one-half times the regular rate at which he is employed.

(2) No employer shall employ any of his employees who in any workweek is engaged in commerce or in the production of goods for commerce, or is employed in an enterprise engaged in commerce or in the production of goods for commerce, and who in such workweek is brought within the purview of this subsection by the amendments made to this Act by the Fair Labor Standards Amendments of 1966—

(A) for a workweek longer than forty-four hours during the first year from the effective date of the Fair Labor Standards Amendments of 1966,

(B) for a workweek longer than forty-two hours during the second year from such date, or

(C) for a workweek longer than forty hours after the expiration of the second year from such date,

unless such employee receives compensation for his employment in excess of the hours above specified at a rate not less than one and one-half times the regular rate at which he is employed.

(b) No employer shall be deemed to have violated subsection (a) by employing any employee for a workweek in excess of that specified in such subsection without paying the compensation for overtime employment prescribed therein if such employee is so employed—

*(1) in pursuance of an agreement, made as a result of collective bargaining by representatives of employees certified as bona fide by the National Labor Relations Board, which provides that no employee shall be employed more than one thousand and forty hours during any period of twenty-six consecutive weeks, or

*(2) in pursuance of an agreement, made as a result of collective bargaining by representatives of employees certified as bona fide by the National Labor Relations Board which provides that during a specified period of fifty-two consecutive weeks the employee shall be employed

---

[42]Section 7 as amended by section 7 of the Fair Labor Standards Amendments of 1949, and as further amended as noted. Single asterisk (*) indicates provision amended by the 1949 Act; double asterisk (**) indicates provision added by the 1949 Act. Bold face type indicates amendment made by the Fair Labor Standards Amendments of 1961. Italic type indicates amendment by the Fair Standards Amendment of 1966.

not more than two thousand two hundred and forty hours and shall be guaranteed not less than one thousand eight hundred and forty hours (or not less than forty-six weeks at the normal number of hours worked per week, but not less than thirty hours per week) and not more than two thousand and eighty hours of employment for which he shall receive compensation for all hours guaranteed or worked at rates not less than those applicable under the agreement to the work performed and for all hours in excess of the guaranty which are also **in excess of the maximum workweek applicable to such employee under subsection (a) or** two thousand and eighty in such period at rates not less than one and one-half times the regular rate at which he is employed; or

(3)[43] *by an independently owned and controlled local enterprise (including an enterprise with more than one bulk storage establishment) engaged in the wholesale or bulk distribution of petroleum products if—*

(A) the annual gross volume of sales of such enterprise is less than $1,000,000 exclusive of excise taxes,

(B) more than 75 per centum of such enterprise's annual dollar volume of sales is made within the State in which such enterprise is located, and

(C) not more than 25 per centum of the annual dollar volume of sales of such enterprise is to customers who are engaged in the bulk distribution of such products for resale,

and such employee receives compensation for employment in excess of forty hours in any workweek at a rate not less than one and one-half times the minimum wage rate applicable to him under section 6,

and if such employee receives compensation for employment in excess of twelve hours in any workday, or for employment in excess of fifty-six hours in any workweek, as the case may be, at a rate not less than one and one-half times the regular rate at which he is employed.

(c) For a period or periods of not more than ten workweeks in the aggregate in any calendar year, or fourteen workweeks in the aggregate in the case of an employer who does not qualify for the exemption in subsection (d) of this section, any employer may employ any employee for a workweek in excess of that specified in subsection (a) without paying the compensation for overtime employment prescribed in such subsection if such employee (1) is employed by such employer in an industry found by the Secretary to be of a seasonal nature, and (2) receives compensation for employment by such employer in excess of ten hours in any workday, or

---

[43]Section 212 of the Fair Labor Standards Amendments of 1966 substituted this provision for the complete exemption from overtime contained in former section 13(b)(10) enacted in the 1961 amendments. Former clause (3) of section 7(b) as enacted in the 1938 Act was replaced by new section 7(c) as enacted by section 204(c) of the Fair Labor Standards Amendments of 1966.

for employment by such employer in excess of fifty hours in any workweek, as the case may be, at a rate not less than one and one-half times the regular rate at which he is employed.

(d) For a period or periods of not more than ten workweeks in the aggregate in any calendar year, or fourteen workweeks in the aggregate in the case of an employer who does not qualify for the exemption in subsection (c) of this section, any employer may employ any employee for a workweek in excess of that specified in subsection (a) without paying the compensation for overtime employment prescribed in such subsection, if such employee—

(1) is employed by such employer in an enterprise which is in an industry found by the Secretary—

(A) to be characterized by marked annually recurring seasonal peaks of operation at the places of first marketing or first processing of agricultural or horticultural commodities from farms if such industry is engaged in the handling, packing, preparing, storing, first processing, or canning of any perishable agricultural or horticultural commodities in their raw or natural state, or

(B) to be of a seasonal nature and engaged in the handling, packing, storing, preparing, first processing, or canning of any perishable agricultural or horticultural commodities in their raw or natural state, and

(2) receives compensation for employment by such employer in excess of ten hours in any workday, or for employment in excess of forty-eight hours in any workweek, as the case may be, at a rate not less than one and one-half times the regular rate at which he is employed.

**(*e*) As used in this section the "regular rate" at which an employee is employed shall be deemed to include all remuneration for employment paid to, or on behalf of, the employee, but shall not be deemed to include—

**(1) sums paid as gifts; payments in the nature of gifts made at Christmas time or on other special occasions, as a reward for service, the amounts of which are not measured by or dependent on hours worked, production, or efficiency;

**(2) payments made for occasional periods when no work is performed due to vacation, holiday, illness, failure of the employer to provide sufficient work, or other similar cause; reasonable payments for traveling expenses, or other expenses, incurred by an employee in the furtherance of his employer's interests and properly reimbursable by the employer; and other similar payments to an employee which are not made as compensation for his hours of employment;

**(3) sums paid in recognition of services performed during a given period if either, (a) both the fact that payment is to be made and the amount of the payment are determined at the sole discretion of the employer at or near the end of the period and not pursuant to any prior contract, agreement, or promise causing the employee to expect such payments regularly; or (b) the payments are made pursuant to a bona fide profit-sharing plan or trust or bona fide thrift or savings plan, meeting the requirements of the Secretary of Labor[44] set forth in appropriate regulation which he shall issue, having due regard among other relevant factors, to the extent to which the amounts paid to the employee are determined without regard to hours of work, production, or efficiency; or (c) the payments are talent fees (as such talent fees are defined and delimited by regulations of the Secretary[45]) paid to performers, including announcers, on radio and television programs;

**(4) contributions irrevocably made by an employer to a trustee or third person pursuant to a bona fide plan for providing old-age, retirement, life, accident, or health insurance or similar benefits for employees;

(5) extra compensation provided by a premium rate paid for certain hours worked by the employee in any day or workweek because such hours are hours worked in excess of eight in a day or **in excess of the maximum workweek applicable to such employee under subsection (a) or in excess of the employee's normal working hours or regular working hours, as the case may be;

*(6) extra compensation provided by a premium rate paid for work by the employee on Saturdays, Sundays, holidays, or regular days of rest, or on the sixth or seventh day of the workweek, where such premium rate is not less than one and one-half times the rate established in good faith for like work performed in nonovertime hours on other days;[46] or

*(7) extra compensation provided by a premium rate paid to the employee, in pursuance of an applicable employment contract or collective-bargaining agreement, for work outside of the hours established in good faith by the contract or agreement as the basic, normal, or regular workday (not exceeding eight hours) or workweek (not exceeding **the maximum workweek applicable to such employee under subsection (a)**), where such premium rate is not less than one and one-half times the rate established in good faith by the contract or agreement for like work performed during such workday or workweek.[47]

(f) No employer shall be deemed to have violated subsection (a) by employing any employee for a workweek in excess of **the maximum workweek applicable to such employee under subsection (a) if such employee is employed pursuant to a bona fide individual contract, or pursuant to an

---

[44]See footnote 20.

[45]Ibid.

[46]Paragraphs (6) and (7) together with section 7(g) continue in effect provisions of section 1 of the Act of July 20, 1949 (63 Stat. 446), which Act is repealed as of the effective date of the Fair Labor Standards Amendments of 1949.

[47]Ibid.

agreement made as a result of collective bargaining by representatives of employees, if the duties of such employee necessitate irregular hours of work, and the contract or agreement (1) specifies a regular rate of pay of not less than the minimum hourly rate provided in **subsection (a) or (b) of section 6 (whichever may be applicable) a**nd compensation at not less than one and one-half times such rate for all hours worked in excess of **such maximum** workweek, and (2) provides a weekly guaranty of pay for not more than sixty hours based on the rates so specified.

(g) No employer shall be deemed to have violated subsection (a) by employing any employee for a workweek in excess of **the maximum work-week applicable to such employee under such subsection if, pursuant to an agreement or understanding arrived at between the employer and the employee before performance of the work, the amount paid to the employee for the number of hours worked by him in such workweek in excess of **the maximum workweek applicable to such employee under such subsection—**

(1) in the case of an employee employed at piece rates, is computed at piece rates not less than one and one-half times the bona fide piece rates applicable to the same work when performed during nonovertime hours; or

(2) in the case of an employee performing two or more kinds of work for which different hourly or piece rates have been established, is computed at rates not less than one and one-half times such bona fide rates applicable to the same work when performed during nonover-time hours; or

(3) is computed at a rate not less than one and one-half times the rate established by such agreement or understanding as the basic rate to be used in computing overtime compensation thereunder: *Provided,* That the rate so established shall be authorized by regulation by the Secretary of Labor[48] as being substantially equivalent to the average hourly earnings of the employee, exclusive of overtime premiums, in the particular work over a representative period of time;

and if (i) the employee's average hourly earnings for the workweek exclusive of payments described in paragraphs (1) through (7) of subsection (*e*) are not less than the minimum hourly rate required by applicable law, and (ii) extra overtime compensation is properly computed and paid on other forms of additional pay required to be included in computing the regular rate.

*(*h*) Extra compensation paid as described in paragraphs (5), (6), and (7) of subsection (*e*) shall be creditable toward overtime compensation payable pursuant to this section.[49]

---

[48]See footnote 20.

[49]Amendment provided by section 7 of the Fair Labor Standards Amendments of 1949. See also footnote 45.

(i) **No employer shall be deemed to have violated subsection (a) by employing any employee of a retail or service establishment for a workweek in excess of the applicable workweek specified therein, if (1) the regular rate of pay of such employee is in excess of one and one-half times the minimum hourly rate applicable to him under section 6, and (2) more than half his compensation for a representative period (not less than one month) represents commissions on goods or services.** *In determining the proportion of compensation representing commissions, all earnings resulting from the application of a bona fide commission rate shall be deemed commissions on goods or services without regard to whether the computed commissions exceed the draw or guarantee.*

(j) No employer engaged in the operation of a hospital shall be deemed to have violated subsection (a) if, pursuant to an agreement or understanding arrived at between the employer and employee before performance of the work, a work period of fourteen consecutive days is accepted in lieu of the workweek of seven consecutive days for purposes of overtime computation and if, for his employment in excess of eight hours in any workday and in excess of eighty hours in such fourteen-day period, the employee receives compensation at a rate not less than one and one-half times the regular rate at which he is employed.

WAGE ORDERS IN PUERTO RICO AND THE VIRGIN ISLANDS

SEC. 8.[50] (a) The policy of this Act with respect to industries **or enterprises** in Puerto Rico and the Virgin Islands engaged in commerce or in the production of goods for commerce is to reach as rapidly as is economically feasible without substantially curtailing employment the objective of the minimum wage prescribed in paragraph (1) of section 6 (a) in each such industry. The Secretary of Labor[51] shall from time to time convene an industry committee or committees, appointed pursuant to section 5, and any such industry committee shall from time to time recommend the minimum rate or rates of wages to be paid under section 6 by employers in Puerto Rico or the Virgin Islands, or in Puerto Rico and the Virgin Islands, engaged in commerce or in the production of goods for commerce **or in any enterprise engaged in commerce or in the production of goods for commerce** in any such industry or classifications therein. Minimum rates of wages established in accordance with this section which are not equal to the minimum wage rate prescribed in paragraph (1) of section 6 (a) shall be re-

---

[50]Section 8 as amended by section 8 of the Fair Labor Standards Amendments of 1949, by section 7 of the Fair Labor Standards Amendments of 1961, and as further amended as noted. Paragraphs (b), (c), (d), (e), and (f) as amended by the 1949 Act read substantially the same as paragraphs (b), (c), (except for the parenthetical reference to the minimum wage rate provided in section 6 (a), (d), (f), and (g) in the original Act).

[51]See footnote 20.

viewed by such a Committee once during each biennial period, beginning with the biennial period commencing July 1, 1958, except that the Secretary,[52] in his discretion, may order an additional review during any such biennial period.[53]

(b) Upon the convening of any such industry committee, the Secretary[54] shall refer to it the question of the minimum wage rate or rates to be fixed for such industry. The industry committee shall investigate conditions in the industry and the committee, or any authorized subcommittee thereof, shall after due notice hear such witnesses and receive such evidence as may be necessary or appropriate to enable the committee to perform its duties and functions under this Act.[55] The committee shall recommend to the Secretary[56] the highest minimum wage rates for the industry which it determines, having due regard to economic and competitive conditions, will not substantially curtail employment in the industry, and will not give any industry in Puerto Rico or in the Virgin Islands a competitive advantage over any industry in the United States outside of Puerto Rico and the Virgin Islands.

(c) The industry committee shall recommend such reasonable classifications within any industry as it determines to be necessary for the purpose of fixing for each classification within such industry the highest minimum wage rate (not in excess of that prescribed in paragraph (1) of section 6 (a)) which (1) will not substantially curtail employment in such classification and (2) will not give a competitive advantage to any group in the industry, and shall recommend for each classification in the industry the highest minimum wage rate which the committee determines will not substantially curtail employment in such classification. In determining whether such classifications should be made in any industry, in making such classifications, and in determining the minimum wage rates for such classifications, no classifications shall be made, and no minimum wage rate shall be fixed, solely on a regional basis, but the industry committee[57] shall consider among other relevant factors the following:

(1) competitive conditions as affected by transportation, living, and production costs;

(2) the wages established for work of like or comparable character by collective labor agreements negotiated between employers and employees by representatives of their own choosing; and

---

[52]Act of August 25, 1958 (72 Stat. 844).

[53]As amended by Act of August 25, 1958 (72 Stat. 844).

[54]See footnote 20.

[55]As amended by section 5(b) of the Fair Labor Standards Amendments of 1955.

[56]See footnote 20.

[57]As amended by sections 5(c) and 5(d) of the Fair Labor Standards Amendments of 1955 (eliminating review by the Secretary of Labor of the recommendations of the industry committee).

(3) the wages paid for work of like or comparable character by employers who voluntarily maintain minimum wage standards in the industry.

No classification shall be made under this section on the basis of age or sex.

(d) The industry committee shall file with the Secretary a report containing its findings of fact and recommendations with respect to the matters referred to it. Upon the filing of such report, the Secretary shall publish such recommendations in the Federal Register and shall provide by order that the recommendations contained in such report shall take effect upon the expiration of 15 days after the date of such publication.[58]

(e) Orders issued under this section shall define the industries and classifications therein to which they are to apply, and shall contain such terms and conditions as the Secretary[59] finds necessary to carry out the purposes of such orders, to prevent the circumvention or evasion thereof, and to safeguard the minimum wage rates established therein.[60]

(f) Due notice of any hearing provided for in this section shall be given by publication in the Federal Register and by such other means as the Secretary[61] deems reasonably calculated to give general notice to interested persons.

ATTENDANCE OF WITNESSES

SEC. 9. For the purpose of any hearing or investigation provided for in this Act, the provisions of sections 9 and 10 (relating to the attendance of witnesses and the production of books, papers and documents) of the Federal Trade Commission Act of September 16, 1914, as amended (U.S.C., 1934 edition, title 15, secs. 49 and 50), are hereby made applicable to the jurisdiction, powers, and duties of the Secretary of Labor[62] and the industry committees.

COURT REVIEW

SEC. 10.[63] (a) Any person aggrieved by an order of the Secretary issued under section 8 may obtain a review of such order in the United States Court of Appeals for any circuit wherein such person resides or has his principal place of business, or in the United States Court of Appeals for the District of Columbia, by filing in such court, within 60 days after the entry of such order a written petition praying that the order of the Secretary be modified or set aside in whole or in part. A copy of such petition shall forthwith be transmitted by the clerk of the court to the Secretary, and

---

[58]Ibid.

[59]See footnote 20.

[60]As amended by section 5(e) of the Fair Labor Standards Amendments of 1955.

[61]See footnote 20.

[62]Ibid.

[63]Section 10(a) as amended by section 5(f) of the Fair Labor Standards Amendments of 1955, and as further amended as noted.

thereupon the Secretary shall file in the court the record of the industry committee upon which the order complained of was entered, as provided in section 2112 of title 28, United States Code. Upon the filing of such petition such court shall have exclusive jurisdiction to affirm, modify, or set aside each order in whole or in part, so far as it is applicable to the petitioner.[64] The review by the court shall be limited to questions of law, and findings of fact by such industry committee when supported by substantial evidence shall be conclusive. No objection to the order of the Secretary shall be considered by the court unless such objection shall have been urged before such industry committee or unless there were reasonable grounds for failure so to do. If application is made to the court for leave to adduce additional evidence, and it is shown to the satisfaction of the court that such additional evidence may materially affect the result of the proceeding and that there were reasonable grounds for failure to adduce such evidence in the proceedings before such industry committee, the court may order such additional evidence to be taken before an industry committee and to be adduced upon the hearing in such manner and upon such terms and conditions as to the court may seem proper. Such industry committee may modify the initial findings by reason of the additional evidence so taken, and shall file with the court such modified or new findings which if supported by substantial evidence shall be conclusive, and shall also file its recommendation, if any, for the modification or setting aside of the original order. The judgment and decree of the court shall be final, subject to review by the Supreme Court of the United States upon certiorari or certification as provided in section 1254 of title 28 of the United States Code.

(b) The commencement of proceedings under subsection (a) shall not, unless specifically ordered by the court, operate as a stay of the Secretary's[65] order. The court shall not grant any stay of the order unless the person complaining of such order shall file in court an undertaking with a surety or sureties satisfactory to the court for the payment to the employees affected by the order, in the event such order is affirmed, of the amount by which the compensation such employees are entitled to receive under the order exceeds the compensation they actually receive while such stay is in effect.

INVESTIGATIONS, INSPECTIONS, RECORDS, AND HOMEWORK REGULATIONS

SEC. 11. (a) The Secretary of Labor[66] or his designated representatives may investigate and gather data regarding the wages, hours, and other conditions and practices of employment in any industry subject to this Act, and may enter and inspect such places and such records (and make such

---

[64]Section 22 of the Act of August 28, 1958 (72 Stat. 948).
[65]See footnote 20.
[66]Ibid.

transcriptions thereof), question such employees, and investigate such facts, conditions, practices, or matters as he may deem necessary or appropriate to determine whether any person has violated any provision of this Act, or which may aid in the enforcement of the provisions of this Act. Except as provided in section 12 and in subsection (b) of this section, the Secretary[67] shall utilize the bureaus and divisions of the Department of Labor for all the investigations and inspections necessary under this section. Except as provided in section 12, the Secretary[68] shall bring all action under section 17 to restrain violations of this Act.

(b) With the consent and cooperation of State agencies charged with the administration of State labor laws, the Secretary of Labor[69] may, for the purpose of carrying out his functions and duties under this Act, utilize the services of State and local agencies and their employees and, notwithstanding any other provision of law, may reimburse such State and local agencies and their employees for services rendered for such purposes.

(c) Every employer subject to any provision of this Act or of any order issued under this Act shall make, keep, and preserve such records of the persons employed by him and of the wages, hours, and other conditions and practices of employment maintained by him, and shall preserve such records for such periods of time, and shall make such reports therefrom to the Secretary[70] as he shall prescribe by regulation or order as necessary or appropriate for the enforcement of the provisions of this Act or the regulations or orders thereunder.

(d) The Secretary is authorized to make such regulations and orders regulating, restricting, or prohibiting industrial homework as are necessary or appropriate to prevent the circumvention or evasion of and to safeguard the minimum wage rate prescribed in this Act, and all existing regulations or orders of the Administrator relating to industrial homework are hereby continued in full force and effect.[71]

CHILD LABOR PROVISIONS

SEC. 12. (a) No producer, manufacturer, or dealer shall ship or deliver for shipment in commerce any goods produced in an establishment situated in the United States in or about which within thirty days prior to the removal of such goods therefrom any oppressive child labor has been employed: *Provided,* That any such shipment or delivery for shipment of such goods by a purchaser who acquired them in good faith in reliance on

---

[67]Ibid.
[68]Ibid.
[69]See footnotes 6 and 20.
[70]See footnote 20.
[71]Section 9 of the Fair Labor Standards Amendments of 1949, as amended by Reorganization Plan No. 6 of 1950.

written assurance from the producer, manufacturer, or dealer that the goods were produced in compliance with the requirements of this section, and who acquired such goods for value without notice of any such violation, shall not be deemed prohibited by this subsection: *And provided further,* That a prosecution and conviction of a defendant for the shipment or delivery for shipment of any goods under the conditions herein prohibited shall be a bar to any further prosecution against the same defendant for shipments or deliveries for shipment of any such goods before the beginning of said prosecution.[72]

(b) The Secretary of Labor,[73] or any of his authorized representatives, shall make all investigations and inspections under section 11 (a) with respect to the employment of minors, and, subject to the direction and control of the Attorney General, shall bring all actions under section 17 to enjoin any act or practice which is unlawful by reason of the existence of oppressive child labor, and shall administer all other provisions of this Act relating to oppressive child labor.

(c) No employer shall employ any oppressive child labor in commerce or in the production of goods for commerce **or in any enterprise engaged in commerce or in the production of goods for commerce.**[74]

EXEMPTIONS

SEC. 13.[75] **(a) The provisions of sections 6 and 7 shall not apply with respect to—**

(1) any employee employed in a bona fide executive, administrative, or professional capacity *(including any employee employed in the capacity of academic administrative personnel or teacher in elementary or secondary schools),* **or in the capacity of outside salesman (as such terms are defined and delimited from time to time by regulations of the Secretary, subject to the provisions of the Administrative Procedure Act, except that an employee of a retail or service establishment shall not be excluded from the definition of employee employed in a bona fide executive or administrative capacity because of the number of hours in his workweek which he devotes to activities not directly or closely related to the performance of executive or administrative activities, if less than 40 per centum of his hours worked in the workweek are devoted to such activities); or**

(2) any employee employed by any retail or service establishment

[72]As amended by section 10(a) of the Fair Labor Standards Amendments of 1949.

[73]See footnotes 6 and 20.

[74]Section 10(b) of the Fair Labor Standards Amendments of 1949 as amended by section 8 of the Fair Labor Standards Amendments of 1961.

[75]Section 13 as amended by section 11 of the Fair Labor Standards Amendments of 1949; by Reorganization Plan No. 6 of 1950; and as further amended by the Fair Labor Standards Amendments of 1961 and 1966.

(except an establishment or employee engaged in laundering, cleaning, or repairing clothing or fabrics or an establishment engaged in the operation of a hospital, institution, or school described in section 3(s) (4)), if more than 50 per centum of such establishment's annual dollar volume of sales of goods or services is made within the State in which the establishment is located, and such establishment is not in an enterprise described in section 3(s) or such establishment has an annual dollar volume of sales which is less than $250,000 (exclusive of excise taxes at the retail level which are separately stated). **A "retail or service establishment" shall mean an establishment 75 per centum of whose annual dollar volume of sales of goods or services (or of both) is not for resale and is recognized as retail sales or services in the particular industry; or**

(3) any employee employed by an establishment which is an amusement or recreational establishment, if (A) it does not operate for more than seven months in any calendar year, or (B) during the preceding calendar year, its average receipts for any six months of such year were not more than 33⅓ per centum of its average receipt for the other six months of such year; or

(4) any employee employed by an establishment which qualifies as an exempt retail establishment under clause (2) of this subsection and is recognized as a retail establishment in the particular industry notwithstanding that such establishment makes or processes at the retail establishment the goods that it sells: Provided, That more than 85 per centum of such establishment's annual dollar volume of sales of goods so made or processed is made within the State in which the establishment is located; or

(5) any employee employed in the catching, taking, propagating, harvesting, cultivating, or farming of any kind of fish, shellfish, crustacea, sponges, seaweeds, or other aquatic forms of animal and vegetable life, or in the first processing, canning or packing such marine products at sea as an incident to, or in conjunction with, such fishing operations, including the going to and returning from work and loading and unloading when performed by any such employee; or

(6) any employee employed in agriculture (A) if such employee is employed by an employer who did not, during any calendar quarter during the preceding calendar year, use more than five hundred man-days of agricultural labor, (B) if such employee is the parent, spouse, child, or other member of his employer's immediate family, (C) if such employee (i) is employed as a hand harvest laborer and is paid on a piece rate basis in an operation which has been, and is customarily and generally recognized as having been, paid on a piece rate basis in the region of employment, (ii) commutes daily from his permanent residence to the farm on which he is so employed, and (iii) has been em-

ployed in agriculture less than thirteen weeks during the preceding calendar year, (D) if such employee (other than an employee described in clause (C) of this subsection) (i) is sixteen years of age or under and is employed as a hand harvest laborer, is paid on a piece rate basis in an operation whih has been, and is customarily and generally recognized as having been, paid on a piece rate basis in the region of employment, (ii) is employed on the same farm as his parent or person standing in the place of his parent, and (iii) is paid at the same piece rate as employees over age sixteen are paid on the same farm, or (E) if such employee is principally engaged in the range production of livestock; or

(7) any employee to the extent that such employee is exempted by regulations, *order or certificate* **of the Secretary issued under section 14; or**

(8)[76] **any employee employed in connection with the publication of any weekly, semiweekly, or daily newspaper with a circulation of less than four thousand the major part of which circulation is within the county where published or counties contiguous thereto; or**

(9) any employee employed by an establishment which is a motion picture theater; or

(10) **any switchboard operator employed by an independently owned public telephone company which has not more than seven hundred and fifty stations; or**

(11) **any employee or proprietor in a retail or service establishment which qualifies as an exempt retail or service establishment under clause (2) of this subsection with respect to whom the provisions of sections 6 and 7 would not otherwise apply, engaged in handling telegraphic messages for the public under an agency or contract arrangement with a telegraph company where the telegraph message revenue of such agency does not exceed $500 a month; or**

(12) **any employee employed as a seaman on a vessel other than an American vessel; or**

(13) **any employee employed in planting or tending trees, cruising, surveying, or felling timber, or in preparing or transporting logs or other forestry products to the mill, processing plant, railroad, or other transportation terminal, if the number of employees employed by his employer in such forestry or lumbering operations does not exceed** *eight;*[77] **or**

(14) **any agricultural employee employed in the growing and harvesting of shade-grown tobacco who is engaged in the processing (including,**

---

[76]As amended by the Fair Labor Standards Amendments of 1966 (which deleted the words "printed and" which formerly preceded the word "published").

[77]Changed from "twelve" by the Fair Labor Standards Amendments of 1966.

but not limited to, drying, curing, fermenting, bulking, rebulking, sorting, grading, aging, and baling) of such tobacco, prior to the stemming process, for use as cigar wrapper tobacco.

(b) The provisions of section 7 shall not apply with respect to—

(1) any employee with respect to whom the Interstate Commerce Commission has power to establish qualifications and maximum hours of service pursuant to the provisions of section 204 of the Motor Carrier Act 1935; or

(2) any employee of an employer subject to the provisions of part I of the Interstate Commerce Act; or

(3) any employee of a carrier by air subject to the provisions of title II of the Railway Labor Act; or

(4) any employee employed in the canning, processing, marketing, freezing, curing, storing, packing for shipment, or distributing of any kind of fish, shellfish, or other aquatic forms of animal or vegetable life, or any byproduct thereof; or

(5) any individual employed as an outside buyer of poultry, eggs, cream, or milk, in their raw or natural state; or

(6) any employee employed as a seaman; or

(7) any driver, operator, or conductor employed by an employer engaged in the business of operating a street, suburban or interurban electric railway, or local trolley or motorbus carrier, if the rates and services of such railway or carrier are subject to regulation by a State or local agency; or

(8) any employee employed by an establishment which is a hotel, motel, or restaurant; or any employee who (A) is employed by an establishment which is an institution (other than a hospital) primarily engaged in the care of the sick, the aged, or the mentally ill or defective who reside on the premises, and (B) receives compensation for employment in excess of forty-eight hours in any workweek at a rate not less than one and one-half times the regular rate at which he is employed; or

(9) any employee employed as an announcer, news editor, or chief engineer by a radio or television station the major studio of which is located (A) in a city or town of one hundred thousand population or less, according to the latest available decennial census figures as compiled by the Bureau of the Census, except where such city or town is part of a standard metropolitan statistical area, as defined and designated by the Bureau of the Budget, which has a total population in excess of one hundred thousand, or (B) in a city or town of twenty-five thousand population or less, which is part of such an area but is at least 40 airline miles from the principal city in such area; or

(10) any salesman, partsman, or mechanic primarily engaged in selling or servicing automobiles, trailers, trucks, farm implements, or aircraft if

employed by a nonmanufacturing establishment primarily engaged in the business of selling such vehicle to ultimate purchasers; or

(11) any employee employed as a driver or drivers' helper making local deliveries, who is compensated for such employment on the basis of trip rates, or other delivery payment plan, if the Secretary shall find that such plan has the general purpose and effect of reducing hours worked by such employees to, or below, the maximum workweek applicable to them under section 7 (a); *or*

(12) any employee employed in agriculture or in connection with the operation or maintenance of ditches, canals, reservoirs, or waterways, not owned or operated for profit, or operated on a sharecrop basis, and which are used exclusively for supply and storing of water for agricultural purposes; or

(13) any employee with respect to his employment in agriculture by a farmer, notwithstanding other employment of such employee in connection with livestock auction operations in which such farmer is engaged as an adjunct to the raising of livestock, either on his own account or in conjunction with other farmers, if such employee (A) is primarily employed during his workweek in agriculture by such farmer, and (B) is paid for his employment in connection with such livestock auction operations at a wage rate not less than that prescribed by section 6(a)(1); or

(14) any employee employed within the area of production (as defined by the Secretary) by an establishment commonly recognized as a country elevator, including such an establishment which sells products and services used in the operation of a farm, if no more than five employees are employed in the establishment in such operations; or

(15) any employee engaged in ginning of cotton for market, in any place of employment located in a county where cotton is grown in commercial quantities, or in the processing of sugar beets, sugar-beet molasses, sugarcane, or maple sap, into sugar (other than refined sugar) or syrup; or

(16) any employee engaged (A) in the transportation and preparation for transportation of fruits or vegetables, whether or not performed by the farmer, from the farm to a place of first processing or first marketing within the same State, or (B) in transportation, whether or not performed by the farmer, between the farm and any point within the same State of persons employed or to be employed in the harvesting of fruits or vegetables; or

(17) any driver employed by an employer engaged in the business of operating taxicabs; or

(18) any employee of a retail or service establishment who is employed primarily in connection with the preparation or offering of food or beverages for human consumption, either on the premises, or by such

services as catering, banquet, box lunch, or curb or counter service, to the public, to employees, or to members or guests of members of clubs; or

(19) any employee of a bowling establishment if such employee receives compensation for employment in excess of forty-eight hours in any workweek at a rate not less than one and one-half times the regular rate at which he is employed.

(c)(1) Except as provided in paragraph (2), the provisions of section 12 relating to child labor shall not apply with respect to any employee employed in agriculture outside of school hours for the school district where such employee is living while he is so employed.

(2) The provisions of section 12 relating to child labor shall apply to an employee below the age of sixteen employed in agriculture in an occupation that the Secretary of Labor finds and declares to be particularly hazardous for the employment of children below the age of sixteen, except where such employee is employed by his parent or by a person standing in the place of his parent on a farm owned or operated by such parent or person.

(3) The provisions of section 12 relating to child labor shall not apply to any child employed as an actor or performer in motion pictures or theatrical productions, or in radio or television productions.

(d) The provisions of sections 6, 7, and 12 shall not apply with respect to any employee engaged in the delivery of newspapers to the consumer **or to any homeworker engaged in the making of wreaths composed principally of natural holly, pine, cedar, or other evergreens (including the harvesting of the evergreens or other forest products used in making such wreaths).**

(e) The provisions of section 7 shall not apply with respect to employees for whom the Secretary of Labor is authorized to establish minimum wage rates as provided in section 6(a)(3), except with respect to employees for whom such rates are in effect; and with respect to such employees the Secretary may make rules and regulations providing reasonable limitations and allowing reasonable variations, tolerances, and exemptions to and from any or all of the provisions of section 7 if he shall find, after a public hearing on the matter, and taking into account the factors set forth in section 6(a)(3), that economic conditions warrant such action.[78]

(f) The provisions of sections 6, 7, 11, and 12 shall not apply with respect to any employee whose services during the workweek are performed in a workplace within a foreign country or within territory under the jurisdiction of the United States other than the following: a State of the United States; the District of Columbia; Puerto Rico; the Virgin Islands; outer Continental Shelf lands defined in the Outer Continental Shelf Lands Act

---

[78]Section 3 of the American Samoa Labor Standards Amendments of 1956.

(ch. 345, 67 Stat. 462); American Samoa; Guam; Wake Island; *Eniwetok Atoll; Kwajalein Atoll; Johnston Island;* and the Canal Zone.[79]

LEARNERS, APPRENTICES, STUDENTS, AND
HANDICAPPED WORKERS

SEC. 14.[80] *(a) The Secretary of Labor, to the extent necessary in order to prevent curtailment of opportunities for employment, shall by regulations or by orders provide for the employment of learners, of apprentices, and of messengers employed primarily in delivering letters and messages, under special certificates issued pursuant to regulations of the Secretary, at such wages lower than the minimum wage applicable under section 6 and subject to such limitations as to time, number, proportions, and length of service as the Secretary shall prescribe.*

(b) The Secretary, to the extent necessary in order to prevent curtailment of opportunities for employment, shall by regulation or order provide for the employment of full-time students, regardless of age but in compliance with applicable child labor laws, on a part-time basis in retail or service establishments (not to exceed twenty hours in any workweek) or on a part-time or a full-time basis in such establishments during school vacations, under special certificates issued pursuant to regulations of the Secretary, at a wage rate not less than 85 per centum of the minimum wage applicable under section 6, except that the proportion of student hours of employment to total hours of employment of all employees in any establishment may not exceed (1) such proportion for the corresponding month of the twelve-month period preceding May 1, 1961, (2) in the case of a retail or service establishment whose employees (other than employees engaged in commerce or in the production of goods for commerce) are covered by this Act for the first time on or after the effective date of the Fair Labor Standards Amendments of 1966, such proportion for the corresponding month of the twelve-month period immediately prior to such date, or (3) in the case of a retail or service establishment coming into existence after May 1, 1961, or a retail or service establishment for which records of student hours worked are not available, a proportion of student hours of employment to total hours of employment of all employees based on the practice during the twelve-month period preceding May 1, 1961, in (A) similar establishments of the same employer in the same general metropolitan area in which the new establishment is located, (B) similar establishments of the same employer in the same or nearby counties if the new establishment is not in a

---

[79]Section 1(1) of the Act of August 30, 1957 (71 Stat. 514), as amended by section 21(b) of the Act of July 12, 1960 (74 Stat. 417), and by section 213 of the Fair Labor Standards Amendments of 1966.

[80]As amended by section 12 of the Fair Labor Standards Amendments of 1949 and section 501 of the Fair Labor Standards Amendments of 1966.

metropolitan area, or (C) other establishments of the same general character operating in the community or the nearest comparable community. Before the Secretary may issue a certificate under this subsection he must find that such employment will not create a substantial probability of reducing the full-time employment opportunities of persons other than those employed under this subsection.

(c) The Secretary, to the extent necessary in order to prevent curtailment of opportunities for employment, shall by certificate or order provide for the employment of full-time students, regardless of age but in compliance with applicable child labor laws, on a part-time basis in agriculture (not to exceed twenty hours in any workweek) or on a part-time or a full-time basis in agriculture during school vacations, at a wage rate not less than 85 per centum of the minimum wage applicable under section 6. Before the Secretary may issue a certificate or order under this subsection he must find that such employment will not create a substantial probability of reducing the full-time employment opportunities of persons other than those employed under this subsection.

(d)(1) Except as otherwise provided in paragraphs (2) and (3) of this subsection, the Secretary of Labor, to the extent necessary in order to prevent curtailment of opportunities for employment, shall by regulation or order provide for the employment under special certificates of individuals (including individuals employed in agriculture) whose earning or productive capacity is impaired by age or physical or mental deficiency or injury, at wages which are lower than the minimum wage applicable under section 6 of this Act but not less than 50 per centum of such wage and which are commensurate with those paid nonhandicapped workers in industry in the vicinity for essentially the same type, quality, and quantity of work.

(2) The Secretary, pursuant to such regulations as he shall prescribe and upon certification of the State agency administering or supervising the administration of vocational rehabilitation services, may issue special certificates for the employment of—

(A) handicapped workers engaged in work which is incidental to training or evaluation programs, and

(B) multihandicapped individuals and other individuals whose earning capacity is so severely impaired that they are unable to engage in competitive employment,

at wages which are less than those required by this subsection and which are related to the worker's productivity.

(3)(A) The Secretary may by regulation or order provide for the employment of handicapped clients in work activities centers under special certificates at wages which are less than the minimums applicable under section 6 of this Act or prescribed by paragraph (1) of this subsection and

which constitute equitable compensation for such clients in work activities centers.

(B) For purposes of this section, the term "work activities centers" shall mean centers planned and designed exclusively to provide therapeutic activities for handicapped clients whose physical or mental impairment is so severe as to make their productive capacity inconsequential.

PROHIBITED ACTS

SEC. 15. (a) After the expiration of one hundred and twenty days from the date of enactment of this Act, it shall be unlawful for any person—

(1) to transport, offer for transportation, ship, deliver, or sell in commerce, or to ship, deliver, or sell with knowledge that shipment or delivery or sale thereof in commerce is intended, any goods in the production of which any employee was employed in violation of section 6 or section 7, or in violation of any regulation or order of the Secretary of Labor[81] issued under section 14; except that no provision of this Act shall impose any liability upon any common carrier for the transportation in commerce in the regular course of its business of any goods not produced by such common carrier, and no provision of this Act shall excuse any common carrier from its obligation to accept any goods for transportation; and except that any such transportation, offer, shipment, delivery, or sale of such goods by a purchaser who acquired them in good faith in reliance on written assurance from the producer that the goods were produced in compliance with the requirements of the Act, and who acquired such goods for value without notice of any such violation, shall not be deemed unlawful;[82]

(2) to violate any of the provisions of section 6 or section 7, or any of the provisions of any regulation or order of the Secretary[83] issued under section 14;

(3) to discharge or in any other manner discriminate against any employee because such employee has filed any complaint or instituted or caused to be instituted any proceeding under or related to this Act, or has testified or is about to testify in any such proceeding, or has served or is about to serve on an industry committee;

(4) to violate any of the provisions of section 12;

(5) to violate any of the provisions of section 11(c) or any regulation or order made or continued in effect under the provisions of section 11(d), or to make any statement, report, or record filed or kept pursuant to the provisions of such section or of any regulation or order thereunder,

---

[81]See footnote 20.
[82]As amended by section 13(a) of the Fair Labor Standards Amendments of 1949.
[83]See footnote 20.

knowing such statement, report, or record to be false in a material respect.[84]

(b) For the purposes of subsection (a)(1) proof that any employee was employed in any place of employment where goods shipped or sold in commerce were produced, within ninety days prior to the removal of the goods from such place of employment, shall be prima facie evidence that such employee was engaged in the production of such goods.

PENALTIES[85]

SEC. 16. (a) Any person who willfully violates any of the provisions of section 15 shall upon conviction thereof be subject to a fine of not more than $10,000, or to imprisonment for not more than six months, or both. No person shall be imprisoned under this subsection except for an offense committed after the conviction of such person for a prior offense under this subsection.

(b) Any employer who violates the provisions of section 6 or section 7 of this Act shall be liable to the employee or employees affected in the amount of their unpaid minimum wages, or their unpaid overtime compensation, as the case may be, and in an additional equal amount as liquidated damages. Action[86] to recover such liability may be maintained in any court of competent jurisdiction by any one or more employees for and in behalf of himself or themselves and other employees similarly situated. No employee shall be a party plaintiff to any such action unless he gives his consent in writing to become such a party and such consent is filed in the court in which such action is brought.[87] The court in such action shall, in addition to any judgment awarded to the plaintiff or plaintiffs, allow a reasonable attorney's fee to be paid by the defendant, and costs of the action. **The right provided by this subsection to bring an action by or on behalf of any employee, and the right of any employee to become a party plaintiff to any such action, shall terminate upon the filing of a complaint by the Secretary of Labor in an action under section 17 in which restraint is sought of any further delay in the payment of unpaid minimum wages, or the amount of unpaid minimum wages, or the amount of unpaid overtime compensation, as the case may be, owing to such employee under section 6 or section 7 of this Act by an employer liable therefor under the provisions of this subsection.**[88]

---

[84]As amended by section 13(b) of the Fair Labor Standards Amendments of 1949.

[85]The Portal-to-Portal Act of 1947 relieves employers from certain liabilities and punishments under this Act in circumstances specified in that Act.

[86]Periods of limitation for such actions are established by sections 6-8 inclusive of the Portal-to-Portal Act of 1947.

[87]Amendment provided by section 5(a) of the Portal-to-Portal Act of 1947.

[88]As amended by section 12 of the Fair Labor Standards Amendments of 1961.

(c) The Secretary of Labor[89] is authorized to supervise the payment of the unpaid minimum wages or the unpaid overtime compensation owing to any employee or employees under section 6 or section 7 of this Act, and the agreement of any employee to accept such payment shall upon payment in full constitute a waiver by such employee of any right he may have under subsection (b) of this section to such unpaid minimum wages or unpaid overtime compensation and an additional equal amount as liquidated damages. When a written request is filed by any employee with the Secretary claiming unpaid minimum wages or unpaid overtime compensation under section 6 or section 7 of this Act, the Secretary may bring an action in any court of competent jurisdiction to recover the amount of such claim: *Provided,* That this authority to sue shall not be used by the Secretary in any case involving an issue of law which has not been settled finally by the courts, and in any such case no court shall have jurisdiction over such action or proceeding initiated or brought by the Secretary if it does involve any issue of law not so finally settled. The consent of any employee to the bringing of any such action by the Secretary, unless such action is dismissed without prejudice on motion of the Secretary, shall constitute a waiver by such employee of any right of action he may have under subsection (b) of this section for said unpaid minimum wages or unpaid overtime compensation and an additional equal amount as liquidated damages. Any sums thus recovered by the Secretary on behalf of an employee pursuant to this subsection shall be held in a special deposit account and shall be paid, on order of the Secretary, directly to the employee or employees affected. Any such sums not paid to an employee because of inability to do so within a period of three years shall be covered into the Treasury of the United States as miscellaneous receipts. In determining when an action is commenced by the Secretary under this subsection for the purposes of the *statutes*[90] of limitations provided in section 6(a) of the Portal-to-Portal Act of 1947, it shall be considered to be commenced in the case of any individual claimant on the date when the complaint is filed if he is specifically named as a party plaintiff in the complaint, or if his name did not so appear, on the subsequent date on which his name is added as a party plaintiff in such action.[91]

(d) In any action or proceeding commenced prior to, on, or after the date of enactment of this subsection, no employer shall be subject to any liability or punishment under this Act or the Portal-to-Portal Act of 1947 on account of his failure to comply with any provision or provisions of such

---

[89]See footnote 20.

[90]Amended by section 601 of the Fair Labor Standards Amendments of 1966.

[91]Section 14 of the Fair Labor Standards Amendments of 1949, as amended by Reorganization Plan No. 6 of 1950 and the Fair Labor Standards Amendments of 1966.

Acts(1) with respect to work heretofore or hereafter performed in a workplace to which the exemption in section 13(f) is applicable, (2) with respect to work performed in Guam, the Canal Zone or Wake Island before the effective date of this amendment of subsection (d), or (3) with respect to work performed in a possession named in section 6(a)(3) at any time prior to the establishment by the Secretary, as provided therein, of a minimum wage rate applicable to such work.[92]

INJUNCTION PROCEEDINGS

SEC. 17. The district courts, together with the United States District Court for the District of the Canal Zone, the District Court of the Virgin Islands, and the District Court of Guam shall have jurisdiction, for cause shown, to restrain violations of section 15, including in the case of violations of section 15 (a) (2) the restraint of any witholding of payment of minimum wages or overtime compensation found by the court to be due to employees under this Act (except sums which employees are barred from recovering, at the time of the commencement of the action to restrain the violations, by virtue of the provisions of section 6 of the Portal-to-Portal Act of 1947).[93]

RELATION TO OTHER LAWS

SEC. 18. (*a*) No provision of this Act or of any order thereunder shall excuse noncompliance with any Federal or State law or municipal ordinance establishing a minimum wage higher than the minimum wage established under this Act or a maximum workweek lower than the maximum workweek established under this Act, and no provision of this Act relating to the employment of child labor shall justify noncompliance with any Federal or State law or municipal ordinance establishing a higher standard than the standard established under this Act. No provision of this Act shall justify any employer in reducing a wage paid by him which is in excess of the applicable minimum wage under this Act, or justify any employer in increasing hours of employment maintained by him which are shorter than the maximum hours applicable under this Act.

(b) Notwithstanding any other provision of this Act (other than section 13(f)) or any other law, any employee—

(1) described in paragraph (7) of section 202 of the Classification Act of 1949 (5 U.S.C. 1082(7)) whose compensation is required to be fixed and adjusted from time to time as nearly as is consistent with the public interest in accordance with prevailing rates, and any Federal

---

[92]Section 4 of the American Samoa Labor Standards Amendments of 1956, as amended by section 1(2) of the Act of August 30, 1957 (71 Stat. 514), effective November 27, 1957.

[93]See footnote 88.

employee in the Canal Zone engaged in employment of the kind described in such paragraph (7), or

(2) described in section 7474 of title 10, United States Code, whose rates of wages are established to conform, as nearly as is consistent with with the public interest, with those of private establishments in the immediate vicinity, or

(3) employed in a nonappropriated fund instrumentality under the jurisdiction of the Armed Forces,

shall have his basic compensation fixed or adjusted at a wage rate which is not less than the appropriate wage rate provided for in section 6(a) (1) of this Act (except that the wage rate provided for in section 6(b) shall apply to any employee who performed services during the workweek in a work place within the Canal Zone), and shall have his overtime compensation set at an hourly rate not less than the overtime rate provided for in section 7(a) (1) of this Act.

SEPARABILITY OF PROVISIONS

SEC. 9. If any provision of this Act or the application of such provision to any person or circumstances is held invalid, the remainder of the Act and the application of such provision to other persons or circumstances shall not be affected thereby.

Approved, June 25, 1938.[94]

Additional Provisions of Fair Labor Standards Amendments of 1966

[Sections 101 to 501, inclusive, and section 601 (a) of the Fair Labor Standards amendments of 1966 amended the Fair Labor Standards Act of 1938, and are incorporated in their proper place in the Act.]

STATUTE OF LIMITATIONS

SEC. 601. . . .

(b) Section 6(a) of the Portal-to-Portal Act of 1947 (Public Law 49, Eightieth Congress) is amended by inserting before the semicolon at the end thereof the following: ", except that a cause of action arising out of a willful violation may be commenced within three years after the cause of action accrued".

EFFECTIVE DATE

SEC. 602. Except as otherwise provided in this Act, the amendments made by this Act shall take effect on February 1, 1967. On and after the

---

[94]The Fair Labor Standards Amendments of 1949 were approved October 26, 1949; the Fair Labor Standards Amendments of 1955 were approved August 12, 1955; the American Samoa Labor Standards Amendments were approved August 8, 1956; the Fair Labor Standards Amendments of 1961 were approved May 5, 1961; the Fair Labor Standards Amendments of 1966 were approved September 23, 1966.

date of the enactment of this Act the Secretary is authorized to promulgate necessary rules, regulations, or orders with regard to the amendments made by this Act.

STUDY OF EXCESSIVE OVERTIME

SEC. 603. *The Secretary of Labor is hereby instructed to commence immediately a complete study of present practices dealing with overtime payments for work in excess of forty hours per week and the extent to which such overtime work impedes the creation of new job opportunities in American industry. The Secretary is further instructed to report to the Congress by July 1, 1967, the findings of such survey with appropriate recommendations.*

CANAL ZONE EMPLOYEES AND PANAMA CANAL STUDY

SEC. 604. *The Secretary of Labor, in cooperation with the Secretary of Defense and the Secretary of State, shall (1) undertake a study with respect to (A) wage rates payable to Federal employees in the Canal Zone engaged in employment of the kind described in paragraph (7) of section 202 of the Classification Act of 1949 (5 U.S.C. 1082(7)) and (B) the requirements of an effective and economical operation of the Panama Canal, and (2) report to the Congress not later than July 1, 1968, the results of his study together with such recommendations as he may deem appropriate.*

STUDY OF WAGES PAID HANDICAPPED CLIENTS IN SHELTERED WORKSHOPS

SEC. 605. *The Secretary of Labor is hereby instructed to commence immediately a complete study of wage payments to handicapped clients of sheltered workshops and of the feasibility of raising existing wage standards in such workshops. The Secretary is further instructed to report to the Congress by July 1, 1967, the findings of such study with appropriate recommendations.*

PREVENTION OF DISCRIMINATION BECAUSE OF AGE

SEC. 606. *The Secretary of Labor is hereby directed to submit to the Congress not later than January 1, 1967, his specific legislative recommendations for implementing the conclusions and recommendations contained in his report on age discrimination in employment made pursuant to section 715 of Public Law 88–352. Such legislative recommendations shall include, without limitation, provisions specifying appropriate enforcement procedures, a particular administering agency, and the standards, coverage, and exemptions, if any, to be included in the proposed enactment.*

Approved, September 23, 1966.

Additional Provisions of Fair Labor Standards Amendments of 1961

[Sections 2 to 12, inclusive, of the Fair Labor Standards Amendments of 1961 amend the Fair Labor Standards Act of 1938, and are incorporated in their proper place in the Act.]

EFFECTIVE DATE

SEC. 14 The amendments made by this Act shall take effect upon the expiration of one hundred and twenty days after the date of its enactment, except as otherwise provided in such amendments and except that the authority to promulgate necessary rules, regulations, or orders with regard to amendments made by this Act, under the Fair Labor Standards Act of 1938 and amendments thereto, including amendments made by this Act, may be exercised by the Secretary on and after the date of enactment of this Act.

Approved, May 5, 1961.

Additional Provisions of Fair Labor Standards Amendments of 1949

[Sections 2 to 15, inclusive, of the Fair Labor Standards Amendments of 1949 amend the Fair Labor Standards Act of 1938, and are incorporated in their proper place in the Act.]

MISCELLANEOUS AND EFFECTIVE DATE

SEC. 16. (a) The amendments made by this Act shall take effect upon the expiration of ninety days from the date of its enactment; except that the amendment made by section 4 shall take effect on the date of its enactment.

(b) Except as provided in section 3(o) and in the last sentence of section 16(c) of the Fair Labor Standards Act of 1938, as amended, no amendment made by this Act shall be construed as amending, modifying, or repealing any provision of the Portal-to-Portal Act of 1947.

(c) Any order, regulation, or interpretation of the Administrator of the Wage and Hour Division or of the Secretary of Labor, and any agreement entered into by the Administrator or the Secretary, in effect under the provisions of the Fair Labor Standards Act of 1938, as amended, on the effective date of this Act, shall remain in effect as an order, regulation, interpretation, or agreement of the Administrator or the Secretary, as the case may be, pursuant to this Act, except to the extent that any such order, regulation, interpretation, or agreement may be inconsistent with the provisions of this Act, or may from time to time be amended, modified, or rescinded by the Administrator or the Secretary, as the case may be, in accordance with the provisions of this Act.[1]

---

[1]Effective May 24, 1950, all functions of the Administrator were transferred to the Secretary of Labor by Reorganization Plan No. 6 of 1950, 64 Stat. 1263. See text set out under sec. 4(a) of the Fair Labor Standards Act, p. 3 of this pamphlet.

(d) No amendment made by this Act shall affect any penalty or liability with respect to any act or omission occurring prior to the effective date of this Act; but, after the expiration of two years from such effective date, no action shall be instituted under section 16(b) of the Fair Labor Standards Act of 1938, as amended, with respect to any liability accruing thereunder for any act or omission occurring prior to the effective date of this Act.

(e) No employer shall be subject to any liability or punishment under the Fair Labor Standards Act of 1938, as amended (in any action or proceeding commenced prior to or on or after the effective date of this Act), on account of the failure of said employer to pay an employee compensation for any period of overtime work performed prior to July 20, 1949, if the compensation paid prior to July 20, 1949 for such work was at least equal to the compensation which would have been payable for such work had section 7 (d) (6) and (7) and section 7 (g) of the Fair Labor Standards Act of 1938, as amended, been in effect at the time of such payment.

(f) Public Law 177, Eighty-first Congress, approved July 20, 1949, is hereby repealed as of the effective date of this Act.[2]

Approved, October 26, 1949.

Pertinent Provisions Affecting the Fair Labor Standards Act from the Portal-to-Portal Act of 1947

PART I

FINDINGS AND POLICY

SEC. 1. (a) The Congress hereby finds that the Fair Labor Standards Act of 1938, as amended, has been interpreted judicially in disregard of long-established customs, practices, and contracts between employers and employees, thereby creating wholly unexpected liabilities, immense in amount and retroactive in operation, upon employers with the results that, if said Act as so interpreted or claims arising under such interpretations were permitted to stand, (1) the payment of such liabilities would bring about financial ruin of many employers and seriously impair the capital resources of many others, thereby resulting in the reduction of industrial operations, halting of expansion and development, curtailing employment, and the earning power of employees; (2) the credit of many employers would be seriously impaired; (3) there would be created both an extended and continuous uncertainty on the part of industry, both employer and employee, as

---

[2]The provisions of the repealed statute are now contained in substance in sec. 7(d) (5), (6), (7), and (g) of the Fair Labor Standards Act, as amended. See pp. 9, 10 of this pamphlet.

to the financial condition of productive establishments and a gross inequality of competitive conditions between employers and between industries; (4) employees would receive windfall payments, including liquidated damages, of sums for activities performed by them without any expectation of reward beyond that included in their agreed rates of pay; (5) there would occur the promotion of increasing demands for payment to employees for engaging in activities no compensation for which had been contemplated by either the employer or employee at the time they were engaged in; (6) voluntary collective bargaining would be interfered with and industrial disputes between employees and employers and between employees and employees would be created; (7) the courts of the country would be burdened with excessive and needless litigation and champertous practices would be encouraged; (8) the Public Treasury would be deprived of large sums of revenues and public finances would be seriously deranged by claims against the Public Treasury for refunds of taxes already paid; (9) the cost to the Government of goods and services heretofore and hereafter purchased by its various departments and agencies would be unreasonably increased and the Public Treasury would be seriously affected by consequent increased cost of war contracts; and (10) serious and adverse effects upon the revenues of Federal, State, and local governments would occur.

The Congress further finds that all of the foregoing constitutes a substantial burden on commerce and a substantial obstruction to the free flow of goods in commerce.

The Congress, therefore, further finds and declares that it is in the national public interest and for the general welfare, essential to national defense, and necessary to aid, protect, and foster commerce, that this Act be enacted.

The Congress further finds that the varying and extended periods of time for which, under the laws of the several States, potential retroactive liability may be imposed upon employers, have given and will give rise to great difficulties in the sound and orderly conduct of business and industry.

The Congress further finds and declares that all of the results which have arisen or may arise under the Fair Labor Standards Act of 1938, as amended, as aforesaid, may (except as to liability for liquidated damages) arise with respect to the Walsh-Healey and Bacon-Davis Acts and that it is therefore, in the national public interest and for the general welfare, essential to national defense, and necessary to aid, protect, and foster commerce, that this Act shall apply to the Walsh-Healey Act and the Bacon-Davis Act.

(b) It is hereby declared to be the policy of the Congress in order to meet the existing emergency and to correct existing evils (1) to relieve and protect interstate commerce from practices which burden and obstruct it; (2) to protect the right of collective bargaining; and (3) to define and limit the jurisdiction of the courts.

PART III

FUTURE CLAIMS

SEC. 4. RELIEF FROM CERTAIN FUTURE CLAIMS UNDER THE FAIR LABOR STANDARDS ACT OF 1938, AS AMENDED, THE WALSH-HEALEY ACT, AND THE BACON-DAVIS ACT.—

(a) Except as provided in subsection (b), no employer shall be subject to any liability or punishment under the Fair Labor Standards Act of 1938, as amended, the Walsh-Healey Act, or the Bacon-Davis Act, on account of the failure of such employer to pay an employee minimum wages, or to pay an employee minimum wages, or to pay an employee overtime compensation, for or on account of any of the following activities of such employee engaged in on or after the date of the enactment of this Act—

(1) walking, riding, or traveling to and from the actual place of performance of the principal activity or activities which such employee is employed to perform, and

(2) activities which are preliminary to or postliminary to said principal activity or activities,

which occur either prior to the time on any particular workday at which such employee commences, or subsequent to the time on any particular workday at which he ceases, such principal activity or activities.

(b) Notwithstanding the provisions of subsection (a) which relieve an employer from liability and punishment with respect to an activity, the employer, shall not be so relieved if such activity is compensable by either—

(1) an express provision of a written or nonwritten contract in effect, at the time of such activity, between such employee, his agent, or collective-bargaining representative and his employer; or

(2) a custom or practice in effect, at the time of such activity, at the establishment or other place where such employee is employed, covering such activity, not inconsistent with a written or nonwritten contract, in effect at the time of such activity, between such employee, his agent, or collective-bargaining representative and his employer.

(c) For the purposes of subsection (b), an activity shall be considered as compensable under such contract provision or such custom or practice only when it is engaged in during the portion of the day with respect to which it is so made compensable.

(d) In the application of the minimum wage and overtime compensation provisions of the Fair Labor Standards Act of 1938, as amended, of the Walsh-Healey Act, or of the Bacon-Davis Act, in determining the time for which an employer employs an employee with respect to walking, riding, traveling or other preliminary or postliminary activities described in subsection (a) of this section, there shall be counted all that time, but only that time, during which the employee engages in any such activity which is compensable within the meaning of subsections (b) and (c) of this section.

PART IV

MISCELLANEOUS

SEC. 6. STATUTE OF LIMITATIONS.—Any action commenced on or after the date of the enactment of this Act to enforce any cause of action for unpaid minimum wages, unpaid overtime compensation, or liquidated damages, under the Fair Labor Standards Act of 1938, as amended, the Walsh-Healey Act, or the Bacon-Davis Act—

(a) if the cause of action accrues on or after the date of the enactment of this Act—may be commenced within two years after the cause of action accrued, and every such action shall be forever barred unless commenced within two years after the cause of action accrued, *except that a cause of action arising out of a willful violation may be commenced within three years after the cause of action accrued;*[1]

SEC. 7. DETERMINATION OF COMMENCEMENT OF FUTURE ACTIONS.— In determining when an action is commenced for the purposes of section 6, an action commenced on or after the date of the enactment of this Act under the Fair Labor Standards Act of 1938, as amended, the Walsh-Healey Act, or the Bacon-Davis Act, shall be considered to be commenced on the date when the complaint is filed; except that in the case of a collective or class action instituted under the Fair Labor Standards Act of 1938, as amended, or the Bacon-Davis Act, it shall be considered to be commenced in the case of any individual claimant—

(a) on the date when the complaint is filed, if he is specifically named as a party plaintiff in the complaint and his written consent to become a party plaintiff is filed on such date in the court in which the action is brought; or

(b) if such written consent was not so filed or if his name did not so appear—on the subsequent date on which such written consent is filed in the court in which the action was commenced.

SEC. 10. RELIANCE IN FUTURE ON ADMINISTRATIVE RULINGS, ETC.— (a) In any action or proceeding based on any act or omission on or after the date of the enactment of this Act, no employer shall be subject to any liability or punishment for or on account of the failure of the employer to pay minimum wages or overtime compensation under the Fair Labor Standards Act of 1938, as amended, the Walsh-Healey Act, or the Bacon-Davis Act, if he pleads and proves that the act or omission complained of was in good faith in conformity with and in reliance on any

---

[1]As amended by section 601 of the Fair Labor Standards Amendments of 1966, 80 Stat. 830.

written administrative regulation, order, ruling, approval, or interpretation, of the agency of the United States specified in subsection (b) of this section, or any administrative practice or enforcement policy of such agency with respect to the class of employers to which he belonged. Such a defense, if established, shall be a bar to the action or proceeding, notwithstanding that after such act or omission, such administrative regulation, order, ruling, approval, interpretation, practice, or enforcement policy is modified or rescinded or is determined by judicial authority to be invalid or of no legal effect.

(b) The agency referred to in subsection (a) shall be—

(1) in the case of the Fair Labor Standards Act of 1938, as amended —the Secretary of Labor[2];

SEC. 11. LIQUIDATED DAMAGES.—In any action commenced prior to or on or after the date of the enactment of this Act to recover unpaid minimum wages, unpaid overtime compensation, or liquidated damages, under the Fair Labor Standards Act of 1938, as amended, if the employer shows to the satisfaction of the court that the act or omission giving rise to such action was in good faith and that he had reasonable grounds for believing that his act or omission was not a violation of the Fair Labor Standards Act of 1938, as amended, the court may, in its sound discretion, award no liquidated damages or award any amount thereof not to exceed the amount specified in section 16 (b) of such Act.

SEC. 13. DEFINITIONS.—

(a) When the terms "employer", "employee", and "wage" are used in this Act in relation to the Fair Labor Standards Act of 1938, as amended, they shall have the same meaning as when used in such Act of 1938.

(e) As used in section 6 the term "State" means any State of the United States or the District of Columbia or any Territory or possession of the United States.

SEC. 14. SEPARABILITY.—If any provision of this Act or the application of such provision to any person or circumstance is held invalid, the remainder of this Act and the application of such provision to other persons or circumstances shall not be affected thereby.

SEC. 15. SHORT TITLE.—This Act may be cited as the "Portal-to-Portal Act of 1947".

Approved, May 14, 1947.

---

[2]As amended by Reorganization Plan No. 6 of 1950, 64 Stat. 1263.

LEGISLATIVE HISTORY OF THE
FAIR LABOR STANDARDS ACT*

John S. Forsythe

The roots of the Federal Fair Labor Standards Act of 1938 are deep in a movement that extends back over a period of years,[1] yet it is evident that the closest relationship exists with the wage and hour standards established under the National Industrial Recovery Act. When the N.I.R.A. was invalidated by the Supreme Court, the subject of federal betterment of wages and hours was not allowed to become quiescent. President Roosevelt is said to have insisted on the labor standards in the 1933 legislation and, after the *Schechter* case, to have repeatedly deplored their abandonment.[2] A chance for a bold declaration came in 1936 when the Supreme Court reiterated its stand that wage and hour control was beyond the sphere of state, as well as federal, activity.[3] This decision paved the way for the plank in the Democratic Party platform of the same year urging national action, by constitutional amendment if need be, to eliminate substandard working conditions and child labor. After the Democratic victory at the polls in November, there is evidence that the manner of carrying out this pledge was receiving much attention from the Administration[4] and members of Congress.

The intensity of speculation in this regard increased when the 75th Congress met in January, 1937. Some felt that the drafting of a constitutional amendment was the only method by which the party pledge might be carried out, but in his message to Congress on January 6, the President stated his general opposition to immediate amendment of the Constitution, and asked instead for an "enlightened view" on social legislation from the judiciary in order that democracy might be made to function successfully. Reports of the President's first press conference of the year indicate that plans were being formulated to "do something" about minimum wages as well as judicial opposition to this program.[5] The coincidence of his statements on these two matters was not properly interpreted in the press at the time, but it serves to illustrate the significant fact, namely, the close tie between federal labor standards legislation and the President's plan for "reorganization" of the Supreme Court. It was to become clear during the

---

*Reprinted with permission from a symposium, "The Wage and Hour Law," appearing in *Law and Contemporary Problems,* Vol. 6, No. 3, Summer 1939; published by Duke University School of Law, Duke Station, Durham, N.C. Copyright 1939 by the Duke University Press.

[1] See de Vyver, *Regulation of Wages and Hours Prior to 1938, supra,* p. 323.

[2] N. Y. Times, Jan. 10, IV, p. 6, col. 3.

[3] *Morehead* v. *People ex. rel. Tipaldo,* 298 U.S. 587.

[4] N. Y. Times, Jan. 4, 1937, p. 18, col. 4.

[5] TIME, Jan. 11, 1937, p. 13.

first session of the 75th Congress that each of these plans was being used in the attempt to bring the other into being.

The month of January, 1937, was a period of intense activity behind the scenes so far as wage and hour legislation was concerned. Numerous drafts were being prepared by Administration advisers, Labor Department officials, and even by persons having no public responsibility. General Johnson, of NRA fame, favored a bill making use of the taxing power, while Donald Richberg, his successor, wished to amend the Anti-Trust Laws so as to accomplish the desired end, and make the work under substandard labor conditions an unfair method of competition subject to the jurisdiction of the Federal Trade Commission.[6]

President Roosevelt began his second term of office with conferences with Senator Black of Alabama, chairman of the Senate Committee on Labor, and with Representative Connery of Massachusetts, who held the similar chairmanship in the House. Rumors flew thick and fast as to what was in prospect and, in spite of assurances to the contrary by the President, many felt that a "new NRA" was being prepared which would cover a broad field of trade practices. Then on February 5, 1937, President Roosevelt announced his plan for reorganizing the federal judiciary. It was instantly recognized that here was his answer to the problem of getting social legislation held valid. In fact it was announced that a wage and hour bill and other legislation would follow in the wake of the passage of the Court Plan.[7] The need for control over hours and wages was evidently considered by the President to be one of the strongest weapons available to force passage of the Court Bill. For this reason it was indicated that the legislation would not be submitted until after there had been action on the Court Plan.[8]

Momentous decisions were being announced by the Supreme Court during this period which were to vitally affect both labor standards legislation and the Court Bill. The Supreme Court reversed its stand on minimum wage legislation[9] and upheld the Railway Labor Act[10] and the National Labor Relations Act.[11] These decisions served to take considerable pressure off of the drive to enact the Court Bill, and as the session wore on without any action on this proposed legislation, the Administration decided to go ahead with the introduction of a wage and hour bill. The provisions of the proposal became known several days before the President's speech on May 24, 1938, calling for its enactment, but the bills introduced into the two houses of Congress by Senator Black and Representative Connery, re-

[6]N. Y. Times, Feb. 3, 1937, p. 10, col. 3.
[7]*Id.*, Feb. 8, 1937, p. 1, col. 8.
[8]*Id.*, April 27, p. 1, col. 6.
[9]*West Coast Hotel Co.* v. *Parrish,* 300 U.S. 379.
[10]*Virginian Ry.* v. *System Federation No. 40,* 300 U.S. 515.
[11]*National Labor Relations Board* v. *Jones & Laughlin Steel Corp.,* 301 U.S. 1.

spectively, deviated from those originally announced in that the basic wage and hour standards were left blank instead of being 40 cents an hour and 40 hours weekly.

The President's message[12] to Congress asserted the necessity for governmental control over maximum hours, minimum wages, the evil of child labor and the exploitation of unorganized labor. He stressed the constitutional basis for such legislation in the power of Congress over the channels of commerce and the desirablity of barring goods produced under "unfair" standards from these channels. It is interesting to note that the President did not envisage a uniform raising of standards in all industries and for all regions. He stated that as a practical matter there should be "some differentiation between different industries and localities."

On the same day that the President sent his special message to Congress nearly identical[13] bills, S. 2475 and H. R. 7200, were introduced by Senator Black and Representative Connery. It was to be exactly 13 months and one day from this date before the measure reached the President's desk for signature and only then after having undergone amendment after amendment until practically the only point in common with the original bill was the legislative number. The original bills proposed the creation of a Fair Labor Standards Board of five members to administer the Act and keep goods produced under substandard labor conditions from entering interstate commerce and those conditions themselves from "affecting commerce." Congress was to set statutory minimum wages and maximum hours but the Board would have power to raise or lower these standards.[14] It is important to note that the purpose of the drafters was not to provide a sudden straight-jacket of wages and hours for all industry. Extreme flexibility was the keynote of this draft. The wages and hours provisions were only to become operative when the Board so ordered, and then only to the specific industries covered by the order.[15] In addition to these barely non-oppressive wage and hour standards the Board had authority to fix a minimum "fair" wage and a maximum "reasonable" workweek.[16] Certain statutory objectives

---

[12]SEN. REP. 884, 75th Cong. 1st Sess. (1937) 1.

[13]There were two minor points of difference. *Joint Hearings before the Senate Committee on Education and Labor and the House Committee on Labor on S. 2475 and H. R. 2700,* 75th Cong. 1st Sess. (1937) 44. Hereinafter cited as *Hearings.*

[14]Original Bill, § 4(c). For an explanation of the terminology used in referring to the several bills, see Table of Bills, *infra,* p. 475.

[15]Assistant Attorney General Robert H. Jackson said in this connection: "Portions of the bill relating to wages and hours would become operative as and when the Board created by the act orders this application. This bill does not plunge the nation headlong into rigid and widespread policy of regulating wages and hours. It permits the building up a body of experience and prevents extension of regulations faster than capacity properly to administer is acquired. The investigations of the Board will also present the evidence and the findings upon which the Government can rest its argument if the constitutionality of the act is assailed." *Hearings,* p. 4.

[16]Original Bill, § 5.

were set forth to be used as guides in arriving at those higher standards. However, the Board was restricted to the extent that it could not establish minimum wages of more than $1200 a year or 80 cents per hour except for overtime, night and extra-shift work. The Board was authorized, if its members so wished, to appoint advisory committees in the various industries.[17]

Child labor under the age of 16 was prohibited, with power in the Chief of the Children's Bureau to bar the labor of those under 18 in any occupation which he thought "particularly hazardous" or detrimental to their health or well-being.[18] The child labor provisions were substantially patterned after the Federal Child Labor Law declared unconstitutional in *Hammer* v. *Dagenhart*.[19] The use of strikebreakers and labor spies was included in the oppressive labor practices forbidden in this draft.[20]

Joint hearings on the proposed legislation were held by the House Committee on Labor and the Senate Committee on Education and Labor from June 2 to June 22, 1937. More than twelve hundred pages of testimony was taken from labor leaders, industrialists, trade association representatives, and others. During the hearings on June 15, 1937, William P. Connery, chairman of the House Labor Committee, died, and the leadership for the coming battle in the House passed to Mrs. Mary T. Norton, of New Jersey.

The opening statement at the hearings was made by Assistant Attorney General Robert H. Jackson, who explained the bill section by section and demonstrated the constitutional bases upon which the various sections would be supported.[21] He likewise took great pains in demonstrating the

---

[17]Original Bill, § 14.

[18]Original Bill, § 2(a) (13).

[19]247 U.S. 251 (1918).

[20]Original Bill, § 2(a) (12). This provision was omitted by the Senate Committee on Education and Labor and never revived in subsequent drafts. The committee felt that such matters could best be handled by Amendment of the National Labor Relations Act. SEN. REP. No. 884, 75th Cong., 1st Sess. (1937) 5.

[21]The several prohibitions of the bill probably incorporate more constitutional theories than any other piece of suggested legislation in the history of the country. The idea was, as Mr. Jackson indicated, to invalidate all hopeful approaches to constitutionality. He stated: "This act combines everything, and is an effort to take advantage of whatever theories may prevail on the Court at the time that the case is heard. Of course, that results in a good deal of complication." *Hearings*, p. 54.

The opinions upon which it was stated that the several sections in the original S. 2475 were based are: § 700 (dissenting opinion by Mr. Justice Holmes in *Hammer* v. *Dagenhart*, 247 U.S. 251 (1918)); § 7(b) (*Kentucky Whip & Collar Co.* v. *Illinois Central R. R.*, 299 U.S. 334 (1937)); § 7(c) (*Wilson* v. *New*, 243 U.S. 332 (1917) and *Coronado Coal Co.* v. *United Mine Workers*, 268 U.S. 295 (1925)); § 8(a) (*Shreveport Rate Case, Houston, E. & W. Texas R. R.* v. *United States*, 234 U.S. 342 (1914)); § 8(b) (*Dayton-Goose Creek R. Co.* v. *United States*, 263 U.S. 456 (1924)); § 9(a) (*Federal Trade Commission* v. *Keppel and Bros.*, 291 U.S. 304 (1934)); § 9(b) (*Stafford* v. *Wallace*, 258 U.S. 495 (1927)); § 10(1) (*National Labor Relations Board* v. *Jones & Laughlin Steel Corp.*, 301 U.S. 1 (1937)); § 10(2) (*Stafford* v. *Wallace*, 258 U.S. 495 (1937)); § 10(3) (*Coronado Coal Co.* v. *United Mine Workers*, 268 U.S. 295 (1915)); § 22(b) (*Whitfield* v. *Ohio*, 297, U.S. 431 (1936)). *Hearings*, pp. 58-62.

bill was not "another NRA." John L. Lewis, representing the CIO and the United Mine Workers of America, testified that he was generally in favor of the bill.[22] He suggested that Congress should set a maximum of 35 hours per week and give the Board power to vary the figure up to 40 or down to 30 as the situation required. Strangely enough, Lewis, and not President Green, of the AFL, was strongly opposed to giving the Board discretionary power to raise wages above 40 cents an hour. He urged the abolition of Section 5 and all other sections pertaining thereto. His reason for so objecting seemed to be the fear that such minimum "fair" wages and maximum "reasonable" hours if fixed by the Board would tend to become actually the maximum wage and the minimum hours. It also seems clear that he felt that it would put a powerful propaganda weapon in the hands of employers if unions saw fit to strike for standards higher than had been set by the Board as "fair" and "reasonable."[23]

William Green, president of the American Federation of Labor, announced that his organization, by action of the executive council, endorsed the proposed Fair Labor Standards Act of 1937 but wished to offer several perfecting amendments.[24] These amendments were mainly to strengthen the administrative portions of the act and further protect collective bargaining agreements.[25] Green stated that the AFL wanted no overlapping between collective bargaining activity and governmental control of wages and hours; that he understood the legislation was merely an attempt to encourage collective bargaining and as collective bargaining expanded, government control should abandon the field. Mr. Green would carry this theory to the extent of refusing to let the Board raise standards reached through collective bargaining even if they were below the minimum standards set by Congress.[26] Green recommended a basic 40-hour week with Board having power to vary it down to 30 hours. He also recommended a basic 40 cent minimum, but unlike Lewis he favored leaving the power in the Board to raise wages up to 80 cents per hour.[27] Green also expressly favored a Board of five to administer the act. This is interesting in view of his later position concerning the administrative features.[28]

Sidney Hillman, president of Amalgamated Clothing Workers of America, a CIO union, took an opposite position to Mr. Lewis on the question of

[22]*Hearings,* p. 271.

[23]*Id.,* pp. 279, 285-286.

[24]*Id.,* p. 211. The Executive Council of the AFL had been in session when the bills were first introduced and Green had announced that the organization might oppose a wages and hours bill because there was "strong feeling on the part of some against minimum wages for men." N. Y. Times, May 24, 1937, p. 1, col. 2.

[25]*Hearings,* pp. 221-222.

[26]*Id.,* p. 226; *cf. id.,* p. 227.

[27]*Id.,* pp. 220-221.

[28]See note 46, *infra.*

whether or not under Section 5 the Board should have power to set up "fair" wages and "reasonable" hours higher than the basic standards set by Congress.[29] He wanted the Board to have this discretion. He explained the difference partly on the ground that Mr. Lewis's experience had been with an industry which bargained on a national scale, while his own was in industries such as textiles, garments, and shoes, where collective bargaining cannot cover the whole industry, and the only way to raise standards uniformly is to have it done by the government. Forcing high standards on a few employers at a time would drive those out of business before the rest of the industry could be effectively organized.[30]

Appearing against the bill, George H. Davis, president of the Chamber of Commerce of the United States, criticized it mainly for the uncertainty in future labor costs which it would cause.[31] Mr. James A. Emery, General Counsel of the National Association of Manufacturers, argued that the bill used an unconstitutional view of the commerce power, and was also an invalid delegation of power.[32] Mr. Noel Sargent, economist for the same organization, also appeared in opposition to the bill. His most important arguments were that it would raise the cost of living for the farmer, that it would be impossible to administer such a complicated and cumbersome bill in a satisfactory manner, and that it would be an unfair burden on the manufacturer who has foreign competition either here or abroad.[33] Others appearing against the bill were Guy L. Harrington, National Publishers Association; Arthur Besse, President of the National Association of Wood Manufacturers; Samuel Fraser, Assistant Secretary of the International Apple Association; Claudius Murchison, President of the Cotton Textile Institute; John B. Scott, Anthracite Institute; and Benjamin C. Marsh, Executive Secretary of the People's Lobby.

On July 8, 1937, Senator Black, for the Senate Committee on Education and Labor, favorably reported the Fair Labor Standards Act with amendments. In one sense the Senate Committee Bill was even more flexible than the Original Draft, in others not so flexible. No statutory minimum wages or maximum hours were set up. Instead the Board was given power to set these standards.[34] However, the range of this power had been greatly curtailed from that in the original bill for the minimum wage could not exceed 40 cents an hour and the maximum hours could not be under 40 hours a week. Advisory committees were made mandatory.[35] The child labor standards were lowered so that children under 16 could be employed

---

[29]*Hearings*, pp. 945-946.
[30]*Id.*, p. 498.
[31]*Id.*, pp. 935-943.
[32]*Id.*, pp. 623-645.
[33]*Id.*, pp. 645-664.
[34]Senate Committee Bill, § 4(b) and (c).
[35]*Id.*, § 11.

in occupations which the Chief of the Children's Bureau found would not interfere with their schooling or be detrimental to their health. Finally a provision was added to quiet the opposition which had developed around the fear that higher wages and lower hours would mean higher production costs which in turn would mean an influx of cheap foreign goods.[36] This provision gave the Tariff Commission the power to investigate to see if higher tariff rates would be necessary because of increased costs of production.[37]

The bill as reported by the Senate Committee did not reach the floor of the Senate for debate until July 26. There were no particular developments of importance in the debate aside from the open split that developed in the AFL ranks between President Green and certain of the department heads. A move to recommit the bill was given impetus by the fact that the AFL was said to be opposed to the form the bill had taken. Mr. Green denied that the AFL favored recommitment. He stated that the bill did not meet labor's expectations, but that it seemed advisable to pass it in its present form with the hope that satisfactory amendment could be effected in the House. At the same time that this announcement was read to the Senate a statement was also read urging recommittal of the bill because of alleged interference with the operation of the Walsh-Healey Act. This latter statement was signed by John P. Frey and J. W. Williams, heads of the metal and building trades departments in the AFL.[38] A number of Southern senators attacked the bill, but the statement attracting the most attention was that of Senator E. D. Smith of South Carolina to the effect that it only took 50 cents a day to live reasonably and comfortably in his state.[39]

The Bill passed the Senate on July 31, 1937, by a vote of 52 to 28. The only outstanding change made on the floor of the Senate was the substitution of the so-called Wheeler-Johnson child labor amendment in place of all the child labor provisions of the Senate Committee Bill.[40] This amendment was based on the convict-made goods formula, whereby a state may exclude goods produced under standards lower than those prevailing within the state, which had been severely criticized at the hearings.[41] It may be that one reason for the relatively easy passage in the Senate was that the opponents of the bill, or of specific provisions of the bill, as in the case of the AFL, had decided it would be better strategy to wait and fight the is-

---

[36] See *Hearings,* pp. 75-76.

[37] Senate Committee Bill, § 8(c) and (d).

[38] N. Y. Times, July 30, 1937, p. 1, col. 6; *id.,* July 31, p. 4, col. 2. See also 81 CONG. REC. 8192 (1937).

[39] N. Y. Times, July 31, 1937, p. 1, col. 4.

[40] Senate Bill, § 24. This provision had been reported favorably as a separate bill by the Senate Interstate Commerce Committee. N. Y. Times, June 8, 1937, p. 9, col. 3.

[41] See p. 489, *infra,* for explanation of the theory of this provision.

sues out in the House. The possibility of early adjournment would add to the value of this technique.

Although the prolonged battle over the Court Plan had added to the usual Congressional urge to leave Washington in mid-summer, a group of some thirty members of the House had pledged themselves to fight adjournment until the wage and hour bill was enacted.[42] On August 6, 1937, the Senate bill with amendments of the House Committee on Labor was reported out favorably. The most important change was to replace the Wheeler-Johnson child labor amendment with the child labor provisions in the Senate Committee Bill.[43] The demands of the AFL for protection of collective bargaining agreements were met to the extent of providing that the Board should not have jurisdiction of wages and hours in occupations where collective bargaining facilities were adequate. It would seem that the bill would have passed the House if it could have been brought to a vote at that time, but the Rules Committee, by a combination of Republicans and Southern Democrats, refused to issue a rule to let the House consider the measure. An attempt was made to get action by calling a Democratic caucus but when it met on August 19, 1937, no business could be transacted because a quorum would not answer to their names, and this spelled the doom of the legislation at this session.[44]

President Roosevelt issued a call for a special session to convene on November 15, 1937. On October 12, he made a radio address in which he declared that wage and hour legislation would be one of the matters considered at the special session; and in a special message to Congress on November 15, 1937, he pointed out the need for federal wage and hour legislation.[45]

When the session convened, however, it immediately became apparent that the members of the Rules Committee had not changed their views on the subject and that they would refuse to issue a rule to let the House consider the bill. On November 16, 1937, Mrs. Norton started a petition to discharge the Rules Committee from further consideration of the matter. At first it did not appear that sufficient names would be secured. For one thing during the summer, more opposition had developed in the ranks of the AFL and President Green had been instructed to consult with the heads of the various departments of the Federation before issuing any more statements about the wages and hours legislation. The AFL opposition now

---

[42]N. Y. Times, July 31, 1937, p. 1, col. 4.

[43]H. R. REP., No. 1452, 75th Cong., 1st Sess. (1937) 9.

[44]This can probably be explained by the fact that many members were not in favor of the legislation at that time for one reason or another and did not want it to be brought from committee, though they would have felt compelled to vote for it if it had been brought to the floor where a vote could have been forced. See 82 CONG. REC. 197 (1937).

[45]N. Y. Times, Dec. 1, p. 22, col. 5.

centered on granting discretionary powers to an administrative board.[46]

In an attempt to meet this AFL opposition the House Labor Committee proposed an amendment placing the administration of the act in a newly created wages and hours division of the Department of Labor with an administrator appointed by the President. This second House Committee Bill differed greatly from former bills. Instead of having a Board initiate moves to set minimum wages and maximum hours with the aid of an advisory committee, the new draft provided that the power should be shifted to wage and hour committees[47] to be appointed by the administrator. The committee recommendations were binding on the administrator if supported by evidence and based on certain enumerated guides in the statute. Although the House Labor Committee wished to make these numerous amendments to the Bill held by the Rules Committee, it still did not appear that the chance to make amendments of any sort would be given. Some of the group, who had in the previous session tried to prevent adjournment before action on the Bill, now determined to make use of the practical political expedient of trading votes. The strategy was to block the farm program until the Rules Committee relaxed its stranglehold. This tie-up with the vote on the farm bill, in the drive to secure names on the petition. was apparently successful. Representative Jones of Texas, sponsor of the farm legislation, was induced to sign, and sufficient signatures were secured by December 2 to discharge the Rules Committee. Representative Fish of New York proffered a resolution that an investigation be made of the administration lobbying during this period but it did not receive serious attention.[48]

When it became evident that the House would vote on the Bill the AFL was not satisfied with the changes suggested by the House Labor Committee. A bill drafted at the convention in Denver was brought forward and offered as a substitute bill under the sponsorship of Congressmen Dockweiler and Griswold.[49] It provided for rigid 40 cent minimum and 40 hour maximum, with an 8-hour day. Since no discretion was necessary to administer these provisions the only enforcement was through the Attorney General. Criminal proceedings were to be brought by the various Federal District Attorneys. After this was defeated by 162 to 131, the AFL threw its weight to have the bill recommitted, which was done on December 17 1937, by a vote of 216 to 198.[50]

The combination of conservative Southern Democrats with Republicans and AFL followers explains the vote, although it came as considerable of

---

[46]This is traceable to the attitude taken by the AFL leaders toward the National Labor Relations Board. There had been no previous objection on this point, in fact a board had been specifically approved. See note 27 *supra*.

[47]Second House Committee Bill, § 4.

[48]N. Y. Times, Nov. 30, 1937, p. 9, col. 1; *id.*, Dec. 3, 1937, p. 1, col. 8.

[49]82 CONG. REC. 1591 (1937).

[50]*Id.*, p. 1835.

a surprise after enough names were secured to get the Bill on the floor. Alsop and Kintner in a syndicated column state that the shift of the vote in the Louisiana and New Jersey delegations was crucial and explain the shift on the basis of the ruffled feelings of New Orleans' Mayor Maestri and the desire of Jersey City's Mayor Hague to take a slap at John L. Lewis.[51] The same dispatch indicates, however. that Lewis did not have a lobby actively working against recommittal.[52]

Although the wage and hour bill was quite definitely on the agenda for the Third Session of the 75th Congress, it received very little attention during the early months of that session. Due notice was taken of the defeat of Heflin in the Alabama senatorial election by Lister Hill who, while in the House, had voted for the wage and hour bill. Still, subsequent to this came the defeat of the President's Reorganization Bill by the House and this was widely held to be a personal rebuke to the President and to the New Deal program in general.[53] In the light of this it seems quite unlikely that any legislation of the type of the wage and hour bill would have been enacted at that session if it had not been for Senator Pepper's victory in the Florida Democratic Primary. The House Labor Committee had already reported out a new bill but it was resting in its usual pigeon-hole in the Rules Committee. Senator Pepper's victory, after a campaign in which the Bill had been an issue, served to open the floodgates, and when 'the petition to discharge the Rules Committee was opened for signature the required number of names were secured in two hours and 20 minutes. The favorable poll of the Institute of Public Opinion undoubtedly had its effect also.[54]

The Third Session Bill took a still different approach to the problem of flexibility of standards. This time the administration of the act was to be placed in the Secretary of Labor.[55] His main duty was to decide if a given industry was in interstate commerce (under standards set up by the statute). If he so found, the wages and hours provisions became automatic and were applicable. No regional differentials were provided. The standards this time were on a scale basis which changed from year to year.[56] Of course with the rigid standards there was no need of any advisory committees. This bill without substantial amendment was passed by the House on May 24, 314 to 97.

Before this Third House Committee Bill was introduced Mrs. Norton had appointed a subcommittee of the House Labor Committee under the chairmanship of Representative Ramspeck of Georgia to make a report. Mr.

---

[51]N. Y. Times, Dec. 22, 1937, p. 20, col. 4.
[52]Ibid.
[53]TIME, April 18, 1938, p. 16.
[54]See 83 CONG. REC. 7282 (1938).
[55]Third House Committee Bill, § 6.
[56]Id., § § 4 and 5.

Ramspeck's report, however, was not accepted by the committee. He therefore submitted it to the House as a minority report and asked that it be an amendment. His bill contained some of the provisions of the older bills: A five-man board to administer the act with power to fix minimum wages and maximum hours within the old 40-40 limit. One new thing added was a provision to keep the board from raising the pay more than five cents in any one 12-months period. This was defeated on May 24 by a vote of 139 to 70.

It was necessary now that a conference committee attempt to iron out the differences between the drafts passed by the House and the Senate. There were rumblings from certain Southern Senators of a filibuster unless the differential, omitted in the Bill passed by the house, be restored. This question of regional differential seems to have been all-important during the period that the conference committee was at work. It is interesting to note that Administrator Andrews, then New York Industrial Commissioner, stated his opposition to a statutory regional differential in a radio address delivered at this time.[57]

The deadlock in the conference was holding up adjournment and it was freely predicted that once again the wage and hour legislation would fail. Senators Ellender and Pepper, members of the conference, at first refused to accede to a statutory wage ever going above 30 cents an hour.[58] But compromises as to flexibility in attaining minima and the inclusion of a provision which could be construed to allow regional differentials (although expressly disclaiming it) paved the way to agreement in the conference on a completely rewritten bill. This was adopted by the House on June 13 and by the Senate on June 14 with comparatively little debate. The bill received the President's approval on June 25, 1938.

The Act as signed by the President sets up a rigid scale of wages and hours for workers in interstate commerce or who produce goods for such commerce. A statutory minimum of 25 cents is in effect the first year, then a 30-cent minimum is the standard until October, 1945, when the 40-cent wage becomes operative. (Section 6). Unless there is payment of one and one-half times the regular rate of pay covered employees may not be worked in excess of 44 hours the first year, 42 hours the second and 40 after the second. (Section 7). The enforcement of the Act is under the control of a single Administrator in the Department of Labor. Industry committees, appointed by him, may make recommendations which can be made the basis of a wage order setting a minimum wage in excess of the universal rate but not more than 40 cents an hour. (Section 8). There are numerous exemptions, some outright, some dependent upon administrative regulation. There

[57]N. Y. Times, May 31, 1938, p. 29, col. 4.

[58]N. Y. Times, June 9, 1938, p. 1, col. 1; id., June 10, 1938, p. 1, col. 8.

may be criminal and injunction proceedings against violators and civil recovery of double damages by workers. (Section 16). Child labor under 16 years of age is prohibited except under certain conditions laid down by the Chief of the Children's Bureau, and may even be eliminated in certain occupations up to 18 years of age (Sections 3(1) and 12).

This article is divided into two main sections. The first has outlined the broad general legislative history from the introduction of the bill until its signature by the President. This second section attempts to pick out particular features and follow them through the maze of proposals which make up the very complicated legislative history of this particular act. The second section is itself divided into a number of parts selected arbitrarily to bring out the most important provisions as they were developed.

In all, ten different bills reached the floor of Congress, all with at least a major change from its predecessor and most of them in the form of amendments substituting an entirely different proposal. Even the structure of the bills was completely changed. The original bill contained five main parts with 30 subsections. The final draft was in a completely different form with 19 sections in no way comparable to the original sections. Of necessity there has been a limitation of the discussion to these ten proposals. There is evidence that many more drafts were written which never got to the floor.[59]

For the sake of convenience the bills are summarized here. The terminology indicated is used throughout the article.

1. Original Bill. Introduced May 24, 1937, in the first session of the 75th Congress. In the Senate it was S. 2475; in the House H. R. 7200.

2. Senate Committee Bill. Introduced into the Senate July 8, 1937, S. 2475, 75th Congress, first Session, Calendar No. 905.

3. Senate Bill. Passed by the Senate July 31, 1937, and sent to the House of Representatives, 75th Congress. first session.

4. First House Committee Bill. Senate Bill with amendments added by the House Committee on Labor. Introduced into the House August 6, 1937. S. 2475, 75th Congress, first session, Union Calendar No. 535. This bill did not reach the House floor before the session ended.

5. Second House Committee Bill. Introduced into the House as amendment to the First House Committee Bill December 14, 1937, during the special session. 75th Congress, second session. It was recommitted to the House Labor Committee December 17, 1937.

6. AFL Bill. This amendment was sponsored by the American Federation of Labor as a substitute for the Second House Committee Bill. It was

---

[59]In looking through the files of the House Labor Committee over 25 separate drafts were discovered which had been considered by the Committee, only four of which ever reached the floor.

introduced on December 15, 1937 by Representative Griswold and defeated December 16, 1937, 75th Congress, second session.

7. Third House Committee Bill. This was introduced into the House on April 21, 1938. S. 2475, 75th Congress, third session. Union Calendar No. 804.

8. Ramspeck Bill. This is a minority bill from the House Labor Committee. Introduced May 4, 1938. 75th Congress, third session. This bill had been introduced in the same session of Congress under a different number, H. R. 10538, 75th Congress, third session. It was defeated May 24, 1938.

9. House Bill. This is the third house committee bill with amendments added from the floor of the House. Passed by the House May 24, 1938. 75th Congress, third session.

10. Act. This is the bill rewritten in the conference. Pub. L. No. 718, 75th Congress, third session (June 25, 1938). 52 STAT. 1060, 29 U. S. C. §§201-219 (Supp. 1938).

Although this was one of the most bitterly fought pieces of legislation ever to be enacted by Congress, with the true issues frequently clouded by storms of falsification and propaganda, a calm analysis reveals that there were really only three main points of contention: flexible against rigid wage and hour standards, single administrator against a board to administer the act, and method to be used to enforce the child labor provisions of the act. The detailed analysis to follow is based on this division.

In the ten bills which are being discussed in this article there were no less than five different methods of administering the provisions of the acts. The administrative machinery was naturally closely correlated with the wage and hour provisions and the change in one will partially explain the change in the other.

The original bill[60] created an independent agency called the Labor Standards Board with five members for staggered terms of five years at salaries of $10,000 a year. The members were to be appointed by the President with the advice and consent of the Senate and were eligible for reappointment. In making the appointment the President was to consider industrial and geographical conditions.

Before making a wage order in a given occupation the Board could, "if it considered it necessary or appropriate"[61] appoint an advisory committee to investigate and report upon the fair value of services rendered, on the number of hours reasonably suitable to the nature of the work involved, or both. The committee was to be made up of an equal number of persons representing employers and employees in the occupation as well as not more

---

[60] § 3.
[61] Original Bill, § 14.

than three persons representing the public, the first two groups being selected as nearly as practicable from lists of names submitted by employers and employees in the occupation. If the committee did not report within 60 days a new committee was to be appointed. The Board was to give the committee all available data on the industry involved, and it could accept or reject in whole or in part the committee report, or appoint a new committee. The Senate Committee on Education and Labor made one important change in the advisory committee by making it mandatory on the Board to appoint on advisory committee before a labor standard order could be issued (it had been optional in the original bill). It should be noted, however, that the committee report was not binding on the Board.[62]

The first important change in the manner of selecting the Board came in the first House Committee bill. There an effort was made to give equal representation by providing that the members should be chosen one from the Northeast, one from the Northwest, one from the Southeast, one from the Southwest and one from the Central part of the United States; and further, one of the members was to be a representative of employers and another one to be a representative of employees. To decentralize the administration as much as possible the House Labor Committee provided that the Board should appoint a director for each state, territory, and the District of Columbia.[63]

One of the focal points of attack on the early drafts of the bill was the administrative provisions establishing the independent Labor Standards Board. During the 1st Session of the 75th Congress the opponents of the bill cried "bureaucracy" at every opportunity. When, in the interim between the 1st Session and the Special Session[64] the American Federation of Labor joined in this cry the pressure became irresistible and it was apparent that some change would be necessary before enough support could be secured to discharge the Rules Committee.[65] The revision vested the administration of the act in a wage and hour division to be set up in the Department of Labor with an administrator appointed by the President.[66] Although the administrator was in the Department of Labor he was independent in that his orders were not subject to review by any person in the executive branch of the government.

The most important change, however, was the shift in power from the

---

[62]Senate Committee Bill, § 11.

[63]First House Committee Bill, § 3(a).

[64]See p. 470, *supra.*

[65]Mrs. Norton announced on the floor during the Special Session that many members had promised to sign the petition if the administration was taken from a five-man board and therefore the labor committee was prepared to offer an amendment which would place the administration in a division of the Department of Labor under an administrator. 82 CONG. REC. 357 (1937).

[66]Second House Committee Bill, § § 3(a), 3(b), and 3(c).

Administrator, the lineal descendant of the Board, to the advisory committees, which were called wage and hour committees,[67] and which were to be
appointed by the Administrator in any occupation where he found a substantial number of employees employed at wages and hours inconsistent
with the minimum standards of living necessary for health, efficiency, and
general well-being. Their duty was to recommend minimum wages and
maximum hours for that occupation. Furthermore, the Administrator could
set minimum wages and maximum hours only after the committee made
their recommendation, having no power to set the standards himself although he could reject the committee recommendation and either send it
back or appoint a new committee to consider the problem.

Following the suggestion of the Secretary of Labor,[68] the Administrator
and Chief of the Children's Bureau of the Department of Labor[69] were
granted power to utilize and pay for the services of state and local officials
charged with the administration of state labor laws.[70] This is particularly
advantageous in situations where intimate knowledge of local conditions is
needed such as for the purpose of issuing certificates for child labor or handicapped labor. At the same time it would tend to strengthen the state labor
agencies.

The wage and hour bill which the AFL had introduced at the second
session of the 75th Congress contained the simplest administrative provisions of all the proposed bills. Because of the rigid standards there was no
administrative machinery. Enforcement of the act was in the hands of the
Attorney General who was authorized to petition for injunctions in the
district courts to enjoin violations of the act. The various United States
district attorneys were to be in charge of any criminal prosecutions.

When the Third House Committee Bill appeared it took a fourth approach to the problem. This time the administration of the act was entrusted
to the Secretary of Labor.[71] However, his only important duty was to determine, after a notice and hearing, whether an industry was in interstate
commerce. If he found that it was in interstate commerce his duties were
practically over for that automatically caused rigid standards of wages and
hours to apply.

The Ramspeck amendment at the 3rd session of the 75th Congress was
practically the same as the Senate Bill as far as administrative provisions
were concerned. He proposed a five-man Board to administer the act with
the aid of an advisory committee in setting wages and hours.[72]

---

[67]Second House Committee Bill, § 4.
[68]*Hearings*, p. 184.
[69]See section on child labor, *infra*, p. 487.
[70]Second House Committee Bill, § 3(b); Act, § 11(b).
[71]§ 6.
[72]Ramspeck Bill, § § 3(a), 3(b), 3(c), and 10.

The administrative provisions of the bill passed by the house were substantially the same as those in the Third Committee Bill which had been introduced at that session.[73]

The conference report, presenting a fifth method of administration, was a compromise between the theory of the Senate Bill and that in the House Bill. In many ways it was better than either. A wages and hours division in the Department of Labor was created under an Administrator appointed by the President, with the advice and consent of the Senate. An industry committee, descendant of the advisory committees and wage and hour committees, must be appointed by the Administrator in each industry engaged in interstate commerce as soon as practicable. These committees may set, within certain limits, wage standards higher than the rigid standards in the act, thus providing some flexibility.

Under the original bill the Board was given broad powers of investigation to gather data regarding wages, hours, and other conditions of employment and their effect on interstate commerce to determine whether persons were violating the act, to aid in enforcing the act, or to gather information for the basis of recommendation of further legislation.[74] The usual powers were also granted to subpoena witnesses, take evidence etc. The final Act gave much the same powers to the Administrator, industry committees, and Chief of the Children's Bureau.[75]

Very important to the enforcement machinery of the act are the requirements that employers keep certain records and reports to aid in discovering violations. The original bill required employers subject to the act to make and preserve records prescribed by the Board regulation or order as to conditions and practices of employment and to make a certified copy of the records for the Board whenever requested. Board representatives were to be permitted to examine and copy any books or records pertaining to conditions of employment. Employers subject to a labor standard order were required to keep a copy of the order posted in every room where employees subject to the order were employed.[76] The senate committee bill contained many new regulations as to records, reports, and schedules to be posted in places of employment. Apparently these additions were made at the suggestion of Secretary Perkins who had testified that experience of state labor agencies had found such regulations necessary to facilitate enforcement.[77] The Act contains less detailed requirement, being somewhat similar to the original bill.[78]

---

[73]Act, § § 9 and 11(a).
[74]§ 15(a).
[75]House Bill, § 6.
[76]Original Bill, § 17(a).
[77]*Hearings*, p. 185.
[78]Act, § 11(c).

Probably the most bitter fight in the whole wage and hour legislation developed around the issue of flexible against rigid standards.[79] Not only were personal, ecconomic, and social viewpoints involved but difficult constitutional issues were encountered. Those in favor of flexible standards pointed out that rigid standards would run into serious due-process problems; those favoring rigid standards contended the flexible standards involved unconstitutional delegation of powers.[80]

The various wage and hour provisions run the gamut from extreme flexibility in the early bills to extreme rigidity in the AFL and House Bills, with a compromise in the conference of low rigid standards tempered by the possibility of wage variations within definite bounds through the flexible machinery of industry committees.[81]

The original bill proposed a somewhat complicated wage and hour schedule centered around the concepts of "oppressive wage,"[82] "oppressive workweek,"[83] "substandard wage,"[84] and "substandard workweek."[85]

The standards for an oppressive wage and oppressive workweek were to be filled in by Congress. However, even these standards could be varied in either direction by the Board; in case of wages, if necessary "to prevent the depression of general wage levels below those consistent with the maintenance of a minimum standard of living necessary for health and efficiency, without unreasonably curtailing opportunities for employment" or, in case of hours, where the Board found it necessary "considering the physical and economic health, efficiency, and well-being of the employees and the

---

[79]The problem was much more basic than merely a disagreement over flexible or inflexible standards. In the final analysis the argument was one involving different theories of political science. Those in favor of flexible standards believed that the legislation could be best handled by an administrative body of experts who could devote their whole time to the problem. They argued that Congress did not have the time or facilities to intelligently cope with the situation. On the other hand the persons favoring rigid standards argued that Congress could, and should, set standards which would be fair and just to all concerned. The same problem is at the heart of all government through administrative agencies.

[80]Robert H. Jackson pointed out that wage and hour legislation inherently involves these two constitutional problems and of necessity standards must not be set so rigidly than an extremely harsh case can be brought up under the due process clause, while on the other hand flexible standards must have enough legislative guides to stand up under a delegation of powers argument. *Hearings*, p. 19.

[81]In the discussion of the wage and hour provisions the reader should note that an "order" can only be given after a hearing, while a "regulation" may be issued at the discretion of the administrative agency.

[82]Oppressive wage was a wage lower than......cents per hour unless another minimum wage standard was established by regulation or order of the Board. Original Bill, § 2(a)(10).

[83]Oppressive workweek was a workweek longer than......hours per week unless another standard was established by regulation or order of the Board. Original Bill, § 2(a)(11).

[84]Substandard wage was a wage lower than a minimum fair wage established by an order of the Board. Original Bill, § 2(a)(16).

[85]Substandard workweek was a workweek longer than a maximum reasonable workweek established by an order of the Board. Original Bill, § 2(a)(17).

number of persons available for employment, without unreasonably curtailing the earning power of the employees."[86] But these levels were to be barely nonoppressive, and the Board had authority to set higher standards under Section 5 of the original bill.

When the Board became convinced that "owing to the inadequacy or ineffectiveness of the facilities for collective bargaining, wages lower than a minimum fair wage are paid to employees in any occupation" subject to the act, it could conduct an investigation of the wages paid in such occupation and the value of the services rendered therefor. If the Board found that wages lower than a minimum fair wage were being paid in a substantial part of the occupation and that the establishment of a minimum fair wage would not unreasonably curtail opportunities for employment, the Board could make an order setting a minimum fair wage in that occupation. In determining the minimum fair wage the Board was to consider: (1) the cost of living and all other relevant circumstances affecting the value of the service rendered, such things as would guide a court in a suit for reasonable value of services rentered without a contract as to the amount of the wage to be paid, (3) the wages established for work of comparable character by bona fide collective labor agreements, and (4) wages paid for comparable work by employers who voluntarily maintain fair wage standards in the occupation.

Likewise, under the same conditions, the Board could fix a maximum reasonable workweek where it would not unreasonably curtail the earning power of the employees. In arriving at the maximum reasonable workweek the Board was to consider: (1) the relation of the work to the physical and economic health, efficiency, and well-being of the employees and other relevant circumstances affecting the reasonableness of the period of working time for the work performed; (2) the number of persons available for employment in the occupation to be subject to the workweek order, and also factors (3) and (4) set out to be considered in connection with minimum fair wages.[87] However, the Board could not set an hourly wage of over eighty cents except for overtime, night, or extra shift work, or one which would yield an annual income of more than $1,200; nor could it set a workweek of less than . . . . . hours.

---

[86]Original Bill, § § 4(c) and 4(d).

[87]The original bill recognized that differentials could be established but it was not the expectation that they should arise merely because of geographical location of a particular industry. Jackson explained that, "The differential which the Board would embody in an order is not a differential which the Board established; it is the differential which already exists, but which it recognized, because the Board is required to find the value of the services at the point which is under consideration. . . . The Board is authorized to recognize in each community the factors in its life which produce a differential, and to fix that differential into its minimum as collective bargaining will be expected to fix it in its maximum." *Hearings*, p. 40.

It is not until one examines the broad powers granted to the Board through its authority to issue labor standard orders that the extreme flexibility of this original bill is fully realized.[88] Each order, which could only be made after notice and hearing to interested parties, had to state the provision or provisions of the act on which it was based, and to define the occupation, the territorial limits thereof, and the class, craft, or industrial unit to which it related. In issuing the order the Board could classify employers, employees, and employments within the occupation according to localities, population of communities, number of employees, nature and volume of goods produced, and other differentiating circumstances necessary to carry out the act, and to make appropriate provision for different classes of employers, employees or employment. But it was declared to be the policy of the Board to avoid unnecessary classification. In the case of an order relating to wages, the Board had authority to include such terms and conditions as it considered necessary or appropriate to prevent the established minimum wage becoming the maximum wage and to prevent the discharge or reduction in wages of employees receiving more than the established minimum wage.[89]

The bill as it appeared from the Senate committee had undergone some change in its wage and hour provisions. Instead of a fixed standard set by Congress with power to raise it by Board order, the new bill provided that there should be but one set of standards and those should be set by the Board. The space for variation was drastically reduced because the Board could not fix wages higher than 40 cents an hour or hours lower than 40 per week. The concept of "substandard" wages and hours did not again appear. However, in fixing the standards under the Senate Committee Bill the Board was to consider exactly the same conditions that were to have been controlling under the original bill[90] (and the standards were not to be applied if they would curtail earning power or curtail opportunity for employment). It was declared to be the policy of the Board to reach the maximum wage and minimum hours as quickly as was economically possible. In an effort to quiet the fears of union officials concerning collective bargaining a section was added specifically announcing that nothing in the act was to be construed as interfering or diminishing in any way the right to bargain collectively for standards higher than were set up under the act.[91]

---

[88] Original Bill, § 12.

[89] This attempt to prevent the minimum from becoming the maximum could only be effective as to those employees whose standards were so low that a labor standard order could be issued concerning them. Thus there was nothing to keep an employer from reducing wages of employees outside the coverage of the act. *Hearings,* pp. 38-39, 61, 78.

[90] Senate Committee Bill, § § 4(b), and 4(c).

[91] Senate Committee Bill, § 5.

The Senate retained the wage and hour provisions but added two more factors to be considered in setting minimum wages. Besides the four previously enumerated the Board was to consider (1) discriminatory freight rates, and (2) local economic conditions.

The wage and hour provisions remained substantially the same in the First House Committee Bill but the factors to be considered in fixing the minimum wage were again slightly changed. The provision that discriminatory transportation costs or freight rates were to be considered [was] altered to read "the relative cost of transporting goods from points of production to consuming markets."[93] An additional consideration [included] was the "differences in units costs of manufacturing occasioned by varying local natural resources, operating conditions, or other factors entering into the cost of production. The Bill provided that the wage and hour regulations should apply to workers without regard to sex,[94] and also contained further safeguards for collective bargaining. A labor standard order could [be] issue[d] only if the Board found that existing collective bargaining facilities were inadequate or ineffective or that collective bargaining agreements in that occupation did not cover a substantial portion of the employees.[95] Nor could the order set a lower wage or higher hours than the minimum wage and maximum hours prevailing for like work in the locality where the order was effective unless the local standards were higher than the Board could set under the statute.[96] And finally, the minimum wage and maximum hours established in an occupation by collective bargaining were to be prima facie evidence of the appropriate minimum wage or maximum hours to be established for like work.[97] These are actually further conditions on the issuance of labor standards although not directly in that section of the bill.

When the Second House Committee Bill shifted the authority to set wage and hour standards from the Administrator to the wage and hour committees, it was only natural that the committees should be bound by these same considerations that had guided for the Administrator. In setting up the wage and hour committees the Administrator was directed not to appoint them in occupations where no employees received less than 40 cents an hour or worked more than 40 hours per week.[97a]

The most rigid standards of all were contained in the AFL bill; a mini-

---

[92]Senator Black announced that these provisions were really contained in the conditions set out in the senate committee bill, therefore they added nothing, merely made it certain that the new factors would be considered. 81 CONG. REC. 7892 (1937).

[93]§ 4(b).

[94]§ 2(c).

[95]First House Committee Bill, § 5(b).

[96]§ 5(c).

[97]§ 5(d).

[97a]Second House Committee Bill, Sec. 4(b).

mum wage of 40 cents and a maximum workweek of 40 hours, with no more than 8 hours any one day.[98] The hours provisions were not to apply in certain cases of emergency.

The bill introduced at the regular session contained a rigid progressive scale which required 25 cents for the first year, 30 cents for the second year, 35 cents for the third year, and 40 cents after the third year.[99] Likewise the maximum hour provisions lowered each year from 44 hours the first year, to 42 hours the second year, and 40 hours after the second year, with no more than 8 hours in any one day.[100] This was the first administration bill which did not leave the way open for differentials and that caused a storm of protest on the floor of the House from some of the Southern representatives, the most vocal of whom was Representative Cox of Georgia. This was the first time that the undercover fight which had been going on over the problem of differentials had been carried to the floor.[101]

The Ramspeck amendment contained substantially the same provisions concerning wages and hours as the First House Committee Bill. However, he did introduce a new concept in providing that the Board should calculate "weighted average" minimum wages in a given industry.[102] The minimum set could not be more than five cents per hour more than this weighted average and wages could not be raised more than five cents in any one 12-months period.[103] The Board could not fix maximum hours under 40 nor over 48 per week except in case of certain plans to employ on a yearly basis.[104]

The conference agreement was a compromise between the other bills. The rigid scale of wages and hours was retained in the milder form of 25 cents for the first year, 30 cents for the next six years, and 40 cents after the seven year period. Hours were 44 the first year, 42 the second, and after that 40 per week.[105] However, flexibility was provided for wages by establishing industry committees which have power to investigate and recommend minimum wages (not over 40 cents) higher than provided for in the rigid scale. It is the policy of the act to reach this minimum of 40 cents as soon as economically possible and the rigid scale is merely to be certain that at the end of the seven years all industry will have reached that

---

[98] § 2.

[99] § 4.

[100] § 5.

[101] But see statement by Mrs. Norton that one reason the bill was recommitted at the Special Session was because it contained differentials. 83 CONG. REC. 7275 (1938).

[102] The "weighted average" was calculated by taking the total pay roll and dividing by the total number of workers.

[103] § 4(b).

[104] § 4(c).

[105] No eight hour a day maximum was inserted because of a feeling on the part of the conferees that it was, after all, an individual matter for the employees as long as the total hours per week were controlled. 83 CONG. REC. 9257 (1938).

level.[106] As soon as practicable the Administrator is to appoint an industry committee for each industry engaged in commerce or in the production of goods for commerce. The members are to equally represent employers, employees and the public, and geographical regions in which the industry is located are to be considered in the choice. From time to time the Administrator is to convene the industry committee to consider the question of minimum wages in the industry it represents. The committee has power to make such classifications with an industry as are necessary to fix for each classification the highest minimum rate which will not substantially curtail employment in the classification, and will not give a competitive advantage to any group in the industry. In determining whether such classifications should be made, in making such classifications, and in determining the minimum wage rates for such classification the industry committee shall consider among other relevant factors the following: (1) "competitive conditions as affected by transportation, living, and production costs; (2) the wages established for work of like or comparable character by collective labor agreements negotiated between employers and employees by representatives of their own choosing; and (3) the wages paid for work of like or comparable character by employers who voluntarily maintain minimum-wage standards in the industry." However, no classification shall be fixed solely on a regional basis.[107] As in the previous bills it was provided that no classification should be made on the basis of age or sex.

The industry committee is then directed to file a report containing their recommendations with the administrator, who after notice and hearing to interested parties shall by order make the recommendations effective if he finds that they are made in accordance with the above enumerated standards; otherwise he shall disapprove of the recommendations and shall refer the matter to the same committee or to a different committee. He must either accept or reject the recommendation for he has no authority to alter it. Seven years after enactment of the law wage orders became ineffective except under particular circumstances. In making wage orders the Administrator shall define the industries and classifications therein to which they are to apply and shall contain such terms and conditions as the Administrator finds necessary to carry out the purposes of the orders. No order is effective till due notice has been given by publication in the *Federal Register*.

The final act contained a clause[108] that the act shall not justify any employer in reducing a wage which is in excess of the minimum required by

---

[106]*Id.*, p. 9164.

[107]Congress intended that there might be differentials but they must be based on facts, not on geography. 83 CONG. REC. 9256-9257 (1938).

[108]Act, § 18.

law; or in raising a workweek which is lower than the maximum hours permitted by law.[109]

In examining the exemption provisions in the various bills the first thing which impresses one is the difference between the way the problem was attacked in the original bill and those which followed it. The original bill had few specific exemptions but placed broad discretionary powers in the Board to make necessary exemptions. As the bill progressed the discretion became more and more narrow and the specific exemptions became larger and larger. Probably most of the specific exemptions enumerated in the final act would have been brought under the original bill; but many exemptions which might have been made under the original bill were not provided for in the final act. Of course in a bill of this kind, the section providing for exemptions is the logical point for pressure groups to point their activity.

There are really three general classes of exemptions to be discussed. The first is the exemptions from all the provisions of the bill; the second is the exemptions from the hours provisions; the last is from wages.[110]

In the original bill persons employed in an executive, administrative, supervisory, or professional capacity or as an agricultural laborer were excluded from the terms of the act. It is important to note that these terms were to be defined by the Board.[111] By the definition of "employer"[112] the United States, any State or political subdivision, or any labor organization (exept when acting as an employer) are not included in the act. Small employers were to be exempt from the wage and hour provisions (not child labor) of the original act if the Board so provided by regulation or order. But the Board could bring them under the act if necessary to carry out the act or prevent circumvention of its provisions.[113] The number of employees which would entitle an employer to this exemption was left blank, to be filled in by Congress. An important condition to this exemption was a provision that the Board had power by regulation or order to determine the method of computing the number of employees.[114] Although it was not spe-

---

[109]The clause discussed in note 89 was carried through all the administration bills until the third house committee bill. In that draft there was no provision for labor standard orders as the clause disappeared. The provision added in the final act is much broader, applying to both wages and hours, and also by implication applying to all employees regardless of what wage they receive, or what hours they work. If the conferees had intended it to be construed more narrowly it would seem that they would have made it applicable only when wage orders were issued.

[110]Exemptions from child labor are discussed in the section on that subject.

[111]Original Bill, § 2(a)(7).

[112]Original Bill, § 2(a)(6).

[113]Original Bill, § 6(a).

[114]This was to prevent evasion by cutting large businesses into small units. *Hearings,* pp. 49-50. It was assumed at the hearings that the number of employees would be somewhere between 10 and 20.

cifically mentioned, the original bill was not intended to apply to retailers or service trades.[115]

The Board was authorized to provide by regulation or order that employment at wages below the legal minimum, or at hours above the maximum, or both, would not be an unfair labor practice in the following cases: learners and apprentices could be employed at such wages below standard as the Board should prescribe; persons whose earning capacity is impaired by age or physical or mental deficiency or injury could be employed at wages below standard under Board supervision; Board regulation or order could provide for deductions for board, lodging, and other facilities furnished by the employer if the nature of the work is such that the employer is obliged to furnish and the employee to accept such facilities; overtime employment in periods of seasonal or peak activity, or in maintenance, repair, or other emergency work; where, because of the nature and character of employment special treatment is justified.[116] It is clear from the above that the Board had very broad powers of exemption, in fact it is difficult to think of a case where the Board could not use the last provision as a basis for exemption.

Employers were to be exempt from the hours provisions of the act if they paid for the overtime at the rate of one and one-half times the regular hourly wage rate at which the employees involved were employed.[117] However, this exemption was drastically qualified by the fact that the Board could by order withdraw this exemption in any occupation, or could by order set up such standards of wages and hours as were necessary to carry out the purpose or prevent the evasion of the act.

The bill from the Senate Committee contained a number of new exclusions from the act:[118] employees in local retailing capacity, seamen, railroad employees subject to the Hours of Service Act, persons employed in taking fish, sea foods or sponges, and the definition of agriculture was broadened.[119] But apart from these exclusions the terms of the Senate Committee Bill were substantially the same concerning exemptions with the exception that the provision for exempting small employers was not included.

---

[115]*Hearings,* p. 35.
[116]Original Bill, § 6(c).
[117]Original Bill, § 6(b).
[118]Senate Committee Bill, § 2(a)(7).
[119]It now included: farming in all its branches, cultivation and tillage of the soil, dairying, forestry, horticulture, market grading, cultivation and growing of fruits, vegetables, nuts, nursery products, ferns, flowers, bulbs, livestock, bees, and poultry, or any other agricultural or horticultural commodity, any practice ordinarily performed by a farmer, and finally it included the definition contained in subsection (g) of section 15 of the Agricultural Marketing Act, approved June 15, 1929, as amended.

An attempt was made to replace this exemption by amendment from the Senate floor[120] but the amendment was rejected.[121] The Senate Bill included new exclusions from the hours provisions of the act. These were (1) employees of any common carrier by motor vehicle subject to the maximum hours provisions of the Motor Carrier Act of 1935, (2) air transport employees subject to title II of the Railroad Labor Act of 1936, (3) employees of express companies subject to the provisions of the latter act.[122] A fourth exclusion was made (but from both wages and hours), by broadening the meaning of agriculture to include delivery to market as an incident to farming operations.[123]

Indirectly the meaning of agriculture was broadened in still another manner, by making a definition of "person employed in agriculture" who was excluded from the act.[124] As that term was used to refer to fresh fruits or vegetables, it included persons employed within the "area of production" engaged in preparing, packing, or storing such fresh fruits or vegetables in their raw or natural state.[125]

Numerous exemptions were made from the hours provisions. They included persons employed in connection with ginning or bailing cotton, canning or packing of fish, sea food, sponges, picking, canning, or processing of fruits or vegetables, processing of beets, cane, and maple into sugar and

---

[120]81 CONG. REC. 7888 (1937).

[121]Apparently the committee did not have a very pronounced view either for or against the amendment. One strong point in favor of the exemption was that it made the administrative task much easier for by far the greater number of all employers employ less than ten persons, and yet their total employees are relatively insignificant when compared with the total employees who would come under the act. It was also argued that the high standards were likely to drive many small employers out of business and thus concentrate industry into fewer hands. On the other side it was claimed that the small employers would furnish unfair and cutthroat competition. Most of the opposition to the exemption naturally came from big business. 81 CONG. REC. 7864. (1937).

[122]These amendments were accepted by the committee in conformance with their policy not to put employees under the jurisdiction of two administrative agencies. Apparently action had been taken in these occupations since the committee had drafted their amendment. 81 CONG. REC. 7875 (1937).

[123]This was accepted to clarify the act, the purpose being to make it clear that the exemption included all work done on a farm as long as it was incidental to agricultural purposes. 81 CONG. REC. 7888 (1937).

[124]Senate Bill, § 2(a)(19).

[125]This amendment was introduced by Senator Schwellenbach specifically to protect the small apple grower in his state who had to go to a central unit to get his crop washed and sorted according to Department of Agriculture rules. The large grower could afford to own his own equipment and thus the operation for him would be part of agriculture. 81 CONG. REC. 7876 (1937).

The concept of "area of production" was intended to keep the exemption from applying to large central cold storage and packing houses. However, Senator Schwellenbach, in answer to a direct question, admitted that he couldn't define the term and said that the definition would have to be left up to the Board. 81 CONG. REC. 7879 (1937).

syrup when the services of the person were of a seasonal nature.[126] Further exemptions from hours were made in case of employees in plants located in dairy production areas in which milk, cream or butter fat are received, shipped, or manufactured if operated by a cooperative association as defined in the Farm Credit Act of 1933,[127] and in the case of employees engaged in processing or packing perishable agricultural products during the harvest season.[128]

The most important changes made by the House Labor Committee concerned the exclusion of "outside salesmen" from the act,[129] a specific amendment that independent contractors and their employees engaged in transporting farm products from farm to market were not included in the definition of "person employed in agriculture" (and thus came under the act),[130] further cotton exemptions from hours, this time exempting those employed in ginning, compressing and storing cotton, or processing cottonseed[131] where employment was seasonal, also employees working during the hours from midnight to 6 A.M. in occupations not requiring continuous process operation (i.e., the "graveyard" shift) should be paid time and a half for their work. Women and children were forbidden to work during those hours.[132]

The exemptions and exclusions remained substantially the same in the amendment sent in by the committee at the special session.

A number of new exemptions were added in the Third House Committee Bill, on the floor of the house, and by the conference committee. They will be discussed together, in the form they appeared in the final act.

Some of the new exemptions from both the wages and hours provisions of the Act were:[133] any employee engaged in any retail or service establishment the greater part of whose selling or servicing is in intrastate commerce;[134] any employee employed in connection with the publication of a weekly or semi-weekly newspaper of less than 3,000 circulation the major part of which is within the county where the paper was printed and

---

[126]Senate Bill, § 4(c). The senate committee, because of the difficulty of legislatively drawing the line to seasonal production had given broad discretion to the Board to make seasonal exemptions. Sec. 6(b) of the Senate Committee Bill and Senate Bill. Therefore these specific exemptions did nothing more than make certain what the Board could have done if necessary. But in making the exemptions specific Congress left the way open for chiselers to evade the act.

[127]The definition was changed to that of Section 15 of the Agricultural Marketing Act by § 4(c) of the First House Committee Bill.

[128]Senate Bill, § 4(c).

[129]§ 2(a)(7).

[130]§ 2(a)(7).

[131]§ 4(c).

[132]§ 4(c).

[133]Act, § 13(a).

[134]It had been stated by the supporters of the wage and hour bills that they were not intended to apply to retail or service establishments (see *Hearings*, p. 35), but this amendment was inserted to make certain that none would be included. 83 CONG. REC. 7437-7438 (1938).

published;[135] any employee of a street, suburban, or interurban railway, or local trolley or motor bus carrier;[136] and the definition of agriculture was further broadened, this time with the express intent to exempt everything agricultural. As one senator said, "The definition seems to be all-inclusive, and we tried to make it so."[137]

Employers were to be exempted from the hours provisions (but not wages)[138] without paying extra for time above the maximum of the act if their employees were employed under a collective bargaining agreement (certified as bona fide by the National Labor Relations Board) which provided (a) that no employee shall work more than 1000 hours during any period of twenty-six consecutive weeks,[139] or (b) more than 2000 hours during any fifty-two consecutive weeks.[140] Also the administrator could exempt employers for not more than fourteen weeks in the agrregate in any calendar year in an industry found to be seasonal.[141] The above three exemptions only applied to the extent of 12 hours in any workday, or 56 hours in any workweek and over that wages had to be paid at the usual overtime rate under the act.

Some specific exemptions from the hours provisions were made in certain industries which for special reasons required long hours, as in the first processing of milk; while the aggregate 14 week exemption was specifically applied to certain seasonal occupations, particularly pertaining to agriculture.[142]

---

[135]The main argument in favor of the amendment was that the only effect of the act on such papers would be to force them to stop their out-of-state circulation, which is usually small, consisting mainly of home town folks who have moved away. Then it was also argued that the small weekly did not have an organization which would lend itself to such standards, an example of which was the typical society editor who collects items in her spare time. 82 CONG. REC. 1810 (1937).

[136]This exemption was to provide for the few cases where such businesses would come under the act (lines running interstate from cities on or near state borders). Such occupations have peak times in morning and evening so that the hours are difficult to regulate. Also it was known that they are generally strongly unionized and get relatively high wages. 83 CONG. REC. 7444-7445 (1938).

[137]83 CONG. REC. 9163 (1938).

[138]Act § 7(b).

[139]This provision was to take care of certain special industries with peculiar conditions such as certain lumbering and mining projects where men have to be sent to isolated sections for periods of time, after which they return to civilization. However, while they are working the men desire, and need, to work long hours for there is generally nothing else to do, and they take the jobs in the first place with the intention of working long hours for a short period. 83 CONG. REC. 9257 (1938).

[140]This takes care of the employer who has worked out some scheme of annual employment in which the hours may fluctuate considerably. 83 CONG. REC. 9257 (1938). Representative Barton of New York had introduced a similar provision from the floor, but it had been rejected. 83 CONG. REC. 7442 (1938).

[141]It should be noted that this is an "aggregate" of fourteen weeks and it was not intended that the work need be done in consecutive weeks. 83 CONG. REC. 9164 (1938).

[142]§ 7(c).

From the very beginning the supporters of child labor legislation (which, incidentally, seemed to include practically all members of Congress) divided into two distinct groups. One group favored the administration method of enforcement, to prohibit the interstate transportation of goods produced by child labor, and the other favored the so-called Johnson-Wheeler amendment based on the prison-made goods theory.[143] The Johnson-Wheeler amendment was substituted in the Senate for the administration child labor provisions by a vote of 57 to 28[144] but it was subsequently removed by the House Labor Committee and all efforts of its House proponents, led by Representative Martin of Colorado, to reinsert it were unsuccessful. The attack of the Johnson-Wheeler group did, however, cause certain amendments to be added by the House Labor Committee but the basic philosophy remained unchanged.

The original bill defined "oppressive child labor"[145] as the employment of any children under the age of 16; however, the Chief of the Children's Bureau of the Department of Labor could by the affirmative action of an order or regulation raise the age level to 18[146] in employments which he found to be particularly hazardous for children or detrimental to their health or well-being.

The Senate Committee lowered these standards by granting the Chief of the Children's Bureau power to permit employment of children under 16 in occupations which the Chief of the Children's Bureau should find would not interfere with their schooling or be detrimental to their health. This broad power to exempt children under the age of 16 drew the fire of the advocates of the Wheeler-Johnson amendment in spite of the fact that Senator Black explained on the Senate floor that the provision was only intended to apply during the vacation months when children were not in school. In the face of this continued criticism the House Labor Committee accepted an amendment at the special session to limit the power to exempt to children between 14 and 16.[147]

Another important change was made by the Senate Committee Bill in exempting children employed in agriculture and those employed by "a parent or a person standing in place of a parent."[148] The exemption in cases

---

[143]The reason the child labor section was included with the wage and hour legislation instead of forming a separate act was because of the feeling that it had a better chance to be declared constitutional as an integral part of general legislation intended to remove the burden of unfair labor practices on the free flow of interstate commerce. Alone, child labor may not be a very great burden, but when considered with the other factors, it has a better chance of surviving attack in the courts. *Hearings*, pp. 1-16.

[144]81 CONG. REC. 7951 (1937).

[145]Original Bill, § 2(a)(13).

[146]It should be noted that there is no requirement for a hearing before the Chief of the Children's Bureau can issue an "order." Compare with note 81 *supra*.

[147]82 CONG. REC. 1691 (1937).

[148]Senate Committee Bill, § 2(a)(10).

of parents was removed in part by amendment from the floor during the special session to prohibit parents and those standing in place of a parent from employing children under 16 in manufacturing or mining.[149] It was explained that this was to prevent certain types of industrial work such as tiff mining where the parent might be tempted to employ his own children.[150]

The exemption in case of agriculture was narrowed considerably in the conference bill by a provision that it would only apply when children were not legally required to be in school.[151] This would seem to leave a way open for states to aid in protection of child labor by high compulsory school ages.[152] It must be remembered, however, that this standard is not as rigid as it seems on its face for most states have legal excuses for failure to attend school, and one of the commonest of these is the need to work.

A further exemption was inserted on the floor during the special session to exclude child actors engaged in the production of motion pictures.[153] This exemption was not included in the third house committee bill but was again inserted from the floor in the regular session and this time included children in theatrical productions.[154]

As early as the Senate Committee Bill the Board was directed to utilize the Chief of the Children's Bureau for all investigations and inspections with respect to the employment of minors[155] and to bring all actions to enjoin oppressive child labor practices.[156] This provision was enlarged in the Third House Committee Bill to place all child labor provisions under the administration of the Chief of the Children's Bureau.[157] In the conference bill the Chief's authority to bring injunction suits was limited because he had to act in this capacity under the direction and control of the Attorney General.[158]

The original bill prohibited the interstate shipment of goods on which

---

[149] 82 CONG. REC. 1693 (1937).

[150] 82 CONG. REC. 1822 (1937). A "person in place of a parent" included only those actually in the legal position of a parent. 82 CONG. REC. 1694 (1937).

[151] Act, § 13(c).

[152] It is true that violation of the compulsory school law would be an offense against the state in any case but this extra federal sanction should make evasion much more difficult particularly since the employer would be the one to suffer. The section has more meaning when it is realized that seven states have a compulsory school age of 18; seven of 17; 31 and the District of Columbia have 16; and only three states have under 16.—See testimony of Miss Katherine F. Lenroot, Chief of Children's Bureau of the Department of Labor, *Hearings,* p. 385.

[153] 82 CONG. REC. 1789 (1937).

[154] Members of the house did not feel that child actors were really within the group which child labor legislation was intended to benefit. 83 CONG. REC. 7441 (1938).

[155] Senate Committee Bill, § 15(b).

[156] Senate Committee Bill, § 12.

[157] § 10(c).

[158] § 12(b).

child labor had been used.[159] This was changed slightly in the Senate Committee Bill which carried a separate provision prohibiting the interstate shipment of goods which had been produced in an establishment in the United States in or about which within thirty days prior to removal any oppressive child labor had been used.[160] However, this provision was not to go into effect till 120 days after enactment.

One of the outstanding provisions of the administration child labor scheme was a clause providing that employers should not be guilty of violating the child labor law if the children they employed had a certificate issued under a regulation of the children's bureau certifying that the employee was above the oppressive child labor age, regardless of their true age.[161] This certificate requirement was intended to keep children from entering into employment illegally and protect the employer who was bona fide trying to observe the law. It was claimed that the Johnson-Wheeler amendment was purely penal and only operated after the child labor law had been violated.

The Johnson-Wheeler amendment[162] took three approaches to the child labor problem: (1) it prohibited interstate shipment of goods produced by child labor; (2) it used the prison-made goods theory of the Ashurst-Summers Convict Goods Act upheld in the *Kentucky Whip and Collar* case to prohibit transportation of goods produced wholly or in part by child labor into states for use there in violation of the law of that state; and (3) it required labeling of goods produced by child labor. The advocates of this method of enforcement pointed out that it had an advantage over the administration plan in that it directly challenged the decision in *Hammer* v. *Dagenhart* by its first prohibition, while at the same time it had an alternative method in the convict-made goods approach if the other should be found to be unconstitutional. On the other hand the convict-goods approach was severely criticized by many child labor experts[163] on the ground that it would be extremely complicated law to administer (convict-goods are made in relatively few places); another objection being being that it would require new legislation in practically all states to make it effective, while the approach of the administration through requiring certificates fitted in with most of the state laws.[164] Another distinct advantage of the administration proposal was that the federal government could utilize the trained state

---

[159]§ 7.

[160]See § 23(e).

[161]Senate Committee Bill, § 2(a)(10).

[162]Senate Bill, § 24.

[163]See testimony of Mr. Courtenay Dinwiddie, General Secretary, National Child Labor Committee, *Hearings,* pp. 396-403; and Mrs. Larue Brown, representing a group of national women's organizations, *Hearings,* pp. 389-394.

[164]Mrs. Norton stated on the floor that 43 of 48 states already have the certificate form of child labor law. 82 CONG. REC. 1783 (1937).

child labor agencies to help control the issuance of certificates as had been done so successfully under the Federal Child Labor Act of 1916.

———

From the foregoing analysis it is obvious that few legislative enactments in our history have had such a stormy career and assumed so many different aspects within a comparatively short period of time as has this Act. The history of the Act affords invaluable material to the student of the legislative process in a democracy. In spite of trials and tribulations it is believed that the provisions finally made law are better than those of the original bill—even though admitted weaknesses remain. If greater flexibility and wide administrative discretion have been eliminated in favor of more rigid standards, it should be remembered that, while the original characteristics would have permitted the accomplishment of much good beyond the scope of the present Act, they also contain in themselves the seed of many undesirable results and in the absence of an almost super-human job of administration might have done considerable harm to the cause they were designed to serve.

THE ORIGINS

Report of the House Committee on Labor
June 11, 1938

MRS. MARY NORTON [DEM., N. J.] submitted the Conference Report.

The committee of conference on the disagreeing votes of the two Houses on the amendment of the House to the bill (S. 2475) to provide for the establishment of fair labor standards in employments in and affecting interstate commerce, and for other purposes, having met, after full and free conference, have agreed to recommend and do recommend to their respective Houses as follows: . . .

The managers of the part of the House at the conference on the disagreeing votes of the two Houses on the amendments of the House to the bill (S. 2475) to provide for the establishment of fair labor standards in employments in and affecting interstate commerce, and for other purposes. submit the following statement in explanation of the effect of the action agreed upon and recommended in the accompanying conference report:

The House amendment strikes out all of the Senate bill after the enacting clause. The Senate recedes from its disagreement to the amendment of the House, with an amendment which is a substitute for both the Senate and the House amendment.

SENATE BILL

SUMMARY OF PROVISIONS

SHORT TITLE

Section 1 of the Senate bill provides that it may be cited as the Fair Labor Standards Act of 1937.

LEGISLATIVE DECLARATION

Section 1 of the Senate bill, the legislative declaration, recites the adverse effects upon interstate commerce of the employment of workers under substandard labor conditions in occupations in and affecting interstate commerce. It contains also a declaration that the correction of such conditions affecting interstate commerce requires congressional action prohibiting the shipment in interstate commerce of goods produced under such substandard conditions, and providing for the elimination of substandard labor conditions in occupations in and directly affecting interstate commerce. This section is very similar to the corresponding section of the House amendment.

DEFINITIONS

Section 2 (a) of the Senate bill contains a series of definitions used in the bill.

"Person" is defined to include an individual, partnership, association, corporation, business trust, receiver, trustee, trustee in bankruptcy, or liquidating or reorganizing agent.

"Interstate commerce" is defined to mean trade, commerce, transportation, transmission, or communication among the several States or from any State to any place outside thereof.

"State" is defined to mean any State of the United States or the District of Columbia or any Territory or possession of the United States.

"Board" is defined to mean the Labor Standards Board created by the bill.

"Occupation" is defined to mean an occupation, industry, trade, or business, or branch thereof, or class of work or craft therein in which persons are gainfully employed.

Employer is defined to include any person acting directly or indirectly in the interest of an employer in relation to an employee but does not include the United States or any State or any political subdivision thereof or any labor organization except when that organization acts as an employer.

"Employee" is defined to include any individual employed or suffered or permitted to work by an employer, but does not include any person employed in a bona-fide executive, administrative, professional, or local retailing capacity. It excludes all persons employed as seamen, fishermen, any railroad employee subject to the Hours of Service Act, any employee of a common carrier by motor vehicle subject to the Motor Carrier Act. Air-transport employees subject to title II of the Railway Labor Act are also excluded from the definition of "employee" as are all persons employed in agriculture. "Agriculture" is defined to include, among other things, practices ordinarily performed by farmers or on a farm as an incident to farm operations.

"Oppressive wage" is defined to mean any wage lower than that set by order of the Board under the provisions of section 4 of the bill.

"Oppressive workweek" is defined to mean a workweek or workday longer than that set by order of the Board under the provisions of section 4 of the bill.

"Substandard labor condition" is defined to mean employment under which any employee is employed at an oppressive wage, or any employee is employed for an oppressive workweek.

"Fair labor standard" is defined to mean employment under which no person is employed at an oppressive wage, or no person is employed for an oppressive workweek.

"Unfair goods" is defined to mean any goods produced under "substandard labor conditions" as defined in the bill.

"Produced" means produced, manufactured, mined, handled, or in any other manner worked on, in any State. This definition further provides that any employee shall be deemed to have been engaged in the production of goods if he was employed in producing, manufacturing, mining, handling, transporting, or in any other manner working on such goods or in any process or occupation necessary to the production thereof, in any State.

The term "person employed in agriculture" as used in the bill insofar as it refers to fresh fruits or vegetables, includes persons employed within the area of production engaged in preparing, packing, or storing such fresh fruits or vegetables in their raw or natural state.

"Labor standard order" is defined as an order of the Board under section 4, 6. or 8 of the bill.

"Goods" is defined as goods (including ships and marine equipment), wares, merchandise, or articles or subjects of commerce of any character, or any part of ingredient thereof, but does not include goods after their delivery into the actual physical possession of the ultimate consumer other than a producer, manufacturer, or processor thereof.

"Fair goods" is defined as goods in the production of which no employee has been employed in any occupation under any substandard labor conditions.

"Sale" or "sell" is defined to include any sale, exchange, contract to sell, consignment for sale, shipment for sale, or other disposition.

"To a substantial extent" is defined as meaning not casually, sporadically, or accidentally, but as a settled or recurrent characteristic of the matter or occupation described, or of a portion thereof, which need not be a large or preponderant portion.

EVIDENCE OF EMPLOYMENT UNDER SUBSTANDARD LABOR CONDITIONS

Section 2 (b) of the Senate bill provides that proof that any employee was employed under any substandard labor condition, in any place of employment where goods are produced, within 90 days prior to the removal of goods therefrom, shall be prima facie evidence that such goods were produced by such employee employed under such substandard labor condition.

LABOR STANDARDS BOARD

Section 3 of the Senate bill provides for the creation of a Labor Standards Board composed of five members appointed for staggered terms of 5 years each, except that the members first appointed are appointed for terms of 1, 2, 3, 4, and 5 years respectively. The members of the Board must be appointed with the advice and consent of the Senate. The section contains the usual provisions regarding the filling of vacancies, the salary of the Board members, the maintenance of offices and the filing of reports.

ESTABLISHMENT OF FAIR LABOR STANDARDS

Part II of the Senate bill provides for the establishment of labor standards with respect to minimum wages and maximum hours, the application of such standards to particular employments and classes of employments, and appropriate exemptions from such standards. This part deals only with the fixing of the standards and the consequences of noncompliance. The powers of the Board to require compliance are defined in parts III and IV.

Section 4 (a) of the Senate bill declares, for reasons specified in such section, that it is the policy of the act to maintain, so far as and as rapidly as is economically feasible, minimum-wage and maximum-hour standards consistent with health, efficiency, and general well-being of workers and the maximum productivity and profitable operation of American business.

ESTABLISHMENT OF MINIMUM-WAGE STANDARDS

Section 4 (b) of the Senate bill directs the Board by order to declare from time to time for such occupations as are brought within the operation of the bill, minimum wages which shall be as nearly adequate as is economically feasible without curtailing opportunity for employment, to maintain a minimum standard of living necessary for health, efficiency, and general well-being. The Board's jurisdiction, however, does not include the power to declare minimum wages in excess of 40 cents per hour. but it is the objective of the bill to attain a minimum wage of 40 cents per hour as rapidly as practicable without curtailing opportunities for employment and without disturbance and dislocation of business and industry, and the attainment of higher minimum wages by collective bargaining and otherwise is to be encouraged. In declaring such minimum wages the Board is directed to consider among other relevant circumstances the cost of living, such considerations as would be relevant in a court in a suit for the value of services rendered, wages established for work of like or comparable character by collective labor agreements, and wages paid for like work by employers voluntarily maintaining minimum-wage standards.

ESTABLISHMENT OF MAXIMUM HOUR STANDARDS

Section 4 (c) of the Senate bill authorizes the Board by order from time to time to declare for such occupations as are brought within the provisions of the bill, a maximum workweek (and the maximum workday therein) which shall be as nearly adequate as is economically feasible without curtailing earning power, to maintain health, efficiency, and general well-being. There are exempted from the provisions of this subsection persons employed in connection with the ginning and baling of cotton, canning or other packaging of fish, sea food, or sponges, or picking, canning, or processing of fruits or vegetables, or the processing of beets, cane, and maple into sugar and sirup, when the services of such persons are of a seasonal nature. There are also exempted from the provisions of this subsection employees employed in a plant located in dairy production areas, in which milk, cream, or butterfat are received, processed, shipped, or manufactured, if operated by a cooperative association as defined in the Farm Credit Act of 1933.

The Board's jurisdiction, however, does not include the power to declare a maximum workweek of less than 40 hours; but it is the objective of the bill to attain a maximum workweek of not more than 40 hours as rapidly as practicable without curtailing earning power or reducing production, and the attainment of a shorter workweek by collective bargaining or otherwise is to be encouraged. In declaring maximum hours the Board is directed to consider among other relevant circumstances (1) the relation of the work to the physical and economic health, efficiency, and well-being of the employees; (2) the number of persons available for employment in the occupation; (3) the hours of employment established for work of like or comparable character by collective bargaining agreements; (4) the hours of employment for work of like or comparable character maintained by employers who voluntarily maintained a maximum workweek; (5) the provisions of this subsection shall not apply to employees engaged in processing or packing perishable agricultural products during the harvesting season; and (6) the average minimum wage ordered by the Board to be paid by private employers in any State shall be the minimum wage paid by the Works Progress Administration to its employees in that State.

COLLECTIVE BARGAINING AGREEMENTS PROTECTED

Section 5 of the Senate bill provides that nothing in the act or in any regulation or order of the Board shall be construed to interfere with the right of employees to bargain collectively or otherwise engage in concerted activities to obtain a wage in excess of the applicable minimum under the bill or to obtain a shorter workweek than the maximum workweek under the bill or other benefits or advantages. Minimum wages and maximum workweeks so sought or obtained are not to be construed or deemed to be illegal because they are in excess of the applicable minimum wage or maximum workweek, as the case may be, under the bill.

EXEMPTIONS FROM WAGE-AND-HOUR STANDARDS

Section 6 of the Senate bill provides certain exemptions from the wage-and-hour standards established under the bill. Subsection (a) introduces flexibility in the regulation of hours by authorizing employment for more hours per week than the applicable maximum upon condition that payment for such overtime is made at one and one-half times the regular rate. The board is authorized to remove or qualify this exemption if it finds that the maintenance of the appropriate workweek is necessary or appropriate in order to prevent the circumvention of the act. Subsection (b) authorizes the Board to make appropriate exceptions from the wage-and-hour standards for special cases such as learners and apprentices, and disabled persons, to whom special licenses are to be issued, deductions for board and lodging necessitated by the nature of the work, overtime employment in seasonal or emergency work, and other similar situations.

PROHIBITIONS RELATING TO INTERSTATE COMMERCE; TARIFF PROVISIONS

Part III of the Senate bill contains the provisions (1) barring from interstate commerce goods which were produced under substandard labor conditions set forth in the bill, (2) prohibiting the employment under substandard labor conditions of any employee engaged in interstate commerce or in the production of goods intended for transportation in violation of the provisions of the bill, and (3) protecting interstate commerce from the effect of substandard labor conditions. This part also contains provisions relating to imports.

PROHIBITED SHIPMENTS AND EMPLOYMENT CONDITIONS IN INTERSTATE COMMERCE AND PRODUCTION FOR INTERSTATE COMMERCE

Section 7 of the Senate bill makes it unlawful among other things to sell or ship in interstate commerce any unfair goods, i. e., goods on which any employee has been employed under any substandard labor condition. It also makes it unlawful to employ, under any substandard labor condition, a person engaged in interstate commerce or in the production of unfair goods intended to be sold or shipped in interstate commerce.

PROTECTION OF INTERSTATE COMMERCE FROM EFFECTS OF SUBSTANDARD LABOR CONDITIONS

Section 8 (a) of the Senate bill authorizes the Board to make orders requiring elimination of substandard labor conditions existing in the production of goods which are not sold in interstate commerce but which compete to a substantial extent with fair goods brought in from another State.

Section 8 (b) of the Senate bill makes it unlawful to violate an order issued under section 8 (a).

TARIFF PROVISIONS

Section 8 (c) of the Senate bill provides that the Tariff Commission upon request of the President, or upon resolution of either or both Houses of Congress, or upon request of the Board, or upon its own motion, or when in the judgment of the Commission there is good and sufficient reason therefor, upon application of any interested party, shall investigate the differences resulting from the operation of the bill in the costs of production of any domestic article and any like or similar foreign article, with a view to determining whether or not any increase should be made in the duty upon such foreign article for the purpose of equalizing such difference. All provisions of law applicable with respect to investigations under section 336 of the Tariff Act of 1930 are to be applicable with respect to investigations under this subsection.

GENERAL ADMINISTRATIVE PROVISIONS

Part IV, the last part of the Senate Bill, contains the general administrative, procedural, and enforcement provisions.

LABOR STANDARD ORDER

Section 9 of the Senate bill contains provisions applicable to orders of the Board made under sections 4, 6, and 8. It provides among other things that such orders may be made only after a hearing, shall define the occupations to which they relate, may classify employers, employees, and employment according to localities, population, and other circumstances and make appropriate provisions for different classes. The section provides that it shall be the policy of the Board to avoid any classification which effects an unreasonable discrimination against any person or locality. The Board is directed to avoid unnecessary and excessive classifications. Provision is made for the inclusion in orders relating to wages of such terms and conditions as the Board may consider appropriate to prevent the minimum wage from becoming the maximum wage. And the policy is declared that orders relating to wages shall affect only those employees who need legislative protection and shall not interfere with the voluntary establishment of appropriate differentials and higher standards for other employees in the occupation.

HEARINGS

Section 10 of the Senate bill contains provisions regarding the hearings which are to be held by the Board before orders are made, modified, extended, or rescinded. This section states the conditions under which the Board shall order a hearing.

ADVISORY COMMITTEE ON WAGE AND HOUR STANDARD

Section 11 of the Senate bill requires the Board to appoint advisory committees composed of representatives of employers, employees, and the public before making an order under section 4 establishing a minimum wage or a maximum workweek, and contains provisions regarding the composition and procedure of such committees.

INVESTIGATIONS AND TESTIMONY

Section 12 of the Senate bill authorizes the Board to conduct investigations, subpoena witnesses, and compel testimony.

INJUNCTIONS TO ENFORCE COMPLIANCE WITH ACT

Section 13 of the Senate bill provides for the enforcement of the act and the orders thereunder by authorizing the Board to institute suit in the United States district courts to enjoin violations.

RECORDS AND LABELS

Section 14 of the Senate bill requires employers to keep such records as the Board may prescribe as necessary or appropriate for the enforcement of the bill. It further provides for the posting of orders in each place where employees in any occupation subject thereto are employed.

PROSECUTIONS OF PERSONS OTHER THAN PRODUCERS

Section 14 (c) of the Senate bill provides that no person other than the producer shall be prosecuted for the transportation, shipment, delivery or sale of unfair goods who has secured a representation in writing from the person by whom the goods transported, shipped, or delivered were produced, resident in the United States, to the effect that such goods were not produced in violation of any provisions of this act.

POWERS OF THE SECRETARY OF LABOR

Section 15 of the Senate bill provides that the Board shall, so far as practicable, make its investigations and inspections through the Secretary of Labor and his representatives, and authorizes the Secretary of Labor to make such investigations and inspections. This section further provides that the Secretary of Labor may utilize the services of State and local agencies offices and employees, and reimburse them for such services.

REGULATIONS AND ORDERS

Section 16 of the Senate bill confers upon the Board power to make, issue, amend, and rescind such regulations and orders as it deems necessary or appropriate to carry out the provisions of the act.

VALIDITY OF CONTRACTS

Section 17 (a) of the Senate bill declares void any contract made in violation of any provision of the act.

Section 17 (b) makes void any contract binding on any person to waive compliance with any provision of the act.

REPARATION

Section 18 of the Senate bill provides for the payment of reparation to employees who have been paid a lower wage or employed for longer hours than the applicable standards allow. In the case of wages this reparation amounts to the difference between the wages received, and that which should have been paid. In the case of hours, additional compensation is required for the overtime (where the act requires overtime) at the rate of one and one-half times the regular wage. The right to this reparation is granted when the condition of employment in question is required to be maintained under the act as well as when goods are shipped in violation of the act, but in the latter case the employer is entitled to prove that he had no reasonable ground to believe that the goods would be transported in violation of the act. And the Board may exempt goods from the prohibition against interstate shipment if it is established to the satisfaction of the Board that every person having a substantial proprietary interest in the goods had no reason to believe that any substandard condition existed in the production of the goods, or that the exemption is necessary to prevent undue hardship or waste and is not detrimental to the public interest; but in order to secure such exemption, provision must be made for the payment of reparation by every employer having a proprietary interest in the goods who failed to maintain the required wage or hour standard.

RELATION TO OTHER LAWS

Section 19 of the Senate bill provides that the bill shall not justify non-compliance with any other Federal, State, or municipal regulation imposing higher standards.

COMMON CARRIERS NOT LIABLE

Section 20 of the Senate bill provides that common carriers shall not be liable under the bill for the shipment of goods in the regular course of their business, and shall not be excused by the bill from their obligations to accept goods for transportation.

COURT REVIEW OF ORDERS

Section 21 of the Senate bill provides for review in the circuit court of appeals of orders of the Board.

JURISDICTION OF OFFENSES AND SUITS

Section 22 of the Senate bill confers appropriate jurisdiction on the district courts over civil and criminal proceedings under the act.

PENALTIES

Section 23 of the Senate bill provides appropriate penalties for violation of provisions of the bill.

SEPARABILITY OF PROVISIONS

Section 25 of the Senate bill provides that all of its provisions shall be separable.

EFFECTIVE DATE OF ACT

Section 26 of the Senate bill provides that the bill shall take effect immediately but that no provision requiring the maintenance of any fair labor standard or giving effect to any substandard labor condition shall take effect until the one hundred and twentieth day after the enactment of the act and that no labor standard order shall be effective prior to that day.

HOUSE AMENDMENT

SHORT TITLE

The first section of the House amendment provides that the act may be cited as the Fair Labor Standards Act of 1938.

FINDING AND DECLARATION OF POLICY

Section 2 of the House amendment states that the employment of workers under substandard labor conditions (1) causes commerce to be used to spread among workers of the several States conditions detrimental to their well-being, (2) burdens commerce and a free flow of goods in commerce, (3) constitutes an unfair method of competition in commerce, (4) leads to labor disputes which burden and obstruct commerce, and (5) interferes with orderly and fair marketing of goods.

The House amendment states that the above-described situation requires that Congress exercise its power under the Constitution to regulate commerce among the several States in order to prevent the instrumentalities of interstate commerce to be used to spread and perpetuate such substandard labor conditions, by prohibiting the shipment in interstate commerce of goods produced under substandard labor conditions and providing for the elimination of substandard labor conditions among employers engaged in industries affecting interstate commerce.

DEFINITIONS

Section 3 of the House amendment contains definitions of terms used.

"Person" is defined as an individual, partnership, association, corporation, business trust, legal representative, or any organized group of persons.

"Commerce" is defined to mean trade, commerce, transportation, transmission, or communication among the several States or from any State to any place outside thereof.

"State" is defined as any State of the United States, or the District of Columbia, or any Territory.

"Employer" is defined to include any person acting directly or indirectly in the interest of an employer in relation to an employee, but does not include the United States or any State or political subdivision of a State, or any labor organization (other than when acting as an employer), or anyone acting in the capacity of officer or agent of such a labor organization.

"Employee" is defined to include any individual employed or suffered or permitted to work by an employer.

"Agriculture" is defined to include farming in all its branches, and among other things to include the cultivation and tillage of the soil, dairying, the cultivation, growing, and harvesting of agricultural or horticultural commodities, the raising of livestock, bees, foxes, or poultry, and any practices performed by a farmer or on a farm as an incident to such farming operations, including preparation for market, delivery to storage or to market or to carriers for transportation to market.

"Employees engaged in agriculture" is defined to include individuals employed within the area of production, engaged in the handling, packing, storing, ginning, compressing, pasteurizing, drying, or canning of farm products and in making cheese and butter.

"Employ" is defined as including to suffer or permit to work.

"Industry" is defined to mean a trade, business, industry, or branch thereof, or group of industries in which individuals are gainfully employed.

"Industry affecting commerce" is defined to mean an industry with respect to which an order issued under section 6 is in effect.

"Employer engaged in commerce" is defined to mean an employer in commerce, or an employer engaged, in the ordinary course of business, in purchasing or selling goods in commerce.

"Secretary" is defined to mean the Secretary of Labor.

"Oppressive child labor" is defined as a condition of employment under which (1) any employee under the age of 16 years is employed by an employer (other than a parent or a person standing in place of a parent employing his own child or a child in his custody under the age of 16 years in an occupation other than manufacturing or mining) in any occupation, or (2) any such employee between the ages of 16 and 18 years is employed by an employer in any occupation which the Chief of the Children's Bureau shall from time to time find and by order declare to be particularly hazardous for the employment of such children or detrimental to their health or well-being.

Oppressive child labor is not deemed to exist by virtue of the employment in any occupation of a person with respect to whom the employer shall have on file a certificate issued and held pursuant to the regulations of the Chief of the Children's Bureau certifying that such person is above the oppressive child-labor age. The Chief of the Children's Bureau is to provide by regulation or by order that the employment of employees of or above the age of 14 but under the age of 16 in occupations other than manufacturing and mining shall not be deemed to constitute oppressive child labor if and to the extent that the Chief of the Children's Bureau determines that such employment is confined to periods which will not interfere with schooling and to conditions which will not interfere with health and well-being.

MINIMUM WAGES

Section 4 of the House amendment provides that every employer engaged in commerce in an industry affecting commerce must pay during the first year (computed from the effective date of the original order issued under section 6 with respect to the industry) each employee employed by him a wage at a rate not less than 25 cents an hour, and during each succeeding year increase such wage 5 cents an hour until the wage reaches 40 cents an hour. Hence the 40-cent rate in a particular industry will be reached at the end of 3 years from the effective date of the order under section 6 with respect to the industry.

MAXIMUM HOURS

Section 5 of the House amendment provides that no employer engaged in commerce in an industry affecting commerce shall employ any of his employees for a workday longer than 8 hours, or during the first year (computed from the effective date of the order issued under sec. 6 with respect to the industry) shall employ any of his employees for a workweek longer than 44 hours. In each succeeding year the employer is required to reduce the weekly hours by 2 hours until a 40-hour workweek is reached. No employee is to be deemed to be employed in violation of this section if he receives additional compensation for his overtime employment at the rate of one and one-half times the regular hourly rate at which he is employed, or times the rate applicable under or pursuant to the act, whichever is higher.

In the case of an employer engaged in the first processing of milk, whey, skimmed milk, or cream into dairy products, or in the ginning and compressing of cotton, or in the processing of cottonseed, the provisions of this section are not to apply to his employees in any place of employment where he is so engaged, and in the case of an employer engaged in the first processing of, or in canning, fresh fish or fresh sea food, or perishable fresh fruits or perishable fresh vegetables, or in handling, slaughtering, or dressing poultry or livestock, the provisions of this section are not to apply for 12 workweeks in any calendar year to his employees in any place of employment where he is so engaged.

INDUSTRIES AFFECTING COMMERCE

Section 6 of the amendment directs the Secretary, as soon as practicable after the enactment of the act, to determine the relation of the various industries to commerce. The Secretary is to give due notice to interested persons and an opportunity to be heard. If in the case of any industry the Secretary finds that the activities of the industry are Nation-wide in their scope, or that the industry is dependent for its existence upon substantial purchases or sales of goods in commerce and upon transportation in commerce, or that the relation of the industry to commerce is in other respects close and substantial, the Secretary is required to issue an order declaring the industry to be an industry affecting commerce, but no such order is to be applicable to any retail industry the greater part of whose sales is in intrastate commerce. The order is to take effect at such time not more than 120 days after it is issued as the Secretary designates in the order.

ATTENDANCE OF WITNESSES

Section 7 of the House amendment provides that for the purpose of the hearing to determine the facts upon which an order under section 6 is based, the provisions of the Federal Trade Commission Act relating to the attendance of witnesses and the production of books, papers, and documents, are to be applicable to the jurisdiction, powers, and duties of the Secretary.

COURT REVIEW OF ORDERS

Section 8 of the House amendment provides for the review of an order issued under section 6 by any person aggrieved thereby, in the circuit court of appeals for the circuit in which is situated his principal place of business, or in the Court of Appeals of the United States for the District of Columbia. The court is given exclusive jurisdiction to affirm, or if it is not in accordance with law to modify or set aside, the order in whole or in part.

INVESTIGATIONS, INSPECTIONS, AND RECORDS

Section 9 of the House amendment provides that the Secretary may investigate and gather data regarding the wages, hours, and other conditions and practices of employment in any industry subject to the act, and may enter and inspect such places and records, question such employees, and investigate such facts, conditions, practices, or matters as the Secretary may deem necessary or appropriate to determine whether any person has violated any provision of the act, or which may aid in the enforcement of the provisions of the act. Except in connection with investigations and inspections relating to the employment of oppressive child labor, the Secretary is to utilize the Bureau of Labor Statistics for all investigations and inspections.

The Secretary, for the purpose of making the investigations and inspections above referred to, is authorized, with their consent, to utilize the services of State and local agencies and their employees, and to reimburse such State and local agencies and their employees for services rendered for such purposes.

Every employer subject to the amendment or to any order thereunder is required to make, keep, and preserve such records of the persons employed by him and of the wages, hours, and other conditions and practices of employment maintained by him, and to preserve such records for such periods of time, and to make such reports therefrom to the Secretary as the Secretary shall prescribe by regulation or order.

CHILD-LABOR PROVISIONS

Section 10 of the House amendment provides that no producer, manufacturer, or dealer shall ship or deliver for shipment in commerce any goods produced in an establishment situated in the United States in or about which within 30 days prior to the removal of such goods therefrom any oppressive child labor has been employed. A prosecution and conviction of a defendant for a shipment or delivery for shipment of any goods under the conditions prohibited in this section is to be a bar to any further prosecution against the same defendant for shipment or delivery for shipment of any such goods before the beginning of such prosecution.

Every employer engaged in commerce in an industry affecting commerce is prohibited from employing any employee under any oppressive child-labor condition.

The Chief of the Children's Bureau is to make all the investigations and inspections referred to above with respect to the employment of minors and to bring all actions under section 15 (relating to injunctions to restrain violations of the act) to enjoin any act or practice which is unlawful by reason of the existence of oppressive child labor, and is to administer all other provisions of the act relating to oppressive child labor.

EXEMPTIONS

Section 11 of the House amendment contains the exemptions from its provisions. Exemptions were made in the Senate bill by the device of excluding the individuals to be exempted from the definition of "employee." The wage-and-hour provisions are not to apply to—

(1) Any employee employed in a bona fide executive, administrative, professional, or local retailing capacity, or in the capacity of outside salesman (as such terms are defined and delimited by regulations of the Secretary);

(2) Any employee employed as a seaman;

(3) Any air-transport employee subject to the provisions of title II of the Railway Labor Act;

(4) Any employee employed in the catching, taking, harvesting, cultivating, or farming of any kind of fish, shellfish, crustacea, sponges, seaweeds, or other aquatic forms of animal and vegetable life, including the going to and returning from work, and including employment in the loading, unloading, or packing of such products for shipment, or in propagat-

ing, processing, marketing, freezing, canning, curing, storing, or distributing the above products or byproducts thereof.

(5) Any employee employed in agriculture; or

(6) Any employee to the extent that such employee is exempted by regulations or orders of the Secretary issued under section 12 (relating to partial exemptions for learners, apprentices, and handicapped workers) or to weekly or semiweekly newspapers with a circulation of less than 3,000, the major part of which circulation is within the county where printed and published.

The hour provisions of the act are not to apply to any employee with respect to whom the Interstate Commerce Commission has power to establish qualifications and maximum hours of service pursuant to the provisions of section 204 of the Motor Carrier Act, 1935, or to any employee of an employer subject to part I of the Interstate Commerce Act.

The child-labor provisions are not to apply to any employee employed in agriculture, or to any child employed as an actor in motion pictures or theatrical productions.

LEARNERS, APPRENTICES, AND HANDICAPPED WORKERS

Section 12 of the House amendment requires the Secretary, to the extent necessary in order to prevent curtailment of opportunities for employment, by regulation or by order to provide for (1) the employment of learners, and of apprentices under special certificates as issued pursuant to regulations of the Secretary, at such wages lower than the applicable minimum and subject to such limitations as to time, number, proportion, and length of service as the Secretary shall prescribe, and (2) the employment of individuals whose earning capacity is impaired by age or physical or mental deficiency or injury, under special certificates to be issued by the Secretary, at such wages lower than the applicable minimum and for such period as shall be fixed in such certificates.

PROHIBITED ACTS

Section 13 of the House amendment makes it unlawful for any person—

(1) To violate any of the wage or hour provisions, or any of the provisions of any regulation or order of the Secretary issued under section 12 (relating to learners, apprentices, and handicapped workers);

(2) To transport, offer for transportation, ship, deliver, or sell in commerce, or to ship, deliver, or sell with knowledge that shipment or delivery or sale thereof in commerce is intended, any goods in the production of which any employee was employed in violation of the wage or hour provisions, or in violation of any regulation or order of the Secretary issued under section 12. No provision of the amendment is to impose any liability upon any common carrier for the transportation in commerce in the regular

course of its business of any goods not produced by such common carrier, and no provision is to excuse any common carrier from its obligation to accept such goods for transportation;

(3) To willfully discharge or in any other manner discriminate against any employee because such employee has filed any complaint or instituted or caused to be instituted any proceeding under or related to the act, or has testified or is about to testify in any such proceeding;

(4) To violate any of the child labor provisions; or—

(5) To violate any of the provisions relating to the requirements of keeping records and making reports therefrom, or to make any statement, report, or record filed or kept pursuant to such provisions, knowing such statement, report, or record to be false in a material respect.

For the purpose of the prohibition relating to transportation in commerce of goods produced in violation of the amendment, proof that any employee was employed in violation of the wages-or-hours provision, or in violation of any regulation or order of the Secretary under section 12 (relating to learners, apprentices, and handicapped workers) in any place of employment where goods were produced, within 90 days prior to the removal of the goods therefrom, is to be prima facie evidence that the goods were produced by such employee.

PENALTIES

Section 14 of the House amendment provides that any person who violates any of the provisions of section 13 shall, upon conviction, be subject to a fine of not more than $500, or to imprisonment for not more than 6 months, or both.

INJUNCTION PROCEEDINGS

Section 15 of the House amendment vests the district courts of the United States and the United States courts of the Territories with jurisdiction to restrain violations of section 13.

RELATION TO OTHER LAWS

Section 16 of the House amendment provides that no provision of the act is to justify noncompliance with any other Federal or State law or municipal ordinance establishing a higher minimum wage or a shorter maximum workday or workweek than that established under the act, and that no provision of the act relating to the employment of child labor is to justify noncompliance with any Federal, State, or municipal ordinance establishing a higher standard than the standard established under the act.

SEPARABILITY OF PROVISIONS

Section 17 of the House amendment contains the usual separability clause.

Section 18 of the House amendment provides that no order under section 6 shall take effect prior to 120 days after the enactment of the act.

CONFERENCE AGREEMENT

SHORT TITLE
Section 1 of the conference agreement follows the provisions of the House amendment in providing that the act may be cited as the Fair Labor Standards Act of 1938.

FINDINGS AND DECLARATION OF POLICY
Section 2 of the conference agreement follows generally the provisions of both the Senate bill and the House amendment, except that it states that the existence, in industries engaged in commerce or in the production of goods for commerce, of labor conditions detrimental to the maintenance of the minimum standard of living necessary for health, efficiency, and general well-being, causes the effects on commerce described in the Senate bill and the House amendment. It is declared to be the policy of the act to correct, and as rapidly as practicable to eliminate, these conditions in such industries without substantially curtailing employment or earning power.

This is the policy which has guided the Congress in the prescription of the definite wage, hour, and child labor provisions; this is the policy which the Congress has set to guide the Administrator and the industry committees in working toward progressive improvement of labor standards. It by no means follows that the highest minimum wages or the lowest maximum hours authorized by the act are adequate to maintain what should be regarded as the minimum fair standard of living. But certainly conditions which fail to conform with the requirements of the conference agreement cannot be deemed adequate to maintain even a rudimentary minimum standard of living.

DEFINITIONS
Section 3 of the conference agreement contains definitions of the terms used in the conference agreement.

"Person" is defined in the same way as in the House amendment.

"Commerce" is defined in the same way as in the House amendment.

"State" is defined as in the Senate bill to include any State or the District of Columbia or any territory or possession. But as is the case with all other provisions of the act, each term therein is to be treated as separable.

"Employer" is defined in the same way as in both the Senate bill and the House amendment.

"Employee" is defined as an individual employed by an employer. Taken in conjunction with the definition of "employ," which is defined as including suffering or permitting to work, the substance of the definition of employee in the conference agreement is contained in both the Senate bill and the House amendment.

"Agriculture" is defined in the same way as in the House amendment with the following exceptions: (1) The production of commodities defined as agricultural commodities in section 15 (g) of the Agricultural Marketing Act is included within the definition of agriculture, (2) the raising of all fur-bearing animals is included within the definition of agriculture, and (3) forestry or lumbering operations when performed by a farmer or on a farm as an incident to or in conjunction with farming operations is also included within such definition.

"Industry" is defined in the same way as in the House amendment.

"Goods," "produced," "sale," and "sell," which are defined in the Senate bill but not in the House amendment, are defined in the same way as in the Senate bill.

"Oppressive child labor" is defined in the same way as in the House amendment with minor clerical changes.

"Wage," which was defined in neither the Senate bill nor the House amendment, is defined as including the reasonable cost, as determined by the Administrator, to the employer of furnishing his employee with board, lodging, or other facilities, where it is customary for the employer to furnish such facilities.

ADMINISTRATION

As the conference agreement provides for a limited degree of flexibility in the application of minimum wage rates, it was impossible to avoid the creation of some administrative machinery to administer the act. Section 4 of the conference agreement provides for the creation of a Wage and Hour Division in the Department of Labor, under the direction of an Administrator to be appointed by the President by and with the advice and consent of the Senate.

INDUSTRY COMMITTEES

Under section 5 of the conference agreement the Administrator is empowered to set up an industry committee for each industry engaged in commerce or in the production of goods for commerce. An industry committee is made up of an equal number of persons representing the public, employers, and employees; and its members are to be selected with due regard to geographical considerations.

MINIMUM WAGES

Section 6 of the conference agreement provides for the establishment of minimum wages for employees engaged in commerce or in the production of goods for commerce. The House amendment provided for the establishment of minimum wages if the employer was engaged in commerce in any industry affecting commerce. The conference agreement contains the definite minima of 25 cents and 30 cents per hour prescribed by the House for the first and second year respectively, but allows 7 instead of 3 years for the minimum of 40 cents per hour to be reached, except in the case of an industry in regard to which it is definitely established, by the preponderance of the evidence, that a rate of 40 cents an hour would substantially curtail employment in such industry. After the second year the absolute floor is 30 cents per hour.

Superimposed upon, and constitutionally separable from, these relatively inflexible requirements of the conference agreement is a provision that enables separate, and, when substantial curtailment of employment will not result, requires higher, minimum rates (not exceeding 40 cents an hour) to be fixed industry by industry.

MAXIMUM HOURS

Section 7 of the conference agreement provides for the establishment of maximum hours of employment for employees engaged in commerce or the production of goods for commerce. The House amendment provided for the establishment of maximum hours of employment if the employer was engaged in commerce in an industry affecting commerce. The conference agreement contains in section 7 (a) the definite maximum hours of employment, 44 hours a week for the first year, 42 hours a week for the second year, and 40 hours a week thereafter, with overtime work permissible upon the payment of one and one-half times the regular wage rate. Provision is made for certain exceptions in the provisions of subsections (b) and (c). The validity or invalidity of these exceptions would not, of course, affect the validity of the balance of the act.

The general exceptions in section 7 (b) are drawn so as to encourage under appropriate safeguards continuity or regularity of employment. Thus an exemption is accorded for employees under bona fide collective bargaining agreements which provide that no employee shall be employed more than 1,000 hours during any period of 26 consecutive weeks. A further exemption is accorded for employees employed on an annual basis under bona fide collective bargaining agreements which provide that no employee shall be employed more than 2,000 hours during any period of 52 consecutive weeks. And a further exemption is provided for periods of not more than 14 weeks in the aggregate in any calendar year, for industries found by the administrator to be of a reasonable nature. These exemptions are further restricted by the requirement that employees coming under these exemptions must receive compensation at one and one-half times the regular rate for employment in excess of 12 hours in any workday or in excess of 56 hours in any workweek.

The specific exemptions (beginning with the exemption of the first processing of milk, raw or pasteurized, into dairy products) from the hours provisions which are contained in the hours section of the House amendment have been retained with the following changes other than clerical changes: (1) It is made clear that the processing of sugar beets, sugar beet molasses, sugarcane, or maple sap into sugar (but not refined sugar) or into sirup is included within the absolute exemption, (2) the period of weeks for the partial exemption has been increased to 14, and (3) there is included within this partial exemption the first processing within the area of production as defined by the administrator) of any agricultural or horticultural commodity during seasonal operations.

WAGE ORDERS

Section 8 of the conference agreement provides the procedure to be followed in the establishment of separate minimum wages, industry by industry. Since the rigid minima establish an absolute floor, so long as they are legally effective, the flexible minima in order to serve any useful purpose would have to be higher. With a view to effectuating the declared policy of the act, section 8 requires the administrator to convene the industry committee for each industry from time to time to recommend minimum wages for such industry.

Section 8 (c) of the conference agreement requires an industry committee to make such reasonable classifications within an industry as it determines to be necessary to fix the highest minimum wage rates consistent with the declared policy without substantially curtailing employment in any such classification and without giving a competitive advantage to any group in the industry. In determining whether such classifications should be made in any industry, and in making and determining the minimum rates for such classifications, no classification is to be made and no minimum rate is to be fixed, solely on a regional basis and no classification is to be made on the basis of age or sex, but the industry committee and the administrator are to consider among other relevant factors, competitive conditions as affected by production, living, and transportation costs, wages established by collective bargaining agreements, and wages paid by employers who voluntarily maintain fair minimum wage standards.

Section 8 (d) provides that an industry committee, after investigating conditions in the industry, is to make a report to the administrator containing its recommendations regarding the minimum wage rates to be established for the industry. Upon the filing of the report, the administrator holds a hearing after giving due notice to interested persons. If upon consideration of the evidence submitted by the industry committee and others, he is satisfied that the recommendations are made in accordance with law, are supported by the evidence, and, taking into consideration the same factors as the industry committee is required to consider, carry out the purposes of the Act, then the administrator enters an order putting the recommendations into effect. If the administrator disapproves the recommendations, he must reconvene the same committee or appoint a new industry committee, for further consideration and recommendations.

This carefully devised procedure has a double advantage. It ensures on the one hand that no minimum wage rate will be put into effect by administrative action that has not been carefully worked out by a committee drawn principally from the industry itself and on the other hand that no minimum wage rate will be put into effect by administrative action which has not been found by an administrative official of the Government, exercising an independent judgment on the evidence, and responsible to Congress for his acts, to be in accordance with law.

Section 8 (e) provides that no order is to be made or continued into effect after the expiration of 7 years from the effective date of section 6 unless the industry committee by a preponderance of the evidence before it determines, and the administrator by a preponderance of the evidence adduced at the hearing finds, that such order is necessary to prevent substantial curtailment of employment in the industry. If no order is effective in an industry after the expiration of seven years, the 40 cent rate automatically applies.

Section 8 (f) provides that orders issued under section 8 shall define the industries and classifications to which they are to apply and shall contain terms and conditions necessary to carry out their purposes, to prevent their circumvention or evasion and to safeguard the minimum rates established therein.

Section 8 (f) and (g) provides the method of giving due notice of the putting into effect of orders and of the holding of hearings.

ATTENDANCE OF WITNESSES

Section 9 of the conference agreement confers the necessary powers for the summoning of witnesses and the production of documents for the purpose of any hearing or investigation under the act. It is substantially the same as in the House amendment.

COURT REVIEW

Section 10 provides for the judicial review of orders. It follows substantially the corresponding section of the Senate bill.

INVESTIGATIONS AND INSPECTIONS

Section 11 of the conference agreement provides for investigations, inspections, and records. Its provisions do not substantially depart from the corresponding provisions of the House amendment except that "Administrator" is substituted for the "Secretary of Labor." The Administrator is directed to utilize the divisions and bureaus of the Department of Labor, of which the Wage and Hour Division itself is a part, for investigations, the gathering of data, and inspections necessary under the Act. The Administrator, except in connection with the child labor provisions, is given power to bring all actions to enjoin violations of section 15.

CHILD LABOR PROVISIONS

Section 12 of the conference agreement adopts the child labor provisions of the House amendment, with one exception. In view of the omission from the conference agreement of the principle of section 6 of the House amendment, subsection (b) of section 10 of the House amendment has been omitted.

EXEMPTIONS

Section 13 of the conference agreement contains the same exemptions as were contained in the House amendment with the following changes and additions: (1) It includes an exemption from both the wage and hour provisions of employees of retail or service establishments the greater part of whose business is in intrastate commerce, (2) it includes an exemption from both the wage and hour provisions of employees of any street, suburban, or interurban electric railway, or local trolley or motor bus carrier not included in other exemptions contained in this section, (3) the provisions of the so-called Biermann amendment have been transferred to this section as an exemption from both the wage and hour provisions; in this amendment the administrator is to define the area of production, and the making of dairy products is included within its terms, and (4) a minor change has been made in the exemption of employees employed in agriculture from the child labor provisions; the child will be affected by the exemption only while he is not legally required to attend school. As in the case of other exemptions and exceptions, the validity or invalidity of any of the above exemptions will not affect the validity of the Act.

LEARNERS, APPRENTICES, AND HANDICAPPED WORKERS

Section 14 of the conference agreement makes special provision for learners, apprentices, and handicapped workers. It follows in the main the provisions of the House amendment, but includes within its terms messengers employed exclusively in delivering letters or messages.

PROHIBITED ACTS

Section 15 of the conference agreement makes it unlawful to ship or sell in commerce or to ship or sell with knowledge that shipment of sale thereof in commerce is intended, any goods in the production of which any employee was employed in violation of section 6 or section 7 or section 14, or to violate the provisions of such sections, or to do certain other acts which violate provisions of the Act or obstruct its administration. Except insofar as modification was necessary to conform with other provisions of the conference agreement, the section follows closely the corresponding section of the House amendment.

PENALTIES

Section 16 of the conference agreement provides a fine of not more than $10,000, or imprisonment for not more than 6 months, or both, for violations of the act. No person is to be imprisoned upon conviction for a first offense. This section also provides for civil reparations for violations of the wages and hours provisions. If an employee is employed for less than the legal minimum wage, or if he is employed in excess of the specified hours without receiving the prescribed payment for overtime, he may recover from his employer twice the amount by which the compensation he should have received exceeds that which he actually received.

INJUNCTION PROCEEDINGS

Section 17 relating to the jurisdiction of the courts to restrain violations of the act follows substantially the corresponding provision of the House amendment.

RELATION TO OTHER LAWS

Section 18 which deals with the relation of the act to other laws follows the corresponding provision of the House amendment with the addition of a provision to the effect that nothing in the act is to be deemed as any justification for a reduction in wages or a lengthening of hours.

SEPARABILITY OF PROVISIONS

Section 19 contains the usual separability provision. Illustrations of its application have been discussed supra in connection with various provisions.

AMENDMENTS

Portal-to-Portal Act of 1947
May 14, 1947

JOHN GWYNNE [R., IOWA] from the committee of conference, submitted the following Conference Report.

The committee of conference on the disagreeing votes of the two Houses on the amendments of the Senate to the bill (H. R. 2157) to define and limit the jurisdiction of the courts, to regulate actions arising under certain laws of the United States, and for other purposes, having met, after full and free conference, have agreed to recommend and do recommend to their respective Houses as follows: . . .

STATEMENT OF THE MANAGERS ON THE PART OF THE HOUSE

The managers on the part of the House at the conference on the disagreeing votes of the two Houses on the amendments of the Senate to the bill (H. R. 2157) to define and limit the jurisdiction of the courts, to regulate actions arising under certain laws of the United States, and for other purposes, submit the following statement in explanation of the effect of the action agreed upon by the conferees and recommended in the accompanying conference report:

FINDINGS AND POLICY

Section 1 of the House bill and section 1 of the Senate amendment contained findings and a declaration of policy by the Congress. Section 1 of the bill as agreed to in conference contains findings and a declaration of policy by the Congress in conformity with the substitute agreed on.

EXISTING PORTAL-TO-PORTAL CLAIMS

General Rule

Under the bill as agreed to in conference (sec. 2 (a)), it is provided that no employer shall be subject to any liability or punishment under the Fair Labor Standards Act of 1938, as amended, the Walsh-Healey Act, or the Bacon-Davis Act (hereinafter in this statement referred to as "the three Acts"), on account of the failure of the employer to pay an employee minimum wages, or to pay an employee overtime compensation, for or on account of an activity of an employee engaged in prior to the date of the enactment of the bill, except an activity which was compensable by either (1) an express provision of a written or non-written contract in effect, at the time of such activity, between such employee, his agent, or a collective bargaining representative, and his employer; or (2) a custom or practice in effect, at the time of such activity at the establishment or other place where such employee was employed, covering such activity, not inconsistent with a written or non-written contract, in effect at the time of such activity between such employee, his agent, or collective bargaining representative, and his employer. The above rule is to apply in the case of any action or proceeding (including criminal actions and injunctions) whether heretofore or hereafter commenced. The effect of both the House bill (section 3) and the Senate amendment (section 2) was (as to existing claims) in essence the same as the provisions of the conference bill, except that the House bill did not contain the provision under which an activity, although compensable by custom or practice, is nevertheless not compensable if the custom or practice was inconsistent with the contract.

Clarifying Provisions

The conference agreement (section 2 (b)) contains a provision not stated expressly in either bill, that an activity shall be considered as compensable under the above referred to contract provision or custom or practice only when it was engaged in during the portion of the day with respect to which it was so made compensable. Under this provision, for example, if under the contract provision or custom or practice an activity was compensable only when engaged in between 8 and 5 o'clock but was not compensable when engaged in before 8 or after 5 o'clock, it will not be considered as a compensable activity when engaged in before 8 or after 5 o'clock. So also, if under the contract provision or custom or practice an activity was compensable when engaged in before 8 but was not compensable when engaged in after 5 o'clock, it will not be compensable under the bill as agreed to in conference when engaged in after 5 o'clock. So also, if under the contract provision or custom or practice an activity was compensable during a certain portion of the regular workday but was not compensable when engaged in during other hours of the regular workday, it will not be compensable under the bill as agreed to in conference when engaged in during such other hours.

The bill as agreed to in conference also contains a provision (section 2 (c)) that in the application of the minimum wage and overtime compensation provisions of the three Acts, in determining the time for which an employer employed an employee there shall be counted all that time, but only that time, during which the employee engaged in activities which were compensable, within the meaning of subsections (a) and (b) of this section. This provision, which is in the nature of a clarifying statement, is for two purposes, (1) to emphasize that employers are not relieved from liability for the payment of minimum wages and overtime compensation under the three Acts for any time during which the employee engaged in activities compensable under the rules above stated, and (2) to make it clear that only such time will be counted for the purposes of applying the minimum wage and overtime compensation provisions of the three Acts, and that it therefore will not be possible by judicial or administrative interpretation to include other time which was not made compensable under the rule above stated. The second above-named purpose was the purpose of that portion of section 2 of the Senate amendment which stated that no judicial or administrative interpretation of the three Acts should have the effect of changing a contract so as to make compensable any activities which the previous portion of the section had declared to be not compensable.

The Senate amendment contained a provision (section 2 (b)) that every claim based on past activities not compensable under contract, custom, or practice would be null and void and unenforceable. This provision has been omitted under the conference agreement as surplusage.

The Senate amendment (section 3) provided that the provisions of section 2 of the Senate amendment which made past activities not compensable if not compensable under contract, custom, or practice, should not be deemed to remove penalty or liability under the aforementioned three Acts based on activities other than the ones so declared not to be compensable. This provision is omitted under the conference agreement as surplusage, and as fully covered by the provisions of section 2 (c) of the bill as agreed to in conference, described above under this heading.

COURT JURISDICTION

Under the conference agreement (section 2 (d)) it is provided that no court of the United States or of any State, Territory, or possession of the United States, or of the District of Columbia shall have jurisdiction of any action or proceeding (including criminal actions and injunctions), heretofore or hereafter instituted, to enforce liability or impose punishment for or on account of the failure of the employer to pay minimum wages or overtime compensation under the three Acts, to the extent that such action or proceedings seeks to enforce any liability or impose any punishment with respect to a past activity which was not compensable under contract, custom, or practice as provided in the preceding subsections. The denial of jurisdiction is of course not applicable to actions or proceedings in which judgment has become final prior to the date of the enactment of the bill.

ASSIGNMENT OF CLAIMS

Under the House bill (section 2 (f)) no cause of action or interest therein shall be assignable if it is for wages, overtime compensation, penalties, or damages under the three Acts. The Senate amendment contained no similar provision. Under the conference agreement (section 2 (e)) it is provided that no such cause of action which accrued prior to the date of the enactment of the bill, or any interest in such cause of action, shall thereafter be assignable in whole or in part to the extent that it is based on an activity which was not compensable under contract, custom, or practice within the provisions of the bill above described under the subheading "General Rule".

Under the new subsection it will be impossible for anyone (even though permitted to do so under State law) to buy up existing claims which were not compensable under contract, custom, or practice, with the hope of compromising such claims at a profit under the provisions of section 3 of the bill as agreed to in conference.

COMPROMISE OF EXISTING CLAIMS

Section 3 of the conference agreement provides that any cause of action under the three Acts which accrued prior to the date of enactment of the bill, or any action (whether heretofore or hereafter instituted) to enforce such a cause of action, may hereafter be compromised, in whole or in part, but only if there exists a bona fide dispute as to the amount payable by the employer to his employee. However, even in the case of a bona fide dispute, the compromise is not permitted to the extent that it is based on an hourly wage rate of less than the minimum required by the Act under which the cause of action arose, or on a payment for overtime at a rate less than one and one-half times such minimum hourly wage rate.

Subsection (b) of section 3 of the conference agreement permits an employee hereafter to waive his right under the Fair Labor Standards Act of 1938, as amended, to liquidated damages, in whole or in part, with respect to activities engaged in prior to the date of enactment of the bill.

Subsection (c) of section 3 of the conference agreement provides that any such compromise or waiver, in the absence of fraud or duress, shall, according to the terms thereof, be a complete satisfaction of such cause of action and a complete bar to any action based on such cause of action.

Subsection (b) of section 3 of the conference agreement states that the provisions of the section shall also be applicable to any compromise or waiver made or given before the date of enactment of the bill.

Subsection (e) of section 3 of the conference agreement defines "compromise" to include "adjustment", "settlement" and "release".

It will be noted that this section of the conference agreement lays down no rule as to compromises or waivers with respect to causes of action hereafter accruing. The validity or invalidity of such compromises or waivers is to be determined under law other than this section.

FUTURE PORTAL-TO-PORTAL CLAIMS

General Rule

The House bill in section 3 applied to future causes of action under the three Acts the same rule as in the case of the past, namely, that an activity should not be compensable unless compensable under contract, custom, or practice.

The conference agreement in section 4, subsections (a) and (b), substantially follows the provisions of sections 6 and 7 of the Senate amendment. It is provided that, subject to the qualification stated below, no employer shall be subject to any liability or punishment under the three Acts on account of his failure to pay an employee minimum wages or overtime compensation for or on account of any of the following activities engaged in on or after the date of the enactment of the bill—

(1) walking, riding, or traveling to and from the actual place of performance of the principal activity or activities which such employee is employed to perform and—

(2) activities which are preliminary to or postliminary to said principal activity or activities,

which occur either prior to the time on any particular workday at which such employee commences, or subsequent to the time on any particular workday at which he ceases, such principal activity or activities.

The qualification above referred to is that the employer shall not be so relieved if the above-described activity is compensable by either (1) an express provision of a written or nonwritten contract in effect, at the time of such activity, between such employee, his agent, or collective-bargaining representative and his employer; or (2) a custom or practice in effect, at the time of such activity, at the establishment or other place where such employee is employed covering such activity, not inconsistent with a written or nonwritten contract, in effect at the time of such activity, between such employee, his agent, or collective-bargaining representative and his employer.

Clarifying Provisions

The conference agreement (section 4 (c)) contains a provision not stated expressly in the Senate amendment, that an activity shall be considered as compensable under the above referred to contract provision or custom or practice only when it is engaged in during the portion of the day with respect to which it is so made compensable. The provision is applicable only to walking, riding, traveling, or other preliminary or postliminary activities above described. Under this provision, for example, if under the contract provision or custom or practice such a preliminary or postliminary activity is compensable only when engaged in during the portion of the day prior to the morning whistle but is not so compensable when engaged in after the evening whistle, it will not be considered as a compensable activity when engaged in after the evening whistle. So also, if under the contract provision or custom or practice an activity is compensable only when engaged in during the portion of the day from whistle to whistle and is not made compensable when engaged in before the morning whistle or after the evening whistle, it will not be considered as a compensable activity when engaged in before the morning whistle or after the evening whistle.

Section 4 (d) of the bill as agreed to in conference contains a similar provision to that contained in section 2 (c) of the bill as agreed to in conference previously described in this statement in connection with section 2 (c), except that it is limited to determining the time for which an employer employs an employee with respect to walking, riding, traveling, or other preliminary or postliminary activities described in section 4 (a). The reasons for and the effect of its insertion in the bill are fully described in this statement in connection with section 2 (c).

REPRESENTATIVE ACTIONS BANNED

Section 5 of the bill as agreed to in conference amends section 16 (b) of the Fair Labor Standards Act of 1938, as amended, by repealing the authority now contained therein permitting an employee or employees to designate an agent or representative to maintain an action for and in behalf of all employees similarly situated. Collective actions brought by an employee or employees (a real party in interest) for and in behalf of himself or themselves and other employees similarly situated may continue to be brought in accordance with the existing provisions of the Act. The amendment also adds a new sentence to such section 16 (b), not contained in existing law, providing that no employee shall be a party plaintiff to any such action unless he gives his consent in writing to become such a party and such consent is filed in the court in which such action is brought. The amendment made by this section is to be applicable only with respect to actions which are commenced on or after the date of enactment of the bill. Representative actions which are pending on such date are not affected by this section.

STATUTE OF LIMITATIONS

Under the House bill and the Senate amendment there was a statute of limitations on actions commenced on or after the date of the enactment of the bill to enforce any cause of action for unpaid minimum wages, unpaid overtime compensation, or liquidated damages under the three Acts. Under the House bill the period was one year and under the Senate amendment two years.

Section 6 of the bill as agreed to in conference provides for a two-year statute of limitations (regardless of the period of limitation provided by any State statute) with respect to any action commended on or after the date of enactment of the bill to enforce any cause of action for unpaid minimum wages, unpaid overtime compensation, or liquidated damages, under the three Acts if the cause of action accrues on or after the date of enactment of the bill. If the action is not commenced within two years after the cause of action accrued it is to be forever barred.

If the cause of action accrued prior to the date of the enactment of the bill, action thereon may be commenced within two years after the cause of action accrued or, in the case of a State having a shorter statute of limitations, the period prescribed by the applicable State statute of limitations; but if such action is commenced within one hundred and twenty days after the date of enactment of the bill, the applicable State statute of limitations (whether longer or shorter than two years) will apply to such action. In other words, in such latter case, if a State statute of limitations, applicable to such cause of action, has run, no action on such claim may be commenced within such 120-day period. If the applicable State statute of limitations has not run, action may be so commenced within such 120 days, and may go back as far as permitted by the applicable State statute of limitations whether more or less than two years. If, with respect to a cause of action which accrued under the Walsh-Healey Act or the Bacon-Davis Act, no State statute of limitations is applicable, an action to enforce such a cause of action commenced within such 120-day period will not be limited by any statute of limitations.

DETERMINATION OF COMMENCEMENT OF FUTURE ACTIONS

Section 7 of the bill as agreed to in conference provides a rule for determining when an action is commenced for the purposes of the statute of limitations provided in section 6. It lays down the general rule that, for such purposes, an action commenced on or after the date of enactment of the bill under the three Acts shall be considered to be commenced on the date when the complaint is filed. This is the same rule laid down in the Federal Rules of Civil Procedure. An exception to the general rule is provided in the case of a collective or class action commenced on or after the date of enactment of the bill under the Fair Labor Standards Act of 1938, as amended, or the Bacon-Davis Act (no collective or class action can be instituted under the Walsh-Healey Act). In the case of such a collective or class action (a collective action being an action brought by an employee or employees for and in behalf of himself or themselves and other employees similarly situated, and a class action being an action described in Rule 23 of the Federal Rules of Civil Procedure) the action shall be considered to be commenced in the case of an individual claimant—

(a) On the date when the complaint is filed, if he is specifically named as a party plaintiff in the complaint and his written consent to become a party plaintiff is filed on such date in the court in which the action is brought, or—

(b) If such written consent was not so filed or if his name did not so appear—on the subsequent date on which such written consent was filed in the court in which the action was commenced.

PENDING COLLECTIVE AND REPRESENTATIVE ACTIONS

Section 8 of the bill as agreed to in conference provides in the case of a collective or representative action commenced prior to the date of enactment of the bill under the Fair Labor Standards Act of 1938, as amended, the statue of limitations prescribed in section 6 (b) (two years or State statute, whichever is shorter) applies to an individual claimant who has not been specifically named as a party plaintiff to the action prior to the expiration of 120 days after the date of enactment of the bill. In the application of such statute of limitations the action shall be considered to have been commenced as to him when, and only when, his written consent to become a party plaintiff to the action is filed in the court in which the action was brought.

Under this provision, the statute of limitations in section 6 does not apply to an individual claimant who has been specifically named as a party plaintiff to the action prior to the date of the enactment of the bill. Nor does such statute of limitations apply to any individual claimant who has been so named within the period beginning on the date of enactment and ending on the 120th day after the date of enactment, if the applicable law provides that the date on which the action is deemed to have been commenced as to him is the date on which the collective or representative action was commenced. If he is so named as a party plaintiff within such 120-day period, and the applicable law provides that the action was deemed to have been commenced as to him when he was so named as a party plaintiff, then the period of limitations to be applied to him is the same as is provided in section 6 (c), namely, the one provided by the applicable State statute of limitations.

If such individual claimant is named as a party plaintiff in any such pending collective or representative action on or after the expiration of such 120-day period, the action shall be considered to have been commenced as to him when, and only when, his written consent to become a party plaintiff to the action is filed in the court in which the action was brought, and the statute of limitations applicable with respect to his cause of action is two years, or the applicable State statute of limitations if less than two years.

RELIANCE ON ADMINISTRATIVE RULINGS, ETC.

Section 9 of the bill as agreed to in conference provides that in the case of an action or proceeding (including injunctive and criminal proceedings) heretofore or hereafter commenced, based on any act or omission prior to the date of enactment of the bill, no employer is to be subject to any liability or punishment for or on account of the failure of an employer to pay minimum wages or overtime compensation under the three Acts, if he pleads and proves that the act or omission complained of was in good faith in conformity with and in reliance on any administrative regulation, order, ruling, approval, or interpretation, of any agency of the United States, or any administrative practice or enforcement policy of any such agency with respect to the class of employers to which he belongs. Such a defense, if established, will be a bar to the action or proceeding, notwithstanding that after such act or omission, such administrative regulation, order, ruling, approval, interpretation, practice, or enforcement policy is modified or rescinded or is determined by judicial authority to be invalid or of no legal effect. It will thus be seen that the administrative regulation, order, etc., does not have to be in writing nor does it have to be a regulation, order, etc., of the Federal agency which administers the Act in question. It will be sufficient if the employer can prove that his act or omission was in good faith in conformity with and in reliance on an administrative regulation, order, etc., of any Federal agency.

Section 10 of the bill as agreed to in conference, relating to an action or proceeding based on any act or omission on or after the date of enactment of the bill, contained a rule which is the same as the rule relating to acts or omissions prior to the date of the enactment of the bill, with two exceptions; (1) The regulations, orders, rulings, approvals, or interpretations, which may be relied on must be in writing; and (2) the regulations, practices, enforcement policies, etc., must be those of the Administrator of the Wage and Hour Division of the Department of Labor—in the case of the Fair Labor Standards Act of 1938, as amended; of the Secretary of Labor, or any Federal officer utilized by him in the administration of the Walsh-Healey Act—in the case of the Walsh-Healey Act; and of the Secretary of Labor—in the case of the Bacon-Davis Act.

It should be noted that under both sections 9 and 10 an employer will be relieved from liability, in an action by an employee, because of reliance in good faith on an administrative practice or enforcement policy, only: (1) where such practice or policy was based on the ground that an act or omission was not a violation of the Act, or (2) where a practice or policy of not enforcing the Act with respect to acts or omissions led the employer to believe in good faith that such acts or omissions were not violations of the Act.

However, the employer will be relieved from criminal proceedings or injunctions brought by the United States, not only in the cases described in the preceding paragraph, but also where the practice or policy was such as to lead him in good faith to believe that he would not be proceeded against by the United States.

The effect of the rules stated in the two preceding paragraphs may be illustrated as follows: An employer will not be relieved from liability under the

Fair Labor Standards Act of 1938 to his employees (in an action by them) for the period December 26, 1946, to March 1, 1947, if he is not exempt under the "Area of Production" regulations published in the Federal Register of December 25, 1946, notwithstanding the press release issued by the Administrator of the wage and Hour Division of the Department of Labor, in which he stated that he would not enforce the Fair Labor Standards Act of 1938 on account of acts or omissions occurring prior to March 1, 1947. On the other hand he will, by reason of the enforcement policy set forth in such press release, have a good defense to a criminal proceeding or injunction brought by the United States based on an act or omission prior to March 1, 1947.

It should also be noted that under both sections 9 and 10 the regulations, interpretations, enforcement policies, etc., which may be in good faith relied on must be those of an "agency" and not of an individual officer or employee of the agency. Thus if inspector A tells the employer that the agency interpretation is that the employer is not subject to the Act, the employer is not relieved from liability, despite his reliance in good faith on such interpretation, unless it is in fact the interpretation of the agency.

LIQUIDATED DAMAGES

Section 2 (g) of the House bill authorized the courts, in their discretion, in awarding liquidated damages under the three Acts to award a lesser amount than the amount specified therein. There was no comparable provision in the Senate amendment. Section 11 of the bill as agreed to in conference permits the court, in its sound discretion, to award no liquidated damages or award any amount thereof not to exceed the amount specified in section 16 (b) of the Fair Labor Standards Act of 1938, as amended, in any action under such Act of 1938 commenced prior to or on or after the date of enactment of the bill to recover unpaid minimum wages, unpaid overtime compensation, or liquidated damages, if the employer shows to the satisfaction of the court that the act or omission giving rise to such action was in good faith and that he had reasonable grounds for believing that his act or omission was not a violation of such Act.

AREA OF PRODUCTION

Section 12 of the bill as agreed to in conference is inserted to relieve the situation created by the decision of the Supreme Court in *Addison, et al.* v. *The Holly Hill Fruit Products, Inc.* (322 U. S. 607, decided June 5, 1944), holding invalid certain regulations of the Administrator of the Wage and Hour Division relating to "area of production", and directing him to issue new regulations, which the Administrator did not do for a period of approximately two and one-half years after the date of such decision.

This section relieves an employer from liability and punishment under the Fair Labor Standards Act of 1938 on account of the failure of such employer to pay an employee minimum wages, or to pay an employee overtime compensation, for or on account of an activity engaged in by such employee prior to December 26, 1946, if such employer (1) was relieved from such liability or punishment by reason of a valid definition of "area of production" by the Administrator applicable at the time of the performance of the activity, or (2) would have been so relieved by reason of an invalid definition applicable at the time of the performance if such definition had been valid, or (3) would have been so relieved if the definition finally made by the Administrator on December 18, 1946, and published in the Federal Register of December 25, 1946, had been in force on and after the effective date of the sections of such Act of 1938 providing for minimum wages and overtime compensation.

It should be noted that under the above provision the protection to the employer under the foregoing provisions for acts or omissions up to December 26, 1946, will exist even though hereafter the regulation of December, 1946 is held invalid.

DEFINITIONS

Section 13 of the bill as agreed to in conference contains definitions of the terms "employer", "employee", "wage", and "State". It also contains an official short title of the Walsh-Healey Act and the Bacon-Davis Act.

SEPARABILITY

Section 14 of the bill as agreed to in conference contains the usual separability clause.

SHORT TITLE

Section 15 of the bill as agreed to in conference provides that the bill may be cited as the "Portal-to-Portal Act of 1947".

AMENDMENT TO TITLE OF BILL

The conference agreement amends the title of the bill so as to read: "An Act to relieve employers from certain liabilities and punishments under the Fair Labor Standards Act of 1938, as amended, the Walsh-Healey Act, and the Bacon-Davis Act, and for other purposes."

Fair Labor Standards Amendment of 1949
October 26, 1949

MR. JOHN LESINSKI [DEM., MICH.], from the committee of conference, submitted the following Conference Report.

The committee of conference on the disagreeing votes of the two Houses on the amendment of the Senate to the bill (H. R. 5856) to provide for the amendment of the Fair Labor Standards Act of 1938, and for other purposes, having met, after full and free conference, have agreed to recommend and do recommend to their respective Houses as follows: . . .

STATEMENT OF THE MANAGERS ON THE PART OF THE HOUSE

The managers on the part of the House at the conference on the disagreeing votes of the two Houses on the amendment of the Senate to the bill (H. R. 5856) to provide for the amendment of the Fair Labor Standards Act of 1938, and for other purposes, submit the following statement in explanation of the effect of the action agreed upon by the conferees and recommended in the accompanying conference report:

The Senate amendment struck out all of the House bill after the enacting clause and inserted a substitute amendment. The conferees have agreed to a substitute for both the House bill and the Senate amendment. The substitute agreed to in conference is explained below.

SHORT TITLE

Both the House bill and the Senate amendment provided that it was to be cited as the "Fair Labor Standards Amendments of 1949." The Conference agreement adopts this title.

FINDINGS AND DECLARATION OF POLICY

The House bill amended subsection (b) of section 2 of the act by referring to the power of Congress under the Constitution to regulate commerce with foreign nations as well as commerce among the several States. This technical change was made in conjunction with the change made in subsection (b) of section 3 defining the term "commerce," which is hereinafter discussed. No such provision was included in the Senate amendment of the House bill. The conference agreement adopts the House provision.

DEFINITIONS

Section 3 of the act, relating to definitions, is unchanged by the conference agreement except that definitions of the terms "commerce," "produced" and "oppressive child labor" are amended and new definitive language is provided for the terms "resale" and "hours worked."

Commerce.—The definition of "commerce" in section 3 (b) of the act now covers outgoing foreign commerce "from any State to any place outside thereof" in addition to interstate commerce "among the several States." It does not cover incoming foreign commerce. The House bill amended the definition by substituting the word "between" for the word "from" and the word "and" for the word "to," so that the definition would cover foreign commerce "between any State and any place outside thereof." The Senate amendment did not contain any provision amending this definition. The conference agreement adopts the House provision. The effect of the amendment is to eliminate inequalities under the act between employees engaged in foreign commerce based on whether the flow of such foreign commerce is out of a State rather than into it. The amendment, will, for example, place employees of importers on an equal footing with employees of exporters under the act.

Produced.—The House bill amended the definition of "produced" in section 3 (j) by inserting the words "closely related" before the words "process or occupation" and substituting the word "indispensable" for the word "necessary". The Senate amendment left the definition of "produced" as contained in the present law unchanged. The bill as agreed to in conference follows the House bill except that the words "directly essential" are substituted for the word "indispensable".

Coverage under the act for a large category of employees is determined by the definition of the term "produced". The definition is divided into two parts. The first part, which the conference bill leaves unchanged, covers any employee "producing, manufacturing, mining, handling, transporting, or in any other manner working on . . . goods." Thus the first part covers employees engaged in actual production activities as opposed, for example, to employees engaged in maintenance, clerical, or custodial work. The second part of the present definition, covering any employee engaged in "*any* process or occupation *necessary* to the production" of goods, has been interpreted by the Administrator and the courts to cover employees of many local merchants, because some of the customers of such merchants are producing goods for interstate commerce. It has made no difference that the merchants sell their goods locally and that such goods do not become a part or ingredient of the goods produced by any of their customers (*McComb* v. *Deibert* (E. D. Pa. 1949), 16 Labor Cases Par. 64,982). The courts have also held the act applicable to employees engaged in maintaining and repairing private homes and dwellings where such homes and dwellings are being leased by interstate producers to their employees. Coverage of the act has also been extended to employees of an independently owned and operated restaurant located in a factory (*McComb* v. *Factory Stores,* 81 F. Supp. 403 (N. D. Ohio 1948)).

Under the bill as agreed to in conference an employee will not be covered unless he is shown to have a closer and a more direct relationship to the producing, manufacturing, etc., activity than was true in the above-cited cases. On the other hand, the proposed changes are not intended to remove from the act maintenance, custodial, and clerical employees of manufacturers, mining companies, and other producers of goods for commerce. Employees engaged in such maintenance, custodial, and clerical work will remain subject to the act, notwithstanding they are employed by an independent employer performing such work on behalf of the manufacturer, mining company, or other producer for commerce. All such employees perform activities that are closely related and directly essential to the production of goods for commerce.

The bill as agreed to in conference also does not affect the coverage under the act of employees who repair or maintain buildings in which goods are produced for commerce (*Kirschbaum* v. *Walling,* 316 U. S. 517) or who make, repair, or maintain machinery or tools and dies used in the production of goods for commerce. Likewise, employees of public utilities, furnishing gas, electricity or water to firms within the State engaged in manufacturing, producing, or mining goods for commerce, will remain subject to the act. All the employees mentioned in this paragraph are doing work that is closely related and directly essential to the production of goods for commerce.

The following are some examples of cases in which the Administrator and the courts will no longer be able to hold the act applicable because the activities involved in such cases are not closely related or directly essential to production:

1. A local fertilizer company engaged in selling all of its fertilizer to local farmers within the State for use on land on which sugarcane is grown, which cane is then sold to sugar mills within the State and processed into raw sugar which is sent out of the State (*McComb, Administrator* v. *Super-A Fertilizer Works,* 165 F. (2d) 824 (C. C. A. 1)).

2. Employees of a quarry engaged in mining and processing stone for local use in the construction of a dike located in the same State and who transport such rock from the quarry to the construction site, where the construction of the dike would have the effect of preventing an oil field that produced oil for commerce from being flooded (*Schroeder* v. *Clifton,* 153 F. (2d) 385 (C. C. A. 10); cert. den., 328 U. S. 858).

3. Employees of a local window-cleaning company doing business wholly within the State but many of whose customers are engaged in interstate commerce or in the production of goods for interstate commerce (*Martino* v. *Michigan Window Cleaning Company,* 327 U. S. 173; reh'g den., 327 U. S. 816).

4. Employees of a local independent nursery concern whose duties include mowing the lawn around the plant of a customer within the State engaged in producing goods for interstate commerce (1944–45 W. H. Man., p. 125).

5. Employees of a local architectural firm whose activities include the preparation of plans for the alteration of buildings within the State which are used to produce goods for interstate commerce (1944–45 W. H. Man., pp. 138–139).

6. Employees of a local exterminator service firm, who work wholly within the State exterminating roaches and other pests in private houses,

apartments, hotels, barber shops, colleges, hospitals, and also in buildings within the State used to produce goods for interstate commerce (3 C. C. H., Labor Law Reporter, 4th ed., No. 25,150.385).

All such employees, as well as the employees of the merchant selling his goods locally and employees engaged in providing residential, eating, or other living facilities for factory workers, are quite clearly not performing any activities that are closely related or directly essential to the production of goods.

Oppressive child labor.—Under the bill as agreed to in conference, the definition of "oppressive child labor" in section 3 (1) of the act is amended to include parental employment of a child under 16 years of age in an occupation found by the Secretary of Labor to be hazardous for children between the ages of 16 and 18 years. This provision was contained in substantially the same form in both the House bill and the Senate amendment, except that the House bill substituted the Administrator of the Wage and Hour Division for the Secretary of Labor, who is responsible under the present law for administration of the child-labor provisions. The conference agreement adopts the language of the Senate amendment. This provision closes a loophole in the present definition under which a parent or person standing in place of a parent, who may not employ his child in a hazardous occupation if between 16 and 18 years of age, is permitted to employ the child in such an occupation until he becomes 16 years of age.

Resale.—The House bill in section 3 (1) declared that "resale" shall not include the sale of goods to be used in residential or farm building construction, repair, or maintenance. The Senate amendment added a proviso that the sale must be recognized as a bona fide retail sale in the industry. The conference agreement adopted the Senate amendment. Under the conference agreement a sale of building materials to a building contractor for use in residential or farm construction is not intended as a sale for resale within the meaning of section 13 (a) (2) provided that it is recognized as a bona fide retail sale in the industry.

Hours worked.—The House bill in section 3 (o) added a partial definition of the term "hours worked." The Senate amendment did not contain an amendment on this subject. The conference agreement adopts the House provisions with an amendment. Under the section as passed by the House, for the purposes of the minimum wage and maximum hours provisions of the act, there would be excluded from "hours worked" any time spent by the employee which was excluded from measured working time under a bona fide collective-bargaining agreement applicable to him or custom or practice thereunder. The conference agreement limits this exclusion to time spent by the employee in changing clothes and cleaning his person at the beginning or at the end of each workday.

ADMINISTRATOR

The House bill amended section 4 of the act by changing its title to read "Administration" instead of "Administrator", by increasing the salary of the Administrator of the Wage and Hour Division to $15,000 per annum and by adding a new subsection (e) providing a defense to any alleged violation of the act with respect to "any act done or omitted in good faith in conformity with any written regulation, order or interpretation of the Administrator or the Secretary of Agriculture, as the case may be," notwithstanding the subsequent, rescission or invalidation of such regulation, order or interpretation. Section 4 was not otherwise changed. The Senate amendment made no changes in section 4 of the act.

The conference agreement follows the provisions of the Senate amendment with respect to the act's administration, except that the salary of the Administrator is fixed at $15,000 per annum.

The conference agreement omits the provision for a "good faith" defense since its subject matter is covered in sections 9 and 10 of the Portal-to-Portal Act of 1947.

The present act does not contain any provision relative to the compensation of the Solicitor of Labor, and neither the House bill nor the Senate amendment contained such a provision. In agreeing to the amendment increasing the salary of the Administrator to $15,000 annually, it was the unanimous agreement of the conferees that the salary of the Solicitor of Labor should be increased to a like figure. It is through the Solicitor and his staff that the Administrator brings actions under section 17 of the act and will bring the actions for recovery of unpaid minimum wages and unpaid overtime compensation which are authorized by the new section 16 (c) contained in the conference agreement. The conference agreement omits a provision equalizing the salary of the Solicitor of Labor with that of the Administrator only because of a parliamentary situation which the committee has been advised might subject the conference agreement to a point of order if such a provision were included. It is the unanimous opinion of the committee of conference that the duties of the Solicitor of Labor are of such a nature that his position should receive the highest possible rate of compensation under the new legislation revising the Classification Act (H. R. 5931).

INDUSTRY COMMITTEE FOR PUERTO RICO AND
THE VIRGIN ISLANDS

The House bill amended section 5 of the act by limiting its application to the appointment of special industry committees to recommend the minimum rates or rates of wages to be paid under section 6 of the act to employees in Puerto Rico or the Virgin Islands engaged in commerce or in the production of goods for commerce. The Senate bill made no changes in section 5 of the act.

The conference agreement follows the provisions of the House bill. In order to preserve existing orders of the Administrator restricting industrial homework in certain industries, the conference agreement provides that a new subsection is added to section 11 of the act under which all existing regulations or orders of the Administrator relating to industrial homework are continued in full force and effect, and the Administrator is authorized to issue such regulations and orders regulating, restricting, or prohibiting industrial homework as are necessary to prevent the circumvention or evasion of, and to safeguard, the minimum wage rate prescribed by the act.

MINIMUM WAGE

The House bill provided that every employer would be required to pay to each of his employees who is engaged in commerce or in the production of goods for commerce wages at a rate of not less than 75 cents per hour. The Senate amendment made almost identical changes in subsection (a) of section 6. The conference agreement adopts the provisions of the Senate amendment.

The House bill also made the following changes in subsection (c) of section 6: The minimum wage rates established by existing wage orders for employees in Puerto Rico and Virgin Islands industries were continued in effect unless and until superseded by a wage order issued pursuant to the recommendations of a special industry committee appointed pursuant to section 5; and the rates prescribed in any such order were made applicable to every employee in any Puerto Rican or Virgin Islands industry covered by such order who is within the coverage of and not exempt under the provisions of the act as amended by the House bill, including employees who either were not covered by the law as it existed prior to such amendment or were exempted from its application, but who were brought within the application of the law by the House bill. The Senate amendment provided that existing wage order rates for employees in Puerto Rico and the Virgin Islands should continue in effect until superseded by a wage order issued pursuant to the recommendations of a special industry committee appointed pursuant to section 5. The conference agreement follows the provisions of the House bill with respect to the scope and effect of existing wage orders for employees in Puerto Rican and the Virgin Islands industries.

MAXIMUM HOURS

General explanation.—The House bill completely revised section 7 of the act relating to maximum hours and overtime compensation, including a definition of "regular rate" and other provisions affecting the application of the overtime compensation requirements of the act. The Senate amendment left section 7 unchanged except for the extension of the overtime exemption provided by subsection (c) to include the first processing of buttermilk into dairy products, a provision also contained in the House bill. The conference agreement follows the provisions of the House bill except as hereafter noted. The general requirement of the present act, that employment in excess of 40 hours in a workweek shall be compensated at a rate not less than 1½ times the regular rate at which the employee is employed, is retained. This requirement applies, as under the present act, to employees engaged in commerce or in the production of goods for commerce, except those specifically exempted. Obsolete provisions of the present section 7 and the provision relating to the effective date of the maximum hours provisions of the 1938 act are deleted.

Semiannual and annual employment agreements.—Under the House bill section 7 (b) (1) of the act, providing a partial exemption from the overtime pay requirement of section 7 (a) for employees employed under collective-bargaining agreements limiting employment to 1,000 hours in any period of 26 consecutive weeks, was amended by inserting "one thousand and forty hours" in lieu of "one thousand hours." This would permit employment under such agreements for an average workweek of 40 hours during any 26-week period. The conference agreement adopts the House provision.

The House bill modified the provisions of section 7 (b) (2) of the act, relating to guaranteed annual employment plans established by bona fide collective bargaining, to provide for greater flexibility. The annual employment guaranteed could be either 2,080 hours (the present figure) or a lesser figure down to a minimum either of 1,840 hours or of 46 normal workweeks of not less than 30 hours per week. The exemption from overtime pay for hours worked up to 12 a day or 56 a week would not, as at present, be lost for the entire year with respect to an employee who must be worked at the end of the year for a few hours beyond the present 2,080-hour limit. The House bill permitted employment in excess of the annual period guaranteed, up to a maximum of 2,240 hours, if not less than time and one-half the regular rate is paid for all hours worked in excess of the guaranteed period which are also in excess of 40 in the workweek or in excess of 2,080 hours in the contract year. The conference agreement adopts the provisions of the House bill.

Fourteen workweek hours exemption for first processing and canning of fish.—The House bill added to section 7 (b) (3) of the act a partial exemption from the overtime pay requirements for employees in industries engaged in the first processing or canning of fish in the raw or natural state. This provision was added in lieu of the complete wage and hour exemption provided in section 13 (a) (5), which is discussed below. The conference agreement substitutes for the House provision a new overtime exemption for canning of fish in section 13 (b) discussed below.

Section 7 (c) hours exemptions for processing of farm products.—The conference agreement leaves unchanged the hours exemptions provided by section 7 (c) of the act, except for adding buttermilk to the commodities listed in the hours exemption provided for the first processing of milk, cream, skimmed milk or whey into dairy products. Such a provision was contained in both the House bill and the Senate amendent. The seasonal exemption for the first processing of agricultural or horticultural commodities within the "area of production" was changed in the House bill by transferring the authority to define "area of production" from the Administrator to the Secretary of Agriculture. The Senate amendment did not make this change. The conference agreement leaves this authority in the Administrator.

"Regular rate" and crediting of overtime pay.—The House bill added a new subsection (d) to section 7 of the act containing a comprehensive statutory definition of "regular rate," and a new subsection (g) specifying the payments excluded from "regular rate" which may be credited toward the overtime compensation required by the act. The Senate amendment contained no such provisions. The conference agreement (sec. 7 (d)) adopts the House provisions defining "regular rate" except for revisions of paragraph (3) of subsection (d) indicated below. The conference agreement adopts the crediting provision contained in subsection (g) of the House bill.

The House bill defined "regular rate" as all remuneration for employment except certain specified types of payments. The conference agreement adopts this approach. Each of the seven subdivisions of subsection (d) is intended to provide a separate, carefully defined exclusion from "regular rate." Accordingly, a payment excluded under any one subdivision would not be deemed part of the "regular rate" by reason of the fact that such payment may not be excluded by the language of any other subdivision. The classes of payments excluded under the first four subdivisions are not creditable toward overtime payments required by section 7 of the act.

Payments excluded from "regular rate" and not creditable as overtime pay —Section 7 (d) (1), (2).—The conference agreement adopts the language of the House provisions excluding from the "regular rate" (1) bona fide gifts and payments in the nature of gifts made at Christmas time or on other special occasions under specified conditions, and (2) payments which are not made as compensation for hours of employment, including payments for occasional periods when no work is performed due to vacation, holiday, illness, or failure of the employer to provide sufficient work, and including payments as reimbursement for traveling or other expenses under certain conditions.

Section 7 (d) (3).—Clause (a) of this subsection of the House bill provided for the exclusion from the "regular rate" of certain sums paid at the sole discretion of the employer in recognition of services performed during a given period of time, and not paid pursuant to a prior contract, agreement, or promise causing the employee to expect such payments regularly. The conference agreement adopts the House provision.

The House bill, in clauses (b) and (c) of this subsection, provided for the exclusion from the "regular rate" of certain payments made pursuant to bona fide profit-sharing plans or trusts and of "talent fees" paid to radio and television performers. The conference agreement makes these exclusions, retaining the numbering of the House bill, but adding language giving the Administrator authority to issue appropriate regulations defining the bona fide profit-sharing plans or trusts pursuant to which payments may be made to employees without increasing the "regular rate," and defining "talent fees." Under the conference agreement, similar provision is made in clause (b) for regulations permitting the exclusion from the "regular rate" of payments made by employers pursuant to bona fide thrift or savings plans. Such plans were not expressly mentioned in the House provision.

Section 7 (d) (4).—The conference agreement adopts the language of the House provision excluding from the "regular rate" contributions irrevocably made by an employer to a trustee or third person pursuant to a bona fide plan for providing old-age, retirement, life, accident, or health insurance or similar benefits.

Payments excluded from "regular rate" and creditable as overtime premiums—Section 7 (d) (5t), (6), (7); section 7 (f).—Under the House bill (section 7 (d) (5)) overtime premiums paid for hours worked in any day or workweek because such hours are in excess of 8 in a day or 40 in a workweek or in excess of the employee's normal working hours or regular working hours, as the case may be, were expressly excluded from the employee's regular rate of pay. Section 7 (g) of the House bill provided for the crediting of such premiums toward statutory overtime compensation due for work in excess of 40 hours. In addition, section 7 (c) (6), (7), and 7 (g) of the House bill continued in effect the provisions of section 7 (e) of the present act added by act of July 20, 1949, (Public Law 177, 81st Cong., 1st sess.). These provisions, which constituted a partial definition of "regular rate" in Public Law 177, are repeated here solely because section 7 (d) is entended to constitute a more comprehensive definition of "regular rate." Although by reason of their textual relation to other provisions of the bill sections 7 (d) (6) and 7 (d) (7) differ slightly in wording from Public Law 177, they are intended to solve the identical problems which Public Law 177 was intended to solve, and the discussion and specific examples set forth in House Report No. 121 and Senate Report No. 402, accompanying H. R. 858, are applicable to sections 7 (d) (6) and 7 (d) (7). The provision of the House bill corresponding to section 7 (e) (1) of the present amended act expressly placed premium pay for work on "regular days of rest" in the same category under that provision as premium pay for work on Saturdays, Sundays, holidays, and sixth or seventh days of the workweek. "Regular days of rest" are not mentioned expressly in the present section 7 (e) (1). The conference agreement adopts the language of the House provision.

As explained later in this statement under the heading "Retroactive provisions," the provisions of section 7 (e) of the present act, as retained in section 7 (d) (6), (7), and 7 (g) of the conference agreement, will continue to have retroactive effect as provided in section 16 (e) of the conference agreement which replaces section 2 of the act of July 20, 1949 (Public Law 177, 81st Cong., 1st sess.).

Contract pay plans.—The House bill (sec. 7 (e)) contained a provision specifically providing that no employer should be deemed to have violated the overtime provisions of the act by employing any employee for a workweek in excess of 40 hours if such employee was employed pursuant to either a bona fide individual contract, or a collective-bargaining agreement, if the duties of such employee necessitated irregular hours of work, and the contract or agreement (1) specified a regular rate of pay of not less than the minimum hourly rate provided in the act, and compensation at not less than one and one-half times such rate for all hours worked in excess of 40 in any workweek and (2) provided a weekly guaranty of pay for not more than 60 hours based on the rates so specified. The conference agreement adopts the House provision.

Overtime pay based on rate not obtained by averaging straight-time earnings for workweek.—The House bill (sec. 7 (f)) permitted overtime payments for hours worked in excess of 40 in a workweek to be made, under specific conditions, at time and one-half the bona fide hourly or piece rates applicable to the work performed during such overtime hours. Under this provision, employers and employees could agree, in advance of the performance of work and subject to specified conditions, to calculate overtime pay for such work by increasing the applicable hourly or piece rate for a given kind of work by 50 percent during the hours worked after 40 in the workweek, rather than by paying time and one-half based on average hourly straight-time earnings for the workweek. The Senate amendment contained no such provision. The conference agreement adopts the House provision, with two modifications. The first modification makes it possible for such an employment agreement to meet the requirements of this subsection whenever overtime pay is so calculated for the total number of hours worked by the employee in such workweek in excess of 40 hours, even though some of the hours for which overtime pay is received fall before the fortieth hour. This makes it unnecessary to recompute the amount due under the statute at the end of the workweek where it is clear that overtime pay as permitted under this subsection has been paid for a number of hours of work equivalent to the number worked after 40. The second modification is the addition to the House provision of a new clause (3), permitting the computation of overtime pay at a rate not less than one and one-half times a basic rate established by agreement (which may remain constant from workweek to workweek) if such basic rate is authorized by regulation of the Administrator as being substantially equivalent to the average hourly earnings of the employee, exclusive of overtime premiums, in the particular work over a representative period of time.

WAGE ORDERS IN PUERTO RICO AND THE VIRGIN ISLANDS

The House bill limited the application of the provisions of section 8 of the act to industries in Puerto Rico and the Virgin Islands engaged in commerce or in the production of goods for commerce and made necessary clarifying changes in its subsections to carry out this purpose. Subsection (a) stated the policy of the act to reach an objective of a 75-cent minimum wage for such industries as rapidly as economically feasible without substantially curtailing employment. Subsection (b) specified that the minimum-wage rates which a special industry committee recommends, and the Administrator approves, were not to give any industry in Puerto Rico or in the Virgin Islands a competitive advantage over any industry in the United States outside of Puerto Rico or the Virgin Islands. Except for technical changes made necessary by raising the statutory minimum to 75 cents an hour, subsections (c) and (d) of section 8, setting forth the standards and procedures to govern the issuance of wage orders, were to be the same as under the present act. Subsection (e) of section 8 of the present act was omitted from the House bill because it served no purpose in such bill. Subsections (f) and (g) of the present act were retained as subsections (e) and (f).

The Senate amendment made no changes in section 8 of the act except to insert the figure "75 cents an hour" for the figure "40 cents an hour" wherever it was used in its several subsections. The conference agreement adopts in substance the provisions of the House bill.

As is noted elsewhere, the conference agreement provides for adding a new subsection to section 11 under which existing orders of the Administrator restricting industrial home work in a number of industries, which were originally issued under subsection (f) of section 8 of the present act, are continued in full force and effect.

ATTENDANCE OF WITNESSES

The House bill amended section 9 of the act relating to attendance of witnesses by making a technical correction therein and by taking away from the Secretary of Labor subpoena powers vested in him by Reorganization Plan No. 2 of 1946 in connection with administration and enforcement of the child-labor provisions of the act. The Senate amendment made no changes in section 9.

The conference agreement follows the Senate amendment in this respect, leaving unchanged the act's provisions relating to attendance of witnesses.

COURT REVIEW

The House bill amended section 10 of the act relating to court review of Puerto Rican and Virgin Islands industry wage orders issued by the Administrator under section 8 of the act by inserting in subsection (a) thereof the requirement that the Administrator's findings of fact on which such orders are based must be supported by "a preponderance of the evidence" rather than by "substantial evidence," as at present. In addition, the House bill made certain technical corrections in section 10. The Senate amendment made no changes in section 10. The conference agreement follows the Senate amendment in this respect and leaves unchanged existing law relating to court review of industry wage orders.

INVESTIGATIONS, INSPECTIONS, RECORDS, AND HOMEWORK REGULATIONS

The House bill made changes in section 11 which transferred to the Administrator of the Wage and Hour Division the authority of the Secretary of Labor to make investigations and inspections under the child-labor provisions of the act. The Senate amendment made no changes in section 11. The conference agreement follows the Senate amendment in this respect and leaves unchanged existing law relating to administration and enforcement of the child-labor provisions, including investigations and inspections.

The conference agreement adds to section 11 a new subsection (d) under which all existing regulations or orders of the Administrator relating to industrial homework are continued in full force and effect. The Administrator is authorized to issue such regulations and orders regulating, restricting, or prohibiting industrial homework as are necessary to prevent the circumvention or evasion of, and to safeguard, the minimum wage rate prescribed by the act. The effect of this provision has been explained above in connection with the discussion of the changes made by the conference agreement in sections 5 and 8 of the act. Consistent with the addition of this new subsection, the title of section 11 has been changed by the conference agreement to read "Investigations, inspections, records, and homework regulations."

CHILD-LABOR PROVISIONS

The House bill added a proviso to section 12 (a) of the act which would relieve a purchaser of goods produced in an establishment where oppressive child labor was employed, if such purchaser could prove that he was without knowledge of the employment of oppressive child labor and acted in good faith in reliance on written assurance from the producer, manufacturer, or dealer that the goods were produced in compliance with the child-labor provisions. The Senate amendment contained no similar provision. The conference agreement follows the House bill in this respect but adopts language similar to the Senate amendment of section 15 (a) (1) of the act, discussed below.

The House bill eliminated the provisions of section 12 (b) of the act which authorize the Secretary of Labor, or his authorized representatives, to make investigations and inspections under the child-labor provisions and to institute actions for injunctions under section 17 for violations of the child-labor provisions. The House bill, in section 11 (a), transferred such authority to the Administrator. The Senate amendment made no change in the existing law. The conference agreement follows the Senate amendment and makes no change in existing law in this respect.

The House bill provided a new section 12 (b) which directly prohibited the employment of oppressive child labor in commerce or in the production of goods for commerce. The Senate amendment contained identical language as section 12 (c). The conference agreement includes this language as section 12 (c).

EXEMPTIONS

General statement.—The House bill substantially revised section 13 (a) (2) of the act relating to retail and service establishments, amended section 13 (a) (5) relating to fisheries and sea-food employees, section 13 (a) (8) relating to newspapers, section 13 (a) (10) relating to the processing of agricultural commodities, and added new exemptions affecting employees of taxicab companies, certain telegraph agencies, forestry, logging, and sawmill operators, nonprofit agricultural irrigation companies, and rural home workers. The House bill also amended section 13 (a) (4) relating to carriers by air and enlarged the child-labor exemption contained in section 13 (c). The Senate amendment also substantially revised section 13 (a) (2), amended section 13 (a) (11) relating to telephone-switchboard operators, and added exemptions for certain employees of agricultural irrigation companies and telegraph agencies, employees engaged in the processing or storing of cotton or the processing of cottonseed, employees engaged as home workers in sewing baseballs, and outside buyers of poultry, eggs, cream, and milk. The Senate amendment also exempted newsboys from the wage, hour, and child-labor provisions, and further enlarged the child-labor exemption. Each provision of the House bill and the Senate amendment is discussed below.

Retail and service establishments.—Both the House bill and the Senate amendment contained an identical amendment providing for an exemption for retail and service establishments (sec. 13 (a) (2)). The amendment was continued in the conference agreement.

The amendment (sec. 13 (a) (2)), agreed to in conference clarifies the existing exemption by defining the term "retail or service establishment" and stating the conditions under which the exemption shall apply. This clarification is needed in order to obviate the sweeping ruling of the Administrator and the courts that no sale of goods or services for business use is retail. See *Roland Electrical Co.* v. *Walling* (326 U. S. 657); *McComb* v. *Diebert* ((E. D. Pa. 1949) 16 Labor Cases Par. 64.982); *McComb* v. *Factory Stores* (81 F. Supp. 403 (N. D. Ohio 1948)).

Under paragraph (2) of section 13 (a) as agreed to in conference an establishment is an exempt retail or service establishment if it meets three tests:

First, over 50 percent of the establishment's sales by annual dollar volume of goods or services must be made within the State in which the establishment is located. The requirement that the greater part of the selling or servicing be in intrastate commerce found in the present law is eliminated because of the tendency of the courts to hold that many sales or services made or performed within a State are not intrastate sales or services. See *Kirschbaum* v. *Walling* (316 U. S. 517, 526); *Boutell* v. *Walling* (327 U. S. 463, 467). Under the new test, if the sales are made within the State in which the establishment is located, it is immaterial that the sales (*a*) are made pursuant to prior orders from customers, (*b*) contemplate the purchase of goods by the establishment from outside the State to fill customers' orders, or (c) are made to customers who are engaged in interstate commerce or in the production of goods for interstate commerce. In this connection, see *Walling* v. *Jacksonville Paper Co.* (317 U. S. 564).

The second test provides that in order for an establishment to be exempt not less than 75 percent of its annual dollar volume of sales of goods or services (or of both) must not be for resale. In other words, at least three-fourths of the goods or services (or both) sold must be to purchasers who do not buy for the purpose of reselling. Normally, goods are to be considered as sold for resale even though the purchaser sells them in an altered form. In section 3 (n) there is a special definition of the word "resale" which is applicable in the case of building materials. This has been discussed above.

The third test provides that 75 percent of the establishment's annual dollar volume of sales of goods are services (or of both) must be recognized in the particular industry as retail sales or services. Under this test any sale or service, regardless of the type of customer, will have to be treated by the Administrator and courts as a retail sale or service, so long as such sale or service is recognized in the particular industry as a retail sale or service. Thus, the sale by a farm implement dealer of farm machinery to a farmer will be retail if the sale is recognized as retail in such industry. So, too, sales by the grocery store, the hardware store, the coal dealer, the automobile dealer selling passenger cars or trucks, the clothing store, the dry goods store, the department store, the paint store, the furniture store, the drug store, the shoe store, the stationer, the lumber dealer, etc., whether made to private householders or to business users, will be retail, so long as they are recognized as retail sales or services in such industries. Likewise, sales or services of hotels, restaurants, barber and beauty shops, repair garages, filling stations and the like, whether made or rendered to private householders or to business customers, will be retail so long as they are recognized as retail sales or services in such industries.

The location of the establishment, whether in an industrial plant, an office building, a railroad depot, or a Government park, etc., will make no difference in the application of the exemption. So long as the establishment meets the tests described above, it will be excluded from the minimum wage and overtime provisions of the act.

Up to 25 percent of the establishment's annual dollar volume of sales of goods or services (or of both) may consist of sales for resale and sales that are not recognized as retail sales or services in the particular industry without loss of the exemption.

Paragraph (2) of section 13 (a) of the conference agreement does not exempt large mail-order houses which make most of their sales to out-of-State customers. Not does it exempt warehouses and central offices of chain-store systems. The employees in such warehouses and central offices are not employed "by" any single retail or service establishment in the chain but rather by the chain itself. Since, however, the exemption does apply to any employee employed "by" an exempt retail or service establishment, it is applicable to employees of an exempt retail or service establishment working in a warehouse operated by and servicing such establishment exclusively, whether or not the warehouse operation is conducted in the same building as the selling or servicing activities. For the same reason, the exemption applies to collectors, repair and service men, outside salesmen, merchandise buyers, consumer survey and promotion workers, and delivery men employed by an exempt retail or service establishment, although they do most of their work away from the establishment. The exemption, however, does not apply to any manufacturing activities since any such activities, when conducted by a retail establishment, if exempt, are intended to be exempt under section 13 (a) (4) discussed below. This does not mean, however, that an exempt retail or service establishment will lose its exemption under section 13 (a) (2) if it engages in some incidental work in the nature of processing in connection with its sales and services, e. g., a grocery may grind coffee; a drug store may prepare prescriptions;

a restaurant may process food; a clothing store may make alterations in suits; or a repair garage may grind valves.

The amendment does not exempt banks, insurance companies, building and loan associations, credit companies, newspapers, telephone companies, gas and electric utility companies, telegraph companies, etc., because there is no concept of retail selling or servicing in these industries. Where it was intended that such businesses have an exemption one was specifically provided by the law (sec. 13 (a) (8) (exemption for small newspapers), sec. 13 (a) (11) (exemption for switchboard operators of small telephone exchanges)). The amendment also does not exempt an establishment engaged in the sale and servicing of manufacturing machinery and manufacturing equipment used in the production of goods, because the sale and servicing of such equipment have never been recognized as retail selling or servicing in the industry which distributes or services that type of equipment.

Laundries.—Both the House bill and the Senate amendment contained an identical amendment exempting certain laundries, section 13 (a) (3). The amendment is continued in the conference agreement.

Paragraph (3) of section 13 (a) of the conference agreement grants a specific exemption to laundries and establishments engaged in laundering, cleaning, or repairing clothing or fabrics. This exemption contains two limitations. First, over 50 percent of the establishment's annual dollar volume must be derived from the sales of such services within the State in which it is located. Second, 75 percent of such volume must be derived from the sales of such services to customers who are not engaged in a mining, manufacturing, transportation, or communications business.

The first limitations means that the laundry or cleaning establishment must be primarily engaged in serving customers within its State. If it is primarily engaged in serving customers outside the State of its location, it will not be exempt.

Under the second limitation, no laundry or cleaning establishment will be exempt if more than 25 percent of its business is with such customers as factories, mines, railroad companies, or bus companies. Thus, laundries whose customers consist principally of interstate business, such as a laundry furnishing linens to Pullman trains, will not be exempt. So also, industrial laundries or linen supply companies, more than 25 percent of whose sales of services are to mining, manufacturing, transportation, or communications business organizations, will be unable to qualify for the exemption and will, as at present, remain subject to the act.

On the other hand, the laundry or dry cleaner will be exempt if it meets the two limitations discussed above, whether it launders towels or other linen for barber or beauty shops, doctors' or dentists' offices, or schools, hospitals, restaurants, or hotels, or for the housewife.

Retail establishments making or processing goods.—The House bill contained an exemption from the wage and hour provisions of the act for any employee employed by an establishment which qualifies as a retail establishment under section 13 (a) (2) and is recognized as a retail establishment in the particular industry notwithstanding that such establishment makes or processes the goods that it sells. The Senate amendment added a proviso to such exemption to the effect that more than 85 percent of the establishment's annual dollar volume of sales of goods or services must be made within the State in which the establishment is located. The bill as agreed to in conference (sec. 13 (a) (4)) adopts the House bill as amended by the Senate amendment with three changes. First, it is made clear that the establishment must qualify as an "exempt" retail establishment under section 13 (a) (2). Second, the reference to "services" contained in the Senate amendment is stricken and in lieu there are substituted the words "so made or processed". Third, the goods which the exempt establishment makes or processes must be made or processed at the establishment which sells the goods. An establishment will be exempt under this provision of the conference bill if it meets the following six tests:

1. Over 50 percent of its annual dollar volume of sales of goods must be made within the State in which the establishment is located.

2. Seventy-five percent of its annual dollar volume of sales of goods must not be for resale.

3. Seventy-five percent of its annual dollar volume of sales of goods must be recognized as retail sales in its industry.

4. The establishment must be recognized as a retail establishment in its industry.

5. More than 85 percent of the establishment's annual dollar volume of sales of goods which it makes or processes must be made within the State in which the establishment is located.

6. The goods which the exempt establishment makes or processes must be made or processed at the establishment which sells the goods. This test will be met despite the fact that there is a physical dividing line between the manufacturing portion of an establishment and the selling portion such as a partition, wall, etc. For example, a bakery will meet the test even though it bakes its bread and pastries in a back room and sells same in a front room of its establishment.

This exemption will apply typically to bakery establishments which bake the breads and pastries which they sell, ice plants which manufacture the ice they sell, and ice cream parlors or candy kitchens which make their own ice cream or candy.

As in the case of the exemption provided by section 13 (a) (2) the exemption here applies to any employee employed "by" rather than "in" the establishment. Consequently, the following types of employees of an establishment which meets the tests set forth above will also be exempt, even though they may do most of their work outside the establishment: bill collectors, outside repair and service men, outside salesmen, merchandise buyers, consumer survey and promotion workers and delivery men.

Fish canning.—The House bill contained a 14-workweek exemption from the overtime provisions of section 7 of the act for any industry engaged in the first processing or canning of fish in the raw or natural state. The Senate amendment had no comparable provision. The House bill continued the exemption contained in existing law with respect to fish, shellfish, etc., with the exception that the processing and canning of the products and byproducts specified in the exemption would not have applied to fish. The Senate amendment continued the exemption contained in existing law. The conference agreement (a) strikes out the 14-workweek exemption contained in the House bill, (b) continues the exemption contained in section 13 (a) (5) of the present law with the exception of canning; and (c) transfers the canning exemption from section 13 (a) of the act to section 13 (b), which has the effect of exempting the canning of any kind of fish, shellfish, or other aquatic forms of animal or vegetable life, or any byproduct thereof, from the overtime provisions of the act, but not from the minimum wage requirements. Under the conference agreement "canning" means hermetically sealing and sterilizing or pasteurizing and has reference to a process involving the performance of such operations. It also means other operations performed in connection therewith such as necessary preparatory operations performed on the products before they are placed in bottles, cans, or other containers to be hermetically sealed, as well as the actual placing of the commodities in such containers. Also included are subsequent operations such as the labeling of the cans or other containers and the placing of the sealed containers in cases or boxes whether such subsequent operations are performed as a part of an uninterrupted or interrupted process. It does not include the placing of such products or byproducts thereof in cans or other containers that are not hermetically sealed as such an operation is "processing" as distinguished from "canning" and comes within the complete exemption contained in section 13 (a).

Irrigation workers.—The House bill added a new wage-and-hour exemption as section 13 (a) (16) which applied to any employee employed in connection with the operation or maintenance of ditches, canals, reservoirs. or waterways, not owned or operated for profit, which are used exclusively for supply and storing of water for agricultural purposes. The Senate amendment provided an identical exemption as an additional clause in section 13 (a) (6) with the exception that language was added permitting the employer to operate on a share-crop basis. The conference agreement follows the Senate amendment and includes the exemption in section 13 (a) (6).

Small newspapers.—The House bill amended section 13 (a) (8) of the act relating to weekly and semiweekly newspapers by increasing the permitted circulation of an exempt newspaper from 3,000 to 5,000, by extending the exemption to dailies and by permitting the major part of the circulation to be not only within the county where printed and published, but also within counties contiguous thereto, whether or not within the same State. The exemption was renumbered section 13 (a) (9). The Senate amendment made no change in existing law. The conference agreement follows the House bill but reduces the circulation from 5,000 to 4,000 and retains the numbering of the present section 13 (a) (8).

"Area of production."—The House bill amended section 13 (a) (10) of the act by transferring the authority to define "areas of production" from the Administrator to the Secretary of Agriculture. The exemption was renumbered section 13 (a) (11). The Senate amendment made no change in existing law. The conference agreement follows the Senate amendment in this respect and leaves the present law unchanged, and retains the numbering of the present section 13 (a) (10).

Small telephone exchanges.—The House bill made no change in existing law with respect to the wage-and-hour exemption provided by section 13 (a) (11) of the act for switchboard operators employed in public telephone exchanges which have less than 500 stations, but renumbered this exemption as section 13 (a) (12). The Senate amendment increased the number of stations to not more than 750. The conference agreement adopts the Senate provision, and retains the numbering of the present section 13 (a) (11).

Taxicabs.—The House bill added a new section 13 (a) (13) to the act which provided a wage-and-hour exemption for any employee of an employer engaged in the business of operating taxicabs. The Senate amendment made no change in existing law in this respect. The conference agreement follows the House bill but renumbers the exemption as section 13 (a) (12).

Contract telegraph agencies.—The House bill added a new wage-and-hour exemption as section 13 (a) (14) of the act for any employee or proprietor in a retail or service establishment as defined in the amended section 13 (a) (2) with respect to whom the wage-and-hour provisions would not otherwise apply, who is engaged in handling telegraph messages for the public under an agency or contract arrangement with a telegraph company if the telegraph message revenue of the agency does not exceed $500 a month. The Senate amendment added substantially the same exemption as section 13 (a) (12) of the act. The conference agreement adopts the House provision but renumbers the exemption as section 13 (a) (13).

Logging and sawmilling.—The House bill added a wage-and-hour exemption as section 13 (a) (15) of the act which applied to any employee employed in planting or tending trees, cruising, surveying, or felling, timber, or in preparing, processing, transporting, or sawing logs or other forestry products in and about a sawmill if the number of employees employed by the employer in forestry or lumbering operations does not exceed 12. The Senate amendment made no change in existing law in this respect. The conference agreement adopts the House provision but excludes from the exemption sawmill and other operations in connection with processing of logs or other forestry products. The exemption covers the woods operations and extends through the preparing and transporting of logs or other forestry products to the mill, processing plant, railroad, or other transportation terminal. To be exempt, an employee must be employed by an employer who has not more than 12 employees in forestry or logging operations.

Cotton and cottonseed.—The Senate amendment added a new wage-and-hour exemption as section 13 (a) (13) of the act which applied to employees of any employer engaged in ginning, storing, or compressing of cotton or in the processing of cottonseed, with the proviso that such employees must be employed in, about, or in connection with such operations which are conducted in any county in which cotton is produced as shown in the most recent annual cotton-production report of the Bureau of the Census. The House bill contained no such provision. The conference agreement follows the House bill and makes no change in existing law in this respect.

Rural home workers.—The House bill added a new wage-and-hour exemption as section 13 (a) (17) of the act which applied to any home worker in a rural area who is not subject to any supervision or control by any person whomsoever, and who buys raw material and makes and completes any article and sells the same to any person, even though the article is made according to specifications and the requirements of a single purchaser. The Senate amendment contained no such exemption. The conference agreement follows the Senate amendment in this respect.

Home work on baseballs.—The House bill contained no specific exemption for home workers employed in sewing baseballs and softballs. The Senate amendment contained such an exemption. The conference agreement follows the House bill in this respect.

Air carriers.—The House bill eliminated the minimum-wage exemption now provided in the act for any employee of a carrier by air subject to the provisions of title II of the Railway Labor Act, but continued the maximum-hour exemption as section 13 (b) (3) of the act. The Senate amendment made no change in existing law in this respect. The conference agreement adopts the House provision.

Outside buyers of poultry and dairy products.—The House bill made no change in existing law with respect to outside buyers of poultry or dairy products. The Senate amendment added a maximum hour exemption as section 13 (f) of the act, which applied to any individual employed as an outside buyer of poultry, eggs, cream, or milk in their raw or natural state. The conference agreement follows the Senate amendment but numbers the exemption as section 13 (b) (5).

Child-labor.—Section 13 (c) of the existing law makes the child-labor provisions inapplicable with respect to employees employed in agriculture while not legally required to attend school as well as with respect to any child employed as an actor in motion pictures or theatrical productions. The House bill made no change in existing law in the provision relating to agriculture but broadened the exemption for actors by extending it to performers and by adding the words "or in radio or television productions" after the words "motion pictures or theatrical productions." The Senate amendment changed the child labor agriculture exemption by substituting for the words "while not legally required to attend school" the language "outside of school hours for the school district where such employee is living while he is so employed." The Senate amendment was identical with the House bill with respect to the child-labor exemption relating to actors and performers in motion pictures or theatrical productions, or in radio or television productions. The conference agreement adopts the Senate amendment with respect to the child labor agriculture exemption and adopts the provisions contained in both the House bill and the Senate amendment which broadens the child-labor exemption applicable to motion pictures and theatrical productions, and radio or television productions.

Newspaper carrier boys.—The House bill provided no special exemption for newsboys. The Senate amendment added an exemption as section 13 (e) of the act which provided a complete minimum-wage, maximum-hour, and child-labor exemption with respect to any employee engaged in the delivery of newspapers to the consumer. The conference agreement adopts the Senate provision but renumbers the exemption as section 13 (d).

LEARNERS, APPRENTICES, AND HANDICAPPED WORKERS

Clause (1) of section 14 of the present act permits the employment "of messengers employed exclusively in delivering letters and messages" at subminimum rates, under regulations or orders of the Administrator as prescribed in section 14. The House bill made no change in existing law. The Senate amendment substituted for the above-quoted language the words "and of minor messengers under 18 years of age employed primarily in delivering letters and messages." The conference agreement follows the House bill but adopts that provision of the Senate amendment which substituted the word "primarily" for "exclusively" in the existing provision.

PROHIBITED

Both the House bill and the Senate amendment added language to section 15 (a) (1) designed to make it lawful for a purchaser in good faith of goods produced in violation of the act to sell such goods in commerce. The conference agreement (sec. 13 (a)) inserts in section 15 (a) (1) a proviso containing the language of the Senate amendment. This provision protects an innocent purchaser from an unwitting violation and also protects him from having goods which he has purchased in good faith ordered to be withheld from shipment in commerce by a "hot goods" injunction. An affirmative duty is imposed upon him to assure himself that the goods in question were produced in compliance with the act, and he must have secured written assurance to that effect from the producer of the goods. The requirement that he must have made the purchase in good faith is comparable to similar requirements imposed on purchasers in other fields of law, and is to be subjected to the test of what a reasonable, prudent man, acting with due diligence, would have done in the circumstances.

The conference agreement also provides in section 13 (b) that regulations or orders of the Administrator under the provisions of the new section 11 (d), dealing with industrial homework, may be enforced in the same manner as the Administrator's record-keeping regulations (sec. 15 (a) (5)).

PENALTIES

Both the House bill and the Senate amendment added a new subsection (c) to section 16 authorizing the Administrator to supervise the payment of unpaid minimum wages or overtime compensation due under the act, and providing that agreement by any employee to accept such payment should, upon payment in full, constitute a waiver of his rights under section 16 (b). The Senate amendment, in addition, authorized the Administrator, at the request or with the consent of the employee, to sue for any back wages due, and provided that the Administrator might join in one cause of action the claims of any employees similarly situated who consented thereto. The Senate amendment also provided that the consent of any employee to the bringing of any such action constituted a waiver of his rights under section 16 (b), unless the action be dismissed without prejudice on motion of the Administrator. The Senate amendment also provided that nothing in the subsection should affect the equitable jurisdiction of the courts under section 17. The Senate amendment also made the Portal-to-Portal Act 2-year statute of limitations applicable to such actions brought by the Administrator. The conference agreement adopts the Senate amendment in revised form.

The conference agreement omits from section 16 (c) in the Senate amendment the provision that the Administrator may sue for wages due at the request or with the consent of the employee making the claim. In its place the conference agreement substitutes a requirement that the Administrator can sue for such unpaid minimum wages or unpaid overtime compensation only on the written request of the employee. The conference agreement adds a proviso to prevent the Administrator from using the authority granted in this section to bring test cases involving new or novel questions of law. The Administrator may use his authority under this section to bring a suit for an employee only in cases whre the law has been settled finally by the courts. The proviso is not intended, however, to preclude the Administrator from instituting suits or the court from taking jurisdiction on the basis of existing legal precedents under the Fair Labor Standards Act of 1938 as amended, except to the extent that they are changed by the amendments made by the conference agreement. While the conference agreement omits the provision that the Administrator could join in one cause of action the claims of any employees similarly situated who consented thereto, it is the intention of the conferees under the conference agreement that the Rules of Civil Procedure of the district courts of the United Stages relating to joinder of parties will apply to actions brought by the Administrator under section 16 (c) as such rules would be applicable in any other civil actions brought in the district courts of the United States. In like manner, the rules as to joinder of parties applicable to civil actions in the courts of the several States and Territories will apply to actions brought by the Administrator in the courts of such States and Territories under section 16 (c).

INJUNCTION PROCEEDINGS

The House bill adopted the language of section 17 of the act without change. The Senate amendment altered this section to include a more precise description of the United States courts having jurisdiction of actions to restrain violations. The legal effect of both versions was the same. The conference agreement adopts the Senate version with a proviso to the effect that no court shall have jurisdiction, in any action brought by the Administrator to restrain violations of section 15, to order payment to employees of unpaid minimum wages or unpaid overtime compensation or an additional equal amount as liquidated damages. This proviso has been inserted in section 17 of the act in view of the provision of the conference agreement contained in section 16 (c) of the act which authorizes the Administrator in certain cases to bring suits for damages for unpaid minimum wages and overtime compensation owing to employees at the written request of such employees. Under the conference agreement the proviso does not preclude the Administrator from joining in a single complaint causes of action arising under section 16 (c) and section 17. Not is it intended that if the Administrator brings an action under section 16 (c) he is thereby precluded from bringing an action under section 17 to restrain violations of the act. Similarly, the bringing of an injunction action under section 17 will not preclude the Administrator from also bringing in an appropriate case an action under section 16 (c) to collect unpaid minimum wages or overtime compensation owing to employees under the provisions of the law. Nor is the provision intended in any way to affect the court's authority in contempt proceedings for enforcement of injunctions issued under section 17 for violations occurring subsequent to the issuance of such injunctions. The provision, however, will have the effect of reversing such decisions as *McComb* v. *Scerbo* ((C. C. A. 2) 17 Labor Cases No. 65,297), in which the court included a restitution order in an injunction decree granted under section 17.

RELATION TO OTHER LAWS

The House bill reenacted, but did not change the provisions of section 18 of the act. The Senate amendment made no change in this section. The conference agreement also leaves unchanged the provisions of this section.

SEPARABILITY OF PROVISIONS

The House bill reenacted but did not change section 19 of the act. The Senate amendment made no change in this section. The conference agreement leaves unchanged the provisions of this section.

MISCELLANEOUS AND EFFECTIVE DATE

Effective date.—The House bill provided that the Fair Labor Standards Amendments of 1949 should take effect upon the expiration of 60 days from the date of the enactment thereof, except that the provisions of section 7, relating to overtime compensation, were to be in full force and effect from and after the date of enactment thereof. The Senate amendment provided that its amendments to the Fair Labor Standards Act should become effective upon the expiration of 120 days from the date of enactment thereof. Section 16 (a) of the conference agreement provides that except for the amendment made by section 4 of the conference agreement which is to take effect upon the date of its enactment, the Fair Labor Standards Amendments of 1949 shall become effective 90 days from the date of enactment thereof.

Portal-to-Portal Act.—The House bill (sec. 3 (d)) provided that no amendment made by the new act should be construed as amending, modifying, or repealing any provision of the Portal-to-Portal Act of 1947. The Senate amendment contained an identical provision (sec. 9 (b)) but added an exception with respect to the last sentence of section 16 (c) of the act added by the Senate amendment, dealing with the date for commencement of actions brought by the Administrator with respect to claims for unpaid minimum wages or overtime compensation owing to employees under the act. Section 16 (b) of the conference agreement adopts the Senate provision, amended to exclude the provisions of section 3 (o) of the act from the operation of this section.

Existing orders.—The House bill (sec. 3 (b)) provided that orders, regulations, and interpretations of the Administrator or the Secretary of Labor, and agreements entered into by the Administrator or the Secretary of Labor, in effect under the act on the date of enactment of the Fair Labor Standards Amendments of 1949 should remain in effect as orders, regulations, interpretations, or agreements of the Administrator or the Secretary of Agriculture, as the case might be, except to the extent that any such order, regulation, interpretation, or agreement might be inconsistent with the provisions of the amendments or might from time to time be amended, modified or rescinded by the Administrator or the Secretary of Agriculture, as the case might be, in accordance with the provisions of such amendments. The Senate amendment did not contain any provisions dealing with this matter. Section 16 (c) of the conference agreement follows the provisions of the House bill with respect to this matter, except that in accordance with the decision by the conferees to make no change with respect to administration of the act the references to the Secretary of Agriculture contained in the House bill have been changed to references to the Secretary of Labor.

Existing liabilities.—The House bill (sec. 3 (c)) provided that penalties or liabilities, with respect to any act or omission occurring prior to the effective date of the fair labor standards amendments of 1949, should not be affected by any amendment made therein, except that after 2 years from such effective date no action was to be instituted under section 16 (b) with respect to any liability accruing thereunder for any act or omission occurring prior to the effective date. The Senate Amendment contained no such provision. Section 16 (d) of the Conference agreement adopts the House provisions. This provision will save the rights of the United States in respect to criminal prosecutions and of employees under section 16 (b). Penalties and liabilities for past acts are unaffected; also, injunctions previously issued by the courts under section 17 retain their validity, except to the extent that the acts or omissions upon which the injunctions were based are no longer unlawful under or prohibited by the amendments made by the conference agreement. The 2-year limitation provision is similar to section 6 of the Portal-to-Portal Act of 1947.

Retroactive provisions.—The House bill (sec. 3 (e)) expressly gave retroactive effect to sections 7 (d) (6), 7 (d) (7), and 7 (g), by adding language identical in effect to that of section 2 of the act of July 20, 1949 (Public Law 177, 81st Cong., 1st sess.). The Senate amendment contained no such provision. The conference agreement follows the approach of the House bill in this respect.

Section 16 (e) of the conference agreement provides that no employer shall be subject to any liability or punishment under the Fair Labor Standards Act of 1938, as amended, in any action or proceeding commenced prior to or on or after the effective date of the conference agreement on account of the failure of said employer to pay an employee compensation for any period of overtime work performed prior to July 20, 1949 (the effective date of Public Law 177, 81st Cong., 1st sess.), if the compensation paid prior to that date for such work was at least equal to the compensation which would have been payable therefor had sections 7 (d) (6), 7 (d) (7), and 7 (g) of the Fair Labor Standards Act of 1938, as amended by the conference agreement, been in effect at the time of such payment.

Repeal of Public Law 177, Eighty-first Congress.—Section 16 (f) of the conference agreement contains a new provision repealing the act of July 20, 1949 (Public Law 177, 81st Cong., 1st sess.). The substance of section 1 of said act has been incorporated in section 7 (d) (6) 7 (d) (7), and 7 (g) of the Fair Labor Standards Act of 1938, as amended by the conference agreement. Section 2 of said act is likewise no longer necessary in view of the language contained in section 16 (e) of the conference agreement.

THE DECISION

United States v. Darby
312 U.S. 100 (1941)

MR. JUSTICE STONE delivered the opinion of the Court.

The two principal questions raised by the record in this case are, *first,* whether Congress has constitutional power to prohibit the shipment in interstate commerce of lumber manufacturer by employees whose wages are less than a prescribed minimum or whose weekly hours of labor at that wage are greater than a prescribed maximum, and, *second,* whether it has power to prohibit the employment of workmen in the production of goods "for interstate commerce" at other than prescribed wages and hours. A subsidiary question is whether in connection with such prohibitions Congress can require the employer subject to them to keep records showing the hours worked each day and week by each of his employees including those engaged "in the production and manufacture of goods to-wit, lumber, for 'interstate commerce.' " . . .

The Fair Labor Standards Act set up a comprehensive legislative scheme for preventing the shipment in interstate commerce of certain products and commodities produced in the United States under labor conditions as respects wages and hours which fail to conform to standards set up by the Act. Its purpose, as we judicially know from the declaration of policy in § 2 (a) of the Act, and the reports of Congressional committees proposing the legislation, S. Rept. No. 884, 75th Cong. 1st Sess.; H. Rept. No. 1452, 75th Cong. 1st Sess.; H. Rept. No. 2182, 75th Cong. 3d Sess., Conference Report, H. Rept. No. 2738, 75th Cong. 3d Sess., is to exclude from interstate commerce goods produced for the commerce and to prevent their production for interstate commerce, under conditions detrimental to the maintenance of the minimum standards of living necessary for health and general well-being; and to prevent the use of interstate commerce as the means of competition in the distribution of goods so produced, and as the means of spreading and perpetuating such substandard labor conditions among the workers of the several states. The Act also sets up an administrative procedure whereby those standards may from time to time be modified generally as to industries subject to the Act or within an industry in accordance with specified standards, by an administrator acting in collaboration with "Industry Committees" appointed by him.

Section 15 of the statute prohibits certain specified acts and § 16 (a) punishes willful violation of it by a fine of not more than $10,000 and punishes each conviction after the first by imprisonment of not more than six months or by the specified fine or both. Section 15 (1) makes unlawful the shipment in interstate commerce of any goods "in the production of which any employee was employed in violation of section 6 or section 7." which provide, among other things, that during the first year of operation of the Act a minimum wage of 25 cents per hour shall be paid to employees "engaged in [interstate] commerce or the production of goods for [interstate] commerce," § 6, and that the maximum hours of employment for employees "engaged in commerce or the production of goods for commerce" without increased compensation for overtime, shall be forty-four hours a week. § 7.

Section 15 (a) (2) makes it unlawful to violate the provisions of §§ 6 and 7 including the minimum wage and maximum hour requirements just mentioned for employees engaged in production of goods for commerce. Section 15 (a) (5) makes it unlawful for an employer subject to the Act to violate § 11 (c) which requires him to keep such records of the persons employed by him and of their wages and hours of employment as the administrator shall prescribe by regulation or order.

The indictment charges that appellee is engaged, in the State of Georgia, in the business of acquiring raw materials, which he manufactures into finished lumber with the intent, when manufactured, to ship it in interstate commerce to customers outside the state, and that he does in fact so ship a large part of the lumber so produced. There are numerous counts charging appellee with the shipment in interstate commerce from Georgia to points outside the state of lumber in the production of which, for interstate commerce, appellee has employed workmen at less than the prescribed minimum wage or more than the prescribed maximum hours without payment to them of any wage for overtime. Other counts charge the employment by appellee of workmen in the production of lumber for interstate commerce at wages at less than 25 cents an hour or for more than the maximum hours per week without payment to them of the prescribed overtime wage. Still another count charges appellee with failure to keep records showing the hours worked each day a week by each of his employees as required by § 11 (c) and the regulation of the administrator, Title 29, Ch. 5, Code of Federal Regulations, Part 516, and also that appellee unlawfully failed to keep such records of employees engaged "in the production and manufacture of goods, to-wit lumber, for interstate commerce."

The demurrer, so far as now relevant to the appeal, challenged the validity of the Fair Labor Standards Act under the Commerce Clause and the Fifth and Tenth Amendments. The district court quashed the indictment in its entirety upon the broad grounds that the Act, which it interpreted as a regulation of manufacture within the states, is unconstitutional. It declared that manufacture is not interstate commerce and that the regulation by the Fair Labor Standards Act of wages and hours of employment of those engaged in the manufacture of goods which it is intended at the time of production "may or will be" after production "sold in interstate commerce in part or in whole" is not within the congressional power to regulate interstate commerce.

The effect of the court's decision and judgment is thus to deny the power of Congress to prohibit shipment in interstate commerce of lumber produced for interstate commerce under the proscribed substandard labor conditions of wages and hours. its power to penalize the employer for his failure to conform to the wage and hour provisions in the case of employees engaged in the production of lumber which he intends thereafter to ship in interstate commerce in part or in whole according to the normal course of his business and its power to compel him to keep records of hours of employment as required by the statute and the regulations of the administrator.

The case comes here on assignments by the Government that the district court erred insofar as it held that Congress was without constitutional power to penalize the acts set forth in the indictment, and appellee seeks to sustain the decision below on the grounds that the prohibition by Congress of those Acts is unauthorized by the Commerce Clause and is prohibited by the Fifth Amendment. The appeal statute limits our jurisdiction on this appeal to a review of the determination of the district court so far only as it is based on the validity or construction of the statute. *United States* v. *Borden Co.,* 308 U. S. 188, 193–195, and cases cited. Hence we accept the district court's interpretation of the indictment and confine our decision to the validity and construction of the statute.

The prohibition of shipment of the proscribed goods in interstate commerce. Section 15 (a) (1) prohibits, and the indictment charges, the shipment in interstate commerce, of goods produced for interstate commerce by employees whose wages and hours of employment do not conform to the requirements of the Act. Since this section is not violated unless the commodity shipped has been produced under labor conditions prohibited by § 6 and §7, the only question arising under the commerce clause with respect to such shipments is whether Congress has the constitutional power to prohibit them.

While manufacture is not of itself interstate commerce, the shipment of manufactured goods interstate is such commerce and the prohibition of such shipment by Congress is indubitably a regulation of the commerce. The power to regulate commerce is the power "to prescribe the rule by which commerce is governed." *Gibbons* v. *Ogden,* 9 Wheat. 1, 196. It extends not only to those regulations which aid, foster and protect the commerce, but embraces those which prohibit it. *Reid* v. *Colorado,* 187 U. S. 137; *Lottery Case,* 188 U. S. 321; *United States* v. *Delaware & Hudson Co.,* 213 U. S. 366; *Hoke* v. *United States,* 227 U. S. 308; *Clark Distilling Co.* v. *Western Maryland Ry. Co.,* 242 U. S. 311; *United States* v. *Hill,* 248 U. S. 420;

McCormick & Co. v. *Brown,* 286 U. S. 131. It is conceded that the power of Congress to prohibit transportation in interstate commerce includes noxious articles. *Lottery Case, supra; Hipolite Egg Co.* v. *United States,* 220 U. S. 45; cf. *Hoke* v. *United States, supra;* stolen articles, *Brooks* v. *United States.* 267 U. S. 432; kidnapped persons, *Gooch* v. *United States,* 297 U. S. 124, and articles such as intoxicating liquor or convict made goods, traffic in which is forbidden or restricted by the laws of the state of destination. *Kentucky Whip & Collar Co.* v. *Illinois Central R. Co.,* 299 U. S. 334.

But it is said that the present prohibition falls within the scope of none of these categories; that while the prohibition is nominally a regulation of the commerce its motive or purpose is regulation of wages and hours of persons engaged in manufacture, the control of which has been reserved to the states and upon which Georgia and some of the states of destination have placed no restriction; that the effect of the present statute is not to exclude the proscribed articles from interstate commerce in aid of state regulation as in *Kentucky Whip & Collar Co.* v. *Illinois Central R. Co., supra,* but instead, under the guise of a regulation of interstate commerce, it undertakes to regulate wages and hours within the state contrary to the policy of the state which has elected to leave them unregulated.

The power of Congress over interstate commerce "is complete in itself, may be exercised to its utmost extent, and acknowledges no limitations other than are prescribed in the Constitution." *Gibbons* v. *Ogden, supra,* 196. That power can neither be enlarged nor diminished by the exercise or non-exercise of state power. *Kentucky Whip & Collar Co.* v. *Illinois Central R. Co., supra.* Congress, following its own conception of public policy concerning the restrictions which may appropriately be imposed on interstate commerce, is free to exclude from the commerce articles whose use in the states for which they are destined it may conceive to be injurious to the public health, morals or welfare, even though the state has not sought to regulate their use. *Reid* v. *Colorado, supra; Lottery Case, supra; Hipolite Egg Co.* v. *United States, supra; Hoke* v. *United States, supra.*

Such regulation is not a forbidden invasion of state power merely because either its motive or its consequence is to restrict the use of articles of commerce within the states of destination; and is not prohibited unless by other Constitutional provisions. It is no objection to the assertion of the power to regulate interstate commerce that its exercise is attended by the same incidents which attend the exercise of the police power of the states. *Seven Cases* v. *United States,* 239 U. S. 510, 514; *Hamilton* v. *Kentucky Distilleries & Warehouse Co.,* 251 U. S. 146, 156; *United States* v. *Carolene Products Co.,* 304 U. S. 144, 147; *United States* v. *Appalachian Electric Power Co.,* 311 U. S. 377.

The motive and purpose of the present regulation are plainly to make effective the Congressional conception of public policy that interstate commerce should not be made the instrument of competition in the distribution of goods produced under substandard labor conditions, which competition is injurious to the commerce and to the states from and to which the commerce flows. The motive and purpose of a regulation of interstate commerce are matters for the legislative judgment upon the exercise of which the Constitution places no restriction and over which the courts are given no control. *McCray* v. *United States,* 195 U. S. 27; *Sonzinsky* v. *United States,* 300 U. S. 506, 513 and cases cited. "The judicial cannot prescribe to the legislative department of the government limitations upon the exercise of its acknowledged power." *Veazie Bank* v. *Fenno,* 8 Wall. 533. Whatever their motive and purpose, regulations of commerce which do not infringe some constitutional prohition are within the plenary power conferred on Congress by the Commerce Clause. Subject only to that limitation, presently to be considered, we conclude that the prohibition of the shipment interstate of goods produced under the forbidden substandard labor conditions is within the constitutional authority of Congress.

In the more than a century which has elapsed since the decision of *Gibbons* v. *Ogden,* these principles of constitutional interpretation have been so long and repeatedly recognized by this Court as applicable to the Commerce Clause, that there would be little occasion for repeating them now were it not for the decision of this Court twenty-two years ago in *Hammer* v. *Dagenhart,* 247 U. S. 251. In that case it was held by a bare majority of the Court over the powerful and now classic dissent of Mr. Justice Holmes setting forth the fundamental issues involved, that Congress was without power to exclude the products of child labor from interstate commerce. The reasoning and conclusion of the Court's opinion there cannot be reconciled with the conclusion which we have reached, that the power of Congress under the Commerce Clause is plenary to exclude any article from interstate commerce subject only to the specific prohibitions of the Constitution.

Hammer v. *Dagenhart* has not been followed. The distinction on which the decision was rested that Congressional power to prohibit interstate commerce is limited to articles which in themselves have some harmful or deleterious property—a distinction which was novel when made and unsupported by any provision of the Constitution—has long since been abandoned. *Brooks* v. *United States, supra; Kentucky Whip & Collar Co.* v. *Illinois Central R. Co., supra; Electric Bond & Share Co.* v. *Securities & Exchange Comm'n,* 303 U. S. 419; *Mulford* v. *Smith,* 307 U. S. 38. The thesis of the opinion that the motive of the prohibition or its effect to control in some measure the use or production within the states of the article thus excluded from the commerce can operate to deprive the regulation of its constitutional authority has long since ceased to have force. *Reid* v. *Colorado, supra; Lottery Case, supra; Hipolite Egg Co.* v. *United States, supra; Seven Cases* v. *United States, supra,* 514; *Hamilton* v. *Kentucky Distilleries & Warehouse Co., supra,* 156; *United States* v. *Carolene Products Co., supra,* 147. And finally we have declared "The authority of the federal government over interstate commerce does not differ in extent or character from that retained by the states over intrastate commerce." *United States* v. *Rock Royal Co-operative,* 307 U. S. 533, 569.

The conclusion is inescapable that *Hammer* v. *Dagenhart,* was a departure from the principles which have prevailed in the interpretation of the Commerce Clause both before and since the decision and that such vitality, as a precedent, as it then had has long since been exhausted. It should be and now is overruled.

Validity of the wage and hour requirements. Section 15 (a) (2) and §§ 6 and 7 require employers to conform to the wage and hour provisions with respect to all employees engaged in the production of goods for interstate commerce. As appellee's employees are not alleged to be "engaged in interstate commerce" the validity of the prohibition turns on the question whether the employment, under other than the prescribed labor standards, of employees engaged in the production of goods for interstate commerce is so related to the commerce and so affects it as to be within the reach of the power of Congress to regulate it.

To answer this question we must at the outset determine whether the particular acts charged in the counts which are laid under § 15 (a) (2) as they were construed below, constitute "production for commerce" within the meaning of the statute. As the Government seeks to apply the statute in the indictment, and as the court below construed the phrase "produced for interstate commerce," it embraces at least the case where an employer engaged, as is appellee, in the manufacture and shipment of goods in filling orders of extrastate customers, manufactures his product with the intent or expectation that according to the normal course of his business all or some part of it will be selected for shipment to those customers.

Without attempting to define the precise limits of the phrase, we think the acts alleged in the indictment are within the sweep of the statute. The obvious purpose of the Act was not only to prevent the interstate transportation of the proscribed product, but to stop the initial step toward transportation, production with the purpose of so transporting it. Congress was not unaware that most manufacturing businesses shipping their product in interstate commerce make it in their shops without reference to its ultimate destination and then after manufacture select some of it for shipment interstate and some intrastate according to the daily demands of their business, and that it would be practically impossible, without disrupting manufacturing businesses, to restrict the prohibited kind of production to the particular pieces of lumber, cloth, furniture or the like which later move in interstate rather than intrastate commerce. Cf. *United States* v. *New York Central R. Co.,* 272 U. S. 457, 464.

The recognized need of drafting a workable statute and the well known circumstances in which it was to be applied are persuasive of the conclusion, which the legislative history supports, S. Rept. No. 884, 75th Cong. 1st Sess., pp. 7 and 8; H. Rept. No. 2738, 75th Cong. 3d Sess., p. 17, that the "production for commerce" intended includes at least production of goods, which, at the time of production, the employer, according to the normal course of his business, intends or expects to move in interstate commerce although, through the exigencies of the business, all of the goods may not thereafter actually enter interstate commerce.

There remains the question whether such restriction on the production of goods for commerce is a permissible exercise of the commerce power. The power of Congress over interstate commerce is not confined to the regulation of commerce among the states. It extends to those activities intrastate which so affect interstate commerce or the exercise of the power of Congress over it as to make regulation of them appropriate means to the attainment of a legitimate end, the exercise of the granted power of Congress to regulate interstate commerce. See *McCulloch* v. *Maryland,* 4 Wheat. 316, 421. Cf. *United States* v. *Ferger,* 250 U. S. 199.

While this Court has many times found state regulation of interstate commerce, when uniformity of its regulation is of national concern, to be incompatible with the Commerce Clause even though Congress has not legislated on the subject, the Court has never implied such restraint on state control over matters intrastate not deemed to be regulations of interstate commerce or its instrumentalities even though they affect the commerce. *Minnesota Rate Cases,* 230 U. S. 352, 398 *et seq.,* and case cited; 410 *et seq.,* and cases cited. In the absence of Congressional legislation on the subject state laws which are not regulations of the commerce itself or its instrumentalities are not forbidden even though they affect interstate commerce. *Kidd* v. *Pearson,* 128 U. S. 1; *Bacon* v. *Illinois,* 227 U. S. 504; *Heisler* v. *Thomas Colliery Co.,* 260 U. S. 245; *Oliver Iron Co.* v. *Lord,* 262 U. S. 172.

But it does not follow that Congress may not by appropriate legislation regulate intrastate activities where they have a substantial effect on interstate commerce. See *Santa Cruz Fruit Packing Co.* v. *National Labor Relations Board,* 303 U. S. 453, 466. A recent example is the National Labor Relations Act for the regulation of employer and employee relations in industries in which strikes, induced by unfair labor practices named in the Act, tend to disturb or obstruct interstate commerce. See *National Labor Relations Board* v. *Jones & Laughlin Steel Corp.,* 301 U. S. 1, 38, 40; *National Labor Relations Board* v. *Fainblatt,* 306 U. S. 601, 604, and cases cited. But long before the adoption of the National Labor Relations Act this Court had many times held that the power of Congress to regulate interstate commerce extends to the regulation through legislative action activities intrastate which have a substantial effect on the commerce or the exercise of the Congressional power over it.

In such legislation Congress has sometimes left it to the courts to determine whether the intrastate activities have the prohibited effect on the commerce, as in the Sherman Act. It has sometimes left it to an administrative board or agency to determine whether the activities sought to be regulated or prohibited have such effect, as in the case of the Interstate Commerce Act, and the National Labor Relations Act, or whether they come within the statutory definition of the prohibited Act, as in the Federal Trade Commission Act. And sometimes Congress itself has said that a particular activity affects the commerce, as it did in the present Act, the Safety Appliance Act and the Railway Labor Act. In passing on the validity of legislation of the class last mentioned the only function of courts is to determine whether the particular activity regulated or prohibited is within the reach of the federal power. See *United States* v. *Ferger, supra; Virginian Ry. Co.* v. *Federation,* 300 U. S. 515, 553.

Congress, having by the present Act adopted the policy of excluding from interstate commerce all goods produced for the commerce which do not conform to the specified labor standards, it may choose the means reasonably adapted to the attainment of the permitted end, even though they involve control of intrastate activities. Such legislation has often been sustained with respect to powers, other than the commerce power granted to the national government, when the means chosen, although not themselves within the granted power, were nevertheless deemed appropriate aids to the accomplishment of some purpose within an admitted power of the national government. See *Jacob Ruppert, Inc.* v. *Caffey,* 251 U. S. 264; *Everard's Breweries* v. *Day,* 265 U. S. 545, 560; *Westfall* v. *United States,* 274 U. S. 256, 259. As to state power under the Fourteenth Amendment, compare *Otis* v. *Parker,* 187 U. S. 606, 609; *St. John* v. *New York,* 201 U. S. 633; *Purity Extract & Tonic Co.* v. *Lynch,* 226 U. S. 192, 201–202. A familiar like exercise of power is the regulation of intrastate transactions which are so commingled with or related to interstate commerce that all must be regulated if the interstate commerce is to be effectively controlled. *Shreveport Case,* 234 U. S. 342; *Railroad Commission of Wisconsin* v. *Chicago, B. & Q. R. Co.,* 257 U. S. 563; *United States* v. *New York Central R. Co., supra,* 464; *Currin* v. *Wallace,* 306 U. S. 1; *Mulford* v. *Smith, supra.* Similarly Congress may require inspection and preventive treatment of all cattle in a disease infected area in order to prevent shipment in interstate commerce of some of the cattle without the treatment. *Thornton* v. *United States,* 271 U. S. 414. It may prohibit the removal, at destination, of labels required by the Pure Food & Drugs Act to be affixed to articles transported in interstate commerce. *McDermott* v. *Wisconsin,* 228 U. S. 115. And we have recently held that Congress in the exercise of its power to require inspection and grading of tobacco shipped in interstate commerce may compel such inspection and grading of all tobacco sold at local auction rooms from which a substantial part but not all of the tobacco sold is shipped in interstate commerce. *Currin* v. *Wallace, supra,* 11, and see to the like effect *United States* v. *Rock Royal Co-op., supra,* 68, note 37.

We think also that § 15 (a) (2), now under consideration, is sustainable independently of § 15 (a) (1), which prohibits shipment or transportation of the proscribed goods. As we have said the evils aimed at by the Act are the spread of substandard labor conditions through the use of the facilities of interstate commerce for competition by the goods so produced with those produced under the prescribed or better labor conditions; and the consequent dislocation of the commerce itself caused by the impairment or destruction of local businesses by competition made effective through interstate commerce. The Act is thus directed at the suppression of a method or kind of competition in interstate commerce which it has in effect condemned as "unfair," as the Clayton Act has condemned other "unfair methods of competition" made effective through interstate commerce. See *Van Camp & Sons Co.* v. *American Can Co.,* 278 U. S. 245; *Federal Trade Comm'n* v. *Keppel & Bro.,* 291 U. S. 304.

The Sherman Act and the National Labor Relations Act are familiar examples of the exertion of the commerce power to prohibit or control activities wholly intrastate because of their effect on interstate commerce. See as to the Sherman Act, *Northern Securities Co.* v. *United States,* 193 U. S. 197; *Swift & Co.* v. *United States,* 196 U. S. 375; *United States* v. *Patten,* 226 U. S. 525; *United Mine Workers* v. *Coronado Coal Co.,* 259 U. S. 344; *Local No. 167* v. *United States,* 291 U. S. 293; *Stevens Co.* v. *Foster & Kleiser Co.,* 311 U. S. 255. As to the National Labor Relations Act, see *National Labor Relations Board* v. *Fainblatt, supra,* and cases cited.

The means adopted by § 15 (a) (2) for the protection of interstate commerce by the suppression of the production of the condemned goods for interstate commerce is so related to the commerce and so affects it as to be within the reach of the commerce power. See *Currin* v. *Wallace, supra,* 11. Congress, to attain its objective in the suppression of nationwide competition in interstate commerce by goods produced under substandard labor conditions, has made no distinction as to the volume or amount of shipments in the commerce or of production for commerce by any particular shipper or producer. It recognized that in present day industry, competition by a small part may affect the whole and that the total effect of the competition of many small producers may be great. See H. Rept. No. 2182, 75th Cong. 1st Sess., p. 7. The legislation aimed at a whole embraces all its parts. Cf. *National Labor Relations Board* v. *Fainblatt, supra,* 606.

So far as *Carter* v. *Carter Coal Co.,* 298 U. S. 238, is inconsistent with this conclusion, its doctrine is limited in principle by the decisions under the Sherman Act and the National Labor Relations Act, which we have cited and which we follow. See also *Sunshine Anthracite Coal Co.* v. *Adkins,* 310 U. S. 381; *Currin* v. *Wallace, supra; Mulford* v. *Smith, supra; United States* v. *Rock Royal Co-op., supra; Clover Fork Coal Co.* v. *National Labor Relations Board,* 97 F. 2d 331; *National Labor Relations Board* v. *Crowe Coal Co.,* 104 F. 2d 633; *National Labor Relations Board* v. *Good Coal Co.,* 110 F. 2d 501.

Our conclusion is unaffected by the Tenth Amendment which provides: 'The powers not delegated to the United States by the Constitution, nor prohibited by it to the States, are reserved to the States respectively, or to the people." The amendment states but a truism that all is retained which has not been surrendered. There is nothing in the history of its adoption to suggest that it was more than declaratory of the relationship between the national and state governments as it had been established by the Constitution before the amendment or that its purpose was other than to allay fears that the new national government might seek to exercise powers not granted, and that the states might not be able to exercise fully their reserved powers. See e. g., II Elliot's Debates, 123, 131; III *id.* 450, 464, 600; IV *id.* 140, 149; I Annals of Congress, 432, 761, 767–768; Story, Commentaries on the Constitution, § 1907–1908.

From the beginning and for many years the amendment has been construed as not depriving the national government of authority to resort to all means for the exercise of a granted power which are appropriate and plainly adapted to the permitted end. *Martin* v. *Hunter's Lessee,* 1 Wheat. 304, 324, 325; *McCulloch* v. *Maryland, supra,* 405, 406; *Gordon* v. *United States,* 117 U. S. 697, 705; *Lottery Case, supra; Northern Securities Co.* v. *United States, supra,* 344–345; *Everard's Breweries* v. *Day, supra,* 558; *United States* v. *Sprague,* 282 U. S. 716, 733; see *United States* v. *The Brigantine William,* 28 Fed. Cas. No. 16,700, p. 622. Whatever doubts may have arisen of the soundness of that conclusion, they have been put at rest by the decisions under the Sherman Act and the National Labor Relations Act which we have cited. See also, *Ashwander* v. *Tennessee Valley Authority,* 297 U. S. 288, 330–331; *Wright* v. *Union Central Ins. Co.,* 304 U. S. 502, 516.

Validity of the requirement of records of wages and hours. § 15 (a) (5) and § 11 (c). These requirements are incidental to those for the prescribed wages and hours, and hence validity of the former turns on validity of the latter. Since, as we have held, Congress may require production for interstate commerce to conform to those conditions, it may require the employer, as a means of enforcing the valid law, to keep a record showing whether he has in fact complied with it. The requirement for records even of the intrastate transaction is an appropriate means to the legitimate end. See *Baltimore & Ohio R. Co.* v. *Interstate Commerce Comm'n,* 221 U. S. 612; *Interstate Commerce Comm'n* v. *Goodrich Transit Co.,* 224 U. S. 194; *Chicago Board of Trade* v. *Olsen,* 262 U. S. 1, 42.

Validity of the wage and hour provisions under the Fifth Amendment. Both provisions are minimum wage requirements compelling the payment of a minimum standard wage with a prescribed increased wage for overtime of "not less than one and one-half times the regular rate" at which the worker is employed. Since our decision in *West Coast Hotel Co.* v. *Parrish,* 300 U. S. 379, it is no longer open to question that the fixing of a minimum wage is within the legislative power and that the bare fact of its exercise is not a denial of due process under the Fifth more than under the Fourteenth Amendment. Not is it any longer open to question that it is within the legislative power to fix maximum hours. *Holden* v. *Hardy,* 169 U. S. 366; *Muller* v. *Oregon,* 208 U. S. 412; *Bunting* v. *Oregon,* 243 U. S. 426; *Baltimore & Ohio R. Co.* v. *Interstate Commerce Comm'n, supra.* Similarly the statute is not objectionable because applied alike to both men and women. Cf. *Bunting* v. *Oregon,* 243 U. S. 426.

The Act is sufficiently definite to meet constitutional demands. One who employs persons, without conforming to the prescribed wage and hour conditions, to work on goods which he ships or expects to ship across state lines, is warned that he may be subject to the criminal penalties of the Act. No more is required. *Nash* v. *United States,* 229 U. S. 373, 377.

We have considered, but find it unnecessary to discuss other contentions.

Reversed.

THE TAFT - HARTLEY ACT

(Labor–Management Relations Act)

Paradoxically, organized labor's political and economic successes led to the passage of the Taft-Hartley Act, which most unions castigated as a "slave-labor law." Congress for Industrial Organization President Philip Murray charged that the 1947 bill "was conceived in sin." President Harry S. Truman, in his veto message, argued that the bill would "reverse the basic direction of our national labor policy." Even Senator Robert A. Taft (R., Ohio), sponsor of the bill, became the willing backer of modifying amendments, never adopted, designed to ease the law's impact on unionization.

The unions had grown tremendously during World War II—from a 5 million membership in 1940 to roughly 15 million in 1945. In the early 1930's the ratio of union members at work in nonagricultural establishments was about 1 to 8; by 1945 it was roughly 1 to 3. Membership growth meant increased power both in industry and in politics. When the great strike wave rolled across the country in 1946, involving more than 4.5 million workers in nearly every major industry, many people felt resentful. Wartime strikes such as the one that hit the coal industry were recalled as arrogant demonstrations of power rather than as desperate demonstrations of legitimate grievances. The public responded favorably to press demands for reform of the Wagner Act. Visions of violence danced on editorial pages, even though the 1946 strikes were among the most peaceful in our history. Workers were more likely to be found fishing than milling angrily by the thousands near plant gates as had been characteristic of strikes during the 1930's. Feelings against the unions, however, ran so high that during the national rail strike of 1946 President Truman secured the passage of a House bill empowering him to draft defiant strikers. After the strike emergency passed, the bill died a little noticed death. Still, there was a distinct feeling that something was not quite right with our national labor policy.

Some felt that the courts were too lenient with labor, not to speak of the applications of the Sherman and Clayton Acts to union activities. For example, in *Apex Hosiery Company* v. *Leader,* 310 U.S. 469 (1940), the Supreme Court held that in determining whether union activity violated the Sherman Act, a showing of "restraint on competition or in the course of trade in the merchandising of articles moving in interstate commerce is not enough, unless the restraint is shown to have or is intended to have an effect upon prices in the market or otherwise to deprive purchasers or consumers of the advantages which they derive from free competition." In *United States* v. *Hutcheson,* 312 U.S. 219 (1941), the Court held that Congress, by passing the Norris-LaGuardia Act, in effect, had overruled the construction previously placed on Section 20 of the Clayton Act in the *Duplex* case. Accordingly, the Court held that all union self-help conduct specified in Section 20, occurring in the course of a labor dispute as defined in the Norris-LaGuardia Act, was immune from the Sherman Act prohibitions. However, in *Allen-Bradley Company* v. *Local No. 3,* 325 U.S. 797 (1945), the Court, while adhering to the foregoing principles, held that a union lost its immunity when it combined with non-labor groups to effect some direct commercial restraint.

If the Court's decisions reflected some uncertainty about labor's role in society, large sections of the public and Congress had no doubts at all about the need for a change. As Professor Archibald Cox noted, there were "careful observers sympathetic to organized labor who perceived the need for procedures halting the abuse of power." He summarizes "their bill of particulars" in six specifications:

1. Too many strikes were called under circumstances threatening serious injury to public health or safety—strikes in the coal mines and in public utilities, for example.

2. It was plain that some so-called "labor unions" were little more than rackets.

3. Strikes and picketing were too often marked by violence organized and promoted by union leaders when peaceful measures failed to achieve their objective.

4. During the war many building trades unions refused to admit new members and charged exorbitant fees for issuing working permits to the employees attracted to the industry by defense construction. Later, large projects were tied up for days while labor unions disputed each other's right to job assignments.

5. The secondary boycott had become an exceedingly powerful weapon. The International Brotherhood of Teamsters could tie up any business dependent upon trucking for supplies and outgoing shipments. The United Brotherhood of Carpenters, through its control of construction projects, could force a boycott of materials produced by any firm on which it desired to impose economic pressure. Secondary boycotts were also used as a method of controlling competition among employers in the product markets.

6. Abuses of power under closed- or union-shop contracts, although exceptional, gave force to the attack upon all union security agreements. A good many observers who saw merit in closed- and union-shop agreements felt the need for additional safeguards.

Many people simply felt that the Wagner Act, passed a decade before, was just not suited to the postwar era. Undemocratic union procedures, racketeering, denial of equal rights to Negroes, and other abuses of union power seemed to cry out for legislative relief. In 1946, a Republican resurgence pushed the Eightieth Congress to the right. The union opposed any reform as pure and simple antiunionism. Understandably, the legislative history of the Taft-Hartley Act was a stormy one.

President Truman, in his State of the Union Message to Congress on January 6, 1947, recognized the sentiment for reform and recommended a four-point program to reduce industrial strife. Included were recommendations for legislation to prevent "jurisdictional strikes" and certain types of secondary boycotts. The program also suggested procedures for resolving disputes over the interpretation of both existing agreements and new terms, and recommended that a temporary joint commission be set up to inquire into the entire field of labor-management relations. Throughout the first several months of 1947 extensive hearings were held before the Senate Committee on Labor and Public Welfare and the House Committee on Education and Labor. More than two hundred bills dealing with labor relations were presented to Congress. One of them, introduced by Representative Fred Hartley, (R., N. J.) was passed by the House of Representatives on April 17 and sent to the Senate. On the same day, Senator Robert Taft (R., Ohio) introduced a bill which, after extensive debate, was passed on May 13. A joint conference was appointed, and its report was agreed to by the House on June 4 and by the Senate on June 6. On June 20 the bill was vetoed by President Truman, but by June 23 both houses of Congress had voted to override the veto, and the Taft-Hartley Act became law.

Gerald D. Reilly, former solicitor of the Department of Labor, member of the National Labor Relations Board, and counsel to the Senate Labor Committee during the hearings on Taft-Hartley, illuminates the policy-making process for us:

There remained the complicated task of reconciling in conference the wide differences between S. 1126 and the Hartley bill. The Senate conferees were Taft, Ball, Ives, Murray and Ellender. Ives was included despite his lack of seniority because it was felt that his views would carry weight with the newly elected Republican Senators. The Speaker appointed Hartley, Landis of Indiana, Hoffman of Michigan, Lesinski of Michigan, and Barden of North Carolina as conferees on the part of the House.

Two more weeks of protracted daily meetings were necessary to work out a conference agreement. Contrary to reports circulated in labor circles no persons other than the conference managers themselves, counsel for the respective committees, and Dwyer Sughrue, Ives' administrative assistant, attended. The work of the technicians, because the structure of the two bills was so different, was facilitated by an understanding between the chairmen that amendments would be made within the framework of the Senate bill. Hartley recognized that because of the close votes in the Senate on some of the controversial provisions, much of the House bill would probably have to be discarded. Nevertheless, certain of his colleagues, particularly Barden who was much in favor of a judicial rather than an administrative approach, pressed skillfully for key House positions.

For several days the conferees were deadlocked, except on peripheral matters and perfecting language to carry out objectives common to both bills. It was at this stage of the conference that the anti-Communist policy of the McClellan amendment was made administratively workable by adding to the filing requirements the signing of Communist disclaimers by union officers.

Similarly on the issue of political activity by unions, Ellender persuaded the conferees to agree to an amendment to the Corrupt Practices Act recommended by his Committee on Elections in the preceding Congress. This section made it illegal for labor organizations as well as corporations to make any expenditures or contributions to candidates for federal office in primaries or general elections.

Toward the end of the conference the House managers receded from their insistence on the MacKinnon bill of rights, the ban on industrywide bargaining, the abolition of the existing Board, and the provisions for direct injunctive relief against unions. The House proposal on featherbedding was discarded, but the Senate agreed to accept, in a new unfair labor practice subsection, a provision making it illegal for unions to exact money for services not performed.

The House conferees, being very much opposed to arbitration, eliminated from Title II any language encouraging this practice. This also meant deleting from the Senate bill a provision of the original Morse bill that gave the Board authority to arbitrate contract disputes. Unfortunately, the conferees overlooked the fact that this made section 10(k) superfluous, a drafting oversight which in later years led to controversies over the intent of section 8(b)(4)(D). Finally, the Senate agreed to recognize in principle the House provision which placed the prosecuting and investigating functions of the Board in a separate agency by adopting an amendment making the office of the general counsel a statutory one and giving it some independent power.

On the House floor the conference report was overwhelmingly adopted by a vote of 320 to 79—a larger margin than had passed the Hartley bill. In the Senate, despite the fact they had made very few major concessions, the conferees were attacked by Morse and other opponents of any legislation for surrendering to the House. Pepper engaged Taft in a sharp debate on the asserted ambiguity of the political contributions section and O'Mahoney of Wyoming assailed the powers given to the general counsel as creating a "labor czar." None of these arguments changed any votes, however, and the Senate sent on the conference report to the White House by a vote of 54 to 17.

Up until this time the position of the White House on this extended battle in Congress had been ambiguous, the Labor Board staff being the only executive agency that had injected itself either publicly or behind the scenes. James J. Reynolds, one of the three members of the Board, was known to be sympathetic with the legislation and he, with Secretary of Commerce Harriman and Secretary of Defense Forrestal, favored approval. But President Truman vetoed the measure and in looking for material to use in his veto message, relied upon a staff memorandum of the NLRB attacking the conference bill in the same extreme and irrational terms that characterized the CIO literature on the subject. The result was that the veto message was so partisan and inaccurate that Senator Taft going on the networks that same evening was able to make an effective rebuttal.

The veto was promptly overridden in the House. This meant that the Senate was the last hurdle. A small group of Senators, Pepper, Morse, Murray, Kilgore of West Virginia, and Taylor of Idaho, then started a filibuster. It was generally known that Lucas of Illinois and Sparkman of Alabama, two Democrats who had voted for the conference report, would shift out of loyalty to the Administration. The filibusters hoped that by keeping the issue open over the weekend, sufficient public clamor would be created to gain three more votes. The filibuster began on June 19, lasted throughout the night and ended in late afternoon of the following day, when Senator Taft negotiated a unanimous consent agreement for a vote the following Tuesday. On that day the galleries of the

Senate were filled with thousands waiting to get in from the outer lobby. When the presiding officer, Senator Vandenberg, quieted the crowds, the final roll call proceeded in almost funereal silence. When it was over, Senator Taft had more than the two-thirds necessary to override. The Taft-Hartley Act had become law, the veto of the President notwithstanding.

The Taft-Hartley Act was considerably broader in scope than the Wagner Act. The first title consisted of rather extensive revision of the original National Labor Relations Act (the Wagner Act). The five-employer, unfair labor practices were retained, though some change was made in the extent to which union security agreements were privileged. The closed shop was forbidden, with only a limited form of the union shop permitted. A new section of the law granted greater freedom of expression to employers and, to a lesser extent, unions in matters of organization and collective bargaining. Significantly, the statute added a considerable listing of union unfair practices, outlawing concerted union pressures involving violence and intimidation as well as certain types of secondary boycott. The statute preserved not only the right of organization but the right to bargain collectively. It imposed upon unions the correlative of the employer's duty to bargain in good faith. It defined the concept "bargain collectively," creating certain obligations for parties involved in collective bargaining agreements.

The Wagner Act provisions concerning representation matters were amended to give employers greater privilege in filing to revoke designation of bargaining representatives, and to limit the discretion of the NLRB in certain types of unit determinations.

Administratively, the board was increased from three to five members, and its functions became primarily judicial. The investigatory and prosecuting functions of the act were vested in a newly created General Counsel of the Board, a position to be filled by the President. To a limited extent the use of the labor injunction was revived by permitting, and in some instances requiring, the NLRB (but not private parties) to obtain injunctive relief against unfair labor practices without the restrictions imposed by the Norris-LaGuardia Act.

The Taft-Hartley Act extended labor relations regulation into areas which had not been touched by the Wagner Act. In Title II the Federal Mediation and Conciliation Service was made an independent agency, and a detailed procedure was set forth for the handling of national emergency disputes. Title III contained a number of important provisions: strikes by government employees were made unlawful; restrictions were placed on political contributions or expenditures; certain types of union unfair labor practices, including secondary boycotts, were declared illegal for purposes of damage actions in the courts; and restrictions were placed upon payments to employee representatives. But probably the most important provisions of Title III were those which provided that suits for violation of collective agreements in industries affecting interstate commerce may be brought by or against a labor organization as an entity in an appropriate federal court. Beginning with the landmark decision of the Supreme Court in *Textile Workers Union* v. *Lincoln Mills,* 353 U.S. 448 (1957), a considerable body of law concerning the collective labor agreement has been created by the courts.

Lastly, reference should be made to the controversial Section 14 (b) of the Taft-Hartley Law, which permits states to outlaw any form of compulsory union membership irrespective of the provisions of the National Labor Relations Act. Nearly one-fourth of the states, largely nonindustrial, have enacted and enforced so-called "right-to-work" laws protected by Section 14 (b).

Although the Taft-Hartley Act was greeted with considerable hostility by organized labor, its adverse impact on the unions has been, on the whole, minimal. Unions were not destroyed, as predicted by some union leaders, nor was their ability to make significant gains for their members seriously inhibited. Whatever damage the unions suffered was, by and large, confined to the smaller and weaker unions and to states with right-to-work laws. As a result unionization drives were not severely hampered, especially in the South. Indeed, as Professor Archibald Cox has pointed out, "organized labor received one unexpected bonanza from the Taft-Hartley amendments," that being that the new statutes greatly enhanced the doctrine of federal preemption in labor relations. Briefly stated, under our federal system the power to regulate labor relations is apportioned between the states and the federal government. Until the New Deal era the power was exercised largely by the states, and largely through judicial control of strikes, picketing, and boycotts. The Taft-Hartley Act represented a major legislative effort by the federal government to regulate these activities on a rather comprehensive scale. It then became necessary for the Supreme Court to determine whether the Constitution's so-called "supremacy clause," which makes federal law supreme, precluded state regulation in these areas. Reasoning that the application of state law might create conflict with the national labor policy, the Court decided that state regulation has been preempted to a considerable degree. And it is plain that the Taft-Hartley limitations, as little as they may be savored by labor, are less restrictive than those prevailing in most states.

The Labor Management Relations Act of 1947—the Taft-Hartley Act —is set forth in full below and is followed by materials relevant to the legislative history of the statute. Included is the Report of the Senate Committee on Labor and Public Welfare on S. 1126 to the Senate on April 17, 1947. Since, as stated above, the major portion of the Taft-Hartley Act derives from the work of the Senate Committee on Labor and Public Welfare, the entire report of this committee on the bill which passed the

Senate is reproduced. It, of course, must be borne in mind that some of the statements refer to provisions which were altered or deleted in the law as enacted. The Minority Views of the committee also are reproduced because they fully and aptly crystallize the point of difference between the proponents and opponents of the statute. As Justice Felix Frankfurter observed in one of his opinions on the statute: "It is relevant to recall that the Taft-Hartley Act was, to a marked degree, the result of conflict and compromise between strong contending forces and deeply held views on the role of organized labor in the free economic life of the Nation and the appropriate balance to be struck between the uncontrolled power of management and labor to further their respective interests."

Excerpts from The Report of the House Committee on Education and Labor on H. R. 3020 to the House of Representatives on April 11, 1947, have also been included. Inasmuch as very little of the bill submitted by Representative Hartley found its way into the Taft-Hartley Law as enacted, the total report of the House committee has not been reproduced. The first several sections of the House report are reproduced, as they reflect the tenor and principal thrust of the House bill. Specific comments of the committee have been reproduced only when pertinent to provisions of the bill which were preserved in whole or in substance in the enacted statute. Also reproduced for its historical interest is the Supplemental Minority Report by Hon. John F. Kennedy, then a member of the House committee.

THE TAFT-HARTLEY ACT
June 23, 1947

To amend the National Labor Relations Act, to provide additional facilities for the mediation of labor disputes affecting commerce, to equalize legal responsibilites of labor organizations and employers, and for other purposes.

Be it enacted by the Senate and House of Representatives of the United States of America in Congress assembled,

SHORT TITLE AND DECLARATION OF POLICY

SEC. 1. (a) This Act may be cited as the "Labor Management Relations Act, 1947".

(b) Industrial strife which interferes with the normal flow of commerce and with the full production of articles and commodities for commerce, can be avoided or substantially minimized if employers, employees, and labor organizations each recognize under law one another's legitimate rights in their relations with each other, and above all recognize under law that neither party has any right in its relations with any other to engage in acts or practices which jeopardize the public health, safety, or interest.

It is the purpose and policy of this Act, in order to promote the full flow of commerce, to prescribe the legitimate rights of both employees and employers in their relations affecting commerce, to provide orderly and peaceful procedures for preventing the interference by either with the legitimate rights of the other, to protect the rights of individual employees in their relations with labor organizations whose activities affect commerce, to define and proscribe practices on the part of labor and management which affect commerce and are inimical to the general welfare, and to protect the rights of the public in connection with labor disputes affecting commerce.

TITLE I—AMENDMENT OF NATIONAL LABOR RELATIONS ACT

SEC. 101. The National Labor Relations Act is hereby amended to read as follows:

FINDINGS AND POLICIES

SEC. 1. The denial by some employers of the right of employees to organize and the refusal by some employers to accept the procedure of collective bargaining lead to strikes and other forms of industrial strife or unrest, which have the intent or the necessary effect of burdening or obstructing commerce by (a) impairing the efficiency, safety, or operation of the instrumentalities of commerce; (b) occurring in the current of commerce; (c) materially affecting, restraining, or controlling the flow of raw materials or manufactured or processed goods from or into the channels of commerce, or the prices of such materials or goods in commerce; or (d) causing diminution of employment and wages in such volume as substantially to impair or disrupt the market for goods flowing from or into the channels of commerce.

The inequality of bargaining power between employees who do not possess full freedom of association or actual liberty of contract, and employers who are organized in the corporate or other forms of ownership association substantially burdens and affects the flow of commerce, and tends to aggravate recurrent business depressions, by depressing wage rates and the purchasing power of wage earners in industry and by preventing the stabilization of competitive wage rates and working conditions within and between industries.

Experience has proved that protection by law of the right of employees to organize and bargain collectively safeguards commerce from injury, impairment, or interruption, and promotes the flow of commerce by removing certain recognized sources of industrial strife and unrest, by encouraging practices fundamental to the friendly adjustment of industrial disputes arising out of differences as to wages, hours, or other working conditions, and by restoring equality of bargaining power between employers and employees.

Experience has further demonstrated that certain practices by some labor organizations, their officers, and members have the intent or the necessary effect of burdening or obstructing commerce by preventing the free flow of goods in such commerce through strikes and other forms of industrial unrest or through concerted activities which impair the interest of the public in the free flow of such commerce. The elimination of such practices is a necessary condition to the assurance of the rights herein guaranteed.

It is hereby declared to be the policy of the United States to eliminate the causes of certain substantial obstructions to the free flow of commerce and to mitigate and eliminate these obstructions when they have occurred by encouraging the practice and procedure of collective bargaining and by protecting the exercise by workers of full freedom of association, self-organization, and designation of representatives of their own choosing, for the purpose of negotiating the terms and conditions of their employment or other mutual aid or protection.

DEFINITIONS

SEC. 2. When used in this Act—

(1) The term 'person' includes one or more individuals, labor organizations, partnerships, associations, corporations, legal representatives, trustees, trustees in bankruptcy, or receivers.

(2) The term 'employer' includes any person acting as an agent of an employer, directly or indirectly, but shall not include the United States or any wholly owned Government corporation, or any Federal Reserve Bank, or any State or political subdivision thereof, or any corporation or association operating a hospital, if no part of the net earnings inures to the benefit of any private shareholder or individual, or any person subject to the Railway Labor Act, as amended from time to time, or any labor organization (other than when acting as an employer), or anyone acting in the capacity of officer or agent of such labor organization.

(3) The term "employee" shall include any employee, and shall not be limited to the employees of a particular employer, unless the Act explicitly states otherwise, and shall include any individual whose work has ceased as a consequence of, or in connection with, any current labor dispute or because of any unfair labor practice, and who has not obtained any other regular and substantially equivalent employment, but shall not include any individual employed as an agricultural laborer, or in the domestic service of any family or person at his home, or any individual employed by his parent or spouse, or any individual having the status of an independent contractor, or any individual employed as a supervisor, or any individual employed by an employer subject to the Railway Labor Act, as amended from time to time, or by any other person who is not an employer as herein defined.

(4) The term "representatives" includes any individual or labor organization.

(5) The term "labor organization" means any organization of any kind, or any agency or employee representation committee or plan, in which employees participate and which exists for the purpose, in whole or in part, of dealing with employers concerning grievances, labor disputes, wages, rates of pay, hours of employment, or conditions of work.

(6) The term "commerce" means trade, traffic, commerce, transportation, or communication among the several States, or between the District of Columbia or any Territory of the United States and any State or other Territory, or between any foreign country and any state, Territory, or the District of Columbia, or within the District of Columbia or any Territory, or between points in the same State but through any other State or any Territory or the District of Columbia or any foreign country.

(7) The term "affecting commerce" means in commerce, or burdening or obstructing commerce or the free flow of commerce, or having led or tending to lead to a labor dispute burdening or obstructing commerce or the free flow of commerce.

(8) The term "unfair labor practice" means any unfair labor practice listed in section 8.

(9) The term "labor dispute" includes any controversy concerning terms, tenure or conditions of employment, or concerning the association or

representation of persons in negotiating, fixing, maintaining, changing, or seeking to arrange terms or conditions of employment, regardless of whether the disputants stand in the proximate relation of employer and employee.

(10) The term "National Labor Relations Board" means the National Labor Relations Board provided for in section 3 of this Act.

(11) The term "supervisor" means any individual having authority, in the interest of the employer, to hire, transfer, suspend, lay off, recall, promote, discharge, assign, reward, or discipline other employees, or responsibly to direct them, or to adjust their grievances, or effectively to recommend such action, if in connection with the foregoing the exercise of such authority is not of a merely routine or clerical nature, but requires the use of independent judgment.

(12) The term "professional employee" means—

(a) any employee engaged in work (i) predominantly intellectual and varied in character as opposed to routine mental, manual, mechanical, or physical work; (ii) involving the consistent exercise of discretion and judgment in its performance; (iii) of such a character that the output produced or the result accomplished cannot be standardized in relation to a given period of time; (iv) requiring knowledge of an advanced type in a field of science or learning customarily acquired by a prolonged course of specialized intellectual instruction and study in an institution of higher learning or a hospital, as distinguished from a general academic education or from an apprenticeship or from training in the performance of routine mental, manual, or physical processes; or

(b) any employee, who (i) has completed the courses of specialized intellectual instruction and study described in clause (iv) of paragraph (a), and (ii) is performing related work under the supervision of a professional person to qualify himself to become a professional employee as defined in paragraph (a).

(13) In determining whether any person is acting as an 'agent' of another person so as to make such other person responsible for his acts, the question of whether the specific acts performed were actually authorized or subsequently ratified shall not be controlling.

NATIONAL LABOR RELATIONS BOARD

SEC. 3. (a) The National Labor Relations Board (hereinafter called the "Board") created by this Act prior to its amendment by the Labor Management Relations Act, 1947, is hereby continued as an agency of the United States, except that the Board shall consist of five instead of three members, appointed by the President by and with the advice and consent of the Senate. Of the two additional members so provided for, one shall be appointed for a term of five years and the other for a term of two years. Their successors, and the successors of the other members, shall be appointed for terms of five years each, excepting that any individual chosen to fill a vacancy shall be appointed only for the unexpired term of the member whom he shall succeed. The President shall designate one member to serve as Chairman of the Board. Any member of the Board may be removed by the President, upon notice and hearing, for neglect of duty or malfeasance in office, but for no other cause.

(b) The Board is authorized to delegate to any group of three or more members any or all of the powers which it may itself exercise. A vacancy in the Board shall not impair the right of the remaining members to exercise all of the powers of the Board, and three members of the Board shall, at all times, constitute a quorum of the Board, except that two members shall constitute a quorum of any group designated pursuant to the first sentence hereof. The Board shall have an official seal which shall be judicially noticed.

(c) The Board shall at the close of each fiscal year make a report in writing to Congress and to the President stating in detail the cases it has heard, the decisions it has rendered, the names, salaries, and duties of all employees and officers in the employ or under the supervision of the Board, and an account of all moneys it has disbursed.

(d) There shall be a General Counsel of the Board who shall be appointed by the President, by and with the advice and consent of the Senate, for a term of four years. The General Counsel of the Board shall exercise general supervision over all attorneys employed by the Board (other than trial examiners and legal assistants to Board members) and over the officers and employees in the regional offices. He shall have final authority, on behalf of the Board, in respect of the investigation of charges and issuance of complaints under section 10, and in respect of the prosecution of such complaints before the Board, and shall have such other duties as the Board may prescribe or as may be provided by law.

SEC. 4. (a) Each member of the Board and the General Counsel of the Board shall receive a salary of $12,000 a year, shall be eligible for reappointment, and shall not engage in any other business, vocation, or employment. The Board shall appoint an executive secretary, and such attorneys, examiners, and regional directors, and such other employees as it may from time to time find necessary for the proper performance of its duties. The Board may not employ any attorneys for the purpose of reviewing transcripts of hearings or preparing drafts of opinions except that any attorney employed for assignment as a legal assistant to any Board member may for such Board member review such transcripts and prepare such drafts. No trial examiner's report shall be reviewed, either before or after its publication, by any person other than a member of the Board or his legal assistant, and no trial examiner shall advise or consult with the Board with respect to exceptions taken to his findings, rulings, or recommendations.

The Board may establish or utilize such regional, local, or other agencies, and utilize such voluntary and uncompensated services, as may from time to time be needed. Attorneys appointed under this section may, at the direction of the Board, appear for and represent the Board in any case in court. Nothing in this Act shall be construed to authorize the Board to appoint individuals for the purpose of conciliation or mediation, or for economic analysis.

(b) All of the expenses of the Board, including all necessary traveling and subsistence expenses outside the District of Columbia incurred by the members or employees of the Board under its orders, shall be allowed and paid on the presentation of itemized vouchers therefor approved by the Board or by any individual it designates for that purpose.

SEC. 5. The principal office of the Board shall be in the District of Columbia, but it may meet and exercise any or all of its powers at any other place. The Board may, by one or more of its members or by such agents or agencies as it may designate, prosecute any inquiry necessary to its functions in any part of the United States. A member who participates in such an inquiry shall not be disqualified from subsequently participating in a decision of the Board in the same case.

SEC. 6. The Board shall have authority from time to time to make, amend, and rescind, in the manner prescribed by the Administrative Procedure Act, such rules and regulations as may be necessary to carry out the provisions of this Act.

RIGHTS OF EMPLOYEES

SEC. 7. Employees shall have the right to self-organization, to form, join, or assist labor organizations, to bargain collectively through representatives of their own choosing, and to engage in other concerted activities for the purpose of collective bargaining or other mutual aid or protection, and shall also have the right to refrain from any or all of such activities except to the extent that such right may be affected by an agreement requiring membership in a labor organization as a condition of employment as authorized in section 8 (a) (3).

UNFAIR LABOR PRACTICES

SEC. 8. (a) It shall be an unfair labor practice for an employer—

(1) to interfere with, restrain, or coerce employees in the exercise of the rights guaranteed in section 7;

(2) to dominate or interfere with the formation or administration of any labor organization or contribute financial or other support to it: Provided, That subject to rules and regulations made and published by the Board pursuant to section 6, an employer shall not be prohibited

from permitting employees to confer with him during working hours without loss of time or pay;

(3) by discrimination in regard to hire or tenure of employment or any term or condition of employment to encourage or discourage membership in any labor organization: Provided, That nothing in this Act, or in any other statute of the United States, shall preclude an employer from making an agreement with a labor organization (not established, maintained, or assisted by any action defined in section 8 (a) of this Act as an unfair labor practice) to require as a condition of employment membership therein on or after the thirtieth day following the beginning of such employment or the effective date of such agreement, whichever is the later, (i) if such labor organization is the representative of the employees as provided in section 9 (a), in the appropriate collective bargaining unit covered by such agreement when made; and (ii) if, following the most recent election held as provided in section 9 (e) the Board shall have certified that at least a majority of the employees eligible to vote in such election have voted to authorize such labor organization to make such an agreement; Provided further, That no employer shall justify any discrimination against an employee for non-membership in a labor organization (A) if he has reasonable grounds for believing that such membership was not available to the employee on the same terms and conditions generally applicable to other members, or (B) if he has reasonable grounds for believing that membership was denied or terminated for reasons other than the failure of the employee to render the periodic dues and the initiation fees uniformly required as a condition of acquiring or retaining membership;

(4) to discharge or otherwise discriminate against an employee because he has filed charges or given testimony under this Act;

(5) to refuse to bargain collectively with the representatives of his employees, subject to the provisions of section 9 (a).

(b) It shall be an unfair labor practice for a labor organization or its agents—

(1) to restrain or coerce (A) employees in the exercise of the rights guaranteed in section 7: Provided, That this paragraph shall not impair the right of a labor organization to prescribe its own rules with respect to the acquisition or retention of membership therein; or (B) an employer in the selection of his representatives for the purposes of collective bargaining or the adjustment of grievances;

(2) to cause or attempt to cause an employer to discriminate against an employee in violation of subsection (a) (3) or to discriminate against an employee with respect to whom membership in such organization has been denied or terminated on some ground other than his failure to

tender the periodic dues and the initiation fees uniformly required as a condition of acquiring or retaining membership;

(3) to refuse to bargain collectively with an employer, provided it is the representative of his employees subject to the provisions of section 9 (a);

(4) to engage in, or to induce or encourage the employees of any employer to engage in, a strike or a concerted refusal in the course of their employment to use, manufacture, process, transport, or otherwise handle or work on any goods, articles, materials, or commodities or to perform any services, where an object thereof is: (A) forcing or requiring any employer or self-employed person to join any labor or employer organization or any employer or other person to cease using, selling, handling, transporting, or otherwise dealing in the products of any other producer, processor, or manufacturer, or to cease doing business with any other person; (B) forcing or requiring any other employer to recognize or bargain with a labor organization as the representative of his employees unless such labor organization has been certified as the representative of such employees under the provisions of section 9; (C) forcing or requiring any employer to recognize or bargain with a particular labor organization as the representative of his employees if another labor organization has been certified as the representative of such employees under the provisions of section 9; (D) forcing or requiring any employer to assign particular work to employees in a particular labor organization or in a particular trade, craft, or class rather than to employees in another labor organization or in another trade, craft, or class, unless such employer is failing to conform to an order or certification of the Board determining the bargaining representative for employees performing such work: Provided, That nothing contained in this subsection (b) shall be construed to make unlawful a refusal by any person to enter upon the premises of any employer (other than his own employer), if the employees of such employer are engaged in a strike ratified or approved by a representative of such employees whom such employer is required to recognize under this Act;

(5) to require of employees covered by an agreement authorized under subsection (a) (3) the payment, as a condition precedent to becoming a member of such organization, of a fee in an amount which the Board finds excessive or discriminatory under all the circumstances. In making such a finding, the Board shall consider, among other relevant factors, the practices and customs of labor organizations in the particular industry, and the wages currently paid to the employees affected; and

(6) to cause or attempt to cause an employer to pay or deliver or agree to pay or deliver any money or other thing of value, in the nature of an exaction, for services which are not performed or not to be performed.

(c) The expressing of any views, argument, or opinion, or the dissemination thereof, whether in written, printed, graphic, or visual form, shall not constitute or be evidence of an unfair labor practice under any of the provisions of this Act, if such expression contains no threat of reprisal or force or promise of benefit.

(d) For the purposes of this section, to bargain collectively is the performance of the mutual obligation of the employer and the representative of the employees to meet at reasonable times and confer in good faith with respect to wages, hours, and other terms and conditions of employment, or the negotiation of an agreement, or any question arising thereunder, and the execution of a written contract incorporating any agreement reached if requested by either party, but such obligation does not compel either party to agree to a proposal or require the making of a concession: Provided, That where there is in effect a collective bargaining contract covering employees in an industry affecting commerce, the duty to bargain collectively shall also mean that no party to such contract shall terminate or modify such contract, unless the party desiring such termination or modification—

(1) serves a written notice upon the other party to the contract of the proposed termination or modification sixty days prior to the expiration date thereof, or in the event such contract contains no expiration date, sixty days prior to the time it is proposed to make such termination or modification;

(2) offers to meet and confer with the other party for the purpose of negotiating a new contract or a contract containing the proposed modifications;

(3) notifies the Federal Mediation and Conciliation Service within thirty days after such notice of the existence of a dispute, and simultaneously therewith notifies any State or Territorial agency established to mediate and conciliate disputes within the State or Territory where the dispute occurred, provided no agreement has been reached by that time; and—

(4) continues in full force and effect, without resorting to strike or lock-out, all the terms and conditions of the existing contract for a period of sixty days after such notice is given or until the expiration date of such contract, whichever occurs later.

The duties imposed upon employers, employees, and labor organizations by paragraphs (2), (3), and (4) shall become inapplicable upon an intervening certification of the Board, under which the labor organization or individual, which is a party to the contract, has been superseded as or ceased to be the representative of the employees subject to the provisions of section 9 (a), and the duties so imposed shall not be construed as requiring either party to discuss or agree to any modification of the terms and conditions contained in a contract for a fixed period, if such modification is to become effective before such terms and conditions can be reopened under the provisions of the contract. Any employee who engages in a strike within the sixty-day period specified in this subsection shall lose his status as an employee of the employer engaged in the particular labor dispute, for the purposes of sections 8, 9, and 10 of this Act, as amended, but such loss of status for such employee shall terminate if and when he is reemployed by such employer.

REPRESENTATIVES AND ELECTIONS

SEC. 9. (a) Representatives designated or selected for the purposes of collective bargaining by the majority of the employees in a unit appropriate for such purposes, shall be the exclusive representatives of all the employees in such unit for the purposes of collective bargaining in respect to rates of pay, wages, hours of employment, or other conditions of employment: Provided, That any individual employee or a group of employees shall have the right at any time to present grievances to their employer and to have such grievances adjusted, without the intervention of the bargaining representative, as long as the adjustment is not inconsistent with the terms of a collective bargaining contract or agreement then in effect: Provided further, That the bargaining representative has been given opportunity to be present at such adjustment.

(b) The Board shall decide in each case whether, in order to assure to employees the fullest freedom in exercising the rights guaranteed by this Act, the unit appropriate for the purposes of collective bargaining shall be the employer unit, craft unit, plant unit, or subdivision thereof: Provided, That the Board shall not (1) decide that any unit is appropriate for such purposes if such unit includes both professional employees and employees who are not professional employees unless a majority of such professional employees vote for inclusion in such unit; or (2) decide that any craft unit is inappropriate for such purposes on the ground that a different unit has been established by a prior Board determination, unless a majority of the employees in the proposed craft unit vote against separate representation or (3) decide that any unit is appropriate for such purposes if it includes, together with other employees any individual employed as a guard to enforce against employees and other persons rules to protect property of the employer or to protect the safety of persons on the employer's premises; but no labor organization shall be certified as the representative of employees in a bargaining unit of guards if such organization admits to membership, or is affiliated directly or indirectly with an organization which admits to membership, employees other than guards.

(c) (1) Whenever a petition shall have been filed, in accordance with such regulations as may be prescribed by the Board—

(A) by an employee or group of employees or any individual or labor organization acting in their behalf alleging that a substantial number of employees (i) wish to be represented for collective bargaining and that their employer declines to recognize their representative as the representative defined in section 9 (a), or (ii) assert that the individual or labor organization, which has been certified or is being currently recognized by their employer as the bargaining representative, is no longer a representative as defined in section 9 (a); or

(B) by an employer, alleging that one or more individuals or labor organizations have presented to him a claim to be recognized as the representative defined in section 9 (a);

the Board shall investigate such petition and if it has reasonable cause to believe that a question of representation affecting commerce exists shall provide for an appropriate hearing upon due notice. Such hearing may be conducted by an office or employee of the regional office, who shall not make any recommendations with respect thereto. If the Board finds upon the record of such hearing that such a question of representation exists, it shall direct an election by secret ballot and shall certify the results thereof.

(2) In determining whether or not a question of representation affecting commerce exists, the same regulations and rules of decision shall apply irrespective of the identity of the persons filing the petition or the kind of relief sought and in no case shall the Board deny a labor organization a place on the ballot by reason of an order with respect to such labor organization or its predecessor not issued in conformity with section 10(c).

(3) No election shall be directed in any bargaining unit or any subdivision within which, in the preceding twelve-month period, a valid election shall have been held. Employees on strike who are not entitled to reinstatement shall not be eligible to vote. In any election where none of the choices on the ballot receives a majority, a run-off shall be conducted, the ballot providing for a selection between the two choices receiving the largest and second largest number of valid votes cast in the election.

(4) Nothing in this section shall be construed to prohibit the waiving of hearings by stipulation for the purpose of a consent election in conformity with regulations and rules of decision of the Board.

(5) In determining whether a unit is appropriate for the purposes specified in subsection (b) the extent to which the employees have organized shall not be controlling.

(d) Whenever an order of the Board made pursuant to section 10 (c) is based in whole or in part upon facts certified following an investigation pursuant to subsection (c) of this section and there is a petition for the enforcement or review of such order, such certification and the record of such investigation shall be included in the transcript of the entire record required to be filed under section 10 (e) or 10 (f), and thereupon the decree of the court enforcing, modifying, or setting aside in whole or in part the order of the Board shall be made and entered upon the pleadings, testimony, and proceedings set forth in such transcript.

(e) (1) Upon the filing with the Board by a labor organization, which is the representative of employees as provided in section 9 (a), of a petition alleging that 30 per centum or more of the employees within a unit claimed to be appropriate for such purposes desire to authorize such labor organization to make an agreement with the employer of such employees requiring membership in such labor organization as a condition of employment in such unit, upon an appropriate showing thereof the Board shall, if no question of representation exists, take a secret ballot of such employees, and shall certify the results thereof to such labor organization and to the employer.

(2) Upon the filing with the Board, by 30 per centum or more of the employees in a bargaining unit covered by an agreement between their employer and a labor organization made pursuant to section 8 (a) (3) (ii), of a petition alleging they desire that such authority be rescinded, the Board shall take a secret ballot of the employees in such unit, and shall certify the results thereof to such labor organization and to the employer.

(3) No election shall be conducted pursuant to this subsection in any bargaining unit or any subdivision within which, in the preceding twelve-month period, a valid election shall have been held.

(f) No investigation shall be made by the Board of any question affecting commerce concerning the representation of employees, raised by a labor organization under subsection (c) of this section, no petition under section 9 (e) (1) shall be entertained, and no complaint shall be issued pursuant to a charge made by a labor organization under subsection (b) of section 10, unless such labor organization and any national or international labor organization of which such labor organization is an affiliate or constituent unit (A) shall have prior thereto filed with the Secretary of Labor copies of its constitution and bylaws and a report, in such form as the Secretary may prescribe, showing—

(1) the name of such labor organization and the address of its principal place of business;

(2) the names, titles, and compensation and allowances of its three principal officers and of any of its other officers or agents whose aggregate compensation and allowances for the preceding year exceeded $5,000, and the amount of the compensation and allowances paid to each such officer or agent during such year;

(3) the manner in which the officers and agents referred to in clause (2) were elected, appointed, or otherwise selected;

(4) the initiation fee or fees which new members are required to pay on becoming members of such labor organization;

(5) the regular dues or fees which members are required to pay in order to remain members in good standing of such labor organization;

(6) a detailed statement of, or reference to provisions of its constitution and bylaws showing the procedure followed with respect to, (a) qualification for a restrictions on membership, (b) election of officers and stewards, (c) calling of regular and special meetings, (d) levying of assessments, (e) imposition of fines, (f) authorization for bargaining demands, (g) ratification of contract terms, (h) authorization for strikes, (i) authorization for disbursement of union funds, (j) audit of union financial transactions, (k) participation in insurance or other benefit plans, and (1) expulsion of members and the grounds therefor;

and (B) can show that prior thereto it has—

(1) filed with the Secretary of Labor, in such form as the Secretary may prescribe, a report showing all of (a) its receipts of any kind and the sources of such receipts, (b) its total assets and liabilities as of the end of its last fiscal year, (c) the disbursements made by it during such fiscal year, including the purposes for which made; and—

(2) furnished to all of the members of such labor organization copies of the financial report required by paragraph (1) hereof to be filed with the Secretary of Labor.

(g) It shall be the obligation of all labor organizations to file annually with the Secretary of Labor, in such form as the Secretary of Labor may prescribe, reports bringing up to date the information required to be supplied in the initial filing by subsection (f) (A) of this section, and to file with the Secretary of Labor and furnish to its members annually financial reports in the form and manner prescribed in subsection (f) (B). No labor organization shall be eligible for certification under this section as the representative of any employees, no petition under section 9 (e) (1) shall be entertained, and no complaint shall issue under section 10 with respect to a charge filed by a labor organization unless it can show that it and any national or international labor organization of which it is an affiliate or constituent unit has complied with its obligation under this subsection.

(h) No investigation shall be made by the Board of any question affecting commerce concerning the representation of employees, raised by a labor organization under subsection (c) of this section, no petition under section 9 (e) (1) shall be entertained, and no complaint shall be issued pursuant to a charge made by a labor organization under subsection (b) of section 10, unless there is on file with the Board an affidavit executed contemporaneously or within the preceding twelve-month period by each officer of such labor organization and the officers of any national or international labor organization of which it is an affiliate or constituent unit that he is not a member of the Communist Party or affiliated with such party, and that he does not believe in, and is not a member of or supports any organization that believes in or teaches, the overthrow of the United States Government by force or by any illegal or unconstitutional methods. The provisions of section 35 A of the Criminal Code shall be applicable in respect to such affidavits.

PREVENTION OF UNFAIR LABOR PRACTICES

SEC. 10. (a) The Board is empowered, as hereinafter provided, to prevent any person from engaging in any unfair labor practice (listed in section 8) affecting commerce. This power shall not be affected by any other means of adjustment or prevention that has been or may be established by agreement, law, or otherwise; Provided, That the Board is empowered by agreement with any agency of any State or Territory to cede to such agency jurisdiction over any cases in any industry (other than mining, manufacturing, communications, and transportation except where predominantly local in character) even though such cases may involve labor disputes affecting commerce, unless the provision of the State or Territorial statute applicable to the determination of such cases by such agency is inconsistent with the corresponding provision of this Act or has received a construction inconsistent therewith.

(b) Whenever it is charged that any person has engaged in or is engaging in any such unfair labor practice, the Board, or any agent or agency designated by the Board for such purposes, shall have power to issue and cause to be served upon such person a complaint stating the charges in that respect, and containing a notice of hearing before the Board or a member thereof, or before a designated agent or agency, at a place therein fixed, not less than five days after the serving of said complaint: Provided, That no complaint shall issue based upon any unfair labor practice occurring more than six months prior to the filing of the charge with the Board and the service of a copy thereof upon the person against whom such charge is made, unless the person aggrieved thereby was prevented from filing such charge by reason of service in the armed forces, in which event the six-month period shall be computed from the day of his discharge. Any such complaint may be amended by the member, agent, or agency conducting the hearing or the Board in its discretion at any time prior to the issuance of an order based thereon. The person so complained of shall have the right to file an answer to the original or amended complaint and to appear in person or otherwise and give testimony at the place and time fixed in the complaint. In the discretion of the member, agent, or agency conducting the hearing or the Board, any other person may be allowed to intervene in the said proceeding and to present testimony. Any such proceeding shall, so far as practicable, be conducted in accordance with the rules of evidence applicable in the district courts of the United States under the rules of civil procedure for the district courts of the United States, adopted by the Supreme Court of the United States pursuant to the Act of June 19, 1934 (U. S. C., title 28, secs. 723-B, 723-C).

(c) The testimony taken by such member, agent, or agency or the Board shall be reduced to writing and filed with the Board. Thereafter, in its discretion, the Board upon notice may take further testimony or hear argument. If upon the preponderance of the testimony taken the Board shall be of the opinion that any person named in the complaint has engaged in or is engaging in any such unfair labor practices, then the Board shall state its findings of fact and shall issue and cause to be served on such person an order requiring such person to cease and desist from such unfair labor practice, and to take such affirmative action including reinstatement of employees with or without back pay, as will effectuate the policies of this Act: Provided, That where an order directs reinstatement of an employee, back pay may be required of the employer or labor organization, as the case may be, responsible for the discrimination suffered by him: And provided further, That in determining whether a complaint shall issue alleging a violation of section 8 (a) (1) or section 8 (a) (2), and in deciding such cases, the same regulations and rules of decision shall apply irrespective of whether or not the labor organization affected is affiliated with a labor organization national or international in scope. Such order may further require such person to make reports from time to time showing the extent to which it has complied with the order. If upon the preponderance of the testimony taken the Board shall not be of the opinion that the person named in the complaint has engaged in or is engaging in any such unfair labor practice, then the Board shall state its findings of fact and shall issue an order dismissing the said complaint. No order of the Board shall require the reinstatement of any individual as an employee who has been suspended or discharged, or the payment to him of any back pay, if such individual was suspended or discharged for cause. In case the evidence is presented before a member of the Board, or before an examiner or examiners thereof, such member, or such examiner or examiners, as the case may be, shall issue and cause to be served on the parties to the proceeding a proposed report, together with a recommended order, which shall be filed with the Board, and if no exceptions are filed within twenty days after service thereof upon such parties, or within such further period as the Board may authorize, such recommended order shall become the order of the Board and become effective as therein prescribed.

(d) Until a transcript of the record in a case shall have been filed in a court, as hereinafter provided, the Board may at any time, upon reasonable notice and in such manner as it shall deem proper, modify or set aside, in whole or in part, any finding or order made or issued by it.

(e) The Board shall have power to petition any circuit court of appeals of the United States (including the United States Court of Appeals for the District of Columbia), or if all the circuit courts of appeals to which application may be made are in vacation, any district court of the United States (including the District Court of the United States for the District of Columbia), within any circuit or district, respectively, wherein the unfair labor practice in question occurred or wherein such person resides or transacts business, for the enforcement of such order and for appropriate temporary relief or restraining order, and shall certify and file in the court a transcript of the entire record in the proceedings, including the pleadings and testimony upon which such order was entered and the findings and order of the Board. Upon such filing, the court shall cause notice thereof to be served upon such person, and thereupon shall have jurisdiction of the proceeding and of the question determined therein, and shall have power to grant such temporary relief or restraining order as it deems just and proper, and to make and enter upon the pleadings, testimony, and proceedings set forth in such transcript a decree enforcing, modifying, and enforcing as so modified, or setting aside in whole or in part the order of the Board. No objection that has not been urged before the Board, its member, agent, or agency, shall be considered by the court, unless the failure or neglect to urge such objection shall be excused because of extraordinary circumstances. The findings of the Board with respect to questions of fact if supported by substantial evidence on the record considered as a whole shall be conclusive. If either party shall apply to the court for leave to adduce additional evidence and shall show to the satisfaction of the court that such additional evidence is material and that there were reasonable grounds for the failure to adduce such evidence in the hearing before the Board, its member, agent, or agency, the court may order such additional evidence to be taken before the Board, its members, agent, or agency, and to be made a part of the transcript. The Board may modify its findings as to the facts, or make new findings, by reason of additional evidence so taken and filed, and it shall file such modified or new findings, which findings with respect to questions of fact if supported by substantial evidence on the record considered as a whole shall be conclusive, and shall file its recommendations, if any, for the modification or setting aside of its original order. The jurisdiction of the court shall be exclusive and its judgment and decree shall be final, except that the same shall be subject to review by the appropriate circuit court of appeals if application was made to the district court as hereinabove provided, and by the Supreme Court of the United States upon writ of certiorari or certification as provided in section 239 and 240 of the Judicial Code, as amended (U. S. C., title 28, secs. 346 and 347).

(f) Any person aggrieved by a final order of the Board granting or denying in whole or in part the relief sought may obtain a review of such order in any circuit court of appeals of the United States in the circuit wherein the unfair labor practice in question was alleged to have been engaged in or wherein such person resides or transacts business, or in the United States Court of Appeals for the District of Columbia, by filing in such court a written petition praying that the order of the Board be modified or set aside. A copy of such petition shall be forthwith served upon the Board, and thereupon the aggrieved party shall file in the court a transcript of the entire record in the proceeding, certified by the Board, including the pleading and testimony upon which the order complained of was entered, and the findings and order of the Board. Upon such filing, the court shall proceed in the same manner as in the case of an application by the Board under subsection (e), and shall have the same exclusive jurisdiction to grant to the Board such temporary relief or restraining order as it deems just and proper, and in like manner to make and enter a decree enforcing, modifying, and enforcing as so modified, or setting aside in whole or in part the order of the Board; the findings of the Board with respect to questions of fact if supported by substantial evidence on the record considered as a whole shall in like manner be conclusive.

(g) The commencement of proceedings under subsection (e) or (f) of this section shall not, unless specifically ordered by the court, operate as a stay of the Board's order.

(h) When granting appropriate temporary relief or a restraining order, or making and entering a decree enforcing, modifying, and enforcing as so modified, or setting aside in whole or in part an order on[1] the Board, as provided in this section, the jurisdiction of courts sitting in equity shall not be limited by the Act entitled "An Act to amend the Judicial Code and to define and limit the jurisdiction of courts sitting in equity, and for other purposes", approved March 23, 1932 (U.S.C., Supp. VII, title 29, secs. 101–115).

(i) Petitions filed under this Act shall be heard expeditiously, and if possible within ten days after they have been docketed.

(j) The Board shall have power, upon issuance of a complaint as provided in subsection (b) charging that any person has engaged in or is engaging in an unfair labor practice, to petition any district court of the United States (including the District Court of the United States for the District of Columbia), within any district wherein the unfair labor practice in question is alleged to have occurred or wherein such person resides or transacts business, for appropriate temporary relief or restraining order. Upon the filing of any such petition the court shall cause notice thereof to be served upon such person, and thereupon shall have jurisdiction to grant to the Board such temporary relief or restraining order as it deems just and proper.

---

[1] So in original.

(k) Whenever it is charged that any person has engaged in an unfair labor practice within the meaning of paragraph (4) (D) of section 8 (b), the Board is empowered and directed to hear and determine the dispute out of which such unfair labor practice shall have arisen, unless, within ten days after notice that such charge has been filed, the parties to such dispute submit to the Board satisfactory evidence that they have adjusted, or agreed upon methods for the voluntary adjustment of, the dispute. Upon compliance by the parties to the dispute with the decision of the Board or upon such voluntary adjustment of the dispute, such charge shall be dismissed.

(l) Whenever it is charged that any person has engaged in an unfair labor practice within the meaning of paragraph (4) (A), (B), or (C) of section 8 (b), the preliminary investigation of such charge shall be made forthwith and given priority over all other cases except cases of like character in the office where it is filed or to which it is referred. If, after such investigation, the officer or regional attorney to whom the matter may be referred has reasonable cause to believe such charge is true and that a complaint should issue, he shall, on behalf of the Board, petition any district court of the United States (including the District Court of the United States for the District of Columbia) within any district where the unfair labor practice in question has occurred, is alleged to have occurred, or wherein such person resides or transacts business, for appropriate injunctive relief pending the final adjudication of the Board with respect to such matter. Upon the filing of any such petition the district court shall have jurisdiction to grant such injunctive relief or temporary restraining order as it deems just and proper, notwithstanding any other provision of law: Provided further, That no temporary restraining order shall be issued without notice unless a petition alleges that substantial and irreparable injury to the charging party will be unavoidable and such temporary restraining order shall be effective for no longer than five days and will become void at the expiration of such period. Upon filing of any such petition the courts shall cause notice thereof to be served upon any person involved in the charge and such person, including the charging party, shall be given an opportunity to appear by counsel and present any relevant testimony: Provided further, That for the purposes of this subsection district courts shall be deemed to have jurisdiction of a labor organization (1) in the district in which such organization maintains its principal office, or (2) in any district in which its duly authorized officers or agents are engaged in promoting or protecting the interests of employee members. The service of legal process upon such officer or agent shall constitute service upon the labor organization and make such organization a party to the suit. In situations where such relief is appropriate the procedure specified herein shall apply to charges with respect to section 8 (b) (4) (D).

INVESTIGATORY POWERS

SEC. 11. For the purpose of all hearings and investigations, which, in the opinion of the Board, are necessary and proper for the exercise of the powers vested in it by section 9 and section 10—

(1) The Board, or its duly authorized agents or agencies, shall at all reasonable times have access to, for the purpose of examination, and the right to copy any evidence of any person being investigated or proceeded against that relates to any matter under investigation or in question. The Board, or any member thereof, shall upon application of any party to such proceedings, forthwith issue to such party subpenas requiring the attendance and testimony of witnesses or the production of any evidence in such proceeding or investigation requested in such application. Within five days after the service of a subpena on any person requiring the production of any evidence in his possession or under his control, such person may petition the Board to revoke, and the Board shall revoke, such subpena if in its opinion the evidence whose production is required does not relate to any matter under investigation, or any matter in question in such proceedings, or if in its opinion such subpena does not describe with sufficient particularity the evidence whose production is required. Any member of the Board, or any agent or agency designated by the Board for such purposes, may administer oaths and affirmations, examine witnesses, and receive evidence. Such attendance of witnesses and the production of such evidence may be required from any place in the United States or any Territory or possession thereof, at any designated place of hearing.

(2) In case of contumacy or refusal to obey a subpena issued to any person, any district court of the United States or the United States courts of any Territory or possession, or the District Court of the United States for the District of Columbia, within the jurisdiction of which the inquiry is carried on or within the jurisdiction of which said person guilty of contumacy or refusal to obey is found or resides or transacts business, upon application by the Board shall have jurisdiction to issue to such person an order requiring such person to appear before the Board, its member, agent, or agency, there to produce evidence if so ordered, or there to give testimony touching the matter under investigation or in question; and any failure to obey such order of the court may be punished by said court as a contempt thereof.

(3) No person shall be excused from attending and testifying or from producing books, records, correspondence, documents, or other evidence in obedience to the subpena of the Board, on the ground that the testimony or evidence required of him may tend to incriminate him or subject him to a penalty or forfeiture; but no individual shall be prosecuted or subjected to any penalty or forfeiture for or on account of any transaction, matter, or thing concerning, which he is compelled, after having claimed his privilege

against self-incrimination, to testify or produce evidence, except that such individual so testifying shall not be exempt from prosecution and punishment for perjury committed in so testifying.

(4) Complaints, orders, and other process and papers of the Board, its member, agent, or agency, may be served either personally or by registered mail or by telegraph or by leaving a copy thereof at the principal office or place of business of the person required to be served. The verified return by the individual so serving the same setting forth the manner of such service shall be proof of the same, and the return post office receipt or telegraph receipt therefor when registered and mailed or telegraphed as aforesaid shall be proof of service of the same. Witnesses summoned before the Board, its member, agent, or agency, shall be paid the same fees and mileage that are paid witnesses in the courts of the United States, and witnesses whose depositions are taken and the persons taking the same shall severally be entitled to the same fees as are paid for like services in the courts of the United States.

(5) All process of any court to which application may be made under this Act may be served in the judicial district wherein the defendant or other person required to be served resides or may be found.

(6) The several departments and agencies of the Government, when directed by the President, shall furnish the Board, upon its request, all records, papers, and information in their possession relating to any matter before the Board.

SEC. 12. Any person who shall willfully resist, prevent, impede, or interfere with any member of the Board or any of its agents or agencies in the performance of duties pursuant to this Act shall be punished by a fine of not more than $5,000 or by imprisonment for not more than one year, or both.

LIMITATIONS

SEC. 13. Nothing in this Act, except as specifically provided for herein, shall be construed so as either to interfere with or impede or diminish in any way the right to strike, or to affect the limitations or qualifications on that right.

SEC. 14. (a) Nothing herein shall prohibit any individual employed as a supervisor from becoming or remaining a member of a labor organization, but no employer subject to this Act shall be compelled to deem individuals defined herein as supervisors as employees for the purpose of any law, either national or local, relating to collective bargaining.

(b) Nothing in this Act shall be construed as authorizing the execution or application of agreements requiring membership in a labor organization as a condition of employment in any State or Territory in which such execution or application is prohibited by State or Territorial law.

SEC. 15. Wherever the application of the provisions of section 272 of chapter 10 of the Act entitled "An Act to establish a uniform system of bankruptcy throughout the United States", approved July 1, 1898, and Acts amendatory thereof and supplementary thereto (U. S. C., title 11, sec. 672), conflicts with the application of the provisions of this Act, this Act shall prevail: Provided, That in any situation where the provisions of this Act cannot be validly enforced, the provisions of such other Acts shall remain in full force and effect.

SEC. 16. If any provision of this Act, or the application of such provision to any person or circumstances, shall be held invalid, the remainder of this Act, or the application of such provision to persons or circumstances other than those as to which it is held invalid, shall not be affected thereby.

EFFECTIVE DATE OF CERTAIN CHANGES

SEC. 102 No provision of this title shall be deemed to make an unfair labor practice any act which was performed prior to the date of the enactment of this Act which did not constitute an unfair labor practice prior thereto, and the provisions of section 8 (a) (3) and section 8 (b) (2) of the National Labor Relations Act as amended by this title shall not make an unfair labor practice the performance of any obligation under a collective bargaining agreement entered into prior to the date of the enactment of this Act, or (in the case of an agreement for a period of not more than one year) entered into on or after such date of enactment, but prior to the effective date of this title, if the performance of such obligation would not have constituted an unfair labor practice under section 8 (3) of the National Labor Relations Act prior to the effective date of this title, unless such agreement was renewed or extended subsequent thereto.

SEC. 103. No provisions of this title shall affect any certification of representatives or any determination as to the appropriate collective bargaining unit, which was made under section 9 of the National Labor Relations Act prior to the effective date of this title until one year after the date of such certification or if, in respect of any such certification, a collective bargaining contract was entered into prior to the effective date of this title, until the end of the contract period or until one year after such date, whichever first occurs.

SEC. 104. The amendments made by this title shall take effect sixty days after the date of the enactment of this Act, except that the authority of the President to appoint certain officers conferred upon him by section 3 of the National Labor Relations Act as amended by this title may be exercised forthwith.

TITLE II—CONCILIATION OF LABOR DISPUTES IN INDUSTRIES AFFECTING COMMERCE; NATIONAL EMERGENCIES

SEC. 201. That it is the policy of the United States that—

(a) sound and stable industrial peace and the advancement of the general welfare, health, and safety of the Nation and of the best interests of employers and employees can most satisfactorily be secured by the settlement of issues between employers and employees through the processes of conference and collective bargaining between employers and the representatives of their employees;

(b) the settlement of issues between employers and employees through collective bargaining may be advanced by making available full and adequate governmental facilities for conciliation, mediation, and voluntary arbitration to aid and encourage employers and the representatives of their employees to reach and maintain agreements concerning rates of pay, hours, and working conditions, and to make all reasonable efforts to settle their differences by mutual agreement reached through conferences and collective bargaining or by such methods as may be provided for in any applicable agreement for the settlement of disputes; and—

(c) certain controversies which arise between parties to collective bargaining agreements may be avoided or minimized by making available full and adequate governmental facilities for furnishing assistance to employers and the representatives of their employees in formulating for inclusion with such agreements provision for adequate notice of any proposed changes in the terms of such agreements, for the final adjustment of grievances or questions regarding the application or interpretation of such agreements, and other provisions designed to prevent the subsequent arising of such controversies.

SEC. 202. (a) There is hereby created an independent agency to be known as the Federal Mediation and Conciliation Service (herein referred to as the "Service", except that for sixty days after the date of the enactment of this Act such term shall refer to the Conciliation Service of the Department of Labor). The Service shall be under the direction of a Federal Mediation and Conciliation Director (hereinafter referred to as the "Director"), who shall be appointed by the President by and with the advice and consent of the Senate. The Director shall receive compensation at the rate of $12,000 per annum. The Director shall not engage in any other business, vocation, or employment.

(b) The Director is authorized, subject to the civil service laws, to appoint such clerical and other personnel as may be necessary for the execution of the functions of the Service, and shall fix their compensation in accordance with the Classification Act of 1923, as amended, and may, without regard to the provisions of the civil service laws and the Classification Act of 1923, as amended, appoint and fix the compensation of such conciliators and mediators as may be necessary to carry out the functions of the Service. The Director is authorized to make such expenditures for supplies, facilities, and services as he deems necessary. Such expenditures shall be allowed and paid upon presentation of itemized vouchers therefor approved by the Director or by any employee designated by him for that purpose.

(c) The principal office of the Service shall be in the District of Columbia, but the Director may establish regional offices convenient to localities in which labor controversies are likely to arise. The Director may by order, subject to revocation at any time, delegate any authority and discretion conferred upon him by this Act to any regional director, or other officer or employee of the Service. The director may establish suitable procedures for cooperation with State and local mediation agencies. The Director shall make an annual report in writing to Congress at the end of the fiscal year.

(d) All mediation and conciliation functions of the Secretary of Labor or the United States Conciliation Service under section 8 of the Act entitled "An Act to create a Department of Labor", approved March 4, 1913 (U. S. C., title 29, sec. 51), and all functions of the United States Conciliation Service under any other law are hereby transferred to the Federal Mediation and Conciliation Service, together with the personnel and records of the United States Conciliation Service. Such transfer shall take effect upon the sixtieth day after the date of enactment of this Act. Such transfer shall not affect any proceedings pending before the United States Conciliation Service or any certification, order, rule, or regulation theretofore made by it or by the Secretary of Labor. The Director and the Service shall not be subject in any way to the jurisdiction or authority of the Secretary of Labor or any official or division of the Department of Labor.

FUNCTIONS OF THE SERVICE

SEC. 203. (a) It shall be the duty of the Service, in order to prevent or minimize interruptions of the free flow of commerce growing out of labor disputes, to assist parties to labor disputes in industries affecting commerce to settle such disputes through conciliation and mediation.

(b) The Service may proffer its services in any labor dispute in any industry affecting commerce, either upon its own motion or upon the request of one or more of the parties to the dispute, whenever in its judgment such dispute threatens to cause a substantial interruption of commerce. The Director and the Service are directed to avoid attempting to mediate disputes which would have only a minor effect on interstate commerce if State or other conciliation services are available to the parties. Whenever the Service does proffer its services in any dispute, it shall be the duty of the Service promptly to put itself in communication with the parties and to use its best efforts, by mediation and conciliation, to bring them to agreement.

(c) If the Director is not able to bring the parties to agreement by conciliation within a reasonable time, he shall seek to induce the parties voluntarily to seek other means of settling the dispute without resort to strike, lock-out, or other coercion, including submission to the employees in the bargaining unit of the employer's last offer of settlement for approval or rejection in a secret ballot. The failure or refusal of either party to agree to any procedure suggested by the Director shall not be deemed a violation of any duty or obligation imposed by this Act.

(d) Final adjustment by a method agreed upon by the parties is hereby declared to be the desirable method for settlement of grievance disputes arising over the application or interpretation of an existing collective bargaining agreement. The Service is directed to make its conciliation and mediation services available in the settlement of such grievance disputes only as a last resort and in exceptional cases.

SEC. 204. (a) In order to prevent or minimize interruptions of the free flow of commerce growing out of labor disputes, employers and employees and their representatives, in any industry affecting commerce, shall—

> (1) exert every reasonable effort to make and maintain agreements concerning rates of pay, hours, and working conditions, including provision for adequate notice of any proposed change in the terms of such agreements;

> (2) whenever a dispute arises over the terms or application of a collective bargaining agreement and a conference is requested by a party or prospective party thereto, arrange promptly for such a conference to be held and endeavor in such conference to settle such dispute expeditiously; and—

> (3) in case such dispute is not settled by conference, participate fully and promptly in such meetings as may be undertaken by the Service under this Act for the purpose of aiding in a settlement of the dispute.

SEC. 205. (a) There is hereby created a National Labor-Management Panel which shall be composed of twelve members appointed by the President, six of whom shall be selected from among persons outstanding in the field of management and six of whom shall be selected from among persons outstanding in the field of labor. Each member shall hold office for a term of three years, except that any member appointed to fill a vacancy occurring prior to the expiration of the term for which his predecessor was appointed shall be appointed for the remainder of such term, and the terms of office of the members first taking office shall expire, as designated by the President at the time of appointment, four at the end of the first year, four at the end of the second year, and four at the end of the third year after the date of appointment. Members of the panel, when serving on business of the panel, shall be paid compensation at the rate of $25 per day, and shall also be entitled to receive an allowance for actual and necessary travel and subsistence expenses while so serving away from their places of residence.

(b) It shall be the duty of the panel, at the request of the Director, to advise in the avoidance of industrial controversies and the manner in which mediation and voluntary adjustment shall be administered, particularly with reference to controversies affecting the general welfare of the country.

NATIONAL EMERGENCIES

SEC. 206. Whenever in the opinion of the President of the United States, a threatened or actual strike or lock-out affecting an entire industry or a substantial part thereof engaged in trade, commerce, transportation, transmission, or communication among the several States or with foreign nations, or engaged in the production of goods for commerce, will, if permitted to occur or to continue, imperil the national health or safety, he may appoint a board of inquiry to inquire into the issues involved in the dispute and to make a written report to him within such time as he shall prescribe. Such report shall include a statement of the facts with respect to the dispute, including each party's statement of its position but shall not contain any recommendations. The President shall file a copy of such report with the Service and shall make its contents available to the public.

SEC. 207. (a) A board of inquiry shall be composed of a chairman and such other members as the President shall determine, and shall have power to sit and act in any place within the United States and to conduct such hearings either in public or in private, as it may deem necessary or proper, to ascertain the facts with respect to the causes and circumstances of the dispute.

(b) Members of a board of inquiry shall receive compensation at the rate of $50 for each day actually spent by them in the work of the board, together with necessary travel and subsistence expenses.

(c) For the purpose of any hearing or inquiry conducted by any board appointed under this title the provisions of sections 9 and 10 (relating to the attendance of witnesses and the production of books, papers, and documents) of the Federal Trade Commission Act of September 16, 1914, as amended (U. S. C. 19, title 15, secs. 49 and 50, as amended), are hereby made applicable to the powers and duties of such board.

SEC. 208. (a) Upon receiving a report from a board of inquiry the President may direct the Attorney General to petition any district court of the United States having jurisdiction of the parties to enjoin such strike or lock-out or the continuing thereof, and if the court finds that such threatened or actual strike or lock-out—

(i) affects an entire industry or a substantial part thereof engaged in trade, commerce, transportation, transmission, or communication among the several States or with foreign nations, or engaged in the production of goods for commerce; and—

(ii) if permitted to occur or to continue, will imperil the national health or safety, it shall have jurisdiction to enjoin any such strike or lock-out, or the continuing thereof, and to make such other orders as may be appropriate.

(b) In any case, the provisions of the Act of March 23, 1932, entitled "An Act to amend the Judicial Code and to define and limit the jurisdiction of courts sitting in equity, and for other purposes", shall not be applicable.

(c) The order or orders of the courts shall be subject to review by the appropriate circuit court of appeals and by the Supreme Court upon writ of certiorari or certification as provided in sections 239 and 240 of the Judicial Code, as amended (U. S. C., title 29, secs. 346 and 347).

SEC. 209. (a) Whenever a district court has issued an order under section 208 enjoining acts or practices which imperil or threaten to imperil the national health or safety, it shall be the duty of the parties to the labor dispute giving rise to such order to make every effort to adjust and settle their difference, with the assistance of the Service created by this Act. Neither party shall be under any duty to accept, in whole or in part, any proposal of settlement made by the Service.

(b) Upon the issuance of such order, the President shall reconvene the board of inquiry which has previously reported with respect to the dispute. At the end of a sixty-day period (unless the dispute has been settled by that time), the board of inquiry shall report to the President the current position of the parties and the efforts which have been made for settlement, and shall include a statement by each party of its position and a statement of the employer's last offer of settlement. The President shall make such report available to the public. The National Labor Relations Board, within the succeeding fifteen days, shall take a secret ballot of the employees of each employer involved in the dispute on the question of whether they wish to accept the final offer of settlement made by their employer as stated by him and shall certify the results thereof to the Attorney General within five days thereafter.

SEC. 210. Upon the certification of the results of such ballot or upon a settlement being reached, whichever happens sooner, the Attorney General shall move the court to discharge the injunction, which motion shall then be granted and the injunction discharged. When such motion is granted, the President shall submit to the Congress a full and comprehensive report of the proceedings, including the findings of the board of inquiry and the ballot taken by the National Labor Relations Board, together with such recommendations as he may see fit to make for consideration and appropriate action.

COMPILATION OF COLLECTIVE BARGAINING AGREEMENTS, ETC.

SEC. 211. (a) For the guidance and information of interested representatives of employers, employees, and the general public, the Bureau of Labor

Statistics of the Department of Labor shall maintain a file of copies of all available collective bargaining agreements and other available agreements and actions thereunder settling or adjusting labor disputes. Such file shall be open to inspection under appropriate conditions precribed by the Secretary of Labor, except that no specific information submitted in confidence shall be disclosed.

(b) The Bureau of Labor Statistics in the Department of Labor is authorized to furnish upon request of the Service, or employers, employees, or their representatives, all available data and factual information which may aid in the settlement of any labor dispute, except that no specific information submitted in confidence shall be disclosed.

EXEMPTION OF RAILWAY LABOR ACT

SEC. 212. The provisions of this title shall not be applicable with respect to any matter which is subject to the provisions of the Railway Labor Act, as amended from time to time.

TITLE III—SUITS BY AND AGAINST
LABOR ORGANIZATIONS

SEC. 301. (a) Suits for violation of contracts between an employer and a labor organization representing employees in an industry affecting commerce as defined in this Act, or between any such labor organizations, may be brought in any district court of the United States having jurisdiction of the parties, without respect to the amount in controversy or without regard to the citizenship of the parties.

(b) Any labor organization which represents employees in an industry affecting commerce as defined in this Act and any employer whose activities affect commerce as defined in this Act shall be bound by the acts of its agents. Any such labor organization may sue or be sued as an entity and in behalf of the employees whom it represents in the courts of the United States. Any money judgment against a labor organization in a district court of the United States shall be enforceable only against the organization as an entity and against its assets, and shall not be enforceable against any individual member or his assets.

(c) For the purposes of actions and proceedings by or against labor organizations in the district courts of the United States, district courts shall be deemed to have jurisdiction of a labor organization (1) in the district in which such organization maintains its principal office, or (2) in any district in which its duly authorized officers or agents are engaged in representing or acting for employee members.

(d) The service of summons, subpena, or other legal process of any court of the United States upon an officer or agent of a labor organization, in his capacity as such, shall constitute service upon the labor organization.

(e) For the purposes of this section, in determining whether any person is acting as an "agent" of another person so as to make such other person responsible for his acts the question of whether the specific acts performed were actually authorized or subsequently ratified shall not be controlling.

RESTRICTIONS ON PAYMENTS TO EMPLOYEE REPRESENTATIVES

SEC. 302. (a) It shall be unlawful for any employer to pay or deliver, or to agree to pay or deliver, any money or other thing of value to any representative of any of his employees who are employed in an industry affecting commerce.

(b) It shall be unlawful for any representative of any employees who are employed in an industry affecting commerce to receive or accept, or to agree to receive or accept, from the employer of such employee any money or other thing of value.

(c) The provisions of this section shall not be applicable (1) with respect to any money or other thing of value payable by an employer to any representative who is an employee or former employee of such employer, as compensation for, or by reason of, his services as an employee of such employer; (2) with respect to the payment or delivery of any money or other thing of value in satisfaction of a judgment of any court or a decision or award of an arbitrator or impartial chairman or in compromise, adjustment, settlement or release of any claim, complaint, grievance, or dispute in the absence of fraud or duress; (3) with respect to the sale or purchase of an article or commodity at the prevailing market price in the regular course of business; (4) with respect to money deducted from the wages of employees in payment of membership dues in a labor organization: Provided, That the employer has received from each employee, on whose account such deductions are made, a written assignment which shall not be irrevocable for a period of more than one year, or beyond the termination date of the applicable collective agreement, whichever occurs sooner; or (5) with respect to money or other thing of value paid to a trust fund established by such representative, for the sole and exclusive benefit of the employees of such employer, and their families and dependents (or of such employees, families, and dependents jointly with the employees of other employers making similar payments, and their families and dependents): Provided, That (A) such payments are held in trust for the purpose of paying, either from principal or income or both, for the benefit of employees, their families and dependents, for medical or hospital care, pensions on retirement or death of employees, compensation for injuries or illness resulting from occupational activity or insurance to provide any of the foregoing, or unemployment benefits or life insurance, disability and sickness insurance, or accident insurance; (B) the detailed basis on which such payments are to be made is specified in a written agreement with the employer, and employees and employers are equally represented in the administration of such fund, together with such neutral persons as the representatives of the employers and the representatives of the employees may agree upon and in the event the employer and employee groups deadlock on the administration of such fund and there are no neutral persons empowered to break such deadlock, such agreement provides that the two groups shall agree on an impartial umpire to decide such dispute, or in event of their failure to agree within a reasonable length of time, an impartial umpire to decide such dispute shall, on petition of either group, be appointed by the district court of the United States for the district where the trust fund has its principal office, and shall also contain provisions for an annual audit of the trust fund, a statement of the results of which shall be available for inspection by interested persons at the principal office of the trust fund and at such other places as may be designated in such written agreement; and (C) such payments as are intended to be used for the purpose of providing pensions or annuities for employees are made to a separate trust which provides that the funds held therein cannot be used for any purpose other than paying such pensions or annuities.

(d) Any person who willfully violates any of the provisions of this section shall, upon conviction thereof, be guilty of a misdemeanor and be subject to a fine of not more than $10,000 or to imprisonment for not more than one year, or both.

(e) The district courts of the United States and the United States courts of the Territories and possessions shall have jurisdiction, for cause shown, and subject to the provisions of section 17 (relating to notice to opposite party) of the Act entitled "An Act to supplement existing laws against unlawful restraints and monopolies, and for other purposes", approved October 15, 1914, as amended (U. S. C., title 28, sec. 381), to restrain violations of this section, without regard to the provisions of sections 6 and 20 of such Act of October 15, 1914, as amended (U. S. C., title 15, sec. 17, and title 29, sec. 52), and the provisions of the Act entitled "An Act to amend the Judicial Code and to define and limit the jurisdiction of courts sitting in equity, and for other purposes", approved March 23, 1932 (U. S. C., title 29, secs. 101–115).

(f) This section shall not apply to any contract in force on the date of enactment of this Act, until the expiration of such contract, or until July 1, 1948, whichever first occurs.

(d) Compliance with the restrictions contained in subsection (c) (5) (B) upon contributions to trust funds, otherwise lawful, shall not be applicable to contributions to such trust funds established by collective agreement prior to January 1, 1946, nor shall subsection (c) (5) (A) be construed as prohibiting contributions to such trust funds if prior to January 1, 1947, such funds contained provisions for pooled vacation benefits.

BOYCOTTS AND OTHER UNLAWFUL COMBINATIONS

SEC. 303. (a) It shall be unlawful, for the purposes of this section only, in an industry or activity affecting commerce, for any labor organization to engage in, or to induce or encourage the employees of any employer to engage in, a strike or a concerted refusal in the course of their employment to use, manufacture, process, transport, or otherwise handle or work on any goods, articles, materials, or commodities or to perform any services, where an object thereof is—

(1) forcing or requiring any employer or self-employed person to join any labor or employer organization or any employer or other person to cease using, selling, handling, transporting, or otherwise dealing in the products of any other producer, processor, or manufacturer, or to cease doing business with any other person;

(2) forcing or requiring any other employer to recognize or bargain with a labor organization as the representative of his employees unless such labor organization has been certified as the representative of such employees under the provisions of section 9 of the National Labor Relations Act;

(3) forcing or requiring any employer to recognize or bargain with a particular labor organization as the representative of his employees if another labor organization has been certified as the representative of such employees under the provisions of section 9 of the National Labor Relations Act;

(4) forcing or requiring any employer to assign particular work to employees in a particular labor organization or in a particular trade, craft, or class rather than to employees in another labor organization or in another trade, craft, or class unless such employer is failing to conform to an order or certification of the National Labor Relations Board determining the bargaining representative for employees performing such work. Nothing contained in this subsection shall be construed to make unlawful a refusal by any person to enter upon the premises of any employer (other than his own employer), if the employees of such employer are engaged in a strike ratified or approved by a representative of such employees whom such employer is required to recognize under the National Labor Relations Act.

(b) Whoever shall be injured in his business or property by reason or any violation of subsection (a) may sue therefor in any district court of the

United States subject to the limitations and provisions of section 301 hereof without respect to the amount in controversy, or in any other court having jurisdiction of the parties, and shall recover the damages by him sustained and the cost of the suit.

RESTRICTIONS ON POLITICAL CONTRIBUTIONS

SEC. 304. Section 313 of the Federal Corrupt Practices Act, 1925 (U. S. C., 1940 edition, title 2, sec. 251; Supp. V, title 50, App., sec. 1509), as amended, is amended to read as follows:

SEC. 313. It is unlawful for any national bank, or any corporation organized by authority of any law of Congress, to make a contribution or expenditure in connection with any election to any political office, or in connection with any primary election or political convention or caucus held to select candidates for any political office, or for any corporation whatever, or any labor organization to make a contribution or expenditure in connection with any election at which Presidential and Vice Presidential electors or a Senator or Representative in, or a Delegate or Resident Commissioner to Congress are to be voted for, or in connection with any primary election or political convention or caucus held to select candidates for any of the foregoing offices, or for any canditate, political committee, or other person to accept or receive any contribution prohibited by this section. Every corporation or labor organization which makes any contribution or expenditure in violation of this section shall be fined not more than $5,000; and every officer or director of any corporation, or officer of any labor organization, who consents to any contribution or expenditure by the corporation or labor organization, as the case may be, in violation of this section shall be fined not more than $1,000 or imprisoned for not more than one year, or both. For the purposes of this section 'labor organization' means any organization of any kind, or any agency or employee representation committee or plan, in which employees participate and which exists for the purpose, in whole or in part, of dealing with employers concerning grievances, labor disputes, wages, rates of pay, hours of employment, or conditions of work.

STRIKES BY GOVERNMENT EMPLOYEES

SEC. 305. It shall be unlawful for any individual employed by the United States or any agency thereof including wholly owned Government corporations to participate in any strike. Any individual employed by the United States or by any such agency who strikes shall be discharged immediately from his employment, and shall forfeit his civil service status, if any, and shall not be eligible for reemployment for three years by the United States or any such agency.

TITLE IV—CREATION OF JOINT COMMITTEE TO STUDY AND REPORT ON BASIC PROBLEMS AFFECTING FRIENDLY LABOR RELATIONS AND PRODUCTIVITY

SEC. 401. There is hereby established a joint congressional committee to be known as the Joint Committee on Labor-Management Relations (hereafter referred to as the committee), and to be composed of seven Members of the Senate Committee on Labor and Public Welfare, to be appointed by the President pro tempore of the Senate, and seven Members of the House of Representatives Committee on Education and Labor, to be appointed by the Speaker of the House of Representatives. A vacancy in membership of the committee shall not affect the powers of the remaining members to execute the functions of the committee, and shall be filled in the same manner as the original selection. The committee shall select a chairman and a vice chairman from among its members.

SEC. 402. The committee, acting as a whole or by subcommittee, shall conduct a thorough study and investigation of the entire field of labor-management relations, including but not limited to—

(1) the means by which permanent friendly cooperation between employers and employees and stability of labor relations may be secured throughout the United States;

(2) the means by which the individual employee may achieve a greater productivity and higher wages, including plans for guaranteed annual wages, incentive profit-sharing and bonus systems;

(3) the internal organization and administration of labor unions, with special attention to the impact on individuals of collective agreements requiring membership in unions as a condition of employment;

(4) the labor relations policies and practices of employers and associations of employers;

(5) the desirability of welfare funds for the benefit of employees and their relation to the social-security system;

(6) the methods and procedures for best carrying out the collective bargaining processes, with special attention to the effects of industry-wide or regional bargaining upon the national economy;

(7) the administration and operation of existing Federal laws relating to labor relations; and—

(8) such other problems and subjects in the field of labor-management relations as the committee deems appropriate.

SEC. 403. The committee shall report to the Senate and the House of Representatives not later than March 15, 1948, the results of its study and investigation, together with such recommendations as to necessary legislation and such other recommendations as it may deem advisable, and shall make its final report not later than January 2, 1949.

SEC. 404. The committee shall have the power, without regard to the civil service laws and the Classification Act of 1923, as amended, to employ and fix the compensation of such officers, experts, and employees as it deems necessary for the performance of its duties, including consultants who shall receive compensation at a rate not to exceed $35 for each day actually spent by them in the work of the committee, together with their necessary travel and subsistence expenses. The committee is further authorized, with the consent of the head of the department or agency concerned, to utilize the services, information, facilities, and personnel of all agencies in the executive branch of the Government and may request the governments of the several States, representatives of business, industry, finance, and labor, and such other persons, agencies, organizations, and instrumentalities as it deems appropriate to attend its hearing and to give and present information, advice, and recommendations.

SEC. 405. The committee, or any subcommittee thereof, is authorized to hold such hearings; to sit and act at such times and places during the sessions, recesses, and adjournment periods of the Eightieth Congress; to require by subpena or otherwise the attendance of such witnesses and the production of such books, papers, and documents; to administer oaths; to take testimony; to have such printing and binding done; and to make such expenditures within the amount appropriated therefor; as it deems advisable. The cost of stenographic services in reporting such hearings shall not be in excess of 25 cents per one hundred words. Subpenas shall be issued under the signature of the chairman or vice chairman of the committee and shall be served by any person designated by them.

SEC. 406. The members of the committee shall be reimbursed for travel, subsistence, and other necessary expenses incurred by them in the performance of the duties vested in the committee, other than expenses in connection with meetings of the committee held in the District of Columbia during such times as the Congress is in session.

SEC. 407. There is hereby authorized to be appropriated the sum of $150,000, or so much thereof as may be necessary, to carry out the provisions of this title, to be disbursed by the Secretary of the Senate on vouchers signed by the chairman.

TITLE V

DEFINITIONS

SEC. 501. When used in this Act—

(1) The term "industry affecting commerce" means any industry or activity in commerce or in which a labor dispute would burden or obstruct commerce or tend to burden or obstruct commerce or the free flow of commerce.

(2) The term "strike" includes any strike or other concerted stoppage of work by employees (including a stoppage by reason of the expiration of a collective bargaining agreement) and any concerted slow-down or other concerted interruption of operations by employees.

(3) The terms "commerce", "labor disputes", "employer", "employee", "labor organization", "representative", "person", and "supervisor" shall have the same meaning as when used in the National Labor Relations Act as amended by this Act.

SAVING PROVISION

SEC. 502. Nothing in this Act shall be construed to require an individual employee to render labor or service without his consent, nor shall anything in this Act be construed to make the quitting of his labor by an individual employee an illegal act; nor shall any court issue any process to compel the performance by an individual employee of such labor or service, without his consent; nor shall the quitting of labor by an employee or employees in good faith because of abnormally dangerous conditions for work at the place of employment of such employee or employees be deemed a strike under this Act.

SEPARABILITY

SEC. 503. If any provision of this Act, or the application of such provision to any person or circumstance, shall be held invalid, the remainder of this Act, or the application of such provision to persons or circumstances other than those as to which it is held invalid, shall not be affected thereby.

Approved, June 23, 1947.

THE ORIGINS

Report of the Senate Committee on Labor and Public Welfare
April 17, 1947 (With Minority Views)

ROBERT TAFT [R., OHIO] submitted the Report.

The Committee on Labor and Public Welfare reports an original bill (S. 1126) to amend the National Labor Relations Act, to provide additional facilities for the mediation of labor disputes affecting commerce, to equalize legal responsibilities of labor organizations and employers, and for other purposes, and recommends that the bill do pass.

The problem of the inadequacy of existing laws on industrial relations is one of grave national concern. The basic Federal law on this subject is contained in two statutes—the Norris-LaGuardia Act of 1932 and the National Labor Relations Act of 1935. Enacted at the time when millions of persons were unemployed and labor organizations were relatively weak and ineffective, these statutes, despite their experimental character, have not been changed in any respect since their original enactment.

While the committee does not believe that social gains which industrial employees have received by reason of these statutes should be impaired in any degree, we do feel that to the extent that such statutes, together with the regulations issued under them, and decisions regarding them, have produced specific types of injustice, or clear inequities between employers and employees, Congress should remedy the situation by precise and carefully drawn legislation.

The need for congressional action has become particularly acute as a result of increased industrial strife. In 1945 this occasioned the loss of approximately 38,000,000 man-days of labor through strikes. This total was trebled in 1946 when there were 116,000,000 man-days lost and the number of strikes reached the unprecedented figure of 4,985.

This bill, formulated by the committee in an attempt to solve some of the more pressing difficulties with which the Nation is confronted, represents the results of numerous hearings before the committee extending over a period of more than 5 weeks. The committee heard 83 witnesses representing not only management, labor organizations, and the Government but also the general public. The actual drafting of the bill was done in executive sessions of the committee during the last 4 weeks, in which almost daily meetings were held. As an indication of the interest in the subject matter, the entire membership of the committee was present at the meetings in which the draft was perfected. Virtually every Senator on the committee made an important contribution to its provisions.

The committee bill is predicated upon our belief that a fair and equitable labor policy can best be achieved by equalizing existing laws in a manner which will encourage free collective bargaining. Government decisions should not be substituted for free agreement but both sides—management and organized labor—must recognize that the rights of the general public are paramount.

The need for such legislation is urgent. Supreme Court interpretations of the Norris-LaGuardia Anti-Injunction Act and the Clayton Act seem to have placed union activities, no matter how destructive to the rights of the individual workers and employers who are conforming to the National Labor Relations Act, beyond the pale of Federal law. Moreover, the administration of the National Labor Relations Act itself has tended to destroy the equality of bargaining power necessary to maintain industrial peace. This is due in part to the one-sided character of the act itself, which, while affording relief to employees and labor organizations for certain undesirable practices on the part of management, denies to management any redress for equally undesirable actions on the part of labor organizations. Moreover, as a result of certain administrative practices which developed in the early period of the act, the Board has acquired a reputation for partisanship, which the committee bill seeks to overcome, by insisting upon certain procedural reforms.

In the course of its deliberations, the committee considered many other proposals, such as restricting alleged monopolistic practices by unions, the formulation of a code of rights for individual members of trade unions, and a clarification of the problem of union-welfare funds. In excluding these matters from the purview of the bill, the majority of the committee should not be understood as regarding such proposals as unsound or unworkable, but rather that the problems involved should receive more extended study by a special joint congressional committee for which the committee bill specifically provides. In other words, the committee in this bill attempted to embody reforms which are long overdue and with respect to which the record of the hearings revealed widespread agreement on the part of informed and impartial persons.

The bill is divided into four titles: Title I amends the National Labor Relations Act to achieve the purposes to which reference has been made. Title II creates a new Federal Mediation Service, which transfers the functions of the Department of Labor in the field of conciliation, along with the property and personnel of the present Service. It also provides special procedures for the Attorney General and the President to utilize in national emergencies. Title III gives labor unions the right to sue and be sued as legal entities for breach of contract in the Federal courts. Title IV establishes a joint Committee of the Congress to make a long-range study of certain aspects of labor relations, concerning which further information was thought desirable by the committee. Title V contains definitions.

The major changes which the bill would make in the National Labor Relations Act may be summarized as follows:

1. It eliminates the genuine supervisor from the coverage of the act as an employee and makes it clear that he should be deemed a part of management.

2. It abolishes the closed shop but permits voluntary agreements for requiring such forms of compulsory membership as the union shop or maintenance of membership, provided that a majority of the employees authorize their representatives to make such contracts. It also protects employees against discharge, if unions deny or terminate their membership for capricious reasons.

3. It gives employers and individual employees rights to invoke the processes of the Board against unions which engaged in certain enumerated unfair labor practices, including secondary boycotts and jurisdictional strikes, which may result in the Board itself applying for restraining orders in certain cases.

4. It reorganizes the central structure of the National Labor Relations Board not only by providing for the addition of four new members to the present Board of three, but by placing upon the members individual responsibility in performing their judicial functions. This would be accomplished by eliminating the review section of the legal staff and the reviewing personnel of the Trial Examining Division.

5. In the interests of assuring complete freedom of choice to employees who do not wish to be represented collectively as well as those who do, it requires the Board to enlarge the rights of petition in representation cases and to give greater attention to the special problems of craftsmen and professional employees in the determination of bargaining units.

6. It prevents the Board from continuing to accord affiliated unions special advantages at the expense of independent labor organizations, by requiring that, under identical circumstances, the Board in complaint cases refrain from any disparity of treatment.

SUPERVISORY PERSONNEL

A recent development which probably more than any other single factor has upset any real balance of power in the collective bargaining process has been the successful efforts of labor organizations to invoke the Wagner Act for covering supervisory personnel, traditionally regarded as part of management, into organizations composed of or subservient to the unions of the very men they were hired to supervise. It was not until 1945, after several changes in position, that the National Labor Relations Board itself by divided vote finally decided that supervisory employees were covered by the National Labor Relations Act. This construction was recently upheld in the Supreme Court in the *Packard Motor Car case* (decided March 10,

1947). It should be noted that the majority of the Court in this case did not approve the policy of the Board's doctrine but, in the absence of any specific limitation upon the word "employee" in the Wagner Act, merely held that the Board had power to reach such a conclusion. This means, as Mr. Justice Douglas pointed out in his dissenting opinion—and as Board counsel conceded in argument—that unless Congress amends the act in this respect its processes can be used to unionize even vice presidents since they are not specifically exempted from the category of "employees."

The Board has placed the issue squarely up to the Congress by stating in one of its recent decisions:

So long as the Congress of the United States imposes no limitation on their choice, it is not for us to do so (*Jones & Laughlin Steel Corp.,* 71 N. L. R. B. 1261).

The folly of permitting a continuation of this policy is dramatically illustrated by what has happened in the captive mines of the Jones & Laughlin Steel Corp. since supervisory employees were organized by the United Mine Workers under the protection of the act. Disciplinary slips issued by the underground supervisors in these mines have fallen off by two-thirds and the accident rate in each mine has doubled. (See testimony of H. Parker Sharp, hearings on S. 55 and S. J. Res. 22, vol. 1, p. 339, *Re Jones and Laughlin Steel Corp.,* 71 N. L. R. B. 1261.)

In drawing an amendment to meet this situation, the committee has not been unmindful of the fact that certain employees with minor supervisory duties have problems which may justify their inclusion in that act. It has therefore distinguished between straw bosses, leadmen, set-up men, and other minor supervisory employees, on the one hand, and the supervisor vested with such genuine management prerogatives as the right to hire or fire, discipline, or make effective recommendations with respect to such action. In other words the committee has adopted the test which the Board itself has made in numerous cases when it has permitted certain categories of supervisory employees to be included in the same bargaining unit with the rank and file. (*Bethlehem Steel Company, Sparrows Point Division,* 65 N. L. R. B. 284 (expediters); *Pittsburgh Equitable Meter Company,* 61 N. L. R. B. 880 (group leaders with authority to give instructions and to lay out the work); *Richards Chemical Works,* 65 N. L. R. B. 14 (supervisors who are mere conduits for transmitting orders); *Endicott-Johnson,* 67 N. L. R. B. 1342, 1347 (persons having the title of foreman and assistant foreman but with no authority other than to keep production moving).)

Before formulating this definition, the committee considered a proposal, occasionally advanced, which would have limited the protection of foremen to joining or organizing unions whose membership was confined to supervisory personnel and not affiliated with either of the major labor federations.

After considerable discussion, the committee decided that any such compromise would be completely unrealistic. There is nothing in the record developed before this committee to justify the conclusion that there is such a thing as a really independent foremen's organization.

It is true that the Foremen's Association of America is nominally independent, but its president admitted in testifying before us that it was the practice of his union to confer with representatives of various CIO and AFL unions to work out a common policy in the event of a strike. (See testimony of Robert H. Keys, id., vol. 3, pp. 232–233.) A number of Board cases are studded with evidence showing collaboration both in the organizing stage and in concerted activity between the Foremen's Association and affiliated unions. (See *Re Chrysler Corp.* 69 N. L. R. B. 182; *Re B. F. Goodrich,* 65 N. L. R. B. 294; and *Re L. A. Young Spring Wire,* 65 N. L. R. B. 298.) It also appeared that the only major company in mass-production industry which has had a collective agreement with the Foremen's Association is the Ford Motor Co. Although this was cited by the Foremen's Association as refuting industry's fears that productivity would suffer if it entered into collective relations with supervisors, it is significant that within the past week this very company has served notice of its termination of its agreement with the association. The termination was accompanied with a statement of the company that—

After 3 years' experience . . . the results have been the opposite of what we have hoped for. Rather than exerting its efforts to bring foremen into closer relationship with management, your association has worked in the opposite direction.

It is natural to expect that unless this Congress takes action, management will be deprived of the undivided loyalty of its foremen. There is an inherent tendency to subordinate their interests wherever they conflict with those of the rank and file. As one witness put it, "Two groups of people working on parallel lines eventually find a parallel interest." (See testimony of James D. Francis, id., vol. 1, p. 239.)

In recommending the adoption of this amendment, the committee is trying to make clear what Congress attempted to demonstrate last year when it adopted the Case bill. By drawing a more definite line between management and labor we believe the proposed language has fully met some of the technical criticisms to the corresponding section referred to in the President's veto of that bill. It should be noted that all that the bill does is to leave foremen in the same position in which they were until the Labor Board reversed the position it had originally taken in 1943 in the *Maryland Drydock case* (49 N. L. R. B. 733). In other words, the bill does not prevent anyone from organizing nor does it prohibit any employer from recognizing a union of foremen. It merely relieves employers who are subject to the national act free from any compulsion by this National Board or any local agency to accord to the front line of management the anomalous status of employees.

COMPULSORY UNION MEMBERSHIP

A controversial issue to which the committee has devoted the most mature deliberation has been the problem posed by compulsory union membership. It should be noted that when the railway workers were given the protection of the Railway Labor Act, Congress thought that the provisions which prevented discrimination against union membership and provided for the certification of bargaining representatives obviated the justification for closed-shop or union-shop arrangements. That statute specifically forbids any kind of compulsory unionism.

The argument has often been advanced that Congress is inconsistent in not applying this same principle to the National Labor Relations Act. Under that statute a proviso to section 8 (3) permits voluntary agreements for compulsory union membership provided they are made with an unassisted labor organization representing a majority of the employees at the time the contract is made. When the committees of the Congress in 1935 reported the bill which became the present National Labor Relations Act, they made clear that the proviso in section 8 (3) was not intended to override State laws regulating the closed shop. The Senate committee stated that "the bill does nothing to facilitate closed-shop agreements or to make them legal in any State where they may be illegal" (S. Rept. No. 573, 74th Cong., 1st sess., p. 11; see also H. Rept. No. 1147, 74th Cong., 1st sess., pp. 19–20). Until the beginning of the war only a relatively small minority of employees (less than 20 percent) were affected by contracts containing any compulsory features. According to the Secretary of Labor, however, within the last 5 years over 75 percent now contain some form of compulsion. But with this trend, abuses of compulsory membership have become so numerous there has been great public feeling against such arrangements. This has been reflected by the fact that in 12 States such agreements have been made illegal either by legislative act or constitutional amendment, and in 14 other States proposals for abolishing such contracts are now pending. Although these regulatory measures have not received authoritative interpretation by the Supreme Court (see *A. F. of L.* v. *Watson,* 327 U. S. 582), it is obvious that they pose important questions of accommodating Federal and State legislation touching labor relations in industries affecting commerce (*Hill* v. *Florida,* 325 U. S. 538; see also, *Bethlehem Steel Co.* v. *N. Y. Labor Board,* decided by the Supreme Court April 7, 1947). In testifying before this committee, however, leaders of organized labor have stressed the fact that in the absence of such provisions many employees sharing the benefits of what unions are able to accomplish by collective bargaining will refuse to pay their share of the cost.

The committee has taken into consideration these arguments in reaching what it considers a solution of the problem which does justice to both points of view. We have felt that on the record before us the abuses of the system have become too serious and numerous to justify permitting present law to remain unchanged. It is clear that the closed shop which requires pre-existing union membership as a condition of obtaining employment creates too great a barrier to free employment to be longer tolerated. In the maritime industry and to a large extent in the construction industry union hiring halls now provide the only method of securing employment. This not only permits unions holding such monopolies over jobs to exact excessive fees but it deprives management of any real choice of the men it hires. Extension of this principle to licensed deck and engine officers has created the greatest problems in connection with the safety of American vessels at sea. (See testimony of Almon E. Roth, id., vol. 2, p. 612.)

Numerous examples were presented to the committee of the way union leaders have used closed-shop devices as a method of depriving employees of their jobs, and in some cases a means of securing a livelihood in their trade or calling, for purely capricious reasons. In one instance a union member was subpenaed to appear in court, having witnessed an assault upon his foreman by a fellow employee. Because he told the truth upon the witness stand, the union leadership brought about his expulsion with a consequent loss of his job since his employer was subject to a closed-shop contract. (See testimony of William L. McGrath, id., vol. 4, p. 1982.)

Numerous examples of equally glaring disregard for the rights of minority members of unions are contained in the exhibits received in evidence by the committee. (See testimony of Cecil B. DeMille, id., vol. 2. p. 797; see also, id., vol. 4, pp. 2063–2071.) If trade-unions were purely fraternal or social organizations, such instances would not be a matter of congressional concern, but since membership in such organizations in many trades or callings is essential to earning a living, Congress cannot ignore the existence of such power.

Under the amendments which the committee recommends, employers would still be permitted to enter into agreements requiring all the employees in a given bargaining unit to become members 30 days after being hired if a majority of such employees have shown their intent by secret ballot to confer authority to negotiate such an agreement upon their representatives. But in order to safeguard the rights of employees after such a contract has been entered into, three additional safeguards are provided: (1) Membership in the union must be available to an employee on the same terms and conditions generally applicable to other members; (2) expulsion from a union cannot be a ground of compulsory discharge if the worker is not delinquent in paying his initiation fee or dues; (3) if a worker is denied membership or expelled from the union because he exercises the right conferred on him by the act to work for the change of a bargaining representative at an appropriate time he cannot be discharged.

It seems to us that these amendments remedy the most serious abuses of compulsory union membership and yet give employers and unions who feel that such agreements promoted stability by eliminating "free riders" the right to continue such arrangements.

UNFAIR PRACTICES BY UNIONS

During the public hearings, testimony was presented relating to practices by labor organizations and their agents, which have seriously interfered with commerce and unduly impinged upon the rights of individual employees, employers, and the public. It was made abundantly clear that the Government, under existing legislation and court decisions, is unable to cope with union practices that injure the national well-being. The committee believes that such practices must be corrected if stable and orderly labor relations are to be achieved. Many and diverse proposals designed to define and correct those union practices which are probably the subject of federal control, have been presented to the committee, by witnesses who appeared before us as well as by members of the committee. Both witnesses and committee members were in substantial accord that many union practices, especially secondary boycotts, jurisdictional disputes, violations of collective bargaining contracts, and strikes and boycotts against certifications of the National Labor Relations Board, should be subject to federal regulation. With respect to other aspects of labor-management relations, there has been a considerable divergence of opinion as to the necessity for federal regulation. Moreover, witnesses and committee members have made numerous suggestions as to the form in which legislative action to remedy unfair practices by unions should be cast.

After a careful consideration of the evidence and proposals before us, the committee has concluded that five specific practices by labor organizations and their agents, affecting commerce, should be defined as unfair labor practices. Because of the nature of certain of these practices, especially jurisdictional disputes, and secondary boycotts and strikes for specifically defined objectives, the committee is convinced that additional procedures must be made available under the National Labor Relations Act in order adequately to protect the public welfare which is inextricably involved in labor disputes.

Time is usually of the essence in these matters, and consequently the relatively slow procedure of Board hearing and order, followed many months later by an enforcing decree of the circuit court of appeals, falls short of achieving the desired objectives—the prompt elimination of the obstructions to the free flow of commerce and encouragement of the practice and procedure of free and private collective bargaining. Hence we have provided that the Board, acting in the public interest and not in vindication of purely private rights, may seek injunctive relief in the case of all types of unfair labor practices and that it shall also seek such relief in the case of strikes and boycotts defined as unfair labor practices. In addition, we have provided that the Board shall be authorized to appoint arbitrators to hear and determine jurisdictional disputes concerning work tasks, if the parties fail to adjust the disputes within 10 days. Pursuant to this authorization, arbitration awards are to have the same force as final orders of the Board.

REORGANIZATION OF THE BOARD

The committee believes that certain changes in the structure and procedures of the National Labor Relations Board are necessary to meet widespread and justifiable criticism. There is no field in which time is more important, yet the Board is from 12 and 18 months behind in its docket. While this condition is due in part to the fact that limited appropriations have made it necessary to curtail the size of the staff in the face of a phenomenal postwar case load, this is not the entire explanation. Much of this delay stems from the fact that the three Board members are so overburdened with the duty of deciding contested cases that they have little or no time to give to problems of internal administration. The result is that the duties of supervision have had to be delegated to subordinate officers who are inured to following a groove of traditional methods. The expansion of the Board from three to seven members, which this bill proposes, would permit it to operate in panels of three, thereby increasing by 100 percent its ability to dispose of cases expeditiously in the final stage, and to leave the remaining member, not presently assigned to either panel, to deal with problems of administration, personnel, expenditures, and the preparation of the budget.

One of the major criticisms of the Board's performance of its judicial duties has been that the members themselves, except on the most important cases, have fallen into the habit of delegating the reviewing of the transcripts of the hearings and findings of trial examiners to a unit of the general counsel's office called the Review Section. This means that after exceptions are filed and oral argument is scheduled, the Board members rely for their knowledge of the cases upon a memorandum submitted by one of the review attorneys. The memorandum sent to each member is identical and has been already reviewed and revised by the supervisory employees of this Section, even though they have not seen the transcripts or familiarized themselves with the briefs and bills of exception. Unless the final memorandum, therefore, differs from the trial examiner's report in major respects, the attention of the Board members may not be focused upon the sharpest issues in the case.

After the Board has voted, it has also been the practice to assign to the Review Section the duty of preparing a draft opinion. Consequently, unless there is a dissent which one of the majority members sees fit to answer, both the decision and the form in which it appears are virtually a product of the corporate personality of this legal section. In other words, the Board, instead of acting like an appellate court where the divergent views of the different justices may be reflected in each decision, tends to dispose of cases in an institutional fashion. To that extent, the congressional purpose in having the act administered by a Board of several members rather than a single administrator has been frustrated.

Since it is the belief of the committee that Congress intended the Board to function like a court, this bill eliminates the Review Section. In its place each Board member may have as many legal assistants of his own as is necessary to review transcripts and assist him in the drafting of the opinions on cases to which he is assigned. Since the Board's function is largely a judicial one, conformance with the practices of appellate courts in this respect should make for decisions which will truly represent the considered opinions of the Board members.

A corollary to this reform relates to the Trial Examining Division. Tremendous responsibility rests upon the judgment of the individual trial examiner who is sent by the Board to the field to hear contested cases, appraise the credibility of the witnesses, resolve conflicts in testimony, make findings of fact and recommendations for Board decision. Under current practice, before a trial examiner issues his report to the parties, its contents are reviewed and frequently changed or influenced by the supervisory employees in the Trial Examining Division. Yet, since the report is signed only by the trial examiner, the Board holds him out as the sole person who has made a judgment on the evidence developed at the hearing. In the first *Morgan case* (298 U. S. 468, at 480–481), one of the leading decisions on administrative law, the Supreme Court enunciated the following principle:

> If the one who determines the facts which underlie the order has not considered evidence or argument, it is manifest that the hearing has not been given . . . The one who decides must hear . . .
>
> This necessary rule does not preclude . . . obtaining the aid of assistants.

It would be difficult to think of a practice which does greater violence to this principle. Consequently, the committee bill prohibits any of the staff from influencing or reviewing the trial examiner's report in advance of publication, thereby obviating the need for reviewing personnel in the Trial Examining Division.

Another questionable practice which the committee has considered has been the attendance of trial examiners at executive sessions of the Board when cases are being decided. Under its rules, the Board gives the parties adversely affected by the trial examiner's report an opportunity to appear by counsel before the Board to argue exceptions. The rules also permit opposing counsel to appear to defend findings in a trial examiner's report which represent his position in the case. It is therefore unfair to the parties to permit a trial examiner, after his findings have alternately been assailed and defended at public hearing, to make a final defense of his publshed determination behind the scenes. It would seem unnecessary to legislate in this matter at all (since the Board has it in its own power to correct these practices) if it were not for the fact that even the present Board has persisted in adhering to such unjudicial practices.

REFORM IN REPRESENTATION PROCEEDINGS

In recent years, the number of cases involving disputes with respect to the choice of bargaining representatives in the units which they should represent have become the major business of the National Labor Relations Board. Cases of this character for the last 4 years have been more than double the number of complaint cases. In view of the tremendous number of such cases, therefore, it is of utmost importance that the regulations and rules of decision by which they are governed be drawn so as to insure to employees the fullest freedom of choice.

The present act contains virtually no directions as to how representation proceedings are to be conducted nor does it furnish any guide to the Board as to the kind of bargaining unit to be established. It gives the Board latitude to select among craft, plant, and employer units, or subdivisions thereof. The only standard which the present act contains is that the unit decided upon must—

insure to employees the full benefit of their right to self-organization and to collective bargaining and otherwise to effectuate the policies of the act.

Many of the current procedures developed administratively are properly subject to the criticism that the Board has made collective bargaining "a one-way street." Despite the absence of discriminatory language in the act, the Board refuses to entertain petitions filed by employees who wish to demonstrate that the current or asserted bargaining representative is not the choice of the majority. The only relief for employees suffering from representation by a radical or racketeering union is to file a petition designating another union as their representative. This, of course, puts a premium upon raiding and jurisdictional rivalries. The committee bill would make it necessary for the Board to entertain petitions from employees irrespective of the kind of relief sought. It does not change the Board's rule of decision with respect to requirements of substantiality in order to obtain a hearing or the rules which militate against a change in bargaining representatives while a lawful collective agreement is in effect.

The present Board rules also discriminate against employers who have reasonable grounds for believing that labor organizations claiming to represent their employees are really not the choice of the majority. It is true that where an employer is confronted with conflicting claims by two or more labor organizations, he may file a petition. But where only one union is in the picture, the Board denies him this right. Consequently, even though a union which has the right to petition and be certified as the majority representative, if it is really such, may strike for recognition, an employer has no recourse to the Board for settlement of such disputes by the peaceful procedures provided for by the act. The one-sided character of the Board's rules has been defended on the ground that if an employer could petition at any time, he could effectively frustrate the desire of his employees to organize by asking for an election on the first day that a union organizer distributed leaflets at his plant. It should be noted that this may be a valid argument for placing some limitation upon an employer's right to petition, but it is no justification for denying it entirely. The committee has recognized this argument insofar as it has point, by giving employers a right to file a petition but not until a union has actually claimed a majority or demanded exclusive recognition. It should be observed that this amendment, like the amendment doing away with disparity of treatment on employee petitions, does not impair the Board's discretion to dismiss petitions by employers where the existence of an outstanding collective agreement or some other special condition makes an election at that time inappropriate.

The committee bill also contains certain standards to guide the Board in unit determinations, thereby meeting some of the valid objections voiced to certain current rules of decision. When Congress passed the National Labor Relations Act, it recognized that the community of interests among members of a skilled craft might be quite different from those of unskilled employees in mass-production industry. Although there has been a trend in recent years for manufacturing corporations to employ many professional persons, including architects, engineers, scientists, lawyers, and nurses, no corresponding recognition was given by Congress to their special problems. Nevertheless such employees have a great community of interest in maintaining certain professional standards. At the hearings, representatives of various professional associations appeared before the committee to protest against the occasional practice of the Board of covering professional personnel into general units of production and maintenance employees or general units of office and clerical employees, despite the fact that their interests in common with such groups was extremely limited. (See testimony of representatives of the American Society of Civil Engineers, American Chemical Association, American Nurses Association, and the American Institute of Architects, hearing, vol. 3, pp. 1702–1715.) Since their number is always small in comparison with production or clerical employees, collective agreements seldom reflect their desires. Under the committee bill, the Board is required to afford such groups an opportunity to vote in a separate unit to ascertain whether or not they wish to have a bargaining representative of their own.

Somewhat similar treatment is provided for members of genuine craft unions. Generally speaking, in plants which have not been organized, the Board has provided an opportunity for craftsmen to vote in a separate unit and thus secure representation of their own if the vote reflects that desire (*Globe Machine and Stamping Company,* 3 N. L. R. B. 294). Where a company has already been organized, however, the Board does not apply this doctrine unless it is consistent with prior bargaining history. Since the decision in the *American Can case* (13 N. L. R. B. 1252), where the Board refused to permit craft units to be "carved out" from a broader bargaining unit already established, the Board, except under unusual circumstances, has virtually compelled skilled artisans to remain parts of a comprehensive plant unit. The committee regards the application of this doctrine as inequitable. Our bill still leaves to the Board discretion to review all the facts in determining the appropriate unit, but it may not decide that any craft unit is inappropriate on the ground that a different unit has been established by a prior Board determination.

Another important procedural change relates to the rules on run-off elections. Under present regulations, if two or more unions are on the ballot and none of the choices receives a plurality in the first elections, the regional directors are authorized to conduct a run-off. Unless the vote for "neither" or "none" is a plurality, however, the employees are limited in the run-off to a choice between two unions, even though one of these unions might have run in third place. The bill proposes to correct this inequity by requiring that, on the run-off, the ballot give the employees an option between the two highest choices. This would make representation proceedings conform more closely to public elections. In order to impress upon employees the solemnity of their choice, when the Government goes to the expense of conducting a secret ballot, the bill also provides that elections in any given unit may not be held more frequently than once a year.

EQUALITY OF TREATMENT FOR INDEPENDENT UNIONS

Another problem to which the committee gave considerable thought was the extent to which independent unions have a real grievance under current policies and practices of the Board. It has been the contention of leaders of the independents for many years that the Board had one rule for independent unions and another one for organizations affiliated with the A. F. of L. or the CIO. There is no doubt that since the passage of the National Labor Relations Act, independent unions have dwindled greatly in numbers. To the extent that this change has come about through the provisions of section

8 (2), which forbids employers to dominate or contribute financial or other support to labor organizations, the committee has not seen fit to make any changes in the present act. It believes that employers should not be permitted to take a hand in the internal affairs of labor organizations, whether affiliated or unaffiliated, or to extend financial assistance to them. In one respect, however, the independent unions do have just cause for complaint under current administrative practice of the Board. If an unaffiliated union gains a foothold in a plant through employer encouragement or support, or if some of the supervisory employees join it—*Brown Company* (65 N. L. R. B. 208)—the Board's practice is to issue a complaint under section 8 (2) and if it finds the allegations to be supported by the evidence, to order the company forever to refrain from recognizing such an organization. (See *Tappan Stove Company,* 66 N. L. R. B. 759, and *Brown Company* (supra).) This is called an order of disestablishment. An organization affected by such an order, no matter if its members and officers purge themselves of the taint of employer domination or interference, is never thereafter permitted recognition. Moreover, neither such an organization nor any successor, no matter how free of employer influence, is subsequently permitted a place on the ballot in a representation case even though, in fact, it may represent the overwhelming choice of the employees.

The Board's policy with respect to affiliated unions is much more lenient. An affiliated union may obtain a collusive contract without representing any of the employees, it may have been organized by supervisors, or it may be receiving a subsidy from an employer. It is true that the Board recognizes that such unions are the beneficiaries of unfair labor practices. Under such circumstances, however, the Board will frame its complaints under subsection 8 (1) and its order will be limited to directing the offending employer to break off relations with the labor organization until such time as it has been certified by the Board. Under current practice, if an employer complies with such an order, an affiliated organization is then permitted to file an election petition 60 days after such a determination. (See *Ohio Valley Bus Co.,* 38 N. L. R. B. 838; *Ace Sample Card Co.,* 46 N. L. R. B. 129; and *Pennsylvania Handbag Company,* 41 N. L. R. B. 1454.) The Board's defense of this disparate practice is that unions affiliated with national organizations stand on a different footing and that a local union chartered by a national body cannot "at least for an extended period of time, be used as a utensil of an employer to deprive employees of free exercise of the rights guaranteed by the act." (See testimony of Chairman Paul M. Herzog, vol. 4, p. 1912.) While this may be true as a general proposition, it is also possible, from the very nature of employee organizational activities, that an independent union which has received employer encouragement may ultimately free itself completely from his control. This is particularly true in view of the fact that what the Board calls domination in independent union cases may merely amount to the mildest kind of support. (See *Brown Company,* supra.) In any event, this is certainly a justiciable issue which should be decided in accordance with the facts of each case and not upon the basis of the a priori reasoning of the Board in 1936. The committee has, therefore, proposed an amendment to section 10 of the act which will assure the application of a fair and uniform rule of decision to both independent and affiliated unions in complaint and representation proceedings.

SETTLEMENT OF LABOR DISPUTES

In dealing with the problem of the direct settlement of labor disputes the committee has considered a great variety of the proposals ranging from compulsory arbitration, the establishment of fact-finding boards, creation of an over-all mediation tribunal, and the imposition of specified waiting periods. In our judgment, while none of the suggestions is completely devoid of merit, the experience of the Federal Government with such devices has been such that we do not feel warranted in recommending that any such plans become permanent legislation.

Under the exigencies of war the Nation did utilize what amounted to compulsory arbitration through the instrumentality of the War Labor Board. This system, however, tended to emphasize unduly the rule of the Government, and under it employers and labor organizations tended to avoid solving their difficulties by free collective bargaining. It is difficult to see how such a system could be operated indefinitely without compelling the Government to make decisions on economic issues which in normal times should be solved by the free play of economic forces. Moreover, the wartime experiment of the 30-day waiting period under the War Labor Disputes Act was not a happy one, since it was too frequently used as a device for bringing to a rapid crisis disputes which might have been solved by patient negotiation. For similar reasons except in dire emergencies the establishment of fact-finding Boards or over-all mediation tribunals also cause dubious results. Recommendations of such bodies tend to set patterns of wage settlements for the entire country which are frequently inappropriate to the peculiar circumstances of certain industries and certain classes of employment.

It is our conclusion that by modifying some of the practices under the Wagner Act which tend to destroy the balance of power in collective bargaining negotiations by restraining one party to a dispute without restraining the other, Congress would go a long way toward making collective bargaining the most effective method of solving the industrial relations difficulties.

The mediation title emphasizes the importance of adjusting disputes through conferences between employers and labor organizations with the Federal Government making available to the parties in the event of an impasse the services of trained mediators. The bill provides for a Federal

Mediation Service under a single Director to be appointed by the President with the advice and consent of the Senate. The personnel and functions of the present Conciliation Service in the Department of Labor are transferred to the new Service, thereby relieving the Secretary of Labor of the burdens incident to the administration of such an agency. In taking this step the committee did not overlook the fact that the prestige of the Secretary, as an adviser to the President, is often an important factor in bringing about the settlement of a dispute of national magnitude. Accordingly, the bill should not be understood as prohibiting the Director of the new Federal Mediation Service from calling upon the Secretary of Labor for assistance in major crises.

While the committee is of the opinion that in most labor disputes the role of the Federal Government should be limited to mediation, we recognize that the repercussions from stoppages in certain industries are occasionally so grave that the national health and safety is imperiled. An example is the recent coal strike in which defiance of the President by the United Mine Workers Union compelled the Attorney General to resort to injunctive relief in the courts. The committee believes that only in national emergencies of this character should the Federal Government be armed with such power. But it also feels that this power should be available if the need arises. It should be remembered that the Supreme Court decision in *U. S.* v. *United Mine Workers* (decided March 6, 1947), did not hold in broad terms that the Government was exempted from the Norris-LaGuardia Act. The majority of the court relied in part upon the fact that the Government had previously seized the mines under the War Labor Disputes Act and that the calling of the strike by the officers of the United Mine Workers was undoubtedly a breach of the criminal provisions contained in that statute. This act, however, is only temporary legislation and expires June 30, 1947.

We concluded, therefore, that the permanent code of laws of the United States should make it clear that the Attorney General should have the power to intervene and secure judicial relief when a threatened strike or lock-out is conducted on a scale imperiling the national health or safety. Recognizing that the right to serve injunctive relief is subject to abuses, this bill is carefully drawn to guard against excessive resort to the courts. It provides that the Attorney General should not petition a Federal court for such relief until he has convened a special board of inquiry to advise him on the matter. It also requires a finding by the court that such drastic measures are necessary as a prerequisite to obtaining a temporary restraining order or other injunctive relief. It makes interlocutory orders subject to appellate review and further provides for the board of inquiry being reconvened during the period in which the Federal Mediation Service is seeking to assist the disputants in reaching a settlement.

Should all such measures prove unavailing after 60 days have elapsed, the

National Labor Relations Board is directed by the bill to poll the employees affected on the question of whether or not they wish to accept or reject the last offer of their employer. When results of such ballot are certified, the Attorney General must then ask the court to vacate the injunction. Under these provisions, any temporary restraining order or injunction would not remain in effect for more than 80 days. In most instances the force of public opinion should make itself sufficiently felt in this 80-day period to bring about a peaceful termination of the controversy. Should this expectation fail, the bill provides for the President laying the matter before Congress for whatever legislation seems necessary to preserve the health and safety of the Nation in this crisis.

ENFORCEMENT OF CONTRACT RESPONSIBILITIES

The committee bill makes collective bargaining contracts equally binding and enforceable on both parties. In the judgment of the committee, breaches of collective agreement have become so numerous that it is not sufficient to allow the parties to invoke the processes of the National Labor Relations Board when such breaches occur (as the bill proposes to do in title I). We feel that the aggrieved party should also have a right of action in the Federal courts. Such a policy is completely in accord with the purpose of the Wagner Act which the Supreme Court declared was "to compel employers to bargain collectively with their employees to the end that an employment contract, binding on both parties, should be made" (*H. J. Heinz & Co.*, 311 U. S. 514).

The laws of many States make it difficult to sue effectively and to recover a judgment against an unincorporated labor union. It is difficult to reach the funds of a union to satisfy a judgment against it. In some States it is necessary to serve all the members before an action can be maintained against the union. This is an almost impossible process. Despite these practical difficulties in the collection of a judgment against a union, the National Labor Relations Board has held it an unfair labor practice for an employer to insist that a union incorporate or post a bond to establish some sort of legal responsibility under a collective agreement.

President Truman, in opening the management-labor conference in November 1945, took cognizance of this condition. He said very plainly that collective agreements should be mutually binding on both parties to the contract:

> We shall have to find methods not only of peaceful negotiations of labor contracts, but also of insuring industrial peace for the lifetime of such contracts. Contracts once made must be lived up to and should be changed only in the manner agreed upon by the parties. If we expect confidence in agreements made, there must be responsibility and integrity on both sides in carrying them out.

If unions can break agreements with relative impunity, then such agreements do not tend to stabilize industrial relations. The execution of an agreement does not by itself promote industrial peace. The chief advantage which an employer can reasonably expect from a collective labor agreement is assurance of uninterrupted operation during the term of the agreement. Without some effective method of assuring freedom from economic warfare for the term of the agreement, there is little reason why an employer would desire to sign such a contract.

Consequently, to encourage the making of agreements and to promote industrial peace through faithful performance by the parties, collective agreements affecting interstate commerce should be enforceable in the Federal courts. Our amendment would provide for suits by unions as legal entities and against unions as legal entities in the Federal courts in disputes affecting commerce.

The amendment specifically provides that only the assets of the union can be attached to satisfy a money judgment against it; the property of the individual members of the organization would not be subject to any liability under such a judgment. Thus the members of the union would secure all the advantages of limited liability without incorporation of the union.

The initial obstacle in enforcing the terms of a collective agreement against a union which has breached its provisions is the difficulty of subjecting the union to process. The great majority of labor unions are unincorporated associations. At common law voluntary associations are not suable as such (*Wilson* v. *Airline Coal Company,* 215 Iowa 855; *Iron Molders' Union* v. *Allis-Chalmers Company,* C. C. A. 7, 166 F. 45). As a consequence the rule in most jurisdictions, in the absence of statute, is that unincorporated labor unions cannot be sued in their common name (*Grant* v. *Carpenters' District Council,* 322 Pa. St. 62). Accordingly, the difficulty or impossibility of enforcing the terms of a collective agreement in a suit at law against a union arises from the fact that each individual member of the union must be named and made a party to the suit.

Some States have enacted statutes which subject unincorporated associations to the jurisdiction of law courts. These statutes are by no means uniform; some pertain to fraternal societies, welfare organizations, associations doing business, etc., and in some States the courts have excluded labor unions from their application.

On the other hand, some States, including California and Montana, have construed statutes permitting common name suits against associations doing business to apply to labor unions (*Armstrong* v. *Superior Court,* 173 Calif. 341; *Vance* v. *McGinley,* 39 Mont. 46). Similarly, but more restrictive, in a considerable number of States the action is permitted against the union or representatives in proceedings in which the plaintiff could have maintained such an action against all the associates. Such States include Alabama, California, Connecticut, Delaware, Maryland, Montana, Nevada, New Jersey, New York, Rhode Island, South Carolina, and Vermont.

In at least one jurisdiction, the District of Columbia, the liberal view is held that unincorporated labor unions may be sued as legal entities, even in the absence of statute (*Busby* v. *Elec. Utility Empl. Union,* U. S. Court of Appeals for the District of Columbia, No. 8548, Jan. 22, 1945).

In the Federal courts, whether an unincorporated union can be sued depends upon the procedural rules of the State in which the action is brought (*Busby* v. *Elec. Util. Empl. Union,* U. S. Supreme Court, 89 Law. Adv. Op. 108, Dec. 4, 1944).

The Norris-LaGuardia Act has insulated labor unions, in the field of injunctions against liability for breach of contract. It has been held by a Federal court that strikes, picketing, or boycotting, when carried on in breach of a collective agreement, involve a "labor dispute" under the act so as to make the activity not enjoyable without a showing of the requirements which condition the issuance of an injunction under the act (*Wilson & Co.* v. *Birlin,* 105 F. (2d) 948, C. C. A. 3).

A great number of States have enacted anti-injunction statutes modeled after the Norris-LaGuardia Act, and the courts of many of these jurisdictions have held that a strike in violation of a collective agreement is a "labor dispute" and cannot be enjoined (*Nevins* v. *Kasmach,* 279 N. Y. 323; *Bulkin* v. *Sacks,* 31 Pa., D and C 501).

There are no Federal laws giving either an employer or even the Government itself any right of action against a union for any breach of contract. Thus there is no "substantive right" to enforce, in order to make the union suable as such in Federal courts.

Even where unions are suable, the union funds may not be reached for payment of damages and any judgments or decrees rendered against the association as an entity may be unenforceable. (See *Aalco Laundry Co.* v. *Laundry Linen Union,* 115 S. W. 2d 89 Mo. App.) However, only where statutes provide for recognition of the legal status of associations do association funds become subject to judgments (*Deeney* v. *Hotel & Apt. Clerks' Union,* 134 P. 2d 328 (1943), California).

Financial statutory liability of associations is provided for by some States, among which are Alabama, California, Colorado, Connecticut, Delaware, New Jersey, North Dakota, and South Carolina. Even in these States, however, whether labor unions are included within the definition of "association" is a matter of local judicial interpretation.

It is apparent that until all jurisdictions, and particularly the Federal Government, authorize actions against labor unions as legal entities, there will not be the mutual responsibility necessary to vitalize collective-bargaining agreements. The Congress has protected the right of workers to organize. It has passed laws to encourage and promote collective bargaining.

Statutory recognition of the collective agreement as a valid, binding, and enforceable contract is a logical and necessary step. It will promote a higher degree of responsibility upon the parties to such agreements, and will thereby promote industrial peace.

It has been argued that the result of making collective agreements enforceable against unions would be that they would no longer consent to the inclusion of a no-strike clause in a contract.

This argument is not supported by the record in the few States which have enacted their own laws in an effort to secure some measure of union responsibility for breaches of contract. Four States—Minnesota, Colorado, Wisconsin, and California—have thus far enacted such laws, and, so far as can be learned, no-strike clauses have been continued about as before.

In any event, it is certainly a point to be bargained over and any union with the status of "representative" under the NLRA which has bargained in good faith with an employer should have no reluctance in including a no-strike clause if it intends to live up to the terms of the contract. The improvement that would result in the stability of industrial relations is, of course, obvious.

Minority Views
April 22 (legislative day, April 21), 1947

ELBERT THOMAS [DEM., UTAH], from the Committee on Labor and Public Welfare, submitted the following Minority Views.

This bill is designed to weaken the effective program of labor legislation which has been, with great pains, built up over the years. It would be destructive of much that is valuable in the prevention of labor-management conflicts. It contains many barriers, traps, and pitfalls that can only make more difficult the settlement of disputes. Its principal results would be to create misunderstanding and conflict, and to aggravate the imbalance between wages, prices, and profits which already endangers our prosperity.

The President in his state of the Union message of January 6, 1947, recommended:

> We should enact legislation to correct certain abuses and to provide additional governmental assistance in bargaining. But we should also concern ourselves with the basic causes of labor-management difficulties.

The President outlined certain immediate steps to be taken: (*a*) Legislation to prevent jurisdictional strikes intended to compel employers to bargain with a minority union instead of the majority union in their plants;

(*b*) legislation to provide for peaceful and binding determinations of jurisdictional disputes over which union is entitled to perform a particular work task; (*c*) legislation to prohibit secondary boycotts when used to further jurisdictional disputes or to compel employers to violate the National Labor Relations Act; and (*d*) legislation to provide for final and binding arbitration of disputes concerning the interpretation of the terms of collective bargaining agreements.

We would support legislation carrying out these recommendations. We are opposed, however, to legislation which goes beyond these recommendations and undermines the foundation laid by the Administration for the promotion of free collective bargaining. We are opposed to legislation such as is included in the committee majority bill which fails to distinguish between justifiable and unjustifiable secondary boycotts and proscribes all boycotts indiscriminnately as unfair labor practices. We are also opposed to those provisions of this bill which instead of merely providing machinery for the binding determination of questions concerning the meaning of contract terms, opens the Federal courts wide to suits for breach of contract without regard to the ordinary prerequisites of Federal jurisdiction.

The President in this State of the Union message recommended as a second point in his program for dealing with labor-management controversies, the strengthening of facilities within the Department of Labor for assisting the processes of free and voluntary collective bargaining. As he stated in his message:

. . . There is need for integrated governmental machinery to provide the successive steps of mediation, voluntary arbitration, and—ultimately in appropriate cases—ascertainment of the facts of the dispute and the reporting of them to the public. Such machinery would facilitate and expedite the settlement of disputes.

The majority bill does not strengthen the facilities of the United States Conciliation Service in the Department of Labor as recommended by the President. On the contrary, it removes the Service from the Department of Labor and establishes a new Federal Mediation Service. This proposal violates sound principles of administration by adding to the already numerous existing agencies handling labor disputes and will promote disorder and confusion in the conduct of the Federal Government's conciliation and mediation activities.

The President also called in his message, as part of his program for dealing with labor disputes, for broadening Federal programs of social legislalation to alleviate the causes of workers' insecurity. The President pointed out:

On June 11, 1946, in my message vetoing the Case bill, I made a comprehensive statement of my views concerning labor-management relations. I said then, and I repeat

now, that the solution of labor-management difficulties is to be found not only in legislation dealing directly with labor relations but also in a program designed to remove
the causes of insecurity felt by many workers in our industrial society. In this connection, for example, the Congress should consider the extension and broadening of our
social-security system, better housing, a comprehensive national health program, and
provision for a fair minimum wage.

The problems involved in attempting to deal with the difficult and complicated labor controversies of this time are not merely matters of governmental machinery. We cannot approach these problems solely on the basis
of prohibitions and restrictions on the activities of private citizens whether
they be employers, labor organizations or their members. The causes of
labor-management controversy lie deep in the complex industrial and financial structure.

Without attention to the problems to which the President directed attention
in his message on the State of the Union such legislation as the Congress may
enact may well take on unwittingly the character of "vindictive," "punitive"
legislation against which the Congress has frequently been warned. Measures
to extend and broaden the social security system, to provide for better
housing, to establish a comprehensive national health program and to raise
the minimum wage under the Fair Labor Standards Act to a level commensurate with present-day conditions are pending before the Congress. In the
absence of action on these measures by this Congress, the proposal of the
majority may well promote instead of resolve the industrial discord and
strife which they, like we, wish to avoid.

The proposal of the committee majority for the formation of a joint congressional committee to study labor-management relations departs in two
important respects from the recommendation of the President with respect
to such a study. He proposed the establishment of a temporary joint commission composed not only of Members of Congress but of representatives
of the public, labor, and management. In so recommending the President
had in mind, as he said, that—

We must not, however, adopt punitive legislation. We must not, in order to punish a
few labor leaders, pass vindictive laws which will restrict the proper rights of the rank
and file of labor. We must not, under the stress of emotion endanger our American
freedoms by taking ill-considered action which will lead to results not anticipated or
desired.

We must remember, in reviewing the record of disputes in 1946, that management
shares with labor the responsibility for failure to reach agreements which would have
averted strikes. For that reason we must realize that industrial peace cannot be achieved
merely by laws directed against labor unions.

Accordingly, the President recommended that the commission which should
study labor relations should have among its members representatives whose

interests are directly involved in all labor disputes, namely, the public, management, and labor.

The President also recommended in his message that the commission which he proposed make its first report, including specific legislative recommendations, not later than March 15, 1947. The majority of the committee, however, have followed an entirely different course of action. They have attempted to deal without prior study by a commission such as that proposed by the President, with a great variety of problems grouped together in an omnibus bill which include not only matters which can properly be dealt with at this time on the basis of presently available experience and study, but also questions which require the full study and investigation which the President felt should be referred to the proposed commission, including: (1) Nation-wide strikes in vital industries affecting the public interest; (2) methods and procedures for carrying out the collective bargaining process; and (3) the underlying causes of labor-management disputes.

The committee has had before it since January 10, 1947, Senate Joint Resolution 22 which would create a temporary Labor Relations Commission to make a study and recommendations concerning labor relations along lines proposed by the President in his message. The undersigned believe that such a study is an essential preliminary to any Federal labor legislation designed to promote labor-management peace and stability which will be fair to the public, to management, and to labor alike. The majority have, however, proceeded without such an investigation and have in a single omnibus bill proposed legislation which will outlaw the closed shop and secondary boycotts, both justified and unjustified, provide for the establishment of a new independent Federal Mediation Service outside the Department of Labor, revive the use of labor injunctions in certain cases, establish complicated procedures for handling disputes in Nation-wide industries and authorize suits by and against labor organizations in the Federal courts without regard to the ordinary requirements of Federal jurisdiction.

Only such completely repressive measures as the Hartley bill (H. R. 3020) could make this measure seem "mild." Judged by the needs of the times, or the ideal of fairness in labor relations, or the evils sought to be reached, it is a harsh bill. Some few of its provisions are useful and progressive; some others are innocuous. But the remainder look backward rather than forward. They would seriously weaken collective bargaining which in recent days has provided dramatic illustrations of its efficacy as the solution of industrial problems. We do not say, and in the work of the committee have not said, that all provisions of this bill are unwise, nor have we taken the position that no legislation can be acceptable. We respect the motives of our colleagues, and on many matters we have found them reasonable and willing to eliminate proposals which to us seemed indefensible. On matters of such moment, however, judgment will differ.

President Truman and the people are aware that our present problem is one of swollen prices and high profits. One marvels at the audacity of those who, drawing to themselves an ever-increasing share of the Nation's wealth, successful with the help of congressional allies in liquidating many of the popular protections against extortion, now call for another "Battle of the Bulge" against workers' last and best protection; their trade-unions. In the name of "fairness" many of them would give more to those who have and less to those who have not; in the name of "equality" they would increase maldistribution of wealth; masquerading as protesters against monopoly they would weaken the remaining barrier to concentration of industrial power. Enough of their position is included in this bill to make it but one further example of a determination to resurrect those mistakes of 1920–29 which led inevitably to the horrors of 1929–33.

The negative attitude of this bill should be replaced by a genuinely affirmative program for the removal of the causes of worker protest and insecurity; higher minimum wages, improved safety legislation, a genuine housing program, expanded protection for the victims of our industrial society. We must go forward rather than stand still.

The bill seems to us a distillate of fears. The successive and creditable rejection by the committee of many extreme proposals (which may be renenewed) evidences a justified fear of worker retaliation at the polls. Yet the retention of many equally unwise provisions manifests a fear that those large corporate interests which have demanded repressive antilabor legislation may not be satisfied with the measure. The necessity for grudging inclusion in the bill of many presently applied rules conceals the fear of admitting that, on the whole, Federal labor policy under the wise leadership of Presidents Roosevelt and Truman has been fair, forthright, and progressive. The adoption, in some measure, as a small segment of the bill, of the program outlined by the President in his state of the Union message illustrates a fear of rejecting present objectives as the policy of the Federal Government.

This bill does not so much turn back the clock as stop it dead. To this point, our labor policy has been premised on the assumption that collective bargaining (and trade-unions which are essential to collective bargaining) are institutions to be strengthened and fostered. We have felt that there is no alternative to collective bargaining if we are to retain a democratic society. While recognizing the imperfections and occasional past failures of collective bargaining, we have sought to improve and develop it. Now this bill calls on industrial relations to mark time, as if we were to say to the medical profession that there should be no further advancement in surgery for a reason. By the denial of well-recognized rights, by hampering restrictions, and by confining rules, this measure, in the interest only of a few industrialists who have never accepted the spirit of the National Labor Relations Act, calls a halt to progress in industrial relations.

It does this in a variety of fashions:

1. It excludes entirely from the number of those who are to benefit under Federal legislation certain "agricultural" workers who are in reality industrial workers, and supervisors, who also have their problems.

2. It slices a wedge out of the Norris-LaGuardia Act by making application for labor injunctions mandatory in certain types of labor disputes.

3. It calls for the splitting up of trade-unions in many industries where collective bargaining is working well.

4. It gives an undue recognition to company-dominated unions by requiring that they be placed on the ballot under certain circumstances.

5. It requires that charges of unfair labor practices be filed within 6 months after their commission—the shortest statute of limitations known to the law thereby offering a premium to those employers who conceal commission of unfair labor practices.

6. It weakens the Conciliation Service by removing it from the Department of Labor, where it properly belongs, for no reason other than the desire to "do something," regardless of merit.

7. It severely limits the right to strike in a variety of circumstances.

8. It requires the holding of elections by the Federal Government on the issue of union security, and the holding of other elections before certain strikes become legal, despite the unhappy experience of the Smith-Connally Act.

9. In a multitude of ways it hampers the effectiveness of the National Labor Relations Board.

10. It requires labor unions to file burdensome reports with the Secretary of Labor under penalty of denial of rights under the National Labor Relations Act.

11. It provides, in the case of union-employer suits alone, that suits may be brought in Federal courts without the ordinary jurisdictional requirement of an investigating commission on labor problems.

12. It disregards in material respects President Truman's suggestions for the establishment of an investigating commission on labor problems. . . .

Report of the House Committee on Education and Labor
April 11, 1947

FRED HARTLEY [R., N. J.] submitted the following Report.

The Committee on Education and Labor, to whom was referred the bill (H. R. 3020) to prescribe fair and equitable rules of conduct to be observed by labor and management in their relations with one another which effect commerce, to protect the rights of individual workers in their relations with labor organizations whose activities affect commerce, to recognize the paramount public interest in labor disputes affecting commerce that endanger the public health, safety, or welfare, and for other purposes, having considered the same, reports favorably thereon with amendments and recommends that the bill as so amended do pass. . . .

The committee's recommendation stems from an exhaustive investigation made by the committee of the causes and effects of industrial strife. In the hearings before the committee, extending over a period of more than 6 weeks, 137 witnesses appeared. They came from all parts of the country, from many walks of life, and represented all points of view.

The committee acknowledges the vast amount of work done on the subject by the many Members of Congress, who prepared and introduced bills for consideration by the committee. They, as well as countless private citizens by correspondence with members of the committee, have made contributions of inestimable value to the formulation of the bill herewith reported.

The committee also had the benefit of the studies of committees of previous Congresses—and particularly that of the Special Committee To Investigate the National Labor Relations Board, created in the Seventy-sixth Congress, many of whose recommendations are included in the bill herewith reported.

NECESSITY FOR LEGISLATION

During the last few years, the effects of industrial strife have at times brought our country to the brink of general economic paralysis. Employees have suffered, employers have suffered—and above all the public has suffered.

The enactment of comprehensive legislation to define clearly the legitimate rights of employers and employees in their industrial relations, in keeping with the protection of the paramount public interest, is imperative.

The bill herewith reported does just that. It prescribes the rights of all parties having a stake in harmonious industrial relations, and requires that each party respect the rights of the others.

The committee believes that the enactment of the bill will have the effect of bringing widespread industrial strife to an end, and that employers and employees will once again go forward together as a team united to achieve for their mutual benefit and for the welfare of the Nation the highest standard of living yet known in the history of the world.

During the 6 years preceding the enactment of the National Industrial Recovery Act of 1933, the United States had an average of 753 strikes a year, involving an average of 297,000 workers; during the next 6 years 2,541 strikes per year involving an average of 1,181,000 workers; and during the next 5 years—that is, through 1944—3,514 strikes a year involving an average of 1,508,000 workers.

In 1945 approximately 38,000,000 man-days of labor were lost as a result of strikes. And that total was trebled in 1946, when there were 116,000,000 man-days lost and the number of strikes hit a new high of 4,985. The resulting loss in national wealth is staggering.

The above figures do not take into account the man-days lost as a result of the indirect effects of these strikes.

In the face of this record there are few who would have the temerity to assert that labor relations in the United States are today satisfactory. The American people, and their representatives of both parties in Congress, are insistent that some means be found by legislation to reverse this alarming trend and to bring about industrial peace.

In approaching the problem of general labor legislation, the committee was impressed by the absolute necessity of steering a course which would recognize the rights of all interested parties in labor relations and which would be scrupulously fair to each—the employer, the employees, and the public. While the right of the public must, in the last analysis, be treated as paramount, it was the belief of the committee, that, except in extraordinary circumstances, the right of the public will be adequately protected if in turn adequate protection is afforded to employers and employees in the exercise of their legitimate rights.

Accordingly the bill herewith reported has been formulated as a bill of rights both for American workingmen and for their employers.

For the last 14 years, as a result of labor laws ill-conceived and disastrously executed, the American workingman has been deprived of his dignity as an individual. He has been cajoled, coerced, intimidated, and on many occasions beaten up, in the name of the splendid aims set forth in section 1 of the National Labor Relations Act. His whole economic life has been subject to the complete domination and control of unregulated monopolists. He has on many occasions had to pay them tribute to get a job. He has been forced into labor organizations against his will. At other times when he has desired to join a particular labor organization he has been prevented from doing so and forced to join another one. He has been compelled to contribute to causes and candidates for public office to which he was opposed. He has been prohibited from expressing his own mind on public issues. He has been denied any voice in arranging the terms of his own employment. He has frequently against his will been called out on strikes which have resulted in wage losses representing years of his savings. In many cases his economic life has been ruled by Communists and other subversive influences. In short, his mind, his soul, and his very life have been subject to a tyranny more despotic than one could think possible in a free country.

The employer's plight has likewise not been happy. He has witnessed the productive efficiency in his plants sink to alarmingly low levels. He has been required to employ or reinstate individuals who have destroyed his property and assaulted other employees. When he has tried to discharge Communists he has been prevented from doing so by a board which called this valid reason for the discharge a mere pretext. He has seen the loyalty of his supervisors undermined by the compulsory unionism imposed upon them by the National Labor Relations Board. He has been required by law to bargain over matters to which it was economically impossible for him to accede, and when he refused to accede has been accused of failing to bargain in good faith. He has been compelled to bargain with the same union that bargains with his competitors and thus to reveal to his competitors the secrets of his business. He has had to stand helplessly by while employees desiring to enter his plant to work have been obstructed by violence, mass picketing, and general rowdyism. He has had to stand mute while irresponsible detractors slandered, abused, and vilified him.

His business on occasions has been virtually brought to a standstill by disputes to which he himself was not a party and in which he himself had no interest. And finally, he has been compelled by the laws of the greatest democratic country in the world—or at least by their administrators— to treat his employees as if they belonged to a different class or caste of society.

This sordid story was unfolded before the committee in its hearings. Those hearings demonstrate the need for action by Congress—and action now.

The bill attacks the problem in a comprehensive—not in a piecemeal—fashion. It is neither drastic, oppressive, nor punitive. It does not restrict or in any manner interfere with employees' rights to organize and to bargain collectively when they wish to do so. It does not restrict in any way employees' rights to engage in lawful strikes. It does not take away any rights guaranteed by the existing National Labor Relations Act.

It does, however, go to the root of the evils and provides a fair, workable, and long-overdue solution of the problem. In brief outline, the bill accomplishes the following:

(1) It abolishes the existing discredited National Labor Relations Board, and creates in lieu thereof a new board of fair-minded members to exercise quasi-judicial functions only.

(2) It establishes a new official to exercise the various prosecuting and investigative functions under the National Labor Relations Act, to be entirely independent of the Board.

(3) It requires the Board to act only upon the weight of credible legal evidence, and it gives to the courts of the United States a real, rather than a fictitious, power to review decisions of the Board.

(4) It outlaws the closed shop and monopolistic industry-wide bargaining.

(5) It exempts supervisors from the compulsory features of the National Labor Relations Act.

(6) It imposes on both parties to labor disputes the duty of bargaining and requires that the employees themselves be given a voice in the bargaining arrangements through the device of providing for a secret ballot of the employees on their employer's last offer of settlement of the dispute.

(7) It protects the existence of labor organizations which are not affiliated with one of the national federations.

(8) It prohibits certification by the Board of Labor organizations having Communist or subversive officers.

(9) It prescribes the rights which an individual member of a labor organization can justly claim of his union, and gives him protection in the exercise of those rights.

(10) It outlaws sympathy strikes, jurisdictional strikes, illegal boycotts, collusive strikes by employees of competing employers, as well as sit-down strikes and other concerted work interferences conducted by remaining on the employer's premises.

(11) It outlaws strikes to remedy practices for which an administrative remedy is available under the bill or to compel an employer to violate the law.

(12) It outlaws mass picketing and other forms of violence designed to prevent individuals from entering or leaving a place of employment.

(13) It outlaws picketing of a place of business where the proprietor is not involved in a labor dispute with his employees.

(14) For unlawful concerted activities it gives the person injured thereby a right to sue civilly any person responsible therefor.

(15) It prescribes unfair labor practices on the part of employees and their representatives as well as by employers.

(16) It creates a new and independent conciliation agency.

(17) It removes the exemption of labor organizations from the antitrust laws when such organizations, acting either alone or in collusion with employers, engage in unlawful restraints of trade.

(18) It makes labor organizations equally responsible with employers for contract violations and provides for suit by either against the other in the United States district courts.

(19) It provides a means for stopping strikes which imperil or threaten to imperil the public health, safety, or interest.

(20) It guarantees to employees, to employers, and to their respective representatives, the full exercise of the right of free speech.

All of the above provisions are explained in detail in the "Analysis of Provisions" portion of this report. Some of them may well be elaborated upon here with the reasons which the committee had for including them.

Report of the House Committee of Conference
June 3, 1947

FRED HARTLEY [R., N. J.] submitted the following Report.

STATEMENT OF THE MANAGERS ON THE PART OF THE HOUSE

The managers on the part of the House at the conference on the disagreeing votes of the two Houses on the amendments of the Senate to the bill (H. R. 3020) to prescribe fair and equitable rules of conduct to be observed by labor and management in their relations with one another which affect commerce, to protect the rights of individual workers in their relations with labor organizations whose activities affect commerce, to recognize the paramount public interest in labor disputes affecting commerce that endanger the public health, safety, or welfare, and for other purposes, submit the following statement in explanation of the effect of the action agreed upon by the conferees and recommended in the accompanying conference report:

SHORT TITLE

The House bill provided that it was to be cited as the "Labor-Management Relations Act, 1947". The Senate amendment (sec. 504) provided that it was to be cited as the "Federal Labor Relations Act of 1947". The conference agreement adopts the short title of the House bill.

DECLARATION OF POLICY

The House bill (sec. 1 (b)) contained an over-all declaration of policy covering all of the various matters dealt with in the bill. There was no corresponding over-all declaration of policy in the Senate amendment. The conference agreement contains the declaration of policy of the House bill with one omission. One of the policies declared in the House bill was to encourage the peaceful settlement of labor disputes affecting commerce by giving the employees themselves a direct voice in the bargaining arrangements with their employers. Since under the conference agreement the provisions relating to a secret ballot on the employer's last offer of settlement (as will be hereafter explained) are not made mandatory, this particular item has been omitted from the over-all declaration of policy in the conference agreement.

TITLE I—AMENDMENT OF NATIONAL LABOR RELATIONS ACT

Both the House bill and the Senate amendment in title I amended the National Labor Relations Act in numerous respects.

In amending section 1 of the National Labor Relations Act (the policy thereof) the House bill omitted from the present law all of the so-called findings of fact, some of which have been so severely criticized as being inaccurate and entirely one-sided. The Senate amendment rewrote the findings and policies contained in section 1 of the National Labor Relations Act so that those findings will not hereafter constitute an indictment of all employers. At the same time the Senate amendment inserted in the findings of fact a paragraph to the effect that experience has demonstrated that certain practices by some labor organizations have the effect of burdening commerce through strikes and other forms of industrial unrest or through concerted activities which impair the interest of the public in the free flow of commerce. The Senate amendment further declared the elimination of such practices to be a necessary condition to the assurance of the rights herein guaranteed. Thus under the Senate amendment the findings and policies of the amended National Labor Relations Act are to be "two-sided." The conference agreement adopts the provisions of the Senate amendment in this respect.

DEFINITIONS

Section 2 of the National Labor Relations Act contains definitions of the terms used therein. Both the House bill and the Senate amendment amended section 2. . . .

ADMINISTRATION

The House bill (secs. 3, 4, and 102) abolished the existing National Labor Relations Board, created a new board of three members, not more than two of whom were to be members of the same political party, and limited the new Board to the performance of the quasi-judicial functions under the act. The investigating and prosecuting functions under the act were to be performed by an Administrator, a new independent office which was created by section 4 of the House bill. The Senate amendment (sec. 3 of the amended Labor Act) retained the existing Board but increased its membership to seven and provided that the Board could assign its duties to groups of not less than three members each. The conference agreement (sec. 3 (a)) retains the existing Board but increases its membership to five. Of the two additional members, who are to be appointed by the President, by and with the advice and consent of the Senate, one is to be appointed for a term of 2 years and one for a term of 5 years. The conference agreement does not make provision for an independent agency to exercise the investigating and prosecuting functions under the act, but does provide that there shall be a General Counsel of the Board, who is to be appointed by the President, by and with the advice and consent of the Senate for a term of 4 years. The General Counsel is to have general supervision and direction of all attorneys employed by the Board (excluding the trial examiners and the legal assistants to the individual members of the Board), and of all the officers and employees in the Board's regional offices, and is to have the final authority to act in the name of, but independently of any direction, control, or review by, the Board in respect of the investigation of charges and the issuance of complaints of unfair labor practices, and in respect of the prosecution of such complaints before the Board. He is to have, in addition, such other duties as the Board may prescribe or as may be provided by law. By this provision responsibility for what takes place in the Board's regional offices is centralized in one individual, who is ultimately responsible to the President and Congress. . . .

RIGHTS OF EMPLOYEES

Both the House bill and the Senate amendment in amending the National Labor Relations Act preserved the right under section 7 of that act of employees to self-organization, to form, join, or assist any labor organization, and to bargain collectively through representatives of their own choosing and to engage in other concerted activities for the purpose of collective bargaining or other mutual aid or protection. The House bill, however, made two changes in that section of the act. *First,* it was stated specifically that the rights set forth were not to be considered as including the right to commit or participate in unfair labor practices, unlawful concerted activities, or violations of collective bargaining contracts. *Second,* it was specifically set forth that employees were also to have the right to refrain from self-organization, etc., if they chose to do so.

The first change in section 7 of the act made by the House bill was inserted by reason of early decisions of the Board to the effect that the language of section 7 protected concerted activities regardless of their nature or objectives. An outstanding decision of this sort was the one involving a "sit down" strike wherein the Board ordered the reinstatement of employees who engaged in this unlawful activity. Later the Board ordered the reinstatement of certain employees whose concerted activities constituted mutiny. In both of the above instances, however, the decision of the Board was reversed by the Supreme Court. More recently, a decision of the Board ordering the reinstatement of individuals who had engaged in mass picketing was reversed by the Circuit Court of Appeals (*Indiana Desk Co.* v. *N. L. R. B.,* 149 Fed. (2d) 987) (1944).

Thus the courts have firmly established the rule that under the existing provisions of section 7 of the National Labor Relations Act, employees are not given any right to engage in unlawful or other improper conduct. In its most recent decisions the Board has been consistently applying the principles established by the courts. For example, in the *American News Company case* (55 N. L. R. B. 1302) (1944) the Board held that employees had no right which was protected under the act to strike to compel an employer to violate the wage stabilization laws. Again, in the *Scullin Steel case* (65 N. L. R. B. 1294) and in the *Dyson case* (decided February 7, 1947), the Board held that strikes in violation of collective bargaining contracts were not concerted activities protected by the act, and refused to reinstate employees discharged for engaging in such activities. In the second *Thompson Products case* (decided February 21, 1947) the Board held that strikes to compel the employer to violate the act and rulings of the Board thereunder were not concerted activities protected by the provisions of section 7. The reasoning of these recent decisions appears to have had the effect of overruling such decisions of the Board as that in *Matter of Berkshire Knitting Mills* (46 N. L. R. B. 955 (1943)), wherein the Board attempted to distinguish between what it considered as major crimes and minor crimes for the purpose of determining what employees were entitled to reinstatement.

By reason of the foregoing, it was believed that the specific provisions in the House bill excepting unfair labor practices, unlawful concerted activities, and violation of collective bargaining agreements from the protection of section 7 were unnecessary. Moreover, there was real concern that the inclusion of such a provision might have a limiting effect and make improper conduct not specifically mentioned subject to the protection of the act.

In addition, other provisions of the conference agreement deal with this particular problem in general terms. For example, in the declaration of policy to the amended National Labor Relations Act adopted by the conference committee, it is stated in the new paragraph dealing with improper practices of labor organizations, their officers, and members, that the "elimination of such practices is a necessary condition to the assurance of the rights herein guaranteed." This in and of itself demonstrates a clear intention that these undesirable concerted activities are not to have any protection under the act, and to the extent that the Board in the past has accorded protection to such activities, the conference agreement makes such protection no longer possible. Furthermore, in section 10 (c) of the amended act, as proposed in the conference agreement, it is specifically provided that no order of the Board shall require the reinstatement of any individual or the payment to him of any back pay if such individual was suspended or discharged for cause, and this, of course, applies with equal force whether or not the acts constituting the cause for discharge were committed in connection with a concerted activity. Again, inasmuch as section 10 (b) of the act, as proposed to be amended by the conference agreement, requires that the rules of evidence applicable in the district courts shall, so far as practicable, be followed and applied by the Board, proof of acts of unlawful conduct cannot hereafter be limited to proof of confession or conviction thereof.

The second change made by the House bill in section 7 of the act (which is carried into the conference agreement) also has an important bearing on the kinds of concerted activities which are protected by section 7. That provision, as heretofore stated, provides that employees are also to have the right to refrain from joining in concerted activities with their fellow employees if they choose to do so. Taken in conjunction with the provisions of section 8 (b) (1) of the conference agreement (which will be hereafter discussed), wherein it is made an unfair labor practice for a labor organization or its agents to restrain or coerce employees in the exercise of rights guaranteed in section 7, it is apparent that many forms and varieties of concerted activities which the Board, particularly in its early days, regarded as protected by the act will no longer be treated as having that protection, since obviously persons who engage in or support unfair labor practices will not enjoy immunity under the act.

UNFAIR LABOR PRACTICES

Both the House bill and the Senate amendment amended section 8 of the National Labor Relations Act by adding thereto unfair labor practices on the part of labor organizations. The practices which under existing law are treated as unfair labor practices on the part of the employer were changed in only two respects by the House bill and in only one respect by the Senate amendment, as will hereafter appear.

Neither the House bill nor the Senate amendment changed the first unfair labor practice on the part of an employer, namely, interfering with, restraining, or coercing employees in the exercise of their rights guaranteed in section 7. What these rights are has already been discussed. The conference agreement contains the provisions of the House bill and the Senate amendment in this respect.

The House bill amended section 8 (2) of the present National Labor Relations Act—the provision making it an unfair labor practice for an employer to dominate the formation or administration of labor organizations —for the purpose of according some protection to labor organizations which were not affiliated with one of the national or international labor organizations. This provision of the House bill had the effect of permitting an employer to do the same kinds of things for independent unions which the Board has permitted him to do for the affiliated unions. The Senate amendment did not change the words of section 8 (2) in existing law.

There were contained, however, in both the House bill and the Senate amendment—in the amendments to sections 9 and 10 of the Labor Act— provisions requiring the Board to treat independent unions in the same manner in which it treats unions which are affiliated with or constitute units of labor organizations national or international in scope. These provisions acted as a limitation on the power of the Board in holding activities to be unfair labor practices under section 8 (a) (2) of the House bill and the Senate amendment. The Board has, for example, in the case of affiliated unions permitted employers to provide bulletin boards in their plants for the union's use, to give union officials preferred treatment in laying off workers and calling them back, and to allow shop stewards without losing pay to confer not only with the employer but with the employees as well, and to transact other union business in the plant. The Board has not permitted the employer to do the same things for nonaffiliated unions, and it was the purpose of the House provision to provide for equality of treatment in this respect.

Since this matter is adequately dealt with in the provisions in sections 9 and 10, the conference agreement omits the provisions of the House bill which amended section 8 (2) of the existing law, and adopts the provisions of the Senate amendment.

Both the House bill and the Senate amendment, in rewriting the present provisions of section 8 (3) of the act, abolished the closed shop. The union shop and maintenance of membership, however, were permitted both under the House bill (sec. 8 (d) (4)) and under the Senate amendment (proviso to sec. 8 (a) (3)). The House bill and the Senate amendment differed in the required procedures for securing the union shop or maintenance of membership. These differences will be hereafter discussed. The conference agreement adopts the language of the Senate amendment in section 8 (a) (3) of the Labor Act with one clarifying omission. Under the provisions of the conference agreement an employer is permitted to enter into an agreement with a labor organization (not established, maintained, or assisted by any action defined as an unfair labor practice) whereby the employer agrees that he will employ only employees who on and after thirty days from the date of their employment (or from the date of the agreement, if that is later) are members of the labor organization concerned. This permission, however, is granted only if, upon the most recent election held under later provisions of the conference agreement (sec. 9 (e)), a majority of the employees in the bargaining unit in question eligible to vote have authorized the union to make such an agreement.

As a protection to the individual worker against arbitrary action by the union, its further provided that an employer is not justified in discriminating against an employee with respect to whom the employer has reason to believe membership in the union was not available on the same terms as those generally applicable to other members, or with respect to whom the employer has reason to believe membership was denied or terminated for reasons other than failure of the employee to tender the periodic dues and the initiation fees uniformly required as a condition of acquiring or retaining membership. In determining whether membership was available on the same terms as those generally applicable to other members, it must be borne in mind that in some unions the dues and initiation fees of pesons who became members many years ago may have been more or less than those currently in effect, or the terms or conditions of membership may have been different. The conference agreement hence does not contemplate availability of membership on the same terms as those applicable to all of the members, nor does it disturb arrangements in the nature of those approved by the Board in *Larus & Brother Co.* (62 N. L. R. B. 1075 (1945)).

Neither the House bill nor the Senate amendment changed the wording of the provisions of section 8 (4) of the existing act, and the conference agreement in section 8 (a) (4) follows the provisions of existing law. The same is true in the case of section 8 (5) of existing law which makes it an unfair labor practice for an employer to refuse to bargain collectively with the representative of his employees, subject to the provisions of section 9 (a).

The Senate amendment contained a provision which does not appear in section 8 of existing law. This provision would have made it an unfair labor practice to violate the terms of a collective bargaining agreement or an agreement to submit a labor dispute to arbitration. The conference agreement omits this provision of the Senate amendment. Once parties have made a collective bargaining contract the enforcement of that contract should be left to the usual processes of the law and not to the National Labor Relations Board.

UNFAIR LABOR PRACTICES OF LABOR ORGANIZATIONS

Both the House bill and the Senate amendment defined, in a new section 8 (b) of the National Labor Relations Act, unfair labor practices on the part of labor organizations and their agents. The House bill also made the unfair labor practices described unfair labor practices on the part of employees.

Under the House bill the following unfair labor practices were set forth:

(1) Intimidating practices to interfere with the exercise by employees of rights guaranteed in section 7 or to compel or seek to compel any individual to be a member of a labor organization.

(2) To refuse to bargain collectively with the employer.

(3) To call or participate in any strike or other concerted interference with an employer's operations, an object of which was to compel the employer to accede to the inclusion in a collective bargaining agreement of matters which under the House bill were not treated as within the proper scope of compulsory bargaining.

Under the new section 8 (b) of the Senate amendment, the following unfair labor practices on the part of labor organizations and their agents were defined:

(1) To restrain or coerce employees in the exercise of rights guaranteed in section 7, or to restrain or coerce an employer in the selection of his representatives for collective bargaining or the adjustment of grievances. This provision of the Senate amendment in its general terms covered all of the activities which were proscribed in section 12 (a) (1) of the House bill as unlawful concerted activities and some of the activities

which were proscribed in the other paragraphs of section 12 (a). While these restraining and coercive activities did not have the same treatment under the Senate amendment as under the corresponding provisions of the House bill, participation in them, as explained in the discussion of section 7, is not a protected activity under the act. Under the House bill, these activities could be enjoined upon suit by a private employer, specific provision was made for suits for damages on the part of any person injured thereby, and employees participating therein were subject to deprivation of their rights under the act. The conference agreement, while adopting section 8 (b) (1) of the Senate amendment, does not by specific terms contain any of these sanctions, but an employee who is discharged for participating in them will not, as explained in the discussion of section 7, be entitled to reinstatement. Furthermore, since in section 302 (b), unions are made suable, unions that engage in these practices to the injury of another may subject themselves to liability under ordinary principles of law. Then, too, under the provisions of section 10 (k) of the conference agreement the Board can seek a temporary injunction enjoining these practices pending its decision on the merits.

In applying section 8 (1) of the existing law, the Board has not held to be unfair labor practices acts which constituted "interference" that did not also constitute restraint or coercion. Section 8 (1) of the present law is written in broad terms, and only by long continued administrative practice has its scope been adequately and properly defined. Concern has heretofore been expressed as to whether such practice would carry over into a corresponding provision of the new section 8 (b) (1), and presumably because of this concern the words "interference with" were omitted from the proposed new section. Omission of these words from the proposed new section was not, however, intended to broaden the scope of section 8 (a) (1) as heretofore defined by the long-continued practice of the Board.

(2) To discriminate against an employee to whom membership in a labor organization has been denied or terminated on some ground other than nonpayment of dues or initiation fees. The purpose of this provision of the Senate amendment was obvious.

(3) To refuse to bargain collectively with an employer, provided the labor organization is the representative of his employees subject to section 9 (a). This provision of the Senate amendment imposed upon labor organizations the same duty to bargain which under section 8 (a) (5) of the Senate amendment was imposed upon employers. What bargaining consists of has already been discussed supra.

(4) To engage in, or induce or encourage the employees of any employer to engage in, a strike or a concerted refusal to use, manufacture, process, transport, or otherwise handle or work on any goods, articles,

materials, or commodities, or to perform any services in the course of their employment, if the purpose thereof was to force the doing of certain things. The proscribed purposes or objectives were described in clauses (A), (B), (C), and (D) of this provision of the Senate amendment.

Under clause (A) strikes or boycotts, or attempts to induce or encourage such action, were made unfair labor practices if the purpose was to force an employer or other person to cease using, selling, handling, transporting, or otherwise dealing in the products of another, or to cease doing business with any other person. Thus it was made an unfair labor practice for a union to engage in a strike against employer A for the purpose of forcing that employer to cease doing business with employer B. Similarly it would not be lawful for a union to boycott employer A because employer A uses or otherwise deals in the goods of, or does business with, employer B.

Clause (B) of this provision of the Senate amendment covered strikes and boycotts conducted for the purpose of forcing another employer to recognize or bargain with a labor organization that has not been certified as the exclusive representative. It is to be observed that the primary strike for recognition (without a Board certification) was not prohibited. Moreover, strikes and boycotts for recognition were not prohibited if the union had been certified as the exclusive representative.

Strikes and boycotts having as their purpose forcing any employer to disregard his obligation to recognize and bargain with a certified union and in lieu thereof to bargain with or recognize another union were made unfair labor practices under clause (C).

Clause (D) covered strikes or boycotts having as their purpose forcing an employer to assign work tests to members of one union when he has assigned them to members of another union. If the employer against whom the strike or boycott was directed was failing to conform to a determination of the Board fixing the representation of employees performing the work tests, then the strike or boycott was not an unfair labor practice.

The matters covered by section 8 (b) (4) in the Senate amendment were dealt with in section 12 of the House bill and in the definitions of illegal boycott and jurisdictional strike.

The conference agreement adopts the provisions of the Senate amendment with clarifying changes, and with one addition to the category of unlawful objectives. Under the conference agreement a strike or boycott to force an employer or self-employed person to become a member of a labor organization will be treated in the same manner as other boycotts.

(5) To violate the terms of a collective bargaining agreement to submit a labor dispute to arbitration.

From the above description of the House bill and the Senate amendment dealing with unfair labor practices on the part of labor organizations and their agents, it is apparent the Senate amendment was broader in its scope than the corresponding provisions of the House bill. The conference agreement adopts the provisions of the Senate amendment with the following changes herein:

(1) Section 8 (b) (2) is expanded so as to prohibit all attempts by a labor organization or its agents to cause an employer to discriminate against an employee in violation of section 8 (a) (3). The latter section, as heretofore explained, prohibits an employer from discriminating against an employee by reason of his membership or nonmembership in a labor organization, except to the extent that he obligates himself to do so under the terms of a permitted union shop or maintenance of membership contract. This provision contained in the conference agreement would, for example, prevent a labor organization from seeking to compel an employer to hire only union foremen or to discharge foremen who were not members of the union, and in this respect it covers matters which, among others, were dealt with under section 12 of the House bill.

(2) A provision which was contained in the Senate amendment in section 8 (b) (2), designed to prevent an employer from discriminating against an employee covered by a union shop agreement, who had been expelled from the union for activities in behalf of another representative, is omitted as unnecessary since there is nothing in the conference agreement which permits an employer to discriminate against an employee who has been expelled for this reason.

(3) Section 8 (b) (4) of the conference agreement has been expanded to cover a matter which was covered by section 12 of the House bill, namely, concerted activity by a union or its agents to compel an employer or self-employed person to become a member.

(4) Two additional unfair labor practices are added which were not contained in the Senate amendment but were contained in the House bill. The first would make it an unfair labor practice for a labor organization or its agents having in effect a permitted union shop or maintenance of membership agreement to require the payment of an initiation fee in an amount which the Board finds excessive or discriminatory under all the circumstances. A similar provision, though broader in its scope, was contained in section 8 (c) (4) of the amended Labor Act in the House bill. It is also made an unfair labor practice for a labor organization or its agents to cause or attempt to cause an employer to pay any money or thing of value, in the nature of an exaction; for services which are not performed or not to be performed. This provision derives from the provisions of the House bill relating to "featherbedding" practices.

(5) Both the House bill and the Senate amendment contained pro-

visions designed to protect the right of both employers and labor organizations to free speech. The conference agreement adopts the provisions of the House bill in this respect with one change derived from the Senate amendment. It is provided that expressing any views, argument, or opinion or the dissemination thereof, whether in written, printed, graphic, or visual form, is not to constitute or be evidence of an unfair labor practice if such expression contains no threat of force or reprisal or promise of benefit. The practice which the Board has had in the past of using speeches and publications of employers concerning labor organizations and collective bargaining arrangements as evidence, no matter how irrelevant or immaterial, that some later act of the employer had an illegal purpose gave rise to the necessity for this change in the law. The purpose is to protect the right of free speech when what the employer says or writes is not of a threatening nature or does not promise a prohibited favorable discrimination.

(6) Section 8 (d) (2) of the amended Labor Act in the House bill contains a provision which is found in section 8 (2) of the existing law and in section 8 (a) (2) of the Senate amendment and the conference agreement. This provides that an employer is not to be prohibited from permitting employees to confer with him during working hours without loss of time or pay. This contemplates payments not only to individual employees but also to employees acting in a representative capacity in conferring with the employer.

Section 8 (d) (3) of the amended Labor Act in the House bill provided that nothing in the act was to be construed as prohibiting an employer from forming or maintaining a committee of employees and discussing with it matters of mutual interest, if the employees did not have a bargaining representative. This provision is omitted from the conference agreement since the act by its terms permits individual employees and groups of employees to meet with the employer and section 9 (a) of the conference agreement permits employers to answer their grievances.

Section 8 (c) of the House bill contained detailed provisions dealing with the relations of labor organizations with their members. One of the more important provisions of this section—that limiting the initiation fees which a labor organzation may impose where a permitted union shop or maintenance of membership agreement is in effect—is included in the conference agreement (sec. 8 (b) (5)) and has already been discussed. The other parts of this subsection are omitted from the conference agreement as unfair labor practices, but section 9 (f) (6) of the conference agreement requires labor organizations to make periodic reports with respect to many of these matters as a condition or certification and other benefits under the act.

Section 8 (d) of the conference agreement (stating what constitutes collective bargaining) has been discussed supra in connection with the treatment of the definition of "collective bargaining", which was contained in the House bill.

REPRESENTATIVES AND ELECTIONS

Except in one respect, neither the House bill nor the Senate amendment made any change in the provisions of section 9 (a) of the existing act (excluding minor textual changes). That section of existing law provides that representatives designated or selected for the purpose of collective bargaining by a majority of the employees in a unit appropriate for that purpose are to be the exclusive representatives of all of the employees in such unit for collective bargaining. The existing law further provides that an individual employee or group of employees will have the right at any time to present grievances to their employer. But, as pointed out in the committee report on the bill in the House, this provision has not been construed by the Board as authorizing the employer to settle grievances thus presented.

Both the House bill and the Senate amendment amended section 9 (a) of the existing law to specifically authorize employers to settle grievances presented by individual employees or groups of employees, so long as the settlement is not inconsistent with any collective bargaining contract in effect. The Senate amendment contained a further proviso, however, to the effect that the bargaining representative be given opportunity to be present at the adjustment of such grievances.

The conference agreement follows the provisions of the Senate amendment.

Section 9 (b) of the existing law—under which the Board is given power to decide the unit which is appropriate for the purpose of collective bargaining—was amended both by the House bill and the Senate amendment. In the Senate amendment the limitations which were described on the Board's powers in establishing such units were contained in a proviso to section 9 (b), while in the House bill the applicable limitations were contained in section 9 (f).

Under section 9 (f) of the House bill the powers of the Board were circumscribed as follows:

(1) With certain exceptions, the Board was prevented from certifying as the representative of employees of one employer a representative that had been certified as the representative of employees of a competing employer. It was this provision of the House bill which, among others, dealt with the question of industry-wide bargaining. It is omitted from the conference agreement.

(2) Under section 9 (f) (2) in the House bill provision was made, upon application of any interested person, for a separate ballot for any craft, department, trade, calling, profession, or other distinguishable group,

and the Board was directed to exclude any such group from the bargaining unit proposed to be established if less than a majority of the employees in it who cast ballots voted for the representative certified by the Board for the rest of the unit. The Board has heretofore, under the so-called "*Globe* doctrine" (3 N. L. R. B. 294 (1937)) provided for separate ballots for crafts and it sometimes applies the same principle to groups other than crafts. It also regularly excludes from larger units groups and individuals whose circumstances differ materially from those of the more numerous members of the unit. The provisions of section 9 (f) (2) of the House bill were designed to establish this principle in the law itself and broaden its application so as to give to groups of employees having common characteristics and interests different from those of the more numerous members of a proposed unit a greater freedom of choice in selecting their representatives than has heretofore been permitted.

The conference agreement, in section 9 (c) (2), covers in specific terms the matter of crafts and professional employees. In the case of the former the conference agreement provides that the Board cannot decide that a craft unit is inappropriate for collective bargaining on the ground that a different unit has been established by a prior Board determination, unless a majority of the employees in the proposed craft unit vote against separate representation. In the case of the latter the Board cannot include both professional employees and employees who are not professional employees in the same unit, unless a majority of the professional employees vote for inclusion therein.

Neither omission from the conference agreement of section 9 (f) (2) of the House bill, nor the particular limitations on the power of the Board under section 9 (b) of the conference agreement, are intended to indicate that only in the specified cases should the Board establish separate units or exclude employees from units for which it certifies representatives. It must be emphasized that one of the principal purposes of the National Labor Relations Act is to give employees full freedom to choose or not to choose representatives for collective bargaining. As has already been pointed out in the discussion of section 7, the conference agreement guarantees in express terms the right of employees to refrain from collective bargaining or concerted activities if they choose to do so. This additional guaranty—recognizing and protecting, as it does, the rights and interests of individuals and minorities—will, it is believed, through wise administration result in a substantially larger measure of protection of those rights when bargaining units are being established than has heretofore been the practice.

The conference agreement, in section 9 (b), contains one further provision covering a particular classification of employees who were dealt with in the House bill in the definition of "supervisor". Under that definition individuals employed for police duties came within the definition of "supervisor". The conference agreement represents a compromise on this matter. It provides that the Board cannot decide that any unit is appropriate for collective bargaining if it includes, together with other employees, any individual employed as a guard to enforce against employees and other persons rules to protect property belonging to the employer or for which the employer is responsible, or to protect the safety of persons on the employer's premises. It is further provided that no labor organization can be certified as the representative of employees in a bargaining unit of guards if such organization admits to membership, or is affiliated directly or indirectly with an organization which admits to membership, employees other than guards.

(3) Under section 9 (f) (3) in the House bill it was provided that, in determining whether a unit is appropriate for collective bargaining, the extent to which employees had organized should not be controlling. There was no comparable provision in the Senate amendment. The conference agreement, in section 9 (c), contains this provision of the House bill.

(4) Under the House bill, in section 9 (f) (4), it was provided that the Board was to apply the same regulations and rules of decision, in determining whether a question of representation affecting commerce exists, regardless of the identity of the person or persons filing the application or the kind of relief sought. It was further provided that employees were not to be denied the right to designate or select a representative of their own choosing by reason of an order of the Board with respect to such representative or its predecessor that would not have issued in similar circumstances with respect to a labor organization national or international in scope, or affiliated with such an organization. The Senate amendment, in section 9 (c) (2), contained a provision having the same purpose. Both the House provision and the Senate provision were directed to the practice of the Board in denying employees the right to vote for independent labor organizations in respect of which orders had been issued by the Board under section 8 (1) or 8 (2) finding employer domination, where under similar circumstances it did not apply the same rule to unions affiliated with one of the national labor organizations. Under the House bill and the Senate amendment the Board was directed to apply the same rules to both. The conference agreement, in section 9 (c) (2), contains a provision having the same purpose and effect.

(5) The House bill, in section 9 (f) (5), provided a new rule for run-off elections. A run-off was not permitted unless within 60 days following the first election a representative receiving votes in the first election furnished to the Board satisfactory evidence that it represented more than 50 percent of the employees in the bargaining unit in question. The run-off was to be between such representative and no representative. The

Senate amendment, in section 9 (c) (3), directed that, where a run-off election was conducted, the ballot should provide for a selection between the two choices receiving the largest and second largest number of valid votes cast in the previous election. The conference agreement adopts the provisions of the Senate amendment.

(6) Under the House bill, in section 9 (f) (6), no labor organization could be certified if one or more of its national or international officers, or one or more of the officers of the organization designated on the ballot, was or ever had been a member of the Communist Party or by reason of active and consistent promotion or support of the policies of the Communist Party could reasonably be regarded as being a member of or affiliated with such party, or believed in or was or ever had been a member of or supported any organization that believed in or taught, the overthrow of the United States Government by force or by any illegal or unconstitutional methods. The Senate amendment, in section 9 (h), contained a similar provision, differing from the House bill only in not imposing the requirement that an officer "never has been" one of the described individuals. The conference agreement, in section 9 (h), contains a provision directed to this problem covered by both the House bill and the Senate amendment, and provides that no investigation shall be made by the Board of any question affecting commerce concerning the representation of employees raised by a labor organization under section 9 (c), no union shop or maintenance of membership agreement petition can be entertained under section 9 (e) (1) (hereafter discussed), and no complaint can be issued pursuant to a charge made by a labor organization under section 10 (b), unless there is on file with the Board an affidavit executed contemporaneously or within the preceding 12-month period by each officer of the labor organization in question and the officers of any national or international labor organization of which it is an affiliated or constituent unit, that he is not a member of the Communist Party or affiliated with such party, and that he does not believe in, and is not a member of, or support, any organization that believes in, or teaches, the overthrow of the United States Government by force or by any illegal or unconstitutional methods. The provisions of section 35 A of the Criminal Code (prescribing penalties for false statements made to induce official action) are to be applicable in respect to such affidavits, and if an officer of a labor organization files a false affidavit with the Board, he will be subject to the penalties prescribed in section 35 A of the Criminal Code.

The "ever has been" test that was included in the House bill is omitted from the conference agreement as unnecessary, since the Supreme Court has held that if an individual has been proved to be a member of the Communist Party at some time in the past, the presumption is that he is still a member in the absence of proof to the contrary.

(7) Under the House bill, in section 9 (f) (7), it was provided that no election should be directed in any bargaining unit or any subdivision thereof within which, in the preceding 12-month period, a valid election had been held, except upon a petition by employees requesting "decertification" of a representative. The Senate amendment, in section 9 (c) (3), contained a similar provision without the exception. The conference agreement adopts the provisions of the Senate amendment. The Senate amendment also contained a provision that employees on strike who were not entitled to reinstatement should not be permitted to vote unless the strike involved an unfair labor practice on the part of the employer. This provision is also included in section 9 (c) of the conference agreement with the "unless" clause omitted. The inclusion of such clause would have had the effect of precluding the Board from changing its present practice with respect to the treatment of "unfair labor practice" strikers as distinguished from that accorded to "economic" strikers.

(8) Under the House bill, in section 9 (f) (8), it was provided that if a new representative were chosen while a collective bargaining agreement was in effect with another repesentative, certification of the new representative should not become effective unless such new representative became a party to such contract and agreed to be bound by its terms for the remainder of the contract period. Since the inclusion of such a provision might give rise to an inference that the practice of the Board, with respect to conducting representation elections while collective bargaining contracts are in effect, should not be continued, it is omitted from the conference agreement.

Both the House bill and the Senate amendment in section 9 (c) of the amended Labor Act provided that petitions under section 9 could be filed by employees or labor organizations wishing an election to designate a representative, by employees or labor organizations wishing to provide for the "de-certification" of an existing representative, and by an employer to whom a representative has presented a claim requesting recognition as the representative for collective bargaining. Investigations of such petitions under the House bill were conducted by the Administrator provided in the House bill. Under the Senate amendment investigations were conducted by the Board. Both under the House bill and the Senate amendment if there was reasonable cause to believe that a question of representation affecting commerce existed a hearing was to be held. Under the Senate amendment it was provided that such hearing could be conducted by an officer or employee in the regional office who, when he reported to the Board with respect thereto, was prohibited from making any recommendations. Both the House bill and the Senate amendment provided that if the Board found upon the hearing that a question of representation existed a secret ballot should be held and the results thereof certified.

The conference agreement, in section 9 (c), follows the provisions of the Senate amendment, most of which, as indicated, were also contained in the House bill. The remaining portions of section 9 (c) of the conference agreement have already been discussed in connection with the treatment of the provisions which were contained in section 9 (f) of the House bill.

Section 9 (d) in the conference agreement, except for clerical changes, is the same as section 9 (e) in the House bill, section 9 (d) in the Senate amendment, and section 9 (d) of existing law.

Section 9 (g) in the House bill, provided for the so-called "union shop" election. This provision, together with the provisions of section 8 (d) (4) in the House bill, provided a somewhat different procedure for authorization of union shop and maintenance of membership contracts than did the Senate amendment. Under the House bill the employer had to agree to a union shop or maintenance of membership provision in the contract before an election with respect thereto could be held. An election under section 9 (g) was for the purpose of authorizing such provision to be carried into effect. The petition for the election was required to be filed under oath and had to state that the agreement of the employer was not secured, neither directly or indirectly, by means of a strike or a threat thereof. The provisions of the agreement providing for a union shop could be carried out only if upon a secret ballot taken a majority of all of the employees in the bargaining unit in question voted in favor thereof, and the election was effective only for the period of the contract in which the union shop agreement was included, or for 2 years if the contract was for a longer period. Under the Senate amendment (sec. 9 (e)) the "union shop" election was to be held for the purpose of authorizing the labor organization to make a union shop or maintenance of membership agreement with the employer and did not have the effect of preventing strikes to secure such an agreement. Like the House bill, the agreement was exempted from the general prohibitions of section 8 (a) (3) (prohibiting discrimination by reason of membership or nonmembership in labor organizations) only if a majority of the employees eligible to vote had authorized the labor organization in question to make such an agreement. Under the Senate amendment, once this authorization had been given, it continued in effect until, upon a secret ballot conducted as a result of the filing of a "de-authorization" petition, a majority of the employees eligible to vote had not voted in favor of the authorization. As in the case of the representation elections, the Senate amendment in section 9 (e) provided that no election in respect of the union shop could be conducted in any bargaining unit or any subdivision thereof within which, in the preceding 12-month period, a valid election had been held.

The conference agreement (sec. 9 (e)) follows the pattern of the Senate amendment with two clarifying changes. The conference agreement requires that the petition for the election (which includes a "de-authorization" petition) must be filed by or on behalf of not less than 30 percent of the employees in the bargaining unit. The conference agreement further provides that the Board can order an election under these provisions only if no question of representation exists. The particular problem dealt with in this latter clarification was provided for in the House bill by the requirement that only certified bargaining agents could make union shop agreements and petition for elections to authorize their execution.

Section 9 (f) of the Senate amendment required labor organizations to file certain information and financial reports with the Secretary of Labor in order to be eligible for certification or have charges processed in their behalf. It was further provided that copies of the financial report be furnished to all members of the labor organization. Provision was made that such information be kept current by annual reports.

The House bill (sec. 303) also contained a provision requiring reports by labor organizations, but did not make the filing of such reports a condition of certification or other benefits.

The conference agreement (sec. 9 (f) and (g)) adopts the provisions of the Senate amendment with three changes therein. *First,* the filing of the information and reports is made a condition of eligibility for requesting a union shop election, in addition to eligibility for filing petitions for representation and eligibility for making changes. *Second,* it is provided that not only the particular labor organization invoking the processes of the act, but also any national or international labor organization of which it is an affiliate or constituent unit, must file the required information and reports. *Third,* there are added to the matters, with respect to which information must be filed, detailed statements of, or reference to, the provisions of the organization's constitution and bylaws, showing the procedure followed with respect to most of the matters which were covered in section 8 (c) in the House bill (the section dealing with the relations between labor organizations and their members). . . .

TITLE II—CONCILIATION OF LABOR DISPUTES IN INDUSTRIES AFFECTING COMMERCE; NATIONAL EMERGENCIES

Title II of both the House bill and the Senate amendment contained provisions creating a new independent conciliation service, and also provisions for the treatment of strikes affecting the national health or safety. Under the House bill the new service was to be known as the Office of Conciliation. Under the Senate amendment it was to be known as the Federal Mediation Service. Both bills provided for a Director to be the head of the new service to be appointed by the President, by and with the advice and consent of the Senate, and to receive compensation at the rate of $12,000 per annum. Both the House bill and the Senate amendment transferred all of the existing functions of the United States Conciliation Service in the Department of Labor to the new independent agency created.

Since the conference agreement in general follows the provisions of the Senate amendment with respect to this service, the Senate amendment in this regard will be described, with changes therefrom made by the conference agreement noted. Section 201 of the Senate amendment contained a statement of policy which also appears unchanged in the conference agreement.

Section 202 of the Senate amendment created an independent agency to be known as the Federal Mediation Service and to be operated by a single official, called the Director, to be appointed by the President, with the advice and consent of the Senate. The functions of the existing Conciliation Service were transferred to the Director, the transfer to take effect upon the sixtieth day after the date of the bill's enactment. The only change made by the conference agreement in this section of the Senate amendment is in the name of the new service. Under the conference agreement the new service is to be known as the Federal Mediation and Conciliation Service.

Section 203 of the Senate amendment described the functions of the new service and emphasized the duty of the Service to interfere only where a dispute threatened to cause a substantial interruption of interstate commerce. It provided that if the parties could not be brought to direct settlement by conciliation or mediation the Service was authorized to seek to induce the parties to submit the dispute to voluntary arbitration. Provision was made for the payment by the United States of not to exceed $500 as a contribution to the cost of an arbitration proceeding. The conference agreement, in section 203, does not mention arbitration as such but provides that if the parties cannot be brought to settlement by conciliation and mediation the Service shall seek to induce them voluntarily to seek other means of settling the dispute without resort to strike, lock-out, or other coercion. The failure or refusal of either party to agree to any procedure suggested by the Director is not to be deemed a violation of any duty or obligation imposed, and the conference agreement omits the provision contained in the Senate amendment relating to the contribution by the United States to defray the costs of arbitration proceedings.

One important duty of the Director which was not included in the Senate amendment is included in the conference agreement and is derived from the provisions of the House bill providing for a secret ballot by employees upon their employer's last offer of settlement before resorting to strike. Under the conference agreement it is the duty of the Director, if he is not able to bring the parties to agreement by conciliation within a reasonable time, to seek to induce them to seek other means of settling the dispute, including submission to the employees in the bargaining unit of the employer's last offer of settlement for refusal or for approval or rejection in a secret ballot.

While the vote on the employer's last offer by secret ballot is not compulsory as it was in the House bill, it is expected that this procedure will be extensively used and that it will have the effect of preventing many strikes which might otherwise take place.

Section 204 of the Senate amendment stated that it should be the duty of employers and employees, and their representatives, to exert every reasonable effort to settle their differences by collective bargaining, and, if this should fail, to utilize the assistance of the Mediation Service. This provision is also included in section 204 of the conference agreement, but there has been omitted therefrom language which appeared in the Senate amendment which indicated that the parties were under a duty to submit grievance disputes to arbitration.

Section 205 of the Senate amendment created an advisory committee for the new Service composed of management and labor representatives. This group was called "The National Labor-Management Panel". The panel was to be composed of 12 members, all appointed by the President, and it was made their duty, at the request of the Director, to advise in the avoidance of industrial controversies in the manner in which mediation and voluntary arbitration should be administered. Section 205 of the conference agreement follows the provisions of the Senate amendment, except that specific reference to "voluntary arbitration" is omitted.

NATIONAL EMERGENCIES

Sections 203 to 206, inclusive, of the House bill gave the President, through the district courts of the United States, power to deal with strikes that resulted in or imminently threatened to result in the cessation or substantial curtailment of interstate or foreign commerce in essential public services. Provision was made for mediation of the dispute after the injunction had issued, and for a secret ballot of the employees on their employer's last offer of settlement if mediation did not result in an agreement. If the employer's last offer was rejected by the employees, provision was made for the convening by the chief justice of the United States Court of Appeals for the District of Columbia of a special advisory settlement board to investigate the dispute and to make recommendations for its settlement. Another secret ballot by the employees was provided on the question whether they desired to accept the recommended settlement. At the conclusion of proceedings provided for, the Attorney General was directed to move the court to discharge the injunction and the injunction was to be discharged. These provisions were not to apply to any person or dispute subject to the Railway Labor Act.

Sections 206 to 210, inclusive, of the Senate amendment contained provisions dealing with this same problem. The Senate amendment was limited in its application to threatened or actual strikes or lockouts affecting an entire industry engaged in trade, commerce, transportation, transmission, or communications among the several States, and the power to invoke these emergency provisions was lodged in the Attorney General rather than in the President. The conference agreement in general follows the provisions of the Senate amendment, with changes therein which will be hereafter noted.

Section 206 of the Senate amendment authorized the Attorney General whenever he deemed that a threatened or actual strike or lock-out affecting an entire industry would imperil the national health or safety, to appoint a board of inquiry to inquire into the issues involved in the dispute. The board of inquiry was directed to investigate the matter and make a report to the Attorney General. The report was to include a statement of facts and a statement of the respective positions of the parties, but was not to contain any recommendations. Under section 206 of the conference agreement the authority is lodged in the President rather than in the Attorney General, and the report which the board of inquiry is to make is to include each party's statement of his own position. Like the provisions of the Senate amendment, the report of the board of inquiry cannot contain any recommendations. Furthermore, under the conference agreement the authority of this section may be invoked not alone when an entire industry is involved but where a substantial part of an entire industry is involved.

Section 207 of the Senate amendment provided for the composition of the board of inquiry, their compensation, and their powers to compel testimony. This section appears unchanged as section 207 of the conference agreement.

Section 208 of the Senate amendment authorized the Attorney General upon receiving the report of the board of inquiry, to apply to the appropriate district court for an injunction enjoining the strike or lock-out, and the court was authorized to issue the injunction if it found that the strike or lock-out affected the entire industry and would imperil the national health or safety. The Norris-LaGuardia Act was made inapplicable. Section 208 of the conference agreement follows the provisions of the Senate amendment except that, as heretofore stated, the authority is lodged in the President rather than in the Attorney General, and the injunction can issue if the strike or lock-out affects an entire industry or a substantial part thereof.

Section 209 of the Senate amendment provided that, after the district court had issued an injunction, it should be the duty of the parties to make every effort to adjust and settle their differences with the assistance of the new Federal Mediation Service. Neither party was to be under any duty to accept, either in whole or in part, any proposal of settlement made by the Service. Furthermore, after an injunction had issued, the Attorney General was directed to reconvene the board of inquiry. At the end of a 60-day period (unless the dispute had been settled in the meantime) the board of inquiry was directed to report to the President the current position of the parties and the efforts which had been made for settlement. Such report was to be made public. Within the succeeding 15 days a secret ballot was to be taken of the employees of each employer involved in the dispute on the question of whether they desired to accept the final offer of settlement made by their employer. The conference agreement, in section 209, follows the provisions of the Senate amendment, with the authority lodged in the President rather than the Attorney General, and with the requirement that the board of inquiry include in its report a statement by each party of his own position. It is provided in the conference agreement that the employees vote on the employer's offer as stated by him.

Section 210 of the Senate amendment provided that upon certification of the results of the balloting under section 309 the injunction was to be discharged, and a full and comprehensive report of the whole matter was to be made to Congress. This provision is also included in the conference agreement, with only textual changes to conform this section to the policy of lodging the authority in the President rather than the Attorney General.

Section 211 of the Senate amendment contained a provision requiring the Bureau of Labor Statistics to maintain a file containing copies of collective agreements and arbitration awards, which would be made available to the public unless involving information received in confidence. There was no comparable provision in the House bill. The conference agreement contains the provisions of the Senate amendment with minor clarifying changes.

Section 212 of the Senate amendment contained a provision stating that title II was not to be applicable with respect to any matter which is subject to the provisions of the Railway Labor Act. As previously noted, a similar provision, more restricted in scope, was contained in section 205 of the House bill. The conference agreement adopts the provision of the Senate amendment.

TITLE III

Section 301 of the House bill contained a provision amending the Clayton Act so as to withdraw the exemption of labor organizations under the antitrust laws when such organizations engaged in combinations or conspiracies in restraining of commerce where one of the purposes or a necessary effect of the combination or conspiracy was to join or combine with any person to fix prices, allocate costs, restrict production, distribution, or competition, or impose restrictions or conditions upon the purchase, sale, or use of any product, material, machine, or equipment, or to engage in an unlawful concerted activity (as defined in sec. 12 of the National Labor Relations Act under the House bill). Since the matters dealt with in this section have to a large measure been effectuated through the use of boycotts, and since the conference agreement contains effective provisions directly dealing with boycotts themselves, this provision is omitted from the conference agreement.

SUITS BY AND AGAINST LABOR ORGANIZATIONS

Section 302 of the House bill and section 301 of the Senate amendment contained provisions relating to suits by and against labor organizations in the courts of the United States. The conference agreement follows in general the provisions of the House bill with changes therein hereafter noted.

Section 302 (a) of the House bill provided that any action for or proceeding involving a violation of a contract between an employer and a labor organization might be brought by either party in any district court of the United States having jurisdiction of the parties, without regard to the amount in controversy, if such contract affected commerce, or the court otherwise had jurisdiction. Under the Senate amendment the jurisdictional test was whether the employer was in an industry affecting commerce or whether the labor organization represented employees in such an industry. This test contained in the Senate amendment is also contained in the conference agreement, rather than the test in the House bill which required that the "contract affect commerce".

Section 302 (b) of the House bill provided that any labor organization whose activities affected commerce should be bound by the acts of its agents and might sue or be sued as an entity in the courts of the United States. Any money judgment in such a suit was to be enforceable only against the organization as an entity and against its assets and not against any individual member or his assets. The conference agreement follows these provisions of the House bill except that this subsection is made applicable to labor organizations which represent employees in an industry affecting commerce and to employers whose activities affect commerce, as later defined. It is further provided that both the employer and the labor organization are to be bound by the acts of their agents. This subsection and the succeeding subsections of section 301 of the conference agreement (as was the case in the House bill and also in the Senate amendment) are general in their application, as distinguished from subsection (a).

Section 302 (c) of the House bill contained provisions describing the venue of suits to which labor organizations were parties and section 302 (d) provided for the manner of service of process upon labor organizations. These provisions of the House bill appear unchanged as section 302 (c) and (d) of the conference agreement.

Section 302 (d) of the House bill made the Norris-LaGuardia Act inapplicable in actions and proceedings involving violations of agreements between an employer and a labor organization. Only part of this provision is included in the conference agreement. Section 6 of the Norris-LaGuardia Act provides that no employer or labor organization participating or interested in a labor dispute shall be held responsible for the unlawful acts of their agents except upon clear proof of actual authorization of such acts, or ratification of such acts after actual knowledge thereof. This provision in the Norris-LaGuardia Act was made inapplicable under the House bill. Section 301 (e) of the conference agreement provides that for the purposes of section 301 in determining whether any person is acting as an agent of another so as to make such other person responsible for his actions, the question of whether the specific acts performed were actually authorized or subsequently ratified shall not be controlling.

RESTRICTIONS ON PAYMENTS TO EMPLOYEE REPRESENTATIVES

Section 302 of the Senate amendment contained a provision making it unlawful for any employer to pay any money or thing of value to any representative of his employees employed in an industry affecting commerce, or for any such representative to accept from the employer any money or other thing of value, with certain specified exceptions. The two most important exceptions are (1) those relating to payments to a representative of money deducted from the wages of employees in payment of membership dues in a labor organization if the employer has received from each employee on whose account the deductions are made a written assignment not irrevocable for a period of more than one year or beyond the termination date of the applicable collective agreement, and (2) money paid to a trust fund established by the representative for the sole and exclusive benefit of the employees of such employer and their families and dependents (or of such employees, families, and dependents jointly with the employees of other employers making similar payments, and their families and dependents). Such a trust fund had to meet certain requirements. Among these requirements were that the fund be held for the purpose of paying for medical or hospital care, pensions on retirement or death, compensation for injuries or illness resulting from occupational activity, or insurance to provide any of the foregoing, or life insurance, disability and sickness insurance, or accident insurance. Furthermore, the detailed basis on which the payments were to be made had to be specified in a written agreement with the employer and the employees and employers had to be equally represented in the administration of the fund. Provision was made for the breaking of deadlocks on the administration of the fund, and the agreement covering the fund had to contain provisions for annual audit, and a statement of the results of the audit were to be made available for inspection by interested persons.

Violations of this section of the Senate amendment were made punishable by a fine of not more than $10,000 or by imprisonment for not more than one year, or both.

Saving provisions were included to protect existing contracts between employers and employees.

The conference agreement adopts the provisions of the Senate amendment with minor clarifying changes.

BOYCOTTS AND OTHER UNLAWFUL COMBINATIONS

Section 303 of the Senate amendment contained a provision the effect of which was to give persons injured by boycotts and jurisdictional disputes described in the new section 8 (b) (4) of the National Labor Relations Act a right to sue the labor organization responsible therefor in any district court of the United States (subject to the limitations and provisions of the section dealing with suits by and against labor organizations) to recover damages sustained by him together with the costs of the suit. A comparable provision was contained in the House bill in the new section 12 of the National Labor Relations Act dealing with unlawful concerted activities. The conference agreement adopts the provisions of the Senate amendment with clarifying changes.

RESTRICTIONS ON POLITICAL CONTRIBUTIONS

Section 305 of the House bill contained a provision placing on a permanent basis the provisions which were contained in the War Labor Disputes Act, whereby labor organizations were prohibited from making political contributions to the same extent as corporations. In addition, this section extended the prohibition, both in the case of corporations and labor organizations, to include expenditures as well as contributions. Moreover, expenditures and contributions in connection with primary elections and political conventions were made unlawful to the extent as those made in connection with the elections themselves. There was no comparable provision in the Senate amendment. The conference agreement adopts the provisions of the House bill, with one change. Under the conference agreements expenditures and contributions in connection with primary elections, political conventions, and caucuses are made unlawful to the same extent as those made in connection with the elections themselves. As a clarifying change the definition of a labor organization has been set forth in full rather than incorporating the provision of the National Labor Relations Act.

STRIKES BY GOVERNMENT EMPLOYEES

Section 207 of the House bill made it unlawful for any employee of the United States to strike against the Government. Violations of this section were to be punishable by immediate discharge, forfeiture of all rights of reemployment, forfeiture of civil-service status, and forfeiture of all benefits which the individual had acquired by virtue of his Government employment. The conference agreement, in section 305, makes it unlawful for any individual employed by the United States or any agency thereof (including wholly owned Government corporations) to participate in any strike against the Government. Violations are to be punishable by immediate discharge and forfeiture of civil-service status, if any, and the individual is not to be eligible for employment by the United States for 3 years.

TITLE IV—CREATION OF JOINT COMMITTEE TO STUDY AND REPORT ON BASIC PROBLEMS AFFECTING FRIENDLY LABOR RELATIONS AND PRODUCTIVITY

Title IV of the Senate amendment created a joint congressional committee consisting of seven members of the Senate Committee on Labor and Public Welfare to be appointed by the President pro tempore of the Senate, and seven members of the House of Representatives Committee on Education and Labor to be appointed by the Speaker. The committee was directed to conduct a survey of the entire field of labor-management relations with particular emphasis upon particular described subjects. The committee was to make a report not later than February 15, 1948, containing the results of the studies, together with its recommendations as to necessary legislation and such other recommendations as it might deem advisable. Authority was granted to hire technical and clerical personnel and to request details of personnel from Federal and State agencies. The committee was granted subpena power and authority to conduct hearings whether or not Congress was in session. An appropriation of $150,000 was authorized to enable the committee to perform its functions.

Title IV of the conference agreement adopts the above provisions of the Senate amendment with one change. The committee is directed to make its final report not later than January 2, 1949.

TITLE V

Section 501 of the Senate amendment contained definitions of terms used in titles II, III, and IV. It should be noted that none of the terms defined, however, have any application to the amendment to section 313 of the Federal Corrupt Practices Act since section 313 of the Corrupt Practices Act is not a part of "this Act".

Section 502 of the Senate amendment contained a provision that nothing was to be construed to require an individual employee to render labor or service without his consent, or to make the quitting of his labor by an individual employee an illegal act. It was further provided that the quitting of labor by an employee or employees in good faith because of abnormally dangerous conditions for work at their place of employment should not be deemed a strike under the act.

Section 503 of the Senate amendment contained the usual separability provision.

Section 501, 502, and 503 of the Senate amendment are contained in the conference agreement with the same section numbers.

THE DEBATE

ROBERT TAFT [R., OHIO]. Mr. President, before taking up any of the miscellaneous matters which were discussed yesterday, I desire to make a comprehensive statement regarding Senate bill 1126, which has been recommended to the Senate by the Committee on Labor and Public Welfare, after 6 weeks of hearings and long consideration in the committee. Members will find the bill on their desks, together with the committee's report, which represent the views of 11 of the 13 members of the committee.

After the preliminary statement the report proceeds to set forth in detail each amendment and what the amendment provides for.

On page 31 of the report is a rewrite of the National Labor Relations Act showing the amendments proposed to be made by the committee bill. That is in accord with the new rule under the La Follette-Monroney Act, and follows the practice which the House has followed for many years, in order that the amendments of an existing act may be clearly understood.

The report also contains the separate views of the Senator from Utah [Mr. Thomas] and supplemental views by myself, the Senator from Minnesota [Mr. Ball], the Senator from Missouri [Mr. Donnell], and the Senator from Indiana [Mr. Jenner] proposing some additional amendments in addition to those which appear in the bill. At this time I do not intend to discuss those amendments. I wish merely to present the committee bill which is a substantial step forward in improving labor relations in the United States, and which redresses many of the injustices which have arisen under the interpretation of past laws.

Mr. President, why is a labor bill necessary? Why is it demanded today by an overwhelming proportion of public opinion? Of course, on the surface it is due to the fact that we have had a large number of strikes, inconveniencing the public, even threatening their safety and welfare. I think even more, the widespread demand for some correction of the existing labor legislation arises because of many injustices which have developed in labor relations, injustices which are perfectly clear to all the people who come in contact with particular disputes which in effect are without remedy in the courts under present laws.

I myself feel that the larger employers can well look after themselves, but throughout the United States there are hundreds of thousands of smaller employers, smaller businessmen, who, under the existing statutes, have come gradually to be at the mercy of labor union leaders, either labor-union leaders attempting to organize their employees, or labor-union leaders interfering with the conduct of their business for one reason or for another.

Mr. President, originally, before the passage of any of these laws, the employer undoubtedly had an advantage in dealing with his employees. He was one man; the employees might be thousands; and he could deal with them one at a time. In negotiations of that character he had such a superior advantage that Congress came to feel that it must legislate specifically in order to correct that situation and bring about a balance. Congress passed the Clayton Act and the Norris-LaGuardia Act in order to limit legal actions against unions. Congress passed the Wagner National Labor Relations Act in order that the employees of a single employer might act as one in dealing with the one employer, in order that they might be on a sound and an equal basis, a principle which I think no one can question, and which certainly is not questioned in the pending bill.

The difficulty with the Clayton Act and the Norris-LaGuardia Act is that they went at the situation with a meat ax. They practically eliminated all legal remedy against unions for any action taken by them. In effect they provide as construed by the courts, at least—that any action by a union taken in order to advance its own interests is proper, and there is no legal recourse against the union. The laws referred to do not discriminate between strikes for justifiable purposes and strikes for wholly illegal and improper purposes. They do not distinguish between strikes for higher wages and hours and better working conditions, which are entirely proper and which throughout this bill are recognized as completely proper strikes, and strikes in the nature of secondary boycotts, jurisdictional strikes, and strikes of the racketeering variety. The acts simply eliminated all remedy against any union, leaving the union leaders free, practically without any control even by their members, to order strikes and boycotts and various kinds of actions that interfered, I believe certainly unlawfully under common law, with the activities of many other persons who were entirely innocent.

The National Labor Relations Act was enacted for a proper purpose, but the result of the actual administration of that act has been completely one sided. It was simply for the one purpose of equalizing, or permitting a large number of employees to act as one; in effect to compel them to act as one if the majority desired such action.

Of course, it was one sided, and the first board that was appointed, I believe, established a method of procedure which was completely prejudiced and completely on the side of labor unions. In 1939 I sat through the hearings for nearly 6 months on the operation of the National Labor Relations Board up to that time, and I do not think I have ever heard, certainly in America, such a series of miscarriages of justice as occurred under the first National Labor Relations Board.

The members of that board were gradually dismissed by President Roosevelt, the protests being so violent against their acts. As their terms expired other men were appointed to take their place, and they disappeared from the picture. The most violent testimony we had in that particular hearing that I remember came from the AFL unions themselves, from Mr. Green and Mr. Padway, who took the position, as I think correctly, that the board regarded themselves not at a judicial board to determine rights under the law in a lawful manner, but as crusaders to put the CIO union in every plant in the United States. In every way they could warp the law to accomplish that purpose, they did so.

Since then they have been succeeded by others who have proved to be much more judicial and who today I think constitute a very fair board. Yet much of the personnel that was appointed under the original law remains. Many of the precedents which were established by the original board still exist, and the result is that in the administration of that law, as testified to before our committee, there were so many injustices that it seemed impossible to correct them without legislation.

The greater part of the bill which is now before the Senate is a revision and amendment of the Wagner Labor Relations Act, which is rewritten from the first section to the last, with amendments dealing with particular injustices which were called to our attention, and which we believe can be corrected by an amendment of the law. These various injustices have been frozen into the law by the fact that for 8 years since the hearings in 1939 there has been no labor bill, no comprehensive consideration of the problem, and nothing for action by the Senate except the Case bill of last year, which was only a partial approach to the problem, and which was vetoed by the President.

Mr. President, the interpretations not only of the laws themselves but of the administrative regulations and the administrative regulations and the administrative rulings, and the decisions of the Supreme Court itself—holding in effect that there was no way in which any court could revise injustices perpetrated by the National Labor Relations Act—resulted in gradually building up the power of the labor leaders, so that today, in my opinion, the weight in collective bargaining negotiations is all on the side of the labor leaders, except perhaps against the very largest companies in the United States. In particular I believe that in dealing with small business, with farmers, and even with the workers themselves, the labor union leaders have acquired a power which today the people resent and which inevitably has been abused. Many of our labor leaders are just as judicial and as fair as anyone could wish them to be, but extreme power, unreasonable power, cannot be granted to any group of men without a large number of them being willing to exercise it to accomplish ends which are not reasonable. Polls taken today show that union members themselves resent the power of labor union leaders. Even on the question of the closed shop, which the union leaders are most vigorously defending, the polls show that more than half their men are actually opposed to the position the leaders are taking, because apparently they feel that today they are at a great disadvantage in dealing with union leaders, and that the power given to the leaders by existing legislation is so great that the individual is unable to exercise their right to free speech, his right to work as he pleases, and their general right to live as he pleases.

As to the proper method of correcting the situation, certainly there is no panacea. I have been interested in talking with employers. A group of employers will say. "This situation must be corrected." When asked, "What is the most important thing?" one man will say one thing, another man will say another thing, and a third man will say something else, because those are the matters that have come to their attention in dealing with labor unions.

The problem is infinitely complicated. I suppose there are at least 50 amendments to the present law in the pending bill. Wherever we found an injustice we tried to correct it; and, of course, the net result of correcting a number of injustices is incidentally to decrease some of the power of the labor union leaders. It seems to me that our aim should be to get back to the point where, when an employer meets with his employees, they have substantially equal bargaining power, so that neither side feels that it can make an unreasonable demand and get away with it. If neither side feels that it can get away with certain demands, I do not believe that the demands will ever be made. If there is reasonable equality at the bargaining table, I believe that there is much more hope for labor peace. That is the method pursued by the bill which is now before the Senate. It is not an antilabor bill. It is not a bill inspired by a desire to wreak vengeance on anyone because of what he may have done. It simply proposes to deal with the causes of labor trouble and the injustices and inequities of the present law.

Basically, I believe that the committee feels, almost unanimously, that the solution of our labor problems must rest on a free economy and on free collective bargaining. The bill is certainly based upon that proposition. That means that we recognize freedom to strike when the question involved is the improvement of wages, hours, and working conditions, when a contract has expired and neither side is bound by a contract. We recognize that right in spite of the inconvenience, and in some cases perhaps danger, to the people of the United States which may result from the exercise of such right. In the long run, I do not believe that that right will be abused. In the past few disputes finally reached the point where there was a direct threat to and defiance of the rights of the people of the United States.

We have considered the question whether the right to strike can be modified. I think it can be modified in cases which do not involve the basic question of wages, prices, and working conditions. But if we impose compulsory arbitration, or if we give the Government power to fix wages at which men must work for another year or for two years to come, I do not see how in the end we can escape a collective economy. If we give the Government power to fix wages, I do not see how we can take from the Government the power to fix prices; and if the Government fixes wages and prices, we soon reach the point where all industry is under government control, and finally there is a complete socialization of our economy.

I feel very strongly that so far as possible we should avoid any system which attempts to give to the Government this power finally to fix the wages of any man. Can we do so constitutionally? Can we say to all the people of the United States, "You must work at wages fixed by the Government"? I think it is a long step from freedom and a long step from a free economy to give the Government such a right.

It is suggested that we might do so in the case of public utilities; and I suppose the argument is stronger there, because we fix the rates of public utilities, and we might, I suppose, fix the wages of public-utility workers. Yet we have hesitated to embark even on that course, because if we once begin a process of the Government fixing wages, it must end in more and more wage fixing and finally Government price fixing. It may be a popular thing to do. Today people seem to think that all that it is necessary to do is to forbid strikes, fix wages, and compel men to continue working, without consideration of the human and constitutional problems involved in that process.

If we begin with public utilities, it will be said that coal and steel are just as important as public utilities. I do not know where we could draw the line. So far as the bill is concerned, we have proceeded on the theory that there is a right to strike and that labor peace must be based on free collective bargaining. We have done nothing to outlaw strikes for basic wages, hours, and working conditions after proper opportunity for mediation.

On page 48 of the bill we have provided for the delay of national emergency strikes. We have provided that when a threatened or actual strike or lock-out affecting substantially an entire industry engaged in trade, commerce, transportation, transmission, or communication among the several States, if permitted to occur or to continue, would imperil the national health or safety, the Attorney General may appoint a board of inquiry to inquire into the issues and make a statement of the issues and report back to him as promptly as he may direct. He may then seek from the court an injunction against striking for a period of 60 days, during which time the Government has another opportunity, through the Mediation Board, to try to bring about an agreement between employers and employees which will prevent a nation-wide strike.

If such mediation should fail, then at the end of 60 days it is provided that there shall be an election by the employees to determine whether or not they accept the last offer made by the employer. If they vote to accept it, of course the strike is terminated. If they vote not to accept it, the injunction is dissolved and they are free to strike. The bill provides that when that happens the Attorney General shall submit to the President a full and comprehensive report of the proceedings, and that the President shall transmit such report, together with such recommendations as he may see fit to make, to the Congress for consideration and appropriate action.

If there finally develops a complete national emergency threatening the safety and health of the people of the United States, Congress can pass an emergency law to cover the particular emergency.

We did not feel that we should put into the law, as a part of the collective-bargaining machinery, an ultimate resort to compulsory arbitration, or to seizure, or to any other action. We feel that it would interfere with the whole process of collective bargaining. If such a remedy is available as a routine remedy, there will always be pressure to resort to it by whichever party thinks it will receive better treatment through such a process than it would receive in collective bargaining, and it will back out of collective bargaining. It will not make a bona-fide attempt to settle if it thinks it will receive a better deal under the final arbitration which may be provided.

We have felt that perhaps in the case of a a general strike, or in the case of other serious strikes, after the termination of every possible effort to resolve the dispute, the remedy might be an emergency act by Congress for that particular purpose.

I have had in mind drafting such a bill, giving power to seize the plants, and other necessary facilities, to seize the unions, their money, and their treasury, and requisition trucks and other equipment; in fact, to do everything that the British did in their general strike of 1926. But while such a bill might be prepared, I should be unwilling to place such a law on the books until we actually face such an emergency, and Congress applies the remedy for the particular emergency only. Eighty days will provide plenty of time within which to consider the possibility of what should be done; and we believe very strongly that there should not be anything in this law which prohibits finally the right to strike.

I have dealt with this question, Mr. President, because it is one of perhaps greater interest and one which affects more than the fundamental philosophy of the bill than the other provisions. It is contained in title 3 as part of the mediation procedure.

But of course the injunctive process does not deal with the main causes of labor trouble, the injustices, and the inequalities of the present law. The bill seeks to restore equality of bargaining power and imposes on the unions the responsibility to balance the power which they have acquired. The bill is not inspired by mere theory or by any hostility to unions. It is based on specific testimony of specific wrongs.

House of Representatives—80th Congress, 1st Session
April 15-17, 1947

FRED HARTLEY [R., N. J.]. Mr. Speaker, I move that the House resolve itself into the Committee of the Whole House on the State of the Union for the consideration of the bill (H. R. 3020) to prescribe fair and equitable rules of conduct to be observed by labor and management in their relations with one another which affect commerce, to protect the rights of individual workers in their relations with labor organizations whose activities affect commerce, to recognize the paramount public interest in labor disputes affecting commerce that endanger the public health, safety, or welfare, and for other purposes.

The motion was agreed to. . . .

Mr. Chairman, during the debate on the rule today, some rather unkind and unfair references have been made to the manner in which this bill has been drafted. This bill was written by the House Committee on Education and Labor. Those of us on the majority side accept full responsibility for what is in this bill. It was our responsibility in the first place and I think we have fulfilled that responsibility.

This committee, as everyone present knows, made the most exhaustive study and held the most exhaustive hearings on this most complicated matter that have ever been held by any Committee on Labor in the history of the Congress of the United States. After the bill was prepared it was presented to the entire committee. It was read line by line and section by section, and no member of the committee was denied the right to amend it in any way he saw fit.

I would also like to make one brief response to the statement made by the gentleman from New York [Mr. Marcantonio] echoing the statement of the president of the CIO and his reference to fascism. As far as I am personally concerned, I am getting sick and tired of hearing those who are not Communists called Fascists. It is too bad that today, if you do not happen to follow the party line, if you do not happen to be a Communist, you have to sit and listen to the charge that if you are not a Communist you must be a Fascist, per se.

We are ready to defend this bill. I am going to, briefly, in a general way, recite what is in the bill. Following me, members of the committee will present in detail all features of the bill. . . .

JOHN KENNEDY [DEM., MASS.]. Mr. Chairman, it is my firm conviction that the House would be making a great mistake to pass this bill in its present form.

I do not think that there are any of us who do not recognize that the 12 years since the passage of the Wagner Act have been marked by turbulence and unrest.

We have seen the growth of powerful unions who have been exempted from judicial and legislative restraint in their relations with their members, with business, and with the Government. They have in their irresponsibility been guilty of excesses that have caused this country great discomfort and concern. Certainly all of us recognize that legislation that will channel the great powers of these unions along lines that will take cognizance of the stake of the public in their activities is needed and should be passed by this House.

But merely because we feel that there are wrongs to be righted, we should not agree to any legislation that is put before us, no matter how high-sounding its language, and how superficially fair it may at first seem, without careful examination.

The bill contains clauses which do much toward guaranteeing each individual union member a square deal from his union. It makes an effort to end feather-bedding, racketeering, and arbitrary combinations of unions which conspire to set prices and conditions which benefit themselves alone. All of these clauses are good, but let us recognize that these clauses are merely window-dressing to secure support from those Members who feel that this Congress has an obligation to correct existing evils. The actual fact is—and I say this with restraint—this bill would in its present form strike down in one devastating blow the union shop, industry-wide bargaining, and so strangle collective bargaining with restraints and limitations as to make it ineffectual. This grave error that the majority of the Committee on Education and Labor have made is that in seeking to destroy what is bad, they are also destroying what is good. There is no need to—there is great need not to—smash the American labor movement to rid ourselves of "feather-bedding," racketeering, and similar evils. Let us look briefly at some of the clauses of this bill.

The majority of this committee in their report have stated. "Important among the provisions of the bill are those that reassure the workers freedom in their organizing and bargaining activities. This concern with the rights of the workers is praiseworthy, but were the majority of the Labor Committee concerned with the rights of the workingman when they outlawed the closed shop and permitted the union shop on only one condition—on condition that the employers give their consent? Is this an example of the bill's concern with the freedom of the workers to organize and bargain? Were the majority of the Labor Committee concerned with the rights of the workingman when they wrote in this bill clauses to outlaw welfare funds, and pension plans, to invalidate in fact two-thirds of the existing welfare plans that are administered jointly by employers and employees? Is it their concern with the rights of the workingman that caused them to do this?

Was it their concern with the rights of the workingman that caused them to outlaw sympathy strikes? Under section 2, if a small number of workers in a plant strike because of any condition, or for any reason, it is forbidden that any of the other workers in the same plant should come to their assistance and strike with them. Is that because of their great concern with the rights of the workingman?

Does section 9 (f) attempt to forbid industry-wide bargaining because it wants to break down as they say "the great labor monopolies," or is it because they recognize that organized plants cannot compete economically with those that are unorganized, and that the latter can, by the sweat of labor, drive out of competition the factories that pay a decent wage, and whose employees work under decent conditions. In order to complete the job, this bill in section 2 (14) (C) will outlaw wholesale any type of boycott, so that the unions cannot protect themselves and their employers against the competition of sweatshops.

Is this bill really concerned with the freedom of the working man to organize and bargain? Under the provision of section 12, together with other sections of the bill, if an employer is guilty of an unfair labor practice by the terms of this bill he would be entitled to a full hearing, findings by the National Labor Relations Board and even by the courts before the findings become legally compelling. Even then the employer is subject only to remedial order and not to punishment. At most he must merely cease and desist and restore the situation to what it was or should have been before he acted. But let us see what happens to the employee. After the bill has outlawed nearly every conceivable type of strike, such as a strike to remedy unfair labor practices, this bill provides that employees who violate certain of these provisions would expose themselves to certain penalties, ex parte injunctions without a hearing, treble damages and loss of his job. Does that honestly show a great concern for the freedom of the working man to organize and bargain freely?

The manifest unfairness of these sections are not isolated. There are others throughout the entire bill.

This bill does not assure the worker freedom and the men who wrote this bill must have known that it does not. It destroys with high-sounding words the power of labor unions to bargain equally with the employers. It will if passed in its present form bring not peace but labor war—a war bitter and dangerous. This bill in its present form plays into the hands of the radicals in our unions, who preach the doctrine of the class struggle. If this bill is passed, this Congress will have fired the opening shot. Where it will lead us no one can say. Have no illusions that you are voting for labor peace and for the protection of the working man. You will be voting for industrial warfare—you will be voting for a bill which seeks to strangle by legal restraints the American labor movement. I urge you to vote against it.

THE VETO MESSAGE
June 20, 1947

The Speaker laid before the House the following veto message from the President of the United States, which was read by the Clerk:

To the House of Representatives:

I return herewith, without my approval, H. R. 3020, the Labor-Management Relations Act, 1947.

I am fully aware of the gravity which attaches to the exercise by the President of his constitutional power to withhold his approval from an enactment of the Congress.

I share with the Congress the conviction that legislation dealing with the relations between management and labor is necessary. I heartily condemn abuses on the part of unions and employers, and I have no patience with stubborn insistence on private advantage to the detriment of the public interest.

But this bill is far from a solution of those problems.

When one penetrates the complex, interwoven provisions of this omnibus bill, and understands the real meaning of its various parts, the result is startling.

The bill taken as a whole would reverse the basic direction of our national labor policy, inject the Government into private economic affairs on an unprecedented scale, and conflict with important principles of our democratic society. Its provisions would cause more strikes, not fewer. It would contribute neither to industrial peace nor to economic stability and progress. It would be a dangerous stride in the direction of a totally managed economy. It contains seeds of discord which would plague this Nation for years to come.

Because of the far-reaching import of this bill, I have weighed its probable effects against a series of fundamental considerations. In each case I find that the bill violates principles essential to our public welfare.

I. The first major test which I have applied to this bill is whether it would result in more or less Government intervention in our economic life.

Our basic national policy has always been to establish by law standards of fair dealing and then to leave the working of the economic system to the free choice of individuals. Under that policy of economic freedom we have built our Nation's productive strength. Our people have deep faith in industrial self-government with freedom of contract and free collective bargaining.

I find that this bill is completely contrary to that national policy of economic freedom. It would require the Government, in effect, to become an unwanted participant at every bargaining table. It would establish by law limitations on the terms of every bargaining agreement, and nullify thousands of agreements mutually arrived at and satisfactory to the parties. It would inject the Government deeply into the process by which employers and workers reach agreement. It would superimpose bureaucratic procedures on the free decisions of local employers and employees.

At a time when we are determined to remove, as rapidly as practicable, Federal controls established during the war, this bill would involve the Government in the free processes of our economic system to a degree unprecedented in peacetime.

This is a long step toward the settlement of economic issues by Government dictation. It is an indication that industrial relations are to be determined in the Halls of Congress and that political power is to supplant economic power as the critical factor in labor relations.

II. The second basic test against which I have measured this bill is whether it would improve human relations between employers and their employees.

Cooperation cannot be achieved by force of law. We cannot create mutual respect and confidence by legislative fiat.

I am convinced that this legislation overlooks the significance of these principles. It would encourage distrust, suspicion, and arbitrary attitudes.

I find that the National Labor Relations Act would be converted from an instrument with the major purpose of protecting the right of workers to organize and bargain collectively into a maze of pitfalls and complex procedures. As a result of these complexities employers and workers would find new barriers to mutual understanding.

The bill time and again would remove the settlement of differences from the bargaining table to courts of law. Instead of learning to live together, employers and unions are invited to engage in costly, time-consuming litigation, inevitably embittering both parties.

The Congress has, I think, paid too much attention to the inevitable frictions and difficulties incident to the reconversion period. It has ignored the unmistakable evidence that those difficulties are receding and that labor-management cooperation is constantly improving. There is grave danger that this progress would be nullified through enactment of this legislation.

III. A third basic test is whether the bill is workable.

There is little point in putting laws on the books unless they can be executed. I have concluded that this bill would prove to be unworkable. The so-called emergency procedure for critical Nation-wide strikes would require an immense amount of Government effort but would result almost inevitably in failure. The National Labor Relations Board would be given many new tasks, and hobbled at every turn in attempting to carry them out. Unique restrictions on the Board's procedures would so greatly increase the backlog of unsettled cases that the parties might be driven to turn in despair from peaceful procedures to economic force.

IV. The fourth basic test by which I have measured this bill is the test of fairness.

The bill prescribes unequal penalties for the same offense. It would require the National Labor Relations Board to give priority to charges against workers over related charges against employers. It would discriminate against workers by arbitrarily penalizing them for all critical strikes.

Much has been made of the claim that the bill is intended simply to equalize the positions of labor and management. Careful analysis shows that this claim is unfounded. Many of the provisions of the bill standing alone seem innocent but, considered in relation to each other, reveal a consistent pattern of inequality.

The failure of the bill to meet these fundamental tests is clearly demonstrated by a more detailed consideration of its defects.

1. The bill would substantially increase strikes.

(1) It would discourage the growing willingness of unions to include "no strike" provisions in bargaining agreements, since any labor organization signing such an agreement would expose itself to suit for contract violation if any of its members engaged in an unauthorized "wildcat" strike.

(2) It would encourage strikes by imposing highly complex and burdensome reporting requirements on labor organizations which wish to avail themselves of their rights under the National Labor Relations Act. In connection with these reporting requirements, the bill would penalize unions for any failure to comply, no matter how inconsequential, by denying them all rights under the act. These provisions, which are irrelevant to the major purposes of the bill, seem peculiarly designed to place obstacles in the way of labor organizations which wish to appeal to the National Labor Relations Board for relief, and thus to impel them to strike or take other direct action.

(3) It would bring on strikes by depriving significant groups of workers of the right they now enjoy to organize and to bargain under the protection of law. For example, broad groups of employees who for purposes of the act would be classed as supervisors would be removed from the protection of the act. Such groups would be prevented from using peaceful machinery and would be left no option but the use of economic force.

(4) The bill would force unions to strike or to boycott if they wish to have a jurisdictional dispute settled by the National Labor Relations Board. This peculiar situation results from the fact that the Board is given authority to determine jurisdictional disputes over assignment of work only after such disputes have been converted into strikes or boycotts.

In addition to these ways in which specific provisions of the bill would lead directly to strikes, the cumulative effect of many of its other provisions which disrupt established relationships would result in industrial strife and unrest.

2. The bill arbitrarily decides, against the workers, certain issues which are normally the subject of collective bargaining, and thus restricts the area of voluntary agreement.

(1) The bill would limit the freedom of employers and labor organizations to agree on methods of developing responsibility on the part of unions by establishing union security. While seeming to preserve the right to agree to the union shop, it would place such a multitude of obstacles in the way of such agreement that union security and responsibility would be largely canceled.

In this respect, the bill disregards the voluntary developments in the field of industrial relations in the United States over the past 150 years. Today, over 11,000,000 workers are employed under some type of union-security contract. The great majority of the plants which have such union-security provisions have had few strikes. Employers in such plants are generally strong supporters of some type of union security, since it gives them a greater measure of stability in production.

(2) The bill would limit the freedom of employers and employees to establish and maintain welfare funds. It would prescribe arbitrary methods of administering them and rigidly limit the purposes for which they may be used. This is an undesirable intrusion by the Government into an important matter which should be the subject of private agreement between employers and employees.

(3) The bill presents the danger that employers and employees might be prohibited from agreeing on safety provisions, rest-period rules, and many other legitimate practices, since such practices may fall under the language defining "feather bedding."

3. The bill would expose employers to numerous hazards by which they could be annoyed and hampered.

(1) The bill would invite frequent disruption of continuous plant production by opening up immense possibilities for many more elections, and adding new types of elections. The bill would invite electioneering for changes in representatives and for union security. This would harass employers in their production efforts and would generate raiding and jurisdictional disputes. The National Labor Relations Board has been developing sound principles of stability on these matters. The bill would overturn these principles to the detriment of employers.

(2) The bill would complicate the collective bargaining process for employers by permitting—and in some cases requiring—the splitting up of stable patterns of representation. Employers would be harassed by having to deal with many small units. Labor organizations would be encouraged to engage in constant interunion warfare, which would result only in confusion.

(3) The bill would invite unions to sue employers in the courts regarding the thousands of minor grievances which arise every day over the inter-

pretation of bargaining agreements. Employers are likely to be besieged by a multiplicity of minor suits, since management necessarily must take the initiative in applying the terms of agreements. In this respect, the bill ignores the fact that employers and unions are in wide agreement that the interpretation of the provisions of bargaining agreements should be submitted to the processes of negotiation ending in voluntary arbitration, under penalties prescribed in the agreement itself. This is one of the points on which the National Labor-Management Conference in November 1945, placed special emphasis. In introducing damage suits as a possible substitute for grievance machinery, the bill rejects entirely the informed wisdom of those experienced in labor relations.

(4) The bill would prevent an employer from freely granting a union-shop contract, even where he and virtually his entire working force were in agreement as to its desirability. He would be required to refrain from agreement until the National Labor Relations Board's work load permitted it to hold an election—in this case simply to ratify an unquestioned and legitimate agreement.

Employers, moreover, would suffer because the ability of unions to exercise responsibility under bargaining agreements would be diminished. Labor organizations whose disciplinary authority is weakened cannot carry their full share of maintaining stability of production.

4. The bill would deprive workers of vital protection which they now have under the law.

(1) The bill would make it easier for an employer to get rid of employees whom he wanted to discharge because they exercised their right of self-organization guaranteed by the act. It would permit an employer to dismiss a man on the pretext of a slight infraction of shop rules, even though his real motive was to discriminate against this employee for union activity.

(2) The bill would also put a powerful new weapon in the hands of employers by permitting them to initiate elections at times strategically advantageous to them. It is significant that employees on economic strike who may have been replaced are denied a vote. An employer could easily thwart the will of his employees by raising a question of representation at a time when the union was striking over contract terms.

(3) It would give employers the means to engage in endless litigation, draining the energy and resources of unions in court actions, even though the particular charges were groundless.

(4) It would deprive workers of the power to meet the competition goods produced under sweatshop conditions by permitting employers to halt every type of secondary boycott, not merely those for unjustifiable purposes.

(5) It would reduce the responsibility of employers for unfair labor practices committed in their behalf. The effect of the bill is to narrow unfairly employer liability for antiunion acts and statements made by persons who, in

the eyes of the employees affected, act and speak for management, but who may not be "agents" in the strict legal sense of that term.

(6) At the same time it would expose unions to suits for acts of violence, wildcat strikes, and other actions, none of which were authorized or ratified by them. By employing elaborate legal doctrine, the bill applies a superficially similar test of responsibility for employers and unions—each would be responsible for the acts of his agents. But the power of an employer to control the acts of his subordinates is direct and final. This is radically different from the power of unions to control the acts of their members—who are, after all, members of a free association.

5. The bill abounds in provisions which would be unduly burdensome or actually unworkable.

(1) The bill would erect an unworkable administrative structure for carrying out the National Labor Relations Act. The bill would establish, in effect, an independent general counsel and an independent Board. But it would place with the Board full responsibility for investigating and determining election cases—over 70 percent of the present case load—and at the same time would remove from the Board the authority to direct and control the personnel engaged in carrying out this responsibility.

(2) It would invite conflict between the National Labor Relations Board and its general counsel, since the general counsel would decide, without any right of appeal by employers and employees, whether charges were to be heard by the Board, and whether orders of the Board were to be referred to the court for enforcement. By virtue of this unlimited authority, a single administrative official might usurp the Board's responsibility for establishing policy under the act.

(3) It would strait-jacket the National Labor Relations Board's operations by a series of special restrictions unknown to any other quasi-judicial agency. After many years of study, the Congress adopted the Administrative Procedures Act of 1946 to govern the operation of all quasi-judicial agencies, including the National Labor Relations Board. This present bill disregards the Procedures Act and, in many respects, is directly contrary to the spirit and letter of that act. Simple and time-saving procedures, already established and accepted as desirable by employers and employees, would be summarily scrapped. The Board itself, denied the power of delegation, would be required to hear all jurisdictional disputes over work tasks. This single duty might require a major portion of the Board's time. The review function within the Board, largely of a nonjudicial character, would be split up and assigned to separate staffs attached to each Board member. This would lead to extensive and costly duplication of work and records.

(4) The bill would require or invite Government supervised elections in an endless variety of cases. Questions of the bargaining unit, of representa-

tives, of union security, of bargaining offers, are subject to election after election, most of them completely unnecessary. The National Labor Relations Board has had difficulty conducting the number of elections required under present law. This bill would greatly multiply this load. It would, in effect, impose upon the Board a 5-year backlog of election cases, if it handled them at its present rate.

(5) The bill would introduce a unique handicap, unknown in ordinary law, upon the use of statements as evidence of unfair labor practices. An antiunion statement by an employer, for example, could not be considered as evidence of motive, unless it contained an explicit threat of reprisal or force or promise of benefit. The bill would make it an unfair labor practice to "induce or encourage" certain types of strikes and boycotts, and then would forbid the National Labor Relations Board to consider as evidence "views, argument, or opinion" by which such a charge could be proved.

(6) The bill would require the Board to "determine" jurisdictional disputes over work tasks, instead of using arbitration, the accepted and traditional method of settling such disputes. In order to get its case before the Board a union must indulge in a strike or a boycott and wait for some other party to allege that it had violated the law. If the Board's decision should favor the party thus forced to violate the law in order that its case might be heard, the Board would be without power over other parties to the dispute to whom the award might be unacceptable.

(7) The bill would require the Board to determine which employees on strike are "entitled to reinstatement" and hence would be eligible to vote in an election held during a strike. This would be an impossible task, since it would require the Board arbitrarily to decide which, if any of the employees had been replaced and therefore should not be allowed to vote.

6. The bill would establish an ineffective and discriminatory emergency procedure for dealing with major strikes affecting the public health or safety.

This procedure would be certain to do more harm than good, and to increase rather than diminish widespread industrial disturbances. I am convinced that the country would be in for a bitter disappointment if these provisions of the bill became law.

The procedure laid down by the bill is elaborate. Its essential features are a Presidential board of inquiry, a waiting period of approximately 80 days— enforced by injunction—and a secret ballot vote of the workers on the question of whether or not to accept their employer's last offer.

At the outset a board of inquiry would be required to investigate the situation thoroughly, but would be specifically forbidden to offer its informed judgment concerning a reasonable basis for settlement of the dispute. Such inquiry therefore, would serve merely as a sounding board to dramatize the respective positions of the parties.

A strike or lock-out might occur before the board of inquiry could make its report, and perhaps even before the board could be appointed. The existence of such a strike or lock-out would hamper the board in pursuing its inquiry. Experience has shown that fact-finding, if it is to be most effective as a device for settlement of labor disputes, should come before the men leave their work, not afterwards. Furthermore, an injunction issued after a strike has started would arouse bitter resentment which would not contribute to agreement.

If the dispute had not been settled after 60 days of the waiting period, the National Labor Relations Board would be required to hold a separate election for the employees of each employer to find out whether the workers wished to accept the employer's last offer, as stated by him. Our experience under the War Labor Disputes Act showed conclusively that such an election would almost inevitably result in a vote to reject the employer's offer, since such action amounts to a vote of confidence by the workers in their bargaining representatives. The union would then be reinforced by a dramatic demonstration, under Government auspices, of its strength for further negotiations.

After this elaborate procedure the injunction would then have to be dissolved, the parties would be free to fight out their dispute, and it would be mandatory for the President to transfer the whole problem to the Congress, even if it were not in session. Thus, major economic disputes between employers and their workers over contract terms might ultimately be thrown into the political arena for disposition. One could scarcely devise a less effective method for discouraging critical strikes.

This entire procedure is based upon the same erroneous assumptions as those which underlay the strike-vote provision of the War Labor Disputes Act, namely; that strikes are called in haste as the result of inflamed passions, and that union leaders do not represent the wishes of the workers. We have learned by experience, however, that strikes in the basic industries are not called in haste, but only after long periods of negotiations and serious deliberation; and that in the secret-ballot election the workers almost always vote to support their leaders.

Furthermore, a fundamental inequity runs through these provisions. The bill provides for injunctions to prohibit workers from striking, even against terms dictated by employers after contracts have expired. There is no provision assuring the protection of the rights of the employees during the period they are deprived of the right to protect themselves by economic action.

In summary, I find that the so-called "emergency procedure" would be ineffective. It would provide for clumsy and cumbersome Government intervention; it would authorize inequitable injunctions; and it would probably culminate in a public confession of failure. I cannot conceive that this procedure would aid in the settlement of disputes.

7. The bill would discriminate against employees.

(1) It would impose discriminatory penalties upon employers and employees for the same offense, that of violating the requirement that existing agreements be maintained for 60 days without strike or lock-out while a new agreement is being negotiated. Employers could only be required to restore the previous conditions of employment, but employees could be summarily dismissed by the employer.

(2) The bill would require the Board to seek a temporary restraining order when labor organizations had been charged with boycotts or certain kinds of jurisdictional strikes. It would invite employers to find any pretext for arguing that "an object" of the union's action was one of these practices, even though the primary object was fully legitimate. Moreover, since these cases would be taken directly into the courts, they necessarily would be settled by the judiciary before the National Labor Relations Board had a chance to decide the issue. This would thwart the entire purpose of the National Labor Relations Act in establishing the Board, which purpose was to confer on the Board, rather than the courts, the power to decide complex questions of fact in a special field requiring expert knowledge. This provision of the bill is clearly a backward step toward the old abuses of the labor injunction. No similar provision directed against employers can be found in the bill.

(3) The bill would also require the Board to give priority in investigating charges of certain kinds of unfair labor practices against unions, even though such unfair labor practices might have been provoked by those of the employer. Thus the bill discriminates, in this regard, in the relief available to employers and unions.

(4) It would impose on labor organizations, but not on employers, burdensome reporting requirements which must be met before any rights would be available under the act.

(5) In weakening the protections afforded to the right to organize, contrary to the basic purpose of the National Labor Relations Act, the bill would injure smaller unions far more than larger ones. Those least able to protect themselves would be the principal victims of the bill.

8. The bill would disregard in important respects the unanimous convictions of employer and labor representatives at the national labor-management conference in November 1945.

(1) One of the strongest convictions expressed during the conference was that the Government should withdraw from the collective bargaining process, now that the war emergency is over, and leave the determination of working conditions to the free agreement of the parties. This bill proceeds in exactly the opposite direction. In numerous ways the bill would unnecessarily in-

trude the Government into the process of reaching free decisions through bargaining. This intrusion is precisely what the representatives of management and labor resented.

(2) A unanimous recommendation of the conference was that the Conciliation Service should be strengthened within the Department of Labor. But this bill removes the Conciliation Service from the Department of Labor. The new name for the Service would carry with it no new dignity or new functions. The evidence does not support the theory that the conciliation function would be better exercised and protected by an independent agency outside the Department of Labor. Indeed, the Service would lose the important day-to-day support of factual research in industrial relations available from other units of the Department. Furthermore, the removal of the Conciliation Service from the Department of Labor would be contrary to the praiseworthy policy of the Congress to centralize related governmental units within the major Government departments.

9. The bill raises serious issues of public policy which transcend labor-management difficulties.

(1) In undertaking to restrict political contributions and expenditures, the bill would prohibit many legitimate activities on the part of unions and corporations. This provision would prevent the ordinary union newspaper from commenting favorably or unfavorably upon candidates or issues in national elections. I regard this as a dangerous intrusion on free speech, unwarranted by any demonstration of need, and quite foreign to the stated purposes of this bill.

Furthermore, this provision can be interpreted as going far beyond its apparent objectives, and as interfering with necessary business activities. It provides no exemption for corporations whose business is the publication of newspapers or the operation of radio stations. It makes no distinctions between expenditures made by such corporations for the purpose of influencing the results of an election, and other expenditures made by them in the normal course of their business "in connection with" an election. Thus it would raise a host of troublesome questions concerning the legality of many practices ordinarily engaged in by newspapers and radio stations.

(2) In addition, in one important area the bill expressly abandons the principle of uniform application of national policy under Federal law. The bill's stated policy of preserving some degree of union security would be abdicated in all states when more restrictive policies exist. In other respects the bill makes clear that Federal policy would govern insofar as activities affecting commerce are concerned. This is not only an invitation to the State to distort national policy as they see fit, but is a complete forsaking of a long-standing constitutional principle.

(3) In regard to Communists in unions, I am convinced that the bill would have an effect exactly opposite to that intended by the Congress. Con-

gress intended to assist labor organizations to rid themselves of Communist officers. With this objective I am in full accord. But the effect of this provision would be far different. The bill would deny the peaceful procedures of the National Labor Relations Act to a union unless all its officers declared under oath that they were not members of the Communist Party and that they did not favor the forceful or unconstitutional overthrow of the Government. The mere refusal by a single individual to sign the required affidavit would prevent an entire national labor union from being certified for purposes of collective bargaining. Such a union would have to win all its objectives by strike, rather than by orderly procedure under the law. The union and the affected industry would be disrupted for perhaps a long period of time while violent electioneering, charges, and countercharges split open the union ranks. The only result of this provision would be confusion and disorder which is exactly the result the Communists desire.

This provision in the bill is an attempt to solve difficult problems of industrial democracy by recourse to oversimplified legal devices. I consider that this provision would increase, rather than decrease, disruptive effects of Communists in our labor movement.

The most fundamental test which I have applied to this bill is whether it would strengthen or weaken American democracy in the present critical hour. This bill is perhaps the most serious economic and social legislation of the past decade. Its effects—for good or ill—would be felt for decades to come.

I have concluded that the bill is a clear threat to the successful working of our democratic society.

One of the major lessons of recent world history is that free and vital trade-unions are a strong bulwark against the growth of totalitarian movements. We must, therefore, be everlastingly alert that in striking at union abuses we do not destroy the contribution which unions make to our democratic strength.

This bill would go far toward weakening our trade-union movement. And it would go far toward destroying our national unity. By raising barriers between labor and management and by injecting political considerations into normal economic decisions, it would invite them to gain their ends through direct political action. I think it would be exceedingly dangerous to our country to develop a class basis for political action.

I cannot emphasize too strongly the transcendent importance of the United States in the world today as a force for freedom and peace. We cannot be strong internationally if our national unity and our productive strength are hindered at home. Anything which weakens our economy or weakens the unity of our people—as I am thoroughly convinced this bill would do—I cannot approve.

In my message on the state of the Union which I submitted to the Congress in January 1947, I recommended a step-by-step approach to the subject of labor legislation. I specifically indicated the problems which we should treat immediately. I recommended that, before going on to other problems, a careful, thorough, and nonpartisan investigation should be made, covering the entire field of labor-management relations.

There is still a genuine opportunity for the enactment of appropriate labor legislation this session. I still feel that the recommendations which I expressed in the state of the Union message constitute an adequate basis for legislation which is moderate in spirit and which relates to known abuses.

For the compelling reasons I have set forth, I return H. R. 3020 without my approval.

Harry S. Truman

THE ENSUING DEBATE

Senate—80th Congress, 1st Session
June 23, 1947

ROBERT TAFT [R., OHIO]. Mr. President, it is now approximately 6 months since this Congress returned to Washington to consider the task which lay before it. Regardless of the issues in the election, there was unquestionably a demand at that time, as there is now, for labor legislation, for a reform of the abuses which had become apparent to the American people. They had been deluged with a series of strikes. They had been deluged with strikes ordered for men who did not desire the strikes. They had been deluged with strikes against companies which had settled all difference with their own men. They had been deluged with strikes in violation of existing collective bargaining agreements. They knew of mass picketing. They knew that in those strikes men had been excluded from their own plants by force and violence. They knew that the men in the unions themselves had been arbitrarily treated by the leaders, and that unless they chose to please the leaders they lost their jobs. They were fired from the union and lost their jobs with the company, and in many cases they found it impossible to continue their own trade. They knew of feather-bedding practices. They knew the limitation on apprentices, so that men could not be obtained for necessary work. They knew of the limitation on the freedom of employers, and they knew of the many unjust provisions of the Wagner Act as administered by the National Labor Relations Board.

There was a demand that we act. I deny completely that there has been politics in the drafting of this legislation. It was participated in by all. Certainly, I felt that with the public demand for reform in this particular field the Republican Party, which happened to have control of the Congress, would be held to be delinquent if it failed to propose a reasonable labor-reform measure. To that extent, if that is politics, the bill is politics.

We went to work. Many bills were introduced. The committee held hearings and heard from labor leaders, from industrialists, from experts— it gave everyone a chance to be heard, until we were criticized for delaying the matter. There was nothing hurried in the development of the legislation.

Finally the committee produced a bill which 11 out of the 13 members of the committee supported when it came to the floor of the Senate. It was amended on the floor. There was an overwhelming vote in favor of some of the amendments. Other amendments were rejected. The bill went to conference, and in conference various provisions of the House bill were accepted. But, Mr. President, after 6 months' consideration, after a thorough debate on the floor of the Senate, after a thorough debate in conference, and

665

another debate on the floor of the Senate on the conference report, the bill was agreed to and sent to the President of the United States.

Last Tuesday the President held a press conference in which he said:

I do not know that there will be a labor veto. I have not made up my mind. I still have to study it.

The President replied to another question that he might act before Friday, but explained that he had not as yet read the bill in the form in which it passed both Houses of Congress. He said: "I am going to study it for the next 2 days."

As the result of 2 days' study by the President of the United States, the work of many hundreds of men, the sincere and careful work of several dozen men who have gone into the details of this legislation from the beginning to the end has been set aside by the veto exercised by the President of the United States. Of course, he has the constitutional right to veto a bill, but it seems to me it is a case in which he might well have withheld the actual exercise of that right. To my good Democratic friends and Republicans who believe in Thomas Jefferson, let me say that Thomas Jefferson never vetoed a bill presented to him by Congress. He felt that that right should be exercisen only in a time of the greatest emergency, and he questioned whether it should be exercised at all.

Mr. President, we have drafted this bill and it is based on the theory of the Wagner Act, if you please. It is based on the theory that the solution of the labor problem in the United States is free, collective bargaining—a contract between one employer and all of his men acting as one man. That is the theory of the Wagner Act, that they shall be free to make the contract they wish to make.

Many people have felt that the Government should come in certain cases and impose compulsory arbitration in the fixing of wages, if the parties cannot agree. Our provision for dealing with Nation-wide strikes has been criticized. After 60 days, if they still want to vote for a strike, we have not forbidden it, because we believe that the right to strike for hours, wages, and working conditions in the ultimate analysis is essential to the maintenance of freedom in the United States. We have rejected every effort to impose upon any men any wages, hours, or working conditions to which they, through their representatives, do not agree.

We have been criticized on the ground that for that reason the bill is too weak. I do not think so. I think that if the Government is going to fix wages it will fix prices and the entire economy. I think our freedom depends upon maintaining the free right to strike. It can be limited. Surely it is not too much to ask men to maintain the status quo for 60 days rather than endanger the safety and health of the Nation. But in the last analysis, if it becomes a political strike, then the Government will have to act through some special emergency legislation for that particular case, as was done in connection with the general strike in England. We have based it upon free collective bargaining and have not modified that right in any material respect.

We have tried to deal with abuses. We tried to get testimony as to just what is wrong in this field, and there is testimony on the record as to each of the things which we have tried to correct.

We have tried to correct secondary boycotts and jurisdictional strikes. The truth is that originally, before the passage of any of the laws dealing with labor, the employer had all the advantage. He had the employees at his mercy, and he could practically in most cases dictate the terms which he wished to impose. Congress passed the Clayton Act, the Norris-LaGuardia Act, and the Wagner Act. The latter act was interpreted by a completely prejudiced board in such a way that it went far beyond the original intention of Congress, until we reached a point where the balance had shifted over to the other side, where the labor leaders had every advantage in collective bargaining and were relieved from any liability in breaking the contract after they had made the bargain. That was a condition under which strikes actually were encouraged and protected, no matter what the purpose or the character of the particular strike.

All we have tried to do is to swing that balance back, not too far, to a point where the parties can deal equally with each other and where they have approximately equal power. I think the largest companies today can deal with their employees throughout the Nation, but the smaller companies are practically at the mercy of the labor-union bosses. Whatever they have insisted upon in the last 4 or 5 years the employers have practically had to give to them. We want to get the situation back to the point where it is fair. If a man does have the power to enforce and obtain an unreasonable demand, he is much less likely to make an unreasonable demand. Strikes have largely been brought about by unreasonable demands to which the employer finally felt he could not possibly yield and at the same time maintain the integrity and independence of his business.

This is a perfectly reasonable bill in every respect. If we are to have free collective bargaining it must be between two responsible parties. Some of the provisions of this bill deal with the question of making the unions responsible. There is no reason in the world why a union should not have the same responsibility that a corporation has which is engaged in business. So we have provided that a union may be sued as if it were a corporation. We have provided that the union must file statements as corporations have had to file them, setting up their methods of doing business and making financial reports to the members and to the Secretary of Labor. That sort of reform actually strengthens the members in their collective bargaining. There will be no free collective bargaining until both sides are equally responsible.

We have set up a Mediation Service. We took it out of the Department of Labor because it was felt, rightly or wrongly, that as long as it was an agency of the Department of Labor it must necessarily take a prolabor slant and therefore could not be as fair in mediating differences between the parties. Then we outlawed secondary boycotts and jurisdictional strikes. There was no testimony in the record anywhere to the effect that secondary boycotts and jurisdictional strikes were justified. We asked the President's representatives as to what kind of secondary boycotts were justified, but we never got a satisfactory answer.

In this bill we prohibit secondary boycotts all over this country. There have been secondary boycotts in which a union has said, "We will not handle the goods of manufacturer X because we do not like the men who make his particular goods"; and in many cases where a manufacturer had a union certified to him—perhaps a CIO union—an AFL union has boycotted it, or vice versa. All over the country such things have occurred; and I know that in my own State, small manufacturers have absolutely been driven out of their business and have been destroyed by unions far off from their concern, unions in which they had no interest whatsoever. Yet the strikes have dragged on. We have tried to prohibit secondary boycotts, and we give the Board the power to decide the controversies.

Here and elsewhere the union leaders have said, "Yes; these are abuses, but leave them to us. We will get together; we will settle these abuses." But never at any time have they suggested legislation.

I say to the Senate that this bill could have been only one-half as strong as it is, if we please to call it strong, and yet there would be exactly the same opposition from every labor leader and we would have exactly the same propaganda that is going out today against this bill. Mr. President, it is not against the provisions of this bill. They try to pick out little things here and there and try to exaggerate their importance. Mr. President, it is not the provisions of this bill that they are concerned about; it is any legislation that would in any way reduce the power of the labor leaders. They have opposed it for 10 years.

I was quoted, perhaps, by the Senator from Wyoming, earlier today, as saying that if this bill does not pass, there will be no legislation. That was not an ultimatum from me; that was a conclusion by the labor leaders, and from the President's own message.

The President did not find one thing to approve in this measure. He has criticized it as he has the Case bill—in every section. Apparently he will veto any bill on the subject.

References have been made to breaking the bill into pieces and enacting the separate pieces. Apparently if that were done, the President would criticize and would veto every piece.

The President has never yet recognized that there are abuses. There is nothing in his message really recognizing that there are abuses, except a little lip service, "Well, there are some things we should do something about." But the President has failed to point out any specific abuses whatever, and he has failed to point out any legislation to accomplish the desired result. His message mentions elimination of jurisdictional strikes and secondary boycotts, but we never got any real recommendation from him about taking care of those problems.

Mr. President, for the last 10 years we have had bills dealing with labor problems and labor legislation. We have in this body, men who know as much about labor legislation as anyone in the Government of the United States or anyone outside the Government of the United States does; and yet they would appoint another commission. That is the recourse of people who do not want any legislation at all.

So we face here the problem of whether, the Senate and the House of Representatives having agreed upon a constructive labor measure, we are going to put that through or whether we are going to say to the labor-union leaders, "No; there is no Congress of the United States, there is no President of the United States, who dares to stand up against your power." Certainly the power they exercise today is a threat to the welfare of the people of the United States.

Certainly the bill is complicated. Why? Because the Wagner Act was complicated; and in order to deal with it, we had to amend every section of the Wagner Act. That is what most of this bill is.

I sat in the hearings on the Wagner Act in 1939, and I can tell the Senate something about the power of the first Board which was set up. Talk about the power of the general counsel under this measure. Just think of the power of that first Board, made up of the two Smiths and Madden—people who regarded themselves as crusaders to put a CIO union, if you please, in every plant in the United States. That was their effort. There was no pretense of fairness or justice. I have never known of any other case in the United States where there were such outrages or such injustices as those which were perpetrated by that Board.

The Board has gradually improved, and today we have somewhat a separation of powers. But at that time the Board was both the judge and the jury. True, the powers against labor unions which they had were not as great as the powers provided in this bill, because the powers that Board had were all against employers. In this bill we have changed that situation, so that now the bill recognizes that there are unfair labor practices on the part of employees, just as the former bill recognized that there were unfair labor practices on the part of employers. We have tried to balance up the two. We have not made unlawful a single act on the part of employees which was not made unlawful on the part of employers in the original bill. Otherwise we have left those provisions alone and untouched, except perhaps for the provision of freedom of speech. In the United States there is a demand that we restore complete freedom of speech to both sides, and that we have done. Otherwise there is no modification. No employer can beat down a union; no employer can discriminate; no employer can refuse to deal with a union with is duly certified to him.

So, Mr. President, I say that in this bill we have simply tried to equalize the Government's power as against the unions and as against the employers. We have tried to abolish special privileges conferred by preexisting legislation, and we have based this measure on freedom of contract and on free collective bargaining.

Mr. President, I have listened with interest to all the criticisms—the petty criticisms of this and the petty criticisms of that. All that we have done with the Board, as referred to by the Senator from Wyoming, is to make a separation of powers. Under this bill the Board is judicial. It is judicial today. Its counsel will be a prosecutor. He will not have any extraordinary powers—nothing like the power of the Attorney General of the United States, who decides whether criminal actions shall be brought against anyone in the United States. Under this bill, the counsel will have the right to make the decision as between employer and employee; but his decision will be subject to the judicial decision of the Board and to provide for the redress of any injustice.

Mr. President, the charges made against this act are wholly unjustified.

I appeal to the Senate of the United States to stand up to the work of the legislative body. This is a case of legislation. It is a case in which the President never should have intervened. It is a case in which the President could well have taken the position that, regardless of whether he liked or did not like the work that had been done, the public desire for equity between employer and employee should prevail, no matter what his personal opinion might be.

Mr. President, I trust that the President's veto will be overridden.

MR. BARKLEY. Mr. President, will the Senator withold that for a moment, to yield to me for one matter?

MR. TAFT. I yield.

MR. BARKLEY. Will the Senator yield, so that there may be read at the desk a brief statement from the Senator from New York [Mr. Wagner], explaining the reason for his inability to be present?

MR. TAFT. I am glad to do so.

MR. BARKLEY. Mr. President, I send the statement to the desk and ask that it be read.

THE PRESIDENT PRO TEMPORE [ARTHUR VANDENBERG, R., MICH.]. That can be done by unanimous consent. Without objection, the clerk will read. The Chief Clerk read as follows:

Senator Wagner, the author of the act which the Taft-Hartley bill will amend, is not able to be present to cast his vote in favor of sustaining the President's veto. Because of his great devotion to the working men and women of this country, and because, in his estimation, this bill will destroy what he has so long labored to develop—industrial peace through democracy—every effort was made and every facility at the disposal of the great city of New York was made available to Senator Wagner in order to have him present here on the Senate floor today. It was Senator Wagner's most ardent hope that the doctors would see fit to let him come. But it was the unanimous and expert decision of his two personal physicians, together with Dr. Edward M. Bernecker, commissioner of hospitals of the city of New York, and Dr. Samuel Frant, of the New York City Health Department, after final and thorough examination this morning, that "he not be permitted to make any trip whatsoever." It is their opinion that if he did so at this moment, it might well prove fatal. Senator Wagner has a heart ailment, and his blood pressure, most unfortunately, at the moment is at such a level that any strain or excitement would be sufficient to result in his death.

From his sick bed he urges those Senators who are about to override the President's veto to reconsider, for he says—and these are his exact words: "The President would not lie at this crucial moment in history."

THE DECISIONS

As previously stated, the Taft-Hartley Act of 1947 amended the Wagner Act in significant respects, perhaps the most important amendments listing a number of union unfair labor practices. In addition the statute proceeded into new areas, dealing with such matters as national emergency disputes and suits for violation of collective agreements. Again, we have set forth a few of the many Supreme Court decisions to illustrate the nature of the problems presented by these provisions.

Lincoln Mills is truly a landmark decision. It upholds the constitutionality of Section 301, which provides for the bringing of suits for violation of labor contracts in the federal courts, on the basis that this section authorizes the federal courts to fashion a body of federal law for the enforcement of collective bargaining agreements. And, the Court holds, included within that federal law is the power specifically to enforce a promise to arbitrate grievances arising under such agreements. Thus the Court spawned a large body of federal law for the enforcement of collective bargaining agreements.

Textile Workers of America v. Lincoln Mills of Alabama
353 U.S. 448 (1957)

MR. JUSTICE DOUGLAS delivered the opinion of the Court.

Petitioner-union entered into a collective bargaining agreement in 1953 with respondent-employer, the agreement to run one year and from year to year thereafter, unless terminated on specified notices. The agreement provided that there would be no strikes or work stoppages and that grievances would be handled pursuant to a specified procedure. The last step in the grievance procedure—a step that could be taken by either party—was arbitration.

This controversy involves several grievances that concern work loads and work assignments. The grievances were processed through the various steps in the grievance procedure and were finally denied by the employer. The union requested arbitration, and the employer refused. Thereupon the union brought this suit in the District Court to compel arbitration.

The District Court concluded that it had jurisdiction and ordered the employer to comply with the grievance arbitration provisions of the collective bargaining agreement. The Court of Appeals reversed by a divided vote. 230 F. 2d 81. It held that, although the District Court had jurisdiction to entertain the suit, the court had no authority founded either in federal or state law to grant the relief. The case is here on a petition for a writ of certiorari which we granted because of the importance of the problem and the contrariety of views in the courts. 352 U. S. 821.

The starting point of our inquiry is § 301 of the Labor Management Relations Act of 1947. . . .

There has been considerable litigation involving § 301 and courts have construed it differently. There is one view that § 301 (a) merely gives federal district courts jurisdiction in controversies that involve labor organizations in industries affecting commerce, without regard to diversity of citizenship or the amount in controversy.[1] Under that view § 301 (a) would not be the source of substantive law; it would neither supply federal law to resolve these controversies nor turn the federal judges to state law for answers to the questions. Other courts—the overwhelming number of them—hold that § 301 (a) is more than jurisdictional—that it authorizes federal courts to fashion a body of federal law for the enforcement of these collective bargaining agreements and includes within that federal law specific performance of promises to arbitrate grievances under collective bargaining agreements. Perhaps the leading decision representing that point of view is the one rendered by Judge Wyzanski in *Textile Workers Union* v. *American Thread Co.,* 113 F. Supp. 137. That is our construction of § 301 (a), which means that the agreement to arbitrate grievance disputes, contained in this collective bargaining agreement, should be specifically enforced.

From the face of the Act it is apparent that § 301 (a) and § 301 (b) supplement one another. Section 301 (b) makes it possible for a labor organization, representing employees in an industry affecting commerce, to sue and be sued as an entity in the federal courts. Section 301 (b) in other words provides the procedural remedy lacking at common law. Section 301 (a) certainly does something more than that. Plainly, it supplies the basis upon which the federal district courts may take jurisdiction and apply the procedural rule of § 301 (b). The question is whether § 301 (a) is more than jurisdictional.

The legislative history of § 301 is somewhat cloudy and confusing. But there are a few shafts of light that illuminate our problem.

The bills, as they passed the House and the Senate, contained provisions which would have made the failure to abide by an agreement to arbitrate an unfair labor practice. S. Rep. No. 105, 80th Cong., 1st Sess., pp. 20–21, 23; H. R. Rep. No. 245, 80th Cong., 1st Sess., p. 21. This feature of the law was dropped in Conference. As the Conference Report stated, "Once parties have made a collective bargaining contract the enforcement of that contract should be left to the usual processes of the law and not to the National Labor Relations Board." H. R. Conf. Rep. No. 510, 80th Cong., 1st Sess., p. 42.

Both the Senate and the House took pains to provide for "the usual processes of the law" by provisions which were the substantial equivalent of

§ 301 (a) in its present form. Both the Senate Report and the House Report indicate a primary concern that unions as well as employees should be bound to collective bargaining contracts. But there was also a broader concern—a concern with a procedure for making such agreements enforceable in the courts by either party. At one point the Senate Report, *supra,* p. 15, states, "We feel that the aggrieved party should also have a right of action in the Federal courts. Such a policy is completely in accord with the purpose of the Wagner Act which the Supreme Court declared was 'to compel employers to bargain collectively with their employees to the end that an employment contract, binding on both parties, should be made . . . .' "

Congress was also interested in promoting collective bargaining that ended with agreements not to strike. The Senate Report, *supra,* p. 16 states:

> If unions can break agreements with relative impunity, then such agreements do not tend to stabilize industrial relations. The execution of an agreement does not by itself promote industrial peace. The chief advantage which an employer can reasonably expect from a collective labor agreement is assurance of uninterrupted operation during the term of the agreement. Without some effective method of assuring freedom from economic warfare for the term of the agreement, there is little reason why an employer would desire to sign such a contract.
>
> Consequently, to encourage the making of agreements and to promote industrial peace through faithful performance by the parties, collective agreements affecting interstate commerce should be enforceable in the Federal courts. Our amendment would provide for suits by unions as legal entities and against unions as legal entities in the Federal courts in disputes affecting commerce.

Thus collective bargaining contracts were made "equally binding and enforceable on both parties." *Id.,* p. 15. As stated in the House Report, *supra,* p. 6, the new provision "makes labor organizations equally responsible with employers for contract violations and provides for suit by either against the other in the United States district courts." To repeat, the Senate Report, *supra,* p. 17, summed up the philosophy of § 301 as follows: "Statutory recognition of the collective agreement as a valid, binding, and enforceable contract is a logical and necessary step. It will promote a higher degree of responsibility upon the parties to such agreements, and will thereby promote industrial peace."

Plainly the agreement to arbitrate grievance disputes is the *quid pro quo* for an agreement not to strike. Viewed in this light, the legislation does more than confer jurisdiction in the federal courts over labor organizations. It expresses a federal policy that federal courts should enforce these agreements on behalf of or against labor organizations and that industrial peace can be best obtained only in that way.

To be sure, there is a great medley of ideas reflected in the hearings, reports, and debates on this Act. Yet, to repeat, the entire tenor of the history indicates that the agreement to arbitrate grievance disputes was considered as *quid pro quo* of a no-strike agreement. And when in the House the debate narrowed to the question whether § 301 was more than jurisdictional, it became abundantly clear that the purpose of the section was to provide the necessary legal remedies. Section 302 of the House bill, the substantial equivalent of the present § 301, was being described by Mr. Hartley, the sponsor of the bill in the House:

MR. BARDEN. Mr. Chairman, I take this time for the purpose of asking the Chairman a question, and in asking the question I want it understood that it is intended to make a part of the record that may hereafter be referred to as history of the legislation.

It is my understanding that section 302, the section dealing with equal responsibility under collective bargaining contracts in strike actions and proceedings in district courts contemplates not only the ordinary lawsuits for damages but also such other remedial proceedings, both legal and equitable, as might be appropriate in the circumstances; in other words, proceedings could, for example, be brought by the employers, the labor organizations, or interested individual employees under the Declaratory Judgments Act in order to secure declarations from the Court of legal rights under the contract.

MR. HARTLEY. The interpretation the gentleman has just given of that section is absolutely correct. 93 Cong. Rec. 3656-3657.

It seems, therefore, clear to us that Congress adopted a policy which placed sanctions behind agreements to arbitrate grievance disputes by implication rejecting the common-law rule, discussed in *Red Cross Line* v. *Atlantic Fruit Co.,* 264 U. S. 109, against enforcement of executory agreements to arbitrate. We would undercut the Act and defeat its policy if we read § 301 narrowly as only conferring jurisdiction over labor organizations.

The question then is, what is the substantive law to be applied in suits under § 301 (a)? We conclude that the substantive law to apply in suits under § 301 (a) is federal law, which the courts must fashion from the policy of our national labor laws. See Mendelsohn, Enforceability of Arbitration Agreements Under Taft-Hartley Section 301, 66 Yale L. J. 167. The Labor Management Relations Act expressly furnishes some substantive law. It points out what the parties may or may not do in certain situations. Other problems will lie in the penumbra of express statutory mandates. Some will lack express statutory sanction but will be solved by looking at the policy of the legislation and fashioning a remedy that will effectuate that policy. The range of judicial inventiveness will be determined by the nature of the problem. See *Board of Commissioners* v. *United States,* 308 U. S. 343, 351. Federal interpretation of the Federal law will govern, not state law. Cf. *Jerome* v. *United States,* 318 U. S. 101, 104. But state law, if compatible with the purpose of § 301, may be resorted to in order to find the rule that will best effectuate the federal policy. See *Board of Commissioners* v. *United States, supra,* at 351–352. Any state law applied, however, will be absorbed as federal law and will not be an independent source of private rights.

It is not uncommon for federal courts to fashion federal law where federal rights are concerned. See *Clearfield Trust Co.* v. *United States,* 318 U. S. 363, 366–367; *National Metropolitan Bank* v. *United States,* 323 U. S. 454. Congress has indicated by § 301 (a) the purpose to follow that course here. There is no constitutional difficulty. Article III, § 2, extends the judicial power to cases "arising under . . . the Laws of the United States . . . ." The power of Congress to regulate these labor-management controversies under the Commerce Clause is plain. *Houston & Texas R. Co.* v. *United States,* 234 U. S. 342; *Labor Board* v. *Jones & Laughlin Corp.,* 301 U. S. 1. A case or controversy arising under § 301 (a) is, therefore, one within the purview of judicial power as defined in Article III.

The question remains whether jurisdiction to compel arbitration of grievance disputes is withdrawn by the Norris-LaGuardia Act, 47 Stat. 70, 29 U. S. C. § 101. Section 7 of that Act prescribes stiff procedural requirements for issuing an injunction in a labor dispute. The kinds of acts which had given rise to abuse of the power to enjoin are listed in § 4. The failure to arbitrate was not a part and parcel of the abuses against which the Act was aimed. Section 8 of the Norris-LaGuardia Act does, indeed, indicate a congressional policy toward settlement of labor disputes by arbitration, for it denies injunctive relief to any person who has failed to make "every reasonable effort" to settle the dispute by negotiation, mediation, or "voluntary arbitration." Though a literal reading might bring the dispute within the terms of the Act (see Cox, Grievance Arbitration in the Federal Courts, 67 Harv. L. Rev. 591, 602–604), we see no justification in policy for restricting § 301 (a) to damage suits, leaving specific performance of a contract to arbitrate grievance disputes to the inapposite procedural requirements of that Act. Moreover, we held in *Virginia R. Co.* v. *System Federation,* 300 U. S. 515, and in *Graham* v. *Brotherhood of Firemen,* 338 U. S. 232, 237, that the Norris-LaGuardia Act does not deprive federal courts of jurisdiction to compel compliance with the mandates of the Railway Labor Act. The mandates there involved concerned racial discrimination. Yet those decisions were not based on any peculiarities of the Railway Labor Act. We followed the same course in *Syres* v. *Oil Workers International Union,* 350 U. S. 892, which was governed by the National Labor Relations Act. There an injunction was sought against racial discrimination in application of a collective bargaining agreement; and we allowed the injunction to issue. The congressional policy in favor of the enforcement of agreements to arbitrate grievance disputes being clear, there is no reason to submit them to the requirements of § 7 of the Norris-LaGuardia Act.

A question of mootness was raised on oral argument. It appears that since the date of the decision in the Court of Appeals respondent has terminated its operations and has contracted to sell its mill properties. All work in the mill ceased in March, 1957. Some of the grievances, however, ask for back pay for increased workloads; and the collective bargaining agreement provides that "the Board of Arbitration shall have the right to adjust compensation retroactive to the date of the change." Insofar as the grievances sought restoration of workloads and job assignments, the case is, of course, moot. But to the extent that they sought a monetary award, the case is a continuing controversy.

The judgment of the Court of Appeals is reversed and the cause is remanded to that court for proceedings in conformity with this opinion.

Reversed.

United Steelworkers of America v. United States
361 U.S. 39 (1959)

SECTIONS 206-210—NATIONAL EMERGENCIES

As previously indicated, the Taft-Hartley Act contains detailed procedures concerning labor disputes which threaten the national health or safety. This decision upholds the constitutionality of the relevant sections and deals with the concept of national emergency as defined by the statute.

PER CURIAM.

The Attorney General sought and obtained in the District Court for the Western District of Pennsylvania an injunction against the continuation of an industry-wide strike of workers in the basic steel industry pursuant to § 208 of the Labor Management Relations Act, 1947, 61 Stat. 155, 29 U. S. C. § 178. We granted certiorari, *post,* p. 878, to review the judgment of the Court of Appeals for the Third Circuit, 271 F. 2d 676, affirming the District Court. In pertinent part, § 208 provides that if the District Court—

finds that . . . [a] threatened or actual strike or lock-out—
   (i) affects an entire industry or a substantial part thereof engaged in trade, commerce, transportation, transmission, or communication among the several States or with foreign nations, or engaged in the production of goods for commerce; and
   (ii) if permitted to occur or to continue, will imperil the national health of safety, it shall have jurisdiction to enjoin any such strike or lockout, or the continuing thereof, and to make such other orders as may be appropriate.

The arguments of the parties here and in the lower courts have addressed themselves in considerable part to the propriety of the District Court's exercising its equitable jurisdiction to enjoin the strike in question once the findings set forth above had been made. These arguments have ranged widely into broad issues of national labor policy, the availability of other remedies to the Executive, the effect of a labor injunction on the collective bargaining process, consideration of the conduct of the parties to the labor dispute in their negotiations, and conjecture as to the course of those negotiations in the future. We do not believe that Congress in passing the statute intended that the issuance of injunctions should depend upon judicial inquiries of this nature. Congress was not concerned with the merits of the parties' positions or the conduct of their negotiations. Its basic purpose seems to have been to see that vital production should be resumed or continued for a time while further efforts were made to settle the dispute. To carry out its purposes, Congress carefully surrounded the injunction proceedings with detailed procedural devices and limitations. The public report of a board of inquiry, the exercise of political and executive responsibility personally by the President in directing the commencement of injunction proceedings, the statutory provisions looking toward an adjustment of the dispute during the injunction's pendency, and the limited duration of the injunction, represent a congressional determination of policy factors involved in the difficult problem of national emergency strikes. This congressional determination of the policy factors is of course binding on the courts.

The statute imposes upon the courts the duty of finding, upon the evidence adduced, whether a strike or lockout meets the statutory conditions of breadth of involvement and peril to the national health or safety. We have accordingly reviewed the concurrent findings of the two lower courts. Petitioner here contests the findings that the continuation of the strike would imperil the national health and safety. The parties dispute the meaning of the statutory term "national health"; the Government insists that the term comprehends the country's general well-being, its economic health; petitioner urges that simply the physical health of the citizenry is meant. We need not resolve this question, for we think the judgment below is amply supported on the ground that the strike imperils the national safety. Here we rely upon the evidence of the strike's effect on specific defense projects; we need not pass on the Government's contention that "national safety" in this context should be given a broader construction and application.

The petitioner suggests that a selective reopening of some of the steel mills would suffice to fulfill specific defense needs. The statute was designed to provide a public remedy in times of emergency; we cannot construe it to require that the United States either formulate a reorganization of the affected industry to satisfy its defense needs without the complete reopening of closed facilities, or demonstrate in court the unfeasibility of such a reorganization. There is no room in the statute for this requirement which the petitioner seeks to impose on the Government.

We are of opinion that the provision in question as applied here is not violative of the constitutional limitation prohibiting courts from exercising powers of legislative or executive nature, powers not capable of being conferred upon a court exercising solely "the judicial power of the United

States." *Keller* v. *Potomac Elec. Power Co.,* 261 U. S. 428; *Federal Radio Comm'n* v. *General Elec. Co.,* 281 U. S. 464. Petitioner contends that the statute is constitutionally invalid because it does not set up any standard of lawful or unlawful conduct on the part of labor or management. But the statute does recognize certain rights in the public to have unimpeded for a time production in industries vital to the national health or safety. It makes the United States the guardian of these rights in litigation. Cf. *United States* v. *American Bell Tel. Co.,* 128 U. S. 315, 370; *Sanitary District of Chicago* v. *United States,* 266 U. S. 405. The availability of relief, in the common judicial form of an injunction, depends on findings of fact, to be judicially made. Of the matters decided judicially, there is no review by other agencies of the Government. Cf. *Gordon* v. *United States,* 2 Wall. 561, 117 U. S. 697. We conclude that the statute entrusts the courts only with the determination of a "case or controversy," on which the judicial power can operate, not containing any element capable of only legislative or executive determination. We do not find that the termination of the injunction after a specified time, or the machinery established in an attempt to obtain a peaceful settlement of the underlying dispute during the injunction's pendency, detracts from this conclusion.

The result is that the judgment of the Court of Appeals for the Third Circuit, affirming that of the District Court, is affirmed. Our mandate shall issue forthwith.

It is so ordered.

THE LANDRUM-GRIFFIN ACT

(Labor–Management Reporting and Disclosure Act of 1959)

Commentary

For a decade organized labor sought to repeal the Taft-Hartley Act without success. Even the combined strength of the American Federation of Labor and the Congress of Industrial Organizations, having merged into the AFL-CIO in 1955, was insufficient to effect the passage of amendments aimed at softening the worst effects of the law. But in 1957 the Senate created a special committee, the Senate Select Committee on Improper Activities in the Labor or Management Field, "to conduct an investigation and study of the extent to which criminal or other improper practices or activities are, or have been, engaged in the field of labor-management relations or in groups or organizations of employees or employers to the detriment of the interests of the public, employers or employees." For over two years, a succession of minor hoods, tough racketeers, and big time mobsters came before the committee chaired by Senator John L. McClellan [Dem., Ark.]. Some took refuge in the Fifth Amendment prohibition against self-incrimination; others talked. Union members fighting corruption within their unions also testified. A picture of labor racketeering, corruption, and the roughshod handling of union members emerged, giving rise to new demands for reform of the labor law.

In its first interim report in 1958, the committee recommended changes in the law that would: (1) regulate and control pension, health, and welfare funds; (2) regulate and control union funds; (3) insure union democracy; (4) curb activities of middlemen in labor-management disputes; and (5) clarify a so-called "no-man's-land" which then existed between state and federal authority over labor relations. Early in the same year President Dwight D. Eisenhower sent a special message to the Congress submitting "recommendations for amendments to the Taft-Hartley Act and for additional legislation to provide greater protections for the rights of individual workers, the public, and management and unions, in labor-management relations." Largely in response to the recommendations of the McClellan Committee, the Kennedy-Ives bill was introduced into the Senate where it was overwhelmingly passed, only to be defeated by a close vote in the House of Representatives.

Before its adjournment in 1958 Congress did, however, enact legislation dealing with the burgeoning area of employee welfare and pension plans. The Welfare and Pension Plans Disclosure Act required publication of plan descriptions and annual reports, and the filing of copies with the Secretary of Labor. By 1962 the original statute was considered deficient on the enforcement side and was strengthened by amendments.

The Eighty-sixth Congress, convening in 1959, went to work in earnest on a labor reform statute. On January 20 Senator John F. Kennedy introduced a revised version of the Kennedy-Ives bill of 1958. After extensive hearings and the incorporation of a number of changes, the Senate Committee on Labor and Public Welfare on April 14 reported out the Kennedy-Ervin bill. There was considerable debate and a number of amendments were made, probably the most important of which was the addition of a bill of rights for union members proposed by Senator McClellan. On April 25 the bill passed by a vote of 90 to 1.

The proceedings in the House of Representatives were more complicated. A number of bills were introduced and after extensive hearings the Committee on Education and Labor on July 30 reported out a bill by a vote of 16 to 14. However, all excepting five of the sixteen said they were voting favorably in order to get a bill on the floor where it might be amended. But there was little agreement among them as to how this should be done. The debate on the House floor involved this bill, the Shelley bill (generally favored by organized labor), and the Landrum-Griffin bill, which incorporated much of the Administration's proposals for reform and which was considered the most restrictive by labor. Early in August, shortly before the commencement of debate in the House, President Eisenhower made an appeal on radio and television for an effective labor reform bill. This reflected his support of the Landrum-Griffin bill, which passed the House on August 14.

A conference was necessary. The conferees from the House and Senate consulted for several days, finally agreeing upon a compromise measure on September 2. After passage of the conference bill by both houses, President Eisenhower signed the bill into law on September 14, 1959.

The Labor-Management Reporting and Disclosure Act of 1959, sometimes referred to as the Landrum-Griffin Act, is made up of seven titles. Title I provides a bill of rights of members of labor organizations. Title II requires certain types of reports from labor organizations, officers and employees of labor organizations, and employers. Title III contains provisions governing union trusteeships. Title IV regulates union elections. Title V declares fiduciary responsibilities of union officers and prohibits Communists and persons convicted of certain crimes within the preceding five years from holding union office. Title VI deals with investigations and a variety of other matters. Title VII consists of amendments to the Taft-Hartley Act, dealing with such matters as federal-state jurisdiction, voting rights of economic strikers, boycotts, and recognition picketing.

The statute is set forth in full below and is followed by materials important to the legislative history of the law.

THE LANDRUM-GRIFFIN ACT
September 14, 1959

To provide for the reporting and disclosure of certain financial transactions and administrative practices of labor organizations and employers, to prevent abuses in the administration of trusteeships by
labor organizations, to provide standards with respect to the election of officers of labor organizations, and for other purposes.

*Be it enacted by the Senate and House of Representatives of the United
States of America in Congress assembled,*

SHORT TITLE

SEC. 1. This Act may be cited as the "Labor-Management Reporting and
Disclosure Act of 1959."

DECLARATION OF FINDINGS, PURPOSES, AND POLICY

SEC. 2. (a) The Congress finds that, in the public interest, it continues
to be the responsibility of the Federal Government to protect employees'
rights to organize, choose their own representatives, bargain collectively,
and otherwise engage in concerted activities for their mutual aid or protection; that the relations between employers and labor organizations and
the millions of workers they represent have a substantial impact on the commerce of the Nation; and that in order to accomplish the objective of a free
flow of commerce it is essential that labor organizations, employers, and
their officials adhere to the highest standards of responsibility and ethical
conduct in administering the affairs of their organizations, particularly as
they affect labor-management relations.

(b) The Congress further finds, from recent investigations in the labor
and management fields, that there have been a number of instances of
breach of trust, corruption, disregard of the rights of individual employees,
and other failures to observe high standards of responsibility and ethical
conduct which require further and supplementary legislation that will afford necessary protection of the rights and interests of employees and the
public generally as they relate to the activities of labor organizations, employers, labor relations consultants, and their officers and representatives.

(c) The Congress, therefore, further finds and declares that the enactment of this Act is necessary to eliminate or prevent improper practices
on the part of labor organizations, employers, labor relations consultants,
and their officers and representatives which distort and defeat the policies
of the Labor Management Relations Act, 1947, as amended, and the
Railway Labor Act, as amended, and have the tendency or necessary effect
of burdening or obstructing commerce by (1) impairing the efficiency,

safety, or operation of the instrumentalities of commerce; (2) occurring in the current of commerce; (3) materially affecting, restraining, or controlling the flow of raw materials or manufactured or processed goods into or from the channels of commerce, or the prices of such materials or goods in commerce; or (4) causing diminution of employment and wages in such volume as substantially to impair or disrupt the market for goods flowing into or from the channels of commerce.

DEFINITIONS

SEC. 3. For the purposes of titles I, II, III, IV, V (except section 505), and VI of this Act—

(a) "Commerce" means trade, traffic, commerce, transportation, transmission, or communication among the several States or between any State and any place outside thereof.

(b) "State" includes any State of the United States, the District of Columbia, Puerto Rico, the Virgin Islands, American Samoa, Guam, Wake Island, the Canal Zone, and Outer Continental Shelf lands defined in the Outer Continental Shelf Lands Act (43 U. S. C. 1331–1343).

(c) "Industry affecting commerce" means any activity, business, or industry in commerce or in which a labor dispute would hinder or obstruct commerce or the free flow of commerce and includes any activity or industry "affecting commerce" within the meaning of the Labor Management Relations Act, 1947, as amended, or the Railway Labor Act, as amended.

(d) "Person" includes one or more individuals, labor organizations, partnerships, associations, corporations, legal representatives, mutual companies, joint-stock companies, trusts, unincorporated organizations, trustees, trustees in bankruptcy, or receivers.

(e) "Employer" means any employer or any group or association of employers engaged in an industry affecting commerce (1) which is, with respect to employees engaged in an industry affecting commerce, an employer within the meaning of any law of the United States relating to the employment of any employees or (2) which may deal with any labor organization concerning grievances, labor disputes, wages, rates of pay, hours of employment, or conditions of work, and includes any person acting directly or indirectly as an employer or as an agent of an employer in relation to an employee but does not include the United States or any corporation wholly owned by the Government of the United States or any State or political subdivision thereof.

(f) "Employee" means any individual employed by an employer, and includes any individual whose work has ceased as a consequence of, or in connection with, any current labor dispute or because of any unfair labor practice or because of exclusion or expulsion from a labor organization in any manner or for any reason inconsistent with the requirements of this Act.

(g) "Labor dispute" includes any controversy concerning terms, tenure, or conditions of employment, or concerning the association or representation of persons in negotiating, fixing, maintaining, changing, or seeking to arrange terms or conditions of employment, regardless of whether the disputants stand in the proximate relation of employer and employee.

(h) "Trusteeship" means any receivership, trusteeship, or other method of supervision or control whereby a labor organization suspends the autonomy otherwise available to a subordinate body under its constitution or bylaws.

(i) "Labor organization" means a labor organization engaged in an industry affecting commerce and includes any organization of any kind, any agency, or employee representation committee, group, association, or plan so engaged in which employees participate and which exists for the purpose, in whole or in part, of dealing with employers concerning grievances, labor disputes, wages, rates of pay, hours, or other terms or conditions of employment, and any conference, general committee, joint or system board, or joint council so engaged which is subordinate to a national or international labor organization, other than a State or local central body.

(j) A labor organization shall be deemed to be engaged in an industry affecting commerce if it—

(1) is the certified representative of employees under the provisions of the National Labor Relations Act, as amended, or the Railway Labor Act, as amended; or

(2) although not certified, is a national or international labor organization or a local labor organization recognized or acting as the representative of employees of an employer or employers engaged in an industry affecting commerce; or

(3) has chartered a local labor organization or subsidiary body which is representing or actively seeking to represent employees of employers within the meaning of paragraph (1) or (2); or

(4) has been chartered by a labor organization representing or actively seeking to represent employees within the meaning of paragraph (1) or (2) as the local or subordinate body through which such employees may enjoy membership or become affiliated with such labor organization; or

(5) is a conference, general committee, joint or system board, or joint council, subordinate to a national or international labor organization, which includes a labor organization engaged in an industry, affecting commerce within the meaning of any of the preceding paragraphs of this subsection, other than a State or local central body.

(k) "Secret ballot" means the expression by ballot, voting machine, or otherwise, but in no event by proxy, of a choice with respect to any election or vote taken upon any matter, which is cast in such a manner that the person expressing such choice cannot be identified with the choice expressed.

(1) "Trust in which a labor organization is interested" means a trust or other fund or organization (1) which was created or established by a labor organization, or one or more of the trustees or one or more members of the governing body of which is selected or appointed by a labor organization, and (2) a primary purpose of which is to provide benefits for the members of such labor organization or their beneficiaries.

(m) "Labor relations consultant" means any person who, for compensation, advises or represents an employer, employer organization, or labor organization concerning employee organizing, converted activities or collective bargaining activities.

(n) "Officer" means any constitutional officer, any person authorized to perform the functions of president, vice-president, secretary, treasurer, or other executive functions of a labor organization, and any member of its executive board or similar governing body.

(o) "Member" or "member in good standing," when used in reference to a labor organization, includes any person who has fulfilled the requirements for membership in such organization, and who neither has voluntarily withdrawn from membership nor has been expelled or suspended from membership after appropriate proceedings consistent with lawful provisions of the constitution and bylaws of such organization.

(p) "Secretary" means the Secretary of Labor.

(q) "Officer, agent, shop steward, or other representative," when used with respect to a labor organization, includes elected officials and key administrative personnel, whether elected or appointed (such as business agents, heads of departments or major units, and organizers who exercise substantial independent authority), but does not include salaried nonsupervisory professional staff, stenographic, and service personnel.

(r) "District court of the United States" means a United States district court and a United States court of any place subject to the jurisdiction of the United States.

TITLE I—BILL OF RIGHTS OF MEMBERS OF LABOR ORGANIZATIONS

BILL OF RIGHTS

SEC. 101. (a) (1) Equal Rights.—Every member of a labor organization shall have equal rights and privileges within such organization to nominate candidates, to vote in elections or referendums of the labor organization, to attend membership meetings, and to participate in the deliberations and voting upon the business of such meetings, subject to reasonable rules and regulations in such organization's constitution and bylaws.

(2) Freedom of Speech and Assembly.—Every member of any labor

organization shall have the right to meet and assemble freely with other members; and to express any views, arguments, or opinions; and to express at meetings of the labor organization his views, upon candidates in an election of the labor organization or upon any business properly before the meeting, subject to the organization's established and reasonable rules pertaining to the conduct of meetings: *Provided,* That nothing herein shall be construed to impair the right of a labor organization to adopt and enforce reasonable rules as to the responsibility of every member toward the organization as an institution and his refraining from conduct that would interfere with its performance of its legal or contractual obligations.

(3) Dues, Initiation Fees, and Assessments.—Except in the case of a federation of national or international labor organizations, the rates of dues and initiation fees payable by members of any labor organization in effect on the date of enactment of this Act shall not be increased, and no general or special assesssment shall be levied upon such members, except—

(A) in the case of a local labor organization, (i) by majority vote by secret ballot of the members in good standing voting at a general or special membership meeting, after reasonable notice of the intention to vote upon such question, or (ii) by majority vote of the members in good standing voting in a membership referendum conducted by secret ballot; or—

(B) in the case of a labor organization, other than a local labor organization or a federation of national or international labor organizations, (i) by majority vote of the delegates voting at a regular convention, or at a special convention of such labor organization held upon not less than thirty days' written notice to the principal office of each local or constituent labor organization entitled to such notice, or (ii) by majority vote of the members in good standing of such labor organization voting in a membership referendum conducted by secret ballot, or (iii) by majority vote of the members of the executive board or similar governing body of such labor organization, pursuant to express authority contained in the constitution and bylaws of such labor organization: *Provided,* That such action on the part of the executive board or similar governing body shall be effective only until the next regular convention of such labor organization.

(4) Protection of the Right To Sue.—No labor organization shall limit the right of any member thereof to institute an action in any court, or in a proceeding before any administrative agency, irrespective of whether or not the labor organization or its officers are named as defendants or respondents in such action or proceeding, or the right of any member of a labor organization to appear as a witness in any judicial, administrative, or legislative proceeding, or to petition any legislature or to communicate with any legislator: *Pro-*

vided, That any such member may be required to exhaust reasonable hearing procedures (but not to exceed a four-month lapse of time) within such organization, before instituting legal or administrative proceedings against such organizations or any officer thereof: *And provided further,* That no interested employer or employer association shall directly or indirectly finance, encourage, or participate in, except as a party, any such action, proceeding, appearance, or petition.

(5) Safeguards Against Improper Disciplinary Action.—No member of any labor organization may be fined, suspended, expelled, or otherwise disciplined except for nonpayment of dues by such organization or by any officer thereof unless such member has been (A) served with written specific charges; (B) given a reasonable time to prepare his defense; (C) afforded a full and fair hearing.

(b) Any provision of the constitution and bylaws of any labor organization which is inconsistent with the provisions of this section shall be of no force or effect.

CIVIL ENFORCEMENT

SEC. 102. Any person whose rights secured by the provisions of this title have been infringed by any violation of this title may bring a civil action in a district court of the United States for such relief (including injunctions) as may be appropriate. Any such action against a labor organization shall be brought in the district court of the United States for the district where the alleged violation occurred, or where the principal office of such labor organization is located.

RETENTION OF EXISTING RIGHTS

SEC. 103. Nothing contained in this title shall limit the rights and remedies of any member of a labor organization under any State or Federal law or before any court or other tribunal, or under the constitution and bylaws of any labor organization.

RIGHT TO COPIES OF COLLECTIVE BARGAINING AGREEMENTS

SEC. 104. It shall be the duty of the secretary or corresponding principal officer of each labor organization, in the case of a local labor organization, to forward a copy of each collective bargaining agreement made by such labor organization with any employer to any employee who requests such a copy and whose rights as such employee are directly affected by such agreement, and in the case of a labor organization other than a local labor organization, to forward a copy of any such agreement to each constituent unit which has members directly affected by such agreement; and such officer shall maintain at the principal office of the labor organization of which he is an officer copies of any such agreement made or received by such labor organization, which copies shall be available for inspection by any member or by any employee whose rights are affected by such agreement. The provisions of section 210 shall be applicable in the enforcement of this section.

INFORMATION AS TO ACT

SEC. 105. Every labor organization shall inform its members concerning the provisions of this Act.

TITLE II—REPORTING BY LABOR ORGANIZATIONS, OFFICERS AND EMPLOYEES OF LABOR ORGANIZATIONS, AND EMPLOYERS

REPORT OF LABOR ORGANIZATIONS

SEC. 201. (a) Every labor organization shall adopt a constitution and bylaws and shall file a copy thereof with the Secretary, together with a report, signed by its president and secretary or corresponding principal officers, containing the following information—

(1) the name of the labor organization, its mailing address, and any other address at which it maintains its principal office or at which it keeps the records referred to in this title;

(2) the name and title of each of its officers;

(3) the initiation fee or fees required from a new or transferred member and fees for work permits required by the reporting labor organization;

(4) the regular dues or fees or other periodic payments required to remain a member of the reporting labor organization; and

(5) detailed statements, or references to specific provisions of documents filed under this subsection which contain such statements, showing the provision made and procedures followed with respect to each of the following: (A) qualifications for or restrictions on membership, (B) levying of assessments, (C) participation in insurance or other benefit plans, (D) authorization for disbursement of funds of the labor organization, (E) audit of financial transactions of the labor organization, (F) the calling of regular and special meetings, (G) the selection of officers and stewards and of any representatives to other bodies composed of labor organizations' representatives, with a specific statement of the manner in which each officer was elected, appointed, or otherwise selected, (H) discipline or removal of officers or agents for breaches of their trust, (I) imposition of fines, suspensions, and expulsions of members, including the grounds for such action and any provision made for notice, hearing, judgment on the evidence, and appeal procedures, (J) authorization for bargaining demands, (K) ratification of contract terms, (L) authorization for strikes, and (M) issuance of work permits. Any change in the infor-

mation required by this subsection shall be reported to the Secretary at the time the reporting labor organization files with the Secretary the annual financial report required by subsection (b).

(b) Every labor organization shall file annually with the Secretary a financial report signed by its president and treasurer or corresponding principal officers containing the following information in such detail as may be necessary accurately to disclose its financial condition and operation for its preceding fiscal year—

(1) assets and liabilities at the beginning and end of the fiscal year;

(2) receipts of any kind and the sources thereof;

(3) salary, allowances, and other direct or indirect disbursements (including reimbursed expenses) to each officer and also to each employee who, during such fiscal year, received more than $10,000 in the aggregate from such labor organization and any other labor organization affiliated with it or with which it is affiliated, or which is affiliated with the same national or international labor organization;

(4) direct and indirect loans made to any officer, employee, or member, which aggregated more than $250 during the fiscal year, together with a statement of the purpose, security, if any, and arrangements for repayment;

(5) direct and indirect loans to any business enterprise, together with statement of the purpose, security, if any, and arrangements for repayment; and

(6) other disbursements made by it including the purposes thereof; all in such categories as the Secretary may prescribe.

(c) Every labor organization required to submit a report under this title shall make available the information required to be contained in such report to all of its members, and every such labor organization and its officers shall be under a duty enforceable at the suit of any member of such organization in any State court of competent jurisdiction or in the district court of the United States for the district in which such labor organization maintains its principal office, to permit such member for just cause to examine any books, records, and accounts necessary to verify such report. The court in such action may, in its discretion, in addition to any judgment awarded to the plaintiff or plaintiffs, allow a reasonable attorney's fee to be paid by the defendant, and costs of the action.

(d) Subsections (f), (g), and (h) of section 9 of the National Labor Relations Act, as amended, are hereby repealed.

(e) Clause (i) of section 8 (a) (3) of the National Labor Relations Act, as amended, is amended by striking out the following: "and has at the time the agreement was made or within the preceding twelve months received from the Board a notice of compliance with sections 9 (f), (g), (h)."

REPORT OF OFFICERS AND EMPLOYEES OF LABOR ORGANIZATIONS

SEC. 202. (a) Every officer of a labor organization and every employee of a labor organization (other than an employee performing exclusively clerical or custodial services) shall file with the Secretary a signed report listing and describing for his preceding fiscal year—

(1) any stock, bond, security, or other interest, legal or equitable, which he or his spouse or minor child directly or indirectly held in, and any income or any other benefit with monetary value (including reimbursed expenses) which he or his spouse or minor child derived directly or indirectly from, an employer whose employees such labor organization represents or is actively seeking to represent, except payments and other benefits received as a bona fide employee of such employer;

(2) any transaction in which he or his spouse or minor child engaged, directly or indirectly, involving any stock, bond, security, or loan to or from, or other legal or equitable interest in the business of an employer whose employees such labor organization represents or is actively seeking to represent;

(3) any stock, bond, security, or other interest, legal or equitable, which he or his spouse or minor child directly or indirectly held in, and any income or any other benefit with monetary value (including reimbursed expenses) which he or his spouse or minor child directly or indirectly derived from, any business a substantial part of which consists of buying from, selling or leasing to, or otherwise dealing with, the business of an employer whose employees such labor organization represents or is actively seeking to represent;

(4) any stock, bond, security, or other interest, legal or equitable, which he or his spouse or minor child directly or indirectly held in, and any income or any other benefit with monetary value (including reimbursed expenses) which he or his spouse or minor child directly or indirectly derived from, a business any part of which consists of buying from, or selling or leasing directly or indirectly to, or otherwise dealing with such labor organization;

(5) any direct or indirect business transaction or arrangement, between him or his spouse or minor child and any employer whose employees his organization represents or is actively seeking to represent, except work performed and payments and benefits received as a bona fide employee of such employer and except purchases and sales of goods or services in the regular course of business at prices generally available to any employee of such employer; and

(6) any payment of money or other thing of value (including reimbursed expenses) which he or his spouse or minor child received directly or indirectly from any employer or any person who acts as a labor relations consultant to an employer, except payments of the kinds referred

to in section 302 (c) of the Labor Management Relations Act, 1947, as amended.

(b) The provisions of paragraphs (1), (2), (3), (4), and (5) of subsection (a) shall not be construed to require any such officer or employee to report his bona fide investments in securities traded on a securities exchange registered as a national securities exchange under the Securities Exchange Act of 1934, in shares in an investment company registered under the Investment Company Act of 1940, or in securities of a public utility holding company registered under the Public Utility Holding Company Act of 1935, or to report any income derived therefrom.

(c) Nothing contained in this section shall be construed to require any officer or employee of a labor organization to file a report under subsection (a) unless he or his spouse or minor child holds or has held an interest, has received income or any other benefit with monetary value or a loan, or has engaged in a transaction described therein.

REPORT OF EMPLOYERS

SEC. 203. (a) Every employer who in any fiscal year made—

(1) any payment or loan, direct or indirect, of money or other thing of value (including reimbursed expenses), or any promise or agreement therefor, to any labor organization or officer, agent, shop steward, or other representative of a labor organization, or employee of any labor organization, except (A) payments or loans made by any national or State bank, credit union, insurance company, savings and loan association or other credit institution and (B) payments of the kind referred to in section 302(c) of the Labor Management Relations Act, 1947, as amended;

(2) any payment (including reimbursed expenses) to any of his employees, or any group or committee of such employees, for the purpose of causing such employee or group or committee of employees to persuade other employees to exercise or not to exercise, or as the manner of exercising, the right to organize and bargain collectively through representatives of their own choosing unless such payments were contemporaneously or previously disclosed to such other employees;

(3) any expenditure, during the fiscal year, where an object thereof, directly or indirectly, is to interfere with, restrain, or coerce employees in the exercise of the right to organize and bargain collectively through representatives of their own choosing, or is to obtain information concerning the activities of employees or a labor organization in connection with a labor dispute involving such employer, except for use solely in conjunction with an administrative or arbitral proceeding or a criminal or civil judicial proceeding;

(4) any agreement or arrangement with a labor relations consultant or other independent contractor or organization pursuant to which such person undertakes activities where an object thereof, directly or indirectly, is to persuade employees to exercise or not to exercise, or persuade employees as to the manner of exercising, the right to organize and bargain collectively through representatives of their own choosing, or undertakes to supply such employer with information concerning the activities of employees or a labor organization in connection with a labor dispute involving such employer, except information for use solely in conjunction with an administrative or arbitral proceeding or a criminal or civil judicial proceeding; or

(5) any payment (including reimbursed expenses) pursuant to an agreement or arrangement described in subdivision (e);

shall file with the Secretary a report, in a form prescribed by him, signed by its president and treasurer or corresponding principal officers showing in detail the date and amount of each such payment, loan, promise, agreement, or arrangement and the name, address, and position, if any, in any firm or labor organization of the person to whom it was made and a full explanation of the circumstances of all such payments, including the terms of any agreement or understanding pursuant to which they were made.

(b) Every person who pursuant to any agreement or arrangement with an employer undertakes activities where an object thereof is, directly or indirectly—

(1) to persuade employees to exercise or not to exercise, or persuade employees as to the manner of exercising, the right to organize and bargain collectively through representatives of their own choosing; or

(2) to supply an employer with information concerning the activities of employees or a labor organization in connection with a labor dispute involving such employer, except information for use solely in conjunction with an administrative or arbitral proceeding or a criminal or civil judicial proceeding;

shall file within thirty days after entering into such agreement or arrangement a report with the Secretary, signed by its president and treasurer or corresponding principal officers, containing the name under which such person is engaged in doing business and the address of its principal office, and a detailed statement of the terms and conditions of such agreement or arrangement. Every such person shall file annually, with respect to each fiscal year during which payments were made as a result of such an agreement or arrangement, a report with the Secretary, signed by its president and treasurer or corresponding principal officers, containing a statement (A) of its receipts of any kind from employers on account of labor relations advice or services, designating the sources thereof, and (B) of its disbursements of any kind, in connection with such services and the purposes thereof. In each such case such information shall be set forth in such categories as the Secretary may prescribe.

(c) Nothing in this section shall be construed to require any employer or other person to file a report covering the services of such person by reason of his giving or agreeing to give advice to such employer or representing or agreeing to represent such employer before any court, administrative agency, or tribunal of arbitration or engaging or agreeing to engage in collective bargaining on behalf of such employer with respect to wages, hours, or other terms or conditions of employment or the negotiation of an agreement or any question arising thereunder.

(d) Nothing contained in this section shall be construed to require an employer to file a report under subsection (a) unless he has made an expenditure, payment, loan, agreement, or arrangement of the kind described therein. Nothing contained in this section shall be construed to require any other person to file a report under subsection (b) unless he was a party to an agreement or arrangement of the kind described therein.

(e) Nothing contained in this section shall be construed to require any regular officer, supervisor, or employee of an employer to file a report in connection with services rendered to such employer nor shall any employer be required to file a report covering expenditures made to any regular officer, supervisor, or employee of an employer as compensation for service as a regular officer, supervisor, or employee of such employer.

(f) Nothing contained in this section shall be construed as an amendment to, or modification of the rights protected by, section 8 (c) of the National Labor Relations Act, as amended.

(g) The term "interfere with, restrain, or coerce" as used in this section means interference, restraint, and coercion which, if done with respect to the exercise of rights guaranteed in section 7 of the National Labor Relations Act, as amended, would, under section 8 (a) of such Act, constitute an unfair labor practice.

ATTORNEY-CLIENT COMMUNICATIONS EXEMPTED

SEC. 204. Nothing contained in this Act shall be construed to require an attorney who is a member in good standing of the bar of any State, to include in any report required to be filed pursuant to the provisions of this Act any information which was lawfully communicated to such attorney by any of his clients in the course of a legitimate attorney-client relationship.

REPORTS MADE PUBLIC INFORMATION

SEC. 205. (a) The contents of the reports and documents filed with the Secretary pursuant to sections 201, 202, and 203 shall be public information, and the Secretary may publish any information and data which he obtains pursuant to the provisions of this title. The Secretary may use the information and data for statistical and research purposes, and compile and publish such studies, analyses, reports, and surveys based thereon as he may deem appropriate.

(b) The Secretary shall by regulation make reasonable provision for the inspection and examination, on the request of any person, of the information and data contained in any report or other document filed with him pursuant to section 201, 202, or 203.

(c) The Secretary shall by regulation provide for the furnishing by the Department of Labor of copies of reports or other documents filed with the Secretary pursuant to this title, upon payment of a charge based upon the cost of the service. The Secretary shall make available without payment of a charge, or require any person to furnish, to such State agency as is designated by law or by the Governor of the State in which such person has his principal place of business or headquarters, upon request of the Governor of such State, copies of any reports and documents filed by such person with the Secretary pursuant to section 201, 202, or 203, or of information and data contained therein. No person shall be required by reason of any law of any State to furnish to any officer or agency of such State any information included in a report filed by such person with the Secretary pursuant to the provisions of this title, if a copy of such report, or of the portion thereof containing such information, is furnished to such officer or agency. All moneys received in payment of such charges fixed by the Secretary pursuant to this subsection shall be deposited in the general fund of the Treasury.

RETENTION OF RECORDS

SEC. 206. Every person required to file any report under this title shall maintain records on the matters required to be reported which will provide in sufficient detail the necessary basic information and data from which the documents filed with the Secretary may be verified, explained or clarified, and checked for accuracy and completeness, and shall include vouchers, worksheets, receipts, and applicable resolutions, and shall keep such records available for examination for a period of not less than five years after the filing of the documents based on the information which they contain.

EFFECTIVE DATE

SEC. 207. (a) Each labor organization shall file the initial report required under section 201 (a) within ninety days after the date on which it first becomes subject to this Act.

(b) Each person required to file a report under section 201 (b), 202, 203 (a), or the second sentence of 203 (b) shall file such report within ninety days after the end of each of its fiscal years; except that where such person is subject to section 201 (b), 202, 203 (a), or the second sentence of 203 (b), as the case may be, for only a portion of such a fiscal year (because the date of enactment of this Act occurs during such person's fiscal year or such person becomes subject to this Act during its fiscal year) such person may consider that portion as the entire fiscal year in making such report.

RULES AND REGULATIONS

SEC. 208. The Secretary shall have authority to issue, amend, and rescind rules and regulations prescribing the form and publication of reports required to be filed under this title and such other reasonable rules and regulations (including rules prescribing reports concerning trusts in which a labor organization is interested) as he may find necessary to prevent the circumvention or evasion of such reporting requirements. In exercising his power under this section the Secretary shall prescribe by general rule simplified reports for labor organizations or employers for whom he finds that by virtue of their size a detailed report would be unduly burdensome, but the Secretary may revoke such provision for simplified forms of any labor organization or employer if he determines, after such investigation as he deems proper and due notice and opportunity for a hearing, that the purposes of his section would be served thereby.

CRIMINAL PROVISIONS

SEC. 209. (a) Any person who willfully violates this title shall be fined not more than $10,000 or imprisoned for not more than one year, or both.

(b) Any person who makes a false statement or representation of a material fact, knowing it to be false, or who knowingly fails to disclose a material fact, in any document, report, or other information required under the provisions of this title shall be fined not more than $10,000 or imprisoned for not more than one year, or both.

(c) Any person who willfully makes a false entry in or willfully conceals, withholds, or destroys any books, records, reports, or statements required to be kept by any provision of this title shall be fined not more than $10,000 or imprisoned for not more than one year, or both.

(d) Each individual required to sign reports under sections 201 and 203 shall be personally responsible for the filing of such reports and for any statement contained therein which he knows to be false.

CIVIL ENFORCEMENT

SEC. 210. Whenever it shall appear that any person has violated or is about to violate any of the provisions of this title, the Secretary may bring a civil action for such relief (including injunctions) as may be appropriate. Any such action may be brought in the district court of the United States where the violation occurred or, at the option of the parties, in the United States District Court for the District of Columbia.

REPORTS

SEC. 301. (a) Every labor organization which has or assumes trusteeship over any subordinate labor organization shall file with the Secretary within thirty days after the date of the enactment of this Act or the imposition of any such trusteeship, and semiannually thereafter, a report, signed by its president and treasurer or corresponding principal officers, as well as by the trustees of such subordinate labor organization, containing the following information: (1) the name and address of the subordinate organization; (2) the date of establishing the trusteeship; (3) a detailed statement of the reason or reasons for establishing or continuing the trusteeship; and (4) the nature and extent of participation by the membership of the subordinate organization in the selection of delegates to represent such organization in regular or special conventions or other policy-determining bodies and in the election of officers of the labor organization which has assumed trusteeship over such subordinate organization. The initial report shall also include a full and complete account of the financial condition of such subordinate organization as of the time trusteeship was assumed over it. During the continuance of a trusteeship the labor organization which has assumed trusteeship over a subordinate labor organization shall file on behalf of the subordinate labor organization the annual financial report required by section 201 (b) signed by the president and treasurer or corresponding principal officers of the labor organization which has assumed such trusteeship and the trustees of the subordinate labor organization.

(b) The provisions of section 201 (c), 205, 206, 208, and 210 shall be applicable to reports filed under this title.

(c) Any person who willfully violates this section shall be fined not more than $10,000 or imprisoned for not more than one year, or both.

(d) Any person who makes a false statement or representation of a material fact, knowing it to be false, or who knowingly fails to disclose a material fact, in any report required under the provisions of this section or willfully makes any false entry in or willfully withholds, conceals, or destroys any documents, books, records, reports, or statements upon which such report is based, shall be fined not more than $10,000 or imprisoned for not more than one year, or both.

(e) Each individual required to sign a report under this section shall be personally responsible for the filing of such report and for any statement contained therein which he knows to be false.

PURPOSES FOR WHICH A TRUSTEESHIP MAY BE ESTABLISHED

SEC. 302. Trusteeships shall be established and administered by a labor organization over a subordinate body only in accordance with the constitution and bylaws of the organization which has assumed trusteeship over the subordinate body and for the purpose of correcting corruption or financial malpractice, assuring the performance of collective bargaining agreements or other duties of a bargaining representative, restoring democratic procedures, or otherwise carrying out the legitimate objects of such labor organization.

UNLAWFUL ACTS RELATING TO LABOR ORGANIZATION UNDER TRUSTEESHIP

SEC. 303. (a) During any period when a subordinate body of a labor organization is in trusteeship, it shall be unlawful (1) to count the vote of delegates from such body in any convention or election of officers of the labor organization unless the delegates have been chosen by secret ballot in an election in which all the members in good standing of such subordinate body were eligible to participate, or (2) to transfer to such organization any current receipts or other funds of the subordinate body except the normal per capita tax and assessments payable by subordinate bodies not in trusteeship: *Provided,* That nothing herein contained shall prevent the distribution of the assets of a labor organization in accordance with its constitution and bylaws upon the bona fide dissolution thereof.

(b) Any person who willfully violates this section shall be fined not more than $10,000 or imprisoned for not more than one year, or both.

ENFORCEMENT

SEC. 304. (a) Upon the written complaint of any member or subordinate body of a labor organization alleging that such organization has violated the provisions of this title (except section 301) the Secretary shall investigate the complaint and if the Secretary finds probable cause to believe that such violation has occurred and has not been remedied he shall, without disclosing the identity of the complainant, bring a civil action in any district court of the United States having jurisdiction of the labor organization for such relief (including injunctions) as may be appropriate. Any member or subordinate body of a labor organization affected by any violation of this title (except section 301) may bring a civil action in any district court of the United States having jurisdiction of the labor organization for such relief (including injunctions) as may be appropriate.

(b) For the purpose of actions under this section, district courts of the United States shall be deemed to have jurisdiction of a labor organization (1) in the district in which the principal office of such labor organization is located, or (2) in any district in which its duly authorized officers or agents are engaged in conducting the affairs of the trusteeship.

(c) In any proceeding pursuant to this section a trusteeship established by a labor organization in conformity with the procedural requirements of its constitution and bylaws and authorized or ratified after a fair hearing either before the executive board or before such other body as may be provided in accordance with its constitution or bylaws shall be presumed valid for a period of eighteen months from the date of its establishment and shall not be subject to attack during such period except upon clear and convincing proof that the trusteeship was not established or maintained in good faith for a purpose allowable under section 302. After the expiration of eighteen months the trusteeship shall be presumed invalid in any such proceeding and its discontinuance shall be decreed unless the labor organization shall show by clear and convincing proof that the continuation of the trusteeship is necessary for a purpose allowable under section 302. In the latter event the court may dismiss the complaint or retain jurisdiction of the cause on such conditions and for such period as it deems appropriate.

REPORT TO CONGRESS

SEC. 305. The Secretary shall submit to the Congress at the expiration of three years from the date of enactment of this Act a report upon the operation of this title.

COMPLAINT BY SECRETARY

SEC. 306. The rights and remedies provided by this title shall be in addition to any and all other rights and remedies at law or in equity: *Provided,* That upon the filing of a complaint by the Secretary the jurisdiction of the district court over such trusteeship shall be exclusive and the final judgment shall be res judicata.

TITLE IV—ELECTIONS

TERMS OF OFFICE; ELECTION PROCEDURES

SEC. 401. (a) Every national or international labor organization, except a federation of national or international labor organizations, shall elect its officers not less often than once every five years either by secret ballot among the members in good standing or at a convention of delegates chosen by secret ballot.

(b) Every local labor organization shall elect its officers not less often than once every three years by secret ballot among the members in good standing.

(c) Every national or international labor organization, except a federation of national or international labor organizations, and every local labor organization, and its officers, shall be under a duty, enforceable at the suit of any bona fide candidate for office in such labor organization in the district court of the United States in which such labor organization maintains its principal office, to comply with all reasonable requests of any candidate to distribute by mail or otherwise at the candidate's expense campaign literature in aid of such person's candidacy to all members in good standing of such labor organization and to refrain from discrimination in favor of or against any candidate with respect to the use of lists of members, and whenever such labor organizations or its officers authorize the distribution by mail or otherwise to members of campaign literature on behalf of any candidate or of the labor organization itself with reference to such election, similar distribution at the request of any other bona fide candidate shall be made by such labor organization and its officers, with equal treatment as to the expense of such distribution. Every bona fide candidate shall have the right, once within 30 days prior to an election of a labor organization in which he is a candidate, to inspect a list containing the names and last known addresses of all members of the labor organization who are subject to a collective bargaining agreement requiring membership therein as a condition of employment, which list shall be maintained and kept at the principal office of such labor organization by a designated official thereof. Adequate safeguards to insure a fair election shall be provided, including the right of any candidate to have an observer at the polls and at the counting of the ballots.

(d) Officers of intermediate bodies, such as general committees, system boards, joint boards, or joint councils, shall be elected not less often than once every four years by secret ballot among the members in good standing or by labor organization officers representative of such members who have been elected by secret ballot.

(e) In any election required by this section which is to be held by secret ballot a reasonable opportunity shall be given for the nomination of candidates and every member in good standing shall be eligible to be a candidate and to hold office (subject to section 504 and to reasonable qualifications uniformly imposed) and shall have the right to vote for or otherwise support the candidate or candidates of his choice, without being subject to penalty, discipline, or improper interference or reprisal of any kind by such organization or any member thereof. Not less than fifteen days prior to the election notice thereof shall be mailed to each member at his last known home address. Each member in good standing shall be entitled to one vote. No member whose dues have been withheld by his employer for payment to such organization pursuant to his voluntary authorization provided for in a collective bargaining agreement shall be declared ineligible to vote or be a candidate for office in such organization by reason of alleged delay or default in the payment of dues. The votes cast by members of each local labor organization shall be counted, and the results published, separately. The election officials designated in the constitution and bylaws or the secretary, if no other official is designated, shall preserve for one year the ballots and all other records pertaining to the election. The election shall be conducted in accordance with the constitution and bylaws of such organization insofar as they are not inconsistent with the provisions of this title.

(f) When officers are chosen by a convention of delegates elected by secret ballot, the convention shall be conducted in accordance with the constitution and bylaws of the labor organization insofar as they are not inconsistent with the provisions of this title. The officials designated in the constitution and bylaws or the secretary, if no other is designated, shall preserve for one year the credentials of the delegates and all minutes and other records of the convention pertaining to the election of officers.

(g) No moneys received by any labor organization by way of dues, assessment, or similar levy, and no moneys of an employer shall be contributed or applied to promote the candidacy of any person in an election subject to the provisions of this title. Such moneys of a labor organization may be utilized for notices, factual statements of issues not involving candidates, and other expenses necessary for the holding of an election.

(h) If the Secretary, upon application of any member of a local labor organization, finds after hearing in accordance with the Administrative Procedure Act that the constitution and bylaws of such labor organization do not provide an adequate procedure for the removal of an elected officer guilty of serious misconduct, such officer may be removed, for cause shown and after notice and hearing, by the members in good standing voting in a secret ballot conducted by the officers of such labor organization in accordance with its constitution and bylaws insofar as they are not inconsistent with the provisions of this title.

(i) The Secretary shall promulgate rules and regulations prescribing minimum standards and procedures for determining the adequacy of the removal procedures to which reference is made in subsection (h).

ENFORCEMENT

SEC. 402. (a) A member of a labor organization—

(1) who has exhausted the remedies available under the constitution and bylaws of such organization and of any parent body, or

(2) who has invoked such available remedies without obtaining a final decision within three calendar months after their invocation,

may file a complaint with the Secretary within one calendar month thereafter alleging the violation of any provision of section 401 (including violation of the constitution and bylaws of the labor organization pertaining to the election and removal of officers). The challenged election shall be presumed valid pending a final decision thereon (as hereinafter provided) and in the interim the affairs of the organization shall be conducted by the officers elected or in such other manner as its constitution and bylaws may provide.

(b) The Secretary shall investigate such complaint and, if he finds probable cause to believe that a violation of this title has occurred and has not been remedied, he shall, within sixty days after the filing of such complaint, bring a civil action against the labor organization as an entity in the district court of the United States in which such labor organization maintains its principal office to set aside the invalid election, if any, and to direct the conduct of an election or hearing and vote upon the removal of officers under the supervision of the Secretary and in accordance with the provisions of this title and such rules and regulations as the Secretary may prescribe. The court shall have power to take such action as it deems proper to preserve the assets of the labor organization.

(c) If, upon a preponderance of the evidence after a trial upon the merits, the court finds—

(1) that an election has not been held within the time prescribed by section 401, or

(2) that the violation of section 401 may have affected the outcome of an election,

the court shall declare the election, if any, to be void and direct the conduct of a new election under supervision of the Secretary and, so far as lawful and practicable, in conformity with the constitution and bylaws of the labor organization. The Secretary shall promptly certify to the court the names of the persons elected, and the court shall thereupon enter a decree declaring such persons to be the officers of the labor organization. If the proceeding is for the removal of officers pursuant to subsection (h) of section 401, the Secretary shall certify the results of the vote and the court shall enter a decree declaring whether such persons have been removed as officers of the labor organization.

(d) An order directing an election, dismissing a complaint, or designating elected officers of a labor organization shall be appealable in the same manner as the final judgment in a civil action, but an order directing an election shall not be stayed pending appeal.

APPLICATION OF OTHER LAWS

SEC. 403. No labor organization shall be required by law to conduct elections of officers with greater frequency or in a different form or manner than is required by its own constitution or bylaws, except as otherwise provided by this title. Existing rights and remedies to enforce the constitution and bylaws of a labor organization with respect to elections prior to the conduct thereof shall not be affected by the provisions of this title. The remedy provided by this title for challenging an election already conducted shall be exclusive.

EFFECTIVE DATE

SEC. 404. The provisions of this title shall become applicable—

(1) ninety days after the date of enactment of this Act in the case of a labor organization whose constitution and bylaws can lawfully be modified or amended by action of its constitutional officers or governing body, or

(2) where such modification can only be made by a constitutional convention of the labor organization, not later than the next constitutional convention of such labor organization after the date of enactment of this Act, or one year after such date, whichever is sooner. If no such convention is held within such one-year period, the executive board or similar governing body empowered to act for such labor organization between conventions is empowered to make such interim constitutional changes as are necessary to carry out the provisions of this title.

TITLE V—SAFEGUARDS FOR LABOR ORGANIZATIONS

FIDUCIARY RESPONSIBILITY OF OFFICERS OF LABOR ORGANIZATIONS

SEC. 501. (a) The officers, agents, shop stewards, and other representatives of a labor organization occupy positions of trust in relation to such organization and its members as a group. It is, therefore, the duty of each such person, taking into account the special problems and functions of a labor organization, to hold its money and property solely for the benefit of the organization and its members and to manage, invest, and expend the same in accordance with its constitution and bylaws and any resolutions of the governing bodies adopted thereunder, to refrain from dealing with such organization as an adverse party or in behalf of an adverse party in any matter connected with his duties and from holding or acquiring any pecuniary or personal interest which conflicts with the interests of such organization, and to account to the organization for any profit received by him in whatever capacity in connection with transactions conducted by him or under his direction on behalf of the organization. A general exculpatory provision in the constitution and bylaws of such a labor organization or a general exculpatory resolution of a governing body purporting to relieve any such person of liability for breach of the duties declared by this section shall be void as against public policy.

(b) When any officer, agent, shop steward, or representative of any labor organization is alleged to have violated the duties declared in subsection (a) and the labor organization or its governing board or officers refuse or fail to sue or recover damages or secure an accounting or other appropriate relief within a reasonable time after being requested to do so by any member of the labor organization, such member may sue such officer, agent, shop steward, or representative in any district court of the United States or in any State court of competent jurisdiction to recover damages or secure an accounting or other appropriate relief for the benefit of the labor organization. No such proceeding shall be brought except upon leave of the court obtained upon verified application and for good cause shown, which application may be made ex parte. The trial judge may allot a reasonable part of the recovery in any action under this subsection to pay the fees of counsel prosecuting the suit at the instance of the member of the labor organization and to compensate such member for any expenses necessarily paid or incurred by him in connection with the litigation.

(c) Any person who embezzles, steals, or unlawfully and willfully abstracts or converts to his own use, or the use of another, any of the moneys, funds, securities, property, or other assets of a labor organization of which he is an officer, or by which he is employed, directly or indirectly, shall be fined not more than $10,000 or imprisoned for not more than five years, or both.

BONDING

SEC. 502. (a) Every officer, agent, shop steward, or other representative or employee of any labor organization (other than a labor organization whose property and annual financial receipts do not exceed $5,000 in value), or of a trust in which a labor organization is interested, who handles funds or other property thereof shall be bonded for the faithful discharge of his duties. The bond of each such person shall be fixed at the beginning of the organization's fiscal year and shall be in an amount not less than 10 per centum of the funds handled by him and his predecessor or predecessors, if any, during the preceding fiscal year, but in no case more than $500,000. If the labor organization or the trust in which a labor organization is interested does not have a preceding fiscal year, the amount of the bond shall be, in the case of a local labor organization, not less than $1,000, and in the case of any other labor organization or of a trust in which a labor organization is interested, not less than $10,000. Such bonds shall be individual or schedule in form, and shall have a corporate surety company as surety thereon. Any person who is not covered by such bonds shall not be permitted to receive, handle, disburse, or otherwise exercise custody or control of the funds or other property of a labor organization or of a trust in which a labor organization is interested. No such bond shall be placed through an agent or broker or with a surety company in which any labor organization or any officer, agent, shop steward, or other representative of a labor organization has any direct or indirect interest. Such surety company shall be a corporate surety which holds a grant of authority from the Secretary of the Treasury under the Act of July 30, 1947 (6 U.S.C. 6–13), as an acceptable surety on Federal bonds.

(b) Any person who willfully violates this section shall be fined not more than $10,000 or imprisoned for not more than one year, or both.

MAKING OF LOANS; PAYMENT OF FINES

SEC. 503. (a) No labor organization shall make directly or indirectly any loan or loans to any officer or employee of such organization which results in a total indebtedness on the part of such officer or employee to the labor organization in excess of $2,000.

(b) No labor organization or employer shall directly or indirectly pay the fine of any officer or employee convicted of any willful violation of this Act.

(c) Any person who willfully violates this section shall be fined not more than $5,000 or imprisoned for not more than one year, or both.

PROHIBITION AGAINST CERTAIN PERSONS HOLDING OFFICE

SEC. 504. (a) No person who is or has been a member of the Communist Party or who has been convicted of, or served any part of a prison term resulting from his conviction of, robbery, bribery, extortion, embezzlement, grand larceny, burglary, arson, violation of narcotics laws, murder, rape, assault with intent to kill, assault which inflicts grievous bodily injury, or a violation of title II or III of this Act, or conspiracy to commit any such crimes, shall serve—

(1) as an officer, director, trustee, member of any executive board or similar governing body, business agent, manager, organizer, or other employee (other than as an employee performing exclusively clerical or custodial duties) of any labor organization, or

(2) as a labor relations consultant to a person engaged in an industry or activity affecting commerce, or as an officer, director, agent, or employee (other than as an employee performing exclusively clerical or custodial duties) of any group or association of employers dealing with any labor organization,

during or for five years after the termination of his membership in the Communist Party, or for five years after such conviction or after the end of such imprisonment, unless prior to the end of such five-year period, in the case of a person so convicted or imprisoned, (A) his citizenship rights, having been revoked as a result of such conviction, have been fully restored, or (B) the Board of Parole of the United States Department of Justice determines that such person's service in any capacity referred to in clause (1) or (2) would not be contrary to the purposes of this Act. Prior to making any such determination the Board shall hold an administrative hearing and shall give notice of such proceeding by certified mail to the State, county, and Federal prosecuting officials in the jurisdiction or jurisdictions in which such person was convicted. The Board's determination in any such proceeding shall be final. No labor organization or officer thereof shall knowingly permit any person to assume or hold any office or paid position in violation of this subsection.

(b) Any person who willfully violates this section shall be fined not more than $10,000 or imprisoned for not more than one year, or both.

(c) For the purposes of this section, any person shall be deemed to have been "convicted" and under the disability of "conviction" from the date of the judgment of the trial court or the date of the final sustaining of such judgment on appeal, whichever is the later event, regardless of whether such conviction occurred before or after the date of enactment of this Act.

AMENDMENT TO SECTION 302, LABOR
MANAGEMENT RELATIONS ACT, 1947

SEC. 505. Subsections (a), (b), and (c) of section 302 of the Labor Management Relations Act, 1947, as amended, are amended to read as follows:

"SEC. 302. (a) It shall be unlawful for any employer or association of employers or any person who acts as a labor relations expert, adviser, or consultant to an employer or who acts in the interest of an employer to pay, lend, or deliver, or agree to pay, lend, or deliver, any money or other thing of value—

"(1) to any representative of any of his employees who are employed in an industry affecting commerce; or

"(2) to any labor organization, or any officer or employee thereof, which represents, seeks to represent, or would admit to membership, any of the employees of such employer who are employed in an industry affecting commerce; or

"(3) to any employee or group or committee of employee of such employer employed in an industry affecting commerce in excess of their normal compensation for the purpose of causing such employee or group or committee directly or indirectly to influence any other employees in the exercise of the right to organize and bargain collectively through representatives of their own choosing; or

"(4) to any officer or employee of a labor organization engaged in an industry affecting commerce with intent to influence him in respect to any of his actions, decisions, or duties as a representative of employees or as such officer or employee of such labor organization.

"(b) (1) It shall be unlawful for any person to request, demand, receive, or accept, or agree to receive or accept, any payment, loan, or delivery of any money or other thing of value prohibited by subsection (a).

"(2) It shall be unlawful for any labor organization, or for any person acting as an officer, agent, representative, or employee of such labor organization, to demand or accept from the operator of any motor vehicle (as defined in part II of the Interstate Commerce Act) employed in the transportation of property in commerce, or the employer of any such operator, any money or other thing of value payable to such organization or to an officer, agent, representative or employee thereof as a fee or charge for the unloading, or in connection with the unloading, of the cargo of such vehicle: *Provided,* That nothing in this paragraph shall be construed to make unlawful any payment by an employer to any of his employees as compensation for their services as employees.

"(c) The provisions of this section shall not be applicable (1) in respect to any money or other thing of value payable by an employer to any of his employees whose established duties include acting openly for such employer in matters of labor relations or personnel administration or to any representative of his employees, or to any officer or employee of a labor organization, who is also an employee or former employee of such employer, as compensation for, or by reason of, his service as an employee of such employer; (2) with respect to the payment or delivery of any money or other thing of value in satisfaction of a judgment of any court or a decision or award of an arbitrator or impartial chairman or in compromise, adjustment, settlement, or release of any claim, complaint, grievance, or dispute in the absence of fraud or duress; (3) with respect to the sale or purchase of an article or commodity at the prevailing market price in the regular course of business; (4) with respect to money deducted from the wages of employees in payment of membership dues in a labor organization: *Provided,* That the employer has received from each employee, on whose account such deductions are made, a written assignment which shall not be irrevocable for a period of more than one year, or beyond the termination date of the applicable collective agreement, whichever occurs sooner; (5) with respect to money or other thing of value paid to a trust fund established by such representative, for the sole and exclusive benefit of the employees of such employer, and their families and dependents (or of such employees, families, and dependents jointly with the employees of other employers making similar payments, and their families and dependents): *Provided,* That (A) such payments are held in trust for the purpose of paying, either from principal or income or both, for the benefit of employees, their families and dependents, for medical or hospital care, pensions on retirement or death of employees, compensation for injuries or illness resulting from occupational activity or insurance to provide any of the foregoing, or unemployment benefits or life insurance, disability and sickness insurance, or accident insurance; (B) the detailed basis on which such payments are to be made is specified in a written agreement with the employer, and employees and employers are equally represented in the administration of such fund, together with such neutral persons as the representatives of the employers and the representatives of employees may agree upon and in the event the employer and employee groups deadlock on the administration of such fund and there are no neutral persons empowered to break such deadlock, such agreement provides that the two groups shall agree on an impartial umpire to decide such dispute, or in event of their failure to agree within a reasonable length of time, an impartial umpire to decide such dispute shall, on petition of either group, be appointed by the district court of the United States for the district where the trust fund has its principal office, and shall also contain provisions for an annual audit of the trust fund, a statement of the results of which shall be available for inspection by interested persons at the principal office of the trust fund and at such other places as may be designated in such written agreement; and (C) such payments as are intended to be used for the purpose of providing pensions or annuities for employees are made to a separate trust which provides that the funds held therein cannot be used for any purpose other than paying such pensions or annuities; or (6) with respect to money or other things of value paid by any employer to a trust fund established by such respresentative for the purpose of pooled vacation, holiday, severance or similar benefits, or defraying costs of apprenticeship or other training programs: *Provided, That the requirements of clause (B) of the proviso to clause (5) of this subsection shall apply to such trust funds."

TITLE VI—MISCELLANEOUS PROVISIONS

INVESTIGATIONS

SEC. 601. (a) The Secretary shall have power when he believes it necessary in order to determine whether any person has violated or is about to violate any provision of this Act (except title I or amendments made by this Act to other statutes) to make an investigation and in connection therewith he may enter such places and inspect such records and accounts and question such persons as he may deem necessary to enable him to determine the facts relative thereto. The Secretary may report to interested persons or officials concerning the facts required to be shown in any report required by this Act and concerning the reasons for failure or refusal to file such a report or any other matter which he deems to be appropriate as a result of such an investigation.

(b) For the purpose of any investigation provided for in this Act, the provisions of sections 9 and 10 (relating to the attendance of witnesses and the production of books, papers, and documents) of the Federal Trade Commission Act of September 16, 1914, as amended (15 U.S.C. 49, 50), are hereby made applicable to the jurisdiction, powers, and duties of the Secretary or any officers designated by him.

EXTORTIONATE PICKETING

SEC. 602. (a) It shall be unlawful to carry on picketing on or about the premises of any employer for the purpose of, or as part of any conspiracy or in furtherance of any plan or purpose for, the personal profit or enrichment of any individual (except a bona fide increase in wages or other employee benefits) by taking or obtaining any money or other thing of value from such employer against his will or with his consent.

(b) Any person who willfully violates this section shall be fined not more than $10,000 or imprisoned not more than twenty years, or both.

RETENTION OF RIGHTS UNDER OTHER FEDERAL AND STATE LAWS

SEC. 603. (a) Except as explicitly provided to the contrary, nothing in this Act shall reduce or limit the responsibilities of any labor organization or any officer, agent, shop steward, or other representative of a labor organization, or of any trust in which a labor organization is interested, under any other Federal law or under the laws of any State, and, except as explicitly provided to the contrary, nothing in this Act shall take away any right or bar any remedy to which members of a labor organization are entitled under such other Federal law or law of any State.

(b) Nothing contained in titles I, II, III, IV, V, or VI of this Act shall be construed to supersede or impair or otherwise affect the provisions of the Railway Labor Act, as amended, or any of the obligations, rights, benefits, privileges, or immunities of any carrier, employee, organization, representative, or person subject thereto; nor shall anything contained in said titles (except section 505) of this Act be construed to confer any rights, privileges, immunities, or defenses upon employers, or to impair or otherwise affect the rights of any person under the National Labor Relations Act, as amended.

EFFECT ON STATE LAWS

SEC. 604. Nothing in this Act shall be construed to impair or diminish the authority of any State to enact and enforce general criminal laws with respect to robbery, bribery, extortion, embezzlement, grand larceny, burglary, arson, violation of narcotics laws, murder, rape, assault with intent to kill, or assault with inflicts grievous bodily injury, or conspiracy to commit any of such crimes.

SERVICE OF PROCESS

SEC. 605. For the purposes of this Act, service of summons, subpoena, or other legal process of a court of the United States upon an officer or agent of a labor organization in his capacity as such shall constitute service upon the labor organization.

ADMINISTRATIVE PROCEDURE ACT

SEC. 606. The provisions of the Administrative Procedure Act shall be applicable to the issuance, amendment, or rescission of any rules or regulations, or any adjudication, authorized or required pursuant to the provisions of this Act.

OTHER AGENCIES AND DEPARTMENTS

SEC. 607. In order to avoid unnecessary expense and duplication of functions among Government agencies, the Secretary may make such arrangements or agreements for cooperation or mutual assistance in the performance of his functions under this Act and the functions of any such agency as he may find to be practicable and consistent with law. The Secretary may utilize the facilities or services of any department, agency, or establishment of the United States or of any State or political subdivision of a State, including the services of any of its employees, with the lawful consent of such department, agency, or establishment; and each department, agency, or establishment of the United States is authorized and directed to co-operate with the Secretary and, to the extent permitted by law, to provide such information and facilities as he may request for his assistance in the performance of his functions under this Act. The Attorney General or his representative shall receive from the Secretary for appropriate action such evidence developed in the performance of his functions under this Act as may be found to warrant consideration for criminal prosecution under the provisions of this Act or other Federal law.

CRIMINAL CONTEMPT

SEC. 608. No person shall be punished for any criminal contempt allegedly committed outside the immediate presence of the court in connection with any civil action prosecuted by the Secretary or any other person in any court of the United States under the provisions of this Act unless the facts constituting such criminal contempt are established by the verdict of the jury in a proceeding in the district court of the United States, which jury shall be chosen and empaneled in the manner prescribed by the law governing trial juries in criminal prosecutions in the district courts of the United States.

PROHIBITION ON CERTAIN DISCIPLINE BY LABOR ORGANIZATION

SEC. 609. It shall be unlawful for any labor organization, or any officer, agent, shop steward, or other representative of a labor organization, or any employee thereof to fine, suspend, expel, or otherwise discipline any of its members for exercising any right to which he is entitled under the provisions of this Act. The provisions of section 102 shall be applicable in the enforcement of this section.

DEPRIVATION OF RIGHTS UNDER ACT BY VIOLENCE

SEC. 610. It shall be unlawful for any person through the use of force or violence, or threat of the use of force or violence, to restrain, coerce, or intimidate, or attempt to restrain, coerce, or intimidate any member of a labor organization for the purpose of interfering with or preventing the exercise of any right to which he is entitled under the provisions of this Act. Any person who willfully violates this section shall be fined not more than $1,000 or imprisoned for not more than one year, or both.

SEPARABILITY PROVISIONS

SEC. 611. If any provision of this Act, or the application of such provision to any person or circumstances, shall be held invalid, the remainder of this Act or the application of such provision to persons or circumstances other than those as to which it is held invalid, shall not be affected thereby.

TITLE VII—AMENDMENTS TO THE LABOR MANAGEMENT RELATIONS ACT, 1947, AS AMENDED

FEDERAL-STATE JURISDICTION

SEC. 701. (a) Section 14 of the National Labor Relations Act, as amended, is amended by adding at the end thereof the following new subsection:

"(c) (1) The Board, in its discretion, may, by rule of decision or by published rules adopted pursuant to the Administrative Procedure Act, decline to assert jurisdiction over any labor dispute involving any class or category of employers, where, in the opinion of the Board, the effect of such labor dispute on commerce is not sufficiently substantial to warrant the exercise of its jurisdiction: *Provided,* That the Board shall not decline to assert jurisdiction over any labor dispute over which it would assert jurisdiction under the standards prevailing upon August 1, 1959.

"(2) Nothing in this Act shall be deemed to prevent or bar any agency or the courts of any State or Territory (including the Commonwealth of Puerto Rico, Guam, and the Virgin Islands), from assuming and asserting jurisdiction over labor disputes over which the Board declines, pursuant to paragraph (1) of this subsection, to assert jurisdiction."

(b) Section 3 (b) of such Act is amended to read as follows:

"(b) The Board is authorized to delegate to any group of three or more members any or all of the powers which it may itself exercise. The Board is also authorized to delegate to its regional directors its powers under section 9 to determine the unit appropriate for the purpose of collective bargaining, to investigate and provide for hearings, and determine whether a question of representation exists, and to direct an election or take a secret ballot under subsection (c) or (e) and section 9 and certify the results thereof, except that upon the filing of a request therefor with the Board by any interested person, the Board may review any action of a regional director delegated to him under this paragraph, but such a review shall not, unless specifically ordered by the Board, operate as a stay of any action taken by the regional director. A vacancy in the Board shall not impair the right of the remaining members to exercise all of the powers of the Board, and three members of the Board shall, at all times, constitute a quorum of the Board, except that two members shall constitute a quorum of any group designated pursuant to the first sentence hereof. The Board shall have an official seal which shall be judicially noticed."

ECONOMIC STRIKES

SEC. 702. Section 9 (c) (3) of the National Labor Relations Act, as amended, is amended by amending the second sentence thereof to read as follows: "Employees engaged in an economic strike who are not entitled to reinstatement shall be eligible to vote under such regulations as the Board shall find are consistent with the purposes and provisions of this Act in any election conducted within twelve months after the commencement of the strike."

VACANCY IN OFFICE OF GENERAL COUNSEL

SEC. 703. Section 3 (d) of the National Labor Relations Act, as amended, is amended by adding after the period at the end thereof the following: "In case of a vacancy in the office of the General Counsel the President is authorized to designate the officer or employee who shall act as General Counsel during such vacancy, but no person or persons so designated shall so act (1) for more than forty days when the Congress is in session unless a nomination to fill such vacancy shall have been submitted to the Senate, or (2) after the adjournment sine die of the session of the Senate in which such nomination was submitted."

BOYCOTTS AND RECOGNITION PICKETING

SEC. 704. (a) Section 8 (b) (4) of the National Labor Relations Act, as amended, is amended to read as follows:

"(4) (i) to engage in, or to induce or encourage any individual employed by any person engaged in commerce or in an industry affecting commerce to engage in, a strike or a refusal in the course of his employment to use, manufacture, process, transport, or otherwise handle or work on any goods, articles, materials, or commodities or to perform any services; or (ii) to threaten, coerce, or restrain any person engaged in commerce or in an industry affecting commerce, where in either case an object thereof is—

"(A) forcing or requiring any employer or self-employed person to join any labor or employer organization or to enter into any agreement which is prohibited by section 8 (e);

"(B) forcing or requiring any person to cease using, selling, handling, transporting, or otherwise dealing in the products of any other producer, processor, or manufacturer, or to cease doing business with any other person, or forcing or requiring any other employer to recognize or bargain with a labor organization as the representative of his employees unless such labor organization has been certified as the representative of such employees under the provisions of section 9: *Pro-*

vided, That nothing contained in this clause (B) shall be construed to make unlawful, where not otherwise unlawful, any primary strike or primary picketing;

"(C) forcing or requiring any employer to recognize or bargain with a particular labor organization as the representative of his employees if another labor organization has been certified as the representative of such employees under the provisions of section 9;

"(D) forcing or requiring any employer to assign particular work to employees in a particular labor organization or in a particular trade, craft, or class rather than to employees in another labor organization or in another trade, craft, or class, unless such employer is failing to conform to an order or certification of the Board determining the bargaining representative for employees performing such work: *Provided,* That nothing contained in this subsection (b) shall be construed to make unlawful a refusal by any person to enter upon the premises of any employer (other than his own employer), if the employees of such employer are engaged in a strike ratified or approved by a representative of such employees whom such employer is required to recognize under this Act: *Provided further,* That for the purposes of this paragraph (4) only, nothing contained in such paragraph shall be construed to prohibit publicity, other than picketing, for the purpose of truthfully advising the public, including consumers and members of a labor organization, that a product or products are produced by an employer with whom the labor organization has a primary dispute and are distributed by another employer, as long as such publicity does not have an effect of inducing any individual employed by any person other than the primary employer in the course of his employment to refuse to pick up, deliver, or transport any goods, or not to perform any services, at the establishment of the employer engaged in such distribution."

(b) Section 8 of the National Labor Relations Act, as amended, is amended by adding at the end thereof the following new subsection:

"(e) It shall be an unfair labor practice for any labor organization and any employer to enter into any contract or agreement, express or implied, whereby such employer ceases or refrains or agrees to cease or refrain from handling, using, selling, transporting or otherwise dealing in any of the products of any other employer, or to cease doing business with any other person, and any contract or agreement entered into heretofore or hereafter containing such an agreement shall be to such extent unenforcible and void: *Provided,* That nothing in this subsection (e) shall apply to an agreement between a labor organization and an employer in the construction industry relating to the contracting or subcontracting of work to be done at the site of the construction, alteration, painting, or repair of a building, structure, or other work: *Provided further,* That for the purposes of this subsection (e) and section 8 (b) (4) (B) the terms 'any employer', 'any person engaged in commerce or an industry affecting commerce', and 'any person' when used in relation to the terms 'any other producer, processor, or manufacturer', 'any other employer', or 'any other person' shall not include persons in the relation of a jobber, manufacturer, contractor, or subcontractor working on the goods or premises of the jobber or manufacturer or performing parts of an integrated process of production in the apparel and clothing industry: *Provided further,* That nothing in this Act shall prohibit the enforcement of any agreement which is within the foregoing exception."

(c) Section 8 (b) of the National Labor Relations Act, as amended, is amended by striking out the word "and" at the end of paragraph (5), striking out the period at the end of paragraph (6), and inserting in lieu thereof a semicolon and the word "and", and adding a new paragraph as follows:

"(7) to picket or cause to be picketed, or threaten to picket or cause to be picketed, any employer where an object thereof is forcing or requiring an employer to recognize or bargain with a labor organization as the representative of his employees, or forcing or requiring the employees of an employer to accept or select such labor organization as their collective bargaining representative, unless such labor organization is currently certified as the representative of such employees:

"(A) where the employer has lawfully recognized in accordance with this Act any other labor organization and a question concerning representation may not appropriately be raised under section 9 (c) of this Act,

"(B) where within the preceding twelve months a valid election under section 9 (c) of this Act has been conducted, or

"(C) where such picketing has been conducted without a petition under section 9 (c) being filed within a reasonable period of time not to exceed thirty days from the commencement of such picketing: *Provided,* That when such a petition has been filed the Board shall forthwith, without regard to the provisions of section 9 (c) (1) or the absence of a showing of a substantial interest on the part of the labor organization, direct an election in such unit as the Board finds to be appropriate and shall certify the results thereof: *Provided further,* That nothing in this subparagraph (C) shall be construed to prohibit any picketing or other publicity for the purpose of truthfully advising the public (including consumers) that an employer does not employ members of, or have a contract with, a labor organization, unless an effect of such picketing is to induce any individual employed by any other person in the course of his employment, not to pick up, deliver or transport any goods or not to perform any services.

"Nothing in this paragraph (7) shall be construed to permit any act which would otherwise be an unfair labor practice under this section 8 (b)."

(d) Section 10 (l) of the National Labor Relations Act, as amended, is amended by adding after the words "section 8 (b)," the words "or section 8 (e) or section 8 (b) (7)," and by striking out the period at the end of the third sentence and inserting in lieu thereof a colon and the following: "*Provided further,* That such officer or regional attorney shall not apply for any restraining order under section 8 (b) (7) if a charge against the employer under section 8 (a) (2) has been filed and after the preliminary investigation, he has reasonable cause to believe that such charge is true and that a complaint should issue."

(e) Section 303 (a) of the Labor Management Relations Act, 1947, is amended to read as follows:

"(a) It shall be unlawful, for the purpose of this section only, in an industry or activity affecting commerce, for any labor organization to engage in any activity or conduct defined as an unfair labor practice in section 8 (b) (4) of the National Labor Relations Act, as amended."

BUILDING AND CONSTRUCTION INDUSTRY

SEC. 705. (a) Section 8 of the National Labor Relations Act, as amended by section 704 (b) of this Act, is amended by adding at the end thereof the following new subsection:

"(f) It shall not be an unfair labor practice under subsections (a) and (b) of this section for an employer engaged primarily in the building and construction industry to make an agreement covering employees engaged (or who, upon their employment, will be engaged) in the building and construction industry with a labor organization of which building and construction employees are members (not established, maintained, or assisted by any action defined in section 8 (a) of this Act as an unfair labor practice) because (1) the majority status of such labor organization has not been established under the provisions of section 9 of this Act prior to the making of such agreement, or (2) such agreement requires as a condition of employment, membership in such labor organization after the seventh day following the beginning of such employment or the effective date of the agreement, whichever is later, or (3) such agreement requires the employer to notify such labor organization of opportunities for employment with such employer, or gives such labor organization an opportunity to refer qualified applicants for such employment, or (4) such agreement specifies minimum training or experience qualifications of employment or provides for priority in opportunities for employment based upon length of service with such employer, in the industry or in the particular geographical area: *Provided,* That nothing in this subsection shall set aside the final proviso to section 8 (a) (3) of this Act: *Provided further,* That any agreement which would be invalid, but for clause (1) of this subsection, shall not be a bar to a petition filed pursuant to section 9 (c) or 9 (e)."

(b) Nothing contained in the amendment made by subsection (a) shall be construed as authorizing the execution or application of agreements requiring membership in a labor organization as a condition of employment in any State or Territory in which such execution or application is prohibited by State or Territorial law.

PRIORITY IN CASE HANDLING

SEC. 706. Section 10 of the National Labor Relations Act, as amended, is amended by adding at the end thereof a new subsection as follows:

"(m) Whenever it is charged that any person has engaged in an unfair labor practice within the meaning of subsection (a) (3) or (b) (2) of section 8, such charge shall be given priority over all other cases except cases of like character in the office where it is filed or to which it is referred and cases given priority under subsection (1)."

EFFECTIVE DATE OF AMENDMENTS

SEC. 707. The amendments made by this title shall take effect sixty days after the date of the enactment of this Act and no provision of this title shall be deemed to make an unfair labor practice, any act which is performed prior to such effective date which did not constitute an unfair labor practice prior thereto.

Approved, September 14, 1959.

THE ORIGINS

Message from the President of the United States transmitting a 20-point program to eliminate abuses and improper practices in labor-management relations, January 28, 1959

To the Congress of the United States:

In the State of the Union message on January 9, I reported again to the Congress on the need for enactment of effective Federal legislation designed—

To safeguard workers' funds in union treasuries against misuse of any kind whatsoever.

To protect the rights and freedoms of individual union members, including the basic right to free and secret election of officers.

To advance true and responsible collective bargaining.

To protect the public and innocent third parties from unfair and coercive practices, such as boycotting and blackmail picketing.

There is submitted herewith for the consideration of the Congress a 20-point program which will eliminate abuses demonstrated by the hearings of the McClellan committee, protect the public interest, and insure the rights and economic freedoms of millions of American workers.

Complete and effective labor-management legislation, not a piecemeal program, is essential to assure the American public that true, responsible collective bargaining can be carried on with full protection to the rights and freedoms of workers and with adequate guarantees of the public interest. These recommendations, when adopted, should do much to eliminate those abuses and improper practices which, I am firmly convinced, the American public expects and believes will be corrected through legislative action. Equally important, they will do so without imposing arbitrary restrictions or punitive measures on the legitimate activities of honest labor and management officials.

I recommend legislation—

1. To require all unions to file detailed annual reports with the Department of Labor and furnish information to their members with respect to their financial operations. These reports would be open to the public, including union members.

2. To require all unions to file with the Department of Labor, as public information, copies of their constitutions and bylaws and information as to their organization and procedures, which would be required to include provisions, which are observed, meeting minimum standards for periodic secret ballot elections of officers, for the removal of officers, and for the imposition of supervisory control over the affairs of subordinate bodies.

3. To require all unions to keep proper records on the matters required

to be reported, open to examination by Government representatives and to permit union members, subject to reasonable conditions and upon request, to see and examine these records.

4. To require unions, union officers and agents, and employers to report and keep proper records with respect to any payments, transactions, or investments which create conflicts of interests or have as their objective the interference with the statutory rights of individual union members and employees.

5. To require that union officers hold and administer union funds and property solely for the benefit of the union members and for furthering the purpose of the union and to make this duty enforceable in any court in a suit for an accounting by the union or by members.

6. To require that unions observe minimum standards for the conduct of the elections of officers, including, in addition to periodic elections, the right of members to vote in secret without restraint or coercion and upon due notice, uniform opportunity for all members to be candidates, procedures to insure an accurate tabulation of votes, a ban upon the use of union or employer funds to promote candidacies for union office, and requiring constitutions and bylaws to contain detailed statements of election procedures and compliance with such procedures.

7. To require unions to observe minimum standards and to conform to the appropriate provisions of their constitution and bylaws in exercising supervisory control over the affairs of subordinate bodies; such control should be limited in purpose to correcting corruption; or the disregard of democratic procedures or other practices detrimental to the rights of the members in the subordinate body, and assuring the performance of duties as a bargaining representative.

8. To place the administration of this legislation in the Secretary of Labor and to provide him with appropriate and adequate authority to issue regulations, investigate, subpena witnesses and records, bring court action to compel compliance and to correct violations, and institute administrative procedures leading to decisions and orders, which would be subject to judicial review, necessary to effectuate the purposes of the legislation.

9. To prescribe criminal penalties for willful violations of the act, for concealment or destruction of records required to be kept, for bribery between employers and employee representatives, for improper payments by employers or their representatives to employees or employee representatives, for embezzlement of union funds, and for false entries or destruction of union books and records.

10. To preserve for union members any present remedies under State or Federal laws, in addition to those provided under this legislation.

11. To amend the secondary boycott provisions of the National Labor

Relations Act so as to cover the direct coercion of employers to cease or agree to cease doing business with other persons; union pressures directed against secondary employers not otherwise subject to the act; and inducements of individual employees to refuse to perform services with the object of forcing their employers to stop doing business with others; and to make clear that secondary activity is permitted against an employer performing "farmed-out struck work" and, under certain circumstances, against secondary employers engaged in work at a common construction site with the primary employer.

12. To make it illegal for a union, by picketing, to coerce an employer to recognize it as the bargaining representative of his employee or his employees to accept or designate it as their representative where the employer has recognized in accordance with law another labor organization, or where a representation election has been conducted within the last preceding 12 months, or where it cannot be demonstrated that there is a sufficient showing of interest on the part of the employees in being represented by the picketing union or where the picketing has continued for a reasonable period of time without the desires of the employees being determined by a representation election; and to provide speedy and effective enforcement measures.

13. To authorize the National Labor Relations Board to decline to take cases where the effect on commerce is relatively insubstantial and to permit the State courts and agencies to act with respect to these cases.

14. To eliminate the statutory prohibition which presently bars certain strikers from voting in representation elections, although their replacements are permitted to vote, and instead to leave the voting eligibility of strikers, as well as all others, to the administrative discretion of the National Labor Relations Board.

15. To authorize the Board, under carefully considered specific conditions, to certify building and construction trades unions as bargaining representatives without an election.

16. In order to speed up the orderly processes of election procedures, to permit the Board under proper safeguards to conduct representation elections without holding a prior hearing where no substantial objection to an election is made.

17. To equalize the onus of the non-Communist affidavit by extending it to employers, as well as unions, wishing to use the processes of the act.

18. To make clear that parties to a valid collective bargaining agreement need not negotiate during the life of the agreement unless they have provided for, or agree to, the reopening of the agreement.

19. To authorize the designation by the President of an acting General Counsel of the Board when vacancies occur in that office.

20. To require that the Board be bipartisan in composition by providing that not more than three members of the Board may be of the same political party.

I urge that Congress give prompt and favorable consideration to this program. Its enactment, in my opinion, would contribute greatly to the protection of the public interest and the basic rights of individual working men and women.

Dwight D. Eisenhower.

Report of the Senate Committee on Labor and Public Welfare
April 14, 1959

JOHN KENNEDY [DEM., MASS.] submitted the Report together with Minority, Supplemental, and Individual Views.

The Committee on Labor and Public Welfare, to whom was referred the bill (S. 1555) to provide for the reporting and disclosure of certain financial transactions and administrative practices of labor organizations and employers, to prevent abuses in the administration of trusteeships by labor organizations, to provide standards with respect to the election of officers of labor organization, and for other purposes, having considered the same, report favorably thereon, with amendments, and recommend that the bill do pass. . . .

PART I—PURPOSE OF THE BILL

The committee reported bill is primarily designed to correct the abuses which have crept into labor and management and which have been the subject of investigation by the Committee on Improper Activities in the Labor and Management Field for the past several years. In its first interim report the McClellan committee made five legislative recommendations. One of these has been implemented in the passage of Public Law 85–836, the Welfare and Pension Plan Disclosure Act of 1958. The remaining recommendations: (1) To regulate and control union funds; (2) to insure union democracy; (3) to curb activities of middlemen in labor-management disputes; and (4) to clarify the "no man's land" between State and Federal authority; were the subject of a bill, S. 3974, which passed the Senate last year by an 88-to-1 vote, but failed to receive the approval of the House of Representatives. The committee-reported bill is based on the legislation approved by the Senate last year and thus it too implements the remaining recommendations of the McClellan committee. In brief, the bill, S. 1555, would accomplish the following:

(1) Full reporting and public disclosure of union internal processes;

(2) Full reporting and public disclosure of union financial operations;

(3) All information required to be reported will be made available to union members in a manner prescribed by the Secretary;

(4) Criminal penalties for failure to make such reports or for filing false reports;

(5) Criminal penalties for false entries in and destruction of union records;

(6) Full reporting and public disclosure of financial transactions and holdings, if any, by union officials which might give rise to conflicts of interest, including payments received from labor relations consultants;

(7) Full reporting and public disclosures by employers of expenditures for the purpose of persuading employees to exercise, not to exercise, or as to the manner of exercising their rights to organize and bargain collectively;

(8) Full reporting and public disclosure by employers of expenditures for the purpose of obtaining information concerning the activities of employees or unions in connection with a labor dispute:

(9) Full reports by employers of any direct or indirect loans to a labor organization or officer or employee of a labor organization;

(10) Criminal penalties for failing to file or falsification of reports required of employers and labor relations consultant;

(11) Provides Secretary with broad investigatory power, including the power of subpena, to prevent violation of the reporting and other provisions of the bill;

(12) Authorizes the Secretary to bring a civil injunction in a district court of the United States to compel compliance with the reporting provisions of the act or any rules or regulations which he promulgates to insure compliance with these provisions;

(13) Criminal penalties for payments by "middlemen" to union officials;

(14) Full reports by employers of any arrangement with a labor relations consultant or other independent contractor by which such person undertakes to persuade employees to exercise or not to exercise or regarding the exercise of their rights to organize or bargain collectively;

(15) Full reports by any person who has an agreement with an employer to persuade employees to exercise or not to exercise or as to the manner of their exercising their rights to organize and bargain collectively; or who supplies information to an employer concerning the activities of employees or labor organizations in connection with a labor dispute;

(16) Prohibits persons who have been convicted of certain crimes from holding union office or employment within 5 years of having served any part of a prison term as a result of such conviction;

(17) Prohibits unions from paying the legal fees or fines of any person indicted or convicted of a violation of the bill;

(18) Full reporting and public disclosure of trusteeships imposed by national or international unions;

(19) Criminal penalties for failure to file or falsification of required reports relating to trusteeships;

(20) Prescribes minimum standards for establishment of trusteeships and sets limits on their duration;

(21) Authorizes Federal court proceedings to dissolve trusteeships when not imposed in accordance with provisions of the bill;

(22) Empowers Federal courts to preserve the assets of a trusteed labor organization and limits the funds which may be transferred from a trusteed labor organization to the international;

(23) Requires election of constitutional officers and members of executive boards of international unions at least every 5 years by secret ballot or by delegates elected by secret ballot;

(24) Requires election of constitutional officers and members of executive boards of local unions at least every 3 years by secret ballot;

(25) Protects freedom of opportunity to nominate candidates in union elections;

(26) Protects members' right to vote in union elections without being subject to improper interference or reprisals;

(27) Insures that every candidate for union office shall be afforded the opportunity to distribute at his own expense literature in support of his candidacy to all the members of the union;

(28) Requires that all candidates shall have the opportunity to have observers present at the balloting and at the counting of the ballots in a union election;

(29) Prohibits use of union funds to promote individual candidacy in union elections;

(30) Procedures whereby a union officer guilty of serious misconduct in office may be removed by a secret ballot vote after court proceedings if the union's constitution does not provide adequate machinery for such removal;

(31) Provides for investigations by the Secretary of members' complaints of improper procedures in union elections and court actions by the Secretary to set aside improperly conducted elections;

(32) Empowers Federal courts to direct new elections to be conducted under supervision of the Secretary where it finds union election was improperly conducted;

(33) Preserves members' rights to enforce union's constitution under State laws with respect to trusteeships and safeguarding fair procedures before an election;

(34) A congressional declaration of policy favoring voluntary self-polic-

ing, through adoption and implementation of codes of ethical practices, by labor organizations and employers;

(35) Establishment of an Advisory Committee on Ethical Practices composed of representatives of the public, labor organizations, and employers;

(36) Eliminates the "no-man's land" in labor-management relations by directing the National Labor Relations Board to exercise jurisdiction directly or with the aid of State agencies in all cases within its competence;

(37) State agencies may, by agreement with the National Labor Relations Board, administer the Federal act in accordance with procedures and substantive law applicable with regard to cases processed by the NLRB;

(38) Subjects shakedown picketing to criminal sanctions;

(39) Bans demand and acceptance by unions or union representatives of payments from interstate truckers of improper unloading fees; shop agreements in the building and construction industry;

(40) Permits with appropriate safeguards, prehire and 7-day union shop agreements in the building and construction industry;

(41) Clarification of the propriety of employer contributions to joint union-management apprenticeship funds;

(42) Restoration of voting rights to economic strikers;

(43) Criminal penalties for embezzlement, conversion, etc., of union funds;

(44) Establishes a prehearing election procedure with respect to labor disputes in which there are no substantive issues present in order to speed up the handling of cases by the National Labor Relations Board;

(45) Authorizes the President to appoint an acting General Counsel to the National Labor Relations Board when a vacancy occurs in that office.

These and other provisions of the bill not included in the foregoing brief summary represent a major attack on the abuses and problems identified by recent investigations. No bill in the committee's view can be written which will close completely the many avenues which the criminal can devise to carry on his nefarious activity, without at the same time wrecking important institutions, violating cardinal precepts of law, and undermining the principles upon which a free society is based.

The bill is designed to prevent, discourage, and make unprofitable improper conduct on the part of union officials, employers, and their representatives by requiring reporting of arrangements, actions, and interests which are questionable. In some instances, the matters to be reported are not illegal and may not be improper. But only full disclosure will enable the persons whose rights are affected, the public and the Government to determine whether the arrangements or activities are justifiable, ethical, and legal.

In addition to comprehensive reporting the bill provides criminal penalties for actions which are clearly improper such as the embezzlement of union funds, tampering with or destroying union records, bribing employee representatives, and violation of the trusteeship or election provisions of the bill.

The Subcommittee on Labor held intensive hearings on all of the relevant bills before it. It considered all of the proposals and suggestions made during the hearings and studied each of the bills pending. S. 505, on which S. 1555 is based, was modified to include those recommendations which strengthened the bill and increased its effectiveness. The Committee on Labor and Public Welfare carefully considered the bill reported by the subcommittee and made a number of substantial changes.

The committee reports this bill favorably after lengthy consideration this year and on the basis of a substantial record and extensive debate on a similar bill in the 85th Congress. The committee recognizes that in addition to the major steps to correct labor and management abuses taken by this bill further attention should be directed to amendments in the laws governing labor-management relations. To assist it in this task, the committee has appointed a distinguished panel of experts to advise it on appropriate modifications in existing law. This advisory panel is expected to make its report later in the session, and it is the intention of the committee to move forward in the area of major revision of our labor-management law as soon as practicable.

PART II—BACKGROUND AND GENERAL APPROACH OF THE BILL

A strong independent labor movement is a vital part of American institutions. The shocking abuses revealed by recent investigations have been confined to a few unions. The overwhelming majority are honestly and democratically run. In providing remedies for existing evils the Senate should be careful neither to undermine self-government within the labor movement nor to weaken unions in their role as the bargaining representatives of employees.

It is plain that the trade union movement in the United States is facing difficult internal problems and—because of these internal problems—tensions with the surrounding community. The problems of this now large and relatively strong institution are not unlike the difficulties faced by other groups in American society which aspire to live by the same basic principles and values within their group as they hold ideal for the whole community. But equal rights, freedom of choice, honesty, and the highest ethical standards are built into changing institutions only after struggle. Trade unions have grown well beyond their beginnings as relatively small, closely knit associations of workingmen where personal, fraternal relationships were characteristic. Like other American institutions some unions have become large and impersonal; they have acquired bureaucratic tendencies and characteristics; their members like other Americans have sometimes become apathetic in the exercise of their personal responsibility for the conduct of union affairs. In some few cases men who have risen to positions of power and responsibility within unions have abused their power and neglected their responsibilities. In some cases the structure and procedures necessary for trade unions while they were struggling for survival are ill adapted to their new role and to changed conditions; they are not always conducive to efficient, honest, and democratic practices.

Whatever the causes, the problems are recognized by those within as well as those outside the union movement. The action of the American Federation of Labor-Congress of Industrial Organizations in recognizing the importance of adherence to traditional principles of ethical conduct and trade union democracy and in formulating and implementing codes of ethical practices to carry out these established principles, is a dramatic and convincing demonstration of the trade union movement's desire to conduct its internal affairs democratically and in accordance with high standards of trust. Nevertheless, effective measures to stamp out crime and corruption and guarantee internal union democracy, cannot be applied to all unions without the coercive powers of government, nor is the present machinery of the federation demonstrably effective in policing specific abuses at the local level.

It is also plain that there are important sections of management that refused to recognize that the employees have a right to form and join unions without interference and to enjoy freely the right to bargain collectively with their employer concerning their wages, working conditions, and other conditions of employment. The hearings of the McClellan committee have shown that employers have often cooperated with and even aided crooks and racketeers in the labor movement at the expense of their own employees. They have employed so-called middlemen to organize "no-union committees" and engage in other activities to prevent union organization among their employees. They have financed community campaigns to defeat union organization. They have employed investigators and informers to report on the organizing activities of employees and unions. It is essential that any legislation which purports to drive corruption and improper activities out of labor-management relations contain provisions dealing effectively with these problems.

The internal problems currently facing our labor unions are bound up with a substantial public interest. Under the National Labor Relations Act and the Railway Labor Act, a labor organization has vast responsibility for economic welfare of the individual members whom it represents. Union members have a vital interest, therefore, in the policies and conduct of union affairs. To the extent that union procedures are democratic they permit the individual to share in the formulation of union policy. This is not to say that in order to have democratically responsive unions, it is necessary to have each union member make decisions on detail as in a New England town meeting. What is required is the opportunity to influence policy and leadership by free and periodic elections.

In acting on this bill the committee followed three principles:

1. The committee recognized the desirability of minimum interference by Government in the internal affairs of any private organization. Trade unions have made a commendable effort to correct internal abuses; hence the committee believes that only essential standards should be imposed by legislation. Moreover, in establishing and enforcing statutory standards great care should be taken not to undermine union self-government or weaken unions in their role as collective-bargaining agents.

2. Given the maintenance of minimum democratic safeguards and detailed essential information about the union, the individual members are fully competent to regulate union affairs. The committee strongly opposes any attempt to prescribe detailed procedures and standards for the conduct of union business. Such paternalistic regulation would weaken rather than strengthen the labor movement; it would cross over into the area of trade union licensing and destroy union independence.

3. Remedies for the abuses should be direct. Where the law prescribes standards, sanctions for their violation should also be direct. The committee rejects the notion of applying destructive sanctions to a union, i.e., to a group of working men and women, for an offense for which the officers are responsible and over which the members have, at best, only indirect control. Still more important the legislation should provide an administrative or judicial remedy appropriate for each specific problem.

The committee does not believe that the record demonstrates that the imposition of indirect sanctions, such as penalizing the union and its members for malpractices of its officers, would be effective in insuring compliance. Moreover, on the basis of information available to the committee, it is clear that the requirements of present law with respect to the filing of financial and other data have hampered the administration of the National Labor Relations Act, have disrupted labor-management relations and have been expensive to administer.

The bill reported by the committee, while it carries out all the major recommendations of the Senate select committee, does so within a general philosophy of legislative restraint. The bill does not spell out in detail all the standards which every trade union should follow. It recognizes the variety of situations to which its provisions must apply and, especially, the inadvisability and injustice of compelling unions to conform to a uniform statutory rule with respect to unimportant details of administration.

The test of a sound bill in this complex and relatively new legislative area is whether it is workable and will produce the desired results without destroying valued free institutions. The committee believes that the bill now reported possesses these attributes. . . .

Report of the House Committee on Education and Labor
July 30, 1959

MR. GRAHAM BARDEN [DEM., N. C.] submitted the Report.

The Committee on Education and Labor to whom was referred the bill (H.R. 8342) to provide for the reporting and disclosure of certain financial transactions and administrative practices of labor organizations and employers, to prevent abuses in the administration of trusteeships by labor organizations, and for other purposes, having considered the same, report favorably thereon and recommend that the bill do pass.

PART I. PURPOSE OF THE BILL

The committee reported bill is primarily intended to correct the abuses which have crept into the labor and management field and which have been the subject of investigation by the Senate Committee on Improper Activities in the Labor and Management Field for the past several years.

During the executive sessions the committee worked primarily from four major bills which were before the committee for consideration. Those bills were: S. 1555, as passed by the U.S. Senate, H.R. 4473, H.R. 7265, and H.R.7680. Among other bills which were also referred to from time to time were S. 1137, H.R. 3540, S. 505, and H.R. 4474.

The committee bill H.R. 8342, which finally emerged from the deliberations of the committee after many executive sessions occurring during a period of more than 5 weeks, covers substantially the same areas of the labor-management field that are treated in S. 1555 as passed by the Senate.

Each of the two bills has seven titles and deals with the following major subjects.

    1. Democratic procedures and basic rights of union members within labor organizations (title I of each bill).

    2. Reporting of union financial and administrative practices by labor unions, and by officials and employees of unions relative to matters involving possible conflict of interest situations. Such reports to be made to the Secretary of Labor (title II of both bills).

    3. Reports by employers and labor relations consultants in respect to certain activities involving labor-management relations. Such reports to be filed with the Secretary of Labor (title II of both bills).

4. Criminal penalties for failure to file and for falsification of reports and records.

5. Procedures to compel compliance with the reporting requirements.

6. Trusteeships-standards are established with respect to the establishment and continuance of such trusteeships, and reports thereon are required to be filed with the Secretary of Labor (title III of both bills).

7. Elections of union officers—Provisions to insure fair and honest elections at specified intervals (title IV of both bills).

8. Fiduciary and bonding requirements—Each bill imposes fiduciary responsibilities upon union representatives and requires bonding of representatives and employees of unions and of trusts in which labor organizations are interested, who handle or control funds or property of such organizations (title V of H.R. 8342 and title VI and III of S. 1555).

9. Amendments to the National Labor Relations Act, as amended, dealing with the no man's land problem, organization picketing, secondary boycotts, prehire agreements in the building and construction industry, voting by economic strikers, prehearing elections by the National Labor Relations Board in representation cases, appointment of an acting general counsel of the National Labor Relations Board by the President (title VII of both bills) and increasing the Board from five to seven members.

In some instances corresponding provisions of the two bills are identical. In other instances minor differences exist between corresponding provisions. In certain areas, however, major differences between the two bills do exist. Some of the latter variances involve substantive matter while others relate to procedures and remedies.

The Committee on Education and Labor after careful and lengthy consideration reports this bill favorably.

PART II. BACKGROUND AND NEED FOR LEGISLATION

The disclosures of the Committee on Improper Activities in the Labor and Management field resulting from the investigations conducted by that committee in the labor and management field during the past several years have revealed shocking abuses. Those abuses involve segments of the trade union movement and certain sections of management.

It is a fact beyond question that the trade union movement in the United States is facing difficult internal problems. Those problems have brought about tensions and repercussions which affect not only the trade unions and employers but the public as well.

Trade unions, during the past 30 years, have grown far beyond their beginnings as relatively small, closely knit associations of workingmen. Many unions today number their members in the hundreds of thousands. Some of our trade unions now have in excess of 1 million members.

Some trade unions have acquired bureaucratic tendencies and characteristics. The relationship of the leaders of such unions to their members has in some instances become impersonal and autocratic. In some cases men who have acquired positions of power and responsibility within unions have abused their power and forsaken their responsibilities to the membership and to the public. The power and control of the affairs of a trade union by leaders who abuse their power and forsake their responsibilities inevitably leads to the elimination of efficient, honest and democratic practices within such union, and often results in irresponsible actions which are detrimental to the public interest.

Recognizing the need to bring about reforms in the trade union movement the American Federation of Labor-Congress of Industrial Organizations, formulated codes of ethical practices to guide its affiliated organizations in the conduct of their affairs in accordance with traditional principles of ethical conduct and democratic procedures. Nevertheless, effective measures to stamp out crime and corruption and guarantee internal union democracy cannot be applied to all unions except through the powers of Government nor is the federation demonstrably effective in policing specific abuses within its affiliated organizations. Furthermore, a large segment of the American trade union movement is not affiliated with the American Federation of Labor-Congress of Industrial Organizations.

The hearings of the McClellan committee have also disclosed evidence that some sections of management have refused to recognize that employees have a right to form and join unions without interference and to enjoy freely the right to bargain collectively with their employer concerning their wages, hours, and other conditions of employment. The hearings of the McClellan committee have shown that some employers have cooperated with crooks and racketeers in the labor movement at the expense of their own employees and contrary to the public interest. Some employers have employed so-called middlemen to organize "no-union committees" and engage in other activities to prevent union organization among their employees. It is essential that any legislation which purports to drive corruption and improper activities out of labor-management relations contain provisions dealing effectively with these problems.

The internal problems currently facing the labor unions are bound up with a substantial public interest. Under the National Labor Relations Act and the Railway Labor Act a labor organization has vast responsibility for the economic welfare of the individual members and other employees whom it represents. Union members and employees who are represented by labor unions have a vital interest, therefore, in union affairs. Thus it is essential that union practices and procedures be democratic and that they recognize and protect the basic rights of the union members and the employees represented by unions. . . .

Report of the House Committee of Conference
September 3, 1959

GRAHAM BARDEN [DEM., N. C.] submitted the Report.

The committee of conference on the disagreeing votes of the two Houses on the amendment of the House to the bill (S. 1555) to provide for the reporting and disclosure of certain financial transactions and administrative practices of labor organizations and employers, to prevent abuses in the administration of trusteeships by labor organizations, to provide standards with respect to the election of officers of labor organizations, and for other purposes, having met, after full and free conference, having agreed to recommend and do recommend to their respective Houses as follows: . . .

STATEMENT OF THE MANAGERS ON THE PART OF THE HOUSE

The managers on the part of the House at the conference on the disagreeing votes of the two Houses on the amendment of the House to the bill (S. 1555) to provide for the reporting and disclosure of certain financial transactions and administrative practices of labor organizations and employers, to prevent abuses in the administration of trusteeships by labor organizations, to provide standards with respect to the election of officers of labor organizations, and for other purposes, submit the following statement in explanation of the effect of the action agreed upon by the conferees and recommended in the accompanying conference report:

The House amendment strikes out all of the Senate bill after the enacting clause and inserts a substitute. The Senate recedes from its disagreement to the amendment of the House, with an amendment which is a substitute for both the Senate bill and the House amendment. The differences between the House amendment and the substitute agreed to in conference are noted in the following outline, except for minor, technical, and conforming changes.

SECTION 3—DEFINITIONS

The House amendment makes many changes in the definitions the Senate bill contains. In all major respects the compromise the conference agreed on adopts the House versions. However, in the conference substitute, the definition of "labor organization" and the specification of which labor organizations that are engaged in an industry affecting commerce are changed to include "general committees." This refers to organizations of the type commonly found in the railway unions that designate general committees.

SECTION 101—BILL OF RIGHTS

This section of the Senate bill and the House amendment, for the most part, contain similar provisions. In all instances where there are differences between the Senate bill and the House amendment the conference substitute follows the House amendment.

In this section there is a matter that must be explained. In paragraph (5), relating to safeguards against improper disciplinary action, it should be noted that the prohibition on suspension without observing certain safeguards applies only to suspension of membership in the union; it does not refer to suspension of a member's status as an officer in the union.

SECTION 201—REPORT OF LABOR ORGANIZATIONS

The conference substitute is the same as the House amendment, except that it makes clear that the Secretary of Labor may prescribe the different categories of financial data that labor organizations must report.

SECTION 203—REPORTS OF EMPLOYERS

The conference substitute substantially rewrites section 203 of the House amendment.

Subsection (a) of both the House amendment and the conference substitute require employers to make detailed reports to the Secretary of Labor of payments, expenditures, or agreements described below.

First, both the House amendment and the conference substitute require employers to report payments and loans to unions and union officers and employees; and they both except payments that section 302(c) of the Labor Management Relations Act, 1947, permits. The substitute also contains an exception, taken from the Senate bill, for payments and loans made by credit institutions, such as banks.

Second, the substitute requires reports of all payments by an employer to his employees, or to a group or committee of his employees, for the purpose of causing them to persuade other employees to exercise or not to exercise, or as to the manner of exercising, the right to organize and bargain collectively through representatives of their own choosing. This requires reporting payments to "front organizations" that employers set up purportedly as spontaneous employee committees or groups. Payments of this type would not have to be reported if they were disclosed to such other employees when they were made or before they were made.

Third, the substitute requires reports of expenditures by an employer made to interfere with, coerce, or restrain employees in exercising their statutory rights to organize and bargain collectively, or to purchase information not otherwise available concerning activities of employees, or of a union, in connection with a labor dispute involving such employer, unless the information is for use solely in connection with an administrative or arbitral proceeding or a civil or criminal judicial proceeding. It should be noted that an employer is not required to report expenditures to obtain information in connection with labor dispute in which he is not involved.

Fourth, the substitute requires reports of all agreements with independent contractors, such as Nathan Shefferman, pursuant to which the independent contractor undertakes to persuade employees to exercise or not to exercise, or as to the manner of exercising, their statutory right to organize and to bargain collectively, or undertakes to supply the employer with information concerning activities of employees, or of a union, in connection with a labor dispute involving such employer, unless the information is for use solely in connection with an administrative or arbitral proceeding or a criminal or civil judicial proceeding.

Fifth, the substitute requires reports of payments under the agreements the preceding paragraph describes.

Subsection (b) of section 203 of the substitute agreed upon in conference deals with reports by labor relations consultants.

It requires reports from a consultant who enters into an agreement with an employer to engage in any of the activities that, under section 203(a)(4), must be reported by the employer.

Subsection (c) of section 203 of the conference substitute grants a broad exemption from the requirements of the section with respect to the giving of advice. This subsection is further discussed in connection with section 204.

Subsection (d) of section 203 makes it clear that reports are required only where an expenditure, payment, loan, or agreement of the kinds described has been made.

Subsection (e) of section 203 makes it clear that no regular officer, supervisor, or employee is required to file a report in connection with services rendered to his employer. Similarly, no employer is required to file a report of expenditures made to any of his regular officers, supervisors, or employees for their services as such.

Subsection (f) of section 203 makes it clear that this section does not impair the free speech that is described in section 8(c) of the National Labor Relations Act, as amended.

Subsection (g) of section 203 provides that the term "interfere with, restrain, or coerce" has the same meaning when used in this section as it has when used in the National Labor Relations Act. The House amendment contains a similar provision.

SECTION 204—ATTORNEY-CLIENT COMMUNICATIONS EXEMPTED

The Senate bill provides that an attorney need not include in any report required by the act any information which was lawfully communicated to such attorney by any of his clients in the course of a legitimate attorney-client relationship.

The conference substitute adopts the provisions of the Senate bill, but in connection therewith the conferees included, in section 203(c), a provision taken from the Senate bill that provides that an employer or other person is not required to file a report covering the services of such persons by reason of his giving or agreeing to give advice to such employer or representing or agreeing to represent such employer before any court, administrative agency, or tribunal of arbitration or engaging or agreeing to engage in collective bargaining on behalf of such employer or the negotiation of an agreement or any question arising thereunder.

SECTION 205—REPORTS MADE PUBLIC INFORMATION

The Senate bill, as a part of subsection (a) of this section, authorizes the Secretary of Labor to publish any information and data which he obtains under the title, and to use it for statistical and research purposes as he deems appropriate. It also allowed him to publish such studies, analyses, reports, and surveys based on information and data obtained under the title as he may deem appropriate. The House amendment contains no comparable provision. The conference substitute includes this provision.

SECTION 401—TERMS OF OFFICE; ELECTION PROCEDURES

Subsection (b) of section 401 of the Senate bill contains a provision making it the duty of each union and its officers to comply with reasonable requests of candidates to distribute, at the candidates' expense, campaign literature to all members of the union, and to refrain from discrimination in favor of or against any candidate with respect to the use of lists of members. The Senate bill also requires that when a union or its officers authorize the distribution to members of campaign literature on behalf of any candidate or of the union itself, similar distribution shall be made by the union and its officers at the request of any other bona fide candidate, with equal treatment as to the expenses of the distribution. The duty so imposed could be enforced by civil action in the Federal courts.

The House amendment omits these provisions, but includes a provision giving every bona fide candidate the right to inspect and copy a list of the names and addresses of all members of the union who are subject to a union shop collective bargaining agreement, which list is to be maintained at principal office of the union.

The substitute agreed upon in conference contains both the provisions of the Senate bill and of the House amendment, except that the provisions from the House amendment are modified to deny candidates the right to copy membership lists and to restrict the right of candidates to inspect such lists to one time within 30 days of the election.

Subsection (d) of section 401 of the Senate bill requires that notice of a union election be mailed to the last known address of each member not less than 15 days before it is held. The House amendment provides that notice of a union election must be given in a manner which is reasonably calculated to inform substantially all of the members eligible to vote of the time and manner of making nominations and of the place and date of the election. Such notice would be given between the 45th and 15th day before the final day on which nominations could be made. The conference substitute accepts the Senate bill on this point.

Subsection (g) of section 401 of the proposed substitute accepts the provision of the Senate bill which permits in union elections, union money to be used for factual statements of issues only if they do not involve candidates.

Subsection (b) of the conference substitute deals with removal of officers guilty of serious misconduct. The Senate bill provides that where the Secretary, upon application of a member of a local union, finds after a hearing that the constitution and bylaws of the local union do not provide an adequate procedure for the removal of an elected officer guilty of serious misconduct, such officer may be removed, for cause shown and after notice and opportunity for a hearing, by the members of the union voting in a secret ballot conducted by the officers in accordance with its constitution and bylaws insofar as they are not inconsistent with this title.

The House amendment provides a procedure which is similar, except that the Federal courts rather than the Secretary of Labor would determine whether the constitution and bylaws provide an adequate procedure for the removal of elected officers guilty of serious misconduct. The House amendment applies to all unions, not just to locals.

The conference substitute adopts the provisions of the Senate bill, and also the final subsection in the Senate bill which gives the Secretary the duty to make rules prescribing minimum standards and procedures for determining the adequacy of removal procedures.

SECTION 402—ENFORCEMENT

Subsections (a) and (b) of section 402 of the Senate bill provide that if a member of a union who has exhausted the remedies available under the constitution and bylaws of the union and its parent body (or has invoked such remedies without obtaining a final decision within 3 months) may file a complaint with the Secretary of Labor alleging a violation of section 401 (which includes a violation of the constitution and bylaws of the union pertaining to the election and removal of officers). The Secretary will investigate each such complaint, and if he finds probable cause to believe that a violation of the title has occurred and has not been remedied, he will bring a civil action against the union in a Federal district court to set aside the invalid election, if any, and to direct the conduct of an election (or hearing and vote upon the removal of officers) under the supervision of the Secretary of Labor. During the course of a proceeding under this section a challenged election will be presumed valid and the affairs of the union will be conducted during such period by the officers elected or in such other manner as its constitution and bylaws may provide. When a civil action is filed, the court will have power to take such action as it deems proper to preserve the union's assets.

The House amendment differs from the Senate bill in that the members of the union, instead of the Secretary, can bring the civil action, and, therefore, there would be no investigation by the Secretary.

The conference substitute is the same as the Senate bill on this point.

In subsection (c) of section 402, the conference substitute adopts the provision of the Senate bill that directs the court to set aside an election if the violation "may have" affected the outcome. Under the House amendment an election could be set aside only if the violation did affect the outcome.

Subsection (d) of section 402 of the Senate bill would not permit the staying of an election during an appeal. The House amendment made this discretionary with the court. The conference substitute adopts the language of the Senate bill.

SECTION 502—BONDING

The House amendment contains a provision which requires the bonding of certain labor union officials in an amount not less than 10 percent of the funds handled by them and their predecessors, if any, during the preceding fiscal year. The conference substitute adopts this provision of the House amendment, but, in addition, provides a maximum limitation so that no such official will be required to be bonded in an amount greater than $500,000.

SECTION 503—LOANS TO OFFICERS OF LABOR ORGANIZATIONS

The Senate bill sets $1,500 as the maximum amount by which an officer or employee could be indebted to his union. The House amendment raised this amount to $2,500. The conference substitute sets this maximum at $2,000.

The House amendment provides that the penalty for violating this section should be a fine of not more than $10,000, or imprisonment for not more than 1 year, or both. The conference substitute adopts the House amendment, except that the maximum fine is reduced to $5,000.

SECTION 504—PROHIBITION AGAINST CERTAIN PERSONS HOLDING OFFICE

The House amendment makes it a crime for a person to hold a union office for a prescribed period after he has been a Communist (or while he is a Communist) or after his conviction of certain offenses. The conference substitute is the same as the House amendment, except that it adds a provision taken from the Senate bill which also makes it a crime for a labor organization or officer thereof to knowingly permit any person to assume or hold any office in violation of the section. A provision has also been added to make it clear that the prohibitions apply regardless of whether the conviction which disqualifies occurred before or after the date of enactment of the act.

SECTION 601—INVESTIGATIONS

The Senate bill contains a provision which directs the Secretary to conduct an investigation when he believes it necessary in order to determine whether any person has, or is about to, violate the act, or any rule or regulation authorized by the act.

The House amendment directs the Secretary to make an investigation when he has probable cause to believe that any person has violated a provision of the act, other than title I.

The conference substitute is similar to the Senate bill, except that the investigation authority is permissive rather than mandatory, no investigation may be made with respect to violations of rules and regulations, and the investigation authority does not extend to title I.

The Senate bill also contains a provision authorizing the Secretary to report to interested persons concerning the facts required to be shown in reports and concerning the reasons for failure or refusal to file a report or any other matter he deems appropriate as a result of an investigation. The conference substitute adopts this provision.

SECTION 611—SEPARABILITY PROVISIONS

The Senate bill provides that if any provision of the act, or its application to any person or circumstances, is held invalid the remainder of the act or the application of such provision to other persons or circumstances, shall not be affected thereby. The House amendment merely provides that if any provision of the act is held invalid, the remainder thereof will not be affected. The conference substitute adopts the provisions of the Senate bill.

SECTION 701—FEDERAL-STATE JURISDICTION

The Senate bill provision relating to this subject amends the National Labor Relations Act, as amended, so as to provide that nothing in that act could be construed to prevent any State or territorial agency, other than a court, from exercising jurisdiction over all cases over which the Board has jurisdiction, but by rule or otherwise has declined to assert jurisdiction provided the State or territorial agency applies and is governed solely by Federal law as set forth in section 8(a) and 8(b) and section 9 of the National Labor Relations Act.

The House amendment contains a provision which authorizes the

Board, in its discretion, by rule of decision or by published rules adopted pursuant to the Administrative Procedure Act to decline to assert jurisdiction over any labor dispute involving any class or category of employers, where in the opinion of the Board, the effect of such labor dispute on commerce is not sufficiently substantial to warrant the exercise of its jurisdiction. The House amendment provides further that nothing in the National Labor Relations Act, as amended, shall be deemed to prevent or bar any agency or the courts of any State or territory (including the Commonwealth of Puerto Rico, Guam, and the Virgin Islands) from assuming and asserting jurisdiction over labor disputes over which the Board, in its discretion, by rule of decision or by published rules adopted pursuant to the Administrative Procedure Act declines to assert jurisdiction.

The substitute agreed upon in conference contains the House amendment with two modifications. The first modification provides that the Board shall not decline to assert jurisdiction over any labor dispute over which it would assert jurisdiction under the standards prevailing upon August 1, 1959. The second modification would amend section 3 (b) of the National Labor Relations Act, as amended, to authorize the Board to delegate to its regional directors its powers under section 9 to determine the unit appropriate for the purpose of collective bargaining, to investigate and provide for hearings, and determine whether a question concerning representation exists, and to direct an election or take a secret ballot under subsection (c) or (e) of section 9 and certify the results of such election, except that upon the filing of a request therefor with the Board by any interested person, the Board may review any action of a regional director delegated to him under section 9, but such a review by the Board would not, unless specifically ordered by the Board, operate as a stay of any action taken by the regional director.

SECTION 702—ECONOMIC STRIKERS

The Senate bill amends the second sentence of section 9(c)(3) of the National Labor Relations Act, as amended, to provide that employees on strike shall vote under such regulations as the National Labor Relations Board shall find to be consistent with the purposes and provisions of the act.

The House amendment amends that sentence by adding a proviso that in any lawful strike in which recognition was not an issue when the strike began, no direction of election pursuant to a petition filed after the commencement of the strike by any person other than the bargaining representative shall issue prior to the termination of such strike as determined by the Board or the expiration of a 6-month period from the commencement of the strike (or for a 12-month period if the petition is filed by an employer), whichever occurs sooner. Under this provision the Board of course, could limit this right to vote even during this 12-month period.

The substitute agreed upon in conference amends the second sentence in section 9(c)(3) to provide that—

Employees engaged in an economic strike who are not entitled to reinstatement shall be eligible to vote under such regulations as the Board shall find are consistent with the purposes and provisions of the National Labor Relations Act, as amended, in any election conducted within twelve months after the commencement of the strike.

SECTION 704(a)—BOYCOTTS

The House amendment contains provisions amending the secondary boycott provisions of section 8(b)(4) of the National Labor Relations Act, as amended. The Senate bill does not contain comparable provisions. The conference committee adopted the provisions of the House amendment with the following changes: (1) the phrase "or agree to cease" was deleted from section 8(b)(4)(B) because the committee of conference concluded that the restrictions imposed by such language were included in the other provisions dealing with prohibitions against entering into "hot cargo" agreements, and therefore their retention in section 8(b)(4)(B) would constitute a duplication of language; (2) a proviso was added which specified that for the purposes of this paragraph (4) only, nothing contained in such paragraph shall be construed to prohibit publicity, other than picketing, for the purpose of truthfully advising the public, including consumers and members of a labor organization, that a product or products are produced by an employer with whom the labor organization has a primary labor dispute and are distributed by another employer as long as such publicity does not have an effect of inducing any individual employed by any person other than the primary employer in the course of his employment to refuse to pick up, deliver, or transport any goods, or not to perform any services at the establishment of the employer engaged in such distribution; (3) no language has been included with reference to struck work because the committee of conference did not wish to change the existing law as illustrated by such decisions as *Douds* v. *Metropolitan Federation of Architects* (75 Fed. Supp. 672 (S.D.N.Y. 1948)) and *NLRB* v. *Business Machine and Office Appliance Mechanics Board* (228 Fed. 2d 553); (4) the amendment adopted by the committee of conference contains a provision "that nothing contained in clause (B) of this paragraph (4) shall be construed to make unlawful, where not otherwise unlawful, any primary strike or primary picketing." The purpose of this provision is to make it clear that the changes in section 8(b)(4) do not overrule or qualify the present rules of law permitting picketing at the site of a primary labor dispute. This provision does not eliminate, restrict, or modify the limitations on picketing at the site of a primary labor dispute that are in existing law. See, for example, *NLRB* v. *Denver Building and Construction Trades Council, et al.* (341 U.S. 675 (1951)); *Brotherhood of Painters,*

Decorators, and Paper Hangers, etc., and *Pittsburgh Plate Glass Co.* (110 NLRB 455 (1954)); *Moore Drydock Co.* (81 NLRB 1108); *Washington Coca Cola Bottling Works, Inc.* (107 NLRB 233 (1953)).

SECTION 704(b)—HOT-CARGO AGREEMENTS

The Senate bill amends section 8 of the National Labor Relations Act, as amended, by adding at the end thereof a new subsection (e) which makes it an unfair labor practice for any labor organization and any employer who is a common carrier subject to part II of the Interstate Commerce Act to enter into any contract or agreement, express or implied, whereby such employer ceases or refrains or agrees to cease or refrain from handling, using, or transporting any of the products of any other employer, or to cease doing business with the same.

The House amendment amends section 8 of the National Labor Relations Act, as amended, by adding at the end thereof a new subsection (e) to make it an unfair labor practice for any labor organization and any employer to enter into any contract or agreement, express or implied, whereby such employer ceases or refrains or agrees to cease or refrain from handling, using, selling, transporting or otherwise dealing in any of the products of any other employer, or to cease doing business with any other person. The House amendment also makes any such agreement heretofore or hereafter executed unenforcible and void.

The committee of conference adopted the House amendment but added three provisos. The first proviso specifies—

that nothing in this subsection (e) shall apply to an agreement between a labor organization and an employer in the construction industry relating to the contracting or subcontracting of work to be done at the site of the construction, alteration, painting, or repair of a building, structure, or other work.

It should be particularly noted that the proviso relates only and exclusively to the contracting or subcontracting of work to be done at the site of the construction. The proviso does not exempt from section 8 (e) agreements relating to supplies or other products or materials shipped or otherwise transported to and delivered on the site of the construction. The committee of conference does not intend that this proviso should be construed so as to change the present state of the law with respect to the validity of this specific type of agreement relating to work to be done at the site of the construction project or to remove the limitations which the present law imposes with respect to such agreements. Picketing to enforce such contracts would be illegal under the *Sand Door* case (*Local 1796, United Brotherhood of Carpenters* v. *NLRB,* 357 U.S. 93 (1958)). To the extent that such agreements are legal today under section 8(b)(4) of the National Labor Relations Act, as amended, the proviso would prevent such legality from being affected by section 8(e). The proviso applies only to section 8(e) and therefore leaves unaffected the law developed under section 8(b)(4). The *Denver Building Trades* case and the *Moore Drydock* cases would remain in full force and effect. The proviso is not intended to limit, change, or modify the present state of the law with respect to picketing at the site of a construction project. Restrictions and limitations imposed upon such picketing under present law as interpreted, for example, in the U.S. Supreme Court decision in the *Denver Building Trades* case would remain in full force and effect. It is not intended that the proviso change the existing law with respect to judicial enforcement of these contracts or with respect to the legality of a strike to obtain such a contract.

The second proviso specifies that for the purposes of this subsection (e) and section 8(b)(4) the terms "any employer," "any person engaged in commerce or an industry affecting commerce," and "any person" when used in relation to the terms "any other producer, processor, or manufacturer," "any other employer," or "any other person" shall not include persons in the relation of a jobber, manufacturer, contractor, or subcontractor working on the goods or premises of a jobber or manufacturer or performing parts of an integrated process of production in the apparel and clothing industry. This proviso grants a limited exemption in three specific situations in the apparel and clothing industry, but in no other industry regardless of whether similar integrated processes of production may exist between jobbers, manufacturers, contractors, and subcontractors.

The third proviso applies solely to the apparel and clothing industry.

SECTION 704(c)—ORGANIZATIONAL AND RECOGNITION PICKETING

Both the Senate bill and the House amendment contain provisions which place certain restrictions on organizational and recognition picketing. The committee of conference adopted a substitute provision, section 704(c), which amends the National Labor Relations Act, as amended, to add a new section 8(b)(7), making it an unfair labor practice to picket or cause to be picketed, or threaten to picket or cause to be picketed, any employer where an object thereof is forcing or requiring an employer to recognize or bargain with a labor organization as the representative of his employees, or forcing or requiring the employees of an employer to accept or select such labor organization as their collective bargaining representative, unless such labor organization is currently certified as the representative of such employees:

(A) Where the employer has lawfully recognized in accordance with this Act any other labor organization and a question concerning representation may not appropriately be raised under section 9(c) of this Act.

(B) Where within the preceding twelve months a valid election under section 9(c) of this Act has been conducted, or

(C) Where such picketing has been conducted without a petition under section 9(c) being filed within a reasonable period of time not to exceed thirty days from the commencement of such picketing: *Provided,* That when such a petition has been filed the Board shall forthwith, without regard to the provisions of section 9(c)(1) or the absence of a showing of a substantial interest on the part of the labor organization, direct an election in such unit as the Board finds to be appropriate and shall certify the results thereof: Provided further, That nothing in this subparagraph (C) shall be construed to prohibit any picketing or other publicity for the purpose of truthfully advising the public (including consumers) that an employer does not employ members of or have a contract with, a labor organization, unless an effect of such picketing is to induce any individual employed by any other person in the course of his employment, not to pick up, deliver or transport any goods or not to perform any services.

The final sentence to the proposed new section 8(b)(7) of the act provides that—

Nothing in this paragraph (7) shall be construed to permit any act which would otherwise be an unfair labor practice under section 8(b) of the Act.

Section 8(b)(7) overrules the *Curtis* and *Alloy* cases to the extent that those decisions are inconsistent with section 8(b)(7).

SECTION 705—BUILDING AND CONSTRUCTION INDUSTRY

The Senate bill amends section 8 of the National Labor Relations Act, as amended, to add a new subsection (e) which provides that it shall not be an unfair labor practice under subsections (a) and (b) of section 8 of that act, for an employer engaged primarily in the building and construction industry to make an agreement covering employees engaged (or who upon their employment would be engaged) in the building and construction industry with a labor organization (not established, maintained, or assisted by any action defined in sec. 8(a) of the National Labor Relations Act, as amended, as an unfair labor practice) of which building and construction employees are members (1) where the majority status of such labor organization has not been established under the provisions of section 9 of the National Labor Relations Act, as amended, prior to the making of such agreement, (2) because such agreement requires as a condition of employment, membership in such labor organization after the seventh day following the beginning of such employment, or the effective date of the agreement, whichever was later, or (3) because such agreement requires the employer to notify such labor organization of opportunities for employment with such employer, or gives such labor organization an opportunity to refer qualified applicants for such employment, or (4) because such agreement specifies minimum training or experience qualifications for employment or provides for priority in opportunities for employment based upon length of service with such employer, in the industry or in the particular geographical area. The Senate provision specifies, however, (1) that nothing in such provision shall set aside the final proviso to section 8(a)(3) of the National Labor Relations Act, as amended, and (2) that any agreement which would not be valid except for this amendment which permits an agreement to be entered into where the majority status of such labor organization has not been established under the provisions of section 9 of that act prior to the making of such agreement, shall not be a bar to a petition filed pursuant to section 9(c) or 9(e) of that act. The Senate provision also specifies that nothing therein shall be construed as authorizing the execution of or application of agreements requiring membership in a labor organization as a condition of employment in any State or territory in which such execution or application is prohibited by State or territorial law.

The conference adopted the provision of the Senate bill permitting prehire agreements in the building and construction industry. Nothing in such provision is intended to restrict the applicability of the hiring hall provisions enunciated in the *Mountain Pacific* case (119 N.L.R.B. 883, 893) or to authorize the use of force, coercion, strikes, or picketing to compel any person to enter into such prehire agreements.

THE DEBATE

Senate—86th Congress, 1st Session
January 20, 1959

JOHN KENNEDY [DEM., MASS.]. Mr. President, I introduce, for appropriate reference, the labor-management reform bill for 1959.

It is my intention to hold prompt hearings on this and related bills, and seek early passage by the Senate and the Congress of an effective measure that will protect workers, employers, honest unions, and the general public from the unscrupulous or dictatorial tactics of the few racketeers. As this bill is considered, I hope several facts will be kept in perspective:

First. This is a bipartisan measure on a nonpartisan subject. Today's bill is a revised version of the measure which passed the Senate last year by a vote of 88 to 1—a bill which was supported by every Member of this body today who was here a year ago, regardless of party.

I also wish to pay tribute to the outstanding work of former Senator Ives, of New York, in connection with this measure. His contribution to labor-management reform legislation will be long and favorably remembered. His conviction as to the necessity for bipartisanship in labor legislation is a principle which should guide us all.

I am taking the liberty of quoting from a letter received by me this week from former Senator Ives:

> I wish you every success in your effort to get this vital legislation on our statute books. This bill represents many months of careful study in committee, the collective judgment of the U.S. Senate as expressed in 5 days and nights of debating and voting, and many, many years of collective experience in the field of labor-management legislation.
>
> Furthermore, it is designed to meet the objectives set forth in the report of the Senate Select Committee on Improper Activities in the Labor or Management Field. It is my firm conviction that this bill not only meets those objectives but does so in a fashion that make it corrective rather than punitive legislation, a measure which will correct abuses without undermining the rights of working men and women.
>
> It is my earnest prayer that, this time, the bill will go through both Houses of Congress without becoming a political football. Throughout my legislative career, I dealt with labor-management matters on a nonpartisan basis because I early learned that it was the only way with which to deal with such matters on a realistic, constructive and equitable basis. The Kennedy-Ives bill is such a nonpartisan measure and deserves nonpartisan consideration and nonpartisan action.

Second. This bill is stronger and clearer than the 1958 version. The Kennedy-Ives bill of 1958, even after it passed the Senate by a vote of 88 to 1, was subject to fantastic distortion by extremists on both sides. Fears of its effects, particularly among businessmen, were unnecessarily aroused by the misinterpretation of isolated sections. To allay such fears and prevent further distortion, the bill has been revised to make it clear that the employer reporting section cannot possibly interfere with normal personnel relations or communications, and that the section on bribes by employers cannot possibly include wage or other normal payments. At the same time, the bill has been strengthened and tightened in other respects— including, for example, the judicial remedies here made available to a rank-and-file member to recover misappropriated dues when his union will not sue; the wider applicability of the provision for union democracy and secret election of officers; and the increased reporting of improper payments to a union or its officers by an employer.

Third. This is primarily a labor-management reform bill, dealing with the problems of dishonest racketeering—it is not a bill on industrial relations, dealing with the problems of collective bargaining and economic power. The two areas of legislation should not be confused or combined. The McClellan committee has been concerned chiefly, as its title states, with "improper activities"—with corruption, conflicts of interest, unethical and undemocratic practices. We have not been concerned primarily with unfair labor practices, union security arrangements and collective bargaining rights, as long as the improprieties I have mentioned were not involved. There are, to be sure, amendments to the Taft-Hartley Act which are necessary to curb racketeering or to facilitate the NLRB's action in this area, and which were approved by the Senate as a part of this bill last year. There are other amendments—such as those dealing with economic strikers and the building trades—which were included as part of last year's package at the insistence of Secretary Mitchell and the Labor and Public Welfare Committee's ranking Republican, former Senator Smith of New Jersey, and which, having wide acceptance as a part of that same package, are included in the bill again this year. But the broad, controversial issues of labor-management relations which that act poses are improperly the subject of an anti-racketeering bill, and can only impede its consideration and passage on its own merits.

I hope, therefore, that this bill will not again be criticized by either labor or management for what it fails to do by way of Taft-Hartley amendments and new collective-bargaining rules. Let us first consider labor-management reform. Let us first stop racketeering without becoming bogged down in the heated and complex issues raised by the entire Taft-Hartley Act. Then let us consider revising that law, proceeding in the manner I outlined in a statement issued last Tuesday—by convening a panel of labor-law experts who can give our committee a fresh but experienced and well-balanced examination of these issues, outline the alternatives and isolate the areas of agreement and disagreement. I shall have more to say on this procedure at a later date.

If this Congress, in its consideration of anticorruption legislation, becomes bogged down in acrimonious controversies over broad and controversial Taft-Hartley revisions, in technical and emotional issues such as boycotts, picketing, and the section 14(b) provisions enabling State right-to-work laws, all of which must be considered this year—if our immediate problem of antiracketeering, on which there is already wide agreement, becomes tied to these other issues before the McClellan committee has made its second report and before our panel of experts has reported—then we can only delay and defeat a vital measure already thoroughly considered and debated. Broad Taft-Hartley revisions, which have been neglected too long, and including such items as boycotts, picketing, and State right to work, should definitely be considered by the Congress this year—and I can assure the Senate that a second labor bill will be reported to the floor this year, with the recommendations of the McClellan committee, the Labor Committee, and our panel of experts. Then all issues can be debated and all amendments considered, with the best information available, and without endangering the passage of a strong antirackets measure.

So let us avoid these unnecessary controversies now—and let us also avoid, in considering this measure, unnecessary partisan politics or uninformed or deliberate distortions, or otherwise it should be clear from last year's record, no antiracket bill at all will pass. The gangsters and hoodlums will continue to prey upon union members and the public. And this Congress will be responsible.

Failure to pass effective reform legislation at this session may please the Hoffas, the Dios, and their ilk. It may please those on the other side who are chiefly interested in keeping a whipping boy alive. But it can only harm our Nation.

Fourth. This is a strong, effective reform bill. It carries out all of the previously unfulfilled recommendations of the McClellan committee. It is aimed at ending the abuses revealed before that committee; and adds other legislative curbs on racketeering as well. It is based upon the bill drafted last year by two members of the McClellan committee, with the strong support of the distinguished chairman of that committee himself. It is broader and stronger than any alternative proposal in this area. It is a bill designed to permit responsible unionism to operate without being undermined by either racketeering tactics or bureaucratic controls. It is designed to strike a balance between the dangers of too much and too little legislation in this field.

I realize that it is always possible to find fault in any bill—to point out omissions—to read in other meanings—or to call indefinitely for further amendments. This is particularly true in the controversial field of labor—which is precisely why no major labor legislation has been passed in the last decade. The extremists on both sides are always displeased—the technical experts will always disagree. No doubt, each Senator, as the Senator from Arkansas [Mr. McClellan] pointed out last year, would draft his own bill differently.

But, as the Senator from Arkansas also emphasized last year, our most important responsibility is "to take what we know all of us want, and pass the bill, and then move on." The Senate did that last year by a vote of 88 to 1—demonstrating, in the words of Business Week magazine, how "wise guidance in the public interest can be substituted for concern over wide apart partisan positions."

I wish to mention the key provisions of the bill introduced today—the basic weapons against racketeering which will be unavailable in the battle against corruption if such a measure is not enacted by the Congress this year:

First. Comprehensive detailed disclosure to members, press, and public and law enforcement agencies of union financial data.

Second. Full reports by union officers on any personal conflict-of-interest transactions.

Third. Criminal sanctions for embezzlement of union funds, false reporting, false entries on books, failure to report, or destruction of union books.

Fourth. Suits by union members for recovery of funds embezzled or misappropriated by union officers.

Fifth. Prohibition of loans by employers or unions to union officers.

Sixth. Secret ballot for the election of all union officers or of the convention delegates who select them.

Seventh. Due notice of all union elections, and real opportunity to nominate opposing candidates.

Eighth. Requirement that union officers be elected by secret ballot every 4 years, by international unions; and every 3 years, by local unions.

Ninth. Prohibition on the use of union funds to support candidacy of any union officer.

Tenth. Prohibition of service as union officers of persons convicted of serious crimes.

Eleventh. Power to Secretary of Labor to institute court action to set aside improper elections, and conduct new elections.

Twelfth. Strict standards for the imposition of trusteeships and a limit of 18 months on their duration.

Thirteenth. Mandatory annual report to Secretary and union members on every trusteeship, the reasons for its establishment, continuance, and operation.

Fourteenth. Prohibition on counting votes of delegates of trustee bodies unless delegates elected by secret ballot, and on transfer of funds from trusteed local union to international except normal dues and assessments.

Fifteenth. Power to Secretary of Labor to begin a court proceeding to break improper trusteeships.

Sixteenth. Prohibition of picketing for extortion or to secure payoff from employer.

Seventeenth. Prohibition of solicitation or payment of fictitious fees for unloading cargo from interstate carriers.

Eighteenth. Public financial reports of the operations of Shefferman-type middlemen; and a prohibition of channeling bribes and improper influence through such middlemen.

Nineteenth. Elimination of the "no-man's land" problem which prevented NLRB action on local labor racketeering by directing the NLRB to exercise its full jurisdiction under the Taft-Hartley Act.

Consider, for example, some of the effects of this bill on Mr. James Hoffa and his hoodlum associates now dominating the vital Teamsters Union. Under our form of government, no act of Congress can specify the elimination of Mr. Hoffa. Like every other citizen, he is entitled to the protection of the fifth amendment, trial by jury, and other constitutional guarantees which he may find it possible to abuse. But passage of this bill will close to Mr. Hoffa and his ilk most of the racketeering opportunities they have exploited—it will stop those practices which, based upon the testimony before our committee, it would appear Mr. Hoffa's career and power are based—and it will, in short, virtually put Mr. Hoffa and his associates out of business:

First. It will no longer be possible for the dues of Teamster members to be paid out to hoodlums posing as business agents, to be invested in improper or risky racetrack or real estate deals, or to be used by Mr. Hoffa and other officers to build their own personal financial empires without the knowledge of the members themselves—or without investigation by the press and public authorities.

Second. Mr. Hoffa would be required to disclose all of his business dealings with insurance agents handling the union's welfare funds, his private arrangements with employers, his hidden partnerships in business ventures foisted upon his members, and all other possible conflicts of interest.

Third. This bill would summarily force from office the extortionists, embezzlers, bribe-takers, and other criminals who have left the penitentiary to find refuge in high positions of trust in the Teamsters Union.

Fourth. Placing a Teamster local in trusteeship would no longer be available as a means of exploiting the dues and privileges of the local members; and Mr. Hoffa would have difficulty repeating power plays such as that at Pontiac, Mich., where as a trustee, he appointed as business agents the very same officials who had been ousted by the local membership on grounds of corruption.

Fifth. Provisions in the Teamster constitution to safeguard free elections and democratic conventions will no longer be a farce, to be waived or ignored at will. Paper locals under Johnny Dio will no longer be able to cast votes in the names of nonexistent or unaware members.

Sixth. The Becks and Hoffas will find future collusion with employers vastly restricted—with no more loans from employer groups, no more attacks on rival unions through middlemen like Nathan Shefferman, and no more secrecy shrouding the use of union funds to bail out a collaborating employer.

Seventh. There will be no more shakedowns and tribute for unloading interstate trucks, no more destruction of union books, and no more falsification of union reports anywhere in the Teamster empire; and honest rank-and-file members will be able to recover funds embezzled or otherwise misappropriated.

This is, in short, a strong bill—a bipartisan measure—a bill that does the job which needs to be done without bogging down the Congress with unrelated controversies. Without doubt, the future course of our action in this area will be plagued with the usual emotional arguments, political perils, and powerful pressures which always surround this subject. But I am confident that our committee will have an effective bill before the Senate early this year; I am confident that the Senate will consider and pass such a measure in the same constructive spirit with which it passed the Kennedy-Ives bill by a vote of 88 to 1 last year; and I am equally confident that such a measure will pass the Congress and become law in 1959. . . .

BARRY GOLDWATER [R., ARIZ.]. Mr. President, I have read with great interest the remarks of the junior Senator from Massachusetts [Mr. Kennedy] which accompanied the introduction of his revised version of the Kennedy-Ives labor reform bill. These remarks contain certain assertions and implications upon which I would like to comment.

Before doing so, however, I wish to advise my colleagues that within the next few days the President will send to Congress his proposals in this field of legislation and that I, as the ranking Republican on the Labor Committee, shall be happy to introduce the bill embodying these proposals.

The statement of the Senator from Massachusetts, referring to his bill, asserts:

This is a bipartisan measure on a nonpartisan subject.

I should like to ask the Senator if his bill is being cosponsored by any of the members of my party. I note that he refers to an approving letter he received from ex-Senator Ives of New York. In my opinion, the support of the ex-Senator does not any more transform this measure from a partisan into a bipartisan one than it did last year, when its sole Republican sponsorship came from the same ex-Senator from New York. I am confident that when I introduce the administration bill, it will be found that the Senators on this side of the aisle will give it their wholehearted support.

It is a nonpartisan subject. We want to treat it that way. But I suggest to the Senator from Massachusetts that honest difference of opinion does not create partisanship. I have sat with him on the McClellan committee and watched and listened to the unfolding of this sordid drama. That our approach to the solutions differs from his does not mean partisanship. It means sincerity in our efforts to give to union members and to the public and to management real relief from the abuses now practiced on them.

Mr. President, the junior Senator from Massachusetts states:

It carries out all of the previously unfulfilled recommendations of the McClellan committee.

I wish to point out most emphatically that the new bill, like its forerunner, the Kennedy-Ives bill of last year, again fails to carry out several of the most important recommendations of the McClellan committee:

First. The new bill does not permit the States to exercise jurisdiction over labor cases which the Labor Board itself has refused to entertain.

Second. It does not impose fiduciary status and character on union funds and union officials handling those funds.

Third. It does not provide democratic voting processes for unions or important matters other than the election of officers.

All three of these were included as recommendations by the McClellan committee, in its interim report, which both the junior Senator from Massachusetts himself and the senior Senator from North Carolina [Mr. Ervin] signed, and thereby endorsed. All three of those recommendations were omitted by the junior Senator from Massachusetts from his bill.

The junior Senator from Massachusetts is emphatic in his insistence that his bill deals "primarily with the problems of dishonest racketeering." At this point let me ask the Senator from Massachusetts whether there is any such thing as honest racketeering—and that it is not a bill on industrial relations, dealing with the problems of collective bargaining and economic power. Those words would seem to indicate that no revision of the Taft-Hartley Act is contemplated in his bill. However, the Senator admits that he has included Taft-Hartley Act amendments "which are necessary to curb racketeering or to facilitate the NLRB's action in this area." He then goes on to concede that he has included other Taft-Hartley Act amendments "such as those dealing with economic strikers and the building trades, which are included as part of last year's package at the insistence of Secretary Mitchell and the Labor Committee's ranking Republican, Senator Smith of New Jersey."

I am delighted at the Senator's willingness to accept Taft-Hartley Act amendments because they have been recommended by the administration and members of the Republican Party, even though they have no bearing upon the problem of racketeering.

But if the junior Senator from Massachusetts is genuinely desirous of cooperating with the administration in his expressed objective of having the Congress enact a bipartisan labor reform bill, why does he fail to include in his bill any provisions imposing necessary limitations on secondary boycotts and certain completely unjustified types of minority picketing? Proposals to correct these two evils were contained in the administration bill last year. They will be in the administration bill this year; and I am confident that the McClellan committee, on the basis of its recent hearings, will recommend remedial legislation dealing with secondary boycotts.

These proposals, unlike those on voting by economic strikers and the building trades, are absolutely essential to any effective curb on racketeerings and racketeers in the labor movement. Anyone with even the slightest familiarity with the racketeering activities of some of the unions investigated by the McClellan committee is aware that the secondary boycott and the minority union picket line are two of the most effective devices used by corrupt union bosses to further their nefarious objectives.

In his statement, the Senator from Massachusetts declares:

Failure to pass effective reform legislation at this session may please the Hoffas, the Dios, and their ilk. It may please those on the other side who are chiefly interested in keeping a whipping boy alive.

Mr. President, I wholeheartedly agree with the junior Senator from Massachusetts that effective reform legislation must be enacted at this session. But I simply fail to understand how anyone who professes to be deeply concerned with eliminating corruption and racketeering from the labor movement can overlook those proposals of the administration which effectively deal with racketeering and yet accept other administration proposals which are totally unrelated to this problem.

Mr. President, in closing I wish to advert to one other matter in connection with the remarks of the junior Senator from Massachusetts [Mr. Kennedy]. In reading his statement it seemed clear to me that it implied that this bill has the approval of the distinguished chairman of the rackets committee, the senior Senator from Arkansas [Mr. McClellan], with whom both of us have the honor of serving in our attempts to root out corruption and racketeering in the labor and management field. This perplexes me. Senator McClellan has declared that he will shortly introduce proposed legislation in this area. I understand that it will include provisions dealing with the secondary boycott and minority picketing, as will the administration's bill, but will go far beyond the latter in imposing on unions additional limitations, prohibitions, and sanctions which the Senator from Arkansas feels are necessary to solve the problems of corruption and racketeering. It is hard for me to understand how the junior Senator from Massachusetts can say that his bill "is broader and stronger than any alternative proposal in this area." Does he mean that it is broader and stronger than the forthcoming bills of the administration and Senator McClellan? I know that this cannot be so with respect to the administration bill, and I have every confidence that it is equally inaccurate with respect to the McClellan bill. . . .

MR. KENNEDY. Mr. President, I wish to make a brief informal report as to the results of our conference, with the understanding that tomorrow, after the language is put together and the staff work is concluded, we will be able to make a formal report to the Senate on the various differences between the House bill and the Senate bill.

I wish particularly to express my appreciation to the minority leader of the Senate [Mr. Dirksen], who, I believe, together with his colleagues the Senator from Arizona [Mr. Goldwater] and the Senator from Vermont [Mr. Prouty], made it possible for us to reach an agreement, an agreement which I find satisfactory and which I wholeheartedly support.

To reach such a result on bills as difficult, on a subject as explosive, on a subject on which emotion runs so high as labor-management relations, and try to bring together bills as different as the bill which passed the Senate and that which passed the House was an extremely difficult task. As Senators know, it occupied the attention of the conferees for 2 weeks.

I speak respectfully of the bill which was passed in the other body, but it seems to me that there were serious shortcomings in the reform bill which passed the House, and the conferees on the Democratic side, the Senator from Michigan [Mr. McNamara], the Senator from West Virginia [Mr. Randolph], and the Senator from Oregon [Mr. Morse], shared my view that we could not under any circumstances have voted for the Landrum-Griffin bill. While many Members of the Senate hold an opposite view, if the Landrum-Griffin bill had come to the floor of the Senate in the form in which it passed the House, in my opinion all the Senators would have regretted it finally. Also, it would have been an extremely close vote, and the bill might not have passed if we had had a chance to debate it.

I say that because I believe that the House of Representatives was not wholly aware of the provisions in the Landrum-Griffin bill. It was not the bill reported by the House committee. It was offered as a substitute on the floor, and after days of debate was passed.

When we view the significant provisions of the Landrum-Griffin bill, one after another, in my opinion we must admit they go far beyond reform, and I will document that tomorrow. They go into an area which I think would limit what we all would consider legitimate activities of men and women who bargain collectively.

Changes which were made, and, speaking from the point of view of Senator McNamara and Senator Randolph, our views have been uniform in this matter. The changes which we believe to be particularly desirable are first, that we protected the working standards, and this was also supported by the Senator from Arizona [Mr. Goldwater], and others, in the garment and apparel industries, do make sure that the hard-won standards in those industries would be protected.

Secondly, the House bill prohibited the union from carrying on any kind of activity to disseminate informational material to secondary sites. They could not say that there was a strike in a primary plant.

We quite obviously are opposed to their affecting liberties in a secondary strike or affecting employees joining, but the House language prohibited not only secondary picketing, but even the handing out of handbills or even taking out an advertisement in a newspaper.

Under the language of the conference, we agreed there would not be picketing at a secondary site. What was permitted was the giving out of handbills or information through the radio, and so forth.

Thirdly, we provide protection for picketing which I believe to be essential, and which can be discussed tomorrow. I believe that under the language on picketing in the House bill, it would be very difficult to organize workers who are unorganized.

We put a limit on no-man's land.

It was the opinion of the Senate that the Federal law should prevail with respect to interstate commerce, and, in order to compromise that feature, it was agreed that the State law could prevail, but only in those areas in which the National Labor Relations Board does not now assume jurisdiction. I understand the Board assumes a good deal of jurisdiction today. I think the House language might have permitted the Board to yield and have permitted State laws to prevail over vast areas of interstate commerce. That cannot be done. We have closed no-man's land.

We have protected the right of employees of a secondary employer, in the case of a primary strike, to refuse to cross a primary strike picket line. The House language was vague.

We have protected the right of the union to follow struck work, in the traditional way provided under the Taft-Hartley Act. That was in doubt under the language of the Landrum-Griffin bill.

We eliminated a section of the Landrum-Griffin bill which would have permitted damage suits against unions which might have picketed for organizational purposes. We have provided regular remedies. Damage suits were the most serious shortcomings of the Landrum-Griffin bill; and yet, as it referred to another section, I doubt if any Member of the House knew that such a provision was in the bill. The Senate conferees did not know it until yesterday afternoon at 2 o'clock.

We have provided protection in respect to membership lists. For example, under the provisions of the Landrum-Griffin bill with respect to membership lists, anyone could have copied down membership lists.

Union membership lists have historically been considered a relatively private affair.

We provided that mailings must be made by the union, and that any member who is a bona fide candidate may inspect the lists, but he may not copy them.

The Landrum-Griffin provision on employer reporting was hopelessly inadequate.

I do not say that everyone will like what we now have, but I will say, having been a member of the Labor Committee of the House or Senate for 13 years, that the bill in its present form is a vast improvement over the Landrum-Griffin bill, from the point of view of reform, and also from the point of view of protecting legitimate employer-union activities.

To accomplish that result required concessions on the part of all of us. The bill as it comes from conference is not a bill which I would have supported originally, but, being faced with the task of reconciling the House and Senate versions, and feeling that any bill brought to the floor of the Senate would have produced a chaotic result, I think we have arrived at a bill which, overall, I can wholeheartedly support.

We have achieved this result because of the work of the Senator from West Virginia [Mr. Randolph], the Senator from Michigan [Mr. McNamara], and the Senator from Oregon [Mr. Morse], who does not agree with us. I understand why he is as disappointed as I am over some sections.

We are also greatly indebted to Members on the minority side. . . .

WAYNE MORSE [DEM., ORE.]. Mr. President, I propose at this time to make my speech setting forth my reasons for not signing the conference report on the labor bill. I prefer to make this speech in advance of the speech of the Senator from Massachusetts [Mr. Kennedy] for two reasons.

First, representatives of the majority have already made public comment in regard to their position on the bill, and I think it is only fair and proper that my reply to them be made at this time.

Second, I think it is appropriate to set forth my detailed objections to the conference report, so that the Senator from Massachusetts, when he presents his discussion on the conference report, will have full knowledge as to the position I have taken in opposition to certain sections of the conference report which he submitted on behalf of the conference over which he so ably presided.

Furthermore, I believe that this course of action will probably prove to be a great time saver in the Senate, because it will spare us from covering again much of the same ground that I would still have to cover in detail if the Senator from Massachusetts were to present his report in the first instance.

At the outset, I am perfectly willing to let the record speak for itself, and let my fellow conferees be my witnesses, as to whether or not, in the long, arduous conference sessions, the senior Senator from Oregon sought to cooperate with the chairman of the conference and his colleagues on the conference; and even though, when we reached certain votes which made it clear that the senior Senator from Oregon could not possibly sign the conference report because of the results of such votes—and so notified the conference—he, however, at the same time made it clear that he would continue to do the best he could to assist the conferees in bringing forth the most acceptable bill, so far as concerned the remaining sections still under discussion.

I hold to the same position today, following my dissent yesterday in conference, which I expressed on television last Sunday to the people of the Nation. At that time I said, in effect, that in my 15 years in the Senate I have never served under a more able chairman of a conference than the Senator from Massachusetts.

We have some very fundamental differences in regard to certain parts of the bill. The Senator from Massachusetts agreed to certain compromises that I could not possibly agree to in order to produce a conference report. I think we have mutual respect, and I think we recognize that each is sincere and intellectually honest in the position he has taken. I believe my chief difference procedurally with the Senator from Massachusetts occurred during the last 2 or 3 days of the conference—in fact, since last Friday, when the Dirksen resolution to ask the Senate for instructions was filed with the Senate. That would have brought the disputed points to the floor of the Senate for instruction.

I have arbitrated a great many labor cases in my professional career, but I have never arbitrated with a strike gun at my head. I have always taken the position that before arbitration on the merits of the issues involved in the case could be conducted impartially, it was necessary for the union to go back to work under a temporary order from the arbitrator; or, if the case involved a lockout, that the employer open the plant or the docks for the continuance of work.

This is an argument by analogy. It is not on all fours, but it has enough common elements to cause me to make it in respect to what I think was the effect of the Dirksen resolution, to have the Senate give instructions on various points on which we were in conflict last Friday.

I was for the resolution. I was satisfied, before the resolution was offered to the conferees, that we had reached the point where the Senate ought to give us instructions. At that time requests were being made for compromises which, in my judgment, affected such important legitimate labor rights that have been won over the decades at great cost to American free labor, that I did not believe a compromise procedure should continue in conference with that resolution hanging over our heads.

I was for going back to the conference, but going back to the conference after the Senate had given us instructions on each of the very difficult points over which, at that time, we were obviously deadlocked. Examples of these important points are the no man's land issue, bonding, hot cargo, organizational picketing, legitimate secondary boycotts, and the like.

I did not prevail; but, as the record of the conference will show, time and time again I moved, prior to a vote or immediately following a vote in conference—and I did it both times on certain occasions—that the Senate conferees stand in disagreement on a particular issue and come to the floor of the Senate for instructions. I did so because I was convinced that we had reached such a point—particularly in view of the Dirksen resolution pending in the Senate—that the Senate as a whole should have been given an opportunity to pass judgment on some of these issues. As I shall point out later in my remarks instructions from the Senate would have been particularly useful in regard to one issue, because it was claimed that the language proposed by the majority of the Senate conferees in connection with situs picketing, for example, would be subject to a point of order in the House; and we were given assurances by the chairman of the House conferees, the distinguished Representative from North Carolina [Mr. Barden], that he would consider it his duty to raise such a point of order in the House.

I pointed out, after I had consulted the parliamentary authorities in the Senate, that under such circumstances, even if the point of order were well taken, it would not make the Senate impotent in the premises. We could have come back to the Senate for instructions, and we could have, in effect, laid aside for the time being further conference consideration until the Senate itself had passed what would have amounted to an independent amendment in regard to the building construction industry, particularly relative to situs picketing. Then we could have sent it to the floor of the House to let the House stand up and be counted as to the position it might wish to take with regard to this very troublesome issue, before we completed the conference work.

I so proposed, but I did not prevail. I say these things because I want the Record to show—newspaper column gossipers to the contrary notwithstanding—that the Senator from Oregon differed with the Senator from Massachusetts primarily upon procedures for conducting the conference during the last 2 or 3 days of the conference. We differed also, as our votes in the conference and our different individual final reports show, on the merits with respect to certain issues.

I make that introductory statement because I have been advised by a newspaper friend this morning—a correspondent, not a columnist, I may say good-naturedly—that there seems to be some question as to what the relationships between the junior Senator from Massachusetts and the Senator from Oregon are at the present moment. I am sure the feeling is mutual, but at least so far as I am concerned the relationships are most friendly.

They are based upon very sincere and honest differences of opinion as to the merits of the conference report. . . .

MIKE MANSFIELD [DEM., MONT.]. In talking with members of the committee of conference on both sides of the aisle, it was my distinct impression that they were all very much impressed and pleased with the many contributions made by the distinguished senior Senator from Oregon. They were very appreciative of the fact that he had at his command probably the greatest amount of knowledge concerning labor law, and that this was of great importance in the consideration of the two bills which were being considered by the conferees.

MR. MORSE. It is very kind of the Senator from Montana to say that, but he was misinformed. The Senator from Oregon did not have at his command—and he wished many times he did have at his command—the legal propositions which he knew existed in the library, if he had had the time to get them, and which he felt would have been more helpful to the conferees if he could have obtained them. But it is the old situation: One cannot be in two places at once. After all, there is only so much time available, and one does the best he can.

But I appreciate the many, many courtesies which were extended to me by both sides of the table, Senate conferees and House conferees, Republicans as well as Democrats, because it developed rather early in the conference that the Senator from Oregon could not possibly sign the conference report. I so stated, for example, when the no-man's-land provision, which was adopted by the conferees, was placed in the bill. I taught constitutional law too long to walk out on my own teachings. I could not think of imposing, not merely on labor, but on the American people as a whole, the provisions of the no-man's-land section of the bill.

In my judgment, as I shall show—and I shall develop this matter in great detail during the afternoon—the no-man's-land issue alone is enough on which to base rejection of the conference report.

I am willing to say on the floor of the Senate today that, although at the present time I recognize that mine is a small minority voice in this country on this issue, in due course of time the position I take today on this issue will come to be recognized generally as a sound legal position.

I apologize to the Senator from Massachusetts for being unable to hand him a carbon copy of all the parts of my remarks, but I should like to have my assistant on the floor proceed to deliver to the Senator from Massachusetts carbon copies of the various sections of the speech I am about to make which are available now. I do not know how many parts are available, because the speech was finished by me, so far as the first few sections are concerned, at about 2:15 o'clock this morning. I started to dictate again a little after 8 o'clock, and a part of my remarks is still in the typewriter and will be delivered from time to time as the speech proceeds.

Mr. President, it was with deep regret that I found it impossible to sign the conference report on the labor bill. There are many good features of the bill. In fact, many sections of the first six titles of the bill were taken directly from the Kennedy-Ervin bill, of which I was a cosponsor. It has been interesting to note that the mail which I have received urging me to support the Landrum-Griffin bill without change came from people who obviously did not know that the first six titles of the Landrum-Griffin bill are very similar to the first six titles of the Kennedy-Ervin bill.

As I shall point out later in this speech, the nationwide propaganda drive conducted against Congress for the adoption of the Landrum-Griffin bill came chiefly from antiunion inspired sources in the country who for a long time have been seeking to weaken or blunt or spike the economic weapons of trade unions. It is because the trade union movement has become effective in advancing the economic welfare of union members in our country that the antilabor forces back of the Landrum-Griffin bill have been so anxious to take advantage of the critical public reaction to labor abuses justifiably aroused by the McClellan committee. It is understandable that at such a time of widespread revulsion of feeling on the part of many people toward unions because of the shameful and inexcusable betrayal of trust on the part of a few crooked and corrupt labor leaders, antiunion forces in our country, spearheaded by such reactionary organizations as the U.S. Chamber of Commerce and the National Manufacturers Association, should wage a Madison Avenue propaganda campaign against unions. One of the results of this tragic setback of the rights of free labor in our country has been to separate true friends of the working people from their fair-weather friends. It has disclosed in the neighborhoods of America, within the business communities of the small and the big towns, within the legislative halls of our cities, States, and Nation, those who, in the name of one rationalization or another, are willing to sacrifice legitimate rights of labor at the altar of political expediency. Yes; when the history of this infamous legislative drive against the hard-earned rights of organized labor has been written, it will record the insincerity of many politicians who followed public clamour rather than tried to mold an intelligent public opinion and lead the public on the basis of the facts to the support of a just labor bill.

However, in my speech today I do not propose to try to fix blame for the sad legislative plight in which labor finds itself or for the political opportunism which motivates so much of the support for this proposed legislation. I am willing to leave those matters to the political reaction of the voters of the country after they have had sufficient time to reflect upon the demerits of this legislation. What I propose to do in this speech is to set out for the record my major reasons for refusing to sign the conference report. I recognize that the conference report will be approved today by an overwhelming vote in the Senate. Political considerations are firmly in the saddle. Most Members of Congress will not take the time to analyze and study the complex abstract illegal implications and concrete economic injustices to labor of this proposed legislation. I shall vote against it because I am convinced that it is not in the public interest.

My mail, which has been voluminous on both the Kennedy-Ervin bill and the Landrum-Griffin bill, leaves no room for doubt that at the present moment a good political vote would be to vote for the conference report bill. However, I will leave that course of action for others who are interested in staying in the Senate even at the cost of sacrifice of principle or who are interested in moving on to higher office, no matter what the cost to labor's legitimate rights and to the long-time best public interest.

As for me, I expect to continue to receive a great deal of personal abuse and political opposition from the reactionary antilabor forces and from some honest and sincere people who justifiably resent the inexcusable abuses which have been practiced by some so-called labor leaders who believe that the way to check those abuses is to pass this unfair piece of legislation. As to this latter group, I would be less than honest if I did not admit that their political declarations of war against me and their bitter personal criticisms set out in their mail make me feel very sad. No Senator enjóys casting a vote on proposed legislation which he knows is bound to cost him many votes at the ballot box, particularly if he is to stand for election in a State immediately following his Senate vote.

However, this political dilemma raises the old, old philosophical question in the field of political science, the answer to which Edmund Burke wrote to my complete satisfaction. As for me, when I come to vote in the Senate on any issue, it is my duty to follow where I think the facts lead, not where political considerations lead whenever the facts cannot be squared with the political advantages of the moment that might flow from a vote against the facts. If one is to follow the philosophy of Edmund Burke that an elected representative of the free people in a parliamentary body owes his constituents the primary obligation to exercise an honest independence of judgment on the merits of issues, in accordance with the facts as he finds them to be, then he must never be afraid to be defeated. He must never lose sight of the fact that it is not important that he or any other politician remain in office; but what is important, if democracy is to remain strong, and if the legislative processes of representative government are to go undefiled, is for each legislator to be true to himself and carry out his trust of voting on each issue in accordance with what he believes the facts show the public interest to be.

This does not mean that if each legislator does that, a legislative body will be unanimous on each vote cast. Sincere and honest differences of opinion on the merits of pieces of proposed legislation are bound to exist among sincere and honest legislators, and will lead them to reach different conclusions as to whether or not a given bill is in the public interest. As the debate on this measure proceeds, we shall see that demonstrated over and over again. But it is also true that, all too frequently, political expediency, political opportunism, compromise of principle, partisan politics, and fear of losing votes influence the votes in legislative halls. Whenever that happens, democratic government suffers and the voters are betrayed. If one is to follow the Burkean philosophy with respect to the principle that the primary obligation of a legislator is to vote on the merits of issues, irrespective of the political consequences, he not only must not be afraid to be defeated, but he also will find strength for standing by his convictions by taking succor from abiding faith that in a democracy, once the voters come to understand a legislator's reasons for voting contrary to an aroused public demand for a given piece of proposed legislation, such as the one now pending in the Senate, they will return their support to him, even though they may not agree with him in entirety.

On the other hand, if they do not find his reasons for his vote satisfactory, along with his overall record of representation in a legislative body, they should defeat him at the polls. That voter power is the essence of self-government. It is no disgrace to be defeated; but it is disgraceful to be afraid to be defeated, and, in an endeavor to avoid it, to follow a legislative course of action of political opportunism and expediency.

Because of the fact that I know that my opposition to the pending labor legislation is both unpopular and misunderstood among many people in my State, I intend to speak at some length today, for the Record, in setting forth my reasons for refusing to sign the conference report and for voting against it here in the Senate, as I probably shall have an opportunity to do before the day is over, or at least by the end of tomorrow.

Those very sincere people in my State who have written or telegraphed to me about my opposition to the Landrum-Griffin bill are entitled to have this official Record to refer to, in reaching a final judgment as to whether I have the political horns which they seem to think I have. It is my belief that many of this group of critics will come to modify their views concerning many of the features of the Landrum-Griffin bill, once they come to understand the harm that such legislation will do to the public interest.

Now just a word about the opposition's abuse that is pouring in from reactionary antilabor forces that would like nothing better than to reduce to economic impotence the free labor movement in the United States. I am pleased to have their opposition. I am glad to be judged by these enemies. Their stand on labor legislation has made their political trusts inflict no deep wounds, and their extremism has no lasting effect on intelligent and thinking voters. I have received telegrams and letters from such extremists by the hundreds in recent weeks, and particularly during the days when the conference committee was in session.

A typical one came from a constituent by the name of Harold G. Cutright, 1000 Southwest Vista Avenue, Portland, Oreg., who apparently thought I might tremble in the political knees if he sent to me a copy of a telegram which he sent to Representative Robert Griffin. His telegram to me reads as follows:

> This telegram sent Robert Griffin: "Urge you fight to bring Landrum-Griffin bill before full Senate for vote. Don't let Wayne Morse lick you. Morse is political dead duck Oregon. He knows it. He is playing labor's racket and seeking votes. He couldn't be elected dog catcher today in Oregon. Northwest people are behind you in your fight to rid labor racketeers, stop organization picketing, and put no man's land cases back in State courts. Keep up the good fight."

In recent days, I have received many such political love messages. I have replied to all of them in about the way I replied to Mr. Cutright. To him I said:

> I am sorry you feel as bitter toward me as you expressed yourself in your wire to Congressman Griffin. I am perfectly willing to let the voters of Oregon judge my record of service to the State and to the Nation, including my votes on labor legislation when I will run for reelection in 1962. I will run for reelection on that record.
>
> By 1962, God willing, I will have given 18 years of legislative service to the people of Oregon in the U.S. Senate. During that entire period of time, my record will show that I have voted for the public interest as I honestly believed it to be in respect to each issue. I have done so by exercising an honest independence of judgment on the merits of issues in accordance with the facts as I have found them in my study of each issue. That voting record shows that I have voted against labor time and time again when the facts convinced me it was wrong on any issue, and I have voted for labor when I thought some legislative proposal sought to injure some legitimate labor right. I have followed the same course of action in connection with every legislative subject matter, no matter what economic group was involved.
>
> Political threats such as yours don't scare me because I don't scare easily.
>
> Sincerely,
>
> Wayne Morse.

Mr. President, I refused to sign the conference report, and I shall vote against the conference committee bill, for the following reasons:

First, in my opinion, a vote for the bill will be to liquidate some of the hard-earned legitimate rights of American free labor. Those rights have been won through long and bitter struggles in this country over the decades. It is regretable that so many Americans, these days, are not familiar with the history of the American labor movement and the heroism of the pioneers in the union movement who won for labor the rights to organize and bargain collectively and effectively with employers for improved wages, hours, and conditions of employment. These rights were long in their winning; and not a single one of them should be lost in a single legislative day, or ever. Part of the responsibility for losing some of them on this legislative day rests squarely on the shoulders of labor itself.

For some time past, organized labor has known that there have been within the house of labor some racketeers and crooks. Labor knew that the house of labor should not be used as a house of sanctuary and refuge for the few labor leaders who had betrayed their trust to the members of their unions, and have sought to escape both the responsibility for and the consequences of their improper conduct.

Organized labor has known for a long time that some union leaders have run their unions as totalitarian economic states, tolerating no opposition or no exercise of democratic rights on the part of the dues-tribute-paying members. It did not require the McClellan committee to disclose to organized labor the ugly fact that a few locals in some unions were ruled by business agents and officers who had shocking criminal records. The scandals of paper unions, the corruption of employer-shakedowns by which a union representative would threaten an employer with various types of illegal, coercive acts if he did not sign a union contract, even if it was well known that the union did not have any members, or, if it had any, had only a few members in the employer's plant, have been known for some time to exist in a few segments of organized labor. The denial of democratic procedures in running union meetings and union conventions, the failure to supply periodic financial reports to union members, the misuse of union funds, the abuse of trusteeship prerogatives, the destruction of perishable goods in secondary boycott cases, conflict of interest practices on the part of a few union officials, and all the other union malpractices which have been disclosed by the McClellan committee did not come as surprising news to most of the leaders of the American labor movement. A sad fact is that the American labor movement should have cleaned its own house long ago. If it had done so, there would have been no need for the McClellan committee and the committee's disclosures of some corruption on the part of some unions and their officials would never have become necessary. The present agitated state of public opinion against organized labor in general would have never developed. Although a part of the responsibility for the present public demand for a legislative housecleaning of the labor movement must be assumed by organized labor itself because of its long delay in cleaning its own house, it does not follow that a destructive legislative bomb should be thrown into the house of labor in order to get rid of a few termites or to open the shutters so that the light of public disclosure can shine in. In fairness to the overwhelming majority of labor leaders in this country trusted with the obligation of serving as officials of international, national, and local unions, it should be said in their defense that there have been many obstacles placed in the way of their doing a better job of housecleaning than was being done until recently. It should be remembered many unions have enjoyed a complete autonomy and independence of any regulatory control in respect to any authority or jurisdiction over their affairs by any federation or organization composed of sister unions. The development of an organization such as now exists in the combined AFL-CIO amalgamation is of recent birth. Great credit is due George Meany and his associate officers of the AFL-CIO for their courage and labor statesmanship in respect to the housecleaning they have been doing within the structures of the affiliated unions that comprise their federation.

As we all know, in some instances they have thrown out corrupt unions which refused to comply with the ethical code of union practices adopted by the AFL-CIO. . . .

MR. MORSE. Mr. President, it is on the basis of that code and the failure of unions such as the Teamsters and others to comply with the ethical standards of the code that George Meany and his officer associates of the combined AFL-CIO had the courage to throw out unions which refused to comply; and I honor them for it.

I hope the day is not far distant when the rank and file membership of the Teamsters Union and the other unions that have been subjected to disciplinary action by the AFL-CIO will bring about the internal reforms necessary to establish democratic procedures and control in those unions, so that they can come back into the house of labor and set as law-abiding units of that family, working shoulder to shoulder with organized labor in general to protect the legitimate rights of free working men and women in this country.

It should be remembered, too, Mr. President, one reason for the rather slow progress that has been made in the past with regard to a general union housecleaning, is that for the past 20 years—and, yes, in some respect prior to that time—the family of American unions has been plagued with family quarrels, jurisdictional and otherwise, with the result that the house of labor has been divided much of the time. This has resulted in lack of discipline. Into such a state of internal union affairs, a few, but only a very few, relatively speaking, unworthy men have connived their way into positions of power in some unions. Their misconduct has reflected adversely on the entire labor movement, and today the entire labor movement is about to suffer the penalty of an unjust and excessive legislative sentence for the wrongdoings and bad practices of a relatively few bad men in the labor movement.

I shall be no party to punishing the innocent for the bad conduct of a few wrongdoers in the labor movement. One of the great strengths of the original Kennedy-Ervin bill, like the Kennedy-Ives bill before it, was to be found in the fact that it directed its legislative controls and penalties against the individual wrongdoer in the labor movement. It sought to avoid punishing the rank and file membership of a union for the wrongdoing of some official, particularly in view of the fact that the evidence brought out before both the McClellan committee and the Senate committee demonstrated time and time again that seldom did the rank and file membership ever have any knowledge of the wrongdoing of corrupt leadership. The evidence shows that in most of those instances in which the rank and file suspected wrongdoing, the membership was immobilized from doing anything about it because they did not have available to them the democratic procedures essential to self-government within the union. Therefore, the Kennedy-Ervin bill sought to penalize the individual wrongdoer within the union. It sought to give the Secretary of Labor, with some appeal provisions from his decisions, the power to investigate and police unions charged with criminal wrongdoings or other violations of the law. Further, and very important, the Kennedy-Ervin bill sought to set up standards and requirements for the establishment of democratic procedures within the unions so that the principles of union self-government would prevail, in keeping with the American ideal of political and economic democratic rights for the individual.

In addition, the Kennedy-Ervin bill sought to make a few emergency, needed amendments to the Taft-Hartley law pending a much broader Taft-Hartley revision program that is expected to follow the completion of the work now being carried on by the so-called special blue ribbon committee appointed by the Senate Labor and Public Welfare Committee to study and recommend Taft-Hartley amendments. . . .

MR. KENNEDY. Mr. President, as I remarked yesterday, no one is fully satisfied with the product of compromise, for in the nature of the process each one gives away something of one's position. This bill is a compromise. I must frankly state that it goes a good deal further in some areas than I think is either desirable or necessary—this is especially true in the Taft-Hartley amendments. On the other hand, the House bill contained some serious weaknesses in the antiracketeering parts of the bill, all of which we were not able to shore up. I regret that it was not possible to close these loopholes.

The point is, nevertheless, that we have before us in this conference report what I believe to be the only bill that it is possible to obtain under all of the circumstances. As it came from the House with the Griffin-Landrum amendment, the bill, in my opinion should not have commanded the support of a majority of the Senate. It contained serious flaws and in the form in which it passed by the other body, unnecessarily restricted normal, legitimate trade union activity.

The Senate conferees had several serious problems with the first six titles of the House bill—but these titles with certain exceptions followed very closely the substance of S. 1555 as it passed the Senate.

The Taft-Hartley amendments in the Griffin-Landrum substitute, however, went far beyond the provisions of the Senate-passed bill.

However, in the 12 days during which the conference met the majority of the Senate conferees secured important changes in the restrictive provisions of the Landrum-Griffin bill, thereby protecting traditional and essential rights of workingmen seeking to improve conditions of employment. It is important that the Senate should note these changes:

First. No-man's land: The Senate conferees insisted upon an amendment which prevents the NLRB from declining to exercise its existing jurisdiction and thereby depriving both employers and employees of the protection of the National Labor Relations Act. The Landrum-Griffin bill would have allowed the Board to surrender unlimited jurisdiction to the States, 35 of which provide no protection to the rights to organize and bargain collectively. The conference report prevents further cession. The current standards of the NLRB assures the widest effective exercise of Federal jurisdiction in the history of the National Labor Relations Act.

Second. Organizational picketing: The House bill would have forbidden virtually all organizational picketing, even though the pickets did not stop truck deliveries or exercise other economic coercion. The amendments adopted in the conference secure the right to engage in all forms of organizational picketing up to the time of an election in which the employees can freely express their desires with respect to the choice of a bargaining representative. When the picketing results in economic pressure through the refusal of other employees to cross the picket line, the bill would require a prompt election. Purely informational picketing cannot be curtailed under the conference report, although even this privilege would have been denied by the Landrum-Griffin measure.

Third. Secondary boycotts: The chief effect of the conference agreement, therefore, will be to plug loopholes in the secondary boycott provisions of the National Labor Relations Act. There has never been any dispute about the desirability of plugging these artificial loopholes. The secondary boycott provisions of the House bill would have curtailed legitimate union activities. Accordingly, the Senate conferees insisted that the report secure the following rights:

(a) The right to engage in primary strikes and primary picketing even though the employees of other employers refused to cross the picket line.

The fact of the matter is that there is some question under the Landrum-Griffin bill whether employees of another employer could have properly refused not to cross a picket line in a primary strike. That has been clarified in the conference report.

(b) The right of employees to refuse to work on goods farmed out from an establishment in which the employees are on strike.

The language in the Landrum-Griffin bill, dealing with how far the employees can go in following struck work was far more restrictive than the present law, and the conference report provision takes us back to present law, which is far more satisfactory.

(c) The right to appeal to consumers by methods other than picketing asking them to refrain from buying goods made by nonunion labor and to refrain from trading with a retailer who sells such goods.

Under the Landrum-Griffin bill it would have been impossible for a union to inform the customers of a secondary employer that that employer or store was selling goods which were made under racket conditions or sweatshop conditions, or in a plant where an economic strike was in progress. We were not able to persuade the House conferees to permit picketing in front of that secondary shop, but we were able to persuade them to agree that the union shall be free to conduct informational activity short of picketing. In other words, the union can hand out handbills at the shop, can place advertisements in newspapers, can make announcements over the radio, and can carry on all publicity short of having ambulatory picketing in front of a secondary site.

MR. GOLDWATER. Mr. President, will the Senator yield at that point for a question?

MR. KENNEDY. I yield.

MR. GOLDWATER. I have been asked by people who are vitally concerned whether there is anything in the conference report which would limit or prohibit the buy-America campaigns which are being carried on by certain unions and business groups, and even by some governmental bodies. I should like to ask the distinguished chairman of the conference committee whether the report was intended to have this effect. It is certainly my own conviction that no such effect was intended, either by the Senate or by the conferees.

MR. KENNEDY. I know that a good deal of effort has been made by some groups of workers, such as those who work on hats, to make sure that their working standards are protected. The answer to the Senator's question is no, it was not intended that the conference report have such an effect. I am glad that we have had the opportunity to establish legislative history in this matter.

MR. GOLDWATER. I thank the Senator.

MR. KENNEDY. I thank the Senator.

(d) The right of labor unions representing employees in the apparel and clothing industry to refuse to work for a jobber or contractor who subcontracts parts of the process of production to nonunion subcontractors. This guarantee, the writing of which into statutory legislation was opposed by the House conferees for 2 weeks, is absolutely essential to the stability of these industries. The bill makes special mention of the industry because it has peculiar problems.

Fourth. Hot cargo: The Landrum-Griffin bill extended the "hot cargo" provisions of the Senate bill, which we applied only to Teamsters, to all agreements between an employer and a labor union by which the employer agrees not to do business with another concern. The Senate insisted upon a qualification for the clothing and apparel industries and for agreements relating to work to be done at the site of a construction project. Both changes were necessary to avoid serious damage to the pattern of collective bargaining in these industries.

Fifth. Economic strikers: The conferees adopted the substance of the provisions of the Senate bill reversing the Taft-Hartley rule that economic strikers who have been replaced should not vote in an NLRB election. This is a highly important change, for the Taft-Hartley prohibition had, in the words of the President of the United States, opened the door to union-busting practices.

The House bill contained a provision on this, but it provided that economic strikers would not have the right to vote if the issue of recognition had been raised before the strike began. It would be extremely difficult for the employer to raise the issue of recognition in almost any economic strike, and in those conditions economic strikers would have been denied the right to vote, we guarantee them the right to vote for at least a year after the strike begins.

Sixth. Prehire agreements: The conference report incorporates the provisions of the Senate bill authorizing labor unions and contractors in the construction industry to negotiate prehire agreements. The Landrum-Griffin bill contains restrictive and unworkable provisions on this point.

Seventh. Employer reports: The conference provision adopts the substance of the Senate bill dealing with the reports to be filed by employers and labor relations consultants, the purpose of which is to disclose to the Government and public opinion any repetition of the unsavory practices brought to light by the McClellan committee. One of the important consequences of these reports will be the full disclosure of sums of money spent by employers to finance "front" organizations distributing propaganda designed to prevent further union organization.

The Landrum-Griffin bill contained a provision whereby if an employer gave $10,000 to a labor relations consultant and asked him to do what he could to see that a union was not organized in his plant, the labor relations consultant could then do anything he wanted with the money, however coercive or corrupt, without the employer's reporting the payment, provided only that the employer was not a party to the consultant's conduct. This was a hole a mile wide in the employer reporting section which was closed by the conference report.

Eighth. Membership lists: The House bill would have required a labor union to open its membership lists to any candidate in connection with an election of officers. Although this requirement might be fair in the case of bona fide candidates, it created grave dangers that stooges would obtain the membership lists for subversive organizations or commercial use. The Senate conferees added the safeguard of limiting the right to one inspection within 30 days prior to an election, without making copies of the list.

In addition to these major changes in the bill, as it came from the House, there are a number of other provisions about which I believe the Senate should be fully informed. This is for the purpose of establishing some legislative history.

PROTECTION OF THE RIGHT TO SUE (SEC. 101(A)(4))

The protection of the right to sue provision originated in the Senate bill and was adopted verbatim in the Landrum-Griffin bill except that the first proviso limiting exhaustion of internal hearing procedures was changed from 6 months to 4 months. The basic intent and purpose of the provision was to insure the right of a union member to resort to the courts, administrative agencies, and legislatures without interference or frustration of that right by a labor organization. On the other hand, it was not, and is not, the purpose of the law to eliminate existing grievance procedures established by union constitutions for redress of alleged violation of their internal governing laws. Nor is it the intent or purpose of the provision to invalidate the considerable body of State and Federal court decisions of many years standing which require, or do not require, the exhaustion of internal remedies prior to court intervention depending upon the reasonableness of such circumstances of a particular case. So long as the union member is not prevented by his union from resorting to the courts, the intent and purpose of the "right to sue" provision is fulfilled, and any requirements which the court may then impose in terms of pursuing reasonable remedies within the organization to redress violation of his union constitutional rights will not conflict with the statute. The doctrine of exhaustion of reasonable internal union remedies for violation of union laws is just as firmly established as the doctrine of exhausting reasonable administrative agency provisions prior to action by courts.

The 4-month limitation in the House bill also relates to restrictions imposed by unions rather than the rules of judicial administration or the action of Government agencies. For example, the National Labor Relations Board is not prohibited from entertaining charges by a member against a labor organization even though 4 months has not elapsed.

DISCIPLINARY ACTION

The so-called bill of rights title also secures important procedural safeguards against improper disciplinary action against union members as members. The Senate should note, however, that all the conferees agreed that this provision does not relate to suspension or removal from a union office.

Often this step must be taken summarily to prevent dissipation or missappropriation of funds. In practice it is usually followed by a hearing.

TIME OF FILING REPORTS—TITLE II

The first financial reports which unions are required to file, and the first reports to be made by union officers, and employees under title II will cover only the period after the date the act becomes effective until the end of their first fiscal year which occurs after such effective date. Activities and transactions which occurred prior to the effective date of the act will not have to be reported.

ELECTIONS AND MEMBERSHIP LISTS

The provisions requiring fair and periodic elections are taken from the Senate bill. The Landrum-Griffin bill would have substituted a variety of suits by individual members for enforcement by the Secretary of Labor. The House conferees receded from this position and the Senate provision was restored.

A second important change in the election title relates to the use of membership lists. The Senate bill requires a union to mail out to all members campaign literature submitted by candidates, at the candidate's expense, but there was no requirement that the candidate be given access to membership lists. Past experience demonstrates that unless lists of union members are kept confidential, they fall into the hands of employers who may use them for the purpose of breaking up the union, and into the hands of subversive organizations and commercial enterprises. The House bill would have required the disclosure of lists of members employed under union security contracts to any candidate despite these dangers. The conference report limits the right of the candidate to inspecting such a list once within 30 days prior to the election, and it prohibits the candidate from copying the names and addresses. The right to inspect will be important as a way of checking the accuracy of the union's mailing list, for the candidate will thus be enabled to ascertain whether the union has in fact mailed his campaign literature to those whom he knows to be union members. The inspection is not to enable him to have a copy. The mere fact that a local union has members covered by such agreements does not mean that the national or international union of which it is a constituent unit is required to keep and make available for inspection a list of all of its members, nor does this section require that federations of labor organizations whose members are composed of national or international unions, rather than individual members, are required to maintain and make available for inspection a list of all their individual members.

I do not wish to detain the Senate unduly, but these matters are extremely important. I think it is important that we have this opportunity to establish clearly the intent of the Senate on some of these points.

FIDUCIARY RESPONSIBILITY—SECTION 501

The general principles stated in the bill are familiar to the courts, both State and Federal, and therefore incorporate a large body of existing law applicable to trustees, and a wide variety of agents. The detailed application of these fiduciary principles to a particular trustee, officer, or agent has always depended upon the character of the activity in which he was engaged. They bear upon a family trustee somewhat differently than a corporate director, upon an attorney quite differently than a real estate agent. The bill wisely takes note of the need to consider "the special problems and functions of a labor organization" in applying fiduciary principles to their officers and agents.

The bill does not limit in any way the purposes for which the funds of a labor organization may be expended or the investments which can be made. Such decisions should be made by the members in accordance with the constitution and bylaws of their union. Union officers will not be guilty of breach of trust under this section when their expenditures are within the authority conferred upon them either by the constitution and bylaws, or by a resolution of the executive board, convention or other appropriate governing body—including a general meeting of the members—not in conflict with the constitution and bylaws. This is also made clear by the fact that section 501(a) requires that the special problems and functions of a labor organization be taken into consideration in determining whether union officers and other representatives are acting responsibly in connection with their statutory duties. The problems with which labor organizations are accustomed to deal are not limited to bread-and-butter unionism or to organization and collective bargaining alone, but encompass a broad spectrum of social objectives as the union may determine.

However, the committee bill also explicitly invalidates any general provision in a union constitution or bylaws purporting to excuse union officials from breaches of trust. The bill follows the well-established distinction between conferring authority upon an agent or trustee, which is permissible and protects him against liability, and attempting to excuse breaches of trust, which is here made void as against public policy.

ORGANIZATIONAL PICKETING—SECTION 704

Two of the three restrictions upon organizational picketing are taken from the Senate bill. Paragraphs (A) and (B) of the new section 8(b)(7), which is added to the National Labor Relations Act, prohibit picketing for union organization or recognition at times when the National Labor Relations Board would not conduct an election. Subdivision (A) covers the situation where a contract with another union is a bar to an election. If the contract is not a bar, either because the incumbent union was recognized improperly or lacked majority support, or because the contract had run for a reasonable period, a question concerning representation could appropriately be raised and subdivision (A) would not bar the picketing. Subdivision (B) bars picketing for organizational purposes or union recognition for 12 months after an election in order to secure the expressed desire of the employees. In both cases the prohibitions relate only to picketing in an effort to organize employees or secure recognition in a bargaining unit covered by the existing contract or the prior election.

The restriction added by the House which was approved in conference prohibits picketing, which involves economic coercion through employees, for more than 30 days without filing a petition for an election.

HOT CARGO—SECTION 704(B)

The first proviso under new section 8(e) of the National Labor Relations Act is intended to preserve the present state of the law with respect to picketing at the site of a construction project and with respect to the validity of agreements relating to the contracting of work to be done at the site of a construction project.

This proviso affects only section 8(c) and therefore leaves unaffected the law developed under section 8(b)(4). The *Denver Building Trades* (341 U.S. 675) and the *Moore Drydock* (92 N.L.R.B. 547) cases would remain in force.

Agreements by which a contractor in the construction industry promises not to subcontract work on a construction site to a nonunion contractor appear to be legal today. They will not be unlawful under section 8(e). The proviso is also applicable to all other agreements involving undertakings not to do work on a construction project site with other contractors or subcontractors regardless of the precise relation between them. Since the proviso does not relate to section 8(b)(4), strikes and picketing to enforce the contracts excepted by the proviso will continue to be illegal under section 8(b)(4) whenever the *Sand Door* case (357 U.S. 93) is applicable.

It is not intended to change the law with respect to the judicial enforcement of these contracts, or with respect to the legality of a strike to obtain such a contract.

It should be particularly noted that the proviso relates only to the "contracting or subcontracting of work to be done at the site of the construction." The proviso does not cover boycotts of goods manufactured in an industrial plant for installation at the jobsite, or suppliers who do not work at the jobsite. . . .

First, the bill is not the bill I should have preferred to see passed by Congress. The House of Representatives went in a different direction from the Senate. The question was, What action should the Senate take? There are those who feel that it would have been wiser if the Senate had never gone to conference and had instead passed the Landrum-Griffin bill 2 weeks ago. Those who may feel that that would have been a wise decision would have made the greatest mistake of their lives if they voted for that bill. They would not have had the vaguest idea of what was in the Landrum-Griffin bill. It took 2 weeks for the conference to fully understand the meaning of all the provisions of the Landrum-Griffin bill.

Second, I think it is fair to say that the House Members of the conference—and I think they will agree—did not know all the implications of the Landrum-Griffin bill.

The fact of the matter is that the Landrum-Griffin bill was not reported by a committee of the House. It was offered as a substitute on the floor of the House. It came up in a debate on the Elliott bill, and both the Shelley and the Landrum-Griffin bill were also before the House. Three conflicting bills, each running dozens of pages in length, and involving cross-references to court decisions and to provisions of laws were before the House. It would not be any wonder that most of the Members of the House could not have known what the provisions of the House bill contained. Therefore, I think if the Landrum-Griffin bill had been passed, it would have been one of the greatest mistakes we could have made.

Once having decided to go to conference, we stayed in conference until we came back here to the Senate Friday night. Four Senate conferees submitted a resolution suggesting what we wanted in title VII. Everything which we wanted in the bill on Friday night, with one exception, is now in the Landrum-Griffin bill, or the Kennedy-Ervin bill, or S. 1555, the labor-management reform bill of 1959, as I would much prefer to call it.

All the provisions and words, with the exception of the words "and other integrated industries," are in the bill. We tried to take care of the problems of other integrated industries, like the garment industry. For example, the Senator from West Virginia [Mr. Randolph] was extremely anxious to protect the practices in the coal industry. The senior Senator from West Virginia objectively approached the problems of the conference from the national aspect. Yet he was keenly aware of and appropriately sought to protect the rights and interests of the dominant industry of his State in proposing amendments to cushion the impact on the labor-management relations between the coal producers and the miners' union. He offered an amendment relating to the coal industry on three different occasions. The Senator from Michigan [Mr. McNamara], the Senator from Oregon [Mr. Morse], and I voted for it. We were unable to persuade the House to accept it. But the point of the matter is that we were able to gain acceptance of the proposals which were in our resolution of last week, Senate Resolution 181, with the one exception that I have mentioned. We were also able to add two additional important provisions.

We have secured a commitment from the leadership of the House and Senate that in January a bill which the Senator from California [Mr. Kuchel] and I will introduce tonight, and which Representative Thompson will offer in the House, on the Denver case, concerning situs picketing, will come to the floors of the House and Senate.

In my opinion, considering the Landrum-Griffin bill and considering what we have now, I think substantial progress was made, progress of the most important kind. It might have been better to have brought the matter to the floor of the Senate a week ago and let the Senate debate it. But the Senate sent us to conference to have us attempt to render our best judgment.

The Parliamentarian has informed me that only once, I believe, in the time he has been here have conferees come back to the Senate for instructions. Therefore, it seems to me it was our job to attempt to do the best we could.

I am frank to say that I do not think the Senate would have reached a more satisfactory solution. It is very possible that after 4 or 5 days of long, drawn-out debate in the Senate, a motion would have been made to have the Senate accept the Landrum-Griffin bill in toto; and in frustration and fear we would have ended with a bill so different from the House bill that we would not have gotten a reform bill. We might have ended with the Landrum-Griffin bill or no bill at all.

So as a member either of the Senate Committee on Labor and Public Welfare or the House Committee on Education and Labor for 13 years, I have no apologies at all for the bill we are now bringing before the Senate.

I believe that any Senator, regardless of his views on these matters, can vote for the conference report. I do not claim that it is a perfect bill or that it is a model of fairness. But, taking it as a whole, it is the best bill we can pass.

I hope that Senators, regardless of any misgivings which they may have concerning some provisions of the bill, and which I have, will see fit to endorse the work which the conference has done. . . .

House of Representatives—86th Congress, 1st Session
July 23—27, 1959

JOHN LANDRUM [R., IND.]. Mr. Chairman, together with the gentleman from Michigan [Mr. Griffin], I have today introduced a nonpartisan bill, dealing with the tremendously vital issue of labor-management reform legislation. We did so only after the most thorough consideration, and in light of what we feel to be absolutely necessary in this field, if free and democratic processes in the industrial relations of our great Nation are to survive.

The Joint Subcommittee on Labor-Management Reform Legislation, of which I had the honor to be cochairman, took extensive testimony in this general area, hearing in all some 98 witnesses, over a 3-month period. Competent persons from all segments of American industrial life were heard—some, several times. Only two argued that reform legislation was unwarranted and unnecessary. I had hoped, therefore, that the Committee on Education and Labor, after its executive sessions, would present to the House a bill which would strike at the roots of the acute problems which were revealed—not only in the testimony given before the joint subcommittee, but also by the dramatic revelations of the select committee in the other body. In my judgment, however, the bill which the House committee reported last Thursday, July 23, fails in several important respects to effectively come to grips with many pertinent matters. Briefly I would like to discuss some of these problems.

Turning to the first title of both the committee bill, and the bill which Mr. Griffin and I have introduced today, "Rights of Members of Labor Organizations," even a cursory reading of the two illustrates the important differences. The committee bill would require that union members "exhaust reasonable remedies" within a 6-month period, which are available under the union's constitution and bylaws. Only then can the member subsequently institute a civil action for relief from infringement of his rights. It is also to be noted that the member would only be entitled to a civil court injunction against further violation. The bill we propose as a substitute would permit a member to seek immediate redress of his basic rights in the courts after 4 months without the further delaying and dilatory route of exhausting union procedures. Our bill would also provide effective criminal penalties against those persons willfully violating such members' rights by force or violence.

That effective and timely relief is needed is shown by a review of certain testimony presented by union members. In one instance, the wife of a union member was called on the telephone, told that her husband was being held, and that he was going to be "cut up" and thrown on the front lawn. Incidentally, the local union, of which this employee was a member, was kept in trusteeship for 10 years, during which $200,000 disappeared from the treasury. In another case, a member was brought up on charges of conduct unbecoming a member, jurors "doubled" for the prosecution, he was denied a lawyer of his own choosing, and the sentence was that he pay a $250 fine, not work in the State for 2 years, and stay away from the union hall for 5 years. In the case of a Teamster local, out of 3,300 members, only 11 were declared to be eligible to run for union office.

I would call to the Members' attention that the interim report of the McClellan committee found that there has been a significant lack of democratic processes in certain unions, that one-man dictatorships have thrived—in some instances for 20 to 30 years—and that through intimidation and fear, the rank and file union member has been deprived of a voice in his own union affairs. In this regard, one of the most significant provisions in title I of the committee bill is that which empowers the union, regardless of the general rights specified, to require of members "loyal observance by every member, of his responsibility toward the labor organization as an institution and toward the labor movement as a whole." Under this, could not the union in Kansas City, which expelled 19 members who resorted to legal action against rigged elections, have done so on the basis of disloyalty. Or what about the union which tried and convicted a member in 1957 for statements made in 1953, 4 years earlier. Could he not also have been disciplined or expelled for disregarding his obligations toward the labor movement as a whole?

I am inclined to agree with Mr. Meany when he said before the Senate committee:

Before the Senate hearings we did not know one one-hundredth of corruption existing in the labor movement.

One of the basic underlying principles of both the Wagner Act of 1935 and the Taft-Hartley Act of 1947 has been the rights of employees—under the first to be free from employer domination, under the second to be free from union domination. That further legislation, however, dealing with union democracy is needed in 1959 cannot be challenged. As one union official put it in his testimony:

We believe that the control of the union by its membership is the best way to insure its democracy and keep the officers in line—I believe that the best demonstration of democracy in action, is where the people directly handle their own union business.

This the substitute bill seeks to accomplish, by insuring effective membership control.

The committee bill also purports to contain reporting provisions, under which the goldfish-bowl approach would enable union members to see for themselves wrongdoing and take effective and corrective action. In actuality, however, it contains an outright exemption for approximately 70 percent of the unions of the country—by exempting those which less than 200 members or gross annual receipts of less than $20,000. Many of the notorious racketeering situations, therefore, such as the Johnny Dio locals would be left untouched, and unhindered. Under the bill we propose, all unions of whatever size would be required to report pertinent financial data, informing the membership of possible conflicts of interest, and other shady deals; while at the same time authorizing the Secretary of Labor to prescribe simplified forms of reporting, if full reporting would be unduly burdensome.

The McClellan committee in this general area found, first, that union financial safeguards have been almost totally lacking; second, destruction of financial records rampant; and third, that misuse of union funds has totaled some $10 million, as of March 24, 1958.

As important as the foregoing problems are, however, I must say in all candor that, in my judgment, two of the most crucial issues confronting the Congress in this labor-management field, are the matters of secondary boycotts, and organizational and recognitional picketing. A blackmail organizational picket line is one wherein a union places a picket or pickets—varying from one to an infinite number—in front of a business establishment, to force the employees of the establishment to join the union. Often there is little or no employee support; or in many instances the employee have said "No" specifically to the union organizers.

What does such a "line" mean to an employee in Missouri or to a small businessman in Los Angeles? The testimony before the joint subcommittee, in a grotesque way, pictured what is meant. In Brownsville, Mo., a bakery was forced out of business after months of such blackmail organizational picketing, although the employees had refused to join. In Peoria, Ill., an employer went broke after 6 months of such daily activity; and a restaurant in that city was picketed for 10 months, although during that entire period no employees were contacted by the union.

In Los Angeles a half-dozen apple processors and packing plants were picketed from 8 to 10 months. A restaurant in San Francisco was picketed continuously for 925 days, or more than 2½ years. An automobile dealer in Galesburg, Mo., underwent this ordeal for 3 years, during which time his showroom was shot up, and new cars received paint jobs of acid and paint removal. In this particular case, the organizer told the employer bluntly:

We realize that we cannot organize your employees, therefore you will have to organize them for us, or we'll break you.

In all these cases, and there are hundreds more, the union puts up a picket line in order to force recognition, to compel the employees to join against their will—in one case brought to our attention a contract with another union had already been signed—and in total disregard of the processes of the National Labor Relations Board.

Yet after months of such testimony, often given at the risk of life and property, the committee bill would not deal with this problem in any way. I repeat, in no way does the committee bill solve the overwhelming problem of blackmail organizational picketing. Our proposed bill would. It would do so by prohibiting picketing when, first, another union has been lawfully recognized; second, where a valid election has been held during the preceding 12 months; third, where the picketing union cannot demonstrate that it has a sufficient showing of interest among the employees to support an NLRB petition for an election; and fourth, where picketing has been engaged in for a reasonable time—not exceeding 30 days—and no petition for an election has been filed.

Basically, the same coercive situation exists on the issue of secondary boycotts. A secondary boycott is a situation where the union, in a dispute with one employer, puts pressure upon another employer or his employees, in order to force the second employer or his employees, to stop doing business with the first employer, and "bend his knee to the union's will." Thus it is called secondary activity.

The committee bill would deal with this problem only in the very narrow way of proscribing the formal execution of "hot cargo" contracts with those employers subject to the Interstate Commerce Act, part II. There of course are thousands of employers not covered by such provisions, with whom the Teamsters, and other unions, could and surely would, execute and effectuate such agreements. By not prohibiting the others, by not naming them, the committee bill would indirectly sanction, if indeed not approve, their execution. I submit if such contracts are bad in one segment of our economy, they are undesirable in all segments.

The reported bill therefore would not touch many of the situations presented to the joint subcommittee. What about the trucking firm in Michigan which had sugar and shellac dumped into its trucks, and its customers driven away, because they feared union trouble? What about the secondary boycott of a company's product in Ohio, which a Member of the other body characterized as a "brazen and coldblooded" move to destroy the business. Or the boycott activity against another trucker of such proportions that the conduct of certain Teamsters leaders were said to "make Attila the Hun appear by comparison to be a very mild mannered and benevolent individual."

What will be our answer to the manufacturer of church furniture in Indiana who had dozens of installation jobs halted at churches from Bunker Hill to Dayton, because its employees had the effrontery to vote against the union? Shall we bow to the union will, and pray only in union-built pews? What about the trucking firm in Los Angeles which was forced out of business after 2½ months of violence and boycotting; or the poultry dealer in Georgia who had customers say: "We like you; we like your poultry; we want to do business with you; but we can't go through the trouble that these unions can cause us. We have done it before, and we'll not do it again." What logical difference is there between union pressure upon secondary employers, and secondary employees? The technique is the same, the result is the same—pressure upon disinterested third parties to make them bring pressure to bear upon the hapless businessman and his pawnlike employee.

I ask: Do they not deserve protection? Do they not merit some relief?

What will be our answer to them? Or to the trucker in Michigan who with his employees was harassed for 3 years because they voted against the Teamsters; or the small filling station operator in Illinois who, when his employees repeatedly stated that they did not wish to belong to the Teamsters, had his customers jeered?

Nor does the full remedy lie, as will be suggested later, in requiring the National Labor Relations Board to take complete jurisdiction over all cases. The Board itself has declared organizational picketing in many instances to be lawful; and would therefore be of little assistance under its interpretation of present law.

The situation in many parts of America has become so ugly and menacing that the joint subcommittee actually heard two union officials testify against picketing abuses. One stated that his organization specifically disapproved of putting a picket line around an employer—to compel the employer to sign a contract with a union that did not represent his employees. Another characterized such situations as bad and immoral.

As one witness said during his appearance:

When the picket line appears, the ballot box disappears. Congress has to make up its mind whether it wants a picket line as a means of forcing union recognition, or whether it wants the ballot box.

In conclusion, Mr. Chairman, let me say that the bill the gentleman from Michigan and I have introduced is not an antiunion bill, it is not a union busting bill, it is not an anticollective bargaining bill. It would not impinge in any way upon the lawful and legitimate purposes and activities of American labor unions.

It is a bill which would restore the control of union affairs to union members. It is a bill which would deal realistically with the life-and-death problems of the small businessman. It is the minimum required to stop blackmail organizational picketing, and secondary boycotts. Here, I submit, is the cancer—the lethal weapon which, in the words of Senator McClellan, ultimately could turn this country "into a jungle," where "we would have to resort to the bullet and to the dynamite for the protection of our property and our loved ones."

It is with a deep sense of responsibility, and not without great deliberation, that I have introduced this bill. I believe that it merits, and hope that it will receive, the support of my fellow Americans, who believe, as I do, that progress can be achieved in our country only through decency and fair play—for the unions, the union members, and the general public. . . .

LEVI GRIFFIN [DEM., MICH.] Mr. Chairman, the subject of labor reform legislation is so serious and the need is so great that surely there can be no room for partisanship. It is in that spirit that I have joined with the distinguished gentleman from Georgia [Mr. Landrum] in sponsoring a reform bill that is truly bipartisan, or nonpartisan.

In our best judgment, as cochairman and ranking minority member, respectively, of the House Labor-Management Reform Subcommittee, our substitute represents the minimum bill that the full Committee on Education and Labor should have reported to the House.

Mr. Chairman, I plead with the Members of both parties to resist the temptation to draw the hard lines of partisanship. This fight for effective reform legislation should not be a battle between the political parties—it must be a battle for the public and for the working men and women of our country. Surely there is plenty of room in both parties for the champions of this great cause.

Our substitute introduced today is a moderate but effective reform bill. It is not punitive or extreme.

However, it may be expected that some will work to defeat this substitute with labels rather than logic.

The Members of the House and the press should be aware that for all practical purposes our substitute is the committee bill, H.R. 8342 with a few very important changes which can be summarized as follows:

First. Title I of the substitute, the bill of rights for union members, is essentially the bill of rights in S. 1555 as it passed the Senate. Those who try to pin a "union-busting" label on our bill of rights will be pinning the same label on 90 Members of the other body.

Second. Titles II, III, IV, V, and VI of the substitute, dealing with reporting, trusteeships, elections, and other safeguards, are almost identical to the provisions in the committee bill except for these important differences: (a) the committee bill automatically exempts nearly 70 percent of all the labor organizations in the country from reporting. The substitute removes the exemption and requires all unions to report but provides that the Secretary may prescribe simplified forms for smaller unions; (b) the substitute restores the language of section 213 in the Senate-passed bill relating to extortionate picketing in place of the confusing revision represented by section 602 of the committee bill; (c) section 607 of the Senate-passed bill which provided criminal enforcement of rights guaranteed under the Act was striken by the House committee. The substitute—in sections 609 and 610—restores the sense of the Senate provision but makes it clear that criminal sanctions apply only when rights are denied through the use of force or violence.

Third. Title VII of the substitute bill contains a number of amendments to the Taft-Hartley Act including provisions to deal with such problems as jurisdictional no man's land, blackmail organizational picketing, hot cargo, and other loopholes in the Taft-Hartley ban against secondary boycotts.

Other amendments to the Taft-Hartley Act in title VII provides: (a) For certification without election of unions in the building and construction industry where there is a prior history of collective bargaining, (b) that a representation election to oust a lawfully recognized union cannot be held during an economic strike for 1 year upon the petition of an employer or for 6 months upon the petition of another union. In general, the provisions of the substitute in this area are in line with the proposals made by the President and the minimum recommendations made by Senator McClellan. The substitute does not go as far in these areas as some advocates of reform legislation have proposed.

Like the committee bill, the substitute repeals the non-Communist affidavit requirement in the Taft-Hartley Act, but makes it a criminal offense for any person to serve as an officer of a union if he is a Communist, or has been a Communist within 5 years prior to such service.

In my opinion those who seek to defeat this substitute with labels will be attacking the position of the President which has already been described throughout the country, and even in the liberal press, as fair, reasonable, and moderate.

Mr. Chairman, the issues are drawn and the question now is whether the American people control the Congress or whether it is controlled by a few labor bosses and special interest groups. I hope the American people will rally now as never before in support of those who are trying to pass effective labor reform legislation. . . .

JOHN SHELLEY [DEM., CALIF.]. Mr. Speaker, I have today introduced H.R. 8490, a labor-management reform measure which is not a pro-labor bill, nor is it an anti-labor bill. At the opening of this Congress it was the general thought of practically all members of both parties that legislation would be enacted which would set up a system of financial accounting and responsibility on the part of both labor and management in connection with their labor relations activities; further, that such legislation would carry provisions which would drive the crooks and the racketeers out of positions with labor and out of positions with management in the labor relations field.

The present situation before the House leaves us to consider two bills, either of which or both of which seek to punish all of the labor movement for the misdeeds of some and which write into the permanent law of the land punitive legislation against labor. Both of these proposals—the Elliott bill and the Landrum-Griffin bill—go far beyond what Congress set out to do —and that is real tough financial accountability legislation. The bill I have introduced seeks to do just this and nothing more. I am setting forth herein a detailed account of what H.R. 8490 does in contrast with the other legislation before us.

PRINCIPAL DIFFERENCES BETWEEN SHELLEY SUBSTITUTE
AND COMMITTEE BILL (H.R. 8342)

First. Unions would be safeguarded in section 101(b) of the Shelley substitute against irresponsible abuse of rights guaranteed in title I—rights of members. No such provision is included in the committee bill.

Second. The encouragement for States to enact union members' bills of rights, which is contained in section 103 of the committee bill, is omitted from the Shelley substitute. Section 103 of the Shelley substitute safeguards union members' rights and remedies under their union constitutions and by-laws and the authority of unions over the conduct of their own internal affairs, except as explicitly provided in the bill.

Third. The employer and labor consultant reporting provisions, which are hardly more than the merest sham in the committee bill, have been made substantially more effective in section 203 of the Shelley substitute.

Fourth. Section 306 of the Shelley substitute omits the confusing language of the committee bill under which the bill's regulations applicable to trusteeships would be superimposed on all of the complicated and varying State regulations and decisions. When actions are filed by the Secretary of Labor to enforce the bill's trusteeship provisions, the district courts would have exlusive jurisdiction under the Shelley substitute.

Fifth. The Shelley substitute omits the provision contained in section 301 (b) of the committee bill, which would make the membership lists of all unions where members are covered by some form of union security agreement available for copying by every bona fide candidate for union office who could in turn give or sell them to an employer, the Communist Party, or commercial advertising concerns. In place of this provision, section 301(b) of the Shelley substitute contains provisions similar to those contained in the Senate-passed bill S. 1555.

Sixth. The Shelley substitute contains in section 501 carefully drafted provisions defining and enforcing the accountability of union officials for embezzled union funds for which they are responsible and for any income or profit they receive in connection with any transaction that conflicts with the interests of their union. This provision takes the place of section 501 of the committee bill under which the propriety of many types of expenditures of union funds could be challenged by members' suits in Federal courts. The Shelley substitute, like the committee bill, makes embezzlement of union funds a Federal crime.

Seventh. Section 502 of the Shelley bill corrects defects in the union officials' bonding requirements contained in the committee bill. Enforcement would be through injunction action brought by the Secretary of Labor in the Federal courts instead of through criminal proceedings, which hardly appear to be appropriate for the enforcement of such types of requirements.

Eighth. The provisions disqualifying persons convicted of certain crimes from serving as officers of unions, as labor relations consultants or as officers or employees of employer associations dealing with unions, which are contained in section 504 of the committee bill, have been broadened in the Shelley substitute to apply in addition to service as employers' labor relations officers or employees or as other personnel officials of employers.

Ninth. The Shelley substitute restores the Senate-passed amendment of section 302(c)(4) of the Taft-Hartley Act permitting the voluntarily authorized checkoff of periodic payments to unions in line of membership dues, as well as the checkoff of union dues, fees and assessments now permitted under existing law.

Tenth. In place of the vague and indefinite language of section 602 of the committee bill, making extortionate picketing a Federal crime, punishable by a prison term of up to 20 years, the Shelley substitute restores improved language from the Senate-passed bill banning shakedown picketing. The penalty for violation would be the same under the Shelley substitute as under the committee bill. Shakedown picketing would also be an unfair labor practice when engaged in by a union under section 705 of the Shelley substitute.

Eleventh. Section 603(a) of the committee bill, which is designed to encourage States to enact State legislation imposing additional restrictions on labor unions' conduct of their own internal affairs, has been omitted from the Shelley substitute.

Twelfth. The provisions contained in section 701 of the committee bill, which would take away from the National Labor Relations Board and confer on the General Counsel authority over the personnel in the Board's regional and field offices, has been omitted from the Shelley substitute.

Thirteenth. The Shelley substitute omits the language contained in section 704 of the committee bill which, by making the prehearing election procedures authorized therein inapplicable whenever the appropriate bargaining unit is in dispute, would largely nullify the value of these procedures.

Fourteenth. Section 705 of the Shelley substitute makes shakedown picketing engaged in by a union an unfair labor practice. Picketing for purposes of extortion is also made a Federal crime under section 602. These provisions take the place of the punitive restrictions which the committee bill would impose on traditional and perfectly legitimate trade union practices under the guise of banning so-called hot cargo agreements and organizational and recognition picketing.

Fifteenth. The Shelley substitute adds to the bill a provision making the bill effective 120 days after the date of enactment.

Technical improvements are also made by the Shelley substitute in the form and language of various provisions of the bill.

At the time of the debate of the labor-reform measure, H.R. 8490 will be offered as an amendment in its entirety or as a substitute for the pending bill. I sincerely appeal to those who believe that a strong democracy needs a strong, clean, honest trade union movement as an integral part thereof, support this proposal on the grounds that it satisfies the needed legislation requirements of the time and does not unduly punish decent, honest American labor.

As of this writing only a few of the issues directly involving provisions of the Landrum-Griffin Act have ripened to a point at which the Supreme Court has accepted review.

American Federation of Musicians v. *Wittstein*
379 U.S. 171 (1964)

DUES UNDER TITLE I

The statute contains a provision prohibiting the increase in dues of an international union except by majority vote of the delegates voting at a regular convention. Does this outlaw the provision of a union constitution that the vote of delegates at a national convention be weighted and counted according to the number of members of the local union that the delegate represents? The Court replied in the negative, stating that such a weighted voting system is wholly consistent with the purpose of the statute to bring about full and active participation by the rank and file in the affairs of the union.

MR. JUSTICE WHITE delivered the opinion of the Court.

The issue presented in these suits is whether § 101 (a)(3) of the Labor-Management Reporting and Disclosure Act of 1959 providing that the dues of an international union "shall not be increased . . . except . . . by majority vote of the delegates voting at a regular convention" prohibits the vote of delegates at a national convention of the union, as authorized by its constitution, from being weighted and counted according to the number of members in the local that the delegate represents.

I.

The petitioner American Federation of Musicians (Federation) is an international labor organization comprising 675 locals in the United States and Canada. As with numerous other national and international labor organizations having many scattered locals of varying size, Federation's constitution and bylaws have long authorized alternative methods of ascertaining the vote of the delegates representing the locals at a union convention. Each local is entitled to one delegate for each 100 members or major fraction thereof, not to exceed three delegates from any one local. Federation's bylaws permit a voice vote of the delegates attending a convention in all cases, which is the method often used on routine noncontroversial matters. When amendments to the union constitution or bylaws are at issue, however, the delegates representing the locals, upon a roll call vote, may

cast as many votes as there are members in the respective locals. A roll call vote is required upon the demand of 10 delegates or five locals. All amendments to the bylaws and constitution approved by a roll call vote are required under the constitution to be referred to a convention committee which may approve or veto the proposal.

At petitioner's 1963 annual convention, a resolution increasing the per capita dues of all members, approximately 255,000, was submitted to the delegates. After the chairman ruled that two voice votes of the delegates were inconclusive, a delegate speaking on behalf of five locals requested a roll call vote in accordance with Federation's constitution. The rules governing a roll call vote were explained to the delegates. Delegates were to cast as many votes as there were members in the local that they represented. If the delegates from a given local were in disagreement, the total votes of that local were to be divided among the delegates. The roll call was taken and the recommendation carried by some 44,326 votes, with less than one-half of the delegates present voting in favor of the proposal.

Respondents, members of several locals whose delegates voted for or against the resolution at the convention, brought these suits against Federation and one of its locals to have the resolution declared null and void and its implementation enjoined. In the District Court, summary judgment in the consolidated actions was rendered for the respondent union members. 223 F. Supp. 27 (D.C.S.D.N.Y.). Finding that the material facts about the enactment of the dues resolution in regard to the issue under § 101 (a)(3)(B) were not in dispute, that court ruled that weighted voting did not comply with § 101 (a)(3)(B)'s requirements of approval by "majority vote of the delegates voting at a regular convention." A divided Court of Appeals affirmed. 326 F. 2d 26 (C. A. 2d Cir.). Although noting that weighted voting "is to all appearances the most 'democratic' method, in the sense that each member is duly 'represented,'" it held that the plain language of § 101 (a)(3)(B) requires that each delegate be allowed but one vote regardless of the number of members he represents. The question being an important one of first impression under the LMRDA, we granted certiorari. 376 U. S. 942. We hold that § 101 (a)(3)(B) does not prohibit a weighted-voting system under which delegates cast a number of votes equal to the membership of the local union from which they are elected.

II.

Under § 101 (a)(3)(B) an international union may increase membership dues or levy an assessment by majority vote of the members voting in a membership referendum, by majority vote of the members of the executive board, effective, however, only to the next regular convention, or "by majority vote of the delegates voting at a . . . convention." The quoted language, it is said, authorizes only one system of voting: a head count of the delegates at a convention. Just as each member and each executive board member is entitled to one vote, so too each delegate may cast only his single vote. There cannot be a majority vote of the delegates voting, the argument proceeds, unless a delegate cast but one vote, no more or less, and the affirmative votes cast add up to a majority of the delegates voting. So far the argument is based solely upon what is said to be the literal meaning of the statutory language; there is no suggestion that § 101 (a)(3)(B) embodies an accepted or preferable system of representation by delegates or that the provision requires any set number of delegates at a convention or any particular relationship between the size of the local and the number of representatives at the convention.

We do not think this is the only fair import of the language in § 101 (a) (3)(B). The section requires a majority *vote* of the delegates voting. It does not state that a dues increase must be approved by a *majority of the delegates voting* at a convention. The respondents' construction renders the key word "vote" entirely superfluous, although that word describes what is to be counted to determine a majority. The provision on its face prescribes only by whom the vote must be cast—a delegate to a convention—and the proportion of votes needed for passage—a majority of the votes cast. The statute does require that those voting at a convention be delegates, but it says nothing about the number of votes each delegate may cast. Where the "vote" cast at a convention is weighted according to the number of people the delegate represents, that vote, we think, is a vote of a delegate. We believe that a majority vote so determined in favor of a dues increase is approval by majority vote of the delegates voting at a convention.

Whatever doubts may be left by sole and plenary reliance on plain meaning are fully resolved by consideration of the legislative history behind § 101 (a)(3)(B) and of other provisions of the LMRDA. This section had its genesis in Senator McClellan's proposals in S. 1137, which would have required a "general vote" on rules relating to the rate of dues and initiation fees and would hve required that the vote of delegates at a convention "be numerically equivalent, or proportionate, to the number of the members of [each] constituent unit." I Leg. Hist. 269, 278. Although S. 1137 was not reported out by the Senate Committee on Labor and Public Welfare, Senator McClellan's requirement that the voting strength of convention delegates be proportionate to the size of their constituency is significant for the reason that it was the outgrowth of the extensive hearings held by the McClellan Committee which uncovered substantial evidence of various forms of internal misgovernment and abuses in several labor organizations. The findings of this committee became the primary basis for the many bills that followed its investigations, an amalgam of which ultimately became the LMRDA. In light of the fact that then as now many large unions had provisions for weighted voting by delegates at a convention, it is very clear that weighted voting was not thought to be one of these abuses or forms of misgovernment.

Senate bill No. 1555, the Kennedy-Ervin bill, was favorably reported out of the Senate Committee on Labor and Public Welfare without any Bill of Rights for union members, now Title I of the Act, of which the provision relating to dues is a part. Senator McClellan soon introduced a comprehensive Bill of Rights provision as an amendment to S. 1555, which was adopted in the Senate by a vote of 47 to 46. In respect to financial exactions, this amendment placed a flat limit on initiation fees and required for approval of a dues increase a majority vote of the members in the case of a local union and a "majority vote of the delegates present" at a general meeting in the case of a national or international union. It is not without significance that this language is susceptible of the same construction that is urged here in respect to § 101 (a)(3)(B), for it is quite clear that the author of this provision, Senator McClellan, did not intend to prohibit weighted voting. A few days later the Kuchel amendment, substituting another Bill of Rights provision, was adopted by a vote of 77 to 14. This amendment eliminated some of the more stringent requirements of Senator McClellan's Bill of Rights, such as the limit on initiation fees, and dealt with voting procedures for approval of a dues increase by a local and an international union in more detail; in the case of a local, majority approval of the members was necessary, while in the case of an international, a "majority vote at a regular convention" was required. Under this language, which was said to be "taken almost verbatim from . . . the McClellan amendment," it is very clear that no question of the permissibility of weighted voting could be raised. And no one expressed the thought that the McClellan proposal on voting was being altered in this or any other respect. S. 1555 passed the Senate with the Kuchel substitute as Title I.

The changes in § 101 (a)(3)(B) in the House support the conclusion that this provision does not bar weighted voting. S. 1555, as passed by the Senate, became the focus of testimony before a Joint Subcommittee of the House Committee on Education and Labor. The gist of the objections to § 101 (a)(3)(B) was that it failed explicitly to allow other methods of ensuring membership participation on proposals of an international or national union to increase dues, and it was too rigid in disallowing action by an executive board of the international or national union. The Committee responded by expanding the permissible methods of raising dues. As reported out in the Elliott bill, § 101 (a)(3)(B) allowed an international to increase dues by majority vote of the members, by majority vote of the members of an executive board, effective only until the next convention, and "by majority vote of the delegates voting at a regular convention." The Committee version was incorporated in identical language in the Landrum-Griffin bill, which prevailed on the floor of the House. In respect to his bill, Representative Griffin observed generally that the "bill of rights in our substitute is essentially the bill of rights in the form passed by the [Senate]. It guarantees to union members, subject to reasonable rules and regulations, . . . that their dues and initiation fees will not be increased arbitrarily." The House Joint Conference Committee Report confirmed the view that the Senate and House versions of Title I contain "similar provisions." Senator Goldwater, a member of the Joint Committee that considered S. 1555 and Landrum-Griffin, stated in his textual analysis of both bills that the House version of § 101 (a)(3)(B) was technically preferable and that the differences were in respect to the expanded methods of approval under the House bill and the applicability of the House bill only to dues increases rather than all changes. And Senator Kuchel, the author of the Senate version of the dues proposal, and a conferee, stated that the Landrum-Griffin bill "adopted substantially the same bill of rights language" as he had earlier authored. In light of the fact that the House changes were in the direction of affording unions more latitude for raising dues and the fact that no one, in the House or Senate, perceived that the House version would restrict voting at a convention to a head count of the delegates, we think it abundantly clear that § 101 (a)(3)(B) was intended to guarantee a member's "right to participate in deciding upon the rate of dues, initiation fees, and assessments," H.. R. Rep. No. 741 on H. R. 8342, 86th Cong., 1st Sess., at 7, I Leg. Hist. 759, 765, but not to bar a well-known system of voting embodied in many union constitutions which well serves that end.

Other provisions of the LMRDA confirm this view. Section 101 (a)(3) (B) is a part of Title I, entitled the "Bill of Rights of Members of Labor Organizations." This Title guarantees to every member of a labor organization equal rights and privileges to vote, to attend meetings, and to participate in the deliberations and business of such meetings. Section 101 (a) (3)(B) forms a part of this framework by requiring participation by all members, either directly or through their elected representatives, on certain union matters thought to be of special importance. We find nothing to indicate that Congress thought this objective would be better fulfilled by allowing a delegate to cast one vote, regardless of the size of his constituency, than by permitting him to cast a vote equal to the number of members he represents. As a part of the Act's purpose of protecting and fostering participation by the rank and file in the affairs of the union, Title IV contains elaborate statutory safeguards for the election of union officers. But nothing in that title prohibits election of union officers by delegates voting at a convention in accordance with the number of members they represent. Respondents do not demonstrate any differences between weighted voting for officers of the union and weighted voting on changes in financial exactions that would support the asserted differences in voting procedures applicable to each. It is argued that delegates may not ascertain or follow the wishes of the members in respect to dues and assessments. But few issues are more likely to arouse active opposition and general membership participation than a proposal to increase dues. Further, this argument is too broad, for it questions the validity of a system of representative union government and has little to do with the manner in which the representative's vote is counted. Section 101 (a)(3)(B), as well as Title IV, authorizes a representative system of government and does not require a town meeting for action by an international or national union. To that end Congress recognized the key role of elections in the process of union self-government and surrounded it with many safeguards to provide a fair election and to guarantee membership participation.

The pervading premise of both these titles is that there should be full and active participation by the rank and file in the affairs of the union. We think our decision today that the vote of an elected delegate may reflect the size of his constituency is wholly consistent with that purpose.

Accordingly, the judgments below are reversed and the case is remanded for proceedings consistent with this opinion.

It is so ordered.

Calhoun v. *Harvey*
379 U.S. 134 (1964)

ELECTIONS UNDER TITLE I AND IV

Both of the above titles contain provisions relating to union elections. The decision below deals with the interplay between these sections. Union members sought to enjoin their union from conducting an election, claiming that their rights under Title I had been violated by union by-laws providing that a member could only nominate himself and that a member was only eligible if he had been a member for five years and had served the required amount of sea time. The Court held that this claim involved no Title I rights and that the challenge to the election could be made only through the procedures of Title IV, which are initiated by the filing of a complaint with the Secretary of Labor.

MR. JUSTICE BLACK delivered the opinion of the Court.

This case raises important questions concerning the powers of the Secretary of Labor and federal courts to protect rights of employees guaranteed by the Labor-Management Reporting and Disclosure Act of 1959.

The respondents, three members of District No. 1, National Marine Engineers' Beneficial Association, filed a complaint in Federal District Court against the union, its president and its secretary-treasurer, alleging that certain provisions of the union's bylaws and national constitution violated the Act in that they infringed "the right of members of defendant District No. 1, NMEBA, to nominate candidates in elections of defendant, which right is guaranteed to each member of defendant, and to each plaintiff, by Section 101 (a) (1) of the LMRDA . . . ." It was alleged that § 102 of Title I of the Act gave the District Court jurisdiction to adjudicate the controversy. The union bylaws complained of deprived a member of the right to nominate anyone for office but himself. The national constitution in turn provided that no member could be eligible for nomination or election to a full-time elective office unless he had been a member of the national union for five years and had served 180 days or more of seatime in each of two of the preceding three years on vessels covered by collective bargaining agreements with the national or its subsidiary bodies. On the basis of these allegations respondents asked that the union be enjoined from preparing for or conducting any election until it revised its system of elections so as to afford each of its members a fair opportunity to nominate any persons "meeting fair and reasonable eligibility requirements for any or all offices to be filled by such election."

The union moved to dismiss the complaint on the grounds that (1) the court lacked jurisdiction over the subject matter, and (2) the complaint failed to state a claim upon which relief could be granted. The District Court dismissed for want of "jurisdiction," holding that the alleged conduct of the union, even if true, failed to show a denial of the equal rights of all members of the union to vote for or nominate candidates guaranteed by § 101 (a)(1) of Title I of the Act, so as to give the District Court jurisdiction of the controversy under § 102. The allegations, said the court, showed at most imposition of qualifications of eligibility for nomination and election so restrictive that they might violate § 401 (e) of Title IV by denying members a reasonable opportunity to nominate and vote for candidates. The District Court further held that it could not exercise jurisdiction to protect § 401 (e) rights because § 402 (a) of Title IV provides a remedy, declared by § 403 to be "exclusive," authorizing members to vindicate such rights by challenging elections after they have been held, and then only by (1) first exhausting all remedies available with the union, (2) filing a complaint with the Secretary of Labor, who (3) may, after investigating the violation alleged in the complaint, bring suit in a United States district court to attack the validity of the election. The Court of Appeals reversed, holding that "the complaint alleged a violation of § 101 (a)(1) and that federal jurisdiction existed under § 102." 324 F. 2d 486, 487. Because the importance of the questions presented and conflicting views in the courts of appeals and the district courts, we granted certiorari. 375 U.S. 991.

I.

Jurisdiction of the District Court under § 102 of Title I depends entirely upon whether this complaint showed a violation of rights guaranteed by § 101 (a)(1), for we disagree with the Court of Appeals' holding that jurisdiction under § 102 can be upheld by reliance in whole or in part on allegations which in substance charge a breach of Title IV rights. An analysis and understanding of the meaning of § 101 (a)(1) and of the charges of the complaint are therefore essential to a determination of this issue. Respondents charge that the bylaws and constitutional provisions referred to above infringed their right guaranteed by § 101 (a)(1) to nominate candidates. The result of their allegations here, however, is an attempt to sweep into the ambit of their right to sue in federal court if they are denied an equal opportunity to nominate candidates under § 101 (a)(1), a right to sue if they are not allowed to nominate anyone they choose regardless of his eligibility and qualifications under union restrictions. But Title IV, not Title I, sets standards for eligibility and qualifications of candidates and officials and provides its own separate and different administrative and judicial procedure for challenging those standards. And the equal-rights language of § 101 (a)(1) would have to be stretched far beyond its normal meaning to hold that it guarantees members not just a right to "nominate candidates," but a right to nominate anyone, without regard to valid union rules. All that § 101 (a)(1) guarantees is that

"Every member of a labor organization shall have equal rights and privileges . . . to nominate candidates, to vote in elections or referendums of the labor organization . . . and to participate in the deliberations and voting . . . subject to reasonable rules and regulations in such organization's constitution and bylaws."

Plainly, this is no more than a command that members and classes of members shall not be discriminated against in their right to nominate and vote. And Congress carefully prescribed that even this right against discrimination is "subject to reasonable rules and regulations" by the union. The complaining union members here have not been discriminated against in any way and have been denied no privilege or right to vote or nominate which the union has granted to others. They have indeed taken full advantage of the uniform rule limiting nominations by nominating themselves for office. It is true that they were denied their request to be candidates, but that denial was not a discrimination against their right to nominate, since the same qualifications were required equally of all members. Whether the eligibility requirements set by the union's constitution and bylaws were reasonable and valid is a question separate and distinct from whether the right to nominate on an equal basis given by § 101 (a) (1) was violated. The District Court therefore was without jurisdiction to grant the relief requested here unless, as the Court of Appeal held, the "*combined* effect of the eligibility requirements and the restriction to self-nomination" is to be considered in determining whether § 101 (a)(1) has been violated.

II.

We hold that possible violations of Title IV of the Act regarding eligibility are not relevant in determining whether or not a district court has jurisdiction under § 102 of Title I of the Act. Title IV sets up a statutory scheme governing the election of union officers, fixing the terms during which they hold office, requiring that elections be by secret ballot, regulating the handling of campaign literature, requiring a reasonable opportunity for the nomination of candidates, authorizing unions to fix "reasonable qualifications uniformly imposed" for candidates, and attempting to guarantee fair union elections in which all the members are allowed to participate. Section 402 of Title IV, as has been pointed out, sets up an exclusive method for protecting Title IV rights, by permitting an individual member to file a complaint with the Secretary of Labor challenging the validity of any election because of violations of Title IV. Upon complaint the Secretary investigates and if he finds probable cause to believe that Title IV has been violated, he may file suit in the appropriate district court. It is apparent that Congress decided to utilize the special knowledge and discretion of the Secretary of Labor in order best to serve the public interest. Cf. *San Diego Building Trades Council* v. *Garmon,* 359 U.S. 236, 242. In so doing Congress, with one exception not here relevant, decided not to permit individuals to block or delay union elections by filing federal-court suits for violations of Title IV. Reliance on the discretion of the Secretary is in harmony with the general congressional policy to allow unions great latitude in resolving their own internal controversies, and, where that fails, to utilize the agencies of Government most familiar with union problems to aid in bringing about a settlement through discussion before resort to the courts. Without setting out the lengthy legislative history which preceded the passage of this measure, it is sufficient to say that we are satisfied that the Act itself shows clearly by its structure and language that the disputes here, basically relating as they do to eligibility of candidates for office, fall squarely within Title IV of the Act and are to be resolved by the administrative and judicial procedures set out in that Title.

Accordingly, the judgment of the Court of Appeals is reversed and that of the District Court is affirmed.

It is so ordered.

CONCLUSION

The Landrum-Griffin Act of 1959 marks the latest direct incursion of the federal government into the labor relations field. But there has been legislation in the 1960's which indirectly bears upon labor relations to a greater or lesser degree. Thus in 1961 the Congress enacted the Area Development Act to stimulate economic activity in "depressed areas." In 1962 Congress passed the Manpower Development and Training Act in an effort to improve the skill capacities of unemployed workers. And the initial steps of a comprehensive program to assist such workers in obtaining necessary skills and to improve the economy so that work would be available appear in the Economic Opportunity Act of 1964, sometimes referred to as the "anti-poverty" act.

In 1964, as part of the new Civil Rights Act, Congress for the first time enacted in Title VII, under the title of Equal Employment Opportunity, the first federal fair employment practice law. It prohibits unions, employers, and employment agencies from engaging in discrimination based on race, color, religion, sex, or national origin in industries affecting interstate commerce. Finally, in 1967 Congress enacted the Age Discrimination in Employment Act, which took effect on June 12, 1968, and which adds age to the prohibited bases of discrimination.

In the field of federal legislation dealing directly with labor relations, one of the most significant phenomena in recent years has been the burgeoning of organization and collective bargaining by government employees at all levels of government. Employers and employees in the public sector have been excluded from the coverage of the major federal statutes, the Wagner Act of 1935, the Taft-Hartley Act of 1947, and the Landrum-Griffin Act of 1959, except to the extent that Taft-Hartley contains in Section 305 an express ban against strikes by federal employees. A considerable number of states have enacted legislation governing in some degree organization and collective bargaining in public employment. At the federal level, however, there has been a minimum of legislation. The Lloyd-LaFollette Act of 1912 protects the right of postal employees to join unions and petition Congress, and from it derives the principle that federal employees may join an organization which does not assert the right to strike against the government. But this Act did little to stimulate any system of collective negotiation for federal employees.

Not until the administration of President Kennedy did pressures for initiation of such a system bear fruit. In June, 1961, the President appointed a task force of high administration officials under the chairmanship of Secretary of Labor Goldberg to report to him concerning employee-management relations in the federal service. In its report of November 30, 1961, the task force made recommendations which provided the basis for subsequent Executive Orders issued by the President. Briefly stated, the Executive Orders give federal employees the right to join or not to join employee organizations, provide for various types of recognition of these organizations, provide that under specified conditions agreements may be entered into with employee organizations, and permit the inclusion in such agreements of provisions for consideration of grievances and for advisory arbitration. However, bargainable issues are limited to a considerable extent since the basic Executive Order 10988 recognizes that employees do not have the right to strike, that the union shop and closed shop are not appropriate for the federal service, that where salaries and other employment conditions are fixed by Congress such matters are not subject to negotiation, and that all agreements must be consistent with merit system principles. In May, 1963, the President supplemented Executive Order 10988 by promulgating certain Standards of Conduct for Employee Organizations, relating largely to the maintenance of democratic internal procedures and fiscal integrity, and a Code of Fair Labor Practices prohibiting both agency management and employee organizations from various types of interference with employee rights.

The Executive Orders have been successful in enlarging union membership and in stimulating collective negotiation. There have been a number of criticisms, mainly from the employee organizations, of certain features of Executive Order 10988, and several bills have been introduced in Congress, presumably in response to the criticism. So far as appears, however, the prospect of passage of federal legislation is not bright. Change, if any, in the immediate future is more likely to result from further executive action.

Returning to the private sector, we are unable to discern any immediate possibility of the enactment of new federal labor legislation on a scale comparable to that reflected by the Railway Labor Act, the Wagner Act, the Taft-Hartley Act, or the Landrum-Griffin Act. Most students of these and related laws acknowledge the desirability of a review and re-codification of these statutes with a view toward eliminating surplusage, conflict, and inconsistency. But the politics involved in legislating in this controversial and inflammatory field are such that it is not likely that such a review, if undertaken, could be successfully completed.

Many specific facets of our existing labor relations law have been and will be the subject of proposed Congressional action. Of these, the aspect most likely to receive prompt attention seems to be the problem of emergency disputes. The provisions of the Railway Labor Act for emergency boards and the Taft-Hartley National Emergency provisions have been subjected to a plethora of searching criticism, and there seems to be a consensus favoring, if not total replacement, substantial modification.

INDEX

A

Adamson Act (1916)
  Beck, James, 244
  constitutionality of
    Wilson v. *New,* 14
  labor disputes
    settlement of, 113
  passage of, 79
  Wilson, Woodrow, 244 ff
  work day, length of
    established by, 78, 84
advisory committees
  Fair Labor Standards Act (1938),
    449–50
age, discrimination by
  Fair Labor Standards Act (1938)
    prohibited, 437
agricultural workers
  Fair Labor Standards Act (1938)
    defined, 485
  Taft-Hartley Act (Labor-Manage-
    ment Relations Act of 1947)
    excluded from, 613
  Wagner Act (National Labor Rela-
    tions Act of 1935)
    excluded from provisions of, 268
agriculture
  Fair Labor Standards Act (1938)
    defined, 401, 485, 492
American Federation of Labor
  actions of, 726, 730
  boycotts by, 4
  communism
    Michener, Earl, 239
  Fair Labor Standards Act (1938)
    attitudes toward, 450
  labor disputes
    railroads, employees of represen-
      tation in, 148
    settlement of, 151
  Meany, George, 763
  Michener, Earl, 239
  Morse, Wayne
    ethical practices of, 763

American Federation of Labor (*cont.*)
  Sabath, Adolph, 346–47
American Liberty League
  Wagner Act (National Labor Rela-
    tions Act of 1935), 265–66
Arbitration Act of 1888
  labor law, 12

B

Bacon-Davis Act
  penalties for violation of, 498–99
  provisions of, 399
  statute of limitations
    actions initiated under, 504–05
Bankruptcy Act
  unions, company
    prohibited under, 290
Barkley, Alben
  Esch-Cummins Act (1920)
    history, 87–88
    provisions of, 87–88
  labor disputes
    arbitration of, 100 ff
    railroads, 80
    wages, 80
    working conditions, 80
  Railway Labor Act (1934)
    congressional debate, 75–109
    importance to public, 75
    public, rights of, 105–07
    transportation industry,
      rights of, 75
  Railway Labor Board
    authority, 88 ff
    failure of, 96 ff
    procedures, 91
  wages agreements
    public excluded from, 107
Beck, Dave
  Kennedy, John F., 748
Beck, James
  Adamson Act (1920), 244

804

F

I

N

S

U